POLITICAL PARTICIPATION OF MINORITIES

Political Participation of Minorities

A Commentary on International Standards and Practice

Edited by
MARC WELLER

Assistant editor
KATHERINE NOBBS

Great Clarendon Street, Oxford OX2 6DP

Oxford University Press is a department of the University of Oxford.
It furthers the University's objective of excellence in research, scholarship,
and education by publishing worldwide in

Oxford New York

Auckland Cape Town Dar es Salaam Hong Kong Karachi Kuala Lumpur Madrid
Melbourne Mexico City Nairobi New Delhi Shanghai Taipei Toronto

With offices in

Argentina Austria Brazil Chile Czech Republic France Greece
Guatemala Hungary Italy Japan Poland Portugal Singapore
South Korea Switzerland Thailand Turkey Ukraine Vietnam

Oxford is a registered trade mark of Oxford University Press
in the UK and in certain other countries

Published in the United States
by Oxford University Press Inc., New York

© The several contributors, 2010

The moral rights of the author have been asserted
Database right Oxford University Press (maker)

Crown copyright material is reproduced under Class Licence
Number C01P0000148 with the permission of OPSI
and the Queen's Printer for Scotland

First published 2010

All rights reserved. No part of this publication may be reproduced,
stored in a retrieval system, or transmitted, in any form or by any means,
without the prior permission in writing of Oxford University Press,
or as expressly permitted by law, or under terms agreed with the appropriate
reprographics rights organization. Enquiries concerning reproduction
outside the scope of the above should be sent to the Rights Department,
Oxford University Press, at the address above

Crown copyright material is reproduced under Class Licence Number
C01P0000148 with the permission of the controller of HMSO
and the Queen's Printer for Scotland

You must not circulate this book in any other binding or cover
and you must impose this same condition on any acquirer

British Library Cataloguing in Publication Data
Data available

Library of Congress Cataloging-in-Publication Data
Political participation of minorities : a commentary on international standards and practice /
edited by Marc Weller.
   p. cm.
   Includes index.
   ISBN 978-0-19-956998-4 (alk. paper)
 1. Minorities–Political activity. 2. Political participation. I. Weller, M. (Marc)
 JF1061.P58 2010
 323'.04208–dc22
                                                                                             2009052045

Typeset by MPS Limited, A Macmillan Company
Printed in Great Britain
on acid-free paper by
Antony Rowe, Chippenhan, Wiltshire

ISBN 978–0–19–956998–4

1 3 5 7 9 10 8 6 4 2

This volume is published under the auspices of the European Centre for Minority Issues and the Centre of International Studies of the University of Cambridge

Like its predecessors, it is dedicated to Professor Sir Elihu Lauterpacht, QC, CBE.

Foreword—The Journey towards the Effective Participation of National Minorities

Developments in the Last 10 Years: A Council of Europe (CoE) Perspective

February 2008 marked the tenth anniversary of the entry into force of the Council of Europe Framework Convention for the Protection of National Minorities (FCNM) and the same month marked the adoption of the second Commentary by the Framework Convention Advisory Committee.

The Framework Convention is the first legally binding multilateral instrument devoted to the protection of national minorities in general, giving effect to the meeting of Heads of State and Government in Vienna in 1993. It called inter alia for the political commitments adopted by the Conference on Security and Cooperation in Europe (CSCE) to be transformed to the greatest extent possible into legal obligations. First and foremost among these for national minorities were the agreements reached at the Human Dimension meeting in Copenhagen in 1990 on national minorities.

Similarly, the Lund Recommendations were founded in the agreements made at the same meeting and both the Lund Recommendations and the FCNM had the same axiomatic base, although they approached the issues from different perspectives. The Lund Recommendations focused on political participation, while the Commentary on Art 15 covered the wider perspective of public affairs and participation in social, economic and cultural life.

The second Framework Convention Commentary is on Art 15 of the Framework Convention, which stipulates that states parties 'shall create the conditions necessary for the effective participation of persons belonging to national minorities in cultural, social and economic life and in public affairs, in particular those affecting them'. Its purpose is to provide a useful tool for state authorities and decision-makers, public officials, organizations of minorities, non-governmental organizations, academics, and other stakeholders involved in minority protection.

The Commentary sets out the Advisory Committee's interpretation of how states should understand and develop the concept of effective participation based on the experience of the Council of Europe (CoE) of monitoring the implementation of the Framework Convention over the last ten years in the thirty-nine states that have ratified the FCNM. The Commentary drew on state reports, opinions formed by the Advisory Committee and comments made by states parties. Consequently, the Commentary can be seen in part as lessons learnt in the practical interpretation of the Lund Recommendations by states, and marks the first ten years in the long journey towards effective participation of national minorities.

The text of the Commentary is explored in various chapters of this book that will not be repeated here. Importantly, it shows that the effective participation of minorities in public services should be fundamental in the development of policies and strategies as well as in their management and delivery. Consultation mechanisms are also a valuable way of taking part in decision-making, though consultation should not be confused with participation. Effective participation should ensure a genuine and substantial influence on decision-making in a regular, permanent, and systematic way with a shared sense of ownership of the decisions and a shared responsibility in rectifying any shortfalls.

Generalizations can be made on national minorities which can be misleading. The Commentary noted the importance of looking at diversity within minority communities and seeking ways to ensure that participation is effective in involving and representing the differences within minority communities, avoiding political and social elitism. This would include balanced representation of women and men, young and old, those living in urban and rural areas, as well as those who are well educated and affluent and those who may have been educationally and economically excluded. This is challenging, but the differentiation is crucial to ensure that participation is effective for all persons belonging to national minorities.

There is a duty among those who represent minorities to avoid hypocrisy in arguing for, and enjoying power on behalf of, their community without then sharing this power with their diverse community. They should ensure that they themselves are genuinely representative, listening to all parts of their community and taking back issues for wider engagement. Their role is not to be a gatekeeper using information for their own power, but to be part of a genuinely democratic and engaging process. Similarly it can be argued that those who are employed in public service should help explain the complexities of decision-making and service delivery and be able to demonstrate a shared ownership in finding responses.

The Council of Europe and its Advisory Committee need to take care that they are not hypocritical, pontificating on the behaviour of others without a self-critical look at how far they promote effective participation in their own operations, and exploring what route they should follow in the future. The structures of the CoE are those of an intergovernmental body which has become well tuned over the years to the active participation of its member states but, as an organization, it has no permanent mechanisms for involving national minorities or for reviewing how many of them are among its staff or committees at different levels. Initially the Framework Convention itself was drafted in camera, without any formal consultation with civil society or minority organizations. It has been argued that the CoE's conduct in drafting the Framework

Convention was not compatible with the effective participation of national minorities in public affairs, as this was an issue that undoubtedly affected them.

The rules of procedure (CoE Committee of Ministers Resolution 97(10)) that elaborated on the monitoring arrangements under Arts 24–6 of the Framework Convention again were not discussed with national minorities. In due course they proved problematic for the Advisory Committee, an independent group of experts that assists in the CoE monitoring of the Framework Convention, as it embarked on its journey seeking to implement the spirit of Art 15 and the philosophy behind the Framework Convention. There was no provision in the rules for information to be sought from a wide range of sources, no authorization to hold meetings with non-governmental bodies and no agreement to encourage country visits. The independent Opinions of the Advisory Committee could be ignored and their publication could be delayed indefinitely.

The Advisory Committee played a leading role in the first five years, adopting a step-by-step approach, encouraging precedents of good practice in certain countries and thereafter using these to persuade all states parties through the CoE Committee of Ministers to adopt a more consultative and transparent approach. More recently, following the Advisory Committee's ten year Impact Review Conference, there have been a number of fresh initiatives. It is likely that most states parties will now release Opinions to National Minorities within four months of their being made available to states parties, though some states have resisted this, while there will be greater involvement of members of national minorities in the third cycle of monitoring that began in 2009.

This legacy of a non-participatory approach is being questioned now by national minorities in a Declaration that was prepared on the Tenth Anniversary of the Framework Convention and presented to various Council of Europe entities. It calls for specific improvements to strengthen the monitoring and implementation of the Framework Convention and to promote the participation of members of national minorities.

The Commentary was led by the Advisory Committee itself, but sought to engage minorities and governments in its development. The substantial practical work was undertaken by the Secretariat with the conceptual thinking undertaken during Committee meetings. The Advisory Committee consulted many minority organizations on the draft and invited some of them and some governmental representatives to a workshop to discuss it. This was a consultative rather than a participatory process, as the decision-making was owned exclusively by the Advisory Committee; nevertheless the draft Commentary was significantly amended to take these views into account.

The Commentary also made observations on the monitoring of the Framework Convention itself. It recommended that when states parties prepare reports, comments on opinions or other communications on the Framework Convention they should consult national minorities inter alia to achieve a balanced and quality outcome. Furthermore, states should go beyond one interlocutor, such as a consultative body, and include a range of other actors, especially minority and/or non-governmental organizations, in the consultation process. This also requires transparency and the wide availability of all monitoring documents, including the texts of opinions and state reports and comments, in local languages, as early as possible.

Furthermore, the Commentary also welcomed alternative reports prepared by non-governmental actors noting that they often constitute a valuable additional source of information. They are a good indicator of a desire on the part of non-governmental actors to engage in a constructive dialogue based on international human rights norms.

It is also important for states parties to set up a system of regular consultations providing an opportunity for minority representatives to discuss their concerns. Such consultations can include follow-up seminars, annual review meetings or discussions within parliamentary committees. This dialogue can respond to specific concerns and can also build trust and confidence in the implementation of the Framework Convention. It creates a climate of tolerance and dialogue which enables diversity to be a source and a factor not of division but of enrichment for each society. Local ownership of the Framework Convention is crucial for its success, bringing together government and civil society in a spirit of goodwill to find practical solutions to often challenging issues. Furthermore the margin of appreciation afforded to states further emphasizes the importance of effective participation in the implementation of the Framework Convention drawing on the court of public opinion nationally and internationally.

This is where international organizations like the European Centre for Minority Issues have an important role to play in this journey. They have undertaken valuable conceptual and practical work over the last decade. Their practical participation programme in a number of European countries that have experienced conflict, their facilitation and support of consultative councils for national minorities and their scholarly work reviewing theory and practice, including the *European Yearbook on Minority Issues* and this Commentary, provide a bedrock for future development. Their work is needed to continue to transform the Lund Recommendations and the new Commentary of the Advisory Committee into effective participation of national minorities in practice.

Alan Phillips
President of the Advisory Committee on the Framework
Convention for the Protection of National Minorities

Foreword—The Lund Recommendations as a Tool for the Work of the OSCE High Commissioner on National Minorities

The effective participation of persons belonging to national minorities in public life is a key factor for their inclusion in society as a whole. Minority participation in decision-making is a twofold asset: first, minorities have a sense of inclusion and feel that they are taken seriously, and in turn their loyalty to mainstream society is reinforced; secondly, it helps states to become more aware of the views of minorities and to take them into account during decision-making, which in turn contributes to a more balanced representation of a society's diversity.

This is why it is of the utmost importance to be aware of international standards and their evolution in this field. It is relevant for all actors involved in the complex kaleidoscope of minority issues—national minorities, states, international organizations, academics and non-governmental organizations (NGOs)—because every action must be guided by existing standards, with a view to making them fully operational. Instruments such as the Lund Recommendations on the Effective Participation of National Minorities in Public Life (Lund Recommendations) and the academic debate surrounding them—of which this book is an important example—are a great help in the practical work of institutions such as the OSCE High Commissioner on National Minorities (HCNM).

The right to effective participation in public life has become deeply embedded, as a general principle applicable to everyone, in modern human rights treaties and commitments undertaken by states participating in the Conference on Security and Cooperation in Europe (CSCE)/Organization for Security and Cooperation in Europe (OSCE) process—notably, in the 1948 Universal Declaration of Human Rights (Art 21), the 1966 International Covenant on Civil and Political Rights (Art 25), the 1990 Document of the Copenhagen Meeting of the Conference on the Human Dimension of the CSCE (paras 6–7), the 1990 Charter of Paris for a New Europe and other CSCE/OSCE documents. More significantly, over the last few decades this right has been envisaged specifically for the needs of national minorities, as is the case in the CSCE Copenhagen Document (para 35), the 1992 United Nations Declaration on the Rights of Persons Belonging to National or Ethnic, Religious and Linguistic Minorities (Art 2) and, above all, the 1995 Council of Europe Framework Convention for the Protection of National Minorities (Art 15).

In light of the HCNM mandate, the fundamental right to effective participation not only has a human rights dimension, but also a security dimension: in the experience of the HCNM, effective participation of minorities in public life considerably reduces tensions and the risk of conflicts involving national minorities. In other words, effective minority participation is as much in the interests of states as it is of national minorities.

This is why the first High Commissioner, drawing upon his day-to-day practical experience of conflict prevention, expressed the need for clear guidelines on instruments for effective participation of persons belonging to national minorities in public affairs. He noted in fact that, previously, 'relatively little attention ha[d] been paid to various methods to ensure the viability of multi-ethnic states'.[1] Rejecting the idea of ethnically homogenous states, which would lead to the creation of new states with new ethnic minorities and the risk of mass migration of populations, he identified a need to search for methods that would help in pursuing another option: to integrate diversity. Against this background, experts were tasked with putting together and categorizing the forms of participation that could be used as tools by the HCNM in his preventive diplomacy: the Lund Recommendations were therefore drafted with a view to 'try[ing] to show that there are other ways to find a mutually acceptable balance between the interests of majority and minority'.[2]

The aim of the Recommendations was 'not to create new norms and standards, but to interpret and elaborate the existing international rules regarding these subjects',[3] with a view to achieving an appropriate and coherent application of relevant minority rights in the OSCE area. The great merit of the Lund Recommendations lies in their bringing together a wide range of forms of effective participation with potential applicability to national minorities. All these forms were previously unknown to politicians, constitutional lawyers and members of civil society, and this is why they were gathered together in one reference document to demonstrate the wide scope of their applicability within diverse domestic frameworks where an appropriate consensus needs to be reached.

Ten years after their adoption, the Lund Recommendations have proven to be an extraordinary tool for a number of reasons. First, they are helpful in the HCNM's daily activities, representing an authoritative document on which further, more specific and country-related recommendations can be based. While not made public, country-specific recommendations on how to better address issues relating to the effective participation of national minorities in public life are often issued by the HCNM and are usually taken extremely seriously by participating states.

---

[1] Max van der Stoel, 'The Hague, Oslo, and Lund Recommendations Regarding Minority Questions' in M Bergsmo (ed), *Human Rights and Criminal Justice for the Downtrodden: Essays in honour of Asbjørn Eide* (2003), 510.   [2] Ibid, 511.
[3] Ibid, 505.

Secondly, the individual HCNM thematic recommendations reinforce one another, because minority rights are closely interconnected as a set of normative rules and as part of human rights as a whole. So far, six thematic recommendations have been drafted and published on issues ranging from education to language, from policing to electoral law, from media to interstate relations. All these thematic recommendations are intended to be read in conjunction with one another. How can participation in public life be effectively granted if the linguistic rights of persons belonging to national minorities are neglected? And how can linguistic rights be enhanced without proper guarantees for the educational rights of persons belonging to minorities? At the same time, linguistic or educational rights cannot be guaranteed without effective participation of national minorities in the decision-making process, particularly on issues of direct concern to them, including education and the use of language. This is why, for the High Commissioner on National Minorities, the Lund Recommendations are more than a set of substantive standards concerning participation of national minorities in public affairs. They also constitute a unique source of procedural rules and guidelines relevant to all other areas of vital importance to national minorities, such as education, language, the media, and policing.

Thirdly, the Lund Recommendations have been the basis for subsequent international documents in the field of minority participation in public life. One just has to think of the Warsaw Guidelines to Assist National Minority Participation in the Electoral Process, developed in 2000 by the OSCE Office for Democratic Institutions and Human Rights (ODIHR) in cooperation with the International Institute for Democracy and Electoral Assistance (IDEA) and the HCNM. The Guidelines were developed directly from Recommendations 7–10 on the issue of elections in the Lund Recommendations and their positive impact has led to further collaboration between the ODIHR and HCNM on a handbook on monitoring and promoting the participation of national minorities in electoral process.

Another striking example of the positive reverberations of the Lund Recommendations and of the mutually reinforcing links with other international documents is the extensive use of the Recommendations in the drafting process of the recently adopted Second Thematic Commentary of the Advisory Committee on the Framework Convention for the Protection of National Minorities on the Effective Participation of Persons belonging to National Minorities in Cultural, Social, and Economic Life and Public Affairs. This valuable text is likely to strengthen the message of the Lund Recommendations in the context of the implementation of the Framework Convention. The documents certainly do not vie with each other and are in fact complementary. The HCNM was consulted during the elaboration process of the Commentary and shared his views on its content.

As a living instrument, the implementation of the Lund Recommendations needs to be continuously assessed. Comprehensive analyses such as this book are particularly helpful in taking stock of state-of-the-art participation issues and in putting forward new input and proposals for a more thorough implementation of the Recommendations throughout the OSCE area. Furthermore, it must be welcomed that this book addresses a number of issues that, for years, were overlooked or even ignored, such as the socio-economic aspects of participation.

This book demonstrates that in the course of the further development and application of the Lund Recommendations they can also serve as a source of reference for extra-European countries and regions seeking reliable and effective examples of good practice for promoting public participation of ethnic and other social groups in the conduct of public affairs.

During the past ten years, official statements and informal voices have suggested certain amendments and adjustments to the Lund Recommendations. However, as a living instrument, the positive development of the Recommendations will be ensured by their careful implementation in practice rather than by amending the text itself. What is required is further practical verification of the impact of the Lund Recommendations and new ideas on how to increase their effectiveness. There is still room for further development and experimentation in some areas, for instance autonomy and kin-state relations, which could tangibly improve participation of national minorities. This book will be a great help in this regard.

Knut Vollebaek
OSCE High Commissioner on National Minorities

Preface

This Commentary is committed to the press almost exactly ten years after the adoption of the *Lund Recommendations on the Effective Participation of National Minorities in Public Life*. The recommendations, generated under the aegis of the High Commissioner on National Minorities of the Organization for Security and Cooperation in Europe (OSCE) and reproduced in Appendix I of this book, have proven to be particularly important in practice. The reasons for this success are twofold. On the one hand, it is widely recognized that political participation issues are foundational in relation to minority rights generally. Hence, there is a strongly felt need for guidance and standards in this area. On the other hand, governments have proven even more reluctant to adopt binding standards in relation to their political system and practices than is the case in relation to other aspects of minority rights. Accordingly, the Lund Recommendations have filled a void in this area.

The Lund Recommendations have now attracted significant implementation practice. Much of this practice is focused around the activities of the OSCE itself. In addition, the Council of Europe has readily drawn upon the recommendations, mainly through the work of the Advisory Committee attached to the Framework Convention for the Protection of National Minorities. Fortuitously for this project, the Committee adopted a substantial *Commentary on the Effective Participation of Persons Belonging to National Minorities in Cultural, Social and Economic Life and in Public Affairs*, reproduced in Appendix II while our work was still ongoing. That Commentary is based on implementation practice under the Framework Convention and we have been able to include it in our analyses.

Our book aims to help crystallize the emerging standards and practices in this area through critical analysis. As was the case with its two predecessors, the chapters in this Commentary first assess the relevance of the specific issue at hand for minority–majority relations more generally. They then consider the legal framework addressing the relevant issue. There follows a review of implementation practice, and concluding observations seek to point to a trend in these developments, aiming to identify emerging standards or best practices in the area of political participation.

In contrast to our previous commentaries, there are however a number of contributions that deviate from this otherwise common structure of legal analysis. In view of the subject area, we have drawn on a number of leading political scientists, in addition to our tried-and-tested team of legal specialists. The progression of analysis naturally differs according to discipline.

We have deliberately limited the focus of this work to the issue of political participation. Clearly, other aspects of participation in public life are also important. However, as the dimensions of this book indicate, political participation in its narrower sense merits weighty consideration in itself. We may well wish to address equal access to economic and social opportunities, or education issues, in a subsequent commentary in this series. For now, we have covered this issue in just one contribution, albeit quite a substantial one.[1]

There is one other area we have somewhat neglected. This is the issue of territorial or functional autonomy. Major works already exist in this field. Indeed, our own project team has considered autonomy in two volumes already,[2] along with a major study on power-sharing aspects of territorial accommodation.[3] Accordingly, we felt justified in emphasizing other aspects of political participation that had yet to be addressed extensively.

We are, once more, greatly indebted to the Carnegie Corporation of New York, which has supported the work of the Cambridge–Carnegie Project on the Settlement of Self-determination Disputes for close to a decade through its States at Risk programme. In addition, we gratefully acknowledge the support of the Danish Ministry of Research and Technology. As before, Katherine Nobbs has done a magnificent job in guiding the outcome of this work through the editorial and production stages. Thanks also to our excellent copy editor, Jeremy Langworthy. At Oxford University Press, we have had the hugely efficient and understanding support of Alex Flach, John Louth, Merel Alstein and Bethan Cousins. Once again, cooperation with the press has been outstanding for what is now the third in this series of Commentaries on Minority Issues.

Marc Weller

Cambridge
August 2009

---

[1] See Kristin Henrard, Ch. 19.

[2] Weller and Wolff (eds), *Autonomy, Self-governance and Conflict Resolution* (Routledge 2005), Weller and Nobbs (eds), *Asymmetric Autonomy Settlement and the settlement of Ethic Conflict* (University of Pennsylvania University Press, forthcoming).

[3] Weller and Metzger (eds), *Settling Self-determination Disputes: Complex power-sharing in theory and practice* (Nijhoff, 2008).

Contents

Table of Cases	xxi
Table of International Treaties and Conventions	xxvii
Table of National Legislation	xxxiii
Table of Recommendations and Expert Advice	xli
List of Abbreviations	xlv
Notes on Contributors	xlix
Introduction—Democratic governance and minority political participation: Emerging legal standards and practice *Marc Weller*	lvii

I. GENERAL ISSUES

1. Ethnic Diversity, Political Exclusion, and Armed Conflict: A quantitative analysis of a global dataset *Andreas Wimmer, Lars-Erik Cederman, and Brian Min*	3
2. Ethnic Domination in Democracies *John McGarry*	35
3. Understanding Minority Participation and Representation and the Issue of Citizenship *Annelies Verstichel*	72
4. The Principles of Non-discrimination and Full and Effective Equality and Political Participation *Zdenka Machnyikova and Lanna Hollo*	95
5. Gendering Minority Participation in Public Life *Karen Bird*	150

II. LEGAL FRAMEWORKS

6. Minorities, Political Participation, and Democratic Governance under the European Convention on Human Rights *Steven Wheatley*	177
7. The Council of Europe Framework Convention on the Protection of National Minorities and the Advisory Committee's Thematic Commentary on Effective Participation *Joseph Marko*	222

8. OSCE Lund Recommendations in the Practice of the High
   Commissioner on National Minorities 256
   Krzysztof Drzewicki
9. Effective Participation by Minorities: United Nations standards
   and practice 286
   Ilona Klímová-Alexander
10. Political Participation Systems Applicable to Indigenous Peoples 308
    Luis Rodríguez-Piñero Royo

III. REPRESENTATION

11. Universal and European Standards of Political Participation
    of Minorities 345
    Andraz A Melansek
12. Electoral Systems and the Lund Recommendations 363
    Brendan O'Leary
13. Making Effective Use of Parliamentary Representation 400
    Oleh Protsyk
14. Power-sharing at the Governmental Level 414
    Florian Bieber
15. At the Heart of Participation and of its Dilemmas: Minorities
    in the executive structures 434
    Francesco Palermo
16. Political Participation and Power-sharing in Ethnic Peace Settlements 453
    Fernand de Varennes

IV. CONSULTATION AND SPECIAL ISSUE PARTICIPATION

17. Minority Consultative Mechanisms: Towards best practice 477
    Marc Weller
18. Special Contact Mechanisms for Roma 503
    Eva Sobotka
19. Participation in Social and Economic Life 524
    Kristin Henrard
20. International Benchmarks: A review of minority participation
    in the judiciary 588
    Katherine Nobbs

V. MINORITY SELF-GOVERNANCE

21. Participation as Self-governance 613
    Yash Ghai
22. Cultural Minority Self-governance 634
    Ephraim Nimni
23. Enhanced Local Self-government as a Means of Enhancing Minority Governance 661
    Bill Bowring
24. Minority Associations: Issues of representation, internal democracy, and legitimacy 682
    Peter Vermeersch

VI. IMPLEMENTATION ISSUES

25. Minority Participation in Bilateral and International Reporting and Monitoring Processes 705
    Emma Lantschner
26. Legal Entrenchment and Implementation Mechanisms 735
    Alain Chablais

Appendix I: The Lund Recommendations on the Effective Participation of National Minorities in Public Life (OSCE) 751

Appendix II: Commentary on the Effective Participation of Persons Belonging to National Minorities in Cultural, Social and Economic Life and in Public Affairs 774

Index 819

Table of Cases

NATIONAL JURISDICTIONS

Austria
VerfSlg 17264/04 (Constitutional Court) 245

Belgium
Court of Arbitration
    Judgments no 7/94 of 20 January 1994 86
    Judgments no 65/93 of 15 July 1993 86
    Judgments no 86/93 of 16 December 1993 86

Bosnia and Herzegovina
Case 5/98 Partial Decision III (1 July 2000) 86
Case U-4/04, Partial Decision, 31 March 2006 602
Case U-5/98, Partial Decision, 1 July 2000 602
Case U-44/01, Partial Decision, 27 February 2004 602

Colombia
Constitutional Court Decision of Constitutionality 136/96, 9 April 1996 330

Germany
BVerfGE Vol 83, 37 (Constitutional Court) 245

India
Sawhney, 16 November 1992 443

Italy
Autonomy Statute (Bolzano/Bozen), Decree 752 444
    Art 89 444
Constitutional Court Judgment 422/1995 444
Corte Cassazione judgment of 24 March 1999, No 11048 247
Decree 99/2005 445

Macedonia
Ruling no Ubrl33/2005-0-1 440

Moldova
Law on Political Parties and Socio-Political Organisations 246

Montenegro
Ruling No 53/06 of 11 July 2006 (Constitutional Court) 237

Poland
Gorzelik, Supreme Court, 18 March 1998 749

Slovenia

Case U-I-283/94 of 12 February 1998 (Constitutional Court) 237
Case U-I-416/98-38 of 22 March 2001 521

United States

Mobile v Bolden 67

INTERNATIONAL COURTS AND TRIBUNALS

African Commission on Human and Peoples' Rights
    Commission Nationale des Droits de l'Homme et des Libertes v Chad, Communication
        no 75/92. 571
    Malawi African Association v Mauritania, Communication no s 54/91, 61/91,
        98/93, 164/97, 196/97 and 210/98..................................... 571
    Social and Economic Rights Action Centre and the Centre for Economic and Social
        Rights v Nigeria, Communication no 155/96.............................. 571
European Committee of Social Rights
    Autisme-Europe v France, Complaint no 13/2002, Decision on the merits of
        4 November 2003 130
    EERC v Greece, Appln 105/2003, 7 February 2005 573
    ERRC v Bulgaria, Appln 31/2005, 30 November 2006.................... 573, 574
    ERRC v Bulgaria, Appln 46/2007 573
    ERRC v Bulgaria, Appln 48/2008 573
    ERRC v France, Appln 51/2008 573
    ERRC v Italy, Appln 27/2004, 21 December 2005...................... 573, 574
    European Committee of Social Rights, Interights v Greece, Appln 49/2008.......... 573
    International Movement ATD Fourth World v France, Appln 33/2006 .... 573, 574
European Court of Justice
    Centrum voor Gelijkheid van Kansen en Racismbestrijding v Firma Feryn NV
        (Case C-54/07), 10 July 2008... 577
    Collins v Secretary of State for Work and Pensions (Case C-138/02) [2004]
        ECR I-2703 582
    Commission v Austria (Case C-147/03), Judgment of 7 July 2005 114
    Grzelczyk v Le Centre public d'aide sociale d'Ottignies-Louvain-la Neuve
        (Case C-184/99) [2001] ECR I-6193 582
    Office Nationale de l'emploi v Ioannidis (Case C-258/04) [2005] ECR I-8275 582
    R (On the Application of Bidar) v London Borough of Ealing (Case C-209/03)
        [2005] ECR I-2119.. 582
    Sala v Bayern (Case C-85/96) [1998] ECR I-2691 582
European Court/Commission of Human Rights
    Aârelâ and Nâkkâlâjârvi v Finland, Communication no 779/1997, 24 October 2001 ... 555
    Abdulaziz, Cabales and Balkandali v United Kingdom, Judgment of
        28 May 1985 .... 119, 120
    Adami v Malta, Appln 17209/02, Judgment of 20 June 2006. 114
    Ahmed v United Kingdom, Reports of Judgments and Decisions 1998-VI 197, 198
    Artyomov v Russia, Appln 17582/05, decision 7 December 2006............. 199, 200
    Association of Citizens Radko and Paunkovski v Former Yugoslav Republic of
        Macedonia, Appln 74651/01, j 15 January 2009. 197
    Aziz v Cyprus, Appln 69949/01, Judgment of 22 June 2004 .... 118, 119, 120,
        133, 143, 216

Table of Cases xxiii

Baczkowski v Poland, Appln 1543/06, Judgment of 3 May 2007 .... 201, 202, 202
Barankevich v Russia, Appln 10519/03, Judgment of 26 July 2000................. 202
Baskaya and Okçuoglu v Turkey, Reports of Judgments and Decisions 1999-IV 201
Belgian Linguistics Case (no 2) (1968) 1 EHRR 252 .... 116, 210
Belgium v Belgium (Merits), Judgment of 23 July 1968..................... 131, 182
Booth-Clibborn v United Kingdom, Appln 11391/85, decision 5 July 1985 674
Boskoski v Former Republic of Macedonia, Reports and Judgments and
    Decisions 2004-VI... 180
Botta v Italy, Reports of Judgments and Decisions 1998-I 209
Chapman v United Kingdom, Appln 27238/95, Judgment of
    18 January 2001 .... 122, 209, 210, 572
Chassagnou v France, Applns 25088/94, 28331/95 and 28443/95 119
Cherepkov v Russia, Appln 51501/99 674
Christian Democratic People's Party v Moldova, Reports of Judgments and
    Decisions 2006-II 195, 198, 199
Church of Scientology Moscow v Russia, Appln 18147/02, Judgment of 5
    April 2007 198
Clerfayt and Legros v Belgium, Appln 10650/83, Decision 17 May 1985 673
Connors v United Kingdom, Appln 66746/01, Judgment of 27 May 2004 ...... 209, 210
Cyprus v Turkey, Reports of Judgments and Decisions 2001-IV................... 195
DH v Czech Republic, Appln 57325/00, Judgment of 13 November 2007 ...... 114, 130,
  131, 572
Doerga v The Netherlands, Appln 50210/99, Judgment of 27 April 2004............ 209
Doyle v United Kingdom, Appln 30158/06, decision of 6 February 2007 217
Dudgeon v United Kingdom, Judgment of 22 October 1981..................... 119
East African Asians, (1973) 3 EHRR 76 .... 120, 195
Evans v United Kingdom, Appln 6339/05, Judgment of 10 April 2007.............. 213
Federación Nacionalista Canaria v Spain, Reports of Judgments and Decisions
    2001-VI.. 216, 673
Freedom and Democracy Party, Reports of Judgments and Decisions 1999-VIII 197
Fryske Nasionale Paetik v The Netherlands (1985) 45 DR 240 202
G and E v Norway (1983) 35 DR 30 .... 209, 210, 572
Gaygusuz v Austria (1996) 23 EHRR 365 .... 120, 573
Georgian Labour Party v Georgia, Appln 9103/04, Judgment of
    8 July 2008.. 185, 189, 190, 192, 193
Glimmerveen and Hagenbeek v The Netherlands 18 DR 187 (1979) 198
Gorisdra v Moldova, Appln 53180/99, 2 July 2002........................... 674
Gorzelik v Poland, Appln 44158/98, Judgment of
    17 February 2004................................. 126, 127, 133,134, 197,
                                                                                                                                                                                       201, 202, 203, 208, 749
Gündüz v Turkey, Reports of Judgments and Decisions 2002-XI 196, 201
Gypsy Council v United Kingdom, Appln 66336/01, decision 14 May 2002.......... 210
Handyside v United Kingdom, [1976] ECHR 5........................... 210, 355
Hatton v United Kingdom, A24 .... 210, 214
Hirst v United Kingdom (No 2), Reports of Judgments and Decisions
    2005-IX [GC].. 182, 187, 213
Hoffman v Austria (1993) 17 EHRR 293................................... 120
Hoogendijk v Netherlands, Appln 58461/00, Judgment of 6 January 2005 114
Howard v Canada, Communication no 579/1999, 26 July 2005 555
Ilaşu v Moldova and Russia, Reports of Judgments and Decisions 2004-VII [GC] 209
Incal v Turkey, Reports of Judgments and Decisions 1998-IV [GC] 196, 201

Ireland v United Kingdom, A25 212
Jordan v United Kingdom, Appln 24746/94, Judgment of 4 May 2001 114
Karataç v Turkey, Reports of Judgments and Decisions 1999-IV 213
Lindsay v United Kingdom, Appln 8364/78, Decision of 8 March 1979 ..... 134, 135, 234
Loizidou v Turkey, A310 .... 178, 213
Lykourezos v Greece, Appln 33554/03, Judgment of 15 June 2006................ 188
Mathieu-Mohin and Clerfayt v Belgium, Appln 9267/81, Judgment of
   2 March 1987................................ 122, 133, 183, 216, 673
Matthews v United Kingdom, Appln 24833/94, Judgment of
   18 February 1999 .... 105, 188, 216
Melnychenko v Ukraine, Reports of Judgments and Decisions 2004-X 189
Mikryukov v Russia, Appln 7363/04, 8 December 2005 674
Moldovan v Romania, Appln 41138/98 and 64320/01, Judgment of 12 July 2005 573
Mólka v Poland, Appln 56550/00, 11 April 2006............................ 674
Nachovo v Bulgaria, Appln 43577/98 and 43579/98, Judgment of 6 July 2005 121
National Union of Belgian Police v Belgium, Appln 4464/70, Judgment of
   27 October 1975.. 112
Noack v Germany, Reports of Judgments and Decisions 2000-VI........... 209, 210, 219
Oberschlick v Austria (no 2), 1 July 1997................................. 356
Ocalan v Turkey, Reports of Judgments and Decisions 2005-IV................. 213
Örhan v Turkey, Appln 25656/94, Judgment of 18 February 2002................. 213
Parti Nationaliste Basque-Organisation Régionale D'Iparralde v France, Appln 71251/01,
   Judgment of 7 June 2007.. 202
Petrovic v Austria, Appln 20458/925, Judgment of 27 March 1998 112
Platform 'Arzte fur das Leben' v Austria, Appln 10126/82, 21 June 1988 357
Podkolzina v Latvia, Appln 46726/99, Judgment of 9 July 2002.......... 121, 133, 188,
                                                        189, 190, 248, 249
Polacco and Garofalo v Italy, Appln 23450/94, decision 15 September 1997......... 209
Pretty v United Kingdom, Reports of Judgments and Decisions 2002-III 209
Py v France, Appln 66289/01, Judgment of 6 June 2005............ 105, 189, 216, 217
Refah Partisi (The Welfare Party) v Turkey, Appln 41340/98, 41342/98,
   41343/98, Grand Chamber, Judgment of 13 February 2003 .... 124, 196, 198,
                                                        200, 201, 218
Rekvényi v Hungary, Reports of Judgments and Decisions 1999, III [GC] 191
Russian Conservative Party of Entrepreneurs v Russia, Appln 55066/00 and
   55638/00, Judgment of 11 January 2007................................ 188
Sahin v Turkey, Reports of Judgments and Decisions 2005-XI................... 208
Santoro v Italy, Appln 36681/97 .... 673, 674
Schmidt and Dahlstrohm v Sweden, Appln 5589/72, Judgment of 6 February 1976.... 112
Schmidt v Germany, Appln 13580/88, Judgment of 18 July 1994 112
Sejdić and Finci v Bosnia and Herzegovina, Appln 27996/06 and
   34836/06 .... 142, 143, 236
Selcuk and Asker v Turkey, Appln 23184/94, Judgment of 24 April 1998........... 573
Sidiropolous v Greece, Appln 26695/95, Judgment of 10 July 1998 .... 125, 209, 233
Silver v United Kingdom, A61 210
Socialist Party v Turkey, Reports of Judgments and Decisions 1998-III........ 195, 196,
                                                        197, 198
Soering v United Kingdom, A161....................................... 213
Stankov and the United Macedonian Organisation Ilinden v Bulgaria,
   Appln 2922/95 and 29225/95, Judgment of 2 October 2001....... 125, 126, 210, 233
Stec v United Kingdom, Appln 65731/01 131

Table of Cases

Sunday Times v United Kingdom [1979] ECHR 1 356
Tnase and Chirtoaca v Moldova, Appln 7/08, Judgment of 18 November 2008 192
Thlimmenos v Greece, Appln 34369/97, Judgment of 6 April 2000 .... 121, 122, 130,
    131, 209, 511, 572
Timishev v Russia, Reports of Judgments and Decisions 2005-XII 188, 194
Timke v Germany, Appln 27311/95, Decision of 12 July 1976 673
Toxo v Greece, Appln 74989/01, Judgment of 20 October 2005 .... 124, 125, 202
Turek v Slovakia, Appln 57986/00, Judgment of 14 February 2006 212
United Communist Party of Turkey v Turkey, Appln 19392/92, Judgment of
    30 January 1998 .... 124, 126, 197, 198
United Communist Party of Turkey v Turkey, Reports of Judgments and
    Decisions 1998-I [GC] 197, 198, 199, 233, 348
United Macedonian Organisation Ilinden and Ivanov v Bulgaria, Appln 44079/98,
    Judgment of 20 October 2005 197
United Macedonian Organisation Ilinden-Pirin v Bulgaria, Appln 59489/00,
    Judgment of 20 October 2005 .... 197, 233
Van Raalte v Netherlands, Appln 20060/92, Judgment of 21 February 1997 112
Vo v France, Reports of Judgments and Decisions 2004-VIII 208
W v United Kingdom, A121 209
Wingrove v United Kingdom, Reports of Judgments and Decisions 1996-V 196
X v Austria, Appln 7008/76, Decision of 12 July 1976 673
X v United Kingdom DR 3 p 165 180
Xuereb v Malta, Appln 52492/99, 2 July 2002 674
Young, James and Webster v United Kingdom [1981] ECHR 4 357
Yumak and Sadak v Turkey, Appln 10226/03, Judgment of 8 July 2008 .... 123, 180, 181,
    183, 184, 185,
    186,187, 189, 1096
Yumak and Sadak v Turkey, Appln 10226/03, Judgment of 30 January 2007 ... 69, 70, 186
Zdanoka v Latvia, Appln 58278/00, Judgment of 16 March 2006 .... 120, 182, 187, 188,
    190, 191, 193,
    194, 195, 213, 680
Zhechev v Bulgaria, Appln 18147/02, Judgment of 5 April 2007 .... 198, 203
Znamenskaya v Russia, Appln 77785/01, Judgment of 2 June 2005 210

Inter-American Commission of Human Rights
    Maya indigenous community of the Toledo District v Belize, Case 12.053 569
    Yanomami Community v Brazil, Case 7615 569

Inter-American Court of Human Rights
    Advisory Opinion 18, 17 September 2003 570
    Advisory Opinion OC-18, 17 September 2003 99
    Indigenous Community of Yakye Axa v Paraguay 570
    Mayagna (sumo) Awas Tingni Community v Nicaragua, 31 August 2001,
        Series C no 79 570
    Moiwana Village v Suriname, 15 June 2005, Series C no 124 570
    Rios Brito v Argentina, Petition no 10109, Resolution no 26/88 124
    Saramaka People v Suriname (Preliminary Objections, Merits, Reparations and
        Costs), Judgment of 28 November 2007, Series C no 172 .... 314, 335
    YATAMA v Nicaragua (Preliminary Objections, Merits, Reparations and Costs),
        Judgment of 23 June 2005, Series C no 127 .... 314, 318, 319, 321, 322, 341

International Court of Justice
    Minority Schools in Albania, Advisory Opinion on (1935) Ser A/B No 64 130
    South West African Cases [1966] ICJ Reports 3 ....100, 101

Permanent Court of International Justice
  Germany v Poland, 25 May 1926, Series A no 7 and 26 April Series A no 15 127
UN Human Rights Committee
  Althammer v Austria, Communication no 998/2001, 21 March 2002. 114
  Aumeeruddy-Cziffra and nineteen other Mauritian women v Mauritius,
    17 September 2009 352
  Ballantyne v Canada, Communication no 359/1989 562
  Costa v Uruguay, Communication no 198/1995. 136
  Debreczeny v The Netherlands, Communication no 500/1992. 117
  Diergaardt v Namibia, Communication no 1760/1996 562
  Gillot v France, Communication no 932/2000, 26 July 2002. .... 117, 217
  Ignatane v Latvia, Communication no 884/1999, 25 July 2001 .... 120, 121, 248
  Jacobs v Belgium, Communication no 943/2000, 7 July 2004 136
  JGA Diergaardt v Namibia, Communication no 460/1997, 25 July 2000 553
  Jonassen v Norway, Communication no 942/2000, 25 October 2002.............. 554
  Kitok v Sweden, Communication no 197/1985, 27 July 1988 .... 146, 147, 553
  Lânsman v Finland, Communication no 511/1992, 26 October 1994.............. 554
  Lânsman v Finland, Communication no 671/1995, 22 November 1996 .... 500, 532,
                                                                         553, 554
  Lovelace v Canada, Communication no R6/24 International
    instruments, 30 July 1981.. 145, 146
  Magnago and Südtiroler Volkspartei v Italy, Appln 25035/94, Decision
    15 April 1996 137
  Mahuika v New Zealand, Communication no 547/1993,
    27 October 2000. .... 131, 482, 553, 554
  Marshall v Canada, Communication no 205/1986 497
  Peitraroia on behalf of Rosa Peitraoia Zapala v Uruguay, Communication
    no 44/1979... 117, 356
  RD Stalla Costa v Uruguay, 17 September 2009............................. 353
  Sister Immaculate Jospeh and Eight Teaching Sisters of the Holy Cross of the
    Third Order of Saint Francis in Menzingen v Sri Lanka, Communication
    no 1249/2004 563
  SWM Broeks v Netherlands, 17 September 2009 352
  Waldman v Canada, Communication no 694/1996............................. 562

Table of International Treaties and Conventions

African Charter of Human and Peoples'
  Rights 346, 351, 570
  Art 2 . . . . 99, 110
  Art 3 . . . . 99, 110
  Art 13 104
American Declaration on the Rights of
  Indigenous Peoples (draft) 314
Berlin Declaration of the OSCE Parliamentary
  Assembly and Resolutions
  (2002) 509, 510
Central European Initiative Instrument for
  the Protection of Minority
  Rights (1994)
  Art 20 480
Charter for European Security
  (Istanbul Summit), 18–19
  November 1999 347
  Art 22 480
Charter of Fundamental Rights
  of the European Union
  (2000) 219, 346, 348
  Art 11 355
  Art 21(1) 352
  Art 52(1) 356, 357
Charter of Paris (1990). 263
CIS Convention on Human Rights
  and Fundamental Freedoms (1995)
  Art 3(1)(b) 362
  Art 3(2) 361
  Art 9(4) 361
  Art 17(1) 361
  Art 18(1)(a) 361
  Art 19(e). 361
Comprehensive Proposal for the Kosovo
  Status Settlement (Ahtisaari plan) 86
  Annex I, Art 3(2)–(3) 86

Congress of Vienna (1814) 4
Convention on Conciliation and
  Arbitration within the CSCE
  (1992) 258
Convention on the Elimination of All
  Forms of Discrimination against
  Women (1976). 102, 110, 301
  Art 1 . . . . 114, 116
  Art 2 353
  Art 4 129
  Art 4(1) 102
  Art 7 . . . . 111, 129, 156, 288
  Art 7(a)-(b). 353
  Art 8 129
  Art 24 353
Convention on the Elimination of All Forms
  of Racial Discrimination
  (1965) 102, 110, 194,
    263, 264, 268, 349, 523,
    536, 706, 736
  Art 1 . . . . 107, 114, 288
  Art 1(1) 115, 116
  Art 1(4) 135
  Art 2(1) 128
  Art 2(2) 558
  Art 2(3) 560
  Art 3 559
  Art 4 126
  Art 5 . . . . 110, 264, 288, 558
  Art 5(b) 349
  Art 5(c) 353
  Art 14 116
Convention on the Participation of
  Foreigners in Public Life at Local
  Level (1992)
  Art 6(1) 92

Convention on the Protection of the Rights of
All Migrant Workers and Members of
their Families (2003) 561, 567, 568
Convention on the Rights of the Child
(1990) 568
Declaration on Principles Guiding Relations
between Participating States of the
Final Act of Helsinki 275
Principle No VII 259
Declaration of Principles for International
Election Observation and Code of
Conduct for International Election
Observers (2005) 365
Draft Convention on Election Standards,
Electoral Rights and Freedoms
(ACEEEO)
Art 2(6) 361
Art 8(1) 361
Art 8(5) 361
Art 9(1) 362
Art 9(2) 362
Art 12(2) 360
Art 17(7) 361
Art 21 361
Draft Declaration on the Rights of Indigenous
Peoples (2008) 569
European Charter of Local
Self-Government 662, 738
Preamble 670
Art 2 738
Art 3 675
Art 4(3) 144, 671, 672, 673
Art 9 670
Art 11 .... 591, 738
European Charter for Regional or Minority
Languages 706
Art 7(4) 481
European Convention for the Protection of
Human Rights and Fundamental
Freedoms (1950) 63, 102, 111,
178, 179, 180, 181, 182,
189, 212, 213, 216, 218, 219,
220, 226, 227, 263, 346,
347, 351, 536,617, 662, 706
Art 1 189
Art 2 .... 180, 208
Art 3 .... 179, 195, 213
Art 4 179
Art 6(1) 180
Art 8 .... 209, 210, 217, 571, 572
Arts 8–11 .... 180, 182, 208, 213
Art 8(2) 210
Art 9 .... 209, 227, 355
Art 10 .... 187, 191, 195, 209, 227, 355
Art 10(1) 196
Art 10(2) 182, 196, 356
Art 11 .... 187, 191, 195, 197, 198,
200, 209, 227, 232, 233, 234, 511
Art 11(1) 197, 357
Art 11(2) 182, 197, 198, 233, 357
Art 13 738
Art 14 .... 99, 110, 111, 112,
118, 119, 120, 121, 126,
130, 136, 142, 149, 183, 188,
190, 194, 208, 209, 264, 352
Art 15(1) 189
Art 15(3) 189
Art 16 208
Art 17 190
Art 19 180
Art 32(1) 178
Art 35 200
Art 46(2) 180
Art 53 .... 194, 216
Art 56(3) 217
Protocol 1
Art 2 209
Art 3 .... 70, 105, 111, 112,
118, 119, 120, 122, 134,
136, 142, 149, 182, 183,
185, 186, 187, 188, 189,
190, 192, 193, 194, 198,
202, 208, 216, 217, 248, 264,
347, 348, 364, 511, 673, 674, 738

Protocol 12............. 99, 100, 110,
    111, 142, 149, 194, 209, 565
  Art 1 .... 142, 194
European Social Charter
    (Revised) 250, 536, 571, 573, 574
  Art E 130
Framework Convention for the Protection
    of National Minorities
    (1995) 1, 65, 77,
    87, 102, 133, 151, 211, 219, 220,
    223, 226, 227, 229, 230, 245, 246,
    253, 254, 271, 272, 280, 282, 284,
    310, 401, 404, 408, 416, 438, 440,
    478, 489, 501, 506, 512, 522, 523,
    526, 527, 528, 535, 536, 537, 549,
    556, 558, 574, 584, 586, 587, 590,
    662, 672, 693, 706, 707, 708, 713,
    714, 715, 717, 718, 721, 723, 725,
    726, 727, 733, 734, 736, 738,
    739, 743, 749
  Preamble 209
  Art 2(2) 512
  Art 3 .... 246, 247, 248, 745
  Art 3(1) 83, 435
  Art 3(2) 225
  Art 4 ...... 89, 99, 112, 132, 133, 224,
    238, 250, 251, 255, 361, 536,
    537, 538, 539, 540, 541, 542,
    544, 551
  Art 4(2) 132
  Art 5 .... 89, 112, 133, 224, 228,
    536, 537, 538, 539
  Art 5(1) 131, 211
  Art 6 .... 537, 538
  Art 7 .... 227, 233, 234
  Art 8 227
  Art 9 .... 227, 353, 538
  Art 10 .... 538, 548, 550
  Art 12 .... 537, 541, 542
  Art 12(1) 538
  Art 12(3) 538
  Art 13 .... 537, 538, 541
  Art 14 .... 224, 537

Art 15 .... 74, 89, 106, 107, 108,
    112, 121, 143, 149, 223, 224, 225,
    226, 228, 230, 232, 249, 250, 254,
    263, 279, 350, 353, 439, 479, 480,
    512, 529, 531, 536, 537, 538,
    539, 540, 541, 542, 544, 672,
    673, 709, 714, 717, 721, 723, 728,
    729, 737, 738, 740, 745, 746
  Art 16 .... 235, 360, 729
  Art 18 .... 728, 729
  Art 20 .... 145, 224
  Art 21 224
  Art 23 227
  Arts 24–26 714
  Art 26 .... 536, 708, 714
General Framework Agreement for Peace
    in Bosnia and Herzegovina
    (Dayton Agreement) 86, 142,
    143, 193
  Art IV 193, 194
  Art V 194
    para 1 236
German-Ukrainian Agreement
  Art 15 719
Gruber-Degasperi Agreement (1946) ... 446
Hungarian-Croatian Convention
  Art 16 .... 719, 720
Hungarian-Macedonian Agreement
  Art 14 720
Hungarian-Romanian Agreement
  Art 11 720
Hungarian-Slovenian Convention
  Art 15 719
Hungary-Ukrainian Declaration
  Art 16 720
ILC Draft Articles on State
    Responsibility (21001)
  Art 33(2) 179
ILO Convention on Discrimination
    (Employment and Occupation) (1958)
    (No 111) 585
ILO Convention on Forced Labour
    (1930) (No 29).............. 585

ILO Convention on Indigenous and Tribal
    Peoples in Independent Countries (1957)
    (No 107) 585, 626
ILO Convention on Indigenous and Tribal
    Peoples in Independent Countries (1989)
    (No 169) 313, 334, 482,
        528, 585, 614, 620, 626, 739
    Art 1(a) 328
    Art 1(b) 328
    Art 4 313
    Art 6(1a). 313
    Art 6(1b) 313
    Art 7(1) 313
    Art 13(1) 329
    Arts 13–17 329
ILO Convention on Migrant Workers
    (1949) (No 97). 585
ILO Convention on Migrant Workers (1975)
    (No 143) 585
Indigenous and Tribal Peoples Convention
    (1989) 219
Inter-American Convention on Human
    Rights 346, 351, 569
    Art 1 . . . . 99, 110
    Art 23 104
    Art 24 . . . . 99, 110
    Art 26 569
    San Salvador Protocol 569
Inter-American Democratic Charter (2001)
    Art 5 319
International Covenant on Civil and Political
    Rights (1966) 115, 117, 219,
        268, 280, 301, 346, 348,
        349, 351, 706, 736
    Art 1 . . . . 288, 291, 312, 553
    Art 1(1) 215
    Art 2 . . . . 110, 146, 248
    Art 2(1) 110, 349, 352
    Art 2(3) 591, 738
    Art 3 146
    Art 12 92
    Art 12(4) 92
    Art 18 355
Art 19 356
Art 19(1) 355
Art 19(2) 355
Art 19(3) 356
Art 20 . . . . 126, 145
Art 21 357
Art 22 92
Art 22(1) 357
Art 25 . . . . 92, 99, 103, 110, 117,
        263, 288, 301, 353, 364,
        614, 615, 619, 738
Art 26 . . . . 114, 146, 288, 349, 561, 562
Art 27 . . . . 91, 106, 131, 145, 146,
        147, 149, 211, 223, 225, 264,
        288, 304, 310, 349, 553, 554,
        555, 562, 572, 586, 614, 619, 626, 637
International Covenant on Economic, Social
    and Cultural Rights (1976) . . 563, 736
    Art 1 312
    Art 1(1) 215
    Art 2(2) 99
    Art 12 563
    Art 12(3) 563
    Art 15(1)(a) 294
IPU Universal Declaration on Democracy
    (1997) 181
    para 12. 203
Stability Pact for Europe (Paris, 20 and 21
    March 1995)
    Art 5 37
Statute of the Council of Europe
    Preamble. 208
Taif Agreement (1989) 86, 443
Treaty on Conventional Armed Forces in
    Europe (1990) 258
Treaty of Lausanne (1923) 73
Treaty on Open Skies (1992) 258
Treaty of Sèvres 73
Treaty of Versailles (1919) 4
Treaty of Waitangi (1840). 317
UN Charter 641
    Art 1(3) 194
    Art 4(1) 258

Art 55c 194
Art 73e 215
UN Committee on the Elimination of
  Discrimination against Women
  General Recommendation 23 129
  General Recommendation 25 . . . 101, 102
UN Declaration on the Right to Development
  (1986) 289, 297
  Art 1(1) 289
  Art 2(1) 289
  Art 2(2) 289
  Art 8(2) 289
UN Declaration on the Rights of Indigenous
  Peoples (2007) 298, 309, 313,
                              328, 482, 556
  Art 2 556
  Art 3 . . . . 312, 556
  Art 4 . . . . 328, 557, 619
  Art 5 . . . . 556, 619
  Art 10 . . . . 313, 556
  Art 14 556
  Art 17(3) 556
  Art 19 313
  Art 23 556
  Art 25 329
  Arts 25–29 329
  Art 26 556
  Art 29(2) 313
UN Declaration on the Rights of Persons
  Belonging to National or Ethnic,
  Religious and Linguistic Minorities
  (1992) 76, 77, 91, 144, 288,
                291, 298, 299, 304, 305, 306,
                309, 349, 479, 480, 536,
                571, 620, 626, 662, 718, 739
  Art 1 . . . . 112, 131
  Art 2 . . . . 106, 263, 349, 417, 510,
                                      511, 709
  Art 2(2) 74, 288, 290, 291, 531,
                              656, 710, 718, 719
  Art 2(3) 74, 144, 288, 292,
                                      293, 670

Art 2(4) 2912
Art 2(5) 291
Art 3 . . . . 349, 655
Art 3(2) 83
Art 4 . . . . 106, 112,
                                      131, 655
Art 4(1) 131
Art 4(5) 288, 293
Art 5 . . . . 106, 655
Arts 5–7 718
Art 5(1) 288, 293
Art 5(2) 718
Art 6 718
Art 7 719
Art 11 619
Art 22 619
Art 23 619
UNESCO Convention against
  Discrimination in Education
  Art 5.1 647
Universal Declaration of Human Rights
  (1948) 210, 280, 346, 351,
                              362, 614, 739
  Art 2 . . . . 99, 352
  Art 4 207
  Art 4(2) 131
  Art 5 207
  Art 7 . . . . 99, 207
  Art 18 355
  Art 19 355
  Art 20(1) 357
  Art 21 . . . . 103, 346
  Art 21(1) 346
  Art 21(3) 180, 346, 364
  Art 27 614
  Art 29(2) 207, 357
  Art 21 263
Vienna Convention on the Law of
  Treaties (1969)
  Arts 26–33 258
  Art 31(1) 212

Table of National Legislation

Aceh
    Law 11–2006 on the Governing of
        Aceh, 11 June 2006. 337
        Art 1.10 337
        Art 1.7 337
        Art 16 337
        Art 17 337
        Art 51 337
        Art 96 337
        Art 98 337
    Law 18/2001, 9 August 2001 337
Argentina
    Law 23302 on Indigenous Policy
        and Support to Aboriginal
        Communities, 30 September 1985,
        amended by Law 25.799, 5
        November 2003
        Art 5 324
    Resolution of the National Institute
        for Indigenous Affairs 152/2004,
        establishing the Council for Indigenous
        Participation, amended by Decree
        301/04 324
Australia
    Aboriginal and Torres Strait Islander Act
        1989 325
    Human Rights and Equal Opportunity
        Commission Act 1986 (Cth), July 2008
        s 46C.1b 325
    Native Title Act, 1993, no 110, 24
        December 1993, amended by the Native
        Title Amendment Act 2007, no 61
        Pt 11 327
Austria
    Autonomy Statute (1976) 81, 745
    Constitution (1983)
        Art 86 597
    Equal Treatment Act, as amended . . . 598

Belgium
    Constitution (1970)
        Art 151 597
Bolivia
    Art 192. 336
    Political Constitution
        (2009) 320, 323, 335
        Art 146(7) 321
        Art 191 336
        Arts 196–204 318
        Art 208 320
    Popular Participation Law (Amendments
        and Additions to Law no 1551) . . . 319
    Popular Participation Law no 1551
        (20 April 1994). 319, 320, 321,
        323, 334
    Project of Law of Justice of Indigenous
        Peoples and Indigenous-Peasant
        Communities (2001) 335
Bosnia and Herzegovina
    Constitution 141, 142, 193
        Art II.4. 602
        Art III.3.b. 602
        Art VI.1.a. 601
        Art VI.1.b. 601
    Electoral Code 141
    Law on National Minorities (2003)
        Art 19 448
Brazil
    Constitution, 5 October 1988
        Arts 231–232 333
    Indian Statute Act 6001 of 19 December
        1973, as amended
        Arts 17–33 333
Bulgaria
    Constitution
        Art 11 233
    Decree no 333 of 2004 484

Canada
  British North American Act 1867 ... 330
  Constitution Act 1867 330
    s 91.24 330
  Constitution Act 1982 331
  Indian Act 146
  Nunavut Act 1993 333
    Art 11 333
    Art 12 333
    Art 31 333
Chile
  Law 19253 establishing norms for the protection, promotion and development of indigenous peoples and creating the National Commission on Indigenous Development, amended by Law 19587, modifying Law 19253 regarding the constitution of the dominion in the Easter Islands for the members of the Rapa Nui community, 13 November 1993 ... 324
Colombia
  Decree 2164 (Indigenous Lands), 7 December 1995 330
  Law 89, 25 November 1890 330
    Art 1 330
    Art 5 330
    Art 40 330
  Law 160, 3 August 1994
    Art 6 330
  Political Constitution (1991)
    Art 171 316
    Art 176 316
  Project of Statutory Law on Indigenous Special Jurisdiction (2003) 335
Costa Rica
  Draft Law of Autonomous Indigenous Development, 22 November 1994 ... 325
  Indigenous Act, Act 6172 of 17 November 1977
    Art 4 334
Croatia
  Constitution
    Art 15 139

Constitutional Law on the Rights of National Minorities (2002) 743
  Art 20 449
  Art 22 .... 80, 450
  Art 22.2 .... 448, 449, 604
Law on Amendments to the Law on the Election of Members of Representative Bodies of Local and Regional Self-Government Units (2003) 449
Law on the Census of Population, Households and Dwellings, Law no 64/2000, 27 June 2000 603
Law on Civil Servants (2005)
  Art 42.2 449
Law on the Election of Representatives to the Croatian Parliament 83
Law on Elections of Parliamentarians to Sabor (2003)
  Art 15 139
  Art 16 139
Law on Local and Regional Self-Government
  Art 56.a.2 450
Law on the State Administration System
  Art 8 449
Cyprus
  Constitution
    Art 63 118
    Art 123 443
    Art 124 443
    Art 125 443
Ecuador
  Law on the Administration of Justice by Indigenous Authorities (2001) ... 335
  Political Constitution (28 September 2008)
    Arts 109–112 320
    Art 117 321
  Special State Decentralization and Social Participation Law of 1997 323
    Art 42 320

Table of National Legislation

European Community
  Commission Communication on Immigration, Integration and Employment (2003) 580
  Commission Decision 2006/33/EC of 20 January 2006 establishing a high-level advisory group on social integration of ethnic minorities and their full participation in the labour market ... 579
  Directive 2003/86/EC of 22 September 2003 on the right to family reunification 581
  Directive 2003/109/EC on the Status of third-country nationals who are long-term residents 581
    Art 5 581
    Art 11 581
    Art 11(4) 581
    Art 14 581
  Directive 2004/38 of 29 April 2004 on the right of citizens of the Union and their family members to move and reside freely within the territory of the Member States 582
  EC Treaty
    Art 39(4) 245
  Employment Equality Directive 2000/78/EC 576, 577
  Racial Equality Directive 2000/43/EC 576, 577, 578, 587
  Treaty of Amsterdam 580
    Art 13 576
  Treaty on European Union (Maastricht Treaty) (1992) 348
  Treaty of Lisbon 575, 577
Finland
  Act on the Sami Parliament, Act 974, 17 July 1995, amended by decrees of 22 December 1995 and 2 March 1996 .... 338, 340
    Art 1 339
    Art 4 339
    Art 5 339
    Art 8 339
    Art 9 339
  Cabinet Decree on the Sami Council 9 November 1973 338
  Constitution of Finland, 11 June 1999
    s 17 338
    s 121 338
  Finnish Language Act 423/2003 485
France
  Constitution
    Art 1(2) 438
Germany
  Constitution (1949)
    Art 94 597
Greenland
  Constitutional Act of Greenland, 5 June 1953, as amended
    Art 28 332
  Home Rule Act 577, 29 November 1978 332
Hungary
  Act on Local Governments 520
  Constitution
    Art 68 489
  Law LXXVII on the Rights of National and Ethnic Minorities (1993) 82, 679, 680, 698, 743
India
  Constitution (9th Amendment) Act 2006
    Art 33 316
  Constitution (1949) 316
    Art 16 443
    Art 332 316
    Art 335 443
    Art 336 443
  Constitutional Act 1995 443
Indonesia
  Law on General Elections (2003) 48
Italy
  Constitutional law no 2 of 31 January 2001 .... 86, 740

Kosovo
  Constitution of the Republic of
    Kosovo (2008)
    Art 61 447
    Art 81 741
    Art 96 427
    Art 102(4) 600
    Art 103(3) 600
    Art 103(6) 600
    Art 104(3) 600
    Art 108(2) 600
    Art 108(6) 600
    Art 108(9) 601
    Art 108(10) 601
    Art 114(3) 600
    Art 148 86
  Constitutional Framework for Provisional
    Self-Government in Kosovo (2001)
    Art 9.3.5 427
  Rules of Procedure, Government of
    Kosovo (2008)
    Art 7 427
  UNMIK Administrative Direction no
    2003/2 447
  UNMIK Regulation 2001/36 on the
    Kosovo Civil Service 447
Lebanon
  Constitution
    Art 95 .... 86, 443
  Law on Minority Rights and Freedoms
    (2006) 443
Macedonia
  Constitution (1991) 38
    Art 8.2..................... 447
    Art 69 440
    Art 109.2 440
  Law on the Territorial Division of the
    Republic of Macedonia 1996 55
  Law on the Use of Flags of
    Communities 440
Mexico
  Code of Political Institutions and Electoral
    Procedures of the State of Oaxaca, Decree
    no 185 (12 February 1992), as amended
    by Decree 203, 1 October 1997,
    Decree 205, 9 October 1997 and
    Decree 723, 31 October 2008
    Arts 131–143 323
  Law of the National Commission for
    the Development of Indigenous Peoples
    (21 May 2003)
    Art 5 324
    Art 11 324
    Art 12 324
  Political Constitution of the Free
    and Sovereign State of Durango,
    as amended, 26 November 2000
    Art 2(A)(VII) 323
  Political Constitution of the State of
    San Luis Potosi, as amended, 15
    August 2006
    Art 9 323
  Political Constitution of the United
    States of Mexico (31 December 1917),
    as amended by Decree
    (14 August 2001) 328
    Art 2.A..................... 335
Moldova
  Law on the Special Legal Status of
    Gagauzia, no 344-XIII (1994)
    Art 22 601
Montenegro
  Constitution
    Art 79 448
  Law on Minority Rights and
    Freedoms (2006)
    Art 25 448
    Art 25(2) 448
Nepal
  National Foundation for
    Development of Nationalities
    Act (2002)
    Art 7 325
    Art 10 325
New Caledonia
  Institutional Act (1999) 216

New Zealand
  Maori Fisheries Act 2004,
    no 78, 25 September 2004
      ss 30–50 327
  Maori Land Act 1993, as amended by
    Maori Land Amendment Act 2004
      ss 6–16 327
  Treaty of Waitangi Act 1975
      s 5(2) 317
      Sch 1 317
  Treaty of Waitangi Amendment Act
    2008 317
Nicaragua
  Autonomy Statute (1987) 322
      Art 19 322
  Communal Land Law 445, 13
    December 2002 327
      Arts 4–10 334
      Art 41 327
      Art 42 327
  Electoral Law no 331 (19 January
    2000) 319
      Art 82 320
  Law of Additions to Art 3 of Law 331
      Art 77 319
Nigeria
  Constitution
      Art 14 442
      Art 153 442
  Decree 34 of 1996
      s 4(1c) 442
Northern Ireland
  Fair Employment (Northern Ireland) Act
    1989 442
      s 31 442
  Ministerial Code of the Executive
      Art 2.12 432
Norway
  Act Concerning the Sami Assembly and
    Other Sami Matters, Act no 56 of 12
    June 1987 .... 338, 657
      Art 1.1 339
      Art 2.7 340

  Art 3 657
  Art 12 657
  Act relating to the legal relations and
    management of land and natural
    resources in the county of
    Finnmark, Act 85, 17
    June 2005 .... 338, 339
  Constitution of the Kingdom of Norway,
    16 May 1816, as amended
      Art 110a 338, 656, 657
Panama
  Law no 2, 23 September 1938, amended
    by Law no 16 332
  Law no 10, 11 March 1997 332
  Law no 22, 17 January 1984 332
  Law no 3428 July 2000 332
  Political Constitution, 4 June 1904, as
    amended by Legislative Acts of 5
    November 1924 and 25 September
    1928
      Art 4 331
  Political Constitution, 1941
      Art 5 331
Papua
  Preamble, para e 337
  Act 21/2001 on Special Autonomy
    for the Papua Province, 23 October
    2001 337
      Art 1.d 337
      Art 1.l 337
      Art 1.p 337
      Art 19 337
      Art 43 337
      Arts 56–66 337
  Law 45/1999 concerning the
    Establishment of the Provinces of
    Central Irian Jaya, West Irian Jaya,
    Regencies of Paniai, Mimika,
    Puncak Jaya and Municipality of
    Sorong 337
  Presidential Decree 1/2003 concerning
    the Acceleration of the Implementation
    of Law 45/1999 337

Peru
  Draft Law on Constitutional Development
    of Art 191:4 335
  Draft Law establishing the Permanent Table
    of Negotiation with Native Communities
    and Aboriginal Peoples, 9 October
    2008 325
  Law 27734, 28 May 2002
    Art 103 322
  Municipal Election Law 2684, 26
    September 1997
    Art 10 322
  Regional Election Law 27683, 14
    March 2002
    Art 12 322
Philippines
  Indigenous Peoples Right Act of 1997
    s 50 325
Romania
  Draft Law on the Statute of
    National Minorities Living in
    Romania 742
  Justice System Act, Law no
    247/2005 597
Russian Federation
  Constitution
    Chapter 1, Art 12 675
    Chapter 8
      Art 131 675
      Art 130 675
  Federal Law on Political Parties
    (2001)
    Art 9.3..................... 48
  Law on General Principles of Organization
    of Local Self-Government in the
    Russian Federation of 6
    October 2003............ 676, 677
    Art 2 677
  Law on General Principles of Organization
    of Local Self-Government in the
    Russian Federation of 28 August
    1995 676

Law on Local Self-Government of 6 July
    1991 676
Law on Local Self-Government of
    1990 676
Serb Republic
  Constitution
    Art 77.2................... 447
    Art 92 431
  Law on Parliamentary Elections
    Art 81 744
  Law on the Protection of Rights and
    Freedoms of National Minorities
    (2002)
    Art 21 447
Slovenia
  Constitution
    Art 64 440
    Art 64(5) 741
    Art 80 440
Spain
  Constitution 651
    Art 1 654
    Art 2 652
    Art 3 .... 652, 654
Sri Lanka
  Constitution (1947)
    s 29.2c..................... 63
  Constitution (1972) 63
    s 18.2...................... 63
  Constitution (1978) 48
    s 157A..................... 48
Sweden
  Constitution of Sweden: Instrument of
    Government, 28 February 1974
    Art 20 338
  Sami Parliament Act, Act 1433,
    17 December 1992 338
    Art 1 339
    Art 2.1.................... 339
United Kingdom
  Canada Act 1982............... 649
    s 35 331

Government of Ireland Act 1920..... 63
   s 5.1....................... 63
Northern Ireland Constitution
   Act 1973 49
Race Relations Act 1976.......... 692
United States
   Constitution of Maine 316
   Voting Rights Act 1965 .... 37, 63, 64, 365

Venezuela
   Bolivarian Constitution (2009)
     Art 125 316
   Organic Law of Public Municipal Power, 8 June 2005
     Art 67 323
     Art 279 323
   Transitional Provision 7 (2002) 317
     Art 8 316

Table of Recommendations and Expert Advice

ACFC Commentary on Effective
    Participation 75, 151, 153,
        288, 305
    para 9 90
    paras 13–15 89
    para 16 89
    para 17 89
    paras 18–21 77
    para 38 305
    para 101 . . . . 92, 93
    para 141 76
Bolzano/Bozen Recommendations on
    National Minorities in Inter-State
    Relations (2008) 266, 709, 710
    para 19 . . . . 712, 713
Code of Good Practice in Electoral Matters:
    Guidelines and Explanatory Report
    (2002) (Venice Commission) 273,
        362, 744
    Art 2(2)(iv) 362
    Art 2(2)(vii) 362
    Art 3(1)(b)(iii) 361
    para 2.4(a)-(c) 273
Committee on the Elimination of Racial
    Discrimination General
    Recommendations
    No XXIII 314
Congress of Local and Regional Authorities
    Recommendation 43 (1998) 671
Council of Europe Recommendations
    No 563 512
    No 1201 (1993) 65, 91
    No 1203 512
    No 1255 (1995) 91
    No 1492 (2001) 91
    No 1557 . . . . 512, 513

Draft General Principles on Freedom and
    Non-Discrimination in the Matter of
    Political Rights
    principle V 352
European Commission against Racism and
    Intolerance
    General Policy Recommendation
    no 8 658
Geneva Report of the CSCE Meeting of
    Experts on National Minorities
    (1991) 263, 264, 266, 277, 280
Guidelines and Good Practice for Policing in
    Diverse Societies (OHCHR) 296,
        304, 306
Guidelines for National Periodic Reports
    (African Commission for Human and
    Peoples' Rights) 571
Guidelines to Assist National Minority
    Participation in the Electoral Process
    (2001) 74, 282, 360
Guidelines on the Use of Minority Languages
    in the Broadcast Media
    (2003) 107, 266
Hague Recommendations Regarding the
    Education Rights of National Minorities
    (1996) 107, 220, 266, 473, 474
Helsinki Document (1992) 259, 275,
        277, 710, 711
    para 24 . . . . 709, 710
    para 25 . . . . 710, 713
    para 26 711
Human Rights Committee General Comments
    No 10 . . . . 356, 564
    Art 13 564
    No 11 564
    No 12 619

No 14 563
No 15 564
  Art 16 564
No 18 .... 98, 100, 114,
              115, 116, 128, 352
No 20
  Art 1 350
  Art 5 350
No 21 .... 294, 306
No 22 355
No 23 .... 91, 106, 131, 264,
          288, 310, 314, 349, 353, 528,
          553, 564, 614, 619, 637
No 25 .... 92, 101, 103, 181,
              360, 361, 615
  Art 16 351
  Art 19 351
  Art 20 351
No 27 92
No 28 145
No 30 560
International Electoral Standards Guidelines for reviewing the legal framework of elections (2001) 352
International Seminar on Cooperation for the Better Protection of the Rights of Minorities Recommendations..... 294
  recommendation 22.............. 294
  recommendation 25.............. 295
  recommendation 26.............. 295
  recommendation 27.............. 295
  recommendation 33.............. 295
Lund Recommendations on the Effective Participation of National Minorities in Public (1999) 35, 64, 65, 69,
      107, 109, 144, 145, 150, 151, 152, 153,
      156, 157, 178, 179, 181, 199, 211, 215,
      220, 224, 225, 254, 256, 257, 261, 262,
      266, 267, 268, 273, 277, 280, 281, 282,
      283, 284, 285, 305, 308, 311, 318, 324,
      336, 340, 342, 360, 364, 365, 374, 385,
      401, 447, 467, 468, 472, 473, 474, 489,
      501, 505, 506, 507, 526, 527, 533, 534,
      536, 614, 616, 617, 620, 622, 623, 628,
      633, 635, 636, 637, 638, 640, 641,
      642, 643, 646, 654, 662, 669,
      681, 709, 710, 736, 747
  Introduction 179
  para 1................... 311, 466
  para 3....................... 278
  para 4....................... 435
  para 5....................... 711
  para 6........ 268, 438, 534, 587, 590
  paras 6–10 .... 268, 669
  paras 6–13 .... 468, 469, 470
  para 7........ 179, 181, 269, 438, 669
  para 8..... 125, 199, 275, 318, 438, 669
  para 9. 181, 269, 321, 374, 385, 438, 669
  para 10........... 181, 269, 374, 669
  para 11............... 324, 669, 670
  para 12... 278, 438, 493, 516, 533, 711,
              712, 713
  para 13... 278, 438, 499, 516, 713, 7110
  para 14.... 144, 215, 472, 643, 669, 670
  paras 14–21 .... 468, 469, 470
  para 15...................... 643
  para 16...................... 215
  para 17................. 215, 657
  para 18........... 215, 645, 654, 657
  para 19....... 179, 215, 282, 472, 669
  para 20................ 282, 622, 669
  para 21............... 145, 282, 622
  para 22..... 90, 468, 469, 470, 736, 737
  para 23..... 90, 468, 469, 470, 736, 737
  para 24........... 591, 713, 736, 749
  Explanatory Note..... 69, 90, 144, 145,
              156, 179, 385, 517,
              520, 643, 644, 646, 737
  General Principles 144, 151
  s 1................... 224, 622
  s 8....................... 69
  s 14..................... 622
OSCE Copenhagen Document (1990) 75, 76, 77, 144, 203,
              219, 226, 259, 268, 271, 273,
              284, 346, 347, 480, 512, 710, 736

para 5.1 . . . . 104, 145, 347	Recommendation 24 115
para 5.2 . . . . 104, 145, 347	Recommendation 27 . . . . 128, 129
para 5.6 364	UN Development Programme Resource
para 5.9 352	Guide on Minorities in
para 6 . . . . 104, 347, 351	Development 297, 306
para 7 . . . . 104, 105, 347	Warsaw Guidelines to Assist National
para 7.1 105	Minorities in the Electoral
para 7.2 105	Process (2001) 74, 113, 270, 271
para 7.3 105	World Conference against Racism, Racial
para 7.4 105	Discrimination, Xenophobia and
para 7.6 . . . . 105, 203	Related Intolerance Declaration
para 7.7 . . . . 105, 351, 355	(2001) 289, 303, 306
para 7.8 . . . . 105, 355	para 4 290
para 7.9 105	para 32 289
para 8 . . . . 105, 347	para 34 289
para 9.1 355	para 43 290
para 9.2 357	para 47 290
para 9.3 357	para 50 290
para 9.4 355	para 74 290
para 24 357	para 98 290
para 24.4 352	para 108 289
para 30 . . . . 591, 711	para 112 290
para 31 . . . . 112, 131	para 113 290
para 32 83	para 190 290
para 33 . . . . 112, 132, 144	World Conference against Racism, Racial
para 35 . . . . 74, 109, 144, 263, 479, 708	Discrimination, Xenophobia and
para 35(1) 710	Related Intolerance Outcome
para 40 508	Document 305
Oslo Recommendations Regarding the	para 70 290
Linguistic Rights of National Minorities	para 110 291
(1998) . . . 107, 220, 266, 466,473, 474	para 111 291
PACE Recommendation 1500 (2001) on the	para 113 291
Participation of Immigrants and Foreign	para 124 291
Residents in Political Life in the Council	para 127 291
of Europe Member States 92	World Conference against Racism, Racial
Recommendations on Policing in Multi-Ethnic	Discrimination, Xenophobia and
Societies (2006) 266	Related Intolerance Programme of
UN Committee on the Elimination of Racial	Action (2001) 289, 303, 306
Discrimination	para 190 290

List of Abbreviations

AC	Advisory Committee on the Framework Convention for the Protection of National Minorities
AfrCh	African Charter on Human and Peoples' Rights
ACHR	Inter-American Convention on Human Rights
AK	Justice and Development Party
ATSIC	Aboriginal and Torres Strait Islander Commission
AV	alternate vote
BDI	Albanian Democratic Union for Integration
BDN	Unity Party for Human Rights
BiH	Bosnia and Herzegovina
BIA	Bureau of Indian Affairs
BSP	Bulgarian Socialist Party
CAHMIN	Ad Hoc Committee for the Protection of National Minorities
CDI	Commission on Indigenous Development
CoE	Council of Europe
CEDAW	Convention on the Elimination of All Forms of Discrimination against Women
CEE	Central and Eastern Europe(an)
CERD	Convention on the Elimination of All Forms of Racial Discrimination
CESCR	Committee on Economic, Social and Cultural Rights
CHR	Commissioner for Human Rights
CHT	Chittagong Hill Tracts
CLNM	2002 Constitutional Law on the Rights of National Minorities
CLRAE	Congress of Local and Regional Authorities of the Council of Europe
CODENPE	Council for the Development of the Nationalities and Peoples of Ecuador
CONADETI	National Commission on Demarcation and Titling
CONADI	National Commission on Indigenous Development
CRC	Convention on the Rights of the Child
CSCE	Conference on Security and Cooperation in Europe
DAC	Development Assistance Committee
DEHAP	People's Democratic Party
DH-MIN	Committee of Experts on Issues relating to the Protection of National Minorities

List of Abbreviations

DINEB	National Direction of Bilingual Intercultural Education
DINSI	National Direction of Indigenous Health
DPS	Turkish Movement for Rights and Freedoms
ECHR	European Convention for the Protection of Human Rights and Fundamental Freedoms
ECtHR	European Court of Human Rights
ECJ	European Court of Justice
ECLSG	European Charter of Local Self-government
EED	Employment Equality Directive
EN	Explanatory Note
ERTF	European Roma and Travellers Forum
EU	European Union
EZLN	Zapatist National Liberation Army
fYROM	former Yugoslav Republic of Macedonia
FCNM	Framework Convention for the Protection of National Minorities
FPIC	free, prior, and informed consent
FUNAI	Federal National Foundation of the Indian
GEPG	Gender Equality in Political Governance Program
HADEP	People's Democracy Party
HCNM	High Commissioner on National Minorities
HDZ	Croat Democrat Community
HRC	Human Rights Committee
ICCPR	International Covenant on Civil and Political Rights
ICESCR	International Covenant of Economic, Social and Cultural Rights
ICG	International Crisis Group
IDEA	International Institute for Democracy and Electoral Assistance
IDF	Israeli Defence Forces
ILO	International Labour Organization
INAI	Institute for Indigenous Affairs
IPU	Inter-parliamentary Union
LR	Lund Recommendations
LTTE	Liberation Tigers of Tamil Eelam
MDGs	Millennium Development Goals
MKP	Hungarian Coalition Party
MMP	mixed member proportional voting
MRGI	Minority Rights Group International
MP	Member of Parliament
MSG	minority self-governments

List of Abbreviations

NDSV	National Movement Simeon II
NGO	non-governmental organization
NFDIN	National Foundation for Indigenous Development of Nepal
OHCHR	Office of the High Commissioner for Human Rights
ODIHR	Office for Democratic Institutions and Human Rights
OECD	Organisation of Economic Co-operation and Development
OSCE	Organization for Security and Cooperation in Europe
PBDNJ	Unity for Human Rights Party
PKK	Kurdistan Workers' Party
PR	proportional representation
PSD	Social Democratic Party
RED	Racial Equality Directive
RUC	Royal Ulster Constabulary
SCMR	special contact mechanisms for Roma
SFP	Swedish People's Party
SMR	single-member districts
SR	Serb Republic
STV	single transferable vote
TCN	third-country nationals
THAC	Traveller Health Advisory Committee
TRS	two-round system
UDF	Union of the Democratic Forces
UDMR	Democratic Alliance of Hungarians in Romania
UDR	Ulster Defence Regiment
UK	United Kingdom
UN	United Nations
UNDHR	United Nations Declaration of Human Rights
UNDP	United Nations Development Programme
UNDRIP	United Nations Declaration on the Rights of Indigenous Peoples
UNIEMI	United Nations Independent Expert on Minority Issues
UNIFEM	United Nations Development Fund for Women
UNMO	United Nations Military Observer
UNODC	United Nations Office on Drugs and Crime
US	United States
USAID	United States Agency for International Development
UUP	Ulster Unionist Party
Venice Commission	European Commission for Democracy through Law
WNC	Women's National Coalition
WTA	winner-takes-all

Notes on Contributors

Ilona Klímová-Alexander is an associate human rights officer at the Indigenous Peoples and Minorities Unit of the Office of the United Nations High Commissioner for Human Rights. She holds a PhD in international relations from the University of Cambridge and has taught and/or developed courses on international relations, nationalism and minority rights at the Charles University in Prague, University of New South Wales, Macquarie University, University of Sydney, and the University of Cambridge. Previously, she worked as a consultant for the World Bank, Organization for Security and Cooperation in Europe (OSCE), Council of Europe, European Union's Monitoring Centre on Racism and Xenophobia and International Centre for Migration Policy Development. She has published on issues of human and minority rights, nationalism, political participation, and migration, including a monograph entitled *The Romani Voice in World Politics: The United Nations and non-state actors* (2005).

Florian Bieber is a lecturer in East European politics at the University of Kent, Canterbury, UK. He received his MA in political science and history and his PhD in political science from the University of Vienna, as well as an MA in South-east European studies from Central European University (Budapest). In 2009 he held the Luigi Einaudi chair in European and international studies at Cornell University, New York. Between 2001 and 2006, he has been working in Belgrade (Serbia) and Sarajevo (Bosnia-Herzegovina) for the European Centre for Minority Issues. He is also a visiting professor at the Nationalism Studies Program at Central European University, at the Regional Masters Program for Democracy and Human Rights at the University of Sarajevo and the Interdisciplinary Master in East European Studies, University of Bologna. He has been an international policy fellow of the Open Society Institute. He is the editor-in-chief of *Nationalities Papers*. His research interests include institutional design in multiethnic states, nationalism and ethnic conflict, as well as the political systems of South-eastern Europe.

Karen Bird is associate professor of political science at McMaster University in Hamilton, Canada. She specializes in comparative politics, with particular attention to gender, ethnic diversity, and the politics of multiculturalism. She is currently working on two research projects. One examines the impact of gender parity laws in France, which require equal numbers of male and female candidates in most elections. The second examines ethnic minority representation in comparative perspective, focusing on differences in the political opportunity structure for minority candidates and representatives in different countries, and at different levels of elective office. Her new book, with Thomas Saalfeld and Andreas M Wüst, is entitled *The political Representation of Immigrants and Minorities: Voters, Parties and Parliaments in Liberal Democracies (2010).*

Bill Bowring is a professor of law at Birkbeck College, University of London, and is a practising barrister, taking cases against Russia and other former Soviet states to the European Court of Human Rights. His research interests include human rights, minority rights, international law and Soviet, post-Soviet, and Russian law. He has more than seventy scholarly publications; his recent book is *The Degradation of the International Legal Order?* (2008). He regularly acts as an expert and trainer for the Organization for Security and Cooperation in Europe, Council of Europe, and European Union on human and minority rights issues, and as a consultant on legal and judicial reform. He has fluent Russian, and has visited Russia and other FSU countries regularly since 1983.

Lars-Erik Cederman has taught at the Graduate Institute of International Studies in Geneva, Oxford, UCLA, and Harvard. He is now professor of international conflict research at ETH Zurich. His main research interests include computational modelling, quantitative and GIS-based conflict research, nationalism, integration and disintegration processes, and historical sociology.

Alain Chablais obtained a PhD from the University of Fribourg (Switzerland) in 1996 and worked for the Swiss Ministry of Justice to prepare a new Federal Constitution until 1998. In 1999 he moved to the Council of Europe in Strasbourg (France) and was given the opportunity to take part in the development of the monitoring mechanism of the Framework Convention for the Protection of National Minorities. Before his departure from the Council of Europe in 2009, he also worked for three years for the Venice Commission, including on national minority issues. Since 2009, he has been working as a judge with the Administrative Federal Court of Switzerland.

Krzysztof Drzewicki is senior legal adviser to the OSCE High Commissioner on National Minorities, The Hague. He holds a LLD and Dr Habilitus in international public law, and served as professor of the University of Gdańsk, Poland (on leave since 1997). In 1994 the minister of foreign affairs appointed him the Agent of the Government of Poland before the European Commission and Court of Human Rights. In his capacity as the government agent he was seconded as minister counsellor to the Permanent Representation of Poland in the Council of Europe in Strasbourg from 1999 till 2003 where he had continued to plead before the European Court of Human Rights. He has written more than ninety scholarly contributions on the international protection of human rights and international humanitarian law.

Yash Ghai was educated at Oxford and Harvard. He was awarded a doctorate of civil law by Oxford in 1990 and elected fellow of the British Academy in 2000. He was called to the English Bar and was admitted to practice law in Tanzania. He has been a law teacher for most of his professional life. He taught for ten years at the University College, Dar es Salaam (a constituent college of the University of East Africa) from 1963 to 1972, ending as the first East African Dean of the Law Faculty. His most recent academic appointment was as the first Sir YK Pao professor of public law at the University of Hong Kong (until the end of 2006). He has been a visiting professor at the Yale Law School, University of Toronto, Melbourne University, the National University of Singapore, University of Wisconsin, and the Harvard Law School. He has published extensively on public law, including human rights, and has advised various governments and political parties on constitutional matters, and was a consultant on the independence constitutions of Papua New Guinea, Solomon Islands, and Vanuatu. He was senior adviser on constitution-making in Afghanistan, Iraq and Nepal, chaired the Kenya Constitution Review Commission and the Kenya Constitution conference between

2000 and 2004, and is currently adviser on the constitutional making process in Somalia. Between 2005 and 2008, he was the Special Representative of the Secretary-General on human rights in Cambodia.

Kristin Henrard is professor in minority protection at the Erasmus University of Rotterdam (EUR) as well as associate professor in constitutional law. She teaches human rights, comparative human rights, minority protection, and constitutional law. Since February 2005 she has been working on a VIDI-project approved by the Netherlands Organization for Scientific Research (NOW) regarding the implications for minority protection of the Race Directive. Since 2005 she has been a member of the Young Academy of the Royal Dutch Academy of Sciences. In 2008 she established the Minority Research Network which has an ever-growing global and interdisciplinary membership.

Lanna Yael Hollo, director of Hollo Human Rights Consulting, holds an LLB from McGill University in Montreal and a Master's degree in political science from the University of Toronto, Canada. She specializes in minority rights and equality law and policy. For a number of years she worked as a legal and policy researcher at the European Commission against Racism and Intolerance. Her ongoing consulting work has recently focused on discrimination and security questions as well as minorities in Western Europe.

Emma Lantschner is a senior researcher at the Institute for Minority Rights at the European Academy Bolzano/Bozen (Italy) and of the Centre for South-east European Studies at the University of Graz. She attained her PhD in law at the University of Graz with a thesis on standard-setting and conflict management through the monitoring mechanisms of bilateral and multilateral instruments. She has worked as an expert for the Council of Europe on the implementation of the Framework Convention for the Protection of National Minorities in Kosovo. She is co-managing editor of the *European Yearbook of Minority Issues*. Her current research focuses on the practice of minority protection in Central Europe.

Zdenka Machnyikova is legal and political adviser to the global initiative on Conflict Prevention through Quiet Diplomacy, Human Rights Centre at the University of Essex, UK. She is an expert in the international protection of minorities, including via legislation, policy, and practice to guarantee linguistic, educational, cultural rights and participation in political processes. She advises governments regarding legislative and institutional design in ethnically diverse societies. She previously served as senior legal adviser to the OSCE High Commissioner on National Minorities and also as legal adviser at the International Law Department of the Czech Ministry of Foreign Affairs. She has worked with governments and minority communities on peace settlements, constitutions, and legislation in the Balkans, the Baltics, Central Asia, Northern Ireland, and Iraq. Ms Machnyikova has published in the field of minority rights and is an author of the forthcoming *Handbook on Managing Linguistic and Religious Diversity for Conflict Prevention Actors*.

Joseph Marko is full professor for comparative public law and political sciences at the Faculty of Law and director of the Centre for South-east European Studies at Graz University/Austria. He also is director of the Institute of Minority Rights at the European Academy Bozen/Bolzano in Italy. From 1997 to 2002 Prof Marko served as one of the three international judges at the Constitutional Court of Bosnia-Herzegovina.

From 1998 to 2002 and from 2006 to 2008 he was a member of the Advisory Committee of the Council of Europe's Committee of Ministers under the Framework Convention for the Protection of National Minorities. His writings and research focuses on comparative federalism/regionalism, minority protection, post-conflict reconstruction and ethnic diversity management.

John McGarry is professor and Canada Research Chair in Nationalism and Democracy in the Department of Political Studies at Queen's University (Kingston, Ontario). During 2008–9, he served as 'Senior Advisor on Power-Sharing' to the Mediation Support Unit of the United Nations. He is the editor, co-editor, and co-author of several books, including *European Integration and the Nationalities Question* (2006), *The Future of Kurdistan in Iraq* (2005) and *The Northern Ireland Conflict: Consociational engagements* (2004). He has also published in journals such as *Ethnic and Racial Studies, Ethnopolitics, Government and Opposition, Nationalism and Ethnic Politics, Nations and Nationalism, Parliamentary Affairs*, and *Political Studies*.

Andraz Melansek completed an MPhil in international relations at Cambridge University and is presently working as a consultant in Slovenia. He worked with the United Nations as electoral administrator in Iraq out-of-country voting and Afghanistan parliamentary elections. With the Organization for Security and Cooperation in Europe he acted as international electoral supervisor in Kosovo elections. He also served as an electoral observer with the European Union in several instances and academically has specialized in electoral issues. He published several articles on the topic of post-conflict reconstruction.

Brian Min is a PhD candidate in the Department of Political Science at the University of California, Los Angeles. His research examines the provision of public goods, particularly in ethnically diverse societies. He holds a BA from Cornell University and an MPP from the Kennedy School of Government at Harvard University.

Ephraim Nimni is reader at the School of Politics and International Studies at Queen's University in Belfast. His areas of research are theories of nationalism, the Israeli–Palestinian conflict and new modalities of ethnic conflict resolution. Recent publications include 'Stateless nations in a world of nation states', in Karl Cordell and Stefan Wolff (eds) *The Routledge Handbook of Ethnic Conflict* (2010); Nationalism, ethnicity and self determination, a paradigm Shift?', in 9 *Studies of Ethnicity and Nationalism* (2009); 'National cultural autonomy as an alternative to minority nationalism', in David Smith and Karl Cordell (eds), *Cultural Autonomy in Contemporary Europe* (2008); 'Constitutional or agonist patriotism? The dilemmas of liberal nations-states', in Per Mouritsen and Knud Erik Jørgensen (eds), *Constituting Communities, Political Solutions to Cultural Conflict* (2008); and *National-Cultural Autonomy and its Contemporary Critics* (2005). His new book, *Multicultural Nationalism*, will be published by Routledge in 2010.

Katherine Nobbs is project associate at the European Centre for Minority Issues (ECMI) in Pristina, Kosovo, and co-managing editor of the *European Yearbook of Minority Issues*. Previously, she worked as research associate and legal adviser at ECMI headquarters in Flensburg, Germany. She holds an MPhil in international relations with distinction from the University of Cambridge, a graduate diploma in law from the College of Law, Bloomsbury, and a BA in politics from the University of Nottingham.

Other publications include *The Protection of Minorities in the Wider Europe* (ed, with Marc Weller and Denika Blacklock) (2008) and *Asymmetric Autonomy and the Settlement of Ethnic Conflicts* (ed with Marc Weller) (forthcoming).

Brendan O'Leary, BA (Oxon), PhD (LSE), is Lauder Professor of political science and director of the Penn Program in Ethnic Conflict at the University of Pennsylvania. Recent books include *How to Get Out of Iraq With Integrity* (2009); *Terror, Insurgency and the State* (2007); *The Future of Kurdistan in Iraq* (2005); *The Northern Ireland Conflict: Consociational Engagements* (2004); and *Right-sizing the State: The politics of moving borders* (2001). Prof O'Leary has acted as a constitutional and political advisor to governments, parties, and international organizations on and in Northern Ireland, Somalia, Kwa-Zulu Natal, Nepal, and Kurdistan, and currently serves as senior adviser on power-sharing for the Mediation Support Unit of the United Nations' Department of Political Affairs.

Francesco Palermo, PhD, is professor of comparative constitutional law in the Faculty of Law, University of Verona and Director of the Institute for Studies on Federalism and Regionalism, European Academy, Bolzano/Bozen. Currently he is senior legal adviser to the OSCE High Commissioner on National Minorities and a member of the Advisory Committee on the Framework Convention for the Protection of National Minorities. His research focuses mostly on comparative federalism, minority rights, constitutional adjudication, and EU integration.

Alan Phillips has been the UK-nominated independent expert to the Council of Europe Advisory Committee on the Framework Convention for National minorities since 1998. He was first elected its president in 2006 and re-elected once again in 2008. Between 1989 and 2001 he was the executive director of Minority Rights Group International and since then he has acted as an adviser and consultant to a range of governments, intergovernmental and non-governmental organization. The primary focus of this work has been in the Western Balkans, often concentrating on the realization of the social and economic rights of national minorities and in particular the Roma. This has included developing training programmes and leading the participatory monitoring and evaluation of programmes for Roma inclusion.

Oleh Prostyk is senior research associate at the European Centre for Minority Issues in Flensburg, Germany. His research interests include ethnic conflict regulation, representation and political parties, and executive–legislative relations. His articles recently appeared in *European Journal of Political Research*, *Political Studies*, and *Post-Soviet Affairs*.

Luis Rodríguez-Piñero Royo is Ramón y Cajal Researcher at the University of Seville (Spain) Law Department, and part of the faculty of the European Master on Human Rights and Democratization in Venice (Italy). He obtained his PhD in law at the European University Institute in Florence. A specialist in indigenous peoples' rights, he worked as an adjunct professor at the University of Arizona Indigenous Peoples Law and Policy Programme. He has served as human rights officer at the United Nations Office of the High Commissioner for Human Rights in Geneva, and acts as a consultant on human rights-related issues for a number of inter-governmental and non-governmental organizations, including the Inter-American Commission on Human Rights and the

United Nations Economic Commission for Latin America. His publications include *Indigenous Peoples, Postcolonialism and International Law: The ILO regime* (2005).

Eva Sobotka, PhD, is working as human rights and networking coordinator at the European Union Agency for Fundamental Rights in Vienna. She is the author of several journal articles on Roma, national minorities, and human rights. Her research has focused on the influence of international norms on policymaking, migration, multilevel governance of human rights, conflict resolution, and EU enlargement.

Fernand de Varennes, PhD, is former director of the Asia–Pacific Centre for Human Rights and the Prevention of Ethnic Conflict and the founding editor-in-chief of the *Asia-Pacific Journal on Human Rights and the Law*. He is one of the world's leading legal experts on language rights and was awarded the 2004 Linguapax Award for his work in the field of linguistic diversity and multilingual education, as well as the Tip O'Neill Peace Fellowship at INCORE (Initiative on Conflict Resolution and Ethnicity) in Derry, Northern Ireland. He has received extensive recognition for his research work on international law, human rights, minorities, and ethnic conflicts and has been involved with numerous international organizations including the United Nations' Working Group on the Rights of Minorities, UNESCO and the OSCE's High Commissioner on National Minorities.

Peter Vermeersch is professor of Political Science at the Social Science Faculty of the University of Leuven in Belgium (KU Leuven) and a former visiting scholar at the Minda de Gunzburg Center for European Studies, Harvard University. His research interests include minority policies, ethnic mobilization, anti-discrimination, and nationalism. He is the author of the book *The Romani Movement: Minority politics and ethnic mobilization in contemporary Central Europe* (2006), which studies the recent attempts of Romani activists in Central Europe to influence domestic and international politics and policies. Other work by Peter Vermeersch has appeared in academic journals such as *Ethnic and Racial Studies, Europe-Asia Studies, Communist and Post-Communist Studies*, and *East European Politics and Societies*.

Annelies Verstichel, LLM (Columbia Law School), PhD (European University Institute), is a Belgian diplomat and has worked as a legal officer for the OSCE High Commissioner on National Minorities and as a policy adviser on community rights for the International Civilian Office and EU special representative in Kosovo. Her PhD investigated the right of persons belonging to minorities to effective participation in public affairs and won the Mauro Cappelletti Annual Prize 2008. She has published on human and minority rights, conflict prevention, and crisis management, and teaches on a regular basis. On several occasions, she has worked as an expert for the Council of Europe, the EU Network of Independent Experts on Fundamental Rights, and the Organization for Security and Cooperation in Europe.

Knut Vollebaek was appointed to the post of High Commissioner on National Minorities of the OSCE for a three-year term on 4 July 2007. As Norway's foreign minister (1997–2000), Mr Vollebaek was the chairman-in-office of the OSCE in 1999. He played a key role in attempting to find a peaceful solution to the Kosovo situation in the run-up to the war, and led the efforts by the international community to establish a presence in Kosovo and to assist in its reconstruction and rehabilitation in the aftermath of hostilities. High Commissioner Vollebaek is internationally recognized for his role in the promotion of peace and security and the protection of human rights, which have been a constant theme in his political and diplomatic career.

Marc Weller is reader in International Law at the University of Cambridge, and a fellow of the Lauterpacht Research Centre for International Law and Hughes Hall. He is also the director of the Carnegie Project on Resolving Self-determination Disputes through Complex Power-sharing, and of the Cambridge Rockefeller Project on Restoring an International Consensus of the Rules Governing the Use of Force. His writings focus mainly on conflict management, international law, and minority rights. He has acted as legal advisor to several governments and organizations, and has been a member of international peace processes. Dr Weller is also former director of the European Centre for Minority Issues in Flensburg, Germany.

Steven Wheatley is reader in international law and director of the Centre for International Governance at the University of Leeds. He is the author of *Democracy, Minorities and International Law* (2005) and *The Democratic Legitimacy of International Law* (2010), in addition to numerous articles exploring the relationship between the idea and practice of democracy and the rights of minorities and indigenous peoples. He is a member of the International Law Association International Research Committee on Rights of Indigenous Peoples, which is working on a commentary to the UN Declaration on the Rights of Indigenous Peoples (GA Res 61/295). He has lead responsibility for the section concerning autonomy and rights of political participation.

Andreas Wimmer is professor of sociology at the University of California, Los Angeles. His research aims to understand the dynamics of nation-state formation, ethnicity, boundary making, and political conflict from a comparative perspective. He has pursued various methodological and analytical strategies, including anthropological fieldwork, network analysis, comparative historical work, and cross-national statistical analysis.

Introduction

Democratic governance and minority political participation: Emerging legal standards and practice

Power denotes the ability to control people and events. In the modern age, we believe in the equal dignity of all human beings. This includes, at least in Western liberal societies, the belief in individual autonomy and freedom when it comes to the fundamental decisions that determine the basic parameters of our lives. Nevertheless, we also recognize that power can, and must, be exercised over us. We accept that the agents of organized society, or the state, can ultimately direct our conduct and even deprive us of our liberties. This is generally seen as a necessary condition for living in community with others.

The two conflicting doctrines of individual free will, and of power exercised by the agents of society over individuals are reconciled through the doctrines of the social contract, of democratic governance, of the rule of law, and of human rights. This is the grand bargain that underpins modern societies. The social contract supposedly bases the exercise of authority over us on the exercise of our own free will. By opting into the state, we are meant to have freely consented to the exercise of its powers. The doctrine of democracy claims that both the framework for decision-making of the state organs, and the actual decisions that emanate from the organs, represent us and our interests. They are democratically mandated. The rule of law ensures that public decisions are indeed compliant with the constitutional and legal structures that are meant to regulate the exercise of public power according to the social contract and the democratic mandate. Human rights offer a final safeguard against abuse of public powers.

This of course, is a rather simplistic view. Generally, individuals have little or no choice over whether or not they wish to opt into a particular society organized as a state. The social contract is a legitimizing myth for the exercise of state power. Democracy rarely operates in a way that lets us trace public acts back to our individual preferences and choices. The rule of law is itself limited by the legal framework it is meant to safeguard, and therefore reinforces, rather than overcomes, any deficiencies in it. And the view of human rights as being purely defensive safeguards against state abuse seems somewhat outdated in view of our understanding of rights as positive entitlements.

Hence, the strands of legitimization for the state and its powers appear somewhat frayed where it comes to the link between the free will of its individual constituents and the exercise of public authority. Of course, we tend to regard this defect as an acceptable one. We understand why individual interest may have to yield to the 'common good'. While we tend to grumble about the lack of genuine representativeness of the state organs and their decisions, few revolutions have ensued, at least in the wider Europe of the post-cold-war era.

Of course, the transition from the cold-war period was indeed marked by a clamour for more genuine democracy based on constitutional governance according to the rule of law in the Western liberal mould. In most instances, this desire was satisfied. But the transition also generated a strong challenge for those content with liberal democracy. In some instances, communist centralist rule was replaced with the exercise of ethnic dominance. In the Caucasus and the Balkans, and to a far lesser extent in the Baltic states, the majoritarian principle was turned into a tool of dominance and control by one ethnic community over others.

As was noted above, previously human rights were meant to protect individuals from abuse by the state. However, human rights regimes, where they existed, proved powerless to combat the exclusion of entire groups from parts of the state (Baltic Republics), their repression (Kosovo), and in some cases even their expulsion (Georgia, Croatia, Kosovo) or attempted extermination (Bosnia and Herzegovina). It became apparent that majority rule might result in tyranny over minorities.[1]

Of course, the dramatic events in the Caucasus and the Balkans of the 1990 merely put into sharp relief what was known already. By definition, government through majority decision can serve to disenfranchise an ethnic minority. This will tend to be the case if two conditions are fulfilled. First, the decisions in question are taken according to group appurtenance, instead of cross-cutting interests. Democratic delegates see themselves as agents of the group they represent and act accordingly. The second necessary condition for turning the state into a means of repression of non-dominant groups, instead of a means of equal representation of all, lies in the absence of effective mechanisms to protect minority interests.

This realization led European and other actors involved in the attempt to engage the ethnic conflicts of the 1990 to try and repair the democratic model in these instances by devising complex power-sharing solutions.[2] These consisted of five principal elements. First, ethnic communities were given territorial autonomy in areas where they lived. Secondly, ethnic communities were given guaranteed rights of co-decision (or veto) in the central institutions of the state. Thirdly, they were also offered roughly proportionate representation in the executive and other organs of state authority. Fourthly, ethnic groups were offered wide-ranging human and minority rights provisions, guaranteeing their

---

[1] See Chapter 2 in this volume by John McGarry.
[2] See, at length, Weller and Metzger (eds), *Settling Self-determination Disputes: Complex power-sharing in theory and practice* (2008).

ethnic identity throughout the state. And finally, certain functions of governance were delegated upwards, to international actors, or at least supervised by them.

These consociationalist settlements did, by and large, help to preserve ethnic peace.[3] However, it was also argued that they retrenched, rather than overcame, ethnic divisions. This debate among consociationalist and integrationist approaches to post-conflict state-building had wider repercussions. It became generally accepted that what was then known as 'minority governance' is an important issue for maintaining the integrity of existing states. In view of the dramatic consequences of ethnic conflict that had been observed in Europe, minority accommodation within the state became 'securitized'. While states had previously been very reluctant to engage with minority issues as human rights issues, they had fewer hesitations when engaging them as issues of conflict prevention or conflict transformation.

Hence, provisions concerning minorities and their role within the state were adopted both in relation to individual post-conflict societies, and in a more general sense. The establishment of the office of the (OSCE) High Commissioner on National Minorities (HCNM), his standard-setting efforts, and the creation of the Council of Europe Framework Convention for the Protection of National Minorities (FCNM) can be best understood against this backdrop.

While reference to the security dimension was helpful in generating international standards and mechanisms on minority issues (at least in the wider Europe), the emphasis since then has been to try and move minority rights out of this particular corner. After all, considering minorities under the heading of security somehow implies that they are a latent or active security threat. This view is of course precisely the one that more advanced thinking about minorities seeks to overcome. This also applies to the problem of access of minorities to the state—or the issue of political participation.

It has now been conclusively demonstrated that the exclusion of minority communities from the state organs and from public decision-making is indeed likely to contribute to ethnic tension or even ethnic conflict.[4] But it is generally accepted that political participation issues are also relevant and important outside of the security dimension. If security concerns are the first dimension of the debate surrounding political participation, then the second dimension extends into a more advanced discussion of non-discrimination. This concerns particularly what is known as indirect discrimination. Indirect discrimination occurs where rules or practices appear to apply equally to all. However, the features or characteristics of a given group are sufficiently different to put them into a position of inequality if that practice or rule is applied equally to them. For instance, a rule stipulating that only parties gaining 10 per cent or more in national elections are eligible for representation in parliament might be applied

---

[3] See Chapter 16 in this volume by Fernand de Varennes.
[4] See Chapter 1 in this volume by Andreas Wimmer, Lars-Erik Cederman, and Brian Min.

equally to all. But a national minority that constitutes just 8 per cent of the national population will in fact be permanently excluded from seeking representation in parliament through its 'own' ethnic minority party.

The third level of debate on political participation is related to the more conceptual issues raised at the beginning of this introduction. The doctrine of democratic representativeness of the Western liberal state cannot coexist easily with instances of structural exclusion of entire groups from the state. In that sense, effective political participation issues concern the legitimacy of the state as such. In summary, therefore, political participation discourse is based on three main strands: the sense that exclusion from the functions of the state fosters conflict, while shared ownership will strengthen it; considerations of what it means to achieve real equality in all aspects of life, including public life; and references to the philosophical underpinnings of the authority and legitimacy of the state.

Of course, beyond these general findings, a number of more specific initial issues arise. The first might be the question of why we focus on political participation of minorities. Among the legal community, the term 'minority' has a fairly specific meaning. While there is no formal and legally binding positive definition, the concept is at least circumscribed in a negative way. That is to say, migrant communities (so-called 'newcomers') are not normally covered. While such communities face many of the same problems encountered by 'traditional' minorities (ie, those traditionally present within the state, or 'autochthonous' minorities), governments have been reluctant to extend to them the full panoply of minority rights.[5] Of course, the considerations of security, discrimination, and political legitimacy or philosophy that underpin participation entitlements now accepted for traditional minorities apply in the same way to more recently arrived communities. Hence, it may be unwise to insist for too long on what may become a somewhat artificial distinction. Instead, the approach of extending minority rights to such communities where they can be usefully applied will undoubtedly prevail over the longer term.

The other challenge to participation discourse may come in relation to groups other than ethnic, national, religious, or linguistic ones. Should there not also be debate about participation rights of women, or the disabled, or gays and lesbians, or others? Surely the right of members of such groups to representation in the sate are of no less value than that of individuals appertaining to minorities? The answer would appear that there certainly should be such debate, taking account of both similarities and differences in these cases. Some of the participation mechanisms, in particular in relation to consultation and special governmental contact, are being applied to such groups in practice. Hence, it would appear that practice in relation both to migrant communities and in relation to other groups is increasingly informed by the experience gained in

---

[5] See Chapter 22 in this volume by Ephraim Nimni.

respect to national minorities. On the other hand, it would also seem unlikely that the entire armoury of political participation tools devised in the context of minorities would be applied in other contexts as such. For instance, no argument could be made in favour territorial autonomy of women within the state, while guaranteed representation of women in public life through quotas in parliament and elsewhere is becoming increasingly accepted.

There are additional threshold issues to be considered. One concerns the distinction between minorities and indigenous peoples. The latter often vigorously resist being classed as minorities. On the other hand, in terms of substantive entitlements, minority rights and indigenous rights often overlap. Certainly, the understanding of certain minority rights was significantly developed through international jurisprudence on indigenous rights. The development of indigenous rights, on the other hand, has benefited from innovations first made in the area of minority rights. Accordingly, it seems worthwhile to recognize the fruitful relationship between these two branches of human rights law.

There is also the problem of double disenfranchisement. For instance, in some instances, women from minority communities may face exclusion by virtue of both their gender and their appurtenance to a minority. However, it is also evident that problems of this nature can be rather complex, making simple solutions applicable to all situations that appear superficially similar less attractive.[6]

A final general problem relates to the question of access to political participation entitlements. Are these rights reserved for those who have formally opted into the social contract—for citizens? Or should anyone regularly subject to the exercise of public authority of the state not also be entitled to share in the control of such authority? Again, international practice on this issue appears to be progressing, granting increasing rights of participation to long-term residents, without offering the full range of participation entitlements.[7]

This development illustrates well the dynamic nature of minority rights. In view of the hesitancy of states to set hard legal standards, the approach has been to start by identifying best practices among some states. These have then been consolidated into soft law documents, like the Lund Recommendations. Or, where there was at least a foothold in hard law (say, Art 15 of the FCNM), implementation practice has been consolidated over time into far more detailed guidance, such as the Advisory Committee (AC)'s Commentary. Much of this development has taken the form of dialogue among governments and minority constituents, often mediated or channelled through international institutions such as the OSCE HCNM.

While the FCNM, the principal instrument on minority rights in Europe is not subject to the 'hard' jurisprudence of the European Court on Human Rights, its interpretation has benefited from some pronouncements by the

---

[6] See Chapter 5 in this volume by Karen Bird.
[7] See Chapter 3 in this volume by Annelies Verstichel.

Court. Similarly, the development of minority rights through the FCNM and its AC has influenced the Court.

Moreover, the activities of the OSCE High Commissioner, the originator of the Lund Recommendations, have strengthened their legal stature. The HCNM will routinely rely on the Recommendations generated under his own aegis in his dialogue with states. The authority of such instruments is very rarely questioned in practice.

It has to be admitted, though, that this development through mediated practice and soft jurisprudence has mainly taken place in the OSCE and CoE area. Developments in other regions have remained more hesitant. However, at the universal level, it is noteworthy that the UN Independent Expert covering minority issues is following a rather similar path. Best practices are being collected with a view to developing initially soft law standards that might later be codified. Indeed, it is understood that political participation is one of the priority areas of work in this respect.

What, then, are the principal tools that can be deployed to share ownership over, and participation in, the state. Generally one can distinguish several key types:

1. At the macro level, there is the issue of state design, which may be modified to accommodate minority self-government. This can range from confederal solutions to local autonomy or even mere decentralization.[8] In particular, the adoption of enhanced local self-government mechanisms (also under the doctrine of subsidiarity) offers an opportunity to accommodate minorities without having to effect major constitutional change.[9]
2. A further approach focuses on anti-discrimination. Through the application of the very well-developed approaches to anti-discrimination to participation issues, full and effective equality can also be realized in that respect.[10]
3. Another way of engaging the issue is by generated enhanced chances for, or even guaranteed rights of, representation by certain groups in state organs. This may include top-level government,[11] or the administration[12] and the justice sector.[13] Often, however, the main focus lies in securing parliamentary representation.[14]
4. Even where representation has been obtained, the question of 'the powers of presence' arises. To give weight to effective representation, certain procedural rules can be adopted to the benefit of minority representatives who may not

---

[8] See Chapter 21 in this volume by Yash Ghai.
[9] See Chapter 23 in this volume by Bill Bowring.
[10] See Chapter 4 in this volume by Zdenka Machnyikova and Lanna Hollo.
[11] See Chapter 14 in this volume by Florian Bieber.
[12] See Chapter 15 in this volume by Francesco Palermo.
[13] See Chapter 20 in this volume by Katherine Nobbs.
[14] See Chapter 12 in volume by Brendan O'Leary.

otherwise find an effective voice.[15] A more enhanced mechanisms would turn presence into powers of co-decision, or even veto, that may be exercised on behalf of minority communities.

5. Engagement is a further tool that may be deployed. Engagement often takes the form of standing minority consultative councils or other mechanisms.[16] These bodies will offer less formal avenues of influence and persuasion to minority representative groups. Minority consultative mechanisms may also be applied as contact facilities just in relation to certain issue areas (education) or in relation to certain groups with particular needs (Roma).[17]

6. Finally, inclusion of minority representative in international contacts offers a useful way of inclusion of minority groups. This includes international negotiations or discussions of particular relevance to the respective groups, and especially their participation in international monitoring of the performance of the state organs.[18]

Overall, therefore, the Lund Recommendations and related documents offer a very substantial tool kit for addressing political participation issues. These opportunities for participation need to be balanced, however, by measures to ensure genuine representativeness of those who profess to exercise this role. Minority representative organizations, in particular, owe a duty of transparency and internal democracy and accountability to their own constituents.[19]

As for significant developments in the area of minority participation, it has to be admitted that international practice has been reluctant to be altogether too specific when considering which mechanisms should be applied to what extent in a given state. There has been wide room for the recognition of national particularities. Even the European Court on Human Rights, the most powerful human rights implementation body anywhere, has been ultra-cautious when addressing the democratic organization of states. It has offered a (very) wide margin of appreciation to governments when considering questions of access to the political system. However, the very significant range of practice reviewed here does confirm that the requirement for full, equal, and effective participation of minorities has real meaning. Generally, it is expected that states will dip into all of the available mechanisms to generate a comprehensive system of participation for minorities. Moreover, there is now increasing acceptance that such mechanisms are not merely temporary concessions of the government of the day, but must become part of the formal constitutional compact that underpins the state.[20]

---

[15] See Chapter 13 in this volume by Oleh Protsyk.
[16] See Chapter 17 in this volume by Marc Weller.
[17] See Chapter 18 in this volume by Eva Sobotka.
[18] See Chapter 25 in this volume by Emma Lantschner.
[19] See Chapter 24 in this volume by Peter Vermeersch.
[20] See Chapter 26 in this volume by Alain Chablais.

PART I
GENERAL ISSUES

1

Ethnic Diversity, Political Exclusion, and Armed Conflict: A quantitative analysis of a global dataset[1]

Andreas Wimmer, Lars-Erik Cederman, and Brian Min

I. Introduction: Ethnic Diversity or Ethnic Politics?	4
II. Ethnicity and Conflict: Getting the Relationship Right	6
III. An Institutionalist, Configurational Theory of Ethnic Politics and Conflict	11
A. Institutional incentives for ethnic politics	11
B. Ethno-political configurations of power and types of ethnic conflict	12
C. War-prone configurations: hypotheses	14
IV. The Ethnic Power Relations (EPR) Dataset, 1946–2005	17
A. Politically relevant ethnic groups and access to power	17
B. War coding	19
V. Variables and Data Sources	20
A. Exclusion, centre segmentation, state cohesion	20
B. Other variables	21
VI. Models and Findings	22
A. Explaining armed conflict	22
B. Explaining ethnic conflict	23
C. Explaining rebellion and infighting	26
D. Explaining secessionist and non-secessionist conflicts by rebels and infighters	28
VII. Conclusions	30

Quantitative scholarship on civil wars has long debated whether or not ethnic diversity breeds armed conflict. In this chapter, we go beyond this debate and show that highly diverse societies are not more conflict prone, but rather states

---

[1] Adapted from A Wimmer, L-E Cederman, and B Min, 'Ethnic politics and armed conflict: A configurational analysis of a new global dataset' (2009) 74 *American Sociological Review* 316–37.

characterized by certain ethno-political configurations of power. First, states that exclude large portions of the population on the basis of their ethnic background are likely to be challenged by armed rebellions. Secondly, segmented states where power is shared between a large number of competing ethnic elites risk violent infighting between them. Thirdly, incohesive states with a short history of direct rule are more likely to experience secessionist conflicts. We test these hypotheses with a new dataset on Ethnic Power Relations (EPR) in all independent states since 1945. Cross-national analysis shows that once properly conceived and measured, ethnic exclusion is as powerful and robust in predicting civil wars as is a country's level of economic development. We then show through multinomial logit regressions that rebellion, infighting, and secession result from high degrees of exclusion, segmentation, and incohesion respectively. More diverse countries, on the other hand, are not more likely to suffer from violent conflict. The conclusion draws some lessons for prevention policies.

I. Introduction: Ethnic Diversity or Ethnic Politics?

Karl Marx predicted that the twentieth would be the century of revolutionary class struggles. Instead, it turned out to be the age of ethno-nationalist conflicts: wars fought in the name of national liberation or ethnic autonomy counted for only one fifth of the wars fought between the Congress of Vienna (1814) and the Treaty of Versailles (1919). From Versailles to 2001, however, the share of ethno-nationalist wars rose to 45 per cent, and to 75 per cent since the cold war ended.[2] Ethnic demands and grievances play a prominent role in most conflicts that make it into the daily news—from Iraq to Darfur, Kenya to Tibet, Israel/Palestine to Burma. What can the social sciences offer to our understanding of these conflicts? When do lines of conflict follow ethnic divides and what are the causal mechanisms linking ethnicity to conflict?

No satisfactory answer can be found in the burgeoning quantitative literature on civil wars that has emerged over the past decade. The most influential school of thought dismisses ethnicity as an explanatory factor altogether, arguing that ethnic grievances are too widespread to explain the rare event of civil war. Rebels will fight when the government is militarily weak or wherever lootable resources can feed an insurgent organization (the 'greed and opportunity' perspective). Other scholars maintain that ethnicity *does* matter, and try to show that more ethnically diverse countries are more likely to see conflict (the 'diversity breeds conflict' tradition). A third group of authors has studied the conditions under which discriminated ethnic minorities will rebel (the 'minority mobilization' school).

---

[2] These figures are based on the dataset assembled by Wimmer and Min and relate to wars with more than 1000 battle deaths. A Wimmer and B Min, 'From empire to nation-state: Explaining wars in the modern world, 1816–2001' (2006) 71 *American Sociological Review* 867–97.

We argue that all three traditions misconceive the relationship between ethnicity and conflict.

To get this relationship right, we first need to realize that the modern state is not an ethnically neutral actor or a mere arena for political competition, but a central object of and participant in ethno-political power struggles. Why is this the case? Our answer takes an institutionalist point of departure: contrary to empires, nation states are governed in the name of 'their peoples', which provides incentives to align political loyalties along ethnic divides. To gain legitimacy, political elites in control of executive-level state power will favour co-ethnics when deciding with whom to ally and to whom to distribute public goods. Politics will then centre on the question of which ethnic group controls which share of executive-level government, and the struggle over state power will pit ethnically defined actors against each other. Ethnic politics thus is not exclusively a struggle to rectify the grievances of minority groups, as the 'minority mobilization' school assumes, but more generally and fundamentally about the distribution of state power along ethnic lines. The 'diversity breeds conflict' school relies on demographic indices of heterogeneity which overlook how ethnicity relates to the state. Rather than high degrees of diversity, it is ethnic exclusion from state power and competition over the spoils of government that breed ethnic conflict.

We propose a configurational theory that identifies three constellations in which this struggle over the state is most likely to escalate into armed conflict. First, when large sections of the population are excluded from central state power on the basis of their ethnic background, armed rebellions against such an ethnocratic regime are more likely. Secondly, when government power is shared between a large number of ethnic elites engaged in a competitive rivalry, the likelihood of infighting increases. Thirdly, both rebellion and infighting will be more likely and take on secessionist forms where segments of the population have a short and troubled history of direct rule by the centre.

We support this argument with quantitative analysis of a new dataset on Ethnic Power Relations (EPR) in all states since the Second World War. This dataset records all politically relevant ethnic groups, minorities and majorities, and their degree of access to executive-level state power—from total control of the government to overt political discrimination and exclusion. The EPR dataset overcomes the limitations of existing datasets, especially the widely used Minorities at Risk dataset, which focuses exclusively on disadvantaged minorities and is thus unable to capture the dynamics of ethnic politics at the power centre. The EPR dataset also improves upon conventional demographic indices of diversity which are only tangentially related to the ethno-political struggle over the state.

We show that once properly conceived and measured, ethnic politics helps in explaining the dynamics of war and peace, contrary to what the 'greed and opportunity' school maintains. Secondly, our results also demonstrate that more diverse countries are not more war prone, in contrast to the expectations of the 'diversity breeds conflict' school. Thirdly, disaggregated analysis using multinomial logit regressions shows that different kinds of ethnic conflicts result from different causal processes: rebellions are more likely the higher the share of the excluded population, the chances of infighting increase with the number of power-sharing elites, and secessions are more frequent in incohesive states that lack a long history of direct rule by the centre. We thus follow in the footsteps of other scholars in the quantitative literature who argue that different types of wars have different causes[3] and support a recent trend to more closely investigate the various mechanisms leading to armed conflicts.[4]

II. Ethnicity and Conflict: Getting the Relationship Right

Two major shortcomings characterize the quantitative literature on ethnicity and violence. First, the mechanisms linking ethnicity to conflict are specified in theoretically problematic and empirically unsatisfactory ways. Secondly, quantitative approaches tend to over-aggregate the dependent variable and treat ethnic conflicts as if they were caused by uniform factors. We discuss the problem of specifying relevant mechanisms first. We discuss the three most prominent traditions of quantitative research on the outbreak of civil wars: the 'greed and opportunity', the 'ethnic diversity breeds conflict' and the 'minority mobilization' schools.

The most influential papers have argued that ethnicity plays no role in predicting the onset of civil wars. The increase in the number of ethnic conflicts that we report in the opening paragraph does not capture any meaningful trend, authors in this tradition argue, but is due to the unfortunate tendency of both scholarly observers and rebels themselves to attribute conflict to primordial ethnic identities—a collective delusion of sorts.[5] More important than ethnic identity or political exclusion along ethnic lines are the material and organizational incentives to stage a rebellion against government. According to Fearon and Laitin's well-known insurgency model, wars erupt where governments are weak and rebels have ample opportunities to hide from troops while recruiting unemployed young men for whatever cause: national liberation, revolutionary progress, the spread of true religion, or rich bounty.[6] Similarly, Collier and Hoeffler maintain that civil wars occur where rebellions are most feasible,

---

[3] M Sambanis, 'Do ethnic and nonethnic civil wars have the same causes?' (2001) 45 *Journal of Conflict Resolution* 259–82; H Buhaug, 'Relative capability and rebel objective in civil war' (2006) 43 *Journal of Peace Research* 691–708.
[4] SN Kalyvas, 'Civil wars' in C Boix and SS Stokes (eds), *Handbook of Political Science* (2007), 416–34. [5] D Laitin, *Nations, States, and Violence* (2007), 22–7.
[6] JD Fearon and DD Laitin, 'Ethnicity, insurgency, and civil war' (2003) 97 *American Political Science Review* 1–16.

rather than where actors are motivated by ethnic inequality or social marginalization.[7] More specifically, they argue that lootable economic resources make organizing and sustaining a rebel organization easier.[8]

A second group of scholars insists that ethnicity *does* matter, and suggest various reasons why ethnically diverse countries experience more conflict. Some researchers state that high degrees of ethnic diversity contradict the assumption of cultural homogeneity on which modern nation states are based, thus triggering waves of separatist wars and ethnic cleansings.[9] Tatu Vanhanen, the most ardent proponent of the 'diversity breeds conflict' argument, relies on van den Berghe's theory of ethnic nepotism, according to which humans tend to favour kin and quasi-kin such as co-ethnics over others.[10] As a result, more ethnically heterogeneous countries will have more conflict. Finally, Sambanis draws on organizational economy models in maintaining that more ethnically divided societies face higher risks of ethnic war because shared ethnicity decreases the collective action costs associated with organizing a rebel force.[11]

Both the 'greed and opportunity' school and the 'diversity breeds conflict' tradition rely on the same type of demographic-diversity indicators to test whether or not ethnicity explains conflict. Many use a linguistic fractionalization index, calculated as the likelihood that two randomly drawn individuals would speak a different language. Obvious to any scholar with minimal country expertise, this is a rather poor indicator to capture the political dynamics associated with ethnic conflict: first, not all ethnic groups matter for politics;[12] secondly, ethnic conflicts are not the outcome of everyday encounters between individuals, but of the interactions between the state and ethno-political movements that challenge its authority.[13]

Given these conceptual and measurement problems, it is not surprising that empirical studies using fractionalization indices have produced conflicting results. Some find that ethnic fractionalization does *not* explain high intensity conflicts with more than 1,000 battle deaths per year.[14] Others show

---

[7] P Collier and A Hoeffler, 'Greed and grievance in civil war' (2004) 56 *Oxford Economic Papers* 563–95.

[8] Cf also P Collier, A Hoeffler, and D Rohner, 'Beyond greed and grievance: Feasibility and civil war' *Centre for the Study of African Economics Working Paper*, no 10 (2006).

[9] T Nairn, 'All Bosnians now?' (1993) *Dissent* 403–10; E Gellner, 'Nationalism and politics in Eastern Europe' (1991) 189 *New Left Review* 127–43.

[10] T Vanhanen, 'Domestic ethnic conflict and ethnic nepotism: A comparative analysis' (1999) 36 *Journal of Peace Research* 55–73.

[11] Sambanis, 'Do ethnic and nonethnic civil wars have the same causes?', (n 3 above); see also W Easterly and R Levine, 'Africa's growth tragedy: Policies and ethnic divisions' (1997) *The Quarterly Journal of Economics* 1203–50, 1223.

[12] As discussed by D Posner, 'Measuring ethnic fractionalization in Africa' (2004) 48 *American Journal of Political Science* 849–63; K Chandra and S Wilkinson, 'Measuring the effect of "ethnicity"' (2008) 41 *Comparative Political Studies* (2008) 515–63.

[13] L-E Cederman and L Girardin, 'Beyond fractionalization: Mapping ethnicity onto nationalist insurgencies' (2007) 101 *American Political Science Review* 173–85.

[14] Collier and Hoeffler, 'Greed and grievance in civil war' (n 7 above); Fearon and Laitin, 'Ethnicity, Insurgency, and Civil War' (n 6 above).

that it matters very much if *low-intensity* wars are included in the dependent variable,[15] or if we focus on *ethnic* wars,[16] or *secessionist* conflicts only.[17] Some find a parabolic relationship between ethnic fractionalization and the prevalence of civil war,[18] while others maintain that polarization between two equally sized ethnic groups, rather than fractionalization, helps to explain conflict.[19]

In this chapter, we move beyond these demographic indicators of ethnic diversity and introduce a new dataset that records politically relevant groups and their access to executive-branch state power for all countries since the Second World War. This allows for a direct test of how ethnic politics affect war and peace, rather than via demographic proxies far removed from how ethnicity works in political practice. Once the political dynamics of ethnic exclusion and competition are accounted for, diversity in and of itself has no effect on the likelihood of civil conflict.

The third major approach to be discussed here is the 'minority mobilization' school. It analyses the relationship between ethnicity and conflict at the group level, rather than the country level. Coming from a political mobilization perspective, Ted Gurr and others explored the conditions under which ethnic minorities protest or rebel.[20] Various factors familiar to students of social movements (from the strength of communal grievances to the political opportunity structure provided by different political regimes) are found to account for the political behaviour of ethnic groups.

Ted Gurr and his associates have also assembled a large dataset on such 'Minorities at Risk' (MAR) around the world. This dataset has produced a quantum leap in the quantitative study of ethnic politics and has provided the research community with an invaluable service. It has been widely used in political science[21] and sociology[22] to explain a variety of outcomes, including ethnic mobilization and rebellions.

---

[15] H Hegre and N Sambanis, 'Sensitivity analysis of empirical results on civil war onset' (2006) 50 *Journal of Conflict Resolution* 508–35.
[16] Sambanis, 'Do ethnic and nonethnic civil wars have the same causes?' (n 3 above).
[17] H Buhaug, 'Relative capability and rebel objective in civil war' (2006) 43 *Journal of Peace Research* 691–708.
[18] N Elbadawi and N Sambanis, 'Why are there so many civil wars in Africa? Understanding and preventing violent conflict' (2000) 9 *Journal of African Economics* 244–69.
[19] JG Montalvo and M Reynal-Querol, 'Ethnic polarization, potential conflict and civil wars' (2005) 95 *American Economic Review* 796–816. Ellingsen finds support for both a linear relationship to fractionalization and a U-shaped relationship to polarization. T Ellingsen, 'Colorful community or ethnic witches' brew? Multiethnicity and domestic conflict during and after the cold war' (2000) 44 *Journal of Conflict Resolution* 228–49.
[20] TR Gurr, *Minorities at Risk: A global view of ethnopolitical conflict* (1993).
[21] SM Saideman and RW Ayres, 'Determining the causes of irredentism: Logit analyses of minorities at risk data from the 1980s and 1990s' (2000) 62 *The Journal of Politics* 1126–44; B Walter, 'Information, uncertainty, and the decision to secede' (2006) 60 *International Organization* 105–35; Z Elkins and J Sides, 'Can institutions build unity in multi-ethnic states?' (2007) 101 *American Political Science Review* 693–708; M Toft, *The Geography of Ethnic Violence: Identity, interests, and the indivisibility of territory* (2003).
[22] S-K Chai, 'Predicting ethnic boundaries' (2005) 21 *European Sociological Review* 375–39; S Olzak, *The Global Dynamics of Race and Ethnic Mobilization* (2006).

The minority mobilization perspective undoubtedly comes much closer to the empirically observable mechanisms linking ethnicity to conflict, and we incorporate some of the major insights of this tradition into the model of ethnic politics developed further below. However, the minority mobilization perspective is limited by its focus on minority groups only, reflected in the group selection criteria underlying the MAR dataset. This has two consequences. First, the state itself appears as ethnically neutral, making it impossible to grasp the dynamics of ethnic politics in the power centre. Secondly, the MAR coding scheme does not fit countries with ruling minorities or with complex coalitions of ethnically defined elites, as Nigeria, India, or Chad.[23] In such countries, ethnic conflict will be pursued in the name of excluded majorities (rather than minorities) or ethnic groups that share power (and are thus not 'at risk'). Roughly half of the observations in our dataset conform to such ethno-political constellations and thus escape the logic of the MAR approach. In other words, the minority mobilization model over-specifies the conditions under which ethnicity leads to conflict by reducing its focus to the political mobilization of discriminated minorities.

Thus, all major schools in the quantitative literature have failed to specify convincing mechanisms linking ethnicity and conflict by either relying on a version of the ethnic diversity argument that is unrelated to the logic of ethnic politics or by defining ethnic conflicts too narrowly as a matter of minority mobilization. A second problem in the existing literature is that it conceives ethnic conflict as a unitary phenomenon caused by uniform factors. Qualitative comparative work, however, has shown how important it is to take different ethno-political constellations into account and to acknowledge the causal heterogeneity of the processes that lead to ethnic conflict. The following four vignettes of well-known ethnic conflicts illustrate the point.

When segments of the Irish Catholic educated middle class, inspired by the American civil rights movement, started to mobilize against their long-lasting exclusion from power, the state apparatus, entirely controlled by Protestant elites who ruled Northern Ireland as an outpost of the British state, reacted with repression and intimidation. The ensuing spiral of escalation led to the reinvigoration of the Irish nationalist underground army who fought to unite the northern parts with the rest of the island and to the emergence of Protestant militias and terrorist groups opposed to this nationalist project.[24]

---

[23] The MAR dataset tries to address these limitations by including five 'advantaged' minorities who benefit from political discrimination and control a state apparatus. MAR also comprises a series of 'communal contenders' mostly in Africa, ie groups that share power with others while at the same time mobilizing in protest or rebellion (cf T Gurr, 'Why minorities rebel: A global analysis of communal mobilization and conflict since 1945' (1993) 14 *International Political Science Review* 161–201). Other ethnically defined elites that do not mobilize their constituencies in protest are left out of the picture, however.   [24] J Bardon, *A History of Ulster* (2001).

In Bosnia shortly before independence, the leadership of the Serbian territories pulled out of the provincial government that they had shared with Croatian and Bosniak politicians, and the seats of Serbian parliamentarians were vacated. Mobilization for war proceeded quickly on both sides, and soon Serbian militias, supported by the army of neighbouring Yugoslavia, started to attack Croatian and Bosniak villages that they intended to incorporate into the territory of a future Serbian state.[25]

In January 1994, the now iconic Commandante Marcos led a group of masked men and women to the main square of San Cristobal de la Casas and announced that the indigenous peoples of Chiapas and Mexico were no longer prepared to accept their fate as second-class citizens and demanded profound constitutional, economic, and political change. His rebellion was preceded by decades of political mobilization by left-wing organizations fighting for land reform as well as by members of the lower clergy inspired by liberation theology. The central government reacted to this provocation by sending the army southwards and occupied indigenous villages supposedly harbouring members of the Zapatista army. After a series of armed encounters, the Zapatistas eventually withdrew into the Lacandon jungle.[26]

Most recently in Iraq after the fall of Saddam Hussein, former Baathist officers and high level functionaries joined Sunni clerics, tribal leaders from the Sunni triangle and foreign *jihadists* in a fragile alliance to fight the new power holders from the Shiite south of the country. They struggled against what they perceived as an illegitimate government controlled by Shiite apostates and Kurdish separatists and opposed any federalization and power-sharing on the national level, dreaming of restoring the ethnocratic regime they once controlled. Meanwhile, factions within the Shiite block jockeyed for power, exploiting the unpopularity of the new government and its dependence on American military power. The 'Sadr Army' harnessed the support of marginalized urban youth to oppose power-sharing with Sunni and Kurdish political parties, advocating instead a strong, central state under Shiite command.[27]

Obviously, the factors affecting these four conflict histories and the mechanisms at play are quite different. While Catholics and indigenous *Chiapanecos* represented excluded groups that were mobilized against the state, representatives of Bosnian Serbs and Shiite Arabs were partners in coalitional

---

[25] SL Burg and PS Shoup, *The War in Bosnia-Herzegowina: Ethnic conflict and international intervention* (1999).

[26] A Wimmer, 'Die erneute Rebellion der Gehenkten, Chiapas 1994' (1995) 3 *1999. Zeitschrift für Sozialgeschichte des 20. und 21. Jahrhunderts* 59–68; G Collier and E Lowery Quaratiello, *Basta! Land and the Zapatista rebellion in Chiapas* (1994).

[27] O Bengio, 'The new Iraq: Challenges for state building' in C Peter et al (eds), *Regime Change in Iraq: The transatlantic and regional dimensions* (2004); J Cole, 'The United States and Shi'ite religious factions in post-Ba'thist Iraq' (2003) 57 *The Middle East Journal* 543–66; A Wimmer, 'Democracy and ethno-religious conflict in Iraq' (2003) 45 *Survival. The International Institute for Strategic Studies Quarterly* 111–34.

governments. Serbian Bosniak elites and Iraqi ethno-religious factions faced a disorganized and ethnically fragmented state while Catholics in Northern Ireland and the Zapatistas in Mexico had to oppose a well entrenched state apparatus. The IRA and Bosnian Serb nationalists developed a separatist agenda aimed at joining established neighbouring states, while the Zapatistas and Iraqi groups focused on changing ethnic power relations within existing states.

It seems doubtful that these different ethno-political dynamics can be grasped by any single indicator. The power configurations are different, as are the mechanisms and logic relating ethnicity to conflict. In the following, we introduce a configurational approach that links different ethno-political constellations with distinct causal pathways leading to specific types of ethnic conflict.

III. An Institutionalist, Configurational Theory of Ethnic Politics and Conflict

Our theory of ethnic politics and conflict is based on two pillars: first, we rely on institutionalist theories that show how established structures of political legitimacy provide incentives for actors to pursue certain types of political strategies over others; secondly, our model is of a configurational nature: even with similar political institutions, different configurations of political power can lead to dissimilar consequences, while similar outcomes can be the consequence of dissimilar constellations of power. The institutionalist part of the argument specifies the conditions under which political loyalties will align along ethnic cleavages; the configurational part explains when we expect such ethnic politics to lead to armed violence.

A. Institutional incentives for ethnic politics

The institutionalist part of the argument is derived from Wimmer's theory of nation-state formation and ethnic politics.[28] It states that ethnicity does not matter for politics because of a universal, naturally given tendency to favour (ethnic) kin over non-kin (as socio-biologists argue), nor because of a primordial attachment of individuals to their identities, nor because it provides lower costs for political organization (as the political-economy tradition maintains). Rather, ethnicity matters because the nation state itself relies on ethno-national principles of political legitimacy: the state is ruled in the name of an ethnically defined people and rulers should therefore care for 'their own people'. As a result, ethnicity and nationhood have much greater political significance in nation states compared to other types of polities such as empires or city states.

---

[28] A Wimmer, *Nationalist Exclusion and Ethnic Conflicts. Shadows of Modernity* (2002).

Given this institutional environment, political office-holders have incentives to gain legitimacy by favouring co-ethnics or co-national over others when it comes to the distribution of public goods and government jobs; judiciary bodies have incentives to apply the principle of equality before the law for co-ethnics or co-nationals, but less for others; the police force has incentives to provide protection for co-ethnics or co-nationals, but less for others, and so forth. The expectation of ethnic preference and discrimination works the other way too: voters prefer parties led by co-ethnics or co-nationals; delinquents hope for co-ethnic or co-national judges; and citizens prefer to be policed by co-ethnics or co-nationals.

Not all modern nation states are characterized by such ethnic/national favouritism, however. As we have discussed elsewhere, it is more likely and widespread in poor states that lack the resources for universal, non-discriminatory inclusion, and in states with weak civil society institutions where other, non-ethnic ways of aggregating political interests and rewarding political loyalty are scarce.[29] In such states, political leaders and followers orient their strategies towards avoiding dominance by ethnic or national others—and strive for the 'self-determination' and 'self-rule' that is at the core of nationalist ideology. This motive is at the same time material, political, and symbolic: 'adequate' or 'just' representation in a central government offers material advantages such as access to government jobs and services; legal advantages such as the benefits of full citizenship rights, a fair trial and protection from arbitrary violence; and symbolic advantages such as the prestige of belonging to a 'state-owning' ethnic or national group. The aggregate consequence of these strategic orientations is a struggle over control of the state between ethnically defined actors—or ethnic politics for short.[30]

Such ethnic politics may lead to a process of political mobilization, counter-mobilization and escalation: political leaders appeal to the ideal of self-rule and fair representation enshrined in the nation-state model to mobilize their followers against the threat of ethnic dominance by others. Their demands might stir up the fear of ethnic dominance among other political elites and their ethnic constituencies and result in a process of counter-mobilization. The conflicting demands might finally spiral up into armed confrontation. Our theory does not explicitly address the logic of this escalation process itself,[31] but rather seeks to specify the ethno-political configurations that make it more likely.

B. Ethno-political configurations of power and types of ethnic conflict

In order to accomplish this task, we first need to introduce some conceptual tools to describe different configurations of actors and the power relations

---

[29] Ibid.
[30] J Rothschild, *Ethnopolitics: A conceptual framework* (1981); M Esman, *Ethnic Politics* (1994).
[31] See S Tarrow and C Tilly, *Contentious Politics* (2006); S Olzak, *The Global Dynamics of Race and Ethnic Mobilization* (2006).

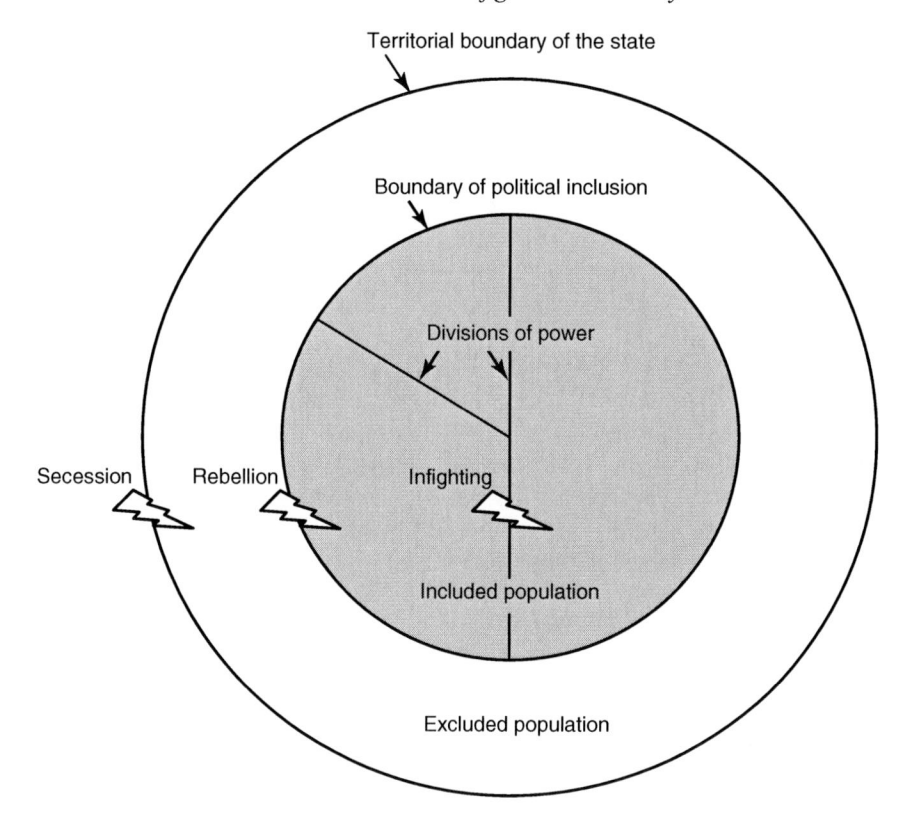

Figure 1.1. Ethno-political constellations of power and conflict

between them (see figure 1.1.). Borrowing from Charles Tilly's polity model, we distinguish between various social groups that control/have access to the central government (the inner circle in grey), those that are excluded from government but still citizens of the country (the next circle in white), and, finally, the social world beyond the territorial boundaries of the state.[32] Each ethno-political constellation of power is thus defined by three types of boundaries: The *territorial boundaries* of a state which define which ethnic communities are considered a legitimate part of a state's citizenry; the *boundary of inclusion* separating those who share government power from those who are not represented at the highest levels of government; the *division of power* and the number of ethnic cleavages among the included sections of the population.

Each of these boundaries can become the focus of ethno-political conflict: who is included or excluded from state power, how power is shared among

[32] C Tilly, *From Mobilization to Revolution* (1978).

ethnic elites and their constituencies, and which ethnic communities should be governed by a state. We can thus distinguish between three types of ethnic conflict, depending on which of these boundaries is at stake and who the actors are that challenge each other over its location. When excluded segments of the population fight to shift the boundaries of inclusion, we call these conflicts *rebellions*. When ethnic elites in power are pitted against each other in a struggle over the spoils of government, we speak of *infighting*. *Secession* aims at changing the territorial boundaries of a polity and can be pursued by both excluded and included groups.

C. War-prone configurations: hypotheses

Following the logic of our configurational argument, we propose separate hypotheses for rebellions, infighting, and secession. First, *high degrees of ethnic exclusion will increase the likelihood of rebellion* (H1) because it decreases the political legitimacy of a state and thus makes it easier for political leaders to mobilize a following among their ethnic constituencies and challenge the government.[33] We expect that the most war-prone configurations are ethnocracies—the rule of an elite with a small ethnic constituency (such as the Tutsi in Burundi, white settlers in Rhodesia, or Sunni rule under Saddam Hussein).

Secondly, we assume that infighting is more likely to occur the more partners share government power, or in other words in states characterized by a segmented centre. Higher numbers of partners increases the possibility and likelihood of alliance shifts and thus the fear of losing out in the ongoing struggle over the distribution of the spoils of government.[34] Thus, it is more likely that an elite faction will mobilize ethnic followers and challenge the other power-sharing partners by demanding a bigger share of the government cake. In countries with only one ethnically defined elite in power, such ethnic infighting is logically impossible. Thus, *the higher the number of power sharing elites, the higher the likelihood of violent infighting* (H2). We expect countries characterized by a high degree of *centre segmentation*, such as Lebanon or India, to be particularly conflict-prone.

Thirdly, we hypothesize *that states with a long history of indirect rule are more likely to see secessionist conflicts* (H3). In such states, large segments of the

---

[33] For additional specifications of the mechanisms leading to successful ethnic mobilization, see M Hechter and M Levi, 'The comparative analysis of ethnoregional movements' (1979) 2 *Ethnic and Racial Studies* 260–74; T Gurr, 'Why minorities rebel: A global analysis of communal mobilization and conflict since 1945' (n 23 above); and A Wimmer, 'Who owns the state? Understanding ethnic conflict in post-colonial societies' (1997) 3 *Nations and Nationalism* 631–65.

[34] Donald Horowitz's magnum opus offers many insights into the mechanisms through which such elite competition escalates into violent conflict, including mutual outbidding of ethnic parties, the holding of a close election that resembles an ethnic census, or the logic military coups and counter-coups. D Horowitz, *Ethnic Groups in Conflict* (1985); cf also S Wilkinson, *Votes and Violence: Electoral competition and ethnic riots in India* (2004).

population are not accustomed to being governed directly by the political centre, and thus can be more easily mobilized for a secessionist project with the argument that only independence will avoid the danger or reality of alien rule.[35] An example is Bosnia, which spent the nineteenth and most of the twentieth century under Ottoman, Habsburg and later Yugoslavian rule. Fourthly, we postulate that *secession is more likely in large states* (H4). Large states are less likely to have penetrated the outer reaches of their territory in the past and accustomed the population to direct rule. Imperial past and population size are thus both measurements of *state cohesion*, ie the degree to which the population takes a state's territorial borders for granted and identifies with a state *independent* of who controls its government. An earlier literature in political anthropology referred to this aspect of an ethno-political configuration as 'institutional pluralism'.[36] States that lack coherence will more likely be challenged by secessionist groups that claim to represent either power-sharing partners or excluded populations. Low state cohesion thus reinforces the dynamics of exclusion and segmentation and leads challengers onto secessionist paths.

Additional factors come into play that may halt the spiral of mobilization, counter-mobilization, contestation, and escalation and instead lead to a path of accommodation and de-escalation. First, governments of rich countries are more able to accommodate protest movements through redistributionist policies and by co-opting their leadership into the power elite, such as in the aftermath of the civil rights movement in the United States. The same holds true for dissatisfied members of a power-sharing arrangement: new government institutions can be created and staffed with their followers, and new infrastructural projects can be directed toward their ethnic constituency. Conformingly, both rebellions and infighting *should be less likely the higher the level of development of a country* (H5).

---

[35] Cf M Hechter, 'Containing nationalist violence' in A Wimmer, D Horowitz, R Goldstone, U Joras, and C Schetter (eds), *Facing Ethnic Conflicts: Toward a new realism* (2003).

[36] Existing typologies are also based on exclusion, elite segmentation and state cohesion as main aspects of ethnopolitical configurations of power. Hechter and Levi, Horowitz, Lustick, and Wimmer distinguish highly exclusionary states and those with high levels of elite segmentation. M Hechter and M Levi, 'The comparative analysis of ethnoregional movements' (1979) 2 *Ethnic and Racial Studies* 260–74; D Horowitz, *Ethnic Groups in Conflict* (1985); I Lustick, 'Stability in deeply divided societies: Consociationalism versus control' (1979) 31 *World Politics* 325–44; and A Wimmer, *Nationalist Exclusion and Ethnic Conflicts: Shadows of modernity* (2002). Anthropologists working in 'complex societies' have analysed different degrees of 'institutional pluralism', thus referring to the cohesion dimension. MG Smith, 'Institutional and political conditions of pluralism' in L Kuper and MG Smith (eds), *Pluralism in Africa* (1969), 27–66; LA Despres, 'Anthropological theory, cultural pluralism, and the study of complex societies (1968) 9 *Current Anthropology* 3–26; JC Simpson, 'Pluralism: The evolution of a nebulous concept' (195) 38 *American Behavioural Scientist* 459–77. Cohen combines cohesion and exclusion, and Schermerhorn segmentation and exclusion. R Cohen, 'Ethnicity: Problem and focus in anthropology' (1978) 7 *Annual Review of Anthropology* 397–403; and RA Schermerhorn, *Comparative Ethnic Relations: A framework for theory and research* (1970). The most comprehensive typologies building on all three aspects are offered by C Young, *The Politics of Cultural Pluralism* (1976); and J Rothschild, *Ethnopolitics: A conceptual framework* (1981), Ch 3.

Our model thus incorporates one of the most robust findings in the civil war literature[37]—that civil wars happen in poor countries—and gives it a new interpretation in line with theories of contestation and violence.[38]

Secondly, the likelihood that a particular actor instigates conflict depends on the entire power configuration, not only on that actor's position within that configuration. More specifically, we expect that power-sharing partners are *less* likely to fight each other when there is at the same time a high risk of rebellion by the excluded population. We thus assume that the *higher the degree of exclusion, the less likely infighting will be* (H6); and *the larger (and thus more incoherent) a state, the less likely infighting will be* (H7). Our configurational theory therefore posits that exclusion and cohesion will have opposite effects on different types of ethnic conflict: ethnocracies will have more rebellions (H1), but less infighting among the included population (H6); incoherent states will have more secession (H4), but less infighting (H7). Only a disaggregated research design distinguishing between different types of ethnic conflicts will be able to test these hypotheses.

Our configurational theory incorporates and reconciles two sets of theoretical propositions that are usually conceived as mutually exclusive. First, much debate has centred on whether exclusion and segregation[39] or 'competition' and increased contact[40] are more conflict-prone. Our theory maintains that both hierarchical exclusion and vertical competition are relevant mechanisms that link ethnic politics to violence, but that they affect different types of actors, as defined by their position in the ethno-political power configuration. Our theory also specifies what competition and exclusion are about: they are not primarily about individual goods such as housing or jobs (as maintained by competition theory) or more generally the fruits of modernization,[41] but rather about control over the state and the public goods and services at its disposal.

Our approach also avoids the popular distinction between 'greed' and 'grievance' theories of civil war.[42] While the alliteration is certainly seductive and the dichotomy resonates well with Western traditions of opposing the material to the ideal, it makes little empirical sense. As argued above, ethnic politics simultaneously concerns 'material' interests such as access to government-controlled jobs, services, and contracts; 'idealist' motives such as the recognition of one's ethnic heritage by the state, and genuine political goals; and, most importantly, access to state power. Because political domination by ethnic others also affects one's economic, legal, and symbolic standing, it is pointless to

---

[37] Hegre and Sambanis, 'Sensitivity analysis of empirical results on civil war onset' (n 15 above).
[38] Cf S Tarrow and C Tilly, *Contentious Politics* (2006), 145.
[39] Cf Hechter's 'internal colonialism' model. M Hechter, *Internal Colonialism: The Celtic fringe in British national development, 1536–1966* (1975).
[40] S Olzak and J Nagel (eds), *Competitive Ethnic Relations* (1986); D Horowitz, *Ethnic Groups in Conflict* (1985). [41] As argued in Horowitz, *Ethnic Groups in Conflict* (n 36 above).
[42] Introduced by Collier and Hoeffler, 'Greed and grievance in civil war'(n 7 above).

try to disentangle these intertwined and mutually reinforcing motives from each other.[43] The crucial question is thus not so much whether rebels are coolly calculating materialists or hot-blooded idealists fighting for a cause, but rather what causal dynamics will lead actors with complexly intertwined motives down the path towards conflict. To investigate this dynamic properly, we need data that measure degrees of competition and exclusion in appropriate ways.

IV. The Ethnic Power Relations (EPR) Dataset, 1946–2005

The Ethnic Power Relations (EPR) dataset identifies all politically relevant ethnic categories around the world and measures access to executive-level state power for members of these ethnic categories in all years from 1946 to 2005. For the sake of brevity, we introduce only the major aspects of the dataset here and refer readers to the online supplement for more details about coding procedures and rules. The dataset contains two parts. The first is a country–year dataset that codes all politically relevant ethnic groups and the degree of access to central state power.[44] The second is a conflict dataset, based on the widely used PRIO/Uppsala Armed Conflict Dataset that includes all armed conflicts with more than twenty-five battle deaths. We extend the dataset with new codings of whether rebels pursued ethnic or non-ethnic goals as well as whether they aim at secession or not; we also link conflicts to politically relevant ethnic groups when rebels claim to fight in the name of a particular ethnic community.

A. Politically relevant ethnic groups and access to power

Following the constructivist, Weberian tradition of ethnicity studies, we define ethnicity as any subjectively experienced sense of commonality based on the belief in common ancestry and shared culture. Ethnolinguistic, ethno-somatic (or 'racial') and ethno-religious groups are included in this definition of ethnicity, but not tribes and clans which conceive of ancestry in genealogical terms, as well as regions which do not define commonality on the basis of shared ancestry. Ethnic categories might be hierarchically nested, ie comprise several levels of differentiation, not all of which might be politically relevant at a particular point in time.[45]

An ethnic category is politically relevant if at least one significant political actor claims to represent the interests of an ethnic group in the national political

---

[43] See also S Tarrow and C Tilly, *Contentious Politics* (2006).
[44] The dataset includes all 155 sovereign states with a population of at least 1 million and a surface area of at least 500,000 km² as of 2005.
[45] On the notion of ethnicity underlying this project, see A Wimmer, 'The making and unmaking of ethnic boundaries: A multi-level process theory' (2008) 113 *American Journal of Sociology* 970–1022.

arena, or if members of an ethnic category are systematically and intentionally discriminated against in the domain of public politics. We did not distinguish between degrees of representativity of political actors who claim to speak in the name of an ethnic group, nor did we code the heterogeneity of political positions voiced by leaders claiming to represent the same community.[46] The coding scheme allowed for the identification of countries or specific periods in which political objectives, alliances, or disputes were never framed in ethnic terms. This avoids using an ethnic lens for countries such as Tanzania and Korea which are not characterized by ethnic politics.

Because politically relevant categories and levels of access to political power may change over time, coders were asked to divide the 1946 to 2005 period and provide separate codings for each sub-period. This was also necessary when the list of politically relevant categories changed from one year to the next, either because certain categories cease to be or become relevant for the first time or because higher or lower levels of ethnic differentiation became salient. The next important step was to code the degree of access to power enjoyed by political leaders who claim to represent these various groups. We focus on executive level power only, ie representation in the presidency, the cabinet, and senior posts in the administration including the army. The weight given to these different institutions depended on their de facto power in a given country. In all cases, coders were to focus on absolute access to power irrespective of the question of under- or over-representation relative to the demographic size of an ethnic category.

All politically relevant ethnic groups were categorized according to the degree of access to central state power by those who claim to represent them. Some hold full control of the executive branch with no meaningful participation by members of any other group, others share power with members of other groups, and some are excluded altogether from decision-making authority within the halls of state power. Within each of these three basic categories, coders were asked to differentiate between further subtypes, choosing between 'monopoly power', 'dominance', 'senior' or 'junior partner' in a power-sharing arrangement, 'regional autonomy', 'powerless', and 'discriminated'. The details of the coding scheme can be found in the online appendix (section 1). For the purpose of the present analysis, we only distinguish between power-holding groups (whatever their share of power), and the excluded population not represented at the centres of state power. A disaggregated analysis at the group level using the full array of power categories is currently in preparation.[47]

---

[46] Cf R Brubaker, 'Ethnicity without groups' in A Wimmer et al (eds), *Facing Ethnic Conflicts: Toward a new realism* (2004).

[47] L-E Cederman, A Wimmer, and B Min, *Understanding Ethno-Nationalist Conflict: from factors to actors* (forthcoming).

B. War coding

The conflict dataset created for this project is based upon the widely used Uppsala/PRIO Armed Conflicts Dataset (ACD).[48] ACD defines armed conflict as any armed and organized confrontation between government troops and rebel organizations or between army factions that reaches an annual battle-death threshold of twenty-five. Massacres and genocides are not included because the victims are not organized and armed, and communal riots and pogroms are excluded because the government is not directly involved.

This dataset has so far been of limited use for the analysis of ethnic conflict because it does not contain information on whether a conflict should be classified as ethnic or not. We conducted new research to overcome this limitation and coded for each conflict whether rebel organizations pursued ethno-nationalist aims and recruited along ethnic lines. We also coded whether or not they aimed at establishing a new independent state.

Ethnic/non-ethnic conflicts were distinguished first by the aims of the armed organization and secondly by their recruitment and alliance structures, in line with other ongoing coding projects.[49] We identified as 'ethnic' the aims of achieving ethno-national self-determination, a more favourable ethnic balance of power in government, ethno-regional autonomy, the end of ethnic/racial discrimination, language and other cultural rights, and so forth. In ethnic wars, armed organizations also recruit fighters predominantly among the ethnic group of their leaders and forge alliances on the basis of ethnic similarity.

We looked at the aims and recruitment patterns of each armed organization involved in a conflict separately. In some complex cases (as in Afghanistan, Burma, Chad, Uganda, Angola, Zaire, and so on), we disaggregated a conflict into sub-conflicts when different ethnic claims were made on the non-governmental side and rebel organizations acted independent from each other. Our dataset thus comprises a higher number of conflicts than the original ACD dataset.

All ethnic conflicts were then linked to the politically relevant ethnic category in the EPR dataset. To avoid endogeneity problems, we made sure that the coding of ethnic power relations reflected the power constellation *before* the outbreak of conflict in cases where political changes occurred in the same year as a conflict. In order to test our configurational theory of ethnic conflict, we then divided ethnic conflicts into those fought in the name of ethnic groups that were excluded from central government power (*rebellions*) and those that were fought in the name of power holders (*infighting*). We further subdivide rebellions and infighting depending on whether they were fought with the aim of establishing a

---

[48] NP Gleditsch et al, 'Armed conflict 1946–2001: A new dataset' (2002) 39 *Journal of Peace Research* 615–37.
[49] N Sambanis, *What is an Ethnic War? Organization and Interests in Insurgencies* (nd).

Table 1.1. The conflict dataset

	Ethnic conflicts		Non-ethnic conflicts	Total
	Infighting	Rebellions		
Secessionist	9	48	3	60
Non-secessionist	11	42	102	155
Total infighting rebellions	20	90		
Total	110		105	215

separate, independent state or joining another existing state. This produces a fourfold typology with separatist rebellions, non-separatist rebellions, separatist infightings, and non-separatist infightings.

Our dataset includes 215 armed conflicts fought between 1946–2005, 110 of which were ethnic conflicts. Secessionist aims were pursued in 60 of these conflicts, the vast majority of which were also ethnic in character. Among the 110 ethnic conflicts, 20 were fought by groups in power, 90 by excluded groups. One-half of the conflicts reached the standard threshold of civil war defined as a conflict with more than 1,000 battle deaths in a year.

V. Variables and Data Sources

A. Exclusion, centre segmentation, state cohesion

To test hypothesis H1, we compute the share of the excluded population in the total population that is ethno-politically relevant. We call this the *share of the excluded population* for short. We assume that increases in the share of the excluded population have a greater effect on the likelihood of conflict at lower levels of exclusion compared to higher levels and therefore use a logged transformation of this variable. We measure the degree of centre segmentation (which according to H2 is associated with higher conflict probability) by counting the number of power-sharing groups represented by ethnic elites. The *number of power-sharing partners* ranges from one to fourteen (in India). Following hypothesis H3, the cohesion of a state decreases the longer the pre-independence history of indirect rule in an empire and the larger the size of the population. We rely on a measure of a country's *past imperial history*, which calculates the percentage of years spent between 1816 and independence under imperial rule.[50] We counted as 'under imperial rule' all years during which a territory was either a colonial or imperial dependency (including of the Soviet Union and other communist empires) or the heartland of a land-based empire such as Turkey

---

[50] A Wimmer and B Min, 'From empire to nation-state' (n 2 above).

under the Ottomans or Austria under the Habsburgs (but not the 'mother country' of an empire with seaborne colonies like Portugal).

B. Other variables

We control for other variables found to be robustly significant in civil war research, especially in the meta-analysis conducted by Hegre and Sambanis.[51] *Linguistic fractionalization*[52] is included to show its limited significance once ethnic politics variables are included. *GDP per capita* and a state's *population size* play an important role in our own theory of ethnic politics (according to H5 and H4).

'Democratic civil peace' theory states that democracies are better able to solve internal disputes. Autocracies on the other hand can suppress rebellions by the use of force or by threatening mass violence. Civil wars should therefore be less likely in strongly democratic and autocratic societies.[53] We use Polity IV data and the widely adopted cut-offs of +6 and −6 to identify democracies, autocracies, and anocracies.

Fearon and Laitin's 'insurgency model' maintains that wars break out if government forces are weak and if mountainous terrain allows rebels to hide and retreat.[54] We included measures of *mountainous terrain* and *previous regime change* (which should weaken the government vis-à-vis rebels) to evaluate their main argument. The mountainous terrain data are adopted from their dataset; regime change is defined as any change in the polity score of three points or more over the prior three years.

Michael Ross has developed a theory of how the availability of natural resources affects different types of conflict.[55] He expects that when the extraction of natural resources can be obstructed by rebels, as with oil, the likelihood of secessionist movements increases.[56] Buhaug, on the contrary, argues that oil should matter for conflicts over control of an existing state, because oil resources

---

[51] Hegre and Sambanis, 'Sensitivity analysis of empirical results on civil war onset' (n 15 above).

[52] As found in the Fearon and Laitin dataset. Fearon and Laitin, 'Ethnicity, insurgency, and civil war' (n 6 above).

[53] Müller and Weede, Mansfield and Snyder, Hegre et al, Ellingsen, Sambanis, and Reynal-QUerol confirm this hypothesis for ethnic wars. EN Müller and E Weede, 'Cross-national variation in political violence: a rational action approach' (1990) 34 *Journal of Conflict Resolution* 624–51; ED Mansfield and J Snyder, *Electing to Fight: Why emerging democracies go to war* (2005); H Hegre, T Ellingsen, S Gates and NP Gleditsch, 'Toward a democratic civil peace? Democracy, political change, and civil war, 1816–1992' (2001) 95 *The American Political Science Review* 33–48; T Ellingsen, 'Colorful community or ethnic witches' brew?' (n 19 above); Sambanis, 'Do ethnic and nonethnic civil wars have the same causes?' (n 3 above); and M Reynal-Querol, 'Ethnicity, political systems, and civil wars' (2002) 46 *Journal of Conflict Resolution* 29–54.

[54] Fearon and Laitin, 'Ethnicity, insurgency, and civil war' (n 6 above).

[55] M Ross, 'Oil, drugs, and diamonds. How do natural resources vary in their impact on civil war?' in K Ballentine and J Sherman (eds), *Beyond Greed and Grievance: The political economy of armed conflict* (2003).

[56] Cf also Collier and Hoeffler, 'Greed and grievance in civil war' (n 7 above).

are usually controlled by the central government, thus increasing the incentives to capture a state, rather than to secede from it.[57] To measure the impact of oil, we generate an *oil production per capita* variable based upon data from Wimmer and Min.[58]

VI. Models and Findings

Our dataset includes 7,155 country–year observations covering 155 sovereign states in all years after independence from 1946–2005. We use the standard modelling approach in the literature on civil war, regressing a range of independent variables on a binary dependent variable coded as 1 in the first year of an armed conflict and 0 otherwise. We create a civil-conflict onset variable which includes both ethnic and non-ethnic onsets as well as a more narrow ethnic-conflict onset variable. For the ethnic-conflict onset variable, we disaggregate further to distinguish between the political status of the groups instigating the conflict (excluded or power sharers) and the aims of these parties (whether secession or not).[59]

Our analysis proceeds in four steps, each one leading to a more fine-grained, disaggregated analysis of conflict onset. First, we determine whether ethnic politics matters at all in predicting the onset of armed civil conflicts. In the second step, we focus on ethnic conflicts only while maintaining our global purview and keeping all country–years in the analysis. Thirdly, we evaluate whether exclusion and segmentation predict rebellions and infighting respectively. In the fourth step, we disaggregate further and determine in how far state cohesion affects both rebellion and infighting and drives them toward secessionist goals.

A. Explaining armed conflict

We first test whether ethnic politics matters for understanding conflict and peace (H1–H3). To make sure that our results do not depend on our coding of civil conflicts, we also run our model on high-intensity wars only as well as against

---

[57] H Buhaug, 'Relative capability and rebel objective in civil war' (2006) 43 *Journal of Peace Research* 691–708.   [58] A Wimmer and B Min, 'From empire to nation-state' (n 2 above).
[59] We control for possible time trends by including the number of peace years since the outbreak of a war as well as a cubic spline function on peace years following Beck, Katz, and Tucker. N Beck, JN Katz, and R Tucker, 'Taking time seriously: Time-series-cross-section analysis with a binary dependent variable' (1998) 42 *Journal of Political Science* 1260–88. We also add a calendar-year variable in order to capture possible changes in the geopolitical climate over time. For the sake of space, we do not show the time control variables in the following tables. As a robustness check, we tested our models with regional controls and also without time controls and found no large differences in our main findings. Throughout, we specify robust standard errors clustered by country to account for the non-independence of observations from the same state. Since armed conflict is a rare event, we also ran our models using the 'rare events' logit estimator and found no substantive differences to our main findings.

war codings from the well-known civil war datasets assembled by Fearon and Laitin and Sambanis.[60]

Table 1.2 shows that ethnic politics is an important part of the puzzle to explain civil wars. The results challenge 'greed and opportunity' theories of civil war according to which ethnicity is unrelated to conflict. It also demonstrates that once ethnic politics is measured directly, the ethnic diversity index loses any significance—contrary to what the 'diversity breeds conflict' school assumes. Rather than diversity as such, it is political exclusion along ethnic lines that breeds ethnic conflict.

The share of the excluded population, the central variable of our configurational model of ethnic conflict, is significant for all model specifications: when using Fearon and Laitin's or Sambanis' coding of dependent variables (ie excluding low-intensity wars); when dropping all ongoing war years from the sample or leaving them in; and with or without additional control variables. Ethnic exclusion is as consistently related to conflict as GDP per capita, one of the most robust explanatory factors in the study of civil wars.[61]

In contrast, the number of power-sharing partners (H2) does not have a robust impact on civil war onset. This is not surprising, given that only 20 of the 200 conflicts in this analysis are initiated by actors representing ethnic groups in power. Moreover, since high degrees of exclusion have a mitigating effect on the likelihood of infighting (H6), we expect to see the effects of centre segmentation only when we disaggregate the dependent variable. The imperial-past variable is positive but insignificant (H3). We demonstrate further below that the lack of state coherence substantially increases the likelihood of ethnic secessionist conflicts.

B. Explaining ethnic conflict

This is the first time that the ethnic-exclusion argument has been statistically confirmed based on a global dataset that measures degrees of exclusion directly, and at the polity rather than the group level. The robustness of this finding is remarkable, given that we regress on all civil conflicts in our dataset. Our model of ethnic politics obviously makes no claims to explain non-ethnic wars such as the civil war in Korea or army coups in Brazil. Since half of the conflicts in the above analysis are not fought in the name of ethnic groups, a more focused investigation needs to exclude non-ethnic conflicts, as we do in the second panel in Table 2 (models 6 to 9). We thus follow in the footsteps of Sambanis who has

---

[60] Fearon and Laitin, 'Ethnicity, insurgency, and civil war' (n 6 above); and N Sambanis, 'What is civil war? Conceptual and empirical complexities of an operational definition' (2004) 48 *Journal of Conflict Resolution* 814–58.
[61] Hegre and Sambanis, 'Sensitivity analysis of empirical results on civil war onset' (n 15 above).

Table 1.2. Ethnicity matters for explaining armed conflict

	DV: Onset of conflicts					DV: Onset of ethnic conflict			
Model no	1	2	3	4	5	6	7	8	9
Conflict dataset	ACD	ACD	ACD High intensity	Fearon and Laitin	Sambanis	ACD	ACD	ACD High intensity	Fearon and Laitin
Ethnic politics variables									
Excluded populations	0.1887**	0.1291*	0.2859**	0.2564**	0.2792**	0.4192**	0.3191**	0.5347**	0.3667**
	(0.0513)	(0.0558)	(0.0834)	(0.0779)	(0.0808)	-0.0862	-0.0875	-0.1351	-0.1214
Centre segmentation	0.0862**	0.0587	0.0562	0.0771	0.0177	0.1554**	0.1120**	0.1272*	0.0969
	(0.0295)	(0.0389)	(0.0455)	(0.0586)	(0.0491)	-0.0312	-0.037	-0.053	-0.0747
Imperial past	0.2075	0.4579	0.7285	0.7899*	0.5932	0.6401	0.9301*	1.1793	1.5761**
	(0.2614)	(0.2886)	(0.4441)	(0.3568)	(0.3307)	-0.4477	-0.4426	-0.6304	-0.4244
Other Variables									
Linguistic fractionalization		0.6298	0.1244	-0.0283	0.0261		1.2800**	0.2563	0.599
		(0.3227)	(0.4597)	(0.4274)	(0.3989)		-0.3997	-0.4974	-0.6156
GDP per capita	0.1239**	-0.1093**	-0.1902**	-0.1267**	-0.1750**	-0.1446**	-0.1256**	-0.1921**	-0.1554**
	(0.0271)	(0.0276)	(0.0546)	(0.0374)	(0.0472)	-0.0415	-0.0448	-0.0746	-0.0585
Population size	0.1556**	0.1397**	0.0865	0.2354**	0.2135**	0.2171**	0.2102**	0.1884**	0.3609**
	(0.0559)	(0.0532)	(0.0636)	(0.0672)	(0.0616)	-0.0714	-0.0656	-0.0757	-0.0894
Mountainous terrain		0.1241*	0.1901	0.1581*	0.1320		0.1749	0.3258*	0.0701
		(0.0601)	(0.1117)	(0.0794)	(0.0765)		-0.0984	-0.1483	-0.109

	DV: Onset of conflicts						DV: Onset of ethnic conflict		
Model no	1	2	3	4	5	6	7	8	9
Conflict dataset	ACD	ACD	ACD High intensity	Fearon and Laitin	Sambanis	ACD	ACD	ACD High intensity	Fearon and Laitin
Political instability		0.3454	0.4555	0.2693	0.2655		0.1544	0.2979	-0.0441
		(0.1764)	(0.2852)	(0.2754)	(0.2412)				
Anocracy		0.4292**	0.4014	0.7218**	0.6478**		0.4469*	0.5681	0.9738**
		(0.1625)	(0.2511)	(0.2369)	(0.1863)				
Oil production per capita		0.0171**	0.0051	0.0056	0.0176*		0.0180*	0.0277**	-0.2614
		(0.0063)	(0.0162)	(0.0165)	(0.0078)				0.0064
Ongoing war	0.9832**	-0.9678**	-1.2732**	-2.1655**	-1.4045**	0.0359	-0.0091	-0.0083	-0.0284
	(0.3620)	(0.3733)	(0.4690)	(0.4277)	(0.4435)		-0.0697	-0.7636	-2.2861**
Constant	-16.1544	-14.2810	-9.0225	-49.4749**	-46.1852**	-0.6123	-0.6166	-0.6271	-0.5551
	(10.2646)	(10.5160)	(13.5435)	(14.6798)	(14.8129)	-37.1296*	-32.6393*	-26.7855	-80.7809**
						-14.6291	-15.1798	-17.9573	-17.4279
No of observations	6938	6865	6865	6034	5818	6938	6865	6865	6034
No of conflict onsets	200	197	82	97	121	103	102	50	66

Time controls not shown; robust standard errors in parentheses; ** $p<0.01$, * $p<0.05$

shown that ethnic civil wars and non-ethnic civil wars are caused by different factors and therefore need to be analysed separately.[62]

As one would expect, once we focus on ethnic conflicts only, the other two ethnic-politics variables become statistically significant. The share of the excluded population is again highly significant in all model specifications. The number of power-sharing groups is significant in all models except in regressions on Fearon and Laitin's coding of high-intensity wars. The imperial-past variable, which measures the degree of state cohesion and should predict secessionist conflicts only, reaches significance in some models (we revisit this result further below).

Exclusion, segmentation, and incohesion are also *substantively* important for the dynamics of war and peace. Increasing the share of the excluded population from 6 per cent to 32 per cent (an increase of one standard deviation from the mean) results in a 25 per cent increase in the probability of ethnic conflict (calculated on the basis of model 7). A one standard-deviation increase in centre segmentation leads to a 9 per cent increased risk of conflict while a similar increase in years under imperial rule between 1816 and independence increases the chance of armed conflict by 13 per cent. One standard-deviation increase in GDP per capita and population size, the two most robustly significant variables in the civil war literature, influence the war probability by 22 per cent and 13 per cent respectively.

The strength and robustness of the exclusion, segmentation, and cohesion variables is all the more remarkable since the dependent variable here does not distinguish between different types of ethnic conflict. However, our theory assumes that infighting, rebellion, and secession are caused by different ethnopolitical configurations and that the same variable might therefore have *opposite* effects on the likelihood of different types of conflict (see H1 and H6 and H4 and H7). In order to test this, we disaggregate the dependent variable further and use multinomial logit regressions to predict the onset of different types of ethnic conflicts.

C. Explaining rebellion and infighting

In the first step, we distinguish between ethnic conflicts fought in the name of excluded groups (rebellions) and those begun by power-sharing partners (infighting). We expect that the two principal aspects of ethnic politics affect rebellions and infighting differently: the higher the number of power-sharing elites and the more unstable their alliance, the more likely they will fight wars against each other (H2), while centre segmentation should have no effect on rebellions by the leaders who claim to represent excluded groups. The size of the

---

[62] Sambanis, 'Do ethnic and nonethnic civil wars have the same causes?' (n 3 above), 259–82; but see Fearon and Laitin, 'Ethnicity, insurgency, and civil war' (n 6 above).

Table 1.3 Explaining onsets of ethnic conflicts by actor type (infighting and rebellion)

Type of ethnic conflict	Infighting by power holders	Rebellion by excluded	Infighting by power holders	Rebellion by excluded
Ethnic politics variables				
Excluded population	-0.0379	0.5212**	-0.3146	0.5146**
	(0.1659)	(0.0808)	(0.1802)	(0.0848)
Centre segmentation	0.3583**	0.0468	0.3285**	0.0648
	(0.0568)	(0.0387)	(0.0684)	(0.0433)
Imperial past	2.8363	0.4000	3.7934*	0.4520
	(1.5424)	(0.4405)	(1.8819)	(0.4836)
Other variables				
Linguistic fractionalization	-0.8215	1.5463**	1.1132	1.4589**
	(1.1411)	(0.4868)	(1.1328)	(0.4450)
GDP per capita	-0.2628	-0.0921*	-0.2148	-0.0967*
	(0.1493)	(0.0391)	(0.1248)	(0.0437)
Population size	-0.2531*	0.3832**	-0.4172**	0.3818**
	(0.1184)	(0.0765)	(0.1517)	(0.0826)
Mountainous terrain			0.6026**	0.0767
			(0.2179)	(0.1189)
Political instability			0.1255	0.1751
			(0.6731)	(0.3150)
Anocracy			0.4277	0.4566
			(0.4815)	(0.2374)
Oil production per capita			0.0198	0.0196
			(0.0113)	(0.0116)
Ongoing war	0.5618	-0.0881	0.2301	-0.1307
	(1.2172)	(0.6913)	(1.1056)	(0.6827)
Constant	-93.2683*	-23.6030	-88.1487*	-26.0182
	(37.7776)	(15.9535)	(42.1082)	(16.3912)
No of observations	6935	6935	6865	6865
No of conflict onsets	20	83	19	83

Time controls not shown; robust standard errors in parentheses; ** $p<0.01$, * $p<0.05$

excluded population, on the other hand, should have opposite effects on included and excluded groups: it should increase the likelihood of rebellion (H1), and therefore provide a disincentive for infighting (H6).

Table 1.3 shows that the higher the number of groups that share power, the higher the likelihood that they will fight each other on the battlefield. There is some evidence that infighting is less likely when large sections of the population are excluded from power (H6), but the finding is not statistically significant. Infighting is also influenced, and again *negatively*, by population size (H7). The larger (and thus more incoherent) a state's population, the less likely elites can afford to fight each other to increase their share of power. Contrary to our expectations, infighting is not significantly less likely in richer countries (inconsistent with H5), though the sign of the coefficient points in the expected direction.

Rebellions by excluded groups are indeed influenced by the size of the excluded population (H1). They are less likely in rich countries (H5) where governments can afford to redistribute state resources and/or co-opt the leaders of protest movements. H5 therefore receives mixed support. More populous and linguistically heterogeneous states are more likely to see rebellions—a finding that is mostly driven by secessionist wars, as we will see in the next section when we further disaggregate the dependent variable by actor's aims. State coherence (measured through the imperial-past variable) does not consistently predict rebellions or infighting, a result also to be revisited below.

D. Explaining secessionist and non-secessionist conflicts by rebels and infighters

We now further differentiate between secessionist and non-secessionist wars. Combining actor types with war aims generates four kinds of ethnic conflict: secessionist wars fought in the name of excluded groups (or secessionist rebellions for short), non-secessionist rebellions, secessionist conflict started by power-sharing groups (or secessionist infighting for short) and non-secessionist infighting. We now run multinomial logit regressions using these four types of ethnic conflict as possible outcomes.

The results displayed in Table 1.4 support our expectations quite clearly. Exclusion and centre segmentation have the same effects on the likelihood of rebellions and infighting as before and they also predict the onset of secessionist wars. How does state cohesion affect conflict? Conforming to H3, having spent more years in imperial polities over the past two centuries increases the likelihood of secessionist conflict instigated by both power sharers and the leaders of excluded groups but has no effect on non-secessionist ethnic conflicts. The size of a state's population is also linked with secessions (H4). Both a long imperial past and a large population size suggest the presence of population segments accustomed to self-rule who are likely to resent the shift to direct rule that the modern nation state brings about. As we expect, population size is significant and positive for excluded populations only and the sign of the coefficient is negative for power-sharing partners (H7).[63]

Our expectations regarding the effects of levels of economic development, however, are again not fully confirmed. While the governments of richer countries are able to avoid non-secessionist rebellions because they can afford to co-opt the leadership of ethnic protest movements, they do not experience less non-secessionist infighting. That said, the frequency of violent infighting is rare

---

[63] The fact that population size is totally insignificant in regressions on the onset of non-ethnic wars (results not shown) supports our interpretation of the population size variable as a proxy for state coherence—contrary to the interpretation of, eg, Fearon and Laitin, who hypothesize that large populations are logistically and militarily more difficult to control by the government. Fearon and Laitin, 'Ethnicity, insurgency, and civil war' (n 6 above).

Table 1.4 Explaining onset of ethnic conflict, by actor and aim

War type	Secession by power holders	Secession by excluded	Infighting by power holders	Rebellion by excluded
Ethnic politics variables				
Excluded population	-0.2032	0.2554*	-0.4504	0.7501**
	(0.3306)	(0.1109)	(0.3156)	(0.1277)
Centre segmentation	0.4956**	0.0008	0.3176**	0.0689
	(0.1164)	(0.0417)	(0.0960)	(0.1001)
Imperial past	14.6269**	1.9524*	1.1870	-0.8041
	(2.8503)	(0.8152)	(1.6311)	(0.7777)
Other variables				
Linguistic fractionalization	1.4433	1.9997**	0.9991	0.9796
	(1.2707)	(0.6431)	(1.6116)	(0.8709)
GDP per capita	-0.6017	-0.0226	-0.1914	-0.1833*
	(0.3302)	(0.0584)	(0.1750)	(0.0814)
Population size	-0.1882	0.4835**	-0.7321**	0.2498
	(0.1925)	(0.1256)	(0.1841)	(0.1329)
Mountainous terrain	0.6948	0.3943	0.5656*	-0.0913
	(0.3751)	(0.2211)	(0.2815)	(0.1608)
Political instability	-35.2497**	0.3655	1.0312	0.0291
	(0.6728)	(0.5128)	(0.7487)	(0.4485)
Anocracy	1.4050	0.2931	0.0115	0.6333
	(0.9854)	(0.3892)	(0.7129)	(0.3639)
Oil production per capita	-0.3692	0.0016	0.0126	0.0296**
	(0.4031)	(0.0452)	(0.0088)	(0.0085)
Ongoing war	2.6879	-0.1664	-0.5972	-0.0502
	(2.9776)	(1.0923)	(1.7814)	(0.9068)
Constant	-290.3441**	-15.6566	12.0956	-45.2199
	(41.4419)	(22.4369)	(68.2112)	(23.1803)
No of observations	6865	6865	6865	6865
No of conflict onsets	9	41	10	42

Time controls not shown; robust standard errors in parentheses; ** p<0.01, * p<0.0

(nine for secessionist and ten for non-secessionist cases). These results therefore should be interpreted with some caution.

Table 1.4 again includes linguistic fractionalization as a control variable. With a disaggregated measure of ethnic conflict as the dependent variable, we find that linguistic diversity is significant only in predicting secessionist rebellions (and only in models that include ongoing war years. We therefore suggest that linguistic fractionalization captures—in an indirect and rough way—an aspect of state coherence. It expresses how far the central state has managed to assimilate its population linguistically in past centuries and thus provides an indicator of a state's capacity to extend its reach over a territory over a prolonged timeframe. Conformingly, linguistic fractionalization should be linked with the consequences of low state cohesion like a higher risk of secessionist conflict.

Table 1.4 shows that once ethnic politics is measured in more adequate and direct ways, and once we have reached the appropriate level of disaggregation, the effects of linguistic fractionalization are very limited.

Among other control variables, anocracy and regime change again have no significant effects on any of the four types of conflict, while mountainous terrain again is associated with infighting rather than rebellion. Oil resources increase the likelihood of non-secessionist wars fought by excluded groups, consistent with Buhaug's hypothesis that oil resources provide incentives to capture the state, but not to secede from it.

Overall, the results of these tables demonstrate that a configurational approach to the study of civil wars yields important insights about the different mechanisms that generate violence and war. Measures of ethnic politics have heterogeneous effects on different types of ethnic conflict, as do other key variables such as population size and oil. Our configurational approach now allows us to better understand why ethnic conflicts and wars might erupt in such widely different ethno-political constellations as in Bosnia, Northern Ireland, and Mexico.

Bosnian Serbs were part of a segmented power-sharing arrangement within which elite competition for control over the newly founded state quickly escalated to incompatible positions and demands. The weak coherence of the former Yugoslav state and the high degree of disidentification of all but the Bosniak segments of the population further increased the likelihood of conflict and gave it a secessionist form. In Northern Ireland, however, the conflict erupted as a struggle over the political exclusion of the large Catholic population. Ireland was long ruled as an internal colony of Great Britain, and conformingly the northern parts of the island disidentified with the British state, increasing the likelihood that rebels would pursue secessionist aims. In 1994 in Mexico, Comandante Marcos led a group of former peasant activists into a rebellion against the exclusion suffered by the indigenous populations of Chiapas for centuries. In contrast to Northern Ireland and Bosnia, however, the Mexican state had enough time over the past two centuries to project its symbolic and political power over the population, who thus had learned to see their membership in the state as self-evident and legitimate. The rebellion thus did not develop into a separatist endeavour, even though ample opportunities for solidarity with neighbouring Guatemaltecan Mayas and their rebel organizations existed.

VII. Conclusions

This chapter identifies the conditions under which struggles over state power may lead to ethnic conflict. The higher the proportion of the population that is excluded from access to the state because of their ethnic background and the more ethnically segmented the centre of power, the more likely the struggle over control of the state will escalate into armed confrontation. These conflicts will be even more likely and will take on secessionist forms in incoherent states in which the population is not accustomed to direct rule by the political centre.

These results represent a major challenge to the 'greed and opportunity' school, which denies that ethnicity is a relevant factor in explaining civil war. To be sure, our argument is not that ethnic 'identity' or 'grievances' motivate people to found and join armed organizations, as opposed to 'interests' and 'greed'. Rather, ethnicity may channel the pursuit of power and prestige along certain pathways such that the factions that struggle over control of the state will align along an ethnic cleavage. Ethnicity is not an aim in itself, but rather the organizational means through which individuals struggle to gain access to state power. Our approach specifies the incentive structures under which this political logic of ethnic solidarity comes into play as well as the conditions under which it leads to armed conflict.

Contrary to what the 'diversity breeds conflict' school assumes, we have shown that ethnic conflicts are not more likely in more diverse countries: ethno-demographic diversity indices rarely achieve significance and do so only for a circumscribed subset of conflicts. Ethno-demographic indices, and many theories of conflict and peace that rely on them, bracket the crucial fact that the state is not a neutral actor, nor a passive arena within which ethnic actors operate, but both the prize over which contending political actors struggle and a power instrument for those who control it.

Our study also goes beyond the 'minority mobilization' model by showing that ethnic mobilization and conflict involve not only discriminated minorities fighting for their rights, but often concern the entire configuration of power, most importantly the question of who has access to state power and controls which share of it. Our results lend themselves to a broader perspective that is not exclusively focused on demographic minorities 'at risk', but on the dynamics of ethnic politics at the centre of the state: contrary to the expectations of the minority-mobilization model, it is excluded majorities, rather than minorities, among which challengers are most likely to find an armed following. In addition, an important number of conflicts are instigated by groups in power—rather than discriminated minorities.

We conclude by pointing out some implications of our research for conflict prevention and intervention. Obviously, this project was not designed to answer the question of how best to avoid the escalation of ethno-political competition into full scale civil war or which power-sharing formulas are more likely to deliver enduring peace.[64] Nevertheless, our analysis speaks to the literature on conflict prevention in important ways.

First, our findings support a recent trend in the debate on prevention and intervention underlining the need to analyse individual conflicts in its own specific terms in order to determine the best strategy of intervention and to find

---

[64] B Walter, *Committing to Peace: The successful settlement of civil wars* (2002).

the institutional arrangements most likely to promote a lasting peace.[65] According to the configurational approach advocated here, it is plausible that conflicts caused by segmentation might need a different solution to those where exclusion or incohesion are the main factors. More precisely, our findings suggest that 'electoral engineering'—eg choosing the appropriate electoral system that maximizes the chances for cross-ethnic alliance building between competing ethnic elites[66]—is the most appropriate instrument for conflict prevention when elite infighting is the main danger to be avoided. It would increase the likelihood of a 'de-ethnicization' of politics and mobilizes the integrative potential of cross-cutting cleavages. Power-sharing in its various forms—from reserved seats in the parliament to consociational arrangements in the executive branch—could be a strategy to overcome the dynamics of exclusion and violent mobilization against such exclusion—though in specific contexts more inclusion might increase segmentation, a point to which we will return below. Substantial forms of self-rule, or even the possibility of independent sovereignty,[67] might prove to be the only durable solution to conflicts that are related to a low degree of state cohesion—although self-rule might increase exclusion and thus increase the likelihood of conflict along new lines, as discussed below.

Secondly, the above indicates that exclusion, segmentation and cohesion are not independent from each other, but interact in complex and often unexpected way. Our research thus explains why outside interventions and attempts at preventing violence might well *produce* violence as an unintended consequence, a theme that has recently been reflected upon by policymakers.[68] The dilemmas associated with peacemaking therefore result from the interrelationship between exclusion and segmentation on the one hand, and exclusion and cohesion on the other hand. We address each of these dilemmas subsequently.

Including hitherto discriminated ethnic groups in a power-sharing arrangement might well decrease the propensity of ethnic conflict along the exclusion dimension. However, the newly included groups might now compete with existing elites for the distribution of state power and thus increase the degree of segmentation. To put this dilemma in provocative terms, under which conditions will more inclusion *increase* the likelihood of conflict? According to our model, this depends on the number of groups already sharing power as well as

---

[65] Cf A Wimmer et al (eds), *Facing Ethnic Conflicts: Toward a new realism* (2004).
[66] Eg, A Ellis, 'The politics of electoral systems in transition' in A Wimmer et al (eds), *Facing Ethnic Conflicts: Towards a new realism* (2003); D Horowitz, 'Some realism about peacemaking' in A Wimmer et al (eds), *Facing Ethnic Conflicts: Toward a new realism* (2003).
[67] H Hannum, 'Territorial autonomy: Permanent solution or step toward secession?' in A Wimmer et al (eds), *Facing Ethnic Conflict: Toward a new realism*, (2003); T Chapman and PG Roeder, 'Partition as a solution to wars of nationalism: The importance of institutions' (2007) 101 *American Political Science Review* 677–91.
[68] Cf M Lund, 'Operationalizing the lessons from recent experience in field-level conflict prevention strategies' in A Wimmer et al (eds), *Facing Ethnic Conflicts: Toward a new realism* (2003); W Kymlicka, *Multicultural Odysseys: Navigating the new international politics of diversity* (2007).

the stability of the relationships between them. The following three examples demonstrate this interrelationship between inclusion and segmentation. For illustrative purposes, we calculated expected war probabilities for various ethnopolitical configurations in Iraq, Mexico, and Bosnia based on the analytical results from Table 1.2, model 7, about p24 above.

Applying the estimated model parameters to contemporary Iraq, the regression model calculates that including the Sunni in the power-sharing arrangement between Shia and Kurdish elites would halve the risk of conflict from 2.2 per cent to 1.0 per cent (the average risk of war in the entire world sample being 1.5 per cent).[69] That said, these risks are still lower than the predicted 3.1 per cent risk of conflict under a Sunni-led ethnocratic regime as under Saddam Hussein. Indeed, that era was characterized by an uninterrupted series of insurgencies by Kurdish nationalist and Shia rebels.[70] Meanwhile, in Mexico, the inclusion of the indigenous population into a genuine power-sharing arrangement would reduce ethnic exclusion within the central spheres of political power and diminish an already low likelihood of war from 0.8 per cent to 0.4 per cent. Indeed, the Zapatista uprising in Chiapas represents the only ethnic conflict in Mexico's post-war history. In Bosnia, finally, the current power-sharing arrangement between Bosniak, Serbian, and Croatian is associated with a conflict risk of 2.2 per cent, less than half the risk of any other possible configuration in that country. Power-sharing arrangements that exclude at least one of the three groups from power are linked with likelihoods of conflict ranging from 7.0 per cent under a Croat ethnocratic regime to 4.6 per cent when Serbs and Bosniaks share power.

Such calculations are obviously not meant to represent 'predictions' in any meaningful sense of the term—there are simply too many other influential factors, including historical contingencies, that are not captured by our theory and data. Correspondingly, the total variance explained by our regression models remains characteristically low and precludes any attempt at prediction. Even so, these calculations are in line with past experiences by negotiators and peacemakers across the world according to which the prevention of ethnic conflict cannot always and automatically be achieved by increasing participation and granting rights to minorities.[71] That these policies can stir up new tensions within the centre of power has been recognized by even the most ardent defendants of minority rights regimes and power-sharing policies.[72] Our research shows why this might be the case: ethnic conflicts can result not only

---

[69] We used the beta coefficients derived from the full sample and then plugged in the values for all independent variables for the appropriate country in 2003 and varied only the value on the excluded population and segmentation variables.

[70] A Wimmer, *Nationalist Exclusion and Ethnic Conflicts: Shadows of modernity* (2002), Ch 6.

[71] M Lund, 'Operationalizing the lessons' (n 68 above).

[72] W Kymlicka, *Multicultural Odysseys: Navigating the new international politics of diversity* (2007).

from exclusion along ethnic lines, but also because of polarizing competition between ethnic elites that share power, or because of the disidentification of peripheral populations that cannot be accommodated even by the most generous minority-rights regime.

Similarily, the granting of local autonomy as a solution to the disidentification of a particular ethnic community might *increase* rather than decrease the likelihood of violence because it can increase levels of exclusion in the autonomous region.[73] When newly autonomous regions are introduced, members of the majority population of a state can suddenly find themselves to be second-class citizens in the new region. The prospects for lasting peace in independent Kosovo, for example, are dim as long as the Serbian minority is excluded from access to power. In addition, partition produces the well-known moral hazard problem of instigating other groups that disidentify with their state to take up arms as well.[74]

A realistic view on the possibility of negotiating peace thus needs to take the complex interweaving of three different dimensions of ethnic politics into account and carefully consider the possible side effects of particular policy options. Beyond these rather sober assessments and cautious recommendations regarding prevention and intervention, our research supports the view that a permanent solution to ethnic conflicts might need to touch the very fundamentals on which a nation state is built, both the definition of the people in whose name a state is governed and the way ethnic backgrounds shape access to central state power. From the political sociology perspective developed in this chapter, therefore, incentives for young fighters to give up their Kalashnikovs and the co-opting and political 'buying off' of rebel leaders might not be enough for a lasting and sustained peace. If ethnic civil wars are the result of certain ethno-political configurations, as we maintain in this chapter, then nothing less than a rearrangement of these configurations will suffice to bring durable peace to war-torn states and their populations.

---

[73] Cf N Sambanis, 'Partition as a solution to ethnic war: An empirical critique of the theoretical literature' (2000) 52 *World Politics* 437–83. Full independent statehood decreases recurrence of violence, however, according to Chapman and Roeder. T Chapman and PG Roeder, 'Partition as a solution to wars of nationalism: The importance of institutions' (2007) 101 *American Political Science Review* 677–91.   [74] Cf RK Schaeffer, *Warpaths: The politics of partition* (1999).

2

Ethnic Domination in Democracies

John McGarry

I. Ethnic Domination and Democracy	36
II. The Institutional and Policy Basis of Ethnic Domination in Democracies	41
A. Demographic domination: right-sizing and right-peopling the state	41
B. Electoral domination	44
C. Domination of political (executive and legislative) institutions	51
D. Territorial domination	54
E. Coercive and legal domination	58
III. The End of Domination?	64
IV. Conclusion	70

This chapter is concerned with ethnic domination in formally democratic states. On the face of it, such domination appears to be in fundamental tension with democracy. Democracy, after all, developed in opposition to hierarchical forms of government, such as monarchy and aristocracy, and is deeply tied to the idea that everyone is a moral equal, and entitled to equal political standing, equal rights, and an equal say in the governance of the society. However, as this chapter shows, the formal institutional mechanisms of democracy, justified by and embodying the notion of individual equality, have lent themselves in many cases to domination of one ethnic community by another.

Many scholars and lawyers who are concerned with the domination of minorities throughout the world, including those who framed the Lund Recommendations, have pinned their hopes on international legal instruments and liberal democratic norms as mechanisms by which minority rights can be promoted. This optimism has been misplaced in most circumstances. International laws have had limited geographic reach in practice. They have also been relatively modest in scope, stretching only to the promotion of liberal individual rights, such as non-discrimination on the basis of ethnicity or freedom of religion, association and expression, but not to the substantive group rights that many minority communities seek, such as territorial self-government, power-sharing in central and regional governments, and the public recognition of and meaningful support for minority cultures, including languages. The failed promise of international laws can be partly explained by realist international relations theory. International laws are made by states and protect state sovereignty, so the protection they offer to minority communities is non-substantive (non-threatening) in nature. Moreover, these laws often lack coercive sanctions, and can be ignored by states, particularly those that are powerful or pariahs. 'Recommendations', such as the Lund proposals, may be more generous to minorities than laws, but they are not laws because they are more generous, and they are even easier to ignore, unless, as in the case of accession to the EU, they can be used as preconditions for membership of a desirable international organization. The spread of liberal democratic norms has not led to the substantive accommodation of minorities, because such accommodation is a profoundly contested good. Several prevailing norms, including those associated with liberalism, democracy, and republicanism (national unity) are in tension with the accommodation of minorities, and even consistent with the continuing domination of minorities.

This chapter is divided into three parts. The first part shows briefly that practices of political, symbolic, cultural, and economic domination are not limited to non-democratic states. The second part, which is the bulk of the chapter, offers a detailed account of the methods and institutions that are used to maintain domination in formally democratic states. The chapter ends by suggesting that domination is resilient, not just for reasons of international realpolitik, but because several prevailing norms are consistent with domination. This represents a clear problem for those who believe that legal instruments and ascendant values offer an answer to the plight of subordinated communities.

I. Ethnic Domination and Democracy

Domination is a fundamentally relational concept, which speaks to the relative power of one person or one group over other persons or groups.[1] In the context of this chapter, it refers to hierarchies of privilege within a political system, where one group can exert power over another, stamping its culture and authority on the collective life of the state. In this way, relations between groups can be conceptualized as ones of domination and subordination, which are mediated and reinforced in the state's basic institutions. Domination can vary in its extent, ranging from a relatively benign privileging of one community in certain areas of public policy to the profound coercive repression of a subordinate community.

---

[1] P Pettit, *Republicanism* (1999).

Several of the world's states are clearly dominated by particular ethnic communities, which operate as '*staatsvolks*', '*herrenvolks*', 'titular nations', 'ethnocrats', '*bumiputra*', or 'charter peoples'. In many cases, as might be expected, these states are not democracies. Before 2003, Iraq was an authoritarian state dominated by its Sunni Arab minority, while Iraq's neighbour Syria remains an authoritarian state dominated by its Alawite minority. Between 1948 and 1994, South Africa was presided over by Afrikaners, and although it gave the franchise to all whites and held competitive elections among white parties, it was not a democracy, as it denied the franchise to the majority of its citizens. China and Myanmar are authoritarian regimes led by particular communities, the Han Chinese and Burmans, respectively. Both are currently engaged in the coercive repression of their minority communities.

In many other cases, however, ethnic domination takes place in states that are formally or institutionally democratic, with a universal franchise, competitive elections, regular turnovers of government, and a varying range of personal freedoms. In Sri Lanka, the Sinhalese dominate Tamils, while in Malaysia, the Malay *bumiputra* dominate Chinese and Indian citizens. Most of post-communist Eastern Europe is comprised of states that are formally democratic but which are dominated by particular ethnic, or ethno-national communities, including Croatia, Estonia, Latvia, Romania, Russia, Serbia, and Slovakia. Israel is a democratic state in which Jews are ascendant over Palestinian Arabs. Domination also takes place in regions of democratic states, such as the Deep South of the United States in the period from post-bellum 'reconstruction' to the Voting Rights Act of 1965, or later. Northern Ireland, a region of the United Kingdom, was a site of domination of Catholics (nationalists) under its unionist regime between 1921 and 1972.[2] In all of these cases, the dominated communities are nationalities, or 'homeland peoples', that have long roots in the polities in question. In many other democracies around the world, 'native' communities dominate more recently arrived immigrant communities.

These facts indicate clearly that whatever success democracy has had in preventing war between neighbouring states, it has not, on its own, delivered equal citizenship for minorities or protection from majority tyrannies. They show that we should not expect the spread of democracy per se to produce the accommodation of minorities.[3] The record also shows that ethnic domination is not a problem that is limited to 'democratization', although democratization may be

---

[2] This shows that federation and autonomy are not panaceas for ethnic domination, although it is not true that autonomy for cultural or ethno-national communities inexorably leads to ethnic domination. Ethnic domination also exists in some unitary states, as the cases reviewed in this chapter show, and it does not exist in many cases where cultural/ethno-national groups enjoy autonomy, such as post-1998 Northern Ireland.

[3] This has been a common belief. See, for example, Art 5 of the Stability Pact in Europe on the Initiative of the European Union (Paris, 20 and 21 March 1995), which looks forwards to the promotion of democracy as the way to maintain good relations between states and between states and their minorities. Available at <http://www.cna.lu/> (accessed 31 July 2009).

conducive to regimes of domination.[4] Domination also develops after democratic transitions, as happened in Sri Lanka where domination was exerted from the mid-1950s, and it can last for decades after such transitions, as has happened in Israel, Sri Lanka, and Northern Ireland.

Domination has political, symbolic, cultural, and economic dimensions. Political domination provides the foundation for the others. It is reflected in the core community's control of the state's central political institutions, including the executive, legislature, judiciary, and bureaucracy, as well as whatever decentralized institutions exist. Minorities are excluded from government, or when included, as in the case of Malaysia's Chinese community, their participation is token in nature and falls short of a genuine partnership in decision-making. The core community's control of political institutions is a reflection of its greater numbers, but is often, as we will see, reinforced by a range of institutional rules and practices that discriminate against subordinated groups and their political representatives.

Symbolic ownership of the state is formally asserted through constitutions or laws. Macedonia's 1991 Constitution declared in its preamble that it was the 'national state of the Macedonian people'. According to Amal Jamal, all of Israel's eleven Basic Laws emphasize its Jewish character.[5] Less formal claims to ownership are asserted in the speeches of dominant community elites who describe their people as 'sons of the soil' and others as outsiders and interlopers, irrespective of how long their ancestors have lived there. As Sri Lanka's development minister declared in 1983, 'Sri Lanka is inherently and rightfully a Sinhalese state. This must be accepted as a fact and not as a matter of opinion to be debated', or as Northern Ireland's first prime minister, James Craig declared, the region had a 'Protestant parliament and a Protestant state'.[6] Israel's leaders regularly pronounce that it is a 'Jewish state', and have recently made recognition of this by Palestinian Arabs a precondition for the resumption of peace negotiations. States, and often their cities and towns, including those in minority inhabited regions, are named after the core people, which also stamps its ethnic impress on the state's anthems, flags, stamps, symbols, and public holidays.

Cultural domination involves the state's public (and sometimes its private) sector, including its political institutions, schools, and public media, functioning in only the language of the dominant community, or a clearly privileged position for this language. While Hebrew and Arabic are both official languages in Israel, the former is clearly dominant in public life. Slovakia has just passed a new language law which imposes fines on its citizens, including native Hungarian-speakers, who break rules promoting the use of Slovak in public.[7] In some cases, a dominant community's religion may also be privileged. Sri Lanka followed its

---

[4] J Snyder, *From Voting to Violence: Democratization and nationalist conflict* (2000).
[5] A Jamal, 'On the morality of Arab collective rights in Israel' (2005) *Adalah's Newsletter* 12, fn 20.
[6] O Yiftachel, *Ethnocracy: Land and identity politics in Israel/Palestine* (2006), 23; and B O'Leary and J McGarry, *The Politics of Antagonism: Understanding Northern Ireland*, 2nd edn (1996) 107.
[7] 'It's a war over words in Slovakia', *Toronto Star*, 3 August 2009.

Sinhala-only language policy of 1956 with a revised constitution in 1972 that gave a special position to Buddhism, the religion of the Sinhalese minority. Cultural domination can extend to public and coercive promotion of the dominant group's lifestyle, customs, dress, and foods, and especially its names.

Economic domination implies the unfair, ethnocentric, allocation of public resources, including education and public sector employment. Privilege results from direct discrimination through discriminatory-action policies which favour, or recruitment policies that are limited to, the core community. It also follows from indirect discrimination, as when benefits or jobs are tied to command of the core community's language or to educational standards in contexts where educational goods are unfairly (ethnocentrically) distributed. Both Sri Lanka and Estonia have required competence in the dominant group's language as either an advantage or prerequisite for public jobs.[8] The state may also direct disproportionate funding towards regions occupied by the dominant group, and privilege its ownership of land, which is usually seen as a strategic and symbolic as well as a material resource. Estonia's post-communist government offered financial incentives to privatize land ownership while restricting the benefits to ethnic Estonians.[9] Israel uses a wide range of techniques to deprive its Palestinian minority of land, and to ensure that land owned by Jews receives better services, including irrigation and communications infrastructure.[10] Malaysia offers lower mortgage rates, and public housing prices, to *bumiputra* and even better mortgage rates to public servants, who are also ethnic Malays.[11] Discrimination in private sector employment may be socially (privately) originated rather than state-sponsored, but state authorities that practice domination shy away from the corrective action necessary to level the playing field when they are not actively promoting discriminatory practices. Economic privileges do not necessarily entail, of course, that politically dominant communities are economically dominant. States may permit politically subordinated communities a strong role in the marketplace, even while discriminating against them, if this brings economic benefits. This describes the situation of the Chinese in Malaysia and Russians in the Baltic states of Estonia and Latvia.[12]

Domination is directed at one of two major conflict-regulation strategies: control or coercive assimilation.[13] Control involves the repression of a

---

[8] N DeVotta, 'Illiberalism and ethnic conflict in Sri Lanka' (2002) 13(1) *Journal of Democracy* 84–98, 86.

[9] S Smooha, *The Model of Ethnic Democracy* (2001), 44; Yiftachel, *Ethnocracy* (n 6 above), 30–1.

[10] Yiftachel, *Ethnocracy* (n 6 above),131–58; Smooha, *The Model of Ethnic Democracy* (n 9 above), 44.

[11] B Shoup, 'Dollars and sense: The nation-building logics of ethnic redistribution', paper presented at workshop on 'Democratization and ethnic communities: Conflict, protection, and accommodation', Munk Centre for International Studies, University of Toronto (2009).

[12] M Commercio, 'Systems of partial control: Ethnic dynamics in post-Soviet Estonia and Latvia' (2008) 43(1) *Studies in Comparative International Development* 81–100.

[13] J McGarry and B O'Leary, 'The macro-political regulation of ethnic conflict' in J McGarry and B O'Leary (eds), *The Politics of Ethnic Conflict Regulation* (1993), 16–22, 23–6.

subordinate community so that it does not threaten the dominant group's privileges.[14] Coercive assimilation is aimed at the destruction of the subordinate community's culture and the coerced incorporation of its members into the ranks of the dominant community. These strategies can be respectively seen as exclusionary and inclusionary versions of domination. Whether control or assimilation is chosen as a strategy by dominant communities depends on a range of factors, including the feasibility of either approach and the nature of the differences between superordinate and subordinate communities. In some cases, as in Israel or Turkey, it is clear what strategy the state seeks. Israel's Jewish community makes no secret of its aversion to assimilating Arabs,[15] while Turkey, operating on Kemalist principles, has been engaged in a long-term campaign of coercively assimilating Kurds and other minorities. In other cases, including most of those in Eastern Europe, it is more difficult to discern the state's aims, particularly as many of the strategies used in coercive assimilation, including banning minority parties, centralized government, the subordination of the minority's language and culture, and the moving of majority groups into and minority groups out of minority regions, are consistent with both strategies of control and coercive assimilation. As the contrast between Israel and Turkey suggests, ethnolinguistic minorities are more likely to be the object of assimilation policies than ethno-religious minorities, a result in part of the perceived feasibility and normative defensibility of linguistic acculturation policies.

The subject matter of this chapter clearly overlaps substantially with that covered in the 'ethnic democracy' literature associated with Sammy Smooha.[16] This literature highlights the presence of ethnic privilege, and thereby upsets regime defenders who prefer to see their states as simply 'democracies'. However, Smooha is less critical of ethnic hierarchies than I am, and more likely to see them as the best alternative in the circumstances. While he claims that his concept of ethnic democracy is analytical and descriptive, his work is also seen as a normative defence of the practice of ethnic democracy. Ethnic democracy, in Smooha's view 'excels' in some of its democratic properties.[17] It is treated by him as a 'model' that is available to states to adopt, and as better than genocide and ethnic cleansing.[18] He draws a favourable distinction between ethnic democracy and 'undemocratic' practices like 'control' and 'domination',[19] and,

---

[14] I Lustick, 'Stability in divided societies: Consociationalism versus control' (1979) 31(3) *World Politics* 325–344; O'Leary and McGarry, *The Politics of Antagonism* (n 6 above), 107–80.
[15] Smooha, *The Model of Ethnic Democracy* (n 9 above), 45.
[16] S Smooha, 'The model of ethnic democracy' in S Smooha (ed), *The Fate of Ethnic Democracy in Post-Communist Europe* (2005), 5–60; 'The Non-emergence of a viable ethnic democracy in post-communist Europe', ibid, 241–58; 'The model of ethnic democracy: Israel as a Jewish and democratic state' (2002) 8(4) *Nations and Nationalism* (2002) 475–503; 'Minority status in an ethnic democracy: The status of the Arab minority in Israel' (1990) 13(3) *Ethnic and Racial Studies* 389–413. [17] Smooha 'The model of ethnic democracy' (n 16 above), 22.
[18] Ibid, 6, 37. [19] Ibid, 21, 29.

echoing Lustick[20] who draws no such distinction,[21] sees normative merit in the ability of ethnic democracies to maintain political stability.[22] My perspective in this chapter is different. Ethnic democracy and ethnic domination are treated as synonyms. While domination can deliver stability, this is an unjust stability, and the resentment and polarization that it promotes can give rise to instability when opportunities arise. Only minorities that have no choice accept domination. Domination is unquestionably superior to genocide and ethnic expulsions, but there is a danger that one may lapse into the other, as happened in Rwanda in 1994 and Croatia in 1995. Moreover, the political choices are not limited to domination on the one hand and harsher methods on the other. There are a range of other mechanisms that can accommodate minorities in ways that are, in principle, consistent with substantive political equality, including civic integration, territorial pluralism and consociational democracy.[23]

II. The Institutional and Policy Basis of Ethnic Domination in Democracies

How do dominant communities implement and maintain ethnic hierarchies in democracies? They do so through a range of political practices and institutions described here under five headings: demographic domination (right-sizing and right-peopling the state); electoral domination; the domination of political institutions; territorial domination; and legal and coercive domination.[24]

A. Demographic domination: right-sizing and right-peopling the state[25]

Core communities can dominate minorities democratically as long as the former comprise a clear majority of the state's citizenship and electorate. While demographic dominance may result from natural or cultural causes, including higher

---

[20] Lustick, 'Stability in divided societies: Consociationalism versus control' (n 14 above), 336.
[21] For a discussion of Israeli 'control' of its Palestinian minority, see A Jamal, 'Strategies of minority struggle for equality in ethnic states: Arab politics in Israel' (2007) 11(3) *Citizenship Studies* 265–6; S Jiryis, *The Arabs in Israel* (1976); I Lustick, *Arabs in the Jewish State: Israel's control of a national minority* (1980); E Zureik, *The Palestinians in Israel: A study in internal colonialism* (1979); and Yiftachel, *Ethnocracy* (n 6 above).
[22] Smooha, 'The model of ethnic democracy' (n 16 above), 36–7.
[23] J McGarry, B O'Leary, and R Simeon, 'Integration or accommodation? The enduring debate in conflict regulation' in S Choudhry (ed), *Constitutional Design for Divided Societies?* (2008), 41–90.
[24] The emphasis on political institutions in my account distinguishes it from Yiftachel's. See Yiftachel, *Ethnocracy* (n 6 above), 36–7.
[25] The terms 'right-sizing' and 'right-peopling' are drawn from B O'Leary, 'The elements of right-sizing and right-peopling the state' in B O'Leary, I Lustick, and T Callaghy (eds), *Right-Sizing the State: The politics of moving borders* (2001), 15–73.

birth rates, it also follows from, and is maintained by, state action, purposively designed to cement the core community's position. One tactic involves 'right-sizing' the state's territory, at the point of state formation or later, so that it comprises an area in which the dominant community exercises clear demographic dominance. Just before the partition of Ireland, Protestants, concentrated in the north east, rejected retaining the nine counties of historic Ulster as a self-governing region within the United Kingdom because it would have meant a slender Protestant majority of 55 per cent. Instead, they persuaded the British government to limit Northern Ireland to six of Ulster's nine counties, which gave Protestants a reasonably comfortable majority of 65 per cent and allowed them to dominate Catholics (nationalists) for the next fifty years. Israel's Likud government abandoned its policy of annexing the West Bank and Gaza Strip during the 1980s when it became clear that the higher Arab birth rate would threaten a Jewish majority in the enlarged state. Incorporation of these territories would either have converted (greater) Israel into an Arab majority state or its Jewish community would have been forced to abandon formal democracy by depriving Palestinians of the vote. One of Israel's current leaders, foreign minister Avigdor Lieberman, has proposed land swaps between Israel and a future Palestinian state as a way to maintain Jewish demographic hegemony in Israel. If he had his way, parts of Israel that are occupied by Arabs would be transferred to the new Palestinian state, while Jewish settlements in the West Bank would be incorporated into Israel.[26]

States also maintain demographic dominance by downsizing minorities, or 'right-peopling' the state. One tactic is expulsion, although opportunities for this tend to be restricted to wartime—see, eg, the conduct of the Balkan states of Serbia, Greece, and Bulgaria during and after the Balkan wars of 1912–14. Israel's security forces and Jewish irregulars expelled Arabs in 1948 to strengthen Jewish dominance of the state, while Croatia expelled most of its Serb minority during 'Operation Storm' in 1995. Serbia attempted to expel Kosovo's Albanian community in 1999, but was prevented from doing so by the intervention of NATO. In some cases, genocide has been used as a right-peopling tool in formal democracies, as happened in Rwanda in 1994, and genocide is sometimes used in combination with expulsions.[27] Alternatively, and when such extreme measures are not desirable or feasible, states have adopted immigration policies that favour the dominant group's diaspora or immigrants that are culturally-related to the core group. Israel allows a 'Right of Return', meaning Israeli citizenship, to all Jews, while denying any such right to the Palestinians who were expelled or fled in 1948 or their heirs. Over 1 million Russians were permitted to immigrate to Israel in the 1990s, many of whom do not appear to have been Jews but were even more clearly not Arabs. States may also seek to

---

[26] 'What does Netanyahu mean for peace?', *Globe and Mail*, 7 April 2009, A13.
[27] M Mann, *The Dark Side of Democracy: Explaining ethnic cleansing* (2005).

maintain demographic domination by influencing birth rates among the dominant and dominated groups. Macedonia sought to control growth in the Albanian population by adopting a four-person nuclear family policy.[28] In 1956 Northern Ireland's unionist regime tried to change British family allowance policy in a way that would have privileged smaller families over larger ones, although it is unclear if its aim was simply to privilege Protestant families which were traditionally smaller than their Catholic counterparts, or discourage larger Catholic families, or both.[29]

A related technique is to downsize the minority's share of the citizenry and electorate as opposed to its share of the population. Upon regaining independence in the early 1990s, Estonia 'denaturalized' most of its Russian-speakers. Estonia's Citizenship Law of 1992 granted citizenship only to its pre-1940 citizens and their descendants, thus stripping citizenship rights from the large number of Russians who had settled in the country during the Soviet era. The denaturalized Russian-speakers were prevented from voting for the state's political institutions or in the 1992 referendum on the new Estonian Constitution, which ensured that ethnic Estonians drove policy. Naturalization was made difficult, and required a demanding language test, five years' residency and a pledge of allegiance to the state and its ethnically partisan arrangements. The result was that by 1999, 62 per cent of Russian-speakers living in Estonia lacked citizenship, while 43 per cent were stateless. Ethnic Estonians, who constituted only 65 per cent of the population, made up 81 per cent of the citizenry.[30] Latvia followed a similar trajectory. Sri Lanka disenfranchised its so-called 'Indian Tamils' (Tamils of Recent Indian Origin/Plantation Tamils/Estate Tamils) through the Indian Citizenship Act of 1949.[31] The policy not only converted the Sinhalese from 74 per cent of Sri Lanka's population into 80 per cent of its citizens, but also had the advantage, from the Sinhalese perspective, of introducing intra-Tamil distinctions.[32] Denaturalization and other policies of domination are often aimed at 'soft expulsion', ie at 'encouraging' minorities to leave. Sri Lanka's denaturalization of 'Indian' Tamils was accompanied by negotiations with India to 'repatriate' them. 130,000 Russians left Estonia during the 1990s, while a disproportionate number of Northern Ireland's Catholics emigrated during the period of the unionist regime.[33]

---

[28] Smooha, 'The non-emergence of a viable ethnic democracy in post-communist Europe' (n 16 above), 248.   [29] O'Leary and McGarry, *The Politics of Antagonism* (n 6 above), 178 fn 7.
[30] Yiftachel, *Ethnocracy* (n 6 above), 29–31.
[31] U Phadnis, 'The Indo-Ceylon Pact and the "stateless" Indians in Ceylon' (1967) 7(4) *Asian Survey* 226–36.
[32] Devotta, 'Illiberalism and ethnic conflict in Sri Lanka' (n 8 above), 85; M Chadda, 'Between consociationalism and control: Sri Lanka' in U Schneckener and S Wolff (eds), *Managing and Settling Ethnic Conflicts* (2004), 94–114.
[33] The Northern Ireland government also set stricter residency requirements before citizens of the Republic of Ireland could vote in Northern Ireland elections than existed in Great Britain.

B. Electoral domination

Parties that represent demographically dominant communities can win elections straightforwardly, if ethnicity is the main political cleavage and if the dominant community remains politically united. These provisos provide incentives for manipulating elections and electoral systems to prevent dominant group fissures, or to prevent non-ethnic or minority parties from becoming electorally pivotal. States may also seek to reduce the representation of particular sorts of minority parties to promote stability and state unity, or for reasons of ethnocentrism or racism. Tactics used towards these ends include (i) reducing the minority's share of the vote; (ii) implementing electoral formulae which underrepresent minorities; (iii) drawing electoral boundaries to underrepresent minorities; (iv) adopting anti-competitive practices that make it difficult for minority parties and politicians to compete for office; and (v) post-election measures that discriminate against elected minority politicians.

1. Reducing the Minority Vote

The denaturalization of minorities in Estonia, Latvia, and Sri Lanka was aimed at disfranchising them, but a range of other measures have also been used to erode minorities' share of the vote. In Northern Ireland before 1968, owners of business premises and university graduates, both of which groups were predominantly Protestant, were given two votes in regional parliamentary elections.[34] In the United States, African Americans in the South (and new immigrants in the North) were deprived of the ballot by a bewildering litany of measures, including literacy tests, property qualifications, residency requirements, provisions which barred petty criminals from voting (although not, strangely, murderers), and poll taxes.[35] By 1904, the payment of poll taxes was a prerequisite for voting in all eleven Southern states that had made up the Confederacy. Illiterate whites, by contrast, were protected from disfranchisement by 'grandfather' and 'fighting grandfather' clauses. Requirements for frequent registration in relatively inaccessible locations also penalized African Americans, who were more likely to lack transportation. As registration required a signature, it became an additional de facto literacy test.[36] Polling stations in the South were consolidated, and located away from minority districts. They were also routinely moved, sometimes 'ten times in as many

---

[34] J Whyte, 'How much discrimination was there under the Unionist regime, 1921–1968?' in T Gallagher and J O'Connell (eds), *Contemporary Irish Studies* (1983), 1–36.

[35] In five states, the poll tax accumulated for more than one year. In Georgia after 1877 and Alabama after 1901, it accumulated indefinitely. Some states made the poll tax due several months before elections were to be held, on the assumption that this would *reduce* payments. JM Kousser, 'The undermining of the first reconstruction: Lessons for the second' in C Davidson (ed) *Minority Vote Dilution* (1984), 32–5. Also see JM Kousser, 'Poll tax' in R Rose (ed), *The International Encyclopedia of Elections* (1999), 208–9.   [36] Kousser, 'Poll tax' (n 35 above), 33–4.

elections'.[37] Receipts for registration or for paid poll taxes were required before ballots could be cast, which de facto discriminated against those elements of the population less likely to retain such documents.[38] Two-stage majoritarian run-off elections made it doubly difficult for poorer blacks to cast their ballots, and sometimes resulted in a black majority in the first stage being converted into a minority by the second stage.[39] African American voters who sought, in spite of these measures, to cast their ballots were routinely deterred by intimidation and violence from organizations like the Ku Klux Klan and Red Shirts, organizations which, when they were not organized by the authorities, were not sufficiently restrained by them.[40] Those who managed to vote found their votes disproportionately cast out by white election officials, as allegedly happened in the 2000 presidential election in Florida. Alternatively, ballot boxes were stuffed with votes for white (Democratic) candidates.[41]

Such policies, and the others detailed in the second part of this chapter, affected minority turnout indirectly. In Northern Ireland between 1921 and 1972, nationalists boycotted elections because they were alienated from the state, or abstained on the understanding that elections results were a foregone conclusion.[42] In Israel, domination has produced a steady decline in Arab participation in elections since the 1980s.[43] In the United States, the courts have recognized that difficulties associated with voting, and the unlikelihood of electing the desired candidate, helps to explain the culture of voter apathy that continues to mark electoral behaviour among blacks.[44]

2. *Underrepresenting Minorities through Plurality or Majority Electoral Formulae*

Minorities, particularly if they are geographically dispersed, have been easily deprived of fair representation by the pluralitarian and majoritarian electoral systems for legislative and executive elections that are used in former British and

---

[37] L Guinier, *The Tyranny of the Majority* (1993), 11. Lani Guinier was President Clinton's nominee for Assistant Attorney General in 1992. She was forced to withdraw her nomination following Republican attacks on her candidacy. These attacks employed many of the arguments that are used to legitimize domination, and that are briefly discussed in the final section of this chapter to explain its resilience.
[38] Kousser, 'The undermining of the first reconstruction' (n 35 above), 33.
[39] According to Guinier, Blacks regarded the majority run-off 'as simply a tool to "steal the election" – a tool that had the effect of demobilizing black political participation, enhancing polarization rather than fostering debate, and in general excluding black interests from the political process' (Guinier, *The Tyranny of the Majority* (n 37 above), 11).
[40] JM Kousser, 'The voting rights act and the two reconstructions' in B Grofman and C Davidson (eds), *Controversies in Minority Voting* (1992), 141–2. [41] Ibid, 143.
[42] O'Leary and McGarry, *The Politics of Antagonism* (n 6 above), 123.
[43] For a discussion of how domination has eroded Palestinian Arab participation in Israeli elections from the 1980s on, see A Jamal, 'Strategies of minority struggle for equality in ethnic states: Arab politics in Israel' (2007) 11(3) *Citizenship Studies* 276–7.
[44] See the court cases listed in Guinier, *The Tyranny of the Majority* (n 37 above), fn 113.

French colonies around the world. These electoral systems are often selected precisely for their 'integrationist' advantages, ie because the effective thresholds required to win make it difficult for politically dispersed minorities to elect their own political parties, or select their own candidates. Such electoral systems are justified on the grounds that they produce 'catch-all' or ethnically neutral parties that reach out to all voters, but their effect in bipolar and divided polities is often to give seat 'bonuses' to the party or parties of the dominant ethnic group, ie a larger share of seats in the legislature than its share of the vote would warrant.[45]

Plurality electoral systems also make it less likely that dominant (or other) ethnic communities will fragment politically, with their members supporting a number of smaller ethnic parties or non-ethnic parties. A concern with fragmentation appears to have been the main reason why Northern Ireland's Ulster Unionist party (UUP) switched from proportional representation to single member plurality for elections to the Northern Ireland parliament in 1929. The UUP had been losing support to smaller unionist parties, and to a party that stressed working class politics. Its concern was to maintain the salience of ethnic politics, and its position as the dominant unionist party, as these two conditions —when combined with the Westminster system of government—assured it a monopoly of executive office. As the unionist Prime Minister, James Craig, put it at the time, 'What I want to get in this house and what I believe we will get very much better in this house under the old-fashioned plain and simple system, are men who are for the Union on the one hand, or who are against it and want to go into a Dublin parliament in the other.'[46]

When minorities are territorially concentrated and capable of winning seats under pluralitarian or majoritarian electoral systems, they can be deprived of a proportional share of seats in the legislature if a high statewide quota (threshold) of votes is required before seats can be won. Such thresholds exist in many countries, including Germany and New Zealand, but the most obvious example occurs in Turkey, which has an unusually high electoral threshold of 10 per cent, and which, unlike Germany and New Zealand, does not have provisions which set the threshold aside if a party wins local constituencies. In the 2002 election in Turkey, the main Kurdish party, the People's Democracy Party (Halkın Demokrasi Partisi—HADEP) obtained approximately 45.95 per cent of the vote (47,449 votes) in Sirnak province, but failed to win one of its three seats in parliament, as it failed to win 10 per cent of the total vote across Turkey. Two of the seats went to the Turkish Islamist AK (Justice and Development) Party and the other to an independent, with the three winning candidates gaining 25 per cent of the regional vote among them.[47] In Slovakia,

---

[45] See Brendan O'Leary, Chapter 12 in this volume.
[46] O'Leary and McGarry, *The Politics of Antagonism* (n 6 above), 123.
[47] Text available at <http://sim.law.uu.nl/SIM/CaseLaw/hof.nsf/233813e697620022c125686 4005232b7/10c6098b3315ccf5c125727400367fea?OpenDocument> (accessed 31 July 2009).

just before the 1998 elections, the Slovakian nationalist Prime Minister Meciar adopted a 5 per cent threshold for statewide elections as a tactic to reduce the representation of opposition parties, including Hungarian parties, in Slovakia's legislature.

3. *Underrepresenting Minorities through the Drawing of Electoral Boundaries (Gerrymandering)*

Parties of territorially concentrated minorities can be deprived of fair (proportional) representation by the manipulation of electoral boundaries. These are drawn either to divide the minority community across several constituencies, so that it is a minority in each, or by packing it into one or a few overly populous constituencies where it constitutes an overwhelming local majority. Widespread gerrymandering of this sort was used to underrepresent Southern blacks in the US Congress and in several state legislatures. While South Carolina had a black majority in the 1880s, only one of its seven congressional districts had a secure black majority. Similar gerrymanders prevailed in congressional districts throughout North Carolina, Alabama, and Mississippi.[48] At the municipal level, blacks were underrepresented by the tactic of switching from local ward-based to at-large (city-wide) elections. This was a move that was widely introduced across Northern American cities during the 'progressive' period on the grounds that it would produce positive city-wide rather than parochial perspectives, and government by business-minded people rather than by populists. At-large elections not only made African American candidates dependent on white urban majorities for winning seats, but made elections more expensive, making it less likely that African Americans would prevail or even run.[49]

Alternatively, cities avoided African American representation by the technique of down-sizing the city—expelling black-populated areas[50]—or, where there were fluctuating political-racial majorities, by annexing the city to a neighbouring white-dominated region when the opportunity arose.[51] In Northern Ireland, the opportunity for reapportionment brought about in 1929 by the switch from nine multi-member (proportional) constituencies to forty-eight single-member constituencies allowed Unionists to divide the nationalist majority county of Fermanagh into three constituencies, two of which came to be won consistently by unionists.

4. *Anti-competitive Practices*

The measures described hitherto are indirect attacks on competitive elections, as they undermine the vote won by minority politicians and political parties. But

---

[48] Kousser, 'The undermining of the first reconstruction' (n 35 above), 32.
[49] Guinier, *The Tyranny of the Majority* (n 37 above), 7, 50.
[50] The term used for this practice is 'de-annexation'.
[51] Kousser, 'The undermining of the first reconstruction' (n 35 above), 32, 35.

states also take direct steps to directly reduce competition from minority parties. Several states, including most African states, ban parties which seek to organize on an ethnic or religious basis or compete in only a part of the state, a measure which favours large parties that identify with the state and the political status quo.[52] The sixth amendment to the (current) Sri Lankan Constitution of 1978 outlawed separatism and led to the Tamil parties being thrown out of parliament for over a decade on the grounds that they were 'acting against the state'.[53] This step decimated the moderate Tamil leadership and paved the way for the emergence of the Liberation Tigers of Tamil Eelam (LTTE).[54] Several states also require elections to be contested only by 'national' parties that are organized across the state's territory, and that have a certain number of registered members or can gain a certain number of signatures in most of the state's regions. These are conditions that privilege parties belonging to the dominant community, as it is more likely to be able to meet the conditions than minority parties. In Russia, political parties can compete in federal elections only if they have regional branches in more than half of the federation's eighty-nine regions, and not less than 500 members in each of these regions.[55] Indonesia's Law on General Elections of 2003 requires that new parties must have executive committees (and permanent offices) in two-thirds of its provinces and two-thirds of the regencies/cities in those provinces, and either 1,000 members in each regency/city where the party is organized or one-thousandth of the population of the regency/city, whichever is smaller. The two tactics—party bans and requirements for national organization—frequently go together. Russia requires national registration and outlaws parties which form on an 'ethnic, religious or national basis'.[56] In Africa, twenty-two countries combine the policies of party bans and national registration.[57]

A variation on anti-competitive behaviour is to limit participation to parties that endorse central elements of the political status quo. Parties in Israel are not allowed to compete in elections if they deny Israel as the homeland of the Jewish people, a requirement that attempts to make it difficult for political parties to

---

[52] M Bogaards, 'Democratization and diversity: Ethnic party bans in Nigeria', paper presented at workshop on 'Democratization and ethnic communities: Conflict, protection, and accommodation', Munk Centre for International Studies, University of Toronto (2009).
[53] Constitution of the Democratic Socialist Republic of Sri Lanka 1978, s 157.A: '(1) No person shall, directly or indirectly, in or outside Sri Lanka, support, espouse, promote, finance, encourage or advocate the establishment of a separate State within the territory of Sri Lanka. (2) No political party or other association or organization shall have as one of its aims or objects the establishment of a separate State within the territory of Sri Lanka.' Available at <www.commonlii.org/lk/legis/const/2000/22.html> (accessed 31 July 2009).
[54] R Coomaraswamy, 'The politics of institutional design: An overview of the case of Sri Lanka' in S Bastian and R Luckham (eds), *Can Democracy Be Designed* (2003), 157.
[55] Available at <http://www.cikrf.ru/eng/politparty/> (accessed 31 July 2009).
[56] Federal Law on Political Parties 2001 (Russian Federation) Art 9.3, <http://www.cikrf.ru/eng/law/fz95_en_110701.jsp> (accessed 31 July 2009).
[57] M Bogaards, 'Democratization and diversity' (n 52 above).

question domination.⁵⁸ In the US Deep South, anti-competitive practices included 'White Democratic primaries' which were the de facto election in most of the region. Not only did the primaries exclude blacks, but losing white candidates who might otherwise have decided to ally with blacks to oppose the primary winner, were required to agree in advance not to compete in the election itself.⁵⁹

5. Post-election Measures that Penalize Elected Minority Politicians

Minority politicians who win elections in spite of the foregoing can find themselves subject to a series of post-election measures that have the effect, and often the aim, of obstructing their access to office. In the case of the UK Parliament, Irish republicans can stand for election, and, if successful, be recognized as the elected member for the relevant constituency, but not take up their seats in the House of Commons (or get paid) unless they swear an oath of allegiance to the Crown.⁶⁰ Northern Ireland's four currently elected Sinn Fein MPs refuse to take this oath and therefore do not sit at Westminster.⁶¹ A similar oath of allegiance was required for sitting in the Northern Ireland parliament after 1921, and even in its local councils.⁶² The oath was abolished in 1973 by the Northern Ireland Constitution Act on the grounds it constituted political discrimination, but it has been retained at Westminster. In the US South, expensive bonds for office holders were designed to keep out poor blacks.⁶³ Like discriminatory oaths of allegiance, they also served as deterrents to standing for office in the first place.⁶⁴ African Americans who won office, or white politicians who were disposed to take up their cause, were also impeached or forced to resign. When one elected black republican judge refused to resign, the Alabama legislature abolished the court over which he presided. Elected local offices were also made appointive, with Alabama abolishing the post of elective commissioner in a number of counties dominated by African American voters.⁶⁵ Alternatively, where whites were in a majority, political power was

---

⁵⁸ S Smooha, 'The model of ethnic democracy' (n 16 above), 46; Jamal, 'On the morality of Arab collective rights in Israel' (n 5 above).
⁵⁹ Kousser, 'The undermining of the first reconstruction' (n 35 above), 33.
⁶⁰ The oath discriminates on political grounds—against republicans, and on religious grounds, against Catholics, as the monarch cannot be, or marry, a Catholic.
⁶¹ UK House of Commons, *The Parliamentary Oath*, HC Research Paper 01/116, 14 December 2001.
⁶² I am grateful to Brian Feeney of the *Irish News* for giving me this information.
⁶³ Kousser, 'The undermining of the first reconstruction' (n 35 above), 32, 35.
⁶⁴ An oath of allegiance would deter participation in elections because a candidate might not bother to stand if s/he was not prepared to sit. In the case of the Northern Ireland parliament election deposits of £150 were retained if the oath was not taken, adding another deterrent to participation.
⁶⁵ Kousser, 'The undermining of the first reconstruction' (n 35 above), 36. Such measures are not just used against ethnic minority groups. Faced with socialist local governments in Wales, Margaret Thatcher established a large number of appointed bodies, quangos, to govern the principality.

transferred from single commissioners to the commission voting collectively, a warning to those who see an unalloyed good in the doctrine of 'collective responsibility'.[66]

Such practices exist during relatively 'normal' times. During minority rebellions, which give rise to emergency legal regimes, elected minority-controlled local governments may be suspended and replaced by military law. During a Sikh rebellion in the Indian state of Punjab in the 1980s, the state legislature and executive was suspended by the central government which implemented 'president's rule'. Elected minority representatives have also been detained or jailed for a variety of political offences, including links to insurgents. In April 2009, the Kurdish Mayor of Diyarbakir, south-eastern Turkey's largest city, was jailed for ten months for 'spreading PKK propaganda'.[67]

Not all such measures are equally successful in excluding minorities and some are more symbolic than others. Bans on parties are sometimes not enforced, and may be easily got around, by changing the name of the party. In Turkey, the Kurdish members of the Democratic Society Party get around the rule that political parties must pass a 10 per cent threshold of votes statewide before winning seats in Turkey's parliament by running as 'independents'. Twenty-two 'independent' members of this party won seats in the 2007 parliamentary elections. The Magyar minority parties, and other opposition parties in Meciar's Slovakia responded to his 5 per cent electoral threshold by coalescing. Oaths of allegiance can also usually be got around, although this may be easier in secular societies. In Northern Ireland, nationalist members of the regional parliament *signed* the oath of allegiance to the Crown after 1927 without holding a Bible. They followed in the footsteps of Eamon De Valera, the republican leader in the Irish Free State, which also had an oath of allegiance to the Crown. De Valera signed the oath in 1927 while famously suggesting it was not an oath but 'a form of words'. Previously, however, the issue had caused a civil war in the republic, when De Valera's side had objected to the oath, so it was an effective bar to office for some at that time. After 1927, nationalists in Northern Ireland signed the oath to get paid, while continuing to abstain from parliament for much of the time, which indicated that their failure to take their seats had wider causes than the oath itself, and was related to Northern Ireland's position as part of the United Kingdom, and its general failure to accommodate its nationalist minority. The ability of Irish nationalists to sign objectionable oaths when it suits them suggests that the oath of allegiance is not the main reason why Sinn Fein members do not currently sit at Westminster.

---

[66] When the first Latina was elected to a Texan local school board, it quickly decided to increase the number of votes necessary to place an item on the agenda from one to two (Guinier, *The Tyranny of the Majority* (1993), (n 37), 9).

[67] 'Turkey's Kurdish parliamentarians on hunger strike', *Press TV*, 3 May 2009, <http://www.presstv.ir/detail.aspx?id=93475&sectionid=351020204> (accessed 31 July 2009).

Other exclusionary tactics have had more substantive impacts on minority representation, including the disfranchising of Russian minorities in Estonia and Lativa and the various tactics used by Southern white racists. Morgan Kousser reports that the requirement for registration and, ironically, the introduction of the secret ballot, which was a de facto 'literacy' test, 'devastated' the black vote in Tennessee 'as it was intended to'.[68] Poll taxes were also decisive in the South, and were, according to contemporary observers around the turn of the century, 'the most effective bar to Negro suffrage ever devised' and 'the most effective instrumentality of Negro disfranchisement'.[69] The 'white primary' made the other restrictions redundant as it cut African Americans out of the South's most important elections altogether.

C. Domination of political (executive and legislative) institutions

Even when minorities have perfectly proportional representation in the legislature, and indeed in the executive, it is consistent with domination by the majority community if the state's political institutions make decisions on an ethnocentric and majoritarian basis. This is one of the reasons why some US civil rights activists have been frustrated by the limits of the Voting Rights Act, which improved black representation in Congress but left the latter's majoritarian voting procedures intact.[70] This problem suggests it is disingenuous of Smooha to claim that Israel's Arab minority's proportional representation in the Knesset is of much other than symbolic importance.[71] As an Israeli Arab political scientist has noted:

Arab participation in the Knesset creates the impression that Arab MKs are genuine participants in the Israeli moral community, and participants in the definition of the moral order that dominates Israeli public culture. However, Israeli representative politics is based on ethnic majoritarianism that is translated into an automatic Jewish majority in cases of major dispute. Most of the crucial decisions are made in institutions, representative or administrative, in which there is Jewish hegemony.[72]

Similarly, the key problem for nationalists in Northern Ireland between 1921 and 1972 or Tamils in Sri Lanka since independence was not that they were underrepresented in the legislature, but that the governing institutions were controlled by the dominant unionist majority.

Both Northern Ireland and Sri Lanka were governed for long periods under the Westminster system, the political institutions of which are particularly conducive to majority domination. Unlike political systems that divide power between the legislature and executive, the Westminster system fuses both

---

[68] Kousser, 'The undermining of the first reconstruction' (n 35 above), 34.
[69] Kousser, 'Poll tax' (n 35 above).   [70] Guinier, *The Tyranny of the Majority* (n 37 above).
[71] Smooha, 'The model of ethnic democracy' (n 16 above), 45.
[72] Jamal, 'On the morality of Arab collective rights in Israel (n 5 above), 6.

executive and legislative power in the party or parties that win a simple majority of seats in parliament.[73] The Westminster model also facilitates ethnic domination because it is associated with a deferential judiciary, no codified bill of rights, a plurality electoral system that underrepresents dispersed groups, a centralized state structure, and a weak or non-existent second chamber that would act as a check on the first chamber. What the model does not facilitate is universal allegiance to the state: excluded minorities in both Northern Ireland and Sri Lanka were given little stake in the system and eventually turned to civil disobedience and armed rebellion.

Ethnic domination can also be maintained through presidential systems, as the experience of Rwanda before 1994 and Sri Lanka since 1978 indicates. This is in spite of an argument favoured by some American political scientists that the separation of powers associated with presidential regimes provide checks and balances against chauvinistic abuse, and multiple access points (in the executive, legislature, and judiciary) for minorities to gain political power and influence.[74] The first reason why this may not happen in practice is that many presidential systems are executive–centred, ie the presidential executive, the only institution directly elected by all of the state's people and enjoying an unparalleled legitimacy, comes to dominate the other legislative and judicial institutions, removing effective checks and balances. This is the case in Sri Lanka, where the president in addition to heading the army and cabinet, is endowed with wide-ranging emergency powers, and the power to dissolve the legislature. In Coomaraswamy's view, the president is 'the pivotal figure among constitutional institutions', while, according to a recent report by the International Crisis Group, his powers are 'excessive'.[75] The second reason is that a dominant community, particularly if it enjoys a strong majority of the electorate, can easily dominate all three branches of government in a presidential regime, even if it splits into more than one political party. This has been true not just of Sri Lanka, but also of Roeder's favourite case study, the Russian Federation, and of his homeland, the United States. In the latter case, blacks were excluded from the presidency until 2009, and there was not a single black Supreme Court Justice until 1967, or black Senator until 1993. At the state level, there have only been two elected black governors in the history of the United States.[76]

---

[73] Sri Lanka has a Westminster-type electoral and executive system from independence until 1978, when it switched to an electoral system based on proportional representation and a directly elected strong presidency combined with a parliamentary executive similar to that which exists in France.

[74] P Roeder and D Rothchild (eds), *Sustainable Peace: Power and Democracy after Civil Wars* (2005).

[75] Coomaraswamy, 'The politics of institutional design' (n 54 above), 151; International Crisis Group (ICG), 'Sri Lanka's judiciary: Politicised courts, compromised rights' (2009) 172 *Asia Report*, ii.

[76] There have only been two black Supreme Court Justices in total, Thurgood Marshall and Clarence Thomas. The first Latina Supreme Court Justice, Sonia Sotomayor, was not confirmed until 2009. The two black governors were Douglas Wilder in Virginia 1990–4 and Deval Patrick in Massachusetts, 2007–present.

The failure of blacks to take advantage of the US political system's 'multiple access points' helps to explain why one prominent black activist has called for weighted (super-majority) voting and 'proportionate interest representation' (ie where a minority gets to make a proportionate share of important decisions).[77]

There are solid prima facie grounds for believing that presidential systems are even more consistent with ethnic domination than parliamentary systems. Most presidencies are single-person in nature and, unlike most parliamentary regimes, are based on majoritarian electoral systems that in divided societies tend to give a monopoly of executive power to the leader of the dominant community. Even when elected by a majority rule plus a geographic distribution rule that requires some support in minority regions, as happens in some countries and is recommended by Donald Horowitz,[78] single-person presidencies still favour dominant communities, as it is they who are most likely to satisfy the double electoral requirements. Parliamentary systems, by contrast, are at least open to the possibility of multi-party and inter-ethnic executive coalitions, particularly if they are based on proportional electoral systems which fragment majorities and create spaces for minorities to gain a share of executive office. In recent years, minority political parties in the parliamentary systems of Slovakia, Romania,[79] and Macedonia have been able to gain access to governing coalitions. The problems of (single-person) executive presidencies can be avoided or mitigated by rotating and collective presidencies, as happens within Bosnia and Herzegovina and within the European Union, and would have happened within Cyprus if the Annan plan had been accepted.[80] The problems may also be avoided or mitigated by 'split' executives, which divide executive power between a president and prime minister. This is what happens in Lebanon, and happened recently in Kenya and Zimbabwe.[81]

Parliamentary and presidential executives that are the exclusive domain of dominant communities are straightforwardly conducive to ethnic domination. However, domination can also exist within more inclusive coalitions, ostensibly based on power-sharing, if the decision-making procedures consistently reflect the will of the dominant community rather than a consensus. Such arrangements are sham rather than genuine consociations, and based on tokenism and co-optation rather than partnership. Malaysia is governed by a multiethnic

---

[77] Guinier, *The Tyranny of the Majority* (n 37 above), 78–9.
[78] DL Horowitz, *A Democratic South Africa? Constitutional engineering in a divided society* (University of California Press, 1991).
[79] Romania has a 'split' executive system which includes a directly elected president and a prime minister accountable to parliament.
[80] Rotation can be adapted to provide shares to each community that are proportionate to their share of the electorate.
[81] There are other problems with the design of the executive in all three of these countries. Lebanon has a flawed 'corporate' consociational system which allocates the presidency and prime-ministership to Christians and Sunni Muslims respectively. Kenya and Zimbabwe have split executives in theory, but in practice the president remains clearly predominant.

coalition (UMNO) in which the Chinese minority has been consistently represented. However, effective power lies with the dominant Malay (*bumiputra*) party within the coalitions. Genuine power-sharing requires informal or formal rules that require consensus.

D. Territorial domination

Dominant communities seek to control all of the state's territory. This is because of concerns that if a part of this territory falls under a minority's control, it will facilitate a bid for secession or irredentism, or permit the minority to reproduce its culture and resist assimilation. There are also sometimes fears that minorities, converted into local majorities, will be able to dominate and discriminate against those from the state's core community who live in the minority-controlled region, or be able to interfere with the extraction of resources from the region. These concerns overlap, and their relative importance depends on context, including the minority's size; whether its territory is adjacent to the state's borders; whether it has a 'kin state'; whether the territory has a homogenous population; and on whether it is of material value. Concerns about secession and irredentism have been uppermost where states are confronted with sizeable ethno-national minorities and with neighbours that have designs on part of the state's territory, as is the case throughout Eastern Europe. Elsewhere, as in the US Deep South, or where indigenous communities are too weak to launch secession bids, territorial domination has been aimed more at preventing local members of the dominant community from being governed by others, and/or at facilitating resource exploitation.

The most straightforward way for a dominant community to achieve territorial domination is through a centralized or unitary political structure, in which there is administrative 'deconcentration' rather than political decentralization. Most examples of democratic domination, such as those in Eastern Europe, or Israel, Turkey, and Sri Lanka, are indeed unitary states.[82] But territorial domination is also consistent with decentralization, within federations or unitary states, as long as the statewide minorities are also minorities in whatever political regions exist. Local/regional boundaries are purposively drawn, or gerrymandered, to achieve this effect. What O'Leary and I have elsewhere termed 'national federations', such as the United States, Mexico, Venezuela, and Brazil, drew their internal political boundaries, among other reasons, to avoid giving self-government to minorities.[83] The boundaries were constructed in the interests of their dominant 'national' community.

---

[82] The Sri Lankan government went to the trouble of explicitly stating in its 1972 and 1978 Constitutions that Sri Lanka was a unitary state, although it had already functioned as one since independence. Coomaraswamy, 'The politics of institutional design' (n 54 above), 152.

[83] J McGarry and B O'Leary, 'Federation as a method of ethnic conflict regulation' in SJR Noel (ed), *From Power-sharing to Democracy: Post-conflict institutions in ethnically divided societies* (2005), 263–96.

In 1996, Slovakia's government responded to calls from the minority Magyar community for modest 'local self-government' and 'community rights' by dividing the state into eight administrative regions that ran in a north—south direction.[84] This had the effect of making the Magyar minority, which was territorially concentrated in an area which runs in an east—west direction along the border with Hungary, into a small minority in all eight regions, and less than 20 per cent in all but two of them. One hundred and twenty-one subdistricts (obvod), in seventeen of which Magyars were a majority, were abolished.[85] The new administrative regions were not themselves self-governing, but it was anticipated that they would become the basis for a future round of decentralization. Bratislava appears to have been concerned that autonomy for a Magyar region or regions would promote secession and irredentism, particularly given that Hungary had annexed Slovakia's Hungarian-speaking area in the Second World War. The concerns were exacerbated by recent irredentist statements from the Hungarian Prime Minister, Josef Antall, and the fact that three communist federations, including that in which Slovakia had been a member, had recently disintegrated along their internal boundaries. The new regional boundaries were also aimed at eroding linguistic protections for the minority, as these protections were predicated on Magyars constituting at least 20 per cent of the regional population. Similarly, in Macedonia, a 1996 Law on the Territorial Division of the Republic of Macedonia sought to check the demographic power of the Albanian minority in the western part of the country, which abuts Albania, by redrawing administrative boundaries so that the larger and more-developed municipalities would have more Macedonians and the less-developed municipalities more Albanians.[86] The internal boundary revisions turned the ethnic Macedonians from minorities into majorities in the towns of Kicevo and Struga.[87]

Shortly after the formation of Northern Ireland in 1921, the unionist government engaged in a significant gerrymander of Northern Ireland's local governments to augment its territorial control. Twenty-five of the nearly eighty councils had nationalist majorities, and many of them were on the border with the Irish Free State and had declared their allegiance to its parliament. There was also an agreement between the British and Irish governments to revise the border, and to establish a commission to report on this. In this threatening context, the Northern Ireland government appointed a judicial commission under Sir John Leech. Leech's work included gerrymandering the boundaries of the local

---

[84] Z Csergo, *Talk of the Nation: Language and conflict in Romania and Slovakia* (2007).
[85] 'Slovak parliament approves laws on territorial reform' *Open Media Research Institute* (hereafter *OMRI*, temporary replacement of *RFE/RL*) 8 July 1996. Also M Brusis, 'Ethnic rift in the context of post-Soviet transformation: The case of the Slovak Republic' (1997) 5(1) *International Journal on Minority and Group Rights* 3–32.
[86] E Friedman, 'The ethnopolitics of territorial division in the Republic of Macedonia' (2009) 8 (2) *Ethnopolitics* 215.   [87] Ibid, 216, Table 1.

councils, as well as their internal ward boundaries. By the time he had completed his work, the number of nationalist controlled councils had dropped to two, with an average of ten to eleven over the subsequent fifty years.[88] While nationalists were 35 per cent of Northern Ireland's population they normally controlled only around 15 per cent of the local councils. Leech's gerrymanders helped to ensure that the boundary commission did not recommend significant change.[89] The most spectacular example of his work was in Northern Ireland's second city of Derry/Londonderry, which was close to the border and had a decisive nationalist electoral majority of around 65 per cent. A gerrymander packed most nationalists into one very large, and virtually homogeneous, ward, which elected eight councillors. The rest of the city was divided into two smaller wards, with twelve councillors, and small but decisive unionist majorities. The result was that a unionist minority of about 35 per cent won a majority of Derry's council at every election from the 1920s to the 1960s.[90] The gerrymandering of local boundaries was supplemented by the sort of electoral devices that have already been referred to, including a local ratepayers (property) franchise; multiple votes for business people (mostly unionists);[91] a switch from PR to plurality rule in local elections; and a requirement that local councillors swear an oath to the Crown.

Formally democratic states have also sought to gain or maintain territorial control by moving (settling) members of dominant communities in minority regions, enticing them there with the promise of cheap or free land and housing, while moving dominated communities off the land.[92] The aim of these settlement policies is to induce assimilation, by diluting the minority's homeland and weakening its ability to reproduce its culture, or to control and weaken the minority's claim to the territory (and to self-government). During the 1970s and 1980s, the Sinhalese-dominated government of Sri Lanka encouraged ethnic Sinhalese to settle in the island's central and eastern regions, which had been previously dominated by Tamils. By 1993, 1.1 million people had been settled in areas which the Tamils considered part of their 'Eelam' homeland.[93] In the United States—in Hawaii and the Southwest—statehood was delayed until the region's long-standing residents were swamped with enough white Anglo-Saxon Protestant (WASP) settlers. Israel has long had a policy of privileging Jewish settlement not just in the West Bank and Gaza but also, through its 'Judaization' policy, in parts of pre-1967 Israel inhabited by Arabs such as Bedouin regions in

---

[88] Nationalists won control of only two councils at the next local government elections in 1924, but much of this was due to an election boycott.
[89] O'Leary and McGarry, *The Politics of Antagonism* (n 6 above), 113.   [90] Ibid, 120–1.
[91] This aspect of the franchise was part of the general law of the United Kingdom, but although it was abolished in Great Britain in 1945, it was retained in Northern Ireland until 1968.
[92] J McGarry, '"Demographic engineering": The state-directed movement of ethnic groups as a technique of conflict regulation' (1998) 21(4) *Ethnic and Racial Studies* 613–38.
[93] Yiftachel, *Ethnocracy* (n 6 above), 24–5; R Muggah, *Relocation Failures in Sri Lanka: A short history of internal displacement and resettlement* (2009).

the Negev.[94] Turkey imposed territorial control over the south-eastern Kurdish region during the PKK insurgency in the 1990s by moving Kurds from rural areas and villages into urban areas, depriving the insurgents of a local support base and facilitating military exercises.[95]

States which practice ethnic domination, when they are not coercively assimilationist, have sometimes conceded cultural (or corporate) autonomy for minorities, ie autonomy that is based on a particular community rather than on a territory. The demise of Marxism–Leninism in Eastern Europe led to several states in the region introducing cultural autonomy regimes for certain minorities, including Estonia in 1993, Hungary in 1993, and Russia in 1996.[96] Israel continues to endorse arrangements, inherited from the Ottoman empire's 'millet' system, whereby religious minorities are self-governing in some matters of religion and family law.

Cultural autonomy in these cases is permitted precisely because it does not threaten the state's control of its territory, and it also has propaganda value, as it allows states and defenders of 'ethnic democracy' to argue that their states 'accommodate' minorities. Smooha uses Israel's system of cultural autonomy to argue that Israel is more accommodating of its minorities than 'liberal republican democracies', while Hungary, which has no significant minorities, seems to have adopted cultural autonomy to help persuade its neighbours to protect their Magyar minorities. Cultural autonomy in Eastern Europe and the Middle East is usually non-substantive and consistent with ethnic hierarchy. It is akin to the Ottoman empire's millet system, under which Christians and Jews were given autonomy but were clearly underprivileged in relation to Muslims.[97] In the case of Estonia, cultural autonomy applies only to citizens and not to the large community of 'Russian-speakers' who had been denaturalized in the early 1990s. It also appears to be consistent with the closing and the de-funding by the state of Russian-language schools and other public institutions as part of its nation-building policy.[98] In other cases, the schemes do not appear to involve autonomy at all, even on a non-territorial basis, but rather the creation of an officially recognized agency to lobby or advise the government on the minority's behalf. Codagnone and Fillipov argue that the influence of these agencies in Russia—the National Cultural Associations—have been minimal.[99] While the position of the Roma in Russia and Hungary may be better with cultural

---

[94] Smooha 'The model of ethnic democracy' (n 16 above), 46.
[95] AT Aker et al, *The Problem of Internal Displacement in Turkey: Assessment and policy proposals* (2005).
[96] J McGarry and M Moore, 'Karl Renner, power-sharing and non-territorial autonomy' in E Nimni (ed), *National Cultural Autonomy and its Contemporary Critics* (2005), 74–94.
[97] B Ye'or, *The Dhimmi: Jews and Christians under Islam* (1985).
[98] D Laitin, *Identity in Formation: The Russian-speaking populations in the near abroad* (1998).
[99] C Codagnone and V Fillipov, 'Equity, exit and national identity in a multinational federation: The "Multicultural Constitutional Patriotism" project in Russia' (2000) 26(2) *Journal of Ethnic and Migration Studies* 263–88.

autonomy than without, their position remains 'marginal' in spite of these reforms.[100]

E. Coercive and legal domination

States use their security sectors to enforce ethnic hierarchies, particularly when minorities violently resist. The army in such cases is used against internal as well as external enemies, while the police becomes a political or state police, under the close control of the political authorities rather than at arm's length, and charged with defending the political order (ethnic domination) as well as combating crime.

In such situations, the dominant community does not just dominate the security sector, but is invariably disproportionately (over-)represented in it, particularly in senior ranks. In Israel, only Jews and Druze Arabs, a minor community, are conscripted into the Israeli Defence Forces (IDF). Palestinian Arabs are technically eligible to volunteer, but do so in negligible numbers. While the absolute size of the IDF is unknown, Palestinian Arabs, nearly 20 per cent of Israel's pre-1967 population, constitute less than 1 per cent of its membership.[101] In Northern Ireland, Catholics, who represented 35 per cent of Northern Ireland's population at the start of the conflict in 1969, comprised just 10 per cent of the police force, the Royal Ulster Constabulary (RUC). While the Catholic share of the population grew to 43 per cent by the time of the 1998 Belfast Agreement, its share of RUC regulars dropped to 8.3 per cent.[102] Sri Lanka's police was comprised without regard to ethnicity in the first decade after independence, but with the onset of domination from the late 1950s, proficiency in Sinhala was made a criterion for appointment and recruitment was skewed towards the Sinhalese.[103] Burger describes the 'rapid Sinhalization of the police at all levels'.[104] By the early 1960s, Tamil police officers in Tamil areas were replaced with 'militant Buddhists'. Jaffna, which had a Tamil population of 90 per cent, had a police force that was 60–70 per cent Sinhalese.[105]

---

[100] P Vermeersch, 'Roma political participation and racism: Reflections on recent developments in Hungary and Slovakia' (2000) 4 *Roma Rights* 43–9.
[101] Knesset, Research and Information Center. Data on Recruitment over Years (Hebrew) (2007).
[102] Report of the Independent Commission on Policing for Northern Ireland, 'A new beginning: Policing in Northern Ireland' (1999), <http://www.nio.gov.uk/a_new_beginning_in_policing_in_northern_ireland.pdf> (accessed 2 September 2009).
[103] A Burger, 'Policing a communal society: The case of Sri Lanka' (1987) 27(7) *Asian Survey* 822–33, 824. [104] Ibid, 826.
[105] Ibid, 825–7. It is difficult to find recent figures on the ethnic composition of SL's police, and Burgess's figures are dated. However, as the violent conflict between the SL government and Tamils broke out after she wrote, it is very likely that the Tamil composition of the police declined further, at least until a split in the Tamil Tiger ranks in 2005 when the TMVP broke away to ally with the government. Available at <http://news.bbc.co.uk/2/hi/south_asia/8124836.stm> (accessed 31 July 2009).

Additionally, the composition of regular security forces may tell only part of the story. There are often reserve and auxiliary forces that are even more dominated by the core community, and more ethnocentric in their practices than the regulars. While in the Baltic states of Latvia, Estonia, and Lithuania, Russians 'citizens' appear to be reasonably well-represented in the army, although not in its senior ranks,[106] there are voluntary paramilitary defence units where the participation of Russian-speakers is minimal.[107] In Northern Ireland, the 'B Specials', an auxiliary police force which existed from 1920 to 1969, and which was comprised of approximately 10,000 members, were exclusively Protestants, and the RUC Reserve and UDR, which effectively replaced the 'specials', were also more Protestant in composition than the regular police.[108]

Compounding problems of underrepresentation, members of subordinate communities who are in the security sector tend not to be representative of their community's political mainstream, and may be ostracized from their communities and seen as traitors. In Ireland, before partition, and in Northern Ireland after it, Catholics who joined the police were known derogatorily as 'Castle' Catholics, with the Castle in question being Dublin Castle, the seat of the British administration in Ireland prior to 1921.

Minority underrepresentation in the security sector is frequently not caused by direct and formal discrimination on the part of the state, except that entry is restricted to citizens. Minorities are usually unwilling to take part in a security sector that is associated with, and defends, an unjust regime. They may also be dissuaded from joining because of indirect discrimination, including language and educational qualifications, because of offensive oaths of allegiance, or because the cultural ethos of the security sector is that of the dominant community. Catholics in Northern Ireland refused to join the Royal Ulster Constabulary in part because of its name: 'Royal' suggested a link with the British Crown, while 'Ulster' is a partisan term for Northern Ireland that is used by Protestants but not Catholics. The fact that the RUC was dominated by members of the anti-Catholic Orange Order, flew the Union Jack atop, and displayed portraits of the Queen in, their police stations, and that police offers had to swear an oath of allegiance to the Queen upon enlisting, also helped to

---

[106] My thanks to Aruna Molis, a Lithuanian specialist on the subject, who supplied this information. He attributes it to informal subjective discrimination.

[107] It is very difficult to get figures on the numbers and breakdown involved here. For this information, I have relied on email communications with Andras Racz, a Hungarian specialist on these matters.

[108] At the time of the Belfast Agreement in 1998, the RUC Reserve was 6.9 per cent Catholic. Report of the Independent Commission on Policing for Northern Ireland 'A new beginning: Policing in Northern Ireland' (1999), <http://www.nio.gov.uk/a_new_beginning_in_policing_in_northern_ireland.pdf> (accessed 31 July 2009). Ellison and Smith report that the part-time RUC Reserve was only 3.8 per cent Catholic (at 174); the Catholic representation in the UDR, while 17 per cent when it was first formed in 1970, settled down to an average of 3 per cent (at 138). G Ellison and J Smyth, *The Crowned Harp: Policing Northern Ireland* (2000).

keep Catholic numbers low. Defenders of the regime pointed out that Catholics did not join because they would have been singled out for attack by co-ethnic radicals, which had a ring of truth about it, but was not the only or the most important reason.[109]

Ethnically skewed composition of the security sector may be reinforced by close political control. After the 1950s, Sri Lanka's top police officer was 'chosen for his political reliability rather than his professional abilities', and he and his fourteen deputies were directly appointed by the governor general on the advice of the government, and later by the president.[110] The Sri Lankan police, in Burger's account, were neutral in their policing role but only between the two large Sinhalese parties that alternated in government. In relations with the minority Tamils, they performed like a 'communal' police, with ethnic background straightforwardly conditioning behaviour.[111] In Northern Ireland, British politicians who visited the province in the 1960s were shocked by the close control that the Unionist regime exercised over the police.[112] In Turkey, there are also close relations between the state and the security sector, but it is less clear that the civil authorities have the upper hand there.

Security-sector domination is complemented by legal domination. In the cases under review here, judges, like soldiers, policemen, and elected officials tend to be drawn disproportionately from dominant communities, and to mix in informal networks with political and security elites. Israel had no Arab judges on its Supreme Court during its first fifty years. It has had two since 1999, with one of these, Abdel Rahman Zuabi, a temporary appointment, serving for only nine months. In the United States, there have been only two black Supreme Court Justices from a total of 114, and one of these, Clarence Thomas, had political opinions that were not representative of blacks in general.[113] Of President Reagan's 366 appointees to the federal judiciary, over half of the total federal bench, only seven were black.[114] In Northern Ireland, six of the region's seven High Court judges in 1969 were Protestant, and Catholics held only seven of sixty-eight senior judicial appointments.[115] Judicial opinions are supposed to be informed by professional (impartial) legal judgments, but they are also influenced by cultural background, and sometimes by overt ethnic or racial bias. As recently as the 1960s, the US Southern courts were bastions of white privilege, 'beyond redemption' as President Johnson's Attorney General Katzenbach put it.[116]

---

[109] J McGarry and B O'Leary, *Policing Northern Ireland: A new start* (1999).
[110] Burger, 'Policing a communal society' (n 103 above), 825.   [111] Ibid, 826.
[112] McGarry and O'Leary, *Policing* (n 109 above), 29.
[113] L Epstein et al, *The US Supreme Court Justices Database* (Northwestern University School of Law, 2007), <http://epstein.law.northwestern.edu/research/justicesdata.html> (accessed 31 July 2009).   [114] Guinier, *The Tyranny of the Majority* (n 37 above), 24.
[115] O'Leary and McGarry, *The Politics of Antagonism* (n 6 above), 128.
[116] A Thernstrom, 'The odd evolution of the Voting Rights Act' (1979) 55 *Public Interest* 52.

The judiciary may also enjoy little independence from the society or the state. In the US, some judges depend for their positions on election. In Sri Lanka, according to a recent report, the bench is heavily 'politicized', 'stacked to favour the government', and possessed with 'an unflinching vision of Sinhala nationalism, political centralisation and the unitary state that runs counter to effective forms of devolution of power and power-sharing'.[117] This politicization results importantly from the current (1978) Constitution which 'vested unfettered control of judicial appointments in presidential hands'.[118] Judges in Sri Lanka are not promoted on grounds of seniority, or by lot from a pool of qualified personnel, but because of political opinion.[119] While a 2001 constitutional amendment sought to increase judicial independence by transferring power over some judicial appointments from the executive to a Constitutional Council, since 2005 Presidents Kumaratunga and Rajapaksa have 'wilfully ignored' this constitutional limit by refusing to convene the council.[120] Judges who step out of line, as well as human rights lawyers, have, apparently, been subject to intimidation or worse from agencies of the state or the 'deep' state.[121]

Courts may also be culturally disposed, or legally obliged, to be passive, permitting the government a free hand in maintaining domination. Those which operate under the Westminster system, including courts in Northern Ireland from 1921 to 1972 and in Sri Lanka from 1947 to 1972, tend to take passive positions that are deferential to the wishes of elected officials, and refuse to comment on, never mind criticize, ethnocentric legislation. In Sri Lanka, the post-independence courts were 'very weak [and] effectively subordinate to parliament'.[122] Both Northern Ireland and Sri Lanka's courts failed to take advantage of admittedly rather meagre constitutional rights provisions to challenge the executive or legislature. In Sri Lanka, only one law was challenged by the courts between 1947 and 1972, and this challenge was abortive. As a result, according to the International Crisis Group, 'the possibility that Sri Lanka's courts might have restrained rising communal tensions of the 1950s and 1960s went unrealised and is today largely forgotten'.[123]

While the step might have been considered redundant, Sri Lanka's second Constitution (1972–8) took away the courts' right to review legislation or question executive action, and abolished appeals to the Judicial Committee of the Privy Council in London.[124] Constitutional review was assigned instead to a five-member constitutional 'court' appointed by the president.[125] Judicial

---

[117] ICG, 'Sri Lanka's judiciary' (n 75 above), i.   [118] Ibid.
[119] The recently retired Chief Justice, Sarath Silva, apparently used his powers of appointment over lower courts to 'punish judges out of step with his wishes and to reward those who toed the line' (ibid, i).   [120] Ibid, i.
[121] Ibid, 4.
[122] Coomaraswamy, 'The politics of institutional design' (n 54 above), 149, 151.
[123] ICG, 'Sri Lanka's judiciary' (n 75 above), 3.
[124] Coomaraswamy, 'The politics of institutional design' (n 54 above), 149, 151; ICG, 'Sri Lanka's judiciary' (n 75 above), 3.   [125] ICG, 'Sri Lanka's judiciary' (n 75 above), 3.

independence was strengthened by the 1978 (current) Constitution, which includes a fundamental human rights chapter, but 'key constraints on judicial power' have been maintained.[126] The constraints include the ability of parliament to overturn the Supreme Court's determinations by a majority of two-thirds, an absolute ban on suits against an incumbent president, and a provision that gives the Supreme Court alone the right to hear suits against the government.[127]

In cases of rebellion, or the threat of it, legal domination is reinforced by emergency powers. These either enlist courts in the suppression of minority rights, or remove jurisdiction from courts to military tribunals. While 'emergency' suggests something that is temporary, extraordinary legal regimes have been used for long periods in Israel, Northern Ireland, Sri Lanka, and Turkey. Israel's emergency regime, which was based on military law, lasted from 1948 to 1967. In Northern Ireland, the Civil Authorities (Special Powers) Act of 1922, which gave the government wide-ranging powers, including the power to intern without trial and arrest people without warrant, issue curfews, and refuse inquests, was renewed annually at first, but then made permanent in 1933, and repealed only in 1972 when the regime collapsed. In Sri Lanka, the chief emergency instrument was the Public Security Ordinance of 1949, supplemented by the Prevention of Terrorism Act of 1979. According to Coomaraswamy, Sri Lanka has been ruled by these emergency powers 'for most of the time since independence' in 1948.[128] These powers are 'used disproportionately in Tamil areas and against Tamil suspects', while their legal framework is administered by the Ministry of Defence rather than the Justice Ministry.[129] While the 1978 Constitution introduced a human rights chapter, several parts of the country have been run since this under emergency law, which exempts them from the framework of the Constitution's protections.[130] In south-eastern Turkey, an emergency legal regime (Olaganüstü Hal or OHAL) was in place between 1987 and 2002. The regime permitted regional governors to suspend political rights. It also provided the legal basis for the forced evacuation of thousands of Kurdish villages, in an effort to establish 'territorial control' of Kurdish areas.[131]

Legal domination can exist even alongside various legal 'protections' for minorities. Some of the reasons have already been alluded to: courts may be 'indifferent' to the minority because of bias or subordination to the state.[132] The rights may not be justiciable, because of costs or because filing a suit requires long trips to the court, whether to the European Court in Strasbourg or the

---

[126] Ibid.   [127] Ibid, 5.
[128] Coomaraswamy, 'The politics of institutional design' (n 54 above), 162.
[129] ICG, 'Sri Lanka's judiciary' (n 75 above), i—ii.
[130] Coomaraswamy, 'The politics of institutional design' (n 54 above), 161.
[131] D McDowall, *The Kurds: A nation denied*, 7th edn (1996), 140.
[132] Thernstrom, 'The odd evolution of the Voting Rights Act' (n 116 above), 49.

Sri Lankan Supreme Court in Colombo.[133] The rights may be limited in their nature, applying to individuals rather than communities, or clumsily worded. Even when a court finds for a minority, its ruling may apply too narrowly to a particular case and have no general effect unless accompanied by legislation and executive enforcement. The US courts failed to remedy the subordination of blacks for almost a century in spite of the fourteenth and fifteenth amendments which provided for racial equality. Sri Lanka's courts could not protect Tamils even though the independence Constitution of 1947 to 1972 prohibited any law that conferred 'on persons of any community or religion any privilege or advantage which is not conferred on persons of other communities or religions'.[134] The 1972 Constitution contained a chapter on fundamental rights, but these were made subject to 'such restrictions as the law prescribes in the interests of national unity and integrity, national security, national economy, public safety, public order, [and] the protection of public health or morals'.[135] Unsurprisingly, not one rights case was brought before the courts under the 1972 Constitution.[136] The Government of Ireland Act 1920, which served as Northern Ireland's 'constitution', outlawed discrimination on the basis of religion, and prohibited the endowment of any religion.[137] The difficulty with this was that, in a politically and nationally divided society, it allowed the regime to discriminate on the basis of political opinion and national identity. Catholics, moreover, were wary of bringing cases under the Act's provisions because, as worded, they threatened the existence of publicly funded Catholic schools.[138] It was to deal with the various limits of judicial protections in the US that the Voting Rights Act of 1965 established the principle of federal oversight over the South's electoral arrangements and handed significant enforcement powers to an administrative agency, the Civil Rights Division of the Justice Department. Case-by-case jurisprudence had been ineffective in preventing innovative and racist jurisdictions from establishing discriminatory electoral arrangements, so the Act required that new arrangements in listed areas be administratively pre-cleared. The result was a significant increase in black registration, voting, and,

---

[133] During the Northern Ireland conflict, suits filed under the European Convention on Human Rights had to be filed at Strasbourg. The International Crisis Group recently identified the fact that human rights suits in Sri Lanka had to be filed in Colombo as an impediment (ICG, 'Sri Lanka's judiciary (n 75 above), ii).

[134] Constitution of Sri Lanka 1947, s 29.2.c, <http://www.tamilnation.org/srilankalaws/46constitution.htm> (accessed 31 July 2009).

[135] Constitution of Sri Lanka 1972, s 18.2, <http://www.tamilnation.org/srilankalaws/72constitution.htm#CHAPTER%20VI> (accessed 31 July 2009).

[136] Coomaraswamy, 'The politics of institutional design' (n 54 above), 150.

[137] The Government of Ireland Act stated that neither the Parliament of Southern Ireland nor that of Northern Ireland 'shall make a law so as either directly or indirectly to establish or endow any religion, or prohibit or restrict the free exercise thereof, or give a preference, privilege, or advantage or impose any disability or disadvantage, on account of religious belief'. Government of Ireland Act 1920 s 5.1, <http://cain.ulst.ac.uk/issues/politics/docs/goi231220.htm#5> (accessed 31 July 2009).   [138] O'Leary and McGarry, *The Politics of Antagonism* (n 6 above), 116–17.

eventually, office-holding. Although disputes involving federal voting rights are normally taken to local courts, those arising under the Voting Rights Act are heard by the District Court of the District of Columbia, and beyond that, the Supreme Court of the United States.[139]

III. The End of Domination?

Some scholars have argued that ethnic domination is becoming less sustainable given the emergence of an international legal and normative regime that promotes the protection of minorities.[140] Yet, a decade after the Lund Recommendations, there is little concrete evidence, particularly outside the European context, that legal instruments or norms have led to the substantive accommodation of minorities, whether through power-sharing in central governments, territorial self-government, official bilingualism or minority language institutions of higher learning.[141] In Israel, Sri Lanka and the Russian republic of Chechnya, the plight of minorities has either remained unchanged over this period or it has worsened. Even in Slovakia, since 2004 a member of the European Union, a new language law was introduced ten years after Lund that arguably worsened the position of the Magyar minority rather than improved it.[142] In some cases, such as Northern Ireland, Sudan, and Iraq, minorities have won substantive accommodation from the state, including power-sharing, autonomy and the public accommodation of minority languages, but this has arguably resulted from factors that have little to do with international laws or norms, including a military stalemate, a change in the domestic balance of power brought about by demographic change, or, as in Kurdistan's case, an international intervention that had little to do with concerns about minority rights. In other cases, norms, international legal instruments or outside pressures have produced improvements for minorities but these have not been of a substantive kind and have not fundamentally altered ethnic hierarchies. OSCE pressure in the context of EU accession led Estonia and Latvia to relax its

---

[139] Thernstrom, 'The odd evolution of the Voting Rights Act' (n 116 above), 52.

[140] Ilan Peleg refers to the 'emergence of a new global governing code', based on democracy, human rights and self-determination, that will place 'enormous pressure' on regimes that repress minorities to 'transform'. I Peleg, *Democratizing the Hegemonic State: Political transformation in the age of identity* (2007), 15. Ted Gurr sees an 'emerging regime of managed ethnic heterogeneity', particularly in democratic states, that will lead to improved inter-ethnic relations. TR Gurr, *Peoples Versus States: Minorities at risk in the new century* (2000), 277–81.

[141] For an explanation of 'accommodation', see McGarry, O'Leary and Simeon, 'Integration or accommodation?' (n 23 above).

[142] Available at <http://www.spectator.sk/articles/view/35906/2/slovakia_and_hungary_clash_again_over_language.html> (accessed 31 July 2009). For good measure, Slovakia's current government has also recognized the 'Benes Decrees', which led to the expulsion of ethnic Germans and Hungarians from Czechoslovakia between 1945 and 1947. 'It's a war over words in Slovakia', *Toronto Star*, 3 August 2009.

naturalization process and allow Russian speakers to acquire citizenship after a language test. However, many Russians have still not qualified or applied for citizenship, and in 2004 the Latvian government moved to substantively erode public education in the Russian language. Pressure from the EU, combined with the emergence of a new moderately Islamist political movement with support in Kurdish areas, has led Turkey to relax some of the strictures of Kemalism, permitting a state-run (ie state-controlled) television station in the Kurdish language and the teaching of Kurdish in private schools. The EU has focused on promoting freedom of expression and association in Turkey rather than a plurinational partnership based on Kurdish self-government or power-sharing, or even public education in Kurdish. All of these latter steps seem a very long way off.

One reason why international law has not produced the substantive accommodation of minorities is that international law does not prescribe such accommodation. International law, formulated by states, has been largely integrationist in character, and has usually focused on promoting individual rights and freedoms rather than power-sharing, territorial self-government, or official bilingualism. The only sort of 'international' documents that have gone substantively beyond integration, to recommend power-sharing or territorial autonomy, such as the Lund Recommendations, have been recommendations rather than law.[143] Even if international law was more generous towards minorities than it is, it is not clear how—lacking coercive sanctions—it could persuade dominant communities, many of which regard the accommodation of minorities as portending the disintegration of their country, or an existential threat, or a reversal of positions. It is also difficult to see how international law could be implemented in the absence of such persuasion. In addition to these realist arguments, however, norms have not produced the substantial accommodation of minorities because prevailing normative standards, based on democracy, liberalism, and republicanism, are not obviously inconsistent with domination. The chapter concludes by treating these three norms in sequence.

The fact that domination occurs in democracy, paradoxically, is one of the reasons why it endures. The most common understanding of democracy is majority rule. Democracy is conceived of as individuals coming together to decide on the collective conditions of their existence, and majority rule is seen as the fairest decision-making rule for sorting out disagreements among them. In divided polities, this rule, intended to protect individual equality and predicated

---

[143] Recommendation 1201 of the Council of Europe Parliamentary Assembly, adopted in 1993, proposed that national minorities should have access to 'appropriate local or autonomous authorities' providing that this was 'in accordance with' domestic laws. This was not legally binding and the subsequently adopted 1995 Framework Convention on National Minorities, which was legally binding, contained no reference to self-government rights. See W Kymlicka, 'Reply and conclusion' in W Kymlicka and M Opalski (eds), *Can Liberal Pluralism be Exported: Western political theory and ethnic relations in Eastern Europe* (2001), 371–3.

on the notion that majorities fluctuate, allows majority tyrannies. As democracy and majority rule are normatively desirable, ethnic communities that dominate in democracies feel justified and are not subject to the sort of internal self-doubts that befell the apartheid (minority rule) regime in South Africa, which excluded the vast majority of the state's population from the franchise and ran afoul of democratic norms.[144] Such communities may also escape criticisms from outsiders, who may not even see domination, unless it is vigorously contested by the minority in question. This is one of the reasons why dominant majorities may consider the radical step of territorial down-sizing rather than become dominant *minorities*, as this would strip them of their democratic credentials.

At a more detailed level, many of the mechanisms and practices that are used to dominate minorities and that were reviewed in the second part of this chapter are seen as necessary to defend and promote democracy, which makes them easier to justify. Electoral rules that reward large parties and discriminate against small parties can be viewed, not as injurious to minorities, but as necessary for 'functional' government and for preventing 'Italian scenarios' where the formation of governments or passage of legislation is difficult. Similarly, single-person presidencies and majoritarian single-party governments are seen as facilitating decisiveness, whereas power-sharing coalitions or minority vetoes are said to obstruct it. Such performance-related variables are commonly seen as important, not just for promoting economic development, but for protecting democracy against the threat of authoritarianism. Majority governments are also said to deliver accountability, whereas power-sharing coalitions including minorities are seen as lacking democratic oppositions and as providing a 'macabre parody of democracy'.[145] The frequent registration of voters, and the secret ballot, both of which were used to discriminate against blacks in the Deep South, were (and are) justified on the grounds that the former was necessary to prevent fraud while the latter, which released voters from the shackles of landlords and employers, underwrote a free vote. Literacy tests have been justified, not on racial grounds, but as necessary for the responsible exercise of the franchise. In republican circles, a unitary state, and a majoritarian parliament free from interference from rights-protecting courts, is seen as necessary for popular sovereignty (the rights of the people as a whole). For some democratic theorists, a common-language policy is important for the creation of a community that can collectively deliberate, and as necessary for trust. All of these 'democratic' arguments have been used to sustain mechanisms that permit domination.

---

[144] Northern Ireland's unionist majority reacted to demands from the nationalist minority in the 1970s for power-sharing by arguing that the latter was undemocratic (as well as being un-British). See A Lijphart, 'Review article: The Northern Ireland problem: Cases, theories, and solutions', (1975) 5 *British Journal of Political Science* 83–106.

[145] R McCartney, 'Devolution is a sham', *Observer*, 20 February 2000; P Brass, *Ethnicity and Nationalism: Theory and comparison* (1991), 334.

Liberalism is usually conceived of as a way, indeed the primary way, to address ethnic domination. In the standard liberal view, domination results from the capture of the state by a dominant ethnic community. The liberal response is a neutral state that separates state and culture (privatizes culture), bans discrimination on the basis of ethnicity, and promotes individual freedoms and equality.[146] In many ways, liberalism's focus on individual freedoms and equality has improved the lot of minorities. Freedom of religion has allowed minorities to practise their religion, while freedom of expression and association has allowed them to mobilize and organize their own political parties. It is these liberal values that have been focused on by the European Union with respect to Turkey's minorities (and its Muslim majority). However, traditional understandings of liberalism do not support the substantive accommodation of minorities. The liberal insistence on the privatization of culture is better than coercive assimilation, but it is still biased towards large communities who have the resources to dominate minority cultures. And while liberalism proscribes the establishment of a state religion, it has had little to say about the neutrality of a state language, which is invariably that of the dominant community.

The promotion by liberals of individual equality and non-discrimination has helped minorities combat direct and formal discrimination, but it has had less success in dealing with mechanisms of domination that are 'facially neutral' and 'indirectly' discriminatory and therefore consistent with a formal or narrow understanding of individual equality. The problem here is that most of the mechanisms of domination reviewed in the second part of this chapter fall into this latter category. Several of them, such as multiple votes for businessmen in Northern Ireland, or the poll tax in the US South, were not directly aimed at Catholics or blacks, but were class-based and discriminated indirectly. The South's literacy tests could be said to test the qualifications of individuals rather than blacks. Facial neutrality applied to virtually all of the Jim Crow regime, which was one of the reasons why it survived court challenges for nearly a century after the fourteenth and fifteenth amendments of the US Constitution. At large electoral systems in the US South did not rest on the direct exclusion of black representatives. They were argued for during the 'progressive era' on the grounds that they would encourage city-wide perspectives and lead to government by business people (boosters) who could ably run cities, compete against neighbouring urban centres, attract investment, resist profligacy, and so on. As a consequence, the US Supreme Court, as recently as 1980 in *Mobile v Bolden* argued that such systems were not discriminatory ipso facto, and that, to show discrimination, litigants would have to prove discriminatory 'intent'. As we have seen, other types of electoral systems that hurt minorities affect small parties in general and can also be justified on a number of non-discriminatory (democratic) grounds, while minorities can easily be kept out of the state's security

---

[146] McGarry, O'Leary and Simeon, 'Integration or accommodation?' (n 23 above).

sectors, or wider public sector, by facially neutral measures that do not directly discriminate.

Liberals generally oppose mechanisms that accommodate minority groups qua groups, which makes it easier for dominant groups to resist such concessions. The standard liberal argument with respect to public institutional protection for ethnic groups is that this promotes ethnocentrism and discrimination against dissenting individuals. This applies to group-based vetoes, group participation in political institutions, and to territorial self-government for minorities. Andreas Wimmer worried that 'ethnically based' autonomy in Iraq 'may heighten, rather than reduce the risks of gross human rights violations, especially for members of ethnic minorities living under the rule of the majority government in a federal unit'.[147] Angela Burger, in an article that pointed to clear flaws with Sri Lanka's centralized police force, nonetheless pointed out that a decentralization of police services would 'doubtless translate into rule by the dominant local ethnic group, which would have had no experience in trying to control the police and scant reason to protect and defend minority rights or prevent police brutality'.[148] Even Eric Nordlinger, who supports power-sharing, refused to support federalism on the grounds that it would allow the region's 'dominant segment to ignore or negate the demands of the minority segment'.[149] Similarly, many liberals have opposed affirmative action as a mechanism for reversing discrimination against minorities on the grounds that it constitutes a form of reverse discrimination that is inconsistent with the merit principle and the notion of careers open to talent. These standard liberal arguments are used by people who genuinely seek a neutral state which stands above ethnicity, but they are also pressed into service by the representatives of dominant communities to justify their failure to address minority aspirations.

Republicans emphasize as a good the achievement of a single public or national identity within the state's frontiers. They espouse integrationist policies as necessary not just for state unity and solidarity but also political stability, and oppose policies that will produce national fragmentation or *dis*integration. These arguments lead to tactical support for, or advocacy of, many of the mechanisms set out in the second part of this chapter.

Republicans have been prepared to ban sectional or ethnic parties on the grounds that they are disintegrative. They also support all of the electoral systems that favour large parties over small (minority) parties because these encourage aggregation, and they may support national registration of parties on the 'positive'[150] grounds that this encourages these parties to reach out beyond a

---

[147] A Wimmer, 'Democracy and ethno-religious conflict in Iraq' (2003) 45(4) *Survival* 111–34, 123. [148] Burger, 'Policing a communal society' (n 103 above), 832.
[149] E Nordlinger, *Conflict Regulation in Divided Societies* (1972), 21.
[150] Bogaards distinguishes between policies that 'block' the organization of parties, ie that ban them, and what he calls 'positive' measures that add 'an important positive incentive for aggregation'. M Bogaards, 'Democratization and diversity' (n 52 above).

single ethnic base (and to take minority interests into account. Such republican arguments can be found in the Lund Recommendations: 'Ideally parties should be open and should cut across narrow ethnic issues; thus, mainstream parties should seek to include members of minorities to reduce the need or desire for ethnic parties. The choice of electoral system may be important in this regard'.[151] In the United States, (small r) republicans have spoken out against black 'majority districts' that help to ensure black representation in state legislatures and in Congress, or ward-based municipal elections, on the grounds that this ghettoizes blacks and allows majority white parties to ignore black interests.[152] Integration, it is argued, is in the interests of the minority, because if it relies on its own ethnic resources, it will always be a minority.[153] The argument rests on the weak assumptions that, in a divided polity, a party that is predominantly of the majority group and needs majority more than minority support, will nonetheless protect minority interests; that the minority will want to vote for politicians of the majority rather than its own; and that a minority party in the legislature cannot be protected by institutional arrangements that allows it to share in power and influence, or make some decisions. Republicans oppose self-government for minorities not so much for the liberal reasons that it promotes discrimination against minorities, but because it allows the reproduction of the minority's culture and identity, threatening the political stability and unity of the state. The (French and Turkish) republican response is a centralized unitary state. The (American) republican response, influenced by liberalism, permits federation, because of its power-dispersing benefits, but only if it is based on non-ethnic principles, and promotes heterogeneous units that, in Madisonian style, permit alliances that cut across ethnic lines.[154] It is not difficult to see how such arguments reinforce the mechanisms discussed under 'territorial domination' in part two of this chapter, including the gerrymandering of internal boundaries so that they cut across ethnic groups.

We can see how these considerations of international realpolitik and norms of democracy, liberalism, and republicanism can come together to prevent redress for minorities by considering a ruling of the European Court of Human Rights in 2007, entitled *Yumak and Sadak v Turkey*.[155] The case concerned Turkey's high electoral threshold of 10 per cent, one of the effects of which was to make it difficult for small parties, including Kurdish parties, to win representation in Turkey's legislature. The plaintiffs, two Kurdish politicians, argued that this

---

[151] Project Unit Office of the High Commissioner on National Minorities, 'The Lund Recommendations on the Effective Participation of National Minorities in Public Life and Explanatory Note' (The Hague: Office of the High Commissioner on National Minorities, 1999). See explanatory note, General Principles, s. 8.
[152] Guinier, *The Tyranny of the Majority* (n 37 above), 65.
[153] Thernstrom, 'The odd evolution of the Voting Rights Act' (n 116 above).
[154] P Roeder, *Where Nation-States Come From: Institutional change in the age of nationalism* (2007). [155] *Yumak and Sadak v Turkey*, Appl 10226/03, Judgment of 30 January 2007,

threshold infringed Art 3 of Protocol 1 to the European Convention on Human Rights (the right to free elections), as it constrained the people's ability to select their representatives. In its ruling upholding the threshold, the Court acknowledged that it was for the 'Turkish authorities, both judicial and legislative', and not international courts, to decide what sort of electoral system was appropriate for Turkey, and that the Turkish authorities had not overstepped its 'wide margin of appreciation' with respect to Art 3. This was an argument that upheld state sovereignty.

The Court nowhere mentioned the discriminatory effect of the threshold on Kurdish representation, but argued rather that the 'purpose of the measure' was to establish 'stable parliamentary majorities' and to 'avoid excessive parliamentary fragmentation and reinforce government stability, regard being had in particular to the period of instability which Turkey had been through in the 1970s'. This part of the ruling suggested the electoral threshold was non-discriminatory, and that it had a reasonable democratic objective—namely to prevent the sort of instability that had prompted a military coup in Turkey in 1980. The Court noted, implicitly in agreement, that Turkey's Constitutional Court had ruled that fair representation could legitimately be balanced with concerns about governmental stability. It did not state that the exclusion of Kurdish political representatives from Turkey's parliament might also be a source of political instability, even though the alienation of Kurds from Turkey's political system had recently resulted in a violent insurrection in which thousands had died.

Finally, the Court noted 'with interest the Government's argument that the aim of the electoral threshold was to give small parties the possibility of establishing themselves nationally and thus form part of a national political project'. This suggested support for the republican and nation-building arguments made by the Turkish authorities. The Court did not note with interest that the threshold meant that small parties that wanted to represent their ethnic community would find it difficult to win seats under this system. The Court's ruling in the case of *Yumak and Sadak v Turkey* offers general support for my argument that it may be too optimistic to expect international legal instruments and liberal democratic norms to provide substantial redress to ethnic minorities faced with domination.

IV. Conclusion

As this chapter details, one should not expect democratic institutions to automatically deliver minorities from domination. Many formally democratic political systems permit one community to dominate another, or others, and to do so using conventional mechanisms that appear uncontroversial. This is why the extension of democracy to places like Eastern Europe has not fundamentally altered relations between majorities and minorities. Nor is international law likely to come to the rescue of minority communities. International law is made by states, which in many, if not most, cases means the majority communities that control states. The spread of new liberal-democratic norms is also unlikely to lead to a substantive improvement in the position of minority communities, as many of these norms are consistent with domination, and, in some cases, bolster it.

All of this suggests that minorities that resist domination will, in most cases, have to rely on their own resources, or on help from outsiders who are motivated by reasons other than a general concern for minority communities, such as concern for their ethnic kin or regional stability, or a desire to weaken a rival state.

3

Understanding Minority Participation and Representation and the Issue of Citizenship

Annelies Verstichel

I. Introduction	73
A. Participation, representation, and ethnic, religious, and linguistic identity	73
B. The right of persons belonging to minorities to effective participation in public affairs	73
II. 'Effective Participation in Public Affairs': A Broad Concept, Less So in its Implementation and Monitoring	75
III. Justification and Aims of Effective Participation of Minorities in Public Affairs	77
A. Rights v security perspective	77
B. Participation v representation	79
IV. The Nature of Minority Participation and Representation and Possible Problematic Aspects	81
A. Mirror representation, authorization, and accountability	81
B. Essentialism, multiple identities, and the opting-out principle	83
C. Group proliferation and social cohesion at risk	86
V. The International Right to Effective Participation of Persons Belonging to Minorities in Public Affairs	87
VI. Citizenship	90
VII. Concluding Remarks	93

I. Introduction

A. Participation, representation, and ethnic, religious, and linguistic identity

Organizing participation and representation along ethno-national, religious, or linguistic lines is not new. Examples of countries and regions are Lebanon, Bosnia and Herzegovina, Belgium, and Northern Ireland. There are, in addition, a lot of countries where participation and representation is not organized completely along ethno-national, religious, or linguistic lines but where mechanisms are in place which promote or even guarantee the participation and representation of ethnic, religious, or linguistic groups. In the United States, for example, boundaries of electoral districts may be adapted on the basis of the Voting Rights Act to promote the election of a representative of an underrepresented and historically marginalized group, mostly African-Americans. In Germany, the voting threshold is removed for political parties of the Danish national minority in Schleswig-Holstein. In Slovenia, the Italian and Hungarian minorities are each guaranteed one seat in parliament. Finally, there are countries where a minority, which constitutes a majority locally, has been granted autonomy, such as in Finland to the Swedish-speaking Aaland Islands.

B. The right of persons belonging to minorities to effective participation in public affairs

What is new, however, is the appearance of an international right for persons belonging to minorities to effective participation in public affairs in the minority rights instruments of the 1990s.[1] The codification of minority rights at the international level was novel to start with. In addition, compliance with minority rights became an accession criterion for international organizations, such as the

---

[1] Only certain treaties concluded in 1919–20 between the allied and associated powers and the states defeated in the First World War, such as those signed in Sèvres with Turkey, Greece, and Armenia, recognized the right of ethnic minorities to proportional or fair representation in the elected bodies of the state. The treaties concluded with Greece and Armenia required these states merely to establish an electoral system which took into account the rights of minorities. The treaty with Turkey was more stringent in that it stipulated that the electoral system was to be founded on the principle of proportional representation of ethnic minorities. However, the Treaty of Sèvres was never ratified, and was in 1923 replaced by the Treaty of Lausanne, which did not contain any guarantees of this kind (F Benoît-Rohmer and H Hardeman, 'The representation of minorities in the parliaments of Central and Eastern Europe' (1994) 2 *International Journal on Group Rights* 95–111).

As a result, one can conclude that the right of minorities to effective participation in public affairs was stipulated for the first time in a general way in the minority rights documents of the 1990s. Moreover, the emphasis lies on *effective* participation: not only presence but also influence on the outcome of the decision-making process is at stake. Finally, the concept of participation is broader: not only representation in parliament but also participation in public affairs is envisaged by the provisions on effective participation of minorities in public affairs.

Council of Europe (CoE) and the European Union (EU). An international right to effective participation in public affairs, as advanced in the Concluding Document of the Copenhagen Meeting of the Conference on the Human Dimension held in November 1990 (hereinafter 'CSCE Copenhagen Document') (para 35) and the 1992 UN Declaration on the Rights of Persons Belonging to National or Ethnic, Religious, and Linguistic Minorities (hereinafter 'UN Declaration on Minorities') (Art 2(2) and (3)), and as guaranteed by the Framework Convention for the Protection of National Minorities (hereinafter, 'FCNM') (Art 15), means that states bind themselves politically—in the case of the CSCE Copenhagen Document and the UN Declaration on Minorities—and legally—in the case of the FCNM—to secure persons belonging to minorities effective participation in decision-making relating to matters which affect them. The effective participation of minorities has become a matter of international concern.

Furthermore, the right of persons belonging to minorities to effective participation in public affairs has been singled out from among other minority rights for further elaboration and exploration in the organizations having elaborated international minority rights catalogues (Organization for Security and Cooperation in Europe (OSCE), United Nations (UN) and CoE). It was developed in the 1999 Lund Recommendations[2] (and further in the Warsaw Guidelines[3]) under the auspices of the OSCE High Commissioner on National Minorities (HCNM). The UN Working Group on Minorities decided to draft a general comment on it[4] and to include it in regional guidelines or codes of practice.[5] The Advisory Committee on the Framework Convention (ACFC) has dedicated its second thematic commentary to effective participation.[6] It reflects the importance of this right among other minority rights, the need to give more concrete content to a broadly formulated provision, and the arrival at a point in time that is ripe, after the first years of monitoring, for more general conclusions and an assessment of best or good practice.

This chapter aims to explore the concepts of effective minority participation and representation. What is their content? What is their justification and what

---

[2] The Lund Recommendations on Effective Participation of Minorities in Public Life (1999), <http://www.osce.org/documents/hcnm/1999/09/2698_en.pdf> (accessed 31 July 2009).

[3] OSCE Guidelines to Assist National Minority Participation in the Electoral Process, Warsaw, 2001, <http://www.osce.org/documents/hcnm/2001/01/240_en.pdf> (accessed 31 July 2009).

[4] See Report of the Working Group on its 10th Session, 2004, E/CN4/Sub2/2004/29, para 66. However, the UN Working Group was abolished before it drafted such a general comment.

[5] See R Letschert, 'Review of the 8th Session of the United Nations Working Group on Minorities' (2002/3) 2 *EYMI* 500–2; and T Hadden, *Towards a Set of Regional Guidelines or Codes of Practice on the Implementation of the Declaration*, 2003, E/CN4/Sub2/AC5/2003/WP1, para 38. However, the UN Working Group was abolished before such regional guidelines or codes of practice were elaborated.

[6] Council of Europe Advisory Committee on the Framework Convention for the Protection of National Minorities, Commentary on Effective Participation of Persons Belonging to National Minorities in Cultural, Social, and Economic Life and in Public Affairs, adopted on 27 February 2008, ACFC/31/DOC(2008)001.

are they aiming for? Are there any limits to their effectiveness and what kind of problematic issues are involved? The results of this examination will then be compared to the concepts underlying the implementation and monitoring practice of the international right of persons belonging to minorities to effective participation in public affairs. Particular attention will be paid to the OSCE HCNM Lund Recommendations and the ACFC Commentary on Effective Participation. Finally, a section will be dedicated to the role of citizenship in relation to minority participation and representation.[7]

II. 'Effective Participation in Public Affairs': A Broad Concept, Less So in its Implementation and Monitoring

'Effective participation in public affairs' has a broad meaning, including political participation in the narrow sense, namely participation in elected bodies such as parliament or regional and local councils, as well as participation in the executive, the administration, law enforcement institutions, advisory bodies, public councils, boards, and committees; as well as participation in semi-state bodies, such as chambers of commerce and industry, in bodies representing agriculture or labour, in social insurance bodies, in trade unions, employers unions and tripartite bodies, and in boards of public broadcasting companies. In addition, all sorts and degrees of autonomy, including federalism, cultural autonomy, and local self-administration, can also be seen as possible methods of implementation of the right to effective participation.

In addition, the qualifier 'effective' in the right of persons belonging to minorities to effective participation in public affairs refers to the fact that the 'presence' of minority representatives in decision-making processes should be translated into 'influence' on the outcome of the decision-making. With a few reserved seats in parliament, for example, minorities can still be out-voted. Autonomy would signify the ultimate influence on the outcome of decision-making as it implies 'control' over it. Admittedly, presence will already imply influence to a certain extent. However, it is useful to be aware of the distinction between the two concepts. Mechanisms related to the presence of minorities in decision-making processes are sometimes not enough for the implementation of the right to effective participation of minorities in public affairs.

However, in reality, at the national level, there are more mechanisms regarding political participation and fewer regarding the broader concept of

---

[7] This article draws to a large extent on the research done for and on some of the main ideas elaborated in the doctoral thesis of the author Representation and Identity: The right of persons belonging to minorities to effective participation in public affairs: Content, justification and limits, which was defended at the European University Institute (Florence) on 13 December 2007. The thesis was awarded the Mauro Cappelletti Annual Prize 2008 and will be published by Intersentia (Antwerp) in the course of 2009.

participation in public affairs. In addition, there are more mechanisms related to the *presence* of minorities in decision-making processes and fewer related to the *influence* of minorities on the outcome of these processes. Moreover, international bodies advancing the implementation of the right of minorities to effective participation in public affairs, and monitoring it, also reflect this focus. In the monitoring of the FCNM by the ACFC, for example, the stress lies on political participation in the narrow sense (representation in parliament and other elected bodies), and to a certain extent on consultation as well, but to a much lesser extent to representation on executive, administrative, judicial and other bodies. Representation on executive, administrative, judicial, and other bodies is also underdeveloped in the OSCE HCNM Lund Recommendations and in the 2005 Commentary on the UN Declaration on Minorities[8] and leaves room for further elaboration. None of the relevant bodies have, to date, considered participation in semi-state bodies, such as chambers of commerce and industry or trade unions, employers unions, and tripartite bodies.[9] Furthermore, most attention goes to the presence of minorities in the decision-making, and hardly any to the *influence* of minorities on the outcome of it. No mention is made in the OSCE HCNM Lund Recommendations or in the Commentary on the UN Declaration on Minorities, for example, of qualified majority voting or veto mechanisms. The ACFC discusses existing mechanisms, but does not suggest or recommend the introduction of any. With regard to consultation mechanisms, however, the ACFC has always stressed that they should have real influence on decision-making[10] and, if there is no obligation to consult, the ACFC recommends that states consult these bodies in a more consistent manner[11] and give reasons when they decide not to follow the advice given.[12] In its commentary on effective participation, the ACFC highlights the importance of the effectiveness of participation, which implies that states should ensure that

---

[8] Commentary of the Working Group on Minorities to the UN Declaration on Rights of Persons belonging to National or Ethnic, Religious, and Linguistic Minorities, UN Doc E/CN4/Sub2/AC5/2005/2, 4 April 2005.

[9] Except for the Venice Commission in its *Questionnaire* on Participation of Members of Minorities in Public Life (by Mr Ergun Özbudun), Strasbourg, 19 December 1995, CDL-MIN (1995)002e-rev-restr, Section II and the ACFC highlighting the importance of the inclusion of persons belonging to minorities in supervisory boards of public service broadcasts, auditors' councils, and other media-related bodies (ACFC, Commentary on Effective Participation (n 6 above), para 141).

[10] Second ACFC Opinion on Finland, ACFC/INF/OPII(2006)003, 20 April 2006, paras 155–6. All ACFC opinions and state reports are available at <http://www.coe.int/t/dghl/monitoring/minorities/3_FCNMdocs/Table_en.asp#Finland> (accessed 31 July 2009).

[11] The Slovak Republic is commended in this respect, see First ACFC Opinion on the Slovak Republic, ACFC/INF/OP/I(2001)001, 22 September 2000, para 46. Otherwise see, First ACFC Opinion on Romania, ACFC/INF/OP/I(2002)001, 6 April 2001, para 66; First ACFC Opinion on Estonia, ACFC/INF/OP/I(2002)005, 14 September 2005, para 57; and Second ACFC Opinion on Croatia, ACFC/INF/OP/II(2004)002, 13 April 2005, para 169.

[12] First ACFC Opinion on Romania (n 11 above), para 66.

persons belonging to minorities have a substantial influence on decisions which are taken and not merely formally provide for their participation.[13]

The lack of, or limited, attention paid to the extent to which minorities have influence on decision-making throughout the UN, OSCE, and Council of Europe begs the question to what extent the 'effectiveness' of participation of minorities is implemented. The adjective 'effective' in the right of minorities to effective participation in public affairs is the most important qualifier of the nature of this right. In this respect, it seems that there is considerable room for improvement in the implementation of the right to effective participation in public affairs. Both the stress on political participation in the narrow sense, and the attention on mechanisms enhancing the presence of minorities in the decision-making rather than their influence on the outcome, reflect that the monitoring (still) largely sticks to commenting on existing mechanisms.

III. Justification and Aims of Effective Participation of Minorities in Public Affairs

A. Rights v security perspective

Effective participation of minorities in public affairs can be justified both from a rights perspective and from a security perspective. Peace and stability concerns led to the elaboration of catalogues of minority rights at the international level in the 1990s. From the preambles and drafting history of the three major minority-rights instruments (the CSCE Copenhagen Document, the UN Declaration on Minorities, and the FCNM), it is clear that they were written at a time of big historical change and the raging of wars and conflicts in which ethnicity and majority–minority relations were central. The idea was, and is, that long-term peace and stability are built on, inter alia, the respect for human rights, including minority rights. Such a comprehensive security concept is, for example, essential to the OSCE as a regional security organization. In this security framework, the effective participation of minorities in public affairs is important as the exclusion of minority groups from the decision-making processes, especially those affecting them, is a potential root cause of conflict. Nevertheless, it should be taken into account that implementing the right of minorities to effective participation in public affairs can also create unrest and social instability in the short term. Empowering marginalized groups is often perceived as a threat by those in power and contrary to their interests. Recommendations related to the participation of minorities in public affairs aimed at creating a 'stable' society might therefore differ from recommendations aiming at creating a 'just' society, in which the right of minorities to effective participation in public affairs is duly implemented.

---

[13] ACFC, Commentary on Effective Participation (n 6 above), paras 18–21.

For an example of different recommendations, see the discussion related to proportional representation with open lists or closed lists.[14]

From a rights perspective, the ultimate goal of minority representation is substantive equality. This goal of substantive equality is, first of all, aimed at overcoming structural inequality and systemic discrimination. Inclusion in decision-making processes should help to break the circle of socio-economic inequality. Minorities should be able to take part in public life as an implementation of the general principle of participatory democracy. Under-representation should be remedied through temporary affirmative action. This justification of group representation is not typical for ethnic, linguistic, or religious minorities alone. Remedying the underrepresentation of women in parliament by setting quota for women on political party lists is another example.

In the second place, the goal of substantive equality is aimed at enabling minorities to protect and promote their identity. Culture, language, and religion are constitutive elements of a person's identity and autonomy. Minorities, like majorities, have a right to the preservation and promotion of their identity. Therefore, minorities should be effectively involved in decision-making processes that have an impact on their identity. It is important that they are involved during the drafting, interpretation, implementation, and evaluation of laws and policies affecting them and their identity. As such, the effective participation and representation of minorities is a precondition for sound minority protection and the right to effective participation in public affairs can be seen as a procedural right.

It might not always be necessary to provide for special representation mechanisms. A given political situation might provide for a climate in which minorities are represented and their interests are duly taken into account. However, when voting patterns generally run along ethnic, religious, or linguistic lines or, at least, when matters are decided which are of particular importance to the identity of a minority, special representation mechanisms will be necessary. The salience of ethnic, religious, and linguistic characteristics in voting behaviour and decision-making processes might evolve over time. A situation in which special mechanisms are needed at the outset, such as after violent conflict, might evolve into a situation where these are no longer needed as people start to vote along other lines, such as ideological convictions. The reverse is also possible. Finally,

---

[14] Open lists generally favour minorities, unless there is a political will or regulation to allocate eligible seats to minority candidates. The open-list recommendation differs from the recommendation Arend Lijphart makes with regard the constitutional design of divided societies. He recommends List PR with closed lists as these encourage the formation and maintenance of strong and cohesive political parties (A Lijphart, 'Constitutional design for divided societies' (2004) 15(2) *Journal of Democracy*, 99–106). The explanation for the difference in recommendations is found in the fact that Lijphart seeks to make recommendations which enhance the stability of a society, whereas the search for effective representation of minorities seeks to combat under-representation of minorities. It should be noted that Lijphart's recommendations target divided societies and are based on the presumption that voting patterns follow ethnic divisions and that parties are generally established along ethnic lines.

it should be recalled that minority rights cannot be short-circuited by political representation. Without firm legal safeguards for minority rights, minority representatives must permanently negotiate these rights.[15]

B. Participation v representation

As stated, under the goal of substantive equality, one can distinguish between, on the one hand, mechanisms to promote or guarantee the participation of minorities as temporary affirmative action in order to compensate for systemic discrimination and, on the other hand, special representation mechanisms aimed at the protection and promotion of minority identity. Or, put differently, one can make the distinction between, on the one hand, the aim of integration and inclusion in order to reverse discrimination, and, on the other hand, the aim of preserving and promoting minority identity, in order to reverse assimilation. This distinction is important as it helps to clarify the difference between minority participation and minority representation.

Admittedly, this conceptual differentiation is a simplification of reality in which processes are more complex and interconnected. Nevertheless, it is essential to be aware of these differences in order to devise minority participation and representation mechanisms suitable for and tailored to their specific purposes. This distinction is, however, not clearly made in the implementation and monitoring of the right to effective participation of minorities in public affairs by the relevant international bodies. Some examples will be given later on to illustrate this.

Mechanisms intended to compensate for systemic discrimination and reverse underrepresentation in different areas of public life—including in parliament, the administration, and law enforcement institutions—constitute temporary affirmative action. In this case, the *participation* of persons belonging to minorities is to be taken literally. It involves minority persons actually sitting in parliament, taking up positions as civil servants or working for the police service, in order to contribute to the aim of combating underrepresentation and discrimination. On the other hand, mechanisms intended to further the participation and representation in decision-making processes affecting minorities, in order to protect and promote minority identity, constitute minority *representation*. What is essential here is that the minority representatives are authorized to represent a minority or minorities and that there is a link of accountability between the minority representatives and the minority or minorities they represent.

---

[15] See F Bieber, 'Balancing political participation and minority rights: The experience of the Former Yugoslavia' in *Minorities in Democracy* (2002) 44. See also S Spiliopoulou-Åkermark, 'Minority protection is not only about political participation and democratic governance' and 'Democracy is inadequate' in S Spiliopoulou-Åkermark, Justifications of Minority Protection in International Law (1997) 31, 32; and A Eide, 'In search of constructive alternatives to secession' in Christian Tomuschat (ed), *Modern Law of Self-Determination* (1993) 155.

The differentiation between, on the one hand, mechanisms to promote or guarantee the *participation* of minorities as temporary affirmative action in order to compensate for systemic discrimination and, on the other hand, special *representation* mechanisms aiming at the protection and promotion of minority identity, is relevant in parliament, the administration, and the judiciary. To illustrate this distinction, several examples can be given. A minority member of parliament (hereinafter 'MP') is not necessarily a minority representative elected to protect and promote the minority identity. He or she might have been offered an eligible position on the list of a mainstream party, among others, as the result of required intra-party quotas to combat underrepresentation of minorities in parliament. Such an MP could be interested in all sorts of fields, such as corporate governance or foreign relations and is not necessarily there to take part in committees working on issues important to the identity of the minority he or she belongs to. The Italian and Hungarian minority representatives in the Slovenian parliament have, on the other hand, both been elected to a reserved seat by voters registered on a special minority voter register. These two MPs each have a veto right regarding laws and other acts concerning minority rights issues. The difference between these two examples is that, in the second case, the MPs are elected to protect and promote minority identity and there is and always should be a link of accountability between minority representatives and the minority they represent.

Secondly, with regard to minority representation in the administration, persons belonging to a minority might be recruited to a civil service position in the administration, as a result of targets set to combat under-employment of minorities resulting from discrimination. For example, Croats of Serb ethnicity might be recruited to the Croatian state administration on the basis of targets set out in the Civil Service Employment Plan in order to implement Art 22 of the 2002 Constitutional Law on the Rights of National Minorities. This is different from the consultation procedure carried out by the administration with minority advisory bodies—elected or appointed by the minority community—during the elaboration of policies that could impact on minority identity. For example, the Ministry of Education of a country might be legally obliged to consult a minority advisory body regarding the elaboration of school curricula. The difference between the first and second situation is that, in the second, the minority advisory body represents the interests of the minority, ie the protection and promotion of its identity, and that there should be a link of accountability between the minority advisory body and the minority it represents.

Finally, the participation of persons belonging to minorities in the judiciary is important in the light of the aim to reverse discrimination and underrepresentation. By contrast, judges belonging to a minority are not appointed to protect and promote minority identity; they have to be impartial.

In reality, it is sometimes hard to distinguish between, on the one hand, mechanisms to promote or guarantee the participation of minorities as temporary affirmative action in order to compensate for systemic discrimination and underrepresentation, and, on the other hand, special representation mechanisms aimed at the protection and promotion of minority identity. Sometimes, these measures become entangled. For example, it might be that measures are originally argued for on the basis of elimination of the effects of discrimination, but they become perceived as enhancing the ability to preserve identity and remain in place as if a permanent measure.[16]

IV. The Nature of Minority Participation and Representation and Possible Problematic Aspects

Based on the previous section regarding the justification and goals of minority participation and representation, this section aims to look further into the nature of minority participation and representation and to discuss its problematic aspects. This should reveal possible limitations to the concept, which have to be taken into account when designing implementing institutions and mechanisms.

A. Mirror representation, authorization, and accountability

What is the defining feature of minority participation and representation? Is an authentic minority representative a person who belongs to that minority and looks like his or her constituents or is it a person who acts in the interest of his or her minority constituents and is elected or appointed by them? Or are both elements required? The idea of 'mirror representation'—also called 'self-representation',[17] 'descriptive representation', or 'microcosmic representation'[18]—entails that the legislature is said to be representative of the general public if it mirrors the ethnic, gender, or class characteristics of the public. This contrasts with the more familiar idea in democratic theory, which

---

[16] For example, the proportional representation in the administration of Italian-, German- and Ladin-speakers in South Tyrol was originally introduced as an act of reparation for the Italianization during the fascist regime. The implementing regulations of the Autonomy Statute of 1976 aimed at determining the jobs in a way that by 2002 (or between 2002 and 2006 for the state administration, according to Palermo) it would be possible to achieve appropriate representation of all linguistic groups in all areas. However, this measure does not seem to be perceived as temporary any more. See K Rainer, 'The Autonomous Province of Bozen/Bolzano – South Tyrol' in K Gàl (ed), *Minority Governance in Europe* (2002), at 96; and F Palermo, 'Self-Government (and Other?) Instruments for the Prevention of Ethnic Conflicts in South Tyrol' in M Žagar, Boris Jesih and Romana Bešter (eds), *The Constitutional and Political Regulation of Ethnic Relations and Conflicts. Selected Papers* (1999), at 305.
[17] See MS Williams, *Voice, Trust and Memory: Marginalized groups and the failings of liberal representation* (1998), 28.
[18] See H Pitkin, The Concept of Representation (1967), 87; and AH Birch, Representation (1971), 54–9.

defines representation in terms of the procedure by which the office holders are elected, rather than their personal attributes.[19]

Minority participation was defined in the previous section as aimed at compensating for systemic discrimination and reversing underrepresentation in different areas of public life—including in parliament, the administration and law enforcement institutions—and constituting temporary affirmative action. As stated, the *participation* of persons belonging to minorities is to be taken literally. In that case, the defining feature of minority participation is mirror representation.

Minority representation, on the other hand, refers to mechanisms intended to further participation and representation in decision-making processes affecting minorities in order to protect and promote minority identity. What is essential here is that minority representatives are authorized to represent a minority or minorities and that there is a link of accountability between the minority representatives and the minority or minorities they represent. This accountability is not determined by the characteristics of the representative, but by the characteristics of the represented. In other words, it is not mirror or descriptive representation which is essential for minority representation—although in most cases persons belonging to minorities will choose a person who shares their minority characteristics to represent them—but the link of accountability.

Three examples can be cited to illustrate the necessity of such a link of accountability as the defining feature for minority representation in order to protect and promote minority identity over mirror or descriptive representation. The first is the election of local minority self-governments ('MSG') in Hungary, which is discussed both in the First and Second ACFC Opinions on Hungary.[20] Originally, the legislation provided that all Hungarian citizens could vote for the members of these local MSGs, as minorities had been reluctant to register on a minority-voter register. However, it was often the majority, ethnic Hungarians voting out of a sense of sympathy, who determined who would represent the minority. Consequently, members of local MSGs were often not regarded as legitimate minority representatives. Since the 2005 amendments to Law LXXVII of 1993 on the Rights of National and Ethnic Minorities, minority voters are now obliged to register on a special voter register, thus establishing a link of accountability between the minority representative and the minority voters.

The second example illustrates that mirror or descriptive representation is *not sufficient* for minority representation. If a minority boycotts elections, as the Kosovo Serbs did in the 2004 and 2007 parliamentary elections in Kosovo, then the minority representatives elected by the few voters who did not boycott the

---

[19] W Kymlicka, Multicultural Citizenship: A liberal theory of minority rights (1995), 138. See also C Casonato, *La tutela delle minoranze etnico-linguistiche in relazione alla rappresentanza politica: un' analisi comparata*, Quaderni del CDE (Centro di documentazione europea) no 1 (1998), section 3.

[20] First ACFC Opinion on Hungary (2000), ACFC/INF/OP/I(2001)004, 22 September 2000, para 52; and Second ACFC Opinion on Hungary, ACFC/INF/OP/II(2004)003, paras 24–30.

elections—such as the Serb representatives occupying the ten reserved seats in parliament—are not considered to be legitimate representatives by the community as a whole, even though mirror representation is in place.

A final example should illustrate that mirror representation is *not even necessary* for minority representation. In Croatia, for example, several minorities have to share one reserved seat in parliament, as they are numerically too small to win a seat each. There is, for example, one joint seat for the Ruthenian, Ukrainian, German, Austrian, Bulgarian, Polish, Roma, Romanian, Russian, Turkish, Vlach, and Jewish minorities.[21] In such a case it would be impossible to institute mirror representation as a single representative cannot simultaneously belong to all these minority communities. What is important is that there is a link of accountability between the minority representatives and the minorities they represent.

B. Essentialism, multiple identities, and the opting-out principle

There is always diversity within each electorate, and this applies also to a minority electorate. Each individual has a multi-layered identity, of which the layer related to culture, language, or religion is only one of many. The unifying process required by group representation inappropriately freezes fluid identities into a unity and can create oppressive segregations. Any institutionalization of minority representation is best kept fluid and dynamic, with evaluation moments at more or less regular intervals. Individuals should have the freedom of choice whether or not to be identified with a minority and whether or not to participate in a special representation mechanism to protect and promote the minority identity. This 'opting out' principle is in line with the liberal view of the autonomy of the individual and has been incorporated into the international minority rights instruments.[22]

One of the consequences is that minority representation mechanisms should allow for the representation of diversity within groups and that authorities should be aware of such diversity and actively seek and take into account the different opinions. For example, in Hungary, the electoral rules for the national minority self-governments were switched from a winner-takes-all electoral system to proportional representation. It prevented a single minority faction from taking control of the national MSG. This is especially important in the light of the fact that these national MSGs were considered by the authorities to be legitimate negotiating partners.

Persons should be free to affiliate with a minority or not and should be free to participate in a minority representation mechanism or not. Consequently,

---

[21] Since the 2003 amendments to the Law on the Election of Representatives to the Croatian Parliament. Croatia, Second State Report, ACFC/SR/II(2004)002, 13 April 2004, 19.
[22] See CSCE Copenhagen Document, para 32; UN Declaration on Minorities, Art 3(2); and FCNM, Art 3(1).

a person should never be obliged to vote for a minority representative in parliament or on an advisory body. In Croatia, for example, persons belonging to a minority can choose between voting for a mainstream party list or for a minority representative. In Slovenia, persons belonging to the Italian and Hungarian minorities have, besides their vote for mainstream party lists, an optional second vote for a minority representative.

Another consequence relates to the extent to which representation is based on ethnicity, language or religion. If representation on the basis of ethnicity, language or religion pervades all aspects of public life, which is typically the case for consociational mechanisms,[23] persons are to a large extent reduced to one aspect of their identity, be it ethnicity, language, or religion, and there is not much room for doing justice to multiple identities or for opting out.

A whole range of mechanisms exists at the national level, spanning from non-existent or very minimal to extensive. Whether there are mechanisms available or not depends on the national (political) choice as to whether ethnic difference is recognized (in the constitution) or not. Such institutions and mechanisms contributing to effective participation of persons belonging to minorities in public affairs can be outlined on a double continuum related to 'presence', on the one hand, and 'influence', on the other.[24]

First, the legal instruments which provide for the 'presence' of minorities in decision-making processes can be arranged on a scale between two poles, namely the individual right to vote and to stand for election on the one hand, and the equal representation of groups on the other. Between these two poles, institutions and mechanisms can be situated which indirectly (eg through proportional representation) or directly (eg through reduced registration requirements for minority parties or exemption of voting threshold) promote or even guarantee (eg through reserved seats) minority representation.

---

[23] One can contest that consociational arrangements are an example of minority protection and an implementation of the right to effective participation. However, in my opinion they are. For my argumentation in the framework of a discussion of the Opinion of the Venice Commission on Possible Groups of Persons to which the Framework Convention for the Protection of National Minorities Could Be Applied in Belgium (CDL-AD(2002)1, Strasbourg, 12 March 2002), see A Verstichel, 'The personal scope of application of the FCNM: An open, inclusive and dynamic approach – the FCNM as a living instrument' in A Verstichel et al (eds), The FCNM: A useful pan-European instrument? (2008) 151–5.

[24] This distinction aims at complementing the usual categorization of institutions and mechanisms in either contributing to participation in the decision-making in the central state authorities at national, regional or local level or as autonomy or self-governance arrangements, as, for example, in the OSCE HCNM Lund Recommendations. (See, eg, J Packer, 'The origin and nature of the lund recommendations on the effective participation of national minorities in public life' (2000) 4 *Helsinki Monitor* 39) This distinction is inspired by the distinction made by Joseph Marko, whose first continuum reflects the legal instruments which provide for the 'representation' of minorities and the second the 'participation' of minorities in decision-making processes (J Marko, 'General presentation on the representation and participation of national minorities in decision-making processes' in *Participation of National Minorities in Decision-making Processes*, Seminar held in Brno, Slovenia, 1–2 December 1997, 18–19).

PRESENCE:

<--->
right to vote and   equal representation of groups
to stand for election

INFLUENCE:

<--->
non-binding advice   absolute veto power

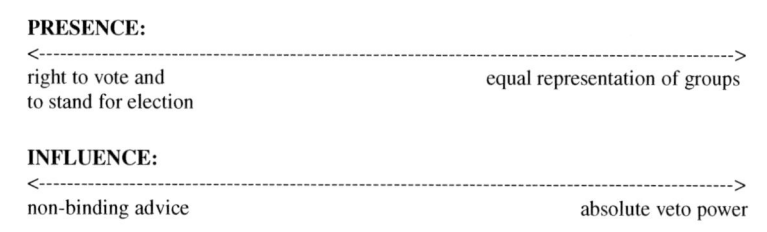

Fig 3.1 Presence and influence scales

Secondly, the legal instruments which provide for the 'influence' of minorities in decision-making processes can also be arranged on a scale between two poles, namely that of non-binding advice on the one hand, to absolute veto power on the other. Between these two poles, institutions and mechanisms can be established to provide, for example, binding advice, the right to legislative initiative under reduced requirements, qualified majority voting, double majority voting, or suspensive veto powers.

Both scales, related to 'presence' and to 'influence', visualize the increasing encroachment upon the right to formal political equality by the institutions and mechanisms of effective participation in order to realize substantive equality in the decision-making process. At the outer end of the spectrum of the presence and influence scales, representation on the basis of ethnicity, language or religion pervades all aspects of public life. As stated above, this is typically the case for consociational mechanisms, where persons are largely reduced to one aspect of their identity, making it difficult to express multiple identities or to opt out.[25] If there is such an opting-out possibility, persons opting out of the main categories—because they do not want to belong to one of them or do not know to which one they belong to because they are children of mixed marriages—are generally divided into a remainder category which is often left out of consociational arrangements or whose votes count less.[26] Persons belonging to the

---

[25] In Belgium, for example, both the House of Representatives and the Senate are divided into a French-speaking and a Dutch-speaking language group. The division into language groups of the members of the House of Representatives is made on the basis of the objective criterion of territory for members whose electoral college is entirely part of the Dutch language region (the Dutch language group) or of the French or German language regions (the French language group) (Art 43.1 of the Constitution), with the exception of the bilingual electoral district Brussels-Hal-Vilvorde. There is no remainder category for persons with another mother tongue—representatives of the German language region are put in the French language group, for example—or for persons who are bilingual and do not want to choose just one language group. In addition, linguistic minorities from the different language regions are not given the opportunity to opt for the language group of their mother tongue.

[26] For example, for important legislation a majority is needed in both the French-speaking and the Dutch-speaking language group in the Belgian federal and the Brussels-Capital parliaments; also within the Bosniac, Croat, and Serb factions of the parliament of Bosnia Herzegovina; and finally also among both registered nationalists and unionists in the parliament of Northern Ireland (or 40 per cent support for both groups, with an overall majority of 60 per cent). The votes of

smaller communities in society, which do not take part in the consociational arrangements, are often excluded from major positions in all branches of government. A typical example is the situation of the 'Others' in Bosnia and Herzegovina.[27]

Consociational arrangements might be the best solution for a country at a given moment. However, there should be a possibility for adapting such mechanisms to changed relationships between and within groups and to allow for individual rights of citizens. There should be a dynamic, process-oriented approach to institutional design in ethnically, religiously or linguistically plural states. There should be means for regular domestic cross-community review of the existing arrangements, which can allow for fine-tuning and development.[28] The initiative for change might be assigned to parliament, government, courts[29] and/or the population at large. According to Bieber, it is not the finality of change that should be defined—as institutional accommodation of ethnic groups can never be finite or conclusive—but the parameters of change.[30]

C. Group proliferation and social cohesion at risk

Finally, when devising mechanisms of special minority representation, one should take into account that it may cause an unworkable proliferation of claims

---

'Others' in Bosnia and Herzegovina and in Northern Ireland (in Belgium, there is no option to belong to 'Others') are counted for the overall majority but no majority is needed among them for important legislation.

[27] Another example is the case for the Ladins in South Tyrol before 2001. For example, the Ladin linguistic group was de facto excluded from the highest offices of the provincial government because the offices of president and vice-president rotated between the German and the Italian linguistic group. The Italian Constitutional Law no 2 of 31 January 2001 removed several discriminations.

[28] A review clause can be found, eg, in the Good Friday Agreement for Northern Ireland (see para 36 of Strand One 'Democratic Institutions in Northern Ireland' and para 5 of the 'Validation, Implementation and Review' section, under review procedures following implementation) and in Art 95 of the Lebanese Constitution as amended by the 1989 Taif Agreement, which reiterates the temporary nature of the power-sharing arrangements and elaborates a procedure for the abolition of 'political sectarianism'.

Such a review clause has not been included in either the Dayton Agreement or the Ohrid Agreement. The Comprehensive Proposal for the Kosovo Status Settlement (also known as the 'Ahtisaari plan') did not foresee a review clause either but provided for a change in the parliamentary reserved seats mechanisms after two electoral mandates (Art 3(2)–(3) of Annex I—see Art 148 Constitution), which entails a decrease in the overrepresentation of minority representatives.

[29] Examples of courts taking the initiative to change consociational arrangements include the Constituent Peoples' Decision of the Constitutional Court of Bosnia and Herzegovina (Constituent Peoples' Decision, Case 5/98 Partial Decision III (1 July 2000), <http://www.ohr.int/ohr-dept/legal/const/default.asp?content_id=5853>, accessed 31 July 2009), and the cases of the Belgian Constitutional Court regarding the representation of all philosophical and ideological tendencies in the cultural public sector (Court of Arbitration, Judgments no 65/93 of 15 July 1993, no 86/93 of 16 December 1993 and no 7/94 of 20 January 1994).

[30] F Bieber, 'The challenge of institutionalizing ethnicity in the Western Balkans: Managing change in deeply divided societies' (2003/4) 3 EYMI 100–1.

for special representation. In addition, demands for self-government or special representation rights might pose risks for social cohesion and create unrest and instability. On the other hand, it might also enforce social cohesion as persons belonging to a minority might feel that they belong to a society which recognizes their existence and their distinct identity. When persons belonging to a minority can take part effectively in the decision-making processes which affect them, they will not consider—or will consider to a lesser extent—undemocratic ways of making their concerns heard. In all cases, claims of stability should be weighed against claims of equality, fairness and justice.

V. The International Right to Effective Participation of Persons Belonging to Minorities in Public Affairs

As stated already, the right of persons belonging to minorities to effective participation in public affairs has been singled out among other minority rights for further elaboration and exploration in the organizations that have developed international minority rights catalogues (OSCE, UN, and CoE). This reflects the importance of this right among other minority rights, the need to give more concrete content to a broadly formulated provision, and the arrival at a point in time, after the first years of monitoring, that is ripe for general conclusions and an assessment of best or good practice.

In all three organizations, the content of the right of minorities to effective participation in public affairs is approached in a balanced way and is based on a broad concept of public affairs. However, as already stated, the stress is still on political participation in the narrow sense and attention to mechanisms enhancing the presence of minorities in the decision-making rather than their influence on the outcome. It reflects that monitoring (still) largely sticks to commenting on existing mechanisms.

With regard to the monitoring of the right to effective participation in public affairs, only the FCNM is provided with a proper monitoring mechanism. As the FCNM is the only multilateral legally binding instrument containing a provision on effective participation of minorities in public affairs, the monitoring by the ACFC (and the Committee of Ministers) of the FCNM is the single most important source for learning about the content of this right. In addition, the work of the Venice Commission and the intergovernmental Committee of Experts on Issues relating to the Protection of National Minorities (DH-MIN) contribute to an enhanced understanding of this right. It is important, though, that these bodies coordinate effectively in order to avoid diverging interpretations of this right. The Venice Commission, in particular, can have an important impact through its opinions on draft legislation of relevance to the effective participation of minorities in public affairs.

Furthermore, in the context of the OSCE, the HCNM is the institution which actively promotes the effective participation of minorities in public affairs in the context of its conflict prevention mandate. As the work of the High Commissioner is confidential—apart from what is known from his speeches or publications by his staff—it is difficult to assess the HCNM's approach to effective participation of minorities in concrete cases. However, it is clear that the HCNM has a potentially big impact through its specific political and legal recommendations of relevance to the effective participation of minorities in public affairs. It is important that the HCNM coordinates with the relevant Council of Europe bodies in order to avoid diverging recommendations regarding the effective participation of minorities in public affairs and to avoid 'forum-shopping' by the different member states.

Whereas the ACFC examines the implementation of minority rights and adopts a rights approach from the perspective of minorities (eg the non-retrogression clause),[31] the underlying concern of the HCNM's work is the achievement of a well-integrated and peaceful society, in which the interests of the state and those of the minority groups are balanced. Nevertheless, the ACFC also conducts its monitoring clearly and in a constructive way so as not to scare off concerned governments with an activist attitude. The UN Working Group merely constituted a yearly forum at which papers were presented, minority representatives and non-governmental organizations (NGOs) could voice their concerns, and government representatives could reply. It remains to be seen how the new Forum on Minority Issues will implement its mandate of providing 'a platform for promoting dialogue and cooperation on issues pertaining to national or ethnic, religious, and linguistic minorities, which shall provide thematic contributions and expertise to the work of the independent expert on minority issues'.[32]

With regard to the nature of minority participation and representation and their limits, none of the above-mentioned bodies has adopted an explicit elaborate theory. However, one can distil an underlying concept or vision from the monitoring process, the recommendations, published reports, commentaries, and other documents. It is an incomplete picture, with the ACFC's puzzle being the most advanced, as exposed in its thematic opinion on effective participation. The ACFC makes a distinction between the two aims of the right to effective participation, namely full and effective equality—as enshrined in Art 4—and preservation and promotion of national minorities' identity and culture—as

---

[31] As the ACFC regularly criticizes the tendency towards reducing the level of protection, such as the abolition of the exemption for minority parties of the 5 per cent voting threshold and the prohibition on using minority languages in television and radio election campaigns and on ballot slips (eg, First ACFC Opinion on Lithuania (2003), ACFC/INF/OP/(2003)008, 21 February 2003, paras 75–6, 79), one can conclude that the ACFC has adopted an implicit stand-still clause.

[32] Human Rights Council Resolution 6/15 of 28 September 2007, para 1. The Forum held its inaugural session on 15–16 December 2008 on the right to education, available at <http://www2.ohchr.org/english/bodies/hrcouncil/minority/forum.htm> (accessed 1 July 2009).

enshrined in Art 5. It states that Arts 4, 5, and 15 can be seen as the three corners of a triangle, which together form the main foundations of the FCNM.[33] None of the other bodies has made an explicit distinction between the two aims of minority participation and representation, and none seems very clear about what constitutes the essence of minority participation and representation and the relationship between mirror representation and accountability. From some country opinions it is clear that the ACFC is of the opinion that mirror representation alone does not mean that persons belonging to minorities are effectively represented and that accountability is the important criterion.[34] However, the relationship between mirror representation and accountability, and the debate as to which determines the essence of minority representation, is less clear in other opinions.[35] Even though the ACFC underlines in its thematic opinion that persons belonging to national minorities should also have a say on issues which are not of exclusive concern to them but affect society as a whole,[36] the Committee does not go as far as linking this statement to the previous section in its Commentary on the two aims of effective participation or to drawing conclusions for the design of participation and representation mechanisms. Nevertheless, the ACFC has an appreciation of existing diversity within minority groups and recommends that states take it into account when devising and using special mechanisms for minority representation.[37]

[33] ACFC, Commentary on Effective Participation (n 6 above), paras 13–15.
[34] Eg, Second ACFC Opinion on the Czech Republic, ACFC/INF/OP/II(2005)002, 26 October 2005, para 172; and Second ACFC Opinion on Croatia, ACFC/INF/OP/II(2007)004, para 162.
[35] For instance, the ACFC has expressed its concern in its First ACFC Opinion on Hungary with regard to the so-called 'cuckoo-problem', 'the situation where persons not belonging to a given minority, through the openness of the electoral system, nevertheless manage to get themselves elected as representatives of that minority' (First ACFC Opinion on Hungary, ACFC/INF/OP/I (2001)004, 22 September 2000, para 52). The Advisory Committee considered that the Hungarian authorities should actively pursue remedies in order to avoid the credibility of the system as a whole being undermined. In my opinion, the ACFC insufficiently made clear why an elected representative, who does not belong to that minority, would not make a good representative of the interests of the persons belonging to that minority. It of course wanted to criticize the fact that there existed no direct link of accountability between the representatives elected in minority self-government and the minority they represented, as everyone could vote in the elections for the minority self-governments, with the result that ethnic Hungarians' votes were often decisive for the representatives finally elected. However, the ACFC gave the impression that the absence of mirror representation was the main flaw in the system. In its Second Opinion on Hungary, the ACFC is clearer in that it criticizes 'candidates … in elections for a local self-government of a minority with which they had no *link* whatsoever' (emphasis added). Further, it welcomed the proposed amendments to the legal provisions on the elections of the minority self-governments providing that only persons belonging to minorities would be able to elect their self-governments (Second ACFC Opinion on Hungary, ACFC/INF/OP/II(2004)003, 14 December 2005, paras 24–30).
[36] ACFC, Commentary on Effective Participation (n 6 above), paras 16–17.
[37] See, for example, with regard to parties and electoral legislation, Second ACFC Opinion on Romania, ACFC/INF/OP/II(2005)007, 23 February 2006, paras 105–8 and 190–1; and with regard to consultative bodies, First ACFC Opinion on Moldova (2002), ACFC/INF/OP/I(2003) 002, 1 March 2002, para 89; First ACFC Opinion on Armenia (2002), ACFC/INF/OP/I(2003) 001, 16 May 2002, para 80 and Second ACFC Opinion on Romania (2005), paras 188–9 and 194.

With regard to the importance of keeping any institutionalization of minority representation fluid and dynamic, with evaluation moments at more or less regular intervals, only the OSCE HCNM Lund Recommendations highlights this explicitly. In its Recommendation 22, it provides for the '[p]eriodic review of arrangements for self-governance and minority participation in decision-making' as these can provide 'useful opportunities to determine whether such arrangements should be amended in the light of experience and changed circumstances'. The Explanatory Note to the Lund Recommendations furthermore underlines that in order to achieve the desired balance between stability and flexibility, it may be useful to specify some reconsideration at fixed intervals, thereby depoliticizing the process of change in advance and making the review process less adversarial. In addition, Lund Recommendation 23 suggests:

[t]he possibility of provisional or step-by-step arrangements that allow for the testing and development of new forms of participation ... These arrangements can be established through legislation or informal means with a defined time period, subject to extension, alteration, or termination depending upon the success achieved.

The Explanatory Note to the Lund Recommendations clarifies that this recommendation differs from Recommendation 22 insofar as it encourages the testing of new and innovative regimes, rather than specifying terms for alteration of existing arrangements.

Of all relevant bodies, the OSCE HCNM dedicates most attention to the issue of social cohesion. Its conflict prevention mandate tasks it with providing early warning and early action regarding tensions involving minority issues which have not yet developed into a conflict. It aims at stable and peaceful societies, which do not constitute a security threat to the wider OSCE area. Its guiding principle is 'integration with respect for diversity'. The ACFC also highlights in its thematic opinion the importance of effective participation for enhancing social cohesion.[38]

VI. Citizenship

The role of citizenship with regard to the right of minorities to effective participation in public affairs should be considered in light of the role of citizenship with regard to access to minority rights in general.

There have been several failed attempts to come up with a common definition of the term 'minority', which is capable of mustering widespread state support both at European and international levels. None of the relevant minority rights instruments define their personal scope of application. Nevertheless, it is currently the position of the international bodies dealing with minority

---

[38] ACFC, Commentary on Effective Participation (n 6 above), para 9.

rights that citizenship should not be an a priori requirement for the enjoyment of minority rights and that their applicability to non-citizens is the rule.[39] Even those international bodies, which originally were against the inclusion of non-citizens in the concept of a minority, have evolved in their point of view regarding the issue.[40]

There are very few individual rights explicitly reserved for citizens in the various international instruments that are relevant to persons belonging to minorities.[41] The most frequently quoted example concerns the field of political

---

[39] For a good overview of the different positions, see European Commission for Democracy Through Law (Venice Commission), Report on Non-Citizens and Minority Rights, adopted by the Venice Commission at its 69th plenary session, Venice, 15–16 December 2006, CDL-AD (2007)001.

The UN HRC has stated in its General Comment no 23 on Art 27 ICCPR: 'A State party may not, therefore, restrict the rights under article 27 to its citizens alone' (para 5.2). In its Commentary on the UN Declaration on Minorities, the Working Group on Minorities stated, 'As the Declaration is inspired by article 27 of the International Covenant on Civil and Political Rights, it may be assumed that the Declaration has at least as wide a scope as that article ... States parties are under an obligation to respect and ensure the application of article 27 to everyone within its territory and under its jurisdiction, whether the person—or group of persons—are citizens of the country or not.' (E/CN4/Sub2/AC5/2005/2, 4 April 2005, para 9.) See also the third annual report of the UN Independent Expert on Minority Issues, which is dedicated to minorities and the discriminatory denial or deprivation of citizenship. (Promotion and Protection of all Human Rights, Civil, Political, Economic, Social and Cultural Rights, including the Right to Development, Report of the Independent Expert on Minority Issues, Gay McDougall, 28 February 2008, A/HRC/7/23, paras. 41–3 and 81.)

Also the ACFC has adopted an inclusive approach and systematically recommends that states consider, on an article-by-article basis, the inclusion of groups other than those which the state in question has recognized, in consultation with those concerned, and frequently mentions non-citizens explicitly. Furthermore, the OSCE HCNM's position is that citizenship is not a basis upon which to exclude the enjoyment of minority rights a priori. By considering the Russian-speaking population of the Baltic States, for example, the OSCE HCNM considers non-citizens in the exercise of his mandate.

[40] Whereas the Venice Commission originally included a citizenship criterion in the definition of a minority contained in its Proposal for a European Convention for the protection of national minorities (Art 2, para 1, Doc CDL(1991)007), it has for some time in several of its opinions on draft legislation on minority protection of CoE member states taken the position that citizenship should not be an a priori requirement for minority protection (eg, *Opinion on the Constitutional Law on the Rights of National Minorities in Croatia*, Doc CDL(2001)74, para 4; and *Opinion on Two Draft Laws amending the Law on National Minorities in Ukraine*, Doc CDL-AD(2004)013, paras 16–22). See also Venice Commission, Report on Non-Citizens and Minority Rights (n 39 above), para 144.

Furthermore, the Parliamentary Assembly of the Council of Europe also included a citizenship criterion in the definition of a minority in its Recommendation 1201 (1993) (and reconfirmed this in Recommendations 1255 (1995) and 1492 (2001)). However, its Committee of Legal Affairs and Human Rights stated in its Report on Rights of National Minorities that, '[i]t would be rather unfortunate if the European standards of minority protection appear to be more restrictive in nature than the universal standards, the more so that, as mentioned above, article 27 of ICCPR is anyway binding for all state parties to the Framework Convention'. Parliamentary Assembly of the Council of Europe, Rights of National Minorities Report, Committee on Legal Affairs and Human Rights, Rapporteur Boriss Cilevičs, Doc 9862, 19 July 2003, para 94.

[41] Venice Commission, Report on Non-Citizens and Minority Rights (n 39 above), para 138.

rights.[42] Article 25 of the UN International Covenant on Civil and Political Rights, which deals with the right to participate in public affairs, voting rights, and the right of equal access to the civil service, addresses 'every citizen' and not 'everyone' or 'every person' as in other provisions of the same treaty.[43] According to the ACFC Commentary on Effective Participation, it is legitimate to impose certain restrictions on non-citizens concerning the right to vote and to stand for election.[44]

However, there is a tendency in Europe to extend active and passive voting rights to non-citizens at the local level, provided they have been lawful residents for a certain period of time.[45] The 1992 Council of Europe Convention on the Participation of Foreigners in Public Life at Local Level requires five years (Art 6.1),[46] whereas a residency requirement of three years is proposed for granting the right to vote and to stand for elections to immigrants in local elections in PACE Recommendation 1500 (2001).[47] The ACFC also encourages state parties to provide non-citizens belonging to national minorities with a possibility to vote and to stand as candidates in local elections.[48] Apart from local voting rights after a certain period of residence, the UN Working Group on Minorities recommends states to develop still other forms of participation by resident non-citizens, such as the inclusion of elected non-citizen observers in municipal, regional and national legislative and decision-making assemblies.[49]

---

[42] Another example is the right to return to his or her own country, contained in Art 12(4) ICCPR. See, however, HRC General Comment no 27(67) on Art 12 ICCPR, para 20, which stresses, 'the scope of "his own country" is broader than the concept "country of his nationality". It is not limited to nationality in a formal sense.'

[43] See, Venice Commission, Report on Non-Citizens and Minority Rights (n 39 above), para 139; The Rights of Non-Citizens, Final report of UN Special Rapporteur Mr David Weissbrodt, E/CN4/Sub2/2003/23, 26 May 2003, para 19; and UN HCR General Comment no 25 on Art 25 ICCPR, 12 July 1996, CPR/C/21/Rev1/Add7, para 3.

[44] ACFC, Commentary on Effective Participation (n 6 above), para 101. See also, ACFC Second Opinion on Croatia, 1 October 2004, ACFC/INF/OP/II(2004)002, paras 28–9; and ACFC Second Opinion on Slovakia, 26 May 2005, ACFC/OP/II(2005)004, para 21.

[45] Venice Commission, Report on Non-Citizens and Minority Rights (n 39 above), para 140. See also, Venice Commission, Opinion on the Draft Law on the Statute of National Minorities living in Romania, adopted by the Venice Commission at its 64th Plenary Session (Venice, 21–2 October 2005) on the basis of the comments by Mr Sergio Bartole (Substitute Member, Italy), Mr Pieter van Dijk, (Member, Netherlands), CDL-AD(2005)026, paras 55–7.

[46] See also, Venice Commission, Explanatory Report of the Code of Good Practice in Electoral Matters of 23 May 2003 (CDL-AD(2002)23rev), Part I, item 1.1 (b): 'a tendency is emerging to grant local political rights to long-standing foreign residents, in accordance with the Council of Europe Convention on the Participation of Foreigners in Public Life at Local Level. It is accordingly recommended that the right to vote in local elections be granted after a certain period of residence.'

[47] See PACE Recommendation 1500 (2001) on the Participation of Immigrants and Foreign Residents in Political Life in the Council of Europe Member State, para 11. See also PACE Resolution 1527 (2006) on the Rights of National Minorities in Latvia, 21 November 2006, paras 12 and 17(5). [48] ACFC Commentary on Effective Participation (n 6 above), para 101.

[49] UN Working Group on Minorities, Commentary on the UN Declaration on Minorities, E/CN4/Sub.2/AC5/2005/2, 4 April 2005, para 50.

With regard to equal access to the civil service, the restriction to citizens seems to be legitimate and proportionate for the higher functions only.[50] When, for example, commenting on the Armenian draft law on citizenship, the Venice Commission member, Mr Tuori, stated that, as EC law allows for citizenship-based limitations only with regard to positions involving the exercise of public authority or touching on national interests, the general requirement of Armenian citizenship for all civil service positions is too strict.[51]

Furthermore, the ACFC and the Venice Commission encourage state parties to provide non-citizens belonging to national minorities with the possibility to vote and to stand for elections for governing boards of cultural autonomies.[52] Generally, one can state that the possibility to participate in minority advisory or consultative bodies set up by the state should not be restricted to citizens. An example of a body open to non-citizens is the representative organ of the Muslim community in Belgium. There is only a residence requirement of one year to vote and of five years to stand for elections.

According to the ACFC, citizenship should also not be a condition for persons belonging to national minorities to join trade unions and other civil society associations.[53]

To conclude, the right to vote and to stand for election at the national level and access to the police and posts in the civil service in which sovereignty is exercised can legitimately be restricted to citizens. However, there are varying degrees of being inside the polity. It can be argued, for example, that non-citizens who are lawful permanent residents for a certain period—three or five years—are entitled to active and passive voting rights at the local level. States increasingly accord voting rights to permanent residents in municipal elections. Also, the lowest levels of the civil service need not be restricted to citizens, nor should minority advisory or consultative bodies or governing boards of cultural autonomies.

VII. Concluding Remarks

This chapter sought to investigate the right of persons belonging to minorities to effective participation in public affairs in the light of the implementation and monitoring practice, and in all its aspects: content, justification and aims, and

---

[50] Venice Commission, Report on Non-Citizens and Minority Rights (n 39 above), para 141.
[51] Venice Commission, Comments on the Draft Civil Service Law of the Republic of Armenia by Mr Kaarlo Tuori (Member, Finland), CDL (2001) 87, 18 September 2001, para 8.
[52] ACFC, Commentary on Effective Participation (n 6 above), para 101; and ACFC, First Opinion on Estonia, ACFC/INF/OP/I(2002)005, 14 September 2001, para 29. See also, Venice Commission, Opinion on the Draft Law on the Statute of National Minorities living in Romania, adopted by the Venice Commission at its 64th Plenary Session (Venice, 21–2 October 2005) on the basis of the comments by Mr Sergio Bartole (Substitute Member, Italy), Mr Pieter van Dijk, (Member, Netherlands), CDL-AD(2005)026, para 30.
[53] ACFC, Commentary on Effective Participation (n 6 above), para 101.

possible limits. Ethnic, religious, and linguistic identity constitutes a reality which needs to be taken into account. However, there are limits. This chapter has tried to describe the problematic aspects of minority participation and representation, which must be taken into account when devising special minority participation and representation mechanisms. To paraphrase Joseph Marko, the civic versus ethnic dichotomy should be superseded and a good mixture of both elements should be aimed at.[54]

---

[54] J Marko, '"United in Diversity?" Problems of state and nation-building in post-conflict situations: The case of Bosnia and Herzegovina' (2006) 30(3) Vermont Law Review 546.

4

The Principles of Non-discrimination and Full and Effective Equality and Political Participation

Zdenka Machnyikova and Lanna Hollo

I. Introduction	95
A. Background	95
B. Full and effective equality and political participation of national minorities	96
II. International Standards	98
A. Non-discrimination and full and effective equality	98
B. The right to political participation	103
C. Equality and non-discrimination and the right to political participation	109
III. Analysis: Specific Issues	113
A. Obligation not to discriminate	113
B. Obligation to ensure equality in law and fact: the need to take positive action	128
C. Self-governance and non-discrimination	143
IV. Conclusion	147

I. Introduction

A. Background

Political participation is increasingly recognized not only as key to the full and effective enjoyment of rights by all minorities, but also as a crucial element contributing to the political stability of a state. Where minorities have the opportunity of participating freely and effectively in all aspects of governance, they are likely to feel co-ownership in the state—in such an environment, a sense of alienation and exclusion from the state, characteristic of ethnically diverse societies, is less likely to emerge.

Within the framework of international human rights law, the principles of non-discrimination and equality are essential to guaranteeing to national minorities such full and effective political participation. These principles are fundamental aspects of the right to political participation that provide important guarantees to members of minority groups. They protect members of minority groups against exclusion from decision-making processes and public life and also require measures that will guarantee their full inclusion—as individuals and members of minority groups with distinct identities.

This chapter examines the extent to which the system of international protection of human rights provides an adequate framework for national minorities to participate fully on an equal footing in political life. More specifically, it looks into the international norm-setting regarding the rights to political participation, equality, and non-discrimination; examines the relationship between these rights; elaborates upon states obligations in order to fully guarantee these rights to national minorities; and assesses the adequacy of this protection.

B. Full and effective equality and political participation of national minorities

The existing system of protection of minorities is built on two foundational doctrines: non-discrimination applied in connection with minorities and with enjoyment of their individual human rights and the respect, protection, and promotion of distinct minority cultural identity secured through minority rights.

The first pillar includes the right to equality before the law and equal protection of the law and the prohibition of discrimination based on membership of a national minority or other relevant characteristics. The prohibition of discrimination is secured in international standards through provisions prohibiting discrimination with respect to enjoyment of the specific rights guaranteed in human rights treaties as well as through provisions prohibiting discrimination in a more general manner, with respect to the enjoyment of any rights and freedoms. Equality and non-discrimination also establish states' obligations to undertake special or adequate measures in order to promote full and effective equality in all areas of life between persons belonging to national minorities and those belonging to majorities. Such positive measures that are needed to eliminate the effects of past discrimination and to achieve full and effective equality for these groups should not be considered discrimination.

The second pillar relates to the recognition of the value of plurality and cultural diversity of society. In this respect the recently developed international standards require states to provide national minorities with the conditions needed to allow them to transmit, maintain and develop their culture and to preserve the essential elements of their identity. The creation of such conditions goes beyond the special measures required to achieve equal enjoyment of rights or a level playing field with members of the majority; it requires states to facilitate the maintenance, reproduction, and further development of minority cultures. These rights are sometimes labelled as minority identity rights.

1. The Right to Effective Participation of Minorities in Political Life

In the context of the right to political participation, a key element for the protection of the rights of members of minority groups as well as for the preservation of their distinct cultural identity, is access to and full participation of national minorities in decision-making. Participation of minorities makes it possible to hear and effectively take into account the concerns and needs of persons belonging to minorities in achieving full and effective equality and their right to preservation and development of their specific identities.

What does the current normative system offer to national minorities to secure their effective participation in various aspects of governance? In the exercise of their right to political participation minorities are protected from discrimination based on grounds such as race, colour, religion, language, and ethnic, or national origin.[1] This protection stems from the general prohibition of discrimination as such (independent or self-standing non-discrimination provisions), as well as from the prohibition of discrimination taken together with the right to political participation and other human rights carrying democratic functions (accessory non-discrimination provisions).

In addition, specific minority rights standards, recognizing the centrality of this issue to the protection of national minorities, provide an obligation for states to create the conditions necessary for the effective participation of minorities in cultural, social, and economic life and in public affairs, in particular as concerns matters directly affecting them. In this respect minority rights standards put a special emphasis on political participation as one of the central pillars of minority protection. Political participation provides an effective mechanism against assimilation and provides minorities with opportunities to maintain their distinct identities within the majority culture, as well as allowing minorities to participate in society on an equal footing. The principal concern in this regard is to ensure the access of national minorities to decision-making regarding wider public policy and regarding matters of special concern to these communities. In this respect, the basic electoral representation is often not enough and a minority is simply disenfranchised by the operation of majority rule. In order to ensure that minorities have an adequate voice to secure their rights and equal opportunities, special facilitation of minority representation in legislatures and other decision-making and executive bodies may be required.

---

[1] It should be noted that this is an illustrative and not comprehensive list of grounds. The words 'such as' included in many non-discrimination provisions indicate an open list of grounds.

II. International Standards

A. Non-discrimination and full and effective equality

As noted above, the principles of non-discrimination and equality provide an important guarantee to national minorities, as they constitute fundamental aspects of the enjoyment of the right to political participation.

The United Nations Human Rights Committee (HRC) has made clear the centrality of the principles of non-discrimination and equality to all rights in its General Comment 18, stating that:

> Nondiscrimination, together with equality before the law and equal protection of the law without any discrimination, constitute a basic and general principle relating to the protection of human rights. Thus, article 2, paragraph 1, of the International Covenant on Civil and Political Rights obligates each State party to respect and ensure to all persons within its territory and subject to its jurisdiction the rights recognized in the Covenant without distinction of any kind, such as race, colour, sex, language, religion, political or other opinion, national or social origin, property, birth or other status. Article 26 not only entitles all persons to equality before the law as well as equal protection of the law but also prohibits any discrimination under the law and guarantees to all persons equal and effective protection against discrimination on any ground such as race, colour, sex, language, religion, political or other opinion, national or social origin, property, birth or other status.[2]

Thus non-discrimination is very much a part of other rights, establishing a cross-cutting condition that each right must be guaranteed—in a non-discriminatory manner—to all individuals and groups regardless of identity, personal characteristics or situation. The principles of non-discrimination and equality are firmly anchored in international law and in regional human rights systems. They are also part of customary law and as such bind all states whether or not a state has ratified a particular treaty.[3]

It is important to highlight that the principles of non-discrimination and equality are included in all major international and regional treaties. Provisions

---

[2] United Nations Human Rights Committee (HRC), General Comment 18: Non-discrimination, 37th session (1989), para 12.

[3] In a 2003 Advisory Opinion on the rights and legal status of undocumented migrants, the Inter-American Court has expressed its opinion that the principles of equality and non-discrimination—on the basis of any ground—have reached the status of jus cogens norms. It stated:

> this Court considers that the principle of equality before the law, equal protection by the law and non-discrimination, belongs to jus cogens, because the whole legal structure of national and international public order rests on it and it is a fundamental principle that permeates all laws.
>
> Nowadays, no legal act that is in conflict with this fundamental principle is acceptable, and discriminatory treatment of any person, owing to gender, race, color, language, religion or belief, political or other opinion, national, ethnic or social origin, nationality, age, economic situation, property, civil status, birth or any other status is unacceptable. This principle (equality and non-discrimination) forms part of general

take two forms. The first form involves self-standing or independent provisions, guaranteeing non-discrimination, equality before the law and equal protection of the law as rights valid in themselves—applying to all rights and freedoms, beyond the scope of the specific rights set out in a given convention. The second form involves accessory provisions, applying to the rights set out in a given convention. In addition, the principle of non-discrimination is sometimes included as part of a particular substantive article, such as its inclusion in Art 25 (right to political participation) of the International Covenant on Civil and Political Rights (ICCPR).[4]

The aim of minority protection is to guarantee to members of minority groups equality in law and fact. This implies a broad range of obligations on states requiring in the first place conformity with the principle of 'non-discrimination', but also extending to ensuring that members of minority groups may enjoy substantive or 'real' equality.

1. Obligation Not to Discriminate

The starting point for protection is the negative obligation not to discriminate on grounds such as race, colour, sex, language, religion, political or other opinion, national or social origin, property, birth, or other status. This obligation requires states to take a range of immediate measures to ensure that legislation, policy and practice do not discriminate against any individuals or groups of individuals with respect to their enjoyment of any rights and freedoms. With respect to political participation, this basic level of protection is particularly important to minority groups as it asserts the illegality of regulations, procedures, criteria, or other factors that exclude or restrict the participation of members of minority groups. This is discussed below in section II.A.2.

2. Obligation to Ensure Equality in Fact

It is important to emphasize that the non-discrimination obligations on states extend beyond formalistic guarantees of equality. It is evidently essential that

> international law. At the existing stage of the development of international law, the fundamental principle of equality and non-discrimination has entered the realm of jus cogens.

Inter-American Court of Human Rights, Juridical Condition and Rights of the Undocumented Migrants, Advisory Opinion OC-18 of 17 September 2003, para 101, available at <www.corteidh.or.cr/docs/opiniones/seriea_18_ing.doc> (accessed 31 July 2009).

[4] Other self-standing provisions include inter alia: Art 7 of the Universal Declaration of Human Rights (UDHR), Art 4 of the Council of Europe Framework Convention for the Protection of National Minorities (FCNM), Art 3 of the African Charter of Human and People's Rights (AfrCh), Art 24 of the American Convention on Human Rights (ACHR), Protocol 12 of the European Convention for the Protection of Human Rights and Fundamental Freedoms. As concerns accessory provisions, see also Art 2 of the UDHR; Art 2.2 of the International Covenant on Economic, Social and Cultural Rights (ICESCR); and on the regional level Art 1 of the ACHR, Art 2 of the AfrCh, and Art 14 of the European Convention for the Protection of Human Rights and Fundamental Freedoms (ECHR).

laws, regulations, and policies do not in their content discriminate against members of minority groups. However, this is not sufficient. Application of laws, regulations, and policies must also conform to the principle of non-discrimination. Equality in fact requires that steps be taken to ensure that there is no discrimination in practice. As such in its General Comment 18, the HRC has emphasized that:

> Reports of many States parties contain information regarding legislative as well as administrative measures and court decisions which relate to protection against discrimination in law, but they very often lack information which would reveal discrimination in fact… While such information is of course useful, the Committee wishes to know if there remain any problems of discrimination in fact, which may be practised either by public authorities, by the community, or by private persons or bodies. The Committee wishes to be informed about legal provisions and administrative measures directed at diminishing or eliminating such discrimination.[5]

Guaranteeing equality in fact requires states to take extensive measures to identify discrimination, eliminate its immediate and underlying causes, address the significant effects of past discrimination, and prevent future discrimination.

With respect to political participation, states will therefore need to put in place the required measures to ensure that members of minority groups may in practice enjoy this right. As will be discussed in detail in section III.B below, this may require that states take a range of positive action measures that account for the particular situation in which members of minority groups find themselves.

3. Equal and Differential Treatment

The different obligations arising from the principles of non-discrimination and equality all arise from the basic equality principle, well-established in international law, that 'what are equal are to be treated equally and what are different are to be treated differently'.

This principle was eloquently expressed in Judge Tanaka's dissenting judgment in the *South West Africa Cases*, considering whether apartheid policies violated the equality principle, and has since been repeated by many courts and international human rights bodies.[6] He stated that:

> The principle of equality before the law requires that what are equal are to be treated equally and what are different are to be treated differently. The question arises: what is equal and what is different.

---

[5] United Nations Human Rights Committee (HRC), General Comment no 18: Non-discrimination, 37th session (1989), para 9.

[6] The Explanatory Report to Protocol 12 of the European Convention for the Protection of Fundamental Rights and Freedoms (ECHR) clearly articulates this principle: 'the principle of equality requires that equal situations are treated equally and unequal situations differently. Failure to do so will amount to discrimination unless an objective and reasonable justification exists', para 15.

All human beings, notwithstanding the differences in their appearance and other minor points, are equal in their dignity as persons. Accordingly, from the point of view of human rights and fundamental freedoms, they must be treated equally.

The principle of equality does not mean absolute equality, but recognises relative equality, namely different treatment proportionate to concrete individual circumstances. Different treatment must not be given arbitrarily; it requires reasonableness, or must be in conformity with justice, as in the treatment of minorities, different treatment of the sexes regarding public conveniences, etc. In these cases, the differentiation is aimed at the protection of those concerned, and it is not detrimental and therefore not against their will.

Discrimination according to the criterion of 'race, colour, national or tribal origin' in establishing the rights and duties of the inhabitants of the territory is not considered reasonable and just. Race, colour, etc. do not constitute in themselves factors which can influence the rights and duties of the inhabitants as in the case of sex, age, language, religion, etc. If differentiation be required, it would be derived from the difference of language, religion, custom, etc., not from the racial difference itself. In the policy of apartheid the necessary logical and material link between difference itself and different treatment, which can justify such treatment in the case of sex, minorities, etc., does not exist... [7]

In other words, when individuals are in similar situations they are to be treated in the same manner and when they are in different situations they are to be treated in a different manner. Different treatment is necessary when concrete individual circumstances place a person or group of persons in a position whereby they require that specific account be taken of their different characteristics, identities, or situation in order to be treated equally. Different treatment must not be given arbitrarily; it requires reasonableness, or must be in conformity with justice. A failure to treat individuals in similar situations in the same manner and individuals in different situations in a different manner will result in discrimination. This is of great importance for national minorities, whose differences of language or way of life, or long-standing experience of discrimination, may require 'different treatment' in order to be treated equally. This is elaborated further under sections II.A.2 and III.B below discussing positive and special measures with respect to political participation of national minorities.

In an illustrative example with respect to women, General Recommendation 25 on temporary special measures, the United Nations Committee on the Elimination of Discrimination against Women commented:

In the Committee's view, a purely formal legal or programmatic approach is not sufficient to achieve women's de facto equality with men, which the Committee interprets as substantive equality. In addition, the Convention requires that women be given an equal start and that they be empowered by an enabling environment to achieve equality of results. It is not enough to guarantee women treatment that is identical to that of men. Rather, biological as well as socially and culturally constructed differences between women and men must be taken into account. Under certain circumstances,

---

[7] The International Court of Justice (ICJ), *South West Africa Cases* [1966] ICJ Reports 3.

non-identical treatment of women and men will be required in order to address such differences. Pursuit of the goal of substantive equality also calls for an effective strategy aimed at overcoming under-representation of women and a redistribution of resources and power between men and women.[8]

In practice, this means that in order to have equal access to the enjoyment of their rights, certain individuals or groups of individuals may require that additional or specifically targeted measures—sometimes different from what is considered to be normal or standard—are taken for their benefit.

There are many examples of such measures. Generally, they are of two kinds:

1. positive measures, that is, measures designed to counter the effects of past discrimination as well as to compensate for ongoing discrimination; and[9]
2. special measures, that is, measures designed to treat equally in fact members of groups who are in a disadvantaged position due to their factual differences with the majority or dominant groups in society (physical differences, cultural, religious, traditions, linguistic, etc).[10]

In practice, in some instances, it is difficult to distinguish positive from special measures, in particular when it comes to political participation of minorities. These measures, designed to respond to the circumstances, specificities and particular needs of members of non-dominant groups, are not privileges but necessary actions that enable members of these groups to enjoy the same rights and services as others.[11]

---

[8] The UN Committee on the Elimination of Discrimination Against Women, General Recommendation 25 on Art 4, para 1 of the CEDAW, on temporary special measures, 30th session (2004).

[9] What are here referred to as 'positive measures' are designated by a range of different names in international and national contexts. Some of the more widely used other labels include: temporary special measures (eg Convention on the Elimination of Discrimination against women—CEDAW), special measures (eg Convention on Elimination of Racial Discrimination—CERD), positive action (eg ECHR), adequate measures (FCNM), affirmative action, and 'positive discrimination'. The term 'positive discrimination' is misleading because positive measures are 'not' discrimination. Discrimination cannot be positive. Discrimination is by definition arbitrary and unjust treatment.

[10] In order to not themselves fall foul of the non-discrimination principle, such measures should be carefully designed with close attention paid to the particular situation to be addressed and a clear articulation of the goals to be achieved. Furthermore, such measures must not result in segregation. Measures designed to counter the effects of past discrimination or compensate for ongoing discrimination should only be continued until such time as the objectives for which they were developed have been achieved. Measures designed to respond to factual differences with the dominant group or majority are not subject to the same time constraint—they may be continued as long as needed to ensure de facto equality, which means that they may well be permanent.

[11] In this text, we have chosen to use two terms—'positive measures' and 'special measures'—in order to clarify the differences between these measures. The first, positive measures, arises from the circumstances in which members of a particular group find themselves and the second arise from differences internal to the group (differences of language, traditions, customs, religion, etc). In practice, it is sometimes difficult to distinguish positive from special measures, in particular when it comes to political participation of minorities. For these instances we use in the text the joint term 'positive action measures'.

B. The right to political participation

For the purposes of providing the specific context for application of the principles of non-discrimination and effective equality the following section will briefly focus on the substantive right to political participation and delineation of the content of the international standards regarding the right to political participation with respect to national minorities.

Persons belonging to national minorities are guaranteed, as any citizen, enjoyment of the right to political participation as an individual right. The right to political participation is defined as the right of citizens to take part and to seek to influence public affairs. The foundational articulation of this right is embodied in Art 21 of the Universal Declaration of Human Rights, which prescribes that '[t]he will of people shall be the basis of the authority of government'. This has been further formalized and elaborated in later treaties, most notably in Art 25 of the ICCPR that defines the specific aspects of political participation as follows:

(a) to take part in the conduct of public affairs, directly or through freely chosen representatives;
(b) to vote and to be elected at the genuine periodic elections which shall be by universal and equal suffrage and shall be held by secret ballot, guaranteeing the free expression of the will of the electors;
(c) to have access, on general terms of equality, to public service in this country.

Political participation is described here in a general but also in a more specific form. In general terms the Covenant refers to the conduct of public affairs. In General Comment 25 on Art 25, the HRC clarifies that:

The conduct of public affairs ... is a broad concept which relates to the exercise of political power, in particular the exercise of legislative, executive and administrative powers. It covers all aspects of public participation, and the formulation and implementation of policy at international, national, regional and local levels.[12]

In this respect public affairs involve formal procedures of government, including the exercise of governance on different levels of authority, but also include activities of non-governmental civic associations, social movements, and advocacy groups, as they participate and influence public policies or often take part in their implementation. Consequently although participants in public affairs should be primarily citizens, as foreseen in the Covenant, they may also include non-citizens. As the sphere of activities included within the notion of public affairs is not restricted to the formal political institutions of a state but also includes social and civic activities of a public nature, this implies an extension

---

[12] HRC, General Comment no 25: The right to participate in public affairs, voting rights and the right of equal access to public service (Art 25), 57th session (1996), CCPR/C/21/Rev1/Add7, para 5.

of the right to participate to non-citizens. Thus although the right to political participation requires the existence of a political community with individual members, most commonly citizens, and an organizational form (government) as a precondition for the exercise of this political right, the scope of activities with respect to the conduct of public affairs goes beyond the formal government institutions and processes which do not require strict adherence to a citizenship.[13]

Aside from the general concept of taking part in the conduct of public affairs, the Covenant defines directly more specific forms of such participation: direct democracy, taking place for example through referendums;[14] elections; and representation in the civil service. Special importance is given to elections in the treaty. Most of the governments incorporate this mechanism of public participation within their political system, either as a central mode of participation or as a partial element of their political system.[15]

The identical aspects of the right to participation are echoed in the regional standards, such as Art 23 of the Inter-American Convention on Human Rights (ACHR). Another example is Art 13 of the African Charter on Human and Peoples' Rights (AfrCh), which refers to the right to participate in the government of a country, either directly or through freely chosen representatives, as well as to the right of equal access to public service. Both standards delegate to national legislation the adoption of conditions for exercise of the three elements of the right to political participation. However, the ACHR expressly stipulates that such conditions should be limited to grounds based on age, nationality, residence, language, education, civil and mental capacity, or sentencing by a competent court. Perhaps the most detailed articulation of the right to political participation can be found in the politically binding commitments of the Organization for Security and Cooperation in Europe (OSCE) in paras 5.1 and 5.2 and paras 6 and 7 of the Document of the Copenhagen Meeting of the Conference on the Human Dimension of the Conference on Security and Cooperation in Europe (CSCE).[16] Of special relevance are paras 6 and 7 since they contain the most comprehensive list of guarantees regarding representative

---

[13] For a more detailed discussion of the relationship between minority political participation and citizenship, please see Chapter 3 in this volume by Annelies Verstichel. It should be noted that at the level of the Council of Europe, a Convention has been adopted on the Participation of Foreigners in Public Life at Local Level.

[14] For various forms of direct democracy, see Direct Democracy: The International IDEA Handbook, issued on 27 November 2008, available at <www.idea.int/publications/direct_democracy/index.cfm> (accessed 31 July 2009).

[15] For state practice regarding electoral systems and various combinations with direct democracy see the International IDEA Table of Electoral Systems Worldwide, issued in January 2005, available at <http://www.idea.int/esd/world.cfm> (accessed 31 July 2009).

[16] Second Conference on the Human Dimension of the CSCE, Document of the Copenhagen Meeting of the Conference on Human Dimension of the CSCE, Copenhagen, 1990.

government, the conduct of free elections,[17] and, most importantly, the international monitoring system of national elections.[18]

The European Convention on Human Rights and Freedoms (ECHR), however, only deals with the right to hold free elections under conditions which will ensure the free expression of the people in the choice of legislature under Art 3 of Protocol 1. Compared with other universal and regional standards, the ECHR therefore provides relatively limited protection as it restricts electoral representation to the legislature.[19]

In principle, the universal and regional international standards cover three basic aspects of the right to political participation:

1. the right to take part in the conduct of public affairs at all levels either directly or indirectly,
2. the right to vote and stand for elected office in genuine periodic elections, and
3. the right to have an equal access to the civil service.

The prohibition of discrimination combined with the right to political participation may imply positive action measures for persons belonging to national minorities in order to ensure their equal opportunities to participate in the public life of a society. The extent to which such general human rights guarantees provide specific obligations either in terms of states' duties of forbearance or performance regarding political participation of national minorities will be discussed in much greater detail later under specific issues.

---

[17] Paragraph 7 of the Document of the Copenhagen Meeting of the Conference on Human Dimension of the CSCE calls upon the participating states: '(7.1)—hold elections at reasonable intervals, as established by law; (7.2)—permit all seats in at least one chamber of the national legislature to be freely contested in a popular vote; (7.3)—guarantee universal and equal suffrage to adult citizens; (7.4)—ensure that votes are cast by secret ballot or by equivalent free voting procedure, and that they are counted and reported honestly with the official results made public; (7.60)—respect the right of individuals and groups to establish, in full freedom, their own political parties or other political organizations with the necessary legal guarantees to enable them to compete with each other on a basis of equal treatment before the law and by the authorities; (7.7) —ensure that law and public policy work to permit political campaigning to be conducted in a fair and free atmosphere in which neither administrative action, violence nor intimidation bars the parties and the candidates from freely presenting their views and qualifications, or prevents the voters from learning and discussion them or from casting their vote free from fear or retribution; (7.8)—provide that no legal or administrative obstacles stands in that way of unimpeded access to the media on a non-discriminatory basis for all political groupings and individuals wishing to participate in the electoral process; (7.9)—ensure that candidates who obtain the necessary number of votes required by law are duly installed in office and are permitted to remain in office until their term expires or is otherwise brought to an end in a manner that is regulated by law in conformity with democratic parliamentary and constitutional procedures.'

[18] See para 8 of the Document of the Copenhagen Meeting of the Conference on Human Dimension of the CSCE.

[19] The European Court on Human Rights confirmed that the electoral representation applies to elected bodies and legislatures at all levels of state administration, even extended such participation to the European Parliament, see ECtHR, *Py v France*, Appl 66289/01, Judgment of 6 June 2005, Reports 2005–1, para 36; ECtHR, *Mathews v United Kingdom*, Appl 24833/94, Judgment of 18 February 1999, para 43.

The second pillar of protection is provided through minority rights recognizing the need for enhanced protection for national minorities and articulating a specific right to effective participation of national minorities in public life. While political participation is a key mechanism for the effective participation of minorities, these standards encompass participation in all forms of public life of the national society.[20] The international minority standards, in particular Arts 2 and 5 of the United Nations Declaration on the Rights of Persons Belonging to National or Ethnic, Religious, and Linguistic Minorities (UN Declaration on Minorities)[21] and Art 15 of the Framework Convention for the Protection of National Minorities (FCNM)[22] refer to participation in cultural, religious, social, economic, and public life. Also the application of Art 27 of the ICCPR at the universal level implies some obligations on states to ensure participation of national minorities in decision-making with regard to enjoyment of their culture.[23] Often the scope of public life intersects with, as well as covers, the other spheres of life of a society specifically cited in the provision of Article 15 of the FCNM and Art 2 and 5 of the UN Declaration on Minorities. This broad scope of public life has also been stressed in the Commentary of the Working Group on Minorities to the United Nations Declaration on the Rights of Persons

---

[20] See para 35 of the Commentary of the Working Group on Minorities to the United Nations Declaration on the Rights of Persons Belonging to National or Ethnic, Religious, and Linguistic Minorities, (4 April 2005, E/CN4/Sub2/AC5/2005/2), which emphasized that: 'The right to participate in all aspects of the life of the larger national society is essential, both in order for persons belonging to minorities to promote their interests and values and to create an integrated but pluralist society based on tolerance and dialogue. By their participation in all forms of public life in their country, they are able both to shape their own destinies and to contribute to political change in the larger society.'

[21] Articles 2 and 4 of the Declaration on the Rights of Persons Belonging to National or Ethnic, Religious, and Linguistic Minorities, adopted by UN GA on 18 December 1992, GA Res 47/135, state: '2(2) Persons belonging to minorities have the right to participate effectively in cultural, religious, social, economic and public life'; '2(3) Persons belonging to minorities have the right to participate effectively in decisions on the national and, where appropriate, regional level concerning the minority to which they belong or the regions in which they live, in a manner not incompatible with national legislation'; '4(5) States should consider appropriate measures so that persons belonging to minorities may participate fully in economic progress and development of their country.'

[22] Article 15 of the Framework Convention for the Protection of National Minorities, adopted on 1 February 1998, ETS no 157, states: 'The Parties shall create the conditions necessary for the effective participation of persons belonging to national minorities in cultural, social, and economic life and in public affairs, in particular those affecting them.'

[23] Although Art 27 of the ICCPR does not refer expressly to the political participation of national minorities, the UN Human Rights Committee noted that such participation is necessary for enjoyment of cultural rights. In General Comment 23: The right of minorities (Article 27) (adopted on 8 April 1994, CCPR/C/12/Rev1/Add.5) in para 7 the Committee observed that: 'With regard to the exercise of the cultural rights protected under article 27, culture manifests itself in many forms, including a particular way of life associated with the use of land resources, especially in the case of indigenous peoples. This right may include such traditional activities as fishing or hunting and the right to live in reserves protected by law. The enjoyment of those rights may require positive legal measures of protection and measures to ensure the effective participation of members of minority communities in decisions which affect them.'

Belonging to National or Ethnic, Religious, and Linguistic Minorities, where in para 36 Asbjorn Eide affirms that:

The words 'public life' must be understood in the same broad sense as in article 1 of the International Convention on the Elimination of All Forms of Racial Discrimination, though much is covered already by the preceding words 'cultural, religious, social and economic'. Included in 'public life' are, among other rights, rights relating to election and to being elected, the holding of public office, and other political and administrative domains.

The Lund Recommendations on the Effective Participation of National Minorities,[24] that attempted to elaborate the substance of the existing standards and which form a background to this publication, concentrate particularly on participation in public life. They provide recommendations directed at the enhancement of political representation and participation of minorities in the legislative processes, government, administration, and in the conduct of public affairs. The Recommendations pay less attention to participation of persons belonging to national minorities in social and economic life and deal with participation in cultural life only through the democratic entitlement to local governance and cultural autonomy. The narrower focus of the Lund Recommendations must be seen in the context of the other thematic recommendations generated by the OSCE High Commissioner on National Minorities, which deal with linguistic rights, education, access to media, and which include recommendations and good practices for minority participation and representation in these areas.[25]

Clarifying the forms of political participation the Lund Recommendations identify two broad areas: participation in decision-making in the governance of the state as a whole, and self-governance. The first prong is concerned with both representation, elaborating specific measures for minorities to be undertaken with respect to elections, and participation in decision-making through arrangements at the level of the central government and the regional and local levels as well as through advisory and/or consultative bodies. The second prong encompasses non-territorial and territorial arrangements for self-government, minorities having jurisdictional control over their own affairs through cultural or personal autonomy and territorial autonomy.

With respect to political participation of national minorities, Marc Weller, in his commentary on Art 15 of the FCNM, distinguishes three layers of entitlement. The first, he argues, concerns 'a voice in governance of a state as a

---

[24] The Lund Recommendations on the Effective Participation of National Minorities in Public Life (Lund Recommendations), OSCE HCNM, September 1999.
[25] See Oslo Recommendations Regarding the Linguistic Rights of National Minorities and explanatory note, OSCE HCNM, February 1998; The Hague Recommendations Regarding the Education Rights of National Minorities and explanatory note, OSCE HCNM, October 1996; Guidelines on the use of Minority Languages in the Broadcast Media, OSCE HCNM, October 2003.

whole'.[26] This means that minorities have equal opportunities in electoral terms, including registration of political parties and election campaigns. Importantly this may also include positive measures to arrange political decision-making in such a way as to ensure effective representation of minorities in the decision-making processes where they would be disqualified or seriously disadvantaged due to their non-dominant position.

The second layer, he claims, relates to:

> the entitlement of minorities to the auto-determination issues that are of particular relevance to them. On the one hand, this includes the rights to arrange issues that are of direct relevance to the expression and development of minority identity—cultural autonomy. On the other hand, it is claimed that minorities must also have the right to organize and maintain political processes in areas where they are a local majority—territorial autonomy.[27]

He concludes that territorial autonomy has not been accepted as a genuine entitlement, however in practice states widely accept the principle of subsidiarity and give substantial control to minorities through decentralized or local forms of government, including control over regions and enhanced forms of self-government.

Interestingly, Weller adds a third layer to minority political participation, 'the internal democracy of minority communities'.[28] As he correctly points out this area is often overlooked and very little attention has been paid to issues of genuine representation of members of minority communities. In his view this layer has two aspects: one relates to the state responsibility to allow communities to decide how they will organize themselves and how they undertake decisions; the other concerns the need for minority organizations to follow genuine democratic principles of accountability and transparency.

The FCNM Commentary on the Effective Participation of Persons Belonging to National Minorities in Cultural, Social, and Economic Life and Public Affairs, in the examination of state practice by the Advisory Committee, divides the implementation of Art 15 of the FCNM by the particular aspects of life identified in the provision. The Advisory Committee interpreting and examining the effective participation in 'public affairs' defined the following forms and areas of political participation of minorities:

- participation of persons belonging to national minorities in legislative process, meaning participation in elections, representation of minorities through electoral design and parliamentary procedures and representation,
- representation and participation of persons belonging to national minorities in public administration, in the judiciary and in the executive,

---

[26] M Weller, 'Article 15' in Marc Weller (ed), *The Rights of Minorities: A Commentary on the European Framework Convention for the Protection of National Minorities* (2005), 432–3.
[27] Ibid. [28] Ibid.

- participation of persons belonging to national minorities through specialized governmental bodies,
- participation of persons belonging to national minorities through consultative mechanisms,
- participation of persons belonging to national minorities through sub-national forms of government, and
- participation of persons belonging to national minorities through autonomy arrangements.[29]

In addition the Commentary underlined the importance of media as a vital source for the effective participation of persons belonging to national minorities in public affairs. It should be noted that the OSCE Copenhagen Document is the only international standard which expressly noted in para 35 that one of the possible means to achieve such effective participation of minorities is through the establishment of local or autonomous administrations.

As the focus of the publication is on political participation of minorities, and more specifically on the Lund Recommendations, this chapter will focus specifically on the application of the principle of full and effective equality with regard to the areas and forms of political participation identified above.

C. Equality and non-discrimination and the right to political participation

The principles of equality and non-discrimination provide important guarantees for members of national minority groups with respect to their right to political participation. This protection concerns them in the same way as other citizens as well as in specific ways as members of groups who require minority protection. It is clear in international law that the principles of equality and non-discrimination apply to all three aspects of the right to political participation: the right to take part in the conduct of public affairs at all levels, either directly or indirectly, to vote and stand for elected office in genuine periodic elections, and to have equal access to the civil service. As noted above, non-discrimination and equality are widely agreed to be principles of customary international law and therefore bind states regardless of their ratification of a particular convention. In addition, equality provisions are specifically included in all the major international and regional legal instruments that set out states' obligations to guarantee the right to political participation.

---

[29] The FCNM Commentary on the Effective Participation of Persons Belonging to National Minorities in Cultural, Social, and Economic Life and Public Affairs, adopted on 27 February 2008, ACFC/31DOC(2008)001, paras 69–74.

The International Covenant on Civil and Political Rights, for instance, contains an accessory equality provision—applicable only with respect to the rights set out in the Covenant—in Art 2.1:

> Each State Party to the present Covenant undertakes to respect and to ensure to all individuals within its territory and subject to its jurisdiction the rights recognised in the present Covenant, without distinction of any kind, such as race, colour, sex, language, religion, political or other opinion, national or social origin, property, birth or other status.

It also contains a self-standing or independent equality provision—a right valid in itself beyond the ambit of the other rights set out in the Covenant—in Art 26:

> All persons are equal before the law and are entitled without any discrimination to the equal protection of the law. In this respect, the law shall prohibit any discrimination and guarantee to all persons equal and effective protection against discrimination on any ground such as race, colour, sex, language, religion, political or other opinion, national or social origin, property, birth or other status.

Similar provisions are replicated in the African Charter on Human and Peoples' Rights (Arts 2 and 3), the American Convention on Human Rights (Arts 1 and 24) and the European Convention for the Protection of Human Rights and Fundamental Freedoms (Art 14 and Protocol 12).

The interlinkage between non-discrimination and the right to political participation is specifically highlighted in Art 25 of the International Covenant on Civil and Political Rights, which provides that:

> Every citizen shall have the right and the opportunity, without any of the distinctions mentioned in article 2 and without unreasonable restrictions:
>
> (a) To take part in the conduct of public affairs, directly or through freely chosen representatives;
> (b) To vote and to be elected at genuine periodic elections which shall be by universal and equal suffrage and shall be held by secret ballot, guaranteeing the free expression of the will of the electors;
> (c) To have access, on general terms of equality, to public service in his country.

This specific reference to Art 2 emphasizes the need for states to ensure that the different aspects of the right to political participation are guaranteed in a non-discriminatory manner.

In addition, legal instruments relating to specific minority groups, such as the Convention on the Elimination of All Forms of Racial Discrimination (CERD) and the Convention on the Elimination of All Forms of Discrimination against Women (CEDAW), that require states to ensure non-discrimination and factual equality, provide an additional framework of protection for national minorities. For instance, Art 5 of the CERD stipulates:

> States Parties undertake to prohibit and eliminate racial discrimination in all its forms and to guarantee the right of everyone, without distinction as to race, colour, or national

or ethnic origin, to equality before the law, notably in the enjoyment of the following rights:

...

(c) Political rights, in particular the right to participate in elections—to vote and to stand for election—on the basis of universal and equal suffrage, to take part in the Government as well as in the conduct of public affairs at any level and to have equal access to public service;

Similarly CEDAW, although not strictly connected to national minorities, provides a general framework and an example of applying an equality and non-discrimination principle to a category of persons. Art 7 provides that:

States Parties shall take all appropriate measures to eliminate discrimination against women in the political and public life of the country and, in particular, shall ensure to women, on equal terms with men, the right:

(a) To vote in all elections and public referenda and to be eligible for election to all publicly elected bodies;
(b) To participate in the formulation of government policy and the implementation thereof and to hold public office and perform all public functions at all levels of government;
(c) To participate in non-governmental organizations and associations concerned with the public and political life of the country.

The fact that each of the elements of the right to political participation needs to be applied in a manner consistent with the principles of non-discrimination and equality is not a controversial matter today.

There may be limits as to the application of the protection provided by a particular legal instrument, however. This problem arises in the context of the ECHR, in particular due to the limited scope of the right to political participation included in this Convention (Art 3 of Protocol 1) as compared to other universal and regional standards—addressing only the right to free elections (see discussion above under section II.B).

More specifically, the problem is whether a situation relating to discrimination concerning an element of political participation not covered by Art 3 of Protocol 1, such as the right to take part in the conduct of public affairs, within the scope of protection provided by the ECHR. The issue is further complicated by the fact that the ECHR's long-standing non-discrimination provision, Art 14, is only an accessory provision (relating to convention rights). The more recent Protocol 12 (adopted 26 June 2000) is an independent non-discrimination provision, extending beyond the ambit of rights specified in the Convention. If the situation occurs in a state which has ratified Protocol 12, discrimination in relation to other elements of political participation would be covered by the ECHR. However, if the state has not ratified Protocol 12, the issue is trickier. Thus far, Court jurisprudence does not address a case that provides clear guidance on this matter. The Court consistently holds that:

> Article 14 of the Convention complements the other substantive provisions of the Convention and its Protocols. It has no independent existence since it has effect solely in relation to 'the enjoyment of the rights and freedoms' safeguarded by those provisions. Although the application of Article 14 does not presuppose a breach of those provisions – and to this extent it is autonomous – there can be no room for its application unless the facts in issue fall within *the ambit* of one or more of the latter.[30]

It has also stated on many occasions that Art 14 comes into play whenever 'the subject-matter of the disadvantage … constitutes one of the modalities of the exercise of a right guaranteed',[31] or the measures complained of are 'linked to the exercise of a right guaranteed'.[32] Based on this guidance, it seems unlikely that other elements of the right to political participation, not in some way related to elections, would be held by the Court to fall within the scope of Art 14 in combination with Art 3 of Protocol 1. This is guesswork, as a specific situation would need to be interpreted by the Court, but it is consistent with the Court's track record of a relatively restricted application of Art 14.

The second layer of protection vis-à-vis equality and non-discrimination is provided by the minority-specific standards. Art 15 of the FCNM is a key provision dedicated to the right to effective participation. Art 4 guarantees the prohibition of discrimination based on membership in a minority group and also requires special measures to ensure real equality. Art 5 requires the creation of conditions to secure and promote the distinct minority culture and identity. These three articles can be seen 'as the three corners of a triangle which together form the main foundations of the Framework Convention',[33] as noted in the FCNM Commentary on the Effective Participation of Persons Belonging to National Minorities in Cultural, Social, and Economic Life and Public Affairs. Similarly, the prohibition of discrimination and the obligation to adopt positive-action measures with respect to political participation of minorities is embodied in Arts 1 and 4 of the UN Declaration on the Rights of Persons Belonging to National or Ethnic, Religious, and Linguistic Minorities and paras 31 and 33 of the Copenhagen Document.

---

[30] ECtHR, *Petrovic v Austria*, Appl 20458/92, Judgment of 27 March 1998, Reports 1998–II, para 22. See also, among many other authorities, *Karlheinz Schmidt v Germany*, Appl 13580/88, Judgment of 18 July 1994, Series A no 291–B, p 32, para 22; and *Van Raalte v The Netherlands*, Appl 20060/92, Judgment of 21 February 1997, Reports of Judgments and Decisions 1997–I, p 184, para 33.

[31] See ECtHR, *National Union of Belgian Police v Belgium*, Appl 4464/70, Judgment of 27 October 1975, Series A no 19, p 20, para 45.

[32] See the ECtHR, *Schmidt and Dahlström v Sweden*, Appl 5589/72, Judgment of 6 February 1976, Series A no 21, p 17, para 39.

[33] The FCNM Commentary on the Effective Participation of Persons Belonging to National Minorities in Cultural, Social, and Economic life and Public Affairs, adopted on 27 February 2008, ACFC/31DOC(2008)001, para 13.

III. Analysis: Specific Issues

A. Obligation not to discriminate

As mentioned above, the starting point for the protection provided by the non-discrimination and equality principles is the negative obligation not to discriminate based on prohibited grounds. Given its clear application to all three elements of political participation, this means that there should be no discrimination in the conditions established for: taking part in the conduct of public affairs at all levels; voting and standing for elected office in genuine periodic elections; and having equal access to civil service, as well as other political rights important for participation of national minorities, such as freedom of association, assembly and expression.

It is not uncommon that in the practice of states various conditions and restrictions are imposed on the enjoyment of the above-mentioned rights. The conditions and restrictions are often linked to specific criteria for the registration and functioning of political parties and minority associations, election campaigns, registration of electoral lists, or employment. In some instances these conditions intentionally aim to exclude certain individuals or groups from representation or participation in public affairs. Often, however, minorities are affected by indirect discrimination, where conditions that are meant to be neutral and are not specifically aimed or directed at any given community, will result in the disadvantage or possible exclusion of individuals or communities from political participation.

For instance, conditions that are seemingly neutral with respect to national minorities may have exclusionary effects upon such minorities due to their distinct features or due to specific disadvantageous conditions in which they find themselves due to being in a minority position. In this regard the OSCE Warsaw Guidelines to Assist National Minorities in the Electoral Process note that a number of eligibility requirements for registering as a voter may have discriminatory effects upon persons belonging to a national minority. In general they refer to requirements such as citizenship for the right to vote, for instance if national origin is a requirement for acquiring citizenship; residency requirements, in particular in situations when minorities have been persecuted and have become refugees or are internally displaced; prescription of a particular language for electoral campaigns or language proficiency used for eligibility to register as a voter or to stand for public office.[34] The extent to which some of these conditions have been considered discriminatory in the practice of the international

---

[34] For a more detailed list of various requirements that may have a discriminatory impact on minorities see 'The prohibition of discrimination' in the Warsaw Guidelines to Assist National Minorities in the Electoral Process, adopted by the OSCE Office for Democratic Institutions and Human Rights (ODIHR), March 2001, 13–15.

bodies in concrete situations will be discussed later in the text under sections III.A.1 and III.A.2.

The obligation not to discriminate spans both direct and indirect forms of discrimination. The non-discrimination provisions in the core international human rights instruments all cover both direct and indirect discrimination. In some cases, such as Art 1 of CERD or CEDAW, the reference to the effect of unfavourable treatment in the wording of the non-discrimination provision itself makes clear that the prohibition includes indirect discrimination.[35] More frequently this has been clarified through interpretive commentary and jurisprudence.[36] For instance, in the *Althammer* case the Human Rights Committee stated that it 'recalls that a violation of article 26 can also result from the discriminatory effect of a rule or measure that is neutral at face value or without intent to discriminate'.[37] Likewise, the case law of the European Court of Human Rights (ECtHR) makes clear 'that if a policy or general measure has disproportionate prejudicial effects on a group of people, the possibility of its being considered discriminatory cannot be ruled out even if it is not specifically aimed or directed at that group'.[38] The European Court of Justice (ECJ) has also recently confirmed that the principle of equal treatment prohibits not only overt discrimination but also all covert forms of discrimination.[39] In General

---

[35] Art 1 of ICERD defines racial discrimination as 'any distinction, exclusion, restriction or preference based on race, colour, descent, or national or ethnic origin which has the purpose *or effect* of nullifying or impairing the recognition, enjoyment or exercise, on an equal footing, of human rights and fundamental freedoms in the political, economic, social, cultural or any other field of public life' (italics added). CEDAW adopts similar language in its definition of 'discrimination against women' (Art 1).

[36] HRC, General Comment 18 notes that 'the term "discrimination" as used in the Covenant should be understood to imply any distinction, exclusion, restriction or preference which is based on any ground such as race, colour, sex, language, religion, political or other opinion, national or social origin, property, birth or other status, and which has *the purpose or effect of nullifying or impairing the recognition, enjoyment or exercise by all persons, on an equal footing, of all rights and freedoms*' (italics added), para 7.

[37] HRC, *Althammer and ors v Austria*, (Communication no 998/2001, 21 March 2002). The case concerned an amendment in regulations governing retirement benefits that decreased the amount of monthly household entitlements in households without children under the age of twenty-seven. The applicants claimed 'that although the amendment of the Regulations is objective on the face of it, it is discriminatory in effect, considering that most retirees are heads of households with a spouse as dependent and no longer have children under the age of 27. The impact of the amendment is therefore greater for retired than for active employees as it effectively abolishes the supplement for retirees' dependants altogether' (para 3.1). The HRC found no violation as, even if a disproportionate impact could be shown, the measure was based on objective and reasonable grounds (para 10.2).

[38] ECtHR, *Hugh Jordan v United Kingdom*, Appl 24746/94, Judgment of 4 May 2001, para 154; and *Hoogendijk v The Netherlands*, Appl 58461/00, Judgment of 6 January 2005; *Zarb Adami v Malta*, Appl 17209/02, Judgment of 20 June 2006, para 80; *DH and ors v The Czech Republic*, Appl 57325/00, Judgment of 13 November 2007, para 175.

[39] ECJ, *Commission v Austria*, Case C147/03, Judgment of 7 July 2005, para 41.

Recommendation XIV, the Committee on the Elimination of Racial Discrimination explained that:

> In seeking to determine whether an action has an effect contrary to the Convention, it will look to see whether that action has an unjustifiable disparate impact upon a group distinguished by race, colour, descent, or national or ethnic origin.[40]

This approach is also followed by other human rights bodies.

In practice, this implies that regulations, procedures, conditions, practices, or other factors relating to these rights of political participation should not in purpose or effect discriminate against any individuals or groups of individuals. Thus even conditions that may appear neutral at face value, may in fact be discriminatory if they have a disparate negative impact on members of certain minority groups.

1. Non-discrimination and the Right to Political Participation

(a) Application of the principle of non-discrimination to particular situations

While it is clear in international law that direct and indirect discrimination are prohibited with respect to all aspects of political participation, the application of the non-discrimination principle to particular situations is more complex. It requires establishing conformity with the principle of non-discrimination of factors such as: electoral rules, the manner by which electoral districts are divided, conditions for holding certain positions in the civil service, decision-making with respect to financing of political parties, etc. A specific context-based assessment is required in every situation in order to assess whether there is discrimination in purpose or effect against certain persons or groups of persons. The following discussion of the definition and legal tests of discrimination seeks to clarify the legal guidelines for the assessment of individual situations. Evidently, these guidelines apply to situations involving members of national minority groups as they do to other individuals and members of other groups.

The definition of discrimination is well-established in international law and clearly articulated by the United Nations Human Rights Committee in General Comment 18. It states that:

> the term 'discrimination' as used in the Covenant [ICCPR] should be understood to imply any distinction, exclusion, restriction or preference which is based on any ground such as race, colour, sex, language, religion, political or other opinion, national or social origin, property, birth or other status, and which has the purpose or effect of nullifying or impairing the recognition, enjoyment or exercise by all persons, on an equal footing, of all rights and freedoms.[41]

---

[40] Committee on Elimination of Racial Discrimination, General Recommendation XIV on Art 1, para 1 of the CERD, 42nd session (1993). See also discussion in K Kitching, *Non-discrimination in International Law: A handbook for practitioners* (2005), 82–90.

[41] United Nations Human Rights Committee (HRC), General Comment 18: Non-discrimination, 37th session (1989), para 7.

Discrimination is similarly defined in conventions dealing with specific types of discrimination. For instance Art 1.1 of the CERD provides that:

the term 'racial discrimination' shall mean any distinction, exclusion, restriction or preference based on race, colour, descent, or national or ethnic origin which has the purpose or effect of nullifying or impairing the recognition, enjoyment or exercise, on an equal footing, of human rights and fundamental freedoms in the political, economic, social, cultural or any other field of public life.[42]

According to these definitions, discrimination involves a form of different treatment based on a prohibited ground. However, international, regional and national level jurisprudence has provided guidance about the definition of discrimination that goes well beyond these definitions. The HRC comments as follows in General Comment 18:

not every differentiation of treatment will constitute discrimination, if the criteria for such differentiation are reasonable and objective and if the aim is to achieve a purpose which is legitimate under the Covenant.

The European Court of Human Rights has further clarified that:

the principle of equality of treatment is violated if the distinction has no objective and reasonable justification. The existence of such a justification must be assessed in relation to the aim and effects of the measure under consideration, regard being had to the principles which normally prevail in democratic societies. A difference of treatment in the exercise of a right laid down in the Convention must not only pursue a legitimate aim: Article 14 is likewise violated when it is clearly established that there is no reasonable relationship of proportionality between the means employed and the aim sought to be realised.[43]

With respect to the right to political participation, this legal test provides guidance in establishing whether a particular regulation, procedure, condition or other factor relevant to any element of political participation is discriminatory—and therefore illegal. This is highly relevant, as discussed later in the text, when it comes to an assessment of whether certain conditions established with respect to electoral systems or public positions do in fact create disadvantageous or exclusionary limitations and constitute discrimination against members of national minorities. The most difficult and controversial aspect of any determination is applying the proportionality principle—in other words considering whether there is an objective and reasonable justification for the distinction at hand.

---

[42] See also Art 1 of the CEDAW: '"discrimination against women" shall mean any distinction, exclusion or restriction made on the basis of sex which has the effect or purpose of impairing or nullifying the recognition, enjoyment or exercise by women, irrespective of their marital status, on a basis of equality of men and women, of human rights and fundamental freedoms in the political, economic, social, cultural, civil or any other field'.

[43] ECtHR, *Belgian Linguistics Case (no 2)*, 1 EHRR 252, 10 (1968).

(b) **International jurisprudence applying the non-discrimination principle to participation in elections**

The UN Human Rights Committee examined discrimination in relation to the right to vote in the case of *Gillot and ors v France*.[44] The applicants were a group of twenty-one authors of French nationality, resident in New Caledonia. They claimed that criteria established in order to determine the electorate for the November 1998 referendum and future referendums, that excluded them from participation, constituted discrimination against them on the basis of ethnic origin or national extraction.

In considering their complaint the HRC recalled:

its decisions in relation to article 25 of the Covenant, namely that the right to vote is not an absolute right and that restrictions may be imposed on it provided they are not discriminatory or unreasonable.[45]

It also noted that:

In order to determine the discriminatory or non-discriminatory character of the criteria in dispute, in conformity with its above-mentioned decisions, the Committee considers that the evaluation of any restrictions must be effected on a case-by-case basis, having regard in particular to the purpose of such restrictions and the principle of proportionality.[46]

The Committee observes that in this case the criteria determining the electorate in the referenda draw a differentiation between persons having the right to participate and those not having the right based on their links with the territory whose institutional development is at issue. The Committee 'recalls that not all differentiation constitutes discrimination if it is based on objective and reasonable criteria and the purpose sought is legitimate under the Covenant'.

It finds that the criteria used to determine the electorate in the 1998 referendum established 'a differentiation between residents as regards their relationship to the territory, on the basis of length of residence requirement … whatever their ethnic origin or national extraction'.[47] It therefore considered that 'the criterion used for the 1998 referendum did not have the purpose or effect of establishing different rights for different ethnic groups or groups distinguished by their national extraction'.[48]

The Committee further considered another aspect of the applicants' complaint alleging discrimination on the basis of descent and family ties in determining the electorate for future referendums from 2014 onwards relating to the option of independence. Conditions for participation in these referendums

---

[44] HRC, *Gillot and ors al v France*, Communication no 932/2000, Views of 26 July 2002, CCPR/C/75/D/932/2000.
[45] Ibid, para 12.2. The Committee here referred specifically to the following decisions: *J Debreczeny v The Netherlands*, Comm no 500/1992; *Alba Pietraroia on behalf of Rosario Pietraroia Zapala v Uruguay*, Comm no 44/1979. [46] Ibid, para 13.2.
[47] Ibid, para 13.10.   [48] Ibid, para 13.11.

included, in addition to the length of residence condition, alternate conditions relating to possession of customary civil status, the presence in the territory of moral and material interests, combined with birth of the person concerned or his parents in the territory.[49] The Committee noted that residents who fulfil criteria relating to descent and family ties are in a situation that is objectively different from that of the authors whose link to the territory is based on length of residence. It further notes that length of residence is taken into account for participation in future referenda and that these criteria may be used alternately.[50]

The Committee also emphasizes that, in its view:

> the restrictions on the electorate resulting from the criteria used for the referendum of 1998 and referendums from 2014 onwards respect the criterion of proportionality to the extent that they are strictly limited ratione loci to local ballots on self-determination and therefore have no consequences for participation in general elections, whether legislative, presidential, European or municipal, or other referendums.[51]

It finds 'that the criteria for the determination of the electorates for the referendums of 1998 and 2014 or thereafter are not discriminatory, but are based on objective grounds for differentiation that are reasonable and compatible with the provisions of the Covenant'.[52]

The European Court of Human Rights has also examined a case of alleged discrimination with respect to the right to vote in *Aziz v Cyprus*.[53] The applicant, Mr Ibrahim Aziz, complained that he was prevented from exercising his voting rights on the grounds of national origin and/or association with a national minority in violation of Art 3 of Protocol 1 (right to free elections) in conjunction with Art 14 (non-discrimination) of the Convention.

Mr Aziz is a Cypriot national who is a member of the Turkish Cypriot community living in the government-controlled area of Cyprus. He was denied the possibility of being registered on the electoral role in order to vote in the parliamentary election of 27 May 2001. In answering his request for registration the Ministry of Interior specified that, by virtue of Art 63 of the Constitution, members of the Turkish-Cypriot community could not be registered on the Greek electoral roll.[54] The Cypriot Constitution came into force in 1960 and Art 63 provided for two separate electoral lists, one for the Greek-Cypriot community and one for the Turkish-Cypriot community.[55] The Court of Human Rights noted, however, that:

> the participation of the Turkish-Cypriot members of parliament was suspended as a result of the anomalous situation that began in 1963. From then on, the relevant Articles of the Constitution providing for the parliamentary representation of the Turkish-Cypriot

---

[49] Ibid, para 13.7.   [50] Ibid, para 13.12.   [51] Ibid, para 13.17.
[52] Ibid, para 13.18.
[53] ECtHR, *Aziz v Cyprus*, Appl 69949/01, Judgment of 22 June 2004.   [54] Ibid, para 11.
[55] Ibid; see more detailed description of the system in the Cypriot government's submission at para 20.

community and the quotas to be adhered to by the two communities became impossible to implement in practice.[56] ... Despite the fact that the relevant constitutional provisions have been rendered ineffective, there is a manifest lack of legislation resolving the ensuing problems.[57]

As a member of the Turkish-Cypriot community, Mr Aziz is therefore unable to vote in elections.

In its judgment, the Court recalled that:

while Article 3 of Protocol No. 1 is phrased in terms of the obligation of the High Contracting Party to hold elections which ensure the free expression of the opinion of the people, the Court's case-law establishes that it guarantees individual rights, including the right to vote and to stand for election.[58]

After finding a violation of Art 3 of Protocol 1 taken alone, the Court examined whether there was also a violation of this article taken together with Art 14. It noted that according to its case law:

a difference of treatment is discriminatory, for the purposes of Article 14 of the Convention, if it 'has no objective and reasonable justification', that is if it does not pursue a 'legitimate aim' or if there is not a 'reasonable relationship of proportionality between the means employed and the aim sought to be realised' (see Abdulaziz, Cabales and Balkandali v. the United Kingdom, judgment of 28 May 1985, Series A no. 94, pp. 35–36, § 72).[59]

It further noted that:

Where a substantive Article of the Convention has been relied on, both on its own and in conjunction with Article 14, and a separate breach has been found of the substantive Article, it is not generally necessary for the Court to consider the case under Article 14 also, though the position is otherwise if a clear inequality of treatment in the enjoyment of the right in question is a fundamental aspect of the case (see Dudgeon v. the United Kingdom, judgment of 22 October 1981, Series A no. 45, p. 26, § 67, and Chassagnou and Others v. France [GC], nos. 25088/94, 28331/95 and 28443/95, § 89, ECHR 1999-III).[60]

In this case, it found that the Art 14 complaint was a fundamental aspect of the case, observing that:

the difference in treatment in the present case resulted from the very fact that the applicant was a Turkish Cypriot. It emanated from the constitutional provisions regulating the voting rights between members of the Greek-Cypriot and Turkish-Cypriot communities that had become impossible to implement in practice.[61]

While taking into account the government's explanations for the situation, the Court found that:

---

[56] Ibid, para 26.
[57] Ibid, para 29.
[58] Ibid, para 25.
[59] Ibid, para 34.
[60] Ibid, para 35.
[61] Ibid, para 36.

they cannot justify this difference on reasonable and objective grounds, particularly in the light of the fact that Turkish Cypriots in the applicant's situation are prevented from voting at any parliamentary election.[62]

The Court found a violation of Art 14 taken in conjunction with Art 3 of Protocol 1.

Both of these cases concern conditions that govern the exercise of the right to vote. They demonstrate the manner in which the proportionality principle is applied to the particular conditions in order to establish whether they create permissible or illegal discriminatory distinctions. Proportionality is assessed by international and regional jurisdictions based on a close examination of the facts at hand. This examination will reflect very specific local considerations. In many cases, even if unfavourable treatment pursues a legitimate aim (ie, protecting public order), if there are alternative means of achieving the aim that do not adversely affect particular groups, then the unfavourable treatment will be found to be disproportionate. Certain jurisdictions consider that unfavourable treatment based on certain grounds of discrimination requires a particularly strong justification in order not to fall foul of the non-discrimination principle. For instance, the ECtHR has made clear that when unfavourable treatment is based on the grounds of race, ethnicity, religion, nationality, birth, sex or sexual orientation, particularly weighty reasons will have to be advanced for the treatment to be considered compatible with the non-discrimination principle.[63] This is particularly significant for national minorities as it means that very weighty reasons would have to be provided to justify unfavourable treatment against members of national minority groups due to their belonging to such groups.

In addition, a case alleging indirect discrimination with respect to the right to be elected of a person belonging to a national minority has been brought before international bodies.[64] Both the HRC in *Ignatane v Latvia* and the ECtHR in *Podkolzina v Latvia*, however, avoided delving into the indirect discriminatory aspects of the case.[65] However, the FCNM Commentary on the Effective

---

[62] Ibid, para 37.

[63] ECommHR and ECtHR, *East African Asians*, 3 EHRR 76 (1973), para 207 ('a special importance should be attached to discrimination based on race'); *Hoffman v Austria*, 17 EHRR 293, (1993) para 36 ('a distinction based essentially on a difference in religion alone is not acceptable'); *Abdulaziz, Cabales and Balkandali v United Kingdom*, Appl 9214/80; 9473/81; 9474/81, Judgment of 28 May 1985, para 78 ('very weighty reasons would have to be advanced before a difference of treatment on the ground of sex could be regarded as compatible with the Convention'); *Gaygusuz v Austria*, 23 EHRR 365, (1996) para 42 ('very weighty reasons would have to be put forward before the Court could regard a difference of treatment based exclusively on the ground of nationality as compatible with the Convention').

[64] In comparison with the right to vote, it is notable that the ECtHR held that stricter requirements may be imposed on eligibility to stand for elections. See ECtHR, *Zdanoka v Latvia*, Appl 58278/00, Judgment of 16 March 2006, para 115.

[65] The applicants claimed that conditioning of the right to stand as a candidate for a parliamentary position or in municipal councils on specific linguistic requirements infringes their right to be elected. Both the HRC and the ECtHR decided not to deal with the possible indirect discriminatory effects of the language proficiency. The ECtHR confirmed again the wide margin of

Participation of Persons Belonging to National Minorities in Cultural, Social, and Economic Life and Public Affairs noted with regard to linguistic requirements contested in these cases that, in general, 'language proficiency requirements imposed on candidates for parliamentary and local elections are not compatible with Art 15 of the Framework Convention'.[66]

(c) A second legal test of discrimination

A second legal test of discrimination has also been established that applies to cases where discrimination involves a failure to treat those in a different situation in a different manner. This test complements the first test whereby discrimination involved a failure to treat those in a similar situation in a similar manner without a reasonable and objective justification. These two tests in fact reflect the two faces of the equality principle, 'what are equal are to be treated equally and what are different are to be treated differently'.

While the first test has been widely applied, the second is a more recent development in international law. The judgment by the European Court of Human Rights in the *Thlimmenos* case, that clearly articulated these two tests and applied the second, was a pivotal decision.[67] In a key paragraph the Court states that it:

has so far considered that the right under Article 14 not to be discriminated against in the enjoyment of the rights guaranteed under the Convention is violated when States treat differently persons in analogous situations without providing an objective and reasonable justification (see the Inze judgment cited above, p. 18, § 41). However, the Court considers that this is not the only facet of the prohibition of discrimination in Article 14. The right not to be discriminated against in the enjoyment of the rights guaranteed under the Convention is also violated when States without an objective and reasonable justification fail to treat differently persons whose situations are significantly different.[68]

The facts of the case involved a Jehovah's Witness who claimed that he had suffered discrimination with respect to his religious beliefs in being refused an

---

appreciation of states when it comes to establishing their democratic system and said that it cannot contest the government's submission, 'that the obligation for a candidate to understand and speak Latvian is warranted by the need to ensure the proper functioning of Parliament, in which Latvian is the sole working language. They emphasised in particular that the aim of this requirement was to enable MPs to take an active part in the work of the House and effectively defend their electors' interests.' See the ECtHR, *Podkolzina v Latvia*, Appl 46726/99, Judgment of 9 July 2002, paras 34, 36. However, in both cases it was confirmed that the applicant's right to stand as a candidate has been violated on the procedural grounds. See, HRC, *Antonia Ignatane v Latvia*, Communication no 884/1999, Views of 25 July 2001, paras 7.4 and 7.5.

[66] The FCNM Commentary on the Effective Participation of Persons Belonging to National Minorities in Cultural, Social, and Economic Life and Public Affairs, adopted on 27 February 2008, ACFC/31DOC(2008)001, para 102.

[67] See also ECtHR, *Nachovo and Others v Bulgaria*, Appl 43577/98 and 43579/98, Judgment of 6 July 2005, para 160.

[68] ECtHR, *Thlimmenos v Greece*, Appl 34369/97, Judgment of 6 April 2000, para 44.

appointment as a chartered accountant on the basis of a law regulating appointments to the profession that excluded persons convicted of a serious crime.[69] The law did not distinguish between persons convicted as a result of their religious beliefs (refusing to serve in the army) and persons convicted on other grounds. The court found that by not taking into account the complainant's specific situation connected with his religious beliefs, and by not having an objective and reasonable justification for this omission, the Greek state violated the principle of non-discrimination. It stated that:

> [t]he right not to be discriminated against in the enjoyment of the rights guaranteed under the Convention is also violated when States without an objective and reasonable justification fail to treat differently persons whose situations are significantly different.[70]

The *Thlimmenos* decision is especially significant for its clear articulation of the second legal test of discrimination. This is very important in the context of positive and special measures that need to be taken in order to treat equally national minorities who are in a different situation than members of the majority. A failure to take such measures when they are needed to bring about equality is a form of discrimination. As this is a recent jurisprudential development in international law, to date there is lack of case law considering the failure of states to take positive action under non-discrimination provisions. This in no way reflects a satisfactory situation as concerns states' actions to take the required measures. See further discussion below under the section on positive action in III.B.

(d) The complexity of examining discriminatory effects of electoral systems

This issue certainly becomes very intricate when it comes to possible discriminatory effects of electoral systems on members of national minorities. The electoral systems are by their nature fairly complex, aiming to balance diverse, often competing interests. From the perspective of the position of national minorities in the electoral system, the position of the ECtHR provides some guiding principles. In *Mathieu-Mohin and Clerfayt v Belgium*, the Court noted that:

> [t]he rights [enshrined in Article 3 of the Additional Protocol to the Convention] are not absolute ... the Court ... has to satisfy itself that the conditions do not curtail the rights in question to such an extent as to impair their very essence and deprive them of their effectiveness; that they are imposed in pursuit of a legitimate aim; and that the means employed are not disproportionate ... In particular, such conditions must not thwart 'the free expression of the opinion of the people in the choice of the legislature'.[71]

---

[69] Ibid. The applicant's complaint to the ECtHR did not concern his initial conviction for insubordination. It focused on the law regulating access to the profession of chartered accountant. See para 33.

[70] Ibid, paras 39–49. See also ECtHR, *Chapman v United Kingdom*, Appl 27238/95, Judgment of 18 January 2001, para 129.

[71] ECtHR, *Mathieu-Mohin and Clerfayt v Belgium*, Appl 9267/81, Judgment of 2 March 1987, para 52.

Notable for minorities is the statement that it does not automatically follow, however, that all votes must necessarily have equal weight as regards the outcome of the election[72] as will be also discussed in greater detail in the section on positive action in III.B.

In terms of the possible positive obligations of a state to take into account the specific situation of minorities, the ECtHR considered the negative effects of the electoral rules on minorities, *inter alia* on Kurdish parties. In this case, it should be noted that the system has been criticized by different Council of Europe bodies, as well as the OSCE.[73] In *Yumak and Sadak v Turkey*, the Court held that the 10 per cent threshold applied in Turkey's elections was perhaps excessive. In that connection it concurred with the other organs of the Council of Europe saying the threshold was exceptionally high and should be lowered. However, in the specific context of the particular elections, the Court sided with the state's argument and said that states can pay due attention to the general exigencies of the national electoral policies in conformity with historical and political factors. The Court was persuaded by specific 'correctives and other guarantees which have limited its [threshold] effects'.[74] It therefore found the threshold to be acceptable in this specific case of elections, given the fact that as a result of the other guarantees the applicant parties could have used the steps that would have allowed them to achieve parliamentary representation.

2. Non-discrimination and Other Political Rights Necessary for Participation of Minorities

As has been widely demonstrated in the practice of international bodies, equally important to enjoyment of the right to political participation is also application of the principle of non-discrimination with respect to enjoyment of other political rights, such as freedom of expression, association, and assembly, as they create the prerequisite conditions for the participation of persons belonging to national minorities in public life. It is not uncommon that, in the practice of states, various restrictions are imposed on enjoyment of these rights. The conditions and restrictions are often linked to specific criteria for the registration and functioning of political parties and minority associations, election campaigns, and employment. In some instances these conditions aim to exclude certain individuals or groups from representation or participation in public affairs, through, for instance, prohibiting registration of a minority political party or association. Often, however, minorities are affected by indirect discrimination, where conditions that are meant to be neutral, and are not specifically aimed or

---

[72] Ibid. See, inter alia, para 54.
[73] Ad hoc Committee of the Parliamentary Assembly of the Council of Europe, Report: Observation of the Parliamentary Elections in Turkey (22 July 2007); OSCE, Office for Democratic Institutions and Human Rights, Assessment Report: Republic of Turkey Parliamentary Elections (2002).
[74] ECtHR, *Yumak and Sadak v Turkey*, Appl 100226/03, Judgment of 8 July 2008, para 147.

directed at the community, will result in the disadvantage or possible exclusion of individuals or a community from political participation. These conditions are often linked to the free enjoyment of these rights and therefore their exercise under conditions of full equality is crucial to securing the protection of national minorities, allowing them to pursue their interests collectively with others through their associations, political parties, and assemblies. Although the supervisory bodies of international instruments give a wide margin of appreciation to states to design their democratic system and electoral rules for political participation, in relation to the infringement of the abovementioned political rights of freedom of association, assembly and expression they apply strict scrutiny, as there must be convincing and compelling reasons to justify interference with these rights.[75]

Due to constrains of space, the authors will provide only a brief summary of the principal jurisprudence concerning the discriminatory effects of the conditions and limitations placed on those rights by states affecting full enjoyment of the right to political participation by national minorities.

Perhaps the most contested issue before the international bodies are restrictions on political parties and minority associations. The importance of the role played by political parties enjoying freedom of association and expression in democratic processes has been confirmed by many international human rights bodies,[76] in particular the ECtHR statement in *United Communist Party of Turkey and ors v Turkey* is of great significance when it comes to acceptance of the existence of minority organizations and their political parties:

The State is under the obligation, among others, to hold, in accordance with Article 3 Protocol No. 1, free elections at reasonable intervals by secret ballot under conditions which will ensure the free expression of the opinion of the people in the choice of the legislature. Such expression is inconceivable without the participation of a plurality of political parties representing the different shades of opinion to be found within a country's population. By relaying this range of opinion, not only within political institutions but also—with the help of the media—at all levels of social life, political parties make an irreplaceable contribution to political debate, which is at the very core of the concept of a democratic society ... [77]

From the relevant jurisprudence and state practice, two main types of restrictions can be observed: first, the state denies registration to a party because it does not want to recognize the existence of a particular minority or it prohibits ethnically based parties, using an argument that such representation is detrimental

---

[75] See, eg, ECtHR, *Ouranio Toxo and ors v Greece*, Appl 74989/01, Judgment, 20 October 2005, para 36.

[76] See, eg, ECtHR, *Refah Partisi (The Welfare Party) and ors v Turkey*, Appl 41340/98, 41342/98, 41343/98, Grand Chamber, Judgment of 13 February 2003. Paragraph 87, Inter-American Court of Human Rights, *Rios Brito v Argentina*, Petition no 10109, Resolution no 26/88, para 10.

[77] ECtHR, *United Communinist Party of Turkey and ors v Turkey*, Appl 19392/92, Judgment of 30 January 1998, para 44.

to civic principles of a state (as opposed to a state of ethnic communities) and equal rights of citizens; secondly, the state denies registration to a party arguing that minority parties and associations would endanger public order, or the territorial integrity or security of the state by seeking to advance minority interests.

In this regard the prohibition of an association or political party purely on the grounds that it seeks to assert minority identity has been considered incompatible with freedom of association. In the noteworthy case of *Sidiropolous and ors v Greece*, the ECtHR held:

> Territorial integrity, national security, and public order were not threatened by the activities of an association whose aim was to promote a region's culture, even supposing that it also aimed partly to promote the culture of a minority, the existence of minorities and different cultures in a country was a historical fact that a 'democratic society' had to tolerate and even protect and support according to the principles of international law.[78]

Similarly in *Stankov and the United Macedonian Organization Ilinden v Bulgaria*, the Court established that:

> The inhabitants of a region in a country are entitled to form associations in order to promote the region's special characteristics. The fact that a minority asserts a minority consciousness cannot in itself justify an interference with its rights under Article 11 of the Convention …[79]

Although states frequently impose strict requirements on registration of political parties, they cannot prohibit ethnic political parties or parties seeking to promote and protect minority identity. In this regard in *Ourani Toxo and ors v Greece*, the ECtHR noted that:

> mention of the consciousness of belonging to a minority and the preservation and development of a minority's culture cannot be said to constitute a threat to democratic society, even though it may provoke tensions … The emergence of tensions is one of the unavoidable consequence of pluralism, that is to say the free discussion of all political ideas.[80]

This view is also supported by the Lund Recommendations which note in Recommendation 8 that:

> The regulation of the formation and activity of political parties shall comply with the international law principle of freedom of association. This principle includes the freedom to establish political parties based on communal identities as well as those not identified exclusively with the interests of a specific community.

The ECtHR provides further guidance as to where the limits of democratic pluralism fall in this regard. In principle unless the party promotes the use of

---

[78] ECtHR, *Sidiroupoulos and ors v Greece*, Appl 26695/95, Judgment of 10 July 1998, para 41.
[79] ECtHR, *Stankov and the United Macedonian Organization Ilinden v Bulgaria*, Appl 29221/95 and 29225/95, Judgment of 2 October 2001, para 89.
[80] ECtHR, *Ouranio Toxo and ors v Greece*, Appl 74989/01, Judgment of 20 October 2005, para 40.

violence or acts undemocratically or incites to ethnic hatred[81] to achieve its objectives, the restrictions imposed by states would most likely be found to be illegitimate. The ECtHR in *United Communist Party of Turkey and ors v Turkey* established:

that there can be no justification for hindering a political group solely because it seeks to debate in public the situation of part of the State's population and to take part in the nation's political life in order to find, according to democratic rules, solutions capable of satisfying everyone concerned ...[82]

Even if a party had advocated secession this would not automatically disqualify it from registration. The fact that the political programme may call for recognition of a Kurdish nation and creation of a Kurdish-Turkish Federation in the *United Communist Party of Turkey and ors v Turkey* does not itself prove that it promoted terrorism. As was later noted in *Stankov and the United Macedonian Organization Ilinden* case:

An essential factor to be taken into consideration is the question whether there has been a call for the use of violence, an uprising or any other form of rejection of democratic principles.

The Court in this respect reiterated that:

the fact that a group of persons calls for autonomy or even requests secession of a part of the country's territory—thus demanding fundamental constitutional and territorial changes—cannot automatically justify prohibition of its assemblies.[83]

With respect to the application of Art 14 protecting against discrimination, in most cases the Court found a violation of the substantive article and did not proceed with examination of the discriminatory effects of the restrictions on minorities.

This was also the case in the very important application of *Gorzelik v Poland* relating to this issue. The state had refused to register the 'Union of People of Silesian Nationality' based on the argument that the name of the organization automatically made them eligible to benefit from special electoral rules for minorities (which according to Polish electoral law are freed from the 5 per cent threshold of votes cast to gain seats in the parliament). Its refusal was based additionally on the suspicion that the group wanted to register precisely for the purposes of gaining the electoral privileges which the Constitution and law restrict to purely 'national' minorities and the argument that such a privilege would derogate from the constitutional principle requiring equality before the

---

[81] See the obligations under Art 20 of the ICCPR and Art 4 of the ICERD.
[82] ECtHR, *United Communist Party of Turkey and ors v Turkey*, Appl 19392/92, Judgment of 30 January 1998, para 57
[83] See ECtHR, *Stankov and the United Macedonian Organization Ilinden v Bulgaria*, Appl 29221/95 and 29225/95, Judgment of 2 October 2001, paras 90, 97; and *Socialist Party and ors v Turkey*, Appl 20/1997/804/1007, Judgment of 25 May 1998, para 47.

law. The government had contested the existence of a Silesian nation according to its understanding of 'national minority' within the Constitution. The Court did not examine this issue[84] but pointed out that there is a lacuna in Polish law. It focused instead on whether the legitimate aim pursued by the Polish state was proportional to its refusal to register the association. The ECtHR in this respect asserted that given that the association was provided with an opportunity to remove the reference to an 'organisation of a national minority' from the memorandum of association, which would give them the automatic right to electoral privileges, the interference was not disproportionate. It held that:

> the refusal was not a comprehensive, unconditional one directed against the cultural and practical objectives that the association wished to pursue, but was based solely on the mention, in the memorandum of association, of a specific appellation for the association. It was designed to counteract a particular, albeit only potential, abuse by the association of its status as conferred by registration. It by no means amounted to a denial of the distinctive ethnic and cultural identity of Silesians or to a disregard for the association's primary aim, which was to 'awaken and strengthen the national consciousness of Silesians'.... On the contrary, in all their decisions the authorities consistently recognised the existence of a Silesian ethnic minority and their right to associate with one another to pursue common objectives.... All the various cultural and other activities that the association and its members wished to undertake could have been carried out had the association been willing to abandon the appellation set out in paragraph 30 of its memorandum of association.[85]

Importantly, from the perspective of the application of the principle of non-discrimination, the Court accepted the state's argument on rather loose grounds. No substantive evidence had been provided as to how the gaining of the privilege by the Silesian minority would actually abuse the democratic system and how the registration of an association would have adverse effects on the rights of other ethnic groups or the majority in Poland. The Court avoided dealing with this issue and simply accepted the legitimate aim of the government, which was in a better position to assess the domestic situation and historical and social circumstances. Comparing the situation of the relevant group with others lies at the heart of the matter when it comes to the examination of discrimination by

---

[84] See the comments in the Joint Concurring Opinion of Judges Costa and Zupančič, joined by judge Kovler that stated that in the ECtHR *Gorzelick and ors v Poland*, Appl 44158/98, Judgment of 17 February 2004, 8. Admittedly, we would not venture to contest the argument regarding the lack of a Silesian 'nation', or the Polish Court of Appeal's view that, in order to constitute a 'national' minority, a group must be linked to a majority from outside Poland, such as the Germans, Ukrainians, Lithuanians, or others. That is a political choice and a matter on which an international court could not dictate to a contracting state without infringing upon the subsidiarity principle. Besides which, even though the Permanent Court of International Justice delivered two famous judgments concerning Polish Upper Silesia in 1926 and 1928 (*Germany v Poland*, 25 May 1926, Series A no 7, and 26 April 1928, Series A no 15), questions relating to national minorities are complex and still somewhat vague.
[85] ECtHR, *Gorzelick and ors v Poland*, Appl 44158/98, Judgment of 17 February 2004, para 105.

the ECtHR. The Court in many cases, as already noted above, has held that the granting of privileges to certain individuals, groups or institutions is not a violation of the Convention if it is done in a non-discriminatory way. The question is whether the government's argument would have passed this test had it been examined by the Court. As noted by the applicants, conversely the refusal to be recognized as a minority with respect to election privileges may entail discrimination directed against the Silesian minority in comparison to other recognized groups.

B. Obligation to ensure equality in law and fact: the need to take positive action

As already noted in the introductory part of this chapter, the equality principle requires that states not only guarantee equality in law, but that they also guarantee equality in fact. Equality in fact implies taking account of the particular factual situation in which members of minority groups find themselves and taking the necessary measures to ensure that they may in fact benefit from equal enjoyment of their rights. These measures may include positive measures and special measures.[86]

In General Comment 18 on non-discrimination, the Human Rights Committee clearly articulated states' obligations to take positive measures:

> The Committee also wishes to point out that the principle of equality sometimes requires States parties to take affirmative action in order to diminish or eliminate conditions which cause or help to perpetuate discrimination prohibited by the Covenant. For example, in a State where the general conditions of a certain part of the population prevent or impair their enjoyment of human rights, the State should take specific action to correct those conditions. Such action may involve granting for a time to the part of the population concerned certain preferential treatment in specific matters as compared with the rest of the population. However, as long as such action is needed to correct discrimination in fact, it is a case of legitimate differentiation under the Covenant.[87]

Article 2.2 of the CERD imposes an explicit obligation on states to adopt positive measures in the social, economic, cultural and other fields when 'the circumstances so warrant'.[88] In line with Art 2.2 of CERD, General Recommendation

---

[86] It is sometimes difficult to distinguish positive from special measures, in particular when it comes to political participation of minorities. For these instances we use in the text the joint term 'positive action measures'. [87] HRC, General Comment 18, para 10.

[88] Article 2.2 provides that: 'States Parties shall, when the circumstances so warrant, take in the social, economic, cultural and other fields, special and concrete measures to ensure the adequate development and protection of certain racial groups or individuals belonging to them, for the purpose of guaranteeing them the full and equal enjoyment of human rights and fundamental freedoms. These measures shall in no case entail as a consequence the maintenance of unequal or separate rights for different racial groups after the objectives for which they were taken have been achieved.'

27 on discrimination against Roma[89] specifically discusses positive-action measures to guarantee equal enjoyment by Roma of the right to political participation.[90]

In the context of positive measures, General Recommendation 23 of the Committee on the Elimination of All Forms of Discrimination against Women specifically relates to 'political and public life'. Therein it describes in detail the role of positive measures in promoting women's equality in political and public life:

> While removal of de jure barriers is necessary, it is not sufficient. Failure to achieve full and equal participation of women can be unintentional and the result of outmoded practices and procedures which inadvertently promote men. Under article 4, the Convention encourages the use of temporary special measures in order to give full effect to articles 7 and 8. Where countries have developed effective temporary strategies in an attempt to achieve equality of participation, a wide range of measures has been implemented, including recruiting, financially assisting and training women candidates, amending electoral procedures, developing campaigns directed at equal participation, setting numerical goals and quotas and targeting women for appointment to public positions such as the judiciary or other professional groups that play an essential part in the everyday life of all societies. The formal removal of barriers and the introduction of temporary special measures to encourage the equal participation of both men and women in the public life of their societies are essential prerequisites to true equality in political life. In order, however, to overcome centuries of male domination of the public sphere, women also require the encouragement and support of all sectors of society to achieve full and effective participation, encouragement which must be led by States parties to the Convention, as well as by political parties and public officials. States parties have an obligation to ensure that temporary special measures are clearly designed to support the principle of equality and therefore comply with constitutional principles which guarantee equality to all citizens.[91]

---

[89] Committee on the Elimination of Racial Discrimination, General Recommendation 27: Discrimination against Roma, 57th session, 2000, paras 41–9.

[90] It recommends to states parties: to take the necessary steps, including special measures, to secure equal opportunities for the participation of Roma minorities or groups in all central and local governmental bodies (para 41); to develop modalities and structures of consultation with Roma political parties, associations and representatives, both at central and local levels, when considering issues and adopting decisions on matters of concern to Roma communities (para 42); to involve Roma communities and associations and their representatives at the earliest stages in the development and implementation of policies and programmes affecting them and to ensure sufficient transparency about such policies and programmes (para 43); to promote more awareness among members of Roma communities of the need for their more active participation in public and social life and in promoting their own interests, for instance the education of their children and their participation in professional training (para 44); to organize training programmes for Roma public officials and representatives, as well as for prospective candidates to such responsibilities, aimed at improving their political, policymaking and public administration skills (para 45); to take special measures to promote the employment of Roma in the public administration and institutions, as well as in private companies (para 28).

[91] The Committee on the Elimination of All Forms of Discrimination against Women, General Recommendation no 23, 16th session (1997), para 15.

As discussed above in section II.A, special measures may also be required in order to treat equally in fact members of minority groups who are in a disadvantaged position due to their factual differences with the majority or dominant groups in society. While this obligation clearly flows from the equality principle, and more specifically the need to treat differently what are different, states' obligations to take such measures have, to date, been given little attention in case law relating to non-discrimination and equality provisions. This is consistent with the relatively recent development of the second legal test of discrimination relating to the failure to treat in a different manner persons whose situations are significantly different (see discussion of *Thlimmenos* judgment above in III.A.1).

An important ruling relating to special measures was issued by the International Court of Justice (ICJ) in 1935 in the *Albanian Schools* case. Ruling on the possibility for 'racial, religious or linguistic' minority groups in Albania to continue to establish and maintain private schools, with the right to use their own language and exercise their religion therein, the ICJ stated that: 'there would be no true equality between a majority and a minority if the latter were deprived of its own institutions, and were consequently compelled to renounce that which constitutes the very essence of its being a minority'.[92] The Court emphasized that 'equality in fact may involve the necessity of different treatment in order to attain a result which establishes an equilibrium between different situations'.[93]

The European Committee of Social Rights made a noteworthy decision relating to special measures in 2003. Relying upon the *Thlimmenos* judgment, it found that Art E of the Revised European Social Charter (which provides that the rights of the Charter shall be recognized without discrimination)

> not only prohibits direct discrimination but also all forms of indirect discrimination. Such indirect discrimination may arise by failing to take due and positive account of all relevant differences or by failing to take adequate steps to ensure that the rights and collective advantages that are open to all are genuinely accessible by and to all.[94]

This decision opens the way for an obligation to carry out special measures to be read into basic non-discrimination clauses.

In the recent case of *DH v Czech Republic*, the ECtHR has acknowledged this possibility ruling that:

> Article 14 does not prohibit a member State from treating groups differently in order to correct 'factual inequalities' between them; indeed in certain circumstances a failure to attempt to correct inequality through different treatment may in itself give rise to a breach of the Article ('Case relating to certain aspects of the laws on the use of languages

---

[92] The International Court of Justice (ICJ), *the Advisory Opinion on Minority Schools in Albania*, (1935) Ser A/B no 64, 14. [93] Ibid, 17.
[94] European Committee of Social Rights, Collective, *Autisme-Europe v France*, Complaint no 13/2002, Decision on the merits of 4 November 2003, para 52.

in education in Belgium' v. Belgium (Merits), judgment of 23 July 1968, Series A no. 6, § 10; Thlimmenos v. Greece [GC], no. 34369/97, § 44, ECHR 2000-IV; and Stec and Others v. the United Kingdom [GC], no. 65731/01, § 51, ECHR 2006 ...).[95]

States' obligations to adopt special measures that take into account the specific needs and identities of minority groups is most clearly articulated in legal provisions and instruments specifically related to minority rights. For instance, Art 27 ICCPR stipulates that:

In those States in which ethnic, religious or linguistic minorities exist, persons belonging to such minorities shall not be denied the right, in community with the other members of their group, to enjoy their own culture, to profess and practice their own religion, or to use their own language.

In General Comment 23, the UN Human Rights Committee has made clear that this article also imposes positive obligations on states to:

protect the identity of a minority and the rights of its members to enjoy and develop their culture and language and to practise their religion, in community with the other members of the group.[96]

More specifically vis-à-vis special measures and political participation of minorities, the HRC in the case of the rights of indigenous communities held that:

the enjoyment of the right to one's own culture may require legal measures of protection by a state party and measures to ensure the effective participation of members of minority communities in decisions which affect them. In this case law under the Optional Protocol, the committee has emphasized that the acceptability of measures that affect or interfere with the culturally significant economic activities of a minority depends on whether the members of the minority in question have had the opportunity to participate in the decision-making process in relation to these measures and whether they will continue to benefit from their traditional economy.[97]

Demands for positive and special measures are present inter alia in Arts 1 and 4 of the UN Declaration on Declaration on the Rights of Persons Belonging to National or Ethnic, Religious, and Linguistic Minorities,[98] as well as in paras 31

---

[95] ECtHR, *DH v Czech Republic*, Appl 57325/00, Judgment of 13 November 2007, para 175.

[96] HRC, General Comment no 23: Art 27 (Rights of Minorities), 50th Session (1994), para 6.2. See also Art 5(1) of the FCNM, which places an obligation upon states parties to 'undertake to promote the conditions necessary for persons belonging to national minorities to maintain and develop their culture, and to preserve the essential elements of their identity, namely their religion, language, traditions and cultural heritage'. See also Art 4.2 of the UDHR which provides that: 'States shall take measures to create favourable conditions to enable persons belonging to minorities to express their characteristics and to develop their culture, language, religion, traditions and customs, except where specific practices are in violation of national law and contrary to international standards.'

[97] HRC, *Apirana Mahuika and ors v New Zealand*, Comm no 547/1993, Views of 27 October 2000, para 9.6.

[98] See, *inter alia*, Art 4 of the UN Declaration on Declaration on the Rights of Persons Belonging to National or Ethnic, Religious, and Linguistic Minorities: 4(1) States shall take measures where required to ensure that persons belonging to minorities may exercise fully and

and 33 of the Copenhagen Document.[99] However, when it comes to minority rights instruments, positive action for benefiting minorities is most clearly established in the legally binding FCNM. Art 4 of the FCNM calls for promotion of full and effective equality for persons belonging to national minorities in all areas of life. This implies the right to equal protection of the law and before the law, and the right to be protected against all forms of discrimination based on belonging to national minority. More specifically Art 4(2) of the FCNM expressly commits states:

> to undertake to adopt, where necessary, adequate measures in order to promote, in all areas of economic, social, political and cultural life, full and effective equality between persons belonging to a national minority and those belonging to the majority. In this respect, they shall take due account of the specific conditions of the persons belonging to national minorities.

As already noted in the FCNM Commentary on the Effective Participation of Persons Belonging to National Minorities in Cultural, Social, and Economic life and Public Affairs:

> full and effective equality also implies the need of the authorities to take specific measures in order to overcome past or structural inequalities and to ensure that persons belonging both to national minorities and to majority have equal opportunities in various fields.[100]

The state practice shows that many countries frequently implement positive action measures for minorities ensuring their adequate electoral representation through altering the election system, adjusting an electoral formula or securing specific participation of minorities in the process of decision-making, establishing cultural or functional autonomy and special representation in local self-government. What is important is that such political participation must be 'effective'. This would suggest a duty to create conditions that would provide a level playing field for minorities by creating equal opportunities for such participation but possibly also specific measures aimed at equality of results.[101]

---

effectively all their human rights and fundamental freedoms without any discrimination and in full equality before the law. (2) States shall take measures to create favourable conditions to enable persons belonging to minorities to express their characteristics and to develop their culture, language, religion, traditions and customs, except where specific practices are in violation of national law and contrary to international standards. (5) States should consider appropriate measures so that persons belonging to minorities may participate fully in the economic progress and development in their country.

[99] See, inter alia, para 31 of Copenhagen Document which stipulates: 'The Participating States will adopt, where necessary, special measures for the purpose of ensuring to persons belonging to national minorities full equality with the other citizens in the exercise and enjoyment of human rights and freedoms.'

[100] The FCNM Commentary on the Effective Participation of Persons Belonging to National Minorities in Cultural, Social, and Economic life and Public Affairs, adopted on 27 February 2008, ACFC/31DOC(2008)001, para 14.

[101] In order to obtain the substantive or real equality, such measures focus on the equality of outcome, often reached by various quota systems.

The positive measures foreseen in the FCNM are not necessarily time-limited; as the Explanatory Report to the FCNM notes, these measures normally 'do not extend, in time or in scope, beyond what is necessary in order to achieve the aim of full and effective equality'. The positive measures are temporary as they are supposed to serve until the discriminatory patterns have been eliminated. However, as noted by Gudmundur Alfredsson in his commentary on Art 4 of the FCNM, these measures may need to be in place in nation states for a long time in order to achieve equal treatment and equal opportunities in relation to a position of the dominant majority.[102]

With respect to special measures Art 5 implies an obligation for states parties to:

promote the conditions necessary for persons belonging to national minorities to maintain and develop their culture and to preserve the essential elements of their identity, namely their religion, language, traditions and cultural heritage, in order to guarantee effectively their right to identity.

This article would require special measures for minority participation regarding the facilitation of the above-mentioned conditions.

1. Positive Action Measures and Right to Political Participation

The following section will examine in greater detail the extent to which positive and special measures have been accepted as obligations under general human rights standards with respect to the application of the equality principle and the right to political participation vis-à-vis national minorities.

It should be stated at the outset that the supervisory mechanisms have taken a rather reluctant and cautious approach towards enforcing state duties to facilitate special minority representation or participation in decision-making under these general standards. This is largely due to the position adopted by the supervisory bodies of the general human rights standards which involves granting a wide margin of appreciation to states in determining their electoral system and the composition of the legislative bodies. This position is based on the view that states are better placed to reflect on their particular historical and political factors.[103]

However, the ECtHR, itself referring to the importance of pluralism as one of the hallmarks of a 'democratic society', has underlined the importance of special measures as a building block of pluralism. In the relatively recent case of *Gorzelick v Poland*, concerning participation in the system of special minority

---

[102] See G Alfredsson, 'Article 4' in M Weller (ed), *The Rights of Minorities* (n 26 above), 149.
[103] See ECtHR, *Mathieu-Mohin and Clerfyat v Belgium*, Appl 9267/81, Judgment of 2 March 1987, para 52; also ECtHR *Podkolzina v Latvia*, Appl 46726/99, Judgment of 9 April 2002, Reports 2002–II, para 33; and ECtHR *Aziz v Cyprus*, Appl 69949/01, Judgment of 22 June 2004, para 28.

electoral representation, the ECtHR supported the concept of special measures needed for adequate minority protection stating:

> although individual interests must on occasion be subordinated to those of a group, democracy does not simply mean that views of the majority must always prevail: a balance must be achieved which ensures the fair and proper treatment of minorities and avoids any abuse of a dominant position …[104]

This has been even more clearly demonstrated by the direct reference by the ECtHR to the FCNM. The Court recognized:

> that, as laid down in the Preamble to the Council of Europe's Framework Convention, 'a pluralist and genuinely democratic society should not only respect the ethnic, cultural, linguistic and religious identity of each person belonging to a national minority, but also create appropriate conditions enabling them to express, preserve and develop this identity'.[105]

In addition to special measures being recognized as an important element of a pluralist society, in *Lindsay and ors v United Kingdom* the ECtHR expressly accepts the collective dimension of the protection of minorities. It also accepts that the application of the principle of substantive equality may imply differential treatment within the electoral system. This key judgment concerned an exception granted to Northern Ireland regarding the electoral law, involving the introduction in Northern Ireland of an election system different from the 'first past the post'[106] system that is applied generally across the United Kingdom.' The system introduced involved a proportional voting system for elections to the legislature[107] aimed at increasing the chances of gaining seats for communities that would not be a majority in any electoral district. The applicants alleged that using a different electoral system in Northern Ireland as compared with the rest of the United Kingdom interferes with the right of the majority, whose vote would be treated differently in the remaining area of the United Kingdom. They therefore claimed that this system violated their rights under Art 3 of Protocol 1 of the ECHR, in particular the condition that elections shall ensure the free expression of the opinion of the people. In this case, the European Commission strongly confirmed the principle of substantive equality, stating—contrary to the applicant's claim—that taking into account a minority position actually provides for better expression of the free opinion of people.

---

[104] ECtHR, *Gorzelik and ors v Poland*, Appl 44158/98, Judgment of 17 February 2004, para 90. [105] Ibid, para 93
[106] 'First past the post' is the electoral system in which the person winning the most votes in a constituency is elected. It is also known as simple plurality electoral system, referred to as a majoritarian or as the simple majority system, when the candidate must win the majority. In practice, however, it means winning plurality (ie, the most votes). The system is thought to penalize small parties both in the aggregation of votes into seats and electorate voting tactically large parties.
[107] The proportional voting system delivers highly proportional election results as the number of votes won are proportional to the number of seats gained. This system benefits minorities and dispersed communities, likely ensuring representation of even small minorities.

Analysis: Specific Issues 135

This is one of the foundational statements of the need for differential treatment of minorities with respect to the right to political participation, given the specific position of the minorities. It is therefore worth reproducing the full finding of the Commission on this point:

> A simple proportional representation will lead to the minority being represented in situations where people vote generally on ethnic or religious lines and one group is in a clear minority through all electoral districts. Where such a situation exists only in a specific region of a country—as it does in Northern Ireland—the Commission cannot find that the application of a system, more favourable to the minority in this part of the country, is not in line with the condition that the people should be able to express its opinion freely. Rather on the contrary, a system taking into account the specific situation as to majority and minority existing in Northern Ireland must be seen as making it easier for the people to express its opinion freely...[108]

The decisions of the supervisory bodies under general human rights standards relating to the right to political participation and the principle of non-discrimination does not go so far as to impose any positive obligations upon states to take particular special measures in order to enhance minority political participation. It does, however, recognize special measures as a means of achieving substantive equality. It is also noteworthy that such measures are viewed as legitimate to the extent that they serve a legitimate aim and are proportionate.

As in other situations, the proportionality principle is key to determining whether positive and special measures aimed at furthering the enjoyment of the right to political participation by members of minority groups conform to the principle of non-discrimination. Both positive and special measures have legitimate aims in that they seek to promote equality and are often even essential to bringing about equality for discriminated and/or minority groups. Thus, as long as the measures taken are proportionate to the goal they seek to achieve, they will not be discriminatory. This implies that positive measures should only be continued until such time as the objectives for which they were developed have been achieved.[109] In the case of special measures there is no time limitation—they may be continued as long as they are needed to ensure de facto equality, which means they may well be permanent.

This brings us to the limits of the application of the principle of substantive equality by the supervisory bodies. Although these bodies have in general shown

---

[108] EcommHR, *Lindsay and ors v United Kingdom*, Appl 8364/78, Decision of 8 March 1979, para IX. 1.

[109] Art 1.4 of CERD makes clear that positive measures are not discrimination as long as they respect the proportionality principle. It provides that: 'Special measures taken for the sole purpose of securing adequate advancement of certain racial or ethnic groups or individuals requiring such protection as may be necessary in order to ensure such groups or individuals equal enjoyment or exercise of human rights and fundamental freedoms shall not be deemed racial discrimination, provided, however, that such measures do not, as a consequence, lead to the maintenance of separate rights for different racial groups and that they shall not be continued after the objectives for which they were taken have been achieved.'

rather divergent attitudes towards the acceptance of positive and special measures, it may nonetheless be asserted, based on their decisions, that such measures are permissible if they meet the 'reasonable and objective' test. This means that such measures should serve a legitimate aim and be proportionate to that aim. This approach has been confirmed by the Commission in the *Lindsay* case wherein it considered whether differential treatment aimed at protecting minorities in the electoral system amounted to discrimination of the individuals seeking redress under Art 14 combined with Art 3 of Protocol 1 of the ECHR. It concluded that:

the United Kingdom has specific reasons for applying a different electoral system in one part of the country, namely the protection of the rights of a minority. The electoral system complained of is, therefore, based on reasonable and objective criteria which justify the differentiation applied. Moreover it does not appear that there is no reasonable relationship of proportionality between the means employed and the aim sought to be realised.[110]

In a detailed discussion of positive action under international law, Kevin Kitching notes that the HRC has:

supported preferential treatment for disadvantaged groups applying for educational, public service, or other positions. It has upheld preferential treatment policies even when other individuals have felt disadvantaged or discriminated by them. For example, in *Stalla Costa v Uruguay* (No. 198/1995, ICCPR) the applicant complained that preference was given to certain public officials in getting admitted to the public service. Those officials had previously been unfairly dismissed on ideological, political or trade-union grounds. The HRC observed that in light of previous discrimination against these individuals, the alleged discrimination was found to be permissible affirmative action.

He further notes that:

the HRC has approved the use of quotas in several of its country reports. For example, in its concluding observations on India, it approved a constitutional amendment in India that reserves one third of seats in elected local bodies for women. It also approved the practice of reserving elected positions for members of certain tribes and castes (see UN Doc. CCPR/C/79/Add.81, paragraph 10).[111]

---

[110] ECommHR, *Lindsay and ors v United Kingdom*, Appl 8364/78, Decision of 8 March 1979, para III and IV.2.

[111] Kitching, *Non-discrimination in International Law* (n 40 above), 97. See also HRC findings in *Guido Jacobs v Belgium*, Communication no 943/2000, Views of 7 July 2004, CCPR/C/81/D/943/2000. The *Jacobs* case dealt with a Belgian quota system for the appointment of High Council of Justice members to ensure an adequate number of elected candidates of each sex. The HRC found this to be a permissible positive measure noting that 'a reasonable proportionality is maintained between the purpose of the gender requirement, namely to promote equality between men and women in consultative bodies; the means applied and its modalities, as described above; and one of the principal aims of the law, which is to establish a High Council made up of qualified individuals' (para 9.5).

2. Proportionality Principle and the Legality of Positive Action Measures

We will now further examine the limits of full end effective equality regarding enhanced minority participation. More specifically, we will examine how far positive action measures have been accepted with respect to different elements of the right to political participation, such as equal suffrage, the equal right to stand for elections, the conduct of public affairs, and decision-making in legislative and executive bodies. These issues have been examined to some extent in the work of the European Commission for Democracy through Law (Venice Commission).[112] In particular, the issue of positive action measures regarding the electoral system has been addressed in a number of its country opinions as well as specific thematic reports such as the Report on Electoral Rules and Affirmative Action for National Minorities' Participation in Decision-Making Processes in European Countries.[113]

More specifically the Commission examined the compatibility of special rules for electoral representation, such as reserved minority seats, lower thresholds for minority political parties or dual vote, with the principle of *equal suffrage*. There are two main aspects of this principle: (1) equal voting right, and (2) equal voting power. Regarding the first aspect, each voter has one vote. If the electoral system provides persons with more than one vote, each voter should then have the same number of votes. When it comes to equal voting power, this means that seats should be evenly distributed between the constituencies. This is usually done via an electoral system formula that converts votes into seats. However, in practice different systems are often used that lead to different outcomes in the distribution of seats and there is no strict requirement that the votes have equal weight.[114]

The Commission noted that there are also other aspects of equal suffrage such as equality of opportunity. This entails a neutral attitude by the state authorities to candidates and parties with regard to an election campaign, coverage in media and public funding of parties and campaigns. It is noteworthy that when it comes to equal suffrage and equality of opportunity the Commission's Code of Good Practice in Electoral Matters refers to strict and proportional equality.

---

[112] The European Commission for Democracy through Law, better known as the Venice Commission, is the Council of Europe's advisory body on constitutional matters. Established in 1990, the Commission has played a leading role in the adoption of constitutions that conform to the standards of Europe's constitutional heritage. For more on its mandate and membership see <http://www.venice.coe.int/site/main/Presentation_E.asp> (accessed 31 July 2009).

[113] European Commission for Democracy through Law (Venice Commission), Report on Electoral Rules and Affirmative Action for National Minorities' Participation in Decision-Making Process in European Countries (Study no 307/2004 adopted on 15 March 2004) CDL-AD(2005) 009.

[114] See EcommHR, *Silvus Magnago and Südtiroler Volkspartei v Italy*, Appl 25035/94, Decision of 15 April 1996. The Commission noted: 'What must be guaranteed is the principle of equality of treatment of all citizens; without however that it follows that all votes must necessarily have equal weight as regards the outcome of the election.'

It explains that if strict equality is applied 'political parties are treated on an equal footing irrespective of their current parliamentary strength or support among the electorate'.[115] However, in electoral matters proportional equality is accepted when political parties are treated according to the results achieved in the elections. This applies in particular to their treatment regarding radio and television air time and distribution of public funding. More importantly from the perspective of our specific subject of examination, among the aspects of equal suffrage the Code also includes application of the equality principle vis-à-vis national minorities. Regarding the special measures for national minorities it concludes that:

> b. Special rules guaranteeing national minorities reserved seats or providing for exceptions to the normal seat allocation criteria for parties representing national minorities (for instance, exemption from a quorum requirement) do not in principle run counter to equal suffrage.[116]

The Venice Commission stressed that such special rules may impact especially on the two aspects of equal suffrage mentioned above: equal voting rights and equal voting power. Following the case law of the ECtHR, the Venice Commission affirmed that:

> states may deviate from the principle of equal suffrage by adapting their electoral systems in the narrow sense (way of translating votes into seats) in a legitimate fashion and adopting special systems in respect of minorities if their purpose is lawful and necessary, and the method chosen is proportionate to the outcome sought.[117]

Such differences would be disproportionate if the voting inequalities were significant. In this respect, the Venice Commission asserted that positive action measures would not violate the principle of equality if and as far as they are necessary to cover the gaps and difficulties which hamper the participation of minorities in public life.[118] Of course, as will be shown below, their legitimacy must always be considered within the context of the concrete and particular situation of a country.

The Venice Commission, similar to the ECtHR, confirmed states' large margin of appreciation by stating that:

> the states are allowed to adopt solutions which are coherent with their constitutional systems, and they can introduce special exceptions to these systems according to the principles of rationality and proportionality. Therefore, votes need not necessarily have equal weight as regards the outcome of the election.[119]

---

[115] European Commission for Democracy through Law (Venice Commission), Code of Good Practice in Electoral Matters, Opinion no 190/2002, adopted on 23 May 2003, CDL-AD(2002) 023rev, para 2.3.   [116] Ibid, para 2.4.
[117] European Commission for Democracy through Law (Venice Commission), The Protection of National Minorities and Elections (Study no 387/2006, adopted on 16 May 2008), CDL-EL (2008)002rev*, para 48.   [118] Ibid, para 47
[119] Ibid, para 53.

Specific debate had arisen around the issue of a dual vote for minorities,[120] a measure that would mean departure from the principle of one person—one vote. This issue has been raised with the Venice Commission by the OSCE High Commissioner on National Minorities, who in his comments regarding the double vote asserted that: '[s]tates enjoy less flexibility in altering the "one person—one vote" principle, than in designing the methods that translate votes into seats of parliament'.[121] The question was posed whether such an exception (to the principle of one person—one vote) is completely inadmissible. The argument was raised that the departure from equal voting right affects the essence of the right and that such an exemption must be really rare. It could only be justified by the impossibility of reaching the result through other available means, such as measures concerning conversion of votes into seats. The Venice Commission has rejected the argument that such a measure is totally inadmissible. It noted that '[s]uch an absolute character (of the equal voting right), however, would be a peculiarity in electoral or human rights law, if not in law in general'.[122] The second argument for inadmissibility, based on the assumption that other measures allowing for minority representation were always at hand, was examined in detail by two members of the Commission with very diverse outcomes and views. Ms Durrieu concluded that in principle the exemption to

---

[120] The Report of European Commission for Democracy through Law (Venice Commission) on Dual Voting for Persons belonging to National Minorities, Study no 387/2006, adopted 16 June 2008, CDL-AD(2008)013, mentions the following examples of dual vote: '10. Slovenia is currently the only country that grants dual voting rights to members of national minorities: two representatives of the Italian and Hungarian minorities elected on special lists have full status as members of parliament. In 1998, the Slovenian constitutional court found that this arrangement was compatible with the principle of equality because it was enshrined in bilateral treaties with Italy and Hungary. Granting members of minorities dual voting rights would be disproportionate if there was too much deviation from the one person one vote principle. 11. In Cyprus, further to their general right to vote as members of the Greek community, the members of each of the Maronite, Armenian and Latin religious groups elect a deputy to the House of Representatives, with a consultative status. Each representative is entitled to submit the views of his or her group on any matter relating to such group or to make necessary representations on such matters relating to his or her group before any organ or committee of the House of Representatives or any organ or authority of the Republic, with regard to the matters which fell within the competence of the Greek Communal Chamber before this Chamber was abolished and its legislative functions were undertaken by the House of Representatives in 1965.12. Article 15 of the Croatian Constitution grants equal rights to members of all national minorities, stipulating that the law might give them the right—besides the general voting right—to elect their representatives to the Croatian Sabor (parliament), but such a dual voting was not introduced up to now. Articles 15 and 16 of the Law on elections of parliamentarians to Sabor (2003) stipulate that the national minorities have 8 seats in the Sabor, elected by a specific electorate covering the whole territory of Croatia. The Serbian national minority votes for three representatives; the Italian and Hungarian ones for 1 each; while the Czech and Slovak minorities elect together one representative; the Austrian, Bulgarian, German, Polish, Roma, Romanian, Rusinian, Russian, Turkish, Ukrainian, Valachian and Jewish minorities elect together one representative, and so do the members of the Albanian, Bosniak, Montenegrin, Macedonian and Slovene minorities.' [121] Ibid, para 56.
[122] European Commission for Democracy through Law (Venice Commission), The Protection of National Minorities and Elections, Study no 387/2006, adopted on 16 May 2008, CDL-EL (2008)002rev*, para 53.

equal voting rights was inadmissible and could be justified only in very exceptional circumstances for minorities which were in a really vulnerable position, and then only for a brief transition period in which no special adaptation mechanism would be satisfactory. Prof Bartole, on the other hand, considered that the mere fact that other measures were at hand did not justify concluding in the abstract that a dual vote was inadmissible; concrete historical circumstances could justify such an exemption. In particular he considered that:

> the dual voting system for persons belonging to national minorities can reconcile the requirement of providing for a reserved representation of a minority, especially if a State comes from a totalitarian experience, with the necessity of favouring the integration of the minority in the national political life. It is an example of reverse discrimination which may be justified by the history of a country, especially if it is provided for as a temporary arrangement until the effects of the repression and of the totalitarian regime are satisfactorily (even if only partially) cancelled. It may be the only system to ensure, on the one side, that the minority has the guarantee of being represented in public affairs, and, on the other side, that the persons belonging to the national minorities are allowed, on an equal basis, to take part in the national political debate. Admittedly, other measures to ensure participation of minorities in public life exist which do not impinge, or impinge less, on other voters' right to equal suffrage. However, the mere fact that other measures than dual vote exist, and indeed have been adopted by other States, does not call for the conclusion in abstracto that the dual vote is unacceptable as such. Dual vote could only be found inadmissible in concreto that is if in a particular case it failed to pass the proportionality test.[123]

The authors find the arguments of Prof Bartole more persuasive. It is true that in order to balance differing public interests and human rights, authorities should look for means that would be the least intrusive. However, the simple possibility of implementing measures other than a dual vote cannot demonstrate that such measures will have the impact required to meet the objective of integrating minorities in the national political life in the specific conditions of a country.

It is noteworthy that the Commission stressed in its final remarks that such specific measures involving exemptions to electoral rules, in particular with regard to a dual vote, should be of a transitional nature.[124] In this regard the Commission set specific conditions as to when measures such as dual voting would be acceptable:

The Commission concludes that dual voting is an exceptional measure, which has to be within the framework of the Constitution, and may be admitted if it respects the

---

[123] Ibid, para 55.
[124] The Report of European Commission for Democracy through Law (Venice Commission) on Dual Voting for Persons belonging to National Minorities, Study no 387/2006, adopted 16 June 2008, CDL-AD(2008)013, in para 63 concludes that: 'If after a certain time this aim can be pursued by other less restrictive measures which do not infringe upon equal voting rights, the system of dual voting is no longer justified.'

principle of proportionality under its various aspects. This implies that it can only be justified if:

- it is impossible to reach the aim pursued through other less restrictive measures which do not infringe upon equal voting rights;
- it has a transitional character;
- it concerns only a small minority.[125]

Of course, as already stressed above, the principle of proportionality must be reflected in each concrete situation, assessing the impact of foreseen measures on securing the necessary representation and participation of minorities in political life and decision-making.

It is also noteworthy that the Venice Commission study considered the issue of positive action measures in electoral processes in light of the integration of minorities into society. In this context, it expressed the view that the long-term interests and needs of minorities, as well as of society, are better served through representation under ordinary electoral systems which guarantees equal rights to citizens, irrespective of their initial national or ethnic affiliation. Nonetheless, it also confirmed that positive action measures, such as exceptions to rules on the threshold, reserved seats and over representation of districts in which the minority is in a majority, are sometimes needed to ensure proper representation of minorities.

Another issue concerning the limits of application of special electoral rules concerns reserved seats in the power-sharing systems. Power-sharing arrangements involve broad-based governing coalitions of a society's significant groups in a political system that provides influence to legitimate representatives of minority groups. Such arrangements often serve to alleviate tensions in a divided society by offering an alternative to simple majoritarian governance in which minority ethnic groups may be permanently excluded from power.[126] The issue under consideration is whether reserving seats for representatives of a limited number of ethnic groups, with the possible exclusion of others, is compatible with the principle of non-discrimination in connection with the right to stand for office. Such a situation arose in connection with the provisions of the Constitution of Bosnia and Herzegovina (BiH) and the corresponding regulations in the country's Electoral Code, which prevent persons not belonging to one of the three constituent peoples from standing for election to the presidency and the House of Peoples of the Parliamentary Assembly of Bosnia and

---

[125] Ibid, para 71.
[126] Power-sharing provisions refer to a more general concept of consociational democracy that is characterized by multiparty cabinets and systems; reserving legislative or executive seats for minority parties; proportional representation; proportionality in the distribution of civil service positions, public funds, and legislative seats; political decentralization; a minority veto on vital issues; and written constitutions that recognize certain non-dominant group rights.

Herzegovina.[127] The issue is now pending before the ECtHR. The applicants, Mr Sejdić and Mr Finci, allege that these electoral rules violate their rights under Art 14 of the European Convention on Human Rights, read in conjunction with Art 3 of Protocol 1 and Art 1 of Protocol 12 to the ECHR.[128] The issue has already been examined by the Venice Commission in its Opinion on the constitutional situation in Bosnia and Herzegovina and the powers of the High Representative. The Venice Commission confirmed in this concrete case that power-sharing norms that may be problematic from the point of view of non-discrimination of other members of a society may be legitimate to the extent that they are necessary to achieve peace and stability, as in BiH. However, it called for reconsideration of the system to reflect the positive developments of the country after its entry into the Council of Europe and the adoption of its standards.[129] In its recent *Amicus Curiae Brief* for the ECtHR concerning the abovementioned applications, the Venice Commission scrutinized the issue in greater depth. Although it confirmed that such a system may satisfy a legitimate aim, it did not find it justifiable to exclude others from political dialogue and

---

[127] The Federation of BiH, which was created in April 1994 in order to stop the war between Muslims/Bosniaks and Croats, as well as the political entity Republika Srpska were recognized as entities of BiH. The BiH Constitution, result of the Dayton peace agreement introduced a system of ethnic representation and veto powers on behalf of the three constituent peoples (Bosniaks, Croats, and Serbs). The consociational system introduced the special ethnic representation for the three constituent peoples in the second chamber, the House of Peoples in the bi-cameral parliamentary system, and the three-member presidency of BiH. The House of Peoples is composed of five Bosniaks, five Croats and five Serbs to be selected by the respective Bosniak and Croat caucuses in the House of Peoples of the Federation Parliament, whereas the Serb delegates have to be selected by the National Assembly of Republika Srpska. The presidency is composed of one Bosniak and one Croat to be directly elected from the territory of the Federation of BiH, and one Serb to be directly elected from the territory of Republika Srpska.

[128] ECtHR, *Mr Sejdić and Mr Finci v Bosnia and Herzegovina*, Appl 27996/06 and 34836/06.

[129] European Commission for Democracy through Law (Venice Commission), Opinion on the constitutional situation in Bosnia and Herzegovina and the powers of the High Representative, adopted on 11 March 2005, CDL-AD(2005)004. The Commission asserted that: '74. In the present case, the distribution of posts in the State organs between the constituent peoples was a central element of the Dayton Agreement making peace in Bosnia and Herzegovina possible. In such a context, it is difficult to deny legitimacy to norms that may be problematic from the point of view of non-discrimination but necessary to achieve peace and stability and to avoid further loss of human lives. The inclusion of such rules in the text of the Constitution [of Bosnia and Herzegovina] at that time therefore does not deserve criticism, even though they run counter to the general thrust of the Constitution aiming at preventing discrimination. 75. This justification has to be considered, however, in the light of developments in Bosnia and Herzegovina since the entry into force of the Constitution. Bosnia and Herzegovina has become a member of the Council of Europe and the country has therefore to be assessed according to the yardstick of common European standards. It has now ratified the [European Convention on Human Rights] and Protocol no 12 [thereto]. As set forth above, the situation in Bosnia and Herzegovina has evolved in a positive sense but there remain circumstances requiring a political system that is not a simple reflection of majority rule but which guarantees a distribution of power and positions among ethnic groups. It therefore remains legitimate to try to design electoral rules ensuring appropriate representation for various groups. 76. This can, however, be achieved without entering into conflict with international standards ...'

from certain parts of the political decision-making process on a permanent basis. It stated that:

> Even if special constitutional arrangements are still deemed necessary for the inter-action between the constituent peoples, this does not justify the complete exclusion of third persons. On the contrary, the inclusion of third persons might help to overcome the stalemate in Bosnia-Herzegovina. The long time that has elapsed since the elaboration of the Dayton Peace Treaty proves that the solution found in 1995 does not really help to overcome the problems in Bosnia-Herzegovina. It is not proportionate to nullify rights guaranteed in the Convention in order to preserve a constitutional structure that has not helped to acquire the desired results within a period of about 13 years.[130]

In conclusion, the practice of the international bodies provides a wide margin of appreciation to states in designing their electoral systems, taking into account differences in historical development, cultural diversity, and political thought. However, this does not allow states to exclude some persons or groups of persons from participating in the political life of the country, particularly as concerns the choice of the legislature.[131] If exemptions are made that affect the very essence of the right, they must be imposed in pursuit of a legitimate aim and the means employed must not be disproportionate. It remains to be seen whether the ECtHR will find continuation of the election rules excluding 'Others' from standing for the presidency and the House of Peoples of the Parliamentary Assembly of Bosnia and Herzegovina to be proportionate in the current circumstances of the country. The issue is particularly uncertain given that it gives a wide margin of appreciation to states, considering them to be in better position to assess their historical and political circumstances.

C. Self-governance and non-discrimination

Effective participation of national minorities can be facilitated in a number of ways as already described in the section on the political participation of minorities above. The minority specific standards, including Art 15 of the FCNM, require states to create the conditions necessary for the effective participation of national minorities in public affairs in general as well as more specifically 'in matters affecting the communities'. Besides various arrangements to ensure minority input—such as through electoral representation or establishment of consultative mechanisms and processes—the practices of some states have shown that participation in decision-making about minority issues is well served by self-governing arrangements. Particular forms include cultural or personal autonomy arrangements, devolution of certain powers to local self-government, or territorial

---

[130] European Commission for Democracy through Law (Venice Commission), *Amicus Curiae Brief in the case of Sejdić and Finci v Bosnia and Herzegovina*, Appl 27996/06 and 34836/06, Opinion no 483/2008 adopted on 22 October 2008, CDL-AD(2008)027, para 33.
[131] ECtHR, *Aziz v Cyprus*, Appl 69949/01, Judgment of 22 June 2004, para 28.

autonomy arrangements. In this regard, the Lund Recommendations explain that 'the term of self-governance implies a measure of control by a community over matters affecting it'.[132]

Although the right to autonomy has not been confirmed by international legal standards, local minority self-governance and autonomous regimes have been cautiously referred to in the political commitments of the OSCE Copenhagen Document and the UN Declaration on Minorities. The Copenhagen Document emphasizes that protection and promotion of the ethnic, cultural, linguistic, and religious identity of national minorities has in state practice also been achieved through appropriate local or autonomous administrations corresponding to the specific historical and territorial circumstances of such minorities.[133] The UN Declaration on Minorities refers to the right of persons belonging to minorities 'to participate effectively in decisions on the national and, where appropriate, regional level concerning the minority to which they belong or the regions in which they live'.[134] Support for devolution of powers and local self-government is also contained in the general principle of subsidiarity which states that decisions shall be taken by those authorities closest to those who are affected by them.[135]

The issue of participation of national minorities through local self-government is discussed in great detail elsewhere in this book.[136] In the context of this chapter, we will now examine the issue of protection of the rights of others and non-discrimination among the members of a community in the implementation of minority self-governing regimes. In this regard the Lund Recommendations in their 'General Principles' expressly note that:

3) When specific institutions are established to ensure effective participation of minorities in public life, which can include exercise of authority or responsibility by such institutions, they must respect the human rights of all those affected.

This principle is rooted in the provisions of the Copenhagen Document which in para 33 requires that any positive action measures 'be in conformity with the principles of equality and non-discrimination with respect to other citizens of the participating State concerned'. In a more general way, the Framework Convention places an obligation on persons belonging to national minorities to respect 'the national legislation and the rights of others, in particular those of persons belonging to the majority or to other national minorities', in the exercise

---

[132] Explanatory note to the Lund Recommendations, Recs 14.
[133] At para 35, Copenhagen Document.   [134] Art 2.3.
[135] This principle has been reiterated in the European Charter of Local Self-government, Art 4 (3) states: 'Public responsibilities shall generally be exercised, in preference, by those authorities which are closest to the citizen. Allocation of responsibility to another authority should weigh up the extent and nature of the task and requirements of efficiency and economy.'
[136] See, in particular, the chapters by Yash Ghai, (Chapter 21), and Bill Bowring (Chapter 23) in this volume.

of rights guaranteed in the Convention.[137] With respect specifically to the transfer of authority in the context of territorial self-government and functional or cultural autonomy, the Lund Recommendations reiterate these principles. Recommendation 16 stipulates that 'Institutions of self-governance ... must be based on democratic principles to ensure that they genuinely reflect the views of the affected population.' Among other things, the fulfilment of this condition requires the local authority in the autonomous territory to secure the democratic rights to participate of members of groups that find themselves in the position of a minority in the autonomous territory, but who may be part of the majority in the state as a whole.[138]

Regarding the protection of the rights of all persons under the administrative authority of local self-government or autonomy, Recommendation 21 of the Lund Recommendations stresses that 'Local, regional and autonomous authorities must respect and ensure the human rights of all persons, including the rights of any minorities within their jurisdiction.'

Besides protecting and securing the rights of groups who may be a majority within the state as whole but who find themselves in a minority position within the self-governing unit, this principle also applies to 'minorities within minorities' situations. Its scope includes protection against discrimination among the members of the minority community and respect for the human rights of women and their equal treatment. Regarding prohibition of gender discrimination in relation to protection of minority rights the HRC General Comment 28 on Equality of rights between men and women (Art 3) indicates that:

the rights which persons belonging to minorities enjoy under Article 27 of the Covenant in respect of their language, culture and religion do not authorize any State, group or person to violate rights to equal enjoyment by women of any Covenant rights, including the rights to equal protection of law.[139]

The issue of exclusion from membership of a group and denial of the enjoyment of specific rights to certain members of a minority community has been dealt with by the Human Rights Committee. It addressed such issues in cases concerning indigenous people that enjoy specific governing regimes and autonomy over their land and way of life. The most significant in this respect is the case of *Sandra Lovelace*, a Malliseet Indian woman, who lost her status as a member of

---

[137] See Art 20 of the FCNM.
[138] Explanatory note to the Lund Recommendations with regard to Recs 21 notes: 'Where powers may be devolved on a territorial basis to improve effective participation of minorities, these powers must be exercised with due account for the minorities with these jurisdictions. Administrative and executive authorities must be accountable to the whole population of the territory.' This follows from paragraph 5.2 of the Copenhagen Document which commits OSCE Participating States to assure at all levels and for all persons 'a form of government that is representative in character, in which the executive is accountable to the elected legislature or the electorate.'
[139] HRC, General Comment 28: Equality of rights between men and women (Art 3), adopted on 29 March, 2000CCPR/C/21/Rev1/Add10, para 32.

an Indian band by marrying a non-Indian man—and thus the right to live on the Indian reserve. This condition in the Canadian Indian Act only applied to women, thereby creating a distinction on the ground of gender. Although the HRC admitted that an issue of disadvantage arises regarding Indian women in comparison with Indian men to whom the same rule does not apply, it was not able to rule on this condition as the Covenant was not applicable to Canada at the time. However, after her marriage ended the effects of denying her the right to live on a reserve continued, and the Covenant was now applicable to Canada. The Committee confirmed that there was no doubt that the applicant was a member of a minority as understood by Art 27[140] and that the continuous denial of her rights to enjoy her culture and language in community with others as foreseen in Art 27 had been violated. In this regard the Committee examined whether the statutory restrictions affecting her rights had a reasonable and objective justification and were consistent with a legitimate aim.[141] The Committee did not find the denial of the right to reside on the reserve reasonable, or necessary to preserve the identity of the tribe. It therefore found a violation of Sandra Lovelace's rights under Art 27. The Committee did not go on to examine the inequalities predating the coming into force of the Covenant for Canada, concerning the prohibition of discrimination under Arts 2, 3, and 26 of the ICCPR. It is noteworthy, however, that at the time the *Lovelace* case was being considered by the HRC, the government of Canada was preparing recommendations for legislative changes involving the delegation of powers to Band Councils to pass by-laws concerning membership in the band. These recommendations specifically stipulated that such by-laws would be required to be non-discriminatory on the grounds of sex, religion and family affiliation.

In a different case, *Kitok v Sweden*, the HRC addressed another situation whereby legislation aimed at protecting the rights of a minority as whole, in its application excluded a single member of that minority. The matter considered was whether the Swedish legislation had resulted in Ivan Kitok, a Sami from Sweden, being deprived of his right to carry out reindeer husbandry. The reindeer grazing legislation had the effect of dividing the Sami population of Sweden into reindeer herding and non-reindeer herding Sami. Reindeer herding was reserved as a right of Sami who were members of a particular Sami village (Sameby), which is a legal entity under Swedish law. Mr Kitok, although a Sami who sometimes practised reindeer herding, did not live in Sameby on a permanent basis and therefore did not meet the conditions established in order to

---

[140] HRC, *Lovelace v Canada* (Communication no R6/24*/, Views adopted on 30 July 1981), see para 14: 'Persons who are born and brought up on reserve who kept ties with their community and wish to maintain these ties must normally be considered as belonging to that minority within the meaning of Covenant. Since Sandra Lovelace is ethnically a Malisset Indian and has been only absent from her home reserve for a few years during the existence of her marriage, she is, in the opinion of the Committee, entitled to be regarded as "belonging" to this minority and to claim benefits of Article 27 of the Covenant.' [141] Ibid. See paras 12 and 16.

be able to herd reindeer as of right. In practice he was nonetheless able to continue herding reindeer (although not as of right). In accordance with its consistent practice, the HRC considered whether the restriction upon the right of an individual member of the group had a reasonable and objective justification and was necessary for continued viability and welfare of the minority as a whole. Importantly the Committee found that by ignoring objective ethnic criteria (being a Sami) in determining membership of the minority group benefiting from reindeer herding rights, the reindeer husbandry law was disproportionate to the aims it sought to achieve. However, it did not find that Mr Kitok's rights under Art 27 had been infringed given the fact that he was permitted, 'albeit not as of right, to graze and farm his reindeer, to hunt and fish', i.e. to enjoy his minority culture.[142]

As was already mentioned in the section on the right to political participation, the obligations upon states imply state responsibility to allow communities to decide how they will organize themselves and how they undertake decisions. In addition, states are responsible for encouraging minority organizations to follow genuine democratic principles of accountability and transparency, as well as to respect human rights. This includes respect for non-discrimination, including in situations where administrative and legislative powers have been transferred to minority communities' institutions.

IV. Conclusion

As this chapter has described, the starting point when it comes to national minorities and the application of the principles of non-discrimination and equality is prohibition of discrimination. States' obligations, however, extend to achieving real equality between persons belonging to minorities and majorities. This fuller protection is the ultimate goal of the minority-protection framework. These two aspects of the principles of non-discrimination and equality, are articulated and firmly rooted in all universal, as well as regional human rights instruments. In considering these obligations with respect to the right of national minorities to democratic governance, the relevant framework of protection is completed by international standards relating to the right to political participation. In this regard, there are three basic entitlements recognized in the international standards which are applicable to all persons, including persons belonging to national minorities: the right to take part in the conduct of public affairs at all levels either directly or indirectly, the right to vote and stand for elected office in genuine periodic elections, and the right to have equal access to

---

[142] HRC, *Kitok v Sweden*, Communication no 197/1985, Views adopted on 27 July 1988, paras 9.7 and 9.8.

the civil service. The full scope of protection provided by the principles of non-discrimination and equality applies to all three of the above entitlements.

Put differently, it is clearly accepted in international law and practice that persons belonging to national minorities must be given full and effective opportunities to exercise and benefit from all aspects of the right to political participation. Furthermore, membership in a national minority cannot be a basis for restricting individuals' rights to political participation. This is not a controversial matter today. The matter becomes more complicated when it comes to the actual interpretation and application of these rights with respect particular national situations. The complexity lies in two rather contradictory trends: on the one hand international judicial and supervisory bodies of human rights instruments grant states a wide margin of appreciation in designing their democratic systems; on the other hand these bodies practise a relatively high level of scrutiny when it comes to classifications on the basis of characteristic minority features, such as ethnicity, race, language, and religion. It is in the interplay between these contrasting trends that the protection for national minorities to fully enjoy their right to political participation has evolved.

International standards and decisions of international bodies reveal progressive, albeit hesitant and broken, movement towards ensuring that members of national minorities are not discriminated with respect to their right to political participation and towards imposing obligations upon states to adopt positive action measures to ensure that national minorities may enjoy this right in fact.

Particularly important has been the articulation by international bodies of the illegality of indirect discrimination. In this connection, international bodies have clearly established that if a policy or general measure (neutral at face value) has disproportionate prejudicial effects on a group of people, the likelihood of it being considered discriminatory cannot be ruled out—even if it is not specifically aimed or directed at that group. This is of great importance for the enjoyment by national minorities of the right to political participation, as conditions relating to these rights, although neutral, frequently have the effect of excluding or restricting the rights to political participation of members of national minority groups. This is especially due to the fact that minorities' factual differences of language, way of life, or minority position are often not, or insufficiently, taken into account when it comes to such conditions central to the practical enjoyment of rights to political participation.

Also important have been recent developments in jurisprudence strengthening obligations for states to make use of positive action measures to guarantee national minorities full enjoyment of the right to political participation. For instance, articulation of the second legal test of discrimination in the practice of the ECtHR (the obligation to treat those differently situated in a different manner) provides an important legal anchor for positive action measures. However, this in no way reflects strong endorsement of the positive obligation of states to take special measures regarding political participation of minorities under the Convention. Again this is connected with the approach of the supervisory bodies to grant states a wide margin of appreciation in developing their democratic systems. However, the legitimacy of special measures regarding political participation of national minorities have been confirmed in the case law of the ECtHR as a means of achieving substantive equality by national minorities.

However, the ECtHR provides a relatively a weak level of protection. Given the limitations of Art 3, Protocol 1, the ECHR's non-discrimination provision (Art 14) would not extend protection to the elements of political participation not relating to the exercise of elections. This is especially so given the Court's track record of a relatively restrictive application of Art 14. This limitation is partly resolved by the recently adopted Protocol 12 to the ECHR; this is an independent non-discrimination provision, therefore extending ECHR protection against discrimination beyond the ambit of rights specified in the Convention. Thus for those states that have ratified Protocol 12, the ECtHR may examine the issue of discrimination with respect to all elements of the right to political participation. However, as of 2 August 2009 only seventeen Council of Europe member states had ratified the protocol.

The conventions with issue-specific focus on discrimination provide greater scope for protection to achieve the substantive equality for national minorities vis-à-vis political participation. In particular CERD and CEDAW clearly establish obligations of states to adopt positive action measures regarding minority groups with respect to their political participation. Also, obligations under the minority-specific Art 27 of the ICCPR require special measures, in particular to ensure consultation with national minorities regarding matters affecting their culture and way of life. It could be concluded that there are efforts across the board towards higher levels of protection against discrimination from which minority groups can benefit in access to and full enjoyment of political participation rights. However, given that the legally binding standard with respect to the obligation on states to adopt special measures for the full and effective enjoyment by national minorities of their participation in public life exists only at the European level, in Art 15 of the FCNM, the protection provided in this respect to minorities remains a complicated and complex matter. The protection is provided through an array of different standards and doctrines of equality and discrimination and it will take some time before these become fully rooted in the practice of international bodies and, through them, provide a firm basis for full minority participation in political life in state practice.

5

Gendering Minority Participation in Public Life

Karen Bird

I. Intersectionality and the 'Targeted' Approach to Women's and Minority Rights	152
II. Making the Personal Political: Women's Movements and the Engendering of Ethnic Nationalisms	159
III. Engendering Outcomes?	165
A. Nunavut	165
B. Belgium	167
C. Fiji	168
D. Afghanistan	170
IV. Conclusions and an Agenda for Future Research	172

This chapter begins from the perspective that women must always be included in working out arrangements for the effective participation and representation of ethnic and national minorities in state governance. Including women in this process, and ensuring that women are fairly represented in the resulting state structures is a crucial step towards promoting women's equal rights in society. More broadly, women's inclusion can serve to strengthen the commitment to democracy among all parties involved in developing constructive solutions to ethnic-related tensions.

Unfortunately, women have not been the focus within the international agenda concerning ethnic minority rights. Rather, they remain at the periphery, largely invisible. Where they are visible, the message is that minority women need to be protected. They are understood as vulnerable subjects and only rarely as potential agents of ethnic conflict resolution and democratization.

In the Lund Recommendations on the Effective Participation of National Minorities in Public Life, women are barely mentioned. Where they are, it is in the context of concerns that national minorities must respect and protect the rights of 'minorities within minorities' including women.[1] The recent Commentary of the Council of Europe Advisory Committee on the Framework Convention for the Protection of National Minorities (FCNM) goes somewhat further, stressing at several points the importance of attention to the 'multiple discrimination' experienced by minority women, and to the need for balanced representation of women and men belonging to national minorities.[2] However, the normative emphasis of both documents is the same. They recognize the dual disadvantage of minority women, but locate the source of the additional burden carried by these women as lying entirely within their minority culture. Minority women, as minority men, are disadvantaged where multinational states fail to ensure effective inclusion of national and ethnic minority groups. But minority women, it is implied, are additionally oppressed by the patriarchal elements of their culture. The main concern reflected in the Lund Recommendations and in the Commentary is that policies and specific arrangements to facilitate the political inclusion of national minorities, and to enable them to maintain their own identity and characteristics, might shore up the power base of men within the community and thereby undermine women's equality.

This is an incomplete picture of the political exclusion experienced by ethnic minority women, and their capacity to overcome this exclusion. An alternative approach would conceptualize minority women as potentially significant agents of ethnic conflict resolution and democratization. Moreover, documents such as the Lund Recommendations and the Advisory Committee Commentary should contain constructive, practical advice on including women actors in the negotiations between states and minorities, as well as strategies to promote women's descriptive and substantive representation within new mechanisms for minority representation. Gender equality needs to be a central rather than a peripheral objective within the resulting political systems.

I take up this argument in three stages. First, drawing on the theory of intersectionality, I show how institutions and rules that are based on mistaken expectations about the sources of oppression experienced by minority women can serve to reinforce their marginalization. I argue furthermore that the failure to reflect on the lessons of intersectionality, and the incomplete picture of the political experiences of ethnic minority women that emerges, is partly a consequence of the 'targeted' approach to group rights that has come to characterize this domain. In the second part of this chapter, I turn to feminist research on social movements. I show how, through collective action, women have been able to have a significant positive impact on conflict settlement and transitions to

---

[1] See General Principles, part 3 of the Explanatory Note to the Lund Recommendations on the Effective Participation of National Minorities in Public Life (September 1999).

[2] Council of Europe Advisory Committee on the Framework Convention for the Protection of National Minorities, Commentary on the Effective Participation of Persons Belonging to National Minorities in Cultural, Social, and Economic Life and in Public Affairs (27 February 2008).

democracy. In addition, I confront the assumption that minority women are highly constrained in their capacity to acquire a feminist conscience and to mobilize in an autonomous fashion. While I acknowledge that there is a problematic relationship between women's emancipation and some forms of nationalism, I show that these goals are not necessarily incompatible. In the third part of the chapter, I briefly examine a number of countries where new governance arrangements have been worked out to promote ethnic peace and equality. In each of these cases, I examine the extent to which gender equality concerns have been included in the process, and in resulting governance arrangements. Drawing on these examples, I speculate about the conditions that might best facilitate the effective inclusion of women and gender equality concerns, in the context of advancing the political rights of ethnic and national minorities.

I. Intersectionality and the 'Targeted' Approach to Women's and Minority Rights

Where women and women's rights are mentioned in the Lund Recommendations and in the Advisory Committee Commentary, there is one principal concern. It is that policies and specific arrangements to facilitate the political inclusion of national minorities, and to enable them to maintain their own identity and characteristics, might shore up the power base of men within the community and thereby undermine women's equality.

While there is certainly some validity to this concern about women's rights in a context of expanded protection for minority cultures, what is absent here is the more sophisticated understanding of the intersectionality of race/ethnic and sex-based discrimination. The idea of intersectionality has been advanced by Kimberle Crenshaw,[3] Patricia Hill Collins,[4] bell hooks,[5] Anne Phillips[6] and others to denote the various ways in which race and gender interact to shape multiple dimensions of minority women's experience. Crenshaw remarks that the tendency of feminist politics and of antiracist politics has been to address issues of sexism and racism as though they occur on mutually exclusive terrains, and the result serves to marginalize and to misrepresent the experiences of minority women. Drawing on minority women's employment experiences, and on their experiences of sexual violence, she details how patterns of sexual and racial subordination intersect. This intersection is 'frequently the consequence of one

---

[3] K Crenshaw, 'Mapping the margins: Intersectionality, identity politics, and violence against women of color' (1991) 43(6) Stanford Law Review 1241–99.
[4] PH Collins, *Black Feminist Thought: Knowledge, consciousness and the politics of empowerment* (1990).   [5] b hooks, *Ain't I a Woman? Black women and feminism* (1981).
[6] A Phillips, *Multiculturalism without Culture* (2007).

burden that interacts with pre-existing vulnerabilities to create yet another dimension of disempowerment'.[7] In some cases, these new dimensions of disempowerment are the result of interventions by well-intentioned actors and institutions that focus either on the vector of gender inequality, or the vector of racial inequality, but that fail to understand how the two vectors (and others such as class) intersect in minority women's lives.

Crenshaw cites the example of 1990 amendments to the marriage fraud provisions of the US Immigration and Nationality Act, showing how these regulations produced new obstacles for immigrant women seeking to escape abusive spouses. A more recent example concerns the French decision in 2004 to ban girls from wearing Islamic headscarves in public schools. The law was imposed ostensibly to protect Muslim girls and young women from patriarchal elements in Islamic family life, thereby promoting individual rights through integration. The law focuses exclusively on the gender dimension of oppression experienced by Muslim girls and women. It dismisses any possibility that these girls might choose to wear the headscarf as a deliberate and gendered act of cultural resistance to shared experiences of racial and socio-economic marginalization within the French post-colonial setting. Though the ban applies only to students in public schools, Joan Wallach Scott describes growing public disapproval of Muslim women wearing headscarves in any setting. She quotes one woman who explains: 'The veil is a 100 percent handicap in French society. You don't see veiled women [working] anywhere, even at the checkout counters of supermarkets in our neighbourhoods. In the end it's not because of Islam that we stay at home, but because of French society.'[8] Ultimately, Scott concludes that rather than resolving the problem of integrating Muslims into French society, the law banning headscarves has exacerbated it. In both the case of US immigration regulations on marriage fraud, and the French headscarf ban, we see that institutions and rules that are based on mistaken expectations about minority women's lives may serve to reinforce their marginalization.

The Lund Recommendations and the Advisory Committee Commentary reflect similar mistaken assumptions about the structures of oppression experienced by minority women. The main message conveyed about minority women is that they are susceptible to the patriarchy of their communities, and that extending rights to national minorities could make them more vulnerable. There is nothing in the text of these documents that acknowledges the intersectional nature of discrimination experienced by minority women, or that provides any concrete strategies for advancing minority women's political participation.

This view may not characterize international human rights organizations as a whole. For example, the non-governmental organization (NGO) Minority Rights Group International has argued that current international standards are

---

[7] Crenshaw, 'Mapping the margins' (n 3 above), 1249.
[8] JW Scott, *The Politics of the Veil* (2007), 179.

insufficient in that they do not take an appropriately holistic approach to redress the position of minority and indigenous women. They explicitly call for more attention to intersectionality, and recommend that states, intergovernmental organizations, and NGOs take strategic actions that include:

making minority and indigenous women visible through research, within statistics and accounts; ensuring political participation; addressing violence against women; protecting the knowledge, innovations and practices of indigenous women; developing with their participation education programmes that respect their history, culture and language; ensuring access to all levels of formal and non-formal education.[9]

I think that this critique is essentially correct. Rather than pursue an intersectional or holistic approach that might more effectively identify and redress the position of ethnic minority women, the international legal and normative framework that has emerged reflects a 'targeted' approach to group rights. Under this approach, the conceptual frameworks and actual advances for different marginalized groups—for women, national minorities, indigenous minorities, immigrants—have developed largely in isolation from each other. For each group, we have seen the emergence of distinctive normative standards regarding appropriate remedies for achieving political inclusion, separate intergovernmental bodies and networks of policy experts, and separate international documents and 'best practice' recommendations.

Will Kymlicka has offered the most comprehensive argument for this targeted approach to group rights. He argues that there should be a different set of standards for women, immigrants, national minorities, and indigenous peoples, because each group tends to have distinctive historic experiences and political aspirations. Kymlicka begins to develop this argument in his earliest writing on multicultural theory, and it represents an important advance on the lack of careful differentiation among group-based rights seen in earlier works of normative theory.[10] Kymlicka argues for special measures of group representation as a remedy for discrimination on the one hand, and self-government rights for national and indigenous minorities on the other. Special representation measures are 'a form of political "affirmative action"' that are intended as a response to oppression or systematic disadvantage that might be experienced by ethnic and racial minorities, as well as by women, sexual minorities, handicapped, the poor, and so on.[11] They are, in principle, temporary. Their purpose is to produce full inclusion of group members into the national political community, at which point the special measures cease to be necessary. Institutional mechanisms for self-government, on the other hand, are based on inherent rights and therefore permanent. They entail a transfer of power from one governmental

---

[9] F Banda and C Chinkin, 'Gender, minorities and indigenous peoples', *Minority Rights Group International Report*, August 2004, 27.
[10] Eg, IM Young, *Justice and the Politics of Difference* (1990).
[11] W Kymlicka, *Multicultural Citizenship* (1995), 141.

body to another, and consequently reduced influence for the national minority (on some issues) in the former legislative arena. Kymlicka explains: 'Both claims reflect a desire for "empowerment", but the sort of power being claimed is significantly different.'[12] As his work has developed, Kymlicka has made this categorical—some have called it hierarchical—treatment of group rights a central element of his multicultural theory. He writes:

> this targeted element is not marginal or peripheral. On the contrary, the entire infrastructure of liberal multiculturalism is often built around it ... We cannot hope to understand the theory and practice of liberal multiculturalism without coming to grips with its targeted or group-differentiated character. Any attempt to articulate liberal multiculturalism as if it were purely a matter of generic minority rights is doomed to failure.[13]

In assessing global developments on minority rights, Kymlicka argues that one of the main obstacles to the formulation and diffusion of good international norms has been this problem of categories.[14] He believes that international organizations started on the correct path, initially adopting a targeted logic. Responding to the escalating threat of ethnic conflict in Central and Eastern Europe following the end of communism, Kymlicka argues that the OSCE and the Council of Europe appropriately sought to normalize the idea of territorial autonomy as a best practice for accommodating homeland minorities. They developed a bold set of new institutional mechanisms to monitor the treatment of national minorities and to recommend changes in the direction of greater political autonomy. Kymlicka laments that international organizations have more recently retreated from this targeted approach. They have more or less abandoned the key right that actually distinguishes national minorities from other ethnic minorities—that is, the right to territorial autonomy. At the same time, a variety of human rights advocates have sought to extend the framework of provisions for national minorities, to cover otherwise unprotected groups, such as the Roma or immigrant minorities. A typical argument in this vein is made by John Packer, who has criticized the narrow conceptual understanding of minority rights and the limited scope for action of the OSCE High Commission for National Minorities, noting the incapacity (or unwillingness) of the organization to address simmering resentments and violent disruptions emerging among the alienated descendents of immigrant communities in Europe.[15]

Kymlicka is strongly critical of these developments—both the retreat from territorial autonomy arrangements in international legal norms, and the attempt to extend protection to non-territorial groups through the back door. His

---

[12] Ibid, 144.
[13] W Kymlicka, *Multicultural Odysseys: Navigating the new international politics of diversity* (2007), 78–9.
[14] Ibid.
[15] J Packer, 'Confronting the contemporary challenges of Europe's minorities' (2005) 3 *Helsinki Monitor* 227–31.

preferred alternative is a differentiated legal framework for each group: territorial groups, immigrant minorities and Roma peoples. He recognizes that this ideal may be practically impossible given the present European backlash against both immigrants and multiculturalism policies. But if the current direction in international legal norms is politically inevitable it is also, he fears, ultimately unstable. The only way forward, he argues, is to encourage the international community to attend closely to the differences in types of groups and geopolitical conditions: 'If we cannot build targeting and sequencing [of minority rights] into international legal norms, we will have to build them into international democratization policies, development policies, peace and stability policies, and so on.'[16]

It is certainly important to understand that the political conditions and needs of different groups will differ. However, there is a danger in over-differentializing among groups. For Kymlicka, for example, women's representational rights are apparently such a distinctive issue from minority representational rights that the former merit virtually no mention in a study of the latter. Whereas his recent book addresses at length the range of international instruments developed to promote the political inclusion of national, indigenous and immigrant minorities, there is nary a word on the parallel international framework to promote the political participation and representation of women. Likewise, the drafters of the Lund Recommendations may have felt that women's representational rights and needs are simply too different from the issues facing national minorities to merit any lengthy consideration. Moreover, they could simply refer to another, roughly parallel set of guarantees for women's rights to participate in the political and public life of the country—those stipulated at Art 7 of the 1979 Convention on the Elimination of All Forms of Discrimination against Women.[17]

Certainly women and ethnic minorities do have different experiences of marginalization, and they do seek different practical remedies to political underrepresentation. But, as Anne Phillips argues, this difference 'arises as much from ... practical considerations of what is possible as from any more theoretically driven contrast between the politics of gender and the politics of race'.[18] Moreover, in her recent work, Phillips calls our attention to the problematic consequences of the targeted approach to minority rights we see manifest in the Lund Recommendations. The main problem she sees is a failure to adequately problematize cultural difference, in other words a tendency to over-differentialize among groups. It is, she says, 'one of the ironies of the multicultural

---

[16] Kymlicka, *Multicultural Odysseys* (n 13 above), 314.
[17] See General Principles, part 3 of the explanatory note to the Lund Recommendations on the Effective Participation of National Minorities in Public Life and explanatory note (September 1999).
[18] A Phillips, *The Politics of Presence: The political representation of gender, ethnicity and race* (1995), 95.

project that in the name of equality and mutual respect between peoples, it has encouraged us to view peoples and cultures as more systematically different than they are'.[19] There are three ways in which cultural over-differentialization is manifest in the Lund Recommendations. One is its exclusive focus on *national* minorities, the second is its relative silence regarding women's political participation and representation, and the third is its normative message regarding the status of women within ethnic minority communities, and the prevailing apprehension that women's rights will be further eroded under minority self-governance arrangements.

It is this last problem that I wish to focus on here, and Phillips provides useful insight as to how this is related to the targeted approach to group rights. She argues that the failure to adequately 'de-essentialize notions of culture' has especially pernicious implications for how we view women in minority cultural groups. There is a tendency, Phillips says, to see cultures as bounded and static, 'as neatly wrapped up, sealed off, and identifiable by core values and practices that separate it from all others'. The more reasonable understanding of cultures, she contends, is that they are hybrid, internally contested, inherently malleable, and in a continuous process of change. An essentialized notion of culture leaves little room to recognize the many ways in which individual members—but notably women—do contest power hierarchies within their cultural groups. It also seriously discounts the potential value and meaning that women may attach to membership in any non-dominant identity community. The essentialist view, Phillips contends, leads us to treat minority women as 'victims without agency'.[20] Essentialist notions of culture lie at the heart of growing worries about the compatibility between women's rights and multiculturalism, and appear to be playing an important role in the current retreat from multiculturalism, especially in Europe.[21] These views are fully reflected in the normative orientation of the Lund Recommendations concerning ethnic minority women.

The separate trajectories in approaches to women's and ethnic minorities' representation are not only a consequence of a normative theory of multiculturalism. There have also been distinctive historical developments and political pressures that have determined one course for women and another for ethnic minorities. Initiatives for enhanced women's representation have arisen largely via the growth and discourse of the international women's movement. Gender quotas—which have now been adopted in over a hundred countries—are the result of a rapid and highly effective transnational diffusion of new norms, equating gender-balanced decision-making with democratic legitimacy. The success of the gender quota movement is largely attributable to information sharing, normative framing, and mobilization among women's groups and

---

[19] Phillips, *Multiculturalism without Culture* (n 6 above), 25.   [20] Ibid, 26–7.
[21] A Phillips and S Saharso, 'The rights of women and the crisis of multiculturalism' (2008) 8 (3) *Ethnicities* 291–301.

NGOs across national borders.[22] For ethnic minorities, it has been quite a different story. With the exception of indigenous groups, ethnic minorities are sometimes in direct conflict with each other regarding representational issues. Even where they are not, the challenges facing different groups are sufficiently distinct that ethnic groups simply have far less capacity than women for coordinated transnational advocacy. International advances in minority representational rights over the last ten to twenty years have thus come about through quite a different process. In most instances, it has been less a matter of 'bottom-up' pressures as is the case for women, but rather 'top-down' democratization and conflict prevention strategies initiated by international organizations and policy networks.

Empirical research on the obstacles to women's and ethnic minority representation in politics has also evolved along two quite separate tracks. Research on each group has been based on distinctive conceptual and methodological frameworks. Women's representation tends to be theorized in terms of macro-level factors such as electoral rules, or broad cultural beliefs about the role of women in society. This has facilitated extensive cross-national research on women's representation, and a set of fairly comprehensive 'best practices' guidelines on how to advance women's political participation and representation around the world.[23] In contrast, ethnic minority representation is shaped by a wide range of contextual factors. There are differences at the national level in rules concerning naturalization and voting rights for immigrants, or in historic regimes of slavery, colonization, and racial stigmatization. There are also local differences related to an ethnic group's size and geographic distribution, alignment with electoral boundaries, capacity for community mobilization, and so on. For many ethnic groups, there are also important transnational or diasporic factors to consider. The varying local, national, and transnational structures of ethnic politics have made it very difficult to comprehensively compare ethnic minority representation across countries, or even to compare different groups within countries. Consequently, while there are a few 'best practices' guides for minority representation,[24] they are far more tentative and contextually limited than is the case for women.

Multicultural theory, political events and pressures, and empirical research methods have all reinforced a stark separation in approaching representational challenges for each group. We now have two distinct columns of international normative, legal, and empirical endeavours—one for women, the other for

---

[22] ML Krook, *Quotas for Women in Politics: Gender and candidate selection reform worldwide* (2009); P Paxton, MM Hughes, and JL Green, 'The international women's movement and women's political representation, 1893–2003' (2006) 71(6) *American Sociological Review* 898–920.

[23] Eg, S Larserud and R Taphorn, *Designing for Equality: Best-fit, medium-fit and non-favourable combinations of electoral systems and gender quotas* (2007).

[24] Eg, D Horowitz, 'Electoral systems: A primer for decision makers' (2003) 14(4) *Journal of Democracy* 115–27.

ethnic minorities. In this context, ethnic minority women have fallen through the gap, receiving only marginal attention within one or the other column. Gradually, we are seeing a correction of this negligence, through the emergence of descriptive accounts of patterns of political participation and representation among ethnic minority women in specific state or local contexts. But until this work expands, our ability to develop valid and comprehensive explanations of the obstacles and opportunities for political participation among ethnic minority women will remain limited.

II. Making the Personal Political: Women's Movements and the Engendering of Ethnic Nationalisms

One area of significant progress has come through feminist literature on women's agency and social-political practices. Feminist studies of social mobilization have shown how the exclusion of women from certain forms of power has led to adaptive efforts to create new spheres for women's collective action. This affects what women do in social movements, in turn shaping both the movement's destiny and the political identity of women engaged in the movement. Particularly interesting for our purposes here are studies of women's movements and political agency within ethnic minority communities and in the context of ethnic nationalism. Research that concentrates on minority women's political agency has helped us to see how these women navigate the complex intersection of gender and culture in their lived experiences.

For example, in her account of immigrant Muslim women in Norway, Line Nyhagen Predelli shows how these women have worked to establish new forms of participation and citizenship through their mosques.[25] Predelli details how Muslim women in Norway have been marginalized both by the migration process, and by patriarchal features of their religion. But what is especially interesting is how these vectors of exclusion work together, creating new challenges for women, but also new opportunities to participate and to develop alternative forms of associational life. Predelli notes that in rural Pakistan, it is uncommon for women to go to mosque; rather they pray at home. In the urban centres of immigrant settlement in Norway, however, Muslim homes are modest and far less spacious, and women do not have access to their ready network of friends and relatives. Women thus choose to attend the mosque and to create there a much more public religious and social community of women. Predelli explains 'issues that would previously have been discussed among women relatives are now being talked about among women who share their religious faith and the experience of migration'.[26] While initially constrained to participating

---

[25] LN Predelli, 'Religion, citizenship and participation' (2008) 15(3) *European Journal of Women's Studies* 241–60.   [26] Ibid, 253.

according to rules established by men, women have gradually achieved some reforms. For example, women have obtained larger prayer spaces, added female Qur'an teachers in the education of women and children, become members of the board of some mosques, and have obtained the right to vote within some congregations.[27] While it is important not to exaggerate the signs of development toward gender equality in this instance, what is clear from this account is that the process of social mobilization and autonomy-building among minority women is closely tied to the specific conditions of gender, ethnic, and class disadvantage that they experience.

Applications of the theory of intersectionality at the level of social practice and citizenship conceive of minority women as active agents who express overlapping identities, and who struggle in different venues and with different resources to create new political, social and family norms.[28] Nevertheless, women's capacity to organize autonomously and to employ feminist ideologies might be quite limited in some contexts.

One prevailing assumption is that there are unique or heightened risks to women, where powers of self-government are devolved to minorities in 'non-Western' or democratically 'underdeveloped' settings. There are, in fact, two concerns here. One is that the oppression of women's rights tends to be especially severe in the context of minority nationalism.[29] The other is that women's capacity for autonomous mobilization is profoundly compromised where demands for territorial autonomy and self-government arise in the absence of a democratic political culture or well-functioning state institutions—for example, in a post-colonial or post-communist context. This second concern arises in part from the problematic association, in many non-Western settings, of feminism with colonialism, modernity and western individualism. The upshot of these two concerns is that 'feminist' consciousness and autonomous political mobilization will be especially limited, and abuses against women's rights more widespread, where minority nationalism emerges in 'non-Western' contexts. According to Will Kymlicka, this is a problem of sequencing: that is, minority rights demands coming *before* the consolidation of democracy and entrenchment of fundamental human rights.[30] For Kymlicka, this is one of the main reasons why it has been quite difficult to expand the principles and practices of multiculturalism beyond the west.

I do not wish to understate the challenges to women's autonomy in such contexts. However, I think that this argument provides a highly simplistic picture

---

[27] Ibid, 254.
[28] B Siim, 'The challenge of recognizing diversity from the perspective of gender equality: Dilemmas in Danish citizenship' (2007) 10(4) *Critical Review of International Social and Political Philosophy* 491–511.
[29] N Yuval-Davis and F Anthias, *Woman-Nation-State* (1989); C. Enloe, *Bananas, Beaches and Bases: Making feminist sense of international politics* (1990).
[30] Kymlicka, *Multicultural Odysseys* (n 13 above).

and conceals enormous variance and complexity in women's organizing capacity in the context of minority nationalism and transitions to democracy.[31] The argument also reflects a broader lack of attention to women within comparative politics.[32]

There is now a significant body of literature examining women's mobilization across a broad range of nationalist contexts—in the Middle East, Latin America, Africa, Asia, Central and Eastern Europe, as well as in Western Europe and North America. An important pattern emerging across this literature is that while feminists of the dominant nation tend to believe in autonomous feminism organized around gender justice, women in dominated nations tend to adopt a more complex, hyphenated ideology and approach that encompasses goals of national liberation *and* women's liberation.[33] The outcomes for women differ widely across these cases. In some instances the results have been disappointing, while in others women have achieved quite positive gender outcomes. There is not space here to review in detail the extent to which women have succeeded or failed to incorporate gender concerns within nationalist movements.[34] However, a few general findings can be noted.

First, it is clear that there are contradictions between Western feminist ideologies and ideas of national liberation, and that women involved in anti-colonial and anti-modern revivalist national movements will tend to reject Western feminism as individualistic or imperialistic. If we look only to Western indicators of women's rights we will certainly miss all or most of what women do achieve in these contexts.

Secondly, women engage in a range of strategies to make their individual and collective struggles visible and to reform the patriarchal status quo. For example, women may use their spatial exclusion and their subordinate status as non-political subjects as opportunities to share information, discuss their struggles, and in the process politicize their shared identity as women.[35] Demands for equality may be framed in traditional terminology, for example by showing how women's rights accord with scriptural or customary principles.[36] Women may

---

[31] J Vickers, 'Bringing nations in: Some methodological and conceptual issues in connecting feminisms with nationhood and nationalisms' (2006) 8(1) *International Feminist Journal of Politics* 84–109; G Waylen, 'Women's mobilization and gender outcomes in transitions to democracy: The case of South Africa' (2007) 40(5) *Comparative Political Studies* 521–46.

[32] AM Tripp, 'Why so slow? The challenges of gendering comparative politics' (2006) 2(2) *Politics and Gender* 249–63.   [33] Vickers, 'Bringing nations in' (n 31 above).

[34] R Miller and R Wilford. *Women, Ethnicity and Nationalism: The politics of transition* (1998); Waylen, 'Women's mobilization' (n 31 above).

[35] M Navarro, 'The personal is political: Las Madres de Plaza de Mayo', S Eckstein (ed), *Power and Popular Protest: Latin American social movements* (1989); L Bayard de Volo, 'Analyzing politics and change in women's organizations' (2003) 5(1) *International Feminist Journal of Politics* 92–115.

[36] TA Jacoby, 'Feminism, nationalism, and difference: Reflections on the Palestinian women's movement' (1999) 22(5) *Women's Studies International Forum* 511–23; T Minor, 'Political participation of Inuit women in the government of Nunavut' (Spring 2002) *Wicazo SA Review* 65–90.

also use their role as 'mothers' and the privileged access this provides within the structure of the family, orphanages, schools, health clinics, and so on, to articulate an alternative vision to patriarchal nationalism. Notable examples include the anti-war and pan-ethnic organization 'Women in Black' founded by a group of mothers in mourning over sons lost to the war in Yugoslavia,[37] and the Revolutionary Association of the Women of Afghanistan.[38] These strategies may of course reinforce some traditional gender roles. Yet even in these cases, where women's organizations do not explicitly adopt a 'feminist' ideology and do not set out to change gender power relations, there tend to be many unplanned small-scale effects for women that can have profound effects on their lives and that can, over time, yield significant structural shifts in gender relations.

Thirdly, the kinds of transformations that we are discussing rarely involve only national identity. Rather these tend to be highly complex transformations that may involve, to varying degrees, significant social, economic, political, and religious changes. Women are subject to multiple cross-currents of change, the dimensions of which will vary from one context to the next. The nature of women's experiences, the forms of their resistance, and the degree of policy success of the women's movement will therefore vary. Briefly, I shall describe just three dimensions of transformational shifts and their unique impact on women's collective identity and organization. (1) Women may face rapid loss of job security or access to agricultural land in the context of market-based economic reforms. Women's rapid economic marginalization may then serve to refocus the objectives of women's movements towards providing basic domestic-family needs. But it may also produce a specifically gendered critique of international development perspectives.[39] (2) There may be rapid changes in the dynamics of civil society, which may force women's movements to adapt their goals and strategies. For example, in communist Poland, the Catholic Church performed a crucial civil society function and provided an alternative power structure to the socialist state, and so it made sense that women's mobilization took place largely within this space. In the transition from communism, the role of the Church shifted to fulfilling an increasingly important welfare role in an economically unstable society. This meant that Polish women could begin to form organizations and create a political subjectivity outside of the influence of the Church and the domestic sphere. The post-communist transition in Central and Eastern Europe is generally viewed as undermining women's rights,[40]

---

[37] B Einhorn and C Sever, 'Gender and civil society in Central and Eastern Europe' (2003) 5(2) *International Feminist Journal of Politics* 163–90.

[38] JL Fluri, 'Feminist-nation building in Afghanistan: An examination of the Revolutionary Association of the Women of Afghanistan (RAWA)' (2008) 89 *Feminist Review* 34–54.

[39] AM Tripp, 'Women's movements, customary law, and land rights in Africa: The case of Uganda' (2004) 7(4) *African Studies Quarterly* 1–20.

[40] V Sperling, *Organizing Women in Contemporary Russia: Engendering transition* (1999); G Waylen, *Engendering Transitions: Women's mobilization, institutions, and gender outcomes* (2007).

nevertheless our analysis of gains and losses will not be accurate unless we understand such contextual shifts in the location and strategies of the movement.[41] (3) The strength and capacity of the state may change across the transition and post-transition period, and this in turn will impact the strategies and achievements of the women's movement. In the extreme case of failed states, women's organizations will tend to shift their focus away from the state, towards addressing immediate local needs in the face of enormous poverty and insecurity.[42] In cases where the state is merely weak or unstable—for example in postcommunist Russia—the women's movement may remain focused on achieving broad women-friendly reforms, but will find the state a highly unreliable interlocutor with limited capacity to implement policy initiatives.[43]

The overall lesson here is that we must place concepts such as 'women's movement', 'civil society', 'feminism', and so on, in specific historic and cultural context in order to assess whether or not women make gains in the context of ethnic nationalism.

A fourth general finding from comparative research on women's mobilization in the context of nationalism concerns the specific conditions that tend to contribute to positive gender outcomes. From a variety of sources we can identify several hypotheses regarding the circumstances under which organized women may be able to assert feminist values within a nationalist project, and achieve positive gender outcomes.[44] This is most likely: (H1) where there is a long-standing history of women's organizing that is seen as a legitimate part of the opposition or nationalist movement; (H2) when the nation-building project is more open and pluralistic, as opposed to being militaristic or fascist; (H3) when there is a good discursive fit between the ideology of the women's liberation and that of the national liberation movement; (H4) when there is a scarcity of men, making women important allies/actors in the nation-building project; (H5) where women are able to get in 'on the ground floor' as institutions are being created or reformed; (H6) where there is a relatively lengthy, formal process of transition, providing ample opportunities for women's groups to strategize and articulate coherent demands at various steps in the process; (H7) where women's organizations are able to establish themselves as legitimately autonomous from political parties, and to articulate their demands independently; and (H8) where women's organizations enjoy good connections to the future governing elite, so as to facilitate implementation of women-friendly policy in the post-transition phase.

Georgina Waylen has shown that many of these conditions were in place in the transition to democracy in South Africa, allowing the women's movement to

---

[41] Einhorn and Sever, 'Gender and civil society in Central and Eastern Europe' (n 37 above).
[42] I Gough and G Wood, *Insecurity and Welfare Regimes in Asia, Africa and Latin America* (2004). [43] Sperling, *Organizing Women* (n 40 above).
[44] Vickers, 'Bringing nations in' (n 31 above); Waylen, 'Women's mobilization' (n 31 above); Waylen, *Engendering Transitions* (n 40 above).

play a key role in negotiating the terms of the new constitution, and to achieve a number of positive policy outcomes for women in the post-transition period.[45] There was a long-standing history of women's organizing in South Africa. And the goals of the women's movement were generally compatible with the left-leaning African National Congress' ideological beliefs favouring equality rights for all. But a crucial factor for South African women was the lengthy, formal process of a pacted transition, in which elites from the non-democratic regime negotiated the settlement with the opposition. Waylen argues that this process provided ample time for women to collectively strategize, and then effectively intervene throughout the negotiations. Specifically, it allowed for women academics, politicians, and activists across party and racial lines to develop a broad-based, mass women's movement, the Women's National Coalition. The leaders of the WNC were able to articulate a clear distinction between national liberation and women's liberation, showing that the first does not automatically guarantee the second, and proposing a set of constitutional provisions most likely to promote gender equality. Importantly, the organization was also able to establish itself as legitimately autonomous from the main opposition, the African National Congress, and to articulate its demands independently, though it enjoyed good connections to the future governing party. According to Waylen, the WNC 'contained within it a critical mass of experienced feminist activists and academics from all races who had clear ideas about a range of gender issues such as women's political representation, the nature of the future constitution, and a national gender machinery'. Furthermore, the WNC 'facilitated a "triple alliance" of key women activists, academics, and politicians of all races, many of them elite members who were well connected in the ANC, to engage with the transition processes and achieve what none could have done on their own'.[46]

The final contribution of this literature on women's movements in the context of ethnic nationalism is that it shifts the normative perspective from women as real or potential victims, to women as real or potential political actors. Women's engagement in ethnic conflict resolution and democratic transition may take many forms. But in almost all cases, their engagement opens new channels and opportunities for change. It can provide a key civil society agenda for conflict resolution and peaceful transition. It can foster a deeper commitment to democratic equality among both majority and minority nationalist groups. It can produce new ways of thinking about gender roles. Finally, and perhaps most importantly, engaging women in the process of building new, post-conflict institutions can be part of the solution to de-ethnicize politics. Women's engagement and mobilization around feminist issues may encourage people to think about their identities and interests in ways that cut across ethnic lines, and that reduce the intransigence of ethnic divisions. This may contribute

---

[45] Waylen, *Engendering Transitions* (n 40 above).   [46] Ibid, 531.

to a more stable political system and can be part of a long-term transformative movement towards ethnic reconciliation.[47]

III. Engendering Outcomes?

I shift now to a brief sketch of four countries where electoral or governance arrangements have been developed to promote ethnic equality and peace. The purpose here is to examine the extent to which women's representation and substantive gender equality concerns have been addressed within these arrangements. The sketches are highly selective, and cannot begin to represent the wide range of countries in which ethnic and gender inequalities intersect. What they can do is point to the importance of context, and the need for much further study in this domain. It is clearly impossible to propose any 'one-size-fits-all' strategy for addressing women's and ethnic minority representational needs. Rather, appropriate arrangements must depend on a close understanding of the structure of both ethnic relations and gender relations within a given society.

A. Nunavut

On 1 April 1998, the self-governing territory of Nunavut was established out of the eastern and northern portions of the Northwest Territories, in Canada. Nunavut contains a population of 29,000 people (of whom 85 per cent are Inuit), and one fifth of Canada's landmass. It is headed by the Nunavut Legislative Assembly which, like other territorial governments in Canada, exercises powers delegated to it by the federal government. The creation of Nunavut marked the conclusion of land claims negotiations between the Inuit Tapirisat of Canada and the federal government, making this the most ambitious of the Canadian aboriginal proposals for self-government. Of particular interest in the Nunavut story was the attempt to achieve gender balance in the new legislative assembly. In 1994, the Nunavut Implementation Commission recommended gender parity, through a voting system in which one man and one woman would be elected as legislative representatives from each electoral district. The Commission believed that the creation of the new territory provided a unique chance to ensure equal participation and incorporate the different approaches of men and women in elite politics. It also felt that gender parity was an effective way to increase the size of the legislature, and that the territory's geographically large constituencies could be more effectively served by two rather than just one representative. The proposal was brought to a plebiscite, and was defeated in

---

[47] SG Simonsen, 'Addressing ethnic divisions in post-conflict institution building: Lessons from recent cases' (2005) 36(3) *Security Dialogue* 297–318.

May 1997. Just 39 per cent of people eligible to vote participated, and gender parity was rejected by 57 per cent of those who cast ballots.

Despite the failure of the initiative, the parity debates struck a unique chord in the soon-to-be autonomous territory. As Elana Wilson documents, the public and politicians on both sides of the issue consistently discussed gender parity through nationalist language 'namely focusing on tradition, unity and the concept of home'.[48] In particular, debates reflected a conceptualization of the new legislative assembly as the public 'home' of the Inuit nation and identity. Wilson argues: 'While the government of Nunavut is a public one, it is also meant to be a place where the Inuit nation or "family" is to be protected and promoted. Thus the opportunity arose for the incorporation of a gendered concept of "home" into formal politics.'[49]

For supporters of the parity proposal, this conceptualization allowed them to reaffirm traditional ideas of the Inuit home as a site of subsistence and cooperation in which men and women each played important roles and all aspects of group livelihood intertwined. This interdependence and gender complementarity was seen as key to Inuit survival during the pre-contact period, but as having broken down as the Inuit moved away from their traditional way of life and, in particular, as Euro-Canadian administrators became more involved in the organization of Inuit social and political life.[50] From this perspective, supporters of the proposal argued that gender parity provided a way of ensuring that Nunavut's form of government was uniquely suited to its cultural history, and that southern institutions of governance did not bring new inequalities as part of their structural baggage.[51]

Opponents of the proposal also advanced their arguments through nationalist language, maintaining that gender parity undermined the traditional sense of unity between the sexes, and created divisive feelings of difference where none had existed previously. For opponents, parity reflected individualist values. These went against the 'Inuit spirit' that was based on collective identity, and that was crucial both to the history of struggle and survival in the north, and to the principle of collective rights and collective ownership of lands that was central to the Nunavut Land Claims Agreement.[52]

Nunavut is an example where ethnic minority claims were advanced through a territorial arrangement of self-governance. In such cases, it appears that the issue of women's representation will necessarily be addressed through the language of nationalism and cultural identity. While the gender parity proposal was rejected in this instance, it is nevertheless clear that many people will view gender equality and cultural identity as fully compatible. A further dimension in

---

[48] E Wilson, 'Gender, nationalism, citizenship and Nunavut's Territorial 'House': A case study of the gender parity proposal debate' (2005) 42(2) *Arctic Anthropology* 82–94, 85.
[49] Ibid, 89.
[50] Minor, 'Political participation of Inuit women in the government of Nunavut' (n 36 above).
[51] Wilson, 'Gender, nationalism, citizenship' (n 48 above), 88.   [52] Ibid, 87.

such contexts is that members of the ethnic minority are in the position of creating a completely new representative system. It may therefore be possible to advance quite far-reaching proposals for gender equality, for part of their appeal will lie in the argument that they represent a significant democratic improvement over the political structures of the dominant ethnic group.

B. Belgium

Belgium is a case where accommodation of ethnic diversity has been developed using a consociational model of elite power-sharing. Belgian political institutions have been designed with a focus on proportionality as a means of accommodating diverse linguistic groups in decision-making processes. Notably, constitutional provisions introduced in 1970 provided for the creation of three linguist communities (Flemish-, French-, and German-speaking) and three regions (Flanders, Wallonia, and Brussels). The Flemish and French communities were given autonomy in cultural matters, the use of language and certain educational matters. In matters where they do not enjoy autonomy (areas of jurisdiction reserved to the central government), linguistic communities can exercise a 'soft veto' through their members of parliament—effectively referring a problematic bill or motion to the federal cabinet as a step towards reaching a decision that is agreeable across communities. The federal cabinet itself must, by constitutional requirement, contain an equal number of French- and Flemish-speaking ministers. Proportionality also applies to members of the highest courts, and to officers in the upper ranks of the military.

In the lower house, seats are distributed in a fashion that ensures proportional representation of distinctive linguistic communities and regions. Elections at this level are carried out using party lists and proportional representation with semi-closed lists, in multi-member constituencies with large district magnitudes. Parties, which are split along ethnic and ideological lines, must meet a minimum threshold of 5 per cent of all valid votes cast in the constituency in order to win seats. The Senate consists of two types of members—those elected directly, and those appointed—but in all cases the number of seats per linguistic groups is established beforehand. In total, forty-one seats are reserved for Flemish speakers, twenty-nine seats are reserved for French speakers, and one seat is reserved for German speakers. European elections also involve reserved seats for the Flemish, Francophone, and German-speaking communities.

Overall then, the Belgian system embodies a high degree of 'pillarization', in which linguistic identities are firmly entrenched throughout all aspects of social and political organization. It is in this context that the Belgian debate over quotas for women must be understood. Quotas were initially introduced by various Belgian political parties in the 1980s and 1990s. At the initiative of the government, legislative quotas were passed by parliament in 1994, mandating that women comprise at least 25 per cent of all electoral lists until 1999, after which the requirement would be raised to 33 per cent. Following the passage of a new law on equality between men and women, parliament revisited the measures and increased the quota to 50 per cent in 2002. The main point of contention during these debates was whether sex was a category of representation on a par with linguistic identities,[53] and this led to extensive bargaining over the form that the new quotas might take. Advocates argued that sex was a defining social characteristic equivalent to other social characteristics that underlay traditional cleavages. Opponents wondered why gender should constitute a basis for representation when many other social characteristics (for example, age) carried no such entitlement to particular attention. The governing parties agreed to gender parity (ie, a 50 per cent quota) for women, but ensured that this was distinct from the guarantees for linguistic groups. The result is that gender quotas apply to electoral lists, and thus only to candidates for office, while seats for linguistic groups are guaranteed.

The Belgian case provides further illustration of the way that gender equality and cultural identity claims intersect. As in Nunavut, the issue of gender parity was framed in relationship to the predominant form of group identity. Aware that even those opposed to gender quotas accepted the idea of linguistic proportionality, parity advocates stressed that balanced representation of key social groups was an essential legitimizing feature of the political system and mobilized on the basis of this norm to justify the adoption of parity for women. Yet the historic context of parity reform in Belgium is quite different from that in Nunavut. Rather than introducing a wholly new legislative body and system of representation, Belgian reforms came in steps, with women's representation being added after the establishment of ethnic representation. This offered a key advantage for women, as some of the procedures to ensure proportionality for linguistic communities had incidentally also promoted the inclusion of women. This was notably the case for legislative elections, which were held using party lists, PR, and large magnitude districts—all mechanisms that are known to favour higher representation of women. Not surprisingly under these conditions, most Belgian parties had already voluntarily adopted gender quotas in the composition of their lists. This meant that there was already both a significant number of female legislators ready to advocate for legislative quotas, and a base of public familiarity with such measures. Belgium thus presents a strong example where gender equality and cultural identity are viewed as quite compatible.

C. Fiji

Fiji represents a very different case than the two just discussed. Rather than devolve power to an ethnic minority (Nunavut) or introduce consociational

---

[53] P Meier, 'The Belgian paradox: Inclusion and exclusion of gender issues', J Lovenduski and C Baudino (eds), *State Feminism and Political Representation* (2005).

measures for elite power-sharing (Belgium), Fiji has instead concentrated on the need to *reduce* the salience of ethnicity so as to promote ethnic peace. Fiji is also distinct in that its minority governance arrangements have evolved in the context of limited democratic stability.

Fiji is a racially divided society, comprised mainly of indigenous and Indo-Fijians, the latter being descended from indentured labourers brought from Southern India in the nineteenth century under British colonialism. Since independence in 1970, Fiji has experienced a series of military coups, interspersed by constitutional reforms and electoral experiments intended to diminish ethnic conflict and promote democratic stability. The most recent round of reforms in 1997 included an innovative package of electoral and power-sharing arrangements.[54]

A notable feature of these provisions is an 'alternative vote' (AV) system that allows voters to indicate how they would vote if their favoured candidate was defeated and they had to choose among those remaining. The basic underlying logic of this system, as applied in a multiethnic setting, is that it promotes reciprocal vote pooling, bargaining, and accommodation across ethnic lines. Especially in deeply divided contexts where no single ethnic group dominates, candidates within an AV system cannot count only on first-preference votes from their own ethnic community; they must appeal for second-choice support from other ethnic groups as well. To attract second-level support, candidates need to make cross-ethnic appeals and demonstrate their capacity to represent groups other than their own. AV is thus thought to be preferable to strictly proportional forms of ethnic representation which, when implemented in highly divided societies (eg, Fiji 1990–7; Bosnia and Herzegovina under the Dayton Peace Accords), have deepened ethnic divisions.

Another interesting feature of the 1997 electoral reforms was the implementation of both 'communal' and 'open' seats. Representatives in communal seats are elected using ethnic voter rolls. There are forty-six such seats, with twenty-three reserved for indigenous Fijians, nineteen for Indo-Fijians, three seats for European and other ethnic minorities, and one for Rotuman Islanders. In addition, there are twenty-five open seats whose members are elected by universal suffrage open to members of any ethnic group. While the constitutional review commission initially proposed a reverse ratio of forty-five open to twenty-five communal seats, this was opposed by Fijian ethnic nationalists who view the communal seats as their power base. Many Indo-Fijians, feminists, as well as parties claiming to be multiethnic, advocate for more open seats.

---

[54] B Reilly, 'Electoral systems for divided societies' (2002) 12(2) *Journal of Democracy* 156–70; S Kumar and CP Biman, 'Preferential voting and electoral engineering: The case of Fiji's 1999 and 2001 general elections' (2004) 42 *Commonwealth and Comparative Politics* 312–32; S Ramesh, 'Preferential voting and Indo-Fijian minority strategy' (2007) 10(10) *Journal of Peace Conflict and Development* 1–27, available at <www.peacestudiesjournal.org.uk> (accessed 17 July 2009).

Initially, the new electoral system appeared promising.[55] However it was ultimately unable to secure a stable ethnic democracy, and two military coups have since occurred. The main problem is that AV is a majoritarian system, based on single-member electoral districts, that produces highly disproportionate results. Like any majoritarian system, AV over-rewards the winning party (whose candidates tend to win the preference vote in many districts), while it under-rewards smaller parties (whose candidates may come in second in a district, but are rewarded no differently than if they had come in last). A preference system based on multi-member districts (STV or 'single transferable vote') had been considered, but was deemed inferior to AV for the reason that the proportional system has a lower threshold for election. Smaller thresholds are known to promote the formation of smaller, single-issue (or single ethnic) parties, which can rarely win seats under a majoritarian electoral system.

A second problem is that Fiji's electoral system tends to underrepresent women. It is at this point that we can address the intersection between gender equality concerns and the peaceful accommodation of ethnic diversity. There are no gender quotas in Fiji, and women have fared quite poorly in electoral politics since Fijian independence. More troubling still, the fact of women's political underrepresentation has been virtually absent from discussions of electoral reform in Fiji. Even the numerous scholarly papers on Fijian electoral design fail in most instances to address the political exclusion of women.

Had women's underrepresentation been taken seriously by scholars and reformers in the Fijian case, it is probable that STV would have been advocated over AV. At the very least, it would have been necessary to weigh the benefits of AV (higher thresholds to discourage single issue/ethnicity parties) against those of STV (better proportionality and better representation of women). They might have also pushed harder for more open seats, in which women and multi-ethnic parties both achieve relatively better rates of electoral success.[56] Finally, it merits investigation whether including more women in Fijian politics, through a quota measure for example, might be a further step towards de-ethnicizing politics.

D. Afghanistan

This may yet be the most important 'gender' question for deeply divided societies: can improved women's representation be an effective component of an ethnic peace-building strategy? There is certainly growing pressure for women's participation in post-conflict state-building. This is evidenced in the UN

---

[55] Reilly, 'Electoral systems for divided societies' (n 54 above).
[56] S Siwatibau, 'Women and minority interests in Fiji's alternative electoral system' in J Fraenkel and S Firth (eds), *From Election to Coup in Fiji* (2007), 384, available at <http://epress.anu.edu.au/fiji/pdf/ch29.pdf> (accessed 17 July 2009).

Security Council Resolution 1325 on Women, Peace and Security, passed in October 2000. In the debate introducing Resolution 1325 in 2000, Kofi Anan stated that 'peace is inextricably linked to equality between women and men ... maintaining and promoting peace requires equal participation in decision-making'. This new 'gendered' peace-building discourse has been joined by expansive efforts by women's INGOs to include women in post-conflict reconstruction and peace building,[57] and to promote women's political participation and inclusion in positions of leadership in emerging democracies throughout Latin America, Africa, the Pacific, and Middle East. Initiatives include the Democracy and Gender Program of the International Institute for Democracy and Electoral Assistance (IDEA), as well as the United Nations Development Fund for Women's (UNIFEM) Gender Equality in Political Governance Program (GEPG). Both of these programmes have organized regional and state-focused workshops on electoral reform and measures to increase women's representation in national parliaments. Quotas for women's representation have thus been implemented in a number of post-conflict and ethnically divided states. Notably, in Iraq and Afghanistan, women now comprise 33 per cent and 27 per cent (respectively) of each country's national assembly.

We have yet to assess whether women's presence in the new governance structures of these states might serve to de-ethnicize politics, but there are some positive signs. In Afghanistan, presidential candidate Massouda Jalal is known to begin her speeches with the call to 'vote for your mother', and to remind Afghan voters that 'voting for your sister is voting for development, peace and a plentiful life'. Jalal's gendered discourse can be read as a strategy for confronting cultural resistance to a woman candidate, while at the same time broadening her appeal across both gender and ethnic lines.[58] Women in the Loya Jirga (Afghanistan's lower house) have also been the only voices to openly criticize the presence of regional warlords in parliament.[59] While female parliamentarians could apparently not stop the passage of a recent recommendation related to Shiite personal law, they have helped to call international attention to the contradiction between women's rights and minority rights protections that are enshrined in the Afghanistan Constitution. They have made it more difficult for President Karzai and other leaders to openly pander to ethnic interests.[60]

---

[57] SA Whittington, 'Financing for gender equality: Post-conflict reconstruction and peace-building' in *Financing Gender Equality: Commonwealth perspectives*, Commonwealth Women's Ministers Affairs Meeting (WAMM), Kampala, Uganda (June 2007), available at <http://www.peacewomen.org/resources/Reconstruction/FinancingGender.doc> (accessed 17 July 2009).
[58] A Wendle, 'Empowerment for peace: Afghanistan's unlikely presidential candidate', *The Women's International Project* (29 April 2009), available at <http://thewip.net/contributoros/2009/04/empowerment_for_peace_afghanis.html> (accessed 17 July 2009).
[59] A Gopal, 'Afghanistan: Women lawmakers battle warlords', Interpress Service News Agency, 9 March 2009, available at <http://ipsnews.net/news.asp?idnews=46028> (accessed 17 July 2009). [60] 'Women, Extremism and Two Key States', *New York Times*, 14 April 2009.

While the inclusion of women in peace- and democracy-building in countries such as Afghanistan is certainly an important achievement, there is a long way to go both towards women's rights and ethnic peace. We do, in any case, need more research on what enhanced women's representation can contribute in such contexts.

IV. Conclusions and an Agenda for Future Research

I have argued in this chapter that we have, as yet, an incomplete picture of the political exclusion experienced by ethnic minority women. This has resulted from a failure to draw sufficiently upon theories of race/ethnic and gender intersectionality, and to adequately recognize the political capacity of minority women in contexts of ethnic nationalism. Early normative work on group recognition argued that the under-representation of women and minorities was equally problematic for any theory of democracy, and postulated a unified concept of inclusion based on fairness.[61] Useful as this was in terms of expanding our understanding of democratic theory, this work failed to grapple with the enormously different obstacles to inclusion facing different kinds of groups. Subsequently, more empirically focused work on multicultural theory has moved in the opposite direction. This work—particularly the 'targeted' approach to group rights—tends to over-differentiate between women and minorities with regard to the standards and appropriate remedies for under-representation of each group. The result is that research on women's and ethnic minority representation in politics has evolved along two quite separate tracks. Both normatively and empirically, ethnic minority women have fallen through the gap.

Yet the fact remains that ethnic minority women everywhere are implicated by both gendered and ethnic forms of exclusion. And increasingly, as we have seen above, actual proposals for representational fairness in countries around the world are being made with *both* women and ethnic minorities in mind. This is not to say that women and ethnic minorities are equally successful in terms of the outcomes of these proposals. Resulting reforms often benefit one group and not the other, but it is increasingly difficult to have a debate about representational fairness for one group without at least considering the other. Unfortunately, our normative and empirical frameworks have not kept pace with the reality on the ground. What we need then are more conversations between researchers focusing on women's representation and those focusing on ethnic minority representation, and more points of contact between advocates working towards advancing political inclusion for each group. We need to be highly

---

[61] J Mansbridge 'Should blacks represent blacks and women represent women? A contingent "yes"' (1999) 61(3) *Journal of Politics* 628–57.

sensitive to historical and political differences in the management of ethnic diversity, and in the relationships between women's claims and those of minorities. While there may be no general formula for adjudicating the representational needs of women and ethnic minorities simultaneously, further comparative analysis of the solutions that have been worked out, with careful attention to contextual circumstances, will help us to develop better knowledge in this domain. This is not simply an academic challenge: there is a pressing need for practical recommendations to ensure fair outcomes for both women and ethnic minorities. And there is a possibility that advancing this agenda will produce more stable and peaceful forms of democratic governance.

PART II
LEGAL FRAMEWORKS

6

Minorities, Political Participation, and Democratic Governance under the European Convention on Human Rights

*Steven Wheatley**

I. The Lund Recommendations in Global Governance	178
II. Democratic Elections	180
A. The nature of the electoral system	183
B. The right to vote in elections	187
C. The right to stand in elections	188
III. Rights of Political Participation in Democratic Politics	195
A. The right to freedom of political expression	196
B. The right to freedom of political association	197
C. Political parties	198
D. Ethnic political parties	199
E. Civil society organizations	201
F. Privileges which follow the fact of association	202
IV. The Democratic Society and the Need for 'Democratic Law'	204
V. The 'Minority' Right to be Different (Art 8)	207
Deliberating on the rights of minorities	210
VI. 'Self-governance'	214
A. Territorial self-government: 'autonomy'	215
B. Non-territorial self-government	217
VII. Conclusion	219

This chapter examines the rights of persons belonging to national minorities to political participation and democratic governance under the European

---

* Thanks to Professor Bill Bowring, Birkbeck College, University of London for his comments on the chapter; the usual caveat applies.

Convention on Human Rights (ECHR), as interpreted by the European Court of Human Rights (ECtHR),[1] in light of the schema suggested by the Lund Recommendations on the Effective Participation of National Minorities in Public Life ('Lund Recommendations'). Following some initial comments on the position of the Lund Recommendations and ECHR in the European system of governance on minorities, the work proceeds with an examination of the Convention rights to political participation in democratic elections and democratic politics, before evaluating the extent to which substantive 'democratic' laws must accommodate the interests of ethno-cultural minorities and the idea of 'self-governance' for (national) minorities.[2] The chapter concludes by reflecting on the fact of fragmentation in the European law on minorities, and the extent to which this creates opportunities for minority activists, advocates, and representatives to develop the international law protection of minorities.

I. The Lund Recommendations in Global Governance

According to the positive orthodoxy, international lawmaking is the preserve of states and international courts (and other judicial-like bodies) that provide authoritative interpretations as to the meaning, scope and extent of inter-state obligations.[3] Instruments such as the Lund Recommendations are dealt with under the rubric of 'soft law', which is not (apparently) (international) 'law'. Soft law norms may point to the future direction of international law (*lex ferenda*), or be evidence of existing customary international law, but they are not themselves regarded as a source of international law obligation.[4] The problem with this argument is that it fails to explain why soft international law standards are framed in terms of 'law', or the influence of soft law norms on the behaviour of state and non-state actors. Both 'hard' and 'soft' forms of international law define legitimate state behaviour by reference to 'law' norms; both influence domestic politics, as actors seek to rely on global governance norms in democratic debates; both rely on domestic governmental institutions for their effective implementation; and both rely on a complex 'interpretive community' of formal judicial bodies and other international law actors to 'judge' conduct against

---

[1] The European Court of Human Rights has the final and thus 'constitutionally' decisive say on the interpretation of the Convention: Art 32(1) of the Convention for the Protection of Human Rights and Fundamental Freedoms, CETS no 005 (as amended). The European Court of Human Rights has described the ECHR as a constitutional instrument of European public order in the field of human rights: *Loizidou v Turkey*, A310, para 75.

[2] Whilst the focus of OSCE instruments is the position of 'national minorities', the ECHR does not distinguish between 'minorities' and 'national minorities'.

[3] See A Orakhelashvili, *The Interpretation of Acts and Rules of Public International Law* (2008), 287–8.

[4] D Shelton, 'Introduction' in D Shelton (ed.) *Commitment and Compliance: The role of non-binding norms in the international legal system* (2000), 6.

international 'law' norms, and in doing so develop the law. The distinctive characteristic of 'soft law' is not that it is 'soft', but that it is 'law': a system of communications ('directives') framed in terms of law, ie coded legal/illegal or other binary equivalent, issued by an authority to subjects of a legal regime, with law actors capable of interpreting the content and application of law norms and consequently of developing the law. The idea does not only include state law and international law, but any exercise of legitimate political authority framed in terms of law.[5]

The Lund Recommendations were developed to assist the OSCE High Commissioner on National Minorities in his conflict prevention role, as the High Commissioner seeks, where he is involved, to ensure the compliance of OSCE participating states with their international law obligations, including 'soft' OSCE standards. The Recommendations were drawn up at a meeting of international experts brought together by the High Commissioner, including international lawyers, political scientists, and sociologists, with the objective being 'to elaborate recommendations and outline alternatives, in line with the relevant international standards'.[6] The authority and influence of the Recommendations rests, in part, on the fact of expert deliberation and that they reflect, to some extent, existing international law standards.[7] The Recommendations are largely framed in terms of 'good practice': 'States *should favourably consider* such territorial devolution of powers, including specific functions of self-government.'[8] A number are though framed in terms of 'law', and capable of resulting in a determination that impugned conduct is not consistent with the norms contained in the Recommendations: 'States *shall guarantee the right* of persons belonging to national minorities to take part in the conduct of public affairs, including through the rights to vote and stand for office without discrimination.'[9]

By contrast, the European Convention on Human Rights is an instrument of 'hard' international law: it creates international law obligations that engage the responsibility of states parties to each other, and to individuals subject to their jurisdiction.[10] The Convention provides for the protection of human rights in the context of democracy; its objective is the establishment of a 'democratic society' in each of the states parties, in which both the individual and collective aspects of self-determination are respected. A number of Convention rights are absolute;[11]

---

[5] See N Luhmann, *Law as a Social System*, K Ziegert (trans) (2004); G Teubner, 'How the law thinks: Toward a constructivist epistemology of law' (1989) 23 Law and Society Review 727–57; B Tamanaha, *A General Jurisprudence of Law and Society* (2001); and J Raz, *The Authority of Law* (1979). See further S Wheatley, 'Indigenous peoples and the right of political autonomy in an age of global legal pluralism', in M Freeman and D Napier (eds.) 12 *Current Legal Issues* (2009) 351.
[6] Lund Recommendations, 'Introduction'.
[7] See Recommendations and Explanatory Note.
[8] Lund Recommendations, para19 (emphasis added).   [9] Ibid, para 7 (emphasis added).
[10] See Art 33(2) of the International Law Commission, Draft Articles on State Responsibility, with Commentaries, Report of the International Law Commission, 53rd session, UN Doc A/56/10 (2001), 59.   [11] Eg, Arts 3 (torture) and 4 (slavery).

others are conditional, in the sense that they can be subject to interference only in defined and limited circumstances;[12] others require that the interests of the individual are 'balanced' against those of the wider society (Arts 8–11).[13] Interferences in the private autonomy rights, ie the right to private life, and rights to freedom of religion, expression and association, must be 'prescribed by [democratic] law' and 'necessary in a democratic society'.

The function of the Court established under the ECHR is to ensure the observance of the engagements undertaken by states parties,[14] not to suggest examples of good practice.[15] The Court is constrained by its constitutive instrument, the Convention; it is not a 'legislature', or an expert advisory body. Two further points: the Court is a supranational body and not a domestic constitutional court, a fact that significantly limits any potential role in disputes between the state authorities and minorities; secondly, in the absence of coercive enforcement mechanisms, the ability of the Court to 'command' compliance is dependent on the extent to which its authority is accepted by states parties, both individually and collectively,[16] a fact it will be aware of in any judgments concerning politically sensitive issues, such as the nature of an electoral system, or treatment of persons belonging to minorities. The margin-of-appreciation doctrine is, in part, a recognition by the Court that it operates within political boundaries, and, in contrast to national authorities, without direct democratic legitimacy.

II. Democratic Elections

There is an acceptance in the international community that democracy is the only legitimate form of domestic government.[17] Central to the practice of democracy is the holding of free and fair elections to a legislative assembly.[18] The right of the citizen to participate directly in formal democratic processes under the ECHR applies only in relation to elections to 'legislative' bodies; it does not, for example, (automatically) apply to elections to an executive presidency,[19] or in the case of referenda.[20] One function of elections is to determine the identity of representatives. The liberal principle of consent to law norms provides that all those subject to the law have the right to be represented in the formal processes that lead to their adoption. The implementation of this right is

---

[12] Eg, Art 2 (life).   [13] See also Art 6.1 of the ECHR.   [14] Art 19 of the ECHR.
[15] Cf *Yumak and Sadak v Turkey*, Appl 10226/03, Judgment, 8 July 2008 [GC], (below).
[16] Cf Art 46.2 of the ECHR.
[17] See GA Res 60/1, adopted 16 September 2005, '2005 World Summit Outcome', para 135.
[18] Art 21(3) of the Universal Declaration of Human Rights: GA Res 217(III)A, adopted 10 December 1948, 'International Bill of Human Rights'.
[19] Cf *Boskoski v Former Yugoslav Republic of Macedonia*, Reports of Judgments and Decisions 2004–VI.   [20] *X v United Kingdom*, DR 3, at 165.

particularly important for those members of society whose life experiences are different from those of the dominant majority. The composition of the legislative body should ensure, as far as possible (consistent with the practical requirements of democratic lawmaking), that those subject to the law are represented in law-making debates.

The European Court of Human Rights has referred to the 'crucial role played in a representative democracy by parliament, which is the main instrument of democratic control and political responsibility'.[21] According to the Universal Declaration on Democracy, adopted by the Inter-parliamentary Union, democracy requires the existence of a parliament in which 'all components of society are represented'.[22] Non-dominant minorities cannot be represented by (dominant) 'others', who attempt to take their interests into account. The Lund Recommendations provide that states 'shall' guarantee the right of persons belonging to national minorities to vote and stand for office without discrimination, but only that the system 'should' facilitate minority representation and influence.[23] In relation to elections, they note that experience in Europe and elsewhere 'demonstrates the importance of the electoral process for facilitating the participation of minorities in the political sphere'.[24] Depending on the particular circumstances, single-member districts, proportional representation, or preference voting may facilitate minority representation; moreover, '[l]ower numerical thresholds for representation in the legislature may enhance the inclusion of national minorities in governance'.[25] No particular electoral system is necessarily more beneficial to minorities than another; both first-past-the-post and proportional systems of voting may facilitate greater minority representation.

The ECHR was established to preserve the rule of law and the principles of democracy, and protect the democratic systems of Western Europe states from threats from the totalitarian right and left through the establishment of a supranational legal order. Democracy is central to the ECHR regime; it is the

---

[21] *Yumak and Sadak v Turkey*, Appl 10226/03, Judgment 8 July 2008 [GC], para 140.

[22] Inter-parliamentary Union's Universal Declaration on Democracy, adopted without a vote by the Inter-parliamentary Council at its 161st session (Cairo, 16 September 1997), para 11. See also Human Rights Committee, General Comment 25, 'Article 25 (Participation in public affairs and the right to vote)', adopted 12 July 1996, reprinted 'Compilation of General Comments and General Recommendations', 167, para 22.

[23] Lund Recommendations, para 7. The Lund Recommendations also argue that geographic boundaries of electoral districts should facilitate the equitable representation of national minorities: para 10. See also OSCE Office for Democratic Institutions and Human Rights' report, 'Existing Commitments for Democratic Elections in OSCE Participating States' (Warsaw, 2003), available at <http://www.osce.org/item/13587.html> (accessed 17 September 2009), para 2.4: 'The system for direct election of legislators and other public officials is a matter for national determination, provided the system operates transparently; is based on universal and equal suffrage of voters; and does not discriminate among candidates and political parties. In choosing an electoral system, states should take into account to what extent it gives effect to the will of the voters, preserves political pluralism, and protects the interests of minorities and other groups in society.'

[24] Lund Recommendations, para 7.   [25] Ibid, para 9.

only political model compatible with the ECHR,[26] although it is, in the words of the ECtHR, 'for each Contracting State to mould into their own democratic vision'.[27] The relevant provision is Art 3 of the Protocol to the Convention for the Protection of Human Rights and Fundamental Freedoms (1952) (hereafter P1-3):

The High Contracting Parties undertake to hold free elections at reasonable intervals by secret ballot, under conditions which will ensure the free expression of the opinion of the people in the choice of the legislature.[28]

It is not clear from the *travaux préparatoires* whether the states parties intended to create individual rights of participation in free and fair elections in the ECHR, and P1-3 is framed in terms of obligations, ie to hold free elections at reasonable intervals by secret ballot. The European Court of Human Rights has, though, interpreted the provision to include implied rights for individuals to vote and to stand in elections: 'the unique phrasing was intended to give greater solemnity to the Contracting States' commitment'.[29] In *Hirst v United Kingdom (no 2)*, the Grand Chamber observed that individual rights of political participation in democratic elections are 'crucial to establishing and maintaining the foundations of an effective and meaningful democracy'.[30] Those rights are not absolute, but subject to implied limitations, with states parties accorded a margin of appreciation—a recognition that the compliance of states parties with their obligations under the ECHR, including the organizing of electoral systems, may be achieved in a number of ways depending on the priorities of the relevant states parties.[31] Given that P1-3 does not specify or limit the aims that a restriction must pursue, a wide range of purposes may be compatible with the provision,[32] and the aims of any limitations are not restricted to those prescribed in Arts 10(2) and 11(2), concerning the rights of (political) expression and association.[33] The Court has established the following principles: any limitation must not curtail the rights in question to such an extent as to impair their very essence and deprive them of their effectiveness; the limitation must pursue a legitimate aim and must not be disproportionate; and finally, any restrictions 'must not thwart the free expression of the people in the choice of the legislature —in other words, they must reflect, or not run counter to, the concern to

---

[26] *Ždanoka v Latvia*, Reports of Judgments and Decisions 2006-IV [GC], para 98.
[27] *Hirst v United Kingdom (no 2)*, Reports of Judgments and Decisions 2005–IX [GC], para 61.
[28] Art 3 of the Protocol to the Convention for the Protection of Human Rights and Fundamental Freedoms (1952) CETS no 009.
[29] *Hirst v United Kingdom (no 2)*, Reports of Judgments and Decisions 2005–IX [GC], para 57.
[30] Ibid, para 58.   [31] Ibid, para 61.   [32] Ibid, para 74.
[33] In *Ždanoka v Latvia*, the Grand Chamber noted that P1-3 concerns the 'institutional order of the State'. It is framed in 'very different terms' from Arts 8–11 and 'must therefore be considered to be less stringent than those applied under Arts 8–11 of the Convention': *Ždanoka v Latvia*, Reports of Judgments and Decisions 2006-IV [GC], para 115.

maintain the integrity and effectiveness of an electoral procedure *aimed at identifying the will of the people through universal suffrage*.[34]

A. The nature of the electoral system

P1-3 is expressed in collective and general terms; it does not require the introduction of any particular electoral system, and there is no requirement to ensure the (proportionate) representation of national, ethnic, religious, linguistic, or other (democratic) minority. The objective of Art 3, Protocol 1 to the ECHR (1952) is an electoral system that ensures 'the free expression of the opinion of the people in the choice of the legislature'. The position of the Court in relation to P1-3 was established in *Mathieu-Mohin and Clerfayt*, which arose out of the complex political settlement in Belgium, designed to accommodate the interests of the Flemish (Dutch-speaking) and Walloon (French-speaking) language groups. The district of Halle-Vilvoorde was in the French district for national elections, but the Flemish district for elections to the regional council. A candidate elected to the national parliament who took the parliamentary oath in French could not be a member of the Flemish council; likewise, an elected representative who took the parliamentary oath in Dutch could not belong to the French-language group in parliament, which played 'an important role in those areas in which the Constitution requires special majorities'.[35] The Court of Human Rights accepted that the aim of the constitutional settlement was the defusing of language disputes 'by establishing more stable and decentralised organisational structures'. One consequence was that linguistic minorities were required to vote for candidates 'willing and able to use the language of their region'. French-speaking voters in Halle-Vilvoorde enjoyed the same right to vote and stand as Dutch-speaking electors, albeit that they had to vote 'either for candidates who will take the parliamentary oath in French and will accordingly join the French-language group in [Parliament], or else for candidates who will take the oath in Dutch and so belong to the Dutch-language group in the House of Representatives or the Senate and sit on the Flemish Council'. This was not a 'disproportionate limitation' on the rights recognized in P1-3, even when taken with Art 14 of the ECHR.[36]

In its judgment, the Court noted that electoral systems 'seek to fulfil objectives which are sometimes scarcely compatible with each other: on the one hand, to reflect fairly faithfully the opinions of the people and on the other, to channel currents of thought so as to promote the emergence of a sufficiently clear and coherent political will'. The principle of political equality of citizens does not though require that 'all votes must necessarily have equal weight as regards the

---

[34] *Yumak and Sadak v Turkey*, Appl 10226/03, Judgment 8 July 2008 [GC], para 109 (emphasis added). [35] *Mathieu-Mohin and Clerfayt*, A 113 (1987), para 56.
[36] Ibid, para 57.

outcome of the election or that all candidates must have equal chances of victory'.[37] The dissenting minority disagreed, concluding that the interference did in fact constitute a violation of Convention rights, given that elected members of parliament for Halle-Vilvoorde could not, if they took the parliamentary oath in French, sit on the Flemish council, and were consequently 'unable to defend their Region's interests in a number of important fields whereas elected representatives who take the oath in Dutch are automatically members of the Flemish Council'. In the case of French-speaking voters, unless they voted for Dutch-speaking candidates, they would not be represented on the Flemish council.[38]

No system is capable of mirroring the plurality of identities, interests and perspectives in society; the design of an electoral system reflects an exercise of political choice that has a significant impact on the identity of those who gain and hold power, and those represented in the national parliament. The need to ensure the emergence of a 'clear and coherent' political will might lead the national authorities (ie political parties in control of national lawmaking bodies) to seek to exclude significant political minorities from electoral representation. The electoral system in Turkey, for example, has a 10 per cent threshold for representation in the national parliament, the justification for which is the perceived need to prevent excessive and debilitating parliamentary fragmentation, and thus strengthen governmental stability.[39] In the 2002 elections, eighteen parties stood for election; only three succeeded in passing the 10 per cent threshold, with the AKP (*Adalet ve Kalkınma*, Justice and Development Party, a party of the conservative right),[40] obtaining two-thirds of the seats in the national assembly on one-third of the votes cast.[41]

The 10 per cent threshold was challenged before the ECtHR in *Yumak and Sadak v Turkey*. Electoral thresholds fall within the margin of appreciation of states parties, and are an area in which they enjoy 'considerable latitude'.[42] The margin is not unlimited, however, with the Court focusing mainly on two issues: whether there has been arbitrariness or a lack of proportionality, and whether the restriction has interfered with the free expression of the opinion of the people.[43] In this case, the applicants stood unsuccessfully in the parliamentary elections of 3 November 2002 as candidates of the People's Democratic Party (DEHAP), known for its interest in the 'Kurdish question'. The election produced the least representative parliament in Turkey since the introduction of the multi-party system in 1946, with 45.3 per cent of the electorate, around 14.5 million voters, not represented in parliament, in addition to the 22 per cent of registered voters, who had abstained from voting.[44] DEHAP polled 6.22 per cent

---

[37] Ibid, para 54.
[38] Joint Dissenting Opinion of Judges Cremona, Bindschedler-Robert, Bernhardt, Spielmann and Valticos (Translation).
[39] *Yumak and Sadak v Turkey*, Appl 10226/03, Judgment 8 July 2008 [GC], para 125.
[40] Ibid, para 16. [41] Ibid, para 17. [42] Ibid, para 64. [43] Ibid, para 109.
[44] Ibid, para 19.

of the national vote, and 46 per cent of votes cast in the constituency of Şırnak, but failed to obtain parliamentary representation as a result of the 10 per cent threshold.[45]

The ECHR affords states parties a wide margin of discretion in the design of electoral systems, and does not require that minorities are represented on a (roughly) proportionate basis: P1-3 'goes no further than prescribing "free" elections held at "reasonable intervals" "by secret ballot" and "under conditions which will ensure the free expression of the opinion of the people". Subject to that reservation, it does not create any "obligation to introduce a specific system" such as proportional representation or majority voting with one or two ballots.'[46] In *Yumak and Sadak*, the Court observed that whilst P1-3 does not, in principle, impose any obligation to adopt an electoral system guaranteeing parliamentary representation to parties with an 'essentially regional base', ie political parties representing a territorial or national minority, that 'a problem might arise if the relevant legislation tended to deprive such parties of parliamentary representation'.[47] The function of the Court is to examine whether electoral laws have the effect of excluding certain persons or groups, 'and whether the discrepancies created by a particular electoral system can be considered arbitrary or abusive or whether the system tends to favour one political party or candidate by *giving them an electoral advantage at the expense of others*'.[48] In a democracy, the rules of the electoral game should be known to all participants and administered in a way which is transparent, impartial, and independent from political manipulation.[49] In its judgment in *Yumak and Sadak v Turkey*, the Grand Chamber noted that the effects of any electoral threshold may differ from one state party to the next, and that different electoral systems may pursue 'different, sometimes even antagonistic, political aims. One system might concentrate more on a fair representation of the parties in parliament, while another one might aim to avoid a fragmentation of the party system and encourage the formation of a governing majority of one party in parliament[.] None of these aims can be considered unreasonable in itself.'[50]

The 10 per cent electoral threshold was the highest of any European system, and well above the 3 per cent recommended by the Parliamentary Assembly of the Council of Europe.[51] The Grand Chamber observed that an electoral threshold 'of about 5 per cent' would correspond more closely to the common practice of states parties.[52] The Chamber and Grand Chamber both concluded

---

[45] Ibid, para 125. [46] Ibid, 110. [47] Ibid, 124.
[48] Ibid, para 121 (references omitted) (emphasis added).
[49] *Georgian Labour Party v Georgia*, Appl 9103/04, Judgment 8 July 2008, para 101. The Court went on to assert that 'the raison d'être of an electoral commission is to ensure the effective administration of free and fair polls in an impartial manner, which, in the Court's opinion, would be impossible to achieve if that commission becomes another forum for political struggle between election candidates': ibid, para 108.
[50] *Yumak and Sadak v Turkey*, Appl 10226/03, Judgment 8 July 2008 [GC], para 131.
[51] Ibid, para 52–3. [52] Ibid, para 132.

that the threshold was excessive,[53] with the Chamber noting that it would be 'desirable' for it to be lowered, or for 'corrective counterbalances to be introduced to ensure optimal representation of the various political tendencies without sacrificing the objective sought (the establishment of stable parliamentary majorities)'.[54]

The argument of the government before the Court was that the applicants could have been elected had they stood as independent candidates, or entered an electoral coalition with a larger political party.[55] The Grand Chamber noted that political parties in Turkey had managed to develop strategies to 'attenuate' certain of the effects of the electoral threshold.[56] When evaluated in light of the political context of the elections in question, 'and attended as it is by correctives and other guarantees which have limited its effects in practice', the threshold did not (in the view of the Grand Chamber) impair the essence of the rights guaranteed by Art 3, Protocol to the ECHR.[57] Judges Tulkens, Vajić, Jaeger, and Šikuta dissented, noting that the voting system failed to accommodate 'the interests and opinions of a large part of the electorate that identifies strongly with a particular region, or with a national or other minority'.[58] They also criticized the reliance by the majority of the Court on 'stratagems' or 'ruses' used by political parties to avoid finding a violation of P1-3, concluding that it was difficult to see how the fundamental goals underlying the Convention could be achieved 'if based on electoral rules that need to be circumvented in order to be compatible with the Convention'.[59]

The democratic principle that all those affected by the law have a right participate in the making of the law requires that all groups are represented in the national legislature. The principle must be balanced against the realities of the practice of democracy (there is, for example, a limit to the number of representatives) and other democratic principles, including the need to design an electoral system that can provide a clear expression of the 'will of the people'. The design of the electoral system is an area in which states parties are accorded a wide margin of appreciation, consistent with the aim of holding free and fair elections to 'ensure the free expression of the opinion of the people in the choice of the legislature' (P1-3). In relation to Turkey, there must be a degree of concern about the high percentage of 'wasted votes' in the 2002 elections;[60] the real concern is the suspicion that the electoral system is designed to exclude the

---

[53] Ibid, para 147.
[54] *Yumak and Sadak v Turkey*, Appl 10226/03, Judgment 30 January 2007, para 77.
[55] *Yumak and Sadak v Turkey*, Appl 10226/03, Judgment 8 July 2008 [GC], para 133.
[56] Ibid, para 143. [57] Ibid, para 147.
[58] Joint Dissenting Opinion of Judges Tulkens, Vajić, Jaeger and šikuta, para 5.
[59] Ibid, para 6 (references omitted).
[60] The Court observed that, with the exception of the 2002 elections, the proportion of the votes cast for ultimately unsuccessful candidates never exceeded 19.4 per cent and the proportion of votes for candidates who failed to secure a seat fell to 13.1 per cent in the elections of 22 July 2007: *Yumak and Sadak v Turkey*, Appl 10226/03, Judgment, 8 July 2008 [GC], para 142.

minority Kurdish population from effective and proportionate electoral representation, an issue that *Yumak and Sadak* does not directly confront.

B. The right to vote in elections

Democracy is a system of government that seeks to give expression to the will of the people on a basis of political equality: 'one person–one vote', etc. In *Hirst v United Kingdom (no 2)*, the Grand Chamber observed that '[u]niversal suffrage has become the basic principle'.[61] Any departure 'risks undermining the democratic validity of the legislature thus elected and the laws which it promulgates',[62] implying a distinction between law and 'democratic' law. The right to vote is not however absolute; it is subject to implied limitations,[63] and states parties enjoy a margin of appreciation.[64] The limitations permitted by P1-3 are not the same as those in relation to Arts 10 and 11; states parties may additionally rely on an aim not provided in those provisions, provided that the aim in question is compatible 'with the principle of the rule of law and the general objectives of the Convention'.[65] Any restrictions must not curtail the right to such an extent as to impair its very essence, and must pursue a legitimate aim; the means employed must not be disproportionate.

Limitations on the right to vote must not thwart the free expression of the people in the choice of the legislature: they must 'maintain the integrity and effectiveness of an electoral procedure aimed at identifying the will of the people through universal suffrage'. Acceptable limitations include minimum age requirements, to ensure the maturity of those participating in the electoral process, and residence requirements, to identify those with sufficiently continuous or close links to, or a stake in, the country concerned. In *Hirst v United Kingdom (no 2)*, an application concerning the general and automatic disenfranchisement of convicted prisoners, the Grand Chamber noted that the rights in P1-3, 'which enshrines the individual's capacity to influence the composition of the lawmaking power', do not exclude the possibility of imposing restrictions on the rights of political participation in the case of individuals and associations 'whose conduct threatened to undermine the rule of law or democratic foundations'.[66] The exclusion of any group or category of individuals from the right to vote must, however, be consistent with the underlying purposes of P1-3.[67] A restriction affecting all convicted prisoners in custody exceeded any acceptable margin of appreciation, resulting in a finding of a violation of the Article.[68]

---

[61] *Hirst v United Kingdom (no 2)*, Reports of Judgments and Decisions 2005–IX [GC], para 59.
[62] *Yumak and Sadak v Turkey*, Appl 10226/03, Judgment 8 July 2008 [GC], para 109.
[63] *Hirst v United Kingdom (no 2)*, Reports of Judgments and Decisions 2005–IX [GC], para 60.
[64] Ibid, para 61.
[65] *Ždanoka v Latvia*, Reports of Judgments and Decisions 2006–IV [GC], para 115.
[66] *Hirst v United Kingdom (no 2)*, Reports of Judgments and Decisions 2005–IX [GC], para 71.
[67] Ibid, para 62.   [68] Ibid, paras 84–5.

The arbitrary exclusion of one part of the population from the right to vote is not consistent with the rights recognized under the ECHR. There is no reason to consider that a group defined by reference to ethno-cultural identity could be denied the right to vote on the basis of national, ethnic, religious, or linguistic identity—certainly not when read with Art 14 of the ECHR, which provides that the enjoyment of Convention rights shall be secured without discrimination on any ground.[69] Art 14 makes express reference to race, colour, language, religion, and association with a national minority as prohibited grounds. Discrimination on the basis of ethnic identity is a form of racial discrimination,[70] and the Court has affirmed that no difference in treatment based on ethnic origin is capable of being objectively justified in a contemporary democratic society.[71] No individual may be denied the right to vote on account of association with a national or ethnic, religious, or linguistic minority.

C. The right to stand in elections

The 'active' aspect of the rights under P1-3, ie the right to vote, is accompanied by a 'passive' aspect, the right to stand in elections.[72] Once elected, the individual and the electorate have a legitimate expectation that a representative will not be arbitrarily removed from office.[73] The right to vote does not include an implied right to vote for a particular candidate or political party: the right to vote does not provide 'a general guarantee that every voter should be able to find on the ballot paper the candidate or the party he had intended to vote for'.[74] The right to stand for election to the legislature is implied separately by P1-3; it is not unlimited, with the Court recognizing a wide margin of appreciation.

The potential exclusionary effects of restrictive criteria for minorities can be seen in *Podkolzina v Latvia*, where the applicant complained that the denial of the right to stand in parliamentary elections because of insufficient knowledge of

---

[69] See *Matthews v United Kingdom*, Reports of Judgments and Decisions 1999–I [GC]; also *Aziz v Cyprus*, Reports of Judgments and Decisions 2004–V, para 28: 'Although the Court notes that States enjoy considerable latitude to establish rules within their constitutional order governing parliamentary elections and the composition of the parliament[,]...these rules should not be such as to exclude some persons or groups of persons from participating in the political life of the country and, in particular, in the choice of the legislature.' Art 14 of the ECHR: 'The enjoyment of the rights and freedoms set forth in this Convention shall be secured without discrimination on any ground such as sex, race, colour, language, religion, political or other opinion, national or social origin, association with a national minority, property, birth or other status.'
[70] *Timishev v Russia*, Reports of Judgments and Decisions 2005–XII, para 56. Whilst the idea of race 'is rooted in the idea of biological classification of human beings into subspecies[,] ethnicity has its origin in the idea of societal groups marked by common nationality, tribal affiliation, religious faith, shared language, or cultural and traditional origins and backgrounds': ibid, para 55.
[71] Ibid, para 58.
[72] *Ždanoka v Latvia*, Reports of Judgments and Decisions 2006–IV [GC], para 106.
[73] Cf *Lykourezos v Greece*, Appl 33554/03, Judgment, 15 June 2006.
[74] *Russian Conservative Party of Entrepreneurs and ors v Russia*, Appl 55066/00 and 55638/00, Judgment, 11 January 2007, para 79.

Latvian constituted a violation of the rights recognized in P1-3. The Court reaffirmed its position that the right to stand in elections may be subject to limitations, provided those limitations do not curtail the rights to such an extent as to impair their very essence and deprive them of their effectiveness, that they are imposed in pursuit of a legitimate aim and that the means employed are not disproportionate.[75] States parties have a 'broad latitude to establish constitutional rules on the status of members of parliament, including criteria for declaring them ineligible'. The criteria will vary in accordance with the 'historical and political factors specific to each State'. In an expression that is much repeated, although without clear explication, the Court concluded that *'features that would be unacceptable in the context of one system may be justified in the context of another'*, and that electoral systems that would not be acceptable in one context might be acceptable in another, provided that the system ensures the 'free expression of the opinion of the people in the choice of the legislature'.[76]

The reasoning is unclear. According to the doctrine of the rule of law, the application of law to substantially the same set of facts should *ceteris paribus* lead to the same conclusion—either impugned conduct is lawful, or it is unlawful (principles of equality before the law and legal certainty). The ECHR obliges states parties to secure to everyone within their jurisdiction the Convention rights recognized in section I, ECHR,[77] subject to the application of the margin of appreciation doctrine, with the exception of rights that have been derogated in times of 'war or other public emergency threatening the life of the nation'.[78] Reference to 'historical and political factors' justifying 'features that would be unacceptable in the context of one system may be justified in the context of another' suggests the introduction of an intermediate category without any determination as to the circumstances in which such an exception might apply, or procedural requirement that the state party declare that its case is 'exceptional':[79] the determination is made *ex post facto* by the ECtHR.

In many cases, historical factors relate to the transition to democracy in states parties in Central and Eastern Europe. In *Georgian Labour Party v Georgia*, the Court noted the 'shortcomings in the new system for the registration of voters', but concluded that 'it would have been an excessive and impracticable burden to expect from the authorities an ideal solution to the problem of chaotic electoral rolls given the time constraints'. It was more important that the national authorities acknowledged the existence of the problem and 'spared no effort in

---

[75] *Podkolzina v Latvia*, Reports of Judgments and Decisions 2002–II, para 33.
[76] Ibid, para 33 (emphasis added). See also *Melnychenko v Ukraine*, Reports of Judgments and Decisions 2004–X, para 56; *Py v France*, Reports of Judgments and Decisions 2005–I (extracts), para 46; *Georgian Labour Party v Georgia*, Appl 9103/04, judgment 8 July 2008, para 89; and *Yumak and Sadak v Turkey*, Appl 10226/03, Judgment, 8 July 2008 [GC], para 111.
[77] Art 1 of the ECHR.   [78] Art 15.1 of the ECHR.
[79] Cf Art 15.3 of the ECHR: 'Any High Contracting Party availing itself of this right of derogation shall keep the Secretary General of the Council of Europe fully informed of the measures which it has taken and the reasons therefor.'

tackling it so that the repeat election could be fairer'.[80] In a 'post-revolutionary' political situation, and in the transition to democracy, imperfections in the system might not justify a finding a violation under P1-3—'features that would be unacceptable in the context of one system may be justified in the context of another'.[81] In relation to the positive obligations under P1-3, the Court has referred to the need for states parties to do 'everything that could reasonably have been expected of them'.[82]

Podkolzina v Latvia concerned indirect discrimination: the exclusion of certain members of a linguistic minority (ethnic Russians) by reference to a language test. In its judgment, the Court observed that the obligation for a candidate to understand and speak Latvian was 'warranted by the need to ensure the proper functioning of Parliament, in which Latvian is the sole working language'; the requirement therefore pursued a legitimate aim.[83] The process by which the candidate was deemed to have insufficient knowledge of Latvian was however procedurally deficient, leading to a finding of a violation.[84] The imposition of mandatory language requirements is not itself a violation of the rights contained in P1-3, even taken with Art 14 of the ECHR: the issue falls with the margin of appreciation accorded to states parties, who may exclude candidates with insufficient knowledge of the language(s) used in the national parliament, provided that the substantive grounds are clearly established and subject of parliamentary and public debate.

In *Ždanoka v Latvia*, the Court was required to examine electoral laws that directly excluded one part of the population from the right to stand in parliamentary elections—persons who had actively participated in the Communist Party of Latvia after 13 January 1991, when the Soviet Union sought to repress moves towards Latvian independence (again, principally the ethnic Russian minority).[85] The Court accepted the possibility that a group of persons might seek to rely on Convention rights in order to destroy the rights set forth in the ECHR; 'any such destruction would put an end to democracy'. It was this concern that led to the introduction of Art 17, 'Prohibition of abuse of rights'.[86] The Court reaffirmed its position that the ECHR did not prevent the

---

[80] *Georgian Labour Party v Georgia*, Appl 9103/04, Judgment, 8 July 2008, para 87.
[81] Ibid, para 89.   [82] Ibid, para 125.
[83] *Podkolzina v Latvia*, Reports of Judgments and Decisions 2002–II, para 34.
[84] Ibid, para 36.   [85] See *Ždanoka v Latvia*, Dissenting Opinion of Judge Zupančič.
[86] *Ždanoka v Latvia*, Reports of Judgments and Decisions 2006-IV [GC], para 99. The Court continued (ibid, para 100): 'in order to guarantee the stability and effectiveness of a democratic system, the State may be required to take specific measures to protect itself… Every time a State intends to rely on the principle of "a democracy capable of defending itself" in order to justify interference with individual rights, it must carefully evaluate the scope and consequences of the measure under consideration, to ensure that the aforementioned balance is achieved.' Art 17 of the ECHR reads 'Nothing in this Convention may be interpreted as implying for any State, group or person any right to engage in any activity or perform any act aimed at the destruction of any of the rights and freedoms set forth herein or at their limitation to a greater extent than is provided for in the Convention.'

introduction of legislative measures that treated a certain group of individuals differently from another group, or from others.[87] It had previously concluded that a class of persons could be excluded provided the definition of the categories of persons affected (members of the armed forces, police and security services), the scope of any restriction sufficiently clear and precise, and the restriction was compatible with the proportionality requirements under Arts 10 and 11 of the ECHR (freedom of political expression and association).[88] Provided the statutory restriction applied to the group was proportionate and not discriminatory, the function of domestic courts might be limited to establishing whether a particular individual belonged to the relevant group.[89]

In *Ždanoka v Latvia*, the Court accepted that it had been 'even more cautious' in its assessment of restrictions on the right to stand in elections than it had been in relation to the right to vote, limiting its role 'largely to a check on the absence of arbitrariness in the domestic procedures leading to disqualification of an individual from standing as a candidate'.[90] That limited role was, however, dependent on the state party engaging in a democratic review of the impugned measure: national authorities are better placed than the Court to evaluate the necessity of any impugned interference, but they must undertake that evaluation and keep the issue under review. The Court noted that the relevant law had been periodically reviewed by the Latvian parliament, most recently in 2004, and, 'more importantly', by the constitutional court, which had 'carefully examined' the historical and political circumstances that gave rise to the enactment of the law in Latvia.[91] To avoid a finding of a violation in the future, the Latvian parliament would need to keep the restriction under 'constant review, with a view to bringing it to an early end'.[92]

The imposition of a mandatory language requirement on candidates for elective office precludes the possibility of the electorate voting for persons not proficient in the official or working language(s) of the state. In most cases, both the candidate and those who vote for the candidate will be members of a linguistic minority. In a strong Dissenting Opinion, Judge Rozakis made the following argument concerning the role of a representative in a democracy: 'parliamentarians represent, by definition, the opinions and the positions of their electorate—that is, those who have voted for them. They replace them in expressing opinions and positions within and outside parliament and, as a fiction, act instead of them in a system which'.[93] Accountability is guaranteed by the fact of electoral support, and the possibility that the electorate may remove the individual from office at the next opportunity. The criterion of eligibility is provided by the 'real representativeness of his or her ideas vis-à-vis even a very

---

[87] Ibid, para 112.
[88] Ibid, para 113. Reference to *Rekvényi v Hungary*, Reports of Judgments and Decisions 1999-III [GC].   [89] Ibid, para 114.
[90] Ibid, para 115.   [91] Ibid, para 134.   [92] Ibid, para 135.
[93] Dissenting Opinion of Judge Rozakis, 49, 50.

small segment of society. Accordingly, if a politician is prevented from representing part of society's ideas, it is not only he or she who suffers; it is also the electorate which suffers, it is democracy which suffers. For these reasons, prohibitions on eligibility to stand for election should be very exceptional and very carefully circumscribed.'[94]

The argument is that the right to stand in elections can be derived from the right to vote, ie from the right to vote for a particular candidate. If that were the case, a state party would be under a positive duty to facilitate the participation of political parties with some support in the population. No such obligation inheres in the theory or practice of democracy. Rozakis' argument follows from a misunderstanding of the role of a representative. Members of the national parliament are not 'agents' in the sense that they represent only those who voted for them; they also represent themselves, in relation for example to 'issues of conscience'; supporters of their political party; their constituents; 'sectoral' interests, for example business or the environment; and the population of the state as a whole. In this way the plurality of interests and perspectives is (imperfectly) 'represented' in the national assembly, but representativeness is not provided or guaranteed by any direct relationship between voters and (successful) candidates.

In *Georgian Labour Party v Georgia*, the Court observed that 'the effectiveness of the right to stand for election is undoubtedly contingent upon the fair exercise of the right to vote'.[95] The disfranchisement of voters, 'especially if it is an arbitrary act, can impede the effective exercise by an election candidate of its right to stand for election'.[96] The issue also arose in *Tnase and Chirtoaca v Moldova*, where the applicant complained that while domestic legislation permitted the holding of dual or multiple nationalities, electoral law (subsequently) prohibited persons holding multiple nationalities from being elected to parliament, resulting in a significant proportion of the population being excluded 'from actively participating in senior positions in the administration of the State, failing renunciation of an acquired additional nationality, [and also facing a] limitation on its choice of representatives in the supreme forum of the country'.[97] In its judgment, the Court noted that its case law distinguished between the active and passive aspects of the rights recognized in P1-3, to vote and stand for election:

it cannot be overlooked that both of those aspects make up, mutually, the decisive components of the guarantee underlying that Article, namely the free expression of the people in the choice of the legislature [:] there is an interdependence and the Court must be vigilant so as to ensure that impediments to the right to be elected to parliament do not rebound

---

[94] Ibid, 51.
[95] *Georgian Labour Party v Georgia*, Appl 9103/04, Judgment, 8 July 2008, para 83.
[96] Ibid, para 121.
[97] *Tnase and Chirtoaca v Moldova*, Appl 7/08, Judgment, 18 November 2008, para 112. (Referred to the Grand Chamber.)

negatively on *citizens' right to vote in accordance with their perception of which candidate will best promote their interests in Parliament*.[98]

The Court was not satisfied that the domestic legislation could be justified—a view 'strengthened by the fact that this far-reaching restriction was introduced approximately a year or less before the general elections[,] [and] the recommendations of the Council of Europe in the field of elections concerning the stability of the electoral law'.[99] The means employed for the purpose of achieving the aim pursued were disproportionate, and there was a violation of P1-3.[100] Elsewhere, the Court has affirmed that 'as a matter of policy, it would indeed be preferable to maintain the stability of electoral law'.[101]

Rozakis is correct in his conclusion that 'prohibitions on eligibility to stand for election should be very exceptional'. Candidates for elective office should be permitted to present themselves to the electorate and to seek their support in the market-place of democratic politics: 'a voter's preference is not static but may evolve in time, influenced by political events and electoral campaigning'.[102] It is for the electorate, not the authorities, to determine the suitability of a candidate for office. Constitutional and democratic rights to political participation are a 'higher' form of Convention rights. The only acceptable limitations are those that seek to protect the democratic system from non-democratic forces, or that are required to promote a more effective system of democracy, and it is not clear that either criteria applies on the facts of *Ždanoka v Latvia*.

One problematic issue remains, in relation to the idea of 'historical and political factors' justifying 'features that would be unacceptable in the context of one system may be justified in the context of another': there is no a priori reason to conclude from the Court's jurisprudence that political factors such as serious political conflict, including violence between majorities and minorities or between different ethnic groups, would be incapable of justifying the introduction of an electoral system that—absent the 'historical and political factors'— would not fall within the margin of appreciation accorded to states parties. Take the example of the Constitution of Bosnia and Herzegovina, established under the General Framework Agreement for Peace in Bosnia-Herzegovina (Dayton Peace Agreement).[103] Article IV provides for an upper House of Peoples, comprising fifteen delegates, 'two-thirds from the Federation (including five

---

[98] Ibid, para 113 (emphasis added)   [99] Ibid, para 114.   [100] Ibid, para 115.
[101] *Georgian Labour Party v Georgia*, Appl 9103/04, Judgment 8 July 2008, para 88. The position is reflected in the OSCE/ODIHR report, 'Existing Commitments for Democratic Elections in OSCE Participating States' (n 23 above), para 2.5 (references omitted): '[a] clear and detailed legislative framework for conducting elections must be established through statutory law[.] Except in extraordinary cases ... amendments to the law may not be made during the period immediately preceding elections, especially if the ability of voters, political parties, or candidates to fulfil their roles in the elections could be infringed.'
[102] See *Georgian Labour Party v Georgia*, Appl 9103/04, Judgment, 8 July 2008, para 120.
[103] The General Framework Agreement for Peace in Bosnia-Herzegovina, (1996) 35 ILM 89.

Croats and five Bosniacs) and one-third from the Republika Srpska (five Serbs)'.[104] Article V provides for a three member presidency, comprising 'one Bosniac and one Croat, each directly elected from the territory of the Federation and one Serb directly elected from the territory of the Republika Srpska'.[105] The provisions exclude the possibility of any person not belonging to one of the relevant groups (ie Bosniacs, Croats, Serbs) standing for elective office in relation to the House of Peoples or presidency, including members of the Roma and Jewish (national) minorities.

Ždanoka v Latvia suggests that a class of individuals may be excluded from the right to stand for election provided the class of persons may be clearly and precisely defined; the restriction is not arbitrary and is proportionate to the legitimate aims; that it is compatible with the principle of the rule of law and the general objectives of the Convention; and subject to domestic parliamentary review. Even if it were possible to overcome the statement by the Court in *Timishev v Russia*, that 'no difference in treatment which is based exclusively or to a decisive extent on a person's ethnic origin is capable of being objectively justified',[106] there are significant problems in applying the criteria in *Ždanoka* to the constitutional arrangement in Bosnia and Herzegovina: it is not possible to clearly and precisely define membership of an ethno-cultural group; discrimination on racial grounds is not consistent with the rule of law (equality before the law); and it is not consistent with the objectives of the ECHR—it is, after all, difficult to accept that provisions that effectively exclude persons belonging to the Roma and Jewish minorities from public office are consistent with the objectives of the ECHR, drafted as it was in the aftermath of the Second World War.[107] This is particularly the case when taken with Art 14 of the ECHR; even more so in relation to Protocol 12 to the ECHR (to which Bosnia and Herzegovina is a party).[108] Discrimination on the grounds of race (and ethno-cultural identity) is not consistent with the ECHR, and the Court has concluded that it can, in certain circumstances, amount to 'degrading

---

[104] Art IV (Parliamentary Assembly), Annex 4, 'Constitution', The General Framework Agreement for Peace in Bosnia-Herzegovina.

[105] Art V (Presidency), ibid. The Court of Human Rights has accepted the possibility of applying P1-3 to presidential elections: *Boskoski v Former Yugoslav Republic of Macedonia*, Reports of Judgments and Decisions 2004–VI.

[106] *Timishev v Russia*, Reports of Judgments and Decisions 2005–XII, para 58.

[107] See also Art 53 of the ECHR: 'Nothing in this Convention shall be construed as limiting or derogating from any of the human rights and fundamental freedoms which may be ensured under the laws of any High Contracting Party or under any other agreement to which it is a Party.' See in particular Arts 1.3 and 55.c of the UN Charter; also International Convention on the Elimination of All Forms of Racial Discrimination, adopted by GA Res 2106 (XX), 21 December 1965, into force 4 January 1969.

[108] 'The enjoyment of any right set forth by law shall be secured without discrimination on any ground such as sex, race, colour, language, religion, political or other opinion, national or social origin, association with a national minority, property, birth or other status.' Art 1.1 of the Protocol 12 to the Convention for the Protection of Human Rights and Fundamental Freedoms, CETS no 177.

treatment' within the meaning of Art 3 of the ECHR.[109] There is little (if any) examination in the literature as to the circumstances in which 'racial discrimination' could be justified under the ECHR, affirming the evident conclusion that direct discrimination on grounds of race is inconsistent with the object and purpose of the European Convention on Human Rights.

III. Rights of Political Participation in Democratic Politics

The idea of democracy is not defined or exhausted by electoral competition. Democratic legitimacy for the exercise of political authority through law is not guaranteed by the holding of free and fair elections, but by a system of government in which laws result from processes of opinion- and will-formation in accordance with the principle of public reason. Parliamentary bodies do not provide the sole locus for democratic deliberations, and legislative bodies must remain open to interests and perspectives emerging from the public sphere. Consequently, citizens must enjoy extensive constitutional rights concerning freedom of political expression and association, rights that are universally guaranteed by the requirements of democratic politics. In addition to the right to participate in free and fair elections, the ECHR recognizes rights to freedom of political expression,[110] and association.[111] In *Ždanoka v Latvia*, the Grand Chamber noted that there is 'undoubtedly a link between all of these provisions, namely the need to guarantee respect for pluralism of opinion in a democratic society through the exercise of civic and political freedoms'.[112] The existence of democracy reflects both the fact of disagreements in society and a willingness to compromise, affording the possibility of resolving problems through dialogue without recourse to violence.[113] Michel Rosenfeld explains: 'democratic law represents a political compromise among proponents of diverging political interests; these proponents have agreed to set aside their political differences concerning the subject matter of the law and to converge, for the time being, around the legislation.'[114] The following sections examine the rights to freedom of political expression and association, with a particular focus on applications before the European Court of Human Rights involving minorities.

---

[109] *Cyprus v Turkey*, Reports of Judgments and Decisions 2001–IV, para 309. See also *East African Asians* Case, 13 DR 17, 20. Art 3 of the ECHR provides: 'No one shall be subjected to torture or to inhuman or degrading treatment or punishment.'

[110] Art 10 of the ECHR; see *Christian Democratic People's Party v Moldova*, Reports of Judgments and Decisions 2006-II, para 66: 'political debate ... is at the very core of the concept of a democratic society'. [111] Art 11 of the ECHR.

[112] *Ždanoka v Latvia*, Reports of Judgments and Decisions 2006-IV [GC], para 115.

[113] See *Socialist Party and others v Turkey*, Reports 1998–III, para 45.

[114] M Rosenfeld, 'Rethinking constitutional ordering in an era of legal and ideological pluralism' (2008) 6 International Journal of Constitutional Law 415, 421.

A. The right to freedom of political expression

A democratic state is a community of citizens and others under the rule of law, in which legitimacy for the exercise of political authority is provided by collective acts of opinion- and will-formation. The European Court of Human Rights has affirmed that an expression of the opinion of the people would be inconceivable 'without the assistance of a plurality of political parties representing the currents of opinion flowing through a country's population[,] not only within political institutions but also, thanks to the media, at all levels of life in society'. Political debate is 'at the very core of the concept of a democratic society'.[115] Although freedom of political debate is important for all citizens, it is particularly important for political parties, elected officials and the media. Political parties and their active members represent their electorate, draw attention to their preoccupations and defend their interests.[116] Interferences with their freedom of expression call, in the words of the Court, 'for the closest scrutiny'.[117]

In *Socialist Party and ors v Turkey*, the Court of Human Rights observed that democracy 'thrives on freedom of expression'.[118] A right to freedom of expression is provided in Art 10(1), which may only be subject to limitations which are prescribed by law and necessary in a democratic society for defined and limited purposes.[119] Any interference must be proportionate to the legitimate aim pursued, with the national authorities enjoying a certain margin of appreciation.[120] There are limited circumstances in which the Court will accept that interferences in the right to freedom of political expression on issues of public interest are justified;[121] this includes political debate on the position of minorities: 'there can be no justification for hindering a political group solely because it seeks to debate in public the situation of part of the State's population'.[122]

Political parties may seek to debate and make policy proposals on any issue of public interest on two conditions: 'firstly, the means used to that end must be legal and democratic; secondly, the change proposed must itself be compatible with fundamental democratic principles'.[123] The right to freedom of political

---

[115] *Yumak and Sadak v Turkey*, Appl 10226/03, Judgment 8 July 2008 [GC], para 107.
[116] *Socialist Party and ors v Turkey*, Reports 1998–III [GC], para 41.
[117] *Incal v Turkey*, Reports 1998–IV [GC], para 46.
[118] *Socialist Party and ors v Turkey*, Reports 1998–III [GC], para 45.
[119] Art 10.2 of the ECHR: 'The exercise of these freedoms, since it carries with it duties and responsibilities, may be subject to such formalities, conditions, restrictions or penalties as are prescribed by law and are necessary in a democratic society, in the interests of national security, territorial integrity or public safety, for the prevention of disorder or crime, for the protection of health or morals, for the protection of the reputation or rights of others, for preventing the disclosure of information received in confidence, or for maintaining the authority and impartiality of the judiciary.'
[120] *Gündüz v Turkey*, Reports of Judgments and Decisions 2003–XI, para 38.
[121] *Wingrove v United Kingdom*, Reports 1996–V, para 58.
[122] *Refah Partisi (The Welfare Party) and ors v Turkey*, Reports of Judgments and Decisions 2003–II [GC], para 97.
[123] Ibid, para 98.

expression applies not only ideas that are favourably received, but also those that offend, shock or disturb: such are the demands of pluralism, tolerance and broadmindedness 'without which there is no "democratic society" '.[124] There can be no justification for hindering a political group solely because it seeks to debate contentious issues or propose solutions to difficult problems.[125] As the European Court of Human Rights has noted, 'it is of the essence of democracy to allow diverse political projects to be proposed and debated'.[126]

The wide scope of protection afforded by the right to freedom of political expression is important for persons belonging to minorities and their representatives, affirming a right to campaign for political and constitutional change that is unpopular with government authorities, and/or a majority of the population, and/or inconsistent with existing constitutional norms.[127] In cases involving the Macedonian minority in Bulgaria, the Court has, for example, observed that, in a democratic society based on the rule of law, 'political ideas which challenge the existing order and whose realisation is advocated by peaceful means must be afforded a proper opportunity of expression'.[128] The fact that a political party proposes autonomy, 'or even requests secession', is not by itself a sufficient basis to justify its dissolution on national security grounds.[129]

B. The right to freedom of political association

Art 11 of the ECHR provides that everyone has the right to freedom of peaceful assembly, and to freedom of association with others.[130] Interferences must be prescribed by law, and necessary in a democratic society for defined and limited reasons.[131] They must be proportionate to the legitimate aim pursued, and the reasons adduced by the national authorities to justify any interference 'relevant and sufficient'.[132] The power of the state to impose restrictions must be used 'sparingly', and 'only convincing and compelling reasons' are capable of

---

[124] *Ahmed and ors v United Kingdom*, Reports 1998–VI, para 55.
[125] *Socialist Party and ors v Turkey*, Reports 1998–III [GC], para 45; also, *United Communist Party of Turkey and ors v Turkey*, Reports 1998–I [GC], para 57.
[126] *Freedom and Democracy Party*, Reports of Judgments and Decisions 1999–VIII [GC], para 41.
[127] See, eg, *Association of Citizens Radko and Paunkovski v Former Yugoslav Republic of Macedonia*, Appl 74651/01, Judgment 15 January 2009.
[128] *The United Macedonian Organisation Ilinden and Ivanov v Bulgaria*, Appl 44079/98, Judgment 20 October 2005, para 115.
[129] *The United Macedonian Organisation Ilinden-Pirin and ors v Bulgaria*, Appl 59489/00, Judgment 20 October 2005, para 61. [130] Art 11.1 of the ECHR.
[131] Art 11.2, ibid: 'No restrictions shall be placed on the exercise of these rights other than such as are prescribed by law and are necessary in a democratic society in the interests of national security or public safety, for the prevention of disorder or crime, for the protection of health or morals or for the protection of the rights and freedoms of others. This article shall not prevent the imposition of lawful restrictions on the exercise of these rights by members of the armed forces, of the police or of the administration of the State'.
[132] *Gorzelik and ors v Poland*, Reports of Judgments and Decisions 2004–I [GC], para 96.

justifying restrictions on the right to freedom of association. The idea of 'necessary' in the limitation clause provided by Art 11(2) 'does not have the flexibility of such expressions as "useful" or "desirable"'.[133]

In both *Socialist Party and ors v Turkey* and *United Communist Party of Turkey v Turkey*, political parties had been proscribed, in part, because of their advocacy of policies aimed at establishing a federal system 'in which Turks and Kurds would be represented on an equal footing and on a voluntary basis'. The fact that a political programme is incompatible with existing constitutional principles and structures does not make it incompatible with democracy.[134] In the words of the Court, '[i]t is of the essence of democracy to allow diverse political programmes to be proposed and debated, even those that call into question the way a state is currently organised, *provided that they do not harm democracy itself*'.[135] The only limits on the rights to freedom of political expression and association are those that seek to protect democracy and the democratic system. The state may legitimately restrict those rights only where the interference facilitates a more effective democracy,[136] or in order to protect the democratic system from non-democratic associations.[137]

C. Political parties

Political parties are of central importance in a democracy as they provide organizational structures though which individuals can both participate effectively in political debate, and seek to gain political office.[138] They are the only forms of association that can come to power, and consequently put in place the 'overall societal model which they put before the electorate'.[139] The Court has observed that the 'free expression of the opinion of the people in the choice of the legislature' (P1-3) would be 'inconceivable without the participation of a plurality of political parties representing the different shades of opinion to be found within a country's population'.[140]

Although not expressly mentioned in Art 11, the European Court of Human Rights has confirmed that, as a form of association essential to the proper

---

[133] *Church of Scientology Moscow v Russia*, Appl 18147/02, Judgment, 5 April 2007, para 75.
[134] See *Zhechev v Bulgaria*, Appl 57045/00, Judgment 21 June 2007, para 47.
[135] *Socialist Party and ors v Turkey*, Reports 1998–III [GC], para 47 (emphasis added).
[136] Cf *Ahmed and ors v United Kingdom*, Reports 1998–VI, para 54; also *Refah Partisi (The Welfare Party) and ors v Turkey*, Reports of Judgments and Decisions 2003–II [GC], para 94.
[137] The Strasbourg authorities have repeatedly found inadmissible complaints from neo-Nazi organizations regarding limits on their freedom of expression: see, eg, *Glimmerveen and Hagenbeek v The Netherlands*, 18 DR 187 (1979).
[138] *United Communist Party of Turkey and ors v Turkey*, Reports 1998–I [GC], para 44.
[139] *Refah Partisi (The Welfare Party) and ors v Turkey*, Reports of Judgments and Decisions 2003–II [GC], para 87.
[140] *Christian Democratic People's Party v Moldova*, Appl 28793/02, Judgment, 14 February 2006, para 66.

functioning of democracy, political parties fall within the scope of the Article.[141] Exceptions to the right will be strictly construed,[142] and, in most instances, the proscription of a political party will not be consistent with states parties' obligations under the ECHR. The position applies also in relation to temporary interferences. In *Christian Democratic People's Party v Moldova*, the application concerned a temporary ban on a political party following its holding of unauthorized gatherings to protest against government plans to make the study of Russian compulsory for school children. The Court noted that the issue was of public interest and that the applicant was an opposition parliamentary political party; consequently, the states parties' margin of appreciation was narrowed, with only 'very compelling reasons' capable of justifying the interference.[143] Those compelling reasons were not present;[144] nor was the temporary nature of the ban of 'decisive importance[,] since even a temporary ban could reasonably be said to have a "chilling effect" on the party's freedom to exercise its freedom of expression and to pursue its political goals'.[145]

D. Ethnic political parties

Political parties that claim to represent the interests of a particular national, or ethnic, religious, or linguistic group are problematic from the perspective of democratic theory, which emphasizes the competition of ideas, and the possibility that citizens will be persuaded by the arguments of others. Where politics is dominated by parties divided along ethno-cultural grounds, the system can be both unstable and ineffective, resulting in 'zero-sum' bargaining between the representatives of the various groups. It is self-evident that the existence of political parties representing the interests of an ethno-cultural majority would be harmful to the practice of pluralist and deliberative democracy in a number of ways; the same cannot be said about parties that represent the interests of minorities, and the establishment of 'ethnic parties' may be the most effective way for persons belonging to minorities to advance their interests within the political system.

The Lund Recommendations are clear on this issue: participating states 'shall comply with the international law principle of freedom of association. This principle includes the freedom to establish political parties based on communal identities.'[146] The provision does not distinguish between majority and minority 'communal identities', although the Lund Recommendations concern the effective participation of *national minorities* in public life. The position under the European Convention on Human Rights is more equivocal. In *Artyomov v*

---

[141] *United Communist Party of Turkey and ors v Turkey*, Reports 1998–I [GC], para 25.
[142] Ibid, para 46.
[143] *Christian Democratic People's Party v Moldova*, Appl 28793/02, Judgment, 14 February 2006, para 71. [144] Ibid, para 76.
[145] Ibid, para 77.   [146] Lund Recommendations, para 8.

Russia, the Court declared inadmissible a complaint concerning the refusal of the authorities to register as a political party the 'Russian All-Nation Union', an association declaring affiliation with the majority ethnic Russian population. The decision was taken in accordance with domestic legislation that prohibited the establishment of political parties based on 'ethnic or religious affiliation'. The European Court of Human Rights noted the conclusion of the Russian Constitutional Court, that the prohibition was based on a belief that the existence of political parties based on ethnic or religious grounds would be deleterious to the 'peaceful co-existence of nations and religions in the Russian Federation and would undermine the principles of a secular state and equality before the law'. The Court accepted that the interference pursued the legitimate aims of preventing disorder and protecting the rights and freedoms of others, noting that 'it is hardly conceivable that a party standing for the furtherance of the interests of one ethnic group or religious denomination would be able to ensure the fair and proper representation of members of other ethnic groups or adherents of other faiths'. The prohibition both 'served to implement the guarantee of equality [in] the Russian Constitution, as well as to ensure the fair treatment of minorities in the political process'. Given the principle of 'respect for national specificity in electoral matters', the Court did not find the reasons to be either arbitrary or unreasonable.[147] The application was 'manifestly ill-founded' in terms of Art 35 of the ECHR.

Artyomov v Russia should not be read as providing a general right for states parties to proscribe ethnic or religious parties. The Court has on another occasion (*Refah Partisi*) concluded that 'a political party animated by the moral values imposed by a religion cannot be regarded as intrinsically inimical to the fundamental principles of democracy, as set forth in the Convention'.[148] The issue can only be decided on a case-by-case basis by an application of the right to freedom of association (Art 11), in light of the margin of appreciation accorded to states parties.

One particular issue that has emerged in Turkey is the position of political parties representing the interests of Muslims, and arguing for the introduction of Sharia. In *Refah Partisi (The Welfare Party) and others v Turkey*, the Court concluded that Sharia was not compatible with democracy, as it is based on 'dogmas and divine rules laid down by religion', which cannot be subject to democratic debate and contestation. A political party which proposed the introduction of Sharia could 'hardly be regarded as an association complying with the democratic ideal that underlies the whole of the Convention'.[149] The judgment does not allow for a general proscription of political parties arguing for the introduction of Sharia, however, particularly in the other Council of Europe states which do not

---

[147] *Artyomov v Russia*, Appl 17582/05, decision 7 December 2006.
[148] *Refah Partisi (The Welfare Party) and ors v Turkey*, Reports of Judgments and Decisions 2003–II [GC], para 100.   [149] Ibid, para 123.

have a Muslim majority population. In *Refah Partisi*, there existed the very real possibility that *Refah* would take power and implement its policies; consequently, the interference (in the banning of the party) could be regarded as proportionate.[150] Given that political parties representing minorities have (almost) no chance of implementing their policies,[151] unless in coalition (when they are dependent on the acceptance of their policies by coalition partners), there can be limited circumstances in which interferences in the rights of political participation for parties representing minorities, including Muslim minorities, including those advocating the introduction of Sharia, could be justified.[152] The mere fact of calling for the introduction of Sharia does not justify any such restriction, particularly when the individuals or associations concerned have no opportunity or possibility of implementing their political beliefs.[153]

E. Civil society organizations

Elections provide one mechanism through which citizens are able to participate in democratic politics, enabling them to express policy preferences and sanction office holders for poor performance by removing them from office. The centrality of elections to democratic systems results from their ability to provide a (relatively) clear expression of the will of the people, reflected directly in a majority of votes cast, or (indirectly) through the allocation of seats in a representative assembly. Citizens also participate in democracy through participation in civil society organizations that contribute to debate in the public sphere. Whilst the European Court of Human Rights has often referred to the essential role played by political parties, it has accepted that 'associations formed for other purposes, including [those] seeking an ethnic identity or asserting a minority consciousness, are also important to the proper functioning of democracy'. In *Gorzelik and ors v Poland*, it noted that 'where a civil society functions in a healthy manner, the participation of citizens in the democratic process is to a large extent achieved through belonging to associations in which they may integrate with each other and pursue common objectives collectively'.[154]

The responsibility of a state party is not simply one of non-interference. In *Bączkowski and ors v Poland*, the authorities refused to grant permission for a

---

[150] The European Court of Human Rights concluded that, at the time of its dissolution, there was the very real possibility that *Refah* would seize political power without being restricted by the compromises inherent in a coalition: 'its monopoly of political power would have enabled it to establish the model of society envisaged in that programme': *Refah Partisi (The Welfare Party) and ors v Turkey*, Reports of Judgments and Decisions 2003–II [GC], para 108.
[151] The unlikely exception would a first-past-the-post system in which the minority vote was concentrated, with the votes of the majority divided between two or more political parties.
[152] Cf *Baskaya and Okçuoglu v Turkey*, Reports of Judgments and Decisions 1999–IV [GC], para 62; and *Incal v Turkey*, Reports 1998–IV [GC], para 58.
[153] See *Gündüz v Turkey*, Reports of Judgments and Decisions 2003–XI, para 51.
[154] *Gorzelik and ors v Poland*, Reports of Judgments and Decisions 2004–I [GC], para 92.

march and meetings to protest against homophobia. The Court concluded that the obligations of states parties 'cannot be reduced to a mere duty ... not to interfere'. There may be positive obligations to secure the effective enjoyment of the rights, and these positive obligations will be 'of particular importance for persons holding unpopular views or belonging to minorities, because they are more vulnerable to victimisation'.[155] The role of the state in conditions of pluralism 'is not to remove the cause of tension by eliminating pluralism, but to ensure that the competing groups tolerate each other'.[156] The Court has reaffirmed the point in a number of cases involving minorities. In *Ouranio Toxo and ors v Greece*, for example, it noted that 'mention of the consciousness of belonging to a minority and the preservation and development of a minority's culture cannot be said to constitute a threat to "democratic society", even though it may provoke tensions'. Tensions between groups are 'one of the unavoidable consequences of pluralism, that is to say the free discussion of all political ideas'.[157] The actions of the *Ouranio Toxo* party in affixing a sign to the front of its headquarters, with the party's name written in Macedonian, could not be regarded as 'reprehensible or considered to constitute in itself a present and imminent threat to public order'.[158] Instead of inciting the population to gather in protest, 'it would have been more in keeping with [the values of a democratic society] for the local authorities to advocate a conciliatory stance, rather than to stir up confrontational attitudes'.[159]

F. Privileges which follow the fact of association

It is difficult to envisage circumstances in which the proscription of a political party seeking to advance by peaceful means the interests of a national or ethnic, religious, or linguistic minority could be regarded as compatible with the Convention rights to political participation. The same point does not apply in relation to privileges that follow the fact of association. Individuals associate with political parties and civil society organizations in order to seek power and influence domestic politics, and in order to do so they require recognition by the domestic legal system. Where recognition is not forthcoming, the right of association may be ineffective. *Gorzelik and ors v Poland* illustrates the point.[160]

---

[155] *Bączkowski and ors v Poland*, Appl 1543/06, Judgment, 3 May 2007, para 64.
[156] *Barankevich v Russia*, Appl 10519/03, Judgment, 26 July 2000, para 30.
[157] *Ouranio Toxo and ors v Greece*, Report of Judgments and Decisions 2005–X, para 40.
[158] Ibid, para 41.   [159] Ibid, para 42.
[160] *Gorzelik and ors v Poland*, Reports of Judgments and Decisions 2004–I [GC]. In other cases the Court has accepted limits on the funding of minority political parties from overseas: *Parti Nationaliste Basque-Organisation Régionale D'Iparralde v France*, Appl 71251/01, Judgment, 7 June 2007, para 47. The judgment is significant for minority groups who rely on financial support from 'kin states', or populations with which they share a sense of ethno-cultural identity. See also *Fryske Nasionale Partij and ors v The Netherlands* (1985) 45 DR 240, 242, where the Commission concluded that P1-3 did not guarantee the right to use a particular language in electoral proceedings, or to submit the names of candidates in a minority language.

The relevant domestic law applied an electoral threshold of 5 per cent to obtain representation in parliament, but exempted associations registered as 'national minorities'. The authorities refused to register the 'Union of People of Silesian Nationality' as a 'national minority', as a result of concerns that the applicants might attempt to claim 'unwarranted privileges' under the electoral law, in particular an exemption from the 5 per cent threshold. The Court concluded that the dispute 'was essentially concerned with the label which the association could use in law—with whether it could call itself a "national minority"'.[161] It was not the right to freedom of association per se that was restricted, but the description of the group as a 'national minority' under domestic law, and the electoral privileges that would inevitably follow;[162] there was no violation of the right to freedom of association.

In *Zhechev v Bulgaria*, the Court observed that because political parties seek to participate in democratic elections and accede to office and power, it might be necessary to require them to register as political parties, 'so as to make them subject to, for instance, stricter rules concerning party financing, public control and transparency'.[163] This is an area in which it is difficult to provide detailed rules that can apply in all circumstances. The OSCE Copenhagen Document refers to the need to respect the right of individuals and groups to establish their own political parties, 'and provide such political parties and organizations with the necessary legal guarantees to enable them to compete with each other on a basis of equal treatment before the law and by the authorities';[164] the Universal Declaration on Democracy refers to the right to organize political parties and carry out political activities, and the principle that '[p]arty organisation, activities, finances, funding and ethics must be properly regulated in an impartial manner in order to ensure the integrity of the democratic processes'.[165] A democratic system must regulate political parties effectively in order to ensure the proper functioning of democracy, but this must not be done in an arbitrary and discriminatory manner. While accepting that states parties enjoy a margin of appreciation in relation to the positive rights that follow the fact of association, the Court must remain vigilant to ensure that any restrictions can be justified by reference to objective and reasonable criteria, and that they do not impede the effective participation of persons belonging to national or ethnic, religious, or linguistic minorities, who are already disadvantaged in democratic systems by virtue of being (democratic) minorities.

---

[161] *Gorzelik and ors v Poland*, para 105.   [162] Ibid, para 106.
[163] *Zhechev v Bulgaria*, Appl 57045/00, Judgment 21 June 2007, para 56.
[164] OSCE Document of the Copenhagen Meeting of the Conference on the Human Dimension, 29 ILM (1990) 1318, para 7.6.
[165] IPU's Universal Declaration on Democracy (n 22 above), para 12.

IV. The Democratic Society and the Need for 'Democratic Law'

The focus thus far has been on the procedural rights necessary for the practice of democratic politics: the rights to participate in competitive elections, to organize politically, and deliberate and debate all issues of public concern. Democratic legitimacy cannot, however, be understood exclusively in terms of process; it is not possible to accept the legitimacy of all outcomes of democratic processes simply on the basis that law norms were agreed through properly constituted democratic processes of law-making. There is, though, an inherent problem in any process of review (at whatever level) that permits the democratic will of the people to be set aside by reference to contestable and (often) indeterminate rules and principles, a problem reflected in Alexander Bickel's 'counter-majoritarian difficulty', which exists where the position of a majority of the 'here and now' people is rejected by reference to 'higher' constitutional law principles, as interpreted by a constitutional court, including constitutional provisions for the protection of human rights.[166] The difficulty can only be overcome where constitutional law norms, including human rights norms, are subject to the democratic will of the people. Courts should not intervene where the results of political processes are (subjectively) 'wrong', but where there is a deficit in the practice of democracy.

The argument is made most persuasively by Jürgen Habermas, who develops a sophisticated argument that democracy should be understood in deliberative terms.[167] The idea of deliberative democracy requires that laws result from a process of reasoned deliberation amongst equal participants who reach a consensus. The assumptions are that deliberative mechanisms will result in better law-making, as decision-making will be more informed, free from factual errors, and participants aware of the interests and preferences of all those subject to the law. The idea of deliberation precludes recourse to self-interested arguments, with disagreements settled through the exchange of reasons. Those seeking to demonstrate the (political) 'truth' of their positions must rely on reasoned arguments if they are to convince others: the idea of public reason. The requirement for reasoned arguments follows the need to orientate language towards mutual understanding: participants must explain their positions by reference to reasons that others might accept in order to reach a consensus. Where an argument is not accepted, there is a shift from justification to discourse in search of agreement, with arguments tested through reasoned deliberations. Where consensus is not possible, the relationship shifts again from discourse to bargaining, in which each participant engages in strategic argumentation. Bargaining is permissible to the extent that the process is deliberative, ie rational, and compromises acceptable in principle to all participants, who may agree for different reasons.

---

[166] A Bickel, *The least dangerous branch: the Supreme Court at the bar of politics* (1962), 17.
[167] J Habermas, *Between Facts and Norms*, William Rehg (trans) (1986).

According to the deliberative model, policies are 'just', 'correct', or 'right' to the extent that they are consistent with the requirements of right process and substantive democratic principles, concerning, for example, political equality and public reason. The democratic legitimacy of laws depends on an institutionalization of the principle of discourse in a constitutional order that recognizes the equality of citizens. The law must grant equal liberties to all: the freedom of each citizen must 'coexist with the freedom of all.'[168] For this to be the case, the subjects of law norms must, at the same time, 'understand themselves, taken as a whole, [to be] the rational *authors* of those norms'.[169] The legal order draws its legitimacy from this idea of collective self-determination: citizens must think of themselves as authors of the law to which they are subject as addressees, 'and it is only participation in the practice of politically autonomous lawmaking that makes it possible for the addressees to have a correct understanding of the legal order as created by themselves'.[170] If all possibly affected persons are able to participate in deliberations, with an equal opportunity to influence others, any consensus position may be regarded as 'right' or 'just' for that political community.

The deliberative model provides that a law is legitimate only if all who are possibly affected could assent to it as participants in rational discourses. It is an application of Habermas' principle of discourse: 'Just those action norms are valid to which all possibly affected persons could agree as participants in rational discourses.'[171] Deliberative politics must be conducted in accordance with the requirements of deliberative democracy: the language of politics must recognize the principle of political equality and the importance of private autonomy; the welfare of all must be the central argument in political discourses; political argument should be conducted in a way that attempts to persuade others by the force of better argument; all laws, including justice norms, framed in terms of constitutional rules and principles and human rights norms must be worked out through democratic politics. In contrast to liberal theories that hold rights to be both prior and superior to democratic laws, Habermas regards private autonomy (individual self-determination) and public autonomy (political participation in democratic lawmaking) to be 'co-original'; they are 'internally related'.[172] The framework of rights and liberties that structures the social context of human life is established through democratic politics in accordance with the principle of public reason. Non-discrimination norms are central to arguments around public reason, as any difference of treatment must be capable of rational justification. The norms passed by the legislature and applied by the courts 'prove their "rationality" by the fact that addresses are treated as free and equal members of an association of legal subjects': the principle of equal treatment. This includes both the idea of equality before the law, and the broader principle of substantive legal

---

[168] Ibid, 32. [169] Ibid, 33 (emphasis in original). [170] Ibid, 121.
[171] Ibid, 107. [172] Ibid, 275.

equality, 'which holds that what is equal in all relevant respects should be treated equally, and what is unequal should be treated unequally. But what counts in each case as the *"relevant respect"* requires justification.'[173] The scope and content of human rights norms must be worked out on a case-by-case basis in a collective act of democratic self-determination, the aim of which is to promote the public and private autonomy of equal citizens. The ideal suggests the possibility of an objective model of judicial review that evaluates the democratic legitimacy of law norms: judicial review of law norms should reinforce rather than contravene the processes of democratic will-formation; its function is to ensure the development of effective processes for democratic law-making.

The idea of deliberation and practice of deliberative democracy has a number of advantages for minorities in democratic politics, not least the (hypothetical) requirement for the consent of all those affected to law norms. The model acknowledges the interrelationship between public and private autonomy, without giving either a priori priority over the other; refuses to designate an idea of the 'good life', beyond the fact of deliberation; and given the centrality of consent, admits the possibility of reconciling the rights of minorities with the principle of democratic self-determination: human rights—with the exception of the rights to equal political participation—are not prior to constitutional dialogue, but a consequence of and therefore constituted by, constitutional dialogue. The exact scope of individual private rights, including the rights of persons belonging to minorities to a distinctive 'way of life', cannot be formulated in the absence of public deliberations. The difficulty in the analysis lies in the requirement that all participants must enter democratic deliberations accepting that they may be persuaded to change their position where faced with the force of better argument, with Habermas arguing that modern societies 'expect their members to take a reflexive attitude toward their respective cultural traditions':[174] cultural and religious freedoms can be guaranteed only where they are enacted as the result of a deliberative process of legislation, 'the mode of which provides grounds for the reasonable expectation of rationally acceptable outcomes'.[175]

The argument is problematic for orthodox religions, which may require 'inflexible commitment to an external authority or to faith achieved through revelation'.[176] According to Habermas, commitment to the laws of a religion or acceptance of the cultural norms of a minority identity are no different from any other perspective or preference, and persons belonging to such minorities must accept that their position may be subject to change where faced with a 'better argument'. Minorities cannot simply make reference to their distinctive ethnocultural identity as a reason for refusing to engage in democratic discourses; but

---

[173] Ibid, 414 (emphasis in original). [174] Ibid, 312.
[175] J Habermas, 'Intolerance and discrimination' (2003) 1 *International Journal of Constitutional Law* 2–12, 6.
[176] R. Gordon, 'The dangers of deliberation' (1997) 106 *Yale Law Journal* 1313, 1316.

neither can the state assert a privileged position in debates by reference to the fact that it can command majority support on questions of culture and cultural rights. It is not possible for the democratic state to ignore the perspectives of 'unreasonable others'. Joseph Raz observes that the interests of persons with 'unreasonable views', those who 'stubbornly fail to see what the reasonable see',[177] are just as likely to be affected by the exercise of political authority as those of 'reasonable' persons, 'and if the other people's agreement is required, so should theirs be'.[178] Disagreement is evidence that at least one of the parties is wrong and the authorities are obliged to consider whether it is their position. Much will depend on whether disagreement can be assigned to bias or ignorance, or acting against expert advice, or acting in circumstances where the life experiences of the minority group 'are foreign to those in power'.[179] The participation and consent of all those who might reasonably be affected is required to establish legitimacy for the exercise of political authority through law. Habermas appears to concede this when he argues that 'deficits [in democratic legitimacy] will always result when the circle of all those involved in democratic decision making does not extend to cover the circle of all those affected by those decisions'.[180] In constitutional and political debates, ethno-cultural minorities have the right to direct participation in decision-making processes that affect their way of life, with consultations conducted in accordance with the principles of deliberative democracy: political equality; the right to direct participation; the right to equal influence; and the need to orientate decision-making processes toward a consensus of all those who will be subject to the law norms.

V. The 'Minority' Right to be Different (Art 8)

The political conception of justice suggested by the deliberative model of democracy is consistent with the body of international human rights law that has emerged in the global system. The Universal Declaration of Human Rights, for example, contains a limited number of absolute provisions,[181] and 'rights' that may be subject to such limitations as are necessary for protecting the rights and freedoms of others, and 'meeting the just requirements of morality, public order and the general welfare in a democratic society'.[182] International human rights law provides the language with which domestic societies deliberate about the nature and content of (domestic) human rights norms, but, with the exception of a limited number of absolute prohibitions, international human rights laws are

---

[177] J Raz, 'Disagreement in politics' (1998) 43 *American Journal of Jurisprudence* 25–52, 34.
[178] Ibid, 33.   [179] Ibid, 51.
[180] J Habermas, 'Toward a cosmopolitan Europe' (2003) 14 *Journal of Democracy*, 86, 90.
[181] Prohibitions on slavery (Art 4) and torture (Art 5), and equal protection under the law (Art 7): GA Res. 217(III)A, adopted 10 December 1948, 'Universal Declaration of Human Rights'.
[182] Art 29(2), ibid.

universal only in the sense of framing the social, economic and political questions that all democratic societies must address, ie the relationship between private autonomy (individual self-determination) and public autonomy (democratic law-making). The ECHR, as interpreted by the European Court of Human Rights, relies on something close to a deliberative understanding of the democracy. While the Statute of the Council of Europe refers only to the idea of a 'genuine democracy',[183] the declared aims of the organization are 'to protect human rights, *pluralist democracy* and the rule of law'.[184] The preamble to the ECHR refers to 'effective political democracy', whilst P1-3 refers to the need to hold elections to 'ensure the free expression of the opinion of the people in the choice of the legislature'. The principle of equality is applied to rights of political participation.[185] In relation to the substantive 'Convention rights', a number are absolute, or may be subject to interferences only in very limited circumstances, ie they are not issues for democratic deliberation and choice.[186] Other rights (Arts 8–11) may be subject to an interference where 'necessary in a democratic society'. In relation to the legitimacy and acceptability of democratic law norms, the European Court of Human Rights has stated that 'democracy does not simply mean that the views of the majority must always prevail: a balance must be achieved which ensures the fair and proper treatment of minorities and avoids any abuse of a dominant position'.[187] Established laws and public policy positions must be based on 'dialogue and a spirit of compromise necessarily entailing various concessions on the part of individuals or groups'. It is this 'constant search for a balance between the fundamental rights of each individual which constitutes the foundation of a "democratic society"'.[188] The ECHR removes a limited number of issues from democratic debate, but in relation to the qualified autonomy rights (Arts 8–11), the Convention operates principally by framing the terms of domestic democratic debates, and, in those political discussions, each state party must recognize and accommodate its own multiethnic (or 'plural') identity.

In *Gorzelik and ors v Poland*, the Grand Chamber observed that respect for national minorities is 'a condition *sine qua non* for a democratic society'.[189] A pluralist and genuinely democratic society must respect the ethnic, cultural, linguistic, and religious identity of persons belonging to national minorities and 'create appropriate conditions enabling them to express, preserve and develop

---

[183] Preamble, Statute of the Council of Europe (1949) CETS no 001.
[184] <http://www.coe.int/T/e/Com/about_coe/> (accessed 17 September 2009) (emphasis added).
[185] Art 14 of the ECHR. States parties may impose restrictions on the political activity of aliens under Art 16.
[186] Cf *Vo v France*, where the ECtHR appeared to grant states parties a certain 'margin of appreciation' in defining the scope of application of Art 2 (right to life): *Vo v France*, Reports of Judgments and Decisions 2004–VIII, para 85.
[187] *Gorzelik and ors v Poland*, Reports of Judgments and Decisions 2004–I [GC], para 90.
[188] *Leyla Sahin v Turkey*, Reports of Judgments and Decisions 2005–XI [GC], para 108.
[189] *Gorzelik and ors v Poland*, Reports of Judgments and Decisions 2004–I [GC], para 68.

this identity'.[190] In *Sidiropoulos and ors v Greece*, the Court affirmed that the existence of minorities and different cultures is a 'historical fact that a "democratic society" [must] tolerate and even protect and support according to the principles of international law'.[191] The ECHR contains a number of rights of particular relevance to persons belonging to minorities;[192] it does not 'guarantee rights that are peculiar to minorities',[193] although in reading the idea of private life (Art 8) in terms of individual autonomy,[194] the Court has recognized the right of persons belonging to minorities to a particular 'way of life'.[195] Interferences in the right occur where a state party regulates cultural practices,[196] or ostensibly neutral laws impact disproportionately on minorities: the right not to be discriminated against in the enjoyment of Convention rights 'is also violated when states without an objective and reasonable justification fail to treat differently persons whose situations are significantly different'.[197] The Court has accepted that there may be positive obligations inherent in the effective respect for private life,[198] although these should not be interpreted in such a way 'as to impose an impossible or disproportionate burden'.[199] Positive obligations might include state funding for cultural activities central to a minority's way of life. Art 8 also contains a procedural aspect. Where the views and interests of the individual are not sufficiently taken into account to provide them with the requisite protection of their interests, 'there will have been a failure to respect their [rights] and the interference resulting from the decision will not be capable of being regarded as "necessary"'.[200]

To avoid a violation of the right to respect for private life, states parties must demonstrate that any interference is in accordance with the law,[201] and necessary

---

[190] Ibid, para 93 (quoting the preamble to the Framework Convention for the Protection of National Minorities).

[191] *Sidiropoulos and ors v Greece*, Reports of Judgments and Decisions 1998–IV, para 41.

[192] The ECHR contains rights to freedom of thought, conscience and religion (Art 9), expression (Art 10), assembly and association (Art 11), and non-discrimination in the enjoyment of Convention rights, inter alia on grounds of race, language, religion and 'association with a national minority' (Art 14). See also Art 2 of the (First) Protocol to the ECHR (freedom of religious education), and Protocol no 12 to the ECHR (non-discrimination).

[193] *Noack and ors v Germany*, ECHR 2000–VI (translation).

[194] *Pretty v United Kingdom*, Reports of Judgments and Decisions 2002–III, para 61. See, also, *Connors v United Kingdom*, Appl 66746/01, Judgment 27 May 2004, para 82.

[195] See, eg, *Chapman v United Kingdom*, ECHR 2001–I, para 73. For a more detailed elaboration, see Wheatley, 'Minorities under the ECHR and the construction of a '"democratic society"' (2007) Winter *Public Law* 770. [196] See *G and E v Norway*, 35 DR 30 (1983).

[197] *Thlimmenos v Greece*, Reports of Judgments and Decisions 2000–IV [GC], para 44. A state party may introduce measures for the benefit of persons belonging to minorities without such measures being considered a violation of the non-discrimination provision (Art 14 ECHR): *Polacco and Garofalo v Italy*, Appl 23450/94, decision 15 September 1997.

[198] *Botta v Italy*, Reports of Judgments and Decisions 1998–I, para 33.

[199] *Ilaşcu and ors v Moldova and Russia*, Reports of Judgments and Decisions 2004–VII [GC], para 332.   [200] *W v United Kingdom*, A121, para 64.

[201] See *Doerga v The Netherlands*, Appl 50210/99, Judgment 27 April 2004, paras 49–50.

in a democratic society for defined and limited purposes.[202] It is the practice of the Court to decide applications principally on the question as to whether an impugned interference is 'necessary in a democratic society', ie whether the interference corresponds to a 'pressing social need', and is 'proportionate to the legitimate aim pursued'.[203] According to the Court, Art 8 requires that a 'fair balance' must be struck between the competing rights of the individual and the interests of the community as a whole.[204] The Court accepts that national authorities are in principle in a better position to determine the necessity of any interference, and, moreover, that they enjoy 'direct democratic legitimation'. On matters of general policy, on which opinions within a democratic society may reasonably differ widely, 'the role of the domestic policy maker should be given special weight'.[205] States parties are accorded a certain, but not unlimited, 'margin of appreciation'.[206] In the few cases on the right to a distinctive way of life, the Strasbourg authorities have accepted the balance struck by the national authorities in favour of the general interest:[207] the fact that the Court has read a minority right to a distinctive way of life into the ECHR has not, at the supranational level, resulted in an increased protection of minorities.

Deliberating on the rights of minorities

There is a general acceptance in the international instruments on the position of minorities that each situation is different and context specific. The Universal Declaration of Human Rights does not, for example, contain a provision directly concerning minorities,[208] as it was considered 'difficult to adopt a

---

[202] Art 8(2) of the ECHR: 'There shall be no interference by a public authority with the exercise of this right except such as is in accordance with the law and is necessary in a democratic society in the interests of national security, public safety or the economic well-being of the country, for the prevention of disorder or crime, for the protection of health or morals, or for the protection of the rights and freedoms of others.'

[203] *Silver v United Kingdom*, A61, para 97. See also *Stankov and the United Macedonian Organisation Ilinden v Bulgaria*, Reports of Judgments and Decisions 2001–IX, para 87.

[204] *Znamenskaya v Russia*, Appl 77785/01, Judgment 2 June 2005, para 28. In the *Belgian Linguistics Case*, the ECtHR observed that the Convention 'implies a *just* balance between the protection of the general interest of the Community and the respect due to fundamental human rights *while attaching particular importance to the latter*': *Case relating to certain aspects of the laws on the use of languages in education in Belgium*, A6, para 5 (emphasis added).

[205] *Hatton and ors v United Kingdom*, Reports of Judgments and Decisions 2003–VIII [GC], para 97.

[206] *Handyside v United Kingdom*, A24, para 48–9. For reasons beyond the scope of this chapter, the Framework Convention for the Protection of National Minorities does not define the content of Art 8 in relation to the position of (national) minorities: see Wheatley, 'Minorities under the ECHR and the construction of a "democratic society"' (2007) *Public Law* 770, 778–9.

[207] See *G and E v Norway*, 35 DR 30 (1983); *Chapman v United Kingdom*, Reports of Judgments and Decisions 2001–I; *Gypsy Council and ors v United Kingdom*, Appl 66336/01, Decision 14 May 2002; *Noack and ors v Germany*, Reports of Judgments and Decisions 2000–VI. Cf *Connors v United Kingdom*, Appl 66746/01, Judgment 27 May 2004.

[208] Universal Declaration of Human Rights: GA Res 217(III)A, adopted 10 December 1948, 'International Bill of Human Rights'.

uniform solution of this complex and delicate question, which has special aspects in each State in which it arises'.[209] Art 27 of the International Covenant on Civil and Political Rights provides a limited, albeit absolute, right for persons belonging to minorities 'not to be denied' the right to enjoy their own culture.[210] Following Art 27 of the ICCPR, the UN Declaration on the Rights of Minorities provides that states 'shall adopt *appropriate* legislative and other measures to [protect the existence and ethno-cultural identity of minorities]'.[211] The Commentary by Asbjørn Eide observes that 'it is essential that the State consult the minorities on what would constitute appropriate measures... Different minorities may have different needs that must be taken into account.'[212] The Framework Convention for the Protection of National Minorities, adopted by the Council of Europe, obliges states parties to 'undertake to promote the conditions necessary for persons belonging to national minorities to maintain and develop their culture and to preserve the essential elements of their identity, namely their religion, language, traditions and cultural heritage'.[213] The Explanatory Report notes that in view of the 'range of different situations and problems to be resolved', Council of Europe states adopted a *framework* Convention, leaving states parties 'a measure of discretion in the implementation of the objectives which they have undertaken to achieve, thus enabling them to take particular circumstances into account'.[214]

In the absence of detailed international law norms on the rights of minorities, the focus shifts to the issues of domestic politics and political participation in the processes leading to the adoption of state law norms (in light of the international standards). In developing the Lund Recommendations, the experts proceeded from an understanding that the idea of 'good and democratic governance' follows an awareness that governments should 'seek to ensure the maximum opportunities for contributions from those affected by public decision-making'.[215] The argument is that the inclusion of 'those affected' will result in better regulation and laws that are more acceptable to all members of the community, which in

---

[209] GA Res 217(III)C, adopted 10 December 1948, 'Fate of Minorities'.

[210] Art 27 of the International Covenant on Civil and Political Rights, adopted by General Assembly Resolution 2200A (XXI), 16 December 1966: 'In those States in which ethnic, religious, or linguistic minorities exist, persons belonging to such minorities shall not be denied the right, in community with the other members of their group, to enjoy their own culture, to profess and practise their own religion, or to use their own language.' See S Wheatley, *Democracy, Minorities and International Law* (2005), 38.

[211] Art 1(2), GA Res 47/135, adopted 18 December 1992, 'Declaration on the Rights of Persons belonging to National or Ethnic, Religious, and Linguistic Minorities' (emphasis added).

[212] A Eide, 'Commentary to the Declaration on the Rights of Persons Belonging to National or Ethnic, Religious, and Linguistic Minorities', UN Doc E/CN.4/Sub2/AC.5/2001/2, 2 April 2001, para 30.

[213] Art 5(1) of the Framework Convention for the Protection of National Minorities (1995) CETS no 157.

[214] Explanatory Report on the Framework Convention for the Protection of National Minorities, Council of Europe H(94)10, Strasbourg, November 1994, para 11.

[215] Lund Recommendations, 'Introduction'.

turn will improve the stability of the political system. One example is the provision that calls for the establishment of advisory or consultative bodies 'to serve as channels for dialogue' between national authorities and minorities on issues such as education, language and culture.[216] These bodies should be able to raise issues with the national authorities and 'provide views on proposed governmental decisions that may directly or indirectly affect minorities'. National authorities should regularly consult these bodies, 'in order to contribute to the satisfaction of minority concerns and to the building of confidence'.[217]

Where persons belonging to national or ethnic, religious, or linguistic minorities object to laws or practices that impact on their ability to enjoy a distinctive way of life, the deliberative understanding of democracy provides that the objection of 'those affected' impugns the legitimacy of the measure. In conditions of imperfect knowledge and disagreement, we cannot be certain that the state authorities have drawn an appropriate balance between the putative 'will of the people' and the rights, interests and perspectives of minorities. The function of constitutional review in a democracy is not to evaluate the substantive outcomes of decision-making processes, but (consistent with the principles of deliberative democracy) to examine the extent to which impugned laws are procedurally legitimate and consistent with democratically agreed constitutional law norms (including agreed human rights norms and the rights of minorities). The process of constitutional review takes place within a legal system defined by reference to a rule of recognition, or basic norm, that provides validity for all norms in the legal order and constitutes the legal order as a single system of law.[218] The place of the supranational European Court of Human Rights in (political) conflicts between the state authorities and minorities is not clear; the Court is (evidently) not a (domestic) constitutional court, and it is not a (fourth) court of appeal for applicants alleging violations of Convention rights.[219]

The Court was established under an international treaty to ensure the compliance of states parties with their international law obligations. Those obligations are contained in the text of the ECHR. The basic rule of interpretation of international law norms is provided by Art 31(1) of the Vienna Convention on the Law of Treaties: 'A treaty shall be interpreted in good faith in accordance with the ordinary meaning to be given to the terms of the treaty in their context and in the light of its object and purpose.'[220] The Court has not, though, felt constrained by the ordinary meaning to be given to the terms of the ECHR, or to an interpretation of Convention rights that gives primary importance to the 'sovereignty' of states parties. The Court does not regard the Convention as an international treaty of the 'classic kind', involving the 'mere reciprocal engagements between contracting States'.[221] The object and purpose of the ECHR is

---

[216] Ibid, para 12.   [217] Ibid, para 13.
[218] HLA Hart, *The Concept of Law*, 2nd edn (1994), 233.
[219] Cf *Turek v Slovakia* (2007) Appl no 57986/00, Judgment 14 February 2006, para 114.
[220] 1155 UNTS 331.   [221] *Ireland v United Kingdom*, A25, para 239.

the collective enforcement of human rights and fundamental freedoms,[222] in the light of present day conditions,[223] and in its approach to the interpretation of the obligations of states parties under the ECHR, the Court has engaged in judicial elaboration of Convention rights.[224] The difficulty for the supranational Court is that the ECHR is not a democratically agreed Bill of Rights, and the Court is not situated within a political community with a shared history and legal and political tradition, and it does not possess the political authority and democratic legitimacy to supervise politico-legal settlements in states parties to the ECHR.

The object and purpose of the ECHR is the effective protection of rights in the context of democracy.[225] The means of compliance with the Convention are principally a matter for states parties.[226] Where the Court finds a violation, the state party will be required to amend its laws and/or practices in order to avoid a repetition of the breach; again, the choice of means for responding is principally a matter for the state.[227] The function of the European Court of Human Rights is to hold states parties to their determinate international law obligations, the prohibition on torture (Art 3), for example, and in relation to the more indeterminate or qualified autonomy rights (Arts 8–11), to promote democratic decision-making, in order to ensure that laws result from an inclusive, consensus-seeking process of will-formation. There is evidence that the Court is beginning to adopt a more procedural approach, both in the sense of demanding evidence that the interference in question has been subject to democratic debate at the national level, and that 'those particularly affected' have been able to participate effectively in decision-making procedures.[228] Where the Court finds against a

---

[222] *Soering v United Kingdom*, A161, para 87.
[223] *Loizidou v Turkey* (Preliminary Objections), A310, para 71.
[224] Judge Garlicki has argued that the Court has engaged in 'judicial modifications of the original meaning of the Convention': *Öcalan v Turkey*, Reports of Judgments and Decisions 2005-IV, Partly Concurring, Partly Dissenting Opinion of Judge Garlicki, para 4. In the judgment, the Court suggested that it had the right to formally 'amend', as opposed to 'interpret', the ECHR: *Öcalan v Turkey*, paras 163–5
[225] *Zdanoka v Latvia*, Reports of Judgments and Decisions 2006-IV, para 98.
[226] *Orhan v Turkey*, Appl 25656/94, Judgment 18 February 2002, para 451.
[227] *Hirst v United Kingdom (no 2)*, Reports of Judgments and Decisions 2005-5-IX [GC], para 83.
[228] In *Hirst v United Kingdom (no 2)*, the Court rejected the United Kingdom's position on the rights of prisoners to vote (P1-1-3), where there was '*no evidence* that Parliament has ever sought to weigh the competing interests or to assess the proportionality of a blanket ban on the right of a convicted prisoner to vote': *Hirst v United Kingdom (no. 2)*, Reports of Judgments and Decisions 2005-5-IX [GC], para 79 (emphasis added). In contrast, the Court has deferred to the position of the state party where the issue has been the subject of parliamentary and political debate: see *Evans v United Kingdom*, Appl 6339/05, Judgment 10 April 2007 [GC], paras 86–92. See (controversially) in this context *Ždanoka v Latvia*, Reports of Judgments and Decisions 2006-IV [GC], para 135. Judges Wildhaber, Pastor Ridruejo, Costa, and Baka observed in their dissenting opinion in *Karataş v Turkey* that 'the democratic legitimacy of measures taken by democratically elected governments commands a degree of judicial self-restraint': *Karatač v Turkey*, Reports of Judgments and Decisions 1999-9-IV, Joint Partly Dissenting Opinion of Judges Wildhaber, Pastor Ridruejo, Costa, and Baka.

state party, it destabilizes existing constitutional settlements and contributes to the reconstruction of 'nation' state identity to reflect a more pluralistic sense of 'self'. In this way, the Court can both promote the practical and effective guarantee of Convention rights and the practice of democracy in states parties.

The function of the European Court of Human Rights is to promote the establishment of political justice at the level of the state. The Court may approach the issue in one of two ways in cases relating to minorities: it may determine a violation of a substantive Convention right where there is an absence of effective participation in decision-making procedures; or, while not determining that the relevant state law is incompatible with the obligations of the state party under the ECHR, the Court might affirm the need for inclusive deliberations in the future in order to avoid a violation of the Convention. A particular focus should be on the principles inherent in the practice of deliberative democracy: political equality; processes of democratic deliberation; the inclusion of those (particularly) affected; laws that can be justified in accordance with the principle of public reason. In all cases, the Court should emphasize the importance of parliamentary and public debate, and the participation of 'those affected'. In *Hatton and ors v United Kingdom*, the Court observed that it would 'scrutinise the decision-making process to ensure that *due weight* has been accorded to the interests of the individual'.[229] The formulation suggests that the applicant must have been included in the decision-making process and that their interests and perspectives were in fact capable of influencing the outcome. In the absence of such evidence the state party should remain vulnerable to international criticism and adverse judgment by the European Court of Human Rights.

VI. 'Self-governance'

Part III of the Lund Recommendations addresses the issue of 'self-governance' for minorities: 'Effective participation of minorities in public life may call for non-territorial or territorial arrangements of self-governance or a combination thereof.'[230] The use of the term 'governance' here is misleading. In the literature, the idea of 'governance' is contrasted with 'government', which is concerned with the exercise of coercive political authority though law.[231] In the absence of the institutions of government (courts, executives, etc), governance regimes rely on non-coercive mechanism in order to exercise political authority—hence reference to 'global governance' (not government).[232] Where the Lund

---

[229] *Hatton and ors v United Kingdom*, ECHR 2003–VIII [GC], para 99 (emphasis added).
[230] Lund Recommendations, para 14.
[231] S Roberts, 'After government: On representing law without the state' (2005) 68 *Modern Law Review* 1, 24.
[232] See, eg, J Rosenau, 'Governance, order and change in world politics' in J Rosenau and E-O Czempiel (eds), *Governance without Government: Order and change in world politics* (1992), 1, 4.

Recommendations refer to 'non-territorial or territorial arrangements of self-governance',[233] this should be understood in terms of territorial self-government,[234] and non-territorial regulation of such issues as 'education, culture, use of minority language, religion and other matters crucial to the identity and way of life of national minorities'.[235] Non-territorial self-government is concerned with the establishment of social norms by minorities to regulate aspects of social and economic life, ie with the establishment of cultural norms that define the distinctive 'way of life' for persons belonging to minorities. The Recommendations refer to the need for institutions of self-governance, whether non-territorial or territorial, to be based on democratic principles 'to ensure that they genuinely reflect the views of the affected population'.[236] While cultural norms are often subject to (internal and external) contestation and debate, their validity and authority does not rest on their democratic legitimacy.

A. Territorial self-government: 'autonomy'

The Lund Recommendations do not propose any 'right' of self-government for (national) minorities.[237] The right to self-government is the right to (political) self-determination, which is a right of peoples.[238] The contemporary position of the right of peoples to self-determination is expressed in Art 1, common to the International Covenants, which provides 'all' peoples with a right to self-determination, ie the right to 'freely determine their political status and freely pursue their economic, social and cultural development'.[239] The right of peoples to self-determination is understood as a right of self-government for the people of the state as a whole,[240] and a right of self-determination or self-government through law for groups within the state recognized as 'peoples'. There is an emerging recognition that territorial self-government or autonomy regimes are an importance aspect of the right of (internal) peoples to self-determination. Marc Weller refers to the idea of territorial autonomy as 'self-governance of a

---

[233] Lund Recommendations, para 14. [234] Ibid, para 15. [235] Ibid, para 18.
[236] Ibid, para 16. [237] See Lund Recommendations, paras 14, 17, and 19.
[238] See GA Res 1514 (XV), adopted 14 December 1960, 'Declaration on the granting of independence to colonial countries and peoples'; and GA Res 1541 (XV), adopted 15 December 1960, 'Principles which should guide Members in determining whether or not an obligation exists to transmit the information called for under Art 73e of the Charter'; and GA Res 2625 (XXV), adopted October 24, 1970, 'Declaration on Principles of International Law Concerning Friendly Relations and Co-operation among States in Accordance with the Charter of the United Nations'.
[239] Art 1(1), common to the International Covenant on Economic, Social and Cultural Rights and International Covenant on Civil and Political Rights, adopted by General Assembly resolution 2200A (XXI), 16 December 1966. The formulation in 'common Art 1' reflects the position under general international law; it is right *erga omnes* and a norms of *jus cogens* standing: see S Wheatley, 'The Security Council, democratic legitimacy and regime change in Iraq' (2006) 17 *European Journal of International Law* 531, 538–9.
[240] See Principle VIII, Final Act of the Conference on Security and Co-operation in Europe (1975) 14 ILM 1293.

demographically distinct territorial unit within the state.'[241] An autonomy or self-government regime is established to reflect the distinctive demographic characteristic of the dominant group within a particular territory; it is established within the constitutional structures of the state; establishes its own laws, often including the constitutional laws of the autonomy; and enjoys the competence to legislate and exercise administrative authority in relation to a wide range of domestic policy issues, but has limited (if any) authority in relation to external relations.[242]

The ECHR does not contain a right of peoples to self-determination, and no such right may be read into the Convention.[243] Where a state party introduces a self-government regime, Art 3, Protocol to the ECHR will apply to any 'legislative' body established under the regime.[244] In *Federación Nacionalista Canaria v Spain*, the Court confirmed that the legislative assembly of the Autonomous Community of the Canary Islands was a 'legislature' within the meaning of P1-3, as legislative assemblies in Spain's Autonomous Communities participated in the exercise of legislative power.[245] The idea of autonomy or self-government is concerned with devolved government for national, ethnic, religious, or linguistic minorities within the constitutional structures of the state. The autonomy regime will replicate the institutions of the central government, including the establishment of legislative, executive, and judicial institutions. Given that an autonomy regime that does not enjoy legislative autonomy is not 'autonomy', properly so-called,[246] the principle of democracy applies to any self-government regimes for ethno-cultural minorities.

In *Py v France*, the Court concluded that the New Caledonian Congress was a 'legislature' for the purposes of P1-3. The 1999 Institutional Act described the body as the 'deliberative assembly', although in fact the Congress enjoyed the power to introduce laws in a number of areas in relation to the territory of New Caledonia. The Court observed that 'effective political democracy' must apply in all territories to which the Convention applies, and that the Congress was

---

[241] M Weller, 'Towards a general comment on self-determination and autonomy', UN Doc. E/CN.4/Sub.2/AC.5/2005/WP.5, 25 May 2005, 5.   [242] Ibid, 5–6.

[243] Cf G Gilbert, 'The burgeoning minority rights jurisprudence of the European Court of Human Rights' (2002) 24 *Human Rights Quarterly*, 736, 774, relying on Art 53 of the ECHR. States parties to the ECHR have international law obligations in relation to other international human rights instruments, but the source of those international law obligations is not the ECHR, and those obligations do not flow into the Convention, and they are not subject to the jurisdiction of the Court of Human Rights.

[244] *Mathieu-Mohin and Clerfayt*, A 113 (1987), para 53. See also *Matthews v United Kingdom*, Reports of Judgments and Decisions 1999–I [GC], and *Aziz v Cyprus*, Reports of Judgments and Decisions 2004–V, para 40: 'The Court recalls that the word "legislature" in Article 3 of Protocol no 1 does not necessarily mean the national parliament: the word has to be interpreted in the light of the constitutional structure of the State in question.'

[245] *Federación Nacionalista Canaria v Spain*, Reports of Judgments and Decisions 2001–VI.

[246] Autonomy – 'Of a state, institution, etc.: The right of self-government, of making its own laws and administering its own affairs' (Oxford English Dictionary).

sufficiently involved in the legislative process to be regarded as part of the 'legislature' of New Caledonia for the purposes P1-3.[247] The applicant's complaint concerned a restriction on the right to vote in elections to the New Caledonian Congress, notably the requirement of residence in the territory for more than ten years.[248] The restriction was agreed with the local population who were concerned to limit the participation of recent arrivals in any vote on self-determination and independence; it was also a central part of an agreement to end violent conflict in the territory. Following an Opinion of the UN Human Rights Committee on the same issue,[249] the Court concluded that 'the history and status of New Caledonia are such that they may be said to constitute "local requirements" [cf Art 56(3) of the ECHR] warranting the restrictions imposed on the applicant's right to vote'.[250] There was no violation of P1-3.

New Caledonia is a non-self-governing territory; it is unlikely that similar restrictions on the rights of political participation would be acceptable if applied to self-government regimes (or self-determination claims) within the metropolitan territory. In *Doyle v United Kingdom*, the applicant complained that he had been denied the right to vote in national elections after having lived abroad for more than fifteen years. The Court noted that rules on the right to vote reflected a need to ensure 'both citizen participation and knowledge of the particular situation of the region in question'. Residence requirements were justified, in part, by the 'close connection between the right to vote in parliamentary elections and the fact of being *directly affected by the acts of the political bodies so elected*'.[251] The general principle remains one of universal suffrage: all those ordinarily resident in the territory, whether members of the minority group or not, are entitled to rights of political participation on the basis of equality, *mutatis mutandis*, the application of the democratic rights at the level of the state—the process of democratic lawmaking having moved down a level.[252]

B. Non-territorial self-government

The idea of 'non-territorial self-government' can be understood in one of three ways: first, it can relate to the 'self-government' of a minority in accordance with the cultural norms and practices of the group. This aspect of the right is guaranteed by the human right to a different 'way of life' (Art 8 of the ECHR).

---

[247] *Py v France*, Reports of Judgments and Decisions 2005–I (extracts), para 43.
[248] Ibid, para 49.
[249] *Gillot and ors v France*, Communication no 932/2000, UN Doc CCPR/C/75/D/932/2000, 26 July 2002.
[250] *Py v France*, Reports of Judgments and Decisions 2005–I (extracts), para 64.
[251] *Doyle v United Kingdom*, Appl 30158/06, Decision 6 February 2007 (emphasis added).
[252] In relation to the indigenous peoples of Europe (and/or the OSCE 'region'), different considerations might apply: see GA Res 61/295, adopted 13 September 2007, 'The United Nations Declaration on the Rights of Indigenous Peoples'.

Secondly, it can refer the devolution of executive functions within the state, and a practical recognition that in the administration of programmes of direct relevance to the life experiences of minorities that persons belonging to minorities are best placed to decide on the social and cultural priorities of the group. Weller, for example, argues for the establishment of 'minority representative bodies' with the authority 'disburse public funds and to exercise certain public functions in relation to all members of the respective minority [in areas such as] education, language and culture'.[253] The issue is one of expertise: just as states may disburse funding for the arts through a variety of bodies with specialist knowledge, they may also devolve decision-making in relation to the funding of minority cultural and educational activities to those with intimate knowledge of the group, provided that the administration of the programme is not undertaken in a manner that discriminates against members of other ethno-cultural minorities, or as between persons belonging to the minority in question.

The idea of 'non-territorial self-government' can also be understood in a more extensive way, as providing those recognized with authority within the group the right to 'legislate' for persons defined by reference to a minority ethno-cultural identity. Political authority is exercised on a personal (not a territorial) basis. It is important to distinguish this situation from any recognition of 'exemption rights' for persons belonging to minorities, where the individual remains the unit of self-determination. The right, for example, of Sikh men not to wear a safety helmet does not oblige Sikh men not to wear safety helmets as a matter of law. Cultural norms may justify the exemption of an individual from the application of state law norms, but the recognition of exemption rights does not imply that the individual is subject to the authority of the cultural norms (as a matter of 'law'). The subjection of an individual to the authority of minority religious or cultural law norms is not consistent with the ECHR. In *Refah Partisi*, the Grand Chamber concluded that the introduction of a plurality of legal systems would not be compatible with the Convention. Such a system would 'categorise everyone according to his religious beliefs and would allow him rights and freedoms not as an individual but according to his allegiance to a religious movement'. It would not be consistent with the ECHR for two reasons: first, 'it would oblige individuals to obey, not rules laid down by the State [,] but static rules of law imposed by the religion concerned', and would remove the individual from the effective protection of Convention rights; secondly, such a system 'would undeniably infringe the principle of non-discrimination between individuals as regards their enjoyment of public freedoms, which is one of the fundamental principles of democracy'.[254] The exercise of authority on a

---

[253] M Weller, 'Towards a general comment on self-determination and autonomy', UN Doc E/CN4/Sub2/AC.5/2005/WP5, 25 May 2005, 5.
[254] *Refah Partisi (The Welfare Party) and ors v Turkey*, Reports of Judgments and Decisions 2003–II [GC], para 119.

personal basis removes the individual from the authority of the state law system, subjecting them to laws of a non-state actor, and resulting in different individuals being subject to different legal regimes; it is not consistent with the ECHR.[255]

VII. Conclusion

Forty-seven of the fifty-six OSCE participating states, to whom the Lund Recommendations are implicitly directed, are states parties to the European Convention on Human Rights.[256] This contribution has demonstrated that the normative provisions in the two instruments are not always consistent, and in places may appear to be in conflict. In Europe, the 'law on minorities' appears messy, inconsistent, and in many respects incoherent.[257] Minority activists, advocates and representatives may find the situation unsatisfactory, as it fails to provide certainty and protection (at the international level) for minorities. Coherence could be achieved, but only through some process of 'constitutionalization' of the various international law regimes that regulate the relationship between states and ethno-cultural minorities in Europe: United Nations law, including provisions, for example, of the International Covenant on Civil and Political Rights and International Labour Organization Conventions;[258] European Union law;[259] Council of Europe law, including the ECHR and Framework Convention for the Protection of National Minorities; the 'law' of the Organization for Security and Cooperation in Europe;[260] etc. Any such process would be under the control of states, and would not reflect the interests of

---

[255] The exercise of other forms of customary, cultural or religious 'law' by and within minority groups is beyond the scope of this chapter. See generally B Tamanaha, 'Understanding legal pluralism: past to present, local to global' (2007) 29 *Sydney Law Review* (SSRN).

[256] The exceptions are Belarus, Canada, the Holy See, Kazakhstan, Kyrgyzstan, Tajikistan, Turkmenistan, the United States of America, and Uzbekistan. Belarus is a candidate for membership of the Council of Europe.

[257] Particularly noteworthy is *Noack and ors v Germany*, Reports of Judgments and Decisions 2000–VI, where members of the Sorbian minority complained that their relocation from the village of Horno would deprive persons belonging to the minority of the chance to perpetuate their customs and speak their language and ultimately entail the destruction of Sorbian culture. The Court concluded that the interference was not disproportionate to the legitimate aim pursued (the economic benefits of lignite mining) in view of the margin of appreciation afforded to state parties and held the complaint to be 'manifestly ill-founded'. On the same issue, the Advisory Committee on the Framework Convention concluded that such measures were 'undeniably likely to make the preservation of their identity more difficult' and should be 'taken only as a last resort, when there is no alternative': Advisory Committee on the Framework Convention, Opinion on Germany, ACFC/INF/OPI(2002)008), para 32.

[258] See, eg, Indigenous and Tribal Peoples Convention, 1989 (no 169).

[259] See Charter of Fundamental Rights of the European Union (2000/C 364/01).

[260] See, eg, Copenhagen Document (n 164, above).

minorities—consider, for example, the limited rights recognized in the text of the Framework Convention for the Protection of National Minorities.

Plurality and fragmentation can in fact be beneficial to minorities. The existence of a plurality of law orders in Europe, including state law systems and the legal order established by the Council of Europe and its institutions, allows national, ethnic, religious, and linguistic minorities to participate in the development of the international law norms that influence both the behaviour of states and the conduct of domestic politics. The fact of fragmentation creates opportunities for political participation outside the state; examples include the role of minority activists and advocates as applicants before the ECHR; as participants in the information gathering processes of the Advisory Committee on the Framework Convention; and as actors responsible for the development of 'soft law' norms, such as the Lund Recommendations.[261] Fragmentation also provides incentives and opportunities for political actors that have been unsuccessful at the domestic level to appeal to other legal systems in support of their demands, and participate in the development of international law norms outside of the state. Those international law norms can then be relied on in domestic politics, with disputes between the state authorities and minorities reframed in terms of a conflict of laws: state law and international law, including the 'hard' Convention rights reflected in the ECHR, and 'soft' law norms reflected, inter alia, in the Lund Recommendations. The participation of minorities in European institutions has led to the adoption of 'hard' and 'soft' law norms that require the 'nation' state to recognize and accommodate the fact of ethnocultural pluralism within society, and develop a (domestic) constitutional framework for the development of democratic laws and lawmaking that is acceptable to all those subject to state law norms, in particular those (minorities) whose life experiences are not shared by the dominant majority.

This chapter has demonstrated the limited potential of the European Court of Human Rights to provide a direct mechanism through which minorities can effect change in the nature of domestic electoral systems. Recent literature has questioned more widely the impact of international human rights instruments, whose importance appears to lie more in their ability to construct legitimate standards of behaviour for state and non-state actors than to improve the conditions of actual persons. That should not be taken to underestimate the importance of human rights instruments, including the ECHR: human rights norms serve a (global) expressive function and a (domestic) constitutive function;[262] they both express legitimate standards of behaviour in the international community, and act to constitute domestic constitutional systems. In one sense,

---

[261] In addition to the Lund Recommendations, see also the Hague Recommendations regarding the Education Rights of National Minorities (1996), and Oslo Recommendations regarding the Linguistic Rights of National Minorities (1998),

[262] O Hathaway, 'Do human rights treaties make a difference?' (2002) 111 *Yale Law Journal* 1935–2042, 2021.

the lack of success of applicants before the European Court of Human Rights is less important than the articulation by the Court of international law norms and principles for the establishment of an effective political democracy and democratic society. Those international law norms and principles provide the basis for rhetorical argument, contestation, and challenge at the level of the state, where the political accommodation between the national authorities and minorities must occur. Understood in this way, the judgments of the European Court of Human Rights present a more positive contribution to the European law on political participation for minorities.

7

The Council of Europe Framework Convention on the Protection of National Minorities and the Advisory Committee's Thematic Commentary on Effective Participation

Joseph Marko

I. Introduction: The Relevance of Effective Participation	223
II. Article 15 in Comparison with the Lund Recommendations and the European Convention on Human Rights	225
'Soft jurisprudence': The dual legal and political effect of opinions and thematic commentaries of the Advisory Committee	225
III. Effective Participation in Public Affairs	230
A. Representation in the legislative process	232
B. Representation in the executive, public administration, and judiciary	237
C. Consultation or participation? From representation without participation to veto rights in decision-making	239
D. Autonomy arrangements	244
E. Legal restrictions and problems	245
IV. Effective Participation in Social, Economic, and Cultural Life	249
A. Introduction	249
B. Areas of concern for effective participation in economic, social, and cultural life	251
V. Conclusions	254

I. Introduction: The Relevance of Effective Participation

Both the Thematic Commentary on the Effective Participation of Persons Belonging to National Minorities in Cultural, Social, and Economic Life and in Public Affairs, adopted by the Advisory Committee on 27 February 2008,[1] and academic commentators on the Framework Convention on the Protection of National Minorities (FCNM) agree that Art 15, prescribing the obligation of states parties to 'create the conditions necessary for the effective participation of persons belonging to national minorities in cultural, social, and economic life and in public affairs, in particular those affecting them' is a 'foundational provision'[2] for the entire system of minority protection and thus part of the 'core of the FCNM', alongside language and education.[3] In light of the legal development of minority protection after the Second World War in general[4] and the 'legislative history' of the FCNM and Art 15 in particular,[5] a special provision in an international legal instrument prescribing political participation reflects a shift in the paradigm from 'national minority' protection in the context of state sovereignty and the European nation state models to the management of ethnic diversity within and between states[6] based on the central values and functional prerequisites of (internal) 'integration' and 'co-governance', where national minorities can also serve as a bridge for peaceful cooperation between nation states.[7] Art

---

[1] ACFC/31DOC(2008)001.

[2] M Weller, 'Article 15' in M Weller (ed) *The Rights of Minorities: A Commentary on the European Framework Convention for the Protection of National Minorities* (2005), 429.

[3] F Palermo, 'Domestic enforcement and direct effect of the FCNM' in A Verstichel et al (eds), *The Framework Convention for the Protection of National Minorities: A useful pan-European instrument?* (2008), 206.

[4] See P Thornberry, *International Law and the Rights of Minorities* (1991), 25–54; and E Ruiz Vieytez, 'The history of legal protection of minorities in Europe', University of Derby Working Papers, 1999.

[5] See Weller, 'Article 15' (n 2 above), 431–4; and R Hofmann, 'New standards for minority issues in the Council of Europe and the OSCE' in J Kühl and M Weller (eds), *Minority Policy in Action: The Bonn-Copenhagen Declarations in a European context 1955–2000* (2005), in particular at 242–8.

[6] The 'French' model of 'ethnic indifference' does not recognize ethnic identities in public affairs so that France—in the tradition of this Jacobin nation state model—upholds a reservation with regard to Art 27 of the International Covenant on Civil and Political Rights and does not become a Party to the FCNM. However, the 'non-recognition' of ethnic, ie cultural diversity along the lines of different languages, religion or belief-systems with regard to the 'commonality' of history or culture, has anti-pluralist, assimilationist and/or de facto discriminatory consequences. In contrast, the 'German' model of 'legal institutionalization of ethnic diversity' when it is based on the ideological fiction of 'ethnic homogeneity' of society—which is, by definition, 'the nation' with a right to create its own state, ie a national state—'creates' the political and legal distinction of 'majority' versus 'minority'. See J Marko, 'The law and politics of diversity management: A neo-institutional approach' (2006–7) 6 *European Yearbook of Minority Issues* 251–80.

[7] See Weller, 'Article 15' (n 2 above), 431, but also the preambular provisions of the FCNM referring to 'stability, security and peace in this continent', 'cultural diversity ... a factor, not of division, but of enrichment of each society' and the necessity of 'transfrontier co-operation between regional and local authorities' in addition to cooperation between states.

15 has to be seen in the context of other provisions of the FCNM, in particular Art 4, which requires 'adequate measures' in order to promote 'full and effective equality', and Art 5, which requires the promotion of identity and culture and prohibits policies and practices aimed at assimilation. Hence, the Thematic Commentary speaks about 'effective participation, full and effective equality and promotion of national minorities' identity and culture' as the 'three corners of a triangle which together form the main foundations of the Framework Convention'.[8] In reaction to the normative principles of territorial integrity and non-interference in traditional state sovereignty concepts of international law and the nation-state models referred to above, Arts 8 and 9 of the Thematic Commentary —mirroring the first of the General Principles of the OSCE Lund Recommendations on the Effective Participation of National Minorities in Public Life[9]— declare 'the degree of participation' to be 'one of the indicators of the level of pluralism and democracy of a society… and [an] integral part of the implementation of the principles of good governance in a pluralistic society'. Effective participation is therefore also seen as 'crucial for enhancing social cohesion' since 'marginalization' will lead to 'social exclusion and tensions among groups' with the risk of losing national minorities' 'contribution and additional input to society'.

Therefore, it is essential for the understanding of the underlying 'philosophy' behind the FCNM, as well as the correct interpretation of its provisions, that the structural interrelatedness between identity, equality, and participation is taken seriously through a contextual interpretation. Insofar as Art 5 of the FCNM implies an obligation for states parties to effectively guarantee a 'right to identity' (Art 14), the distinction between 'integration' and 'assimilation' can no longer be seen as an academic construction, for the concept of 'integration' is based on the text of the FCNM itself.

'Effective participation' must be seen as an important instrument in balancing the policies for the promotion of the basic values and functions of cultural diversity on the one hand with social cohesion and political unity on the other.[10] This requires understanding that a strict individualist liberalism[11]—with the consequence that all 'special measures' or 'affirmative action' on behalf of national minorities with regard to the 'effectiveness' of participation—are, by definition, seen as a violation of the principle of individual equality before the

---

[8] At Art 13. This wording and the following phrases on social cohesion follow closely A Eide, 'Towards a pan-European instrument' in A Verstichel et al, *The Framework Convention* (n 3 above), 9, 10.

[9] See K Myntti, *A Commentary to the Lund Recommendations on the Effective Participation of National Minorities in Public Life* (2001).

[10] Again this follows already from a contextual interpretation with Arts 20–1 of the FCNM referring to 'respect' for 'the national legislation an the rights of others, in particular those of persons belonging to the majority or to other national minorities' and 'sovereign equality, territorial integrity and political independence of States'.

[11] See Marko, 'Law and politics' (n 6 above), in particular at 258–68.

law, as will be proven in more detail in the analysis in section III below. Despite the fact that the texts of the FCNM and the Thematic Commentary on Effective Participation usually refer to 'rights of persons belonging to national minorities', it becomes clear that both effective participation through political representation mechanisms, as well as full and effective equality, cannot be considered without a group dimension. You cannot represent an individual in parliament or guarantee effective equality to a single person without making a group-related category the yardstick of comparison. Therefore, not only the Lund Recommendations—which were praised from the very beginning for their distinct group-oriented approach—but also 'effective participation' according to Art 15 of the FCNM cannot seriously be implemented with a certain degree of group orientation[12] so that the ideological dichotomy of individual versus group rights[13] no longer makes sense in this context.

II. Article 15 in Comparison with the Lund Recommendations and the European Convention on Human Rights

'Soft jurisprudence': The dual legal and political effect of opinions and thematic commentaries of the Advisory Committee

Generally speaking, the FCNM as an international treaty with legally binding effect differs in this respect from the OSCE Lund Recommendations on the

---

[12] Art 6 of the Thematic Commentary itself refers to the fact that, first, 'the Framework Convention protects the rights of individual persons belonging to national minorities' and, secondly, that 'the enjoyment of certain rights, including the right to effective participation, has a collective dimension'. Due to the ideological underpinnings of the term 'collective' I prefer, however, the notion of group orientation, which is based on a structural analysis as will be demonstrated below.

[13] See also Marko, 'Law and politics' (n 6 above), 274–6, generally deconstructing the dichotomy into a triadic structure with 'individual rights' implying the de facto existence of a group (as most language rights do), 'constitutional proclamations' on behalf of minorities and, finally, provisions which declare the group itself as bearer of the right with the consequence that representatives of groups—with or without legal personality—are granted legal standing before courts. However, from a structural analysis of various international and national minority protection instruments, this finding goes beyond the cautious political compromise formula to be found in Art 27 of the ICCPR and Art 3.2 of the FCNM that individual rights can be effectively enjoyed only in community with other persons, which is also repeated in Art 6 of the Thematic Commentary. From a deconstructivist perspective, this formula simply camouflages the fact that 'in community with others' usually hints at the existence of a group. Therefore, I prefer to speak of various levels of group orientation so that the phrase 'in community with others' is identical with my first level of group orientation outlined above. Hence, I do not agree with Hofmann that the discussion on the dichotomy of individual or group rights is more or less closed with the formula 'in community with others' (Hofmann, 'New standards' (n 5 above), 257). From the perspective of political theory this position can even be dangerous, as evidenced in R Brubaker, *Ethnicity without Groups* (2004), who strongly argues against the 'essentialization' of what he calls 'groupness' and thereby tries to undermine the political and legal concept of 'integration' and to justify again a 'need' for assimilation.

Effective Participation of National Minorities in Public Life. The Recommendations specify the provisions of the Document of the Copenhagen Meeting of the Conference on the Human Dimension of the CSCE of 29 June 1990, but they have—like all OSCE documents—'only' politically binding effect. The FCNM differs from the European Convention on Human Rights (ECHR) insofar as the ECHR—with the European Court of Human Rights (ECtHR)—foresees a supranational judicial mechanism for the protection of the rights guaranteed under the ECHR. This Court can be addressed by individuals who claim that the authorities of the respective state party of the ECHR have violated their rights under the Convention. In contrast, the implementation of the FCNM is reviewed by a political mechanism, the Committee of Ministers, albeit with the support of an Advisory Committee, composed of eighteen 'independent' experts. But they do not enjoy the guarantees of judicial independence, nor is there an individual complaint mechanism foreseen. This comparison raises two issues of general relevance for the character of the thematic commentaries of the Advisory Committee: what is the 'real' normative 'nature' of the FCNM in terms of effective legally binding effect, and which is 'more' effective—a political or a legal mechanism?

Francesco Palermo has recently proven through an analysis of the case law of national courts[14] that the provisions of the FCNM are certainly more than 'soft law'[15] based on 'programme-type provisions … which will not be directly applicable' as para 11 of the Explanatory Report to the FCNM[16] declares with reference to its character as 'framework convention'. This is also true with regard to the substance of Art 15, ie representation in elected bodies, electoral mechanisms etc, which will be analysed in detail below. The entire problem of the normative power of the document, and in particular its 'judicial potential', eg its legally binding effect, must be subdivided into the following two questions. First, is the FCNM only imposing obligations on states or conferring rights on individuals, thereby creating a 'direct effect'? Secondly, how can the implementation of obligations and/or rights be reviewed and/or enforced, ie effectively guaranteed?

In short, no judgment issued by the national courts analysed by Palermo considered the provision of the FCNM as merely a binding, but not 'self-executing', legal obligation for states parties to this international treaty. Instead, the courts gave the FCNM direct effect in two ways: either by making direct use of the legal provision of the FCNM as a standard of review for domestic law and

---

[14] See F Palermo, 'Domestic enforcement and direct effect of the Framework Convention for the Protection of National Minorities: On the judicial implementation of the (soft?) law of integration' in Verstichel et al, *The Framework Convention* (n 3 above), 187–214.
[15] M Weller, 'Conclusions' in Weller, *The Rights of Minorities* (n 2 above), 633.
[16] Preparatory Work of the Ad Hoc Committee for the Protection of National Minorities (CAHMIN), Explanatory Report to the Framework Convention for the Protection of National Minorities, CAHMIN H(1995)010, 1995.

practice under consideration, or indirectly by referring to the 'spirit' or normative 'principles' of the FCNM as additional textual elements for the interpretation of the domestic legal provisions under review (in some cases even if the FCNM had not yet been ratified, ie entered into force as part of the national legal system). As can be seen from this court practice, most provisions of the FCNM are obviously considered to be specific enough so as to enable courts to give them direct effect as rules containing rights or obligations without the necessity of national legislation for translating 'principles' into 'rules'. This position has also been adopted by the Thematic Commentary on several occasions in its declaration that the FCNM does not prescribe vague programme-style principles, but 'protects the rights of individual persons',[17] and not only if there is a similar right to be found in the ECHR.[18]

Against this legal-theoretical background, the question arises of the normative character of the country-specific opinions of the Advisory Committee (AC), the respective recommendations of the Committee of Ministers and, in particular, the thematic commentaries of the AC. Following the theoretical distinction between 'hard' and 'soft' law, scholars have already created the notion of 'soft jurisprudence' based on hard law.[19] Unlike the case law of courts—which usually have binding effect only *intra partes* and not *erga omnes*, but are nevertheless considered to be 'hard jurisprudence based on hard law'—the opinions and recommendations of the AC and Committee of Ministers do not adjudicate on individual cases, but have to assess the implementation of the FCNM in law and in the practice of states parties. Hence, expectations about their normative 'nature' must be different and can be multiple. Sia Spiliopoulou Akermark has, in my opinion, correctly outlined that the FCNM has at least two functions, and that these are not mutually exclusive as the theoretical distinction between political and legal effects seems to suggest. In a functional sense and following from the title and text of the Convention itself, the protection of the rights of persons belonging to national minorities is the good to be delivered. Hence, a rights-oriented evaluation by the AC and the Committee of Ministers focusing on rights violations could and should be preferred.[20] On the other hand, in an

---

[17] See Arts 6, 13, 14, 65, 75, and 133 (in a negative way).

[18] Also the text of Art 23 of the FCNM itself expressis verbis refers to 'the rights and freedoms flowing from the principles enshrined in the present framework Convention'. The ongoing text of the sentence 'in so far as they are the subject of a corresponding provision in the Convention for the Protection of Human Rights and Fundamental Freedoms or in the Protocols thereto, [they] shall be understood as to conform to the latter provisions' cannot, however, be restrictively interpreted as if only those provisions such as Arts 7, 8, and 9 of the FCNM which correspond to Arts 9, 10, and 11 of the European Convention on Human Rights (ECHR) would contain rights. See also s Spiliopoulou Akermark, 'The added value of the Framework Convention for the Protection of National Minorities (I)' in Verstichel et al, *The Framework Convention* (n 3 above), 82–7.

[19] See Hofmann, 'New standards' (n 5 above), 244; and J Packer, 'Situating the framework convention in a wider context: Achievements and challenges' in Council of Europe (ed), *Filling the Frame: Five years of monitoring the Framework Convention for the Protection of National Minorities* (2004), 49.   [20] See Akermark, 'Added value' (n 18 above), 88.

'Aristotelian mode as agora', as she calls it, international organizations are also places of discussion for continued exchange of views and the ongoing formation of knowledge and opinions. Seen from this perspective, the task of the AC—as its first president, Rainer Hofmann, repeatedly stressed—is a 'permanent dialogue'[21] between the Council of Europe and its organs and the states parties, but also with those directly effected, namely minorities, their members, and representatives.

This ambivalence between (legal) standard-setting through 'soft jurisprudence' for the monitoring task on the one hand, and 'dialogue' in order to raise awareness, enhance legal and empirical knowledge and provide options for legislation and policy formulation on the other, is also reflected in the Thematic Commentary on Effective Participation. Paragraph 10 of the Commentary, for instance, speaks about 'an obligation of result' for the states parties. Paragraph 14 expressly declares that Art 5 of the FCNM implies an obligation on states parties to effectively guarantee the 'right to identity' of persons belonging to national minorities. And para 15 refers expressly to 'the right to effective participation'. From this rights-oriented perspective, para 2 declares that:

> The main objective of this commentary is to highlight the interpretation given by the Advisory Committee, mainly in its country-specific opinions adopted between 1999 and 2007, to the provisions of the Framework Convention relating to the effective participation of persons belonging to national minorities.

The next sentence of the same paragraph, however, mirrors the dialogue- and advice-oriented perspective: 'The commentary aims to provide a useful tool for State authorities and decision-makers, public officials, organisations of minorities, non-governmental organisations, academics and stakeholders involved in minority protection', followed by the statement in para 10: 'This Commentary aims to provide the State Parties with an analysis of existing experiences to help them to identify the most effective options.'

In conclusion, the normative substance of the FCNM and Art 15, in particular in its interpretation by the AC in its Thematic Commentary, is twofold: on the one hand, the 'soft jurisprudence' will serve as a legal standard of review for both the AC itself and national courts, if they make use of it. On the other hand, the statements, assessments, alternative options, and recommendations to be found in the Thematic Commentary serve as a 'toolbox' for governments, legislators, as well as NGOs and minority organizations.

This 'Janus-faced' nature of the work of the AC is not necessarily a contradiction in itself, but fits with the general theory of the sources of public

---

[21] Having been myself member of the AC from 1998 to 2002 and from 2006 to 2008, I can report from participatory observation that this alternative is indeed constantly discussed among the members of the AC. It goes without saying that those experts with a legal-educational background tend to give more weight to a rights-oriented monitoring procedure, whereas experts with an INGO background or with an education in the humanities prefer the dialogue-oriented approach.

international law as can be seen from a detailed analysis of the opinions of the AC from the first and second monitoring cycle with regard to its standard setting activities. Emma Lantschner has thereby identified three types of standards which the AC implicitly uses in its evaluations and recommendations.[22] First is what she calls a 'minimum standard': in several country-specific opinions, the AC comes to the conclusion that the situation regarding legislation or practice is a clear 'violation' of the respective provision of the FCNM. As will be seen in more detail from the assessments regarding the prohibition of political parties below, the evaluation that the situation in a given country amounts to a violation of the FCNM is very often based on a comparison with the standards created by the case law of the European Court of Human Rights. Hence, the 'soft jurisprudence' of the AC is based on the 'hard jurisprudence' of the ECtHR and follows the rights-oriented approach with the possible effect of contributing to the creation of a 'Pan-European' regional customary law of minority protection. Second is an 'emerging standard', which can be deduced from evaluations and recommendations when the AC concludes that the situation in a given country does not amount to a 'violation', but nevertheless recommends an improvement and requires state action either through legislation or governmental policies. On top of the hierarchy of standards are 'best practices', which are recognized by the AC in a given country. Best practices obviously do not follow as a legal obligation from the FCNM, but are highlighted by the AC as coming close to or even fulfilling the 'philosophy' of the FCNM for a 'truly democratic society' based on integration in the 'triangle of effective participation, full and effective equality and promotion of national minorities' identity and culture' in order to provide social cohesion and the integrity of states. 'Emerging standards' and even 'best practices' identified by the AC in its opinions and the thematic commentaries can contribute to the creation of hard customary international law, if this is taken over by the recommendations of the Committee of Ministers of the Council of Europe and/or the states parties themselves as evidence of *opinio juris* and/or state practice.

In conclusion, we must ask: what is more 'effective', the political or the legal approach? This is again a false dichotomy, not taking into account the timelines and interdependence of politics and law in the process of 'standard-setting'. Rainer Hofmann is, of course, right in stressing the importance of a permanent political dialogue as a starting point given the strong legacy of the nation state models in Europe and therefore the necessity of supporting the shift in paradigm from the concept of either the 'neutrality' or ethnic 'homogeneity' of nation states to that of cultural diversity as an added value in both the minds of political elites and the attitudes of populations. However, in addition to dialogue,

---

[22] E Lantschner, *Soft Jurisprudence im Minderheitenrecht. Standardsetzung und Konfliktbearbeitung durch Kontrollmechanismen bi- und multilateraler Instrumente* (2009), in particular at 5–26.

there must be some sort of legal 'institutionalization' in order to make the shift in paradigm sustainable; otherwise, dialogue could be too easily discredited as a 'matter of negotiation on a case-by-case basis',[23] ending up in double-standards[24] and legal insecurity. Rainer Hofmann is again right when he stresses the 'persuasive authority'[25] of country-specific reports, guidelines, etc, of various international monitoring bodies 'in their potential to influence domestic policies and legislation'. However, 'persuasive authority' is certainly a necessary element, but is in no way sufficient to guarantee the effectiveness of the FCNM as a legally binding instrument. The classification of evaluations and recommendations in the AC opinions and thematic commentaries according to the hierarchy of minimum standards, emerging standards and best practices can serve both the 'transition' process of the political shift from the nation state and minority protection concept to the cultural diversity management paradigm, as well as the transformation of 'soft jurisprudence' into hard law.

III. Effective Participation in Public Affairs

At first glance, the Thematic Commentary repeats the cautious approach of the FCNM with regard to state structures. Paragraph 69 of the Commentary speaks rather vaguely about the 'examination' by the AC of 'representation and participation [of national minorities] in various mechanisms', and paras 70–1 generally refer to 'a wide range of possible forms' and 'whatever mechanisms chosen'. Moreover, the Thematic Commentary does not obviously prescribe any 'specific' legal instrument or measure for the effective participation of national minorities in the territorial or functional layering of the exercise of state powers in order to respect the 'various constitutional traditions' of the states parties. Marc Weller has also shown in his analysis of the legislative history of Art 15 that if not the concept then at least the language of functional or territorial 'autonomy' was carefully avoided.[26]

However, a contextual interpretation of the provisions of the FCNM and a comparative, systematic analysis of the 'wide range' of representation and participation mechanisms in political decision-making processes to be found in the national legal systems of states parties, which was undertaken by the AC in its elaboration of the Thematic Commentary, go far beyond the unsystematic and purely demonstrative description of more or less specific instruments

---

[23] See Weller, 'Conclusions' (n 15 above), 635.
[24] See Akermark, 'Added value' (n 18 above), 73 in convincingly contesting the opinion that the FCNM was intended only or mainly for the former communist countries of Eastern Europe.
[25] See Hofmann, 'New standards' (n 5 above), 244.
[26] See Weller, 'Article 15' (n 2 above), 436–7.

enumerated in the Explanatory Report.[27] The concept of 'effective participation' in public affairs—as can be seen from the table of contents of the Commentary —is thus structurally subdivided in three different ways.

First, there is a general subdivision into instruments and measures which enable, foster, or guarantee effective participation. Hence, there are legal instruments, in particular fundamental rights and freedoms, that are supposed to enable effective participation against institutional and legal barriers or obstacles. The individual right to vote or to stand as a candidate, or freedom of association including the freedom to found parties along ethnic lines, are therefore functional prerequisites for any participation which must be guaranteed without undue restrictions and/or discrimination. In a next step, there are 'special' instruments or measures which, for instance, foster the participation of national minorities such as 'exemptions from threshold requirements' in a proportional vote system or 'benign gerrymandering' of electoral districts under a majority vote system without, however, guaranteeing their representation in elected bodies. And finally there are again 'special' instruments or measures which even guarantee, for instance, representation through 'reserved seats', ie irrespective of the number of members of the national minority or even the number of votes cast.

Secondly, there is a general subdivision which refers to different institutional mechanisms on the one hand, and procedures on the other in order to effectively influence the outcomes of decision-making processes. Hence, there might be a need for representation of national minorities *in* the various state bodies of the legislative, executive and judicial powers and/or the creation of bodies outside the organizational structures of state authorities in order to give the interests of national minorities an institutional voice, to aggregate them and to represent them vis-à-vis state authorities. However, this division and the respective institutional set-up do not necessarily decide the 'degree' of procedural influence on decision-making processes and their outcomes. Again from an ideal-typical point of view, the procedural role may be put on a continuum between mere observer status or consultation towards unlimited veto power. Hence, 'consultative' bodies outside the state organization—if they must be consulted in the legislative process—might be 'more' effective than mere representation in state bodies without a chance to effectively influence the outcome of decision-making. In conclusion, the seemingly inconsistent rules elaborated under paras 71–2 of the Thematic Commentary make perfect sense from this perspective: since para 71 regulates that national minorities 'should be given real opportunities to influence decision-making', the Thematic Commentary establishes both the rules as minimum standards that 'mere consultation is, as such, not a sufficient means to be considered effective participation'

---

[27] Such as consultation when adopting legislative or administrative measures likely to affect national minorities; involvement in the preparation and implementation of development plans; studies to assess the impact of development activities; participation in decision-making bodies and elected bodies at all territorial levels; and decentralized or local forms of government.

and, according to para 72, that 'representation and participation… in elected bodies, public administration, judiciary and law enforcement agencies is an essential but not sufficient condition for effective participation'. It thus follows from this neither-nor rule that 'special mechanisms, such as reserved seats, quotas, qualified majorities, dual voting or "veto rights"' or 'specialised governmental structures dealing with minority issues' referred to under para 73 may not only 'be introduced' or 'contribute' to the need of minorities to be integrated into governmental issues, as the Thematic Commentary outlines, but are logically required as necessary additional instruments to either consultation or representation.

Thirdly, from a functional perspective, all instruments of minority protection can be subdivided into instruments serving either the goal of 'integration' through representation and (procedural) participation in decision-making bodies, or 'autonomy' in order to keep the necessary balance for the preservation of their distinct cultural identity.

Seen from this conceptual background, and as will be demonstrated in more detail below, the Thematic Commentary indeed specifies the abstract notion of 'effective participation' on the basis of all the legal instruments to be found in national legal systems so that it is proven beyond doubt that 'effective participation' according to Art 15 of the FCNM is not only a normative principle without imposing any concrete legal obligations, but provides concrete policy options in the form of 'best practices' as well as 'emerging' and even 'minimum' legal standards, which have to be considered as justiciable rights that can be invoked before national courts.

Finally, the Thematic Commentary goes far beyond the vague language and restrictions of the Explanatory Report by specifically referring to participation 'through sub-national forms of government' and 'autonomy arrangements' in Part III.3.(e) and (f).

A. Representation in the legislative process

The first section of Chapter 3 of Part III, dedicated to participation in public affairs, deals with legal instruments and institutions for representation in elected bodies on a continuum between individual freedom of association and the right to vote for proportional representation of national minorities which enable, foster, or guarantee effective participation.

1. Political Parties

Conceptually, freedom of association, in particular the freedom to found political parties, is a functional prerequisite of parliamentary democracy.

However, countries following the French state-nation concept established through their national legal system a prohibition to found political parties along ethnic lines. Examples include Turkey and Greece, as well as Bulgaria and Albania. As follows from Art 11 of the ECHR, any party ban which is not

Effective Participation in Public Affairs 233

'necessary in a democratic society' and not based on one of the substantive criteria for limitations according to para 2 of this provision such as, inter alia, national security, prevention of disorder, or the protection of the rights and freedoms of others, amounts to a violation of this fundamental freedom. Hence, the respective case law of the ECtHR[28] has served as a minimum standard in the evaluation of the AC.

Despite these established international legal obligations, the Bulgarian Constitutional Court banned the political party UMO-Ilinden-Pirin with an ethnic Macedonian orientation with the reasoning that public declarations made by party officials violated the principle of Bulgaria's territorial integrity and thus national security. The ECtHR, however, recalling its established case law, found this party ban to be in violation of Art 11 of the ECHR:

The mere fact that a political party calls for autonomy or even requests secession of part of the country's territory is not a sufficient basis to justify its dissolution on national security grounds. In a democratic society based on the rule of law, political ideas which challenge the existing order without putting into question the tenets of democracy, and whose realisation is advocated by peaceful means must be afforded a proper opportunity of expression through, inter alia, participation in the political process. ... It is of the essence of democracy to allow diverse political programmes to be proposed and debated, even those that call into question the way a State is currently organised, provided that they do not harm democracy itself.[29]

Despite the fact that the AC had nevertheless only cautiously criticized Art 11 of the Bulgarian Constitution as 'problematic', regarding Art 7 of the FCNM which contains the same provision on freedom of association, the Bulgarian government rejected the criticism of the AC as 'unfounded'.[30] Unlike Bulgaria, Albania abolished the possibility of banning parties founded along ethnic lines in 2000, which was explicitly welcomed by the AC in its opinion on Albania.[31]

In conclusion, para 75 of the Thematic Commentary makes it clear that a prohibition on founding political parties or organizations simply because they

---

[28] Already in ECtHR, *United Communist Party of Turkey and ors v Turkey*, Appl 113/1996/752/951, Judgment of 30 January 1998; and ECtHR, *Sidiropoulos and ors v Greece*, Appl 57/1997/841/1047, Judgment of 19 July 1998, the Court established the rule that a justification with reference to the constitutionally enshrined 'unity of the Turkish nation' does not meet the standard of 'national security' according to Art 11.2 of the ECHR and that 'Mention of the consciousness of belonging to a minority and the preservation and development of a minority's culture could not be said to constitute a threat to a "democratic society".' The Court basically entrenched this as established case law in ECtHR, *Stankov and United Macedonian Organisation Ilinden v Bulgaria*, Appl 29221/95, Judgment of 2 October 2001.
[29] ECtHR, 20 October 2005, *United Macedonian Organisation Ilinden – Pirin and ors v Bulgaria*, Appl 59489/00.
[30] Commentary by the Bulgarian Government, published on 5 April 2006, GVT/COM/1 (2006)001.
[31] At Arts 42 and 71. For the full text of all AC Opinions and State Reports, please refer to the Council of Europe website at <http://www.coe.int/t/dghl/monitoring/minorities/3_FCNMdocs/Table_en.asp> (accessed 31 July 2009).

represent minorities, amounts to a violation of Art 7 of the FCNM. According to Art 11 of the ECHR, a limitation or even prohibition of political parties along ethnic lines can only be justified in line with the rules established by the ECtHR so that the case law of the ECtHR prescribes a minimum standard also with regard to Art 7 of the FCNM.

Another important minimum standard can be derived from the normative principle of a 'dual pluralism' embedded in paras 78–9 of the Thematic Commentary. First, para 78 establishes the rule that the inclusion of minority representatives in mainstream political parties may not be sufficient for 'effective' participation so that, as a rule, 'political parties, both mainstream and those formed by persons belonging to national minorities, can play an important role in facilitating participation'. The existence of minority parties cannot therefore be seen as an indicator of ethnic polarization or even division of a country. Secondly, para 79 requires political pluralism within ethnic groups so that one party cannot establish a monopoly on the representation of the interests of a given minority group.

2. Design of Electoral Systems

The design of electoral systems can have a great impact on minority representation in elected bodies at all levels. The case law of the former European Commission on Human Rights, in particular *Lindsay v United Kingdom*,[32] followed the general wisdom that a proportional vote system is in general more favourable to minority representation. In comparison, the Thematic Commentary takes a much more cautious position by declaring in Art 81 that 'State Parties are sovereign to decide on their electoral systems', but that it is 'important to provide opportunities for minority concerns to be included in the public agenda'.

From a comparison of national electoral systems, there are, in principle, two legal instruments which foster the representation of national minorities in elected bodies as 'special measures'. First, every proportional vote system (PR) is balanced by the introduction of thresholds in order to prevent the fragmentation of elected bodies, in particular national parliaments. On average, European countries with a PR system have introduced 3 to 5 per cent thresholds.[33] In effect, only those parties which gain more votes than 3 to 5 per cent of the votes cast can participate in the allocation of seats in the respective elected body. As can be seen from various studies,[34] political parties representing smaller or territorially dispersed national minorities will therefore be disadvantaged by such a threshold

---

[32] ECtHR, 8 March 1979, Appl 8364/78.
[33] See Venice Commission, Comparative Report on Thresholds and Other Features of Electoral Systems which Bar Parties from Access to Parliament, CDL-AD(2008)037.
[34] See recently D Hine, 'Electoral systems, party law and the protection of minorities', Strasbourg, 2 April 2009, Report for the Committee of Experts on Issues Relating to the Protection of Minorities, DH-MIN(2006)013final; and F Bieber, 'Regulating minority parties in Central and South-Eastern Europe' in B Reilly and P Nordlund (eds), *Political Parties in Conflict-Prone Societies: Regulation, engineering and democratic development* (2008), 95–125.

requirement. 'Exemptions from threshold requirements' on behalf of political parties representing national minorities are therefore seen as a 'special measure' to foster minority representation. Secondly, in a majority vote system the geographic design of electoral districts makes the difference. In the past, 'gerrymandering', ie the redrawing of the boundaries of electoral districts, was used by parliamentary majorities in order to discriminate opposition parties. By contrast, 'benign gerrymandering' is thus, again, a possible 'special measure' to foster the representation of minority parties.

The position of the AC with regard to these two possible instruments on behalf of national minorities was and is rather cautious. In general, the exemption from thresholds was welcomed, as can be seen from the opinions on Germany, Poland, and Serbia and Montenegro.[35] However, the withdrawal of the exemption from the threshold requirement by Lithuania in 1996, when legislative changes led to a reduction of minority protection according to the national standard previously achieved, was not criticized by the AC in the usual manner. In effect, Lithuania upheld this reduction of participatory opportunities with the consequence that only two minority representatives were elected in 2004 in contrast to nineteen representatives in 1990. Despite these findings, the language of para 82 of the Thematic Commentary is rather weak when it declares, 'Exemptions from threshold requirements have proved useful to enhance national minority participation in elected bodies.'

As far as benign gerrymandering is concerned, this instrument is referred to in para 88 and 90 of the Thematic Commentary under heading (iii), Administrative and Constituency Boundaries. As far as this instrument is concerned, the AC has criticized Albania, Lithuania, Ukraine, Slovakia, and Denmark,[36] saying that changes in the boundaries of electoral districts, but also in municipalities, have a negative impact on minority representation. But only in relation to Lithuania did the AC state that such changes required consultation with the affected minorities or population. This requirement of consultation was then taken up in para 89 of the Thematic Commentary with the minimum standard following from Art 16 of the FCNM, and was reiterated in para 90 that 'in any case, State Parties should not adopt measures which aim to reduce the proportion of population in areas inhabited by persons belonging to national minorities'.

In conclusion, 'special measures' in electoral systems, in order to foster minority participation, are certainly not required as legal obligations by the

---

[35] First Opinion on Germany, ACFC/INF/OP/I(2002)008, 1 March 2002, para 63; First Opinion on Poland, ACFC/INF/OP/I(2004)005, 27 November 2003, para 86; Second Opinion on Serbia, ACFC/INF/OP/II(2009)001, 25 June 2009, para 102.

[36] First Opinion on Albania, ACFC/INF/OP/I(2003)004, 12 September 2002, para 73; First Opinion on Lithuania, ACFC/INF/OP/I(2003)008, 21 February 2003, para 82; First Opinion on Ukraine, ACFC/INF/OP/I(2002)010, 1 March 2002, para 69; Second Opinion on Slovak Republic, ACFC/INF/OP/II(2005)004, 21 June 2006, para 115; and Second Opinion on Denmark, ACFC/INF/OP/II(2004)005, 11 May 2005, para 154.

FCNM, but they are rather cautiously evaluated by the AC both in its country-specific opinions as well as in the Thematic Commentary. Hence, they cannot be qualified either as recommended 'best practice' or as an emerging standard.

3. Reserved Seats

In contrast to exemptions from threshold requirements and benign gerrymandering, the AC is more positive in its assessment of a 'reserved seats system' as a special measure, which not only fosters, but guarantees minority participation insofar as reserved seats are independent of the number of members of minorities or of votes cast for representatives of national minorities. Again, one can distinguish between two forms: on the one hand, a minimum representation in the sense that each minority will be represented through one seat in the elected body, as is the case in Slovenia (but only for the Italian and Hungarian minority) and Romania, or that even several smaller minorities have to share one seat, as in Croatia. On the other hand, one can find a system of proportional representation of ethnic groups, as in Bosnia and Herzegovina (BiH) and Kosovo.[37] Both systems are also applied on the regional and local level in Slovenia, Croatia, and the autonomous province of South Tyrol.[38] In all of these cases the AC welcomed reserved seats in the form of minimum representation in the respective country-specific opinion, but criticized the system of proportional representation of 'constituent peoples' in BiH at the national level since it leads to the *de jure* exclusion of national minorities.[39] The abolition of reserved seats for Crimean Tatars in the Autonomous Republic of Crimea in Ukraine was criticized by the AC, as was the exclusion of minorities from representation in certain electoral districts in Dagestan in the Russian Federation, since specific minorities were given a monopoly in representation.[40]

The positive assessments in the country-specific opinions are reflected in the Thematic Commentary insofar as para 91–2 declare that such arrangements 'proved to be a useful means to enhance participation' and that such a system 'is

---

[37] For a detailed analysis of these arrangements see recently S Constantin, 'Romania'; A Petričušić, 'Croatia'; M Kmezić, 'Montenegro'; S Milikić, 'Bosnia and Herzegovina'; and A Hajrullahu, 'Kosovo' all in E Lantschner, J Marko, and A Petričušić (eds), *European Integration and Its Effects on Minority Protection in South Eastern Europe* (2008). For Slovenia see I Kristan, 'Die Rechtsstellung der nationalen Minderheiten in Slowenien' in G Brunner and B Meissner (eds), *Das Recht der nationalen Minderheiten in Osteuropa* (1999), 167–8.

[38] On the legal arrangements and their political analysis see recently J Woelk, F Palermo and J Marko (eds), *Tolerance through Law: Self governance and group rights in South Tyrol* (2008).

[39] First Opinion on Bosnia and Herzegovina, ACFC/INF/OP/I(2005)003, 11 May 2005, paras 98–9. At the moment of writing the cases *Sejdic* and *Finci v Bosnia and Herzegovina* are pending before the Grand Chamber of the ECtHR. Both claim to have been violated in their right to stand as candidates in the elections for the presidency of Bosnia-Herzegovina because they belong to a national minority. Art V, para 1 of the Dayton Constitution, however, reserves membership in the Presidency to one Bosniak, one Croat, and one Serb. See also Venice Commission, Amicus Curiae Brief in the cases of *Sejdić* and *Finci v Bosnia and Herzegovina*, CDL-AD(2008)027.

[40] First Opinion on Ukraine (n 36 above), para 70; and First Opinion on Russian Federation, ACFC/INF/OP/I(2003)005, 13 September 2005, para 104.

particularly adapted to the needs of numerically small minorities'. Minimum representation in the form of reserved seats, in particular for small minorities, must be seen, if not as an emerging standard, but as recommended best practice.[41] Also the principle of pluralism is again taken care of, since the AC requires in Art 92 that elected representatives 'should take due care to represent the concerns of all persons belonging to national minorities in the constituency'.

B. Representation in the executive, public administration, and judiciary

As far as representation in the executive, public administration, and the judiciary is concerned, the state reports identified a wide range of possibilities. From a systematic point of view, national minorities can—on the one hand—be represented through persons belonging to these minorities by holding any cabinet post in government or through equitable or even proportional representation in public administration or the judiciary. On the other hand, the alternative is the creation of 'specific' ministries or governmental bodies or departments within the administration for national minorities with or without persons belonging to national minorities, as members of such bodies which will be dealt with below under the heading of 'consultative mechanisms'.[42]

All these possibilities were generally welcomed by the AC in its country-specific opinions, in particular for efforts undertaken by governments in the development of coherent and coordinated minority policies.[43] Hence, steps backwards in this area were firmly criticized, for instance when Albania abolished the Ministry for Minorities[44] or Moldava abolished the Minority Committee within the Presidential Office.[45]

The representation of national minorities in public administration and the judiciary is also considered an important aspect of effective participation so that

---

[41] The Montenegrin Constitutional Court declared reserved seats unconstitutional in its Ruling No 53/06 of 11 July 2006 by arguing that affirmative action measures violated the then still valid Montenegrin Constitution of 1992. Slovenia is the only country where reserved seats system is combined with dual voting. Persons belonging to minorities can thus cast one vote for party lists and another vote for a minority candidate. The Slovene Constitutional Court upheld this regulation against the claim that a dual vote system would violate the fundamental rule of 'one man, one vote'. Case U-I-283/94 of 12 February 1998. A very cautious position is taken by the Venice Commission in the Document, The Protection of National Minorities and Elections, CDL-EL (2008)002rev with one of the two rapporteurs arguing that a dual vote system is in any case a violation of principle of equal voting rights.

[42] Marc Weller labels the latter possibility 'co-ordination mechanism'. M Weller, 'Consultation arrangements concerning national minorities', Report prepared for DH-MIN, Strasbourg 24 February 2006, DH-MIN(2005)011final.

[43] First Opinion on Armenia, ACFC/INF/OP/I(2003)001, 16 May 2002, paras 81–2; First Opinion on Lithuania (n 36 above), paras 77–8; First Opinion on Poland (n 35 above), para 89; Opinion Serbia and Montenegro, ACFC/INF/OP/I(2004)003, 7 November 2003, para 105; First Opinion on Ukraine (n 36 above), para 71.   [44] First Opinion Albania (n 36 above), para 68.

[45] First Opinion on Moldova, ACFC/INF/OP/I(2003)002, 1 March 2002, para 87.

the AC welcomed or criticized countries in their respective opinions.[46] In particular, Roma and Travellers were identified as the most disadvantaged groups. The AC also criticized low employment figures of minority members in law enforcement bodies and the army. Whereas the AC in most cases required states only to examine the situation, Croatia and Bosnia and Herzegovina were required to take affirmative action measures.

Based on these country-specific experiences, the Thematic Commentary tries first to distil a more general normative principle for the representation and participation of national minorities in this area by balancing the basic value that 'public administration should, to the extent possible, reflect the diversity of society' (para 120) with the caveat that 'measures which aim to reach a rigid, mathematical equality in the representation of various groups... should be avoided' (para 123). Secondly, the Thematic Commentary also hints at more 'specific' measures:

- 'Targeted measures can be designed to address the specific circumstances of past inequalities in employment practices of some national minorities', including sufficient training for all and not only minority employees (para 125).
- The promotion of recruitment of persons belonging to minorities can be put on a legal basis including adequate implementation measures (para 121).
- Minority representation in the executive can be advanced at all (territorial) levels.

Since effective participation has to be interpreted in light of effective equality according to Art 4 of the FCNM, the first and second of these 'specific' measures—obviously tailored not to generally promote equal opportunities, but to overcome

---

[46] A Governmental Action Plan for the increase of minority representation was welcomed in First Opinion on BiH (n 39 above), para 112; also positive First Opinion on Italy, ACFC/INF/OP/I(2002)007, 14 September 2001, para 66 with reference to South Tyrol and the Aosta Valley; First Opinion on the former Yugoslav Republic of Macedonia (hereafter, Macedonia), ACFC/INF/OP/I(2005)001, 2 February 2005, para 97–8; First Opinion on Austria, ACFC/INF/OP/I(2002) 009, 16 May 2002, para 68 with reference to the Länder Burgenland and Carinthia; critical comments: First Opinion on Albania (n 36 above), para 75; First Opinion on BiH (n 39 above), para 111; First Opinion on Bulgaria, ACFC/INF/OP/I(2006)001, 5 April 2006, paras 66 and 107; First Opinion on Croatia, ACFC/INF/OP/I(2002)003, 6 April 2001, paras 55–7 with reference to Serbs and Roma; Second Opinion Estonia, ACFC/INF/OP/II(2005)001, 22 July 2005, paras 158 and 160; First Opinion on Italy, above, para 66, and Second Opinion on Italy, ACFC/INF/OP/II (2005)003, paras 139–40 with reference to the Slovene minority; First Opinion on Ireland, ACFC/INF/OP/I(2004)003, 22 May 2003, para 94 with reference to Travellers; First Opinion on Macedonia, above, para 99 with reference to the judicial system; First Opinion on Moldova (n 45 above), para 91, and Second Opinion on Moldova, ACFC/INF/OP/II(2007)002, 9 July 2008, paras 143–5; First Opinion on Romania, ACFC/INF/OP/I(2002)001, 6 April 2001, para 71 with reference to the Hungarian minority; Opinion on Serbia and Montenegro (n 43 above), 103; Second Opinion on Slovak Republic (n 36 above), para 116 and 118; First Opinion on United Kingdom, ACFC/INF/OP/I(2002)006, 30 November 2001, paras 96–9.

past and present *de jure* and de facto discrimination—have to be considered legally binding minimum standards, whereas the third can be seen as an emerging standard. In addition, the Thematic Commentary also refers to language proficiency requirements and the need for statistical data which will be dealt with below in more detail.

C. Consultation or participation? From representation without participation to veto rights in decision-making

As follows from the core considerations of the Thematic Commentary, *effective* participation of minorities requires from states parties 'an obligation of result' (para 10). And para 19 continues that 'it is not sufficient for State Parties to formally provide for the participation of persons belonging to national minorities. They should also ensure that their participation has a substantial influence on decisions which are taken ...' Is 'representation' in state bodies sufficient if minority representatives are members, but cannot participate in the decision-making process itself? It is obvious from the results-oriented approach elaborated in the core considerations that representation without participation cannot meet the standards for *effective* participation. These considerations lead to the conclusion that representation and participation are not identical concepts, but have to be distinguished: representation refers to ('formal') membership in elected bodies; the executive, administration and judiciary as well as other bodies created by or for minorities and the institutional devices for selection of that membership. Participation *stricto sensu* then refers to the process of decision-making in and by such bodies, ie the procedural aspects.[47] Instruments of participation in this sense therefore range on a continuum of 'effectiveness' of

---

[47] Weller, 'Consultation arrangements' (n 42 above), distinguishes consultative bodies with the role of 'hard or soft co-decision' such as minority councils with or without veto power on substance, 'consultation stricto sensu' through minority councils composed of minority members only and through minority governmental bodies with a 'mixed composition' of civil servants and minority members. Finally he identifies 'co-ordination mechanisms' such as interministerial committees with the task to 'mainstream' minority policies in the executive without any minority representation. His typology was, however, not taken over by monitoring bodies of international organizations, not least since a fixed terminology and concepts of legal doctrine for minority protection such as territorial or cultural *autonomy* or *representation* and *participation* would disappear behind his new terminological branding. Hence, the underlying typology of this commentary and my previous writings follow the language used in international documents and tries to systematize legal instruments and institutions on that basis. The term participation, however, is used in international documents and in particular also in the Thematic Commentary in two ways: either as overarching concept or in a narrower sense. The latter distinguishes only procedural possibilities to influence the decision-making processes on a continuum ranging from consultation to veto-powers, ie is process- and result-oriented, whereas the former sometimes confusingly refers both to institutions and their composition, ie to the organizational aspects of representation, as well as to the process-oriented aspects of participation in this narrower sense. See, with further references, Marko, 'Diversity management' (n 6 above).

influence in decision-making from membership, which is the right only to raise one's voice, to absolute veto powers.

The first ideal-typical situation happened in Cyprus[48] and Denmark. In Denmark, the German minority would have lost its representation at the local level through planned reform of the municipalities, but the Danish government proposed to create a reserved seat system without, however, the right to participate in voting in the elected body. This was firmly criticized by the AC, but the Danish government argued that a reserved seat with the right to participate in the decision-making would amount to an 'unjust privilege' for the German minority party. However, the Committee of Ministers of the Council of Europe confirmed the position of the AC.[49] Representation without participation in state bodies cannot therefore be considered to meet the minimum standard required for effective participation. Next on the continuum of participation are thus consultative mechanisms.

1. Consultative Mechanisms

The AC stressed in several country-specific opinions the importance of consultative mechanisms, in particular if there was no effective representation in elected bodies,[50] either in the form of minority councils, usually created by and composed of persons belonging to national minorities, or in the form of 'mixed bodies', ie consultative bodies outside the formal state organization but often created by the government and composed of civil servants and minority representatives. Hence, states parties that had not established consultative bodies were required to form such mechanisms.[51] In several cases, the AC also criticized the representativeness and/or practice of consultative bodies. So, the AC recommended that the appointment of members of consultative bodies should be

---

[48] See the Second Opinion on Cyprus, ACFC/INF/OP/II(2007)004, 9 July 2008, paras 141 and 143 where the AC criticizes the role of the minority representatives in parliament 'as observers' and requires the 'need to identify ways of making the participation of the representatives of the three minority groups in parliament more effective'.

[49] Resolution ResCMN(2005)9, on the implementation of the Framework Convention for the Protection of National Minorities by Denmark, 14 December 2005.

[50] See Opinion on BiH (n 39 above), para 106; Second Opinion on Denmark (n 36 above), para 154; Second Opinion on Finland, ACFC/INF/OP/II(2006)003, 2 March 2006, paras 159–60; Second Opinion on Czech Republic, ACFC/INF/OP/II(2005)002, 24 February 2005, para 172.

[51] See First Opinion on Albania (n 36 above), para 69; First Opinion on BiH (n 39 above), paras 106–7 where existing legislative provisions had not been implemented; First Opinion on Cyprus, ACFC/INF/OP/I(2002)004, para 42; Second Opinion on Denmark (n 36 above), paras 156–7 where the AC welcomes the consultation mechanism for the German minority, but recommends their establishment for other minorities also; First Opinion on Estonia, ACFC/INF/OP/I(2002)005, parah 58; First Opinion on Finland, ACFC/INF/OP/I(2001)002, 22 September 2000, para 149, and Second Opinion on Finland (n 50 above), para 151 with regard to the Russian minority; First and Second Opinions on Italy (n 46 above), paras 64–5 as well as 130–1 and 143–4; First Opinion on Macedonia (n 46 above), para 96; First Opinion on Norway, ACFC/INF/OP/I(2003)003, 12 September 2001, para 61, whereas the AC welcomed the establishment in the Second Opinion on Norway, ACFC/INF/OP/II(2006)006, 16 November 2006, para 138.

made by the minorities themselves or with their close involvement and that at least half of the members of 'mixed' bodies should be minority representatives.[52] In several cases the AC also criticized the effectiveness of the consultation process, insofar as decision-makers contacted consultation mechanisms only on an ad hoc basis, rarely or too late, or did not take their opinions seriously into consideration.[53] Moreover, the AC also required secure financial resources for such bodies, as well as the legal regulation of the status, competencies, and decision-making procedures.[54] Finally, in its country-specific opinions the AC criticized that governments favoured the bodies of usually larger, national minorities or gave one organization a monopoly in representation.[55]

The Thematic Commentary does not create a systematic typology of bodies and procedural mechanisms for consultation. However, it is obvious that the concept of 'consultative mechanisms' used by the Thematic Commentary in paras 106–19 covers both institutions created by and for national minorities, ie representation issues, and process- and results-oriented measures and advice, ie participation issues in the narrow sense which have been evaluated in the country-specific opinions.[56]

Moreover, the Thematic Commentary—based on the experiences of country-specific opinions—develops rather detailed rules for the existence, composition

---

[52] See First Opinion on Austria (n 46 above), paras 68–9; First Opinion on Croatia (n 46 above), para 63; Second Opinion on Czech Republic (n 50 above), para 169; First Opinion on Estonia (n 51 above), para 58 (critical), and Second Opinion on Estonia (n 46 above), para 153 (positive); Second Opinion on Finland (n 50 above), paras 157–8 (positive); Second Opinion on Ireland, ACFC/INF/OP/II(2006)007, 30 October 2006, paras 108–11; First and Second Opinions on Italy (n 46 above), paras 63 and 130–1; First Opinion on Slovak Republic, ACFC/INF/OP/I(2001)001, 22 September 2000, para 46.

[53] See First Opinion on Armenia (n 43 above), para 8, and Second Opinion on Armenia, ACFC/INF/OP/II(2006)005, 24 October 2006, paras 124 and 126; First Opinion on Azerbaijan, ACFC/INF/OP/I(2004)001, 26 January 2004, paras 73–4; First Opinion on BiH (n 39 above), para 109; First Opinion on Estonia (n 51 above), para 57, and Second Opinion on Estonia (n 46 above), para 154; First Opinion on Finland (n 51 above), para 50, and Second Opinion on Finland (n 50 above), paras 155–6; First Opinion on Hungary, ACFC/INF/OP/I(2001)04, 22 September 2000, para 47; First Opinion on Lithuania (n 36 above), para 79; Second Opinion on Norway, ACFC/INF/OP/II(2006)006, 16 November 2006, para 141, 144, and 146; First Opinion on Romania (n 46 above), para 66, and Second Opinion on Romania, ACFC/INF/OP/II(2005)007, 23 February 2006, paras 188 and 194; First Opinion on Sweden, ACFC/INF/OP/I(2003)006, 25 August 2002, para 63; First Opinion on Ukraine (n 36 above), para 72.

[54] First Opinion on Armenia (n 43 above), para 79; First Opinion on Azerbaijan (n 53 above), para 74; First Opinion on BiH (n 39 above), paras 107 and 109; First Opinion on Czech Republic, ACFC/INF/OP/I(2002)002, 6 April 2001, paras 68–9, and Second Opinion on Czech Republic (n 50 above), paras 174–6; First Opinion on Finland (n 51 above), para 50, and Second Opinion on Finland (n 50 above), paras 155–6; First Opinion on Lithuania (n 36 above), para 79; Second Opinion on Slovak Republic (n 36 above), paras 117 and 199; Opinion Serbia and Montenegro, para 108.

[55] First Opinion on Armenia (n 43 above), para 125, and Second Opinion on Armenia (n 53 above), para 127; First Opinion on Croatia (n 46 above), para 64; First and Second Opinion Moldava, para 89 and paras 139–40; Opinion Serbia and Montenegro, para 109; First Opinion on Romania (n 46 above), para 67, and Second Opinion Romania (n 53 above), paras 189–91.

[56] See nn 50–55 above .

and working methods of consultative mechanisms. As a general rule, para 106 stresses that consultative mechanisms are 'particularly important' in countries where there are no representational devices foreseen for national minorities, but adds the caveat that 'consultation alone does not, however, constitute a sufficient mechanism for ensuring *effective* participation …' (emphasis in the original). Paragraphs 107–19 then develop detailed rules for the organization, working methods and institutional relations of consultative bodies, which must also be considered minimum standards in light of the requirement to establish such bodies:

- With regard to organizational structures, there must be a clear legal status (para 107); para 116 even requires legal personality.
- Paragraph 111 regulates that appointment procedures must be transparent and designed in close consultation with national minorities and that there are periodical reviews of appointment procedures.
- Paragraph 109 requires 'appropriate attention' for the "inclusiveness" and "representativeness" of consultative bodies'.

Hence, in the case of mixed bodies, this requires that 'the proportion between minority representatives and officials should not result in the latter dominating the work' without, however, taking recourse here to a quantitive standard. Moreover, the same and the following paragraph require again a 'dual pluralism'. On the one hand, the Thematic Commentary requires that all national minorities should be represented in a consultative body. According to para 112, this implies that the agenda for consultation should not just reflect the concerns of the numerically largest minorities. But when specific consultative mechanisms in respect of an individual national minority are set up, authorities have to take care of the diversity within this group (para 110). Paragraph 111 also requires that authorities take care of the representation of women belonging to national minorities. In addition, para 114 requires that consultative mechanisms with national minorities should not exclude 'parallel consultation with independent experts'.

- In addition to national structures, regional and local consultative mechanisms must be established where decision-making powers have been decentralized (para 115).
- Finally, with regard to organizational matters, para 119 requires authorities to make 'adequate resources' available to support the effective functioning of consultative mechanisms.
- With regard to working methods, para 116 requires clearly defined rules of procedure and publicity of the work of the consultative bodies in order to promote transparency. Paragraph 117 requires that the meetings of these bodies are convened frequently and on a regular basis.
- With regard to institutional relations, the Thematic Commentary requires that the obligation to consult them must be entrenched in law and that the

relevant regulations must be 'detailed enough to provide for efficient and consistent consultation' (para 107); in addition, para 118 specifically regulates that consultative bodies 'need to be duly consulted in the process of drafting new legislation, including constitutional reforms that directly or indirectly affect minorities'.

Consultations cannot be only ad hoc, but must be established on a regular basis 'with a view to institutionalising dialogue between the governments and minority representatives' (para 113) so that 'their involvement in decision-making processes is of a regular and permanent nature' (para 107). Moreover, para 112 requires that consultation cannot be limited to areas with traditional or substantive minority population.

Finally, the Thematic Commentary addresses 'specialised governmental bodies', which are called 'co-ordination mechanisms' by Weller because minority representatives are not involved in such bodies. Paragraph 103 underlines that 'specialised governmental structures ... within national, regional or local authorities can help improve minority participation in public affairs' and requires that states parties establish them or, 'at a minimum', establish contact points for minority issues within public services. Paragraphs 104–5 then determine that specialized bodies cannot substitute, but only complement national minorities' consultative mechanisms, as well as mainstream government institutions on minority-related issues. Again, these rules have to be considered a minimum standard.

In conclusion, this section of the Thematic Commentary obviously offers the most concrete guidelines which must, moreover, be seen as legally binding minimum standards.

2. Participation in Elected Bodies

Based on representation in elected bodies, paras 95–6 of the Thematic Commentary deal with parliamentary practice. The Commentary stresses that 'special parliamentary committees' to address minority issues have proven to be effective in taking minority considerations into account, whereby 'the possibility of using minority languages in these committees has proved particularly effective'. The use of minority languages in parliament cannot, however, be considered a minimum standard with regard to the conclusions from language proficiency requirements dealt with below, but rather a recommendation of best practice. The Commentary also recommends that cooperation across party lines within parliamentary committees strengthens efforts conducive to mainstreaming minority issues into politics.

Finally, paras 97–9 of the Thematic Commentary deal with possible 'veto rights' in the legislative process as the—theoretically—most effective form of influence on the outcome of decision-making processes. Nevertheless, veto rights are criticized—with reference to Slovenia—if they can be invoked only in relation to legal acts concerning exclusively the rights and status of national minorities and not to issues which do not concern them directly or exclusively.[57] The different mechanism of 'vital national interest' vetoes foreseen under the Dayton Constitution for constituent peoples in BiH is criticized for the totally different reason that 'it can lead to a paralysis of State institutions' so that 'other and/or additional ways of enabling persons belonging to national minorities to voice their views in legislative processes' are recommended without, however, giving more specific hints, such as a requirement of dual majorities in place in Switzerland, but also Macedonia as part of the Ohrid compromise.[58] In conclusion, veto rights can neither be considered as best practice recommended by the AC nor as an emerging standard.

D. Autonomy arrangements

The assessment of existing territorial and functional/cultural autonomy regimes by the AC in its country-specific opinions made clear that the AC sees both forms of autonomy as an important contribution to the effective participation of national minorities.[59] Nevertheless, several recommendations for improvement were made with regard to competencies, effective consultation in drafting legislation, and financing.

Despite the cautious approach taken with regard to state structures as outlined above, and against all the political constraints in Eastern and South-eastern European countries against autonomy arrangements, the Thematic Commentary goes beyond the Explanatory Report of the FCNM by referring not only to decentralization, but also to 'subnational forms of government' and—literally—'participation of persons belonging to national minorities through autonomy arrangements'. It repeats the positive assessment of the AC from the opinions in the form of the general advice that 'they can foster a more effective participation of persons belonging to national minorities in various areas of life' (para 133) and even gives—against the hesitation in other sections of the Thematic Commentary for classifications or typologies—a definition of functional/cultural autonomy under para 135:

cultural autonomy arrangements are granted collectively to members of a particular national minority, regardless of a territory. They aim inter alia to delegate to national

---

[57] See First Opinion on Slovenia, ACFC/INF/OP/I(2005)002, 14 March 2005, para 71.
[58] On Macedonia see Z Ilievski, 'Macedonia' in Lantscher et al, *European Integration* (n 37 above), 189–209.
[59] See First Opinion on Denmark, ACFC/INF/OP/I(2001)005, para 36 with regard to Greenland and the Faroe Islands; First Opinion on Finland (n 51 above), para 47 with regard to the Aaland Islands and the Sami parliament; First Opinion on Hungary (n 53 above), paras 46–7 with regard to minority local self-government and cultural autonomy; First Opinion on Italy (n 46 above), paras 61–2 with regard to the autonomous regions of Trentino-South Tyrol and the Aosta Valley; Opinion Norway, para 60 with regard to the Sami parliament; First Opinion on Slovenia (n 57 above), para 69 with regard to local self-government for the Italian and Hungarian minority.

minority organisations important competences in the area of minority culture, language and education and can, in this regard, contribute to the preservation and development of minority cultures.

Due to the fact that a legal obligation to establish autonomy arrangements can certainly not be derived from the FCNM, the following recommendations in the Thematic Commentary on the organization, working methods, and institutional relations are far less specific in comparison to consultative mechanisms, but reflect the recommendations in the opinions. In contrast to the rules concerning consultative mechanisms, they cannot be considered necessary minimum standards either, but—in line with the nature of autonomy regimes—as recommendations for best practice: paras 130 and 136 recommend that the respective competencies of central and sub-national forms of government, as well as of cultural autonomy bodies, should be clearly defined through law. In addition, the legal status of cultural autonomy bodies should also be clarified and appropriate resources and funding should be made available to all forms of autonomy arrangements.

Finally, in an important caveat, para 132 of the Thematic Commentary mentions the usual legal obligation under public international law that 'irrespective of the territorial structure adopted by State Parties, the central authorities should remain committed to their general responsibility resulting from their international obligations' so that states parties are reminded that they have to ensure that sub-national authorities respect these obligations. Hence, the Thematic Commentary recommends 'specific awareness-raising at the local and regional level… to ensure this outcome'.

E. Legal restrictions and problems

1. Citizenship, Residency or Registration Requirements

Political rights, in particular the right to vote and to stand as a candidate in national elections, affected the 'essence' of state-formation and nation-building over the last two centuries.[60] Hence, every democratic system will consider citizenship of the respective country, and the implicit demonstration of loyalty vis-à-vis the political system, a necessary legal condition for the right to participate in the formation of a political community, in particular for employment in the public administration.[61] In the 1990s, for instance, both the German and Austrian constitutional courts declared regional legislation unconstitutional, which had extended the right to vote to non-citizens.[62] The Venice Commission of the Council of Europe also came to the conclusion in a study in 2006 that 'restricting

---

[60] See in particular R Brubaker, *Citizenship and Nationhood in France and Germany* (1992).
[61] As can obviously be seen from the exemption of the individual right to free movement of workers according to Art 39, para 4 of the Treaty of the European Community.
[62] See Decision of the German Constitutional Court, BVerfGE, vol 83, 37; and Decision of the Austrian Constitutional Court, VerfSlg 17264/04.

certain political rights—including those guaranteeing minority representation in the legislature—to citizens who belong to a national minority is also viewed as a legitimate requirement under the FCNM'.[63]

Despite the fact that several countries—when ratifying the FCNM—made a declaration/reservation that only old or 'autochthonous' minorities whose members usually hold citizenship would fall under the scope of application of the FCNM, in order to exclude 'new' immigrant minorities from the application of the legal obligations stemming from the FCNM, the AC argued from the very beginning—on the basis of Art 3 of the FCNM—for an open, inclusive and flexible approach as far as the personal scope of application of the FCNM was concerned.[64] Following this generally inclusive approach, the AC welcomed the electoral provisions in Estonia, which enable non-citizens to participate in local elections. In line with this position, the Thematic Commentary warns in para 100 that citizenship requirements can hamper effective participation and stresses again the need for flexibility and inclusiveness. Hence, despite mirroring the previous position of the Venice Commission that certain restrictions in the right to vote and to be elected might be legitimate at the beginning of para 101, the Thematic Commentary continues with the rule that 'such restrictions should not be applied more widely than is necessary' and particularly recommends that states parties extend the right to vote and to stand as candidates in local elections and in governing bodies of cultural autonomies. Moreover, citizenship requirements for membership in trade unions and 'other' civil society institutions are declared illegitimate.

In addition, residency requirements can restrict effective participation, in particular for an itinerant lifestyle. Therefore, the AC welcomed in its opinion on Ireland, at para 104, that residency requirements were tailored in such a way as not to restrict the rights of Travellers. On the other hand, residency requirements can be introduced for the protection of minorities, as was the case in South Tyrol and this practice has not been criticized by the AC. The Thematic Commentary does not really reflect this as a general issue of concern, but refers to it only in para 84, which requires states parties to take into account the negative impact of residency requirements, in particular for elections at the local level.

As the country Opinions on Moldova, the Russian Federation, and Bulgaria have demonstrated, national legislation can also establish general requirements in the registration process for the foundation of parties or organizations which might amount to a de facto prohibition.[65] Hence para 76 of the Thematic Commentary

---

[63] See Venice Commission, Report on Non-Citizens and Minority Rights, 15/16 December 2006, CD-AD(2007)001, para 139.
[64] See R Hofmann, 'The Framework Convention at the end of the first monitoring cycle' in Council of Europe (ed), *Filling the Frame* (n 19 above), 21–2.
[65] For registration, the Moldovan Law on Political Parties and Socio-political Organizations requires at least 5,000 members who must be residents in half of the districts of the country. Moreover, there must be at least 600 members in each of these districts. See also the critical comment by the Council of Europe Venice Commission, CDL-AD(2002)028.

2. Ethnic Identification Requirements and the Need for Statistical Data

Art 3 of the FCNM is a basic rule strictly requiring that 'every person belonging to a national minority shall have the right freely to choose to be treated or not to be treated as such and no disadvantage shall result from this choice or from the exercise of the rights which are connected to that choice'. If this Article is seen as an axiomatic normative rule for minority protection under liberal and democratic premises, as it is by the AC,[66] there can be no exemption from it. Nevertheless, there are situations which seem to require that persons identify themselves along ethnic lines; for instance, if persons belonging to minorities would like to be elected for reserved seats or if an ethnic quota system more or less strictly reserves jobs for minority members.

The AC evaluated such situations in three countries. The autonomy statute of Trentino-South Tyrol requires that the ethnic affiliation of candidates for election to parliament is known because the number of candidates elected from the three language groups—Germans, Italians, and Ladins—also determines the proportional composition of the executive and the entire public administration and services. Hence, in practice, not only candidates for the elections but all citizen have to fill in a so-called 'language affiliation declaration' at the census every ten years. The language affiliation declaration serves the purpose of minority protection. However, the AC criticized this instrument because the declaration is obligatory for every citizen and a refusal to declare would automatically lead to an exclusion from competition for public jobs or the possibility to stand as a candidate in elections. Moreover, the AC was critical of the fact that these sensitive data were not properly protected, and finally declared the language affiliation declaration incompatible with Art 3 of the FCNM in the way it is used, but without giving advice on how to improve it in order to make it compatible with Art 3.[67]

In its opinion on BiH, the AC even recommended the abolition of the subjective declaration of ethnic affiliation for candidates in elections as a first step in a process of de-ethnification of public offices.[68] In its opinion on Cyprus, the AC strongly criticized the constitutional obligation for persons belonging to the

---

[66] See Hofmann, 'Five years' in Council of Europe (ed), *Filling the Frame* (n 19 above), 21.
[67] According to the standards of the proportionality test which is used by the ECtHR in reviewing limitations of human rights, it is not necessary to require a language affiliation declaration from every person at each census. An ad hoc declaration might serve the same purpose with less burdensome consequences. This was already ruled out by the Italian Corte Cassazione in its judgment of 24 March 1999, No 11048 in the case of Ivan Beltramba. For further details see E Lantschner and G Poggeschi, 'Quota system, census and declaration of affiliation to a linguistic group' in J Woelk et al (eds), *Tolerance through Law* (n 38 above), 219–33.   [68] At para 105.

three minority groups—Armenians, Latins, and Maronites—to affiliate themselves with one of the two national communities: the Greek Cypriot Community or the Turkish Cypriot Community.[69]

Another important problem in this respect, which the AC faced in virtually all state reports, is the problem of the collection of data on ethnic affiliation. Many governments reported that they do not—because of their legal obligation for data protection—collect data on ethnic affiliation at all. However, from the very beginning, the AC made clear in its country-specific opinions that comprehensive data and statistics on ethnic affiliation were crucial for the design of effective legislation and governmental policies to overcome past discrimination or structural barriers in the field of employment in the public and private sector or housing and education, in particular for the most disadvantaged groups such as Roma.

Hence, the problem of ethnic data collection is also addressed in the Thematic Commentary. In light of the experience with State Reports, paras 30–1 establish the rule that 'State Parties should regularly collect data and gather up-to-date information on the socio-economic and educational situation of persons belonging to national minorities …', but that data-collection has to be made in accordance with international standards of personal data protection and in compliance with Art 3 of the FCNM. Moreover, since participation is the overall concern, the Thematic Commentary specifically requires that minority representatives should be involved throughout the process of data collection, and that methods of collection of such data should be designed in close cooperation with them. Paragraph 127 of the Thematic Commentary repeats these rules for minority participation in public administration and services. Both the general requirement of data collection, observing data protection standards, as well as the specific rule on the involvement of minority representatives must be considered minimum standards.

3. Language Requirements

Another legal obstacle which the AC encountered in state reports is language-proficiency requirements for elected bodies or in the field of employment.

Latvia had excluded candidates from parliamentary elections after the State Language Board found that they did not meet the necessary standards of proficiency in Latvian as the official language. In two cases, Russian-speaking candidates were reviewed by the Board despite the fact that they had already been in possession of a certificate proving their knowledge in the official language. Both the UN Human Rights Committee and the ECtHR declared this practice a violation of the respective international legal obligations.[70] The ECtHR

---

[69] Second Opinion on Cyprus (n 48 above), para 11.
[70] See HRC, 31 July 2001, *Ignatane v Latvia*, Communication No 844/1999, violation of Art 25 in conjunction with Art 2 of the ICCPR and ECtHR, 9 April 2002; *Podkolzina v Latvia*, Appl 46726/99, violation of Art 3 of the First Protocol ECHR.

declared in the reasoning in *Podkolzina v Latvia* that 'requiring a candidate for election to the national parliament to have sufficient knowledge of the official language pursues a legitimate aim', but found the renewed language review and procedure incompatible with the requirements for procedural fairness and legal certainty. So when the AC had to deal with similar legislation in Estonia, the AC criticized in its opinion the negative impact on effective participation and required a change of the respective legal provisions. The Estonian parliament indeed abolished the respective language requirements, which was welcomed in the AC's Second Opinion on Estonia.[71]

Going beyond the case law of the ECtHR, para 102 of the Thematic Commentary now rules that 'language proficiency requirements imposed on candidates for parliamentary and local elections are not compatible with Article 15 of the Framework Convention'. This strict rule seems to exclude language requirements constituting a legitimate aim, even if pursued in a proportionate way. In contrast, para 126 of the Thematic Commentary, referring to language proficiency requirements placed on public administration personnel, resembles the balance found by the ECtHR in Podkolzina by declaring that such requirements 'should not go beyond what is necessary for the post or service at issue' so that requirements 'which unduly limit' the access of minority members to employment opportunities in public administration 'are not compatible with the standards embedded in the Framework Convention'.[72] As follows from the rights-oriented language in the Thematic Commentary, the rules developed with regard to language proficiency requirements must be considered minimum standards.

IV. Effective Participation in Social, Economic, and Cultural Life

A. Introduction

A review of the state reports and country-specific opinions revealed that the monitoring activities of the AC in the field of effective participation in the first monitoring cycle were—in order to rephrase the problem—not 'effectively' dedicated to participation in social, economic and cultural life, not least due to the lack of data and statistics. As Alan Phillips reported,[73] almost three-quarters of the paragraphs in the first twenty-four opinions published by September 2003 were devoted to public affairs. Nevertheless, the opinions identified and highlighted in various countries general problems such as the urban-rural divide whereby minorities—who traditionally live in rural areas—are disproportionately affected

---

[71] At para 151.　[72] See also First Opinion on Azerbaijan (n 53 above), para 79.
[73] A. Phillips, 'Commentary: Economic participation of national minorities', in Council of Europe (ed), (n 19 above), 99.

by higher unemployment because of regional disparities not only in East and South-east European transition countries, but also in areas with 'old industries' in Western and Central Europe.[74] Hence, the AC has welcomed and encouraged special measures to enhance economic opportunities for minorities in economically depressed regions.[75] Moreover, a general problem identified was under-representation in public administration and the judiciary,[76] not least in ex-Yugoslav republics due to discrimination and ethnic cleansing during the wars in the 1990s. Land use and property rights were general problems, in particular for Sami in the Scandinavian countries, but also in the conflict-ridden new democracies in the Western Balkans. Roma and Travellers were identified—not least because of racial stereotyping and discrimination—as the most disadvantaged groups in both the public sector and the private labour market, but also in access to education or social services. Finally, the AC criticized multiple discrimination, in particular with regard to ethnicity and gender.[77]

The Thematic Commentary thus responds to these findings and shortcomings by dedicating the first section of Part III of the Commentary, after the introduction and preliminary remarks, to the key findings on economic and social life in paras 23–64.

A systematic analysis of these paragraphs reveals a 'general philosophy' underlying the various general problems addressed in different sectors of economic and social life, as well as the standards and recommendations developed. Para 23 is obviously a response to the shortcoming in the monitoring cycle regarding the review of social and economic life when declaring that 'effective participation in economic and social life is of equal importance to... participation in public affairs, in conformity with the principles of the European Social Charter and the Revised European Social Charter'. Paras 26–8 again pursue an approach which reveals the intimate interrelatedness of Arts 4 and 15 of the FCNM with regard to 'full and effective equality'. Hence, effective participation in social and economic life requires states parties not only 'to remove barriers which prevent persons belonging to national minorities from having equal access to various spheres of economic life and social services' which would only be a more formal anti-discrimination approach, but also 'to promote participation... in benefit and outcomes in the social and economic spheres'. The latter obviously requires affirmative action measures far beyond the goal of simply removing barriers in access to 'adequate housing, health care, social protection (social insurance and social benefits), social welfare services and work' (para 24) in order to achieve formal equality. A second important element of the

---

[74] See First Opinion on Estonia (n 51 above), para 59; First Opinion on Switzerland, ACFC/INF/OP/I(2003)007, 20 Feburary 2003, para 103.
[75] See First Opinion on Ukraine (n 36 above), para 73.
[76] See Second Opinion on United Kingdom, ACFC/INF/OP/II(2007)003, 26 October 2007, para 241; Second Opinion on Croatia, ACFC/INF/OP/II(2004)002, 13 April 2005, paras 156–7.
[77] See Second Opinion on Ireland (n 52 above), paras 50–1.

'general philosophy' in these areas is the horizontal effect, ie the need for prohibiting discrimination by private actors, addressed at several occasions in the Thematic Commentary. A third element is the particular attention paid to the fact of multiple discrimination, in particular with regard to ethnicity and gender.

B. Areas of concern for effective participation in economic, social, and cultural life

As far as anti-discrimination legislation is concerned, para 32 of the Thematic Commentary subdivides different forms of discrimination with which members of national minorities are faced, namely direct and indirect discrimination, but also—in line with the substantive equality approach of Art 4 of the FCNM —'inequalities' which cannot be traced back to discrimination but to 'structural obstacles'. Since missing anti-discrimination legislation is very often also based on a lack of sensitivity not only on the part of society at large, but also of political and other elites, paras 33–6 develop a set of specific rules: first, para 33 requires the existence of 'comprehensive' legislation prohibiting discrimination 'covering the fields of employment, housing, health care and social protection by public *and private actors*' (emphasis JM) as 'a precondition' in any policy aimed at promoting participation. Secondly, para 32 requires that such legislation will also be 'fully implemented' including 'adequate measures ... to raise awareness in the society at large and provide training for all stake-holders, including law-enforcement bodies'. Thirdly, para 35 requires 'appropriate legal remedies' and 'awareness-raising' to make sure that these are easily accessible. Finally, para 36 requires 'targeted measures' against multiple discrimination faced by women belonging to national minorities.

In line with the requirement for 'full implementation' is also the set of standards developed in the Thematic Commentary with regard to capacity-building in the administration and public services in the following paragraphs. Paras 38–41 again require special measures for the 'training of staff' to respond to the special needs of persons belonging to national minorities and 'targeted approaches, which fully take into account cultural and other specific circumstances' (para 38). Moreover, paras 39–40 require a range of 'outreach activities', as well as 'information and advice on public services ... in the languages of national minorities'. Finally, para 41 requires states parties 'to promote the recruitment, promotion and retention in the administration and public services' of persons belonging to national minorities.

All of these rules developed for anti-discrimination legislation and capacity-building in the administration and public services have to be considered minimum standards.

Following the experience of the country-specific opinions, the next areas of concern in the Thematic Commentary for participation in economic and social life are depressed regions, and for access to land and property. Again the AC requires that states parties 'should take specific measures to increase the opportunities for persons belonging to minorities living in peripheral and/or economically depressed areas, such as rural, isolated and border areas, war damaged areas or regions affected by de-industrialisation' (para 42). The requirement to take specific measures must again be seen as a minimum standard going far beyond mere anti-discrimination measures, but to tackle 'structural obstacles' addressed in para 32. Also for post-conflict situations, para 46 requires 'specific measures… to redress the consequences of past discrimination and promote these persons' participation in socio-economic life'. Not only for economic rehabilitation programmes and regional development initiatives (para 44), but for all activities concerning 'the planning, implementation, monitoring and evaluation of policies and projects likely to have an impact on their economic situation and the situation of regions where they live in substantial numbers' (para 45), the Thematic Commentary requires that authorities must ensure that persons belonging to national minorities are 'fully involved'.

As far as access to land and property is concerned, the Thematic Commentary identifies in paras 51–3 privatization processes, armed conflicts and displacement of persons, as well as processes of property restitution which have had 'a disproportionate impact' on national minorities. In comparison to the very concrete rules and standards developed to address 'structural obstacles', the identification of the causes and consequences in this area already reveals an ultra-cautious approach, using the euphemistic language of 'displacement of persons' to refer ethnic cleansing. It comes as no surprise therefore that the remedy requested by the Commentary is rather vague, namely the responsibility of states parties to 'ensure equal and fair access to privatisation and property restitution processes' (para 51) so that they 'do not result in discriminatory outcomes' (para 52).

The next areas of concern for the Thematic Commentary are housing standards and health care. Here, the Commentary is again more specific, requiring that states parties not only 'take effective measures to put an end to discriminatory practices which lead to segregation and marginalisation' (para 58), but also 'develop comprehensive sectoral policies to address problems of substandard housing and lack of access to basic infrastructure' (para 59). As far as health care is concerned, para 63 requires training of medical and administrative staff employed in health services on the cultural and linguistic background of national minorities and, according to para 64, 'equal opportunity policies should not be limited to access to health care only', but 'also aim at the provision of quality services'. For both sectors the Thematic Commentary also requires the effective involvement of minority representatives into the design, implementation, monitoring and evaluation of measures taken.

Finally, the area of cultural life is also more specifically taken into consideration under paras 65–8. Based on the 'triangular' relationship addressed in the core considerations of the Thematic Commentary, para 65 specifies that it is the overall purpose of the FCNM to:

protect both the rights of persons belonging to national minorities to preserve and develop their own cultural heritage and identity and the right for them to take part effectively and interact in mainstream cultural life, in a spirit of tolerance and intercultural dialogue.

This value-oriented goal is then more institutionally specified with regard to cultural autonomy arrangements and media in paras 67–8. Moreover, reference to the importance of establishing minority media, as well as access to mainstream media and their reporting activities through participation in supervisory boards of public service broadcasters, auditors' councils and other media-related bodies is also made in the section of the Thematic Commentary referring to public affairs (paras 140–1). Finally, very sophisticated differentiations are made for the (procedural) participation of minorities in cultural life: when designing and implementing cultural policies, authorities have to carry out adequate consultations. As far as the allocation of public support for cultural initiatives is concerned, they have to be effectively involved in the decision-making process. When specific institutions exist for channelling such support, minorities must be adequately represented and given the opportunity to participate in the decision-making process (para 66).

In conclusion, the Thematic Commentary pursues a process- and results-oriented approach in the areas of economic, social and cultural life, requiring not only anti-discrimination legislation and implementing measures, but also the promotion of effective participation in order to overcome structural barriers against equal opportunities. Whenever rules are developed and 'special measures' required by the Thematic Commentary for this purpose, they have to be considered as minimum standards.

1. Legal Requirements and Obstacles

Similar to the section on public affairs, the Thematic Commentary addresses specific legal requirements and obstacles for effective participation in the social and economic life. Para 54 identifies residency requirements that are imposed by public or private employers as a precondition for recruitment or for registering and running private business. Residency requirements will usually affect national minorities disproportionately, in particular if they are not adapted to an itinerant lifestyle. The same holds true for language proficiency requirements, which can hamper access to certain jobs or the delivery of services and goods. The Thematic Commentary therefore requires under paras 55–6 that states parties take effective measures to remove undue restrictions in these areas and, when language proficiency requirements are a legitimate condition, as is often the case in public administration, that language training courses are made available.

V. Conclusions

In light of the critique at the time of the adoption of the FCNM that it provided no justiciable rights, but only vaguely formulated, programme-type principles, and that the political monitoring mechanism would not be at all effective, the Thematic Commentary of the AC on Effective Participation of National Minorities in fact proves the opposite.

'Effective participation' can no longer be seen as a vague principle that does not provide specific obligations for states parties or individual rights for those affected by violations of these obligations by state and private actors. The comprehensive and systematic analysis of the country-specific opinions and the rules established on that basis by the Thematic Commentary prove beyond doubt that Art 15 of the FCNM entails a set of very concrete minimum standards as legally binding rules which mirror all the solutions that are offered also by the OSCE Lund Recommendations. They will serve the AC and the Committee of Ministers as yardsticks in its further monitoring activities, but they can also be invoked by persons belonging to national minorities before courts at the national level. Moreover, following the Recommendations of the Committee of Ministers as well as the reactions of states parties to the criticisms raised in the country-specific opinions, the Thematic Commentary has also established emerging standards in the field of effective participation so that Art 15 must be seen as a 'useful pan-European instrument' in the development of European customary law for the protection of national minorities. As can be seen from the country-specific opinions as well as the more general rules established by the Thematic Commentary, monitoring and criticism by the AC is not restricted to Eastern and South-eastern European countries, and the FCNM can thus be seen as a truly pan-European.

The Thematic Commentary also makes clear that 'effective participation' bridges the opposition between formal and substantive approaches. Effective participation is, together with effective equality and cultural diversity, one of the 'three corners' of a triangle which together form the main foundations of the FCNM. Seen in the light of this interrelatedness, the Thematic Commentary in many instances goes for beyond the formal anti-discrimination approaches of other international and European anti-discrimination instruments and requires 'special measures', not only in order to remove barriers resulting from past or present direct or indirect discrimination, but also to overcome 'structural' barriers and to promote the identity and culture of national minorities as a *permanent* task within the goal of cultural diversity of society at large. The requirement of 'effective' participation also counters all formalistic and individualistic restrictive interpretations: the Thematic Commentary proves that Art 15 of the FCNM also entails a group-oriented dimension that takes seriously the existence of minorities as groups. Nor can 'participation' be restricted to formal representation in elected bodies or consultation mechanisms only. Finally, seen from this perspective and in relation to Art 4 of the FCNM, the Thematic Commentary also requires that effective participation in economic, social, and cultural life is accorded the same importance as effective participation in public affairs.

In conclusion, 'effective participation' is, beyond doubt, hard law, and the rules established by the Thematic Commentary will also be used by the OSCE High Commissioner on National Minorities and the EU as was previously the case with country-specific opinions. But from a dialogue-oriented perspective the challenge remains for the Thematic Commentary not only to prove itself to be a useful tool for minority representatives, organizations, and NGOs, but—given the 'institutional insensitivity' which the AC encountered in several country visits in Western, Central, and Eastern Europe over the last decade—also for lawmakers and governments at the national level. The main challenge, however, will be the 'effect' that the Thematic Commentary might also have in the long run on the attitudes of majority populations, if the goal of cultural diversity and the need for its management is to become an 'ordinary' task that is sustainable for them.

8

OSCE Lund Recommendations in the Practice of the High Commissioner on National Minorities

Krzysztof Drzewicki

I. Introduction	256
II. The Mandate of the OSCE High Commissioner on National Minorities	257
A. The Organization for Security and Cooperation in Europe	257
B. The High Commissioner on National Minorities	259
III. Origins and Background of the Lund Recommendations	261
A. Conflict prevention considerations	261
B. Normative deficit on national minority standards	263
IV. Application of the Lund Recommendations by the HCNM	267
A. Electoral arrangements	268
B. Political parties	275
C. Consultative and advisory bodies	277
V. Conclusions	280
A. Verification of the tentative submissions	280
B. General observations	283

I. Introduction

The occasion of ten years since the adoption of the Lund Recommendations on the Effective Participation of National Minorities in Public Life in June 1999 affords an excellent opportunity for taking stock of experiences gained and lessons learned from the application of their provisions.¹ Such an exercise can facilitate an assessment of the practical usefulness of the guidelines presented in the Lund Recommendations and identification of their failures, challenges, and successes.

The title of this chapter appropriately reflects these aims by emphasizing its focus upon practice rather than just theory. This should hopefully produce a basis for drawing both theoretical and practical conclusions. However, before attempting to examine the practical experiences of the application of the Lund Recommendations, it is advisable to recall briefly their origins against the background of the broader mandate of the High Commissioner on National Minorities. Furthermore, the Lund Recommendations should be set against the larger perspective of normative developments in international law and international relations in the field of human rights and fundamental freedoms, including the rights of persons belonging to national minorities.

It is tentatively submitted that the Lund Recommendations were adopted under the impact of an acute normative deficit in the field of participation. Entering the area of standard-setting, a role not assigned to him explicitly, the High Commissioner on National Minorities demonstrated that he desperately needed normative recipes for minority participation not as art for art's sake but for conflict prevention purposes. It is also tentatively submitted that the ten-year history of the application and implementation of the Lund Recommendations seems to have shown that they are also viable instruments in the changing circumstances after 1999.

II. The Mandate of the OSCE High Commissioner on National Minorities

A. The Organization for Security and Cooperation in Europe

Established in 1975 by the Helsinki Final Act, the Conference on Security and Cooperation in Europe (CSCE) was renamed the Organization for Security and Cooperation in Europe (OSCE) in 1994 within the context of a move towards

---

[1] The Lund Recommendations were originally reproduced in a booklet in English published by the Foundation on Inter-ethnic Relations (1999), ISBN 90–7598905–9, 1–34 (hereinafter, 'Booklet'). It contains an 'Introduction' (3–6) and normative text of the 'Lund Recommendations' (7–14) followed by the Explanatory Note (15–33) thereto arranged on a recommendation-by-recommendation basis. The whole publication is available on the HCNM's website in twenty-one languages, at <www.osce.org/hcnm> (accessed 31 July 2009). See also the other HCNM thematic instruments in *National Minority Standards: A compilation of OSCE and Council of Europe Texts* (2007), 45–152 (hereinafter, 'Compilation'). For earlier assessments of the Lund Recommendations see K Drzewicki (guest ed), 'The Lund Recommendations on the Effective Participation of National Minorities in Public Life: Five years after and more years ahead' (2005) 12(2–3) *International Journal on Minority and Group Rights* (2005), 123–267.

further institutionalization of the Helsinki process. The Helsinki Final Act was a politically binding agreement. It was the very first European diplomatic arrangement or organization which built a bridge between East and West. It aimed to build a new and comprehensive approach to pan-European cooperation and security.[2]

The Organization was thus brought into being as a diplomatic conference or arrangement, with regular meetings but without a legal treaty basis for cooperation. This practice of undertaking predominantly political commitments has been continued and constitutes a characteristic feature of the organization even after 1990, when the rapid institutionalization of the OSCE started, but still predominantly without resorting to treaty-based instruments and obligations.[3]

Importantly, the process of negotiations on the content of political commitments has been pursued in no less rigid a diplomatic way than in the case of draft legal instruments. It should not be surprising therefore that the outcome of negotiations, notably in the field of the human dimension, results in formulating political commitments in the clear and precise parlance typical of legal instruments. This is a result of the fact that sensitive state interests are at stake and because political commitments, notably in the field of the human dimension, explicitly repeat or reformulate legal provisions. Furthermore, these provisions are subsequently applied and construed by means of interpretation techniques used by lawyers, like those envisaged by the 1969 Vienna Convention on the Law of Treaties (Arts 26–33).

Although born predominantly from political and security considerations, the OSCE also integrated human rights, including minority rights, and humanitarian issues into its agenda, not as a marginally concomitant element but rather as an integrated aspect on an equal footing with security and political dimensions. With its focus on security issues, the OSCE reminds the United Nations of where security considerations prevail over the requirements of democracy and human rights.[4] However, unlike the UN, the OSCE has as its major objective the attainment of democratic governance in all participating states.

---

[2] See K Drzewicki, 'European systems for the promotion and protection of human rights' in C Krause and M Scheinin (eds) *International Protection of Human Rights* (2009), 381–7. On the evolution of the OSCE (until 1994 CSCE) see A Bloed (ed) *The Conference on Security and Co-operation in Europe: Analysis and basic documents, 1972–1993* (1993), 92–5. In 2008, OSCE membership comprised fifty-six participating states from Europe proper, the United States and Canada as well as five Central Asian republics.

[3] In a few instances, the OSCE decided to draw up and adopt treaties which had already been ratified by some of the participating states. An example is the Convention on Conciliation and Arbitration within the CSCE (1992). Another group is made up of treaties of non-OSCE origin but which are linked with the Organization (eg the Treaty on Conventional Armed Forces in Europe 1990) or their link is established by servicing a treaty's implementation body (eg the Treaty on Open Skies of 1992). See *OSCE Handbook* (2007), 96–9.

[4] Art 4(1) of the UN Charter states that: 'Membership in the United Nations is open to all other peace-loving states which accept the obligations contained in the present Charter.' Therefore, it is not required that candidate and actual members of the UN be democratic countries based on the rule of law and respect for human rights.

Probably the most innovative aspect in the OSCE has been the bringing together of all three substantive 'baskets', nowadays called 'dimensions': the politico-security dimension, the economic and environmental dimension, and the human dimension (democratic governance, the rule of law, human rights and fundamental freedoms, and humanitarian issues). Regarded as interdependent and inseparable, all the dimensions reflect the so-called 'comprehensive and co-operative' approach to pan-European security.[5]

As far as human rights and humanitarian issues are concerned, they have been reflected in the four OSCE frameworks. The first is expressed as the politico-security principle embodied in Principle no VII—'Respect for human rights and fundamental freedoms including the freedom of thought, conscience, religion or belief'—of the Declaration on Principles Guiding Relations between Participating States of the Final Act of Helsinki (the Decalogue). The second is identified as part of substantive human dimension commitments which emerged mainly after the demise of the cold war, discernible notably in the Copenhagen Document of 1990.[6] The third framework has evolved as part of human dimension commitments on monitoring compliance in the course of the early 1990s. It was built by designing the Vienna and Moscow mechanisms, establishing the Office for Democratic Institutions and Human Rights, and through the Human Dimension Implementation Meetings. The fourth framework has become part of the conflict prevention mandate of the High Commissioner on National Minorities (HCNM).

B. The High Commissioner on National Minorities

It is within this OSCE set-up that one should understand the establishment of the institution of the High Commissioner on National Minorities. It was launched in the 'CSCE Helsinki Document 1992: The Challenges of Change' as a highly autonomous and independent political body within the OSCE working in confidence as 'an instrument of conflict prevention at the earliest possible stage' (paras 1–2 and 4 of the Helsinki mandate).[7]

The establishment of this arrangement came as a reaction to interethnic conflicts increasingly erupting in Central and Eastern Europe at the end of the

---

[5] For more details see T Buergenthal, 'CSCE human dimension: The birth of a system' in A Clapham and F Emmert (eds) *Collected Courses of the Academy of European Law* (1990) vol I, book 2, (1992), 160–209.

[6] For more comments on the Copenhagen Document see Bloed, *The Conference on Security and Co-operation in Europe* (n 2 above), 92–5; and D Gomien, 'Human rights standard-setting and the CSCE conference on the human dimension: The contribution of the Copenhagen Document', in Z Kędzia, A Korula, and M Nowak (eds), *Perspectives of an All-European System of Human Rights Protection: The role of the Council of Europe, the CSCE, and the European Communities* (1991), 93–102.

[7] See the texts of Helsinki Decisions of 10 July 1992 (Chapter II) and other OSCE documents on the powers of the HCNM in the Compilation (n 1 above), 35–44.

cold war during the course of the painful process of restoring democratic governance to post-communist Europe. Tensions of an interethnic nature need to be addressed using a multi-dimensional approach. The mandate of the High Commissioner was conceived to reflect just such a response through the application of a preventive perspective and means.[8] To this end, when determining the mandate of the HCNM, it was envisaged that the High Commissioner 'will thus be an instrument of conflict prevention at the earliest possible stage' (para 2).

To achieve this end, the High Commissioner is required to provide 'early warning' and, as appropriate 'early action' at the earliest possible stage:

in regard to tensions involving national minority issues which have not yet developed beyond an early warning stage, but, in the judgement of the High Commissioner, have the potential to develop into a conflict within the OSCE area, affecting peace, stability or relations between participating States, requiring the attention of and action by the Council or the CSO. [para 3][9]

The role of the High Commissioner is thus to identify and seek early resolution or de-escalation of ethnic tensions, which may threaten peace and stability. The High Commissioner's mission is basically twofold: 'first, to address and de-escalate tensions before they ignite and, second, to act as a "tripwire", meaning that he is responsible for alerting the OSCE whenever such tensions threaten to develop to such a level that he cannot alleviate them with the means at his disposal'.[10] In other words, the HCNM is expected to contribute to the de-escalation of emerging tensions.

Importantly, he is not to become engaged in all minority-related issues but only in those with security aspects or implications. From such a perspective, the position of the High Commissioner on National Minorities is often characterized as an instrument for international security or conflict prevention rather than a human dimension instrument.

However, such a conclusion seems to be overly categorical and overlooks the momentum accumulated over the course of the operational activities carried out by the HCNM, notably in recent years when high-level tensions have been seriously reduced. This has opened up more opportunities for gradual efforts

---

[8] For more on the background of the post see R Zaagman and H Zaal, 'The CSCE High Commissioner on National Minorities: Prehistory and negotiations' in A Bloed (ed) *The Challenges of Change: The Helsinki Summit of the CSCE and its aftermath* (1994), 95–111.

[9] For more on the content of the mandate see R Zaagman, 'The CSCE High Commissioner on National Minorities: An analysis of the mandate and the institutional context' in Bloed, *The Challenges of Change* (n 8 above), 113–75; J Packer, 'The OSCE High Commissioner on National Minorities' in G Alfredsson et al (eds) *International Human Rights Monitoring Mechanisms: Essays in honour of Jacob Th Möller* (2001), 641–56; and YI Diacofotakis, *Expanding Conceptual Boundaries: The High Commissioner on National Minorities and the protection of minority rights in the OSCE* (2002), 15–29.

[10] See *Annual Report on OSCE Activities 2003: Security and co-operation for Europe* (2003), at 138.

designed to strengthen the infrastructure of the rule of law and human rights from the medium- and long-term perspectives. The overall assessment of the High Commissioner's activities thus demonstrates that the human dimension approach has become an integral part of the 'tool box' for conflict prevention in diplomacy, which in turn often brings with it indirectly a strengthening of the human dimension effects.[11]

The focus of the mandate on conflict prevention has thus neither deprived him of, nor prevented him from, being involved in the concomitant task of monitoring human dimension commitments, most notably those on minority rights. This largely stems from the interpretation of para 6 of the Helsinki mandate, whereby the High Commissioner, in considering a situation, 'will take fully into account the availability of democratic means and international instruments to respond to it and their utilisation by the parties involved'. The potential of para 6 can also be seen from the perspective of the thematic recommendations through which the HCNM has been instrumental in developing minority commitments in the fields of education, use of language, participation in public life, access to broadcast media and, most recently, policing in multi-ethnic societies, and others. The High Commissioner has consequently demonstrated the potential of the concept of 'comprehensive security' with a strong human rights component.

III. Origins and Background of the Lund Recommendations

One may tentatively identify two groups of reasons behind the emergence of the Lund Recommendations and all the other thematic recommendations of the High Commissioner on National Minorities. The first stems from considerations of conflict prevention in response to the political situation in Europe during the 1990s and particularly the instability, disturbances, tensions, and conflicts frequently exhibiting the interethnic components. The second reason is largely embedded in a classic deficit of standards in the field of national minorities.

A. Conflict prevention considerations

The first High Commissioner (Max van der Stoel) observed in general terms that conflict prevention requires a comprehensive approach which combines the various tension-generating factors—both short-term and long-term—within an

---

[11] In this respect, some scholars conclude, in no less strong terms, that 'it goes without saying that the HCNM is deeply involved in the monitoring of minority rights in those states where he has become active'. See A Bloed, 'Monitoring the human dimension of the OSCE' in G Alfredsson, *International Human Rights Monitoring Mechanisms* (n 9 above), 636.

overall strategy. Short-term conflict prevention should be seen and pursued from the perspective of long-term conflict prevention. Long-term conflict prevention is really about building a viable democracy and institutions; about creating confidence between the government and the population and groups within the population; about structuring the protection and promotion of human rights; and about fostering tolerance, understanding, and mutual acceptance in society.[12]

This philosophy explicitly establishes a link between long-term conflict prevention on the one hand and democracy, human rights, and related values on the other. The relationship thus includes the concept of participation of national minorities in public life which constitutes a component part of democracy and human rights, or of good governance more broadly.

As was admitted by the High Commissioner, the Lund Recommendations 'were intended to take a stand against the increasing scepticism about the chances of survival of multi-ethnic States since the dramatic dissolution of Yugoslavia'. Rejecting the idea of ethnically homogenous states, which would lead to the creation of new states with new ethnic minorities and with a risk of mass migration of populations, he identified the need to search for methods that would assist in the pursuit of another option—to attempt 'to integrate diversity'. In this context he noted how amazing it was for him to find out that 'relatively little attention has been paid to various methods to ensure the viability of multi-ethnic States'. Therefore the Lund Recommendations were to 'try to show that there are other ways to find a mutually acceptable balance between the interests of majority and minority'.[13]

After the adoption of the Lund Recommendations the High Commissioner noted his hope that they would open up new horizons for looking at ways of allowing minorities to have a greater say over decisions that affect them, without breaking up states. He said that it was only when members of a minority feel that they were represented in the political bodies of the state at all levels, and could be heard there, that they would identify with the state and regard it as their own.[14]

One can conclude that conflict prevention considerations constitute a strong motivation for the High Commissioner to promote effective participation of persons belonging to national minorities in public affairs. Consequently, any improvements in the participation process by national minorities in public

---

[12] M Merrick Yamamoto (ed), *Preventing Ethnic Conflict and Building Cohesive States: Memorable words of Max van der Stoel First OSCE High Commissioner on National Minorities from his speeches 1992–2001* (2007), 21–2. Note that submissions compiled in the publication referred hereto are drawn entirely from the speeches of Max van der Stoel.

[13] M van der Stoel, 'The Hague, Oslo and Lund Recommendations regarding minority questions' in M Bergsmo (ed), *Human Rights and Criminal Justice for the Downtrodden. Essays in honour of Asbjørn Eide* (2003), 505-12.

[14] Merrick Yamamoto (ed), *Preventing Ethnic Conflict and Building Cohesive States* (n 12 above), 6–7.

affairs are expected to contribute indirectly to de-escalating tensions and increasing the stability of and integration into society. Significantly, drawing upon the practical challenges in his conflict-prevention activities, the High Commissioner addresses participation demands not only in the short- and medium-term but also within the context of a longer perspective.

B. Normative deficit on national minority standards

As recounted above, another reason behind the High Commissioner's decision to draw up a set of recommendations on the participation by national minorities in public life was a classic deficit of standards in the field of national minorities. The deficit in question had two substantive and one procedural dimensions.

1. Normative Deficit in Substantive Standards

The first dimension pertains to the state of substantive international regulations on the right of everyone to effective participation in public life under modern human rights treaties and commitments undertaken by states participating in the OSCE process. Albeit as general normative provisions, they have been deeply embedded in major instruments such as the 1948 Universal Declaration of Human Rights (UDHR) (Art 21), the 1966 International Covenant on Civil and Political Rights (ICCPR) (Art 25), the 1990 Document of the Copenhagen Meeting of the Conference on the Human Dimension of the CSCE (paras 5–7), the 1990 Charter of Paris for a New Europe and other OSCE documents.[15]

The second, and even more significant, dimension is that this right has subsequently become envisaged specifically for the needs of national minorities, as in the case of the CSCE Copenhagen Document (para 35), the 1991 Geneva Report of the CSCE Meeting of Experts on National Minorities, the 1992 United Nations Declaration on the Rights of Persons Belonging to National or Ethnic, Religious, and Linguistic Minorities (Art 2) and above all the 1995 Framework Convention for the Protection of National Minorities (FCNM) (Art 15).[16] In other instruments, such as the 1950 European Convention on Human Rights (ECHR) and the 1965 International Convention on the

---

[15] For the instruments referred to see *Human Rights in International Law: Collected texts*, 2nd edn (2000); and Bloed, *The Conference on Security and Co-operation in Europe* (n 2 above), 537–38, 439–45.

[16] See Compilation (n 1 above), 13–26; and Drzewicki 'The Lund Recommendations' (n 1 above), 124–5. Likewise, see the submission on legal instruments 'which do not spell out issues of minority participation in a great deal of detail' by S Holt, 'The Lund Recommendations in the activities of the HCNM' (20045) 12(2–3) *International Journal on Minority and Group Rights* 169–88, 171. For an extensive examination of the Framework Convention see A Verstichel, 'Elaborating a catalogue of best practices of effective participation of national minorities: Review of the Opinions of the Advisory Committee regarding Article 15 of the Council of Europe Framework Convention for the Protection of National Minorities' (2002–3) *European Yearbook of Minority Issues* 165–95.

Elimination of All Forms of Racial Discrimination (ICERD) certain aspects of participation (eg, the right to free elections) are supported by and linked to the prohibition of discrimination on the ground, inter alia, of 'association with a national minority' (Art 14 of the ECHR and Art 3 of Protocol 1 thereof; and Art 5 of the ICERD).

It is instructive that the formulation of Art 27 of the ICCPR on ethnic, religious, and linguistic minorities, weak in itself by deliberate diplomatic decision, enumerated only the rights 'to enjoy own culture, to profess and practice their own religion, or to use their own language'. However, this provision was negotiated in a period that was still overshadowed by the philosophy of the UN founding San Francisco Conference which had reflected pre-war fears about a need not for the protection of minorities but for the protection *from* minorities.[17]

This is why the provision has failed to include explicitly the participatory rights of national or ethnic minorities. It may be said that only subsequent case law, developed decades later by the Human Rights Committee, has partly remedied this omission through a broader interpretation of Art 27.[18]

It should be recalled that the post-Second World War reticence in both the UN and regional systems to set international standards on national minorities have been often characterized as a 'normative deficit' of minority rules in international law. The above developments show however that the deficit was largely reduced in the 1990s. Thus it has taken more time for the jurisprudence to emerge and be developed.[19]

It is in this context that the question arises as to the main reasons behind the decision by the High Commissioner to launch the very idea of drawing up specific recommendations on minority participation. With the above enumeration of legal and political standards in hand, the High Commissioner could have promoted them in the practice of participating states where he found any symptoms of normative deficit at the domestic level. However, his major problem was that all these legal and political commitments, typically for human rights formulations, were expressed in general and abstract terms which would need to be adjusted to the specificities of domestic circumstances. Furthermore,

---

[17] See J Helgesen, 'Protecting minorities in the Conference on Security and Co-operation (CSCE) process' in A Rosas and J Helgesen (eds), *The Strength of Diversity: Human rights and pluralist democracy* (1993), 86–91.

[18] See M Nowak, *UN Covenant on Civil and Political Rights: CCPR commentary* (1993), 480–505. In its General Comment no 23 (1994) on rights of minorities the Human Rights Committee attempted at integrating participatory rights but narrowly by reference to the exercise of cultural rights and through application of positive legal measures, HRI/GEN/1/Rev9 (Vol I) 209, para 7.

[19] The main contribution to the growing body of instruments and jurisprudence based on minority rights can be attributed to the OSCE (Copenhagen and Geneva Documents), HCNM (thematic recommendations or guidelines), the Council of Europe's Advisory Committee of the Framework Convention (opinions on individual reports and commentaries), the Venice Commission, the European Court of Human Rights, and other organs.

at that time (the 1990s) the jurisprudence of treaty-based bodies, including that of the European Court of Human Rights, was very poorly developed. While having only a general legal and political base for the right to participation by minorities in public life, the High Commissioner could hardly promote the specific forms of its implementation. And it is for this reason that he decided to task a group of experts with attempting to reduce or file that amazing gap by elaborating a set of the different forms of minority participation that existed in the constitutional practice of states, which could be used as a tool by the HCNM in his preventive diplomacy. In other words, experts were not asked to work out innovative approaches but rather to bring together or compile a number of applicable arrangements that could be implanted in or adjusted to states in need of developing mechanisms for the effective participation in public affairs by national minorities.

2. Procedural dimensions of the normative deficit

As concerns the procedural question behind the decision to draw up recommendations on participation by national minorities in public life, one should be aware that the High Commissioner has no formal standard-setting powers. The mandate of the High Commissioner is 'based on CSCE principles and commitments' (para 4 of the Helsinki mandate) and thus has been built into the institutional and functional arrangements of the OSCE. Consequently, the HCNM is obliged to act in accordance with the OSCE principles and commitments. Neither the Helsinki mandate nor any other OSCE documents conferred upon the High Commissioner any explicit powers or authority in the field of standard-setting or interpretation of OSCE commitments.

It is of significance however that while establishing the mandate for the High Commissioner as 'an instrument of conflict prevention at the earliest possible stage', the Helsinki Decisions of July 1992 explicitly gave him the mandate to take fully into account the availability of democratic means and international instruments to respond to it, and their utilization by the parties involved (para 6). It can be inferred from the formulation of this provision that the office is empowered to assess the 'availability' of democratic means and international instruments, eg, whether they exist and can be used, or if they are not available and should probably be established or, in case of international instruments, acceded to. If this interpretation is acceptable, the High Commissioner nonetheless has the power within his conflict prevention mandate to attenuate the formally restrictive parameters of his mandate to allow for standard-setting. There are at least two compelling reasons for the HCNM to undertake certain actions which could facilitate the process of interpretation, application and implementation of the OSCE commitments in general and notably in regard to minority standards.

The first is the practical demand for a clarification of standards in the field of national minorities, particularly when the HCNM discusses specific modalities and recommendations with governments concerning their domestic regulations, policy-making and administrative decision-making. The need for clarification stems largely from the above-mentioned deficit of minority standards. The commendable progress in OSCE standard-setting of the adoption of Copenhagen and Geneva Documents has not only come with delay but has also been insufficient in responding to numerous detailed questions on the scope of minority rights. Only actors, such as the HCNM, who actually apply, construe, and refer to minority standards on a daily basis accumulate a practical and profound sense of their content and gaps.

The second is the practical demand for the effective application and implementation of minority standards. This is not a question of clarifying content, but of identifying the mode of implementation to be recommended. The HCNM suggests that domestic authorities adopt specific measures which should serve as effectively as possible to improve the practical operation of minority standards.

It is within these specific circumstances and demands of his mandate that the High Commissioner initiated proceedings for expert recommendations in a number of substantive areas. In six such cases the end result was the adoption of the following thematic recommendations or guidelines:[20]

- The Hague Recommendations regarding the Education Rights of National Minorities (October, 1996)
- The Oslo Recommendations regarding the Linguistic Rights of National Minorities (February, 1998)
- The Lund Recommendations on the Effective Participation of National Minorities in Public Life (June 1999)
- The Guidelines on the Use of Minority Languages in the Broadcast Media (October 2003)
- The Recommendations on Policing in Multi-ethnic Societies (February 2006)
- The Bolzano/Bozen Recommendations on National Minorities in Inter-state Relations (June 2008).

All these instruments fall into both the above-mentioned categories, characterizing the reasons for the HCNM's involvement in developing interpretation, application, and implementation of national minority commitments. One can therefore legitimately submit that the adoption of thematic recommendations is not tantamount to his encroaching upon or taking over standard-setting activities.

---

[20] For the first five texts of thematic recommendations or guidelines of the HCNM together with explanatory notes see Compilation, above note 1, 45–152. The sixth set is reproduced in *The Bolzano/Bozen Recommendations on National Minorities in Inter-State Relations and Explanatory Note* (2008), 1–27. All these are available on the abovementioned website, above note 1.

None of these recommendations and guidelines set new standards, but they are expressions of good practice. They constitute a set of rules that rearticulate both hard and soft law, and recommend a number of more detailed issues and proposals for domestic application. To a large extent these instruments reflect proposals addressed in country recommendations. Their usefulness lies in their formulation by the HCNM as recommendations of a general nature, thereby investing them with a wider spectrum of potential applicability. According to the first High Commissioner, from a conflict prevention perspective, the recommendations were designed to 'try to show that there are other ways to find a mutually acceptable balance between the interests of majority and minority'.[21] Above all, the High Commissioner needs these recommendations and guidelines to guide him in his dialogue with governments. They may thus be helpful as parameters for policy-makers and law-makers.

It may therefore be said that the HCNM's recommendations and guidelines are not representative of typical standard-setting activity even if some of their provisions seem to be formulated like 'delegated legislation', 'codes of conduct' or 'guidelines'. All the provisions are mere recommendations or guidelines aimed at facilitating the practical implementation of minority standards in specific areas such as education, use of minority language, public participation, broadcasting, and policing in multiethnic societies. Although thematic recommendations do not set new standards, they are nonetheless an influential instrument in the hands of the High Commissioner.[22]

IV. Application of the Lund Recommendations by the HCNM

The viability of the Lund Recommendations can best be tested against the practice of their application over the course of last ten years. Actually a good number of arrangements, which were later transformed into the Lund Recommendations, had been applied by the High Commissioner prior to the adoption of the Recommendations in 1999. The aim of this section is to provide an overview of the most typical or representative cases of their application in the activities of the High Commissioner which will reflect their variety.

Generally, for his part, the High Commissioner on National Minorities has promoted the application of the Lund Recommendations in two ways. One approach has traditionally been used within his conflict prevention mission in

---

[21] M van der Stoel, 'The Hague, Oslo and Lund Recommendations regarding minority questions', in Bergsmo, *Human Rights* (n 13 above), 505–12.
[22] According to SR Ratner, 'Does international law matter in preventing ethnic conflict?' (2000) 32(3) *New York University Journal of International Law and Politics* 668–73, the Office of the HCNM is a 'normative intermediary' as it promotes observance of a norm and induces 'compliance through a hands-on process of communication and persuasion with relevant decision-makers' (at 668).

relations with individual participating states. A large part of this activity has taken place in confidential dialogue with the governments concerned (visits, direct talks, letters with recommendations, and follow-up assessments). Such instances can consequently be referred to below only if their status is not an obstacle to making them public.[23] Exceptionally, in some cases, underlying problems will be mentioned but without any reference to the name of country concerned.

A second manifestation of the practical application of the Lund Recommendations is a general and thematic approach. This is due in large part to the limited accessibility to documents on individual interventions by the High Commissioner, so that more instances of the application of the Lund Recommendations will be given below in thematic terms. Furthermore, due to constraints of space, it has been necessary to select just a few thematic areas: electoral arrangements, political parties, and consultative and advisory bodies.

A. Electoral arrangements

For years, the content of the human right for everyone to take part in public life by means of electoral participation, and specifically for members of national minorities, remained very general in its formulation, and was supported by weak jurisprudence.[24] The first emerging recommendation or guideline for ensuring possible electoral arrangements in practice to foster minority participation and representation in elective bodies at national, regional and local levels have appeared within the OSCE (Copenhagen and Geneva Documents), and most extensively in the Lund Recommendations in 1999. Their content has been a remarkable compilation of election-related provisions. Of the twenty-four Lund Recommendations five have been devoted to electoral issues (6–10). Three of them are expressions of general principles, while two others are detailed rules on various ways electoral systems should facilitate minority representation.

The first electoral recommendation (6) recommends ensuring effective voice for minorities at the level of central government, including through special representation of national minorities, for example, through a reserved number of seats in one or both chambers of parliament or in parliamentary committees or

---

[23] There are only a few dozen confidential letters and other documents from 1993–2001 (duration of all the terms of office of Max van der Stoel) which were made public several years afterwards so that the principle of confidentiality was not adversely affected. These documents can be consulted at the OSCE website (n 1 above). The first fraction of those documents can be found in Bloed, *The Conference on Security and Co-operation in Europe* (n 2 above), 1063–101. To date, subsequent High Commissioners have not decided whether to render older documents publicly accessible.

[24] This may certainly be said about jurisprudence developed by the UN treaty-based bodies under the International Convention on the Elimination of all Forms of Racial Discrimination (ICERD) and the International Covenant on Civil and Political Rights (ICCPR). Bodies of the Council of Europe accelerated their jurisprudential contribution at the end of 1990s.

by other forms of guaranteed participation in the legislative process. Recommendation 7, as a second principle, contains the rather banal observation that '[e]xperience in Europe and elsewhere demonstrates the importance of the electoral process for facilitating the participation of minorities in the political sphere'. That said, the recommendation reiterates the principle that states should 'guarantee the right of persons belonging to national minorities to take part in the conduct of public affairs, including through the rights to vote and stand for office without discrimination'. The third principle-type provision can be found in Recommendation 8 which addresses questions of political parties as a reflection of the international principle of freedom of association, and that of ethnic-based political parties (see section IV.B below).

The second group has reflected a number of arrangements which in proportional, majority and mixed electoral systems are capable of facilitating minority representation (Recommendations 9–10). Recommendation 9 lists four such arrangements which, if applied in specific electoral system, may better facilitate minority representation. In a separate recommendation (10), the geographical boundaries of electoral districts are seen as arrangements that should facilitate the equitable representation of national minorities.[25]

1. Individual Country Approach

For his part, the High Commissioner has been promoting the application of the Lund Recommendations in his relations with a number of countries. Predominantly his intention has been to enter into dialogue on specific issues. For instance, given the extensive history and legal complexity of the issue of national minorities in Croatia, the Commissioner submitted a report on constitutional matters, including electoral developments, for the future reporting on these issues by the Mission to Croatia.[26] Other examples concerned high linguistic requirements to stand for elected office in Latvia, the use of language by elected representatives in the former Yugoslav Republic of Macedonia (fYROM), the lack of citizenship as an obstacle to participation in elections in Russia, the lack of knowledge as to voting process, and others.[27]

A special form of promoting minority representation in electoral bodies has been the participation of HCNM experts in certain election observation missions arranged by the Office for Democratic Institutions and Human Rights (ODIHR). This practice allows for field observation of the degree of participation

---

[25] See the broadest existing provision-by-provision commentary to the Lund Recommendations in K Myntti, *A Commentary to the Lund Recommendations on the Effective Participation of National Minorities in Public Life* (2001), 1–67.
[26] See the public document on the above-mentioned OSCE website (n 1 above): *Background Report on Constitutional Law on National Minorities*, 22 January 2002, 1–10, which focuses primarily on electoral legislation.
[27] For a more extensive examination of these and other cases of the HCNM's intervention in individual countries see Holt, 'The Lund Recommendations' (n 16 above), 177–9.

of minorities in the electoral process as a whole. It has become a regular practice of the ODIHR to consult the HCNM on minority-related issues dealt with by final reports following election observation missions. The importance of this practice is not diminished by the fact that the High Commissioner's participation in election observation has been reasonably limited to some parliamentary and local elections only in participating states of concern to him. To date, one can note a lot of positive accumulated experience resulting from the participation of HCNM advisers in election observation, as it has created better opportunities for assessing the practical side of electoral process (from campaigning through the work of electoral commissions up to appeal procedures), particularly in areas inhabited by national minorities.

2. Impact on the Content of Other International Instruments on Minority Participation

It is entirely comprehensible in itself that in order to maintain the validity and integrity of the Lund Recommendations the High Commissioner has attempted to exert an impact on the content of any international instrument devoted to national minority participation. The prevailing approach has thus been to support in a constructive way any further instruments contributing to the strengthening of minority participation. Consequently, this conduct is expected to avoid or at least reduce the risk of undermining the Lund Recommendations or their interpretation. Two instances reflect such conduct by the High Commissioner.

The first was the remarkable instance of recourse to the Lund Recommendations by an initiative which brought about the elaboration in 2000 of the Warsaw Guidelines to Assist National Minority Participation in the Electoral Process. They were developed by the ODIHR in conjunction with the International Institute for Democracy and Electoral Assistance (International IDEA).[28] They are a set of more specific and detailed statements developing Lund Recommendations 6–10 on the issue of elections. In other words, the Warsaw Guidelines translate the Lund Recommendations on elections into a language of practical arrangements for assisting national minorities in the electoral process. In this sense, they resemble a sort of 'implementing' or 'delegated legislation' and practice-oriented guidance for election observation.

In the course of their application over nearly a decade, the Warsaw Guidelines have proved their usefulness for a number of target groups, notably for election observers from the OSCE and other international organizations, by providing them with substantive and methodological guidance for the assessment of minority participation in elections in accordance with relevant international standards and good practice. Likewise, they are a useful tool for

---

[28] The Office of the HCNM was involved in the finalization of the guidelines. For the full text, with commentary, see *Guidelines to Assist National Minority Participation in the Electoral Process* (2001).

legislators, government authorities, national minorities, political parties, and other non-governmental organizations.

This success has led the ODIHR and HCNM to work together on the second edition which is forthcoming, entitled *The Handbook on Monitoring and Promoting the Participation of National Minorities in Electoral Process*. Of importance for the High Commissioner is that the Warsaw Guidelines and future handbook are 'operationalizing the Lund Recommendations and building on them'.[29]

The second example of the impact of the HCNM was demonstrated by no less remarkable developments in regard to the Commentary (no 2) of the Advisory Committee of the Council of Europe's Framework Convention for the Protection of National Minorities. In addition to its country-specific opinions on the implementation of the FCNM, the Committee also developed a transversal approach by adopting its thematically oriented interpretations and assessments. This pattern was modelled on the practice of other human rights treaty bodies which adopt the so-called 'general comments', 'suggestions and general recommendations', etc. General comments evolved as an extension and conclusion of individual country opinions on thematic issues resulting from the reporting systems. Although under international law they are admittedly characterized as non-binding instruments they nevertheless constitute a sort of quasi-authoritative interpretation and usually enjoy high legal authority.[30]

Thematic commentaries of the Advisory Committee are a fairly recent development. Once it appeared that they were intended to evolve in the same direction as the 'general comments' of other human rights treaty bodies in developing interpretations of minority standards the High Commissioner could not remain indifferent.[31] The HCNM and the Advisory Committee share a special responsibility for the integrity and effectiveness of national minority standards, irrespective of whether their rules are binding legally (FCNM) or politically (HCNM). This responsibility stems from the fact that the Framework Convention followed and was largely inspired by the OSCE Copenhagen Document. In order to fulfil this joint responsibility both bodies have established modes of regular and useful inter-agency cooperation, notably through consultation on matters of common interests. Hence, it came as no surprise that

---

[29] See Opening Address by Knut Vollebaek, OSCE High Commissioner on National Minorities, to the Tenth Anniversary Seminar of the Lund Recommendations on the Effective Participation of National Minorities in Public Life, Lund, Sweden, 18 May 2009, at the OSCE website (n 1 above), 4.   [30] See Nowak, *UN Covenant on Civil and Political* (n 18 above), 576.
[31] As they stem from a treaty-based body, the commentaries of the Advisory Committee should consistently be characterized as case law (jurisprudence) of an autonomous and quasi-judicial entity made up of independent experts, and not as instruments of soft law. The latter position actually undermines the legal significance of commentaries in international law. See the arguments of a proponent of commentaries as soft law in F Palermo, 'The dual meaning of participation: The Advisory Committee's commentary on participation', Conference: Enhancing the Impact of the Framework Convention, 9–10 October 2008, Palais de l'Europe, Strasbourg, 2–5.

they mutually consult their major instruments or documents on thematic issues which are designed to facilitate the interpretation and application of minority standards.[32]

This practice can best be illustrated by the process that led to the adoption of Commentary no 1 on Education under the Framework Convention for the Protection of National Minorities (2006), and Commentary no 2 on the Effective Participation of Persons Belonging to National Minorities in Cultural, Social, and Economic Life and Public Affairs (2008). In both cases, the HCNM was invited to submit his observations on preliminary draft commentaries and his representatives were also invited to meetings of the Advisory Committee for a dialogue on the respective sets of issues.[33]

One should note in conclusion that this mode of cooperation is not art for art's sake. Instead it has created vast opportunities to work out as far as possible a common interpretation of specific standards on minority rights and other commitments. The strength of potential synergy becomes even more important once it is realized that both bodies are mostly competent and active at different stages and use different tools—preventive measures at 'the earliest possible stage' of emerging tensions regarding national minorities (HCNM), and reactive measures at the other end to monitor compliance through a reporting mechanism (FCNM's Advisory Committee and the Committee of Ministers).[34] In this way the Lund Recommendations and Framework Convention reinforce and complement each other. They contribute to avoiding inconsistent or conflicting interpretations thereby strengthening their validity, integrity and effective implementation.

3. Legitimization of Electoral Arrangements through Cooperation with the Venice Commission

The High Commissioner on National Minorities has been regularly following the work of the European Commission for Democracy through Law (Venice Commission) due to its well-established authority in constitutional law, including on issues pertaining to national minorities and electoral law. The Venice Commission is the Council of Europe's advisory body on constitutional matters which has become an internationally recognized independent legal think tank. In addition to its role in promoting the European constitutional heritage,

---

[32] For more on the concepts of 'permeation effect' and 'mutual feedback' see K Drzewicki, 'Framework Convention as a pan-European instrument: A perspective of the OSCE High Commissioner on National Minorities' in A Verstichel et al (eds) *The Framework Convention for the Protection of National Minorities: A useful pan-European instrument* (2008), 222–6.

[33] For more details on the consultation process concerning Commentary no 2 see E Jurado and A Korkeakivi, 'Completing the first decade of monitoring: Latest developments under the Framework Convention for the Protection of National Minorities' (2006–7) 6 *European Yearbook of Minority Issues* 377–8.

[34] Drzewicki, 'Framework convention as a pan-European instrument (n 32 above), 226.

based on the continent's fundamental legal values, the Commission serves as a tool for emergency constitutional engineering and also plays a unique and unrivalled role in crisis management and conflict prevention through constitution-building and advice.[35]

The HCNM's instruments have regularly been referred to in the reports, opinions and studies of the Venice Commission. More advanced links have been established for consultation and seeking opinions. As far as electoral matters are concerned it should be noted that the Venice Commission consulted the HCNM before the adoption of its fundamental document, the Code of Good Practice in Electoral Matters: Guidelines and Explanatory Report. Adopted upon a request by the Parliamentary Assembly, the code has performed an influential role far beyond the Council of Europe in promoting and implementing the principles and rules of genuinely democratic elections. The code contains a few minority-related rules which were earlier reflected in the Copenhagen Document and Lund Recommendations. Paragraph 2.4(a–c) of the code provides that parties representing national minorities must be permitted, special rules should be implemented guaranteeing national minorities reserved seats or providing for exceptions to the normal seat-allocation criteria for parties representing national minorities, and that candidates and voters should be prohibited from revealing their membership of a national minority.[36]

More extensive consultation took place when the Venice Commission debated the Report on Electoral Rules and Affirmative Action for National Minorities' Participation in Decision-making Process in European Countries. The aim behind this report was to review electoral rules on affirmative action in European countries in the context of a motion for a resolution in the Parliamentary Assembly of the Council of Europe. Invited to submit his comments to the draft report, the High Commissioner on National Minorities referred extensively to his experience and conceptual observations. The final version of the report not only took note of the HCNM's input but also commented on his views about such complex issues as the notion and scope of 'affirmative action' or 'special measures' such as policies and mechanism designed to favour groups, including national minorities, which were disadvantaged in electoral representation. The report explicitly took note of the experience of the HCNM in promoting affirmative action electoral rules in local elections. The importance of such arrangements was underlined particularly in territories where national minorities represented a substantial part of the population.[37]

---

[35] For more information, see its website at <www.venice.coe.int> (accessed 31 July 2009).
[36] The code was adopted by the Venice Commission at its 52nd session, Venice 18–19 October 2002, CDL-AD (2002) 23 rev. It also referred to a document of the Venice Commission, entitled *Electoral Law and National Minorities*, CDL-INF (2000) 4, also available on the website (n 35 above).
[37] See Report on Electoral Rules and Affirmative Action for National Minorities' Participation in Decision-making Process in European Countries, adopted by the Council for Democratic Elections at its 12th meeting, Venice, 10 March 2005; and the Venice Commission at its 62nd plenary session, Venice, 11–12 March 2005, CDL-AD(2005)009, notably at 2–3, 11–13.

An even more advanced relationship in promoting specific forms of electoral arrangements for the representative needs of national minorities in elective bodies was the problem of the advisability and lawfulness of so-called 'dual voting'. It was upon the initiative and formal request of the High Commissioner on National Minorities, addressed to the Venice Commission in 2006, that a study was undertaken on the question of dual voting for persons belonging to national minorities. The request by the HCNM for a study on this issue was submitted, together with comprehensive legal and political reasoning. In addition, his representatives actively participated in the debates of the Commission and its Council for Democratic Elections. At the 75th plenary session of the Venice Commission (13–14 June 2008), the final report on this issue was adopted.[38]

What was most significant in the HCNM's motion for a legal opinion was actually the uncertainty surrounding the very permissibility of dual voting. The reasons behind this request stemmed from the practical observation that in some countries the law envisages giving members of national minorities a general voting right for party lists and, additionally, the right to vote for minority representation. For the High Commissioner this arrangement seemed to constitute a useful means of supporting effective participation of minorities and their integration. For the Venice Commission it was an opportunity to comment on a wider range of special measures that may guarantee representation of minorities in parliaments in accordance with the principle of equal suffrage, notably equal voting rights (the 'one person–one vote' principle). In other words, the High Commissioner saw the problem predominantly from a conflict-prevention perspective, while the Venice Commission approached it from the point of view of the fundamental principles of electoral law.

In its final Report the Venice Commission underlined that dual voting could only be admitted as an exceptional and temporary measure when other measures proved unsuitable to achieving integration. It also stated that this had to remain within the framework of the constitution, and respect the principle of proportionality in the context of its various aspects. This implies that it can only be justified if it is impossible to reach the aim pursued through other, less restrictive measures that do not infringe upon equal voting rights; it has a transitional character; and it concerns only a small minority. In addition, the report concluded that the exceptional nature of dual voting means that periodical review is desirable.[39]

---

[38] Report on Dual Voting for Persons Belonging to National Minorities. Adopted by the Council for Democratic Elections at its 25th meeting, Venice, 12 June 2008; and the Venice Commission at its 75th plenary session, Venice, 13–14 June 2008, CDL-AD(2008)013, 1–13. See also K Drzewicki and V de Graaf, 'The activities of the OSCE High Commissioner on National Minorities (July 2006–December 2007)' (2006–7) 6 *European Yearbook of Minority Issues* 447–8.

[39] Report (n 38 above), 3, 12–13. Actually the Commission recalled that dual voting exists at present only in Slovenia, while in Croatia it is provided for by the Constitution but was not introduced and implemented by ordinary legislation.

It may be concluded that the Venice Commission took a very open position on the admissibility of affirmative action or special measures by electoral law, but a restrictive position with regard to dual voting. The admissibility conditions of dual voting render this arrangement extremely difficult in terms of implementation. This is an indication that ensuring effective participation and representation of national minorities in elective bodies should be approached by other means. Conflict prevention is not sufficient justification for departing from the principle of one person–one vote.

B. Political parties

The need to intensify minority participation in the political, economic, social, and cultural life of participating states including through 'democratic participation in decision-making and consultative bodies at the national, regional and local level, inter alia, through political parties and associations' was explicitly underlined by the Helsinki Document of 1992.[40] This provision demonstrates a growing awareness of the participating states that specific forms of participation should be explicitly listed to encourage further and effective participation of minorities.

Lund Recommendation 8 focuses on freedom of association and particularly on the right to establish community-based political parties. Although this provision forms part of a section on elections its importance goes far beyond electoral matters alone. The message in the recommendations is not only in their repetition of the obvious rule whereby regulations about the formation and activity of political parties must comply with international standards on freedom of association. This important but commonplace observation served as an introductory statement for raising the very controversial issue of ethnic parties. Recommendation 8 thus continues by adding that the principle of freedom of association includes 'the freedom to establish political parties based on communal identities as well as those not identified exclusively with the interests of a specific community'.

For the High Commissioner on National Minorities this question, like the one on dual voting, reflected a tension between a fundamental standard (freedom of association) and the demands of conflict prevention. In a number of countries with sizeable minorities certain historical antecedents have generated a reticence, and sometimes even hostility, towards certain ethnic groups and their associations, including political parties. Cases are very serious when an ethnic community has a kin-state which formerly occupied and oppressed the country. We then have to deal with a degree of emotional nationalism by the majority population against the hated former rulers. It is not surprising if, in such

---

[40] See *CSCE Helsinki Document 1992: The challenges of change, decisions: Chapter VI, The human dimension*, para 24. See also Compilation (n 1 above), 27.

circumstances, a ban on establishing ethnic-based parties appears in law and domestic policy. Such a ban runs directly counter to the fundamental principle of freedom of association. However, in some quarters, there is a sense of permissibility in the departure from the demands of freedom of association. This standpoint is often substantiated by fears that ethnic parties will promote and generate a spiralling of tension and conflict, particularly in countries undergoing a transition to democratic governance or those at a post-conflict rehabilitation stage. This approach might suggest then that in the specific circumstances of such a transition considerations of conflict prevention could prevail over respect for freedom of association.

In this context, one cannot ignore empirical social science research which suggests that although ethnic parties mobilize ethnic groups to engage in protest and defend their interests there is no evidence that the appearance of ethnic parties independently promotes communal conflict. These findings seem to 'call into question whether "remedial" actions such as ethnic party bans are effective at all'. The party bans may actually achieve exactly the opposite: greater exclusion and the increased attractiveness of extra-legal action.[41]

The High Commissioner appears to have regarded the dilemma in question (freedom of association versus conflict prevention) as premised on an overly rigid approach. From the beginning he has adopted an approach that both accommodates respect for freedom of association and advocates inter ethnic peace and stability. It was discernible from his experience that the formation of ethnic parties in some countries has contributed to polarization of demands and an increase in tensions (eg, in some Central Asian republics). However, in some other countries the activities of ethnic parties have been instrumental in containing tensions and conflicts with majority community and other ethnic groups (eg, in Central and Eastern Europe).

The wisdom of this approach stems from an understanding that the role of ethnic parties varies from country to country due to essential differences in the traditions of distinct political and legal cultures. This is why on each occasion the HCNM has had to tailor his judgements to fit the specificities of individual countries or regions and adjust his country recommendations accordingly.

The best illustration of the HCNM's preventive diplomacy in the context of political parties has been his consistent promotion of freedom of association in the establishment both of political parties based on communal identity and of those not identified exclusively with the interests of a specific community.[42] The High Commissioner has thus held the view, including prior to the adoption of

---

[41] See J Ishiyama, 'Do ethnic parties promote minority ethnic conflicts?' (2009) 15(1) *Nationalism and Ethnic Politics* 56–83, 78–80. This research examined ethnic parties in eighty-two countries, including those of the OSCE area. The author also points to the role of state responses to ethnic mobilization and other symptoms of ethnification.

[42] This wording comes explicitly from the second sentence of the Lund Recommendation 8. See also the Explanatory Note thereto, Booklet (n 1 above).

the Lund Recommendations, that individuals and groups of ethnic origin should have an opportunity to express their opinions and exert influence upon ethnic political parties as well as on a variety of parties from the left to the right. As emphasized by the Explanatory Note to Lund Recommendation 8, 'Ideally, parties should be open and should cut across narrow ethnic issues; thus mainstream parties should seek to include members of minorities to reduce the need or desire for ethnic parties.'

However, the practical dimension of this option is more problematic than its normative characterization. It is simply not the case that both options need to be followed in each country or are best suited to any country's political system and culture. While it appears to be a widely shared view that the accommodation of minority groups within mainstream parties is an advisable mechanism for increasing participation, controversy has arisen over how to generate such results. Political parties and their leaders should not be compelled by legal means to achieve specific results in this regard, but should be encouraged to demonstrate the political will to open their programmes to minority concerns and their party lists to minority candidates. Several participating states have experienced a failure on the part of political leaders to show willingness to incorporate members of ethnic groups, often resulting in the establishment by those groups of their own ethnic-based parties.[43]

C. Consultative and advisory bodies

During the 1990 Geneva Meeting of Experts, participating states found that 'democratic participation of persons belonging to national minorities or their representatives in decision-making or consultative bodies constitutes an important element of effective participation in public affairs'. Likewise the need to intensify minority participation in the political, economic, social, and cultural life of participating states 'including through democratic participation in decision-making and consultative bodies at the national, regional and local level' was explicitly emphasized by the Helsinki Document of 1992.[44]

As for the Lund Recommendations, they approach this issue through imperative language by pointing out that states 'should establish' advisory or consultative bodies to serve as channels for dialogue between governmental authorities and national minorities. It is further stipulated that such bodies may

---

[43] These practical dilemmas were discussed and conclusions taken with a participation of the HCNM's representative at an OSCE meeting, See *OSCE Human Dimension Seminar on Effective Participation and Representation in Democratic Societies: Consolidated Summary*, Warsaw, 16–18 May 2007, 15–17 (Working Group IV: Participation of persons belonging to national minorities and underrepresented groups in democratic societies. Moderator: Mr Krzysztof Drzewicki (Office of the HCNM); Introducer: Ms Kate Fearon (Office of the High Representative to Bosnia-Herzegovina; and Rapporteur: Mr Mustafa Turan (Permanent Delegation of Turkey to the OSCE).

[44] For the text of 1992 Helsinki Decisions and Chapters III and IV of the Report of the CSCE Meeting of Experts on National Minorities, Geneva, 1991, see Compilation (n 1 above), 20–2, 27.

also include special purpose bodies for addressing specific issues and their composition should reflect their purpose and contribute to more effective communication and the advancement of minority interests (Recommendation 12). The competence of these bodies should be to raise issues with decision-makers, prepare recommendations, formulate legislative and other proposals, monitor developments, and provide views on proposed governmental decisions that may directly or indirectly affect minorities. Government authorities should consult bodies regularly regarding minority-related legislation and administrative measures in order to contribute to the satisfaction of minority concerns and to the building of confidence. It is also provided that the effective functioning of these bodies will require adequate funding (Recommendation 13).

From the beginning of his activities, the High Commissioner has developed the concept of what is termed 'the chain of three objectives': 'communication-participation-integration'.[45] The sequence of these objectives reflects the existence of causal links between them because substantial progress in the integration of minorities must be preceded by the achievement of viable communication and participation. It is clear, therefore, why communication is placed as a starting point for further work on participation and integration; it is a procedural channel and platform for regular dialogue between public authorities and national minority representatives and their organizations.

It seems that one of the weaknesses of Recommendations 12 and 13 is a soft formulation of the composition of these bodies. There is no indication that delegates from national minorities are expected to be representative or even elected by their minority groups or their organizations. It is a well-known fact that a lot of minority groups compete with each other and even show symptoms of open and fierce rivalry (eg, Roma groups). This undermines their opportunities for a single and hence stronger voice in a dialogue with public authorities. Such a situation actually paves the way for a policy of favouritism by public authorities.

As submitted by Holt, these bodies must be carefully created in order to ensure both the inclusion of all minorities in the participatory process, as well as adequate representation of the pluralism within different national minority groups. To remedy a lack of specific rules on the issue of the composition of advisory and consultative bodies, a cross-reference to Principle 3 of the Lund Recommendations was proposed.[46] For its part, Principle 3 says that when specific institutions are established to ensure the effective participation of minorities in public life, which can include the exercise of authority or responsibility by such institutions, they must respect the human rights of all those affected. However, one can hardly share this view entirely because a general clause on respect for the human rights of others is insufficient to introduce a

---

[45] For more comments see Diacofotakis, *Expanding Conceptual Boundaries* (n 9 above), 54–5.
[46] See Holt, 'The Lund Recommendations' (n 16 above), 181.

fully representative system of selecting minority representatives. It can only be hoped that governments will create a system that conforms to the principles of pluralism.[47]

Already in the early 1990s the High Commissioner noted a lack of bodies and mechanisms that could serve as a means for entering into and developing dialogue on the most essential matters in relations between the public authorities and national minority groups. This was a reflection of a high degree of hatred and isolation. In order to remedy this elementary failure, the High Commissioner has widely encouraged governments to establish such bodies and remedy their various weaknesses. For example, in one of the Eastern European countries, a consultative body was established by legislation and set in motion, but after a few years was no longer convened. In his letter the HCNM requested that the authorities reconvene the body and ensure its regular operation, particularly in light of the fact that in the meantime the number of disputed issues between the government and national minority groups had increased. Another difficulty arose regarding an advisory and consultative body in Central Asia. The composition of that body included representatives of national minority organizations appointed de facto by public authorities themselves. The HCNM turned the attention of the authorities to a certain deficit of democratic procedure in the system of electing or appointing the minority representatives. This case was accorded an additional context in that it had been granted certain decision-making powers.

The experience of the High Commissioner has generally been positive with regard to the establishment and functioning of advisory and consultative bodies. These have demonstrated their enormous potential in dealing with minority issues, be they at the national or regional/local level, and the positive role of the activities of both general and specialized bodies for consultation must be noted.[48] In some countries, where schools became a regular ground for externalization of interethnic tensions, school councils made up of parents, headmasters, and other teachers proved to be more effective in the search for negotiated solutions. They contribute to better mutual understanding and positively affect the easing of tensions. It would be useful for the High Commissioner to seek assessment of the activities of such bodies by public authorities and national minorities themselves on a periodic basis.

---

[47] A similar dilemma of fair representation has existed in tripartite relations between trade unions, employers' organizations and government. This problem was largely solved within a concept of 'the most representative organizations', which has been extensively worked out in domestic and international jurisprudence by domestic bodies and the International Labour Organization since 1919. In the field of minorities, some Balkan countries have extensive experience with regard to so-called 'national minority councils'.

[48] For more on practical problems of a similar character but under Art 15 of the Framework Convention see M Weller, 'Creating the conditions necessary for the effective participation of persons belonging to national minorities' (2004) 10(4) *International Journal of Minority and Group Rights* 279–82.

V. Conclusions

As was preliminarily submitted at the beginning of this chapter, in the first place, the Lund Recommendations were adopted under the impact of an acute normative deficit in the field of participation by minorities in public affairs and, in the second place, the application of the Lund Recommendations throughout the last decade seems to have proven their continuing viability in the changing circumstances after 1999.

A. Verification of the tentative submissions

As to the first submission, a brief account of the codification and progressive development of international human rights law, of the OSCE binding human-dimension commitments and of relevant soft law has led to the conclusion that the normative deficit existed mainly at a level below general regulations. These rules have appeared fairly belatedly and as substantive rules within general provisions on the right of everyone to participation in the conduct of public affairs (1948 UNDHR and 1966 ICCPR)—but better late than never. A quality threshold was passed with the first legally and politically binding regulations that directly stipulated the right to participation by person belonging to national minorities (see 1990 Copenhagen and 1991 Geneva Documents, and the 1995 Framework Convention).

Emerging thus with delay and with only general and vague content, these provisions required, for their further implementation, the development of 'delegated' or implementing legislation and of domestic and international jurisprudence. We have had to deal with general legal bases followed by underdeveloped jurisprudence. Filling or narrowing this gap has thus been a goal of the HCNM at the moment when the normative deficit continued to exist, prompting him to initiate a drafting process. Ten years later, one may say that the deficit in question has largely been filled due to the activities of the HCNM, the Advisory Committee of the Framework Convention and other international bodies and domestic authorities. This deficit, together with conflict prevention considerations, thus created strong motivation for the High Commissioner to promote the development of indispensable standards in the field of minority participation.

While these powerful motives appear logical, functional, and convincing it cannot be said that the High Commissioner has performed a typical standard-setting activity, a role not assigned to him explicitly. His sets of thematic recommendations or guidelines serve two purposes: clarification of minority standards for his regular activities and practical demands for the effective application and implementation of minority standards. The conflict prevention mandate of the HCNM includes his empowerment to take fully into account the availability of democratic means and international instruments (para 6 of the

HCNM mandate). This supports the submission that the HCNM has implicit competence to initiate standard-setting designed to facilitate the implementation of minority standards for the purposes of conflict prevention. After all the expectation on the part of the High Commissioner himself was 'not to create new norms and standards, but to interpret and elaborate the existing international rules regarding these subjects'.[49] Likewise, it was declared that the aim of such recommendations was to achieve 'an appropriate and coherent application of relevant minority rights in the OSCE area', so that they could subsequently serve as 'references for policy- and law-makers in a number of States'.[50]

What these conclusions add up to is actually an absence of official protest on the part of any participating state or major OSCE body against the adoption of thematic recommendations or guidelines.[51] In both legal and political terms it can be inferred that a customary rule was established which legitimized the High Commissioner's power to draw up sets of thematic recommendations in the field of minority issues. This characterization is relevant for all six sets of the HCNM's thematic recommendations or guidelines.

Against this background the content and status of the Lund Recommendations needs to be addressed. Their content is made up of a fairly diversified set of statements and provisions. They formulate objectives; value statements; restate binding principles of international law, principles of law or OSCE commitments; issue policy recommendations and guidelines, interpretative guidance for law-makers and policy-makers, rules of conduct and others. Some recommendations constitute a sort of inventory of arrangements borrowed from constitutional law and the policies of numerous models of democratic states. In this sense the Lund Recommendations have been an exercise in a sort of 'creative eclecticism'.

Furthermore, the legal parlance of the Lund Recommendations deliberately resorts to language of 'progressive realization' of specified objectives, suggestions for pursuing specific policies and even self-executing rules. In other words, the language of the Lund instrument reflects the responsibilities, legally speaking, of both conduct and result. And those are indeed the great merits of the Lund instrument, the message of which is instrumental for new thinking and further developments towards ensuring the effective participation of national minorities in public life.

The great merit of the Lund Recommendations lies in their bringing together a wide range of forms of effective participation with potential applicability to

---

[49] See van der Stoel, 'The Hague, Oslo and Lund Recommendations' (n 13 above), 505.
[50] See 'Introduction' in the Booklet reproducing the Lund Recommendations (n 1 above), 4.
[51] This conclusion seems not to be undermined by an incident that occurred at the Istanbul Summit in November 1999. A suggestion of the chairman to include reference to the Hague, Oslo, and Lund Recommendations together 'as useful tools to assist States' was ultimately defeated at the very last moment by the resistance of one state for reasons not directly related to the Lund Recommendations. See J Packer, 'The origin and nature of the Lund Recommendations on the effective participation of national minorities in public life' (2000) 11(4) *Helsinki Monitor* 29–61, 43.

national minorities. Earlier, all these forms were unknown to politicians, constitutionalists, and members of civil societies, but they were brought together to demonstrate the wide scope of opportunities for their applicability in diversified domestic frameworks whenever an appropriate consensus could be reached. A further analytical glance at the content and structure of the recommendations prompts one to conclude that they were drawn up in a very balanced and cautious way without imposing their provisions in strongly demanding terms.[52]

As far as the second tentative submission is concerned, it has been verified upon a chosen class of practical cases of application of the Lund Recommendations. Due to the size of this chapter, the evidence presented here has been confined to a selected list of themes and practical cases, which have been taken predominantly from three thematic fields: electoral arrangements, political practices, and consultative and advisory bodies. Since individual country cases have been extensively examined elsewhere,[53] and post-2001 practice remains largely confidential, the focus was on thematic manifestations of the practical impact of the Lund Recommendations.

The problems reviewed showed a vast range of opportunities for the High Commissioner to seek legitimation of certain controversial arrangements in electoral systems, as in the case of dual voting. Another example demonstrated the usefulness of consultation with other international organs in promoting more effective methods of electoral representation by minority representatives (cases of affirmative action or special measures within electoral process). Furthermore, consultation with other international bodies ensured an essential influence upon documents such as the ODIHR Guidelines to Assist National Minority Participation in the Electoral Process and the Commentary no 2 of the Advisory Committee of the Framework Convention on the Effective Participation of Persons Belonging to National Minorities in Cultural, Social, and Economic Life and Public Affairs. The practical approach of the High Commissioner has proved very successful in encouraging the establishment and functioning of political parties of both ethnic origin and mainstream parties. Regular observation of the activities of consultative and advisory bodies provided the High Commissioner with an opportunity to establish and maintain dialogue between public authorities and national minorities. All the cases under review have demonstrated the high degree of viability of the Lund Recommendations in the activities of the High Commissioner.

---

[52] It was pointed to, for instance, in paras 19–21 of the Lund Recommendations, 'where the word "autonomy" is mostly avoided and instead reference is made to "self-governance"'. See M Weller, 'Article 15' in M Weller (ed), *The Rights of Minorities in Europe: A commentary on the European Framework Convention for the Protection of National Minorities* (2005), 436. One may further indicate an absence of recommendations with regard to semi-public bodies or economic, social, and cultural dimensions of participation. See also Drzewicki 'The Lund Recommendations' (n 1 above), 127–8.   [53] See Holt, 'The Lund Recommendations' (n 16 above).

One must also take note, however, of some new perceptible trends. One is that in order to ensure the integrity of the Lund Recommendations and to continue to promote their effective implementation, the High Commissioner must increasingly rely on inter-agency consultation, cooperation, and coordination. This trend is the result of the fact that in 1999 the Lund Recommendations were the only document with an extensive list of different forms of participation by national minorities in public life. Ten years later, the situation has changed as other actors have appeared on the scene and established themselves, with some becoming active and successful in the promotion of minority participation. It has therefore been wise on the part of the High Commissioner to initiate and pursue regular consultation with them to work out, as far as possible, a common attitude and interpretation of minority standards.[54]

The second trend that must be fairly recorded pertains to cases in which the Lund Recommendations have failed. It must be critically pointed out that in some participating states there is still insufficient representation of minority groups in parliaments and regional or local elective bodies. Worst cases are discernible in states where national minority representatives in the elective bodies are appointed or selected by public authorities, rather than being elected in free and fair elections preceded by consultations with minority groups and their organizations. Another example is the slow pace of development with regard to decision-making bodies and procedures, as well as modest progress in pursuing self-governance, notably territorial autonomies. Both the latter instances reveal a continuously high level of mistrust on the part of domestic authorities. Wider recourse to these arrangements is a challenge for all the actors dealing with minority participation.

B. General observations

Finally, a few general observations on the Lund Recommendations are necessary. After ten years it can safely be concluded that the Lund Recommendations have been a remarkable success. As a precedent among international documents the Lund Recommendations paved the way for the more effective implementation and application of a variety of possible forms of participation of minorities in public affairs. There is no doubt that this document is the most important among a set of thematic recommendations or guidelines endorsed by the High Commissioner. This is largely true because effective participation has two sides:

---

[54] For the record of cooperation with other international bodies see annual reports on the activities of the HCNM in the *European Yearbook on Minority Issues* since 2001. The HCNM's proactive role in this sphere can best be illustrated by his eventually successful diplomatic advocacy introducing a clause on minority rights into the draft European Constitution and subsequently to the draft Treaty of Lisbon. For a detailed account see K Drzewicki, 'The enlargement of the European Union and the OSCE High Commissioner on National Minorities' in M Weller, D Blacklock, and K Nobbs (eds) *The Protection of Minorities in the Wider Europe* (2008), 154–70.

substantive, and instrumental or procedural. The first points to effective participation as a substantive human right translated specifically to the demands of national minorities. The other underlines how much this human right is instrumental to the enjoyment of all other minority rights throughout all the relevant fields. The effective implementation and application of minority rights in education, use of language, access to media, policing and other spheres could hardly be achieved without a decent level of regular minority participation in different forms and at various levels of governance.

In the course of their ten years the Lund Recommendations have actually played an important role, and in the changing circumstances of further decades they are not entirely exhausted and continue to have potential. As demonstrated above, there are provisions which are rarely used or badly implemented and will thus require a reinvigorated approach to their implementation. Other recommendations have been well adjusted to new challenges and thus their usefulness and value continue. In the meantime the High Commissioner has succeeded in contributing to a strengthening the Lund Recommendations through cooperation with other international bodies. The HCNM can do more for the promotion of minority standards and their interpretations, jointly shared with the Advisory Committee via the Copenhagen Document. The High Commissioner can continue to pursue his policy of promoting minority participation in areas, if need be, beyond the reach of the Framework Convention (eg, non-states parties to the FCNM).[55] Although the HCNM's mandate does not formally extend to migrant communities, or the so-called 'new minorities', there are no obstacles on the part of public authorities to apply the Lund Recommendations in larger multi ethnic contexts, notably for the achievement of the more effective integration of migrants. Likewise, the Lund instrument can be referred to by new minorities in their claims for more effective participatory rights.

Amendments to the Lund Recommendations are sometimes proposed.[56] However, international experience confirms how difficult and lengthy such a process can be nowadays and how much it can blur and undermine the integrity of the amendments envisaged. Even if one or more provisions could be added or rephrased, careful consideration should be given to whether adjustment by amendment is the right way.[57] A better solution seems to be to maintain the integrity of the text but improve its implementation and application, and

---

[55] On extending the outreach of the Framework Convention by the HCNM see K Drzewicki, 'Framework Convention as a pan-European instrument' in Verstichel et al, *The Framework Convention* (n 32 above), 226–8.

[56] K Henrard, '"Participation", "representation" and "autonomy" in the Lund Recommendations and their reflections in the supervision of the FCNM and several human rights conventions' (2005) 12(2–3) *International Journal on Minority and Group Rights* 168.

[57] Five years after my initial proposal, I maintain my submission that any decision on possible amendment should be preceded by a thorough examination along a chain of actions which was termed a strategy of four 'A's: Adoption, Application, Assessment and Adjustment. See also Drzewicki 'The Lund Recommendations' (n 1 above), 130–1.

promote whenever possible its extensive functional interpretation (*interpretatio extensiva*).

On the whole, the Lund Recommendations have substantially influenced the legal and political basis for the right of everyone, including persons belonging to national minorities, to effective participation in public life. This sensitive theme was approached in the Lund Recommendations from a practical perspective by listing forms of possible improvements in public participation by national minorities. Experiences during the ten years since their adoption have amply demonstrated their usefulness in the context of the preventive diplomacy of the High Commissioner on National Minorities. In this way the Lund Recommendations have become a powerful tool by which the High Commissioner has been able to contribute to enhancing good governance, stability, security, and peace in the OSCE area. However, their mission has not yet been accomplished.

9

Effective Participation by Minorities
United Nations standards and practice

Ilona Klímová-Alexander[1]

I. Introduction	287
II. Norms and Standards	287
A. Declaration on the Rights of Persons Belonging to National or Ethnic, Religious, and Linguistic Minorities (UN Minorities Declaration) (Adopted by General Assembly resolution 47/135 of 18 December 1992)	288
B. Declaration on the Right to Development (Adopted by General Assembly resolution 41/128 of 4 December 1986)	289
C. World Conference Against Racism, Racial Discrimination, Xenophobia, and Related Intolerance Declaration and Programme of Action	289
D. The Outcome Document of the Durban Review Conference	290
III. Recommendations and Expert Advice	291
A. Commentary of the Working Group on Minorities to the UN Minorities Declaration (E/CN4/Sub2/AC5/2005/2)	291
B. General Comment no 21 on the Right of everyone to take part in cultural life (Art 15.1a of the International Covenant of Economic, Social and Cultural Rights (ICESCR)) (E/C12/GC/21)	294
C. Recommendations of the International Seminar on Cooperation for the Better Protection of the Rights of Minorities regarding participation of minorities in development	294

---

[1] The views expressed in this article are those of the author and are not necessarily shared by the OHCHR.

    D. The Minority Profile and Matrix (E/CN4/Sub2/AC5/
       2006/3)   295
    E. OHCHR Guidelines and Good Practice for Policing
       in Diverse Societies   296
    F. Human rights-based approach to development   296
    G. United Nations Development Programme
       (UNDP) Resource Guide on Minorities in
       Development—towards a policy note   297
    H. UNDP and Inter-parliamentary Union (IPU)
       Project 'Promoting inclusive parliaments: The
       representation of minorities and indigenous
       peoples in parliaments'   298
IV. Monitoring and Implementation   298
    A. The UN Minorities Declaration   298
    B. The treaty bodies   299
    C. Universal Periodic Review (UPR)   301
    D. Special procedures, including the Independent Expert
       on Minority Issues   302
    E. The Durban Declaration and Programme of
       Action   303
V. Advancing the Substance of the Right to Effective
   Participation through UN Norms, Standards,
   Recommendation, and Expert Advice and their
   Implementation?   304

I. Introduction

This chapter provides a brief overview of United Nations (UN) standards and practice in relation to effective participation by minorities. It first lists norms and standards that have been adopted by UN member states, followed by recommendations by expert-based bodies. The second part concentrates on practice in terms of monitoring and implementation by advisory bodies, treaty bodies and special procedures. The conclusion reflects upon the extent and ways in which the substance of the right to effective participation has been advanced through UN norms, standards, recommendations, and expert advice as well as monitoring and implementation.

II. Norms and Standards

While United Nations instruments cover political participation in general and prohibit discrimination in the exercise of rights to political participation on grounds such as gender, race, colour, language, religion, or national origin (eg Arts 1, 25, and 26 of the International Covenant on Civil and Political Rights (ICCPR), Arts 1 and 5 of the International Convention on the Elimination of All Forms of Racial Discrimination (ICERD), Art 7 of the Convention on the Elimination of All Forms of Discrimination against Women (CEDAW)), there is no minority-specific legally binding provision to guarantee the rights to political participation, perhaps with the exception of Art 27 of the ICCPR. Although the Article itself does not refer to political participation, the Human Rights Committee has stated, in its General Comment 23 which interprets this Article, that the enjoyment of cultural rights 'may require positive legal measures of protection and measures to ensure the effective participation of members of minority communities in decisions which affect them'.[2]

A. Declaration on the Rights of Persons Belonging to National or Ethnic, Religious, and Linguistic Minorities (UN Minorities Declaration) (Adopted by General Assembly resolution 47/135 of 18 December 1992)

This Declaration is the only minorities-specific instrument of the United Nations. It contains four provisions that refer specifically to participation rights of minorities—Arts 2.2 (cultural, religious, social, economic, and public life),[3] 2.3 (decision-making),[4] 4.5 (economic progress and development),[5] and 5.1 (national programmes and policies).[6] The rights enumerated under Arts 2.2 and 2.3 have received significant attention, including in fora outside the UN, both in legal instruments and interpretative documents (for example through the Lund Recommendations and the ACFC Commentary). Articles 4.5 and 5.1 have received less attention in other fora. Further interpretation of these articles has been elaborated in a commentary of the UN Working Group on Minorities (see below).

---

[2] General Comment no 23: The rights of minorities (Art 27): 08/04/94, CCPR/C/21/Rev1/Add5, para 7.

[3] Persons belonging to minorities have the right to participate effectively in cultural, religious, social, economic, and public life.

[4] Persons belonging to minorities have the right to participate effectively in decisions on the national and, where appropriate, regional level concerning the minority to which they belong or the regions in which they live, in a manner not incompatible with national legislation.

[5] States should consider appropriate measures so that persons belonging to minorities may participate fully in the economic progress and development in their country.

[6] National policies and programmes shall be planned and implemented with due regard for the legitimate interests of persons belonging to minorities.

B. Declaration on the Right to Development (Adopted by General Assembly resolution 41/128 of 4 December 1986)

The Declaration contains several references to participation of the entire population and all individuals in economic, social, cultural, and political development, most importantly in Arts 1.1,[7] 2.1,[8] 2.2,[9] and 8.2.[10]

C. World Conference Against Racism, Racial Discrimination, Xenophobia, and Related Intolerance Declaration and Programme of Action

These two texts were adopted by UN member states in 2001 at the World Conference in Durban, representing formal commitments arising from a global dialogue and a road map of how the international community was to follow up on these commitments. The preamble of the Declaration recognizes, among other things, that equal participation without discrimination in economic, social, cultural, civil, and political life of peoples of the world, including domestic as well as global decision-making, can contribute to a world free from racism, racial Discrimination, xenophobia, and related intolerance. Two paragraphs (32 and 34) of the Declaration are devoted specifically to participation rights of people of African descent and the necessity of their full participation at all levels in the decision-making process in general and in the design, implementation and development of educational systems and programmes in particular.[11] The Declaration also recognizes the necessity of special measures or positive actions to encourage equal participation of all racial and cultural, linguistic, and religious groups in all sectors of society, including electoral reforms, land reforms, campaigns for equal participation, etc, aimed at achieving appropriate representation in educational institutions, housing, political parties, parliaments, and employment (especially in the judiciary, police, army, and other civil services) (para 108).

---

[7] The right to development is an inalienable human right by virtue of which every human person and all peoples are entitled to participate in, contribute to, and enjoy economic, social, cultural, and political development, in which all human rights and fundamental freedoms can be fully realized.

[8] The human person is the central subject of development and should be the active participant and beneficiary of the right to development.

[9] States have the right and the duty to formulate appropriate national development policies that aim at the constant improvement of the well-being of the entire population and of all individuals, on the basis of their active, free, and meaningful participation in development and in the fair distribution of the benefits resulting therefrom.

[10] States should encourage popular participation in all spheres as an important factor in development and in the full realization of all human rights.

[11] The Declaration and Programme also refer to participation rights of indigenous peoples which are not considered in this contribution.

The Programme of Action urges states to implement the provisions contained in Art 2.2 of the UN Minorities Declaration[12] in order to protect minorities from any form of racism, racial discrimination, xenophobia, and related intolerance (para 47) and to actively recruit all groups, including minorities, into public employment, including the police force and other agencies within the criminal justice system (para 74). In relation to people of African descent, the Programme urges states to facilitate their participation 'in all political, economic, social and cultural aspects of society and in the advancement and economic development of their countries' (para 4). It also calls upon states to facilitate the media's efforts to encourage the participation of 'Roma/Gypsies/Sinti/Travellers' (para 43). Furthermore, it urges states to ensure the participation of women from various disadvantaged groups (such as of African and Asian descent) in the economic and productive development of their communities (para 50). It also recommends that states include in their periodic reports to United Nations human rights treaty bodies statistical information on participation in political life relating to individuals, members of groups and communities (para 98). It encourages states to elaborate national plans with the aim of creating conditions for all to participate effectively in decision-making (para 99). Finally, a whole section relating to policies and practices is devoted to equal participation in political, economic, social, and cultural decision-making. In this section, the Programme urges states and encourages the private sector and international financial and development institutions to promote participation of victims of racism 'in economic, cultural and social decision-making at all stages, particularly in the development and implementation of poverty alleviation strategies, development projects, and trade and market assistance programmes' and in economic life in general (paras 112–13). Lastly, it encourages financial and development institutions and the operational programmes and specialized agencies of the United Nations to regularly report on the participation of victims of racism within their programmes and activities (para 190).

D. The Outcome Document of the Durban Review Conference

The Review Conference took place on 20–24 April 2009 in Geneva to evaluate progress towards the goals set in Durban. The Outcome Document urges states to strengthen measures aimed at improving access to opportunities for greater and more meaningful participation in the political, economic, social and cultural spheres of society, for persons belonging to minorities in general and people of African and Asian descent in particular (para 70). It further calls on states to encourage political parties to work towards fair representation of minorities at all levels of their party system, to ensure that multicultural diversity is reflected in political and legal systems, and to develop more participatory

---

[12] Neither the Article nor the Declaration are explicitly referred to but the content is identical.

and all-inclusive democratic institutions (paras 110–11). The Document also encourages states to adopt strategies, programmes and policies, including special measures, to improve access to political, judicial and administrative institutions for victims of racism, racial discrimination, xenophobia and related intolerance (para 113). The Human Rights Council is requested 'to continue promoting intercultural and interreligious dialogue with enhanced participation of all stakeholders, including from the grass-roots level' (para 127). Lastly the Document calls on states to contribute to the Trust Fund for the Programme of the Decade to Combat Racism and Racial Discrimination for, inter alia, the participation of people of African descent in the work of the Intergovernmental Working Group on the effective implementation of the DDPA (para 124).

III. Recommendations and Expert Advice

A. Commentary of the Working Group on Minorities to the UN Minorities Declaration (E/CN4/Sub2/AC5/2005/2)[13]

According to the Commentary, the Declaration grants minorities neither group rights to self-determination nor to autonomy. It simply suggests that 'the duties of the State to protect the identity of minorities and to ensure their effective participation might in some cases be best implemented by arrangements for autonomy in regard to religious, linguistic or broader cultural matters' (para 20). Should states wish to establish autonomy arrangements, the Commentary advises that these 'can be organized and managed by associations set up by persons belonging to minorities in accordance with article 2.4[14] [of the Declaration]'.

In relation to Art 2.2, the Commentary defines public life in the same broad sense as in Art 1 of the ICERD—ie inclusive of, eg, rights relating to election and to being elected, the holding of public office, and other political and administrative domains (para 36). It links this right to other rights in the Declaration by stating that the ways to ensure participation include the use of minority associations (the already cited Art 2.4) and free contacts both inside the state and across borders (Art 2.5).[15]

---

[13] The Working Group on Minorities functioned between 1995 and 2006 as a subsidiary organ of the Sub-commission on the Promotion and Protection of Human Rights and was composed of five experts, one representing each of the five geographic regions the United Nations uses to apportion seats on UN bodies (for more about this body see, eg, RM Letschert, *The Impact of Minority Rights Mechanisms* (TMC Asser Press: The Hague, 2005). The Commentary was originally drawn up by the working group's former chairperson, Mr Asbjørn Eide, and adopted at the tenth session of the working group, as a commentary of the working group as a whole. It is intended to serve as a guide to the understanding and application of the UN Minorities Declaration.

[14] Persons belonging to minorities have the right to establish and maintain their own associations.

[15] Persons belonging to minorities have the right to establish and maintain, without any discrimination, free and peaceful contacts with other members of their group and with persons belonging to other minorities, as well as contacts across frontiers with citizens of other states to whom they are related by national or ethnic, religious, or linguistic ties.

Art 2.3 deals specifically with participation in decision-making on matters affecting the minority or the region where it lives. The Commentary emphasizes the crucial importance of the phrase 'participate *effectively*' which implies that representatives of persons belonging to minorities should be involved from the initial stages of decision-making in order to be able to make a difference (para 38). In relation to Art 2.3, the Commentary does not propose particular measures but simply cites examples of participatory mechanisms that have been proposed as effective by a Meeting of Experts on National Minorities held by the Conference on Security and Cooperation in Europe in 1991 in Geneva.[16] It acknowledges that it draws extensively on the Lund Recommendations as well as recommendations adopted at the fifth session of the working group in May 1999[17] and that it aims to not only set out 'the minimum rights under article 2.3 of persons belonging to minorities, but also to provide a list of good practices which may be of use to Governments and minorities in finding appropriate solutions to issues confronting them' (para 41). However, in this regard, the Commentary is neither very detailed nor advanced. It simply points out that:

- Effective participation can serve as a means of dispute resolution and ensuring stability in a diverse society.
- The absolute minimum of effective participation boils down to minorities having 'the right to have their opinions heard and fully taken into account before decisions which concern them are adopted' (para 42).
- The most appropriate ways to create conditions for effective participation depend on the composition, needs and aspirations of different types of minorities.[18]
- Effective participation requires representation in legislative, administrative, and advisory bodies and more generally in public life.

In relation to the last point, it elaborates by noting that establishing political parties along ethnic lines is one option that should be available for minorities and in areas where minorities are concentrated territorially, single-member districts may be used to provide sufficient minority representation. It then suggests

---

[16] These are: minority representatives as members of advisory and decision-making bodies, in particular with regard to education, culture, and religion; assemblies for national minority affairs; local and autonomous administration; autonomy on a territorial basis, including the existence of consultative, legislative, and executive bodies chosen through free and periodic elections; non-territorial autonomy; and decentralized or local forms of government.

[17] The working group dealt with the issue of effective participation by minorities at great length at its 5th session in May 1999. It based the discussion on two working papers: one on the question of citizenship and minority rights, prepared by Mr Eide (E/CN4/Sub2/AC5/1999/WP3) and the other (E/CN4/Sub2/AC5/1999/WP4) on the recommendations of the regional seminar on effective participation organized by the European Centre for Minority Issues in Flensburg. It highlighted a number of recommendations presented in the latter document which are virtually all reflected in the Commentary. (For the recommendations highlighted see E/CN4/Sub2/1999/21).

[18] Eg dispersed v compact, small v large, old v new, religious v ethnic, and combinations thereof.

other options including proportional representation systems, some forms of preference voting, decentralization of powers based on the principle of subsidiarity, and advisory or consultative bodies or round tables involving minorities within appropriate institutional frameworks. However, the Commentary emphasizes that public institutions (be it at local, regional, or national levels) should not be based on ethnic or religious criteria. Instead there should be equal access to public sector employment across the various ethnic, linguistic, and religious communities.

Last but not least, in relation to Art 2.3 the Commentary points out that citizenship is an important condition for full and effective participation. Barriers to the acquisition of citizenship for members of minorities should thus be reduced and forms of participation by resident non-citizens (including local voting rights after a certain period of residence and inclusion of elected non-citizen observers in municipal, regional, and national legislative and decision-making assemblies) should be developed.

In relation to Art 4.5, the Commentary points out that under this article the Declaration requires steps to be taken to prevent minorities from being excluded, marginalized, or neglected in the economic life of the society. But at the same time it aims to 'prevent minorities being made into museum pieces by the misguided requirement that they remain at their traditional level of development while the members of the surrounding society experience significant improvements in their standard of living' (para 71). To this end, the article calls for the integration of everyone in the overall economic development of society as a whole, in ways which allow minorities to preserve their own identity (para 72). However, in terms of facilitating this task, the Commentary only suggests that it should be facilitated by 'the existence of active and free associations of minorities which are fully consulted in regard to all development activities which affect or can affect their minority' (para 72).

The Commentary then links Art 4.5 with Art 5.1, stating that Art 4.5 can only be achieved if Art 5.1. is also implemented (ie, interests of minorities are taken into account in the planning and implementation of national policies and programmes). But Art 5.1 goes further than Art 4.5 because it does not concentrate only on economic aspects. The Commentary points out that 'due regard'[19] should be given to the interests of the minorities in the planning of, eg, educational policy, health policy, public nutrition policy, or housing and settlement policies (paras 72–3).

The Commentary ends with a caveat that measures to ensure effective participation, or to ensure that minorities benefit from economic progress in society or have the possibility to learn their own language, should not contravene the principles of equality and proportionality (para 83).

---

[19] Ie, the interests of minorities should be given reasonable weight compared with other legitimate interests that the government has to take into consideration.

B. General Comment no 21 on the Right of everyone to take part in cultural life (Art 15.1a of the International Covenant of Economic, Social and Cultural Rights (ICESCR)) (E/C12/GC/21)

Following a day of general discussion, the Committee on Economic, Social and Cultural Rights (CESCR) was finalizing the above comment at the time of writing, which is likely to address the right of minorities to effective participation in cultural life in several ways. One area covered during the discussions was encouraging states to adopt measures aimed at ensuring that educational programmes for minorities transmit the knowledge necessary for full and equal participation in their own as well as national communities. Another area is expanding the minimum core obligations of states to include the obligation to allow and encourage the participation of persons belonging to minorities in the design and implementation of laws and policies affecting them. Discussion also centred on the issue of states having to obtain informed prior consent of indigenous and minority communities if the preservation of cultural resources, especially those associated with the way of life and cultural expression of the communities, is at risk. Lastly, a discussion took place about including the lack of appropriate measures to remedy the under-representation of persons from cultural minorities in public life among violations of the obligation to fulfil the right of everyone to take part in cultural life.

C. Recommendations of the International Seminar on Cooperation for the Better Protection of the Rights of Minorities regarding participation of minorities in development

The International Seminar on Cooperation for the Better Protection of the Rights of Minorities was organized by the Office of the High Commissioner for Human Rights (OHCHR) in Durban, South Africa, on 1–2 and 5 September 2001 for representatives of international and regional organizations, treaty bodies and specialized agencies. Participants at the seminar adopted a number of recommendations, drawing on those adopted by the Working Group on Minorities at its May 2001 session. Issues of participation were covered mostly in relation to the working methods of the Working Group (and have thus become obsolete with its closure) and to development assistance. The latter were addressed to multilateral trade, finance, and development actors as well as bilateral development actors and are worth detailing here because the topic of effective participation in development assistance has not been addressed much outside UN fora:

- Respect the right of minority communities to set their own priorities for development, in accordance with their own concept of development (Recommendation 22).

- Ensure the effective participation of minorities, especially those subject to multiple forms of discrimination, such as women, persons with disabilities, and older persons, in the formulation, implementation, and evaluation of country strategies, development plans, and programmes that affect them, and to build the capacity of minorities and multilateral actors to implement this effective participation (Recommendation 25).
- Ensure that country offices are working closely with minorities, including through the use of appropriate methodologies to assess the impact of development strategies on the situation of minorities in the country, especially those who are most marginalized, as well as through the equitable representation of minorities within such country offices and the provision of human rights training for staff covering such matters as the need for United Nations staff to engage actively with minorities in their communities (Recommendation 26).
- Establish independent review and complaints procedures that are easily accessible to minorities, to ensure the implementation of the recommendations enumerated above (Recommendation 27).

One related recommendation was also addressed to governments:

- Ensure the effective participation of minorities, especially those subject to multiple forms of discrimination, such as women, persons with disabilities and older persons, in the formulation, implementation, and evaluation of country strategies, development plans, and programmes that affect them, including the 2015 International Development Goals, and build the capacity of minorities and governmental actors to implement this effective participation (Recommendation 33).[20]

D. The Minority Profile and Matrix (E/CN4/Sub2/AC5/2006/3)

Additionally, the Working Group considered the Minority Profile and Matrix on the human rights situation of minorities, which provides a checklist of issues and measures based on the provisions and principles contained in the UN Minorities Declaration and the Commentary. This monitoring and learning tool has been developed by OHCHR minority fellows in 2005 and 2006. It contains several sections on participation rights, each of which contains a series of monitoring questions. The participation rights covered are:

- to participate effectively in cultural life and right to enjoy their own culture (Arts 2.1, 2.2, and 4.2) (see pp 23–6)
- to profess and practise religion and effectively participate in religious life (Arts 2.1, 2.2, and 4.2) (see pp 27–32)

---

[20] E/CN4/2002/92.

- to participate effectively in public life (Art 2.2) (see pp 40–5)
- to participate effectively in social and economic life and participate in development and economic progress (Arts 2.2 and 4.5) (see pp 46–53)
- to participate in decisions concerning the minority within the country, including through policy-making and programming (Arts 2.3 and 5) (see pp 53–5).

Although this tool does not advance standard-setting for effective participation, it provides a useful overview of the existing standards and their applications in a user-friendly checklist form.

A number of other papers dealing with effective participation by minorities and related issues were considered by the working group,[21] however no further specific recommendations were made.

E. OHCHR Guidelines and Good Practice for Policing in Diverse Societies

With a view to offering guidance for technical assistance, and pursuant to para 74 (a) of the Durban Programme of Action (see above), OHCHR is currently finalizing this information tool on the practical application of human rights principles and provisions related to integration with diversity in policing. The tool is based on an expert meeting[22] with senior professionals from the police service of different regions and countries of the world as well as representatives of intergovernmental organizations and civil society, organized in January 2008 in cooperation with the International Labour Organization (ILO), the United Nations Office on Drugs and Crime (UNODC), and the Independent Expert on Minority Issues, as well as an earlier draft of a toolkit aimed at greater integration of members of minorities in the agencies of police, security, and criminal justice at a national or regional level, considered by the Working Group.[23] The Guidelines are intended to assist governments, UN officials, non-governmental organizations, and others, in ensuring that agencies of the criminal justice system and law enforcement agencies are representative of, and responsive and accountable to the community as a whole.

F. Human rights-based approach to development

Human rights-based approach to development, broadly agreed upon by UN agencies, upgrades development from a mere charity to a sustainable process of

---

[21] For the list of documents see <http://www2.ohchr.org/english/issues/minorities/docs/docstable.doc> (accessed 5 September 2009).
[22] An OHCHR report on the expert meeting is available at <www2.ohchr.org/english/issues/minorities/seminar.htm> (accessed 5 September 2009).
[23] T Hadden, 'Integration with diversity in security, policing and criminal justice', Working paper, Queen's University, Belfast, E/CN4/Sub.2/AC5/2006/WP1.

empowering people—'especially the most marginalized—to participate in policy formulation and hold accountable those who have a duty to act'.[24] The principle of participation and attention to vulnerable groups such as minorities, indigenous peoples, women, and others, are two of the main principles of this approach. The approach promotes 'active, free and meaningful' participation (as stipulated in the UN Declaration on the Right to Development, see above) which goes beyond mere formal or 'ceremonial' contracts or consultations with beneficiaries. It advocates process-based development methodologies and techniques, rather than externally conceived 'quick fixes' and imported technical models. It requires that development data are disaggregated, as far as possible, by categories such as race, religion, ethnicity, language, and sex and the most vulnerable groups in each situation are identified.

G. United Nations Development Programme (UNDP) Resource Guide on Minorities in Development—towards a policy note

Among the broader UN family, UNDP has so far taken most interest in the issues of effective participation of minorities. UNDP considers that since at present it does not have a specific policy, guidance, or practice note on how to deal with minorities in its programming processes, the adoption of a UNDP Policy Note on Minorities would be an important tool for UNDP country offices to start and/or to strengthen their work with minorities. A 2006 consultation concluded that such a policy note would also be a step towards establishing a more systematic approach by the UN to promoting minority rights and found that minority communities would be very interested in engaging with the UNDP and other UN agencies as partners in development and in advocacy for their rights. As a result, the UNDP is currently finalizing a Resource Guide/Toolkit which should serve as a resource and practical guide for UNDP practitioners to enable them, among other things, to learn how to increase opportunities for meaningful participation and representation of minorities in development processes.[25] The practical issues discussed in the Guide include, for example, facilitating better the participation of minorities at all stages of designing and implementing poverty reduction strategies and health programmes; supporting the political participation and representation of minorities through electoral reforms, decentralization of governance, building the capacity of local governments, parliamentarian support, and public service reform; facilitation the participation of minorities in peace-building, etc.

---

[24] OHCHR, *Frequently Asked Questions on a Human Rights-Based Approach to Development Cooperation* (New York and Geneva: United Nations, 2006), 15.
[25] Annotated draft outline for 'UNDP Resource Guide/Toolkit on Minorities in Development' (4 October 2007).

H. UNDP and Inter-parliamentary Union (IPU) Project 'Promoting inclusive parliaments: The representation of minorities and indigenous peoples in parliaments'

This recently started project is another UNDP initiative, jointly with the IPU, to advance effective participation of minorities—in this case in parliamentary processes. It aims to provide an analysis of the state of minority and indigenous representation in parliament, including how minority and indigenous representatives are able to make an effective and meaningful contribution to parliamentary work and case studies of how parliaments seek to be inclusive. The practical goals of the project include assisting parliaments in becoming more inclusive of the social diversity of the population, stimulating parliamentary discussion and action in favour of the effective representation of minorities and indigenous peoples in parliament, and promoting greater engagement of UN treaty mechanisms with the issue of minority representation. The outcomes of the project will be available at a dedicated website, <http://www.ipu.org/dem-e/minorities/overview.htm>.

IV. Monitoring and Implementation

The majority of the above-mentioned norms, standards, and recommendations do not have implementing mechanisms, with the exception of the more general provisions in the core international human rights treaties monitored by treaty bodies.[26] Additionally, special procedures also have a monitoring function.[27]

A. The UN Minorities Declaration

The UN Minorities Declaration itself does not have a monitoring or implementation procedure and has not been referred to by the treaty bodies in their country reviews.[28] While the mandates of both the OHCHR and the Independent Expert on Minority Issues (see later in this chapter) include the promotion of the implementation of the Declaration, more systematic monitoring is not carried out. Between 1995 and 2006, the former UN Working Group on Minorities, the mandate of which included reviewing the promotion and practical realization of the Minorities Declaration, attempted to do a more

---

[26] For more information about treaty bodies see <http://www2.ohchr.org/english/bodies/treaty/index.htm> (accessed 6 September 2009).

[27] For more information about special procedures see <http://www2.ohchr.org/english/bodies/chr/special/index.htm> (accessed 6 September 2009).

[28] This is in stark contrast to the much younger Declaration on the Rights of Indigenous Peoples, adopted in 2007, which some treaty bodies started to refer to immediately.

systematic monitoring but lacked the resources and mechanisms to do so in a coherent and effective way. Its monitoring capacity was largely limited to collecting non-governmental organization (NGO) information presented through oral and written interventions at annual sessions, without the ability to verify the information or follow up on the issues, with the exception of occasional dialogue with governments. NGOs from all regions of the world have indeed regularly addressed the issue of effective participation in their statements under the agenda item 'Reviewing the Promotion and Practical Realization of the Declaration on the Rights of Persons Belonging to National or Ethnic, Religious, and Linguistic Minorities' but this on its own has usually not resulted in any further action.

Aware of the severe limitation on its monitoring capacity, since 2001 the Working Group has added country visits to its repertoire. However, since the states did not only have to invite the Working Group but also to pay for the visit, only two visits took place. In 2001 it visited Mauritius and discussed, among other issues, participation by all communities in political, social, and economic life. In its recommendations, it 'stressed the important aspect of participation by all communities in political, social and economic life in the multi-ethnic society of Mauritius' and recommended 'that disaggregated data and information on disadvantaged communities be collected in order to design future policy on the promotion and protection of the rights of minorities'.[29] This issue was also considered during its second country visit—to Finland in 2004—when the Working Group noted 'that the Russian-speaking community called for the establishment of an advisory body to examine integration issues' and suggested that the government of Finland considers this demand.[30]

B. The treaty bodies[31]

The issue of effective participation by minorities in public life is not an easy one to address for treaty bodies as states are often reluctant to provide adequate information on this topic and do not accord it sufficient attention.[32] The Committee on Elimination of Racial Discrimination (CERD) has been the most active of the treaty bodies in drawing attention to the under-representation of minorities in political institutions (and in some cases other state institutions

---

[29] E/CN4/Sub2/AC5/2002/2, paras 48–9. A similar request was made by CERD the same year (CERD/C/ADD106, para 9) and the country has not been reviewed by CERD since.
[30] E/CN4/Sub2/2004/29/Add1, para 46. Finland has since established the Ombudsman for Minorities and the Advisory Board for Minority Issues (A/HRC/8/24, para 43).
[31] I would like to thank Daniel Ruiz de Garibay for his help with the background research on the work of treaty bodies on effective participation of minorities.
[32] N Prouvez, 'Minorities and indigenous peoples' protection: Practice of UN treaty bodies in 2003' (2003/2004) 3 *European Yearbook on Minority Issues* 493.

such as the police).³³ At the same time, it has also relatively frequently commented on positive developments in relation to the political participation of minorities.³⁴ It is indeed encouraging that information on positive developments in relation to political participation of minorities has recently been increasingly included in state reports. For example, in 2001 Vietnam reported a significant number of representatives of minority groups in the national parliament,³⁵ and Estonia reported the elimination of language requirements from the Election Act and the Local Government Council Election Act.³⁶ In 2005, Georgia informed CERD about recent measures to strengthen participation of ethnic minorities in political institutions³⁷ and in 2007, Israel informed CERD that for the first time an Arab Israeli citizen had been appointed to the Cabinet and that affirmative action programmes to ensure better representation of minority groups in the civil service and within government-owned corporations had been adopted.³⁸ The same year, the former Yugoslav Republic of Macedonia reported its adoption of a strategy on equitable representation of members of ethnic communities in state administration and public enterprise.³⁹

The Human Rights Committee (CCPR) has also occasionally addressed the under-representation of minorities in public institutions⁴⁰ and has drawn attention to the exclusion of minorities from enjoying political rights such as standing for elections, employment in public service, and voting rights, under various pretexts such as non-citizenship status, adherence to religious organizations or beliefs, minority status, linguistic requirements, and criminal record. For example in 2003, considering the situation of long-term resident non-citizen Russian-speaking minorities, the CCPR recommended that Estonia consider allowing non-citizens become members of political parties⁴¹ and that Latvia consider enabling them to participate in local elections and to ease other restrictions on their participation in public life.⁴² In the concluding observations to the state report by Germany on 2004, CCPR expressed concern that 'adherence to certain religious organizations or beliefs constitutes one of main grounds for disqualifying individuals from obtaining employment in public service', which, in its opinion, 'may in certain circumstances violate rights

---

³³ Eg, in relation to Crimean Tatars in Ukraine (CERD/C/UKR/CO/18, paras 14 and 18), Roma in Croatia (CERD/C/60/CO/4, para 10), Moldova (CERD/C/MDA/CO/7, para 16) and Slovenia (CERD/C/62/CO/9, para 10), Indo-Fijians in Fiji (CERD/C/62/CO/3, para 18) and Dalits in India (CERD/C/IND/CO/19, para 17) as well as various groups in many other countries from all regions.
³⁴ Eg, in the case of Azerbaijan, Australia, Canada, Estonia, Fiji, Georgia, India, Iran, Israel, Nepal, the former Yugoslav Republic of Macedonia, Slovakia, Slovenia, United Kingdom of Great Britain and Northern Ireland, United States of America, Venezuela, and Vietnam.
³⁵ A/56/18(SUPP), para 413.   ³⁶ Ibid, para 359.
³⁷ CERD/C/GEO/CO/3, para 9.   ³⁸ CERD/C/ISR/CO/13, para 8.
³⁹ CERD/C/MKD/CO/7, para 8.
⁴⁰ Eg, in the case of Brazil, Georgia, Germany, and Israel.
⁴¹ CCPR/CO/77/EST, para 17.   ⁴² CCPR/CO/79/LVA, para 17.

guaranteed in articles 18 and 25 ICCPR'.[43] In the case of the review of Bosnia and Herzegovina in 2006, CCPR expressed concern that the State Constitution and Election Law continue to exclude persons not belonging to one of the state's 'constituent peoples' from being elected to the House of Peoples and to the tripartite presidency of Bosnia.[44] In Namibia (2004), the concerns related to members of the population who only spoke non-official languages being denied access to public service.[45] In the case of the United States of America (2006), the CCPR was concerned that about 5 million citizens could not vote due to a felony conviction, with this practice having significant racial implications.[46] The Committee on Elimination of Discrimination Against Women (CEDAW) has also frequently addressed the lack of minority women in public positions.[47]

In terms of jurisprudence relating to individual complaints to treaty bodies, political participation has been addressed mostly within the specific context of indigenous rights, with the exception of the *Ignatane v Latvia* case dealing with the determination of linguistic competence as a limitation to the right to participate in public life under Art 25 of the ICCPR.[48]

C. Universal Periodic Review (UPR)

The newly established Universal Periodic Review (UPR) procedure of the Human Rights Council[49] is another monitoring mechanism which can engage on the issues of effective participation by minorities. During its first and second session, out of the thirty-two countries reviewed, outcome documents for eleven countries touched upon effective participation of minorities—namely recruitment to police forces (Czech Republic[50] and Switzerland[51]), political representation of minority women (Ecuador[52] and the Netherlands[53]), consultative bodies (Finland[54] and Romania[55]), consultation on national programmes (India[56]), participation in public affairs, including electoral participation and/or participation in public service (the UK,[57] Ukraine,[58] Switzerland,[59] France,[60] and Pakistan[61]). In three instances, these points were raised explicitly on the basis of previous treaty body or special procedures recommendations (CERD for Ecuador, CEDAW for the Netherlands and the Independent Expert on

---

[43] CCPR/CO/80/DEU, para 19. [44] CCPR/C/BIH/CO/1, para 8.
[45] CCPR/CO/81/NAM, para 21. [46] CCPR/C/USA/CO/3/Rev 1, para 35.
[47] Eg, the former Yugoslav Republic of Macedonia, Croatia, China, New Zealand, Czech Republic, Romania, Italy, Phillipines, Turkmenistan, Venezuela, Surinam, Vietnam, and Namibia.
[48] See M Weller, 'Effective participation of minorities in public life' in M Weller (ed), *Universal Minority Rights* (Oxford: Oxford University Press, 2007), 477–516.
[49] For more information see <http://www.ohchr.org/EN/HRBodies/UPR/Pages/UPRMain.aspx> (accessed 6 September 2009). [50] A/HRC/8/33, para 12.
[51] A/HRC/8/41, para 16 and Recommendation 11. [52] A/HRC/8/20, para 32.
[53] A/HRC/8/31, para 50 and Recommendation 19. [54] A/HRC/8/24, para 43.
[55] A/HRC/8/49, para 55. [56] A/HRC/8/26, para 38. [57] A/HRC/8/25, para 43.
[58] A/HRC/8/45, para 45. [59] A/HRC/8/41, para 24.
[60] /HRC/8/47, paras 18 and 37. [61] A/HRC/8/42, paras 12 and 51.

Minority Issues for France). In just two instances, the issues were reflected in specific recommendations for action with Canada recommending that Switzerland recruit minorities into the police and Ghana recommending that the Netherlands strengthen measures to increase the participation by ethnic minority women in politics.

D. Special procedures, including the Independent Expert on Minority Issues

Among special procedures,[62] Ms Gay McDougall, the Independent Expert on Minority Issues, has prioritized participation rights of minorities.[63] Ensuring effective participation of members of minorities in public life, especially with regard to decisions that affect them is one of the four broad areas of concern relating to minorities around the world that Ms McDougall identified as priorities for her mandate. Full and effective participation of minorities in policies and decisions that affect them is a guiding principle of all of the Independent Expert's thematic work. Within her focus on minority communities in the context of poverty alleviation, development and MDGs,[64] she has highlighted the need to work with states and all other development actors, including minorities themselves, to promote programmes, policies, and activities that take fully into account the needs and rights of minorities. Her focus on increasing the understanding of minority issues in the context of promoting social inclusion and ensuring stable societies has concentrated also on the inclusion of minority political voice. In terms of mainstreaming the consideration of minority issues within the work of the UN and other important multilateral forums, the Independent Expert seeks to ensure that minorities are consulted, and are able to participate effectively in decisions that affect them for the planning and implementation of programmes of work. Finally, her thematic focus on minorities and the discriminatory denial or deprivation of citizenship has highlighted the deliberate denial of citizenship as a tool for excluding minorities from political processes, consequences of which are experienced over generations.[65]

In terms of country visits, the Independent Expert has been collecting good practices at local and national levels in relation to political participation of minorities and has often identified the lack of effectiveness of participation measures at the local level and under-representation of minorities in political bodies in all regions of the world.[66] Her most detailed recommendations can be

---

[62] For more on UN special procedures see <http://www2.ohchr.org/english/bodies/chr/special/index.htm> (accessed 6 September 2009).

[63] Many thanks to Graham Fox for his input to the section on the Independent Expert. For more information see <http://www2.ohchr.org/english/issues/minorities/expert/index.htm> (accessed on 7 September 2009).   [64] See A/HRC/4/9/Add1.

[65] See A/HRC/7/23.

[66] See, eg, her report on country visit to Ethiopia (A/HRC/4/9/Add3, para 99).

found in her report on the country visit to Hungary. The most progressive of those are perhaps the ones requesting the government to ensure Romani representation in the national parliament, to emphasize that primary responsibility for meeting the social welfare needs of minority communities rests with municipal majority governments, to strengthen the recruitment of Romani professionals into key government posts and public organizations, and to ensure that all efforts to increase the participation of Roma in public life are carried out with the gender dimension in mind.[67]

Other special procedures mandate-holders also occasionally touch upon the issue of effective participation of minorities.[68] Perhaps most importantly, the Special Rapporteur on freedom of religion and belief pays attention to the obstacles to participation of religious minorities, an issue that is less well covered in other areas of the OHCHR's work. For example, in 2007 the Special Rapporteur expressed concern that in the Maldives constitutional provisions restricted the eligibility to apply for citizenship, to vote, and to restrict certain public offices to Muslims only.[69] In 2008, she shared the concern of CESCR that in the UK Catholic staff is under-represented in the Police Service of Northern Ireland, the prison service and other criminal justice agencies. While welcoming affirmative action strategies to ensure that these agencies can recruit a more representative workforce, she pointed out that such measures should also address adequate representation of *all* religious or belief communities.[70]

E. The Durban Declaration and Programme of Action

A thorough look at the implementation of the Durban Declaration and Programme goes beyond the scope of this chapter, however, there are some indications that, seven years on, the Durban participatory clauses are far from being implemented. Despite the recommendation to states to include in their periodic reports to UN human rights treaty bodies statistical information on participation of minorities in political life, since then frequently reiterated by the treaty bodies (especially CERD) in their concluding observations, many states remain either unable or unwilling to provide such data. Similarly, the recommendation to adopt national plans creating conditions for all to participate effectively in

---

[67] A/HRC/4/9/Add2.
[68] Eg, the Representative of the Secretary-General on the human rights of internally displaced persons in relation to Bosnia and Herzegovina (E/CN4/2006/71/Add4, para 60) and Croatia (E/CN4/2006/71/Add3, para 50); the Special Rapporteur on contemporary forms of racism, racial discrimination, xenophobia, and related intolerance in relation to Japan (E/CN4/2006/16/Add2, para 86) and Brazil (E/CN4/2006/16/Add3, para 84); the Special Rapporteur on freedom of religion or belief in relation to Maldives (A/HRC/4/21/Add3, paras 66–7) and United Kingdom (A/HRC/7/10/Add3, para 63); the Special Rapporteur on the independence of judges and lawyers in relation to Ecuador (E/CN4/2006/52/Add2, para 28) and the Special Rapporteur on the situation of human rights in Myanmar (A/HRC/4/14, paras 87 and 110).
[69] A/HRC/4/21/Add3, paras 66–7.   [70] A/HRC/7/10/Add3, para 63.

decision-making has been taken on board by very few states. The African Group of the UN member states has recently identified '[a]chieving racial equality, in particular participation in political life … of the individuals and various groups and communities in a given society' as a priority theme 'where lack of implementation and dangerous trends are apparent'.[71] Participation of victims of racism and civil society organizations needs to be promoted and enhanced even within the work of the Durban process itself and the follow-up mechanisms created at the UN. Elsewhere in the UN family, progress also remains slow. As the Intersessional Open-ended Intergovernmental Working Group (IGWG) to follow up the work of the Preparatory Committee for the Durban Review Conference recently pointed out, the core principle of participation, among others, remains to be mainstreamed through partnerships spearheaded by the Human Rights Council into the policies and operational activities of the World Trade Organization, the International Labour Organization (ILO) and the International Organization for Migration.[72] A modest contribution of the OHCHR towards the Durban participatory clauses relating to minorities is the development of Guidelines and Good Practice for Policing in Diverse Societies (see above).

V. Advancing the Substance of the Right to Effective Participation through UN Norms, Standards, Recommendation, and Expert Advice and their Implementation?

As can be seen, the UN member states have yet to adopt a binding legal standard on effective participation of minorities. It is only through the expert interpretation of Art 27 of the ICCPR that states can be called upon to enact measures to ensure the effective participation of members of minority communities in decisions which affect them and, in practice so far, this Article has not been invoked for this purpose very regularly. In terms of non-binding standards, adopted by the General Assembly by consensus, the right of persons belonging to minorities to participate effectively in cultural, religious, social, economic, and public life, including in decision-making, planning, development, and economic progress, is well established through the UN Minorities Declaration. Unfortunately, this standard is not frequently invoked or even well known.

It is more in relation to the right to participate in development and in relation to effective participation as a means to fight against racism that the non-binding standards receive attention. However, even in relation to the fight

---

[71] First session of the Intersessional Open-ended Intergovernmental Working Group (IGWG) to follow up the work of the Preparatory Committee for the Durban Review Conference, Geneva, Palais des Nations, 26–30 May 2008, *Non-paper: Outcome Document—Inventory of issues*.
[72] Ibid.

against racism, many states remain reluctant to commit to more progressive measures to facilitate effective participation. While earlier drafts of the Outcome Document of the Durban Review Conference included references, eg to the necessity of quotas in parliaments and recommended establishing mechanisms for collection of disaggregated data on, inter alia, political participation and representation (albeit both in relation to people of African descent only),[73] these have not made it into the final adopted version. Similarly, a reference to best practices in developing frequent consultations with representative bodies of persons belonging to minorities and creating frameworks to encourage active participation of minorities in national and local governments have been omitted.

Significant headway has not yet been made through recommendations and expert advice within the UN fora either. Although the Lund Recommendations build heavily upon many principles of international human rights law codified in UN treaties, the UN has not yet produced a similarly elaborate document on effective participation by minorities, addressing constitutional and legal safeguards as well as remedies. Since there are no detailed provisions in international law regarding the institutions and mechanisms to be adopted for implementing the right to participation for minorities, further expert engagement on this topic within the UN fora is definitely overdue. The very basics of this work have been laid out in the Commentary to the UN Minorities Declaration, which however only scratches the surface. For example, although unlike the Lund Recommendations and the ACFC Commentary that concentrate primarily at the domestic level, the Commentary on the Declaration emphasizes that '[m]inorities should be involved at the local, national and *international* levels in the formulation, adoption, implementation and monitoring of standards and policies affecting them' (emphasis added, para 38), but does not go into much detail regarding the international level, except as relates to issues other than decision-making, eg the right to form international minority associations, have cross-border contacts, and benefit from intergovernmental cooperation and assistance in development and economic matters in general. Similarly, while the Lund Recommendations remain silent on the issue of citizenship, the Commentary proposes certain participatory rights for non-citizens (as does the much younger ACFC Commentary) but again does not go into much detail.

Recognizing this gap in expert advice, the Independent Expert on Minority Issues has chosen the topic of 'Minorities and Effective Political Participation' to be the thematic focus of the second session of the Forum on Minority Issues,[74] scheduled to take place 12–13 November 2009 at the Palais des Nations in

---

[73] See, eg, A/CONF211/PC/WG2/CRP1.
[74] The Forum was established pursuant to Human Rights Council Resolution 6/15 of 28 September 2007 to replace the Working Group on Minorities, providing a platform for promoting dialogue and cooperation on issues pertaining to minorities as well as thematic contributions and expertise to the work of the Independent Expert on Minority Issues. For further detail see <http://www2.ohchr.org/english/bodies/hrcouncil/minority/forum.htm> (accessed 25 September 2009).

Geneva. The Forum will seek to provide thematic recommendations on the topic, which would be of practical value to all stakeholders.

Another encouraging development in terms of expert advice is the recent engagement of treaty body experts with the topic of effective participation for minorities in their work on general comments—for example through the drafting of the CESCR General Comment no 21 on the right of everyone to take part in cultural life. Not only is this comment likely to bring together existing provisions, in some cases it might even go beyond them. For example, should the discussion of the principle of informed prior consent (as relates to the preservation of cultural resources) in connection to minorities be reflected in the final comment, this would represent a significant advance. Similarly, if the final comment includes the lack of appropriate measures to remedy the under-representation of minorities in public life among violations of the obligation to fulfil the right of everyone to take part in cultural life, and if this is taken on board by CESCR in its monitoring practice, this would be a significant step forward as this issue has not really been scrutinized by CESCR much so far. However, the comment is not likely to be progressive on all fronts. For example, issues of cultural autonomy for minorities did not seem to resonate much during the day of general discussion, despite the fact that it was covered in detail by one of the invited experts.[75]

The OHCHR has also recently embarked on providing expert advice on substantive issues relating to the minorities mandate. In this respect, the OHCHR Guidelines and Good Practice for Policing in Diverse Societies will hopefully fill in a gap at the international level which has already been filled at the regional OSCE level through the High Commissioner on National Minorities' Recommendations on Policing in Multi-ethnic Societies upon which the OHCHR guidelines build and expand.

The one area where the UN takes a lead in relation to minority participation is participation in development. This is an important theme not only in the UN Minorities Declaration and the accompanying commentary but also, for example, in the Durban Declaration and Programme of Action. In addition, the principle of participation and attention to vulnerable groups such as minorities are two of the main principles of the human rights-based approach to development, which has been broadly agreed upon by UN agencies. However, a full commitment to this approach has not yet been achieved at the political, intergovernmental level and it is thus premature to analyse its potential any further. Among UN agencies, UNDP is taking lead in promoting meaningful participation and representation of minorities in development processes. Should the issues currently covered in the draft UNDP Resource Guide on Minorities in Development eventually be included in a UNDP policy note, this would

---

[75] See E Nimni, 'Collective dimensions of the right to take part in cultural life', UN Doc E/C12/40/17.

represent significant headway in terms of UNDP's commitment to effective participation of minorities in development.

In terms of monitoring, there is definitely room for greater engagement of the UN treaty mechanisms, special procedures and the UPR with the issue of effective participation by minorities although positive developments are discernible. Given the reluctance of states to provide adequate information on this topic and to prioritize it, the work of the treaty bodies has so far been largely limited to drawing attention to the underrepresentation of minorities in public life and to the exclusion of minorities from enjoying political rights as well as to encouraging states to report on the participation of minorities in public life. Jurisprudence relating to individual complaints to treaty bodies has addressed political participation mostly within the specific context of indigenous rights. There is thus a need to raise awareness of this procedure among persons belonging to national or ethnic, religious, and linguistic minorities outside of the indigenous camp. The UPR itself, as a political process, is not likely to advance the substance of the right to effective participation of minorities much further. It does, however, have the potential to become an important means towards the implementation of existing commitments, if used effectively.

Some positive developments are also discernible in the work of special procedures. Among those, the work of the Independent Expert on Minority Issues is particularly worth mentioning—especially as it relates to her initiative to promote participation of minorities in development processes and poverty alleviation which has stimulated much of the recent UNDP action in this regard.

10
Political Participation Systems Applicable to Indigenous Peoples

Luis Rodríguez-Piñero Royo

I. Introduction	308
II. International Standards Regarding Indigenous Peoples' Right to Participation	311
III. Indigenous Peoples' Participation in Decision-making	315
A. Arrangements at the level of the central government	315
B. Elections	318
C. Arrangements at the regional and local levels	322
D. Advisory and consultative bodies and mechanisms	324
IV. Indigenous Self-governance	328
A. Territorial arrangements	329
B. Non-territorial arrangements	338
V. Critical Assessment	340

I. Introduction

This chapter discusses the relevance of the Lund Recommendations on the Effective Participation of National Minorities in Public Life (Lund Recommendations) of the Organization for Security and Cooperation in Europe (OSCE) in the specific context of indigenous peoples, analysing a number of specific examples of modern legal and institutional arrangements that promote the participation of indigenous peoples in public life in the states in which they live.

As is known, the application of the concept of national minorities to indigenous peoples is essentially contested. Since the mid-1970s, when indigenous peoples started to emerge as distinct voices within the international human rights system, indigenous representatives have consistently refused their categorization as 'minorities', arguing instead their status as 'peoples' on an equal footing with other peoples whose rights have been affirmed in international law.[1] This view, subsequently endorsed by the thriving academic literature that followed and supported indigenous peoples' demands,[2] has been confirmed by international standard-setting processes and by the practice of international human rights mechanisms, in the form of a specific international legal regime on the rights of indigenous peoples that relates to, but is distinct from, the minority rights regime.[3] The adoption in 2007 of the United Nations (UN) Declaration on the Rights of Indigenous Peoples (UNDRIP),[4] parallel to the 1992 Declaration on the Rights of Persons Belonging to National or Ethnic, Religious, and Linguistic Minorities,[5] is a definitive endorsement of the individuality of the indigenous peoples regime in modern international law.

This notwithstanding, it is also a shared view that indigenous peoples' claims and rights under international law do overlap in substantive issues with those ascribed to national and other minorities, and minority rights arguments, instruments and protection mechanisms have indeed been used effectively in order to advance indigenous rights. As argued by Benedict Kingsbury, minority rights is one of several, sometimes conflicting, arguments that have been used simultaneously to advance indigenous peoples' rights in international and domestic legal practice.[6] Despite the limitations of the minority rights approach in the context of indigenous peoples' rights, minority rights mechanisms have, in practice, been a useful tool to advance at least some of the key aspects of

---

[1] See, eg, Intervention by Sharon Venne to the UN Working Group on Indigenous Populations, Eleventh Session, Geneva, 19–30 July 1993 (20 July 1993), 2 ('There is a lot of talk about us ... in terms of ethnic minorities, linguistic minorities and anything else that you can think of but the word PEOPLES. It is as if people have an allergic reaction to the word PEOPLES. They would rather call us something else than what we are ... We are Indigenous Peoples. We are not included in the Declaration on the Rights of Minorities because we are not minorities').

[2] The literature on the rights of indigenous peoples in international law is now massive. Among the most relevant general pieces, see SJ Anaya, *Indigenous Peoples in International Law* (2004); P Thornberry, *Indigenous Peoples and Human Rights* (2002); A Xanthaki, *Indigenous Rights and United Nations Standards: Self-determination, culture and land* (2007). A review on earlier literature is found in BK Roy and G Alfredsson, 'Indigenous rights: The literature explosion' (1987) 13(1) *Transnational Perspectives* 19–24.

[3] For a historical account of a distinct international legal regime regarding the rights of indigenous peoples, see R Barsh, 'Indigenous North America and contemporary international law' (1983) 62 Or L Rev 73; B Clavero, *Derecho indígena y cultura constitucional en América* (1994); R Niezen, *The Origins of Indigenism: Human rights and the politics of identity*(2003); L Rodríguez-Piñero, *Indigenous Peoples, Postcolonialism, and International Law: The ILO regime (1919-1989)* (2005).

[4] United Nations Declaration on the Rights of Indigenous Peoples, adopted by General Assembly resolution 61/295 of 17 September 2007 (hereinafter, UNDRIP).

[5] United Nations Declaration on the Rights of Persons Belonging to National or Ethnic, Religious, and Linguistic Minorities, adopted by General Assembly Resolution 47/135, 18 December 1992. Text available at <http://www.un-documents.net/a47r135.htm> (accessed 31 July 2009).

[6] B Kingsbury, Reconciling five competing conceptual structures of indigenous peoples' claims in international and comparative law (2001) 34(1) *New York University Journal of International Law and Politics* 189–250, 202–16.

indigenous peoples' rights-based claims. A much cited example is the ample jurisprudence developed by the Human Rights Committee under Art 27 of the International Covenant on Civil and Political Rights,[7] touching upon issues of indigenous land and recourse rights as well as participation in decision-making.[8] Both the European Council and the OSCE have taken a similar stand. The European Framework Convention for the Protection of National Minorities[9] does not refer specifically to the situation of indigenous peoples in Europe, ranging from the Sami people in the Nordic countries, to their fellow Sami and other 'small peoples' in the Russian Federation, from the Inuit population in Greenland to the Crimean Tatars in Ukraine. The Advisory Committee, responsible for the supervision of the convention by ratifying states, has taken the view that its provisions apply also to indigenous peoples, a position that has been contested in some countries.[10] Similarly, neither the OSCE standards on national minorities nor the mandate of the OSCE High Commissioner on National Minorities refer explicitly to indigenous peoples, but both the High Commissioner and the OSCE participating states have included the situation of indigenous peoples in the different activities carried out in the framework of the institution's mandate, particularly in countries such as Canada, the United States, the Russian Federation, or Ukraine.

The Lund Recommendations develop a set of standards to promote the effective participation in public and democratic life that are potentially applicable to all national minorities in all OSCE participating states. From a pragmatic approach à la Kingsbury, these standards may be useful to promote the effective participation of indigenous peoples as affirmed in the UNDRIP and other relevant international standards. As the coming sections will show, many of the policy suggestions included in the Lund Recommendations concerning specific state, legal, or institutional arrangements are particularly relevant to the

---

[7] See General Comment 23 on The Rights of Minorities (Art 27), CCPR/C/21/Rev1/Add5, 8 April 1994. Text available at <http://www.unhchr.ch/tbs/doc.nsf/0/fb7fb12c2fb8bb21c12563ed004df111?Opendocument> (accessed 31 July 2009).

[8] For a review of contentious cases dealing with indigenous peoples' lands rights under Art 27 of the ICCPR, see M Scheinin, 'The right to enjoy a distinct culture: Indigenous and competing uses of land' in TS Orlin and M Scheinin (eds), *The Jurisprudence of Human Rights: A comparative interpretative approach* (2000) (Scheinin was a key actor in promoting the Committee's interpretation of Art 27, first as a lawyer in Sami land cases and then as member of the Committee). See also D McGoldrick, 'Canadian Indians, cultural rights and the Human Rights Committee' (1991) 40 *International and Comparative Law Quarterly* 658–69.

[9] Framework Convention for the Protection of National Minorities, ETS no 154 (1 February 1995), entered into force on 1 February 1998, available at <http://conventions.coe.int/Treaty/EN/Treaties/Html/157.htm> (accessed 31 July 2009).

[10] Sami cultural rights in Finland and Sweden, including rights over lands and resources, are monitored by the Advisory Committee of the European Framework Convention for the Protection of National Minorities. See Second Opinion on Finland, ACFC/OP/II(2006)003, 20 April 2006, paras 55, 164; Second Opinion on Sweden, ACFC/OP/II(2007)006, 30 January 2008, paras 68, 178. The Sami people of Norway have taken the formal view that international minority instruments do not apply in their context.

situation of indigenous peoples in OSCE participating states and other parts of the world. Moreover, the comparative experience in the design and implementation of participatory mechanisms for indigenous peoples provides abundant empirical data to confirm the effectiveness of the kind of arrangements advocated by the Lund Recommendations in fostering the expressed objectives of 'inclusion of minorities within the State' while 'maintain[ing] their own identity and characteristics', simultaneously promoting 'the good governance and integrity of the State'.[11] Further, a reflection on the applicability and relevance of the Lund Recommendations for indigenous peoples in the context of relevant international standards and domestic practice may also bring to light some of the limitations or lacuna of these recommendations in the specific circumstances that these peoples face.

While couched in the distinctive conflict prevention language of the OSCE minority protection system, the Lund Recommendations built and elaborated upon existing international standards regarding equality, non-discrimination, and political participation of minority groups.[12] With the same rationale, this chapter starts by analysing the relevant international human rights standards and practice concerning indigenous peoples' right to participation. The chapter goes on to analyse concrete examples of legal or institutional arrangements aimed at promoting the effective participation of indigenous peoples in the countries in which they live, following the categorization coined in the Lund Recommendations. This includes both participation in decision-making and self-government or autonomy systems, where the comparative experiences in OSCE participating states and in other parts of the world provide numerous good practice guidelines. The chapter concludes with a number of reflections regarding the relevance of the Lund Recommendations in the context of indigenous peoples, pointing to a number of areas in which the recommendations, along with existing international minority rights standards, fail to include indigenous peoples' participatory concerns as a channel to prevent social conflicts.

II. International Standards Regarding Indigenous Peoples' Right to Participation

As other minority or marginalized groups in Europe, the Americas, and other parts of the world, indigenous peoples suffer from a chronic lack of access to and participation in the broader societal and institutional structures of the states in

---

[11] Lund Recommendations on the Effective Participation of National Minorities in Public Life, Foundation for Inter-ethnic Relations, (hereinafter, Lund Recommendations), Ch I: 'General principles', para 1. Text available at <http://www.osce.org/documents/hcnm/1999/09/2698_en.pdf> (accessed 31 July 2009). [12] Ibid, para 2.

which they live, where they often feel unrepresented in both pragmatic and symbolic terms. Indigenous peoples' lack of participation in state decision-making processes is inextricably connected to the historical patterns of forced incorporation and assimilation, which resulted in effective deprivation of their capacity to contribute to the constitutional make-up of the countries in which they live. As argued by S James Anaya, one of the conceptual founders of the modern indigenous rights regime, indigenous peoples' denial of their constitutive and ongoing self-determination is at the heart of indigenous peoples' modern demand for self-determination, self-government, and autonomy.[13]

A response to these demands, the UNDRIP is primordially a remedial instrument, seeking to repair 'the ongoing consequences of the historical denial of the right to self-determination and other basic human rights affirmed in international instruments of general applicability'.[14] Art 3 of the UNDRIP reproduces the self-determination clause common to the two UN International Covenants,[15] without prejudicing the principle of state territorial integrity.[16] The link between the overarching right to self-determination and indigenous peoples' right to participation is expressly reflected in the text of the Declaration in the following terms:

Indigenous peoples, in exercising their right to self-determination, have the right to autonomy or self-government in matters relating to their internal and local affairs, as well as ways and means for financing their autonomous functions.[17]

As distinct from other minority or majority groups, the affirmation of indigenous right to autonomy (a term used in the current discussion in Latin America) or self-government (a term more often used in English-speaking countries) is connected to the preservation and development of traditional systems of government and administration of justice, now affirmed in the UNDRIP and other international instruments. The Declaration thus asserts the rights of indigenous peoples to 'maintain and strengthen their distinct political, legal, economic, social and cultural institutions', and to their 'institutional structures [including] juridical systems or customs'.[18] Similar provisions regarding respect for and promotion of indigenous autonomous institutions,

---

[13] See Anaya, 'Indigenous peoples in international law' (n 2 above), Ch III: 'Self-determination: A foundational principle'.
[14] Promotion and Protection of All Human Rights, Civil, Political, Economic, Social and Cultural Rights, Including the Right to Development: Report of the Special Rapporteur on the Situation of Human Rights and Fundamental Freedoms of Indigenous People, SJ Anaya, UN Doc A/HRC/9/9 (11 August 2008), para 36.
[15] International Covenant on Civil and Political Rights, adopted and opened for signature, ratification and accession by General Assembly Resolution 2200A (XXI) of 16 December 1966, entered into force on 23 March 1976 (in accordance with Art 49), Art 1; International Covenant on Economic, Social and Cultural Rights (ICESCR), adopted and opened for signature, ratification and accession by General Assembly resolution 2200A (XXI) of 16 December 1966, entered into force on 3 January 1976 (in accordance with Art 27), Art 1.
[16] UNDRIP (n 4 above), Art 46.1.   [17] Ibid, Art 4.   [18] Ibid, Arts 5, 34.

including the administration of justice, are found in the International Labour Organization (ILO) Convention on Indigenous and Tribal Peoples in Independent Countries (Convention 169), to date the most advanced international instrument regarding indigenous rights with full binding force for states parties.[19]

The endorsement of self-government rights by the UNDRIP and Convention 169 is simultaneous to the affirmation of indigenous peoples' right to participate in the conduct of public affairs in the states in which they live. The UNDRIP underlines the voluntary character of this engagement—in remembrance of the historically enforced incorporation of indigenous peoples into state structures—affirming their 'right to participate fully, *if they so choose*, in the political, economic, social and cultural life of the State'.[20]

An idiosyncratic derivation of the affirmation of participatory rights within the international indigenous peoples' rights regime is the emphasis on their right to participate in, and to be consulted on, all decisions affecting them, particularly in relation to the planning and implementation of development projects in their traditional territories. The 'participation-consultation' principle, originally coined by ILO Convention 169,[21] is further enshrined in the UNDRIP, which additionally stresses the state obligation to obtain indigenous peoples' 'free, prior, and informed consent' (FPIC), at least in relation to state measures having a major impact on indigenous territories.[22] Yet another instance of the remedial character of the indigenous rights regime—the state's duty to consult indigenous peoples with a view to obtain their consent—is to be seen as an administrative procedural requirement stemming from the historical, widespread pattern of disregard to indigenous peoples' own wishes and priorities, particularly with regard to development activities implemented in their traditional territories.

---

[19] International Labour Organization (ILO) Convention on Indigenous and Tribal Peoples in Independent Countries, 1989 (no 169) adopted on 27 June 1989 by the General Conference of the ILO at its 76th session, entered into force on 5 September 1991 (hereinafter, ILO Convention 169), Art 4 ('[s]pecial measures shall be adopted as appropriate for safeguarding the ... institutions [and] cultures ... of the peoples concerned'); Art 6.1.b (governments shall 'establish means by which [indigenous peoples] can freely participate ... at all levels of decision-making in elective institutions'). [20] UNDRIP (n 4 above), Art 5 (emphasis added).

[21] ILO Convention 169 (n 19 above), Art 6.1.a (governments shall '[c]onsult the peoples concerned ... whenever consideration is given to legislative or administrative measures which may affect them directly'); Art 7(1) (indigenous peoples 'shall participate in the formulation, implementation and evaluation of plans and programmes for national and regional development which may affect them directly').

[22] UNDRIP (n 4 above), Art 19 ('States shall consult and cooperate in good faith with the indigenous peoples concerned through their own representative institutions *in order to obtain their free, prior and informed consent* before adopting and implementing legislative or administrative measures that may affect them') (emphasis added). The requirement of FPIC is restated, in compulsory terms, in relation to forced reallocation of indigenous communities, ibid, Art 10 ('No relocation shall take place without the free, prior and informed consent of the indigenous peoples concerned'); and disposal of hazardous waste in indigenous territories, ibid, Art 29.2 ('States shall take effective measures to ensure that no storage or disposal of hazardous materials shall take place in the lands or territories of indigenous peoples without their free, prior and informed consent').

The norm of indigenous participation, with its dual dimension of internal self-government and enhanced participation in state decision-making structures, along with the procedural requirements of consultation-participation and FPIC, has been reinforced and elaborated upon by a number of international human rights bodies and international standards and policies.[23] Of particular relevance in this regard is the jurisprudence of the Inter-American Court of Human Rights. In the case of *YATAMA v Nicaragua*, which will be discussed below, the Court recalled the state duty to adopt 'all necessary measures to ensure that [indigenous peoples] can participate, in equal conditions, in decision-making on matters and policies that affect or could affect their rights', while doing it 'within their own institutions and according to their values, practices, customs and forms of organization'.[24] The Court has further started to elaborate an advanced jurisprudence regarding the state duty to consult, and in some cases, to obtain the free, prior, and informed consent of indigenous communities whenever development projects have an impact on indigenous territories.[25]

---

[23] See, eg Committee on the Elimination of Racial Discrimination (CERD), General Recommendation XXIII: Indigenous Peoples, A/52/18, annex V (1997), reproduced in Compilation of General Comments and General Recommendations adopted by Human Rights Treaty Bodies, UN Doc HRI/GEN/1/Rev7 (2004) (hereinafter, UN Treaty Bodies Compilation), 215, para 4.d (calling upon States parties to 'ensure that members of indigenous peoples have equal rights in respect of effective participation in public life and that no decisions directly relating to their rights and interests are taken without their informed consent'); Human Rights Committee, General Comment 23: Art 27 (1994) reproduced in UN Treaty Bodies Compilation, above, 38, para 7 ('culture manifests itself in many forms, including a particular way of life associated with the use of land resources, especially in the case of indigenous peoples ... The enjoyment of those rights may require positive legal measures of protection and measures to ensure the effective participation of members of minority communities in decisions which affect them'); Proposed American Declaration on the Rights of Indigenous Peoples, adopted by the Inter-American Commission on Human Rights on 26 February 1997, at its 1333rd session, 95th Regular Session, OAS Doc CP/doc2878/97corr1, with amendments as per Record of the Current Status of the Draft American Declaration on the Rights of Indigenous Peoples, 11th Meeting of Negotiations in the Quest for Consensus (United States, Washington DC, 14–18 April 2008), OEA/SerK/XVI, GT/DADIN/doc334/08 rev 3 (30 December 2008), Art XX (right to [autonomy] or [and] self-government); Art XXI (indigenous law and jurisdiction); Art XXII ('contributions' of the indigenous legal and organizational systems).

[24] *YATAMA v Nicaragua* (Preliminary Objections, Merits, Reparations and Costs) I/A Court HR, Judgment of 23 June 2005, Series C no 127 (hereafter *YATAMA v Nicaragua*), para 225. An excellent commentary on the Inter-American Court's decision in this case is found in MS Campbell, 'The rights of indigenous peoples to political participation and the case of YATAMA v Nicaragua' (2007) 24(2) *Arizona Journal of International and Comparative Law* 499–541. See also L González Volio, 'Los pueblos indígenas y el ejercicio de los derechos políticos de acuerdo a la Convención Americana: El Caso Yatama contra Nicaragua' (2005) 41 *Revista Instituto Interamericano de Derechos Humanos* 318–45; V Toldeo Llancaqueo, 'El derecho a la participación política. Reforma al sistema electoral: ¿y los pueblos indígenas?' (2006) 21 *Documentos de Políticas Públicas y Derechos Indígenas*.

[25] *Saramaka People v Suriname* (Preliminary Objections, Merits, Reparations, and Costs) I/A Court HR, Judgment of 28 November 2007, Series C no 172 (hereafter *Saramaka v Suriname*).

III. Indigenous Peoples' Participation in Decision-making

The assertion of a reinforced right to participation for indigenous peoples has led to the development of a number of affirmative action mechanisms to ensure the effective participation of these peoples in the wider global political or societal structures in the countries in which they live. These mechanisms, which are comparable to consocational structures in other multicultural contexts, vary in their degree of effectiveness, and they are often plagued with flaws. However, they represent a significant domestication of the international norm of indigenous participation, which coexist with formal or informal self-government arrangements.

A. Arrangements at the level of the central government

The Lund Recommendations submit a number of specific policy proposals regarding the participatory inclusion of minority groups at the level of central government institutions. Comparative state practice shows plenty of examples of specific arrangements aimed at fulfilling this objective with regard to indigenous peoples, with an ultimate view to remedying, at least partially, the historical underrepresentation in decision-making processes at this level.

One example of this kind of arrangement is the special representation of indigenous peoples through the legislative process by virtue of special parliamentary seats reserved to indigenous representatives. A particularly innovative experience in this regard is the case of New Zealand/Aotearoa, where, since 1867, voters of Maori descent may chose between registering at the general electoral census or registering at a special Maori census.[26] In the second case, they are entitled to elect Maori representatives for a number of special seats in parliament. While this system originated in the colonial system introduced by European settlers—where the vast majority of Maori were not entitled to vote on the general electoral roll[27]—the system has historically evolved as a powerful tool for advancing Maori interests at the level of central government. According to the new proportional system introduced in the 1996 national elections, the boundaries of Maori districts match up with those of the general electoral systems and both elections are held simultaneously.[28] This new system has resulted in an increase in the number of Maori special seats over the last decade.[29]

---

[26] For an overview of the New Zealand electoral system regarding the participation of the Maori population, see CI Magallanes, 'Dedicated parliamentary seats for indigenous peoples: Political representation as an element of indigenous self-determination' (2003) 10(4) *E-Law*, available at <http://www.murdoch.edu.au/elaw/issues/v10n4/iorns104.html> (accessed 31 July 2009). See also R Maaka and A Fleras, 'Engaging with indigeneity: Tino Rangatiratanga in Aotearoa' in D Ivison and D Sanders (eds), *Political Theory and the Rights of Indigenous Peoples* (2000).
[27] Magallanes, 'Dedicated parliamentary seats' (n 26 above), para 17.   [28] Ibid, para 38.
[29] A Reynolds, *Electoral Systems and the Protection and Participation of Minorities* (2008), 14.

A similar system of indigenous representation was introduced early in the nineteenth century in the state of Maine (USA). The Constitution of Maine foresees the participation of two indigenous delegates at the legislature. These delegates represent the two major Indian nations of the state, but do not take part in the voting procedure. With this important limitation, it is a system that is now seen to correspond to the government-to-government relation between the US and Indian nations, coupled with the affirmation of tribal sovereignty.[30]

Another classic example is the quota system operating in India since independence. The 1949 Constitution reserves 20 per cent of parliamentary seats in the *Lok Sabha* to minority groups that experienced historical marginalization and discrimination, including both scheduled castes (*Dalits*) and scheduled tribes (*Adivasis*).[31] These special seats are assigned proportionally according to the relative demographic weight of these groups in the different states. The quota system is replicated by state legislatures.[32]

Similar arrangements have been developed in Latin America in the wave of constitutional reform processes in the last two decades aiming at the affirmation of indigenous rights, within the context of a new paradigm of 'multicultural constitutionalism'.[33] The 1991 Colombian Constitution, which affirms the 'multicultural character of the Colombian nation', established for the first time a quota system with a number of two special Senate seats reserved for indigenous representatives, known as 'indigenous circumscription'.[34] Candidates for these special seats must evidence proof of recognized authority, either by having exercised positions of traditional authority within their own communities or as leaders of indigenous organizations. Five seats of the Chamber of Representatives are also assigned by the Constitution to 'ethnic groups and political minorities', of which one is assigned to an indigenous representative.[35] A similar quota system was instituted in Venezuela by the 1999 Bolivian Constitution, which guarantees 'indigenous representation in the National Assembly and in the deliberative bodies in federal and local entities with indigenous population'.[36] The 'indigenous circumscription' is divided into three electoral regions, each of which is assigned one representative at the National Assembly.[37]

---

[30] Iorns, 'Dedicated parliamentary seats' (n 26 above), para 35.
[31] Constitution of India (26 November 1949), as amended by the Constitution (94th Amendment) Act, 2006, Art 33. On the experience of the Indian reserved parliamentary seats system for Dalits and Adivasis, see Y Ghai, *Public Participation and Minorities* (2003), 15–16.
[32] Constitution of India (n 31 above), Art 332.
[33] The expression 'multicultural constitutionalism' in the context of Latin American constitutional reform process in the 1990s comes from DL Van Cott, *The Friendly Liquidation of the Past: The politics of diversity in Latin America* (2000). For insightful analyses of Latin American recent constitutions with regard to the rights of indigenous peoples, see B Clavero, *Geografía Jurídica de América Latina* (2008); R Sieder (ed), *Multiculturalism in Latin America: Indigenous rights, diversity and democracy* (2002). [34] Political Constitution of Colombia, 6 July 1991, Art 171.
[35] Ibid, Art 176. [36] Bolivarian Constitution of Venezuela, 20 December 1999, Art 125.
[37] Ibid, Transitional Provision 7; Organic Law on the Electoral System, *Gaceta Oficial* 37/573, 19 November 2002, Art 8.

A similar model for enhanced indigenous representation at the national legislatures has also been discussed in Chile, where the establishment of an 'indigenous electoral system' has been proposed as part of the wider reform of the country's binominal electoral system.[38] Likewise, proposals for special seats have been discussed in New South Wales and Queensland in Australia as part of the wider policy initiatives to counter Aboriginal under-representation in political life.[39]

Together with the establishment of special seats in the legislative assemblies, other institutional arrangements to ensure the political participation of indigenous peoples at the central government level entail the involvement of indigenous authorities in judicial decision-making. The involvement of indigenous elders as 'expert witnesses' in order to document issues related to indigenous cultural heritage, land ownership or indigenous customary legal systems is now widespread in countries such as Australia, Canada, Colombia, or Mexico, sometimes dubiously mixed with anthropological expert witnesses.[40]

A step further is the actual inclusion of indigenous authorities in formal judicial institutions responsible for decision-making in areas directly touching upon indigenous rights and interests. A classic example is the Waitangi Tribunal in New Zealand/Aotearoa. Established in 1975, the Tribunal is responsible for interpreting the provisions of the 1860 Treaty between the British Crown and the Maori.[41] Its composition is mixed, including an approximately equal number of Maori and Pākehā (people of European descent). While it does not have powers to settle issues of law, the Tribunal issues recommendations to the Crown and claimants, and it has 'exclusive authority' to interpret the provisions of the Waitangi Treaty.[42]

The last event in the chain of constitutional reform processes in Latin American—the Bolivian Constitution, adopted by referendum in January 2009—goes one step further with a comprehensive reform of all branches of government with a view to promoting indigenous peoples' representation at the highest levels. One of the most advanced aspects of this reform is the

---

[38] See Government of Chile, *Pacto Social por la Multiculturalidad* (1 April 2008), Tit III: 'Plan de Acción y condiciones para su puesta en marcha', Art 1.1. In announcing this proposal, President Bachelet stated, 'We want indigenous representatives in the Parliament'. Daniela Estrada, 'Chile: Bachelet unveils new indigenous policy,' *Inter Press Service*, 2 April 2008.

[39] See Iorns, 'Dedicated parliamentary seats' (n 26 above), paras 45–71.

[40] See Y Betancourt, *La experiencia del peritaje antropológico* (2002).

[41] Treaty of Waitangi/*Te Tiriti o Waintangi* (6 Februrary 1840), reproduced in Sch 1 of the Treaty of Waitangi Act, 1975, no 114 (10 October 1975), last amended by the Treaty of Waitangi Amendment Act 2008 (2008 no 34).

[42] Ibid, s 5.2. On modern settlements lead by the Tribunal of Waitangi, see C Charters, *Report on the Treaty of Waitangi 1840 Between Maori and the British Crown*, Background Paper presented for the Expert Seminar on Treaties, Agreements and Other Constructive Arrangements between States and Indigenous Peoples, Geneva, 15–17 December 2003, organized by the Office of the United Nations High Commissioner for Human Rights, UN Doc HR/GENEVA/TSIP/SEM/2003/BP15 (2003).

establishment of a 'Plurinational Constitutional Court' ('*Tribunal Constitucional Plurinacional*'), responsible for exercising control over the constitutionality and the safeguard of constitutional rights.[43] Indigenous judges can serve as members of the court, and the experience of serving as an authority in the indigenous judicial systems is actually one of the criteria for appointment to the court.

B. Elections

Historically, indigenous peoples have seen their rights denied by the simple mechanism of depriving them of citizenship in the state structures built around their traditional territories. The liberal republics that followed centuries of Iberian or British colonialism, crafted various legal devices to deprive indigenous peoples and other subdued social groups from enjoying basic citizenship rights, including the right to elect and to be elected through the ballot. While formal denial of citizenship continued until recently in some countries—as recent as 1962, in the case of Australia[44]—in other countries the formal requirements for exercising the right to vote, mostly literacy requirements or the ability to express oneself in the 'national language', as in Latin America, actually operated as an exclusion test for indigenous communities and individuals.[45]

The gradual extension of universal adult suffrage to indigenous peoples throughout the twentieth century did not however prove to be a definitive solution to ensuring indigenous peoples' effective participation in electoral politics. One of the most outstanding barriers to indigenous peoples' effective electoral participation is the political party system in the countries in which they live. While the Lund Recommendations advocate a formula based on freedom of association, including 'the freedom to establish political parties based on communal identities',[46] this formula has often proven limited in channelling indigenous peoples' demands, entering into conflict with indigenous forms of social organizations. Recent experiences in countries such as Ecuador, Chile, and Guatemala, in which indigenous candidates ran in the presidential elections with only meagre results, or in Peru, Argentina, or Mexico, in which indigenous political parties unsuccessfully attempted to win local elections, constitute important reminders.[47]

A case in point in this regard is the judgment of the Inter-American Court on Human Rights in the *YATAMA v Nicaragua* case. In this case, the

---

[43] Political Constitution of Bolivia, 25 January 2009, Arts 196–204.
[44] Gay, *Public Participation and Minorities* (n 21 above), 10.
[45] For the specific case of Peru, see B Clavero, 'Estado pluricultural, orden internacional, ciudadanía poscolonial: Elecciones constitucionales en el Perú' (2001) 114 *Revista de Estudios Políticos* 11–40, 20–5.
[46] Lund Recommendations (n 11 above), Ch II: 'Participation in decision-making', para 8.
[47] For a wider analysis of the interaction between indigenous peoples and political party systems, see S Martí (ed), *Pueblos indígenas y política en América Latina* (2007); K Wessendorf (ed), *Challenging Politics: Indigenous peoples experiences with political parties and elections* (2001).

Inter-American Court had to adjudicate the claim put forward by the indigenous political party YATAMA (Miskitu acronym for 'Children of the Modern Earth United') against the regulations passed by the Nicaraguan central government which resulted in preventing YATAMA from participating in the 2000 local elections. The Court found that Nicaraguan electoral law, by imposing the requirement of participation exclusively through political parties,[48] excluding electoral associations—a possibility previously afforded to YATAMA and other indigenous organizations—constituted an undue restriction of indigenous peoples' right to participate in public life. According to the Court, the requirement that candidates running for local elections should be affiliated to political parties was:

[an] undue limitation of the exercise of a political right, entailing an unnecessary restriction of the right to be elected, taking into account the circumstances of the instant case, which are not necessarily comparable to the circumstances of all political groups that may be present in other national societies or sectors of a national society.[49]

The Court went further to provide an open defence of special mechanisms to ensure and encourage the political participation of indigenous peoples and other groups:

There is no provision in the American Convention that allows it to be established that citizens can only exercise the right to stand as candidates to elected office through a political party. The importance of political parties as essential forms of association for the development and strengthening of democracy are not discounted, but it is recognized that there are other ways in which candidates can be proposed for elected office in order to achieve the same goal, when this is pertinent and even necessary to encourage or ensure the political participation of specific groups of society, taking into account their special traditions and administrative systems, whose legitimacy has been recognized and is even subject to the explicit protection of the State. Indeed, the Inter-American Democratic Charter states that '[t]he strengthening of political parties *and other political organizations* is a priority for democracy'.[50]

The Inter-American Court's decision in *YATAMA* reflects a recent trend of legal and institutional reform in Latin American countries that seeks to promote the participation of indigenous organizations in national elections by recognizing electoral subscription groups. The trend was initiated in the mid-1990s with the adoption of the Law of Popular Participation and the reform of the land administration regime in Bolivia,[51] which instituted the territorial grassroots

---

[48] Electoral Law no 331 (19 January 2000), *La Gaceta Diario Oficial*, no 16, amended by the Law of Additions to Art 3 of Law 331, Electoral Law 659, *La Gaceta Diario Oficial* 131, Art 77.
[49] *YATAMA v Nicaragua* (n 24 above), para 129.
[50] Ibid, para 125 (citing Art 5 of the Inter-American Democratic Charter, adopted by the OAS General Assembly in Lima on 11 September 2001). Footnotes omitted. Emphasis added.
[51] Popular Participation Law no 1551 (20 April 1994), Gaceta Oficial 1828, as amended by the Popular Participation Law (Amendments and Additions to Law no 1551), 1702, Gaceta Oficial 1945.

organizations *(organizations territoriales de base)* and the surveillance committees *(comités de vigilancia)* as an alternative to political parties in local affairs.[52] The new Bolivian Constitution now affirms the same status to 'indigenous aboriginal *peasant* organizations'—a complex denomination that reflects the various indigenous identities in the country—'citizen associations', and political parties in order to present candidates to all public elections.[53] Similarly, the 1996 and 1998 constitutional amendments in Ecuador allowed for the participation of candidates not affiliated to political parties, while the 1997 Special State Decentralization and Social Participation Law of 1997 allowed for the participation of indigenous organizations in municipal bodies.[54] The new Constitution of Ecuador, adopted in 2008, grants similar status to political parties and 'political movements',[55] an implicit reference to the major role played by the indigenous movement *Pachacuti* in the country's political life during the last decade.

The *YATAMA* decision is also particularly relevant to the issue of facilitating access to indigenous minority groups to political representation through the redefinition of the electoral system. In this case, YATAMA was prevented from participating in the Nicaraguan local elections, in part, due to the reform of the electoral law promoted by the Nicaraguan central government—in collusion with the major opposition party at the national level. Through an exercise of electoral engineering, the new electoral law incorporated the new requirement that all political parties running for the local elections had to ensure delegates into 80 per cent of the municipalities of the territorial district.[56] Provided that the Miskitu population in Nicaragua—YATAMA's main electoral base—is found predominantly on the Northern Caribbean region (RAAN), YATAMA was eventually unable to meet the requirements introduced by the new electoral system in the Southern Region (RAAS). In its final decision in this case, the Court found that the requirement of the electoral law constituted a 'disproportionate restriction that limited unduly the political participation of the candidates proposed by YATAMA for the municipal elections', failing to take into account that the 'indigenous and ethnic population is a minority in the RAAS'.[57] This requirement, in the Court's opinion, constituted an act of 'legal

---

[52] On the early experience of the Law of Popular Participation in Bolivia, see R Calla, 'Ley de Participación Popular y cambios de gobierno en Bolivia (1994–8); René Orellana, 'Municipalización de pueblos indígenas en Bolivia' in W Assies, G van de Haar and A Hoekema (eds), *El reto de la diversidad. Pueblos indígenas y reforma del Estado en América Latina*. Zamora (Mex, El Colegio de Michoacán, 1999), 149, 326; Campbell, 'The rights of indigenous peoples to political participation' (n 24 above), 532. [53] Political Constitution of Bolivia (n 43 above), Art 208.
[54] Special State Decentralization and Social Participation Law 27 (8 October 1997), Art 42 (Ecuador), cited in Campbell, 'The rights of indigenous peoples to political participation' (n 24 above), 533. [55] Political Constitution of Ecuador (28 September 2008), Arts 109–12.
[56] Electoral Law no 331 (n 48 above), Art 82.
[57] *YATAMA v Nicaragua* (n 24 above), para 223.

and real' discrimination against those communities,[58] ordering the reform of that regulation from the electoral law.[59]

While not yet fully implemented—a new electoral law still awaits adoption by the Nicaraguan National Assembly—the standard set forth in the Inter-American Court's *YATAMA* decision with regard to the exercise of the right of political participation in the context of indigenous peoples is a good example of the kind of arrangements that can facilitate minority representation and influence through the electoral system.[60] These arrangements include the redefinition of electoral districts in order to foster the effective participation of indigenous groups, a formula which has only become feasible in countries in which indigenous peoples represent a considerable percentage of the general population. For instance, the Bolivian Popular Participation Law of 1994 Bolivia fostered the establishment of new municipalities in indigenous-populated areas, a measure which allowed for indigenous organizations to gain control over local governments in areas where they had been previously excluded, particularly in the low lands of the Amazon and Chaco regions.[61] The new Constitution of Bolivia similarly foresees the establishment of a number of 'special *peasant* indigenous aboriginal circumscriptions' in areas in which indigenous peoples represent a demographic minority, yet to be established by the electoral legislation.[62] In Ecuador, the issue was also the subject of discussions at the recent constitution-making process, leading to an initial agreement to establish a new proportional system and a revision of existing electoral circumscriptions.[63]

However, experiences of redistricting to facilitate indigenous representation have not been always successful. Leaving aside the case of New Zealand, discussed above, in which Maori electoral districts are connected to a special representation system at the central government level,[64] in other cases indigenous representation has not been actually enhanced. In the case of Mexico, for instance, a 2006 reform of the electoral system established twenty-eight uninominal districts in indigenous-populated areas. However, the reform did not significantly alter the existing distribution of power among local political parties, mostly because of the failure of these parties to include indigenous persons in their candidate lists.[65] In this connection, another arrangement to ensure the

---

[58] Ibid, para 224.   [59] Ibid, para 275.11.
[60] Lund Recommendations (n 11 above), Ch II: 'Participation in decision-making', para 9.
[61] Nn 51–2 above and accompanying text.
[62] Political Constitution of Bolivia (n 43 above), Art 146.7.
[63] Political Constitution of Ecuador (n 55 above), Art 117 ('[T]he Law shall establish an electoral system based on the principles of proportionality, equality of vote, equity, parity, and alternation between women and men, and shall determine the electoral circumscriptions within and outside the country'—unofficial translation).
[64] (Nn 26–9 above) and accompanying text.
[65] JA González Galván, 'La redistictación electoral y la participación política de los pueblos indígenas en México: Balances y Perspectivas (2006-2009)' (2008) XLI (121) *Boletín Mexicano de Derecho Comparado* 173.

representation of indigenous peoples through the ballot is the quota system. A model case in this regard is Peru, where the reforms to the regional and local electoral laws introduced the requirement that the list of candidates proposed by political parties for those elections should include at least 15 per cent of members of the 'native communities and aboriginal populations' in the respective region or province.[66] Indigenous organizations of that country are now demanding the establishment of a similar quota system for the national elections, aiming at countering the historical under-representation of indigenous peoples at the central government level.[67]

C. Arrangements at the regional and local levels

Other than in relation to the *YATAMA* case, Nicaragua is also a particularly interesting example with regard to the establishment of mechanisms to promote the participation of indigenous peoples at the regional or local levels of government. A product of a bitter civil war that brought the Sandinista regime into conflict with an indigenous guerrilla in the country's Atlantic coast, the Nicaraguan 1987 Constitution established a mechanism of regional autonomy for the coast, divided into two autonomous regions (North and South). The Nicaraguan system is not a system of indigenous self-government as such, insofar as the autonomous bodies are based on a proportional system of representation in an area which is characterized by its multicultural make-up, with a significant indigenous population (Miskitu, Mayangna, and Rama), a no less significant community of people of African descent, and a blooming demographic majority of *Mestizos* of Hispanic descent.[68] However, in order to ensure the representation of each community in the regional autonomous bodies, the Nicaraguan Autonomy Law prescribes the representation of at least one representative of all indigenous or ethnic communities in the respective autonomous region.[69]

Various systems of indigenous representation at the local or municipal level started to appear in Latin America following the 'multicultural' constitutional reforms of the 1990s. A path-breaking reform of the electoral law of the

---

[66] Municipal Election Law 2684, 26 September 1997, Art 10, amended by Law 27734, 28 May 2002, Art 103; Regional Election Law 27683, 14 March 2002, Art 12, cited by Campbell, 'Indigenous peoples' rights to political participation' (n 24 above), 538.

[67] M Salazar, 'Peru: Indigenous organizations aim for the presidency' *International Press Service*, 29 May 2008.

[68] Autonomy Statute of the Two Regions of the Atlantic Coast of Nicaragua, Law 28, 2 September 1987, *La Gaceta Diario Oficial* 238. On the regional system of autonomy in the Nicaraguan Atlantic Coast, see ML Acosta, *Los derechos de las comunidades y pueblos indígenas de la Costa Atlántica en la Constitución política de Nicaragua* (1996); H Díaz Polanco, *Autonomía regional: La autodeterminación de los pueblos indios* (1996), 189–201; M González, *Gobiernos Pluriétnicos: La Constitución de las Regiones Autónomas en la Costa Atlántica de Nicaragua* (1996); J Mattern, *Autonomía Regional en Nicaragua: una aproximación descriptiva*(2003).

[69] Autonomy Statute (n 68 above), Art 19.

Mexican State of Oaxaca, in the mid-1990s, allowed for a system of 'uses and customs' (*usos y costumbres*) in running local elections in municipalities where the indigenous population represent the majority population.[70] The system, praised by indigenous rights advocates and condemned by liberal commentators, was seen by the Inter-American Commission on Human Rights as 'consistent with political pluralism, the right to participation, and freedom of expression'.[71] In 2007, 418 of the 570 municipalities opted for the 'uses and customs' system, thereby demonstrating the strength of that system.[72] While not fully adhering to the Oaxaca model, other Mexican states have introduced reforms into their legal systems to ensure the participation of indigenous representatives in local elected bodies.[73]

Other leading examples are the Bolivian Popular Participation Law of 1994 and the Ecuadorian Special State Decentralization and Social Participation Law of 1997, already mentioned. Both laws granted special access to indigenous communal organizations to decision-making in local bodies in order to ensure that their views were duly taken into account, particularly in decisions concerning local development.[74] Bolivia has now formalized this mechanism in its new constitutional text.[75] Venezuela similarly opened a 'double path' for ensuring indigenous peoples' representation at the municipal level, allowing both for the constitution of 'indigenous municipalities' and for the special representation of indigenous communities where they represent a demographic minority.[76]

---

[70] Code of Political Institutions and Electoral Procedures of the State of Oaxaca, Decree no 185 (12 February 1992), amended by Decree 203, 1 October 1997, by Decree 205, 9 October 1997, and last amended by Decree 723, 31 October 2008, Arts 131–43. The last amendment of the code shifted the terminology of the special indigenous municipal regime from 'uses and customs' (*usos y costumbres*) to 'customary law' (*derecho consuetudinario*). A text of reference on this system is MC Velázquez Cepeda, *El nombramiento. Las elecciones por usos y costumbres en Oaxaca* (2000).

[71] Inter-American Commission on Human Rights, *Informe sobre la situación de los derechos humanos en México*, OAS Doc OEA/SerL/V/II100, doc 7 rev 1 (1998), para 518. Cited in Campbell, 'The rights of indigenous peoples to political participation' (n 24 above), 539.

[72] See <http://www.usosycostumbres.org/2007.html> (accessed 31 July 2009).

[73] Political Constitution of the State of San Luis Potosí, as amended, 15 August 2006, Article 9 (IX) ('Indigenous communities will elect and designate their representatives ... before municipal bodies ... in accordance with their normative systems and forms of community organization'); Political Constitution of the Free and Sovereign State of Durango, as amended, 26 November 2000, Article 2(A)(VII) ('This Constitution recognizes and guarantees the indigenous peoples and communities ... the autonomy to ... elect, in the municipalities with indigenous populations, representatives before the municipal bodies ... in accordance with their traditions and internal norms'). Cited in Campbell, 'The right of indigenous peoples to political participation' (n 21 above), 538 (unofficial translation). [74] See nn 51–5 above, and accompanying text.

[75] The new Bolivian Constitution stipulates that the local indigenous groups that are not constituted into formal indigenous autonomies may elect members of their respective Municipal Councils 'directly [and] in accordance with their own norms and procedures'. Political Constitution of Bolivia (n 43 above), Art 284.2.

[76] Organic Law of Public Municipal Power, 8 June 2005, *Gaceta Oficial* 38.204, Arts 67, 279.

D. Advisory and consultative bodies and mechanisms

The Lund Recommendations propose the establishment of advisory or consultative bodies as potential 'channels for dialogue between governmental authorities and national minorities' which may 'contribute to more effective communication and advancement of minority interests'.[77] In the context of the international regime on indigenous peoples, as affirmed in the UNDRIP, ILO Convention 169, and other relevant legal and policy instruments, consultation is seen as a distinct right belonging collectively to indigenous peoples, and as a corresponding state duty, in relation to all administrative or legislative measures affecting them.[78]

Implementation of the duty to consult indigenous peoples has lead to the establishment of consultative bodies in a number of countries with the participation of indigenous representatives. Many of these bodies are set up at the central government level and are associated with government agencies responsible for indigenous affairs, and they represent indigenous communities' interests and provide technical advice in relation to general policies affecting indigenous peoples, particularly in relation to the design of social or welfare services. One of the first consultative bodies in Latin America, expressly connected to the exercise of indigenous peoples' right to consultation, was the Chilean National Commission on Indigenous Development (CONADI), established by the 1993 Indigenous Law;[79] new proposals are now in place to turn this Commission into a 'Council of Indigenous Peoples', responsible for centralizing consultation procedures in relation to all state measures impacting on the indigenous peoples of the country.[80] Other Latin American countries have followed suit, including among others, the Consultative Council associated with the National Commission on Indigenous Development (CDI) in Mexico,[81] and the Council for Indigenous Participation, associated to the National Institute for Indigenous Affairs (INAI) in Argentina.[82] Similar

---

[77] Lund Recommendations (n 11 above), para 11.
[78] See nn 21–2 above, and accompanying text.
[79] Law 19253 establishing norms for the protection, promotion and development of indigenous peoples and creating the National Commission on Indigenous Development (Indigenous Law), *Diario Oficial* 34683, amended by Law 19587, modifying Law 19253, regarding the constitution of the dominion in the Easter Island for the members of the Rapa Nui community, 13 November 1993, *Diario Oficial* 36213.
[80] Comisionado Presidencial para Asuntos Indígenas, *Minuta de posición sobre los contenidos de la propuesta de proyecto de ley que crea el Consejo de Pueblos Indígenas*, 7 January 2009.
[81] Law of the National Commission for the Development of Indigenous Peoples, *Diario Oficial de la Federación* 21 May 2003, Arts 5, 11–12.
[82] Law 23302 on Indigenous Policy and Support to Aboriginal Communities, 30 September 1985, amended by Law 25.799, 5 November 2003, Art 5; Resolution of the National Institute for Indigenous Affairs (INAI) 152/2004, establishing the Council for Indigenous Participation, amended by Decree 301/04.

mechanisms are now under discussion in countries such as Costa Rica[83] and Peru.[84]

In the Asia-Pacific region, the Australian Aboriginal and Torres Strait Islander Commission (ATSIC), in operation from 1990 to 2005, represented an innovative attempt to centralize consultation to and advice from indigenous peoples in relation to national policies and legislation. The ATSIC was an elected body representing a mixed constituency of Aboriginal communities in Australian mainland and Tasmania, and Torres Strait Islanders.[85] After successive scandals of financial corruption and mismanagement, the ATSIC was formally disbanded by the Howard government and its functions attributed to a new governmental body, the Office of Indigenous Affairs, which is now in the process of establishing a new National Indigenous Representative Body.[86]

In the Philippines, the National Commission on Indigenous Peoples is advised by ad hoc consultative bodies integrated by 'traditional elders, elders and representatives from the women and youth sectors' in issues pertaining to the implementation of the Indigenous Law.[87] A step further is represented by the consultative mechanism established in the National Foundation for Indigenous Development of Nepal (NFDIN), in Nepal. NFIDN, the maximum governmental body responsible for the coordination of policies specifically targeted at indigenous 'nationalities' (*Adivasi Janjati*), is governed by an interesting institutional arrangement that allows for the participation of representatives of the main indigenous organization of the country, the Nepal Federation of Indigenous Nationalities. According to the NFIDN Act, four out of five members of the Foundation's Executive Committee, and eighty-two out of the ninety-two members of its Council, should belong to indigenous communities.[88]

The establishment of this kind of indigenous consultative body at the central government level, while commendable in terms of implementing the state duty to consult in relation to general legislation and policies, has nonetheless given rise to many problems in practice. Representation in these bodies is a constant

---

[83] Draft Law of Autonomous Indigenous Development, File no 12,302, *La Gaceta* 222, 22 November 1994.
[84] Draft Law establishing the Permanent Table of Negotiation with Native Communities and Aboriginal Peoples, File 02767/2008-CR, introduced on 9 October 2008.
[85] Aboriginal and Torres Strait Islander Act (ATSIC), 1989, 150, 27 November 1990, Act Compilation (superseded)–C2004C00150. On the establishment and functioning of the ATSIC, see W Sanders, 'Towards an indigenous order of Australian government: Rethinking self-determination as indigenous affairs policy', *Centre for Aboriginal Economic Research Discussion Paper* 230 (2002).
[86] See *Building a Sustainable National Indigenous Representative Body: Issues for consideration*, Issue Paper prepared by the Aboriginal and Torres Strait Islander Social Justice Commissioner, in accordance with s 46C.1.b of the Human Rights and Equal Opportunity Commission Act 1986 (Cth), July 2008.
[87] Indigenous Peoples Right Act of 1997, Republic Act no 8371, 28 July 1997, S no 1728, H no 9125, s 50.
[88] National Foundation for Development of Nationalities Act, 2058 BS (2002), Arts 7, 10.

object of dissent, and, in the absence of accountability mechanisms, indigenous representatives in these bodies are subject to patrimonialist dynamics, particularly in relation to the allocation of development resources. The scope of their mandate is also subject to controversy, with the tendency, as shown in the case of Chile, to cover processes of consultation regarding specific development projects at the community level, in detriment of the rights pertaining to the communities concerned.[89]

While the number of consultative or advisory bodies with a general mandate regarding indigenous issues is still limited, consultative mechanisms regarding specific policy sectors are more widespread, and, not without limitations, they have proved more effective in putting indigenous peoples' interests on central or regional governments' agendas. A particularly relevant model in this regard is that of the United States, where, since 1994, all federal departments and agencies are instructed to consult with tribal governments 'prior to taking actions that have substantial direct effects on federally recognized tribal governments'.[90] Under this framework, the Bureau of Indian Affairs (BIA) developed a general 'Government to Government Consultation Policy' in 2000,[91] and other relevant federal government ministries and agencies have adopted their own consultation procedures and guidelines.[92]

In other instances, specific consultative mechanisms or procedures have been set up in relation to areas of specific concern for indigenous peoples' rights and interests. One of these key areas is the allocation of land and natural resources. For example, Nicaragua established a system of representation within the

---

[89] See Open letter from the Consejo Nacional Aymara de Mallkus y T'allas and other eight indigenous organizations to Michelle Bachelet, President of Chile, 17 February 2009, available at <http://www.mapuexpress.net/> (accessed 31 July 2009) (criticizing that the proposal to establish a National Council of Indigenous Peoples as 'another bureaucratic body, subordinated to State structures, aiming at reaching endorsements and vitiated consultations, and which supersedes existing Councils that are recognized by our Respective Peoples') (author's translation).

[90] Presidential memorandum for the Heads of Executive Departments and Agencies regarding Government-to-Government relations with Native American Tribal Governments (29 April 1994), 59 *Fed Reg* 22951 (4 May 1994). The main directives of the 1994 Memorandum were extended by Executive Order no 13175: Consultation and Coordination with Indian Tribal Government, 65 *Fed Reg* 67249 (6 November 2000); Executive Order no 13096: American Indian and Alaska Native Education, 63 *Fed Reg* 4268 (6 August 1998); Presidential memorandum for the Heads of Executive Departments and Agencies: Government-to-Government Relationship with Tribal Governments (23 September 2004). Executive Order no 13336: American Indian and Alaska Native Education (30 April 2004); Executive Order no 13084: Consultation and Coordination with Indian Tribal Governments, 63 *Fed Reg* 27655 (14 April 1998).

[91] Bureau of Indian Affairs, Government-to-Government Consultation Policy (13 December 2000).

[92] See, among others, Bureau of Land Management, General Procedural Guidance for Native American Consultation, H-8160-1, 3 November 1994; United States Fish and Wildlife Service, Native American Policy, 28 June 1994; Environmental Protection Agency (EPA), Memorandum to all EPA Employees Reaffirming Indian Policy, 11 July 2001; Department of Housing and Urban Development (HUD), Government-to-Government Tribal Consultation Policy, 28 June 2001; Department of Energy, American Indian and Alaska Native Policy, 21 August 2001.

National Commission on Demarcation and Titling (CONADETI) and regional bodies responsible for the implementation of the Communal Land Act.[93] In New Zealand, the Maori Land Court (*Te Kooti Whenua Maori*), integrated by Maori judges, has jurisdiction over the allocation, management, and preservation of existing Maori lands, applying Maori law to solve internal disputes.[94] Following a similar arrangement, the Treaty of Waintangi Fisheries Commission (*Te Ohu Kai Moana*) is responsible for the allocation of fisheries assets resulting from the Maori fisheries settlement (1989–92), which allots to local Maori groups a percentage of the fishery industry in the country.[95] In Australia, a complex network of Native Title Representative Bodies and Land Councils is in operation, both at the federal and at the state or territory level, with various powers in relation to land allocation, management and development, although their level of representativeness is contested.[96]

Another area where indigenous consultative bodies have proven particularly successful is in the design of policies related to local development and social welfare services. In Australia, for instance, several consultative or advisory bodies exist at the state level, particularly in the realm of education.[97] In Ecuador, three official advisory bodies include representatives of indigenous communities in areas of particular concern for these communities: the Council for the Development of the Nationalities and Peoples of Ecuador (CODENPE), with ministry level; the National Direction of Bilingual Intercultural Education (DINEB); and the National Direction of Indigenous Health (DINSI).[98]

---

[93] Law 445 of Communal Land Regime in the Atlantic Coast of Nicaragua and the Rivers Bocay, Coco, Indio and Maíz, 13 December 2002, *La Gaceta Diario Oficial* 16 (hereafter, Communal Land Law, Nicaragua], Art 41 (establishing the National Commission on Demarcation and Titling, CONADETI, incorporating representatives of all the ethnic groups of the Atlantic Coast and of the Bocay River); Art 42 (establishing three Inter-sectorial Commissions of Demarcation and Titling, CIDTs, incorporating representatives of al ethnic groups of the Atlantic Coast, and of the rivers Coco and Bocay).
[94] *Te Kooti Whenua Maori* Act, 1993/Maori Land Act 1993 (4), 21 March 1993, ss 6–16, last amended by *Te Ture Whenua Maori* Amendment Act 2004/Maori Land Amendment Act 2004 (3) (2004, 108).   [95] Maori Fisheries Act 2004, no 78, 25 September 2004, ss 30–50.
[96] Native Title Representative Bodies are governed by the Native Title Act, 1993, no 110, 24 December 1993, amended by the Native Title Amendment Act, 2007, no 61, Pt 11. On the structure and functioning of Native Title Representative Bodies and Land Councils, see *Building a Sustainable National Indigenous Representative Body* (n 86 above), 32–4.
[97] This is, for instance, the case of the Aboriginal and Torres Strait Islander Education Committee, in Queensland, which is devised as the main mechanism 'consult with Aboriginal and Torres Strait Islander communities' on matters under the jurisdiction of the Queensland Studies Authority. See Queensland Studies Authority, Aboriginal and Torres Strait Islander Education Committee: Terms of reference and membership structure, 12 September 2007, 1. Other examples include the Aboriginal Education Consultative Group, in New South Wales; the Victorian Aboriginal Education Association; the South Australian Education and Training Advisory Committee; the Western Australia Aboriginal Education Training Council, and the Tasmanian Aboriginal Education Association. For a review on these consultative mechanisms, see M-A Bin-Sallik and S Smallacombe, *Review of Indigenous Education Consultative Bodies and Indigenous Support Units: Final report*, Australian Government, Department of Education, Science and Training (2003).
[98] I Almeida, N Arrobo y L Ojeda (eds), *Autonomía indígena frente al Estado Nación y a la globalización neoliberal* (2005), 99–109.

IV. Indigenous Self-governance

If there is a key component of indigenous peoples' demands, subsequently endorsed by state and international practice over the decades, this is the recognition of indigenous self-government or autonomous institutions. As seen, the UN Declaration on the Rights of Indigenous Peoples now explicitly endorses this principle, affirming indigenous peoples' 'right to autonomy or self-government in matters relating to their internal and local affairs' as a direct materialization of their right to self-determination within the boundaries of the states in which they live;[99] the same formulation is now found in the Mexican Constitution after its amendment in 2001.[100]

The 'self-government plus' conferred upon indigenous peoples by international standards—much clearer than the affirmation of self-government rights in the international minority rights regime—derives from the basic historical fact that, despite centuries of colonial rule and assimilation policies, most indigenous peoples have preserved some sort of self-governing structures in managing their own affairs, to the extent that this characteristic has often been linked with the working definition of indigenous peoples in international standards.[101] Modern indigenous self-governing structures are not mere replicas of pre-colonial structures or mere transpositions of colonial institutions, but often a postcolonial hybrid, which has evolved along with the transformations of indigenous cultures and identities.[102] They are typically associated with operating justice systems and customary legal norms.[103] In fewer cases, indigenous self-governing structures have evolved to include policing and the provisions of other public services normally reserved by the state.

From this perspective, in many respects, the demand for autonomy is nothing but a demand for recognition and 'legalization' by the state of the actual spheres of

---

[99] UNDRIP (n 4 above), Art 4.
[100] Political Constitution of the United States of Mexico (31 December 1917), as amended by Decree, *Diario Oficial de la Federación*, 14 August 2001.
[101] See ILO Convention 169 (n 19 above), Art 1.a (defining 'tribal peoples' as peoples 'whose status is regulated wholly or partially by their own customs or traditions'); ibid, Art 1.b (defining indigenous peoples as peoples who 'retain some or all of their own social, economic, cultural and *political institutions*').
[102] On the intersection between colonial practices and the modern recognition of indigenous peoples' rights, see A Martínez de Bringas, *Los pueblos indígenas y el discurso de los derechos* (2003); E Povinelli, *The Cunning of Recognition: Indigenous alterity and the making of Australian multiculturalism* (2000); MT Sierra, 'Esencialismo y autonomía: paradojas de las reivindicaciones indígenas' (1997) 7(14) *Alteridades* 131–43.
[103] For comparative studies on indigenous legal and justice systems, see C Roy (eds), *Defending Diversity: Case studies* (2004); MT Sierra and V Chenaut (eds), *Los pueblos indígenas delante del derecho*(1995); R Stavenhagen and D Iturralde (eds), *Entre la ley y la costumbre. El derecho consuetudinario indígena en América Latina* (1990).

autonomy that indigenous peoples have ceaselessly strived to preserve. Most of the indigenous self-governing structures across the world remain de facto arrangements, which are not formally recognized within the institutional design of the state. With diverging levels of accommodation, these structures are often tolerated by state authorities, under what could be described as some sort of customary constitutional rules, but conflicts between indigenous and state structures often arise, particularly with regard to the operation of traditional justice systems. Together with these widespread de facto systems, a number of countries have historically developed formal arrangements for indigenous self-government, which in some cases coexist and interact with traditional indigenous structures.

A. Territorial arrangements

A distinct characteristic of indigenous peoples' autonomy or self-government arrangements is their territorial base. In the context of the indigenous peoples, territory is not understood solely as an administrative subdivision traced around a given demographic group or a historical or symbolical framework of political demands. It refers to the complete geographical area that indigenous peoples use, or have traditionally used, as a means of material subsistence, cultural reproduction and spiritual practice, to which they are so closely connected that their very identity is defined by that connection. The 'special importance for the cultures and spiritual values of [indigenous] peoples of their relationship with the lands or territories' is now explicitly upheld by international standards,[104] which also affirm substantive rights in relation to the lands, territories and traditional resources traditionally owned, occupied or used by these peoples.[105] From this perspective, indigenous territories are more than a mere space for political participation: they define the scope of jurisdiction of indigenous political, legal and political institutions, while providing the framework for the exercise of their collective rights.

A number of examples of formal state recognition of indigenous territorial arrangements date back to the nineteenth century with the first wave of decolonization in the Americas, where a number of independent republics granted some level of continuity to colonial structures of indirect rule, some of which are still operative today. A case in point is the *resguardo* system in Colombia. The *resguardo*, a Hispanic institution typical of the colonial divide of citizenry and subjects—formalized in the so-called '*Repúblicas de Indios*'—was granted

---

[104] ILO Convention 169 (n 19 above), Art 13.1. Cf UNDRIP (n 4 above), Art 25 ('Indigenous peoples have the right to maintain and strengthen their distinctive spiritual relationship with their traditionally owned or otherwise occupied and used lands, territories, waters and coastal seas and other resources and to uphold their responsibilities to future generations in this regard.')

[105] ILO Convention 169 (n 19 above), Arts 13–17; UNDRIP (n 4 above), Arts 25–9.

recognition by an act of the Colombia legislature in 1889.[106] The Resguardo Act is a typical example of the continuation of colonial civilizing assumptions. Yet, the system was operative throughout the twentieth century and was subsequently endorsed in the 1991 new constitutional makeup, redefined under the new paradigm of multicultural constitutionalism.[107]

A similar dynamic of evolution of a colonial model of seclusion into a modern system of indigenous self-government is the much discredited Indian reservation system in the United States. Created virtually as human deposits during the British and subsequent US expansion, the reservations evolved into the current form with Roosevelt's 'Indian New Deal' throughout the 1940s, becoming self-governing arrangements with complex institutional structures, including codified laws and formalized judicial systems, with a broad set of powers regarding internal affairs, including the provision of social services and policing. The previous relation of colonial dependency with the US federal government has historically evolved into a government-to-government relationship, as well as into a legal barrier against attempts to reduce autonomy powers by federated states.[108] After 1988, with the enactment by the US Congress of the Self-governance Demonstration Project, the reservation system was reinforced with the bilateral negotiations between the US and tribal governments, leading to the signature of Compacts of Self-government and Annual Funding Agreements.[109] The system facilitated tribal governments access to the management and planning of programmes and services previously administered by the BIA.[110]

The experience of the US reservation system was interestingly replicated in other countries. In 1867 the Canadian Constitution Act vested the federal government with exclusive jurisdiction over Indian bands and reserved lands.[111] After several attempts to disband this system, the constitutional discussions starting in Canada in the 1970s lead to the recognition of indigenous

---

[106] Law 89, 25 November 1890, determining the manner in which savages should be governed and reduced into civilized life; Law 160, on the National Agrarian Reform System and Peasant Rural Development, 3 August 1994, *Diario Oficial* 41479, Art 6; Decree 2164 (Indigenous Lands), 7 December 1995, *Diario Oficial* 42140.

[107] Constitutional Court, Decision of Constitutionality 139/96, 9 April 1996 (overturning Arts 1, 5 and 40 of Law 89 of 1890, depicting indigenous peoples as 'savages' and affirming the objective of bringing them into 'civilization').

[108] For analysis of the evolution of the US policy and legislation regarding Indian Nations, see V Deloria Jr and CM Lytle, *The Nations Within: The past and future of American Indian sovereignty* (1998); R Williams Jr, *Like a Loaded Weapon: The Renquish Court, Indian rights, and the legal history of racism in America* (2005).

[109] Tribal Self-governance Demonstration Project, *HJ Res* 395, 100th Congress, 1st Sess, 22 December 1987.

[110] See RC Ryder, 'Resuming self-government in Indian country: From imposed government to self-rule inside and outside the United States of America' (1995) 2(1) *E-Law*.

[111] Constitution Act, 1867 (formerly the British North American Act, 1867), consolidated, with amendments, 27 March 1867, s 91.24.

self-government as an existing Aboriginal right in the 1982 Constitution Act;[112] to the negotiation of 'comprehensive land claim agreements', including aspects of self-government; and, to a renewed phase of treaty negotiations including aspects of governance, jurisdiction, economic resources, and lands.[113] Plagued with controversies of all kinds, both the signature of comprehensive land agreements and the modern treaty process have lead to an important reinforcement of indigenous autonomy powers, involving, among other things, the limitation of federal powers over the management of internal affairs; the recognition of the bands' power to administer and manage lands, education, health and welfare services, financial autonomy, as well as legislative and taxation powers.[114]

In Panama, following the 1925 'Tule Revolution', and with the direct intervention of the US government, the system of indigenous reservations or *comarcas* was introduced in 1928.[115] The Panamanian *comarcas* system has historically evolved into a system of indigenous territorial autonomy, in which,

---

[112] Constitution Act, 1982, enacted as Sch B to the Canada Act, 1982, (UK) 1982 c. 11, entered into force on 17 April 1982, s 35 ('The existing aboriginal and treaty rights of the aboriginal peoples of Canada are hereby recognized and affirmed'). The government of Canada has taken the formal stand that this provision also includes indigenous peoples' self-governing rights. A particularly well-documented review of the evolution of Canadian aboriginal self-government is found in MC Hurley and J Wherrett, 'Aboriginal self-government', *Parliament of Canada, Parliament Research Brach*, Issue Paper 99-19E (1999, 2000).

[113] The main policy milestones in the process of comprehensive land agreements and the self-government negotiations are the 1973 Canadian Statement on Claims of Indian and Inuit People; the 1986 Comprehensive Land Claims Policy; the 1995 Inherent Rights Policy; and the 2007 Specific Claims Policy. See Minister of Indian Affairs and Northern Affairs, Canada, *Comprehensive Land Claim Agreements and Self-Government Agreements*, Ottawa, Indian and Northern Affairs, 2003, 7–9.

[114] See, among others, James Bay and Northern Quebec Agreement, signed between the Gran Council of the Crees, the Northern Quebec Inuit Association, the Government of Quebec, the Government of Canada, et al (11 November 1975), with complementary agreements, amended by the Northeastern Quebec Agreement, signed by the Naskapi Indian Band, the Grand Council of the Cree, the Northern Quebec Inuit Association, the government of Quebec, the government of Canada, et al (31 January 1978); Sechelt Indian Band Self-government Act, 1986, c 27, S-6.6, 17 June 1986, Art 4 ('The purposes of this Act are to enable the Sechelt Indian Band to exercise and maintain self-government on Sechelt lands and to obtain control over and the administration of the resources and services available to its members'); Umbrella Final Agreement between the government of Canada, the Council for Yukon Indians and the government of the Yukon, Whitchorse, 20 May 1993; Memorandum of Understanding: 'The dismantling of the Department of Indian Affairs and Northern Development, the restoration of jurisdictions to First Nations Peoples in Manitoba and the recognition of First Nations governments in Manitoba', Winnipeg, 7 December 1994; Nisga'a Final Agreement, signed by the government of the Nisga'a Nation, the government of Canada, and the government of British Columbia, 23 April 1999; Final Agreement among the Nisga'a Nation, Her Majesty the Queen in right of Canada and Her Majesty the Queen in right of British Columbia, endorsed by the Nisga'a Final Agreement Act, SBC 1999, 26 April 1999.

[115] Political Constitution of the Republic of Panama, 4 June 1904, as amended by Legislative Acts of 5 November 1924 and 25 September 1928, Art 4; Political Constitution of the Republic of Panama, 1941, Art 5.

albeit not without practical limitations, indigenous communities have been able to exercise self-government and preserve their territorial base.[116]

A new wave of indigenous territorial self-government arrangements started with the ground-breaking 1979 Greenland Home Rule Act, whereby this dependent (colonial) territory of Denmark became an autonomous region under the principle of *Rigsfællesskabet* ('Community of the Realm').[117] The Greenland system, coupled with some elements of the Spanish autonomy regime, inspired many of the features of the post-conflict 'multi ethnic' autonomous system in the Nicaraguan Atlantic Coast, discussed above.[118] Both the Greenland and the Nicaraguan systems share the same rationale of autonomy territorial arrangements not specific for indigenous peoples. However, while the demographic majority of the Inuit population is overwhelming in the case of Greenland, ensuring indigenous control over the autonomous institutions, in Nicaragua the demographic trend in recent years has turned the indigenous population into a minority within the broader autonomous region.[119] This majority allows the Inuit people to control the Greenland autonomous institutions, including an autonomous government (*Landsstyre*), and a unicameral parliament (*Landsting*), with broad jurisdiction except for foreign relations, which is retained by government.[120] In addition, two seats at the Danish parliament (*Folketinget*) are constitutionally reserved for Greenland representatives.[121] By referendum held in 2008, the majority of Greenlanders voted in favour of greater autonomy powers, officially becoming a country within Denmark, establishing *Inuktitut* as the only official language, and recognizing the Inuit as a separate people under international law.[122]

The Greenland model was replicated in recent years with the creation of Nunavut ('Our Land', in *Inuktitut*) in the Canadian Arctic region. A vast

---

[116] Five indigenous *comarcas* currently exist in Panama, which are officially recognized as part of the country's administrative map: the Comarca Kuna Yala or de San Blás (established by Law no 2, *Gaceta Oficial* 7873, 23 September 1938, amended by Law no 16, *Gaceta Oficial* 12042, 7 April 1953; Comarca Emberá-Wounan, (Law 22, Gaceta *Oficial* 19976, 17 January 1984; the Comarca Kuna of Madugandí, *Gaceta Oficial* 22951, 15 January 1996; the Comarca Ngöbe-Gublé, Law no 10, *Gaceta Oficial* 23242, 11 March 1997; and the Comarca Kuna of Wargandí, Law no 34, *Gaceta Oficial* 24106, 28 July 2000. Each *comarca* has an organic chart, negotiated with the central government, which defines the jurisdiction of indigenous authorities and the coordination with state institutions. For a case study of the actual functioning of the Comarca Kuna, see V Cabedo, *Constitucionalismo y Derecho Indígena en América Latina* (2004), 242–9.

[117] H Hannum, *Autonomy, Sovereignty and Self-Determination: Accomodating conflicting rights* (1990), 331–46. M Suksi, 'On the entrenchment of autonomy' in M Suksi (ed), *Autonomy: Applications and implications* (1998); I Foighel, 'A framework for autonomy: The case of Greenland' (1979) 9 *Israel Yearbook on Human Rights* 82.

[118] D Polanco, *Autonomía regional* (n 68 above), 185–9.

[119] Programa de Naciones Unidas para el Desarrollo (PNUD), *Nicaragua: Informe de Desarrollo Humano 2005. Las regiones autónomas de la Costa Caribe ¿Nicaragua asume su diversidad?* (2005), 25–8.   [120] Greenland Home Rule Act 577, 29 November 1978.

[121] The Constitutional Act of Greenland, 5 June 1953, as amended, Art 28.

[122] A Cowell, 'Greenland vote favors independence', *The New York Times*, 29 November 2008.

territory covering one-fifth of Canada, with an approximate population of 30,000 people—of which 85 per cent are Inuit—the Nunavut Territory was created in 1993, and started functioning in 1999.[123] Its act of creation grants the Nunavut government similar administrative powers, jurisdiction, and institutions to the North Western Territory.[124] With Inuit control of the Nunavut government institutions through the ballot, government policies have focused on priority areas for the local Inuit population.[125]

The notion of 'indigenous autonomy' in Latin America is at the kernel of a complex set of discourses and practices, somewhere in between formal recognition by state law and actual, 'informal' practice.[126] Indigenous autonomy arrangements in Latin America can be grouped into three main categories. First, the 'multi ethnic' regional system, of which the Atlantic Coast of Nicaragua has been to date the only institutionalized example. However, discussions about this model have continued in other countries in recent years, particularly in the case of Mexico.[127]

The second model, built upon the formal recognition of indigenous territories, typically multi ethnic, is best represented by the *resguardo* model in Colombia and the *comarcas* model in Panama, already discussed. A modern variable of this second model is connected to the processes of indigenous land titling and demarcation in Latin American, particularly in the rainforest. The 'indigenous lands' demarcated in the framework of the 1988 Constitution enjoy an important level of autonomy, albeit subject to the overall supervision of the Federal National Foundation of the Indian (FUNAI);[128] a similar system is in

---

[123] Nunavut Act 1993, c 28, N-28.6, 10 June 1993, entered into force on 1 April 1999; Agreement between the Inuit of the Nunavut Settlement Area as represented by the Tungavik Federation of Nunavut and Her Majesty the Queen in Right of Canada (Nunavut Land Claims Agreement) (Iqaluit, 25 May 1993). On the history of the Nunavut process, see P Jull, 'Reconciliation and Northern Territories, Canadian-style: The Nunavut process and product' (1999) 4(20) *Indigenous Law Bulletin*, available at <http://www.austlii.edu.au/au/journals/ILB/1999/30.html> (accessed 31 July 2009).

[124] Nunavut Act (n 118 above), Arts 11 (Commissioner), 12 (Council), 31 (Supreme Court and Appeal Court).

[125] The statement of policy of the first government of Nunavut was set forth in the so-called 'Bathurst Mandate'. See Nunavut Legislative Assembly (*Qingauq/Bathurst Inlet*), 'The Bathurst Mandate' (21 October 1999). The document reflects four priority areas of government action for the following years, based on Inuit concepts: 'healthy communities' (*Inuuqatigiittiarniq*); 'simplicity and unity' (*Pijarnirnirqsat Katujjiqatiriittiarnirlu*); Self-reliance (*Namminiq Makitajunarniq*) and 'continuing learning' (*Ilippallianginnarniq*). See P Jull, ' A blueprint for indigenous self-government: The Bathurst Mandate' (2000) 4(27) *Indigenous Law Bulletin*.

[126] For general discussions on the topic, see M Aparicio, *Los pueblos indígenas y el Estado: el reconocimiento constitucional de los derechos indígenas en América Latina* (2002); D Polanco, *Autonomía regional* (n 68 above); *Leo Gabriel and Gilberto López y Rivas* (eds), *Autonomías indígenas en América Latina. Nuevas formas de convivencia política*(2003).

[127] See AC Mayor (ed), *Indigenous Autonomy in Mexico* (2002); H Díaz Polanco and C Sánchez, *México diverso: el debate por la autonomía* (2002).

[128] Constitution of the Federal Republic of Brazil, 5 October 1988, Arts 231–2; Indian Statute, Act 6001 of 19 December 1973, as amended, Arts 17–33.

operation in Costa Rica.[129] In Bolivia, the 1994 Popular Participation Law created the category of the Aboriginal Communitarian Lands (*Tierras Comunitarias de Origen*, TCOs), conceived mainly as spaces for indigenous land management but which have increasingly evolved into territorial autonomies comprising vast areas of land.[130] The new system of land titling in Nicaragua is similarly associated with the recognition of indigenous territorial authorities, somehow redefining state-indigenous relationships under the 1997 Autonomy Statute.[131]

The third model of territorial autonomy in Latin America, and certainly the most extended one, is local or communitarian autonomy at the village level. An *indigenization* of the municipal space is ongoing in indigenous-populated areas in several countries, a process through which indigenous peoples and their organizations are increasingly taking control of local government institutions. The case of the State of Oaxaca, already discussed, and Michoacán or Chiapas, in Mexico; the increasing *Mayanization* of rural municipalities in Guatemala, or the successful experiments of indigenous municipalities in Ecuador and Bolivia are only some examples of the exercise of indigenous autonomy government at the local level.[132] Other than that, indigenous autonomy arrangements in Latin American countries are centred around the community or village.

'Communitarian autonomy' is, despite the many debates and proposals for reconstruction of indigenous territories, by far the most common example of indigenous autonomy in Latin America, and also in other parts of the world where legal recognition of indigenous peoples and their collective rights is lacking, particularly in Africa and Asia. In the case of Latin America, however, the right of indigenous peoples to maintain their own institutions and to manage their internal affairs, at least at the community level, is legally recognized. Most Latin American countries are parties of ILO Convention 169. The new 'multicultural' constitutions now affirm those rights, including in most cases the recognition of indigenous customary law and judicial systems. Despite recognition in principle, communitarian autonomy continues to operate de facto in the absence of concrete formal legislative or institutional arrangements. For many indigenous communities, this is indeed a voluntary choice and a barrier against further state intrusion. Yet, the legal limbo is also at the root of not a few conflicts between indigenous autonomies and government institutions.

---

[129] Indigenous Act, Act 6172 of 17 November 1977, Art 4 ('[Indian] reserves shall be regulated by indigenous people, through their communitarian or traditional structures, or by the relevant laws of the Republic, under the coordination and advice of the CONAI [National Corporation of Indigenous Affairs]') (author's translation).   [130] See nn 51–2 above, and accompanying text.
[131] Communal Land Law, Nicaragua (n 93 above), Arts 4–10 (regulating the jurisdiction of communal and territorial authorities, 'with legal representation').
[132] For a comparative study, see W Assies and H Gundermann (eds), *Movimientos indígenas y gobiernos locales en América Latina* (2007).

Historically, one of the most common problems in this regard has been the lack of formal recognition of indigenous communities as part of the state administrative machinery. In Mexico, the 2001 constitutional reform explicitly excluded this possibility, attributing indigenous communities and peoples the status of 'public interest entities',[133] falling short of the commitment to recognize them as collective subjects of rights, as included in the 1996 Peace Accords with the Zapatist National Liberation Army (EZLN).[134] The legal recognition of indigenous peoples and communities was discussed in the recent decision by the Inter-American Court of Human Rights in the case of the *Saramaka People v Surinam*. In this case, dealing with the rights of the Saramaka tribal people over their traditional lands, the Court objected to the Surinam government position that only individual members of the community could receive land titles,[135] explicitly linking the recognition of the collective legal personality of indigenous and tribal people to the recognition of their communal land rights.[136] Accordingly, the Court ordered the state to 'establish ... the judicial and administrative conditions to ensure the [Saramakas'] judicial personality with the aim of guaranteeing them the use and enjoyment of their territory in accordance with their communal property system, as well as the rights to access to justice and equality'.[137]

A second element of controversy regarding the actual functioning of communitarian autonomy refers to indigenous legal and judicial systems. While those systems have generically been recognized in modern Latin American constitutions, in most cases they operate within a legal vacuum, and the lack of concrete regulations regarding the scope of indigenous jurisdiction and its interaction with the state's formal judicial system gives rise to continuous and serious problems.[138] Attempts to formally regulate the 'compatibility' between the indigenous and the state justice systems have failed in countries such as Colombia, Ecuador or Peru.[139] The recent Constitution of Bolivia opened up a new chapter with regard to the recognition of indigenous justice systems. The Constitution recognizes the existence of 'indigenous aboriginal peasant justice'

---

[133] Constitution of the United States of Mexico (n 100 above), Art 2.A.
[134] See 'Common Proposals that the Federal Government and the EZLN Commit to Submit to the National Institutions of Debate and Decision-Making, under Point 1.4 of the Rules of Procedure' (18 January 1996), included in the Accords of San Andrés Larraínzar between the Federal Government and the Zapatist National Liberation Army (EZLN) (16 February 1996), s I.3 (recognition of indigenous peoples as 'subjects of rights').
[135] *Saramaka v Surinam* (n 25 above), para 162.   [136] Ibid, para 172.
[137] Ibid, para 174.
[138] See, generally, Cabedo (n 116 above), 77-14; R Yrigoyen, *Pautas de coordinación entre el derecho indigena y el derecho estatal*(1999).
[139] See Draft Law on Constitutional Development of Art 191.4: Law on the Administration of Justice by Indigenous Authorities (Ecuador) (2001); Project of Law of Justice of Indigenous Peoples and Indigenous-Peasant Communities (Bolivia) (2001); Project of Statutory Law on Indigenous Special Jurisdiction (Colombia) (2003); Draft Law 420/2006-CR and 1265/2006-CR, on the 'Development of Article 149 of the Constitution, that recognizes the special Jurisdiction of Peasant and Native Communities, and that establishes mechanisms of coordination between the

as part of the state's judicial branch, and stipulates the binding force and enforceability of its decisions.[140] The Plurinational Constitutional Court, of multicultural composition, is responsible for hearing appeals of decisions by indigenous judicial authorities.[141]

Last but not least, much in line with the conflict prevention rationale of the Lund Recommendations, a number of territorial arrangements relevant to indigenous peoples have been created in armed conflict situations and as part of comprehensive peace settlement agreements. Both the Panama *comarcas* system and the Nicaraguan 'multi ethnic' autonomy followed armed revolts involving the local indigenous population. In Asia, similar cases are found in Bangladesh and Indonesia. An armed conflict erupted in the Chittagong Hill Tracts (CHT), in South-eastern Bangladesh, during the 1980s and 1990s, following Bangladeshi attempts to promote the influx of Bengali settlers in the traditional territory of indigenous 'hill' tribes. After a bitter conflict, a peace treaty was signed in 1997 between the government and the indigenous rebel force, the Shanti Bahini. The peace treaty incorporated, among other things, the devolution of powers to the Hill District Councils, including jurisdiction over land, police, and education; the establishment of a Regional Council with legislative and administrative jurisdiction over CHT; and the appointment of a Ministry of CHT Affairs, in a sort of indigenous-autonomy arrangement combining the local, regional, and central levels.[142] However, despite indigenous peoples' outcry, the 1997 CHT Peace Agreement remains mostly unimplemented, while many of the abuses that led to the decades-long conflict in the region, including militarization and land-taking, are still ongoing.[143]

Similar post-conflict territorial arrangements can be found in Indonesia, where special autonomy regimes have been established in the provinces of West Papua and Aceh. In Papua, after a low-intensity conflict leading to massive human rights abuses and civil displacement, a Special Autonomy Law was

latter and the Judicial Power'. In contrast, a number of laws regulating the coordination between state and indigenous justice have been passed in other countries. See, eg, Law on Indigenous Justice of the State of Quintana Roo (Mexico), 14 August 1996, as amended; Organic Law on Indigenous Peoples and Communities (Venezuela), *Diario Oficial*, 38344, of 27 December 2005, Art 114–15; Law on the Administration of Indigenous and Communitarian Justice of the State of San Luis Potosí (Mexico), Decree 501, 1 June 2006; Law of Communal Justice of the State of Michoacán de Ocampo (Mexico), 30 March 2007.

[140] Political Constitution of Bolivia (n 43 above), Arts 191–2.

[141] See n 43 above, and accompanying text.

[142] Chittagong Hill Tracts Peace Agreement, signed by the government of Bangladesh and the Parbatya Chattagram Jana Sanghati Samity (PCJSS), Dhaka, 2 December, 1997. For a comment on the context of the Peace Agreement, see D Roy, 'Indigenous rights in Bangladesh: Land rights and self-government in the Chittagong Hill Tracts', Paper submitted at the Indigenous Rights in the Commonwealth Project South and South East Asia Regional Expert Meeting, Indian Confederation of Indigenous and Tribal Peoples (ICITP), New Delhi, 11–13 March 2002, 5–6.

[143] See Asian Indigenous Peoples Network (AIPN), 'The Chittagong Hill Tracts Peace Accord: Squandering the peace and human rights dividends', (2003) III(3) *Indigenous Rights Quarterly*; RC Roy, *Land Rights of the Indigenous Peoples of the Chittagong Hill Tracts, Bangladesh* (Copenhagen, IWGIA, 2000), 171–8.

promulgated in 2001.¹⁴⁴ In Aceh, the armed conflict between the Indonesian military and the indigenous, separatist Free Aceh Movement ended with the signature of a peace agreement in 2005,¹⁴⁵ which included the objective of limited autonomy in the province.¹⁴⁶ Both the Papua and the Aceh special autonomy arrangements share similar characteristics: they are governed by their own government and legislature,¹⁴⁷ with powers over local development and social services, land management, and police.¹⁴⁸ The two regional systems further recognize indigenous local authorities¹⁴⁹ and traditional customary norms and institutions at the local level (*adat*),¹⁵⁰ as well as independent regional authorities with jurisdiction over the implementation of *adat* institutions.¹⁵¹ While the enactment of autonomy regimes in the two provinces opened a window of hope for the Papuan and Acehnese indigenous peoples, many commentators perceived them as an attempt by the Indonesian government to disperse secessionist aspirations and to clarify the political status of these two territories, irregularly incorporated into Indonesia during the decolonization process. Implementation of the two autonomy systems has actually been shady: Papua was divided into two provinces in 2003, in breach of the autonomy regime, and reports of human rights abuses against the Papuan indigenous populations have not ceased.¹⁵² In the meantime, the Aceh autonomy law was

---

¹⁴⁴ Act 21/2001 on Special Autonomy for the Papua Province, 23 October 2001 (hereafter, Papua Autonomy Law). The Act repeals the Law 45/1999 concerning the Establishment of the Provinces of Central Irian Jaya, West Irian Jaya, East Irian Jaya, Regencies of Paniai, Mimika, Puncak Jaya, and Municipality of Sorong.
¹⁴⁵ Memorandum of Understanding between the Government of the Republic of Indonesia and the Free Aceh Movement, Helsinki, 15 August 2005, s 1.1.
¹⁴⁶ Law 11/2006 on the Governing of Aceh, 11 June 2006 (hereinafter, Aceh Autonomy Law). The Act repeals the Law 18/2001, 9 August 2001.
¹⁴⁷ Papua Autonomy Law (n 144 above), Arts 1.d, 1.f; Aceh Autonomy Law (n 146 above), Arts 1.7, 1.10.
¹⁴⁸ Papua Autonomy Law (n 144 above), Arts 49, 56–66; Aceh Autonomy Law (n 146 above), Art 16–17.
¹⁴⁹ Papua Autonomy Law (n 144 above), preambular para e (recognizing 'the natives of the Papua Province' as 'one of the groups of the Melanesian race [with] a variety of culture, history, customs, and its own language'), Arts 1.1 (*kampung* local communities), 1.p (*adat* indigenous communities); Aceh Autonomy Law (n 146 above), 1.16 (*mukim* local communities).
¹⁵⁰ Papua Autonomy Law (n 144 above), Art 43 (*adat* rights and *ayalat* land system), Art 51 (*adat* judicature); Aceh Autonomy Law (n 146 above), Art 98 (*adat* institutions).
¹⁵¹ Papua Autonomy Law (n 144 above), Art 19 (Papua Peoples' Assembly); Aceh Autonomy Law (n 146 above), Art 96 (*Wali Nanggroe*).
¹⁵² Presidential Decree 1/2003 concerning the Acceleration of the Implementation of Law 45/1999. The original plan to divide Papua into three provinces was overturned by the Constitutional Court (Decision 018/PUU-I/2003 concerning the division of the Province of Irian Jaya, 11 November 2003), which however sanctified the creation of the province of West Papua. On the human rights situation in Papua, see J Wing and P King, 'Genocide in West Papua? The role of the Indonesian state apparatus and a current needs assessment of the Papuan people', Report prepared for the West Papua Project at the Centre for Peace and Conflict Studies, University of Sydney, and ELSHAM Jayapura, Papua, August 2005.

criticized as falling short of the expectations raised by the 2005 peace accord, and violence continues to be endemic in the region.[153]

B. Non-territorial arrangements

As noted above, indigenous peoples' self-government structures are typically associated with their traditional territories, and with the special relation they maintain with these territories in political, cultural, spiritual and material terms. This explains why, almost invariably, any discussion on indigenous autonomy or self-government is implicitly connected to territorial arrangements at the regional or local levels. An important exception in this regard is the Sami parliaments system in the Nordic countries, which, while combining elements of special political representation through elected bodies and advisory mechanisms at the level of central government, may be also regarded as a unique system of indigenous non-territorial or personal autonomy.[154]

The Sami parliaments (*Sámediggi*), in their current form of officially recognized bodies with advisory and administrative powers, were established in Finland in 1973;[155] in Norway in 1987;[156] and in Sweden in 1993.[157] In Russia, with an estimated population of 2,000 Samis in the Murmansk region, calls for a similar representative body have not been met with an institutional response.[158] The three Sami parliaments share similar representation, powers, and structures, in a sort of demonstration effect operating from one Nordic country to the other, and in recent years have started a policy of transnational

---

[153] M Renner, 'New Aceh governing law falls short on autonomy promises, triggers protests', *World Watch Institute*, 10 August 2006; R Sukma, 'Insight: Peace, DDR in Aceh cannot be taken for granted', *The Jakarta Post*, 8 November 2008; World Bank/Conflict and Development Program, 'Aceh conflict monitoring update: 1 December 2008–28 February 2009'.

[154] See Hannum, *Autonomy, Sovereignty and Self-Determination* (n 117 above), 247–62; E Josefen, 'The Saami and the national parliaments: Channels for political influence. Sami self-determination in the making?' (2007) 2 *Gáldu Čála – Journal of Indigenous Peoples Rights*; K Mynti, 'The beneficiaries of autonomy arrangements with special reference to indigenous peoples in general and the Sami in Finland in particular' in M Suksi (ed), *Autonomy: Applications and implications* (n 117 above), 277–292; JT Solbakk, *The Sámi People: A handbook* (2006).

[155] Cabinet Decree on the Sami Council, 9 November 1973; Act on the Sami Parliament, Act 974, 17 July 1995, amended by Decrees of 22 December 1995 and 2 March 1996; The Constitution of Finland, 11 June 1999, ss 17 (recognizing the Sami as an indigenous people), 121 (recognizing Sami cultural and linguistic self-government).

[156] Act Concerning the Sami Assembly and Other Sami Matters (Sami Act), Act no 56 of 12 June 1987; The Constitution of the Kingdom of Norway (16 May 1816), as amended, Art 110.a; Act relating to legal relations and management of land and natural resources in the county of Finnmark (Finnmark Act), Act 85, 17 June 2005.

[157] Sami Parliament Act, Act 1433, 17 December 1992; Constitution of Sweden: Instrument of Government (*Regeringsformen*), 28 February 1974, Art 20.

[158] Solbakk, *The Sámi People* (n 154 above), 222–30.

coordination in the form of an annual Sami Parliamentarian Conference and an inter-sessional Sami Parliamentarian Council.[159]

The three Sami parliaments share similar objectives of promoting the Sami language and culture (defined, in the case of Finland, as the promotion of 'cultural autonomy').[160] In order to fulfil these objectives, the three parliaments share similar powers of legislative initiative or proposal with regard to the central government in relation to legislative or policy measures affecting Sami interests in their respective countries (more strongly defined, in the case of Finland, as a process of 'negotiation' between the Sami parliament and the central government[161]), as well as a number of administrative powers in the areas of culture and cultural patrimony, education, language, allocation of development funds, and management of natural resources.[162]

Interestingly, the statutory powers of the three Sami parliaments combine both territorial and non-territorial elements: while their advisory powers in cultural and linguistic matters is not necessarily circumscribed to Sami areas, their administrative powers are typically connected to the management of public educational services, cultural heritage, and natural resource management in Sami-populated areas (or 'Sami homeland' in the terminology of the Finnish Parliament Act[163]). The method of electing representatives to those parliaments is not territorial, but personal: only Sami people or descendants of Sami people, and who are registered in special Sami electoral register, are eligible to elect or to

---

[159] Declaration from the First Sami Parlamentarian Conference (Jokkmokk, 24 Feburary 2005), para 26 (deciding that the Sami Parlamentarian Conference will be held every four years, and organized by a Sami Parlamentarian Council).

[160] Sami Parliament Act (Norway) (n 155 above), Art 1.1 ('The purpose of the Act is to make it possible for the S[a]ami people in Norway to safeguard and develop their language, culture and way of life') (unofficial translation); Sami Act (Finland) (n 156 above), Art 1 ('The purpose of this Act is to guarantee the S[a]ami as an indigenous people cultural autonomy in respect to their language and culture') (unofficial translation); Sami Parliament Act (Sweden) (n 157 above), Art 1 (the Sami parliament is constituted with 'the primary objective of handling issues related to Sami culture in Sweden'), cited in Josefsen, 'The Saami and national parliaments' (n 154 above), 20.

[161] Sami Act (Finland) (n 156 above), Art 9 ('The authorities shall negotiate with the Sami Parliament in all far-reaching and important measures which may directly and in a specific way affect the status of the S[a]ami as an indigenous people') (unofficial translation).

[162] Ibid, Arts 5, 8–9; Sami Parliament Act (Sweden) (n 132 above), Art 2.1, cited in Josefsen, 'The Saami and national parliaments' (n 154 above), 21. In the case of Norway, while the original Sami Act listed a limited number of administrative powers, additional responsibilities have been vested upon the Sami parliament by virtue of subsequent legislation, including the management of the Sámi Development Fund and of the Sami Culture Fund; the allocation of funds to Sami language municipalities and counties and Sami schools; the protection of Sami heritage sites, and the election of 50 per cent of the members of the Finnmark Estate, responsible for the management of land and natural resources under the Finnmark county under the Finnmark Act, 2005 (n 131 above). See Solbakk, *The Sámi People* (n 154 above), 176–9.

[163] Sami Act (Finland) (n 156 above), Art 4.

be elected to the Sami parliaments.[164] However, while representatives to the Sami parliaments in Sweden are elected from a single constituency and from thirteen constituencies in Norway, from across the country, in Finland the Sami parliament is elected exclusively from four constituencies that constitute the Sami homeland.[165] All these characteristics make the Sami parliaments system a unique arrangement for the participation of indigenous peoples that, crafted into the specific realities of the Sami people in the Nordic countries, seeks to advance the exercise of self-government rights beyond within and beyond the traditional Sami territory, and, what is more, beyond the borders of the states in which they now live.

V. Critical Assessment

This chapter has tried to review the applicability of the Lund Recommendations in the specific context of indigenous peoples. While a complete evaluation of the effectiveness of these mechanisms goes beyond the scope of the chapter, the main conclusion is that institutional and legal mechanisms of the kind proposed by the Lund Recommendations are in place in many countries and, notwithstanding their important political and institutional limitations, have contributed to some extent towards (i) enhancement of the political participation of indigenous peoples in the overall government structures in the countries in which they live, (ii) guaranteeing that indigenous peoples' views and rights-based concerns are duly taken into account in government decisions affecting them, and (iii) the defusing of potential conflicts.

As pointed out at the beginning of the chapter, indigenous peoples' rights and concerns overlap significantly with those of minorities. The area of political participation is particularly relevant in this regard. Both minorities and indigenous peoples have been historically excluded from participating in decision-making as a result of the wider legal, institutional, and social structures in the

---

[164] Sami Parliament Act (Norway) (n 155 above), Art 2.7 ('All persons who provide a declaration to the effect that they consider themselves to be Sami, and who either ... have Sami as the language of the home, or ... have or have had a parent or grandparent with Sami as the language of the home may demand to be included in a separate register of Sami electors in their municipality of residence'); Sami Act (Finland) (n 156 above) ('Sami means a person who considers himself a Sami, provided ... that he himself or at least one of his parents or grandparents has learnt Sami as his first language; ... that he is a descendent of a person who has been entered in a land, taxation or population register as a mountain, forest or fishing Lapp; or ... that at least one of his parents has or could have been registered as an elector for an election to the Sami Delegation or the Sami Parliament.'). In Sweden, similarly, the right to vote and to be elected in Sami parliament elections is restricted to the Sami, including both a subjective criterion (whoever consider herself to be a Sami) and an objective criterion (Sami as the home language, or the parents' or grandparents' home language). Solbakk, *The Sámi People* (n 154 above), 195.

[165] The Sami homeland is constituted by the Sami-populated municipalities of Enontekiö, Utsjoki, Inari, and Sodankylä. Sami Act (Finland) (n 156 above), Art 4.

countries in which they live. There is now a growing international normative consensus that the mechanisms for political representation and participation of classical liberal theory are not only insufficient to address the concerns of minority or historically excluded groups within society, but that, as signalled by the Inter-American Court of Human Rights in the *YATAMA* case, these mechanisms may actually have exclusionary effects that contradict modern conceptions of human rights. As in the case of ethnic, national, religious, or linguistic minorities, the kind of special participatory mechanisms proposed by the Lund Recommendations have contributed to countering the deficiencies of the liberal constitutional model vis-à-vis the recognition and social inclusion of indigenous peoples and, most importantly, to transforming the institutional underpinnings of states in ways that accommodate the multicultural fabric of their respective societies.

Is there any relevant difference between indigenous peoples' and minority rights, and the respective state legal and institutional mechanisms for accommodating those rights, in the realm of political participation? The review of relevant international standards and domestic practice shows at least two significant differences, both related to the normative justification of a distinct indigenous peoples' rights regime. One of these differences concerns the primordially remedial character of this regime. Inasmuch as it seeks to repair the historical and ongoing consequences of the processes of conquest and colonization that prevented indigenous peoples from freely determining the conditions of their incorporation into the wider societies in which they now live, their right to participation has a normative plus that goes beyond affirmative action or participatory policy considerations. This is particularly relevant with regard to indigenous peoples' right to be consulted on decisions directly affecting them. International standards and domestic norms recognize that indigenous peoples' right to consultation generates a correlative state duty which, irrespective of the serious problems it faces in practical terms, is normally implemented—at least in those countries in which indigenous peoples are effectively recognized—and judicially enforceable. A myriad of decisions by international human rights bodies and domestic courts show that the state duty to consult indigenous peoples is increasingly seen as part of the due administrative and legal procedures in relation to all government measures affecting indigenous peoples, and lack of consultation may involve the overturning of those measures.

A second idiosyncratic characteristic of the legal mechanisms guaranteeing the participation rights of indigenous peoples is that they are meant to reflect existing and evolving institutional and social forms of internal organization, including legal and judicial systems which, in most cases, predate the existence of modern states. From this perspective, the formal recognition of self-government or autonomous systems for indigenous peoples within state structures is—or should be—more a reflection of societal structures, whose existence is legitimized by the state, than a form of devolution of power or decentralization in order to enhance the participation of minority or excluded groups. Comparative state practice shows that existing formal arrangements for indigenous self-governance are institutional hybrids that combine elements of indigenous traditional forms of organization with state bureaucratic forms. Nonetheless, experience shows that the legitimacy and effectiveness of these arrangements depend mostly on their degree of harmony with indigenous cultural and social patterns.

This dimension further contributes to explaining the relative success of indigenous autonomous arrangements in comparison to the relative difficulties faced in implementing participation mechanisms at the level of central government, including through the establishment of reserved parliamentary seats and by the creation of 'ethnic parties' as suggested by the Lund Recommendations. International and comparative practice suggests the need for more flexible and creative ways of enhancing indigenous participation in state structures including, as suggested by the examples of Ecuador or Bolivia, through the recognition of other channels of participation beyond traditional party systems.

While the pre-existence of internal forms of organization may be a shared characteristic with some minority groups, particularly national or religious minorities, the territorial dimension is certainly unique to indigenous peoples' experiences across the world. The close material, cultural and spiritual relationship that invariably link indigenous peoples to their traditional territories goes beyond the geographical borders of territorial self-government arrangements and is closely linked to a *sui generis* land- and resource-rights regime. From this perspective, the establishment of indigenous political participation systems exceeds the objective of promoting the participation in public life of these previously disenfranchised groups. These systems also serve as procedural safeguards to protect the rights of indigenous peoples to survive and thrive as distinct societies, and to preserve and develop their identities and cultures in close relation with their traditional territories. These objectives have now been endorsed by modern human rights law.

PART III

REPRESENTATION

11

Universal and European Standards of Political Participation of Minorities

Andraz A Melansek

I. Introduction	345
II. The Universal Principles	346
III. Electoral Process and Minority Rights	348
IV. Application of International Legal Principles in Practice	351
A. Equal and universal suffrage	351
B. Genuine elections	353
C. Basic freedoms	354
V. Implementation of International Legal Standards	357
VI. Codification of Practices	360
VII. Conclusion	362

I. Introduction

The substance of the right to political participation is reflected in global human rights treaties, opinions of the UN Human Rights Committee (HRC) and regional tribunals, as well as instruments of the OSCE and other regional bodies. The universal principles of political participation are dispersed across a vast body of norms, practices, principles, comments, and recommendations. There is no single comprehensive document which could describe the universal standards of political participation. In explaining the right of minorities to political participation, it is also important to go beyond written standards and have a look at the current electoral practice. Today, widely accepted global electoral principles that serve as a means of evaluation of democratic elections require that the will of the people must be expressed in periodic and genuine elections, held by universal and equal suffrage and by secret vote or by equivalent free voting procedures.

II. The Universal Principles

The right to political participation first appeared in multilateral human rights instruments after the Second World War.[1] It was first articulated in the Universal Declaration of Human Rights (UDHR), which was adopted unanimously in 1948 by the United Nations. Article 21 is the fundamental article on which the whole body of related electoral law is built. The Article states that 'everyone has the right to take part in the government of his country, directly or through chosen representatives'.[2] This Article is also the cornerstone of establishing legitimacy of the government through free and genuine elections: 'The will of the people shall be the basis of the authority of government; this shall be expressed in periodic and genuine elections which shall be by universal and equal suffrage and shall be held by secret ballot or by equivalent voting procedures.'[3] UDHR firmly entrenches the right to political participation as the basic political right.

Universal validity of the right to political participation has become globally accepted when it became enshrined and reiterated in other international human rights documents. Most prominently, the right to political participation was established by the International Covenant on Civil and Political Rights (ICCPR), which is a widely ratified United Nations human rights treaty, and might be, in principle, directly applicable before domestic courts.[4] It must be noted, however, that the right is essentially a political right and as such restricted to citizens of a particular country. ICCPR codifies, reiterates and expands rights enshrined in the UDHR.

The right to political participation has also become an integral part of regional human rights documents, which shows their regional applicability. Most important among them are the European Convention for the Protection of Human Rights and Fundamental Freedoms (ECHR), the American Convention on Human Rights, the African Charter on Human and Peoples' Rights, the Charter of Fundamental Rights of the European Union (EU) and the Copenhagen Document of the Organisation for Security and Cooperation in Europe (OSCE).

The cornerstone documents protecting the principles of democratic elections in the OSCE region, and one of the most important such documents in the world, is the Document of the Copenhagen Meeting of the Conference on Human Dimension of the Conference on Security and Co-operation in Europe

---

[1] GH Fox, 'The right to political participation in international law' in GH Fox and BR Roth (eds) *Democratic Governance and International Law* (2000), 49–90, 53.   [2] UDHR, Art 21(1).
[3] UDHR, Art 21(3).
[4] C Harland, 'The status of the International Covenant on Civil and Political Rights (ICCPR) in the domestic law of state parties: an initial global survey through UN Human Rights Committee documents' (2000) 22(1) *Human Rights Quarterly* 187–260, 200.

(now OSCE). Known as the Copenhagen Document, and primarily but not solely an election-related document, it contains a wide range of principles, which are important in conducting elections. Although this document is not legally binding, it does express states' understanding of the right to political participation at the highest political level and it does, as such, reveal their political commitment to ensure 'free elections that will be held at reasonable intervals by secret ballot or by equivalent free voting procedure, under conditions which ensure in practice the free expression of the opinion of the electors in the choice of their representatives'.[5] Most of the fundamental principles related specifically to elections are contained in only a few paragraphs,[6] but the principles are also set in the wider context of human rights. The basic commitments seen in other international human rights instruments have been deepened and clarified by the OSCE and cover a wider electoral cycle. The principles cover the holding of free, fair, transparent, and accountable elections by an equal universal and secret suffrage. Furthermore, they also protect the right to establish political parties on the basis of equal treatment by law, ensure that political campaigning can be conducted in a free and fair atmosphere, ensure unimpeded access to the media, protect honest counting and tabulation, as well as timely installation of candidates elected in office.

Apart from the Copenhagen Document, the OSCE has developed a rich body of international obligations and commitments dealing with elections. In 1996, heads of states or governments have recognized electoral fraud in their comprehensive approach to security as a security issue, which continues to endanger the stability in the OSCE region. The commitment to free and fair elections is also an integral part of the Charter for European Security.[7] Moreover, as a specific characteristic of the OSCE area, the participating states have committed themselves to invite observers from other OSCE states to observe their elections.[8] The crucial role they attribute to the Office for Democratic Institutions and Human Rights in developing and implementing electoral legislation only shows the importance these electoral standards play in the OSCE area. In the Istanbul Summit Declaration, states themselves especially committed to 'secure the full right of persons belonging to minorities to vote and to facilitate the right of refugees to participate in elections held in their countries of origin'.[9] This clearly shows how OSCE has gradually codified and expanded relevant international provisions on holding genuine and transparent elections in the area.

Apart from the Copenhagen Document, the most important human rights instrument in Europe is the ECHR. Although the Convention itself does not deal with electoral rights, it does so in Art 3 of its First Optional Protocol where

---

[5] Copehnagen Document (Art 5(1)). [6] Copenhagen Document, para 6–8.
[7] Charter for European Security, Istanbul Summit, OSCE, Istanbul, 18–19 November 1999, 25, available at <http://www.osce.org/documents/mcs/1999/11/17497_en.pdf> (accessed 6 September 2009). [8] Ibid.
[9] Ibid, 26.

it requires states to 'hold free elections at reasonable intervals by secret ballot, under conditions which will ensure the free expression of the opinion of the people in the choice of the legislature'. Although this provision of Art 3 of the First Optional Protocol seems much narrower in scope than other international legal provisions, both the European Commission and the European Court of Human Rights interpreted this provision as providing substantially the same guarantees as other international human rights instruments, such as the ICCPR.[10] Without a doubt, the right to political participation as the cornerstone of democracy has become 'a fundamental feature of the European public order'.[11] As the European Court of Human Rights pointed out, 'democracy thus appears to be the only political model contemplated by the Convention and, accordingly, the only one compatible with it'.[12] Contrary to the case of OSCE political commitments, the Council of Europe's[13] obligations are legally enforceable and individuals can appeal to the European Court of Human Rights when they have exhausted all other domestic legal remedies.

Within Europe it is also important to mention efforts of the EU in the field of electoral standards. With the Treaty of Maastricht,[14] the EU confirms democracy and democratic elections as one of the cornerstones on which it is founded. Based on the constitutional traditions of the EU member states, rights and freedoms recognized by the ECHR, the Council of Europe's Social Charter, and other international human rights instruments to which EU member states are parties, the EU has adopted a European Charter on Fundamental Rights. Despite the still ambiguous legal status of this document, it gives us an indication that democracy and fundamental freedoms are the essence of European legal order. The EU also stresses the importance of protecting democratic rights in principles in its relations with accession countries and third countries.

III. Electoral Process and Minority Rights

Complementary to the body of human rights law protecting the right to political participation, specialized human rights law dealing with minority issues gives

---

[10] GH Fox, 'The right to political participation in international law' in GH Fox and BR Roth (eds), *Democratic Governance and International Law* (2000), 49–90, 53, 59.
[11] *United Communist Party of Turkey and ors v Turkey*, 19392/92 [1998] ECHR 1, Judgment of 30 January 1998, 45.
[12] In the Greek case the ECHR ruled that the existence of representative bodies, elected at reasonable intervals is essential for ensuring the right to political participation. T Franck, 'Legitimacy and democratic entitlement' in GH Fox and BR Roth (eds), *Democratic Governance and International Law* (2000), 66.   [13] Hereinafter CoE.
[14] Treaty on European Union, Official Journal C 191, Maastricht, 29 July 1992, available at <http://eur-lex.europa.eu/en/treaties/dat/11992M/htm/11992M.html> (accessed 31 July 2009).

additional protection to the political rights of minorities. Foundations of special protection of members of minorities stem from the ICCPR. Although Art 27 is framed in the negative, that persons belonging to minorities shall not be denied certain rights, the scope of the Article goes further. It implies that 'the enjoyment of those rights may require positive legal measures of protection and measures to ensure the effective participation of members of minority communities in decisions that affect them'.[15] This Article therefore obliges states to positively protect the right to political participation but leaves the definition of 'rights that affect them' open for states to decide. Alongside special rights protected by Art 27, persons belonging to national minorities enjoy the rights of non-discrimination.[16]

It took the international community thirty-eight years to write and publish the General Comment on Art 27. This indicates that the new understanding of the political rights of minorities, which was developed at the end of the Cold War, has found its way into human rights law through the practice of general comments. This interpretation is supported by the 1992 UN Declaration on the Rights of Persons Belonging to National or Ethnic, Religious, or Linguistic Minorities.[17] The language is similar to what has later been observed by the HRC. The states have declared that persons belonging to minorities have the right to 'participate effectively in decisions on the national and … regional level' in issues of their concern.[18] The right to effective political participation is buttressed by the right to participate effectively in public life,[19] which is one of the cornerstones of political rights in democracies. These documents indicate that the relative importance of protection of political rights has progressively developed to the point where states have an obligation to positively enforce these rights.

Right to political participation of minorities is also protected by the Convention on the Elimination of All Forms of Racial Discrimination (CERD). This nearly universally accepted document,[20] with an even higher number of states parties than the ICCPR, guarantees everyone, without distinction on the basis of ethnic origins, the right of enjoyment of their political rights. It connects the wide body of international electoral standards into one article. The states are obliged to guarantee the right of minorities to vote and to stand for elections, 'on the basis of universal and equal suffrage'.[21] It also protects different freedoms, taking part in the government and in conducting political affairs, as well

---

[15] General Comment no 23: The Rights of Minorities (Art 27), 50th session, CCPR/C/21/Rev1/Add5, Art 7.
[16] International Covenant on Civil and Political Rights, Ga Res 2200A(XXI), 16 June 1966/23 March 1976, Arts 2(1) and 26, <http://www2.ohchr.org/english/law/ccpr.htm>.
[17] Declaration on the Rights of Persons Belonging to National or Ethnic, Religious, or Linguistic Minorities, GaRes 47/135, 18 December 1992, available at <http://www.ohchr.org/Documents/Publications/GuideMinoritiesDeclarationen.pdf> (accessed 17 September 2009).
[18] Ibid, Art 3.   [19] Ibid, Art 2.
[20] On 17 August 2008 the CERD had 173 states parties.   [21] CERD, 5(b).

as equal access to public service. All states are under an obligation to acknowledge and protect these rights, but as the Committee on the Elimination of Racial Discrimination noted, the manner of translation of this provision into domestic legal orders of states may differ.[22] States may, by themselves, decide how the protection of these rights will be achieved, either by use of public institutions or even through activities of private institutions.[23]

These international developments have also had an impact on regional levels where countries have developed regional electoral standards. The most important document to understand this process is certainly the 1990 OSCE Copenhagen Document. It started the process of formalization and codification of political rights of minorities. Participating states have recognized that the rights of national minorities can only be properly guaranteed in a democratic political framework respecting basic rights and fundamental freedoms, which form international electoral standards.[24] Going a step further from this connection between democracy and human rights, states have pledged to 'respect the right of persons belonging to national minorities to effective participation in public affairs'.[25]

Ensuring minorities' effective participation in political affairs of their countries in Europe has been codified in a Framework Convention for the Protection of National Minorities. Parties have the express duty to create the necessary conditions for the 'effective participation of persons belonging to national minorities in public affairs, in particular those affecting them'.[26] Effective participation, as opposed to merely formal participation, on all levels of political life in consequence means that basic democratic standards have to be met. Although the convention contains mostly programme-like provisions and leaves the parties a measure of discretion in the translation and interpretation of provisions, the high number of states that have signed and quickly ratified it shows a high level of agreement with its content. An additional factor, which contributed to the compliance with minority rights provisions and has influenced the development of electoral standards, is the accession policy of the EU. All the standards seen in international human rights documents have become a cornerstone of accession talks with candidate countries. The Copenhagen meeting of the European Council has stated that membership of the EU requires democracy, respect for human rights, the rule of law, and respect for and the protection of national minorities. This conditionality principle was also adopted by the Council of

---

[22] CERD General Comment (XX), Art 1, available at <http://www.unhchr.ch/tbs/doc.nsf/(Symbol)/8b3ad72f8e98a34c8025651e004c8b61?Opendocument> (accessed 6 September 2009).
[23] CERD General Comment (XX), Art 5.
[24] <www.osce.org/item/13992.html> (accessed 6 September 2009), 30. [25] Ibid, 35.
[26] Framework Convention for the Protection of National Minorities, ETS no 157, CoE, Strasbourg, 1 February 1995, available at <http://conventions.coe.int/Treaty/EN/Treaties/Html/157.htm> (accessed 17 September 2009), Art 15.

Europe where new member states had to adopt previous CoE standards, including the standards on minority rights.

IV. Application of International Legal Principles in Practice

As follows from the vast body of international legal practice in the area of elections, today widely accepted global electoral principles of the democratic elections are: periodic and genuine elections, universal and equal suffrage, and secret vote or equivalent free voting procedures. These standards also necessitate the respect of some other basic rights and freedoms in order to protect the substance of the right. Important basic freedoms, which are essential for the conduct of elections, include the freedom of expression, association, and assembly.

In the past, the most comprehensive and widely used principle has been the one of 'free and fair' elections. However, the use of this principle does not have support in the wording of international legally binding documents.[27] Indeed, due to the 'inherent difficulties with the use of the words "free and fair" as a verdict on an election'[28] other democratic principles have been accepted as more appropriate for declaring elections as having been conducted in accordance with international democratic standards. Standards have also progressed since early days of the simple black-and-white free-and-fair characterization elections.

A. Equal and universal suffrage

The principle of universal and equal suffrage addresses the question of who exactly can be permitted to cast the ballot and how important their vote will be. The vote of every citizen who is eligible to vote needs to be given equal weight; this position has been known as the 'one person–one vote' principle.[29] Universal suffrage stipulates that the broadest possible number of citizens be given the right to political participation in elections.[30] In every election, technical

---

[27] A Melanšek, *Uporaba standardov opazovanja volitev po svetu: zaton svobodnih in poštenih volitev?* (2006) 17–40.
[28] *Handbook for EU Election Observation Missions* (*EOM*) (Brussels, 2002), 3, available at <http://europa.eu.int/comm/external_relations/human_rights/eu_election_ass_observ/docs/handbook_en.pdf> (accessed 6 September 2009). Difficulties of this concept have been more extensively elaborated in Melanšek, *Uporaba standardov opazovanja volitev po svetu* (n 27 above). The term 'fair elections' cannot be found in any of the basic documents: ICCPR, UDHR, American Convention on Human Rights, African Charter on Human and Peoples' Rights or the ECHR. The term features only in the Copenhagen Document (Arts 6, 7(7)). General Comment no 25 mentions fairness but does not define it (Arts 16, 19, 20).
[29] *Human Rights and Elections: A handbook on the legal, technical and human rights aspects of elections*, (1994), 68, available at <http://www.ohchr.org/Documents/Publications/training2en.pdf> (accessed 8 September 2009). [30] Ibid, 64.

processes such as constituency delimitation, registration of voters, polling, and counting procedures, need to be given great attention to ensure equality of votes.[31] Each vote must have the same weight and electoral districts must be established on an equitable basis that completely reflects the will of all the voters.[32]

The right to elect and to be elected may, however, be subject to certain limitations such as citizenship, age, residency requirements, mental capacity, and criminal convictions. The Human Rights Council has expressed the view that limitations on the grounds of economic requirements, restrictions on voting by naturalized citizens, excessive residency requirements, language and literacy requirements, and excessive requirements on voting rights of convicted criminals are not in accordance with the principle of equal and universal suffrage[33] and cannot be used to limit the right to vote for citizens falling into any of these categories.

Furthermore, suffrage needs to be exercised without distinction on the grounds of race, colour, sex, language, religion, political or other opinion, national or social origin, property, birth, or other status.[34] The European electoral context also features prohibitions on the basis of genetic features, such as disability, age, or sexual orientation.[35] Every voter and candidate needs to be equally treated by law, election administration, and election procedures. For example, on the day of elections, everyone must have access to voting. Equal voting rights must be guaranteed to the greatest extent possible. No legal requirements are allowed that might violate the principle of non-discrimination of persons in elections.[36]

In order to effectuate this principle, states are under a further obligation during the elections to prohibit and eliminate racial discrimination and to guarantee the right of everyone 'to participate in elections—to vote and to stand

---

[31] Ibid, 68–9.
[32] Draft General Principles on Freedom and Non-Discrimination in the Matter of Political Rights (principle V).
[33] *Human Rights and Elections* (n 29 above), 67; International Electoral Standards: Guidelines for reviewing the legal framework of elections, International Institute for Democracy and Electoral Assistance, Strömsborg, 2001, available at <http://www.idea.int/publications/ies/upload/electoralguidelines-2.pdf> (accessed 9 September 2009), 33.
[34] UDHR (Art 2), ICCPR (Art 2(1)), ECHR (Art 14). The provisions of Copenhagen Document (Art 5(9)) are written in a less specific language but protect the same right. They have to be read together with provision of the Art 24(4).
[35] Charter of Fundamental Rights of the European Union (Art 21(1)). General definition of discrimination can be found in General Comment no 18: Non-discrimination, 37th session, HRC, 10 November 1989, 7, available at <http://www.unhchr.ch/tbs/doc.nsf/(Symbol)/3888b0541f8501c9c12563ed004b8d0e?Opendocument> (accessed 9 September 2009).
[36] *Shirin Aumeeruddy-Cziffra and nineteen other Mauritian women v Mauritius*, available at <http://www.unhcr.org/refworld/docid/3f520c562.html> (accessed 17 September 2009), para 9.2(b)(2)(i)(8). The prohibition of non-discrimination also covers all areas, which are not necessarily covered by the ICCPR as confirmed in *SWM Broeks v The Netherlands*, available at <http://humanrights.law.monash.edu.au/undocs/newscans/172-1984.html> (accessed 17 September 2009), para. 5(3).

Application of International Legal Principles in Practice 353

for election—on the basis of universal and equal suffrage'.[37] They must take all appropriate measures to ensure enjoyment of equal rights for people, which could also be interpreted as a possibility, but not a duty, of affirmative action.[38] States must also ensure that women, on equal terms with men, have the right to vote, are eligible for election and have the opportunity to hold public office and functions.[39] Given that virtually all the OSCE participating states have accepted the ICCPR,[40] it can be concluded that states have a positive obligation in elections to use all appropriate means and all necessary measures to ensure equal rights of men and women in electoral process.[41]

States have further duties with regard to protecting the rights of minorities. Despite the low number of ratifications of the Framework Convention for the Protection of National Minorities,[42] the document advances the European regime of minority protection. It recognizes the fundamental freedoms for every person belonging to a national minority and articulates the corresponding obligation of the state to establish conditions for effective exercise of a person's rights and freedoms.[43] In practice the principle of universal and equal suffrage necessitates representation of national minorities in the electoral process. Political participation of members of national minorities in public debates as well as casting their ballots must not be obstructed.

B. Genuine elections

The principle of genuine elections incorporates each of the previously mentioned electoral principles. The *travaux préparatoires* of the ICCPR indicate that elections can be considered genuine if they reflect the free expression of the will of the electors. Genuine elections give effect to the will of the people and translate their will into elected seats by a pre-arranged and accepted formula. The fulfilment of this requirement might be questioned in situations where the fundamental rights and freedoms have not been respected, there has been no political competition, excessive and unreasonable restrictions have been put on the work of political parties, or if there has been no real prospect that votes will be effectively translated into political seats. The requirement of genuine elections

---

[37] CERD (Art 5(c)).
[38] HRC in *RD Stalla Costa v Uruguay*, available at <http://www.hrlibrary.ngo.ru/undocs/session42/198-1985.htm> (accessed 17 September 2009), para 11, declared that reasonable measures of affirmative action do not constitute a breach of Art 25 of the ICCPR. See, eg, the White paper published by the government of the Republic of South Africa.
[39] The Convention on the Elimination of All Forms of Discrimination against Women (CEDAW) (Art 7(a)–(b)). According to the convention, states must ensure equal participation of women based on their obligations under the ICCPR (General Recommendation no 23 (p 6)).
[40] Among the OSCE Participating states only the Holy See is not a member of this Convention (Division for the Advancement of Women 2006).   [41] CEDAW (Arts 2, 24).
[42] Total number of ratifications and accessions is thirty-nine, whereas four signatures were not followed by ratification (CoE Treaty Office 2007).
[43] Framework Convention for the Protection of National Minorities (Arts 9, 15).

also prescribes a real choice in elections, which presupposes freedom of information and informed choice by the voters. Guarantees of political pluralism and the protection of fundamental rights are the ultimate preconditions for the existence of genuine elections.

In addition, this principle refers to the whole legal electoral framework and all stages of electoral process. In order for an election not to be seen as designed to quell internal dissent or to forego international scrutiny, genuine elections necessitate electoral laws to be drawn up in a manner enabling democratic and effective exercise of the right to political participation. For elections to be genuine, all electoral processes such as constituency delineation, electoral campaign, registration procedures, balloting, counting and inauguration of elected representatives must effectively protect the right to political participation and enable free democratic elections.

Unlike with the principle of 'free election' and 'universal and equal suffrage', international legal documents are of little help in explaining the principle of 'genuine' elections. This term has been interpreted subjectively by states and does not seem to have any easily identifiable content. Similarly, the term itself provides no identifiable or enforceable standard of the election process, since 'every assessment [of genuine elections] must be mediated through [an] observer', often but not always in a context in which even reasonable people may come to different conclusions.[44]

C. Basic freedoms

1. Freedom of Thought, Conscience, Belief, and Opinion

Freedom of thought, conscience, belief, and opinion are essential for guaranteeing meaningful exercise of the right to political participation and contribute to the required democratic atmosphere for conducting elections. International documents are replete with references to free political participation but fail to further specify the methodology for ensuring such freedoms. Applying these freedoms to electoral processes shows that free elections demand an atmosphere where there is no intimidation and a wide range of fundamental freedoms is guaranteed.[45] Special attention to these freedoms must be given in the context of electoral campaigns, election propaganda, voter information campaigns, political meetings, and rallies. Obstacles to full participation must be removed in order to satisfy the principle of free election and special protection of fundamental freedoms extended to political groupings as well as individuals participating in an electoral process.

The principle of free elections stipulates that 'no legal or administrative obstacle stands in the way of unimpeded access to the media' in order to obtain

---

[44] GS Goodwin-Gill, 'Free and fair elections: New expanded version' (2006), 5.
[45] *Human Rights and Elections* (n 29 above), 6.

or disseminate information.[46] States in Europe have accepted the political commitment to ensure that law permits political campaigning to be conducted in a 'free atmosphere in which neither administrative action, violence nor intimidation bars the parties and the candidates from freely presenting their views and qualifications, or prevents the voters from learning and discussing them'.[47]

The fundamental freedoms of thought, conscience, belief, and opinion are absolute rights and must be especially respected as such during election time; they cannot be derogated, not even in time of public emergency or war.[48] Such unconditional protection of the freedom to hold a political opinion is essential in the context of elections as the ultimate expression of popular will, which would be meaningless without these protections. Moreover, individuals also have the right to doubt and to not accept an official ideology at the time of elections. HRC notes that if a set of beliefs is treated as official ideology 'this shall not result in any impairment of the freedoms under article 18 or ... in any discrimination against persons who do not accept the official ideology or who oppose it'.[49] The freedom of thought, conscience, and belief,[50] as well as the right to hold opinions without interference,[51] must be distinguished from the freedom to manifest beliefs, which does not enjoy unconditional protection and are subject to laws of the country that is holding elections.

2. Freedom of Expression and Information

Freedom of expression and information must also be guaranteed throughout a democratic electoral process.[52] Freedom to seek, receive, and impart information through different media are prerequisites for democratic elections.[53] Election parties, candidates, as well as voters, have the right to receive and impart information, regardless of frontiers, 'orally, in writing or in print, in the form of art, or through any other media'. These freedoms pertain not only to 'information or ideas that are favourably received or regarded as inoffensive or as a matter of indifference', but also to those that offend, shock, or disturb the state or any sector of the population.[54] Because of their role in a democratic society,

---

[46] Copenhagen Document (Art 7(8)). [47] Copenhagen Document (Art 7(7)).
[48] General Comment no 22: The right to freedom of thought, conscience and religion (Art 18), 48th session, CCPR/C/21/Rev1/Add4, HRC, 30 July 1993, available at <http://www.unhchr.ch/tbs/doc.nsf/(Symbol)/9a30112c27d1167cc12563ed004d8f15?Opendocument> (accessed 9 September 2009).   [49] Ibid, 10.
[50] UDHR (Art 18), ICCPR (Art 18), ECHR (Art 9), Copenhagen Document (Art 9(4)), EU Charter (Art 10).
[51] UDHR (Art 19), ICCPR (Art 19(1)), Copenhagen Document (Art 9(1)), ECHR (Art 10), EU Charter (Art 11).
[52] UDHR (Art 19), ICCPR (Art 19(2)), ECHR (Art 10), Copenhagen Document (Art 9(1)), EU Charter (Art 11).
[53] *OSCE Election Observation Handbook*, 5th edn (Warsaw, 2005), 65, available at <http://www.osce.org/publications/odihr/2005/04/14004_240_en.pdf> (accessed 9 September 2009).
[54] *Handyside v United Kingdom*, 5493/72 [1976] ECHR 5, ECHR, Judgment of 7 December 1976, 49, available at <http://www.worldlii.org/eu/cases/ECHR/1976/5.html> (accessed 9 September 2009).

print and electronic media, as well as political speech, need to be specially protected.[55] Politicians can also be subject to more public criticism due to the demands of democracy.[56] The right to express and receive partisan ideas and information must be firmly grounded in electoral law. This requirement is crucial: without informed people it is impossible to guarantee democratic elections.

The exercise of these freedoms during the time of elections imposes specific duties and responsibilities on individuals and the state.[57] Freedom of expression can therefore be subject to certain restrictions, which must, however: (a) be provided by law; (b) be in accordance with the provision of the ICCPR (Art 19 (c)); and (c) be justified as being necessary for that state party for one of those purposes.[58] States cannot merely assert that the restriction of a freedom was necessary during the conduct of elections for reasons of national security and use derogation to obstruct democratic electoral process.[59] According to the Copenhagen Document of the OSCE, it is the duty of the participating states to ensure that due to their exceptional character these restrictions are not abused and are not applied in an arbitrary manner.[60] In an electoral context this provision means that citizens must be guaranteed these rights to the greatest extent possible.

Limitations may be imposed only for the purpose of securing due recognition and respect for the rights and freedoms of others, requirements of morality, public order, general welfare in a democratic society,[61] prevention of crime, preventing the disclosure of information received in confidence, or for maintaining the authority and impartiality of the judiciary.[62] The principle of proportionality requires that suspension of obligations must be reasonable in light of what is necessary to address the emergency.[63] Account must also be taken of the public interest when assessing the interference with the exercise of the freedom of expression.[64] In the area of protecting public morals in, for example

---

[55] M Nowak, 'Civil and political rights' in J Symonides (ed), *Human Rights: Concept and standards* (Unesco, 2000), 93.
[56] *Oberschlick v Austria (no 2)* (47/1996/666/852) 1 July 1997, Art 35, available at <http://www.hrcr.org/safrica/expression/oberschlick_austria.html> (accessed 17 September 2009).
[57] ICCPR (Art 19(3)), Copenhagen Document (Art 24).
[58] General Comment no 10 (pp 4). See also EU Charter (Art 52(1)).
[59] *Alba Pietraroia v Uruguay, Communication*, 44/1979, HRC, 1984, available at <http://www1.umn.edu/humanrts/undocs/html/44_1979.htm> (accessed 9 September 2009).
[60] Document of the Copenhagen Meeting of the Conference on the Human Dimension of the CSCE, OSCE, Copenhagen, 29 June 1990, (Art 24), available at <http://www.osce.org/documents/odihr/1990/06/13992_en.pdf> (accessed 9 September 2009).
[61] UDHR (Art 29(2)), ICCPR (19(3)). [62] ECHR (Art 10(2)).
[63] Amnesty International, 2007, Ch 31. For more details and examples see also DF Orentlicher, 'Settling accounts: The duty to prosecute human rights violations of a prior regime' (1991) 100(8) *Yale Law Journal* 2537–615, 2606–12.
[64] *The Sunday Times v United Kingdom*, 6538/74 [1979] ECHR 1, 26, April 1979, available at <http://www.worldlii.org/eu/cases/ECHR/1979/1.html> (accessed 9 September 2009).

election campaigns, states are allowed more discretion due to the absence of common universal moral standards.[65]

3. Freedom of Assembly and Association

Given that the expression of political support is essential for elections, freedom of peaceful assembly needs to be protected by the state holding elections but as soon as the assembly loses its peaceful character, restrictions might be imposed.[66] This freedom is especially relevant in the context of political campaigns and rallies organized in order to gather support for political ideas. Any violent assembly, as well as messages and opinions expressed at the assembly, may be subjected to restrictions while on the other side, the assembly itself may not be altogether prohibited. States are also under a positive obligation to protect demonstrators taking part in a public assembly.[67]

On the other hand, freedom of association[68] guarantees the citizens freedom to associate with others. Within democratic societies, the right to join political parties is an especially prominent expression of this freedom. In turn, this right also protects the freedom not to join associations.[69] The legitimate limitations of this right include a similar tripartite test to the one found in limiting freedom of expression.[70] Freedom of association can be limited for reasons of public order, public safety, national security, or protection of rights and freedoms of others. It is crucial that this freedom is respected in an electoral context since, in democracies, the participation in political life of the country is exercised through political organizations. The ultimate indication as to whether elections have been free is the extent to which elections reflected and fully expressed the political will of the people concerned.

V. Implementation of International Legal Standards

The right to political participation is firmly entrenched in the European politico-legal context. The understanding of international electoral standards has been clarified through practice of international organizations.[71] The organizations observing elections have been at the forefront of their implementation and

---

[65] *Human Rights and Elections* (n 29 above), 7. For issues of perception of morality among states see also *Leo Hertzberg and ors v Finland*.
[66] UDHR (Art 20(1)), ICCPR (Art 21), ECHR (Art 11(1)), Copenhagen Document (Art 9 (2)), EU Charter (Art 12(1)).
[67] *Plattform 'Arzte fur das Leben' v Austria*, Appl no 10126-82, ECHR, 21 June 1988, para 32.
[68] UDHR (Art 20(1)), ICCPR (Art 22(1)), Copenhagen Document (Art 9(3)), ECHR (Art 11 (1)), EU Charter (Art 12).
[69] *Young, James and Webster v United Kingdom*, 7601/76; 7806/77 [1981] ECHR 4, 13 August 1981, para 57(b).
[70] UDHR (Art 29(2)), ICCPR (Art 22(1)), ECHR (Art 11(2)), Copenhagen Document (Art 24), EU Charter (Art 52(1)).
[71] See Goodwin-Gill (n 44 above), 5.

clarification.[72] In the case of election observation the three most notable organizations in Europe are the OSCE, the Council of Europe and the EU. The latter has mainly observed elections outside of Europe but is still rooted in the same European democratic tradition as the other two. The practical development of the regional and international legal standards can be seen from the methodology used to observe elections, as well as from electoral reports and states' reactions to them.

Election observation methodology stresses a few key areas where the rights of minorities deserve special attention. Already as part of the legal review of electoral legislation of the country observed, observers are instructed to pay attention to the way constituencies are drawn up in order to test whether they preserve equal suffrage of members of minorities.[73] Observers also stress that all voters need to have access to an impartial and non-discriminatory registration procedure.[74] They ascertain whether there is a sufficient number of registration centres and whether they are accessible to politically disadvantaged groups, including members of national minorities, especially in remote areas.[75] For that reason observers are given a comprehensive briefing on minority questions since the knowledge of these issues is relevant in ensuring equal and universal suffrage.[76] Thirdly, the methodology stresses the necessity of effective access to polling,[77] especially for national minorities. The three methodological developments show that the right to political participation of minorities is not limited only to the principle of one person equalling one vote. It follows from the election observation methodology that the weight and the quality of votes also matter.

Respecting electoral rights of minorities has become an important election standard when drawing election boundaries and delineating constituencies. Observers emphasize that a constituency that differs excessively in size from other constituencies in the country challenges the principle of equal suffrage.[78] The logic behind this provision is that if constituencies differed greatly in size, the relative weight of a ballot cast in big constituencies would be smaller compared to smaller constituencies. A difference in the size of the electorate is only allowed by organizations observing elections in cases of practical problems with drawing up constituencies and where there is a special need to protect equal suffrage of minorities.[79] The practice of gerrymandering by merging areas with different shares of minorities is heavily criticized[80] and prohibited. Mechanisms

---

[72] A Melanšek, *Election Observation in Europe: A case of the impact of implementation procedures on norm development* (2007), 79–85.   [73] *Handbook for EU EOM* (n 28 above), 69.
[74] OSCE EOM Handbook (n 53 above), 39–40; *Handbook for EU EOM* (n 28 above), 66–9.
[75] K Archer, *Guiding Principles of Voter Registration*, ACE Electoral Knowledge Network, available at <http://aceproject.org/ace-en/topics/vr/vr20> (accessed 17 September 2009).*Guiding Principles* 2006)   [76] *OSCE EOM Handbook*, 30.
[77] Ibid, 19.   [78] OSCE EOM Albania (2005), 4.
[79] OSCE EOM Albania (2007) 15.   [80] CoE EOM Macedonia (1998).

Implementation of International Legal Standards 359

for election observation in general call attention to special characteristics of certain groups of voters such as minorities and internally displaced persons. This practice resulted in the shifting of state attention from ensuring equal and universal suffrage for all citizens to taking positive steps to ensure that under-represented groups of voters were able to effectively exercise their right to vote.

Observers emphasize that special attention needs to be given to voter registration procedures when registering voters from ethnic minorities. The case of the Roma population is of particular concern to them. Roma often lack permanent housing, education and identity documents which makes them less likely to be included in voter registers purely due to practical obstacles preventing registration.[81] Often members of minorities also face administrative difficulties trying to obtain proper documents which would make them eligible to register as voters.[82] To ensure the fulfilment of the principle of equal and universal suffrage, observers recommend that states should adopt special measures to promote equal rights of ethnic minorities. States must actively encourage voter registration,[83] conduct civil education and train members of election bodies to become more sensitive and aware of minority issues.[84] Moreover, observation emphasizes that it is the duty of the state to establish the actual number of citizens lacking identification documents and take adequate measures to secure relevant documents for them.[85]

In voting, election observers emphasize that states have a special duty to ensure effective suffrage of ethnic minorities. Election observation confirms that many members of such minorities are marginalized and socially excluded, which can make them targets for illegal practices such as selling votes in exchange for small sums of money, food, or settlement of minor debts.[86] These practices deny them suffrage on an equal footing with other voters. Throughout its observation efforts the OSCE has received numerous reports of malpractices affecting minority communities and as a result focuses on ensuring effective equal suffrage for their members.

The practice also shows that the protection of language rights of minorities is necessary for the proper exercise of equal and universal suffrage.[87] Observers welcome good practices where the election administration conducts voter education campaigns in minority languages[88] and, drawing on these good practices, recommend other states to do the same in their elections.[89] They especially point out difficulties minorities face where ballots are not produced in their language, particularly when the ballots use a different alphabet.[90] Despite ballots

---

[81] OSCE EOM Albania (2003), 18; OSCE EOM Macedonia (2004), 19.
[82] OSCE EOM Macedonia (2005), 17.   [83] OSCE EOM Albania (2005), 29.
[84] OSCE EOM Macedonia (2004), 26; OSCE EOM Macedonia (2005), 26.
[85] OSCE EOM Macedonia (2005), 25.   [86] OSCE EOM Macedonia (2006), 18.
[87] CoE EOM Macedonia (1998), 44.
[88] OSCE EOM Albania (2005), 17; OSCE EOM Albania (2007), 15.
[89] OSCE EOM Macedonia (1999), 11.   [90] OSCE EOM Macedonia (1998), 8.

being printed in minority languages in some countries in Europe, the OSCE did not at first recommend that minority languages to be included on the ballot as an obligation of the state. In the case of Macedonia it merely recognized that 'the use of languages of minorities is … a complex and sensitive political and legal issue, with constitutional implications'.[91] Later, however, Macedonia included language requirements relating to official election material and documents in its Election Code, and extended such requirements to ballots.[92] This shows that states widely accept the obligation to provide ballots in minority languages.[93] A trend is apparent where election observation extends language requirements to all state areas where minority languages or scripts are used by a significant part of the local population.[94]

The practice of election observation, therefore, shows that respecting the rights of minorities has become one of most important tasks of electoral observers. The importance of their protection is also evident from their codification in international legal documents.

VI. Codification of Practices

States also agree with the obligation to extend the principle of equal and universal suffrage by encouraging effective representation of under-represented groups and providing them with enhanced voting rights. This perception of the principle is recognized by the HRC in its General Comment no 25. The HRC stresses that '[p]ositive measures should be taken to overcome specific difficulties, such as illiteracy, language barriers, poverty, or impediments to freedom of movement which prevent persons entitled to vote from exercising their rights effectively'.[95] As Weller notes, the need for effective participation is especially pronounced in the case of non-dominant groups facing structural disenfranchisement.[96] In line with this perception the Draft Convention on Election Standards, Electoral Rights and Freedoms[97] recognizes the obligation to take further legislative measures to guarantee rights of participation for persons with physical disabilities as well as other categories of the population.[98] States agree to

---

[91] Ibid. [92] OSCE EOM Macedonia (2006), 18.
[93] See also OSCE EOM Montenegro (2006), 15. [94] Ibid, 23.
[95] General Comment no 25, p 11. See also S Joseph, J Schultz and M Castan, *The International Covenant on Civil and Political Rights: Cases, materials and commentary* (2004), pp. 23, 69.
[96] M Weller, *The Rights of Minorities: A commentary on the European Framework Convention for the Protection of National Minorities* (2005), 430.
[97] Convention on Election Standards, Electoral Rights and Freedoms (draft), Association of Central and Eastern European Election Officials, Moscow, 28 September 2002, available at <http://www.venice.coe.int/docs/2003/CDL(2003)057-e.asp> (accessed 9 September 2009).
[98] Draft ACEEEO Convention (Art 12(2)), The Lund Recommendations (B(10)), Framework Convention for the Protection of National Minorities (Art 16), Guidelines to Assist National Minority Participation in the Electoral Process.

undertake special measures ensuring representation of national minorities or ethnic groups in elections. If under-represented groups of society are deprived of the possibility of an equal standing with respect to political and electoral rights compared to the rest of the population, such measures are not considered discriminatory.[99]

A system of mere legal guarantees is therefore not enough and states need to ensure organizational, financial, informational, and other guarantees of election rights and freedoms to ensure that national minorities have 'additional means for participating in elections'.[100] As was well summed up by Joseph, Schultz, and Castan, states have a positive obligation to protect equal and universal suffrage that goes beyond mere provision of electoral facilities.[101] Some specific areas of norm extension through their application in practice can be pointed out in support of this perception.

First, states recognize their obligation to ensure implementation of language rights for national minorities in order to protect their right to vote. In line with election observation recommendations, states codified the need to conduct elections in the languages of the composite parts of the state territory, including languages of 'nations and nationalities, national minorities and ethnic groups in the territories of their compact living'.[102] It is a legal requirement that ballot papers and other election documents need to be published according to these requirements.[103] Also, legal commentaries recognize the need for taking special measures with respect to electoral procedures to ensure effective representation of members of national minorities in the political life of a country.[104]

Secondly, states' obligations to provide adequate access to polling places is codified in international law. In order to protect equality of suffrage every voter must have equal and unimpeded access to polling places for the purpose of voting.[105] This provision reflects the concern of election observers that people with physical disabilities or people living far from polling stations must be ensured access to polling. Moreover, states also recognize the right of everyone to have access to an equitable procedure of state registration of voters,[106] which is the reflection of registration requirements stressed above.

Thirdly, legal instruments allow for a deviation in drawing up electoral boundaries in the form of positive discrimination where nations, national

---

[99] CIS Convention (Art 18(1)(a)). Same provision can be found in the Framework Convention for the Protection of National Minorities (s II/Art 4).
[100] Draft ACEEEO Convention (Art 21(2.2)).
[101] Joseph, Schultz and Castan (2004: pp. 22.24).
[102] CIS Convention (Art 9(4)), Code of Good Practice in Electoral Matters (Art 3(1)(b)(iii)) and Draft ACEEEO Convention (Art 7).
[103] CIS Convention (Art 17(1)), Draft ACEEEO Convention (Art 17(7)), General Comment no 25, p. 12.   [104] Weller, *The Rights of Minorities* (n 95 above), 458.
[105] CIS Convention (Art 3(2)), Draft ACEEEO Convention (Art 2(6)).
[106] Draft ACEEEO Convention (Art 8(1)(5)), CIS Convention (Art 19(e)).

minorities, or ethnic groups live compactly in one area.[107] The Venice Commission has specifically recommended that the permissible departure from the norm is 15 per cent difference in the number of voters in a constituency in order to protect national minorities.[108] The obligation to protect national minorities when drawing electoral boundaries, also pointed out by Weller, is covered in a separate paragraph of the Code of Good Practice in Electoral Matters.[109] It states that when constituency boundaries are defined it must be done 'without detriment to national minorities'.[110] OSCE has observed that, in view of the wide variety of geographical and demographic factors in Europe, it is not advisable to specify and codify the norm any further.[111]

VII. Conclusion

Rights to political participation of minorities have become an integral part of international electoral standards. Derived from the UDHR, they have been extended and clarified by issue specific human rights conventions protecting the rights of minorities. However, the most important development of legal standards has occurred since the end of the Cold War with the spread of the practice of election observation. Observers have, through their practice, clarified and extended international electoral standards. It can therefore be concluded that the political rights of national minorities are protected by the standards of periodic and genuine elections, held by universal and equal suffrage, and by secret vote or by equivalent free voting procedures. Moreover, the standards require that minority rights are given special attention in electoral processes and are positively enforced to protect their right to vote.

---

[107] CIS Convention (Art 3(1)(b)), Draft ACEEEO Convention (Art 9(1)(2)).
[108] Code of Good Practice in Electoral Matters (Art 2(2)(iv)).
[109] Weller, *The Rights of Minorities* (n 95 above), 445.
[110] Code of Good Practice in Electoral Matters (Art 2(2)(vii)).
[111] Existing Commitments for Democratic Elections (Ch II/pp III(3)(2)).

12

Electoral Systems and the Lund Recommendations

*Brendan O'Leary**

'The large prefer the small, and the small prefer the large.'
 Josep M Colomer, *The Micro-Mega Rule*.[1]

'The strong do what they have the power to do and the weak accept what they have to accept.'
 The Athenian Ambassadors to the Melians, Thucydides, *The Peloponnesian War*.[2]

'Those who really deserve praise are the people who, while human enough to enjoy power, nevertheless pay more attention to justice than they are required to do by the situation.'
 The Athenian Ambassadors to the Spartans, Thucydides, *The Peloponnesian War*.[3]

I. Election Systems	365
II. The Classification of Electoral Systems by Formula	367
A. Plurality and majoritarian systems—including WTA-SMD, TRS, the alternative vote, and parallel systems	374
B. Proportional Systems—including list-PR, STV, and MMP	387
C. Districting, geography, and thresholds	394
D. Corporate or reserved systems	395
E. Untried systems	396
III. Concluding Observations	397

---

* Thanks are owed to Marc Weller, Stephan Stohler, and John McGarry. My debts to Patrick Dunleavy, Bernard Grofman, Arend Lijphart, Jack Nagel, and Rein Taagapera should be transparent.
 [1] JM Colomer, '*The Strategy and History of Electoral System Choice*' in JM Colomer (ed) *Handbook of Electoral System Choice*, with a Foreword by Bernard Grofman (2004).
 [2] Thucydides, *Thucydides: History of the Peloponnesian War*, Penguin Classics (1954). Book V, 89. [3] Ibid, Book I, 76.

The Lund Recommendations on the Effective Participation of National Minorities in Public Life advocate two core goals:

(i) promoting the *participation* of national minorities in governmental decision-making at all levels, central, regional, and local
(ii) promoting the self-government of such minorities through functional or territorial autonomy.[4]

Let us call these the *participation* and the *autonomy* goals respectively. Both are admirable, but advisers should warn that appropriately precise electoral system evaluations and recommendations should vary according to which goal is being considered or prioritized. For example, a national minority, by virtue of being a minority, is highly likely to benefit from the use of proportional representation (PR) to elect the federal or central parliament of a state, but in the exercise of self-government in its regional homeland, where it may be a majority, it might prefer winner-takes-all (WTA) in single member districts (SMD) to be the electoral formula.

This chapter focuses comment on *electoral system* designs in the light of the Lund Recommendations, and does not emphasize *electoral regulations*.[5] The latter are, however, very important, and encompass, among other matters, the laws and conventions governing electoral administration, eg laws on the franchise, determining who has the right to vote; regulations on electoral deposits; on the eligibility requirements and signatures required to register and stand for office; the rules on absentee or diaspora ballots; electoral registers and the uses that can be made of them; the roles of independent or partisan electoral commissions; and rules governing campaigning, competition over fund-raising, advertising, and access to public and private media. Surprisingly, the Lund Recommendations present no significant prescriptions for electoral regulations. The original Explanatory Note appended to them observed that states must fulfil their obligations under the Universal Declaration of Human Rights (Art 21.3), the International Covenant on Civil and Political Rights (Art 25), the European Convention on Human Rights (Protocol 1, Art 3), and the Copenhagen Document (para 5–6) 'without discrimination', and with 'as much representativeness as possible'.[6] The authors seem to have had in mind freedom of expression, assembly and association for the effective exercise of the right to vote, rather than the more extensive details of electoral administration. Later, however, the authors of the Explanatory Note recognized that 'ideally, [electoral]

---

[4] Project Unit Office of the High Commissioner on National Minorities, The Lund Recommendations on the Effective Participation of National Minorities in Public Life and Explanatory Note (1999). See II, 8–10, and III, 10–12

[5] The distinction is made in M Gallagher and P Mitchell (eds), *The Politics of Electoral Systems* (2005), 3. For a very useful discussion of the rules governing the conduct of elections see L Massicotte, A Blais, and A Yoshinaka, *Establishing the Rules of the Game: Election laws in democracies* (2004).

[6] The Lund Recommendations (n 4 above), 23.

boundaries should be determined by an independent and impartial body to ensure, among other concerns, respect for minority rights', and noted that this task 'is often accomplished in OSCE ... States by means of standing, professional electoral commissions'.[7] By this standard, of course, the United States is now an international democratic pariah. It does not have an independent federal electoral commission. The states of the federation run the federal elections under their own regulations, do not have independent electoral commissions, and most allow the governing political party to re-draw electoral districts every ten years, with severe consequences for the level of competitiveness of elections to the federal House of Representatives.[8] If the Lund Recommendations were ever revised it would be helpful if an explicit prescription commended an independent electoral commission in each state, at central or federal level, replicated as appropriate with regional or state commissions in federations or union-states. It is the practice of the United Nations Electoral Assistance Unit to recommend the establishment of such commissions at the state level, but separate independent commissions may also be appropriate at the regional level within multinational states: national minorities that govern regions or provinces would then not have state-wide independent bodies imposed on them.[9] Provided such independent bodies are charged with ensuring protections for the electoral rights of all, and are legally accountable for their conduct, there is no reason to believe that regional electoral commissions will behave worse (or better) than state-wide commissions, and their existence would be one way of maintaining federal organizational principles.

I. Election Systems

Analysis of election systems, in political science, now refers to eight key elements. The three that are generally agreed to be most important are as follows:

(1) The *electoral formula* is the rule that converts votes into seats or office (sometimes known as 'the seat allocation rule').
(2) The *district magnitude* is the number of representatives elected in a constituency or district.

---

[7] Ibid, 25.
[8] Though the US does not have an independent federal electoral commission its citizens may appeal directly to the Attorney General of the United States, or the US District Court for the District of Columbia, if they believe their voting rights have been infringed because of racial discrimination, see The Voting Rights Act, (1965), USA, 42, §, 1973, 89–110, 1973, 1965 amended 1982, Denial or Abridgment of Right to Vote on Account of Race or Color through Voting Qualifications or Prequisites; Establishment of Violation
[9] The UN, along with multiple intergovernmental and international governmental organizations, has endorsed guideline principles for the international observation of elections, United Nations Secretariat, Declaration of Principles for International Election Observation and Code of Conduct for International Election Observers, (2005).

(3) The *size of the elected body* is the number of people being elected to an assembly, parliament, executive, or court, which may not be the same as the district magnitude.

The next element (4) the *ballot structure*, is determined by the combination of (1) and (2). The *ballot structure* can be categorical, ie the voter may select just one party or candidate, or ordinal, ie the voter may select more than one party or candidate and may rank them. A further element (5) is the *electoral threshold*, ie the minimum level of support that a party or candidate needs to win office. This threshold is implicit in the combination of (1), (2), and (3), but it may also be specified or modified by statute law, eg a country may require that a party may be required to obtain at least 10 per cent of the votes cast throughout the state, as in contemporary Turkey.[10] Another element (6) is the degree of *malapportionment*, ie the degree to which electoral districts electing the same number of officials are unequally sized in numbers of registered voters. There is always some unintended malapportionment in any country with more than one electoral district simply because of demographic shifts between census periods, or between intervals in composing electoral registers, but malapportionment may also be deliberate—either entrenched, eg through rules that fix districts' entitlements to elect a certain number of persons even if their population falls below what would have been a proportional threshold (eg to ensure that rural, sparsely populated constituencies are not overly large), or the product of deliberate district boundary manipulations. Yet another element (7) is the *nature of the executive*. Whether there is a parliamentary government or a directly elected presidential executive may significantly affect both the behaviour of voters and party system dynamics.[11] A last element of significance (8) is the existence or otherwise of *apparentement*: the ability or otherwise of parties to link their separate votes for the allocation of seats.[12] Each of these eight elements may have significant implications for the participation and autonomy of national minorities in a state.

Before we classify electoral systems into families according to their formulas and consider their likely impact on national minorities we should consider the judgment of Bernard Grofman, perhaps the current serving professorial doyen of electoral systems evaluation in the English language. Having spent several decades engaged in extensive cross-national research on the empirical behaviour

---

[10] This threshold is especially targeted at Kurdish parties, which are additionally banned from organizing under an openly ethnic or national label, *and* required to be organized in at least half of Turkey's provinces, and one third of the districts within these provinces—'distributive requirements' that are targeted at weakening the prospects of such parties.

[11] See M Soberg Shugart and JM Carey, *Presidents and Assemblies: Constitutional design and electoral dynamics* (1992). Here I neglect the consequences of bicameralism and multi-tier governance, though doubtless these elements affect voting behaviour as well—voters, eg, are more likely to be irresponsible, reckless, experimental, or not to turn out for what they deem to be second- or third-order elections.

[12] All eight elements are discussed further in the modern classic A Lijphart (ed), *Electoral Systems and Party Systems: A study of twenty-seven democracies, comparative European politics* (1994), 10–15.

of electoral systems, while also being an *aficionado* of formal or mathematical studies of voting systems, Grofman maintains that there is a consensus among political scientists that 'No electoral system or voting rule is uniformly best under all criteria or in all places (and times)'.[13] That is both because there are so many considerations that we might want to take into account when we judge voting rules and because there are numerous theorems about the impossibility of having one voting rule satisfy all desirable criteria—for instance Kenneth Arrow's impossibility theorem.[14] But Grofman does not imply that political science is a sea of relativism. Some election systems are definitely worse than others on some criteria for unambiguous reasons, as is especially true for the representation and autonomy of national minorities. We can also say which systems are worst if we wish to prioritize certain inputs or outcomes—and that applies to the representation and autonomy of national minorities.

II. The Classification of Electoral Systems by Formula

There are many ways to classify electoral systems.[15] The most common empirical classification distinguishes them by their electoral (or seat allocation) formulas into four types:

(i) plurality
(ii) majoritarian
(iii) proportional
(iv) mixed or hybrid systems

Their names tell their stories. In plurality systems the winner or leader takes all, whether or not the candidate, bloc, or party has a majority. In majoritarian systems the winner(s) must obtain 50 per cent plus one in the final vote count (which may take several rounds, or ballots, and may involve the elimination of those with the lowest vote shares). In proportional systems the seat or office shares allocated are proportional to vote shares. Mixed or hybrid systems combine at least two of the preceding systems, normally through electing some people in districts through plurality or winner-takes-all, and others through proportional representation. In fully compensatory mixed systems the proportional allocation fully compensates for any disproportionality introduced in the districts. But there are also two-tier systems in which little or no compensation takes place—or in which further

---

[13] Public Lecture, Sawyer-Mellon Seminar on 'Power-Sharing in Deeply Divided Places', University of Pennsylvania, 5 February 2008. See also B Grofman, 'Electoral rules and ethnic representation and accommodation: Combining social choice and electoral system perspectives' in J McEvoy and B O'Leary (eds), *Power-Sharing in Deeply Divided Places* (2010 in press).
[14] KJ Arrow, *Social Choice and Individual Values* (1963).
[15] For good surveys see DM Farrell, *Comparing Electoral Systems* (1997), DM Farrell, *Electoral Systems: A comparative introduction* (2001).

disproportionality is added. These are generally known as 'parallel systems'. Fully compensatory systems clearly belong to the species of proportional representation at the level of the state as a whole, whereas parallel systems are kindred in spirit and effects to plurality and majoritarian systems. For this reason some simplify this fourfold classification by formulas into two types; namely, majoritarian systems (including plurality, double-ballot majoritarian, parallel systems and the alternative vote) are distinguished from proportional systems (including list PR, the single transferrable vote, and fully compensatory hybrid systems, now generally known as 'mixed member proportional representation'[16]).

This twofold simplification has one normative fault, which often leads to loose talk. Majoritarian systems, broadly conceived, as we shall see, often generate 'artificial legislative majorities', whereas proportional systems, precisely because they may oblige the formation of multi-party cabinets, are far more likely to generate authentic majority governments, ie governments in which the governing parties were jointly supported by more than 50 per cent of the electorate.[17] For this reason it is quite mistaken to assume that proportional systems solely benefit minorities. They are, in fact, far more likely than plurality systems to benefit majorities (albeit majorities comprised of coalitions of minority parties). Indeed, it is fairer to say that plurality and majoritarian systems are as likely to favour dominant minorities, as they are to favour authentic majorities.

The preceding distinctions are not the only ways to classify electoral systems. Another mode focuses on whether the voter exercises a categorical or X vote through non-preferential voting, or, by contrast, is able to express ranked numerical preferences across candidates or parties. Non-preferential voting systems include X voting in single member districts according to plurality rule, X voting in multi-member districts according to the single non-transferable vote,[18] and X voting in multi-member districts using list proportional representation. Preferential voting systems, by contrast, include both majoritarian systems, such as the alternative vote,[19] and proportional

---

[16] See M Soberg Shugart and MP Wattenberg, *Mixed-member Electoral Systems: The best of both worlds?* (2003).

[17] JH Nagel, 'Expanding the spectrum of *democracies:* Reflections on proportional representation in New Zealand' in MML Crepaz, TA Koelbe, and D Wilsford (eds), *Democracy and Institutions: The life work of Arend Lijphart* (2000).

[18] B Grofman et al (eds), *Elections in Japan, Korea and Taiwan under the Single Non-Transferable Vote: The Comparative study of an embedded institution* (1999). The SNTV system gives the voter just one vote though there are multiple candidates to be elected—its results are often described as 'semi-proportional'). See the discussion of thresholds below, pp 394–5.

[19] C Bean, 'Australia's experience with the alternative vote' (1997) 34(2) *Representation* 103–10; J Fraenkel and B Grofman, 'A neo-Downsian model of the alternative vote as a mechanism for mitigating ethnic conflict in plural societies' (2004) 121 *Public Choice* 487–506; J Fraenkel and B Grofman, 'Does the Alternative vote foster moderation in ethnically divided societies? The case of Fiji' (2006) 39(5) *Comparative Political Studies* 623–51; J Fraenkel and B Grofman, 'The failure of the alternative vote as a tool for ethnic moderation in Fiji? A rejoinder to Horowitz' (2006) 39(5) *Comparative Political Studies* 663–6; A Lijphart, 'The alternative vote: A realistic alternative for South Africa?' (1990) 18(2) *Politikon* 91–101.

representation systems, such as the single transferable vote in multi-member constituencies.[20]

Yet another way we might classify systems is by the number of persons elected per district—single-member, multi-member, single-tier or multi-tier, and so on. Given the eight systemic elements identified earlier it is easy to see why an almost infinite permutation in the classification of systems is possible. But we shall confine the bulk of our focus to the systems discussed in the Lund Recommendations.

Before deepening analysis it is important to reflect briefly on the origins of electoral system choices since these choices decisively shape the fates of national minorities. A fascinating paper from the International Political Science Conference of 1994, focused on the entire world of states, identified four variables that then correlated significantly with electoral system choice in democracies (and in the non-democracies that used elections).[21] André Blais and Louis Massicotte identified colonial background as one key variable. For example, countries subjected to or created by British imperialism tended to use the electoral system used in Great Britain since the eighteenth century, and earlier, namely, plurality or winner takes all in single-member districts (hereafter WTA-SMD), eg the USA, India, Canada, Malaysia, Nigeria, Kenya, Uganda, Sudan, and the formerly British-governed island democracies of the Caribbean, and the states of South Asia, and the South Pacific. Countries once under the French empire were more likely to use double-ballot majoritarianism or the two-round system (hereafter TRS) to elect their legislature, and double-ballot run-offs to elect their presidents, eg Algeria (for its president), the Comoros, the Republic of the Congo, Gabon, Haiti, Mali, Mauritania, Togo, and Vietnam. Countries once governed by the Dutch were more likely to use list proportional representation, eg Netherlands Antilles and Indonesia. And, I would add, countries once controlled by Soviet imperialism are now strikingly more likely to follow the Russian Federation in using parallel systems, eg Armenia, Azerbaijan, Georgia, Kazakhstan, Lithuania, Tajikistan, and the Ukraine.

---

[20] S Bowler and B Grofman (eds), *Elections in Australia, Ireland and Malta under the Single Transferable Vote* (2000); SJ Brams and PC Fishburn, 'Some logical defects of the single transferable vote' in A Lijphart and B Grofman (eds), *Choosing an Electoral System: Issues and alternatives* (1984); M Gallagher, 'Comparing proportional representation electoral systems: Quotas, Thresholds, paradoxes and majorities' (1992) 22 *British Journal of Political Science* 469–96; M Gallagher, 'Does Ireland need a new electoral system ?' (1987) 2 *Irish Political Studies* 27–48; M Gallagher, 'The political consequences of the electoral system in the Republic of Ireland' (1986) 5(3) *Electoral Studies* 253–75; R Katz, 'The single transferable vote and proportional representation' in A Lijphart and B Grofman (eds), *Choosing an Electoral System: Issues and alternatives* (1984).
[21] A Blais and L Massicotte, 'Electoral systems in the world: A macroscopic perspective', paper presented at the International Political Science Association, 16th World Congress, Berlin, 21–5 August 1994.

Table 12.1 Imperial or Hegemon effects in electoral system choice within the OSCE. The apparent impact of a former imperial power or regional hegemon on electoral systems.

Plurality	Majoritarian	Proportional	Hybrid-Mixed	
			Proportional	Parallel
Great Britain	France	Sweden	Germany (MMP)	Russia-USSR
Canada		Norway	Albania	Armenia
USA		Denmark	Hungary	Azerbaijan
		Iceland		Georgia
		Finland		Kazakhstan
				Lithuania
				Tajikistan
				Ukraine

A second key variable noticed by Blais and Massicotte was geography. Electoral systems cluster by world regions. The causal presumption is that states tend to emulate their neighbours in their choice of election systems. Western Europe has become dominated by proportional representation systems, with the exceptions of Great Britain (at state level) and France, and that system choice has now spread throughout much of Eastern Europe as the European Union expanded after Blais and Massicotte wrote their paper. Oceania, by contrast, is the site of non-proportional (both WTA-SMD and TRS) systems. Asia has many examples of WTA-SMD, and of TRS and parallel systems, whereas a state in Spanish- and Portuguese-speaking America is now highly likely to have proportional representation. In Table 12.2, updating and adapting Blais and Massicotte's findings, I show that the member states of the OSCE are dominated by proportional systems in continental Europe, but are flanked to their north-west by broadly majoritarian systems influenced by Great Britain and France, and to their east by majoritarian parallel systems influenced by Russia. Colonial background and geography are inter-correlated: British imperialism was strong in North America, South Asia, Africa, and Oceania; French imperialism in West Africa and the Pacific; and Soviet imperialism dominated central and parts of South-west Asia. But colonialism, geography, or neighbourly emulation does not tell the whole story of system origin. After all, both Iberia's and Latin America's general shift to proportional representation is recent. Before the previous wave of military dictatorships WTA-SMD had been common in Latin America. Geography, the colonial or imperial past, or the current hegemon are not any country's destiny.

A third correlation found by Blais and Massicotte was population density. Densely populated countries were less likely to have PR. The explanation for this variable is not obvious. India, the USA, and Japan are examples of large

Table 12.2 Electoral systems within the OSCE in 2009 showing Continental European proportionality flanked by British, French, and Russian influenced majoritarianism

Plurality (WTA-SMD)	Majoritarian (TRS)	Proportional	Hybrid-Mixed	
			Proportional	Parallel
Canada	Belarus	Austria	Albania (MMP)	Andorra
UK	France	Belgium	Germany (MMP)	Armenia
USA	Kyrgyzstan	Bosnia and Herzegovina	Hungary (MMP)	Azerbaijan
	Turkeministan	Bulgaria		Georgia
	Uzbekistan	Croatia		Kazakhstan
		Cyprus		Lithuania
		Czech Republic		Monaco
		Denmark		Russia
		Estonia		Tajikistan
		Finland		Ukraine
		Greece		
		Iceland		
		Ireland (STV)		
		Italy		
		Latvia		
		Liechtenstein		
		Luxembourg		
		Macedonia		
		Malta (STV)		
		Moldova		
		Montenegro		
		Netherlands		
		Norway		
		Poland		
		Portugal		
		Romania		
		San Marino		
		Serbia		
		Slovak Republic		
		Slovenia		
		Spain		
		Sweden		
		Switzerland		
		Turkey*		

Sources: International IDEA, updated through the Inter-parliamentary Union's website.

* Turkey's double threshold requirement makes its system highly 'majoritarian' in practice. A party must (i) be organized in at least half of Turkey's provinces *and* one-third of the districts within these provinces, and (ii) must obtain at least 10 per cent of the vote cast throughout the state to win seats. **The Holy See is a member state of the OSCE. The election system used for the papacy is a very interesting subject,[22] though the electors appear to believe their God casts the decisive ballot.

[22] See among others JM Colomer and I McLean, 'Electing Popes: Approval voting and qualified majority rule', (1998) 29(1) *Journal of Interdisciplinary History* 1–22; G Tobin, *Selecting the Pope: Uncovering the mysteries of papal elections* (2009).

countries with formally non-proportional systems. Perhaps the explanation may be that big states, or great powers, or former great powers may be less willing to adopt proportional representation. Perhaps great powers prefer to have a strong discretionary executive in foreign affairs, and therefore resist proportional systems, which are held to empower legislatures. During the First World War, in a polemical essay, Max Weber suggested that the institutions of consensual democracy were for the weak, like the Swiss, whereas a Machstaat, such as Germany, would not and should not adopt them. To adapt a recent comparison from international relations we might suggest that PR countries are small wimps from Venus, while majoritarians are big warriors from Mars.[23] But, however interesting this line of speculation might be, no widely agreed causal story exists that fits all the data well, and the correlation may be spurious.

The last variable identified by Blais and Massicotte is more interesting for present purposes. They showed that the higher a state appeared on a series of indicators that measured the depth of its democratization then the more likely the state was to have a proportional representation system. It may be suggested that the relevant indices of democratization are biased toward European models of democracy, but others have found that 'consensus democracies' do better than 'majoritarian democracies' on a range of indicators of democratic performance.[24]

Other cross-state research on founding electoral system choice, and subsequent shifts in choice, suggests that what was most important, when the choice was fully considered—and was not simply a default 'decision' based on an institutional or colonial legacy—was the interests of outgoing authoritarian incumbents, and the bargains they struck with their likely replacements.[25] Where incumbents feared complete loss of power, or revolutionary redistributive programmes, then they favoured proportional representation, to secure for themselves some stake in the new order, and, where possible, to break up the potentially usurpationist popular majority they believed was ranged against them. This is roughly the explanation given for the switch from majoritarian systems under limited suffrage to proportional representation systems with full adult suffrage in Scandinavia in the early twentieth century. It is also the style of explanation provided for communist parties' modes of negotiation of their departures from legislative control in various parts of Eastern Europe. Where they believed themselves to have strong organizational and electoral futures they

---

[23] See M Weber, 'Between two laws' in P Lassman and R Speirs (eds), *Political Writings* (1994), 75–80; see also R Kagan, *Of Paradise and Power: America and Europe in the new world order* (2003).

[24] Notably A Lijphart, *Patterns of Democracy: Government forms and performance in thirty-six countries* (1999).

[25] See S Rokkan et al, 'Electoral systems' in *Citizens, Parties and Elections* (1970) for a discussion of Western European cases; and A Lijphart, 'Democratisation and constitutional choices in Czecho-Slovakia, Hungary and Poland, 1989–91' (1992) 4(2) *Journal of Theoretical Politics* 207–23, for a discussion of post-communist Central European cases. A fairly comprehensive collection of global case-studies on system choices may be found in JM Colomer, *Handbook of Electoral System Choice* (2004).

favoured majoritarian systems, but where they were less confident they favoured proportional representation.

The purpose of this brief commentary on the historical evidence is to emphasize that electoral system choice for a state has rarely been driven by profound concern for national minorities, especially among incumbent elites (though it has often been partly driven by a concern to out-manoeuvre national minorities). Formerly dominant communities that emerge as minorities as a result of secession or decolonization have shaped electoral-system choice far more often than generously accommodationist majorities have deliberately made room for national minorities. During decolonization the British, for example, generally did not propose proportional representation, even when they feared for the subsequent futures of minorities. Their constitutional lawyers usually exported versions of the Westminster model, including WTA-SMD. There was one notable exception. The single transferrable vote system of proportional representation (STV-PR) was imposed on both parts of Ireland as the British government partitioned the island in 1920. The reason was that the British government wished to protect the British national minority in what became the Irish Free State.[26] It has been suggested that Westminster wanted to protect the Irish national minority, as it now became, in the new entity of Northern Ireland, but there is no serious empirical warrant for this claim, and the British government did not subsequently resist when STV-PR was shortly after abolished in favour of WTA-SMD by the Northern Ireland government, first for local government elections, and then for the regional parliament.[27] This case therefore conforms to the rule suggested. The elite of the state in question was far more concerned with the fate of a national minority that was part of its national majority but headed for another jurisdiction than it was with a national minority within its own jurisdiction. This is not to make an Anglophobic remark. Given that post-colonial states in the former British imperial world have had a better record of democratic maintenance than places subjected to other empires,[28] it is rather to emphasize that concern for national minorities was rarely to the forefront in electoral system choice at the foundation of most democratic regimes before the 1970s. (And for the record Great Britain eventually restored PR-STV in Northern Ireland in 1973, though only after the outbreak of sustained armed conflict.) What is exceptional in this particular story is the decision of the Irish Free State to keep STV-PR after it became independent—the system did for a

---

[26] C O'Leary, *The Irish Republic and Its Experimentation with Proportional Representation* (1961).
[27] B O'Leary and J McGarry, *The Politics of Antagonism: Understanding Northern Ireland*, 2nd expanded edn (1996), see especially Ch 3.
[28] See for example K Bollen, 'Issues in the comparative measurement of political democracy' (1980) 45(3) *American Sociological Review* 370–90; K Bollen, 'World system position, dependency and democracy: The cross-national evidence' (1983) 48 *American Sociological Review* 468–79; K Bollen, 'Political democracy and the timing of development' (1979) 44 *American Sociological Review* 572–87.

while benefit the dwindling minority of British Protestants, especially in local government. Inertia might be suggested—winners under any election system are not strongly motivated to change it. Another explanation offered is that because it was a non-British system Irish nationalists were happy to adopt it. Yet another is that leading figures in Sinn Féin, notably Arthur Griffith, were already committed to the system from a principled concern for minorities (though they wanted the system applied to a united rather than a partitioned Ireland).[29]

Both the imposition of PR-STV in favour of British Protestants in 1919–20, and its restoration in favour of Northern Irish Catholics in 1973, suggest that great powers and neighbouring powers can affect the design or redesign of electoral systems in the interests of national minorities—as was the tacit hope of The Lund Recommendations. The European Union, the United States, and the United Nations Election Assistance Unit have all played significant roles in election system choice after the defeat of dictatorships in the Balkans, East Timor, Afghanistan, and Iraq. We are therefore increasingly perhaps in a world in which international interventions, as well as unfolding international norms, may play greater roles in election system choice.

Having suggested that positive concern for national minorities has rarely been a powerful factor in the choice of electoral system, we are now in a position to consider the electoral formulae explicitly cited in the Lund Recommendations, and to assess their merits from the perspective of national minorities.

A. Plurality and majoritarian systems—including WTA-SMD, TRS, the alternative vote, and parallel systems

The Lund Recommendations maintain that the electoral system 'should facilitate minority representation and influence', and observe, 'where minorities are concentrated territorially, single-member districts may provide sufficient minority representation'. Shortly afterwards its authors noted, 'The geographic boundaries of electoral districts should facilitate the equitable representation of national minorities.'[30] The converse propositions are implicit, namely, that where minorities are territorially dispersed single-member districts will not help their prospects of representation, and *a fortiori*, their autonomy; and that the inequitable drawing of constituency boundaries (usually known as 'gerrymandering' in English) has obviously negative repercussions.

The wording of the Lund Recommendations was diplomatic, and no doubt reflected recognition that Canada, the United Kingdom, and the United States, members of the OSCE, all use 'winner-takes-all' in single-member districts; that France, another member, uses the two-round system in single-member districts;

---

[29] For discussions see M Gallagher, 'Ireland: The Discreet charm of PR-STV' in M Gallagher and P Mitchell (eds) *The Politics of Electoral Systems* (2005); B Kissane, *Explaining Irish Democracy* (2002). [30] Lund Recommendations (n 4 above), II B 9, 10.

and that in Russia and some of its neighbours, also members, single-member districts elect the bulk of parliamentarians in majoritarian parallel systems.

The diplomatic wording of the Lund Recommendations avoided the strong social and political science consensus initiated at least for the post-colonial world in the 1960s by the Nobel Laureate Sir Arthur Lewis. In his *Politics in West Africa* he wrote that 'The surest way to kill the idea of democracy in a plural society is to adopt the Anglo-American electoral system of first-past-the-post.'[31] By a plural society he meant a state with multiple nationalities, ethnicities, and religions—in short, one lacking cultural or political homogeneity. Canada, if we leave to one side its treatment of its First Nations before the 1960s, and the United States, if we leave aside its treatment of Native and African Americans, Jews, and Catholics before 1965, and the United Kingdom, if we leave to one side its record in Northern Ireland before 1998 and in Ireland before 1921, now have fair reputations as human- and minority-rights respecting domestic states. But it is surely worth considering whether they have achieved their improved reputations *in spite of* rather than *because of* the electoral formula they use to elect their respective federal and union parliaments.[32]

1. WTA-SMD

WTA-SMD is, in fact, the subject of nine standard criticisms in the social science literature. First, and the point is not banal, WTA-SMD is not accurately characterized by the metaphor preferred by its proponents, namely 'first-past-the-post'. There is in fact no fixed post, ie there is no minimum requirement for a candidate to go past a demarcated threshold, other than winning more votes than his or her rivals. One vote is enough, if everyone else has zero.

Secondly, WTA-SMD is compatible with extraordinarily high levels of disproportionality, especially the radical over-representation of the winning party, and the dramatic underrepresentation of losing parties. In small island democracies or regions of federations or union states with small parliaments, the winning party may in consequence completely eliminate opposition parties and candidates from a particular term of parliament.[33] The potential technical and political horrors that may be occasioned through the use of WTA-SMD can be illustrated through a simple example. Imagine that there are just two political parties, as preferred by proponents of this system, and let us call one the party of

---

[31] WA Lewis, *Politics in West Africa: The Whidden lectures, 1965* (1965), 71.
[32] In the United Kingdom, the homeland of WTA-SMD, plurality rule is now under siege, as Paul Mitchell puts it. The Scottish Parliament, the Welsh National Assembly, and the London Assembly use mixed-member proportionality systems; members of the European Parliament from Great Britain are elected by list-PR; and the Northern Ireland Assembly and Members of the European Parliament from Northern Ireland are elected by STV-PR, as are Northern Ireland's and Scotland's local government councils. See P Mitchell, 'The United Kingdom: Plurality rule under siege' in M Gallagher and P Mitchell (eds) *The Politics of Electoral Systems* (2005).
[33] See R Taagepera and J Ensch, 'Institutional Determinants of the largest seat share' (2006) 25 *Electoral Studies* 760–75.

Hate (H) and the other the party of Love (L). Suppose that they each run one hundred candidates in one hundred constituencies to elect an assembly. Imagine that there are one hundred voters in each district, so there is no deliberate malapportionment, and that all persons vote. Imagine further that the H party wins fifty-one votes in each of fifty-one districts. Then it has won a majority of seats in the assembly with just 2,601 votes or 26 per cent of the vote. By contrast, L wins 7,399 votes, or 74 per cent, through winning one hundred votes in forty-nine seats, and forty-nine votes in each of the other fifty-one. The result is explained by the 'efficient concentration' of Hate's support, and the 'wasteful spread' of Love's support. The extreme disproportionality in this case actually benefits a minority at the expense of a much larger majority, which is why many people refuse to call WTA-SMD a 'majoritarian' system, and mock French speakers for describing plurality as a 'relative majority' formula. But readers will immediately realize that any 'wastefully spread' national minority is far more likely to be a loser from the operation of WTA-SMD than is a majority national community.

Thirdly, and relatedly, WTA-SMD artificially 'manufactures' parliamentary majorities. The approximation known as the 'cube rule' derived from UK elections states that cubing the ratio of votes received by the two major parties, H and L, (V_H/V_L), yields roughly the ratio of parliamentary seats they win (S_H/S_L), ie $(S_H/S_L) = (V_H/V_L)^3$. Though it is not a robust law, its mere discussion is evidence of the extent to which the winning party benefits dramatically from the system.[34]

Fourthly, the system is a useful one, perhaps, if today's majority can become tomorrow's minority (in particular districts), but national minorities are, likely as not, demographically durable minorities. They cannot, generally, be assured of being pivotal or 'swing' voters. Unless their votes are regularly sought by the leading parties they are unlikely to influence government formation or legislative outcomes, and even if their support is sought it is likely to be by parties running on assimilationist or integrationist platforms that seek homogeneity or the privatization of the identity and culture of national minorities.

Fifthly, votes are easily 'wasted' under WTA-SMD. Those who vote for minority party candidates in particular districts cannot have their votes cumulated with voters in other places to affect seat allocations (as they can in some proportional systems). Likewise a partly territorially concentrated minority may be 'over-concentrated'. That makes it likely that it will pile up huge majorities in particular districts for a national minority party, well beyond what is required to win these seats, while at the same time winning no representation in those places

---

[34] See MG Kendall and A Stuart, 'The law of cubic proportion in election results' (1950) 1 *British Journal of Sociology* 183–96; and R Taagepera and M Soberg Shugart, *Seats and Votes: The effects and determinants of electoral systems* (1989), 158 ff.

where they are territorially dispersed, or simply a sizeable minority. These are examples of 'non-additive' and 'non-transferable' wastage in votes.

Sixthly, under WTA-SMD, where there are more than two parties, and no strong incentives for the largest parties to converge on the preferences of moderate voters, then extremist shifts may be possible in public policy, to the potential detriment of national minorities. A hard-line 'integralist party', determined to impose an assimilationist programme to make all conform to the majority ethos, may win strong legislative majorities on the basis of a relatively modest share of the vote. This is not a far-fetched possibility. At several junctures in the last two decades it seemed possible that the Hindu nationalist party, the BJP, and its allies, might win a legislative majority that would be strongly detrimental to the interests of India's very large Muslim minority.

Seventhly, under WTA-SMD there may be a related but different problem, ie extremist governing parties might alternate in power, creating 'adversarial' cycles in policy-making. These are situations in which one party spends its initial time in office undoing the entire legislative program of its predecessor, before embarking on the opposite tack.[35] National minorities face two unpleasant possibilities in such scenarios. In one they may be identified as the allies of one party and therefore the enemy of the other. The enemy party can then be relaxed in attacking the identity, ethos, and institutions of the national minority because it is only interested in pealing away support from the majority community—and will target its major rival as the party that only addresses the concerns of the national minority. In another, and worse scenario, a national minority may become the subject of competition between parties over which party would treat them with most repressive rigour if returned to government, or, similarly, the parties of the majority community may compete over how best to homogenize the political culture of the state. The fate of any such 'securitized minority' may be profoundly unpleasant. Arguably it describes the experience of the Tamil community within Sri Lanka after that country's leading party decided to promote a Sinhala-only language policy in 1956.[36]

Eighthly, under WTA-SMD it is relatively easy for governing majorities to manipulate constituency boundaries, through 'gerrymandering', in ways which adversely affect national minorities.[37] With efficient gerrymandering, targeted at

---

[35] See P Dunleavy, *Democracy, Bureaucracy and Public Choice: Economic explanations in political science* (1991) 133–5; P Dunleavy and C Husbands, *British Democracy at the Crossroads: Voting and party COMPETITION IN The 1980s* (1985), 38–43.

[36] See A Rabushka and KA Shepsle, *Politics in Plural Societies: A theory of democratic instability* (1972), 129–41.

[37] For discussions of gerrymandering in the United States see R Morill, 'Electoral geography and gerrymandering: Space and politics' in G Demko and WB Wood (eds), *Reordering the World: Geopolitical perspectives in the twenty-first century* (1994); D Nieman, *Promises to Keep: African-Americans and the constitutional order, 1776 to the present* (1991); F Shelley, JC Archer, and FM Davidson, *Political Geography of the United States* (1996), and in Northern Ireland see O'Leary and McGarry, *The Politics of Antagonism* (n 27 above), 119–21.

national minorities, the targets are concentrated into small numbers of districts where they are bound to elect the winners, but elsewhere are effectively dispersed across multiple constituencies where they have no prospects of being pivotal voters. Such gerrymandering, it should not be forgotten, can occur without malapportionment, and therefore does not obviously attack the principle of one vote of equal value. Racist gerrymandering was merely one way in which African Americans were excluded from effective participation in the United States, especially in the states of the former Confederacy in the South. Provided boundary drawers have good information about the residential locations of national minorities, eg through knowledge of first names and surnames on electoral registers, or data on the ethnic, religious, and linguistic composition of schools, then in conjunction with geographical information systems a precise science of political engineering is now technologically feasible.

Lastly, WTA-SMD has an important 'psychological effect', first identified by Maurice Duverger.[38] Under WTA-SMD all voters, not just national minorities, are likely to consider whether they should vote tactically or sincerely. If they vote tactically they may vote for the candidate most likely to defeat the candidate of the party they most fear, whereas if they vote sincerely, but for a candidate who has few prospects of success, then their vote may be wasted for the reasons given above. The psychological impact of this pressure on national minorities may be significant, obliging them to vote for a moderate member of the national majority community rather than an authentic representative of their community. The psychological impact may also feed through into party and candidate organization, persuading national minorities that it is not worth standing for office, at least not explicitly as representatives of a national minority party. It may also lead people among national minorities to argue that it is just not worth voting.

This formidable array of criticisms of WTA-SMD suggests that the system scarcely merits the faint and conditional praise given to it in the Lund Recommendations. In a recent survey of specialists on electoral systems WTA-SMD was one of the lowest-ranked systems, though not without its enthusiasts.[39] The reader may therefore ask whether there are any plausible defences to be made of WTA-SMD. The answer is 'yes', especially for those governments intent on promoting assimilation or coercive integration, but that is hardly what the authors of the Lund Recommendations had in mind. The High Commissioner on National Minorities is required to be impartial between governments and their national minorities but the rationale of the office would be wasted if it advised governments on how best to disorganize their national minorities.

---

[38] M Duverger, *Political Parties: Their organization and activity in the modern state*, B North and R North (trans) (1954).
[39] S Bowler, DM Farrell, and RT Pettit, 'Expert opinion on electoral systems: So which choice is best?' (2005) 15(1) *Journal of Elections, Public Opinion, and Parties* 3–19.

Briefly, there are six general arguments to be made in favour of WTA-SMD, but most of these are not addressed to the needs and interests of national minorities, and may well be to the detriment of their efforts to maintain their ethos and identity. First, WTA-SMD is very simple to understand, and therefore easy to use even for non-literate citizens. Secondly, provided it returns a single party with a majority to parliament, WTA-SMD may facilitate a strong government that may be held to account by the electorate at the next general election for its tenure of office. Thirdly, provided that it generates a two-party system, in accordance with 'Duverger's Law', then it may generate a governing party in competition with a responsible opposition party, which may replace it in office.[40] This competition may check the governing party from abusing its tenure of office and through the possibility of regular alternation it makes elections likely to matter in shaping policy through popular pressure. Fourthly, provided that a number of demanding conditions are met, WTA-SMD may generate a two-party system in which political parties converge in pursuit of the 'median voter' with the happy consequence that this two-party competition both has centripetal and integrative effects.[41] Fifthly, some claim that WTA-SMD facilitates a politics of innovation. Precisely because it is easier to win office without having to obtain high levels of consensus the political system is less likely to stagnate. Lastly, some argue that Duverger's psychological effect has a beneficial consequence. It discourages excessive party formation, and low party fragmentation may help voters and public policy by structuring a small number of well-defined choices.

There is, ironically, just one potentially powerful argument in favour of WTA-SMD from the perspective of national minorities, but it is precisely the argument that is least likely to appeal to governments intent on preserving the territorial integrity of their states; namely, WTA-SMD may help secession. Where a national minority is territorially concentrated within a region or province of a democratic federation or union state then it may be able to command

---

[40] For discussions of Duverger's Law see, among others: A Blais and RK Carty, 'The psychological impact of electoral laws: Measuring Duverger's elusive factor' (1991) 21 *British Journal of Political Science*; M Duverger, 'Duverger's Law: Forty years later' in Bernard Grofman and Arend Lijphart (eds) *Electoral Laws and Their Political Consequences* (1986); B Grofman, S Bowler, and A Blais, *Duverger's Law in Canada, India, the US and the UK* (2009); WH Riker, 'Duverger's Law revisited' in B Grofman and A Lijphart (eds), *Electoral Laws and Their Political Consequences* (1986); WH Riker, 'The two-party system and Duverger's Law: An Essay on the history of political science' (1982) 76 *American Political Science Review* 753–66; A Wildavsky, 'A methodological critique of Duverger's *Political Parties*' (1959) 221 *The Journal of Politics* 303–18.

[41] The argument was first set out with some rigour in A Downs, *An Economic Theory of Democracy* (1957) Ch 8, adapting the model of H Hotelling, 'Stability in competition' (1929) 39 *The Economic Journal*. Bernard Grofman has argued that the median voter theorem is in fact a 'knife-edge' result that requires no less than fifteen assumptions to be true for it to work in theory —and in practice. Only three of these fifteen assumptions are likely to be true—the election of a single candidate in a single constituency though the plurality vote, ie the definitional elements of WTA-SMD! See B Grofman, 'Downs and two-party convergence' (2004) 7 *Annual Review of Political Science* 25–46.

a strikingly disproportionate share of the seats in any regional or provincial legislature. It may then use that legislative majority to declare secession, or to organize a referendum seeking independence, using its executive incumbency to significant effect both in timing the referendum and managing its agenda. It is of interest that the Parti Quebecois has twice been able to use a legislative majority in the Province of Quebec, obtained under WTA-SMD, to organize two referendums, in 1980 and 1995, the second of which came within less than a percentage point of leading to the break-up of Canada. (On one of these occasions the Parti Quebecois had won a legislative majority without being the plurality winner of the popular vote). By contrast, Basque parties in the Basque provinces in Spain, the Scottish National Party in Scotland, and the Irish nationalist parties in Northern Ireland, will likely need to get legislative majorities based on actual popular majorities before they are likely to hold and win referendums on secession (or reunification with Ireland in the latter case). The secessions of Slovenia and Croatia from Yugoslavia, and their head-on collisions with Serbia, were preceded by elections in each of the Yugoslav republics based on WTA-SMD. These are present-day illustrations. But it is worth recalling that Sinn Féin's remarkable performance in 1918 in winning an overwhelming majority of the seats that Ireland had in the Westminster Parliament was sufficient to spearhead its successful push for independence even without the prior existence of a regional or home rule parliament.[42] And it is also worth recalling the reflections of Sir Arthur Lewis, whom we cited earlier as the initiator of the formidable assault on WTA-SMD in the post-colonial world,

> Suppose for example that there are equal numbers of yellow and purple, but while all the yellows live in one part of the country, half the purples live there and the other half lives in the rest of the country. Proportional representation gives equal seats to yellows and purples. A single-member constituency system might give (according to its type) one quarter of the seats to purples, and three-quarters to yellows. The country then becomes divided into purple-land and yellow-land. Since the result is obviously unjust, purple-land may well demand to secede, as the Muslims of India did in such circumstances; the single member constituency system is much more likely to break up the country than is proportional representation.[43]

2. The Block Vote

WTA-SMD is not the only majoritarian system, using the latter description in its broad sense. It is not even the worst from the perspective of national

---

[42] For the results and the political use made of them see E de Valera, *'The Foundation of the Republic of Ireland in the Vote of the People' Results of the General Election of December, 1918. A National Plebiscite Held under British Law and British Supervision* (1919); M Laffan, *The Resurrection of Ireland. The Sinn Féin Party, 1916-1923* (1999); C O'Leary, *Irish Elections, 1918-77: Parties, Voters and Proportional Representation* (1977); BM Walker, 'Parliamentary Election Results in Ireland, 1801-1922' in TW Moody, FX Martin and FJ Byrne (eds), *A New History of Ireland: Ancillary Publications IV* (1978).   [43] Lewis, *Politics in West Africa* (n 31 above), 72–3.

minorities. That dubious distinction should perhaps go to the 'party block vote'—in which categorical x voting is combined with plurality rule and party lists in multi-member districts. This system even further aids the winning party, while drastically weakening the opposition. Introduced quite recently in Palestine it gave Fatah a huge legislative majority on the first occasion, which was then reversed in favour of Hamas a few years later, even though there was just a small percentage gap between the two parties' share of the vote.

3. TRS

The best-known formally majoritarian system is that used in France to elect the president, often known as 'the two-round system' (TRS). In the first round there is no restriction on the number of candidates. Anyone obtaining 50 per cent plus one or more of the vote automatically becomes president. But if no one obtains that winning total there is a second round—in which only the two best-placed candidates from the first round are allowed to compete. This restriction ensures that the winner of the second round has a majority among those who vote. Strictly speaking this is a 'majority-majority' double-ballot system. To elect its legislature France, by contrast, uses 'majority-plurality' in its single-member legislative districts. Anyone who wins 50 per cent or more in the first round is elected. If no one wins that total then candidates with vote shares below a certain threshold (which has varied from 12.5 to 17.5 per cent) are eliminated, and those above the threshold are entitled to run in the second ballot. Candidates entitled to run again may drop out, leaving the contest as a two-horse race (in which case a majority will elect the winner). But all those entitled to run may do so, and in a multi-candidate race the winner is the plurality winner.

Like its philosophers, the French voting system has its champions, notably the Italian-American political scientist Giovanni Sartori.[44] The principal arguments for two-round systems are straightforward. Especially in their majority-majority mode they conform to 'majority rule', and are especially useful in ensuring that a single-person executive president has significant legitimacy. The TRS system facilitates governability, especially if its leads to the formation of a competitive two bloc system, with the same virtues as a two-party system under STV-SMD. TRS also discourages excessive party fragmentation, and maintains territorial constituency linkages between representatives and voters. The first round gives voters the opportunity to vote according to their first preferences (their hearts), whereas the second round leaves them with a strategic binary choice among the likely winners (their heads). Sartori especially emphasizes its merits in penalizing 'extremist' and 'anti-system' parties.

The principal arguments against TRS are likely to be more compelling in the eyes of national minorities, especially minorities that are dispersed or small in

---

[44] G Sartori, *Comparative Constitutional Engineering: An inquiry into structures, incentives, and outcomes* (1997), 53–79.

size. The 'majority' created in the second round—often merely the plurality winner—is an artificial rather than a genuine majority. The system, by definition, creates a high threshold for electoral success even if does not create a strong barrier to entry in the first round. The system is likely to give a very large bonus in seats to the winning bloc or party, creating the possibility of unrepresentative and illegitimate super-majorities in assemblies. Though the major blocs or parties may incorporate minorities as candidates, they will not be likely to get elected under their own national or ethnic labels or parties, except where they have very significant territorial concentrations. Supporters of national minorities may well think that Sartori's defence of TRS wrongly presumes that national minorities are 'extremists' and 'anti-system', and might complain that to be excluded or discriminated against in representation under their own parties may make them more likely to become extreme or anti-system. In short, TRS is a system designed to aid assimilationist or integrationist political parties and systems, and not to aid national minorities. It is not an accident that France is its home.

4. AV

In the Anglophone world, notably in Australia, another majoritarian system has been developed, widely and rather curiously known as the 'alternative vote', or 'the instant run-off'. The former expression is curious because there are many electoral systems that provide an alternative to WTA-SMD; the latter because there is in fact no 'run-off' between the two best-placed candidates, and the counting process need not qualify for the description 'instant', though it does spare voters from going twice or more to the polls. It is perhaps better described as a 'majority-preferential' system, because voters are entitled to rank candidates in numerical order of preference, but we shall nevertheless use the better-known expression the 'alternative vote' (AV).

Under AV, ballot instructions may vary in mandating the voter to exhaust all their possible preference rankings. AV may be used both for legislative and single person presidential elections, eg it is used to elect the Australian House of Commons and the president of Ireland. In a single-member district the winning candidate must win an absolute majority of first-preference votes, or a majority of votes after the transfer of lower-order preferences from eliminated candidates.[45] The procedure is to eliminate the last-placed candidate first, and allocate the next valid order of preferences from their voters to the remaining candidates, and to repeat the process until someone has over 50 per cent of the vote.

Advocates of AV maintain that it ensures 'majority rule' at the level of each single-member district, and facilitates a constituency link between the voters and their deputy. As in the TRS, voters are said to be able to deploy both their hearts

---

[45] For critical evaluations see Bean, 'Australia's experience with the alternative vote' (n 19 above); Lijphart, 'The alternative vote: A realistic alternative for South Africa?' (n 19 above).

and their heads—ranking their most favoured candidate first, while strategically allocating their other preferences. Its proponents maintain that AV will usually have a moderating or centripetal effect on party competition—encouraging 'centrist' candidates, parties and blocs (alliances of parties). Since minor, including national minority, parties may run and win first preference votes the 'parties of government' may have inducements to moderate their platforms to encourage the voters of minor parties to give them some of their lower order preferences. Proponents also claim that AV is easy to shift into from WTA-SMD because existing districts can be kept, thereby making it likely that an existing legislature will be less hostile to a change in the electoral system.

Critics of the alternative vote[46] observe first that it not only is likely to generate artificial majorities at the district level, but also highly likely to produce strongly disproportional outcomes in assembly elections. Secondly, they note that because of the high threshold in each district (in effect 50 per cent plus one) national minority parties are very likely to be strongly underrepresented. AV therefore neither favours the participation nor the autonomy goals emphasized in the Lund Recommendations: it is in fact much more of an integrationist than an accommodationist system.[47] Participation is biased toward majority communities, and autonomy is jeopardized by the fact that national minorities may have to rely on moderate members of the majority ethnicity to protect their interests rather than their own parliamentary leaders.

Thirdly, there are three technical objections to AV: (i) it is 'non-monotonic'; relatedly, (ii) it does not treat all preferences equally; and (iii) it does not guarantee a 'Condorcet winner'.

When an election system is non-monotonic a candidate may be harmed if they were to win more votes with the order of all other candidates remaining the same.[48]

The unequal treatment of preferences was polemically observed by Lord Alexander of the UK's Conservative Party during recent debates over the merits of changing the electoral system for the Westminster Parliament:

> AV comes into play only when a candidate fails to secure a majority of first preference votes. It does not, however, then take account of the second preferences of all voters, but only of those who have supported the least successful candidates. So it ignores the second preferences of the voters who supported the two candidates with the highest first preference votes, but allows the voters for the third or even weaker candidates to have their second votes counted so as to determine the result. I find this approach wholly illogical.

---

[46] See n 19 above.

[47] See B O'Leary and J McGarry, 'The politics of accommodation: Surveying national and ethnic conflict regulation in democratic states' in A Guelke (ed) (2010 in press).

[48] Technically 'A choice procedure is *monotonic* if when c_j is chosen with profile p, and when the only voters to change their preferences change them to give c_j a higher ranking (hence, preserving the original relative ranking of the other candidates), then c_j is elected with new profile p.' D Saari, *Geometry of Voting: Studies in economic theory* (1994), 251.

Why should the second preferences of those voters who favored the two stronger candidates on the first vote be totally ignored and only those who support the lower placed and less popular candidates get a second bite of the cherry? Why, too, should the second preferences of these voters be given equal weight with the first preferences of supporters of the stronger candidates? In 1931 Mr Winston Churchill described this proposal as taking account of 'the most worthless votes of the most worthless candidates'.[49]

We do not need to accept Churchill's implicit suggestion that 'national minorities' might have the most worthless candidates or be the casters of the most worthless votes in order to see the unequal treatment of preferences as a problem in the equality of votes.

A Condorcet winner is that candidate who would win all pair-wise majority-vote elections against all other candidates.[50] Consider three candidates: A, B, and C. Consider five voters with preferences across the three candidates that are as follows A>C>B, A>C>B, B>C>A, B>C>A, and C>B>A (where > means preferred to). Under the alternative vote, B will be elected because C would be eliminated in the first round, as it has the lowest first preferences. But C is in fact the Condorcet winner. Three voters prefer C to B, and three voters prefer C to A. The alternative vote may therefore elect a non-Condorcet winner.[51] To understand that this is not just a minor problem, consider whether C might be the moderate candidate, kindly toward national minorities, or indeed the candidate of a national minority.

These three technical objections are truths of logic, which cannot be refuted by proponents of the AV. What they tend to claim instead is that non-monotonicity does not occur very often in real-world cases; that all preferential systems treat lower-order preferences unequally; and that they do not regard reliably producing a Condorcet winner as the definitive criterion by which to evaluate a system.

Fourthly, AV is inferior to TRS in one key respect. Under TRS the voter gets an informed strategic choice if there is a second round. By contrast, under AV the voters cannot know how efficiently strategic their lower-order preference votes will be. They are obliged to rank their preferences in the dark about how other voters appraise the candidates.

Fifthly, and of fundamental importance for national minorities, the alleged centripetal and moderating effect of the alternative vote can only work—in logic and in fact—if voters have particular preference profiles. Donald Horowitz's strong claims for the properties of the alternative vote have been demonstrated to be both theoretically and empirically unwarranted—through detailed

---

[49] See Note of Reservation by Lord Alexander, in The Report of the Independent Commission on the Voting System (HMSO 1998), Ch 9, Recommendations and Conclusions, available at <www.archive.official-documents.co.uk/document/cm40/4090/chap-9.htm>.
[50] Saari, *Geometry of Voting* (n 48 above), 79.
[51] This example is indebted to Grofman, 'Electoral rules and ethnic representation and accommodation: Combining social choice and electoral system perspectives' (n 13 above).

exploration of the case of Fiji.[52] As Horowitz himself recognizes, AV can only have moderating possibilities if there are sufficient numbers of the right types of ethnically heterogeneous districts, because if districts are predominantly inhabited by one ethnic community then they may be able to return hard-liners on the first count, or hard-liners can win on the next count through small numbers of transfers from within their own communities. But what he appears not to have appreciated is that even if constituencies are heterogeneous (ie, lack a predominant ethnic group) is that AV will only plausibly be effective in aiding moderates if voters have preference profiles in which they will transfer lower-order preferences to moderate candidates of ethnic others ahead of hard-line candidates within their own national or ethnic community. In highly polarized states it is just implausible to assume that significant numbers of voters have such preference profiles.

The alternative vote was implemented by the Organization for Security and Cooperation in Europe (OSCE) for presidential elections in Republika Srspka in 2000, on the recommendations of Horowitz. Though this federative entity has a large Serb majority, the OSCE believed that AV would facilitate the election of a moderate Serb by increasing the pivotality of the non-Serb minority. Matters turned out otherwise.[53] Horowitz's arguments also obviously influenced some of the drafters of the Lund Recommendations, written in the same period. The Recommendations carefully state that 'Some forms of preference voting, where voters rank candidates in order of choice, may facilitate minority representation, and inter-communal co-operation.'[54] The Explanatory Note sensibly maintains that states 'should adopt the system which would result in the most representative government in their specific situation'.[55] The foregoing analysis, and arguments to come, enables me to suggest, in line with an emergent consensus among political scientists, that the Lund Recommendations would benefit from the following two emendations:

(i) Among preference-based voting systems, the alternative vote is not as good for national minorities on either the participation criterion, or the autonomy criterion, as numerous other election systems, especially proportional representation election systems, including but not confined to preference-based proportional representation (STV).
(ii) In highly polarized states, with deep national or ethnic divisions, constitutional or electoral system designers, and national minorities, should treat with scepticism the moderating or centripetal claims made for the

---

[52] See Fraenkel and Grofman, 'A neo-Downsian model of the alternative vote as a mechanism for mitigating ethnic conflict in plural societies' (n 19 above); Fraenkel and Grofman, 'Does the Alternative vote foster moderation in ethnically divided societies?' (n 19 above); Fraenkel and Grofman, 'The failure of the alternative vote as a tool for ethnic moderation in Fiji?' (n 19 above).
[53] See S Bose, *Bosnia after Dayton: Nationalist partition and international intervention* (2002).
[54] The Lund Recommendations (n 4 above), II. B. 9.   [55] Ibid, Explanatory Note, B.7.

alternative vote. In the guise of promoting inter-group accommodation the alternative vote may in many real-world cases facilitate majoritarian integrationism, and the effective exclusion of national minority parties from parliaments and assemblies.

No suggestion is made here that Horowitz and the 'centripetalist school' have been anything other than sincere in their desire to promote interethnic accommodation. Rather, the arguments appraised here, suggest that the centripetalist school's claims are greatly overstated, and, in some key respects, have been logically refuted, or shown to be empirically unsupported—except in those few cases where AV is demonstrably superior to WTA-SMD, such as Papua and New Guinea.[56] But for an electoral system to be better than WTA-SMD is not, for the reasons given earlier, praise worth having.

Lastly, there is a fundamental implementation problem with the alternative vote, of crucial importance for national minorities. If AV is to be implemented with the express intention of supporting moderates against hard-liners (who are more likely to have or to use guns) it is not clear why hard-liners should take such a manifest manipulation lying down.[57] Horowitz understands that his centripetal approach faces an 'implementation problem', ie that antagonistic elites are unlikely to accept institutions that overtly favour moderate politicians, but he and his supporters believe that their catch-22 can be overcome with the assistance of outside forces. In 2000, Horowitz suggested that the way out of the dilemma created by the failure of ethnic elites to accept centripetal institutions was for internal parties to put 'constitutional decision-making in other hands', including outside governments and international organizations.[58] More recently, he called for a 'strong American push' in the reshaping of Iraq's just-made Constitution, arguing that the 'departing colonial powers left their

---

[56] B Reilly, *Democracy in Divided Societies: Electoral enginerring for conflict management* (2001); B Reilly, 'Preferential voting and political engineering: A comparative study' (1997) 35(1) *Journal of Commonwealth and Comparative Politics* 1–19. In Papua and New Guinea, geographical isolation and tribalism led to plurality winners who frequently had less than 10 per cent of the vote, whereas the previous use of AV had at least created some in incentive among candidates to win from outside their own village or tribe. This case enables us to conclude that in conditions of deeply dispersed and highly heterogeneous ethnic group-formation AV is better for democratic politics and inter-group accommodation than WTA-SMD—but no more than that.

[57] This is the fundamental reason why in 1998–9 I opposed changing the electoral system to AV in Northern Ireland when such a change was being mooted for the UK as a whole (in the guise of 'AV Plus'). Such a change would then have targeted the hard-line parties whose cooperation or compliance with the recently negotiated Northern Ireland Agreement was essential for the success of its peace process, see B O'Leary, 'The implications for political accommodation in Northern Ireland of reforming the electoral system for the Westminster Parliament' (1999) 35(2–3) *Representation* 106–13. Fortunately, the change did not occur, and the hard-line parties benefited from other institutional incentives to become more moderate—so much so that one might conclude that today the introduction of AV for Westminster elections in Northern Ireland might further weaken the moderate parties!

[58] See DL Horowitz, 'Constitutional design: An oxymoron?' in I Shapiro and S Macedo (eds) *Designing Democratic Institutions* (2000), 277.

imprints on new constitutions all over Asia and Africa, and many of these proved durable'.[59] It 'is time' he said, 'for the U.S. to do the same'.[60,61] Such quasi-imperial advocacy rests centrally upon the belief that centripetal institutions, including AV, once implemented, are likely to be self-sustaining, because they have the right domestic incentive properties to keep them going, and therefore would require minimal external maintenance or intervention. There is, as yet, no solid empirical evidence for these beliefs, outside perhaps of Papua and New Guinea,[62] and good theoretical grounds for doubting them.

5. Mixed or Parallel Electoral Systems

The mixed or parallel electoral systems within the 'majoritarian' family can, fortunately, be tersely treated. From the perspective of national minorities such systems are no better at the district level than WTA-SMD, TRS, or the AV—and indeed do not differ from them. The second or list tier in such systems, provided that the formula in such tiers is proportional, offers some better prospects for the parties of national minorities that have dispersed support, but because there is no intention in such systems to compensate for disproportionality in the districts we may conclude that national minorities will generally much prefer straightforwardly proportional systems, and have good reasons to suspect that parallel systems can easily be engineered against their interests.

B. Proportional Systems—including list-PR, STV, and MMP

The family of proportional representation systems have in common that their formulas endeavour to ensure proportionality between votes cast and seat shares won by political parties and/or candidates. In list-PR voters have a single vote to cast for the party of their choice (and candidates are elected based on their placement on the party's nominated list).[63] Under PR (STV), voters rank-order candidates, as with AV, but this time to elect multiple candidates, who individually need to obtain a quota that is significantly less than a majority of the vote. Mixed-member Proportional (MMP) systems, in principle, may use list-PR, or STV, in conjunction with WTA or AV, in order to modify the disproportional consequences of the latter systems, and for that reason we shall confine our attention mostly to list PR and STV. But before we do that we must briefly explain how proportionality is accomplished through multi-member districts,

---

[59] 'Some' would have been more accurate than 'many'.
[60] See DL Horowitz, 'The Sunni moment', *The Wall Street Journal*, 14 December 2005, A20.
[61] In 2003, Andreas Wimmer, a follower of Horowitz, commended a 'strong dose of outside interference' to establish centripetal institutions in Iraq. See A Wimmer, 'Democracy and ethno-religious conflict in Iraq' (2003–4) 45(4) *Survival* 111–34.   [62] See n 56 above.
[63] This describes 'closed list' PR; in open-list systems voters are able to modify the party's rankings—though usually only with very extensive collective coordination.

and then the use of either quotas or divisors (the pleasantly arcane complexities of combining quotas and divisors shall be avoided).

It is multi-member districts that make proportionality feasible. In list-PR and in STV-PR systems the whole country can be treated as a single but enormous multi-member district. In these cases it therefore matches the size of the parliamentary assembly. Israel uses statewide list-PR, and so did Iraq in its first federal elections of January 2005. It is, however, much more common with list-PR to use regional or provincial districts, as in Sweden, and as in Iraq since December 2005. List-PR systems can have one-tier, two-tier or even multi-tiered districts. Iraq, for example, now elects its parliamentarians in its multi-member governorates (or provinces), but has a second-tier allocation of seats, which compensates for disproportionality within the governorates, but not for disproportionality across Iraq as a whole.[64]

STV-PR systems are employed in Ireland, Northern Ireland, Malta, and the Australian Senate.[65] Only the Australian Senate elections comprise a nationwide electoral district, and here the problem of requiring voters to rank order a very large number of candidates is solved by enabling voters to rank order the parties' lists of offered candidates. In all other usages of STV-PR it is normal to have multi-member districts that range in size between three and six. In MMP systems, of which there are significant variants, the norm is to elect a high proportion of assembly members in single-member districts, and then to allocate a high proportion of seats through a second tier (which might be provincial or national) so that the second-tier allocation compensates fully for any disproportionality introduced at the district level.

Proportionality in seat allocation is mathematically accomplished either through quotas or divisors, and some attendant rules. The use of quotas and divisors is necessary because human beings do not vote in neat proportions, and assembly members cannot be easily dismembered, at least not proportionally. For instance, if a party A seems entitled to 12.4 seats in a hundred-member assembly because it has 12.4 per cent of the vote, the question is should it receive twelve seats or thirteen seats given that it cannot be represented by four-tenths of a person?

There is no one way to achieve proportionality but there are several that are not difficult to appreciate. The use of quotas is easiest to understand. A quota is what is required to win a seat, eg in AV the quota is 50 per cent plus one. When allocating seats proportionally, a quota, which will always be less than 50 per cent, is subtracted from a party's vote share each time that it wins a seat. The simplest or 'natural' quota is the Hare quota, also known as the Niemeyer quota.

---

[64] This novel form of two-tier PR has the unfortunate consequence that provinces with higher voter turn-outs are underrepresented in the federal parliament.
[65] For discussions of STV see Bowler and Grofman (eds) *Elections in Australia, Ireland and Malta under the Single Transferable Vote* (n 20 above).

It is defined as V/M, where V = votes cast, and M = the district magnitude. So, in a five-seat district the quota is (100/5)% = 20%. A more frequently used quota is the Hagenbach-Bischoff quota, V/(M+1). In a five-seat district the Hagenbach-Bischoff quota is therefore (100/(5+1))% = 16.7%. That quota is almost the same as the Droop quota, (V/(M+1))% + 1, which is also widely used. So, in a five-seat district the Droop quota is (100/(5+1))%+1 = 16.7% + 1 (we can drop the 1 in simple examples). Quotas are usually combined with 'a largest remainders' rule to determine final allocations of seats.

Table 12.3 provides worked examples for three parties competing for seven seats in a district. Under Hare, the largest party, A, wins two seats for its two quotas, B wins one seat for its quota, and so does C. Party B, however, wins the remaining seat as it has the largest remainder (twelve). Under the Droop quota there will be the same outcome, though it is obvious that party A comes much closer to winning a third seat than it does under Hare. So, the smaller the quota the better the largest party is likely to do.

The use of divisors to accomplish proportionality is less intuitive. These allocate seats in sequence, awarding a seat on each occasion to the party which has the highest remaining 'average'—that is the number of votes it has won divided by a number indicating the seats it has already been awarded. These sequential allocation systems are also best understood through worked examples. Table 12.4 below illustrates the use of two widely known and widely used systems of divisors, the d'Hondt or Jefferson method (dividing through by the set of positive integers 1, 2, 3, 4, 5, and so on), and the Webster or Sainte-Laguë method (dividing through by the set of positive odd numbers, 1, 3, 5, 7, and so on).

The reader should now be in a position to understand Colomer's 'micro-mega rule', which neatly sums up current political science wisdom, and which forms the epigraph to this chapter. Larger parties prefer small district sizes (especially

Table 12.3 Hare and Droop quotas rules applied to a district electing seven members of an assembly

Hare V/M	Party A (% vote)	[quotas]	Party B (% vote)	[quotas]	Party C (% vote)	[quotas]
20%	(47)	[2] + 7	(32)	[1] + 12	(21)	[1] + 1
Droop (V/M+1)+1 16.7%	Party A (% vote) (47)	[quotas] [2] + 13.6	Party B (% vote) (32)	[quotas] [1] + 15.3	Party C (% vote) (21)	[quotas] [1] +4.3

The quota is divided into each party's vote share. Numbers inside square brackets indicate the number of quotas, and are followed by their remainders.

Table 12.4 The D'Hondt and Sainte-Laguë divisor rules applied to a district electing seven members of an assembly

D'Hondt Divisor	Party A (% vote)	[seat won]	Party B (% vote)	[seat won]	Party C (% vote)	[seat won]
1	(47.00)	[1]	(32.00)	[2]	(21.00)	[4]
2	(23.50)	[3]	(16.00)	[5]	(10.50)	[7]
3	(15.66)	[6]	(10.67)		(7)	
4	(11.75)	[7]				
Sainte-Laguë Divisor	Party A (% vote)	[seat won]	Party B (% vote)	[seat won]	Party C (% vote)	[seat won]
1	(47.00)	[1]	(32.00)	[2]	(21.0)	[3]
3	(15.66)	[4]	(10.67)	[5]	(7.0)	[7]
5	(9.4)	[6]	(6.40)		(4.2)	
7	(6.7)					

Numbers inside square brackets indicate the order in which parties win seats, decided by the declining size of the quotients in question. Under d'Hondt party A wins four seats, B wins two seats, and C wins one seat. By contrast, under Sainte-Laguë, party A wins three seats, B wins two seats, and C wins two seats. The example intentionally illustrates that d'Hondt generally helps the largest parties, whereas Sainte-Laguë generally helps smaller parties.

single-member districts), small assemblies (which have a lower total district magnitude, where they are likely to do better), small gaps between divisors (as in d'Hondt), and smaller quotas (eg, Droop as opposed to Hare). By contrast, smaller parties prefer large district magnitudes (because they will find it easier to win seats with lower effective thresholds), large assemblies (for the same reason), large gaps between divisors (as in Sainte-Laguë) and large quotas (especially the Hare quota). It follows that national minorities, all other things being equal, will prefer large district magnitudes, large assemblies, large gaps between divisors, or large quotas. One partial qualification to that rule will be made later when we consider districting and political geography.

1. List-PR Systems

List-PR systems are strongly normatively supported. They are said to be just, because proportionality treats each voter equally, and minimizes vote wastage. Secondly, as Jack Nagel has emphasized, list-PR systems, like all proportional systems, are truly majoritarian, because they make it far more likely that the legislature will be controlled by a set of parties which jointly have a mandate from the voters that constitutes an actual majority.[66] Thirdly, list-PR enables the election of strong parties, in which strong leaderships have disciplinary controls

---

[66] See Nagel, 'Expanding the spectrum of *democracies*' (n 17 above).

over their elected members (who may lose their places or their ranking on party-lists if they behave irregularly). This feature of list-PR, if true, can be a bonus in trying to sustain power-sharing systems.[67] Fourthly, for those worried that parties may be too authoritarian in list-system PR, proponents point out that 'open lists' can be used, which enable voters in effect to shift the rankings offered by the party leadership or caucuses. Fifthly, list-PR systems are more likely to incentivize parties to accommodate voters' preferences, and thereby correspond to intuitive notions of democratic governments following the public will, whereas non-PR systems provide more extensive opportunities for parties to engage in manipulative or preference-shaping behaviour.[68] Lastly, all list-PR systems facilitate both the participation and autonomy goals of national minorities, provided they are not micro-minorities, ie lower in electoral size than is necessary to win one quota or to cross the effective threshold.

Critics of list-PR electoral systems complain that they may incentivize the formation of multiple parties, and lead more or less inevitably to coalition governments, some of which may not have the prior endorsement of the electorate. They complain that they may empower and entrench medium- to small-sized parties, making them pivotal in government formation, a complaint not likely to worry national minorities that may aspire to such status. Critics also fear that list-PR is likely to encourage party fragmentation, because breakaway factions may not suffer too much of a seat loss after forming their own parties, and that may create difficulties for the governability of the country or region.

2. STV-PR

STV-PR, also known as the 'quota-preferential' or the 'Hare' system, resembles AV in that voters enumerate their preferences across multiple candidates; they are not normally obliged to exhaust their possible preference rankings. The Droop quota is used in all extant systems, so in a five-member district the quota is one-sixth of the vote plus one. Allocation of votes proceeds as follows. First-preference votes are tallied. Any candidates that win quotas are allocated a seat. Then any 'surplus' (votes above the quota) of such candidates is distributed across the remaining candidates, using any second or 'available' preferences specified among the surplus ballot papers. If no candidates win the quotas then the last-placed candidate is eliminated and the next available preferences among their ballot papers are transferred among the remaining candidates. The process of elimination continues until another candidate wins a surplus, and that surplus is then allocated. Sometimes the last seat is allocated to the leading candidate

---

[67] A Lijphart, *Democracy in Plural Societies: A comparative exploration* (1977); A Lijphart, *Thinking About Democracy: Power sharing and majority rule in theory and practice* (2008).
[68] P Dunleavy, *Democracy, Bureaucracy and Public Choice: Economic explanations in political science* (1991), 137, Table 5.2.

who has not yet won a quota once it is clear that no other candidate can win a quota.

Most of the arguments for STV-PR resemble those made for list-PR, so we need not repeat them. There are, however, some distinctive arguments made in its favour. One is that, like AV, it enables transfers across ethnic divisions, but, unlike AV, STV encourages the full participation of both hard-line and moderate parties and voters from among national minorities. A second argument, sometimes contested, is that it facilitates sincere voting—since a transfer may count, voters will not waste their votes in recording their first or indeed second and third preferences. Thirdly, unlike list-PR, STV-PR empowers voters to target the most hard-line or corrupt or undesirable candidates within all parties by placing others within their party ahead of them in their rankings. Lastly, and relatedly, STV-PR permits voters from minority parties, including national minority parties, some power over dominant parties through the preference ranking of candidates.[69]

Critics of STV-PR include populists who complain of its 'complexity', by which they mean the vote transfer process; and party managers, who complain that it weakens party discipline by encouraging candidates from within the same party to run against one another, including against decisions made by their own party in government, and that it strengthens any tendencies toward clientelism in the local political culture. The technical objections to STV include the same complaints made against AV—it allows for non-monotonic outcomes; it allows for the possibility that a 'Condorcet tail' may be elected; that the transfer process does not treat all votes equally; and, in the hand version of the counting process, it is added that there is no guarantee that any surplus that is transferred is an accurate representation of the ballot papers in the pile of the candidate whose surplus it is. This last objection can be met by technical, including computerized, fixes to ensure that the surplus is fully representative,[70] but the others are mathematically robust. Proponents of STV-PR meet them in the same manner as supporters of AV—non-monotonic possibilities are practically rare, and Condorcet-efficiency should not be the sole basis on which to evaluate the merits of an election system.

3. MMP

There is no need to provide any significant analysis of the emergent array of MMP systems. They provide, however, one special possibility for national minorities. Precisely because they enable the majority community and its parties

---

[69] For a detailed discussion see B O'Duffy and B O'Leary, 'Tales from elsewhere and an Hibernian sermon' in H Margetts and G Smyth (eds), *Turning Japanese? Britain with a permanent party of government* (1995).
[70] See N Tideman and D Richardson, 'A comparison of improved STV methods' in Bowler and Grofman (eds), *Elections in Australia, Ireland and Malta under the Single Transferable Vote* (n 20 above).

to maintain single-member districts while conceding overall proportionality through an extra tier of list-based elected members they offer an institutional compromise from which many national minorities may benefit.

All proportional systems—list-PR, STV, MMP—have a particular institutional appeal. In deeply divided places, with which the Lund Recommendations were partly concerned, political leaders in polarized polities are far more likely to agree on consociational[71] (power-sharing) rather than integrationist bargains; and for that reason to prefer proportional to majoritarian electoral systems. After all, power-sharing and proportionality guarantee all the major parties some share of power, and minimize the risk that their rivals will unilaterally dominate them. Their leaders are therefore far more likely to agree to proportional systems rather than systems such as AV, because they can win votes and seats on their own preferred platforms. This is particularly true of radical elites who are the most ready to resist integrationist impositions. Proportionality norms, embedded in consociations, may enhance political stability because they match the rival parties' respective bargaining strengths and conceptions of distributive justice. And as proportional election systems pose fewer barriers to entry for new political forces than plurality and majority-based alternatives, they can also contribute to long-term stability by allowing integrationist forces to emerge organically.

Consociationalists also argue that inclusion in power-sharing coalitions may make radicals less extreme, because it will provide them with opportunities to have their concerns addressed; in short, it gives them a stake in the system.[72] Inclusion may strengthen the position of moderates within radical factions, a possibility that centripetalists tend to omit from their thinking.

---

[71] For discussions of consociation see, inter alia, A Lijphart, 'Consociational democracy' (1969) 21(2) *World Politics* 207–25; A Lijphart, 'Majority rule verse consociationalism in deeply divided societies' (1977) 4 *Politikon* 113–26; A Lijphart, 'The puzzle of Indian democracy: A consociational interpretation' (1996) 90(2) *American Political Science Review* 258–68; IS Lustick, 'Lijphart, Lakatos and consociationalism' (1997) 50 *World Politics* 88–117; J McGarry and B O'Leary, 'Consociational theory, Northern Ireland's conflict, and its agreement. Part Two. What critics of consociation can learn from Northern Ireland' (2006) 41(2) *Government and Opposition* 249–77; J McGarry and B O'Leary, 'Consociational theory, Northern Ireland's conflict, and its agreement. Part One. What consociationalists can learn from Northern Ireland' (2006) 41(1) *Government and Opposition* 43–63; B O'Leary, 'Debating consociation: Normative and explanatory arguments' in SJR Noel (ed), *From Power-Sharing to Democracy: Post-conflict institutions in ethnically divided societies* (2005);Brendan O'Leary, 'The logics of power-sharing, Consociation and pluralist federations' in M Weller, B Metzger, and N Johnson (eds), *Settling Self-determination Disputes: Complex power-sharing in theory and practice* (2008).

[72] See P Mitchell, 'Transcending an ethnic party system? The Impact of consociational governance on electoral dynamics and the party system' in R Wilford (ed), *Aspects of the Belfast Agreement* (2001); P Mitchell, G Evans, and B O'Leary, 'Extremist outbidding in ethnic party systems is not inevitable: Tribune parties in Northern Ireland' (2009) 57(2) *Political Studies* 397–421; P Mitchell, B O'Leary, and G Evans, 'Northern Ireland: Flanking extremists bite the moderates and emerge in their clothes' (2001) 54(4) *Parliamentary Affairs* 725–42; P Mitchell, B O'Leary, and G Evans, 'The 2001 elections in Northern Ireland: Moderating "extremists" and the squeezing of the moderates' (2002) 39(1) *Representation* 23–36.

This survey of electoral systems by their formulas, which is less comprehensive than it may appear to the uninitiated, therefore suggests that further emendations to the Lund Recommendations are in order:

(i) From the perspective of national minorities, the comparative evidence against the use of WTA-SMD is powerful—though appropriate districting for certain groups can in principle, prevent its worst possible outcomes.
(ii) National minorities are more likely to prefer list-PR or STV-PR to WTA-SMD or AV because proportional systems make it more likely that they will be able to represent themselves if they form their own parties and have sufficient supporters—thereby serving the participation goal.
(iii) The emergent consensus is that whereas AV can do a better job than WTA-SMD in certain highly specific (and rare) contexts, it does not in logic provide powerful incentives for accommodative behaviour by political leaders unless there are extraordinarily fortunate patterns of preferences among voters, and equally benign geographical distribution of national minorities and majorities.
(iv) 'Colomer's law' suggests that national minorities, all other things being equal, will prefer large district magnitudes, large assemblies, and large gaps between divisors or large quotas. (They will not, of course, prefer large district magnitudes if they dilute their national territory in which they aspire to self-government.)

C. Districting, geography, and thresholds

A fair inference from what has been said so far is that proportional representation is best for national minorities because they make it easier for them to win seats—because there is a lower effective threshold to be crossed. Bernard Grofman, however, has shown that this reasoning must be qualified. In comparing the effective threshold faced under 'winner takes all' to that faced under proportional representation we must always control for the size of the relevant electoral districts.[73] It may, in some cases, be easier for national minorities to win seats in smaller-sized single-member electoral districts than in larger-sized multi-member districts (size here refers to the number of voters). This point returns us, partly, to the observation made earlier in discussing WTA-SMD: it is a system that may sometimes help appropriately territorially concentrated national minorities. The formal point is that to choose PR over WTA-SMD in the interests of national minorities should only be the recommended choice when the territorial distribution of voters and the district magnitude(s) have been fully considered.

---

[73] B Grofman, 'A note of caution in interpreting the threshold of exclusion' (2001) 20 *Electoral Studies* 299–303.

One other observation must be registered on districting, geography, and effective thresholds. It is the powerful outcome of sustained empirical observation and of mathematical logic, and shows a firm and robust example of cumulative knowledge in political science. It is owed perhaps most to Rein Taagepeera, though other political scientists, notably Bernard Grofman and Gary Cox deserve credit.[74] We have already seen it embedded in what I have called Colomer's law, but it is worth highlighting separately. The result is this: the more seats that are available to be filled per voter then the more proportional the outcome of elections, irrespective of the precise electoral formula. It follows from this important result that the position of national minorities, *ceteris paribus*, will be improved (unless they are accidental beneficiaries of peculiar geography) by an expansion in the number of seats available per voter (provided, of course, there is no malapportionment or gerrymandering). It is equally true, on the same logic, that the larger the assembly size, irrespective of the particular districting system, then the more proportional the outcomes of elections will be, again to the benefit of national minorities.

D. Corporate or reserved systems

The Lund Recommendations are silent on the subject of 'reserved seats', and of a related idea, 'separate electoral rolls'. With reserved seats, a certain number of seats in an assembly or council are specifically set aside for national minorities.[75] North American and Europeans tend to assume that such systems reflect undesirable 'separatism', and to regard them as the functional equivalents of apartheid. But such systems may be sought and negotiated by national minorities themselves. A good example is the Kurdistan Region of Iraq, which since 1992 has reserved seats in addition to its one hundred-member National Assembly: five are reserved for the Christians of Kurdistan (Assyrians, Chaldeans

---

[74] See G Cox, *Making Votes Count: Strategic coordination in the world's electoral systems* (1997); R Taagepera, *Predicting Party Size* (2007); R Taagepera, 'The effect of district magnitude and properties of two-seat districts' in A Lijphart and B Grofman (eds) *Choosing an Electoral System: Issues and alternatives* (1984); R Taagepera, 'The size of national assemblies' (1972) 1(4) *Social Science Research* 385–401; Taagepera and Shugart, *Seats and Votes* (n 34 above).

[75] For references to reserved seats for Maoris in New Zealand, see among others A Armitage, *Comparing the Policy of Aboriginal Assimilation: Australia, Canada and New Zealand* (1995); A Lijphart, 'Proportionality by Non-Pr Methods: Ethnic representation in Belgium, Cyprus, Lebanon, New Zealand, West Germany and Zimbabwe' in A Lijphart and B Grofman (eds), *Choosing an Electoral System: Issues and alternatives* (1986); JH Nagel, 'Social choice in a pluralitarian democracy: The politics of market liberalization in New Zealand' (1998) 28 *British Journal of Political Science*; NS Roberts, 'A period of enhanced surprise, disappointment, and frustration? The Introduction of a new electoral system in New Zealand' in J Elklit (ed), *Electoral Systems for Emerging Democracies: Experiences and suggestions* (1997); J Vowles, 'The politics of electoral reform in New Zealand' (1995) 16(1) *International Political Science Review* 95–115. Maoris chose to preserve their reserved seats, though the number changed, when New Zealand changed its electoral system from WTA-SMD to MMP.

and Syrian Orthodox); five for the Turkmen; and more recently one seat has been reserved for the Armenians. The evidence at present suggests that these reserved seats slightly over-represent the relevant communities in the Kurdistan National Assembly. These reserved seats do not, however, prevent members of national minorities from running on the lists of the major parties running for the non-reserved seats, which they do, but voters must decide on which rolls to be registered. In my interviews with representatives elected to the Kurdistan National Assembly, and with samples of national minorities throughout the Kurdistan Region in the spring of 2009, I found strong support for the maintenance of the reserved seats—I was told they assured representation, enabled internal debate among the affected minorities, and should be maintained. A small number of critics within the minorities observed, however, that the reserved seats had led to fragmentation, especially among the Christian nationalities (as the Assyrians and Chaldeans often describe themselves), into multiple parties—though they did not think this was the result of manipulation by the Kurdish majority. Reserved seats may be especially appropriate for indigenous homeland minorities, fearful minorities, or micro-minorities that would be unlikely to win representation for their own parties even under proportional representation. Provided these are set up because of national minorities' own decisions, and provided individual members of national minorities are free to register on the roll of their choice, these systems are compatible with liberal consociation and self-determination. They should only be condemned if individuals are obliged to participate only within the electoral roll reserved for a national minority.[76]

E. Untried systems

There are several electoral systems that have not yet been extensively tested in real world political systems, and have deliberately not been discussed here. Among these are:

(i) the very new 'méthode majoritaire', invented by Michel Balinski,[77] which cannot (yet) be pithily summarized, though it is modelled on French examination grades—it biases choice in favour of median preferences, but has many interesting properties;

---

[76] See A Lijphart, 'Self-determination versus pre-determination of ethnic minorities in power-sharing systems' in Will Kymlicka (ed) *The Rights of Minority Cultures* (1995); J McGarry and B O'Leary, 'Iraq's Constitution of 2005: Liberal consociation as political prescription' (2007) 5(4) *International Journal of Constitutional Law* 1–29.

[77] See M Balinski and R Laraki, 'A theory of measuring, electing, and ranking' (2007) 104(21) *Proceedings of the National Academy of Science* 8720–5; M Balinski and R Laraki, 'Election by majority judgement: Experimental evidence' (2007) 28 *Ecole Polytechnique: Centre National de la Recherche Scientifique*.

(ii) the system of *approval voting*, invented by Steve Brahms,[78] which seeks to find broadly acceptable winners—voters may express support for as many candidates as they wish up to one less than the number of candidates and the winner has the most approval votes, enabling the least-opposed candidate to win;

(iii) the so-called *anti-plurality* vote, in which voters indicate who they least want elected (the candidate with the least such votes is the winner);

(iv) the *Coombs rule*, which alters the transfer process used in AV and STV—instead of eliminating the last placed candidate, it is the candidate with the largest number of last-placed votes who is first eliminated; and[79]

(v) the Borda method(s), favoured for example by Peter Emerson, which relies on ranking with numbers.[80]

I have not discussed these systems because it remains to be seen whether they will ever be widely used. Like all systems, they have their respective drawbacks. It is also not yet clear what their impacts would be on national minorities—though it may be that the first two and last methods bias outcomes in favour of 'moderates', whereas the third and fourth rule out the most extreme (even if they have fairly high levels of support) from among all communities.

III. Concluding Observations

The political science of electoral systems is now sufficiently advanced, robust, and rigorous that I have been able to report here widely accepted results in the field that have a bearing on the Lund Recommendations. The most contested part of my summary of research results would likely be the report that the arguments once made for the alternative vote in promoting interethnic accommodation are no longer logically—or empirically—plausible. This is not a conclusion to which Donald Horowitz is yet willing to assent.

There is no need to repeat here the proposed modifications to the Lund Recommendations, which I have made at several junctures in the text. Instead I wish to use the conclusion to make certain general observations about electoral systems and national minorities, some obvious, some less so.

First, electoral systems are just one set of institutions that affect the fate of national minorities. They may not, in some cases, be the most important: legislative decision rules requiring qualified majorities where matters affect national

---

[78] For discussions see J Baron, NY Altman, and S Kroll, 'Approval voting and parochialism' (2005) 48(6) *Journal of Conflict Resolution* 895–907; M Regenwetter and B Grofman, 'Approval voting, Borda winners and Condorcet winners: Evidence from seven elections' (1998) 44(4) *Management Science* 520–33.

[79] See B Grofman and SL Feld, 'If you like the alternative vote (aka the instant runoff), then you ought to know about the Coombs rule' (2004) 23 *Electoral Studies* 641–59.

[80] See PJ Emerson, *Defining Democracy: Decisions, elections, and good governance* (2002).

minorities; inclusive executive composition and decision rules, requiring collective presidencies or dual premiers or representative cabinets; and constitutional or supreme courts with mandates to protect national minorities and which operate by consensus, may be separately, and jointly, just as important, or more important (see John McGarry, Chapter 2 in this volume)—likewise, policies of representativeness in security sectors (the military, intelligence services, and the police), or economic policies of affirmative action or of balanced development or of resource autonomy or resource redistribution. In most states of the OSCE, even if proportional systems are used to elect legislatures, regional assemblies, and local governments, there is normally unqualified majoritarianism in legislative and executive decision-making, and this may be of far more consequence than the electoral system. But that said, electoral systems matter, especially overt pathologies that are obvious indicators of the maltreatment of national minorities. OSCE observation teams, INGOs, and NGOs should be on the lookout for gerrymandering, malapportionment, high thresholds, and the use and abuse of electoral regulations to suppress or dilute the voting rights of national minorities.

Secondly, electoral systems tend to be 'sticky'; once chosen they have considerable staying power. Locking them into the constitution or making change to them more difficult, eg through an organic law, is therefore only good if the system being entrenched is good. It is the message of this chapter that from the perspective of national minorities locking in the principle of proportionality (though not any precise system) would be far better than locking in any non-PR system into the constitution.

Thirdly, the empirical consequences of an electoral system in a given country and region are not mechanically deducible from its formal properties. The historical, cultural, and political contexts in which they are introduced matter, as do the electoral regulations and party law regulations that envelop them. Politics is about agency, and local agents respond differently to the same set of institutional incentives. So, in new democracies, or renewing democracies, care should be taken in presuming that an electoral system will import with reliably predictable consequences.

Fourthly, national minorities, especially small ones, will generally be neglected when electoral reform is being considered within a majority community. That was clearly the case with the UK's Jenkins Commission, which focused most of its attention on the big three British and English parties—the Conservatives, Labour, and the Liberal Democrats—with much less care taken over how electoral system changes might impact Scotland, Wales, and Northern Ireland. Legal systems, minority rights commissions, and second legislative chambers, should be staffed with people sufficiently expert to exercise 'voice' when electoral system changes might unintentionally adversely affect national minorities.

Lastly, electoral systems and party systems are highly interactive, and it has been no part of my brief to consider party systems. The Lund Recommendations are slightly hostile to the creation of national minority parties. The references to 'communal' parties', and the desirability of fair treatment to discourage the formation of such parties certainly suggests as much. By contrast, I would suggest that a national minority is not a free *national* minority unless it has at least one nationalist party (with the word nationalist being used here in a non-pejorative way, and with no presumption being made that a nationalist must necessarily have a secessionist as opposed to an autonomist agenda). But, whatever may be the rival assessments on the merits of a statewide party system in which there are no national minority parties, we should all conclude that a fair electoral system, fairly regulated, and transparently designed to provide both participation and autonomy opportunities to national minorities, will reduce the temptations, and the justifications, for parties among national minorities to become 'anti-system'.

13

Making Effective Use of Parliamentary Representation

Oleh Protsyk

I. Agenda-setting	401
A. Partisan control of agenda-setting	402
B. Agenda-setting offices	403
II. Deliberation	405
Legislative arenas for deliberation	407
III. Accountability	409
Monitoring	411
IV. Conclusion	413

The representative nature of modern democracies makes the issues of parliamentary organization and functioning centrally important to our understanding of how minority interests and demands are dealt with in legislative assemblies. Parliamentary rules, norms, and procedures shape the legislative decision-making process and affect accountability relations between representatives and their constituencies. While the extent to which minorities are represented in parliament is mainly determined by electoral rules and party legislation, the effectiveness of minority representation is also shaped by the character of parliamentary institutions. This chapter provides a general conceptual overview of how the institutional design of legislatures and procedural issues impact on the ability of minority representatives to contribute substantively to the legislative decision-making process.

    Parliamentary practices have received considerably less attention than other legislative representation-related issues, such as electoral rules and party regulations, in documents setting international standards for the effective participation of minorities. The Lund Recommendations contain only a passing mention of the committee membership issue in the Explanatory Note attached to the document.[1] Slightly more attention is paid to parliamentary issues in the recent Commentary of the Advisory Committee (AC) to the Framework Convention for the Protection of National Minorities (FCNM) on the effective participation of national minorities.[2] In this latter document, the focus is on the functioning of special parliamentary committees established to address minority issues. At the same time, the two paragraphs that the Commentary devotes to a discussion of parliamentary practice also touch on a number of broader themes pertaining to key aspects of legislative functioning.

This chapter explores these themes in greater detail by analysing how different features of parliamentary organization shape the effectiveness of ethnic minority representation. The chapter discusses the following key aspects of parliamentary functioning in relation to minority interests: agenda-setting, deliberation, and accountability relations. Rules and procedures that regulate parliamentary activity in each of these areas can have a significant impact on how ethnic minority claims and demands are first articulated and then processed within the legislative arena. The section on agenda-setting discusses the possibilities for minority representative participation to set the agenda of the legislature. The section examines both partisan and institutional channels that allow minority representatives to influence the law-making process. The section on deliberation explores how the use of different parliamentary arenas for debate and discussion can enhance the minority cause. The final section highlights the critical importance of transparency and monitoring for enhancing accountability relations between minority communities and their representatives in parliament.

I. Agenda-setting

Agenda-setting is an overarching issue within the organization of the legislative process. It is understood here broadly as any special ability to determine which bills are considered on the floor and under what procedures. The emphasis in this definition is on special, as opposed to general, ability to influence the legislative process—the latter being expressed in the equal power of each legislator's vote on the floor.[3] Control of agenda-setting powers translates into decisions about how the process of law-making in parliament should be organized and what rules and procedures should apply. These rules and procedures include

---

[1] Foundation on Inter-ethnic Relations, 'The Lund Recommendations on the Effective Participation of National Minorities in Public Life and Explanatory Note' (The Hague, 1999), II, A, 6.

[2] Advisory Committee on the Framework Convention for the Protection of National Minorities, Commentary on Effective Participation of Persons Belonging to National Minorities in Cultural, Social, and Economic Life and in Public Affairs, ACFC/31DOC(2008)001, III, 3, v.

[3] On the concept of agenda-setting, see GW Cox, 'The organization of democratic legislatures' in BR Weingast and DA Wittman (eds), *The Oxford Handbook of Political Economy* (2006).

provisions on how draft bills are introduced into the parliament, what stages of legislative consideration these drafts have to go through, and how decisions at each stage are made. These rules also specify how gate-keeping powers—whether to make proposals or to apply vetoes in the legislative process—are distributed among various legislative offices.

A. Partisan control of agenda-setting

Agenda-setting is largely the domain of political parties that control the legislative majority. As long as rules and procedures affect substantive outcomes, parliamentary majorities develop preferences over alternative sets of rules and pursue strategies that enable them to implement the preferred set of rules. As they constitute legislative minorities in parliament, representatives of ethnic minority interests cannot, by definition, control agenda-setting powers. It does not, however, mean that minority representatives are unable to influence both the nature of the bills considered and procedures used for this consideration.

The ability of ethnic minority representatives to influence the legislative agenda is profoundly shaped by their relation with legislative majorities. Being inside the government coalition provides these representatives with significant opportunities for influencing the legislative priorities of the coalition. When minority representatives belong to non-ethnic parties that control the legislative majority, their opportunity to impact on agenda-setting is derived from working inside the legislative caucuses of these parties. The activity of minority representatives involves building intra-party coalitions in support of specific legislative procedures or substantive policy issues that are of interest to ethnic minorities. Being a representative of ethnic minority interests is understood here in substantive or policy representation terms: minority interests could be represented both by legislators who belong to a specific minority group or by those who are not themselves members of the group.

A different set of opportunities, and a different strategic situation, arises when minority representatives enter the government coalition as a distinct political force. This happens when ethnic minority parties are successful in gaining legislative representation through general or special electoral provisions; and/or when reserved seat provisions for ethnic minority representation are in place in a given political system. Constructing legislative support for minority-related issues then becomes an exercise in inter-party coalition-building. The bargaining power of ethnic parties or reserved seats deputies depends in this case on their relative legislative size. When government coalitions depend on ethnic minority parties or reserved seats deputies, with the latter being treated here as distinct legislative parties, for their ability to maintain their majority status in the legislature, the bargaining power of ethnic minority representatives is strongest. When legislative coalitions can sustain their majority status without the support of ethnic minority representatives—that is, when winning coalitions are not minimum majority-sized—the bargaining power of these representatives is significantly weaker.[4]

The chances of ethnic minority parties joining the government might be stronger than one would have expected, given their legislative weight. Political science literature on cabinet formation often expects government coalitions to be formed in a way that increases the coalition partners' share of governmental control—that is, by including into the coalition only those parties that are necessary to maintain the majority status of government. In practice, oversize government coalitions are frequently formed and ethnic minority parties can be part of these coalitions. The case of the Unity Party for Human Rights (BDN), one of the Greek minority parties in Albania, is telling in this respect. The party, which represents an ethnic group whose relative size within the country's total population is around 2 per cent, has been a part of various government coalitions since 1997 and has been consistently granted one of the cabinet ministries in each of the successive governments. Similar examples of ethnic minority parties forming part of oversize government coalitions can be found in other ethnically diverse countries in Central and Eastern Europe.[5]

When they do not form part of the government coalition, either as individual members of the legislative caucuses of non-ethnic parties or as a team of legislators elected on an ethnic party ticket, minority representatives face more difficulties in trying to influence a legislature's policy priorities and procedural rules. Their access to agenda-setting issues in this case is largely determined from outside—by the legislative majority's decision over how many procedural rights should be granted to the legislative opposition. The opposition's ability to influence agenda-setting is further fragmented by the multi-party character of its composition. More than one party can usually be found to share the opposition status in the vast majority of democratic legislatures.

B. Agenda-setting offices

Control over agenda-setting is primarily exercised through various legislative offices. Committees, directory boards and presiding offices are key types of legislative office. The names of these parliamentary bodies and their relative influence vary across legislatures, but most national assemblies have the functional equivalent of the three types of offices identified above. These offices are endowed with different combinations of negative agenda powers (the power to delay or veto the placement of bills on the plenary agenda) and positive agenda powers (the power to hasten or ensure the placement of bills on the plenary

---

[4] For political science literature on government coalitions in parliament see, eg, M Laver and KA Shepsle, *Making and Breaking Governments: Cabinets and legislatures in parliamentary democracies* (1996).

[5] European Centre for Minority Issues (ECMI), ECMI Dataset on Minority Representation, Flensburg.

agenda). They can also have substantial control over the distribution of scarce resources such as staff and operational budgets.

Committees stand out from the system of legislative offices as the institution with the most direct relevance to ethnic minority interests. As their numerical size and subsequent legislative weight are often quite limited, the best chance minority representatives have of gaining positions in agenda-setting offices is through membership of legislative committees. Committee positions not only give legislators the opportunity to influence agenda-setting, but also provide them with the possibility of acquiring or deepening their policy expertise.

The importance of legislative committees for minority interests is reflected in the fact that the authors of the 2008 AC Commentary on Effective Participation of National Minorities singled out legislative committees as a central topic within the brief section on parliamentary practices. The section provides a positive assessment of the role played by specialized committees on minority issues, where such committees exist, in addressing minority issues. It also stresses the importance of the representation of minority interests on other legislative committees whose activities might have an effect on minority-related issues.[6]

While the potential benefits of having a legislative committee on minority issues might be quite substantial, it is very rare that such committees function as permanent and specialized legislative offices. Parliamentary practices around the world do favour a system of permanent and specialized rather than ad hoc and general committees.[7] However, minority issues are not usually considered a policy area that qualifies for separate committee-level status. Minority issues are more often the responsibility of a subcommittee within a committee with a broader jurisdiction. For example, in post-communist parliaments minority issues frequently fall within the jurisdiction of committees on human rights or regional development.[8]

The strength of legislative committee powers varies considerably across political systems. The literature on the agenda-setting powers of legislative offices, which was developed largely in the context of US studies, regards the committees of the US Congress and especially their chairs as very powerful legislative players who can prioritize or delay consideration of bills or their placement for the floor vote.[9] Similar types of procedural powers have an impact on the decision-making process across different legislatures. Therefore, having

---

[6] Advisory Committee on the Framework Convention for the Protection of National Minorities, Commentary on Effective Participation of Persons Belonging to National Minorities in Cultural, Social, and Economic Life and in Public Affairs, ACFC/31DOC(2008)001, III, 3, v.

[7] For a review of the committee system in Western Europe, see I Mattson and K Strom, 'Committee effects on legislation' in H Doring and M Hallerberg (eds), *Patterns of Parliamentary Behaviour* (2004).

[8] On committee structure in the early post-communist legislatures see DM Olson and P Norton, *The New Parliaments of Central and Eastern Europe* (1996).

[9] GW Cox and MD McCubbins, *Setting the Agenda: Responsible party government in the US House of Representatives* (2005).

an office with even the limited institutional status of a subcommittee can provide minority representatives with a modicum of procedural power.

The procedural powers of such an office are enhanced if an extensive system of committee referrals is in place in a legislature.[10] Committee influence depends on whether bills actually go to the committee on their way through the legislative process. Parliamentary practice varies with regard to how frequently bills are sent for review by several committees rather than by the one identified as most relevant for the bill. The system of multiple committee referrals enhances the chances that different types of minority-relevant bills will be scrutinized by committees or subcommittees on minority issues.

However, the extent of committee power should not be exaggerated. Committees cannot prevent bills from entering the floor, or issue bill-related recommendations that would be binding for the floor, in either the US Congress or in the legislatures of other democratic states. Consequently, the suggestion by the 2008 AC Commentary that legislators pay appropriate attention to the recommendations of committees dealing with minority issues does not envision any mechanisms for obligatory enactment of committee recommendations. Committees are also unlikely to be especially successful in another function envisioned for them by the Commentary, namely, to foster cross-partisan consensus on minority-related issues. As one recent comprehensive study of parliamentary behaviour across Western Europe indicates, there is little empirical evidence to suggest that committees can help to resolve partisan conflict.[11] There are few reasons to expect that the same pattern will not hold true for the special case of partisan conflict over minority issues.

Committees or subcommittees on minority issues can nevertheless be of significant benefit to both minority representatives and to legislatures at large. They serve as an important arena where deputies interested in minority issues can articulate policy proposals and conduct their political activities. They constitute one of the primary parliamentary venues for debate and discussion of minority problems. They encourage the exchange of policy ideas, knowledge acquisition, and the development of specialization which contribute to the overall strengthening of the legislature as an institution.

II. Deliberation

Deliberation is an important mechanism for political decision-making. Deliberation refers to decision-making through argumentation and involves the participation of all those affected by the decision or their representatives.

---

[10] See on this topic, eg, Mattson and Strom, 'Committee effects on legislation' (n 7 above).
[11] Doring and Hallerberg, *Patterns of Parliamentary Behaviour* (n 7 above).

Legislatures constitute one of the key public fora for deliberation.[12] This is, of course, true only in the case of democracies. The phrase of the speaker of the lower chamber of Russian parliament, who famously exclaimed in a moment of irritation in December 2003 that 'parliament is not a place for discussion', can symbolize the approach of semi-democratic and non-democratic regimes to the work of representative assemblies.[13]

The irony in the operation of democratic legislatures is that they function under constant time pressure, which imposes serious constraints on legislators' ability to discuss and debate. The scarcity of plenary time as a cause of procedural rules limiting ordinary legislators' powers and creating inequalities among them is a key topic in rational choice-based discussions of legislative organization.[14] Legislative debates and deliberations nevertheless constitute a uniform feature of parliamentary institutions; the analytical content and properties of these debates is increasingly a subject of thorough and detailed empirical investigation.[15]

The interests of ethnic minority communities are greatly served when minority representatives take full advantage of opportunities presented by legislative debate. The utility of these debates for minority representatives stems from the transformative potential that deliberation can have on the preferences of legislative majorities. The support of these majorities is essential for the success of bills and resolutions on ethnic minority issues. The transformation of legislative preferences can be based on two different mechanisms, which are worth outlining briefly here.

Debates can help formulate majority positions on ethnic minority issues. This can be the case when minority issues are not politically salient in a given society. Legislative deliberation in such circumstances serves the goals of informing the majority of legislative deputies who have no position on ethnic minority issues about the needs of minority communities. In this case, providing information on these needs and deliberating over legislative solutions to community requests can help majorities form preferences on ethnic minority issues.

Debates can also try to convince legislative majorities to change their prior positions on minority issues. Where ethnic issues are already politicized, legislative actors are likely to have well-established preferences over alternative policies on minority-related issues. Minority representatives might strive through the process of deliberation to persuade sceptics and opponents of minority-focused policies to change their position. Such a change of position is more likely when it concerns the transformation of second-order or derived

---

[12] JM Carey, 'Legislative organization' in RAW Rhodes, SA Binder, and BA Rockman, *The Oxford Handbook of Political Institutions* (2006).
[13] A Levchenko, 'Not a place for discussion', *Gazeta.ru*, available at <http://www.gazeta.ru/politics/elections2007/articles/2311346.shtml> (accessed 31 July 2009).
[14] GW Cox, 'The organization of democratic legislatures' (n 3 above).
[15] J Steiner et al, *Deliberative Politics in Action: Analysing parliamentary discourse* (2004).

preferences, which are preferences over the best means of realizing shared ends. Deliberation, however, might also help to transform fundamental preferences, which are preferences over ultimate ends.

While the general ability of pure reasoning and deliberation to modify the preference structure of self-interested actors should be rightly viewed with a degree of scepticism, the potential of discussion and deliberation to shape policy outcomes should not be underestimated. The general resurgence of interest in deliberation received a lot of attention in political philosophy literature, which explores what potential benefits other than preference transformation can be generated through 'free and public reasoning among equals'. This literature largely dismisses the idea that public discussion should not be taken too seriously as it is devoid of content or routinely used by political actors in 'cheap talk' practices and in concealing their true underlying preferences.[16]

The deliberative democracy literature points instead to a number of beneficial effects of public discussion, even if that discussion does not reshape actors' preferences. Deliberation induces a particular mode of justifying demands which is rooted in the public goods frame of reference. Deliberation can be creative in the sense that it involves not only a process of choosing among given alternatives, but also a process of generating new alternatives. It might equally constrain or even prevent self-interested proposals from coming onto the voting agenda.[17]

This last argument in favour of deliberation, which Jon Elster calls the 'civilizing force of hypocrisy', is that it makes legislative debates about minority interests easier for proponents of minority rights. The growing normative appeal of minority rights, which are increasingly seen as part of a general human rights agenda,[18] means that it is more difficult for opponents of minority protection policies to justify their policy positions within the public arena. This and the other above-mentioned benefits of public discussion should lead minority representatives to seek to maximize the chances of minority issues being exposed to legislative deliberation, regardless of whether this deliberation promises to change the majority position on the current issues under legislative consideration.

Legislative arenas for deliberation

Legislatures provide several distinct arenas for public deliberation. These include, among others, directory board meetings, governing coalition presidiums and conferences, plenary floor sessions, committee meetings, and

---

[16] J Elster (ed), *Deliberative Democracy* (1998).
[17] J Elster, 'Introduction' in Elster, *Deliberative Democracy* (n 16 above).
[18] M Weller (ed), *The Rights of Minorities: A commentary on the European Framework Convention for the Protection of National Minorities* (2005).

committee hearings. Meetings of parliamentary caucuses of political parties or parliamentary groups of independent deputies can also serve as a forum for deliberation, albeit limited to intra-party or intra-group discussion. Each of these venues has its own advantages and limitations in terms of fostering legislative awareness of minority issues.

Directory board and governing coalition meetings as well as plenary floor sessions are likely to provide more limited opportunities for minority representatives due to the fact that the agendas of these meetings are usually overcrowded and deliberation time is especially scarce, with many different policy issues competing for the participants' attention. At the same time, debating ethnic minority issues in the context of these forums represents the most effective way of communicating minority concerns both to the parliamentary leadership and to the rank-and-file members of the legislature.

The committee environment creates more space for minority-related deliberation. Internal committee meetings allow for a detailed and informed discussion of the issues raised. This discussion usually rests on some base of knowledge accumulated by the committee members who share professional interest and experience in minority issues and by the permanent technical staff of the committee. While deliberations in such meetings are still likely to be dominated by partisan considerations, the committee members might develop some shared in-group norms that make cooperative behaviour more likely. The small size of committee meetings and the face-to-face nature of interaction can also diminish the tendency of using the committee floor for grandstanding and self-promotion.

Minority representatives can take advantage of the special opportunities provided by the committee powers, which usually include the authority to summon experts and executive government officials and to hold official hearings on specific topics. Both meetings with experts/officials and hearings organized by the committees are well suited for achieving one of the AC FCNM Commentary's recommendations, which is to establish 'regular dialogue … between the committees and the relevant authorities as well as between them and minority associations'. Such hearings can serve both as a source of additional expertise for committee members and as a forum for publicizing minority issues inside and outside the parliament. However, provisions for committee hearings, as well as for ad hoc special commissions, vary significantly across the legislatures. Minority interests can be better served when such provisions are well institutionalized.

Another statement of the AC FCNM Commentary related to committee proceedings mentions that it might be desirable to have committee deliberation in minority languages. However, the issue of minority language use in the legislature could be considered in a broader perspective, as part of the general definition of the status of a minority group in a given society. If the group enjoys an especially elevated status, which could be labelled as a constituent nation status, its language might be on an equal footing with the majority language in parliament. The use of French in the Canadian parliament or Albanian in the

Macedonian legislature are examples of such an approach. Otherwise, the use of minority languages in the legislature is a matter of procedure decided by the legislative majorities on a temporary basis. Many post-Soviet parliaments, for example, allow the use of Russian in legislative proceedings and provide translation services for minority deputies who lack titular language skills. These provisions, unless they are based on the constitutionally entrenched status of Russian as a second state language, do not signify some normative commitment to use minority languages. Rather, they reflect the practical need to ensure effective communication in newly established states where the earlier Soviet policies of linguistic 'Russification' made Russian the only available language for communication between titular and minority groups.

Overall, the deliberative and public nature of parliamentary proceedings provides minority representatives with opportunities to advocate and advertise a minority agenda. The existence of different deliberation fora inside the legislature allows these representatives to target different legislative audiences and to engage outside actors such as expert community members, minority organizations, and the media. Making good use of these opportunities is the responsibility of minority representatives and this is a topic to which we will now turn our attention.

III. Accountability

Legislative accountability is a core issue in any democratic polity, due to the centrality of legislatures within the democratic process.[19] Legislative accountability means that elected representatives are responsive to the needs and demands of their constituencies and that the latter have the means to sanction representatives for their lack of responsiveness. This section first discusses briefly the importance of constituency-type relations for the legislative behaviour of ethnic minority representatives. It then focuses on the problem of monitoring the performance of legislators. It is argued that making full use of the tools and mechanisms available for such monitoring will provide minority communities with important leverage for ensuring the responsiveness of their representatives.

Electoral connection plays a key role in the conceptualization within democratic theory of constituency-representative relations and legislative responsiveness. Different constituencies have different things they want their representatives to do. Constituencies are largely defined by electoral rules and, as indicated by the variety of electoral systems employed across the democratic polities, electoral institutions can define constituencies in a number of different ways. What is common across these different institutional rules is the principle

---

[19] For a general discussion of political representation issues see A Przeworski, SC Stokes, and B Manin (eds), *Democracy, Accountability, and Representation* (1999).

of free and regular elections as the primary means of holding representatives accountable.

In terms of organizational form, representation of ethnic minority interests in the legislature can be more party-dominated or individual legislator-based. Electoral rules that encourage the development of strong and disciplined political parties structure parliamentary representation along party lines. Electoral rules that foster direct ties between individual candidates and constituencies emphasize individual-level representation. This distinction does not necessarily coincide with proportional representation (PR) and single-member district (SMD) electoral rules; it constitutes a distinct dimension that cuts across these two main types of electoral systems. Different combinations of the different electoral rules can lead to different forms of representation coexisting in the same legislature.[20] Electoral ties shape how legislators who belong to ethnic minority groups perceive their responsibilities to minority communities. Minority group members can enter the legislature through a variety of institutional channels. They can become legislators through electoral lists or the nomination of mainstream political parties or ethnic minority parties. They can stand as independent candidates in regular SMD elections or in special minority reserved seats elections. These alternative types of electoral ties, as well as a number of other electoral characteristics and party procedures, affect how individual parliamentarians choose their legislative policy priorities, deal with competing demands for their political loyalty, and define their stand on minority-related issues.

In terms of the content of representation, the distinction between descriptive and substantive representation has long occupied a central position within the literature.[21] Substantive representation is essentially about policy representation. It focuses on how responsive representatives are to the basic policy needs of minority communities. It also implies that the policy interests of minority constituencies can be represented by parliamentarians who are not themselves necessarily members of minority communities. Many political theorists, however, have made the case for the importance of descriptive representation which, in the context of parliamentary representation, refers to whether members of parliament look like their constituents.[22] These theorists argue there is distinctive symbolic value in having various community groups represented by their members. They also suggest that there is a relationship between descriptive and substantive representation. Empirical political science research provides some support for this assumed connection: minority group membership of the legislators matters for substantive representation.[23]

---

[20] On the distinction between individual and collective representation see J Carey, *Legislative Voting and Accountability* (2009).   [21] HF Pitkin, *The Concept of Representation* (1972).
[22] A Phillips, *The Politics of Presence* (1998); W Kymlicka, *Multicultural Citizenship: A liberal theory of minority rights* (1996).   [23] D Canon, *Race, Redistricting and Representation* (2002).

Monitoring

While any conceptualizing of representation has at its core the notion that representation implies acting in the interests of the represented, positive political theory makes us aware of a multitude of situations when normatively desirable outcomes are not easily achievable. The central concern of analytical approaches to representation is the problem of politicians' self-interest. As one group of scholars put it, 'politicians have goals, interests, and values of their own, and they know things and undertake actions that citizens cannot observe or can monitor only at a cost'.[24] This is a problem that has been conceptualized more formally in the principal–agent literature that explores the numerous implications of conflict of interest between principals and agents; in our case, minority constituencies are principals and parliamentarians serve as their agents.

There is no reason to believe that politicians who come from ethnic minority groups are less self-interested or somehow different in this respect from politicians of the majority group. One telling example in this respect can be found in recent efforts by the minority reserved seats deputies in the Romanian parliament to change the legislative rules that govern elections to the reserved seats. Through bargaining and log-rolling they secured the support of the legislative majority for much stricter electoral registration rules, which privileged the minority organizations represented by the sitting deputies and made it much more difficult for competing minority organizations to contest the seats. These actions clearly did not serve the best interests of minority communities, whose ability to freely choose their representatives was significantly undermined by the change in the rules.[25]

Monitoring the legislative behaviour of representatives is an important way of addressing informational asymmetry between representatives and their constituencies and of achieving a higher degree of representative compliance with constituency wishes. Legislators might resist efforts to improve the monitoring of their activity and devise strategies to limit the amount of information available about the legislative process. For example, a recent comprehensive study of voting records across a large number of legislatures found considerable differences in the availability of roll-call data records, which the author of the study attributes to the specific preferences of those who control the legislative agenda.[26]

However, growing demands for transparency combined with advances in information technology have rapidly increased the amount of information on

---

[24] B Manin, A Przeworski, and SC Stokes, 'Elections and representation' in Przeworski, Stokes, and Manin (eds), *Democracy, Accountability, and Representation* (n 19 above).

[25] O Protsyk, M Caluser, and M Matichescu, 'Electoral dynamics of minority reserved seats competition in Romania', ECMI Working Paper no 43, April 2009, available at <http://www.ecmi.de/rubrik/58/working+papers/> (accessed 31 July 2009).

[26] J Carey, *Legislative Voting and Accountability* (2009).

legislative activity available to experts, scholars, non-governmental organizations, and the interested public. This includes roll-call data; transcripts of parliamentary debates and hearings; committee decisions and resolutions on individual bills; documentation on committee membership, parliamentary group affiliation, and parliamentary group changes by individual deputies; individual legislators' records of speeches, bill sponsorship, and interpolations/requests to executive agencies.

Roll-call data, which is the record of individual legislators' votes on a given bill, is a major source of information on the behaviour of legislators. This data comes from floor voting, which is a critical procedural element of all democratic legislatures. Monitoring of such votes by interest groups has long been a practice in the US, where 'report cards' based on legislative voting records are issued by groups ranging from pro-gun lobbies to environmental organizations. The positions that parties and individual legislators take on minority-related bills should also be the subject of constant interest to non-governmental organizations and groups advocating minority interests. The number of such bills in ethnically diverse polities can be quite considerable; they can deal with policy issues such as affirmative action, minority education, language use, multiculturalism, special social welfare and economic development programmes.

A lot of important legislative activity takes place outside the voting floor. Much of this activity, which involves negotiation between parliamentary groups and inside the groups between group leadership and rank-and-file legislators, is not observable from outside the legislative arena. Yet there are many other indicators of legislative behaviour which can serve as valuable sources of information on how legislators serve minority community interests. Committee assignments taken up by minority representatives are indicative of policy areas in which they plan to specialize. While committee membership is usually not determined solely by the preferences of legislators, committee assignments indicate in what substantive policy area the legislators' substantive contributions to law-making should be anticipated.

Bill sponsorship or co-sponsorship is another source of information on legislators' commitment to minority issues. Even when some minority-related draft bills stand no chance of being passed, such legislative initiatives have important symbolic value and serve as a register of minority public policy concerns. Efforts made by individual legislators to identify specific policy issues, such as drafting and introducing the bill, signal their attention to ethnic minority concerns. Speeches made in the different venues of parliamentary deliberation, as well as interpolations/requests sent to the executive government agencies regarding specific issues of policy implementation, can also contain important information for evaluating legislators' performance.

Overall, increasing the amount of systematic information about legislative behaviour is highly beneficial for the ability of minority constituencies to hold their representatives accountable. Where such information is not available, its systematic collection and release should be demanded. Greater availability of such information helps to reduce the informational asymmetry between minority legislators and their constituencies, and allows the latter to make informed decisions about sanctioning or rewarding their representatives.

IV. Conclusion

Legislatures are key arenas of representation, deliberation, and policy-making in modern democracies. Whether ethnic minorities are present in national legislative assemblies, whether their voices are heard, and whether their interests are taken into account are all important indicators of the ability of the minority to effectively participate in the political process. This chapter has tried to go beyond the usual dictum of 'majorities rule, minorities have rights' and to explore the various opportunities available to representatives of ethnic minority interests within the framework of national legislative assemblies. It discussed channels and procedures that allow minority representatives to influence legislative agenda-setting and examined the role of legislative offices in promoting minority interests.

This chapter has also pointed to the importance of parliamentary deliberation as a mechanism for advancing an ethnic minority agenda. Effective use by minority representatives of the various deliberation arenas that exist within a legislature can generate multiple benefits for minority communities. Parliamentary deliberation can have a positive effect on majority preferences and perceptions of minority issues. It can help to alleviate the marginal status of these issues and delegitimize assimilationist rhetoric. It can also expand the choice of policy alternatives and generate creative new solutions for policy problems faced by minority communities.

Finally the chapter stressed the importance of accountability in constituent–representative relations. Whether multiple opportunities for advancing minority interests are utilized depends on how faithfully minority representatives exercise their responsibilities in serving the minority community. This chapter has cautioned against assuming the unproblematic nature of this service. It pointed to the conflicting demands faced by representatives. It highlighted the importance of achieving greater transparency in the work of legislative representatives as a means of improving the monitoring capacity of constituencies, and argued that stronger accountability relations are an essential component of minority political participation.

14

Power-sharing at the Governmental Level

Florian Bieber

I. Introduction	414
II. Minority Rights, International Standards, and Executive Power-sharing	416
III. Forms of Minority Inclusion	419
A. Minority representation	420
B. Executive power-sharing	422
C. Hybrid or transitional systems	427
D. Regional executive power-sharing	429
IV. Conclusions	432

I. Introduction

Among different forms of political representation, the participation of minorities in government would appear to be the most advanced form of minority inclusion in a country. While the representation of minorities in parliament through electoral systems or the discrimination against minority inclusion through gerrymandering has received considerable attention in scholarship and among international organizations, the inclusion of minorities in government has often been neglected.[1]

There is a rich record of minority inclusion in the executive in Europe, as more than a quarter of all European countries have experimented with the participation of minority parties in government at the state or regional level. These include countries with long histories of interethnic cooperation, minority inclusion, and stable institutions such as Switzerland, to more recent democracies and, for that matter, countries such as Kosovo. The inclusion of group representatives in the executive authorities of a country or region derives primarily from the political concept of

---

[1] Venice Commission, *Electoral Law and National Minorities*, CDL-INF, 25 January 2000 (2000), 4; CF Juberías, 'Post-communist electoral systems and national minorities: A dilemma in five paradigms' in JP Stein (ed), *The Politics of National Minority Participation in Post-Communist Europe* (2000), 31–64; JK Birnir, *Ethnicity and Electoral Politics* (2006).

power-sharing rather than from minority rights. However, as we shall see, executive power-sharing, while underdeveloped in terms of international minority rights standards, has become an important aspect of minority inclusion across Europe.

Over the years, the term 'power-sharing' has acquired a broad and often contradictory meaning. From majoritarian systems which seek to promote interethnic accommodation through group-specific incentives to broad-based coalitions, many types of governance have been characterized as 'power-sharing'. In a recent study, Pippa Norris argues for power-sharing on the basis of defining it through features such as inclusive governance, a vibrant media and civil society to representative PR-based electoral systems and parliamentary democracy.[2] In addition to this breadth of regimes understood as power-sharing, there is also significant variation in terms of duration. Power-sharing is widely used to describe transitional, inclusive governments after civil conflict,[3] but temporary coalitions between majorities and minorities have also been called power-sharing.[4] As a result, the number of possible cases might increase, but the clarity of the category is increasingly blurred and the concept of power-sharing risks losing its analytical edge. This chapter follows the distinction made by O'Leary and others to adopt a restrictive definition, but to allow for some flexibility by distinguishing between different degrees of power-sharing.[5]

This chapter is not about power-sharing in general, but one aspect of it, namely the representation of groups in the executive. Considering the focus on minorities (or ethno-national groups more broadly), power-sharing between other types of groups, such as the 'pillars' (protestant, catholic and social democratic) in the Dutch sense or between former combatants within a conflict (eg, El Salvador) shall be excluded. For the purposes of this chapter, we will understand executive power-sharing as the inclusion of all major ethno-national groups in the executive. As we shall discuss further on, this representation has to be robust in terms of the timeframe and in terms of the protection it offers to smaller groups. If the inclusion of minorities in the executive falls short of these standards, to be defined as power-sharing, it will be considered just as executive representation. Executive power-sharing will often coincide with other aspects of consociationalism, such as proportional representation, segmental autonomy, and veto mechanisms, but such a combination is not necessary. Thus, executive power-sharing can exist without the political system in question being a consociatonal democracy, but no consociational democracy can exist without executive power-sharing. When discussed as a feature

---

[2] P Norris, *Driving Democracy. Do power-sharing institutions work?* (2008).

[3] C Hartzell and M Hoddie, 'Institutionalizing peace: Power sharing and post-civil war conflict management' (2003) 47(2) *American Journal of Political Science* 312–32.

[4] M Brusis, 'The European Union and interethnic power-sharing arrangements in accession countries' (2003) 1 *Journal on Ethnopolitics and Minority Issues in Europe* (2003), available at <http://ecmi.de/jemie/> (accessed 17 July 2009).

[5] B O'Leary, 'The logics of power-sharing, consociation and pluralist federations' in M Weller and B Metzger (eds), *Settling Self-determination Disputes: Complex power-sharing in theory and practice* (2008); A Lijphart, 'Constitutional design for divided societies'(2004) 15 (2) *Journal of Democracy* 96–109.

of consociationalism, executive power-sharing is often described as a grand coalition. However, as some cases will illustrate, the term 'coalition' might be misleading.

This chapter will argue that while international and European standards in the field of executive representation or power-sharing are few and weak, there is a rich practice across Europe. In discussing the origins and variations of this practice, the chapter will explore the contribution executive power-sharing can make to the effective participation of minorities in political life.

II. Minority Rights, International Standards, and Executive Power-sharing

Executive power-sharing as a form of minority inclusion in the political system derives from two separate sources. While the perspective of this volume focuses on different forms of minority representation and a subset of minority rights, executive power-sharing in fact has stronger foundations elsewhere. Thus, after examining this rather narrow basis in international minority rights standards, we will turn to its origins within domestic legislation and tradition, often based on interethnic accommodation to prevent or address inter-group conflict.

If international minority and human rights standards have stayed mostly clear of political representation of minorities, this applies in particular to the inclusion of minorities in government. International human rights provisions could be interpreted as prohibiting the systematic exclusion of minorities from government, but a wide gap exists between merely rejecting exclusion and executive power-sharing. Together with minority representation in the legislature, minority representation in government is the place where minority rights and considerations of democracy meet. Regulating the representation of minorities in government is inherently controversial and would suggest a particular form of government formation and electoral system. Furthermore, the question arises when and how minorities should be represented in government. For small minorities, inclusion in government might at best be a coincidence based on particular (and temporary) coalition and/or government formation, rather than a legal requirement. Thus, the Framework Convention for the Protection of National Minorities (FCNM) and other relevant standards remain largely silent on executive representation of minorities. However, the Commentary of the FCNM Advisory Committee on the Effective Participation of National Minorities in Public Life notes the benefits of representation of minorities in the executive and notes the possibility of 'posts assigned for minority representatives in the executive at all levels'.[6] Thus, the Committee extends the potential reach

---

[6] Advisory Committee on the Framework Convention for the Protection of National Minorities, Commentary on the Effective Participation of Persons Belonging to National Minorities in Cultural, Social, and Economic Life and in Public Affairs, 27 February 2008, ACFC/31DOC (2008)001, para 128.

of minority inclusion by emphasizing the merit of executive representation at the sub-national level of government.[7] However, it does not discuss the particular options for how such representation could be achieved and which particular type of minority inclusion might be the most effective. Even the Advisory Committee, while noting the merits of minority representation, identifies potential problems: the Commentary warns against the dangers of veto rights and their potential for blocking decision-making. While being discussed in the context of parliamentary voting, veto rights can also be a feature of executive representation.[8] The scepticism of the Advisory Committee is borne primarily out of the experience of Bosnia and Herzegovina, rather than any theoretical or comparative study of these mechanisms. Joseph Marko identifies this tension in the position of the Advisory Committee when he notes that on one hand the Committee has been critical of minority inclusion without granting minority representatives the means to partake in decision-making, while on the other hand it has been critical of excessive minority vetoes.[9] The middle ground between excessive veto rights and tokenistic representation is often hard to find.

In addition to the work of the Advisory Committee, the only other international minority rights document which makes clear reference to the participation of minorities in the executive are the Lund Recommendations, which outline the benefits of including minorities in government:

States should ensure that opportunities exist for minorities to have an effective voice at the level of the central government, including through special arrangements as necessary. These may include, depending upon the circumstances: ... formal or informal understandings for allocating to members of national minorities cabinet positions ...[10]

This recommendation constitutes a clear reference to power-sharing rather than merely the occasional representation of minorities in the executive. As with the work of the Advisory Committee, the Lund Recommendations constitute no binding standards, but can be seen instead as identifying best practice.

However, the representation of minorities in the executive can also be understood as deriving indirectly from other aspects of minority rights. It is widely understood that minority rights in the sphere of language, culture, media, or education require the active and full participation of minorities in the exercise of these rights.[11] Thus, minority rights are not only implemented for, but also

---

[7] Ibid, para 131.   [8] Ibid, para 97–99

[9] J Marko, *Effective Participation of National Minorities: A comment on conceptual, legal and empirical problems*, Committee of Experts on issues Relating to the Protection of National Minorities, DH-MIN(2006)14, Strasbourg, 20 October 2006, 8.

[10] Foundation on Inter-ethnic Relations, 'The Lund Recommendations on the Effective Participation of National Minorities in Public Life, and Explanatory Note', (1999).

[11] Art 2, UN Declaration on the Rights of Persons belonging to National or Ethnic, Religious, and Linguistic Minorities; United Nations, General Assembly Resolution 47/135, 18 December 1992; and K Henrard, *Designing an Adequate System of Minority Protection: Individual human rights, minority rights and the right to self-determination* (2000), 273–4.

by, minorities themselves. This participatory aspect of minority rights can be accomplished in a number of ways, from specific consultative mechanisms—in the development of curricula and textbooks for example—to broader forms of cultural autonomy. Finally, minority participation in the executive can also serve the purpose of securing minority participation in the implementation of minority rights. Thus, a number of countries in Central and South-eastern Europe in particular have often named ministers from minority communities to oversee the ministerial portfolio responsible for minority rights. Montenegro, for example, has had a minister from an Albanian minority party responsible for minority rights since 1998, even though the Albanian parties never formally joined the government.

In addition to minority rights standards, a basis for executive power-sharing can derive from the concept of self-determination. If self-determination is not only understood by its external dimension, ie in regard to the independence of territories, but also as internal self-determination, power-sharing can be viewed as a mechanism to fulfil such a right.[12] As Henrard notes, 'systems of consociational democracy form part of the wide range of possible implementations of the right to internal self-determination'.[13] However, such an understanding of internal self-determination is not widely reflected in international law, but rather left to the domestic legislation of the countries in question.[14] While it might be argued that state policies which repress minorities and aim at forcibly assimilating or expelling minorities would be deemed unacceptable internationally, there are few concrete signposts in terms of the positive measures to include minorities in the political system. The Arbitration Commission of the Conference on Yugoslavia, when asked to assess the claim to self-determination of Serbs in Croatia and Bosnia and Herzegovina, reduced internal self-determination to the protection of minority and human rights, without specifying any right to representation, autonomy, or governance of the country.[15] Arguably, international law has advanced since then, but altogether the basis of executive representation of minorities remains mostly limited to domestic sources of legitimacy, be they laws or political agreements.

Most countries of Europe which have established a form of executive power-sharing, have done so for domestic considerations. While other forms of minority rights might have their basis not only in the domestic reality, the weakness of international standards in the field of executive power-sharing has meant that domestic legislation is not 'only' the transposition of international law into domestic legislation, but is based on domestic 'need'.

---

[12] Ibid, 313–14. [13] Ibid, 314.
[14] D Archibugi, 'A critical analysis of the self-determination of peoples: A cosmopolitan perspective' (2003) 10(4) *Constellations* 488–505, 499.
[15] Opinion 2, Arbitration Commission of the Conference on Yugoslavia, 11 January 1992, (1992) 31 *ILM* 1488.

III. Forms of Minority Inclusion

Although international standards in this field might be scarce, there is a rich practice of inclusion of minorities in the executive of governments at different levels throughout Europe. This experience is sometimes the result of legal requirements, sometimes a consequence of long-established or more recent traditions. In discussing the practice of minority or group inclusion, we need to distinguish between two broad categories: minority representation and executive power-sharing. The overall distinction is immediately clear when comparing two post-communist countries: Macedonia and Slovakia.[16] In Slovakia, the Hungarian Coalition Party (MKP) joined the winning coalition of Prime Minister Mikuláš Dzurinda in 1998 and remained a governing partner for two consecutive legislative periods, until 2006. However, after the electoral victory of the new party *Smer* the MKP left government, which was subsequently formed with only Slovak parties, including the nationalist Slovak National Party. Despite the eight years in government, no tradition developed to include the MKP within government. By contrast, in Macedonia different Albanian parties have been in government since 1992. In recent parliamentary elections in 2008, the nationalist Macedonian VMRO-DPMNE won a resounding victory among its mostly Macedonian constituency and gained, together with some pre-election coalition partners, 63 of the 120 seats in the Macedonian *sobranie*, which would have allowed it to govern alone. However, it invited the Albanian Democratic Union for Integration (BDI) to join the new government. This move was particularly surprising, as both parties had been locked in a tense conflict only a few months earlier. Thus, the tradition of including an Albanian government proved resilient despite adverse political circumstances, unlike in Slovakia. The combination of entitlement, tradition, and duration constitutes an important distinction between mere representation and genuine power-sharing which we need to consider.

However, when discussing different forms of power-sharing, we also need to consider the degree to which the inclusion translates into effective power in government. Here, the focus rests on two aspects. First, to what degree do the minority members in government represent the minority? As minority executive power-sharing has to be more than just the co-option of minorities by the majority, minority members in the executive need to reflect the minority representation in the legislature, rather than being token minority members chosen by the majority. Individuals of minority background have achieved access to governments in Europe without this inclusion being part of a broader policy or tradition of minority inclusion. In fact, a member of a minority community

---

[16] For a comprehensive comparison between the minority policies of Slovakia and Macedonia see E Friedman, 'Electoral system design and minority representation in Slovakia and Macedonia' (2005) 4(4) *Ethnopolitics* 381–96.

might join government, without particular weight given to the degree to which that person actually *represents* the respective community. A recent example would be the inclusion of ministers of immigrant background in the cabinet of French Prime Minister François Fillon.

Brendan O'Leary has distinguished between a complete, concurrent, and weak consociational executive. The first includes all relevant parties, the second parties representing the majority of the community, whereas the last type describes a system where a plurality of the community is represented.[17] This consideration generally[18] only applies to cases where there are multiple parties representing the particular community, thus mostly to countries with larger groups, such Belgium, Bosnia and Herzegovina, and Macedonia. The second consideration is the influence of the minority members within government, ie does government decide by consensus or majority voting? After discussing the different forms of minority inclusion in the executive, we are thus able to map out the emerging patterns of executive power-sharing in Europe.

A. Minority representation

Minority representation is a weaker form of executive inclusion than power-sharing. It is temporary, due to the lack of political or legal safeguards and, as a result, majorities choose to cooperate with minority representatives and to include these in government, but are not required to do so.

There are a number of reasons why minorities are included in government short of an established tradition or legal requirement. The first one is arithmetic: including the minority party secures the majority the necessary parliamentary majority to govern. The inclusion of the primarily Turkish Movement for Rights and Freedoms (DPS) in Bulgaria in government can be explained by such a dynamic. Minority parties become preferred partners to provide for parliamentary majorities in a polarized party system where majority parties are unwilling to enter into coalitions with one other. Furthermore, minority inclusion might be at a lower cost than the inclusion of similar size parties which enjoy electoral support from the majority. As minority parties often seek minority-specific benefits (minority rights, increase in the share of minorities in the public administration), their demands might be more easily satisfied and 'contained' than the broader demands of majority parties. Finally, minority parties might be a moderate coalition partner, which is able to form coalitions with both parties of the left and of the right, as has been the case in both in Romania and Bulgaria. Related is the fact that the alternatives are often more

---

[17] B O'Leary, 'Debating consociational politics: Normative and explanatory arguments' in S Noel (ed), *From Power Sharing to Democracy: Post-conflict institutions in ethnically divided societies*, 12–13.
[18] Kosovo is the exception here as there have been multiple Serb parties represented in parliament, with only smaller ones generally joining government.

extreme parties to the left or the right. The ability to form coalitions domestically is supplemented by the external benefits in terms of reputation such a coalition might signal. In particular EU-accession countries have sought to reaffirm their moderate and pro-European orientation by including minority parties in government.[19] For example, in Croatia the conservative Croat Democrat Community (HDZ) won the 2003 parliamentary elections and had the choice between two very different coalition partners: the staunchly nationalist Croat Party of Right and the Independent Democratic Serb Party. Considering the suspicions many HDZ voters held towards Serbs, the choice for the Serb minority party was by no means obvious.[20] It was ultimately the country's ambition to join the EU that proved decisive in the choice of coalition partner.

Similar patterns can be observed in Serbia, where parties representing the Hungarian and Bosniak minorities have been in government on and off since 2000. All governments have been based on broad coalitions, including at least four parties, and both minority parties have been key in securing the reformist image of the country. For example, Rasim Ljajić, a Bosniak politician who has held a number of ministerial posts, also coordinated the cooperation of the country with the International Criminal Tribunal for the Former Yugoslavia. In addition to such foreign policy considerations, the inclusion of minorities in government can be a reflection of a government policy commitment to multiculturalism or diversity and thus less of a symbolic gesture directed towards the outside, but oriented towards the country itself.

These considerations for minority inclusion can thus be motivated by policies on diversity, as well as other policy considerations. Most importantly, the decision to offer minority inclusion is not the consequence of a legal or political obligation. Majority parties thus make this offer from a position of strength and are able and likely at some point in the future to withdraw their support. The asymmetric power relationship does not allow us to describe this form of minority inclusion as power-sharing. While some have argued that such forms of minority inclusion resemble the model of 'control'—a model of majority control over the minority—such a conceptualization carries strong negative connotations.[21] Furthermore, in countries with relatively small minorities (10 per cent or less), this form of government inclusion is more realistic and appropriate than formal guarantees (unless we consider specific cases, such as Kosovo, where historic circumstances make legal power-sharing guarantees appear more appropriate).

---

[19] Brusis, 'The European Union' (n 4 above).
[20] B Peranic, 'HDZ seek new friends', *Balkan Reconstruction Report*, 8 December 2003.
[21] K D McRae, *Conflict and Compromise in Multilingual Societies*, iii: *Finland* (2000), 249.

B. Executive power-sharing

In contrast to the aforementioned cases of temporary government representation, executive power-sharing can be described as a firm and durable commitment towards the inclusion of different groups within government. Such a commitment might be expressed either by a political agreement, which has evolved over time into a tradition, or a legal requirement.

1. Traditions of Executive Power-sharing

In Europe, there are three examples of executive power-sharing based on traditional models of minority party inclusion: Finland, Switzerland, and Macedonia. Although a tradition of executive power-sharing can be as firm as a legal requirement, it requires a broader commitment on the part of all key political players to endure beyond a change of governing parties. Arguably, a tradition can hold greater weight than law, as a law might be based on a narrower consensus than a tradition of inclusion. Furthermore, inclusion without legal requirements might result in greater flexibility in terms of the specifics of minority inclusion. Nevertheless, traditions can also be vulnerable, as newcomers to a political scene might not respect them. The political representatives of the majority are also in a dominant position, as the inclusion of minorities lacks formal entitlement. It is thus not surprising that in all three cases in Europe of traditions of power-sharing, the largest community amounts to at least two-thirds of the population.

A good example of this pattern is Finland. Here, the Swedish People's Party (SFP) has been a frequent, yet not constant, coalition partner in government since the emergence of an independent Finland after the First World War. An empirical study of government participation demonstrates that the SFP has participated in forty-three of sixty-three governments between 1917 and 1983, while this ratio increased since the 1960s with the party participating in most governments, being out of government between 1968 and 1995 for a total of only twenty-one months. In general, the SFP has been a constant member of governing coalitions, with the exception of caretaker governments, suggesting that executive representation of the Swedish minority has become an established tradition. As Finland illustrates, minority parties might be temporarily excluded from the executive, but this exclusion is not lasting. Thus, long-term minority exclusion is not a realistic scenario and one can consider Finland a case where a tradition of executive power-sharing has emerged.

As a relatively small party (gaining between 4.6 and 5.5 per cent of the vote since 1983[22]) the SFP's share of ministries in government was generally small, ranging between one and two ministerial posts (of a mostly fourteen- to eighteen-

---

[22] Data from Statistics Finland, available at <http://www.stat.fi/til/vaa_en.html>.

member cabinet). Unlike in other countries, where smaller minorities are often excluded from influential ministries or ministries associated with core functions of the state, the SFP often held the foreign affairs, interior, justice and finance portfolios.[23] This informal system of minority inclusion has meant that the Swedish minority lacks any veto powers in the executive.[24] Considering the lack of entitlement for government representation and the clear dominance of the Finnish-speaking majority, McRae considers the Finnish model to be closer to Lustick's system of control than to Lijphart's consociationalism.[25] Considering the small size of the Swedish minority in Finland, executive power-sharing does not translate into other spheres of the administration and the dominance of the Finnish majority remains beyond doubt. While surely not a case of consociationalism, executive power-sharing in Finland suggest that even small minorities can achieve access to decision-making in a country through such traditions.

Switzerland is another classic example of executive power-sharing by tradition. However, the pattern here is quite different: representation of the linguistic communities has not been based on the inclusion of a group-specific party, as in Finland, but instead different parties have represented different linguistic communities. This pattern is a reflection of the cross-community political party system in Switzerland, which differs from most other party systems in diverse societies across Europe, where smaller communities tend to gravitate towards minority-specific parties.

In addition to the adequate representation of linguistic communities, political parties, cantons, and religious communities are part of the consideration for the allocation of seats in the seven-member federal council. Since 1959, a 'magic formula', largely unchanged, has secured seats for the different parties in government and law limits the representation of each canton to one councillor. The representation of linguistic communities, however, is not prescribed by law, but remains a tradition. According to this tradition at least two councils are drawn from the smaller French and Italian communities. While the larger French-speaking community is always represented, sometimes by two councillors, there is not always an Italian-speaking representative in the Federal Council.[26] In fact, the representation of the Italian-speaking canton Ticino is often at the expense of a second Francophone councillor.[27]

---

[23] McRae, *Conflict and Compromise* (n 21 above), 248–9.
[24] This excludes the Aaland Islands which enjoy a special status and decisions affecting the island require consent of Aaland authorities, ibid, 325. [25] Ibid, 249.
[26] P Sciarini and S Hug, 'The odd fellow: Parties and consociationalism in Swizerland' in K R Luther and K Deschouwer (eds), *Party Elites in Divided Societies* (1999), 155. The Swiss Constitution (Art 175, para 4) does require that the regions and linguistic groups are adequately represented (*angemessen vertreten*).
[27] K D McRae, *Conflict and Compromise in Multilingual Societies: Switzerland* (1998), 131.

Altogether, non-German-speakers have generally been over-represented in the Swiss Federal Council, being represented during the period of 1848 and 1981 at a ratio of German to non-German-speakers of about five to two.[28] The share of German-speakers in the federal councils has been 65.7 per cent in the 1970s and 57.1 per cent in the 1990s, considerably lower than in all other federal institutions and than their share in the population.[29] The small Romansh-speaking community, less than 0.5 per cent of the Swiss population, however, is not regularly represented in the executive.

While both Finland and Switzerland often have broad coalitions that are not only based on the inclusion of smaller linguistic communities, Switzerland is set apart by the numerous interlocking mechanisms to balance the representation of different communities in the Swiss executive. The linguistic divide is certainly the closest to ethnic, confessional, and other identity-driven divides elsewhere, but Switzerland cannot be considered a divided or multinational society, as the divide into different language groups does not translate into separate national or ethnic identities.

In some post-communist countries, similar traditions have begun to emerge. As noted previously, it would be premature to consider all of these forms of inclusion to be executive power-sharing, as some have not endured through different governments (Slovakia, Romania) and have not resulted in a clear entitlement for minority party inclusion. The only country where a firm tradition of executive power-sharing has emerged since the transition to democracy in post-communist Europe is Macedonia. Albanian ministers first joined an expert government in 1991 and ever since Albanian parties have participated in all Macedonian governments. This pattern has seen three different Albanian parties participating in government, together with one of the large parliamentary blocks focused on the Left—the Social-democratic Union of Macedonia (SDSM)— and Right (VMRO-DPMNE). Albanian parties have held between four and six ministerial posts (governments usually had eighteen to twenty-seven members) during this period. Albanian ministers were often in charge of ministries of health, education, and social affairs. In the 2008 government, one of the six Albanian ministers was also in charge of the economy. In addition to ministerial posts, Albanians have often been appointed to the post of deputy minister in ministries where Macedonians or others hold the ministerial post. This has been a largely symbolic step, as deputy ministers yield little power.[30] The tradition of

---

[28] Ibid.

[29] Italian- and French-speakers have been accordingly over-represented, with on average 30 per cent French and 12.9 per cent Italian speakers, with a population share of 73.4 per cent German, 20.5 per cent French and 4.1 per cent Italian-speaking Swiss citizens. W Linder and I Steffen, 'Ethnic structure, inequality and governance in Switzerland' in Y Bangura (ed) *Ethnic Inequalities and Public Sector Governance* (2006), 228.

[30] F Bieber 'Power-sharing and the implementation of the Ohrid Framework Agreement' in S Dehnert and R Sulejmani (eds), *Power-sharing and the Implementation of the Ohrid Framework Agreement* (2008), 26–7.

power-sharing was reinforced by the Ohrid Framework Agreement in 2001, which followed a brief conflict between Macedonian government forces and the Albanian National Liberation Army. Although the agreement does not require the participation of Albanian parties in government, it introduces other consociational features, such as proportional representation in the public administration and double majority voting in parliament on issues pertaining to the fundamental nature of the state (ie, constitution) or minorities issues (education, culture). Hence, Albanian parties have argued that the double majority is a de facto commitment to executive power-sharing as the government would lack support for key legislation if a majority of minority representatives opposed the government.[31] Due to the fact that the Albanian community is represented by more than one political party, the question has also emerged of which Albanian party is to be included in government. During the period 2006–8, the second-largest Albanian party joined government, raising the issue of representativeness within the community, with the largest Albanian party BDI, excluded from government, claiming that the government lacked legitimacy among the Albanian community.[32]

With Finland, Switzerland, and Macedonia, three very different countries have developed informal traditions of executive power-sharing. In Switzerland, the roles form part of the larger consensus-based political system, whereas Finland has strong majoritarian tendencies due to its demographic distribution. Macedonia has moved since its independence from a majoritarian towards an increasingly consociational system.

2. Constitutional Executive Power-sharing

The main alternative form of executive power-sharing to a system based on tradition is executive representation by legal requirement. Legally binding executive representation is generally a feature of more deeply divided societies, where legal safeguards protect from abuse. Furthermore, two of the three countries in Europe which are governed by such a system, Belgium and Bosnia lack a large political majority, unlike most other cases under consideration.

Belgium is the only Western European country which has group representation in the state-level executive enshrined in its constitution. Since 1970, the government has been composed of equal numbers of French- and Dutch-speaking cabinet members, whereas the prime minister is 'neutral', although de facto hailing mostly from the larger Flemish community. Deputy ministers in the federal government are from different linguistic communities to that of the ministers. As the government makes decisions by consensus, no one community can be out-voted and the cabinet functions in both languages.[33] The small German community, less than 1 per cent, has not benefited from this formula

---

[31] See several of the contributors in Dehnart and Sulejmani, *Power-sharing* (n 30 above).
[32] Bieber, 'Power-sharing' (n 30 above), 28–9.
[33] K Deschouwer, 'Ethnic structure, inequality and governance of the public sector in Belgium' in Y Bangura (ed), *Ethnic Inequalities and Public Sector Governance* (2006), 148–9.

and is not represented in government.[34] In terms of the allocation of ministerial posts, certain patterns have emerged, such as the allocation of ministerial portfolios that address the need for Walloon ministers, who have traditionally hailed from the left. In addition to representation in the government, the federal structure of the country led to the establishment of the Deliberation Committee for the Government and the Executives, which mediates between the executives of the federal units (regions and communities). This committee is based on the parity of linguistic communities and federal versus regions and decides by consensus. In the complex federal and consociational Belgian system, this mechanism constitutes a second pillar of executive representation and protection of linguistic groups.[35]

Similar to Belgium, Bosnia also boasts a complicated power-sharing arrangement, which secures the representation of all three groups in all state-level institutions.[36] In the Council of Ministers, the central government, all three constituent people (Croats, Bosniaks, and Serbs) have to be equally represented and two-thirds of the ministerial posts are allocated to the federation of Bosnia and Herzegovina and one-third from the Serb Republic. Decisions in the Council which are not submitted for voting in parliament require a consensus of all members present. If this is not reached, decisions can be taken by a majority of all ministers present, with at least one minister from each of the three nations voting in favour.[37] In addition to the representation in the Council of Ministers, Bosnia is the only country in Europe that extends group representation to the presidency. The three-member presidency reserves one seat for each of the three large communities based on elections in the different entities, thus requiring the Croat and Bosniak members to be elected to the federation and the Serb member to be voted for in the Serb Republic. This form of executive representation has been deemed to violate European human rights standards by the Venice Commission and other international actors, as it precludes the representation of minorities and members of the three constituent communities from other parts of the country.[38] Bosnia has, together with Belgium, the most

---

[34] K D McRae, *Conflict and Compromise in Multilingual Societies*, ii: *Belgium* (1997), 185.

[35] L Hooghe, 'Belgium: Hollowing the center' in N Bermeo and U Amoretti (eds), *Does Federalism Matter? Political institutions and the management of territorial cleavages* (2004), 55–92.

[36] For a detailed discussion see F Bieber, *Post-war Bosnia: Ethnicity, inequality and public sector governance* (2006), 52–4.

[37] This later modification was imposed by the Office of the High Representative in late 2007, causing considerable controversy and even leading to a boycott of the joint institutions by Serb representatives. The amendments also lowered the quorum requirements, reducing a blockage of the government by absenteeism. Office of the High Representative, 'Decision Enacting the Authentic Interpretation of the Law on Changes and Amendments to the Law on the Council of Ministers of Bosnia and Herzegovina Enacted by the Decision of the High Representative of 19 October 2007', Sarajevo, 3 December 2007, available at <http://www.ohr.int/decisions/statemattersdec/default.asp?content_id=40931> (accessed 17 July 2009).

[38] Venice Commission, *Opinion on the Constitutional Situation in Bosnia and Herzegovina and the Powers of the High Representative*, CDL-AD 004, 11 March 2005 (2005).

elaborate and complex system of executive representation. This experience highlights the tendency of executive power-sharing to marginalize smaller communities, which are left out from the division of offices. Consequently, group representation might actually disadvantage minority representation.

Kosovo is the third European country where minority representation in the executive is constitutionally enshrined. The 2001 Constitutional Framework and the 2008 Constitution stipulate that if the government consists of less than twelve ministers, it must include one Serb and one other minority member; if there are twelve or more ministers, an additional minority member must be included. Furthermore, the government needs to include two Serb and two other minority deputy ministers for governments smaller than twelve and one more of each for larger governments.[39] The representation of minority communities has been mostly the result of international pressure and with the exception of the period between 2002 and 2004, most significant Serb parties have boycotted the work of Kosovo institutions, resulting in the inclusion of less representative Serb parties in government. Considering the relatively small size of the non-Albanian communities in Kosovo and the fact that decisions in government are taken by majority vote,[40] the impact of the minority members in government decision-making has been limited.

Of the three legally required systems of minority inclusion, only Bosnia and Belgium are also otherwise consociational arrangements. Kosovo is unusual in requiring executive representation without displaying other features of consociational power-sharing, such as veto rights. The limited nature of Kosovo's power-sharing is largely a function of the small size of the minorities. Although the legal safeguards would place Kosovo in the same category as Bosnia and Belgium, the influence minority members yield does not. Thus, minority members of government might hold influence over the ministries they head, but the impact on other ministries and governmental agencies is likely to be limited.

C. Hybrid or transitional systems

In addition to the two types of minority executive representation, inclusion and power-sharing, we can identify a hybrid or transitional model. This hybrid model does not contain any requirement for minority inclusion, but there has been a considerable tradition of minority inclusion in government. Three countries in Europe, Albania, Romania, and Bulgaria, fall into this category. These countries have experienced considerable periods of minority party inclusion and minority parties have participated in different coalitions. The latter is particularly important, as it suggests that minority inclusion is not only

---

[39] Art 9.3.5, Constitutional Framework for Provisional Self-government in Kosovo, 2001; Art 96, paras 3–4, Constitution of the Republic of Kosovo, 2008.
[40] Art 7, Rules of Procedure, Government of Kosovo, 2008.

achievable through just one coalition constellation, based on only one party or ideological stream. Such a restricted form of minority party inclusion, as discussed above in the case of Slovakia, does not provide security to the minority and risks policy reversals. However, the duration of minority inclusion notwithstanding, minority representation is not broadly understood as a requirement for governing coalitions and we cannot (yet) consider them cases of executive power-sharing.

Romania and Bulgaria have followed a similar pattern of minority inclusion since the onset of democratic governance in the 1990s. In Bulgaria, the Movement for Rights and Freedoms (DPS) supported the first post-communist government led by the conservative Union of the Democratic Forces (UDF) in 1991–2. After the party withdrew its support for the government, it took a leading role in establishing an expert government, also supported by the Bulgarian Socialist Party (BSP) between 1992 and 1994. Due to the central role of the DPS, it was even described by some UDF officials as a 'Turkish government'.[41] Following a seven-year interlude, it formally entered government for the first time in 2001, first with the National Movement Simeon II (NDSV) and, after 2005, jointly with the BSP and the NDSV. Following the electoral victory of the right-wing Citizens for European Development of Bulgaria in 2009, the DPS was no longer included in government, suggesting that the tradition of inclusion had not been sufficiently consolidated to secure continuity of minority inclusion. The weight of the party has been relatively limited, gaining only the Ministry of Agriculture, a Minister without Portfolio, and a Deputy Minister for Defence in 2001, but holding more power in the public administration and regional functions.[42]

In Romania, the Democratic Alliance of Hungarians in Romania (UDMR) joined government first in 1996, along similar lines as in Slovakia, as part of a broad centre–right coalition against a left-leaning nationalist semi-authoritarian regime. Unlike in Slovakia, the Hungarian party continued to support the government between 2000 and 2004, lead by the Social Democratic Party (PSD) even after its coalition partners lost the elections. Despite an alliance with the PDS for the 2004 elections, it formed a coalition with the liberal and conservative winners of the elections and remained in government until 2008. While supporting different governments, it has not been continuously represented in government, most notably between 2000 and 2004. When in government, it has, however, yielded greater weight than its Bulgarian counterpart. Thus, in the last government the UDMR held four (of eighteen) seats in

---

[41] RV Vassilev, 'Post-communist Bulgaria's ethnopolitics' (2001) 1(2) *The Global Review of Ethnopolitics* 37–53, 51.

[42] Brusis, 'The European Union' (n 4 above), 6. The government after 2006 included more substantial DPS representatives, including three ministers (agriculture and deputy prime minister, environment, and disasters). M Spirova, 'Bulgaria' (2007) 46(7–8) *European Journal of Political Research* 901–8.

government, including portfolios such as environment, communication, development, and the State Ministry for European Integration.[43]

Albania is the weakest hybrid case of the three. Here, the Unity for Human Rights Party (PBDNJ), representing mostly the Greek minority, has been in government between 1997 and 2009. It first supported a socialist-led government, but switched its support in 2005 to the conservative Democratic Party. During the legislative period 2005–9, the party held one ministrial post (the Ministry of Labour, Social Affairs and Equal Opportunities), as well as a number of other lower-ranking political appointments in the administration, such as the Head of the State Committee for Minorities.[44] The relatively small share of the Greek minority in executive power is a function of the small size of the minority,[45] making the relatively durable inclusion of the Greek minority remarkable. Despite its duration for more than ten years and the change of government, the inclusion of the Greek minority cannot yet be considered an enduring tradition, not least due to the small and thus insecure representation of the PBDNJ in parliament (usually just two seats, only one in 2009) and due to the fact that following its pre-election coalition with the Socialist Party, it failed to re-enter government in 2009.

As we have seen from these three examples, minority parties have achieved a considerable record of executive inclusion, just short of a legal or political 'right' to representation. They thus fail to qualify for the second category of power-sharing. Nevertheless, they extend beyond merely occasional inclusion in the executive. Some cases might be transitional, as Bulgaria and Romania might head towards a consolidated tradition of executive power-sharing, following the Macedonian model. At the same time, recent elections in both countries suggests that they are more likely to revert to the Slovak pattern.[46]

D. Regional executive power-sharing

A final category which merits our attention is regional power-sharing arrangements.[47] A number of regional autonomies across Europe, from Northern Ireland to the Federation of Bosnia and Herzegovina, have instituted varying forms of executive power-sharing. In some cases, they supplement state-level

---

[43] L Stan and R Zaharia, 'Romania' (2008) 47(7–8) *European Journal of Political Research* 1115–26.

[44] G Sinani, 'Minorities in Albanian and their participation in public life', *Political Parties and Minority Participation* (2008), 213.

[45] There are no reliable statistics for the number of Greeks in Albania, as the last census asking about national affiliation, held under Communist rule in 1989, cannot be considered reliable. It gives 2.01 per cent of Greeks, ibid, 202.

[46] In fact, since the UDMR move to the opposition in 2008, Romania appears to head towards the Slovak model.

[47] S Wolff, 'The institutional structure of regional consociations in Brussels, Northern Ireland, and South Tyrol' (2004) 10 *Nationalism and Ethnic Politics* 387–414.

power-sharing, as in Belgium or Bosnia, while in others they offer minority inclusion where it would be impractical or impossible at the state level, as in Italy or Great Britain. The four most significant cases are Northern Ireland, South Tyrol, Brussels, and the Federation of Bosnia and Herzegovina.[48] In two cases—Brussels and the Bosnian Federation—the regions are also federal units, giving them considerable say at the state level. The other two cases are examples of regional autonomies in otherwise unitary states.

South Tyrol is an example of a regional autonomy with guaranteed representation of the two largest population groups in the executive. The regional statute requires the representation of the different linguistic groups according to their strength in parliament in government, with an Italian- and German-speaking Deputy President of the region, who is in practice from the German-speaking community.[49] In addition to the representation of the groups in government, the linguistic groups also enjoy considerable autonomy in community matters, such as language, culture, and education, for which separate members of the regional government are responsible. However, voting takes place by majority, which creates tensions between the cultural autonomy that government members embody and the voting system.[50]

In Belgium, the power-sharing in the region of Brussels mirrors the state-level power-sharing. Statewide the Dutch-speaking population has a clear majority, while they find themselves in a minority in Brussels. In the Brussels executive, an equal number of members represent both linguistic communities, two of each, with a fifth government member hailing from the largest language group in parliament, de facto giving the Francophone population a permanent majority. Of the three state secretaries, one also has to hail from the less numerous, ie Dutch-speaking, community.[51] The ministers derive separately from the colleges of the two language groups, which exercise group-specific powers in Brussels. Jointly, these two colleges form the unified college, identical in composition to the government but acting as a coordination and mediation body between the communities, and ministers are equal members without portfolio in

---

[48] Some Swiss cantons have weak forms of minority inclusion, thus one member of the government of the canton of Bern has to be from the French-speaking Jura, but the member is elected by all cantonal voters, while Valais ensures the representation of a German-speaker in government through special electoral units. T Fleiner, 'Switzerland: Constitution of the federal state and the cantons' in LR Basta Fleiner and T Fleiner (eds), *Federalism and Multiethnic States: The case of Switzerland*, 2nd rev edn (2000), 139.

[49] The small Ladin community can be represented even if this is not a reflection of proportionality, ie a positive measure to include the community is allowed. Art 50, Vereinheitlichter Text der Gesetze über das Sonderstatut für Trentino-Südtirol, 31 August 1972.

[50] G Pallaver, 'Ethnische Konkordanzdemokratie. Südtiroler Autonomie zwischen "Gemeinschaft" und "Gesellschaft"' in S Salzborn (ed), *Minderheitenkonflikte in Europa. Fallbeispiele und Lösungsansätze* (2006), 73–4.

[51] See Présentation de la Région, available at <http://www.rbc.irisnet.be/crisp/fr/b4.htm> (accessed 17 July 2009)

this body.[52] Thus, as in South Tyrol, executive power-sharing also contains a form of cultural autonomy.

In the predominantly Bosniak and Croat Federation of Bosnia and Herzegovina, one of the country's entities, a complex system secures executive representation. As in Belgium, the system largely mirrors the state-level institutions. In the Federation, a three-member presidency shares executive functions with the government, which has to be composed of eight Bosniaks, five Croats, and three Serbs, ie proportionality based on the 1991 census. In addition, the prime minister can allocate one governmental position from the larger, ie Bosniak, contingent to a member from the 'others', a catch-all term to describe smaller minorities and citizens who refuse identification with the three large ethnic groups.[53] The president and vice-presidents require consent from all three communities in the upper chamber of parliament and rotate on an annual basis.[54] Some weaker forms of executive representation exist in the other entity, the Serb Republic, where eight ministers are Serbs, five Bosniaks, and three Croats. In addition the directly elected president, presumably Serb, has two vice-presidents, one Croat and one Bosniak. Due to the dominance of the Serb community in the entity, these forms of representation have not translated into power-sharing in practice.[55]

The final example of regional executive power-sharing is Northern Ireland. Executive power-sharing was established in the 1998 Good Friday Agreement, but has been repeatedly interrupted by the suspension of regional autonomy by the British government. Similar to South Tyrol, executive representation in Northern Ireland is based on proportionality; however, this is not proportionality based on the size of the communities but on the size of the political parties represented in parliament. Parties can pick portfolios according to their size, determined by the D'Hondt formula commonly used for the allocation of seats in elections. As a result, it is not just some parties from each community that are represented in government, but all larger parties.[56] The first minister, the equivalent of the prime minister, and the deputy first minister are elected jointly by a 60 per cent majority with 40 per cent support

---

[52] F Delpérée and S Depré, *Le système constitutionnel de la Belgique* (1998), 109.

[53] According the 2002 amendment, the system will change once the refugee return process is completed, when each community has the right to 15 per cent of the ministerial posts, one is reserved for 'others' and two constitution people jointly must hold at least 35 per cent. Amendment XLIV Decision on Constitutional Amendments in the Federation, Office of the High Representative, 19 April 2002, available at <http://www.ohr.int/decisions/statemattersdec/default.asp?content_id=7475> (accessed 17 July 2009).   [54] Amendment XLII, ibid.

[55] Art 92, Constitution of the Serb Republic. When the RS President Milan Jelić died in office in 2007, the president of parliament became the acting president, rather than one of the two non-Serb vice-presidents. D Maksimovic, 'Republika Srpska: Streit um Wahl des Interimspräsidenten', *Fokus Ost-Südost*, 18 October 2007.

[56] J McGarry and B O'Leary, 'Consociational theory, Northern Ireland's conflict, and its agreement. Pt 1: What consociationalists can learn from Northern Ireland' (2006) 41(1) *Government and Opposition* 43–63, 61–62.

from both communities.[57] Within the Executive Committee, the Northern Ireland government, decisions are generally taken by consensus. While majority voting is possible in cases where a consensus cannot be reached, three members can request cross-community support, which constitutes a veto right for communities in government.[58]

The four cases of regional executive power-sharing highlight that firm executive inclusion of groups is not limited to state-level governance and in some cases might be more elaborate and better developed at the sub-state level.

IV. Conclusions

Minority political parties have been included in governments across Europe, giving rise to a rich diversity of experience (see Table 14.1). Once included,

Table 14.1 Power-sharing at government level

	Long Duration	Un-interrupted	Legal Guarantee	Consensus	Broad Inclusion	Consociational System
Minority Representation						
Slovakia	N	N	N	N	Y	N
Serbia	N	N	N	N	Y	N
Montenegro	N	Y	N	N	N	N
Croatia	N	Y	N	N	Y	N
Hybrid Systems						
Bulgaria	Y	Y	N	N	Y	N
Romania	Y	N	N	N	Y	N
Albania	Y	Y	N	N	Y	N
Executive Power-sharing						
Tradition of Power-sharing						
Switzerland	Y	N	N	Y	Y	Y
Finland	Y	Y	N	N	Y	N
Macedonia	Y	Y	N	N	N	Y
Legal Requirement						
Bosnia and Herzegovina	Y	Y	Y	Y	Y	Y
Belgium	Y	Y	Y	Y	Y	Y
Kosovo	N	Y	Y	N	N	N
Regional Power-sharing						
Northern Ireland	Y	Y	Y	Y	Y	Y
South Tyrol	Y	Y	Y	N	Y	Y
Brussels	Y	Y	Y	Y	Y	Y
Federation of Bosnia and Herzegovina	Y	Y	Y	Y	Y	Y

[57] Good Friday Agreement, 10 April 1998, available at <http://www.intstudies.cam.ac.uk/centre/cps/documents_ireland.html> (accessed 17 July 2009).
[58] Art 2.12. Ministerial Code, Northern Ireland Executive.

minorities have often remained in government for considerable periods of time, even without legal requirements. In particular, nearly all South-east European countries have included minorities within their governments for varying periods of time. In a number of cases, such as Bulgaria and Romania, participation in government by the Turkish and Hungarian party respectively might develop into a tradition, as it has in Macedonia and Finland.

When looking at the different patterns of group inclusion in executives, we can identify two types: executive power-sharing in multiethnic or multilingual states, which are governed by larger consociational arrangements, such as Switzerland, Belgium, and Bosnia and Herzegovina; and countries with clear population majorities where executive power-sharing is a form of minority inclusion, but does not lead to veto rights or other forms of co-decision-making, such as Finland, Bulgaria, or Kosovo. Macedonia is possibly an example of a country in between, with a strong majority but other consociational features. In terms of duration, Finland would be the model for the latter type. Born out of different circumstances in terms of the demographic distribution and political and social power, the inclusion in government of the Swedish minority has been very enduring even in the absence of other requirements. In some cases, for example the regional arrangements in Brussels and South Tyrol, executive power-sharing is closely intertwined with the cultural autonomy of the community, while in most other cases, such as Finland or Switzerland, representatives from the communities administer ministries in domains unrelated to the particular concerns of their community.

As a result, executive power-sharing or minority representation has been a tool to allow minorities to shape the implementation of minority rights. At the same time, it has also been a mechanism for securing the inclusion of minorities which might otherwise have no access to executive posts except for a twist in electoral fate, and allowed them to become co-decision-makers in areas beyond narrow minority concerns. Without other aspects of consociationalism, executive power-sharing cannot by itself give sufficient access to decision-making and, without minority rights, it cannot protect minorities. However, as part of a larger arrangement—informal or otherwise—minority inclusion in government can be crucial in broadening minority 'ownership' in the state and a sense of inclusiveness.

15

At the Heart of Participation and of its Dilemmas

Minorities in the executive structures

*Francesco Palermo**

I. Introduction	434
II. The Dilemma of Participation	435
A. Effective participation as pluralist inclusion	435
B. Effective participation in public life vs. parliamentary representation?	437
III. Participation of Minorities in the Executive Branch: A Theoretical Reflection	438
IV. Selected Case Studies of Enhanced Minority Participation in the Civil Service	441
A. Lessons from a consolidated experience: the case of South Tyrol	444
B. Cases from countries in transition: the experience of the Western Balkans	446
V. Concluding Remarks	450

I. Introduction

What do minorities want and how can they achieve it? While much practical and academic energy is devoted to the ultimately vain attempt to agree on a definition of the concept of 'minority', too little attention is paid to these basic, and yet no less essential, questions. They are, however, at the heart of the debate on minority representation and participation in social, economic, cultural, and public life. By focusing on a limited but essential part of the broad phenomenon of minority participation—their representation in executive structures—this

---

* The views expressed in this article are those of the author and are not necessarily shared by the High Commissioner or the OSCE.

chapter contends that the focus of political claims and academic research with regard to minority participation in public life should shift from the parliamentary to the executive dimension. This implies, more importantly, that further reflection is required on what really matters when it comes to minority participation in public life and that we should begin to question some of the most deeply rooted assumptions in this regard. More generally, it requires proper awareness of the instruments available to improve effective minority participation in each particular area.

The following pages will therefore first address some fundamental issues regarding minority participation, pointing out some of its unresolved dilemmas (section II). The analysis will then move to the forms of minority representation in the executive power structures, notably within the administration (section III). Subsequently, a few indicative case studies of minority representation in the executive structures will be analysed in more detail (section IV) and, finally, some concluding remarks will be drawn with regard to the instruments available for enhanced minority representation in the civil service, to their shortcomings and to the trends that can be observed in this matter (section V).

II. The Dilemma of Participation

A. Effective participation as pluralist inclusion

Each group—including national minorities—is identified as such because its members share one characteristic that the legal system acknowledges as a justified ground for differential treatment.[1] This by no means implies that interests, aspirations, and goals of persons belonging to minorities are the same simply because they share one characteristic out of many.[2] When it comes to participation, it can be presumed that (persons belonging to) minorities want to participate, ie to be given an effective voice in social, cultural, economic, and

---

[1] This is what the famous definition of a minority provided by Francesco Capotorti already highlights, by identifying it with a group of people 'numerically inferior to the rest of the population of a State, in a non-dominant position, whose members—being nationals of the State—possess ethnic, religious, or linguistic characteristics differing from those of the rest of the population and show, if only implicitly, a sense of solidarity, directed towards preserving their culture, traditions, religion or language'. UN, 'Study on the rights of persons belonging to ethnic, religious, and linguistic minorities', E/CN4/Sub2/384/Add1-7 (1977). See also R Toniatti, 'Minorities and protected minorities: Constitutional models compared' in T Bonazzi and M Dunne (eds), *Citizenship and Rights in Multicultural Societies* (1995), 195–219.

[2] This is why Art 3.1 of the Framework Convention for the Protection of National Minorities (FCNM) affirms that 'every person belonging to a national minority shall have the right freely to choose to be treated or not to be treated as such ... ' and Principle 4 of the Lund Recommendations on the Effective Participation of National Minorities in Public Life endorsed by the OSCE High Commissioner on National Minorities in 1999 go even further by providing that 'the decision as to whether an individual is a member of a minority, the majority, or neither rests with that individual and shall not be imposed upon her or him'.

political life, but at the same time they might differ profoundly as to the understanding and the kind of participation that each group and (groups of) individuals within each group might look for.

Minority participation thus faces an intimate dilemma: on the one hand, it is essential to any minority governance—as it is self-evident that minority policies cannot be elaborated, implemented and monitored over the head of the concerned groups—that minority rights are not benevolently imposed from the top down without the effective participation of those concerned, as this attitude is both paternalistic and ineffectual; on the other hand, involving minorities always brings about the risk of involving only *some* groups, *some* of their representatives, *some* of their views, *some* of their interests, and neglecting many other factors that might emanate from a complex social formation like a minority group.

In modern, pluralist societies this problem acquires a more general significance related to the very concept of democracy, which is facing tremendous challenges to its core principle of majority representation. And this is due not least to the fact that minority issues have acquired increasing importance with respect to the traditional concepts of democracy and representation, which are subject to profound debate.

Like democracy more generally, minority participation is therefore forced to develop devices to address the extremely complex issue of selecting and determining the will of the respective group: merely relying on the minority's political elite, or even on the majority within the minority group would contradict the pluralist essence of minority rights and is per se at odds with the very *raison d'être* of minority rights. But what are the alternatives? Is the democratic system ready to attenuate its very foundations (majority rule and democratic accountability) in order to achieve more effective minority participation, or should minority participation adjust to the majority principle and accept never to be determinant?

There is no doubt that a solution should be found through balancing potentially conflicting principles, such as majority rule versus the inclusion of minorities and ultimately democratic versus effective participation. And while there is no universal recipe for achieving such balance, it is clear that it becomes more effective the more it can include pluralist solutions. Therefore the instruments that could make minority participation more effective need to be as pluralist as possible, ie they should allow for the participation of the largest possible number of persons belonging to minorities, representing as many views as possible: the more effective participation is, the more inclusive it is of the different interests and needs of persons belonging to minority groups, and the closer it comes to fair representation of the whole spectrum of interests of the involved groups. It follows that, for the purpose of this analysis, the benchmark of effectiveness of participation is its degree of pluralism: the more pluralist the procedures for (involving persons belonging to minorities in the) decision-making are, the more effective the participation.

B. Effective participation in public life vs. parliamentary representation?

In this context, political participation, as an essential part of minority inclusion in society, needs to be approached in pluralist terms.[3] The Western legal tradition has usually focused primarily on elections as the main (and often exclusive) legitimizing democratic factor. Consequently, when it comes to the representation of minorities, the bulk of attention (of both majorities and minorities as well as of scholars) has been devoted to representation in parliament.

This is essential, but not sufficient. Not only are parliaments losing their political and institutional significance due to structural changes in representative democracy, but within parliaments minorities are by definition in a non-decisive position. Their influence is therefore limited twofold: as part of bodies whose influence is declining overall and as minorities within those bodies. In addition, as stated above, the selection of representatives through election inevitably leads to the appointment of representatives of 'the majority within the minority', thus reducing the degree of pluralism in representation.

This is not to say, of course, that guaranteed minority representation in elected bodies is not important. The point is that it is less effective than many believe,[4] including very often minority leaders. Effective participation means a more pluralist presence in public life, and the positive measures required for minority protection have to be proportionate and therefore often do not allow for fully fledged representation of minorities in all sectors of public life. Therefore, the choice is very often between (a focus on) one form of minority participation and another, as both together are not possible to the same extent if we want to (as we have to) accept that minority rights have to be developed within the framework of the democratic principle. Thus, privileging representation in parliament might often mean reducing the opportunity of obtaining participation in other areas of public life such as the civil service, which, in the long run, might turn out to be more effective as they are more pluralist and place participation where it matters more.

Proper attention should be devoted to effective minority participation in public life, a phenomenon far bigger, more complex and more challenging than representation in parliament. This chapter suggests that increased attention to representation in the executive structures as compared to representation in parliaments is not only required for academic purposes, but is in the best interest of minorities—although not always of their leaders.

---

[3] See also R Hofmann, 'Political participation of minorities' (2006–7) 6 *European Yearbook of Minority Issues* 5–17, who argues, from the standpoint of the scope of application, that at least some participatory rights in public life should be extended to persons belonging to 'new' minorities.

[4] W Kymlicka, *Multicultural Citizenship: A liberal theory of minority rights* (1995), 150: 'representation in the legislature needs to be situated within the context of other mechanisms for representing the views or interests of a group'.

III. Participation of Minorities in the Executive Branch: A Theoretical Reflection

From a comparative analysis it is clear that guaranteed minority representation is a lot more recurrent in the legislative branch than in the executive or in the judiciary. This is due to the phenomenon described above, which led to the overall assumption that positive measures (as they are usually required for minority representation) are more 'acceptable' within the electoral process than in the composition of, for instance, the civil service. Such an assumption is often mirrored in the (constitutional and ordinary) legislation of several states, where positive measures are provided in the electoral system but are excluded from the composition of the civil service.[5]

The international actors and the documents they produce are also influenced by this attitude. An outstanding example of this is provided by the Lund Recommendations, which first present all the potential options to 'ensure that opportunities exist for minorities to have an effective voice ... including through special arrangements as necessary' (which, unsurprisingly, begin with special representation in parliament and end with participation in the civil service)[6] and then develop further only on electoral arrangements (Recommendations 7–9) and on advisory bodies (Recommendations 12–13), neglecting the other measures. A similar approach is followed by the Commentary on the Effective Participation of Persons belonging to National Minorities in Cultural, Social, and Economic Life and in Public Affairs, adopted by the Advisory Committee on the Framework Convention for the Protection of National Minorities in 2008,[7] although this is much more detailed and also devotes some attention to the forms of minority representation in public administration (paras 120–8).[8]

---

[5] These rules derive primarily from the traditional French approach to administrations as specialized and neutral bodies. However, even France has recently allowed for (previously unthinkable) positive measures for promoting minority groups and women, although this has been limited to the electoral arena and to management, while the principle of formal equality (ie, legal equality vis-à-vis minorities) still dominates the sphere of public administration: Art 1.2 of the French Constitution after the amendment in 2000 reads: 'La loi favorise l'égal accès des femmes et des hommes aux mandats électoraux et fonctions électives, ainsi qu'aux responsabilités professionnelles et sociales.'

[6] These include (Recommendation 6): 'special representation of national minorities ... in Parliament or parliamentary committees and other forms of guaranteed participation in the legislative process'; 'allocating to members of national minorities cabinet positions, seats on the supreme or constitutional court or lower courts, and positions on nominated advisory bodies'; 'special measures for minority participation in the civil service'.

[7] ACFC/31DOC(2008)001, adopted on 27 February 2008.

[8] In this regard, it must be noted that the Commentary also contains general principles regarding this particular form of representation. Paragraph 123 states in fact that 'measures which aim to reach a rigid, mathematical equality in the representation of various groups, which often implies an unnecessary multiplication of posts, should be avoided. They risk undermining the effective functioning of the State structure and can lead to the creation of separate structures in the society.'

There is, of course, nothing wrong with this approach, nor does this chapter propose to reverse it. What is suggested is a conscious approach to participation rather than one based on inertia, which entails a critical reflection on its principles, rationales, and instruments, including against the background of the effectiveness of minority participation. There are good reasons to consider that special measures are 'less special' and therefore 'more acceptable' when it comes to the rules on the election of assemblies rather than on the composition of governments, administrations, and judicial bodies. These include the fact that assemblies are the 'front door', the first stage of legitimacy, that they are political in nature, and that governments usually depend on them; by contrast, the administration and the judiciary, as neutral bodies, should in principle not include criteria for selection other than the professional requirements. While it is not demonstrated that participation in public life needs to be identified with political representation, it is also clear that representation in the political process has a fundamental symbolic importance as it testifies to the inclusion of minorities in society.

In any event, it is essential that these issues are not approached by inertia and that sufficient attention is paid to the reasons why minority participation in public life has so far meant primarily special electoral arrangements, while very little attention and very high suspicion has been attached to minority participation in other branches of government. In a way, there is a sort of 'unwritten hierarchy' among measures for enhanced minority participation in public life: at the bottom of the pyramid, where special measures are more easily accepted, is representation in parliament; above it comes representation in government, then in administration and, finally, in the judiciary. Civil service and the judiciary are thus the fields where reserved posts for persons belonging to minorities are less recurrent and more strictly scrutinized. This chapter does not contend that this is right or wrong: it only acknowledges that this is happening, that it (too) often happens in an uncritical way and that this might negatively affect the effective participation of minorities, as participation in elected bodies is usually far less effective in terms of minority involvement in decision-making than it is in other branches of government.[9]

In other words, minority participation is to be found to a greater extent in areas where it is less effective (in elected bodies), and scarce attention is dedicated to other forms of participation in public life, even if these forms are more

---

[9] Similarly, it can be said that an analogous hierarchy (which is however much less justified) is to be observed with regard to the relationship between participation in cultural, social, and economic life on the one hand and in public affairs on the other. While the former can be considered as a factual (and to some extent also legal) precondition for the latter, political and scholarly attention is devoted to a much higher degree to participation in public affairs. For some reflections on this phenomenon see F Palermo, 'The dual meaning of participation: The advisory committee's commentary to Article 15 FCNM', to be published in *European Yearbook on Minority Issues* 2009.

promising both because public administration (including the government and the courts) is more influential than parliament, and because representation in non-parliamentary bodies is more pluralist (thus eventually more representative and therefore more effective) as it affects larger numbers of persons belonging to minorities.

Not least, when it comes to minority participation, it is worth noticing that its effectiveness is also contingent on the powers conferred to minority representatives in the decision-making process. When participation does not go beyond mere representation,[10] ie where it simply consists of a decorative presence without a substantial voice or real power for minority representatives, then it is not helpful. While from a legal point of view, minority MPs usually represent the whole nation like any other parliamentarian—and it is uncommon that they enjoy veto rights on issues of concern to minorities[11]—they clearly have a political constituency and/or a party to which they are politically accountable. Conversely, persons belonging to minorities who are employed in the civil service or in the judiciary are there as individuals and are not accountable to any particular group.[12] In some way, the presence of persons belonging

---

[10] While the terms 'participation' and 'representation' are often used interchangeably, it has been correctly pointed out that, as in contrast to mere representation, participation needs to be active and inclusive. See A Verstichel, *Representation and Identity: The right of persons belonging to national minorities to effective participation in public affairs—content, justification and limits* (PhD, EUI, Florence, 2007). As some authors have noted, however, representation can be understood as both 'descriptive' and as 'active': see HF Pitkin, *The Concept of Representation* (1967). For some notes on the meaning (and the divergent interpretation) of these terms see K Henrard, '"Participation", "representation" and "autonomy" in the Lund Recommendations and their reflections in the supervision of the FCNM and several human rights conventions' (2005) 12 *International Journal on Minority and Group Rights* 133–68.

[11] For instance, in Slovenia, pursuant to Arts 64 and 80 of the constitution and the respective laws on elections (national and local), the Hungarian and Italian minorities elect their own deputies to the National Assembly (as well as to eight municipal councils covering the ethnically mixed territories, three Italian and five Hungarian). The minority MPs have veto rights on issues affecting the national minorities. An overview of the different mechanisms for minority representation in parliament and their powers can be found in European Commission for Democracy through Law (Venice Commission), *Opinion on the Constitutional Law on the Rights of National Minorities in Croatia*, adopted by the Venice Commission at its second plenary session, Venice, 18–19 October 2002, CDL-AD (2002) 30, paras 27–31, available at <www.venice.coe.int/site/interface/english.htm> (accessed 31 July 2009).

[12] In a few cases their appointment is linked to a particular group but this does not mean that they have to represent that group after they are appointed. As an interesting example, take the former Yugoslav Republic of Macedonia, the constitution of which provides for enhanced majorities in parliament in order to approve some legislation (Art 69 Constitution) and to appoint three constitutional judges (Art 109.2 Constitution), but these judges do not represent 'their groups', even if in some case they might politically feel that they do: when in 2007 the court struck down some of the key provisions of the 2004 law on the use of flags of the communities (ruling no Ubr133/2005-0-1), the three ethnic Albanian judges (who voted against) resigned. The same goes for the appointment of judges in the Constitutional Court of Bosnia and Herzegovina: while each constituent group appoints two judges, legally they do not represent either 'their' people or the entity which they come from. In some exceptional cases, the legislation does establish a link

to national minorities in the civil service and in the judiciary only relates to the participation of minorities and not to their representation.

This might constitute an additional reason for considering that enhanced minority presence in the civil service is more 'exceptional', because in such cases it is extremely difficult to determine the collective impact and the powers of the group as such. Unlike in elected bodies, in public administration the collective component of the presence of persons belonging to minorities is indirect only, and collective participation is the outcome of the numerical presence of several individuals who, as such, are not accountable (either legally or politically) to a group. Minority participation in public administration and the judiciary constitutes 'meta-participation', a second level of participation, which can only be derived from an aggregate of individuals participating in a non-collective way. Consequently, minority participation in the civil service and in the judiciary is conceptually difficult to handle and it often 'scares' decision-makers.

The following part of this chapter deals with one particular form of minority participation in the administration—that is, the rules on enhanced participation of persons belonging to national minorities in the civil service, not including government or the judiciary.

IV. Selected Case Studies of Enhanced Minority Participation in the Civil Service

At a closer look, the enhanced participation of minorities in public administration is more widespread than might first appear, especially if certain specific areas such as the police are also considered.[13] Nevertheless, as a logical consequence of the above-mentioned link between guaranteed minority representation and the democratic pattern, the provision of specific rules on minority quotas in the civil service is (or rather was) a distinctive feature of power-sharing structures or ethnic consociational democracies, ie of the governmental

---

between persons belonging to national minorities in administrations and the groups they belong to, but the real meaning of such provisions is far from clear: one could think of the law on the protection of rights of members of national minorities of Bosnia and Herzegovina, which establishes that 'representatives of national minorities in public administration bodies shall represent all national minorities and are bound to protect the interests of all national minorities' (Art 20). In practice, this only refers to elected bodies and implies that a minority representative has to take care of the concerns of all minority groups and not only of his/her own.

[13] In many countries, there are special plans for recruitment of more 'diverse' police forces, even when formally it has nothing to do with national minorities or with recognized minorities as such. One example of many is the Netherlands, where the police carry out an affirmative action programme for recruiting police staff with a view to ensuring by 2011 that 8 per cent of the national police force is from an 'ethnic' background. This kind of special arrangement in limited areas of the civil service and for particular groups that do not qualify as (national) minorities will not be considered in this chapter, nor will general affirmative action programmes for vulnerable groups as these, while conceptually part of the same phenomenon, are inherently different from the core subject of this study.

technique aimed at overcoming the majority–minority spill-over by tying all groups involved to institutional cooperation beyond their numerical ratio or on the basis of it.[14] Consequently, all the countries that provide for some (national) minority quotas in the civil service also comprise rules designed to allow for some form of guaranteed participation of minorities in elected bodies and in the composition of the government.

This is why, traditionally, it can be affirmed that guaranteed representation of minorities in elected bodies is also often provided in systems of promotional inspiration, ie in those with the predominance of a national group (the majority) and the presence of one or several minority groups,[15] while guaranteed minority representation in the civil service is a typical attribute of power-sharing arrangements in multinational states, where the constitutional order aims at integrating and reflecting the different groups within all its structures.[16] One can think of examples of countries like Nigeria,[17] Northern Ireland,[18]

---

[14] For a comprehensive analysis and the detailed illustration of several case studies see M Weller and S Wolff (eds), *Autonomy, Self-governance and Conflict Resolution: Innovative approaches to institutional, design in divided societies* (2005). Power-sharing can be paritarian (ie, the groups have the same number of representatives in the power-sharing institutions, such as, eg, in the case of the Belgian government and of the Cour d'Arbitrage (since May 2007, Constitutional Court), in Bosnia and Herzegovina for the presidency, the Council of Ministers and the House of Peoples, etc), or proportional (ie, the representation of the groups is proportional to their numerical consistency, such as, eg, in South Tyrol for the composition of the provincial and regional governments, in Canada for the composition of the Supreme Court, in Belgium for the Senate, in Switzerland for the Federal Council as well as for the Federal Tribunal, etc).

[15] For this classification and definition see Toniatti, 'Minorities and protected minorities' (n 1 above), 45–81.   [16] Ibid, 65.

[17] Art 14 of the Nigerian Constitution provides that '(3) The composition of the Government of the Federation or any of its agencies and the conduct of its affairs shall be carried out in such a manner as to reflect the federal character of Nigeria and the need to promote national unity, and also to command national loyalty, thereby ensuring that there shall be no predominance of persons from a few State or from a few ethnic or other sectional groups in that Government or in any of its agencies. (4) The composition of the Government of a State, a local government council, or any of the agencies of such Government or council, and the conduct of the affairs of the Government or council or such agencies shall be carried out in such manner as to recognise the diversity of the people within its area of authority and the need to promote a sense of belonging and loyalty among all the people of the Federation.' Art 153 of the Constitution establishes the Federal Character Commission, with the task to 'work out a formula for the redistribution of jobs and to establish, by administrative fiat, the principle of proportionality within the Federal Civil Service' (Decree 34 of 1996, s 4(1c)).

[18] In Northern Ireland, beside the power-sharing composition of the government, the Fair Employment (Northern Ireland) Act 1989 also extends to the private sector the rules on the community representation. Section 31 of the Act affirms: '(1) In the case of each registered concern, the employer shall from time to time review the composition of those employed in the concern in Northern Ireland and the employment practices of the concern for the purposes of determining whether members of each community are enjoying, and are likely to continue to enjoy, fair participation in employment in the concern. (2) In a case where it appears to the employer in the course of the review that members of a particular community are not enjoying, or are not likely to continue to enjoy, such participation, he shall as part of the review determine the affirmative action (if any) which would be reasonable and appropriate.'

India,[19] and many other historic or current experiences including Cyprus[20] and Lebanon.[21]

However, the experience of the Western Balkan countries over the last decade in particular proves that this clear-cut division between 'promotional' and 'multinational' states with regard to minority representation in the civil service

---

[19] The Indian case is extremely complex in this regard. Suffice it to mention here that the constitutional provisions, particularly Art 16, provide for a long list of 'exceptions' to the principle of formal equality in access to civil service: '(1) There shall be equality of opportunity for all citizens in matters relating to employment or appointment to any office under the State. ... (4) Nothing in this article shall prevent the State from making any provision for the reservation of appointments or posts in favour of any backward class of citizens which, in the opinion of the State, is not adequately represented in the services under the State. (4A) Nothing in this article shall prevent the State from making any provision for reservation in matters of promotion, with consequential seniority, to any class or classes of posts in the services under the State in favour of the Scheduled Castes and the Scheduled Tribes which, in the opinion of the State, are not adequately represented in the services under the State (added with Constitutional Act 1995, 16-9-1995, see also Supreme Court of India, case of Indira Sawhney, 16-11-92). (5) Nothing in this article shall affect the operation of any law which provides that the incumbent of an office in connection with the affairs of any religious or denominational institution or any member of the governing body thereof shall be a person professing a particular religion or belonging to a particular denomination.' Moreover, Arts 335–6 of the Constitution provide respectively for claims of Castes and Tribes to services and posts and for special provisions for Anglo-Indian community in certain services, two provisions related to the initial years of the Constitution.

[20] The 1960 Cyprus Constitution designs a multinational state, which, however, was never realized due to well-known historic events. In this context it is worth mentioning some of the provisions that only remained on paper in this regard, such as Art 123 ('1. The public service shall be composed as to seventy per centum of Greeks and as to thirty per centum of Turks. 2. This quantitative distribution shall be applied, so far as this will be practically possible, in all grades of the hierarchy in the public service. 3. In regions or localities where one of the two Communities is in a majority approaching one hundred per centum the public officers posted for, or entrusted with, duty in such regions or localities shall belong to that Community'), Art 124 ('1. There shall be a Public Service Commission consisting of a Chairman and nine other members appointed jointly by the President and the Vice-President of the Republic. 2. Seven members of the Commission shall be Greeks and three members shall be Turks') and Art 125 ('1. Save where other express provision is made in this Constitution with respect to any matter set out in this paragraph and subject to the provisions of any law, it shall be the duty of the Public Service Commission to make the allocation of public offices between the two Communities').

[21] Before the constitutional change subsequent to the so-called 'Taif Agreement' of 1989 (Constitutional Law of 21 September 1990), Art 95 of the Lebanese Constitution stated that 'A titre transitoire et dans une intention de justice et de concorde, les communautés seront équitablement représentées dans les emplois publics et dans la composition du ministère sans que cela puisse cependant nuire au bien de l'Etat.' After the above-mentioned constitutional amendment (which could nevertheless be implemented only to a limited extent), the same Article reads: 'La règle de la représentation confessionnelle est supprimée. Elle sera remplacée par la spécialisation et la compétence dans la fonction publique, la magistrature, les institutions militaires, sécuritaires, les établissements publics et d'économie mixte et ce, conformément aux nécessités de l'entente nationale, à l'exception des fonctions de la première catégorie ou leur équivalent. Ces fonctions seront réparties à égalité entre les chrétiens et les musulmans sans réserver une quelconque fonction à une communauté déterminée tout en respectant les principes de spécialisation et de compétence.' The 2006 Law on Minority Rights and Freedoms still provides that 'Minorities shall have the right to proportional representation in public services, state bodies and local self government bodies. Competent bodies in charge of human resources, in cooperation with the Councils of minorities, shall look after the representation of persons belonging to minorities ...'

no longer mirrors reality and that the model of 'proportional' or 'equitable' representation of national minorities in all state structures, including notably the civil service, is spreading into 'promotional' states as well, as will be elaborated further below. In other words, minority participation in the civil service is no longer a typical facet of multinational, power-sharing governments but has spread out as a more general and wide-ranging form of minority inclusion.

In this context, the chapter will look at two different European cases of enhanced participation of minorities in the civil service. One refers to an 'older' and more consolidated system, in place at the sub-national level of government as the result of an internationally guaranteed power-sharing agreement (South Tyrol), while the other is an overview of the most recent provisions on this form of minority participation in a regional comparative perspective (Balkan countries). Finally, some tentative conclusions will be drawn from the analysis.

A. Lessons from a consolidated experience: the case of South Tyrol

The autonomous province of Bolzano/Bozen (South Tyrol) in Northern Italy has a (comparatively) old, well-established and deeply rooted quota system in the public service.[22] The ethnic quota system at all levels of the administration is the most visible consequence of the institutionalized separation between the linguistic groups of the region (German-speakers, Italian-speakers and Ladins). The autonomy statute[23] provides that jobs in the civil service in South Tyrol are 'distributed among the three linguistic groups based on their numerical strength as it results from the declaration of affiliation to them rendered in the population census' (Art 89). This rule tends to privilege the interest of each group to 'control' a portion of public jobs over the interest of each individual to access the civil service on the basis of equal opportunity.[24]

---

[22] For an extensive analysis of the main elements of the South Tyrol constitutional design see J Woelk, F Palermo and J Marko (eds), *Tolerance through Law: Self governance and group rights in South Tyrol* (2008). For details on the quota system see E Lantschner and G Poggeschi, 'Quota system, census and declaration of affiliation to a linguistic group' in ibid, 219–33. It has to be noticed that, overall, the Italian constitutional system does not follow a multinational approach, but rather a classical promotional one, meaning that quotas for specific groups including in the administration are admissible, but under strict conditions (for instance quotas are in place for persons with disabilities, for university recruitment and to some extent for female electoral representation—but see Constitutional Court Judgment 422/1995). The legal system of South Tyrol is therefore exceptional with regard to the rest of the country, as it provides for strictly regulated power-sharing mechanisms.
[23] The autonomy statute is the constitution of the province (and of the whole region including the southern province of Trento). It has constitutional rank within the Italian legal system and is internationally guaranteed as to its essential features. Its original text dates back 1948, although it was entirely revised in 1972. Most of the provisions on the quota system currently in place are laid down in a specific by-law to the statute, adopted in 1976 (Decree 752).
[24] Se A Pizzorusso, *Il pluralismo linguistico tra Stati nazionali e autonomie regionali* (1975), 206.

Based on the last population census (2001)[25] the German-speaking group accounted for 69.15 per cent of the population of South Tyrol, Italian-speakers for 26.47 per cent and Ladins for 4.38 per cent: public jobs and cultural resources (including for schools) are distributed accordingly among the groups.[26] There is no doubt that the system has proven effective in increasing the participation of persons belonging to the German-speaking minority in all branches of the civil service.[27] The quotas have been introduced gradually, in order to have the least possible impact on individual rights: no civil servant was fired and the new posts were simply ethnically earmarked according to the new system.[28] Moreover, civil servants of all groups are required to show sufficient knowledge of both official languages, Italian and German—and Ladin in the Ladin valleys.

In practice, the selection of civil servants is based on separate tracks, and each candidate only competes for the jobs reserved for his/her group (eg seven positions for the German speakers, two for Italians and one for Ladins). More recently, as the proportion of the population groups in all sectors of the civil service has been achieved, flexible practices have been introduced which enable candidates belonging to the 'wrong' group to be hired under exceptional circumstances, as long as the overall proportion is respected.[29]

The case of the quota system in South Tyrol is of outstanding importance because it provides extremely useful hints for other, more recent experiences of enhanced minority representation in public life and in the civil service in particular. Albeit extremely detailed on technical issues, the legal rules in place in

---

[25] In the meantime, however, the rules on the census have changed. Decree 99/2005 makes the figures of the 2001 census 'permanent', as there will be no further general collection of individuals' ethnic affiliation. Instead, each person who turns eighteen has to declare his/her belonging to one of the groups and everyone can change this declaration at any time, although the change will only take effect after eighteen months.

[26] The same rule applies at the municipal level. In each municipality, the proportion is based on the composition of the groups in that very municipality. For instance, therefore, in the capital city of Bolzano/Bozen (72 per cent of Italian-speakers) the vast majority of municipal jobs are reserved to the Italian group.

[27] In 1972, when the current, more rigid quota system was introduced, German-speakers in the state offices (ie not including the provincial and municipal administrations) were 662 out of 7,131. Today, they represent 69.2 per cent of the entire civil service: 70.8 per cent in the provincial administration (by far the biggest employer in South Tyrol), 66.8 per cent in the municipalities, 69.1 per cent in the health services, 68 per cent of teachers. The quota system also applies to some private jobs when they perform a public function, such as the postal service, the railroad, pharmacies, etc.

[28] This has, however, created some disappointment among the Italian population: as Italians largely dominated the public sector in the early 1970s, readdressing the balance implied that the German-speaking group was assigned practically all new jobs, particularly in some areas of the civil service, considerably reducing the chances for the new generation of Italian-speakers to access the civil service.

[29] This has, however, no legal basis and only happens as a matter of fact and of 'common sense'. While this might be helpful in order to hire the best candidate irrespective of his/her ethnic affiliation, this has negative repercussions on other jobs, as in the end the mathematical proportion has to be re-established through future hirings.

South Tyrol do not provide any answer to the most basic questions of enhanced minority participation in the civil service. One of those concerns for instance the so-called 'vertical' quota system, ie the distribution of jobs in the various ranks of the administration. As a consequence, there are several complaints (mostly from within the Italian group) about the distribution of key jobs in the public sector, although it is often argued in the political discourse that the quota system, designed to protect the weaker group (originally the German-speakers), has now become an instrument for the protection of Italians in South Tyrol.

Another, much more fundamental question left unresolved by the legal rules on ethnic quotas in South Tyrol is the issue of its nature and future. Is such a system to remain in place now that it has achieved its goal? If yes, under what conditions? Are quotas an exceptional, and thus temporary, measure or can they be considered an ordinary, and thus permanent, instrument? Politically there is consensus among the German-speaking group (as well as among the majority of Italians) that the system has to continue; therefore, no substantial change should be expected in the coming years. Legally, however, the issue is far more complex[30] and the basic question remains. The very fact that even the oldest, most developed and most sophisticated rules on minority quotas do not provide any answers as to their essence proves that participation is a living process and one which is ultimately extremely difficult to measure in numeric terms. Paraphrasing Churchill, it could be said that quotas are the worst form of minority participation, except for all those other forms that have been tried from time to time.

B. Cases from countries in transition: the experience of the Western Balkans

1. Second-generation Representation Clauses

Over the last decade, several countries have adopted specific rules at the constitutional and legislative level for minority participation in the civil service.

---

[30] The question is not only one of constitutional law (how exceptional are quotas vis-à-vis the principle of equality?) but also, in the case of South Tyrol, one of international law. The so-called 'Gruber-Degasperi Agreement' of 1946, which lays the foundations of the South Tyrolean autonomy, provides that some sort of link between the consistency of the groups and their representation in the civil service must be provided. The text (English original) reads: 'the German-speaking citizens will be granted in particular ... (d) equality of rights as regards the entering upon public offices with a view to reaching a more appropriate proportion of employment between the two ethnical groups'. No unilateral change of this principle will be possible without the consent of the German-speaking population, and ultimately of Austria as the international guarantor of the agreement. An additional complicating factor might originate from European law, as the quota system might not be compatible with the freedom of movement and establishment. For further considerations see G Toggenburg, 'Regional autonomies providing minority rights and the law of European integration: Experiences from South Tyrol' in Woelk, Palermo and Marko, *Tolerance through Law* (n 22 above), 177–200.

This has been especially the case in the vast majority of the countries of the Western Balkans, and the time coincidence clearly shows a link between this form of minority involvement and the process of European and international conditionality.[31] It is not by chance, in fact, that all the provisions at stake were enacted after the adoption of the Lund Recommendations.[32]

With the exception of Albania,[33] all other countries in the region have legislation in place with a view to providing for an enhanced presence of national minorities within the civil service both at the national and the local level. While the incidence of these provisions, their rank, and above all their implementation, varies from country to country, the stipulations are quite similar, including in their wording, and clearly show a process of cross-fertilization in the region. Seen from a comparative perspective, both regionally and with older legislation on quotas in the civil service in Europe and in the world, the provisions adopted in the Western Balkans can be defined as the 'second generation' of special measures for minority participation in the civil service. Unlike other cases, most of these provisions are designed in a more flexible way, particularly by introducing the new concept of 'equitable representation' of national minorities in the civil service:[34] this term indicates that the minority presence should not be

---

[31] See C Pinelli, 'Conditionality and Enlargement in Light of EU Constitutional Developments' in 10(3) *European Journal of Law* 2004, 354-362.

[32] Although the Lund Recommendations, as stated above, are extremely cautious as to this form of minority participation in decision-making (only one bullet point under Recommendation 6 refers to 'special measures for minority participation in the civil service'), they have played a key role in spreading awareness of minority participation and its instruments. See, among others, J Packer, 'The Origin and Nature of the Lund Recommendations on the Effective Participation of National Minorities in Public Life' in 11(4) *Helsinki Monitor* (2000), 29-45; and K Drzewicki, 'The Lund Recommendations on Effective Participation of National Minorities in Public Life – Five Years After and More Years Ahead', 12(2-3) *International Journal on Minority and Group Rights* (2005), 123-131.

[33] In Albania, efforts in this regard are limited to the area of police, albeit in the absence of a clear plan. According to the Advisory Committee Second Opinion on Albania, adopted 28 May 2008 (ACFC/OP/II(2008)003), para 96, 'efforts are being made to recruit persons belonging to minorities into the police in "minority zones"; in particular, competitions are being organised on an *ad hoc* basis with a view to appointing candidates belonging to national minorities'.

[34] The term is used in the former Yugoslav Republic of Macedonia (Art 8.2 Constitution: '*equitable* representation of persons belonging to all communities in public bodies at all levels and in other areas of public life'), in Kosovo (Art 61 of the Constitution: 'communities and their members shall be entitles to *equitable* representation in employment in public bodies and in publicly owned enterprises at all levels' as well as UNMIK Regulation 2001/36 on the Kosovo Civil Service, 2.1 lit. h, and subsequent UNMIK Administrative Direction no 2003/2 implementing it, 3.3, 7.2, and 10.1). Similarly, Art 77.2 of the Serbian Constitution provides that 'when taking up employment in state bodies, public services, bodies of autonomous province and local self-government units, the ethnic structure of population and *appropriate* representation of members of national minorities shall be taken into consideration' and the 2002 Law on the Protection of Rights and Freedoms of National Minorities stipulates that 'in the course of employment in public services, including the police, it is obligatory to take care of the national composition of the population, *adequate* representation and the knowledge of the languages spoken in the territory of the authority or service' (Art 21).

an arithmetical factor, but rather a general goal.[35] In other words, 'equitable representation' poses a political goal rather than an arithmetic one. This obviously makes it more flexible, but at the same time a lot more difficult to measure. Therefore, while it avoids the excessive rigidity of other experiences such as in the case of South Tyrol, the concept of 'equitable representation' simultaneously opens the door to potentially endless claims, as it is per se an indefinable notion. This might well be one of the reasons why the implementation of this requirement proves so difficult in practice.[36]

Other countries of the region refer to proportionate or proportional representation.[37] These terms, while not necessarily synonymous, are de facto interpreted in a rather flexible way, and the (so far, largely incomplete) implementation seems to link the concept to an approximate, 'equitable' minority presence in the civil service rather than on an arithmetic proportion.

2. In Particular: The Case of Croatia

In Croatia, as the most advanced Balkan country on the way to EU accession,[38] the issue of guaranteed participation of national minorities in the national, local,

---

[35] For this reason, para 123 of the AC Commentary on Participation, which expressly discourages 'measures which aim to reach a rigid, mathematical equality in the representation of various groups', should be considered to perfectly represent the second generation of norms.

[36] For more details, see the opinions of the Advisory Committee under the Framework Convention in the respective countries. See in particular the critical remarks in the First Opinion on Croatia (ACFC/INF/OP/I(2002)003, 6 April 2001, para 57), in the First Opinion on Bosnia and Herzegovina (ACFC/INF/OP/I(2005)003, 11 May 2005, para 112), in the Opinion on (then) Serbia and Montenegro (ACFC/INF/OP/I(2004)002, 27 November 2003, para 103) and in the Second Opinion on Croatia (ACFC/INF/OP/II(2002)003, 6 April 2001, paras 155–9).

[37] In Montenegro, Art 79 of the Constitution provides national minorities with the 'right to *proportionate* representation in public services, state authorities and local self-governments', while Art 25 of the 2006 Law on Minority Rights and Freedoms stipulates that 'minorities shall have the right to *proportional* representation in public services, state bodies and local self-government bodies'. At the same time, para 2 of the same article provides that 'bodies in charge of human resources, in cooperation with the councils of minorities, shall *look after* the representation of persons belonging to minorities'. In Croatia, as it will be further explained below, Art 22.2 of the 2002 Constitutional Law on the Rights of National Minorities provides national minorities with the right to 'be ensured representation in the state administration and judicial bodies in compliance with the provisions of a special law, *taking into account* the share of members of national minorities in the total population at the level at which the state administration or the judicial body was established'. In Bosnia and Herzegovina, also given the overall ethnicization of public life, the relevant provision (referring to national minorities only and not to constituent peoples) of Art 19 of the 2003 Law on National Minorities seems to underpin a more rigid, mathematical proportion: 'persons belonging to national minorities ... have the right to be represented in the bodies of public authorities and other civil services at all levels, *proportionally* to their share in the population of BiH, in accordance with the last census'.

[38] In fact, the participation of minorities is a key priority for the European Commission in its negotiations with Croatia toward future accession to the European Union. In this area, the EU has painted a mixed picture in its last progress report, with some progress in terms of adoption of the 2008 employment plans and the establishment of the national minorities department in the Central State Office for Administration. SEC(2008) 2694, available at <http://ec.europa.eu/enlargement/pdf/press_corner/key-documents/reports_nov_2008/croatia_progress_report_en.pdf> (accessed 31 Juy 2009).

and regional administration, as well as in the judiciary, has been ongoing for some time.

The provision of Art 22.2 of the 2002 Constitutional Law on the Rights of National Minorities (CLNM)[39] stipulates that members of national minorities are 'guaranteed representation in state administration and judicial bodies in compliance with provisions of a special law, taking into account the share of members of national minorities in the total population at the level at which the state administration body or judicial body has been established, as well as the acquired rights'.[40] Para 4 of the same article foresees that national minority members be given priority, under equal conditions, while filling up work posts in the aforementioned bodies. In compliance with Art 8 of the Law on the State Administration System:[41]

members of ethnic or national communities or minorities are guaranteed representation in ministries and state administrative organizations, taking into account their total participation in the population of the Republic of Croatia and, with regard to state administration offices in regional self-government units, taking into account their total participation in the population of the county.

Furthermore, the provision of Art 42, para 2 of the Law on Civil Servants[42] stipulates that:

the Civil Service Employment Plan will also determine the percentage of members of national minorities to be employed in vacant posts in state bodies, as well as plan the employment of the necessary number of civil servants who are members of national minorities for the purpose of achieving representation in compliance with the Constitutional Law and the law regulating the state administration system.

In compliance with this provision, the Central State Administration Office has been established as the main government agency responsible for overseeing the

---

[39] Constitutional Law on the Rights of National Minorities, Official Gazette 155/2002. On the law see A Petričušić, 'Constitutional law on the rights of national minorities in the Republic of Croatia' (2002–3) 2 *European Yearbook of Minority Issues* 607–29.

[40] It is worth noting that, according to the law, representation in the civil service shall be determined 'taking into account' (*vodeći računa*) the share of members of national minorities in the population, which equals to an 'equitable' form of representation, whereas in governments the minority representation shall be 'proportional' to the ethnic composition of the assemblies (*treba osigurati srazmjerna zastupljenost članova*) if minorities have achieved proportional representation in the representative body of that unit. Proportional representation of national minority members in the representative body of a unit is determined by Art 20 CLNM and exercised solely by those national minorities which amount to a share of at least 15 per cent in the population of a local self-government unit or if they amount to a share of more than 5 per cent in the population of a regional self-government unit. Furthermore, Art 3 of the Law on Amendments to the Law on the Election of Members of Representative Bodies of Local and Regional Self-government Units (Official Gazette 45/03) stipulates that the statute of a local or regional self-government unit determines the number of members of its representative body from the ranks of Croatian citizens who are members of national minorities in compliance with the provisions of the Constitutional Law. [41] Official Gazette no 75/93, 92/96, 48/99, 15/00, 59/01, and 199/03.
[42] Official Gazette 92/05.

implementation of Art 22 of the CLNM concerning employment of national minorities in the state administration. Moreover, national minority representatives who have the right to proportional representation in representative bodies of local and regional self-government units, also have the right to representation in the executive and administrative bodies of those units.[43] The authorities of local units determine in the Employment Plan the vacancies in the units' administrative bodies, and plan for the employment of the necessary number of national minority members for the purpose of achieving national minority representation in those bodies.

In spite of these detailed provisions, the implementation of enhanced minority participation in the civil service is still rather slow. Not only has the practice made representation even more flexible than is provided for in the law —avoiding strict quotas and focusing instead on an 'equitable' form of representation[44]—but a number of important questions remain unresolved. For instance, it is not clear how the figures for minority recruitment in the Employment Plan are calculated, or how the plan strikes the balance required by the notion of equitable representation to not focus exclusively on approximate figures but to be grounded in a qualitative approach, which helps ensure that there is representation of national minorities at all levels of public administration, including from first-time hires to middle- and upper-level positions.

The case of Croatia, which is indicative of the experience of almost all other countries in the Balkans, shows that the combination of clear rules and flexibility which characterizes the 'second generation' of representation clauses, does not provide entirely satisfactory answers to the basic dilemmas of minority representation in public administration as identified by this paper.

V. Concluding Remarks

In sum, all types of legal response to the challenge of minority representation in the executive structures show some deficits. Those of the 'first generation', based on a strict numerical correspondence between the share of national minority population and their reflection in the civil service, prove too rigid and they lack a

---

[43] Art 56.a.2 of the Law on Local and Regional Self-government.
[44] Generally to the detriment of national minorities: according to the Civil Service Employment Plan 2007 elaborated by the Central State Administration Office, in 2007 of approximately 21,000 civil servants employed at national level (excluding the Ministry of Interior) approximately 3 per cent belong to national minorities, while the overall proportion of minorities in the country amounts to 7.5 per cent. At county level, the share is 6 per cent. Of more than sixty local and regional self-governments obliged to produce employment plans for local administration based on the 2001 census, only eleven had done so by 2007, and according to the Croatian government all local and regional self-governments taken together employ minorities at approximately 65 per cent of proportionality. See OSCE Mission to Croatia, Status Report no 18 on Croatia's Progress in Meeting International Commitments Since June 2006, 19 July 2007.

vision of what comes next. This is mostly due to the fact that the regulations have been adopted as a measure for conflict resolution within the framework of a power-sharing system that has been designed to stop or to prevent a conflict. Moreover, dating back to times when formal equality and parliamentary democracy based on majority rule were considered the overarching and undisputable principles, they have been designed as exceptional, temporary measures and have gradually become permanent, thus creating a conundrum when it comes to their interpretation.

The 'second generation' tries to resolve the dilemma by setting political rather than numerical goals. This makes them more flexible and less exceptional, and thus easier to reconcile with the constitutional foundations of equality and majoritarian democracy, and potentially permanent. Moreover, the second generation of clauses on minority representation in the public administration is spreading across countries with systems of government that are not necessarily based on power-sharing between equally constitutive nations. By doing so, they respond to the need for more effective participation of minorities where they can better contribute to the diversity of a country and more effectively influence the decision-making process. At the same time, however, their implementation is more exposed to political will, as a relatively wide margin of discretion is accorded in the interpretation of concepts such as 'equitable', 'proportionate', 'appropriate' representation, which makes it very difficult to make these clauses justiciable in courts. Eventually, they represent a weaker guarantee for minorities, as political actors are left with a great deal of discretion in their implementation. In sum, while the second generation of norms represents an overall improvement, it still faces severe problems both at the theoretical and the practical level.

It can thus be said, in general, that the legal system has not yet found a clear way of addressing and effectively regulating the issue of effective participation of minorities in public life. Among the reasons for this, the unresolved conceptual issues sketched out above might also play a role, as ultimately this most effective form of minority participation is still regarded with suspicion and considered exceptional. It is paradoxical, however, that as long as representation in the executive structures remains exceptional, too little attention—including by decision-makers—is devoted to it, and as long as there is insufficient attention it will remain exceptional. In this respect, it is undeniable that focusing on representation in elected bodies is a lot less problematic for the system, more rewarding for minority leaders and easier for majorities as it does not pose structural questions to the foundation of the society, including to majority rule.

Nevertheless, the trends of the last decade clearly show that there is strong demand for this form of minority participation as the most pervasive, pluralist, and therefore ultimately effective participation, including and probably even more so in countries that are not based on the coexistence of equally constitutive nations. Minority participation in the civil service is no longer a typical facet of multinational, power-sharing governments, but has spread out as a more general and wide-ranging form of minority inclusion.

Effective participation has to find its way through guaranteed participation in the civil service, and generally through the branches of government other than the legislature, in a consistent way. There is still much work to do to identify the most effective instruments for achieving this. Perhaps it will take a third generation of rules on enhanced representation to successfully address this extremely complex but unavoidable issue.

16

Political Participation and Power-sharing in Ethnic Peace Settlements

Fernand de Varennes

I. Introduction	453
II. A Struggle for Power: Why Minorities Are Involved in Conflicts	454
A. The non-neutrality of states and minorities	455
B. State preferences and their significance in political participation	458
C. Participation *simpliciter* versus effective participation: why it matters	460
D. Exclusion, participation and conflicts involving minorities	461
III. Peace Agreements and Effective Participation of Minorities	464
A. The Lund Recommendations and power-sharing: redressing the underrepresentation and 'under-participation' of minorities	465
B. The resonance of the Lund Recommendations in peace agreements	467
IV. Conclusion	473

I. Introduction

The Gileadites captured the fords of the Jordan leading to Ephraim, and whenever a survivor of Ephraim said, 'Let me cross over', the men of Gilead asked him, 'Are you an Ephraimite?' If he replied, 'No', they said, 'All right, say "Shibboleth".' He said, 'Sibboleth', because he could not pronounce the word correctly, they seized him and killed him at the fords of the Jordan. Forty-two thousand Ephraimites were killed at that time. [Judges 12]

This story from Judges in the Old Testament—or *Shoftim* in Hebrew—is perhaps the first recorded instance in human history of an ethnic conflict, and it is remembered for the killing of the fugitive Ephraimites who were identified by their accent; a linguistic or ethnic difference. In some ways it is almost frighteningly similar to more recent incidents and history is peppered with not too dissimilar situations: in the thirteenth century, native Sicilians used the word *ceci* (chickpeas) to identify Norman French soldiers during an uprising in Palermo (known as the Sicilian vespers) against Charles d'Anjou's rule, and the sentence *Setze jutges d'un jutjat mengen fetge d'un penjat* (sixteen judges of a court eat the liver of a hanged man) was used during the War of Spanish Succession (1701–14) to distinguish speakers of Castilian (Spanish) and others from the Catalan-speaking population.

The twentieth and twenty-first centuries are not immune to similar tensions, in that ethnic differences remain one of the salient fault lines along which conflicts continue to erupt throughout the world. Most of today's conflicts can be categorized as ethnic,[1] usually but not always involving national minorities, and it is for this reason that the standard-setting activities of the High Commissioner on National Minorities, including obviously but not exclusively the Lund Recommendations on the Effective Participation of National Minorities in Public Life and Explanatory Report, must be understood as part of conflict-prevention efforts, because ultimately they provide for ways in which political power can be spread out more fairly and effectively so as to alleviate conflict.

Other chapters in this book deal with specific standards set out in the Lund Recommendations. This chapter attempts to consider more broadly the extent to which issues of political participation and power-sharing, as articulated in the Lund Recommendations, figure prominently in ethnic peace settlements. This will be done by first explaining why national minorities find themselves so frequently as one of the antagonists in violent conflicts worldwide. There will then follow an examination of how political participation and power-sharing are of any relevance in situations of ethnic conflict involving national minorities, set against the Lund Recommendations. The chapter will conclude with an overall assessment of the 'effectiveness' of the Lund Recommendations by looking at peace agreements which incorporate political participation and power-sharing provisions and which can be claimed to have brought ethnic conflicts to an end, or at least to have led to a much-reduced state of violence and conflict.

II. A Struggle for Power: Why Minorities Are Involved in Conflicts

[T]he state is more than a passive register of citizen preferences, and in policy deliberation state leadership and initiative are critical … Here we encounter another paradox: the state is the arbiter and broker of cultural difference, yet the state is unlikely to be wholly neutral in ethnic terms. In

---

[1] Ethnic/ethnicity is used in this chapter in its broader portmanteau sense and includes not only cultural but also linguistic, religious, or racial connotations.

the distribution of power within their structures, states inevitably reflect the dominant groups within civil society (by class and interest, as well as ethnic derivation). As noted earlier, many states invest their national personality with the cultural attributes of the leading ethnic community. Even in countries with predominantly civic forms of nationalism, such as the United States, the argument that different communal segments (racial in this instance) were neutrally treated would be impossible to sustain historically. States are thus asked—figuratively speaking—to leap out of their own skins, to transcend their own cultural nature. Notwithstanding the intrinsic difficulties of this task, and the improbabilities of complete success, we contend that the larger requirements of statecraft—the imperative necessities of stability and comity within the polity—make partial realization possible.[2]

Most conflicts today are internal conflicts within states, usually involving ethnic groups which often have human rights grievances against the government. They are massively costly in human terms, with some studies suggesting that since the end of the Second World War perhaps 17 million people have died in internal conflicts, compared with less than 4 million in wars between countries. About 125 internal wars have raged since 1945, compared with something like 25 conventional wars.[3] While on one hand there is no doubt about the pre-eminence of minority concerns or claims in most of the world's conflicts since the end of the Second World War, there is less consensus as to why this is the case. Though points of view on these matters often diverge according to the commentators' particular background, a number of observations from a legal perspective might highlight why the Lund Recommendations affect some fundamental issues that come up repeatedly in terms of the tensions leading up to many of these conflicts.

A. The non-neutrality of states and minorities

> Community of language and culture ... does not necessarily give rise to political unity, any more than linguistic and cultural dissimilarity prevents political unity.[4]

States are never completely neutral in terms of ethnic, religious, linguistic, or cultural preferences. Most states worldwide make an unambiguous, if sometimes mainly symbolic, affirmation of the dominant position of the majority's religion (Nepal, Pakistan, Ireland, etc), ethnicity/culture (Macedonia, Myanmar, etc), or, more commonly, language (France, Nepal, El Salvador, Slovakia, Bangladesh, etc) in its constitution.

---

[2] C Young, *Ethnic Diversity and Public Policy: An overview* (1994).
[3] See, eg, L Harbom and P Wallensteen, 'Armed conflict and its international dimensions, 1946–2004' (2005) 42 *Journal of Peace Research* 623–5.
[4] A Lijphart, 'Self-determination versus pre-determination of ethnic minorities in power-sharing systems' in W Kymlicka (ed), *The Rights of Minority Cultures* (1995), 277.

Even in states portrayed as secular, there are always direct or indirect preferences in terms of religious traditions and preferences. Models of secularism such as the United States of America and France still indirectly or directly favour the religious traditions of the Christian majority. Public holidays decreed by these governments still coincide with Christian holy days, giving to Christians a number of advantages which individuals who happen to be members of a religious minority do not enjoy to the same degree. Muslims, Hindus, and other faiths in most European countries do not have the benefit or advantage of having their most venerated holy days as official public holidays, whereas most Christians in Europe do.

These holidays/holy days may be described as secular, but in reality they involve the state indirectly granting certain advantages linked to the religious and cultural traditions of the ethnic or religious majority. The same applies conversely to non-Muslims in countries such as Saudi Arabia, Bangladesh, and Iran, non-Jews in Israel, etc.

Whereas absolute state neutrality in terms of religious preferences is difficult to achieve in most countries, absolute state neutrality in terms of language preferences is simply not possible. All states must—for practical reasons if nothing else—choose one or a few languages in which to conduct administrative and other state activities and interact with their population. In a very real sense, no state is able to respond in all of the languages used by every single person on its territory. Unavoidably, there are necessary language preferences which are made, and this usually takes the form of the state having one official language— usually the language shared by the dominant linguistic group in the country—or at most a few official languages spoken by the most numerous linguistic groups, though this is not always the case.[5]

Some countries are however in a permanent state of denial. Rather than acknowledge that there are deliberate linguistic choices made, and that these language preferences will impact differently upon individuals according to whether it is the language in which they are most fluent, some states prefer either not to have any official language or to have only one and assert that all individuals are treated 'equally', 'without discrimination' since the language preference applies to everyone.

In the area of language preferences, one could also give as examples cases of countries like Australia, Japan, and the United States which do not have an official language. Despite having no official language, the state machinery in practice operates almost exclusively in English or Japanese (obviously, for Japan), showing a definite preference for the majority of their inhabitants that share the same language (and indirectly cultural background), while at the same

---

[5] Indonesia has Bahasa Indonesia as its official language, a language which is not the mother tongue of most of the country's population. Many African states have maintained the language of their former colonial masters as the lingua franca official language.

time disadvantaging those who have no or limited fluency in this non-official language, especially Aborigines (in Australia) Native Americans and Hispanics (in the US), and Koreans (in Japan).

The Thai-only language preferences applied by state officials in Thailand are clearly serious and real obstacles for access to public services, state-provided education, and employment opportunities in the civil service for the Malay-speaking minority in the south of the country who are not fluent in Thai, as are similar language requirements in the United States for Hispanics. Similarly, the official 'Turkish language only' policies of the government of Turkey (which are now beginning to change) also constituted severe and concrete obstacles to the advancement of many Kurds, who were not all perfectly fluent in the only official language of the state.

Rather than examples of 'equality', the language preferences of these and other states result in quite the reverse: one language for all does not guarantee equality for all if it is not a language in which everyone is equally fluent, in the same way as one religion 'for' all does not guarantee equality if not everyone is of the same religion.

These and other state preferences may have a concrete impact on an individual's freedom of action (businesses may not be allowed to operate on public holidays, thus reflecting a concrete and marked preference for the religious values of the majority), or disadvantage individuals who are not native speakers of the official language(s) in terms of educational success or access to public employment.

If, however, a minority's language (or religious) preferences are taken into account and actually integrated into the activities of the state—to the extent that this is practically possible—it would often result in benefit to the minority. In the case of language preferences, using a minority language in the conduct of state activities usually requires the necessary hiring of functionally bilingual officials. More often than not, these tend to be members of the minority, as in the case of Canada (French-speaking minority), Macedonia (Albanian-speaking minority), etc.

From the above, three points should be borne in mind which will later explain why the issues of power-sharing and political participation figure prominently in both the Lund Recommendations and ethnic peace agreements that address the sources of conflicts:

1. Absolute state neutrality in terms of religious, linguistic, or cultural preferences is impossible.
2. Since absolute neutrality is impossible, this means that in reality a modern state does not necessarily or automatically treat all individuals in exactly the same way. Some individuals (usually members of the religious, linguistic, or cultural majority) receive, directly or indirectly, advantages and benefits which other individuals (usually members of the religious, linguistic, or cultural minority) do not or cannot enjoy to the same extent.

3. In most states, there are therefore in practice competing interests within the state between members of the religious, linguistic, or cultural majority and those of the religious, linguistic, or cultural minority because in many areas the state cannot be absolutely neutral in its policies or conduct.

Although it is normally the members of an ethnic, religious, or linguistic majority who control the state machinery and can therefore see their own language, religion, or culture reflected or favoured in the operations of the state, in modern times there are well-known examples of a minority being politically dominant, the political exclusion of the non-white majority in Apartheid South Africa and the traditional dominance of the Sunni minority in Iraq being perhaps the most well known.

One point ought to be made clear: there is nothing in international human rights or international law which automatically prevents a state from having cultural, religious, or linguistic preferences. However, while human rights do not automatically prohibit such preferences, there are situations where state cultural, religious, or linguistic preferences will not be permitted if they amount to a violation of fundamental human rights such as freedom of religion, non-discrimination, etc.

B. State preferences and their significance in political participation

> Only on the basis of respect of one group for another can what binds us be sought, a kind of common world-wide minimum whose binding nature makes it possible for mankind to co-exist on a single planet. It could only work if the commitment grew out of a climate of equality and a common quest. It is no longer possible for one group to force it upon others. [Vaclav Havel, New Delhi, February 1994][6]

The above is important because it means that, in most states, governments tend in their activities to grant advantages linked to the preferences of the religious, ethnic, or linguistic majority, meaning that the minorities need to be able to defend their own interests or risk being seriously disadvantaged if not excluded from certain benefits.

Minorities are in most countries of the world vastly underrepresented in terms of elected officials sitting in national parliaments and other representative political bodies. In other words, the political weight they carry is almost always much weaker than their actual demographic strength and numbers. Essentially, the problem faced by members of ethnic, religious, or linguistic minorities is that in a non-neutral state—in practical terms, this means most, if not all, states—their interests may be neglected or completely set aside because they are not interests shared by the majority which tends to monopolize power through sheer numbers.

---

[6] Quoted in JF Perea, 'Demography and distrust: An essay on American languages. Cultural pluralism and official English' (1992) 77 *Minnesota Law Review* 269–373, 355.

In historical terms, citizens who belong to linguistic, ethnic, or religious minorities—and sometimes citizens who belong to majorities who were politically powerless, such as non-Whites in Apartheid South Africa and women in many countries—were often not allowed to become, or were seriously disadvantaged in becoming, voters or in taking part in the conduct of public affairs.

In the past, a variety of techniques were used in different parts of the world to disenfranchise members of linguistic, ethnic, or religious minorities (and sometimes majorities). These could include the requirement of demonstrating an ability in the official or national language in order to be registered or entitled to vote, a requirement as to land ownership, or even being able to understand the national constitution to the satisfaction of state officials (who happened to be mainly members of the linguistic, ethnic, or religious majority or dominant community). For example, before the turnover to majority rule in present-day Zimbabwe, there was a period when only citizens who were fluent in English and who had a certain level of education could vote. This resulted in the exclusion of the vast majority of citizens—who happened at that time to be black, and spoke little English—from voting and from being able to participate effectively and be represented in the political life of their country. Even to this day, a number of states prevent their own citizens from being elected on the basis of being unable to speak or write the official language to a particular level—a case of the people needing to reflect the state, rather than the state having to reflect the reality of the composition of the people.

To put it crudely, minorities have tended to be out-voted in terms of political representation, and more often than not have found themselves excluded or severely disadvantaged in most spheres of public and political life.

In most states, and perhaps particularly in democratic ones as Alexis de Tocqueville warns in *Democracy in America*,[7] there is the danger of a tyranny of the majority which may have the effect of excluding or rendering politically powerless and invisible members of most ethnic, religious, or linguistic minorities in terms of participation in public and political life.

This danger appears to have been recognized in the Northern Ireland Peace Agreement,[8] for example, where both Ireland and the United Kingdom agreed that the will of the democratic majority in Northern Ireland had to be tempered with provisions to ensure that the Catholic minority was not consistently outvoted. It therefore contained a variety of measures requiring 'cross-community' agreement on key decisions instead of simple, pure liberal-democratic control by the majority. Additionally, a large and increasing number of states acknowledge this 'democratic deficit', and attempt to increase the effectiveness of the political participation of minorities through a variety of institutional or consultative

---

[7] A de Tocqueville, *Democracy in America* (1899), Bk I, Ch 15.
[8] The Northern Ireland Peace Agreement ('Belfast Agreement'), 10 April 1998, available at <http://www.intstudies.cam.ac.uk/centre/cps/documents_ireland.html> (accessed 31 July 2009).

means. Essentially, these measures represent a recognition that the equal right to vote and free elections do not ensure that persons who belong to minorities will be effectively represented or will be able to effectively participate in public affairs under the usual democratic rule of the majority. Unless participation is 'effective', minorities risk being completely set aside in the electoral lottery where they are almost consistently outvoted.

C. Participation *simpliciter* versus effective participation: why it matters

> Minorities are entitled to the fullest justice.
>
> Mahatma Gandhi

It could be argued that the underrepresentation or out-voting of persons who belong to minorities would not have serious consequences if the fiction of a neutral or ethnically, religiously, or linguistically blind modern state were true, and all citizens were to be treated equally without any disadvantages because of these personal characteristics. But this is an intellectual delusion: all states usually tend to reflect and protect the interests of the majority to a greater extent, including in some cases by demonstrating definite cultural, linguistic or religious preferences.

Minorities therefore tend to suffer disproportionately from a 'democratic deficit' in terms of numbers and influence in many, if not most, political systems, and therefore run the risk of seeing their interests often ignored or rejected by most governments and of subsequently being disadvantaged. While a democratic society does allow citizens to participate in choosing those who govern and in devising the laws governing society, it does not automatically offer any assurances that those with divergent interests from the majority will actually be represented effectively or heard in public or political life.

And that is the crux of the matter. There are divergences of interest because all states are more or less 'non-neutral' in terms of religious, cultural, or linguistic preferences. Some of the states' preferences will impact negatively on minorities that have different religious, cultural, or linguistic preferences. At the same time, the ability of these minorities to address or redress any negative impact in political and practical terms may often be severely limited because of their weak political weight and influence. Thus, while they are permitted to participate, minorities are often unable to change significantly the religious, cultural, or linguistic preferences of the state in the strictly 'winner-takes-all' arrangements characteristic of most political, majoritarian systems. They tend to run the risk of not being able to effectively make the case for respect for or compliance with their own preferences as opposed to those of the majority by the institutions of the state. Their voice in the world of political representation, even in completely democratic systems, tends to be either weak or barely audible, and their presence almost invisible. Consequently, they may be unable to successfully defend their interests where they diverge from those of the majority, reflected in the preferences of the state in religious, cultural, and linguistic terms.

It is often when these divergences of preferences and interests are disregarded—especially when these involve corresponding denials of the basic human rights of minorities—that ethnic tensions are likely to escalate and potentially explode into violent conflict.

D. Exclusion, participation and conflicts involving minorities

> But the imperial city has endeavoured to impose on subject nations not only her yoke, but her language, as a bond of peace, so that interpreters, far from being scarce, are numberless. This is true; but how many great wars, how much slaughter and bloodshed, have provided this unity!
>
> Saint Augustine, City of God, XIX.

There are of course a multitude of explanations as to why conflicts erupt. This chapter does not pretend to summarize these or to offer an all-encompassing explanation in this regard. It seeks more modestly to highlight what appear as common denominators in many of the world's ethnic conflicts, common denominators which are simultaneously also addressed in the approaches put forth in the Lund Recommendations as conducive to resolving or avoiding conflicts.

Contrary to what some primordialists may claim, the vast majority of ethnic conflicts do not involve innate antagonism between different groups within a state nor, as constructivists would have it, are they simply the result of the use of ethnicity as a tool for political power by elites. States with minority or ethnic conflicts tend to have in common an extended period leading up to the conflict during which minorities are excluded or marginalized and find their interests and preferences disregarded in ways that are probably in breach of human rights standards, and it is usually the extended period of refusal or inability to respond to the legitimate demands of these minorities, and the inability of minorities to change this state of affairs despite their participation in public life, which eventually create the conditions for instability leading to violence. Minorities usually revert to violence in frustration at not being able to change their government's policies because they are outnumbered and out-voted. They usually react to defend their interests in a legal and political environment which they believe they cannot control, or even influence significantly. In other words, it is often because a state appears unable or unwilling to respond to the needs and demands of minorities within the existing political and legal structures that instability emerges, often linked to violations of the rights of minorities in areas of language, religion, or culture. This is not to suggest that these are the only causes of instability. In most cases of conflict there is a consistent context, a certain background which seems to act as a precondition in most cases of instability:

I. Conflicts are more likely where one ethnic minority is fairly large or constitutes a substantial percentage of the population.
II. Conflicts are more likely if an ethnic group is concentrated in a specific territory which is considered 'traditional'.
III. The more a government favours identification with the ethnic majority and their interests through its laws and policies, the more the counter-reaction risks being violent, especially from a large indigenous people or national minority.

The above are symptomatic of states where, despite the participation of minorities—and this is especially true of large, territorially concentrated minorities—in public life, they remain unable to sway government policies significantly to redress perceived or real deficiencies. In this sense, it is arguable that most ethnic conflicts do not begin as a quest for territorial sovereignty or independence.[9] On the contrary, what you have in most of these is not a 'minority problem' but a 'majority problem', or rather the refusal of state authorities to abide by basic principles of human rights and minority rights in ways that, among others, would tend to facilitate their effective participation in public life.

One clear example of such a failure involves Sri Lanka, one of the countries viewed as 'most likely to succeed' at the time of its independence in 1948, but which would within a few decades spiral into an ethnic conflict some forty years ago that is still continuing today. The Tamils constitute more than 18 per cent of the total population of the country, and the Sinhalese majority perhaps 74 per cent, though these percentages are also a source of disagreement. Despite some initial promises around the time of independence that both the Tamil and Sinhalese languages would be used by the government, it finally adopted only Sinhalese as an official language, with English. In 1956 another government removed English as an official language, and only Sinhalese remained.

In practical terms, the Tamil minority were increasingly excluded from many if not most jobs in the state civil service because of linguistic preferences, and by the 1970s the Tamils were seriously underrepresented in the civil service. This remains true to this day, as shown in Table 16.1.

In legal terms, an exclusive language policy, which in effect disadvantages and even excludes a large percentage of the population from a variety of services, benefits, or employment, could be regarded as discrimination under human

---

[9] F de Varennes, 'Recurrent challenges to the implementation of intrastate peace agreements: The resistance of state authorities' in M Boltjes (ed) *Implementing Negotiated Agreements, The real challenges to intrastate peace* (2007), 50.

Table 16.1 Proportion of Tamil- and Sinhalese-speaking government employees 1946–2004

	Sinhalese	Tamil
1946		
Civil Service	44.5%	20%
Judicial Service	46.7%	28.9%
1980		
Civil Service	85%	11%
2004 (est)		
Civil Service	90%	8.5%

rights treaties such as Art 26 of the International Covenant on Civil and Political Rights.[10]

There were other measures in terms of access to jobs and education that continued to create a tense situation. In education, the government adopted a policy which required higher marks from Tamil students for admission to some university programmes than from Sinhalese students. This would possibly be discriminatory today under international law. There was also a government-sponsored 'transmigration' policy which began in the 1930s and gave mainly Sinhalese individuals land in traditional Tamil regions. Once again, there is a distinct probability that certain aspects of these last measures would now constitute discrimination under international law. The violent ethnic conflict only erupted after 1956 in reaction to the anger and frustration caused by the government with policies that breached the human rights of minorities, mainly non-discrimination, in areas such as employment, education, access to and ownership of land, or even citizenship.[11]

The ethnic conflict in ancient Ceylon did not occur overnight. There was in fact a gestation of almost a couple of decades of policies which violated minority rights. In other words, there was a gradual process of increased frustration by members of the Tamil minority which led to eventual instability. The reasons for the slide towards ethnic conflict, from a minority-rights perspective, were clear: continued discrimination such as the Sinhalese-only rule, combined with the role of political entrepreneurs, the rise of intolerance against the other and a gradual polarization of the whole ethnic scene, led to the civil war in Sri Lanka. Since the Tamils were such a significant percentage of the population, territorially concentrated and culturally, linguistically, and religiously distinct from the

---

[10] GA res 2200A (XXI), 21 UN GAOR Supp (no 16), 52; UN Doc A/6316 (1966), 999 UNTS 171.

[11] Around 500,000 'Indian Tamils' were denied citizenship until 1988, at which time almost half of them eventually received Sri Lankan citizenship, and about 200,000 Indian citizenship. Some 75,000 remain stateless in Sri Lanka.

Buddhist Sinhalese majority, the discriminatory practices by the state in areas such as language and possibly religion were an invitation to violence and eventual demands for secession, since the democratic regime was unable to respond to their interests and preferences, and their participation in the existing political and legal frameworks was completely ineffective in changing the blatant denial of their rights.

III. Peace Agreements and Effective Participation of Minorities

> [It] is not difficult to establish that violations of the rights of free exercise [of religion] and non-discrimination intensify conflict in divided multi-ethnic societies, nor to project with reasonable confidence that the observance and implementation of those norms will serve to reduce conflict.[12]

As shown in a number of comparative studies of ethnic conflicts that have been ended or at least dramatically abated through the application of peace agreements,[13] most of these provide for some form of power-sharing (usually some form of autonomy) between state authorities and the ethnic minority involved in the conflict, as well as provisions for protecting their rights. This normally takes the form of provisions enshrined in the constitution or specific rights legislation dealing mostly with language use or religion, and the prohibition of discrimination in specific areas of contention.

This is no coincidence. Autonomy arrangements directly address the asymmetry of power and influence between the dominant group within a state and a minority. More to the point, they often seek to redress the underrepresentation of the minority in political and public life, and in many cases its vulnerability to discriminatory practices. In other words, there is a tendency for peace agreements to give to an ethnic group an increased structural and political control that—at least theoretically—should lead to the minority either de facto forming a majority in a sub-unit of the state, or at least through some other form of power-sharing (as in the case of Northern Ireland[14]), increased participation and representation as well as a measure of control on the levers of government to ensure that its interests are better reflected in the linguistic, religious, or cultural preferences, operations, and structures of government. To give one more example, the 2001 Ohrid Framework Agreement which ended the violent conflict between segments of the Albanian minority and the government of Macedonia involved a combination of greater local autonomy, guaranteed status, and the use of the Albanian language in

---

[12] D Little, 'Belief, ethnicity and nationalism' (1995) 1 *Nationalism and Ethnic Politics* 284–301.
[13] F de Varennes, 'Recurrent challenges to the implementation of intrastate peace agreements' (n 9 above); and C Bell, *Peace Agreements and Human Rights* (2001).
[14] J Darby, *Northern Ireland: The background to the peace process* (2003), available at <http://cain.ulst.ac.uk/events/peace/darby03.htm> (accessed 31 July 2009).

municipalities where they constituted more than 20 per cent of the population, as well as quotas in areas where the Albanian minority was hugely underrepresented such as the police force and universities.[15]

Situations such as Northern Ireland and Macedonia, where peace agreements can be deemed to have been largely successful, generally include measures to guarantee a minority's higher presence and participation in, and indeed even control over, some aspects of the state's activities. Autonomy and other forms of guaranteed representation and power-sharing arrangements thus appear as preferred means for addressing grievances in a general climate of distrust and animosity. Nor are these two examples exceptional. From Mindanao in the Philippines[16] to the Nicaraguan Atlantic coast,[17] agreements that have either stopped or dramatically decreased conflict often have, if not similar, at least some form of recognizable autonomy and/or power-sharing mechanism in place.

It is this common thread that is also the link with the objectives ingrained in, and the measures proposed by, the Lund Recommendations.

A. The Lund Recommendations and power-sharing: redressing the underrepresentation and 'under-participation' of minorities

> Linguistic and cultural diversity never causes conflict, it is the refusal of some people to adapt or accept diversity that causes problems and strife.
>
> Member of European Parliament Eileen Lemass, 1987.

As shown elsewhere in this book, the OSCE High Commissioner on National Minorities was primarily established as 'an instrument of conflict prevention at the earliest possible stage'. Max van der Stoel, the first High Commissioner, quickly identified a number of recurrent themes which, if not necessarily causes of conflict themselves, seemed frequently to come up as grievances that could lead to further escalations. This led to the bringing together of groups of internationally recognized independent experts to elaborate sets of recommendations covering these themes: first in 1996 with the Hague Recommendations regarding the Education Rights of National Minorities, followed by the Oslo Recommendations regarding the Linguistic Rights of National Minorities in 1998. These were to serve as subsequent references for policy-makers and law-makers.

---

[15] Text of the Ohrid Agreement available at <http://www.coe.int/t/e/legal_affairs/legal_co-operation/police_and_internal_security/OHRID%20Agreement%2013august2001.asp> (accessed 17 July 2009).

[16] See, eg, 'Mindanao conflict: In search of peace and human rights' (2008) 42 *Hurights Osaka Focus Asia-Pacific* 2–4.

[17] C Chapman, 'In Nicaragua, a historic—and unlikely—alliance for peace', 21 September 2006, available at <http://us.oneworld.net/places/nicaragua/-/article/in-nicaragua-a-historic-and-unlikely-alliance-peace> (accessed 31 July 2009).

The third recurring theme was undoubtedly the effective participation of national minorities in the governance of states, or more accurately its absence in countries that could become susceptible to tensions that would eventually lead to violence. Thus a third group of international experts were brought together in Lund, Sweden, to elaborate recommendations dealing specifically with the various mechanisms which should be put into place to render the participation of minorities more 'effective'. As the Explanatory Note to the Lund Recommendations on the Effective Participation of National Minorities in Public Life itself confirms:

> The purpose of the Lund Recommendations, like The Hague and Oslo Recommendations before them, is to encourage and facilitate the adoption by States of specific measures to alleviate tensions related to national minorities and thus to serve the ultimate conflict prevention goal of the HCNM.

The Lund Recommendations on the Effective Participation of National Minorities in Public Life attempt to reach this purpose by building upon previous recommendations and the content of minority rights to set out what exactly would provide for greater, more effective participation of minorities in public life, essentially following two main avenues: some recommendations suggest a number of arrangements that may be put into place to increase minority participation in the governance of a state generally, while others suggest a number of options with regard to granting to minorities an increased likelihood of participation in public life through various forms of devolved powers or—even though the word appears to have been avoided intentionally—autonomy.[18]

What is also noteworthy in the very first recommendations contained in the General Principles section is the implication that steps need to be taken to ensure the 'effective' participation of minorities, as opposed to their participation *simpliciter* in a democratic state. Recommendation 1 essentially sets the tone by stating that, without effective participation of minorities, there is a higher likelihood of instability and even conflict:

> Effective participation of national minorities in public life is an essential component of a peaceful and democratic society. Experience in Europe and elsewhere has shown that, in order to promote such participation, governments often need to establish specific arrangements for national minorities. These Recommendations aim to facilitate the inclusion of minorities within the State and enable minorities to maintain their own identity and characteristics, thereby promoting the good governance and integrity of the State.

It is a strong if somewhat coded admission that in many states great care must be taken to avoid the exclusion—or at least serious disadvantage—of minorities

---

[18] The twenty-four Lund Recommendations are divided into four subheadings covering general principles, participation in decision-making, self-governance, and how the effective participation of minorities in public life can be guaranteed.

from public life, lest some minorities see violent opposition and even secession as the only option available to them and to redress their lack of voice and influence in public life. In a sense, it admits the scenario which seems to be at the centre of most peace agreements in situations of ethnic conflict: that the exclusion from real, effective participation in a state's public life may lead to conflict, and that therefore measures such as guaranteed minority rights or even some form of devolution of powers or autonomy are needed to buttress or even quarantine a minority's ability to participate beyond a token or ineffective level in public life.

Rather than an exception to individual human rights, the second general principle which underlines the drive behind the Lund Recommendations is that the underrepresentation and 'under-participation' of minorities in public life must be redressed by building upon these human rights, and in particular non-discrimination, since it is strongly hinted that discriminatory policies by states themselves may hinder the 'rights of national minorities to participate in public life and to enjoy other political rights'.[19]

One may argue with the validity of these premises, but what remains interesting—and perhaps involves more than a hint of practical utility to be found in the Lund Recommendations—is that the same premises would appear to be validated by their inclusion in peace agreements generally. In other words, it is more than a coincidence that what is presented as the basis of the Lund Recommendations, essential steps that can assist in maintaining a peaceful and democratic society that avoids the disintegration of a country, is to be found so frequently in peace agreements.

B. The resonance of the Lund Recommendations in peace agreements

> Autonomy arrangements also contribute to constitutionalism in that they divide power. The guarantees for autonomy and the modalities for their enforcement emphasise the rule of law and the roles of independent institutions. The operation of the arrangements, particularly those parts governing the relationship between the center and the region, being dependent on discussions, mutual respect, and compromise, frequently serve to strengthen these qualities. They help break up the hegemony of the dominant group and give the minority some influence at the center, depending on the precise institutional arrangements, and integrate it in the state.[20]

There are many examples of ethnic peace agreements that are broadly in line with the premises behind and the specific arrangements contained in the Lund

---

[19] See on the link between discrimination against minorities and the eruption of ethnic conflicts F de Varennes, 'Recurrent challenges to the implementation of intrastate peace agreements' (n 9 above), 54–5.

[20] Y Ghai, 'Autonomy as a strategy for diffusing conflict' in P Stern and D Druckman (eds), *International Conflict Resolution after the Cold War* (2000), 497.

Recommendations. As indicated earlier, specific recommendations in the Lund Recommendations focus on means to ensure that minorities can be heard and participate more tangibly and effectively in a state's public institutions ('participation in decision-making'), and in addition suggest that some form of devolved powers or autonomy may be necessary. To a large degree, this is indeed mirrored in numerous peace agreements. Though it is not feasible in this chapter to exhaustively explore the content of the hundreds of peace agreements involving minorities concluded since the end of the Second World War, it is nevertheless possible to give a broad outline from a number of cases around the world to highlight their similarity of approach, despite the extremely diverse conditions and settings involved. It should be pointed out that some of these peace agreements were never fully implemented or may not have been entirely 'successful' for reasons that will not be explored here. What is significant in the context of this study of the Lund Recommendations is the unavoidable observation that most of these peace agreements are consonant with the approaches put forth in the Lund Recommendations as arrangements conducive to avoiding violent conflict.

There are many more ethnic peace agreements which broadly follow similar principles that focus on the sharing of power and measures to facilitate participation—of attempting to ensure that minorities are not simply outvoted or excluded—enshrined in the Lund Recommendations, including those relating to the conflicts in Azerbaijan, Bosnia, Palestine, the Philippines, etc. Whether there are lessons to be learned from all of these examples is perhaps premature, as much more in-depth consideration of the complexities and differences involved would undoubtedly be useful. Nevertheless, there are a few general preliminary conclusions that can be tentatively put forward.

The vast majority of peace agreements above, as well as others involving ethnic conflicts—meaning in fact most of the world's conflicts in the last sixty years—clearly tend to privilege some form of power-sharing or political participation formula for minorities that can be found in the Lund Recommendations. While it is somewhat precocious to make too many conclusions on the basis of a rather small sample, what is striking is the extent to which most of the Lund Recommendations are actually found in almost all of these agreements. As the above shows, most peace agreements contain measures dealing with the three main themes of the Lund Recommendations: measures to increase or otherwise ensure the effective participation of minorities in public life (Lund Recommendations 6–13 on participation in decision-making), measures for a devolution of power or some other form of autonomy that would specifically benefit minorities (Lund Recommendations 14–21 on self-governance), and finally measures that would form a type of legislative or constitutional cement to attempt to consolidate the rights and guarantees such as autonomy in place to ensure a minority's effective participation in public life (Lund Recommendations 22–3 on guarantees).

Table 16.2 Measures in Peace Agreements that Mirror Arrangements in Lund Recommendations

Agreement	Measures for increased/effective minority participation in public life (Lund Recommendations 6–13)	Measures for devolution of power or autonomy (Lund Recommendations 14–21)	Legislative or constitutional guarantees (Lund Recommendations 22–3)
Chittagong Hill Tracts (CHT) Accord, 1997 (Bangladesh)[21]	Reserved seats in district and regional councils. Advisory role for traditional chiefs. Job quotas.	Creation of district and regional councils. Additional powers to councils. Jurisdiction to CHT councils over customary law.	Proposed legislative amendments. Language rights protection.
Ohrid Framework Agreement, 2001 (Macedonia)[22]	Job quotas (public administration). Requirement of minority support in parliament for certain laws affecting language, culture, etc. Requirement of minority support for appointment of Public Attorney, Judicial Council, etc. Committee for Inter-community relations where minority views and proposals must be considered Security Council must reflect composition of population.	Increased local powers and autonomy.	Proposed constitutional and legislative amendments. Human rights and language rights protection.
1969 Package of measures in favour of the population of South Tyrol (in conjunction with the 1946 De Gaspari-Gruber Agreement) (Italy)[23]	Proportional representation in local parliaments. Ethnic proportionality and linguistic parity in South Tyrol for employment in all public institutions (except national police and defence).	Creation of two autonomous provinces. Extensive powers.	Special legislation (quasi-constitutional).
National Reconciliation Charter, 1989 (Lebanon)[24]	Equal parliamentary representation between Muslims and Christians, and proportional representation as between sects.		Constitutional and legislative provisions.

Agreement	Measures for increased/effective minority participation in public life (Lund Recommendations 6–13)	Measures for devolution of power or autonomy (Lund Recommendations 14–21)	Legislative or constitutional guarantees (Lund Recommendations 22–3)
Good Friday Agreement of 1998 (Northern Ireland, UK)[25]	Requirement of 'cross-community consent' in regional authority for certain decisions. Requirement of 'parallel consent' in regional authority for certain decisions. First minister and deputy first minister of the government acting together as heads of the executive government, one of which to be from minority. Executive government selected on basis of D'Hondt formula, guaranteeing minority appointments in government.	Creation of regional authority for Northern Ireland. Powers in a number of areas, though not exhaustive (nothing about human rights or linguistic diversity).	Numerous legislative steps to implement agreement.
San Andrés Larráinzar Agreements, 1996 (Chiapas, Mexico)[26]	Right of indigenous populations to participate in plans, projects, and programmes of their communities and municipalities. Mechanisms for proportional representation of indigenous populations in municipalities. Right to reject decisions of municipalities.	Setting up autonomy for indigenous collectivities. Increased autonomy and powers (described as self-determination). Creation of indigenous councils with certain powers.	Numerous constitutional and legislative amendments. Legal protection of customary law and language rights.
Agreement on Identity and Rights of Indigenous Peoples, 1995 (Guatemala)[27]	Equal representation of indigenous peoples on joint commissions. Right of communities to participate in the use, administration and conservation of the natural resources existing in their lands. Consultation of indigenous representations in drafting legislation on culture and resources.	Development of rules for indigenous communities to manage their own internal affairs. Consideration of institutional forms of individual and collective participation in the decision-making process.	Legislative and constitutional amendments.

Protocol between the Government of Sudan and the Sudan People's Liberation Movement (SPLM) on Power-sharing, 2004 (Sudan)[28]	National electoral representation of south based on proportionality. Affirmative action in civil service to assure appropriate level of representation. Target of 20–30 per cent representation for south Sudan population. No less than 25 per cent and a target of 30 per cent upper levels of national civil service for southern Sudanese.	Devolution of power to local and regional levels. Creation of a government of Southern Sudan, with judicial, legislative and executive powers.	Legislative amendments. Commitment to ratifying international human rights treaties.
Transitional Period Charter, 1991 (Ethiopia)[29]	Council of Representatives made up of, among others, national liberation leaders. Head of state, the prime minister, vice-chairperson and secretary of the Council of Representatives made up of different ethnic groups.	Right to territorial autonomy, including self-determination local and regional councils defined on the basis of nationality.	Legislative and constitutional guarantees, including right of secession.

---

[21] Available at <http://www.lcgbangladesh.org/CHT/reports/The%20Chittagong%20Hill%20Tracts%20Peace%20Accord%20of%201997.doc> (accessed 17 July 2009).

[22] See n 15 above.

[23] Annex 4, Italian Peace Treaty (1950) 49 UNTS 184.

[24] Available at <http://www.monde-diplomatique.fr/cahier/proche-orient/region-liban-raef-en> (accessed 31 July 2009)

[25] See n 8 above).

[26] Available at <http://www.usip.org/files/file/resources/collections/peace_agreements/agreement_960216.pdf> (accessed 17 July 2009).

[27] Full text available at <http://www.c-r.org/our-work/accord/guatemala/identity-rights.php> (accessed 31 July 2009).

[28] Available at <http://www.unsudanig.org/docs/Protocol%20Between%20GoS%20&%20SPLM%20on%20Power%20Sharing%20May%202004.pdf> (accessed 31 July 2009).

[29] Available at <http://www.intstudies.cam.ac.uk/centre/cps/documents_erit_trans.html> (accessed 31 July 2009).

This is perhaps to be expected, as the Lund Recommendations are made up of a quite extensive list of possible measures, so it may have been unavoidable that measures for participation in decision-making, and some type of legal or constitutional guarantees, would find their way into most peace agreements. One of the more surprising recurrences is perhaps that despite a few exceptions (such as the Northern Ireland peace agreement which is a non-territorial power-sharing arrangement), one of the recurrent modes of ensuring the effective participation of minorities in public life in the more violent or long-standing conflicts appears to be territorial autonomy, or 'territorial arrangements of self-governance or a combination thereof' to use the terminology adopted in Lund Recommendation 14, which is then elaborated further in other recommendations, and particularly Recommendation 19.

It is clear that the Lund Recommendations themselves do not demonstrate a particular preference for territorial autonomy as a means of ensuring the effective participation of minorities in public life; it is just one of the many listed options that could play an important role in creating conditions for the effective participation of persons belonging to national minorities. It would seem however, as other European institutions dealing with minority issues have tended to agree, that provisions only dealing with participation in decision-making and legislative or constitutional guarantees are on the weaker end of the scale of measures aimed at creating these conditions, and that 'stronger' measures involving territorial autonomy are quite often necessary, perhaps even fundamental, in agreements aimed at ending a conflict:

Consultation mechanisms are an additional way to enable persons belonging to national minorities to take part in decision-making processes. However, just as representation in elected bodies alone may be insufficient to ensure substantial influence on the decision-making, mere consultation does not constitute a sufficient mechanism for ensuring effective participation of persons belonging to national minorities.[30]

While the Lund Recommendations were not influential—as far as this author is aware—in the final form or content of the peace agreements referred to, it is still striking how the principles and 'goalposts' which the various recommendations represent can in fact be systematically found when one looks more closely at the actual content of numerous peace agreements, both pre- and post-1999. This would suggest, at least indirectly, that the development of the Lund Recommendations as a 'tool for conflict resolution' may indeed have succeeded, at the very least, in that the type of measures they offer are frequently and extensively present in many peace agreements. In other words, practice in the real world of conflict prevention and resolution confirm the prominence of what the Lund

---

[30] Advisory Committee on the Framework Convention for the Protection of National Minorities, 'Commentary on the effective participation of persons belonging to national minorities in cultural, social, and economic life and in public affairs', 28 February 2008, ACFC/31DOC(2008) 001, 7.

Recommendations propose: the peace agreements by and large 'resonate' with the types of measures put forward to try to alleviate the tensions that could lead to violent conflict by urging measures that might—by guaranteeing the more effective participation of minorities in public life—help avoid or stop a conflict, and thus ensure a state's stability and even its own integrity.

In a way, to use a quaint colloquial expression, if the proof of the pudding is in the eating, then the Lund Recommendations are passing the test: the issues of political participation and power-sharing which they advance as one of the main themes in conflict prevention are indeed also central issues in ethnic peace settlements.

IV. Conclusion

> Full respect for human rights, a working democracy and the existence of the rule of law, are the best guarantees for a positive situation for national minorities ... To confront the root causes of excessive nationalism, one has to break down 'nationalist' issues to their core elements. More often than not, these concern political participation, education, language, culture or resource allocation ...
>
> Max van der Stoel, former OSCE High Commissioner on National Minorities

The Lund Recommendations were intended as a tool to assist the OSCE High Commissioner on National Minorities in his conflict prevention endeavours. That role continues today, and has been confirmed as other parties have in recent years referred to the Lund Recommendations, as well as to the Oslo and the Hague Recommendations, to address minority issues and ethnic conflicts which still persist in many parts of the OSCE region and beyond.

As this chapter has sought to highlight, the Lund Recommendations have, if at times indirectly and in terms that are both diplomatic and practical, sought to provide authorities and others with a panoply of measures to redress a recurrent deficiency in many European democratic settings: the *manque à gagner* or inability of minorities to participate effectively in the public life of their country, and the resulting tensions and ethnic strife that this may create.

That is what an examination of peace agreements in this chapter confirms. The road towards settling ethnic conflicts invariably involves a mix of the three main themes for measures identified in the Lund Recommendations for assuring a minority's more effective participation in public life. More than a mere coincidence, this would seem to confirm the basic premises outlined in the Lund Recommendations. Peace and stability require a balance, a balance within a state that properly and reasonably reflects the reality on the ground. Especially when a state is made up of a substantial minority population, their preferences and interests cannot be disregarded or discounted, even if this is the will of the majority. The path towards peace and stability in such situations is one which takes account of the preferences and interests of minorities, something which was fully understood by the OSCE High Commissioner during the preparation of the Oslo, the Hague, and the Lund Recommendations.

By redressing this 'democratic deficiency', the Lund Recommendations share what most peace agreements acknowledge and attempt to redress: that all too often, conflicts appear because minorities in certain contexts are relatively speechless or powerless in matters of public life, and that measures that provide for a minority's more effective participation may correct this deficiency, especially through some form of power-sharing, if a situation reaches the explosive level of violent ethnic conflict.

PART IV
CONSULTATION AND SPECIAL ISSUE PARTICIPATION

17

Minority Consultative Mechanisms
Towards best practice

Marc Weller

I.	Legal Framework	479
	A. General reference to political participation	479
	B. Specific reference to minority consultation	480
	C. Conclusion	482
II.	Types of Minority Consultative Bodies	482
	A. Types of activities	483
	B. Areas of activities	486
	C. Complex systems	488
III.	Legal Establishment	488
IV.	Mandates and Functions	489
	A. Functions of organizations representing national minorities	490
	B. Involvement in the drafting of legislation pertaining to national minorities	491
	C. Involvement in programming	491
	D. Relations with international organizations	492
V.	Membership	493
VI.	Working Methods and Resourcing	497
VII.	Quality of Outcome	500
VIII.	Conclusion	500

The understanding of the right to effective participation of persons belonging to national minorities in public affairs has developed significantly over the past few years. There have been four phases in this development. Initially, minority participation was mainly conceived as an inward-looking entitlement of a group. It was understood in the sense of minority self-government, either by way of cultural autonomy or possibly even through elements of territorial autonomy—a non-dominant group would be given a space, either in terms of subject matter jurisdiction or geographically, where it could dominate the one or other layer of decision-making. This understanding meant that the issue of minority participation often came loaded with undesirable ballast. The concerns of government that often accompany debates about autonomy became entangled with this issue as well.

A second phase in the development of the concept of minority participation is reflected in the wording adopted in several international standards, referring to participation of minorities in relation to 'areas where they live' or 'matters or particular concern to them'. This language goes beyond minority self-governance. It accepts that minorities have a role to play in determining the public policy of the overall state, rather than just in relation to internal decision-making within the group. However, this role is once again focused mainly on decisions that are specifically targeted at the group.

The third phase of discourse about minority political participation has come about as a result of the post-modern discovery that minorities require more than just legal space within which to exist and retain their identity. If minorities are to be integrated, it is necessary to offer to their members a sense of shared ownership of the state. This requires not only space for minority-self governance and participation in central decisions of relevance to minorities, but guarantees for full and effective participation of persons belonging to minorities in all aspects of public policy and governance of the state. This discovery was accelerated by the attempts of conflict transformation that followed violent ethno-political conflict in Eastern Europe. Where control over the state, or its continued existence, had been the subject of armed contestation, it was seen as essential to offer to each group a slice of control over the polity, if its existence was to be maintained. Complex power-sharing techniques were developed to help generate a sense of shared ownership over the state.

Complex power-sharing combines autonomy with mechanisms that spread control over state organs among diverse constituencies. It also adds an international layer of control or arbitration in order to prevent collapse or deadlock of the system during its initial phase of tenuous operation. Power-sharing techniques include guaranteed representation of nominated groups in the top level of government, in the executive, and in the judiciary. It also ensures that non-dominant groups can obtain representation in elected bodies, from the state parliament to regional assemblies and municipal councils. Moreover, in addition to securing representation, steps are taken to ensure that minority voices can be heard, and matter, within the central institutions.

The Advisory Committee (AC) attached to the Council of Europe Framework Convention for the Protection of National Minorities (FCNM) has noted that minority consultative bodies will be a particularly relevant part of the toolkit of participation mechanisms for minorities where they are not fully represented in elected and other bodies. In such instances, the lack of powers of co-decision is to be compensated for by the softer process of consultation before decisions are taken. However, even where minorities are directly represented in the legislature or in the government or senior executive, consultative mechanisms will not generally lose their relevance. Often, minorities will only be able to exercise quite limited influence in relation to legislative and other projects, given their non-dominant position in society and hence also in elected bodies. While mechanisms to facilitate representation by minorities are important, also for symbolic reasons, consultative mechanisms often prove more effective in transmitting the interests of minority constituencies into the chain of legislative or political decision-making.

This also concerns participation and consultation in relation to the 'fourth generation' of debates about participation of minorities in public life. This concerns participation in relation to economic and social issues. It is now increasingly observed that the integrationist project will fail if exclusive emphasis is placed on formal mechanisms to secure participation in the political process, defined in a narrow sense. According to that view, persons belonging to minorities will not be able to claim a share of ownership of, and control over, the polity, if they are not also fully integrated in the economic and social spheres. Or, to put it the other way around, where minorities are structurally excluded from economic and social opportunities, they will also be alienated from the political sphere of the state. Hence, Art 15 of the FCNM includes an important reference to this dimension—a reference that is only now beginning to be imbued with meaning in scholarship and in implementation practice. Again, it is mainly the AC that has started to give more specific meaning to this element of participation. This includes consultative mechanisms covering the economic and social dimension.

Before considering the different types and varieties of minority consultative mechanisms, it will be convenient to set out the international legal framework within which they operate.

I. Legal Framework

A. General reference to political participation

The development of the relevant international legal basis of the right to full and effective participation of national minorities in public affairs was presaged in the OSCE Copenhagen Document of the Conference on the Human Dimension of 1990. This document affirms the need to respect the right of persons belonging to national minorities to effective participation in public affairs.[1] This right has been fleshed out in greater detail in a number of subsequent OSCE documents.[2] At the universal level, the United Nations Declaration on the Rights of Persons

---

[1] Copenhagen Document, para 35.
[2] In particular, the Lund Recommendations on the Effective Participation of National Minorities in Public Life that will be considered in greater detail below.

Belonging to National or Ethnic, Religious, and Linguistic Minorities confirms—albeit in soft law— the right to effective participation in public life, stating that:

> Persons belonging to minorities have the right to participate effectively in decisions on the national and, where appropriate, regional level, concerning the minority to which they belong or the regions in which they live, and in a manner not incompatible with national legislation.[3]

In relation to the Council of Europe area, the Framework Convention for the Protection of National Minorities is the first international instrument that introduces this right in hard law. Under Art 15 of this Convention, states parties commit themselves to create:

> the conditions necessary for the effective participation of persons belonging to national minorities in cultural, social and economic life and in public affairs, in particular those affecting them.

At a sub-regional level, the Central European Initiative Instrument for the Protection of Minority Rights of 19 November 1994 confirms that states shall guarantee 'the right of persons belonging to national minorities to participate without discrimination in the political, economic, social and cultural life of the State ... and shall promote conditions for the exercising of those right'.[4] This is to be achieved, in particular, by opening the decision-making process to national minorities and creating conditions for the promotion of the ethnic, cultural, linguistic, and religious identity of national minorities through appropriate measures.[5]

B. Specific reference to minority consultation

Minority consultative mechanisms as a specific means of enhancing participation was already mentioned in the CSCE Copenhagen document. That instrument required that states should take 'the necessary measures to that effect, after due consultation, including contacts with organizations or associations of ... minorities, in accordance with the decision-making procedures of each State'.[6]

The official Explanatory Report attached to the FCNM expands upon the terms of Art 15 of the Convention, providing detailed guidance on how effective participation can be achieved. Particular emphasis is placed on minority consultative mechanisms and their mandate and functions:[7]

> consultation with these persons [belonging to minorities], by means of appropriate procedures and, in particular, through their representative institutions, where Parties and contemplating legislation or administrative measures likely to affect them directly.

---

[3] General Assembly Resolution 47/135, 18 December 1992, Art 2, para 3.   [4] Art 20.
[5] Art 22.   [6] Para 33.
[7] Council of Europe, Secretariat of the FCNM, Framework Convention for the Protection of National Minorities and Explanatory Report, (undated), 46.

The AC has repeatedly referred to the issue of national minority consultative mechanisms. These recommendations will be drawn upon in greater detail below. Generally, the Committee has recommended the firm legal entrenchment of consultative mechanisms, a broad mandate for them, widely representative membership, and the taking of steps to ensure their effective functioning. Where such bodies contain a significant number of governmental representatives, these bear a special responsibility for ensuring that the relevant mechanism contributes effectively to their participation in decision-making.[8] The general absence of any provision for minority consultative mechanisms, or the failure to establish such bodies if they have been provided for in legislation, has been criticized by the AC and the Committee of Ministers on a number of occasions, and the governments so criticized have generally taken measures to improve performance.[9]

As will be noted in greater detail later, this practice has most recently been consolidated in the AC's Commentary on the Effective Participation of Persons Belonging to National Minorities in Cultural, Social, and Economic Life and in Public Affairs of 27 February 2008.[10] In its Commentary, the AC stresses that consultation mechanisms are an 'additional way to enable persons belonging to national minorities to take part in the decision-making process'.[11] Arguing that consultative mechanisms may be particularly important where there is no direct representation in elected bodies, it emphasizes that consultation needs to be seen as part of a whole armoury of participation mechanisms.

The OSCE HCNM expanded on this requirement in the Lund Recommendations for the Effective Participation of National Minorities in Public Life of 1999:

12. States should establish advisory or consultative bodes within appropriate institutional frameworks to serve as channels for dialogue between governmental authorities and national minorities. Such bodies might also include special purpose committees for addressing such issues as housing, land, education, languages and culture.

Outside of the context of indigenous peoples, consultation mechanisms may be required in relation to certain issue areas addressed by special instruments, especially those concerning minority identity and culture. For instance, the European Charter for Regional or Minority Languages of the Council of Europe indicates that states shall take into consideration the needs and wishes expressed by groups using such languages in determining their language policy. To this end, 'they are encouraged to establish bodies, if necessary, for the purpose of advising the authorities on all matters pertaining to regional or minority languages'.[12]

---

[8] See M Weller, *The Rights of Minorities* (2005), 446–50.
[9] Eg, Armenia, Azerbaijan, Bosnia, and Herzegovina.
[10] ACFC31DOC)2008)001, 27 February 2008.   [11] Ibid, 7.   [12] Art 7, para 4.

Particularly intensive consultative and co-decision mechanisms were also established in the ILO Convention (169) relating to indigenous peoples, on which one might draw by analogy in this instance.[13] These references have recently been echoed and enhanced through the United Nations Declaration on the Rights of Indigenous Peoples. This concerns general consultation requirements through the representative institutions of indigenous peoples so as to obtain free, prior, and informed consent before adopting and implementing legislative and administrative measures that may affect them.[14] A similar consultation requirement is also expressed in relation to specific issues, such as the protection of indigenous children from exploitation or the issue of land use.[15]

The Human Rights Committee has also addressed indigenous peoples' issues in some detail. It has found that:

the acceptability of measures that affect or interfere with the culturally significant economic activity of a minority depends on whether the members of the minority in question have had the opportunity to participate in the decision-making process in relation to these measures and whether they will continue to benefit from their traditional autonomy.[16]

C. Conclusion

One may therefore note that full and effective participation of national minorities in public life has established itself as a right in international documents concerning the protection of national minorities. The establishment of minority consultative mechanisms is referred to in these authoritative documents and in international practice as one of the key mechanisms towards achieving this aim. However, one may also note that minority consultative bodies are only one of several mechanisms that should be deployed in order to ensure full and effective participation of national minorities in public life.

II. Types of Minority Consultative Bodies

Minority consultative bodies can be best distinguished according to the type of consultation activity, and to the subject area to which it relates.

---

[13] ILO Convention (no 169) concerning Indigenous and Tribal Peoples and Tribal Peoples in Independent Countries.
[14] UNGA Resolution 61/295, 13 September 2007, para 19.
[15] Ibid, paras 17.2, 32.
[16] ARC Communication no 547/1993, *Apirana Aahuika and ors v New Zealand*, UN Doc CCPR/C/70/D/547/1993, para 9.6.

A. Types of activities

There are four principal categories of minority consultative mechanisms. These are:

- co-decision mechanisms
- consultation mechanisms
- coordination mechanisms
- minority self-governance mechanisms.

It will be convenient to consider each of these separately.

1. Co-decision Mechanism

Co-decision occurs where minority consultative councils must be heard before certain decisions can be made, or where minority consultative councils have genuine decision-making powers. Co-decision in the former sense will take place mostly where consultative councils are attached to national or regional parliaments. Generally, minority consultative councils attached to parliaments, and often also those attached to government, will at least have the right to review draft legislation of special interest to them and to provide views on such draft legislation. Where the legislation cannot be adopted without such views at least having been obtained and considered, one may speak of a soft form of co-decision. In some instances, minority representative groups or minority consultative councils will have a right of legislative initiative, and possibly even blocking powers where the adoption of sensitive legislation affecting their interests is concerned. The latter would be considered hard powers of co-decision.

In some instances, minority consultative councils will exercise principal decision-making powers, rather than merely powers of co-decision. Such functions may relate to programming, planning and funding issues in relation to minority self-governance. While the central government will set the general framework of, and funding level for, minority policy and programmes, decisions relating to their implementation may be left to the relevant minority consultative council. For instance, in its Second Opinion on Croatia, the AC observed that the newly established Council for National Minorities had enhanced the role of minorities in the decision-making process in the allocation of funds to minority organizations.[17]

2. Consultation Mechanisms

The mechanisms of consultation can be organized in a variety of ways. At the central level, there tends to be three principal models. First, there are minority

---

[17] Para 166.

consultative councils that are principally composed and organized by minority representative organizations. These consultative councils will assist in coordinating and articulating minority interests from among the broad spectrum of minorities within the state and to represent these jointly to government or parliament. Such bodies will be mainly self-organized. While at times enacted in legislation, the minority representative groups themselves set up conditions of membership, working methods and activities. In addition to the external representation of minority interests, such consultative councils will also perform an important function in mobilizing minority communities and in streamlining their own ability to represent themselves through umbrella organizations.

A sub-group of national minority councils organized principally by the minorities themselves comprises those that serve to organize and mobilize just one particular national minority. In a number of cases, provision has been made for national minority councils that are composed, in the first instance, of various NGOs and other bodies representing one particular minority. Either, these minority councils will then have direct access to a governmental contact office or to a minority consultative mechanism also involving governmental representatives set up specifically for that specific minority, or the representatives of the individual national minority council will nominate representatives to a consultative body where other minorities are represented as well.

A second model would establish a minority consultative council around a high-ranking governmental official, or a governmental contact office for minority issues. This official will often be affiliated with the office of the state president or prime minister or federal chancellor, or he or she may hold office as a minister of minority issues or national coordinator for minority affairs. The membership of such councils tends to be mixed, being composed both of governmental representatives and minority representative groups. This kind of body gives minorities access to high-level officials in the governments.

A third type of coordination mechanism would be led by governmental representatives. These may constitute the majority of the membership and may dominate the process of selection of other members and the working process. An example of such a mechanism is provided by the Bulgarian Decree no 333 of 2004, establishing a National Council for Cooperation on Ethnic and Demographic Issues at the Bulgarian Council of Ministers. This body, led by the deputy prime minister, is composed of fourteen ministries and six state agencies and the secretariat lies in the hands of a governmental directorate. Membership of minority representative organizations, on the other hand, is left fairly open, and there is as yet no practice to indicate whether minority representation will be open and broad. While it is of course beneficial to place a significant number of high-ranking members of government at the disposal of minorities, consultative councils of this kind may be at risk of coming close to mechanisms of coordination of governmental policy, rather than of genuine consultation with the minorities.

Similarly, the establishment of contact offices, at the office of the prime minister or in individual ministries, can only be regarded as a partial answer to the issue of minority consultation. In some instances, such contact offices proved to be very effective. For instance, the German minority in Denmark benefits significantly from a contact facility at high governmental level. In this way, it can influence policy directly and often effectively. Such a mechanism may be appropriate where provision needs to be made to a limited number of minority groups, or perhaps only one. In cases where contact offices are accessible to a larger number of minorities, or minorities that do not have the ability to represent themselves through one strong, central representative body, this model will be less effective. Even where contact offices have the proactive mandate of searching out minority views and engaging with various minority representative organizations, one can really speak only of minority consultative mechanisms where these organizations have a formal role in an established joint institutional setting. However, to deal with this deficiency, such contact offices are often complemented by the parallel establishment of minority consultative councils.

The case may arise where there is competition between bodies set up by the government and by the minorities themselves. For instance, in the First Opinion of the AC on Armenia, it was pointed out that there was a certain tension between a minority consultative council which comprises representatives of eleven minorities and headed by a presidential adviser, and the Union of Nationalities, representing twelve national minority cultural organizations.[18]

3. Coordination Mechanisms

Mechanisms of coordination are not genuine minority consultative bodies. Instead, these will be interministerial working parties, charged with ensuring that minority policy is delivered in a consistent way throughout all relevant branches of government. For instance, Cyprus reports that the permanent secretary of the Ministry of the Interior acts as the coordination point for minority issues across government. Similarly, within individual ministries, there may be coordination points with a view to mainstreaming concern for minority issues in relation to governmental policy. For instance, the Finnish Ministry of Justice, the lead agency for the implementation of the Finnish Language Act (423/2003) has established an Advisory Board on Language Affairs. This body serves to help mainstream language policy according to the requirements of relevant legislation.

Occasionally, such expert bodies will be given a limited role of consultation, for instance by inviting minority representative organizations to give presentations at meetings, or by maintaining contacts with relevant NGOs. It should be noted that in a number of answers to the questionnaire, governments have

---

[18] Para 79.

referred to coordination mechanisms, instead of genuine minority consultative mechanisms, which may have been lacking.

In some instances, less formal processes of coordination may be established, for instance in the form of presidential round-tables. The AC has found that to the extent to which such expert bodies, intended to advise the executive, are lacking in representativeness of minority organizations and in the ability to influence legislation, they cannot be considered to be genuine consultative mechanisms.[19]

4. Minority Self-governance Mechanisms

Where a minority council has been established in order to organize or mobilize individual minorities, such bodies will often have functions that go beyond the external representation of minority interests. Such minority councils may be provided with decision-making powers in an internal sense. This will generally be the case where there is provision for setting up of functional or cultural autonomy for minorities at the national, regional, or local level. In such instances, national councils will function as the executive organ of the respective cultural autonomy. Particular procedures apply where indigenous populations enjoy extensive powers of self-governance (eg the Sami parliament). In such instances, minority self-governance will be involved in maintaining regular contacts between the bodies of self-governance and both the state parliament and the executive.[20]

B. Areas of activities

In addition to these above-mentioned categories of mechanisms, it is also necessary to distinguish between the modalities of consultations and the specialization of the consultative body. Three further categories may be identified: these relate to multilevel consultation, to specialized consultative mechanisms, and to particular mechanisms focusing on just one minority group.

1. Multilevel Consultation

Multilevel consultation concerns what is known as the vertical layering of public authority. That is to say, most of the modalities of consultation outlined above can be applied throughout the different layers of public authority, from the central government to the local one. For instance, within a particular state there may be a national minority consultative council, a regional minority consultative

---

[19] Eg, the comments of the AC in its First Opinion on the Presidential Round Table in Estonia, ACFC/INF/OP/II(2002)005, 14 September 2001, para 8, that were answered by the establishment of a Chamber of Representatives of National Minorities, Second Opinion on Estonia, ACFC/INF/OP/II(2005)001, 22 July 2005, para 153. See also First Opinion on Norway, ACFC/INF/OP/I (2003)003, 12 September 2002, para 61.

[20] A lack of such provision was noted by the Committee of Ministers in relation to Norway, ResCMN (2003), 6.

council as part of a devolved authority, and local consultative councils on education, language, and culture. Good practice of minority consultation would suggest that provision should be made at all levels, depending, of course, on the demographic and geographic distribution of the relevant minority within the state.

2. Specialized Consultative Mechanisms

A second feature that is common to most modalities for minority consultation is that they may also be arranged according to specific issue areas, or horizontally. Hence, in addition to general mechanisms for minority consultation, one will often find an additional layer of consultative mechanisms, addressing specific issue areas that are of special concern to minorities. These issue areas will typically include education or cultural policy. The relevant state ministries and regional or local authorities will often establish specific consultative mechanisms in these areas with an expert membership from government and minority representative group. For instance, the Hungarian Ministry of Education has established a National Committee of Minorities, as provided for in the Public Education Act. In addition to providing advice and undertaking consultations, this body even has certain powers of co-decision. Each national minority delegates one member.

3. Mechanisms Focusing on Particular Groups

A third feature concerns specialization according to minority groups. Again, in addition to general consultative mechanisms, a special process may be established in relation to minorities that face unique, or particularly pronounced problems. Often, this is the case where large Roma communities are at risk of structural disenfranchisement within a given society. Such mechanisms may exist at all levels of governance, and they may also consist of specialized consultative mechanisms focusing on one particularly vulnerable group (eg Roma education). However, a number of states also maintain extensive consultative structures in parallel, for each of the main national minorities. Germany, for instance, provides individual consultative mechanisms for Sorbs, Frisians, and Danes at the level of both the parliament and the executive body. Such separate provision should not detract, however, from the need to provide the respective minorities the opportunity to represent their interests together, in a joint consultative setting. It is good practice to balance statewide mechanisms focusing on one particular minority with regional bodies of that kind, where a particular minority is territorially compact, or where it is threatened with particular difficulties in particular geographic areas (for instance, Finnish practice relating to Roma populations).

Rather than just providing for separate consultative bodies limited to certain groups that may be at particular risk of exclusion, a number of states have provided for the establishment of a separate consultative council to each of them. In Austria, for instance, there is provision for *Volksgruppenraete*. Hungary has developed an extensive system of minority self-governance for Armenian, Bulgarian, Croatian, German, Greek, Polish, Roma, Romanian, Ruthenian, Serbian, Slovak, Slovenian, and Ukrainian minorities. Generally this practice is followed by states favouring concepts of 'national cultural autonomies'.

C. Complex systems

There may also exist systems that feature a mixture of different consultation mechanisms. Bulgaria, for instance, has established a national contact office with a somewhat limited consultative function. However, it has also generated a Commission on the Integration of Roma (a body focused on one particular group), a Centre on Educational Integration of Children and Pupils Belonging to Ethnic Minorities (a subject specific means of consultation located at a specific ministry), and a number of other specialized mechanisms. In addition, there is a layering of mechanisms, also stretching from regional councils for cooperation on ethnic issues to local councils. While it is not clear that this structure performs as yet in a fully integrative and effective way, it offers some glimpse of the increasingly interlocking nature of different types of mechanisms. In addition to the developing system in Bulgaria, a significant number of other replies indicate that there exist quite complex, multilayered and interlocking consultative mechanisms covering all of the types indicated above. Such examples were provided, inter alia, by Croatia, Finland, Germany, Hungary, the Slovak Republic, Slovenia, and the United Kingdom.

This complexity of provision suggests that it may be useful to devise a matrix that relates the type of state (centralized, devolved, federal), demographic conditions (number and location of minorities), the level of representation of minorities in decision-making bodies, and to particular problems encountered by them (eg in educational, cultural, and linguistic matters). One may then relate this data and draw conclusions regarding the kinds of minority consultative bodies that good practice would suggest for each type of situation.

III. Legal Establishment

The AC Commentary emphasizes that 'it is important to ensure that consultative bodies have a clear legal status'.[21] In practice, the degree of legal establishment of minority consultative bodies varies greatly between states. At the top end, there is the constitutional entrenchment of the existence,

---

[21] Para 107.

membership, and mandate of such bodies. This may be the case in relation to consultative bodies attached to national parliaments, or bodies established by agreements following violent ethnic conflicts. Hungary provides in Art 68 of its constitution for collective representation of minorities and enacts this requirement through the Minorities Act. In federal states, the constitution of those constituent republics where minorities reside may offer specific provision for them (eg, Germany).

In other cases, minority consultation will be entrenched in superior legislation, eg minority laws of constitutional rank, which is the case of Serbia and Montenegro. This will often be either an omnibus law on national minority questions, or it will be a specific law on the establishment of minority consultative mechanisms. The AC on the Framework Convention has repeatedly emphasized that such entrenchment in legislation is preferable, if not necessary, if confidence in the effectiveness and seriousness of the consultative process is to be achieved.

While main legislation is certainly the preferable way of establishing consultative bodies, a significant number of mechanisms have been established by governmental decrees. These will at times, however, tend to be mechanisms that are billed as being focused on minority consultation, while they may actually serve more in the nature of governmental coordination bodies with some minority representation attached to it.

Legally unestablished consultative mechanisms remain the exception and have been the subject of criticism by the AC.

IV. Mandates and Functions

The Lund Recommendations provide for the following functions of minority consultative bodies:

13. These bodies should be able to raise issues with decision-makers, prepare recommendations, formulate legislative and other proposals, monitor developments and provide views on proposed governmental decisions that may directly or indirectly affect minorities. Governmental authorities should consult these bodies regularly regarding minority related legislation and administrative measures in order to contribute to the satisfaction of minority concerns and to the building of confidence.[22]

The Explanatory Report attached to the Framework Convention for the Protection of National Minorities adds:

– consultation with these persons [belonging to national minorities], by means of appropriate procedures and, in particular, through their

---

[22] Lund Recommendations for the Effective Participation of National Minorities in Public Life of 1999.

representative institutions, when Parties are contemplating legislation or administrative measures likely to affect them directly;
– involving these persons in the preparation, implementation and assessment of national and regional development plans and programmes likely to affect them directly;
– undertaking studies, in conjunction with these persons, to assess the possible impact on them of projected development activities;
– effective participation of persons belonging to national minorities in the decision-making processes and elected bodies both at national and local levels.

The nature of the respective consultative mechanisms (national, regional or local; co-decision, consultation or coordination; general, issue-specific, focused on just one particular group) will clearly have an impact on the mandate and functions of these bodies. However, a review of state practice reveals that the following functions should be covered in relation to each layer of governance (national and, where minorities are present, regional or local), every minority, and all issue areas of concern to the respective minorities. These concern (1) the organization, mobilization, and coordination among minority representative organizations; (2) contribution to legislation; (3) contribution to governmental programming; and (4) participation in reporting to international mechanisms.

A. Functions of organizations representing national minorities

This function includes:

- assisting in organizing and mobilizing individual minority communities
- enhancing capacity-building among minority representative groups
- ensuring coordination of interests among different minority groups and minority representative organizations
- contributing to the standards of democratic and transparent governance of minority representative organizations in seeking representation in consultative bodies
- requesting and receiving information and data from public authorities
- assisting in maintaining contacts between minorities and other populations across borders.

The role of consultative mechanisms in enhancing the competence of minority representative organizations and in assisting minority communities in generating umbrella bodies that can be engaged by the state represents an interesting recent development (see for instance, the Finnish Advisory Board for Ethnic Relations). It is observed that the effectiveness of minority consultation, even in countries where reliable mechanisms were established, is severely hampered by the inability of minorities to ensure the effective representation of their own interests in these bodies. Another benefit arising from this function is the facility of interethnic dialogue that is particularly useful in states where ethnic tensions persist.

B. Involvement in the drafting of legislation pertaining to national minorities

This function includes:

- undertaking legislative initiatives
- reviewing and commenting on legislative initiatives which are of relevance to minorities
- campaigning to support the drafting of legislation which is of relevance to minority communities
- contributing to the awareness-raising on adopted legislation pertaining to national minorities and campaign in favour of its implementation.

It should be noted that almost all minority consultative mechanisms functioning at central/general level provide for some involvement in relation to legislative initiatives. The AC commentary therefore emphasizes that 'consultative bodies need to be duly consulted in the process of drafting new legislation, including constitutional reforms that directly or indirectly affect minorities.[23] Good practice would indicate that such a right should be clearly established, and it needs to be meaningful. That is to say, advice given by the consultative councils should be followed or, where this is not the case, at least substantive dialogue should be pursued.

C. Involvement in programming

This function includes:

- participating in surveys and needs assessment exercises relating to minorities
- participating in establishing policy priorities in areas which are of relevance to minorities
- educating public officials about sensitive issues, concerns, and perspectives pertaining to minorities
- participating in governmental programming in relation to minorities, or in relation to issues of particular relevance to them (eg education, culture, etc)
- participating in decisions regarding the funding to be allocated to the implementation of programmes

---

[23] Para 118.

- monitoring, supervising, and evaluating the implementation of various programmes
- strengthening relations between central, regional, and local governments when minority issues are in question
- highlighting minority concerns in relation to the general public and support programmes aimed at combating discrimination and assisting the integration of minorities
- contributing to awareness-raising and other information campaigns.

The involvement of consultative bodies in programming contributes to the reinforcement of the minority participation in public life. First, it ensures that minority communities develop the technical competences needed for carrying out activities such as needs assessment, programme development, implementation, and evaluation. Secondly, it ensures that minority constituencies are involved in decision-making processes, especially on issues affecting or targeting them. Thirdly, minority constituencies will start sharing a sense of responsibility in relation to such policies and programmes. In this way, rivalry amongst minority consultative groups can be avoided and unrealistic demands or expectations vis-à-vis the government may be reduced. It is to be noted that the government will be also involved in a permanent dialogue with minorities and will be under higher pressure to be more efficient and make the resources which may have been budgeted at the outset, available.

D. Relations with international organizations

This function includes:

- engaging in consultations with international funders of programmes relevant to minorities (EU, UNDP, etc) in relation to programming priorities, even where the recipient of such programmes is the government in the first instance
- contributing to the development of international standards affecting minorities, in particular the drafting of minority rights standards, through national authorities and representation at the international level as may be facilitated by them
- contributing to reporting to international human and minority rights monitoring bodies.

It is already standard practice for minority organizations to play a role in preparing reports on minority policy to international bodies. They may either be involved in the drafting of reports, or may attach separate statements to it. However, even in cases where there exists such formal involvement, there is still a need for shadow reports aimed at providing international bodies with a perspective other than the one provided by governments. Minority consultative councils have met the AC members in the course of various country visits and it should be emphasized that their views are an important source of information for the AC.

Minority consultative councils may also be invited to give views on the drafting of international treaties concerning national minorities and their subsequent signatures and ratifications by states. The inclusion of representatives of minorities in international delegations addressing issues of special concern to minorities, including human and minority rights treaties, discrimination, subregional developments, or international programmes aimed at supporting particular minorities (such as the Roma Decade) is considered to be good practice.

It is of course unlikely, and probably undesirable, that one single minority consultative body could fulfil all these functions. Accordingly, these will ordinarily be distributed across different types of bodies that have been considered in the previous section. In this context, the AC has stressed that it is not sufficient to propose consultation only in some areas, such as education and culture.[24] Hence, governments should ensure that all above-mentioned aspects, even if they are distributed among several consultative bodies, are presently covered by the existing bodies.

V. Membership

The Lund Recommendations stipulate:

12. The composition of such bodies should reflect their purpose and contribute to more effective communication and advancement of minority interests.

The AC Commentary adds that:[25]

Appropriate attention should be paid to the 'inclusiveness' and 'representativeness' of consultative bodies. This implies, inter alia, that whether there are mixed bodies, the proportion between minority representatives and officials should not result in the latter dominating the work. All national minorities should be represented, including numerically smaller national minorities.

The balance of membership from among minority representative bodies and the government or other public bodies depends on the type of minority consultative organization as well as on its function. Bodies of minority self-governance, or umbrella fora of a specific minority or a coordination body of national minorities, will generally be composed only of minority representatives. The Sami parliament whose members are elected is one such example. It is to be pointed out that compliance with principles of internal democracy, transparency, and accountability is to be expected even in less wide-ranging minority

---

[24] First Opinion on Moldova, ACFC/INF/OP/I(2003)002, 1 March 2002, para 88.
[25] Para 109.

self-administration such as associations or other minority organizations. It is up to the minority representative organizations to create such criteria of conduct rather than to leave it to governments.

Where consultative bodies are assigned to parliaments with a view to contributing to the drafting of legislation touching upon national minorities, they will usually be composed entirely of minority representatives, members of minority representative groups, minority representatives from parliament (where there are any), and other members of parliament. There are also mixed mechanisms, where a minority group is given access to a joint committee composed of parliamentarians and governmental agencies (eg Germany). Consultative bodies with mixed minority and governmental membership may be established with a view to ensuring regular exchange of views between the government and minorities.

In consultative councils that are composed of a significant number of representatives of government and minority representative organizations, best practice would suggest a preponderance of minority representatives, or at least equality of representation. This issue is a difficult one, as it may well be in the interests of the minorities themselves to be represented on the consultative council together with representatives of all of the ministries and governmental agencies that are of relevance to them. On the other hand, as was already noted above, a preponderance of governmental representation can significantly impact on the functioning of the consultative council, turning it rather into a body of governmental coordination. In some situations, minority representatives may well feel intimidated by broad and dominant high-level governmental representation. The working process, which may then resemble that of government agencies, may also not be conducive to producing uninhibited and effective participation of minority representatives.

When considering the First State Report of Germany, the AC noted that members of the Sorbian minority constituted only a minority of members on the relevant Sorbian consultative body, and did not possess veto powers in relation to the decisions of that body.[26] Germany explained that the body had decision-making powers relating to funding issues, where the government concerned would be unable to assign principal decision-making powers to the relevant minority.[27] This episode proves that minority communities should generally be able to play a decisive role in the consultative bodies and should be in the majority. Similarly, the AC recommended that the Slovak Republic change its arrangements with a view to ensuring that the majority of members of the Council of National Minorities and Ethnic Groups are composed of minority representatives.[28] Subsequently, it was reported that fifteen out of eighteen members in the Council of National Minority

---

[26] AC, First Opinion on Germany, ACFC/INF/OP/I(2002)008, 1 March 2002, para 65.
[27] Germany, Second State Report, ACFC/SR/II(2005)002, 13 April 2005, para 805.
[28] AC, First Opinion on Slovak Republic, ACFC/INF/OP/I(2001)001, 22 September 2000.

and Ethnic Groups are persons belonging to national minorities. The Czech Republic has also taken measures to ensure that a majority of members in the consultative council are nominated by the national minority associations.

In addition, the question of the determination of which minorities are to be represented in such consultative bodies can cause disagreements. It is considered in general terms that all national minorities should be entitled to be represented in the consultative bodies.

With respect to state control over minority representation, a number of following problematic issues may arise:

- The legislative act or decree on the establishment consultative bodies enumerates exclusively the minorities which are to be represented. Such legislation can lead to the exclusion of other groups.
- The relevant instrument draws on the wider definition by the state of which groups it considers to be national minorities. This can be general definition of the term minority (eg, Serbia and Montenegro), or an enumeration of groups. Such definitions may be found in the constitution, national minority laws, or declarations made in connection with the ratification of international treaties. Again, this may exclude certain groups, including autochthonous minorities that plainly exist according to objective criteria, but have not been accorded 'recognition' by the relevant government.
- The relevant instrument limits representation to minority representative bodies that qualify according to a rather restrictive and at times subjective catalogue of criteria that are administered by the government.
- The relevant instrument limits minority representation to their achievement of representation in other bodies, for instance in parliament (Romanian National Minorities Council). Such an attitude would be controversial, given the particularly pronounced need for representation in consultative bodies of those minorities that do not have access to processes of co-decision.
- The relevant instrument does not appear to restrict membership to certain groups, but in practice, certain minority communities are not invited to participate.

The AC has repeatedly urged states to ensure full and comprehensive representation of all national minorities, including non-autochthonous minorities, whether recognized by the respective state or not.

A formulae for representation has been established in some cases, For instance, the Lithuanian Council of National Communities which is composed of members of individual minorities according to their number (three seats for national minorities of more than 100,000 members, two for communities comprising from 10,000 to 100,000 members, and one for less numerous minorities). In the same way, Croatia reports arranging representation according to the relative numerical size of minorities.

There are also different models concerning the selection process of representatives in minority consultative councils. As already noted, a fully democratic process can be expected in minority self-governance. Minority associations should equally ensure that their candidates for national minority consultative councils have been selected democratically and according to a transparent process.

Where the membership in a minority consultative body depends on appointment by government, it is good practice to ensure that minority representatives are automatically appointed if they are nominated by their respective communities. If there are grounds for the refusal of an appointment (eg, a criminal record of the nominee), best practice would let the matter be addressed by the minority consultative council in question rather than the government.

In some cases, the government itself will select the representatives of such consultative bodies. The lack of consultation with minorities with respect to the designation of minority representatives was criticized by the AC (see for example, the ACFC Opinion on Lithuania).[29] This is not in accordance with good practice. However, such a procedure of designation appears to occur mainly with respect to coordination bodies rather than consultative mechanisms. Coordination bodies are usually composed of external members who are experts in the field rather than representatives of minorities.

In some cases the government concerned will establish criteria for the selection of minority representative groups to be represented in the respective consultative council. Such selection criteria may include, as is the case of the Finnish Advisory Board on Ethnic Relations:

- their ability to represent the relevant communities
- the size of the group they represent
- their expertise as it relates to the respective council's mandate
- the risks of exclusion of the group represented by an association or non-governmental organization (NGO)
- the organizational capacity of the relevant association or NGO

Such criteria may add to the transparency when decisions need to be made about the selection of just some representative groups in relation to the limited spaces available on a consultative council. However, overly restrictive criteria, or criteria that may have the effect of excluding a particular minority group from representation, are to be avoided.

Where full representation of all major groups representing minority communities, or the establishment of umbrella organizations, is not possible, the AC has proposed representation according to a rotation system of seats.[30] Another way of spreading representation is the establishment of topical working groups, in addition to the principal consultation mechanisms. Membership in these

---

[29] First Opinion on Lithuania, ACFC/INF/OP/I(2003)008, 21 February 2003, para 79.
[30] UK, ACFC/OP/II(2007)003, para 248.

groups can be arranged according to specific interests and capacities of representative groups seeking to offer input.[31]

As mentioned above, where the organization representing a national minority is concerned, it is up to the relevant communities to arrange for their own minority representative structures. Difficulties may arise in cases where there is just one representative organization that is accepted by the members of the minority as their umbrella organization. However, in circumstances where there is no centralized representation comprising minorities, NGOs, and representative organizations, the selection procedure becomes difficult (eg, the Czech Republic). In such circumstances, the government may be well advised to encourage the relevant community to seek consensus on its representatives or to form an umbrella organization for the purpose of its representation (eg, Serbia and Montenegro reported that the proliferation of minority organizations requires that such a step be taken).

The UN Human Rights Committee has ruled, however, that smaller groups do not have a right to have their specific views represented through an umbrella organization. If the consultative process encompasses one or more umbrella organizations representing a wide spectrum of groups, discussions with these may fulfil a consultation requirement that may exist in relation to a specific issue.[32]

In circumstances where there are fewer but competing organizations representing a particular minority, the AC stressed that governments should avoid selecting just some of these organizations to represent a particular minority. Where there are objective reasons for being unable to accommodate all major groups in such circumstances, good practice would suggest that the criteria for selection should be public and the selection process transparent. An appeal procedure, perhaps administered through the relevant minority consultative council itself, should be made available. In this context, reference may be made once more to double-layered systems, where each minority will itself, first generate its own representative council at the local, regional, and/or national level. The leaders of these councils can in turn constitute the core membership of the national minority consultative council at the state level. This method is in line with good practice and places the burden of selection on the minorities themselves.

VI. Working Methods and Resourcing

The AC criticized the failure of consultative councils to meet on a regular basis and to ensure frequent consultations and permanent dialogue on the issues

---

[31] Ibid, para 252.
[32] HRC, Communication no 205/1986, *Marshall v Canada*, CCPR/C/43/D/205/1986, para 5.5.

pertaining to national minorities.[33] In this context, it is to be pointed out that there is an expectation of significant and substantive use of minority consultative processes.

Consultative bodies with dominant or significant minority representation will be in charge of determining their own working procedures. In some instances, governmental decrees establishing the mechanism will provide for procedural guidance. In general, such documents will assign the chairmanship of the body to a senior governmental representative. As far as the state-level consultative mechanisms are concerned, this will be a minister or a senior representative of the prime minister or the president. It is good practice to ensure that at least the deputy chair is assigned to a minority representative. It is unusual that a more detailed working practice, such as the setting up of working groups within a consultative council, is anticipated in a decree (eg, Romania). It is expected that decisions of this kind will be made by the relevant body itself with the support of the majority of minority representatives.

Where working procedures are drawn up by governments and, at the same time, there is strong governmental representation on the consultative council, it is also good practice to make sure that these procedures provide measures to ensure genuine minority consultation. It can be mentioned as an example that such procedures will ensure that individual members can propose items to be considered and that minority representatives have the possibility to ensure their inclusion on the agenda. In this respect, minority representative groups should also be able to propose information surveys to be carried out, experts who may be nominated, and any sources of information relevant to be taken into account by the councils.

There should be transparency in the work of the council: while it may be sometimes necessary to discuss a specific item *in camera*, good practice revealed in the questionnaires and other documents indicates that the outcome of all deliberations should be made public. Provision should be made for regular press briefings and information on activities relating to the work of the council.

In general, a work programme will be drawn up by minority consultative bodies themselves. This programme should be the result of consultation and should be agreed by consensus among the members rather than simply reflecting the priorities of the government of the day. Work programmes will generally cover a review of legislative provisions on a given area, suggestions for improvements in that area, needs assessments, programming, related programme evaluation, and dissemination activities. These steps will normally be accompanied by an agreed set of milestones of achievement that is envisaged, and projected dates for such achievements.

Many minority representative councils will set up working groups that function under the authority of the overall consultative council. Such working

---

[33] First Opinion on Ukraine, ACFC/INF/OP/I(2002)010, 1 March 2002, para 72.

groups carry out the more detailed work according to the work programme approved by the plenary. Good practice requires that steps are taken to ensure that the less numerous minorities that have limited representation in the minority council can contribute fully to the work of such working groups.

Good practice would also indicate that the dominant position of governmental representatives in the decision-making process should be avoided. In addition, if minority representatives do not have a majority on the consultative council, they should have the possibility to inhibit decisions to which a significant number of their members objects. It is a general practice to adopt special provisions for decisions that have resource implications beyond those means that have been assigned to the council in the state, regional, or local budget for disposition within its regular mandate. Similarly, it is clear that consultative councils cannot make decisions that are ulta vires of the functions or mandate granted to them in their constituent instruments.

The effective functioning of these bodies will require that they have adequate resources.[34] Some may be weary of governmental funding granted to minority groups fearing that this may reduce their independence from governments. It is a positive obligation of governments to provide financial means to minority organizations in order to support the effective participation of minorities in public life. Such funding must be granted unconditionally. It is up to the governments to ensure that decisions related to funding are not used in a way that might stifle genuine minority representation. Good practice would propose that some decisions on the allocation of funds are put into the hands of the minority councils themselves.

Funding should be available in three areas: (a) costs covering the technical support ensuring the functioning of the consultative councils itself, (b) funds of projects and activities to be obligatorily implemented by the consultative councils, and (c) funds for minority representative groups and associations which should be channelled through the minority consultative councils. The lack of funding affects, to a great extent, the effective functioning of minority consultative councils. In some cases no minimum technical support was made available to the councils which hampered their effective operation. There was a lack of funds available for various projects. It was also observed that some funding previously budgeted was not ultimately made available which may have had a negative effect on the credibility of the relevant consultative body.

In cases where decisions about the funding of minority representative organizations and associations are made by the relevant consultative council, good practice requires that particular attention is paid to ensuring transparency in the decision-making process. There should be objective criteria for assessing applications for funding. A conflict of interests may arise in cases where some of the potential recipients of such funds are members of the council while others are

---

[34] Lund Recommendations, Section D, para 13.

not. Provision should be made to avoid situations of conflict of interest and an appeals procedure should be made available.

VII. Quality of Outcome

An important element for the credibility of consultative councils is whether their advice or decisions are actually acted upon, or at least taken into consideration by the relevant state bodies. Where the decision does not follow the advice given, it is to be expected that this fact is at least explained by the relevant state body.[35]

Participation through consultation does not, however, mean a right to veto, according to the Committee. If the authorities have gone through a genuine process of hearing and considering the interests of the relevant constituencies, they can act even against their advice as long as they have gone through the process of 'weighting the author's interests' against other (in this case economic) interests.[36]

The actual meaning of consultation or negotiation requirement has been raised in connection with the Sami parliament in Finland. The AC has pressed for action to ensure that the views of the Sami representation are 'fully taken into account in decision-making affecting the protection of the Sami'.[37]

VIII. Conclusion

The legal obligation to provide for effective participation of national minorities in public life is now entrenched in minority rights law. Besides many other aspects, including those relating to direct participation of minorities in decision-making processes, the principle of effective participation includes the establishment of minority consultative mechanisms. In cases where minorities have no access to decision-making in areas of special relevance to them in the legislative, governmental, or administrative process, the requirement for effective consultation mechanisms is even more important.

Minority consultation can no longer be achieved through the establishment of a single mechanism. Instead, each state needs to consider, in cooperation with minority representative groups, a spectrum of measures needed to be taken to ensure effective participation through consultative mechanisms. This relates to vertical mechanisms covering all layers of governance within a particular state, including the national, regional, and local one. In addition to general mechanisms covering all aspects of minority interests, special—issue-specific—mechanisms

---

[35] AC, First Opinion on Romania, ACFC/INF/OP/I(20020)001, 6 April 2001, para 66.
[36] HRC, Communication no 671/1995, *Jouni E Laensman andors v Finland*, CCPR/C/58/D/671/1995, para 10.5.   [37] ACFCOP/II(2006)003, para 157.

are increasingly becoming a standard feature, in particular in the areas of education, language, and culture. Moreover, where particular minority groups are subject to structural exclusion, either generally or in relation to certain issue areas, it is also appropriate to establish consultative bodies focusing particularly on that group.

The AC has identified a number of elements of good practice in its opinions. This guidance is already reflected in a number of examples of practice provided in the replies of governments to the questionnaire.

First, good practice suggests entrenchment of the main minority consultative bodies (for example, those operating at national level) in the Constitution or in primary legislation. Principal regional mechanisms in regions where minorities reside can be similarly entrenched in the Constitution of the respective constituent republics in the case of federations or in regional statutes. Provisions for local consultative mechanisms can be best contained in the legislation related to local governance adopted at national level.

It is important not to confuse governmental coordination bodies and minority consultative bodies. Coordination bodies will mainly comprise governmental representatives and will operate according to the procedural rules established by the relevant governmental agencies. In addition, the coordination bodies may be chaired by governmental officers. Minority representative groups will often be invited to participate in their meetings and related activities. However, their role appears subordinate to the aim of interministerial coordination. Genuine minority consultative bodies have a wider mandate. Their membership will typically be dominated by representatives of minority groups, and nominated by the respective minority representative groups. Access to genuine minority consultative processes should be available to all relevant groups, whether or not these are recognized as national minorities by the state in question.

On the basis of the practice reported by governments, the guidance contained in the OSCE Lund Recommendations, the Explanatory Report to the Framework Convention and the Commentary of the AC, this chapter has identified a broad range of functions of minority consultation. First, these functions relate to the organization, mobilization, and governance of minority communities. Secondly, they concern participation in drafting legislation at the national, regional and local levels. Third, they concern participation in programming, programme monitoring, and evaluation. Finally, they concern effective participation in the development of and reporting to international legal instruments and mechanisms of relevance to minority communities.

As far as working methods are concerned, genuine minority consultative arrangements, including those comprising significant numbers of governmental representatives, will provide for the right of initiative on the part of minority representatives. It is important that minority consultative bodies are able to work in an atmosphere of consensus. If a decision needs to be made, good practice would suggest that the minority representative should have the possibility to adopt such a decision within the established mandate of the respective consultative body. Representatives of particular minority representative groups, as well as government representatives, should have the opportunity to dissociate themselves publicly from decisions which they do not endorse. The work and adopted decisions or recommendations of minority consultative bodies should be transparent and communicated to the general public.

Funding provided to minority consultative bodies needs to be established to ensure the effective functioning of the respective mechanism. This contains technical services, such as meeting costs—secretariat and dissemination as well as financial resources for capacity building of its member organizations—including funds related to programming, programme implementation, and their monitoring and evaluation. Funds may need to be made available to consultative mechanisms in order to be able to acquire external expertise with respect to research, surveys, and assessments. As far as the distribution and use of public funds devoted to minority communities are concerned, a budget should be prepared in advance in consultation with the relevant minority groups, ideally while the preparation of the national, regional, or local budget is underway.

18

Special Contact Mechanisms for Roma

Eva Sobotka

I. Introduction	503
II. Roma Political Participation and Special Contact Mechanisms for Roma	504
III. Lund Recommendations and Special Contact Mechanism for Roma	507
IV. Other Relevant Provisions in Universal and Regional Human Instruments	508
A. Organization for Security and Cooperation in Europe	508
B. UN standards for the protection of minority rights for political participation	510
C. European Convention on Human Rights	511
D. Council of Europe	512
V. Special Contact Mechanisms for Roma in the Implementation Practice of States	514
A. Parliamentary representation as SCMR	514
B. Advisory bodies and consultative bodies	516
C. Arrangements at regional and local levels	520
VI. Concluding Remarks: Overall Assessment of the Effectiveness of Special Contact Mechanisms for Roma	522

I. Introduction

The political participation of Roma[1] at the legislative and executive levels of the state has been identified by various organizations operating in national security,

---

[1] The term 'Rom/Roma' has been used as a broad categorization, and has been increasingly employed by transnational organizations, activists and social scientists to refer to a variety of communities. Over centuries, Romani communities have adopted names closely related to their occupation and today Romani subgroups are mostly differentiated on the grounds of anthropology, ethnography, history, linguistics, and musicology: Lovari, Kalderashi, Romungro, Bergitka, Cerhari, Ciuirari, Manush, Kale, Xoraxane, Sinti, Laleri, etc. Hence, the term Roma, as used in political science, international relations, and in political discourse generally, has to be understood as referring to a variety of peoples with a variety of histories and lifestyles.

conflict prevention and/or human rights paradigms as a prerequisite for the healthy functioning of a democratic political system and as a way of increasing security and compliance with human rights.[2] The effective participation of minorities in public affairs is necessary to ensure that minorities are respected, recognized, and heard. Simple majority rule, often used as a tool for democratic decision-making, with its principle of one vote per person, can risk injustice by its failure to accommodate minority-specific needs and interests. This chapter examines different models for including Roma in the process of political participation. Under the heading 'special contact mechanisms for Roma' (SCMR), the chapter looks at mechanisms that range from consultation to the preparation, implementation, and assessment of national and regional programmes, plans to participate in decision-making process and elections, as well as the right to be represented and to hold office. Roma special contact mechanisms most resemble Lund recommendations 6, 11, 12, and 13, which will be analysed in this chapter.

II. Roma Political Participation and Special Contact Mechanisms for Roma

Following the end of global bipolarity in 1989, Roma were recognized as a national minority in a number of countries of post-communist Europe.[3] Human rights violations, ranging from racially motivated attacks to discrimination in all areas of life became an everyday reality for many diverse Romani communities within the Central and Eastern European (CEE) region. At the same time, Roma have intensified their process of ethnic mobilization and emancipation, combating racism and discrimination, demanding equality, and political participation and representation.[4] Some have also mobilized politically

---

[2] US Central Intelligence Agency, 'Global trends 2015: A dialogue about the future with non-government experts' 2000; US Statement on National Minorities and Roma at OSCE Human Dimension Implementation Meeting, 20 September 2002; Council of Europe, Committee of Ministers, Recommendation 1557 (2002), available at <http://assembly.coe.int/Main.asp?link=http%3A%2F%2Fassembly.coe.int%2FDocuments%2FAdoptedText%2Fta02%2FEREC1557.htm> (accessed 31 July 2009); Report on the Situation of Roma and Sinti in the OSCE Area, 7 April 2000; Roma (Gypsies) in the CSCE Region: Report of the High Commissioner on National Minorities; Statement of HCNM on his Study of the Roma in the CSCE Region, 23 September 1993; Mr M. Van der Stoel High Commissioner on National Minorities of the Conference on Security and Cooperation in Europe, CSCE Human Dimension 'Seminar on Roma in the OSCE Region', Warsaw, 20 September 1994; Address by Max van der Stoel OSCE High Commissioner on National Minorities to the Supplementary Human Dimension Meeting on Roma and Sinti Issues, Vienna, 6 September 1999.

[3] MS Rooker, *The International Supervision of Protection of Romani People in Europe* (2002), 347.

[4] P Vermeersch, *The Romani Movement: Minority politics and ethnic mobilization in contemporary Central Europe* (2006); N Gheorghe, 'Roma-Gypsy ethnicity in Eastern Europe' (1991) 58 *Social Research* 829–44, 831.

within ethnic Romani political parties or mainstream political parties.[5] Hence, political participation has become an important element for Romani leaders and actors advocating improvement in human rights implementation.[6]

The concept of SCMR has been developed in order to remedy the absence of a 'Roma voice' in public affairs.[7] Based largely on the outcome of discussions between Roma activists, international organizations, and governments regarding the terms of political participation and representation, SCRM developed typically as advisory bodies on Roma or national minorities policy-making. These have focused in a narrow sense on providing advice on specific issues at the national, regional or local levels, but also constitute a broader effort at including Roma in public life and obtaining effective representation of minority groups at the highest level of public life in their respective countries.[8] A number of consultations among Romani elites have taken place over the 1990s on the issue of Roma political participation, in an international as well as national context.

In fact, the Lund Recommendations were preceded by earlier efforts to support effective Romani political participation. In the context of the 1997 Human Dimension Implementation meeting of ODIHR, a Roundtable on Strategies of Implementing the Minority Rights of Roma and Sinti took place, which pointed out that Romani movement functions at different levels, more or less independently, with loose structures of competence and communication.[9] The meeting called for urgent dialogue between Romani activists and leaders, both intellectual and more traditional, as a necessary step towards strategizing political participation and representation of Romani groups. Questions such as legitimate leadership and mobilization at the transnational and domestic levels were identified as long-term interests of Romani communities.

In 1999, perhaps inspired by the Lund Recommendations which were adopted on 1 September 1999, the Supplementary Human Dimension meeting

---

[5] E Sobotka, 'Roma in politics in the Czech Republic, Slovakia and Poland' (2003) 4 *Roma Rights*, available at <http://www.errc.org/cikk.php?cikk=1354> (accessed 31 July 2009); E Sobotka, 'Political representation of the Roma: Roma in politics in the Czech Republic, Slovakia and Poland', International Policy Fellowship Programme (2003), available at <www.policy.hu/document/200808/sobotka.pdf&letoltes=1> (accessed 31 July 2009); A Jurová, *Vývoj rómskej problematiky na Slovensku po roku 1945* (1993); I Klímová, 'Political representation of Roma and Central and Eastern Europe' (2002) 12(2) *Romani Studies* 103–47; Vermeersch, *The Romani Movement* (n 4 above); J Majchrák, 'Rómovia ako téma politických strán' in M Vašečka (ed), *Súhrnná správa o Rómoch na Slovensku* (2002).

[6] European Roma Rights Centre, *Political Participation and Democracy in Europe: A short guide for Romani activists* (2001).

[7] E Sobotka, 'Crusts from the table: Policy formation towards Roma in the Czech Republic and Slovakia (2001) 6 (2–3) *Roma Rights*, available at <http://www.errc.org/cikk.php?cikk=1698> (accessed 31 July 2009).

[8] K Myntti, *A Commentary to the Lund Recommendations on the Effective Participation of National Minorities* (2001), 5; Klímová, 'Political representation of Roma' (n 5 above).

[9] Roundtable: Strategies for Implementing Minority Rights of Roma and Sinti, OSCE Human Dimension Implementation Meeting Warsaw, 19 November 1997, 2.

on Roma and Sinti Issues of the OSCE/ODIHR proposed recommendations for increasing political participation through a survey of 'best practices' in Romani policy identified among OSCE states. In particular, focus was devoted to central arrangements in the form of advisory bodies on Romani policy.[10] Recommendations for increasing the participation of Romani women at the local level and in administrative positions were also put forward, alongside a plea for increased numbers of Roma policemen, judges, and prosecutors.[11] Discussions were shaped in large part by the introductory speech of the High Commissioner on National Minorities (HCNM), Max van der Stoel, who identified the improvement of political participation and Romani interest representation as the next step forward.[12]

HCNM key notes on political participation/representation included:

[M]echanisms that are set up to allow for Roma participation must be genuine in their intentions and meaningful in their endeavours; ... The effectiveness of consultative mechanisms can be measured by a number of criteria: allowing for early involvement of Roma in Roma-related policy formation; the extent to which the process is broadly representative; transparency; and the involvement of Roma in implementation and evaluation of Roma-related programs. Effective participation of Roma at all levels of government, the development and refinement of mechanisms to alleviate tension and conflict between Romani and non-Roma communities, and combating racism and discrimination within public administrations.

... [The] effective participation of national minorities in public life is an essential component of a peaceful and democratic society. In the Roma case, more than most, ways have to be found of facilitating them within the State while enabling them to maintain their own identity and characteristics.[13]

Since the adoption of the Lund Recommendations and the landmark speech of the High Commissioner on National Minorities, which identified criteria for measuring the effectiveness of political participation, discussions have taken place continuously. The OSCE High Commissioner and the Contact Point on Roma and Sinti Issues within the Office of Democratic Institutions and Human Rights (ODIHR), and the Expert Committee on Roma and Travellers, the Advisory Committee on the Framework Convention on National Minorities (FCNM) and the Commissioner for Human Rights (CHR) and the Parliamentary Assembly in the Council of Europe, have been at the forefront of efforts to remind member states of the need to include Roma and Travellers within the political participation processes of the state, at the national and local levels. The most recent effort, strongly supported by Finland, was the establishment of the European Roma and Travellers Forum, a Special Contact Mechanism on Roma

---

[10] OSCE/ODIHR Supplementary Human Dimension Meeting, Roma and Sinti Issues, Vienna, 6 September 1999.   [11] Ibid.
[12] Address by Max van der Stoel to the OSCE/ODIHR Supplementary Meeting on Roma and Sinti Issues, Vienna, September 6, 1999.   [13] Ibid.

and Travellers par excellence, which built up a close relation with the Council of Europe. The forum represents a peak in international efforts and has devoted the last years to improving representation of Roma.[14] At the EU level, three Romani women candidates were included on the electoral list of political parties in Hungary, and two were subsequently elected to the European Parliament. Most recently, conclusions reached at the Roma Summit, organized by the European Commission in September 2008, proposed the possibility of a Roma Platform, a mechanism which would allow Roma and pro-Roma actors to coordinate more closely and improve participation between Roma and the EU.[15]

III. Lund Recommendations and Special Contact Mechanism for Roma

The purpose of the Lund Recommendations is to encourage and facilitate the adoption by states of specific measures to alleviate tensions related to national minorities. They attempt to clarify the content of minority rights, encourage respect and implementation of human rights, and freedom from discrimination in particular. The most relevant Lund Recommendation to SCMR is Recommendation 6, which is concerned with the specific recognition of minorities in public life through a mechanism for dealing with minority issues through high level ministerial advisory bodies and the formal inclusion of such groups within the political decision-making structure through special measures.[16] Recommendation 11 brings in the local and regional level, which is important in building up minority political participation at a level of government below the national or central authorities, such as provinces, departments, districts, prefectures, municipalities, cities, and towns, whether they be units within a unitary state or constituent units of a federal state, including autonomous regions and other authorities. The consistent and equal enjoyment of all human rights means that entitlements enjoyed at the level of the central government should also be enjoyed at the regional and local levels.[17] Lastly, Recommendations 12 further spells out the rules on minority advisory and consultative mechanisms that the state may decide to set up in order to facilitate dialogue on relevant issue areas, thereby promoting participatory democracy. It is concerned with so-called

---

[14] R Kristof, *Finská iniciativa— návrh na ustavení Evropského romského fóra* ('Finnish initiative —proposal to establish European Roma Forum') (2004), available at <http://aa.ecn.cz/img_upload/ea85d6c87301f0a7507b0e8d7b873b63/erf.pdf> (accessed 31 July 2009); E Sobotka, 'Mobilising international norms: Issue actors, Roma and the state', unpublished PhD thesis, Lancaster University (2004). For more on ERTF see <http://www.coe.int/t/dg3/romatravellers/FERV/default_en.asp> (accessed 31 July 2009).

[15] For more information on Roma Summit see <http://ec.europa.eu/social/main.jsp?catId=88&langId=en&eventsId=105> (accessed 31 July 2009).

[16] Myntti, *A Commentary to the Lund Recommendations* (n 8 above), 11.   [17] Ibid, 28.

'participatory democracy'. According to the ideals of participatory democracy, all voices should be heard so that governments can govern in the interest of the population as a whole, including minority groups. Ideally, different groups should have their own representative or non-representative institutions; these institutions should receive subsidies from public funds if necessary, and should be consulted by the authorities prior to the adoption of any legislative or administrative measures that directly affect the relevant groups or the regions in which they live.

IV. Other Relevant Provisions in Universal and Regional Human Instruments

There have been provisions in universal and regional instruments, such as the UN system and the regional system of rights protection of the Council of Europe and political process of the OSCE, which are of relevance to Special Contact Mechanisms for Roma.

A. Organization for Security and Cooperation in Europe

As stated earlier, political processes within the OSCE were instrumental in setting and shaping the discussion concerning the need and content of SCMR. OSCE commitments, essentially political, are not legally binding, yet mechanisms of interaction within the OSCE, such as the OSCE Human Dimension for example, goes much further in linking human rights and the rights of national minorities with the institutional and political system of a state. The distinction is between 'legal' and 'political' and not between 'binding' and 'non-binding'. First, explicit concerns relating to the situation of Roma were raised in the Concluding Document of the Human Dimension meeting in Copenhagen on the 29 June 1990. Para 40 reads:

> The participating States clearly and unequivocally condemn totalitarianism, racial and ethnic hatred, anti-semitism, xenophobia and discrimination against anyone as well as persecution on religious and ideological grounds. In this context, they also recognise the particular problems of Roma (gypsies).[18]

The Copenhagen Document further specified that:

> among those elements of justice which are essential to the full expression of the inherent dignity and of the equal and inalienable rights of all human beings ... [belongs] the respect of the right of persons belonging to national minorities to effective participation

---

[18] Document of the Copenhagen Meeting of the Conference on the Human Dimension Meeting of the OSCE, OSCE/ ODIHR, 2001, 104, available at <http://www.osce.org/documents/odihr/1990/06/13992_en.pdf> (accessed 31 July 2009).

in public affairs, including participation in the affairs relating to the protection and promotion of the identity of such minorities.

At the OSCE Summit in Budapest in December 1994 (at which the CSCE became the OSCE), a decision was taken to create an office within ODIHR that would deal with the issue of Roma and Sinti and, more importantly, obtained a commitment from member states to provide sufficient resources. The Concluding Document dated 6 December 1994 reads:

> The participating States decide to appoint within the ODIHR a contact point for Roma and Sinti (Gypsies) issues. The ODIHR will be tasked to: act as a clearing-house for the exchange of information on the implementation of commitments pertaining to Roma and Sinti (Gypsies); facilitate contacts on Roma and Sinti (Gypsies) issues between participating States, international organisations and institutions and NGOs; maintain and develop contact on these issues between CSCE institutions and other international organisations and institutions. To fulfil this task, the ODIHR will make full use of existing resources. In this context they welcome the announcement made by some Roma and Sinti (Gypsies) organisations of their intention to make voluntary contributions. The participating States welcome the activities related to Roma and Sinti (Gypsies) issues in other international organisations and institutions, in particular those undertaken in the Council of Europe.[19]

During the ministerial meeting in Oslo in 1998, the Ministerial Council on Enhancement of the OSCE's Operational Capabilities issued a decision regarding Roma and Sinti, which de facto enhanced the role of the OSCE, declared that the Contact Point should deal solely with matters concerning Roma and Sinti, and finally tasked the Permanent Council with devising appropriate ways of ensuring that adequate resources were available to implement this decision.[20] In the Ministerial Council meeting in Bucharest in 2001, the parties agreed to Decision no 7 (MC(9) DEC/7 on continuing support of the Contact Point for Roma and Sinti, and tasked the ODIHR with:

> elaborat[ing] an Action Plan of targeted activities as mandated by the Istanbul Summit, as one of the ways the ability of the Contact Point can be strengthened to assist participating States in fulfilling their commitments to improve the situation of Roma and Sinti ...[21]

In the Resolution on Roma Education in the Berlin Declaration of the OSCE Parliamentary Assembly and Resolutions, adopted during the eleventh annual

---

[19] Budapest Concluding Document 1994, 'Towards a genuine partnership in a new era', available at <http://www.osce.org/documents/mcs/1994/12/4050_en.pdf> (accessed 31 July 2009).

[20] Seventh Meeting of the Ministerial Council, Declaration on Kosovo, 2–3 December 1998, Oslo, available at <http://www.osce.org/documents/mcs/1998/12/4168_en.pdf> (accessed 31 July 2009).

[21] Ninth Meeting of the Ministerial Council, Ministerial Declaration, 3 and 4 December 2001, available at <http://www.osce.org/documents/mcs/2001/12/4173_en.pdf> (accessed 31 July 2009).

session in Berlin on 10 July 2002, the parties agreed to develop anti-discrimination legislation and welcomed the Finnish initiative to set up a democratically elected European Roma Consultative Forum that would be able to articulate and transmit the voice of Romani individuals and communities.[22] For several years, the OSCE has tried to mobilize Roma participation during elections by running campaigns such as 'Roma, Use Your Ballot Wisely!' Last but not least, it has convened the meetings during which standards such as the Lund Recommendations in 1999 and the Warsaw Guidelines to Assist National Minority Participation in the Electoral Process in 2001 were drafted.

B. UN standards for the protection of minority rights for political participation

The Universal Declaration of Human Rights provides that the 'will of the people shall be the basis of the authority of the government', whereas the International Covenant on Civil and Political Rights (ICCPR) guarantees the right and opportunity, without distinction of any kind (such as race, colour, sex, language, religion, political or other opinion, national or social origin, property, birth, or other status), to take part in the conduct of public affairs, directly or through freely chosen representatives; to vote and be elected at genuine periodic elections by universal and equal suffrage, held by secret ballot; and to have access on general terms to equality to public service in one's country (Art 25). With regard to the exercise of the cultural rights protected under Art 27, the Committee has observed that the enjoyment of those rights may require positive legal measures of protection and measures to ensure the effective participation of members of minority communities in decisions which affect them.

Article 5 of the Convention on the Elimination of All Forms of Racial Discrimination (ICERD) obliges states to prohibit and to eliminate racial discrimination in all its forms and to guarantee the right of everyone to (among other rights) 'political rights, in particular the right to participate in elections—to vote and stand for election—on the basis of universal and equal suffrage; to take part in the government as well as in the conduct of public affairs at any level; and have equal access to public service'.

Article 2 of the UN Declaration on the Rights of Persons Belonging to National or Ethnic, Religious, or Linguistic Minorities states that:

(2) Persons belonging to minorities have the right to participate effectively in cultural, religious, social, economic and public life.

---

[22] See Berlin Declaration of the OSCE Parliamentary Assembly and Resolutions adopted during the 11th annual session Berlin, 10 July 2002, available at <http://new.oscepa.org/images/stories/documents/declarations/2002_-_berlin_declaration_-_english.2301.pdf> (accessed 31 July 2009). The Finnish Initiative later developed into the European Roma and Travellers Forum.

(3) Persons belonging to minorities have the right to participate effectively in decisions on the national and, where appropriate, regional level concerning the minority to which they belong or the regions in which they live, in a manner not incompatible with national legislation.
(4) Persons belonging to minorities have the right to establish and maintain their own associations.
(5) Persons belonging to minorities have the right to establish and maintain, without any discrimination, free and peaceful contacts with other members of their group and with persons belonging to other minorities, as well as contacts across frontiers with citizens of other States to whom they are related by national or ethnic, religious, or linguistic ties.

C. European Convention on Human Rights

When it comes to regional mechanisms, Art 3 of Protocol 1 to the European Convention on Human Rights specifies that the High Contracting Parties undertake 'to hold free elections at reasonable intervals by secret ballot, under conditions which will endure the free expression of the opinion of the people in the choice of legislature'. Interestingly, according to several rulings of the European Court of Human Rights (ECtHR), this Article guarantees electoral rights only with regard to the choice of legislature. Minority groups need to be able to participate effectively in cultural, religious, social, economic, and public life (Art 11 and Protocol 1, Art 3). Formal or de facto exclusion from participation in the political processes of the state is contrary to the democratic principles espoused by the Council of Europe. It is the essence of democracy to allow diverse political projects to be proposed and debated, even those that call into question the way a state is organized, providing they do not undermine democracy or human rights. Also, the ECtHR has held that if a state takes positive measures to enhance the status of a minority group (for example, with respect to their participation in the democratic process), the majority cannot claim discrimination based on such measures. In general, 'a balance must be achieved which ensures the fair and proper treatment of minorities and avoids any abuse of a dominant position'.[23] However, the ECtHR, has declared inadmissible complaints concerning the methods by which organs of local or regional communities are formed, which exercise no more than regulatory power delegated by parliament and so are ultimately subject to the supervision of the latter; examples include the municipal councils and councils of public social assistance in Belgium, and the county councils and district councils in the United Kingdom.

---

[23] ECtHR, *Thlimmenos v Greece*, Judgment of 6 March 2000.

D. Council of Europe

1. Framework Convention on the Rights of National Minorities

The Framework Convention on the Rights of National Minorities (FCNM) builds upon the 1990 Copenhagen Document of the OSCE by containing important innovations regarding substantive provisions for minorities, including the rights to self-identification, religious belief and practice, access to media, use of minority languages, use of minority names, learning of and in the mother tongue, effective participation in cultural, social, and economic life and in public affairs. To a large extent, the FCNM transformed the political commitments of the OSCE Copenhagen Document into legal obligations. The FCNM was adopted by the Committee of Ministers of the Council of Europe in 1994 and entered into force in 1998. The Committee of Ministers is tasked with monitoring the implementation of the FCNM, with the assistance of the Advisory Committee composed of independent expert members.[24] With regard to political participation, Arts 2(2) and 15 of FCNM stipulate that member states need to create the conditions necessary for the effective participation of persons belonging to national minorities in cultural, social, and economic life and in public affairs, in particular those affecting them. In May 2008 the Council of Europe's Advisory Committee on the Framework Convention for the Protection of National Minorities adopted a Commentary on the Effective Participation of Persons belonging to National Minorities in Cultural, Social, and Economic Life and in Public Affairs, pointing out that Roma and Travellers are often particularly underemployed in public administration and that this issue requires the specific attention from the authorities. Their employment in public administration can contribute to a better image and increased awareness of such minorities in society at large, which in turn is likely to improve their participation at all levels. Besides increasing focus on the participation of minorities in public life, it is worth noting some of the innovative approaches that have been adopted to make the FCNM a more powerful force in the effective implementation of minorities' rights.[25]

2. Council of Europe Roma-specific Recommendations

Council of Europe Recommendation 563 on the situation of Gypsies and other travellers in Europe of 1969, Recommendation 1203 on Gypsies in Europe of 1993, and Recommendation 1557 on the legal situation of Roma in Europe of

---

[24] See Resolution 97/10 of the Committee of Ministers of the Council of Europe, Rules Adopted by the Committee of Ministers on the Monitoring Arrangements Under Arts 24–6 of the Framework Convention, 17 September 1997.

[25] A Phillips, 'Monitoring human rights conventions: Can lessons be learnt from the New Council of Europe Framework Convention for the Protection of National Minorities' in RF Jorgensen and K Slavensky *Implementing Human Rights: Essays in honour of Morten Kjaerum* (2007), 349.

2002 were more instructive with regard to the political representation of Roma.[26] In particular, Recommendation 1557 stipulated that member states of the Council of Europe should encourage Roma to set up their own organizations and participate in the political system as voters, candidates, or members in national parliaments. At the same time, incentives should be provided to mainstream political parties to include Roma on their electoral lists, in electable positions. There were also specific guidelines for SCMR, while states were encouraged to devise and implement policies aiming at the full participation of Roma in public life at all levels of administration and to strengthen democratic Romani constituencies. Romani communities, organizations, and political parties should be given the full opportunity to take part in the process of elaborating, implementing, and monitoring programmes and policies aimed at improving their present situation.[27]

3. European Roma and Travellers Forum

The issue of the European Roma and Travellers Forum (ERTF),[28] as a body that represents Roma, was raised on a number of occasions and in various contexts, with the political support of the President of Finland. In 2001, President Tarja Halonen, in an address to the Parliamentary Assembly of the Council of Europe, proposed the setting up of a consultative assembly for the Roma at the European level. From 2001 until July 2004, several dozen meetings took place in Strasbourg, during which Roma and Traveller representatives negotiated with the Council of Europe over the creation of the ERTF, and a group of eminent personalities examined the added value of such initiatives. In July 2003, France and Finland made a common contribution to the GT-ROMS consideration.[29] These two countries considered that, although the need to promote the participation of Roma and Travellers had been recognized, discussions had shown that some delegations were hesitant to establish a forum, raising the issue that it might entail definitions of minority groups that were incompatible with domestic legislation.[30] They had therefore worked together to find a model that was acceptable to all the governments of the Council of Europe, as well as to Roma and Travellers. The model proposed was based on an independent

---

[26] For a full range of Roma specific Recommendations, please see the Recommendations and Resolution of the Council of Europe Committee of Ministers, available at <http://www.coe.int/t/dg3/romatravellers/documentation/recommendations/default_en.asp> (accessed 31 July 2009).
[27] Recommendation 1557(2002) on the Legal Situation of Roma in Europe, available at <http://www.coe.int/t/dg3/romatravellers/documentation/recommendations/parec1557(2002)_en.asp> (accessed 31 July 2009).
[28] Official website at <http://www.coe.int/t/dg3/romatravellers/FERV/default_en.asp> (accessed 31 July 2009).
[29] European Roma and Travellers Forum, Final Activity Report, Appendix III, available at <http://www.coe.int/t/dg3/romatravellers/FERV/cm2004179rapportfinal_en.asp> (accessed 31 July 2009).
[30] Kristof, *Finská iniciativa* (n 14 above); Sobotka, 'Mobilising international norms' (n 14 above).

consultative, international association, which would have regular cooperation and working relations with the Council of Europe. The ERTF was eventually registered in July 2004 as an association under French law, and in November 2004 the Council of Europe Committee of Ministers agreed to establish close and privileged relations with the ERTF through a Partnership Agreement which was signed on 15 December 2004.[31]

V. Special Contact Mechanisms for Roma in the Implementation Practice of States

As advised in Lund Recommendation 6, several states have established special representation of national minorities, for example through reserved seats in one or both chambers of parliament or in parliamentary committees, and other forms of guaranteed participation in the legislative process, such as parliamentary and other committees, which have at times served as SCMR.

A. Parliamentary representation as SCMR

The participation of Roma at the parliamentary level remains fairly modest throughout Europe. Yet, there are a few exceptions (Bulgaria, Hungary, Romania, Serbia, and 'the former Yugoslav Republic of Macedonia'). Only special arrangements (lower thresholds, reserved seats, etc) seem to be able to provide a minimum degree of representation. In Albania and Serbia, parties representing minority groups benefit from a lower electoral threshold, while the lower chambers of Germany and Poland remove the threshold completely. In Germany, legislation provides for the possibility that political parties defending minority interests to receive funding from a kin state.[32] Bosnia and Herzegovina, Croatia, Romania, and Slovenia have a system of reserved seats for representatives of minorities. In addition, the Constitutional Framework for Provisional Self-government of Kosovo provided for reserved seats for minorities in the Assembly. The current situation shows that it is only in Romania, Kosovo, and Croatia that a reserved seat in the national parliament is actually occupied by a Roma.[33]

---

[31] Partnership Agreement between the Council of Europe and the ERTF, available at <http://www.coe.int/t/dg3/romatravellers/FERV/partnershipagreementscan_en.pdf> (accessed 31 July 2009). [32] Roma, having no kin-state, cannot benefit from this provision.
[33] Under the electoral law, a seat is reserved in the Chamber of Deputies for a Roma organization (*Partida Romilor*) if it obtains at least 5 per cent of the average number of votes required for the election of an 'ordinary' MP. In Romania, non-governmental organizations representing national minorities may stand for election in order to enter parliament. Each national minority (except the Hungarian minority) may obtain only one seat, but the total number of representatives of minorities sitting in parliament is not restricted (it varies according to the number of minorities that obtain enough votes in the elections). In the Assembly of Kosovo, there are twenty seats

Parliamentary committees focusing specifically on Roma issues, such as the parliamentary committee for Kale (Gitanos) issues in Spain or the sub-committee on employment of Roma in Hungary, ceased to exist.[34] Yet, there are many parliamentary committees and subcommittees in Europe which are mandated to deal with minority issues, and can therefore be considered as having a potential role to play as a SCMR: human rights committees (and minority rights and/or religious affairs committees, etc) exist in Albania, Bulgaria, Croatia, the Czech Republic, Finland, Greece, Hungary, Ireland, Lithuania, Moldova, Romania, Slovakia, 'the former Yugoslav Republic of Macedonia', and Ukraine; an interethnic relations committee exists in Serbia; a justice and equality committees exists in Ireland; domestic affairs committees exist in Germany and Slovenia; social affairs committees exist in Greece and Latvia; legal affairs committees exist in Estonia, Germany, and Ireland; education and cultural affairs committees exist in Estonia and Latvia; and a migration and integration committee exists in Denmark. In practice, where members of the Roma community have been elected to parliament, they tend to sit on these committees (Bulgaria, Hungary, Serbia, 'the former Yugoslav Republic of Macedonia') or even to chair them (Romania). In Croatia, for example, a Roma representative (not an elected MP) sits on the Subcommittee for National Minority Rights of the Parliamentary Committee for Human Rights and National Minority Rights. Likewise, in Slovakia, there is an advisory body on the rights of the Roma minority, whose members are not parliamentarians; this body advises the Parliamentary Committee on Human Rights. In Bosnia and Herzegovina, the Law on Protection of National Minority Rights provides for the establishment of National Minority Councils, including a Roma representative, responsible, inter alia, for working in close cooperation with the

---

reserved for different minorities. Representatives of the Roma, Ashkali, and Egyptians are entitled to four of these seats. At the moment, all the seats are occupied by members of these communities. In Croatia, national minorities have been entitled to reserved seats in the single-chamber parliament since 1992. The Roma were elected for the first time into the Croatian parliament (*Sabor*) in November 2007. Following changes to the law on parliamentary elections in 2003, the minorities, including the Roma, are permitted to elect a total of eight members of the Croatian parliament. There are eight seats reserved for twenty-two minorities. One minority can elect three representatives (Serbs), two minorities one representative each (Hungarians and Italians), and nineteen other minorities may together elect three representatives according to certain groupings. Roma belong to a group of twelve minorities entitled to elect one deputy. Since the Roma community is the largest of the group of twelve minorities, in principle it has a real chance of electing a representative. However, where there are a number of candidates from the same minority (which was often the case for Roma), the chance of electing an MP from that minority is smaller.

[34] In 1999 Spain experimented with a parliamentary subcommittee which looked specifically into Kale (Gitanos) issues (under the authority of the Committee on Social Employment Policy); this committee no longer meets. Regional parliaments (in Andalusia, Aragon, Catalonia, and Murcia) have tabled or indeed adopted a number of parliamentary motions concerning Kale (Gitanos). Likewise, in Hungary, there used to be a subcommittee dealing specifically with the employment of Roma (Cigany) under the authority of the Committee on Employment Issues but it stopped functioning in 2006. Currently, at least one subcommittee dealing with integration and equal opportunities at schools is concentrating on Roma issues.

parliaments of the entities. In September 2007, the Committee on Interethnic Relations of the Serbian Parliament formed a new subcommittee for considering and improving situation of Roma and on the Decade of Roma Inclusion 2005–15. This subcommittee is meant to function as a body that will take care of realizing the Decade of Roma Inclusion goals and other issues important for improving the situation of Roma, their social emancipation and integration. In countries with a federal structure such as Germany, the committees of each *Länder* parliament responsible for dealing with Roma issues are those in charge of monitoring the affairs of the ministry with a central role in the defence of national minorities. This varies from one *Länder* to another.

In some countries, there is also the possibility of appointing representatives of minorities or religious groups as observers in parliament with an advisory function in religious and educational matters, but this does not appear to concern Roma. In Cyprus, 'minorities' are defined as religious groups who have been asked to choose between membership of the Greek community or the Turkish community in order to make the Constitution applicable. It appears that the Roma have not been recognized as a fully fledged religious group, but that 'because of their religion (Muslim) [they are] considered as members of the Turkish-Cypriot community'. An alternative solution for involving Roma in parliamentary consultation is to hold parliamentary hearings, to which Roma representatives are invited if the topics under discussion affect them. This system is practised in Finland.

B. Advisory bodies and consultative bodies

Lund Recommendations 12 and 13 spell out the rules on minority advisory and consultative mechanisms. Forms of these advisory mechanisms vary from a single Roma adviser—usually placed at the level of the ministries—to expert committees that advise governments on policy-making on issues of relevance to Roma, eg human rights, social inclusion, minorities, and, specifically, the situation of Roma.

1. *Roma Advisers*

Posts for Roma advisers currently exist at the ministerial level in eight countries. They are usually appointed by the ministries on the basis of merit with a view to providing the ministry in question with expert advice on Roma issues; in some instances, this advisory function might even extend to the cabinet or the presidency. In Bosnia and Herzegovina there is a Roma adviser at the cantonal level in Tuzla. In the Czech Republic, Roma advisers are established at the Ministry of the Interior; the Ministry of Education, Youth and Sport; and the Ministry of Labour and Social Affairs. Three Roma officials work in the Human Rights Department of the government bureau. In Finland, there is a Secretary General of the Advisory Board on Romani Affairs in the Ministry of Social Affairs and

Health, cultural secretaries in the Romany Educational Unit in the National Board of Education, and Roma advisers to the Ministry of Foreign Affairs. In Hungary, there is a state secretary for Roma issues who heads the Office for Roma Affairs under the authority of the Minister without Portfolio for equal opportunities. There is also a Roma ministerial commissioner in the Ministry of Education and Roma desk officers in the Ministries of Education; National Cultural Heritage; the Interior; Information and Communication; Defence; Economic Affairs; Employment; Health, Social, and Family Affairs; Agriculture and Rural Development; the Environment; and the Office for National and Ethnic Minorities. In Romania, there are several advisers in place: the Under-Secretary of State heading the National Office for Roma under the Department for Interethnic Relations in the Prime Minister's office, the Roma adviser to the president of the Republic and adviser within the Prime Minister's office, and the Roma adviser at the Ministry of Culture and Religious Affairs. In Slovakia, the Plenipotentiary of the Government of the Slovak Republic for Roma Communities works closely with a Roma adviser to the minister of the interior. In Slovenia, there is a Roma officer in the Ministry of Culture. In the former Yugoslav Republic of Macedonia there is a Roma adviser at the Ministry of Education and Science and an adviser/translator in parliament. In Croatia, the national programme for Roma, which was approved in October 2003, includes posts earmarked for Roma within the Ministry of the Interior and provides for Roma advisors within public administration and local self-government.

2. Roma Advisory Bodies

Advisory and consultative bodies can be permanent or ad hoc, part of or attached to the legislative or executive branch, or independent from both. Aside from advice and counsel, they can offer special expertise and constitute a useful intermediary institution between decision-makers and minority groups at all levels of government, including self-government arrangements.[35] At times, they are also in charge of implementing Roma-specific national or regional programmes.[36] In most European countries there is at least one ministry which is

---

[35] The Lund Recommendations 1999, Explanatory Note, II. D. 12.
[36] Albania: a government strategy for improving the Roma minority's living conditions was in the process of being adopted (2003); Belgium: in the Walloon region, guidelines for the reception of Travellers were issued in February 2000; Bosnia and Herzegovina: on 14 November 2002, the Framework Work Programme of the Committee for Roma (body within the Council of Ministers) for the period 2002–6 was adopted and serves provisionally as a medium-term national programme for Roma; Croatia: national programme for Roma was adopted on 16 October 2003; Czech Republic: the concept of political integration of Roma at the national level was adopted on 14 June 2000, and revised in 2002 and 2003; some regions have adopted their own political integration concepts; Finland: Strategies under the Policy for Roma were published in 1999, followed by a working group memorandum published in 2001; Hungary: a package of medium-term measures

mandated to deal with Roma issues, and which therefore plays a more active internal role as an SCMR.

In Albania, the interministerial commission under the Deputy Minister for Labour and Social Affairs includes Roma representatives appointed from a network of Roma organizations. In Bosnia and Herzegovina, the Committee for the Roma within the Council of Ministers, composed of eighteen members, including nine Roma representatives, was appointed in July 2002 at the proposal of the twenty-one Roma NGOs in existence at the time. The Committee is chaired by a Rom.

In Croatia, the Committee for Monitoring the Implementation of the National Programme for Roma, chaired by the Deputy Minister for Social Affairs and Human Rights, is made up of representatives of the relevant ministries and governmental bodies, representatives of the two regions with the largest Roma communities, a representative of a human rights non-governmental organization (NGO) and seven Roma representatives drawn from Roma councils at the local and regional levels and from Roma associations.

In the Czech Republic, there are three councils that are directly involved in monitoring the concept of Roma integration; they are the Council for Human Rights, the Council for National Minorities, and, above all, the Council for Roma Community Affairs. The latter is made up of representatives of the relevant ministries and fourteen Roma representatives (from each of the country's fourteen regions), appointed by the Deputy Minister for Research and Development,

---

for improving Roma living conditions was adopted in 1997, amended in 1999 and 2001 (accompanied each year by an action plan), and a new package of measures was drawn up in 2003; Ireland: several theme-based strategies, ie the National Travellers' Health Strategy 2003–5, were launched in February 2002, and the Traveller Education Strategy was scheduled for the end of 2004—moreover, the Housing (Traveller Accommodation) Act of 1988 provides for specific measures concerning Travellers' accommodation; Lithuania: a government programme for the integration of Roma for the period 2000–4 was issued on 1 July 2000 (the initial phase covered the central regions, but was to be extended to the entire country in 2005–9); Moldova: the government took a decision on 16 February 2001 on measures in support of Moldova's Roma population for 2001–10 (the framing of a national programme for Roma is currently under discussion); Poland: a pilot government programme for the Roma community of the province of Malopolska, for the period 2001–3, was adopted on 13 February 2001 and was to be extended to the entire country in 2004; Romania: a Romanian government strategy for improving the situation of Roma was adopted on 25 April 2001 for the period 2001–10, together with an action plan to implement it covering the period 2001–4; Slovak Republic: the first national-level stage of a government strategy for the solution of the Roma national minority's problems, and a set of measures for implementing it, was adopted in September 1999, and a second stage for regional and local levels was adopted in May 2000 (the basic theses of the policy conception of the government of the Slovak Republic on the integration of Roma communities was adopted in April 2003); Slovenia: a programme of measures to assist Roma was adopted on 30 November 1995 (with additional measures adopted on 1 July 1999); Spain: the Gypsies Development Programme was adopted on 3 October 1989; Ukraine: a regional programme (*Zakarpattia*), 'Roma population for the period 2003–2006', was adopted on 25 September 2002. In Italy there is no national programme, but several regions have drafted specific laws protecting the 'Roma', 'Sinti', 'Gypsies', or 'Travellers' (according to the term used in each region). Other countries (Luxembourg) address these issues in accordance with Art 13 of the Treaty of European Union on discrimination on grounds of ethnic origin.

human resources, and human rights. Half of these representatives are NGO activists, and the other half are local Roma government officials. All are entitled to vote (in the same way as the deputy ministers representing the ministries). Three Roma also sit on the Council for National Minorities (they are appointed by the government on a proposal from Roma organizations). The Government Commissioner for Human Rights is required to submit regular progress reports on implementation of the political integration concept.

In Hungary, the Interdepartmental Committee, chaired by the Minister without Portfolio for equal opportunities, with, as vice-chair, the State Secretary for Roma Issues. The president of the National Roma Self-government, the secretary of the Council for Roma Affairs, the minorities ombudsman, and the public foundations in charge of Roma issues all participate in the work of the committee as permanent guests. In addition to the above-mentioned interdepartmental committee an Advisory Council for Roma Issues was set up in 2002. It has twenty-one members, including the president of the National Roma Self-government, the State Secretary for Roma Issues and Roma, and non-Roma public figures. The council is chaired by the Prime Minister.

In Ireland, representatives of Travellers' organizations participate (along with representatives of the relevant ministries) in the work of four committees:

a) the interdepartmental committee responsible for monitoring implementation of the recommendations of the Task Force on the Travelling Community, set up in 1995
b) the Advisory Committee on Traveller Education set up in 1998
c) the Traveller Health Advisory Committee (THAC), also set up in 1998
d) the National Traveller Accommodation Consultative Committee, set up in April 1999, and the Local Traveller Accommodation Consultative Committees.

Moreover, there is a group of senior officials on social inclusion, consisting of the relevant ministers, which sometimes deals with Traveller-related issues.

In Lithuania, there is an interdepartmental commission responsible for implementing the Roma Integration Programme (it includes representatives of the main Roma NGOs). In Poland, the Committee for Roma Issues is open to Roma representatives. In Romania, the Joint Committee (Interministerial) for Implementing and Monitoring the National Strategy on Roma is chaired by the Roma advisor to the prime minister. In Slovakia, the Inter-sectoral Commission for Roma Community Affairs advises the government on Roma issues, and is similar to the Slovenian Interdepartmental Committee for the Protection of the Roma Ethnic Community. In Spain, there is an Advisory Commission for Monitoring the Gypsies Development Programme, composed of representatives of the Ministry of Labour and Social Affairs, of the Autonomous Communities and of regional federations of Gypsy associations.

Although they have no national programme for the Roma, several countries have established joint committees to deal with Roma issues specifically. In

Sweden, a Council for Roma Issues has been set up; its members include sixteen representatives of Roma organizations. It also includes various government bodies and is chaired by the Minister for Minority Issues. However, the appointment of the Roma members, who are proposed by Roma organizations, can be vetoed by the minister. In Finland, the Advisory Board on Romani Affairs in the Ministry of Social Affairs and Health is appointed by the government. It has a maximum of eighteen members, half of whom are Roma representatives. The other half is composed of representatives of various ministries. The general secretary is of Roma origin. In France, a National Advisory Commission for Travellers was set up in August 1999 and includes a ten-member college of Travellers. In Belgium, in the Walloon region, a Mediation Centre for Travellers was set up in September 2001; it includes Travellers' associations and is responsible for public information and for mediating in disputes. In Ireland, the Traveller Monitoring Group organized by the Department of Justice, Equality, and Law Reform is responsible for monitoring progress made on Traveller-related policies. The NGO Pavee Point Traveller Centre is represented on this group, but Roma representatives are not. Lastly, there are other types of ministerial commissions or governmental councils for minorities as a whole, which in principle include Roma or Traveller representatives.

C. Arrangements at regional and local levels

As advised in Lund Recommendation 11, the consistent, equal, and universal enjoyment of all human rights means that the entitlements enjoyed at the central government level should also be enjoyed at all lower levels of government, even though the criteria used to create structures at the lower levels may be different. Different needs or desires may be accommodated with variations on a general scheme through the establishment of asymmetrical structures.[37]

Concrete measures to improve the participation of minorities in public life at the local level have been amply demonstrated by the Hungarian example. Local government duties include minority protection and the enforcement of minority rights in their respective settlements and at the county level. As most public services are delivered at the local level, local public administrations play a major role in distributing resources and providing equal access to public services. Furthermore, local governments are responsible for cooperating with elected minority self-governments (MSG).[38] According to the Act on Local Governments, candidates can run as minority representatives for seats in the local

---

[37] The Lund Recommendations 1999, explanatory note, II.C.11.
[38] The rules for this cooperation are spelled out in the Law on Local Government and the Minority Act. However, due to the unequal distribution of power and financial dependence of MSGs, the level of participation of minorities in local policymaking really depends on the goodwill of the local authorities.

government.³⁹ Slovenia assures autochthonous minorities seats on municipal councils in areas where they are sufficiently numerous. Some Roma candidates are elected at municipal and/or regional level.

In Hungary, four Roma have been elected to the position of mayor and there are 545 Roma representatives in local authorities. In Slovakia, 158 Roma parliamentarians (out of 756 Roma candidates) and ten Roma mayors have been elected to local self-government (out of twenty-one Roma candidates for the office of mayor in towns and villages). In Slovenia, three laws were amended in 2002 to enable Roma to participate in local affairs. Roma now have the right to elect a councillor in twenty municipalities. Accordingly, the Slovenian Constitutional Court stated that 'it is not in conflict with the Constitution if a municipal statute determines that the autochthonous minority [ie, Italians] is directly represented in the council of a local community'. For the Constitutional Court, it is unconstitutional that a local community council who resigns is automatically replaced by the candidate who was second in the elections. Concerning the prohibition of a Roma candidate to stand for municipal elections in the Slovenian municipality of Novo Mesto, the Constitutional Court stated that the municipal statute was unconstitutional for not including the Roma among the autochthonous communities, since they are entitled to a constitutional right to be represented in the municipal council.⁴⁰

In Finland, advisory boards on Romani affairs were made permanent in four provinces by government decree at the beginning of 2004. Their mode of operation and membership are identical to those of the national board (see above). Some of these boards employ Roma secretaries. In Romania, county offices on Roma are placed under the authority of the Ministerial Commission on Roma under the Ministry of Local Administration; they are responsible for implementing the strategy at local level. At least one of the three or four people employed by these offices must be of Roma origin (forty-two regions altogether). There are also posts of local experts on Roma affairs in the municipalities, but these duties are combined with the existing duties of municipal officials and accordingly do not guarantee membership of the Roma community. In the Czech Republic there are Roma advisers at the level of each region. In Denmark, Roma issues are addressed at the local level, where necessary, through integration councils. In Ireland, a liaison office for Traveller accommodation in Galway belongs to the Traveller community. Moreover, the Public Service Commission,

---

[39] In 1998 a total of 1,055 minority deputies were elected, most of them belonging to the two largest groups (the Roma and German minorities). J Kaltenbach, 'From paper to practice in Hungary: The protection and involvement of minorities in governance' in A-M Bíró and P Kovács (eds) *Diversity in Action: Local public management of multi-ethnic communities in central and Eastern Europe* (2001), 181.
[40] Slovenian Const Court, U-I-416/98-38 of 22 March 2001. Only 40 per cent of the Roma population in Slovenia is considered autochthonous, and only one representative of that group was elected.

liaising with Traveller organizations, is currently studying solutions to promote recruitment of Travellers into the civil service.

VI. Concluding Remarks: Overall Assessment of the Effectiveness of Special Contact Mechanisms for Roma

The aim of effective political participation is to interrupt the dominance of one nation or group over another through the adoption of an inclusive approach and by according minorities a fair chance for their interests to be heard, considered and taken into account.[41] While there has been an increase of Romani participation in formal political communities at different levels, both at the local level and in representative organs of government and international institutions, the effectiveness of participation remains unsatisfactory due to the fact that, proportionally, Roma remain largely underrepresented. SCMR therefore continue to play a significant role in facilitating Roma inclusion.

The monitoring bodies of the Council of Europe, such as the Advisory Committee on the FCNM, concluded in many of its state monitoring reports that the situation of the Roma is still a matter for concern, both in terms of their equality and their effective participation in public life.[42] In the view of the Commissioner for Human Rights of the Council of Europe, proactive measures are absolutely necessary.[43] By way of example, reserved seats for Roma representatives in national or local assemblies have been tried in Bosnia and Herzegovina, Croatia, Romania, and Slovenia with largely positive results. In Slovenia, the practice of reserving one seat in local assemblies had created a channel in some municipalities between the Roma communities and the authorities. Another example of good practice is to have various consultative bodies for Roma affairs, or for general minority issues with Roma inclusion, at the government or ministry level. This type of solution is especially important in countries with dispersed and numerically small Romani populations like Finland, the Czech Republic, or Poland.

Advisory bodies on Roma policy-making are heavily influenced by the cultural and institutional attributes of each country. They can transform into bodies operating further down at the level of regions or districts, and the future

---

[41] F Palermo and J Woelk, *No Representation without Recognition: The right to political participation of national minorities* (2003).

[42] The Advisory Committee is the independent expert committee responsible for evaluating the implementation of the Framework Convention in states parties and advising the Committee of Ministers. The outputs of this evaluation are detailed country-specific opinions adopted after a monitoring procedure. This procedure involves the examination of state reports and other sources of information as well as on-the-spot meetings with government interlocutors, national minority representatives and other relevant actors.

[43] See Commissioner for Human Rights, 'Roma representatives must be welcomed into political decision-making', 1 September 2008, available at <http://www.coe.int/t/commissioner/Viewpoints/080901_en.asp> (accessed 31 July 2009).

involvement of local Roma and local administration staff is necessary if human rights implementation is to be improved. Roma participation will not be successful at the national level unless it is also encouraged in the municipalities and taken as a prerequisite of cohesive communities, where human rights are enjoyed by all. It seems that more structured genuine and meaningful consultation on concrete problems is needed, for instance in the municipalities between the local authorities and the Roma population. While human rights instruments such as ICERD or FCNM have demonstrated their potential to examine in detail how various SCMR function and how they could be enhanced to increase implementation of the respective provisions on political participation of minorities, it would be worthwhile to evaluate how much of a difference they have made in enhancing the political participation of Roma and what lessons can be learnt. At a very minimum, their recommendations and the results of monitoring of political participation need to be better considered by implementing authorities. With regard to supranational SCMR, such as the European Roma and Travellers Forum, it is still too soon to subject their functioning to rigorous evaluation.

19

Participation in Social and Economic Life

Kristin Henrard

I.	Introduction (and Overview)	525
II.	Participation in Social and Economic Life: The Scope	527
	A. Participation	527
	B. Participation in economic and social life	529
	C. The equality prism	529
	D. Elements of participation in social and economic life	530
	E. Definition of minorities	532
	F. Lund Recommendations on the Effective Participation of National Minorities in Public Life (OSCE)	533
	G. Framework Convention for the Protection of National Minorities	535
	H. Requirements for anti-discrimination legislation	539
III.	General Trend: Increasingly More Detailed Assessments	542
	A. Trends regarding (un)employment	543
	B. Trends regarding education	544
	C. Trends regarding access to health care	547
	D. Trends regarding access to housing	547
	E. Trends regarding access to social services/public services/ public facilities/ basic facilities (water, electricity etc)	548
	F. Special attention for Roma	548
	G. Instrumental issues	549
	H. Governments' response?	551
IV.	Other Relevant Universal and Regional Instruments and Supervisory Practice	553
	A. United Nations	553
	B. Regional instruments	568
	C. European Union documents	574
V.	Other Actors	583
	A. UN: UNIEMI and the Forum on Minority Issues	583
	B. International Labour Organization	585
	C. Organisation of Economic Co-operation and Development (OECD): Development Assistance Committee (DAC)	585
	D. MRG: Minority Rights Group International	586
VI.	Evaluation	586

I. Introduction (and Overview)

Minority-specific instruments tend to focus on issues related to the separate identity of minority groups, for example identity features such as language or religion, or on mechanisms for passing on that separate identity, like education. Consequently, problems relating to minorities are often identified within this same domain, for example, mother tongue education, separate minority schools, or the right to speak one's language in relation to public authorities etc.

In sharp contrast, there are hardly any standards that deal explicitly with socio-economic opportunities for minorities. At the same time, it is hard not to see that minority status is intrinsically connected to a disadvantaged socio-economic position, often related to (systemic) discrimination in these domains, and resultant problematic integration. These dismal circumstances may be glaring in the case of some minorities, such as the Roma, and in relation to several immigrant population groups or new minorities. Incidents with these population groups have also shown that inequality and socio-economic disadvantage may lead to social unrest.[1]

When tying this into the overarching principles of minority protection, the fundamental equality principle and prohibition of discrimination, as well as the theme of integration, also come immediately to mind. The right to identity does not seem to feature prominently here, and thus neither does the 'integration without forced assimilation' credo. However, as we will see, there are definitely both (some) direct and (mostly) indirect connections between participation in social and economic life on the one hand and the right to identity

---

[1] UNIEMI, Thematic Priorities, 1, available at <http://www2.ohchr.org/english/issues/minorities/expert/objectives.htm> (accessed 10 September 2009). See also Human Rights Council Resolution 7/7, Mandate of the independent expert on minority issues, 3rd preambular paragraph. See also Veenman who underscores that 'labour market participation is a manifestation of formal bonding, and as such, can contribute to a joint definition of the situation of those who take part in this bonding ... conversely, ... limited participation on the labour market can threaten social cohesion. ... Limited labour market participation implies a lack of reciprocity, which puts social cohesion under pressure' (J Veenman, 'Social cohesion, social integration and labour market exclusion' (2003–4) *European Yearbook on Minority Issues* 279–80, 275). Cf Jonathan Wheatley who underscores that 'unequal access to employment, education, health and housing has ... undermined political and economic stability in regions as diverse as the Balkans, Northern Ireland, South Tyrol and Cyprus' and that 'economic under-development and especially the economic marginalization of a particular identity group increase the likelihood of inter-ethnic conflict' (J Wheatley, 'The economic dimension of minority participation in Europe', ECMI Issue Brief 15, available at <http://www.ecmi.de/download/brief_15.pdf> (accessed 31 July 2009), 3–4). The UN press release of 10 December 2008 entitled '"Economic, social and cultural rights: Legal entitlements rather than charity" say UN human rights experts' also emphasizes that 'widespread violations of economic, social and cultural rights are often root causes of social unrest and conflict', available at <http://www.unhchr.ch/huricane/huricane.nsf/0/C5486C42747EC60BC125751B005B08B3?opendocument> (accessed 31 July 2009), 2.

on the other hand.² In other words, adequate protection of minorities (and potential problems relating to minorities) is also concerned with questions of socio-economic opportunity, and thus with participation in social and economic life.

This brings me to the theme of this book: political participation as a foundational issue for adequate minority protection (and the review of relevant international standards and practice). Indeed, when discussing participatory rights for persons belonging to minorities, a lot of attention is accorded to the various dimensions of political participation. Nevertheless, the editors agreed to include a contribution on participation in social and economic life, which would highlight the links with political participation. It can be argued in any event that the economic empowerment of minorities, and the concomitant reduction of economic inequality, leads to increased participation of minorities in public life.³

Of course, the relevant minority-specific standards do have cursory references to this dimension of participation. There is however no detailed enumeration of relevant themes, nor of standards of assessment in this respect. In other words there are no explicit standards concerning access to housing, land, natural resources, food, health, and a healthy environment for persons belonging to minorities.⁴ While the same may seem to be true for political participation, several themes and sub-requirements have in fact crystallized over recent years, and can be found, inter alia, in the Lund Recommendations on the Effective Participation of Minorities in Public Life, developed by the High Commissioner on National Minorities (HCNM) of the Organization for Security and Cooperation in Europe (OSCE), and the Commentary on the Effective Participation of Persons belonging to National Minorities in Cultural, Social, and Economic Life and in Public Affairs put forward by the Advisory Committee (AC) of the Framework Convention on National Minorities (FCNM) (the central reference points for this edited volume).

In any case, in view of the paucity of explicit standards delineating the terms of minority participation in social and economic life, developments in this area are contingent on the interpretation of other norms, such as related minority-specific standards, as well as general human rights.

This chapter will investigate the extent to which issues of participation in social and economic life are taken up in the supervisory practice of general

---

² See below: the direct link with the right to identity is present where indigenous people are obstructed to engage in and/or benefit from their traditional economic activities because of exploitation activities by or supported by the government. These economic activities are intrinsically related to their own culture and identity. A more indirect link is the necessity of having a basic level of living conditions to be able to invest energy in the maintenance and promotion of a particular ethnic identity.   ³ Wheatley, 'The economic dimension' (n 1 above), 4.
⁴ M E Salomon, 'Socio-economic rights as minority rights' in M Weller (ed), *Universal Minority Rights: A commentary on the jurisprudence of international courts and treaty bodies* (2007), 431.

human rights and minority rights standards. A first definitional section (including thoughts on the concepts of 'participation', 'participation in social and economic life' and 'minorities') also contains some basic theoretical considerations on equality, non-discrimination and minorities. In line with the rest of the book, the rest of the chapter is an analysis of what can be gleaned from the Lund Recommendations and the practice of the AC of the FCNM, as captured by the Commentary. In addition to the Commentary, the (complete set of) AC opinions are also examined for reference to participation in social and economic life. Government reactions to the Lund Recommendations, as well as the practical constructive dialogue approach of the AC (as emanating from the second-cycle opinions), are also analysed.

Other global and regional instruments are then reviewed for a greater understanding of advisory practice. At the UN level, minority-specific standards and related practice are assessed, followed by supervision by the relevant UN treaty bodies. At the regional level, the three regional human rights conventions are discussed, as well as the European Social Charter in the Council of Europe, and the various instruments of the European Union. The concluding comments are preceded by a succinct overview of relevant activities undertaken by 'other actors' (bodies and organizations that are not established by an instrument for its supervision) like the United Nations (UN) Independent Expert on Minority Issues (IEMI), the International Labour Organization (ILO), and Minority Rights Group (MRG).

II. Participation in Social and Economic Life: The Scope

A. Participation

The lack of a generally agreed upon, let alone legal, definition of the concept 'participation' does not make it impossible to indicate that it is potentially very far-reaching. The Lund Recommendations already reveal the broad range of issues that can be included: consultation, representation, self-governance, all serve as container concepts for a myriad of different matters. Arguably, the emphasis of these concepts is on political participation. And as the focus of the present volume confirms, the emphasis on participatory rights in academic writing rests indeed on participation in public (read, political) life. Nevertheless, as will be explained more fully below, the existing standards pertaining to participation for persons belonging to minorities do not only cover participation 'in public life' and 'in public affairs', but also mention 'participation in cultural, religious, social, and economic life'. Participation in the latter dimensions of 'societal life' is arguably concerned with related and sometimes overlapping, but generally distinct issues, to those addressed by political participation.

Participation, and particularly political participation, is in any event of central importance to minority protection.[5] It has often been emphasized that political participation is a foundational value for adequate minority protection, in the sense that it is an essential instrument of minority protection. This rather instrumental reading of political participation underlines its contribution to the protection and promotion of other group interests, in the sense that it is important for the actual enforcement and realization of these other rights.[6]

The Commentary by the AC of the FCNM also confirms this foundational understanding of effective participation[7] by underscoring that the lack of participation in public life can lead in turn to the exclusion of all sorts of rights and benefits,[8] including those pertaining to the economic and social domain. This idea that effective enjoyment of minority rights requires effective participation is also reflected in the Human Rights Committee's General Comment 23(50) on Art 27 of the International Covenant on Civil and Political Rights (ICCPR) (para 7). While it is only mentioned in relation to cultural rights, the reasoning is arguably more broadly applicable.[9]

The importance of involving persons belonging to minorities in the decision-making process and in the taking of decisions is also relevant to participation in economic and social life. It is debatable whether such consultation, and the related right to be taken seriously, is a component of political participation or is (also) a procedural aspect of participation in economic life.[10] In any event, the central importance of consultation, and even more active involvement of minorities in relation to policies of (direct or indirect) relevance to them, can be

---

[5] In the words of Alan Phillips, 'participation is a foundation right' (A Phillips, 'The Framework Convention for the Protection of National Minorities and the Protection of Economic Rights of Minorities', (2003–4) *European Yearbook on Minority Issues* 287–306, 288.

[6] F Bieber, *Balancing Political Participation and Minority Rights: The experience of the former Yugoslavia* (2002–3), 2–3, available at <http://pdc.ceu.hu/archive/00001819/01/Bieber.pdf> (accessed 31 July 2009); K Henrard, *Devising an Adequate System of Minority Protection: Individual human rights, minority rights and the right to self-determination* (2000), 271–2. See also P Thornberry, 'Images of autonomy and individual and collective rights in international instruments on the rights of minorities' in M Suksi (ed), *Autonomy: Implications and applications* (1998), 110.

[7] AC, Commentary on the Effective Participation of Persons Belonging to National Minorities in Cultural, Social, and Economic Life and in Public Affairs (ACFC/31DOC(2008)001), 9. See also M Weller, 'Report: A critical evaluation of the first results of the monitoring of the Framework Convention on the Issue of Effective Participation of Persons belonging to National Minorities' in *Filling the Frame: Five years of monitoring the FCNM* (2004), 71.

[8] S Holt, 'The Lund Recommendations in the activities of the HCNM' (2005) 12(2–3) *IJMGR* 169–88, 178.

[9] A Verstichel, 'Recent developments in the UN Human Rights Committee's approach to minorities, with a focus on effective participation' (2005) 12(1) *IJMGR* 25–42, 30.

[10] See also Salomon, 'Socio-economic rights' (n 4 above), 439–40. For an excellent overview in terms of jurisprudence of the HRC, the ILO Convention no 169 on Indigenous and Tribal Peoples and the Recommendation on Indigenous Peoples by the UN Committee on the Elimination of Racial Discrimination, see Salomon, 'Socio-economic rights' (n 4 above), 440–1.

explained by its double effect of enhancing minority *integration* while strengthening their *identity*.[11]

B. Participation in economic and social life

While some of the typical aspects of political participation are also relevant to participation in economic and social life—for example, the question of consultation, minority involvement and 'ownership' of the policies designed to enhance participation—participation in economic and social life has a distinctive signature. Even when it has been argued (inter alia in the Explanatory Report to Art 15 of the FCNM) in relation to participatory rights more generally that the goal of effective participation is full or real equality,[12] participation in economic and social life brings us, again through the prism of the equality principle, to the realm of economic and social rights (including particular interpretations of civil and political rights); rights which the indivisibility paradigm claims are equally as important as, and interwoven with, civil and political rights.[13]

C. The equality prism

As the equality principle is central to the following argumentation, it seems sensible to dwell a little longer on its precise meaning and implications (in relation to minority protection).[14]

An important distinction is between formal equality (or equality as consistency), which sets out to treat everybody in exactly the same way, on the one hand, and substantive or real or full equality on the other. Substantive or real equality acknowledges differences in starting positions and might necessitate formal unequal treatment, resulting in the so-called 'paradox of the equality principle'.

Although the equality principle has several dimensions—including the prohibition of discrimination, equality before the law, equal protection of the law, positive action (affirmative action, positive discrimination)—the prohibition of discrimination is the central focus point of legal provisions and academic writing on equality. Positive action also attracts considerable attention, but even this is intrinsically related to the prohibition of discrimination.

The prohibition of discrimination does not prohibit all differences in treatment; it only prohibits differences in treatment for which there is no reasonable

---

[11] Opinion on Moldova, ACFC/INF/OP/I(2003)002, 1 March 2002, 39–40.
[12] Weller, 'Report' (n 7 above), 72. Participation in economic and social life is predominantly concerned with the effective enjoyment of social and economic rights, or the 'social and economic benefits that flow from life within the state'.
[13] See also A Phillips, 'Commentary: Economic participation of national minorities' in *Filling the Frame: Five years of monitoring the FCNM* (2004), 109.
[14] For a more elaborate discussion of the relevant points, see, eg, K Henrard, *Equal Rights versus Special Rights: Minority protection and the prohibition of discrimination* (2007); and 'Equality of individuals', *Max Planck Encyclopedia on Public International Law* (2008).

and objective justification. This justification formula requires both a legitimate aim and a relationship of proportionality between that aim and the differential treatment. This formulation suggests that the prohibition of discrimination does entail the potential for accommodating substantive equality, which is simultaneously one of the foundational principles or *raisons d'être* of minority protection.

In this respect it is important to highlight the ways in which the prohibition of discrimination can embrace substantive equality. One important mechanism is the prohibition of indirect discrimination, which recognizes that seemingly neutral measures can nevertheless amount to discrimination when it affects a particular group disproportionately, without there being a reasonable and objective justification. A good and relevant example here would be the recognition that disproportionate demands (not justified by the nature of the job) as to proficiency in official language for jobs in the private or public service can amount to indirect racial discrimination.[15] Intent is obviously irrelevant in relation to indirect discrimination. Similarly, intent plays no role in so-called 'systemic' or 'institutionalized' discrimination, which flows from ingrained prejudices. The latter can manifest itself clearly at the level of personnel selectors, where cultural differences can trigger a rejection of an otherwise suitable candidate.[16]

A second opening towards substantive equality concerns the duty flowing from the prohibition of discrimination to take differential measures in relation to persons who find themselves in substantively different situations. This duty to take special measures is obviously particularly important for persons belonging to minorities, since they need their special circumstances to be taken into account.[17]

Thirdly, the relationship between positive action and the prohibition of discrimination needs to be clarified, not least because substantive equality also plays a role here. As positive action concerns differential treatment, its legitimacy is determined by the general criteria which distinguish prohibited discrimination from acceptable differential treatment: the need for a legitimate aim and compliance with the proportionality principle. Since the legitimate aim of positive action is substantive equality, the 'only' problem with positive action is its proportionality.

D. Elements of participation in social and economic life

When considering treaties on economic and social rights, the type of rights enshrined therein are those concerning, among other things, access to education, to employment, to housing, to health care, to social security, and to social services in general. It is common knowledge that persons belonging to minorities confront disproportionate problems in effectively accessing education (including quality

---

[15] Eg, B de Witte and E Horvath, 'The many faces of minority policy in the European Union' in K Henrard and R Dunbar (eds), *Synergies in Minority Protection* (2008), 365, 372.
[16] Veenman, 'Social cohesion' (n 1 above), 284–5.
[17] Venice Commission, '*Note de synthèse sur la participation des personnes appartenant à des minorités à la vie sociale*', CDL-MIN(97)3, 2–4.

and segregation), employment, and housing, due to existing prejudices combined with their particularly vulnerable situation.[18] Effective access or substantively equal access points to the need to take the specific characteristics and needs of minorities into consideration. For example, in the context of employment, this would have implications for working conditions, including equal opportunity for advancement.[19] Effective access to public services also has implications for the language of communication and the awareness among public authorities of the specific cultural needs of minorities. In this respect, employment of minorities in the public service is not merely an aspect of political participation but also one of effective participation in economic (it is a form of employment) and social (facilitating effective access to social services) life. In the words of Alan Phillips, 'the employment of minorities within public services can help ensure that service delivery is sensitive to the linguistic and cultural needs of a community, while showing a shared ownership of education, health care, social services'.[20]

The few explicit references in minority rights standards to participation in economic and social life are only elaborated in very general terms.[21] Hence, everything depends on the interpretation of these vague norms, as is the case more generally with human rights, of which minority rights is a component part. In view of the interrelation of social and economic rights, combined with non-discrimination and participation in social and economic life, it is indeed essential to take into account the interpretation of these rights as applied to minority situations.[22] At the same time, it should not be forgotten that the interpretation of civil and political rights has also touched on social and economic issues.[23] Furthermore reference can be made to the third-generation human right of development, which is not only closely related to the second-generation economic and social rights but is gaining increasing focus in relation to minorities.[24]

---

[18] T Bedard, *Participation in Economic Life: An advocacy guide for minorities in South-east Europe* (2005), 13.   [19] Ibid, 14.
[20] Phillips, 'Commentary' (n 13 above), 103.
[21] Art 2(2) of the UN Minorities Declaration and Art 15 of the FCNM.
[22] Bedard, *Participation in Economic Life* (n 18 above), 11–17. See also Henrard and Dunbar, *Synergies in Minority Protection* (n 15 above).
[23] See, eg, I Daugareilh, 'La Convention Européenne de sauvegarde des droits de l'homme et des libertés fondamentales et la protection sociale' (1991) 1 *Revue Trimestrielle des Droits de l'Homme* 123–37, 128–31; O De Schutter, 'The protection of social rights by the European Court of Human Rights' in P Van Der Auweraert et al (eds), *Social, Economic and Cultural Rights: An appraisal of current European and international developments* (2002) 207, 213–39.
[24] See below on the UNIEMI. See, eg, various publications of the Minority Rights Group International in this respect, including P Justino and J Litchfield, *Economic Exclusion and Discrimination: The experiences of minorities and indigenous peoples*; ME Salomon and A Sengupta, *The Right to Development: Obligations of states and the rights of minorities and indigenous peoples*; SC Janet, *Development, Minorities and Indigenous Peoples: A case study and evaluation of good practice*; R Riddell, *Minorities, Minority Rights and Development* (all available at <www.minorityrights.org>). See also the decision of the UN Working Group on Minorities in March 2004 to focus discussions on minorities and development (and action taken by governments for incorporating minority issues in activities to reach the Millennium Development Goals).

Finally, it is also important to mention that this economic and social dimension has an intrinsic link to culture and more obvious identity issues. Not only does a lack of participation in social and economic life, and economic marginalization, erode the ability of minorities to preserve their own way of life,[25] but traditional economic activities are accepted as a component part of their own, distinctive culture.[26] The positive duty to protect minority identity and culture thus also imposes in turn certain limits on the way in which the state can pursue its own economic activities. This has to be done in a way that ensures that, insofar as minorities are affected by these economic activities (eg, logging in relation to reindeer breeding), they can still continue to enjoy their own traditional way of life.[27]

E. Definition of minorities

A final preliminary point which needs to be made concerns the definition of minorities. While the starting point is still that there is no general agreement in this respect, it is generally accepted that minorities are non-dominant groups with a separate ethnic, religious, or linguistic identity, who are less numerous than the rest of the population, and wish to hold on to their separate identity.[28]

While some states still retain a nationality requirement and/or a requirement of traditional residence, migrants are becoming increasingly accepted as minorities.[29] These so-called 'new' minorities could also include internally displaced persons and refugees.[30]

Similarly, while there is no generally accepted definition of the concept of 'indigenous people', it is widely agreed that there is substantial overlap between the two categories. This is also visible in the supervisory practice in relation to minority specific standards.[31]

---

[25] Salomon, 'Socio-economic rights' (n 4 above), 432–4. See also TH Malloy, *The Aspect of Culture in the Social Inclusion of Ethnic Minorities* (2006), which assesses the impact of cultural policies of states in relation to the social inclusion of minorities, available at <http://www.ecmi-eu.org/uploads/media/Inter-Cultural_Indicators.pdf> (accessed 31 July 2009).

[26] As will be elaborated upon below, the Human Rights Committee has in terms of Art 27 of the ICCPR equated traditional economic activities as essential elements of minority (indigenous) culture. See also Salomon, 'Socio-economic rights' (n 4 above), 434.

[27] HRC, Communication no 511/1992, *Länsman and ors v Finland*, UN Doc CCPR/C/52/D/511/1992 (1994), para 9.8.

[28] See also Henrard, *Devising an Adequate System of Minority Protection* (n 6 above), 47–8.

[29] K Henrard 'New minorities and the applicability of minority rights' in E Bakker et al (eds), *'New Minorities': Inclusion and equality: Roundtable conference—October 20, 2003* (2003), 19.

[30] Bedard, *Participation in Economic Life* (n 18 above), 3–4.

[31] See also L Thio, 'Battling Balkanization: Regional approaches toward minority protection beyond Europe' (2002) 43(2) Harvard International Law Journal, 409–68, 420. Adequate attention is given to the supervisory practice in relation to indigenous peoples in terms of general human rights and minority specific rights. No detailed analysis of the standards pertaining explicitly to indigenous peoples is included, however, due to constraints of space. Succinct references in footnotes to these standards are included throughout the text, where relevant.

F. Lund Recommendations on the Effective Participation of National Minorities in Public Life (OSCE)

While the mandate of the High Commissioner on National Minorities of the OSCE does not include standard-setting, a practice developed early on of requesting that international independent experts draft recommendations on themes that recurred in practice. These recommendations have been based on existing human rights and minority-specific standards, but have been more elaborate and specific, thereby providing more insight into practical implications.[32] Their endorsement by the HCNM has tended to strengthen their legitimacy. In any event, it is striking that these recommendations are not only used by academics, but by states to guide their policies and practice.[33]

As indicated in the introduction, the Lund Recommendations are strongly focused on political participation. Their title already points in that direction but the content of the recommendations and the fact that they are structured in two dimensions, one on participation in decision-making and one on self-governance, clearly attests to a focus on political participation. References to the economic, social, and cultural dimensions of participatory rights of minorities feature only marginally.

First of all, para 12 deserves some attention, as it highlights the importance of having channels of dialogue for issues such as housing, education, and land, all of which are relevant to economic and social participation. While this is taken up in the section on participation in decision-making, and concerns consultative and advisory bodies, it should be underscored that the general theme underlying all the Lund Recommendations—namely the need for inclusion, in the sense that the voice of minorities should be heard and taken seriously[34]—actually presupposes dialogue with and consultation of minorities.[35]

Para 12 can then be seen to confirm that consultation mechanisms are also important in relation to issues pertaining to economic and social participation. This involvement of minorities is in turn bound to improve the 'effectiveness' of the resulting participation.

---

[32] Eg, K Henrard, 'The latest recommendations endorsed by the HCNM on ethnic policing: A new development in relation to minority protection?' (2005–6) 5 *European Yearbook on Minority Issues* 67–98, 68–9, 81.

[33] See also specifically related to the Lund Recommendations: Holt, 'The Lund Recommendations' (n 8 above), 169.

[34] See also K Myntti, *A Commentary to the Lund Recommendations on the Effective Participation of National Minorities in Public Life* (2001), 28, who identifies a concern for participatory democracy, and the related importance that all voices should be heard.

[35] See, eg, 'Lund Recommendations on the Effective Participation of National Minorities in Public Life and Explanatory Note' (1999) 25. AC, First Opinion on Norway, ACFC/INF/OP/I (2003)003, 12 September 2002, para 61, where the AC indicates that a consultative council on minority issues which only consists of government representatives is not sufficient as a consolidated structure for minority representatives. The point the AC makes here is that the minorities themselves (also) need to be consulted.

Secondly, the section on self-governance includes references to social and economic dimensions of self-governance in both the heading on non-territorial and territorial arrangements: setting educational standards and determining curricula for teaching minority languages, cultures, etc, for non-territorial arrangements; and education, economic development, housing, health, and other social services for territorial arrangements. While it does not prescribe the inclusion of competences in the socio-economic fields, in relation to territorial arrangements it does underscore that the successful assumption of authority in these fields contributes to a more effective response to the concerns of minorities (para 20).

Thirdly, the section on 'participation in decision-making' has two clauses in (the last bullet point of) para 6 that are relevant to effective access to services for minorities. 'Special measures for minority participation in the civil service' arguably points to measures aimed at promoting employment of persons belonging to minorities in the civil service. The Explanatory Note confirms that this is intended but underscores the importance of equal access to the public service for (other) persons belonging to minorities. The presence of minority members in the public service arguably enhances equal access to the public service and the social services they provide,[36] because they can communicate in the language of the national minority.

Finally, the Explanatory Note to the Lund Recommendations relies heavily on the principle of real, substantive equality to justify the need for special measures adapted to the specific conditions of the minorities concerned.[37] This is equally relevant for participation in socio-economic life.

1. Implementation—Dialogue with Governments?

As the Office of the HCNM endorsed the Lund Recommendations, and considered them a clarification of state obligations in the field concerned, it was anticipated that the High Commissioner would use them in his practice and in his interaction with governments, and he does.

The mandate of the HCNM is focused on preventing conflict. While at first sight the lack of participation in economic and social life might not seem to have considerable implications for conflict potential, in extreme situations—as have arisen in several Roma communities—it has. This High Commissioner has definitely focused on social and economic deprivation and disadvantage in relation to the Roma,[38] which he made one of his priorities.[39] Discussions with

---

[36] See also Holt, 'The Lund Recommendations' (n 8 above), 175–6.
[37] The Lund Recommendations (n 35 above), 18, 21, 26.
[38] OSCE HCNM, 'Report on the situation of Roma and Sinti in the OSCE Area' (2000), 162–3, available at <http://www.osce.org/documents/hcnm/2000/03/241_en.pdf> (accessed 31 July 2009).
[39] The special attention for Roma and their social and economic deprivation is obvious in several of his speeches, but also in the report he commissioned to external experts on Roma migration in Europe.

senior legal HCNM advisers have indicated that he often raises Roma-related issues in meetings with government representatives (of a wide variety of countries, including Germany, Italy, Serbia, Kosovo, Romania and Hungary). The issues centre on integration and inclusion of Roma within national society and have as their overarching theme the need to eliminate discrimination of Roma in areas such as employment, education, and access to social services like housing. Consequently, his recommendations to particular states further clarify the ambit of participation in socio-economic life.

This can also be noticed more broadly in relation to other non-Roma groups. For example the HCHM has made recommendations on the use of minority languages by the public service in Romania, Estonia, and Latvia, which have had a positive impact.[40] In relation to education, the HCHM has asked various Baltic states to adopt a consultative, inclusive approach to education reform, including the language of education,[41] which is considered important for effective access to education.

While the governments accept these recommendations in principle and acknowledge the need to work on these themes, the problem lies (especially in relation to Roma issues) in a lack of the necessary political will needed to adopt the relevant policies and actually implement them.

Be that as it may, the High Commissioner has decided to increase his focus on socio-economic issues, albeit within the limits of the conflict prevention mandate. However, it cannot be a fully fledged strategy, and since lack of participation in social and economic life, with its close interrelation with questions of discrimination, tends to be a big problem for the 'new minorities', this would also raise the contentious and sensitive issue of the extent to which the High Commissioner should become involved with migrant populations.

Nevertheless, it is anticipated that in 2009 the High Commissioner will address socio-economic issues in a more consistent way, so that the socio-economic sources of potential conflict are examined in much more depth that was previously the case.[42]

G. Framework Convention for the Protection of National Minorities

A lot has been written about the FCNM. At least a few interrelated things should be repeated here so as to clarify the focus of this section on the work of the AC. Indeed, while the Convention itself entrusts the Committee of Ministers of the Council of Europe with supervising state implementation of the FCNM, in reality the work of the AC—a body meant to assist the Committee of

---

[40] For an excellent overview see Holt, 'The Lund Recommendations' (n 8 above), 176.
[41] 'OSCE High Commissioner urges implementation of education reform in Kyrgystan', OSCE Press Release, 21 July 2004; Delegation of Latvia, 'Reply to HCNM Ekeus at Permanent Council Meeting No 383', March 2002, OSCE Doc PCDel/142/02.
[42] Discussions with senior legal adviser of the HCNM, Francesco Palermo, 5 December 2008.

Ministers—is decisive. The Committee of Ministers has not only chosen for the members of the AC to consist of independent experts,[43] but has from the outset adopted a practice of confirming the opinions of the AC, to the extent it even refers back its full opinions.[44] This is even more striking when one considers that the AC has adopted rather progressive readings of the framework-like provisions of the FCNM, which initially seemed to leave states with a considerable margin of discretion.[45] The AC is not in a position to oblige states to change their policies or practice, but it continuously invites states to do more, to be more inclusive *ratione personae*, and more generous *ratione materiae*, in accordance with what the committee perceives as being 'more', 'better', etc. In this respect, it is said that the AC focuses on constructive dialogue with states parties: acknowledging and welcoming positive developments, but making suggestions for further improvement and pointing towards outstanding issues. In this way, states do not feel slighted but are continuously reminded of how things could be done differently.[46]

The following analysis is based on all the opinions of the AC, published by December 2008, but will of course link this to the AC's Commentary on the Effective Participation of Persons Belonging to National Minorities in Cultural, Social, and Economic Life and in Public Affairs where appropriate.[47]

It seems important to highlight that participatory rights have strong ties with the central themes of minority protection: full equality, the right to identity, and integration (without forced assimilation). In this respect, the Commentary underscores that the right to equality and the right to identity, as captured in Arts 4 and 5 of the FCNM, constitute together with Art 15 on participation the main foundations of the Convention.[48]

The statement in the Commentary that political participation has repercussions for social cohesion, countering the marginalization in socio-economic life[49] links participatory rights to the integration theme, while integration in turn is understood as 'inclusion in public affairs, cultural, social and economic

---

[43] Resolution (97)10 of the Committee of Ministers, under Art 26 of the FCNM, stipulates this independence requirement for members of the AC.

[44] See also A Eide, 'Towards a pan-European instrument?' in A Verstichel et al (eds), *The Framework Convention for the Protection of National Minorities: A useful pan-European instrument?* (2008), 16.

[45] G Alfredsson, 'A frame with an incomplete painting' (2000) 7(4) *IJMGR* 291–304, 296.

[46] A Verstichel, 'Personal scope of application: An open, inclusive and dynamic approach: The FCNM as a living instrument' in A Verstichel et al (eds) *The Framework Convention for the Protection of National Minorities: A useful pan-European Instrument?* (2008), 133–7.

[47] AC, Thematic Commentary (n 7 above). The Commentary highlights that it provides an integrated analysis of the practice (and thus interpretation) by the AC. However, the Commentary is not confined to the practice under the FCNM but is also influenced by the Lund Recommendations, and the UN Minority Declaration as well as by the (supervisory practice in terms of) CERD, the ECHR, and the European Social Charter (at 10). It remains unclear to what extent that is already done in the actual country-specific opinions of the AC, or only for this Thematic Commentary. [48] Ibid, 11.

[49] Ibid.

life'.⁵⁰ In this respect it can be highlighted that the President of the AC pointed out in a presentation on 12 November 2008⁵¹ that the work of the AC has clarified/shown that employment and economic participation is essential for harmoniously integrated societies.

By way of preliminary remarks, it should be underscored that a clear central theme that emerges from an evaluation of the supervisory practice of the AC is the need to consult with minorities in all matters covered by the FCNM.⁵² The Commentary confirms the central importance of *dialogue* and effective channels of communication for effective participation, which requires as an absolute minimum permanent dialogue through an institutionalized consultative mechanism.⁵³ This dimension of political participation is also recognized as essential in relation to participation in social and economic life (and could be qualified as a procedural dimension of social and economic participation).

In relation to political participation, the Commentary points out that such consultation also carries an obligation of result, in the sense that it should lead to substantial influence on decisions.⁵⁴ It is unclear whether this would be translated into participation in social and economic life and, if so, whether this translation would entail actual access to the labour market and so on.

The issues/domains of relevance for participation enumerated above are all addressed in the practice of the FCNM.⁵⁵ The intrinsic link between effective and substantively equal access (to employment, to education, etc) in this respect confirms that the aim of Art 15 participatory rights is full, real equality between persons belonging to minorities and the majority.⁵⁶ Art 4 also captures the economic and social dimension of participation and this is clearly manifested in the supervisory practice of the AC.⁵⁷ In addition to Arts 15 and 4,⁵⁸ the overview of elements relevant to participation in social and economic life reveals that other provisions should also be taken into account. Since education⁵⁹ is obviously connected to participation in social life, with implications for employment and hence participation in economic life, Arts 12–13 of the

---

⁵⁰ The entire Framework Convention is based on the idea of '*integration*' of minorities in the sense of inclusion in public affairs, cultural, social, and economic life. In this respect it can be highlighted that the President of the AC pointed out in a presentation on 12 November 2008 that the work of the AC has clarified/shown that employment and economic participation is essential for harmoniously integrated societies. J Marko, 'Effective participation of national minorities: A comment on conceptual, legal and empirical problems', DH-MIN(2006)014), 3.
⁵¹ Unpublished, on file with the author.
⁵² See, eg, AC, First Opinion on Armenia, ACFC/INF/OP/I(2003)001, 16 May 2002, para 100; AC, First Opinion on Sweden, ACFC/INF/OP/I(2003)006, 25 August 2002, para 19.
⁵³ See also Marko, 'Effective participation of national minorities' (n 50 above), 7.
⁵⁴ Ibid, 13.   ⁵⁵ AC, Thematic Commentary (n 7 above), 14.   ⁵⁶ Ibid.
⁵⁷ Ibid, 14: without a clear division between the two articles. See also Verstichel, 'Recent developments' (n 9 above), 31–2.
⁵⁸ See also Phillips, 'The Framework Convention' (n 5 above), 292.
⁵⁹ See also AC, Commentary on Education under the Framework Convention for the Protection of National Minorities, ACFC/25DOC(2006)002. Strikingly, also in this Commentary, which primarily deals with Arts 12–14, the relevance of Arts 4, 5 and 6 is highlighted: see 9–10.

FCNM should also be included. Effective and equal access to education, with its broader implications in terms of language of instruction and curriculum issues, is captured in paras 12(1) and (3), while Art 13 protects the right of minorities to establish and run private minority schools.

Furthermore, the Commentary confirms, under the heading of participation in social and economic life, that traditional economic activities, and the right to exercise and benefit from these are component parts of the right to identity, and the related right to one's own way of life. These economic activities are thus protected by Art 5. Under the same heading, the Commentary also underscores the importance of language use, especially the use of minority languages by public authorities in order to guarantee effective access to public services. In other words, Art 10 should also be considered.

While the actual text of the Commentary does not bring this to the fore, its appendix entitled, 'Relevance of other articles of the Framework Convention for the interpretation of Article 15' does show that still other articles of the FCNM[60] have occasionally proven relevant to aspects of participation in social and economic life.[61] This is particularly the case for Art 6 on the importance of mutual tolerance and respect, of intercultural dialogue, and of integration policies more generally.

In view of the central importance of Art 4, and the more indirect relevance of Arts 5–6 of the FCNM, the quasi jurisprudence of the AC will now be expanded upon. In relation to the latter two, at first sight 'protection of minority identity' and 'mutual respect and understanding (through) intercultural dialogue' do not seem self-evident vehicles for the protection and promotion of minority participation in social and economic life. Nevertheless, the AC does regularly address issues in terms of Art 6 that arguably pertain to participation in social and economic life. Sometimes there is a more or less pronounced connection with tolerance, mutual respect etc, but this link is often implied. Problems of systemic and widespread discrimination, often against Roma, are tackled under Art 6.[62]

---

[60] The appendix on 'Relevance of other Articles of the Framework Convention for the interpretation of Article 15, to the Advisory Committee's Commentary on the Effective Participation of Persons Belonging to National Minorities in Cultural, Social, and Economic Life and in Cultural Affairs, also indicates that the possibility under Art 9 to create and use their own media may have indirect social and economic benefits for persons belonging to national minorities, ACFC/31DOC (2008))001, 39–40. This theme has not been taken up here, as it has not been developed in the country-specific opinions so far.

[61] For an even more extensive list, see the full appendix to the Commentary.

[62] While these comments are expected in relation to Eastern European countries, like the Czech Republic (First Opinion, ACFC/INF/OP/I(2002)002, 6 April 2001, para 35: discrimination in employment) and the former Yugoslav Republic of Macedonia (First Opinion, ACFC/INF/OP/I (2005)001, 2 February 2005, para 52: discrimination in relation to housing, education, employment, and access to social assistance), they are also made about Western European countries—Finland (First Opinion, ACFC/INF/OP/I(2001)002, 22 September 2002, para 25: prohibition to enter restaurants) and Portugal (First Opinion ACFC/INF/OP/I(2006)002, 5 September 2007, para 42: unequal access to education, health and other social services).

The First Opinion on Bosnia and Herzegovina underscores more generally the lack of economic opportunities for persons belonging to minorities,[63] which is arguably related to the lack of respect for/understanding of and prejudices against minorities. Similarly the AC calls on Austria to tackle its existing discriminatory practices in the field of employment and to step up its integration policy, while ensuring that the required funds were made available to realize these changes.[64]

In terms of Art 5 it is more obvious what types of issues are addressed:[65] traditional economic activities that are intrinsically related to minority culture. Furthermore, the AC does not shy away for the related question of land rights.[66] Problems in available accommodation/inadequate stopping sites for Travellers[67] and regulation of their itinerant trade, a typical component of the way of life of Travellers,[68] are also understandably assessed here, as these 'housing manifestations' are also bound up with minority identity.[69]

Many opinions underscore the intrinsic connection between discrimination (Art 4) on the one hand, and issues of effective equality as addressed through Art 15 on the other.[70] It is clear that often, if not mostly, the problems concerning participation in economic and social life are addressed under Art 4, sometimes in addition to similar remarks made under Art 15. Especially in relation to Roma, the systemic discrimination they suffer in relation to economic and social rights tends to be addressed within the context of Art 4.[71]

H. Requirements for anti-discrimination legislation

The Advisory Committee underscores the importance of a comprehensive legislative framework to tackle discrimination in the fields of social and

---

[63] AC, First Opinion on Bosnia and Herzegovina, ACFC/INF/OP/I(2005)003, 11 May 2005, para 66.
[64] AC, First Opinion on Austria, ACFC/INF/OP/I(2002)009, 16 May 2002, para 34–5.
[65] AC, First Opinion on Finland (n 62 above), para 22. See also Commentary (n 7 above), 18–19.
[66] The problems of the Sami are noted in relation to several Scandinavian countries: First Opinion on Norway (n 35 above), para 32; First Opinion Sweden (n 52 above), para 30.
[67] AC, First Opinion on Ireland, ACFC/INF/OP/I(2004)003, 22 May 2003, para 48; AC, Opinion on UK, ACFC/INF/OP/I(2002)006, 30 November 2001, para 40–1.
[68] AC, First Opinion on Switzerland, ACFC/INF/OP/I(2003)007, 20 February 2003, para 34.
[69] The central importance of the equality principle (enshrined in Art 4) is also manifested because the issue of traditional economic activities is sometimes dealt with under Art 4 instead of Art 5 (AC, Opinion on Portugal (n 62 above), para 32). Similarly, the high level of unemployment of the Traveller community, related to the fact that their traditional areas of economic livelihood have been eroded, has led the AC to urge the Irish government in terms of Art 4 to examine how to promote both traditional and new economic activities of Travellers (AC, Opinion on Ireland (n 67 above), paras 35–6). Sometimes the lack of stopping places for Roma is also critically assessed in relation to Art 4: AC, Opinion on Norway (n 35 above), para 23. The AC does not seem to have a consistent approach in this respect as is buttressed by the First Opinion on Switzerland: while the problem of lack of stopping places are dealt with in terms of Art 5, land use planning and commerce regulation that does not take into account specific characteristics of Travellers culture and way of life are criticized in terms of Art 4: Switzerland (n 68 above), para 28.
[70] Phillips, 'Commentary' (n 13 above), 101.   [71] Ibid, 105.

economic life.[72] Regularly the Committee highlights the need for coverage in areas such as housing and education,[73] while health care and access to services more generally are also singled out.[74] In addition to the requisite substantive provisions, the AC remarks on the need for appropriate sanctions and effective remedies where acts of racial and ethnic discrimination have been committed, and for proper enforcement of those sanctions.[75]

1. Indirect Discrimination (and Positive Action)

Again in relation to the Roma and their especially disadvantaged situation, the AC recognizes that equal treatment of Roma in a formal sense (without taking their particular circumstances into account) might lead to prohibited indirect discrimination. The AC urges states to adopt special/differential measures to avoid findings of indirect discrimination. Slovenia, for example, is asked to amend legislation to redress the fact that Roma are disproportionally affected by dwellings becoming illegal,[76] while the Russian Federation is urged to adopt effective measures to tackle the disproportionately high unemployment among not only the Roma but also the numerically smaller indigenous peoples.[77] In this respect, the AC welcomes the adoption of special measures/a national plan by Romania and the Serbia, aimed at improving the social, medical and educational situation of the Roma communities.[78]

An evaluation (in relation to Arts 4 and Art 15[79]), which is not focused on Roma but is similarly important when discussing problems of indirect discrimination,[80] concerns the acknowledgement that a country's economic

---

[72] AC, Thematic Commentary (n 7 above), 15.
[73] AC, Opinion on Austria (n 64 above), para 34; AC, First Opinion on Croatia, ACFC/INF/OP/I(2002)003, 6 April 2001, para 23; AC, First Opinion on Cyprus, ACFC/INF/OP/I(2002)04, 6 April 2001, para 23; AC, First Opinion on Estonia, ACFC/INF/OP/I(2002)005, 14 September 2001, para 21; AC, First Opinion on Germany, ACFC/INF/OP/I(2002)008, 1 March 2002, para 22; AC, First Opinion on Norway (n 35 above), para 21; AC, First Opinion on the Russian Federation, ACFC/INF/OP/I(2003)005, 13 September 2002, para 32; AC, Opinion on Slovenia, ACFC/INF/OP/I(2005)002, 14 March 2005, para 26. In its First Opinion on Lithuania the AC promotes the adoption of non-discrimination provisions in relation to the key sectors of social life such as housing, health, and the supply of goods and services: ACFC/INF/OP/I(2003)008, 21 February 2003, para 28.   [74] AC, First Opinion on fYROM (n 62 above), para 28.
[75] AC, First Opinion on the Czech Republic (n 62 above), para 25; AC, Opinion on Denmark, ACFC/INF/OP/I(2001)005, 22 September 2000, para 25; AC, First Opinion on Poland, ACFC/INF/OP/I(2004)005, 27 November 2003, para 30. See also Commentary (n 7 above), 15.
[76] AC, First Opinion on Slovenia (n 73 above), para 30.
[77] AC, First Opinion on the Russian Federation (n 73 above), paras 41–2.
[78] AC, First Opinion on Romania, ACFC/INF/OP/I9(2002)001, 6 April 2001, para 25; AC, First Opinion on Serbia, ACFC/INF/OP/I(2004)002, 27 November 2003, para 42.
[79] No steady practice: issue comes up in relation to Arts 4 or 15: AC, First Opinion on Estonia (n 73 above), para 59.
[80] See also AC, Opinion on Portugal (n 62 above), para 30 in which it is underscored by the AC that persons belonging to the Roma minority seem to be especially disadvantaged in areas such as housing, education, and access to employment in comparison with the majority population.

problems have a disproportionate impact on minorities,[81] which must be countered by tailored and decisive initiatives.[82] Noting that the difficult situation of minorities in relation to employment, housing, education and the like is not compatible with Art 4, the AC calls for the adoption of special, targeted, and comprehensive measures by the authorities[83] to restore full and effective equality.

Arguably the AC even welcomes affirmative action/positive action measures in this respect when it remarks that 'temporary measures targeting specific ethnic groups in order to restore equality of opportunities shall not be considered to be an act of discrimination'.[84] This resonates well with positive action measures in the socio-economic domain (especially employment and education).

It is common knowledge that participation in social and economic life is accorded less attention in comparison to political participation. Nevertheless, several of the relevant issues are addressed explicitly and seemingly in increasing detail, probably because minorities themselves have raised this issue prominently.[85] This is reflected in the Commentary which, although focusing predominantly on political participation,[86] nevertheless dedicates a separate section to participation in social and economic life, taking up the point frequently made by the AC that effective participation cannot be restricted to participation in public affairs, and is equally important in relation to economic and social life.[87]

The preceding analysis has sought to clarify why participation in social and economic life is not only addressed in terms of Art 15 of the FCNM. However, a critical point should be noted here, namely that the evaluation of socio-economic participation issues occurs predominantly in terms of articles other than Art 15. This is to some extent understandable and even logical, for example in the case of adequate non-discrimination legislation (Art 4) and educational issues (Arts 12–13). However, when these issues are highlighted in relation to

---

[81] AC, First Opinion on Albania, ACFC/INF/OP/I(2003)004, 12 September 2002, para 28; AC, First Opinion on Azerbaijan, ACFC/INF/OP/I(2004)001, 26 January 2004, paras 29–30; AC, First Opinion on Croatia (n 73 above), para 54; AC, First Opinion on Estonia (n 73 above), para 24; AC, First Opinion on fYROM (n 62 above), para 102. See also AC, Thematic Commentary (n 7 above), 15. See also Weller, 'Report' (n 7 above), 86, where he emphasizes that in situations of economic divergence the AC has requested that the government develop measures capable of limiting the effects of such structural differences. The AC has more generally encouraged active and decisive measures to address economic opportunities for persons belonging to national minorities, especially in economically depressed regions.
[82] AC, First Opinion on Germany (n 73 above), para 24; AC, First Opinion on Hungary, ACFC/INF/OP/I(2001)004, 22 September 2000, para 18; AC, Opinion on Lithuania (n 73 above), para 35.   [83] AC, First Opinion on Slovenia (n 73 above), para 29.
[84] AC, First Opinion on Portugal (n 62 above), para 33. See also AC, Thematic Commentary (n 62 above), 12.
[85] AC, First Opinion on Bulgaria, ACFC/INF/OP/I(2006)001, 5 April 2006, para 111.
[86] AC, Thematic Commentary (n 7 above), 22.   [87] Ibid, 14.

other articles it is undeniably odd not to mention them at all in terms of Art 15.[88]

III. General Trend: Increasingly More Detailed Assessments

A first general trend concerns the fact that assessments of what amounts to de facto participation in social and economic life are becoming increasingly detailed. In the first cycle, the AC usually confined its evaluation of these issues to very general statements about the low level of participation in economic life (in terms of Art 15), without specifying what aspects were problematic. Unemployment probably featured rather high on the list of problems but this is not made explicit.[89] The AC's concomitant calls to governments to make substantial efforts to ensure effective participation of minorities in economic and social life may be important, but do not provide the contracting parties with much guidance.[90]

Later opinions (often but not only those of the second cycle) deal with problems of participation in economic and social life in much more detail[91] (albeit more frequently in terms of Art 4).[92] The AC is particularly elaborate in its Second Opinion on the UK, where it is critical of educational achievement differentials and, in the field of employment, recommends not only equality mainstreaming in the private sector but also representation in public sector

---

[88] Eg, AC, First Opinion on Poland (n 75 above), in relation to the position of the Roma. The AC in its Second Opinion on Armenia does not mention anything on participation in economic life under Art 15 while in terms of Art 4 it is obvious that Yezedi suffer discrimination in relation to access to social benefits and employment (AC, First Opinion on Armenia (n 52 above), paras 42–3).
[89] AC, First Opinion on Albania (n 81 above), para 75; AC, First Opinion on Bulgaria (n 85 above), para 109; AC, First Opinion on Slovak Republic, ACFC/INF/OP/I(2001)001, 22 September 2000, para 47; AC, First Opinion on Spain, ACFC/INF/OP/I(2004)004, 27 November 2003, para 79.   [90] AC, First Opinion on Slovenia (n 73 above), para 76.
[91] AC, Second Opinion on Armenia, ACFC/OP/II(2006)005, 24 October 2006: nothing is said about participation in economic life under Art 15 while in terms of Art 4 it is obvious that Yezedi suffer discrimination in relation to access to social benefits and employment (paras 42–3). Note the absence of any reference under Art 15 to problems in relation to participation in economic life, also in AC, Second Opinion on Germany, ACFC/OP/II(2006)01, 7 February 2007; and AC, Second Opinion on Hungary, ACFC/INF/OP/II(2004)003, 14 December 2005; AC, Second Opinion on Sweden, ACFC/OP/II(2007)006, 30 January 2008; AC, Second Opinion on Switzerland, ACFC/OP/II(2008)002, 2 September 2008, while in these countries there are significant problems in this regard, as is pointed out in terms of other Articles (Arts 4 and 12, etc).
[92] See also AC, Second Opinion on Slovak Republic, ACFC/OP/II(2005)004, 21 June 2006, para 14 and its elaboration throughout several articles of the FCNM, but not Art 15. Even when there are brief remarks pertaining to participation in economic and social life under Art 15, this is often combined with reference back to analysis in terms of Art 4, and sometimes also others like Art 12: eg AC, Second Opinion on fYROM, ACFC/OP/II(2007)002, 9 July 2008, para 202; AC, First Opinion on Slovenia (n 73 above), para 176 (just mentioning under Art 15 that there are ongoing problems of exclusion and marginalization in fields such as employment, education, and housing, while more elaborate analysis and especially recommendations can be found under Arts 4 and 12).

services, the police, and the judiciary.[93] In its First Opinion on Switzerland, the AC addresses many distinctive employment issues, even to the extent of noting decisions of companies to relocate to 'other' areas (to the disadvantage of persons belonging to minorities).[94] Increasingly the AC acknowledges the central importance of education[95] for subsequent employment possibilities and the negative knock-on effects that inferior education has in this respect.[96]

Especially in its second cycle of opinions, the AC also explicitly highlights problems in relation to access to adequate housing, health, and education, access to social services, etc.[97] It is suggested that governments make a more determined effort to combat related social exclusion.[98]

A. Trends regarding (un)employment

According to the AC, the fact that minorities tend to be disproportionately affected by unemployment[99] needs to be addressed by positive action measures,[100] inter alia by promoting ethnic diversity in working life.[101] Such positive action measures are key to reaching full and effective equality,[102] and should be facilitated and possibly be made compulsory through legislation.[103] Examples of soft positive action measures that are welcomed by the AC include the adoption of training courses for young Roma and counselling and guidance programmes.[104]

---

[93] AC, Second Opinion on the United Kingdom, ACFC/OP/II(2007)003, 26 October 2007, para 235 ff.   [94] AC, First Opinion on Switzerland (n 68 above), para 75.
[95] ENAR also highlights the crucial importance of education, not only because education can foster intercultural societies respectful of difference but also, and this is important here, because 'education is viewed as a major route to economic growth, long-term competitiveness and social cohesion and to the creation of more equal and fair societies': *General Policy Paper No 5: Fighting Racism and Promoting Equal Rights in Education and Training* (November 2008), available at <http://cms.horus.be/files/99935/MediaArchive/pdf/GPP%20No%205%20Education%20-%20EN%20final%20&%20adopted.pdf> (accessed 9 September 2009). Admittedly these considerations transcend the importance of education for the individual advancement of persons belonging to minorities and is more focused on the benefit for society as a whole, but the underlying rationale is the same.
[96] AC, Second Opinion on Ireland, ACFC/OP/II(2006)007, 6 October 2006, para 116.
[97] AC, Second Opinion on Moldova, ACFC/INF/OP/II(2004)004, 24 May 2005 paras 45–7. See also AC, Second Opinion on Norway, ACFC/OP/II(2006)006, 16 November 2006, para 145; AC, Second Opinion on Spain ACFC/OP/II(2007)001, 22 February 2008, paras 47–9.
[98] AC, Second Opinion on Moldova (n 97 above), para 48.
[99] AC, First Opinion on Bulgaria (n 85 above), para 36; AC, First Opinion on Romania (n 78 above), para 70; and explicitly in terms of Art 15: AC, First Opinion on the Russian Federation (n 73 above), para 109; AC, First Opinion on Serbia (n 78 above), para 113.
[100] AC, First Opinion on the United Kingdom, ACFC/INF/OP/I(2002)010, 30 November 2001, para 95.   [101] AC, Second Opinion on Sweden (n 92 above), para 48.
[102] AC, First Opinion on Serbia (n 78 above), para 38.
[103] The AC expands on the implications and limitations of positive measures. While quotas are not the only form of positive action that can be used to redress inequalities, whatever measures taken should not go beyond what is proportional and adequate with respect to their aim of achieving full and effective equality: AC, Second Opinion on Sweden (n 91 above), para 51.
[104] AC, First Opinion on Spain (n 89 above), para 33.

While employment in the public service is an aspect of political participation, for the individuals concerned it also concerns employment and, thus, economic participation. In relation to Ireland the AC urged the state to set targets to include Travellers within its general recruitment strategies.[105] It regards the exclusion of persons belonging to particular minorities from accessing key positions in public life as problematic in terms of Art 4.[106] The requirement that state language proficiency requirements should not go beyond what is necessary for the post at issue (and the ancillary need to have proper language training facilities insofar as a language requirement is a legitimate condition for access to a job)[107] would seem to facilitate representation of minorities in the public service. Any excessive difficulties experienced by persons belonging to minorities in being recruited to public enterprises should also be countered by the authorities.[108]

B. Trends regarding education

In relation to education, the AC recognizes that education and equal access to education is essential/foundational not only for proper participation in public life (Art 15)[109] but also for combating disadvantages in relation to employment and housing,[110] and for the ultimate attainment of full and effective equality.

Equal access to education concerns not only physical access, but broader issues that are important for genuine access to education. No physical access to education can result from a blatant refusal to register persons belonging to minorities,[111] but also from a lack of adequate educational facilities, as in the case of the displaced Ingush and Chechen population in Ingusethia.[112] A minority-specific problem of genuine equal access to education concerns problems with, or a lack of, or a reduction in education in minority languages, since this can have negative repercussions for educational achievements and for equal access to higher education.[113] The funding of private schools is relevant in this regard: when private schools are the only option for receiving education in one's mother tongue, substantively equal access to education would necessitate some level of funding.[114] The prohibition of establishing private educational

---

[105] AC, First Opinion on Ireland (n 67 above), para 37.
[106] AC, First Opinion on Bosnia and Herzegovina (n 63 above), para 39.
[107] AC, Thematic Commentary (n 7 above).
[108] AC, First Opinion on Bosnia and Herzegovina (n 63 above), para 43.
[109] AC, First Opinion on Lithuania (n 73 above), para 84; AC, Second Opinion on Austria, ACFC/OP/II(2007)005, 11 June 2008, para 148.
[110] AC, First Opinion on Austria (n 64 above), para 23; AC, First Opinion on Finland (n 62 above), para 20.
[111] AC, First Opinion on Albania (n 81 above), para 59; AC, First Opinion on Azerbaijan (n 81 above), para 41 (problems of Chechens non-citizens).
[112] AC, First Opinion on the Russian Federation (n 73 above), para 90.
[113] AC, First Opinion on Estonia (n 73 above), para 47. See also AC, First Opinion on Poland (n 75 above), para 84.   [114] AC, Second Opinion on Germany (n 91 above), para 128–30.

institutions furthermore inhibits effective access to education for minorities more generally.[115]

The AC recognizes that the extent to which minority culture is reflected in the curriculum determines genuine access to and benefit from education:[116] adequate recognition should be given to the minority culture, history, and values and their specific needs should be catered for.[117] This also has repercussions for appropriate, adapted textbooks.[118]

In the case of attainment gaps for particular ethnic groups in education, the AC welcomes the adoption of special measures (positive action), possibly even quotas,[119] to improve access to higher education.[120] The AC sometimes has rather specific suggestions for states to promote equal opportunity for minorities to access education at all levels, such as the establishment of a multicultural university.[121]

The opinions of the AC reflect common knowledge concerning the entrenched problems of Roma and the difficulties in providing them with adequate, equal educational opportunities. In several Eastern European countries, the Roma are disproportionately sidelined[122] to so-called 'special schools' for underachievers or mentally disabled students,[123] on the basis of tests that do not take into account the specific needs, social, and cultural characteristics or language skills of the Roma.[124] The AC strongly rejects segregation in education, not only in the form of special schools for particular minority groups but also special classes, as it maintains that separate education for one particular minority risks places the children concerned at a disadvantage.[125] This disapproval extends even to special education groups within the public school system aimed at providing additional support to the pupils concerned.[126] According to the AC, even if it might be necessary to give special support to particular minority students, this should be done in a way that does not hamper their being educated together in an integrated environment, as this is in their long-term interests.[127] The AC even identifies the positive obligations of public authorities

---

[115] AC, First Opinion on fYROM (n 62 above), para 86.
[116] AC, Opinion on Albania (n 81 above), para 60; AC, First Opinion on Croatia (n 73 above), para 49. See also AC, First Opinion on Serbia (n 78 above), para 91; AC, First Opinion on Slovakia (n 89 above), para 40; AC, First Opinion on Slovenia (n 73 above), para 64.
[117] AC, Second Opinion on Italy, ACFC/INF/OP/II(2005)003, 25 October 2005, para 115.
[118] AC, First Opinion on Armenia (n 52 above), para 66.
[119] AC, First Opinion on the United Kingdom (n 100 above), para 79.
[120] AC, First Opinion on Serbia (n 78 above), para 91; AC, First Opinion on fYROM (n 62 above), para 81.
[121] AC, First Opinion on Ukraine ACFC/INF/OP/I(2002)010, 1 March 2002, para 61.
[122] AC, First Opinion on Germany (n 73 above), para 36.
[123] AC, First Opinion on Bulgaria (n 85 above), para 88; AC, First Opinion on the Czech Republic (n 62 above), paras 61–2; AC, First Opinion on Hungary (n 82 above), para 41; AC, First Opinion on Serbia (n 78 above), para 89; AC, First Opinion on Slovenia (n 73 above), para 63.
[124] AC, Opinion on Serbia (n 78 above), para 89.
[125] AC, First Opinion on Sweden (n 52 above), para 53.
[126] AC, First Opinion on Finland (n 62 above), para 37.
[127] AC, First Opinion on Ireland (n 67 above), para 85.

to counter privately induced segregation.[128] In addition to the lack of integrated education with other children, the AC often criticizes such schools for having inferior material conditions and an inferior standard of education.

Throughout its opinions, the AC identifies several special measures that could equalize educational opportunities for Roma, ranging from projects that seek fuller integration of Roma children into the school system (which indirectly contributes to their effective access to education);[129] to better taking into account and accommodating the itinerant culture of Roma (measures to provide stopping places)[130] so as to ensure equal access to education at all levels;[131] special assistance programmes for Roma,[132] including special education programmes; dialogue with families and direct financing;[133] having more Roma teachers and special assistants;[134] using Roma pedagogical advisers,[135] Roma cultural mediators,[136] and Roma school assistants;[137] having 'zero' classes to prepare Roma children for basic school education by improving language skills in majority language;[138] more general increased support for pre-school access;[139] special training for teachers working with Roma children;[140] and free textbooks for Roma pupils.[141]

Acknowledging that problems in levels of minority achievement can have varied and complex causes, the AC advocates a holistic approach which takes into account the precarious financial circumstances of Roma families/parents, as well as the distance and dangerous roads to schools that contribute to the inability of Roma children to attend school due to their extremely poor living conditions.[142] The AC calls on governments to break this vicious circle and 'take

---

[128] AC, First Opinion on Spain (n 89 above), para 71; AC, First Opinion on Hungary (n 82 above), para 43. [129] AC, First Opinion on Bulgaria (n 85 above), para 87.
[130] AC, Opinion on the United Kingdom (n 100 above), para 82.
[131] AC, First Opinion on Norway (n 35 above), para 54.
[132] AC, First Opinion on Albania (n 81 above), para 60.
[133] AC, First Opinion on Lithuania (n 73 above), para 77.
[134] AC, First Opinion on Albania (n 81 above), para 60; AC, Second Opinion on the Czech Republic, ACFC/INF/OP/II(2005)002, 26 October 2005, para 152.
[135] AC, Opinion on the Czech Republic (n 62 above), para 63.
[136] AC, First Opinion on Portugal (n 62 above), para 31.
[137] AC, Second Opinion on Austria (n 109 above), para 147. In view of the success obtained by these assistants the AC suggested in the second cycle to enhance the use of teaching assistants and school mediators: AC, Second Opinion on Spain (n 97 above), para 125; AC, First Opinion on Slovenia (n 73 above), para 123.
[138] AC, First Opinion on the Czech Republic (n 62 above), para 63.
[139] AC, First Opinion on Poland (n 75 above), para 77; AC, Opinion on Portugal (n 62 above), para 33; AC, Second Opinion on the Czech Republicm (n 134 above), para 152. In relation to the former Yugoslav Republic of Macedonia the AC even suggested to turn pre-school education into a strategy of integration: AC, Opinion on fYROM (n 62 above), para 79; while its second opinion on Slovenia underscored the importance of enrolling Roma children in pre-school education for at least two years prior to primary school in order to help them to learn the official language as well as their mother tongue: AC, First Opinion on Slovenia (n 73 above), para 147.
[140] AC, Opinion on Spain (n 89 above), para 68.
[141] AC, First Opinion on Serbia (n 78 above), para 91.
[142] AC, First Opinion on Bosnia and Herzegovina (n 63 above), para 89.

these issues seriously and follow up on related complaints',[143] recognizing that a whole range of long-term measures are required to remedy this situation, including measures aimed at poverty reduction, provision of essential food, etc.[144]

C. Trends regarding access to health care

Problems in relation to substantive access to health care have only been raised in relation to Roma and Travellers, who are said to experience levels of health that fall short of those enjoyed by the population at large.[145] In that respect, the AC welcomes the opening of medical care facilities in Roma populated areas, and suggests or welcomes the use of Roma assistants[146] or health mediators as these would facilitate access to health care for Roma.[147]

D. Trends regarding access to housing

In relation to housing, the precarious situation of the Roma is again singled out, notably in relation to their accommodation and the discrimination they face in this respect.[148] Particularly problematic is the lack of a clear legal status for their settlements and the lack of resources.[149] The AC actually identifies a duty of outcome on the part of the state to provide effective access to adequate housing, in the sense that states have to end discriminatory practices in this sphere and need to promote equal access to adequate housing, inter alia by improved access to subsidized housing.[150]

In addition to problems encountered by the Roma, the AC also notes the problem of occupancy rights after an ethnic conflict and the impact on persons belonging to national minorities. The de facto discrimination which inhibits repossession of one's property merits special attention and needs to be addressed by governments.[151]

---

[143] AC, First Opinion on Albania (n 81 above), para 59; AC, First Opinion on Bulgaria (n 85 above), para 90. Similarly in its first opinion on Lithuania the AC stipulates that 'the Roma are faced with socio-economic difficulties which have considerable influence on their access to education and ... improvements in this situation require determined and coordinated action, with measures taken at various levels (economic, social, linguistic and cultural)': AC, First Opinion on Lithuania (n 73 above), para 64. See also AC, First Opinion on Spain (n 89 above), para 70.
[144] AC, First Opinion on Romania (n 78 above), para 57, AC, Second Opinion on Romania, ACFC/OP/II(2005)007, 23 February 2006, para 158.
[145] AC, First Opinion on Ireland (n 67 above), para 40.
[146] AC, First Opinion on Bulgaria (n 85 above), para 39.
[147] AC, Second Opinion on Romania (n 144 above), para 53.
[148] On Roma, see also AC, First Opinion on Bulgaria (n 85 above), para 36, AC, First Opinion on Croatia (n 73 above), para 28; AC, First Opinion on Sweden (n 52 above), para 74.
[149] AC, First Opinion on fYROM (n 62 above), para 31.
[150] AC, Thematic Commentary (n 7 above), 20.
[151] AC, First Opinion on Croatia (n 73 above), para 22–4.

E. Trends regarding access to social services/public services/public facilities/ basic facilities (water, electricity etc)

Again in relation to Roma, the AC emphasizes that access to social and medical assistance is marred by great obstacles, hence hinting at indirect discrimination in this respect.[152]

Here the question of language (use) in relation to public authorities (enshrined in Art 10) comes up again as a determinant factor in attaining effective access to these services, and the AC hints at the importance of proficiency in minority languages among civil servants.[153]

In addition to effective access to work and economic activities, the need for effective or substantively real access to social services is furthered by the argument (reflected in the Commentary) that the staff of public services must be trained to provide adequate responses to the special needs of persons belonging to national minorities.[154] The Commentary does not clarify whether this goes beyond language training,[155] and would also necessitate training on specific cultures, etc. The latter seems plausible in view of the point made about the importance of representation of minorities in all echelons of public services[156] and the criticism of hampered minority access to health care due to language and cultural differences, which would necessitate training the staff accordingly.[157]

Finally, while it is not something that comes up in many opinions, and is not explicitly seen as a component of participation in social life, trends regarding access to places of entertainment, restaurants and the like are arguably relevant in this respect. This is (again) a recurring problem for Roma and Travellers, which needs to be addressed by the authorities.[158]

F. Special attention for Roma

The preceding overview has clearly shown that while pervasive discrimination in the socio-economic field is a point of concern for several minorities,[159] the AC often highlights the particular problems encountered by Roma and Travellers

---

[152] AC, First Opinion on Albania (n 81 above), para 28.
[153] AC, First Opinion on Germany (n 73 above), para 50; AC, First Opinion on Norway (n 35 above), para 47.   [154] AC, Thematic Commentary (n 7 above), 16.
[155] Ibid, 19.   [156] Ibid, 17.   [157] Ibid, 31.
[158] AC, First Opinion on Ireland (n 67 above), para 43; AC, First Opinion on Norway (n 35 above), para 24; AC, First Opinion on Sweden (n 52 above), para 24.
[159] AC, First Opinion on Albania, ACFC/INF/OP/I(2003)004, 12 September 2002, para 28 mentions national minorities generally; AC, First Opinion on Azerbaijan (n 81 above), para 29 refers also to Kurds and Meskhetians and para 30 to Budukha; AC, First Opinion on the Czech Republic (n 62 above), para 25 mentions 'ethnic groups' in addition to Roma; AC, First Opinion on Serbia (n 78 above), para 38: Albanian, Bosniak, Croatian, and Muslim minorities; AC, First Opinion on Switzerland (n 68 above), para 75: linguistic minorities; AC, First Opinion on fYROM (n 62 above), para 102: Albanians; AC, First Opinion on Ukraine (n 121 above), para 29: Crimean Tatars; AC, Second Opinion on Austria (n 109 above) para 96: immigrants.

across the wide spectrum of socio-economic themes, including elevated levels of unemployment, inadequate access to services and public places, and substandard housing conditions without basic facilities.[160] The Roma undoubtedly constitute an extremely disadvantaged and vulnerable group, which is articulated by the AC as an 'increasing socio economic gap between Roma and the rest of the population',[161] and 'a real socio economic divide between this minority and the rest of the population'.[162]

The AC underscores the need for governments to make further efforts to improve this situation (general statement),[163] including through the adoption of a range of special measures aimed at improving the overall socio-economic situation of the Roma[164] and their living conditions[165] as a matter of priority.[166] This would necessitate attention to both the legislative framework and its implementation.[167] The combination of increased attention to the effectiveness of Roma participation, and the overarching importance accorded by the FCNM to the protection of the right to identity, arguably explains the AC's stated requirement that special support measures concerned should be tailored to the Roma's own culture.[168]

G. Instrumental issues

Finally a few instrumental issues should be mentioned, instrumental in the sense that they (can) constitute preconditions to effective participation in economic and social life, for example: access to land and property, language requirements for jobs, and citizenship. The importance of data collection for monitoring purposes and sound policy development should not be excluded[169] and is in any

---

[160] AC, First Opinion on Bosnia and Herzegovina (n 63 above), paras 45–6; AC, First Opinion on Bulgaria (n 85 above), paras 32–6. See also AC, First Opinion on Serbia (n 78 above), para 39; AC, First Opinion on the Czech Republic (n 62 above), para 29; AC, Opinion on Ireland (n 67 above), para 34 (this is related to the Traveller community, which has several parallels with the Roma community); and AC, First Opinion on Italy, ACFC/INF/OP/I(2002)007, 14 September 2001, para 24; AC, First Opinion on Spain (n 89 above), paras 32–6.
[161] AC, First Opinion on Albania (n 81 above), para 30; AC, First Opinion on Austria (n 64 above), para 71; AC, First Opinion on Slovak Republic (n 89 above), para 18. See also AC, Opinion on Spain (n 89 above), para 31.
[162] AC, First Opinion on fYROM (n 62 above), para 30.
[163] AC, First Opinion on Austria (n 64 above), para 71; AC, First Opinion on Bosnia and Herzegovina (n 63 above), para 44; AC, First Opinion on Finland (n 62 above), para 48; AC, First Opinion on Slovak, Republic (n 89 above), para 20.
[164] AC, First Opinion on Bosnia and Herzegovina (n 63 above), para 45; AC, Opinion on Croatia (n 73 above), para 65; AC, First Opinion on Lithuania (n 73 above), para 33; AC, First Opinion on Norway (n 35 above), para 28.
[165] AC, First Opinion on Spain (n 89 above), paras 31–2.
[166] AC, First Opinion on Poland (n 75 above), para 36.   [167] Ibid, para 50.
[168] AC, First Opinion on Spain (n 89 above), para 37.
[169] See also Weller, 'Report' (n 7 above), 86; and Phillips, 'The Framework Convention (n 5 above), 291–2.

event a general theme featuring in virtually all country-specific opinions of the Committee.

Access to land can be a key factor in ensuring effective participation in social and economic life, as noted by the AC in relation to Ukraine's Crimea.[170] Countering discrimination in relation to land privatization[171] or adequate access to land distribution schemes is essential when land constitutes an important source of income.[172] For indigenous peoples like the Saami, ownership of their ancestral lands is extremely important and any disputes in this respect should be resolved as soon as possible.[173]

1. Language Requirements

In several respects language requirements could hinder participation of minorities in economic (and social) life.

First, according to the AC no language restrictions, let alone prohibitions of using the minority language in signs, posters, or advertisements of a private enterprise should be imposed. Private in this respect would include signs visible to the public as long as they were not official.[174]

Secondly, being able to address authorities providing social services in your minority language is important for effective access to public services/social services. On the other hand, demands about a certain level of proficiency in an official language may be legitimate for public servants, but these requirements should not be overly extensive.[175] In relation to Cyprus the AC welcomes the use of different levels of language skills requirements for entry into the civil service of persons belonging to religious groups, which would facilitate access to employment for the minorities concerned. Disproportionate language requirements can also pose problems in terms of Art 10, and need to be attenuated through special educational programmes.[176]

2. The Importance of Citizenship

As was confirmed in the 2008 Annual Report of the UN Independent Expert on Minority Issues, citizenship remains very important for integration and full economic and social participation.[177] Precisely because non-citizens are especially vulnerable to discrimination and cannot participate fully in economic and

---

[170] AC, First Opinion on Ukraine (n 121 above), para 74.
[171] AC, Second Opinion on Armenia (ACFC/OP/II(2006)005), 24 October 2006, para 47.
[172] AC, First Opinion on Albania (n 81 above), para 28.
[173] AC, First Opinion on Finland (n 62 above), para 22.
[174] AC, First Opinion on the Russian Federation (n 73 above), para 43; AC, Opinion on Estonia (n 73 above), para 43.
[175] AC, First Opinion on Azerbaijan (n 81 above), para 79; AC, First Opinion on Estonia (n 73 above), para 60.   [176] AC, Opinion on Moldova (n 11 above), para 63.
[177] AC, First Opinion on Austria (n 64 above), para 35

social life, states are urged not to exercise undue citizenship requirements, especially in the wake of state dissolution.[178] A similar problem, often noted in relation to Roma, concerns the lack of identity documents, as this also seriously hampers access to a great deal of social and economic rights.[179]

3. Cross-border Cooperation with Kin-states?

Finally, a critical comment should be made: considering the broad range of socio-economic issues that are explicitly addressed in the Commentary, it is surprising that no attention is paid to the possible impact of economic relations with kin-states,[180] especially as there are clear examples (eg Hungary/Romania) where cross-border cooperation between minorities and kin states has proven important in unlocking the economic potential of minority communities. Even though not all minorities would benefit from cross-border ties with kin-states,[181] this line of reasoning remains strangely unexplored.

H. Governments' response?

This assessment of government responses takes as its starting point the results of the constructive dialogue between AC and states that emerges from the second cycle of AC opinions. In line with the general characteristics of constructive dialogue, the AC second opinions begin by highlighting positive developments, as compared with the first cycle findings, then note any outstanding issues, and finally issue recommendations.

Sometimes, the AC notes that there has been no development, no improvement. Croatia was criticized for not having adopted any positive action to redress past discrimination, and the Russian Federation was reprimanded not only because it had yet to make any effort to adopt comprehensive civil and administrative legislation combating discrimination,[182] but also because it did not accommodate the special needs of small indigenous peoples so as to protect them against industrial and commercial expansion.[183] More often, the AC will

---

[178] AC, First Opinion on fYROM (n 62 above), para 37; AC, Second Opinion on Croatia, ACFC/INF/OP/II(2004)002, 13 April 2005, para 16; AC, First Opinion on Slovenia (n 73 above), para 60.
[179] AC, Second Opinion on Romania (n 144 above), para 58; AC, First Opinion on Slovenia (n 73 above), para 72.   [180] Phillips, 'The Framework Convention' (n 5 above), 297.
[181] Wheatley gives the example of Russians in Estonia and Latvia who have been largely unable to exploit their relationship with their ethnic kin in Russia because of declining trade relations between the states and because Russia is poorer then the Baltic republics: Wheatley (n 3 above), 10.
[182] AC, Second Opinion on Croatia (n 178 above), para 60. See also AC, Second Opinion on Switzerland (n 91 above), para 35, noting in terms of Art 4 that there is still a lack of specific provisions against discrimination in key areas such as housing, employment, access to public places and provision of services.
[183] AC, Second Opinion on the Russian Federation, ACFC/OP/II(2006)004, 2 May 2007, paras 43, 102–3.

note that while the appropriate policies are in place, actual implementation is missing.[184]

Overall, however, the data suggest that contracting states are moving (slowly) in the direction indicated by the AC and hence, in the context of participation in economic and social life, are adopting policies and taking measures aimed at improving the economic and social situation of persons belonging to minorities. However, the AC also points out that further improvements are still possible/required, that existing initiatives and programmes need to be stepped up, that new legislation and strategies should be tried, and that adequate resources should be made available.[185]

In follow-up assessments, while considerable attention is paid to the situation of the Roma and the persistent discrimination they face, in the UK similar points are made in relation to 'ethnic communities': although the AC welcomes efforts being made to tackle unemployment and restricted access to health care and housing, it notes that progress is very slow and that public authorities should adopt more rigorous policies and actions.[186]

In the face of persistent problems related to deep-seated and ingrained discrimination (as is often the case in relation to minorities and especially Roma) the AC welcomes the adoption of more comprehensive strategies to counter the socio-economic disadvantages faced by Roma and Travellers, like specific education and employment strategies, and new health and social security measures geared towards the specific situation of Roma.[187] Particular actions that are positively assessed include the use of Roma counsellors in the employment bureau,[188] support programmes to assist in the inclusion of Roma children,[189] mainstreaming equality throughout the curriculum, and special language classes and grants.[190] At the same time, the AC underscores the importance that these programmes and measures be geared towards the specific needs of the Roma.[191]

---

[184] AC, Second Opinion the Czech Republic (n 134 above), para 152, AC, Second Opinion on Switzerland (n 91 above), para 48; AC, Second Opinion on Hungary (n 91 above), para 14; AC, Second Opinion on the Slovak Republic (n 92 above), para 14.

[185] AC, Second Opinion the Czech Republic (n 134 above), para 39; AC, Second Opinion on Croatia (n 178 above), para 42; AC, Second Opinion on Hungary (n 91 above), para 48.

[186] AC, Second Opinion on the United Kingdom (n 93 above), para 69–71.

[187] AC, Second Opinion on Croatia (n 178 above), para 69–74; AC, Second Opinion the Czech Republic (n 134, above), para 48; AC, Second Opinion on Ireland (n 96 above), para 46; AC, First Opinion on Slovenia (n 73 above), paras 63–7. See also Bedard, *Participation in Economic Life* (n 18 above), 51–6 discussing the action plans for Roma taken in several Eastern European countries including Albania, Bulgaria, and Croatia.

[188] AC, Second Opinion on Croatia (n 178 above), para 149.

[189] AC, Second Opinion on fYROM (n 92 above), para 162.

[190] AC, Second Opinion on the United Kingdom (n 93 above), para 195.

[191] Eg, AC, First Opinion on Slovenia (n 73 above), para 73; AC, Second Opinion on the Slovak Republic (n 92 above), para 46. See also AC, Second Opinion on Germany (n 91 above), para 52–4; AC, Second Opinion on Croatia (n 178 above), para 92; AC, Second Opinion the Czech Republic (n 134 above), paras 50, 57.

IV. Other Relevant Universal and Regional Instruments and Supervisory Practice

The following paragraphs do not only provide an overview of the activities of some minority specific supervisory bodies/organizations but also a broad variety of 'instruments', documents, and types of supervisory practice related to a diverse gamut of organizations (with global or regional coverage): minority-specific norms, non-specific human rights with minority specific interpretations, and attention for minorities in the implementation phase of particular (potentially relevant) policies.

The first two subsections concern general human rights and/or minority-specific standards, and the related supervisory practice (respectively with a global and a regional focus), whereas the last subsection covers various bodies with a totally different 'colour', ranging from the UN Independent Expert on Minority Issues to a non-governmental organization (NGO).

A. United Nations

1. Article 27 ICCPR and the HRC[192]

A steady line of jurisprudence, reflected in the HRC General Comment on Art 27, para 7, concerns the recognition, also detected in the quasi jurisprudence of the AC, that the right to enjoy one's own culture includes the right to exercise and benefit from traditional economic activities like hunting and fishing. Actually, this provision is mostly applied in relation to indigenous people, like the Sami in the Scandinavian countries. While traditional economic activities are assured a place within the application of Art 27, the opinions of the HRC in relation to particular complaints reveals that, in the de facto balancing process of state interests on the one hand and minority interests on the other, the HRC gives a lot of weight to state concerns regarding their own economic development.[193] In other words, the actual level of protection of these traditional economic activities, as essential components of the economic participation of the

---

[192] Art 1 of the ICCPR on the right to self-determination of all peoples also enshrines the right of peoples to pursue their own economic and social development. There is no generally accepted definition of the concept 'people' and its relation to the concept 'minority' is similarly not crystallized. According to the HRC Art 1 contains a group right and can thus not be invoked in terms of the individual complaints procedure, but the Committee does acknowledge that this idea of self-determination (Art 1) may be relevant in the interpretation of other rights protected by the Covenant, and in particular Art 27 of the ICCPR, the most basic minority specific provision in international law: eg, HRC, *JGA Diergaardt and orsl v Namibia*, 25 July 2000, no 760/1997, CCPR/C/69/D/760/1997; *Mahuika and ors v New Zealand*, 27 October 2000, no 547/1993, CCPR/C/70/D/547/1993, para 9.2. See also Verstichel, 'Recent developments' (n 9 above), 36.

[193] See also the analysis in Henrard, *Devising an Adequate System of Minority Protection* (n 6 above), 178–85, discussing, eg, *Kitok v Sweden*, *Länsman and ors v Finland I* and *II*.

minorities concerned, is rather modest.[194] In both *Länsman* cases[195] the HRC acknowledged the erosion of reindeer breeding as a result of the impact of extraction activities (mining and logging), but indicated that this erosion was not so bad as to amount to a violation of Art 27.[196] The warning in both cases that further extension of activities and related negative effects on reindeer breeding might result in the finding of a violation carries considerably less weight after the second opinion.[197] Strikingly, the HRC took into account the fact that the Sami community had been consulted as a factor that rendered the interference reasonable, notwithstanding that the Sami themselves denied having meaningfully participated in the decision-making process.[198]

Similar issues can be identified in the *Mahuika and ors v New Zealand* case,[199] which concerned a complaint by a group of Maori that they were unable to freely pursue their economic and social development as a result of a deed settling the fishing quota for the Maori at large. The HRC acknowledged that fishing is one of the main elements of Maori traditional culture, and that it comprises some commercial elements. This is clearly problematic as the commercial element cannot be neatly severed from the non-commercial part.[200]

An important development in that case was that, as a matter of relevant principles, the HRC not only considered the opportunity to participate in decision-making concerning measures which interfere with culturally significant economic activities to be relevant in deciding whether or not there has been a violation of article rights, but also considered it essential that the minority

---

[194] Nevertheless, it has been argued that the principle of effective participation is not only particularly important in the use of economic resources by indigenous groups, but is actually more generally applicable (and expected to be recognized by the HRC) despite the absence of HRC jurisprudence in this area: R. Burchill 'Minority rights' in A Conte, S Davidson, and R Burchill (eds), *Defining Civil and Political Rights: The jurisprudence of the UNHRC* (2004), 183, 196. A few critical words are also in order about the *Jonassen and orsl v Norway* case concerning an alleged failure to recognize and protect their right to let their herds graze on their traditional grazing grounds because the existing regulation of grazing rights does not take into consideration specific features of reindeer herding, nor Sami culture (HRC, *Jonassen and ors v Norway*, 25 October 2002, no 942/2000, CCPR/C/76/D/942/2000, para 3.9). As rightly criticized in the Dissenting Opinion by Henkin, Scheinin, and Yrigoyen, the inadmissibility decision for failure to exhaust local remedies is unjustly formalistic. The Committee could have clarified in its views on the merits its understanding about the positive obligations of states to take minority particularities into account when applying general norms, not only in general but also in relation to the exercise of a traditional economic activity and thus participation in economic life.

[195] HRC, *Ilmari Länsman and ors v Finland*, 26 October 1994, no 511/1992, CCPR/C/52/D/511/1992 (*Länsman I*); HRC, *Jouni E Länsman and ors v Finland*, 22 November 1996, no 671/1995, CCPR/C/58/D/617/1995 (*Länsman II*).

[196] HRC, *Länsman I*, para 9.6; and HRC, *Länsman II*, para 10.5.

[197] Henrard, *Devising an Adequate System of Minority Protection* (n 6 above), 183.

[198] Compare *Länsman I*, para 9.6 with *Länsman II*, para 10.4

[199] HRC, *Mahuika and ors v New Zealand*, 27 October 2000, no 547/1993, CCPR/C/70/D/547/1993.   [200] Ibid, paras 6.2, 9.2.

concerned continued to benefit from its traditional economy.[201] In other words there must be some assurance of actual participation in economic life.

Furthermore, the HRC is swayed not so much by the fact that the Maori were consulted but that their views actually did affect the design of the ultimate arrangement.[202] Indeed during the broad consultation process, special attention was paid to the cultural and religious significance of fishing for the Maori, as well as the sustainability of Maori fishing activities.[203] It therefore did not seem unreasonable that the HRC concluded that, *in casu*, Art 27 had not been violated. The HRC also clarified that it took into consideration minorities within the minority and that for these 'double minorities' a measure of economic participation must be ensured. While it considered it acceptable for the deed to go ahead with substantial, if not complete, Maori support, it did emphasize that measures affecting the economic activities of Maori must generally be carried out in such a way that those who do not agree to the settlement can continue to enjoy their culture, including their traditional economic activities.[204]

The question of adequate consultation in the context of participation in economic life continues to give rise to complaints before the HRC, as evidenced by the *George Howard v Canada* case, concerning the surrendering of traditional hunting and fishing rights by in a particular indigenous people through a treaty.[205] The complainants tried to distinguish the *Mahuika* case because there had not been proper consultation, nor had sufficient attention been paid to the cultural and religious significance of fishing for the traditional community concerned.[206] Unfortunately the HRC did not explicitly assess these arguments because of a disagreement between the parties on the factual circumstances of the case, and arguably gave the government the benefit of the doubt by concluding that it did not have sufficient information to conclude a violation of Art 27.[207] This does not seem to amount to an effective protection of the economic participation of the indigenous people concerned. Exactly the same remarks can be made in relation to *Äärelä and Näkkäläjärvi v Finland*,[208] a case which again concerned the Saami, in which the HRC maintained that it did not have sufficient information to conclude independently that the additional logging and road construction activities in the area concerned would have such an impact on reindeer husbandry as to amount to a denial of the Saami's right to enjoy their own culture.[209]

Arguably, these opinions demonstrate that the HRC is often ready to let 'procedural economic participation' take precedence over substantive economic participation, although it should be noted that its assessment of the procedural

---

[201] Ibid, para 9.5. [202] Ibid, para 9.6 [203] Ibid, para 9.8
[204] Ibid, paras 9.6, 9.9.
[205] HRC, *George Howard v Canada*, 26 July 2005, no 879/1999, CCPR/C/84/D/879/1999.
[206] Ibid, para 11.13. [207] Ibid, para 12.11.
[208] HRC, *Äärelä and Näkkäläjärvi v Finland*, 24 October 2001, no 779/1997, CCPR/C/73/D/779/1997. [209] Ibid, para 7.6.

dimension sometimes pays lip service to the importance of consultation.[210] Furthermore, it can be argued that when the HRC wants to give weight to the consultation process it should do so in an appropriate and transparent way, by developing criteria to evaluate and take on board whether the voice of the relevant minority is being taken seriously and whether the negotiation process has been fair.[211]

2. UN Declaration on the Rights of Persons Belonging to National or Ethnic, Religious, and Linguistic Minorities[212]

Since the UN Declaration does not have a proper supervisory body, its analysis in terms of economic and social participation will be confined to those provisions that are most relevant, while paying attention to the clarifications in the Commentary to the UN Declaration made by the now defunct Working Group on Minorities.[213] The Working Group on Minorities was, inter alia, meant to promote adequate implementation of the UN Declaration, which is now a special task of the United Nations Expert on Minorities Issues.[214]

In addition to two paragraphs that are framed in terms of participatory rights, there are (at least) three others that also address matters pertaining to social and economic participation. Article 2 confirms, in wording very close to Art 15 of the FCNM, that persons belonging to minorities have the right to participate effectively in cultural, religious, social, economic, and public life (para 2). In relation to participation in social and economic life, the Commentary to the Declaration confirms that citizenship remains an important condition for full and effective participation. Consequently, barriers to the acquisition of citizenship for members of minorities should be reduced (para 50). The importance of all communities being 'equally' represented in the public service is similarly highlighted as an important dimension of participation (para 49).

---

[210] Verstichel, 'Recent Developments' (n 9 above), 38.   [211] Ibid, 39.

[212] After a very lengthy negotiation process, the UN Declaration on the Rights of Indigenous Peoples was adopted by the General Assembly in September 2007 (A/61/L67). Even at a first glance it is obvious that the rights enshrined in this declaration are much stronger and more elaborate in comparison with the Declaration on Minorities. While a full blown analysis would go beyond the confines of this contribution, it should be highlighted that there is extensive coverage of rights with a socio-economic focus. Art 3 grants indigenous people the right to self-determination, and thus also the right to freely pursue their own economic development. This is further elaborated upon inter alia in Art 23 which enshrines the right to determine and develop the priorities and strategies in relation to their development, as outlined in social and economic programs. Art 10 protects them against forcible removal of their lands while Art 26 acknowledges their ownership of their ancestral lands. Art 5 underscores that they are at liberty to participate in the economic and social life of the state (in addition to their right to autonomy). In addition to a general guarantee of equal treatment and non-discrimination Art 17(3) also enshrines the right not to be discriminated against in labour conditions and salary. Art 14 enables indigenous peoples to have and administer their own educational systems, with adequate attention for their own culture and language.

[213] See also the report by F de Varennes, entitled 'Towards effective political participation and representation of minorities', E/CN4/Sub2/AC5/1998/WP4, 1 May 1998.   [214] See below.

Art 4 of the UN Declaration also contains a paragraph of particular relevance to economic participation, which to date has not accorded appropriate attention, namely the duty of the state to consider appropriate measures so that persons belonging to minorities may participate fully in the economic progress and development of their country. The Commentary highlights the importance of this state obligation to counter the economic marginalization and exclusion of minorities (para 71). At the same time, the Commentary underscores that the overall economic development of a society should not be compromised by the preservation of the minority identity (para 72).

The Commentary also highlights the importance of mother tongue education for minorities, the feasibility of which depends on the number and territorial concentration of the groups concerned. Pre-school and primary school education should ideally be in the child's own language, ie the minority language, while the importance of adequate knowledge of the official language for optimal integration and participation is also acknowledged (paras 60–1). The Commentary distinguishes between territorial and non-territorial languages in this respect, with the former having the stronger position. New or immigrant minorities tend to be extremely dispersed, and to encompass so many different identities that their entitlements are even weaker than the persons speaking non-territorial traditional languages (para 64).

In relation to the question of curriculum, the Commentary on the UN Declaration promotes intercultural and multicultural education (para 66). It is expected that racial prejudice and intolerance will be reduced when the majority population has adequate knowledge of minorities and their cultures (para 67–8).

It is obvious that, in terms of minority-specific provisions, ample attention is paid to education as an important aspect of participation in social life in itself, and as a foundation for all other dimensions of economic and social participation. Hence, it does not come as a surprise that the education of persons belonging to minorities was also the theme of the first session of the Minority Rights Forum (successor to the UN Working Group on Minorities) in December 2008.

3. *Non Minority-specific Convention Norms and Supervision by UN Treaty Bodies*

In addition to minority-specific provisions, the UN has several human rights conventions which are not minority-specific but which are nevertheless especially important for persons belonging to minorities. Their interpretation by UN treaty bodies has often added an important minority protection gloss to the convention provisions, revealing an added layer of synergy/synergies in the framework of minority protection.[215]

---

[215] See the book edited by Henrard and Dunbar, *Synergies in Minority Protection* (n 15 above).

a. International Convention on the Elimination of All Forms of Racial Discrimination (ICERD)

It is common knowledge that the Convention on the Elimination of Racial Discrimination is particularly relevant to ethnic minorities and this has been confirmed by the supervisory practice of its treaty body, which often addresses minority problems in its opinions and concluding observations, and has even formulated two general recommendations dedicated to a particular minority: the Roma and indigenous peoples.[216]

Art 5 is particularly relevant to the focus of this contribution as it encapsulates the state obligation to guarantee the enjoyment of (inter alia) economic and social rights without racial discrimination. In line with the supervisory practice of the AC, the CERD Committee urges authorities to adopt comprehensive legislation to combat racial discrimination also in relation to social and economic life.[217] The Committee pays considerable attention to the need to make protection effective, which has repercussions for remedies and investigations.[218]

ICERD is known as one of the few international conventions which has clauses explicitly enabling and even obliging positive action, and the committee does not shy away from calling on states to comply with their obligations in terms of Art 2(2) 'to eliminate the persistent disparities in the enjoyment of human rights and fundamental freedoms and ensure the adequate development and protection of members of racial, ethnic and national minorities'.[219]

The importance of adequate representation of minorities in the public service, an issue of direct relevance for the economic participation of the civil servants concerned as well as effective access to state services, is also taken up here, and states are called upon to effectively promote this equitable representation.[220] A further synergy with the advisory practice of the FCNM is the recognition of the problematic nature of overly demanding language requirements, which tend to inhibit effective access to employment, including in the private sector.[221] The CERD Committee also shows awareness of the importance of supportive measures in relation to those jobs for which language

---

[216] CERD Committee, General Comment no 23: Rights of Indigenous Peoples; CERD, General Comment no 27: Discrimination against Roma.
[217] CERD Committee, Concluding Observations on Moldova, CERD/C/MDA/O/7 (2008) para 10.
[218] CERD Committee, Concluding Observation on Belgium, CERD/C/BEL/CO/15 (2008) para 10.
[219] CERD Committee, Concluding Observation on the United States of America, CERD/C/USA/CO/6 (2008) para 15; CERD Committee, Concluding Observation on Sweden, CERD/C/SWD/CO/18(2008) para 13.
[220] CERD Committee, Concluding Observation on Moldova (n 217 above), para 16.
[221] CERD Committee, Concluding Observation on Latvia, CERD/C/LVE/CO/2 (2003) para 9.

requirements would be legitimate, and notes the importance of enhanced education of the official language for persons belonging to minorities.[222]

In line with Art 3 of the ICERD, the Committee urges states to actively counteract de facto segregation, remarking explicitly that problems relating to housing have a negative impact on other socio-economic issues.[223] The Committee underscores the potential danger that linguistic requirements to benefit from social housing are indirectly racially discriminatory.[224] Concerns of indirect discrimination have also been voiced in relation to access to rental housing, when landlords can refuse rental by reference to very vague criteria because these can shield discriminatory motives.[225]

This supervisory body is also strongly opposed to all forms of segregation in education. Authorities are urged to counter segregation by integrating minorities, including new minorities, into regular schools, and if need be to support them through additional training in the official language.[226]

In line with the practice of the FCNM, the CERD Committee pays special attention to Roma and, in line with the practice of the HRC, it accords particular importance to the rights of indigenous peoples. In relation to Roma, the Committee has called on states to adopt comprehensive legislation to eradicate discrimination against Roma.[227] States are also asked to adopt special measures to counter the numerous disadvantages suffered by the Roma and Travellers in relation to housing, education, and employment.[228] The Committee is once again aware of the need for supportive measures, like providing additional training for Roma to enhance their qualifications and thus their employability.[229] In relation to the education of Roma, the Committee follows a holistic approach, also visible in the practice of the AC, whereby authorities are urged to provide financial support to Roma families for school books, transport

---

[222] CERD Committee, Concluding Observation on Moldova (n 217 above), para 18.

[223] CERD Committee, Concluding Observation on Italy, CERD/C/ITA/CO/15 (2008) para 14; CERD Committee, Concluding Observation on Belgium (n 218 above), para 15. In this respect, the assessment of the US is particularly enlightening: the committee notes with concern that racial, ethnic and national minorities are disproportionately concentrated in poor residential areas, characterized by substandard housing conditions, limited employment opportunities, inadequate access to health care facilities, and underresourced schools (CERD Committee, Concluding Observation on USA (n 219 above), para 16).

[224] CERD Committee, Concluding Observation on Belgium (n 218 above), para 16.

[225] CERD Committee, Concluding Observation on Germany, CERD/C/DEU/CO/18 (2008) para 17.

[226] CERD Committee, Concluding Observation on Germany (n 225 above), para 23; CERD Committee, Concluding Observation on Russia, CERD/C/RUS/CO/19 (2008), para 27.

[227] In line with the specification in General Comment No 27 on Discrimination against Roma: see CERD Committee Concluding Observation on Italy (n 223 above), para 12.

[228] CERD Committee, Concluding Observation on Switzerland, CERD/C/CHE/CO/6 (2008) para 19; CERD Committee, Concluding Observation on Sweden (n 119 above), para 18; CERD Committee, Concluding Observation on Germany (n 225 above), para 21; CERD Committee, Concluding Observation on Russia (n 226 above), para 14.

[229] CERD Committee, Concluding Observation on Moldova (n 217 above), para 17; CERD Committee, Concluding Observation on Sweden (n 219 above), para 18.

and other indirect costs of schooling.[230] The inclusion of Roma culture and language in the curriculum also features here as an important means of ensuring genuinely equal access to education, while the use of Roma teachers is also explicitly encouraged in this respect.[231] Finally, positive action to increase Roma presence in higher education is welcomed not only in the form of scholarship schemes but also in quotas.[232]

In relation to indigenous peoples, the CERD Committee acknowledges the problematic impact on their ancestral lands of economic activities like mining and logging, with negative implications not only for their economic activities but also for their health, thus impairing their effective access to economic and social participation. Hence, authorities are urged to ensure that these economic activities do not have unacceptable implications for the indigenous peoples. Prior consultation is seen as a potential means of achieving that effect.[233] Furthermore, and in view of the disproportionate poverty among indigenous peoples and the ensuing limited enjoyment of economic and social rights like housing, education, health, and employment, authorities are called upon to develop special programmes to combat poverty and improve the overall social and economic situation of indigenous communities.[234] Another issue which resonates with the practice of the FCNM's AC concerns the need for land disputes concerning Sami ancestral lands to be settled in a way which does not discriminate indirectly against them.[235] Namibia is similarly urged to recognize ownership of indigenous communities over lands which they traditionally occupied.[236]

An important point that touches on the *ratione personae* scope of ICERD concerns the reach of the exclusion in Art 2.3 of differentiations on the basis of nationality. Gradually, the Committee has come to recognize that such differentiations can amount to indirect racial discrimination. The Committee underscores in its General Recommendation 30 that non-citizens should also be protected against racial discrimination.[237] In its Concluding Observation on Italy of 2008 it 'urges authorities to take measures to eliminate discrimination against non citizens in relation to working conditions and work requirements, including employment rules and practices with discriminatory

---

[230] Ibid, para 19.
[231] Ibid para 19; CERD Committee, Concluding Observation on Sweden (n 119 above), para 18. [232] CERD Committee, Concluding Observation on Moldova (n 217 above), para 19.
[233] CERD Committee, Concluding Observation on USA (n 219 above), para 29; CERD Committee, Concluding Observation on Russia (n 226 above), para 24; CERD Committee, Concluding Observation on Ecuador, CERD/C/ECU/CO/19 (2008), para 16.
[234] CERD Committee, Concluding Observation on Russia (n 226 above), para 15; CERD Committee, Concluding Observation on Namibia, CERD/C/MAM/CO/12 (2008) paras 20–1.
[235] CERD Committee, Concluding Observation on Sweden (n 119 above), para 20.
[236] CERD Committee, Concluding Observation on Namibia (n 234 above), para 18.
[237] See also CERD Committee, Concluding Observation on Moldova (n 217 above), para 10.

purposes or effects'.[238] At times, it even requests that authorities facilitate access to citizenship for long-term residents, without banning double nationality.[239]

A final synergetic development is the consistent suggestion made to states to ratify the Convention on the Protection of the Rights of All Migrant Workers and Members of their Families, which clearly addresses matters of relevance to participation in economic and social life for new minorities.[240]

b. International Covenant on Civil and Political Rights

In its concluding observations when reviewing periodic state reports the Human Rights Committee (HRC) takes up several themes of relevance to the participation of persons belonging to minorities in economic and social life. A first theme is the importance of enacting comprehensive anti-discrimination legislation in all areas and related policies and programmes, thus also covering the socio-economic field.[241] In relation to Art 26 of the ICCPR, which is not minority-specific, the Committee also underscores the positive state duty to combat discrimination against persons belonging to minorities in employment, so as to ensure their equal access.[242] It is generally known that one needs to be proficient in the official language to be eligible for good jobs, hence the emphasis on adequate teaching of the official language to obtain these qualifications and thus to counter marginalization and underrepresentation in different public and private spheres is to be welcomed.[243] Still, in relation to the prohibition of discrimination in Art 26, education is a sore point for the Roma in several respects. The problems of the Roma are exemplified by the still rather prevalent practice of sidelining them to special schools or classes with diminished curricula (often meant for students with mental disabilities or learning difficulties).[244] The HRC joins forces with other treaty bodies and states that, while it cannot be denied that Roma often have special educational needs, these can and should be

---

[238] CERD Committee, Concluding Observation on Italy (n 223 above), para 17. See also CERD Committee, Concluding Observation on Austria, CERD/C/AUT/CO/17 (2008) para 20, in which the Committee notes that the lack of nationality can hinder effective access to economic and social life. In relation to Sweden (above note 119, para 17) the committee also urges the authorities to review health care policies to offer genuine equal access to immigrants, and to improve their employment opportunities.
[239] CERD Committee, Concluding Observation on Germany (n 225 above), para 20.
[240] CERD Committee, Concluding Observation on Moldova (n 217 above), para 22 ; CERD Committee, Concluding Observation on Italy (n 223 above), para 23; CERD Committee, Concluding Observation on Belgium (n 218 above), para 19; CERD Committee, Concluding Observation on Germany (n 225 above), para 27.
[241] HRC, Concluding Observations on the Czech Republic, CCPR/C/CZE/CO/2 (2008) para 16; HRC, Concluding Observations on France, CCPR/C/FRA/CO/4 (2008) para 25.
[242] HRC, Concluding Observations on France (n 241 above), para 25.
[243] HRC, Concluding Observations on Georgia CCPR/C/GEO/CO/3 (2007) para 17.
[244] HRC, Concluding Observations on the Czech Republic (n 241 above), para 17; HRC, Concluding Observations on the former Yugoslav Republic of Macedonia, CCPR/C/MKD/CO/2 (2008) para 19.

tackled without segregation.²⁴⁵ The HRC also confirms the aforementioned connection between the inclusion of information on Roma language and culture in the general curriculum and effective access to education for Roma. Similarly, the importance of mother tongue education for genuinely effective access to education is recognized, as is the concomitant need to have qualified teachers for instruction in the Roma language.²⁴⁶ The supervisory practice of the HRC exhibits more generally particular attention for the Roma and their disadvantaged situation, often entailing segregation and unequal access to social services.²⁴⁷ One of the concerns highlighted by the HRC is residential segregation. Consequently, the authorities are urged to counter skewed residential patterns.²⁴⁸

The HRC not only pays special attention to indigenous communities in its jurisprudence on Art 27; in its concluding observations on Art 26, for example, it also notes and criticizes the unequal access to health and education services for persons belonging to indigenous communities.²⁴⁹ In line with the practice of the FCNM's AC and the CERD Committee, the HRC underscores the need to counter discrimination against non-citizens, which is clearly of benefit to new minorities.²⁵⁰

While Art 27 is undoubtedly the provision of the ICCPR most readily related to minority protection, important decisions pertaining to the economic and social participation of minorities have been decided in terms of other provisions. *Ballantyne and ors v Canada*²⁵¹ clarified that freedom of expression does not permit prohibition of signposting and publicity for companies in a language other than the official language of a province; while in *Waldman v Canada*²⁵² the HRC considered it incompatible with the prohibition of discrimination of Art 26 not to fund a private Jewish school while funding private Catholic schools. In *Diergaardt v Namibia*²⁵³ the HRC sanctions as a violation of Art 26 of the ICCPR a blanket prohibition against using the minority language with citizens, even when the public servants concerned would be perfectly capable of doing so.²⁵⁴ As noted earlier, being able to communicate with public authorities in one's native language has a significant impact on effective/real access to public services.

---

²⁴⁵ HRC, Concluding Observations on the Czech Republic (n 241 above), para 17.
²⁴⁶ HRC, Concluding Observations on Austria (n 238 above), para 21.
²⁴⁷ Eg, HRC, Concluding Observations on the Czech Republic (n 241 above), para 16.
²⁴⁸ Ibid.
²⁴⁹ HRC, Concluding Observations on Panama, CCPR/C/PAN/CO/3 (2008) para 21.
²⁵⁰ HRC, Concluding Observations on the Czech Republic (n 241 above), para 18.
²⁵¹ HRC, *Ballantyne and ors v Canada*, no 359/1989 and 385/1989, A/48/40, Part II (1993), Annex XII, Sect, P (91–101).
²⁵² HRC, *Waldman v Canada*, no 694/1996, CCPR/C/67/D/694/1996.
²⁵³ HRC, *Diergaardt v Namibia*, no 1760/1996, CPR/C/69/D/760/1996.
²⁵⁴ See also K Henrard, 'Charting the Gradual emergence of a more robust level of minority protection: Minority specific instruments and the European Union' (2004) 22(4) *Netherlands Quarterly of Human Rights* 559–84, 575–7.

Finally, the HRC's decision in the case concerning *Sister Immaculate Joseph*[255] shows that a certain protection of participation in economic and social life for minorities can flow from the freedom to religion and a general prohibition against discrimination. While the argument is not formulated in terms of minorities and their entitlements, the case does concern the religious order of a minority which is refused incorporation (for no transparent, objective reason) and hence is inhibited from performing its social and economic activities. This inhibition results from their inability to realize the objects of their order, eg because they cannot hold property, they cannot construct a place of worship (para 7.2). The limitations concerning participation in economic and social life for the order thus impaired their right to manifest their religion. The HRC concluded the absence of a legitimate limitation, and thus a violation of freedom of religion as well as the prohibition of discrimination (paras 7.2–7.3).

c. International Covenant on Economic, Social and Cultural Rights (ICESCR)

The supervision of the ICESCR has been confined to a review of periodic state reports resulting in concluding observations. However, the Committee has been very active in the formulation of (often very detailed) general comments, which often refer explicitly or implicitly to minorities,[256] and these should thus not be excluded from this assessment. A detailed analysis of what is required in terms of social and economic rights arguably amounts to a clarification of participation in social and economic life. The extra translation in favour of persons belonging to minorities was not to be expected and should be welcomed. It is especially important that there are several similarities with issues identified as relevant for participation in social and economic life in terms of minority-specific rights, without explicit focus on social and economic rights.

General Comment 14 (2000) on the right to the highest attainable standard of health[257] does not contain an explicit reference to minorities but does specify that the acceptability of health should also be measured in terms of what is culturally appropriate (Art 12.3), clearly referring to the special needs of persons belonging to minorities to effectively enjoy this aspect of social participation. The General Comment includes quite a lengthy paragraph on elements that would help to define an indigenous peoples' right to health in order to better enable states with indigenous peoples to implement the provisions contained in Art 12 of the Covenant. Again, concerns are expressed about the negative impact of the displacement of indigenous communities because of economic activities that would benefit the country at large (para 27). According to the Committee:

---

[255] HRC, *Sister Immaculate Joseph and Eighty Teaching Sisters of the Holy Cross of the Third Order of Saint Francis in Menzingen v Sri Lanka*, no 1249/2004, CCPR/C/85/D/1249/2004.

[256] MA Martin-Estebanez, 'The UN International Covenant on Economic, Social and Cultural Rights' in Henrard and Dunbar, *Synergies in Minority Protection* (n 15 above), 230–9.

[257] E/C12/2000/4.

[I]ndigenous peoples have the right to specific measures to improve their access to health services and care. These health services should be culturally appropriate, taking into account traditional preventive care, healing practices and medicines. States should provide resources for indigenous peoples to design, deliver and control such services so that they may enjoy the highest attainable standard of physical and mental health. The vital medicinal plants, animals and minerals necessary to the full enjoyment of health of indigenous peoples should also be protected.

The Committee notes that, in indigenous communities, the health of the individual is often linked to the health of the society as a whole and has a collective dimension.

In this respect, the Committee considers that development-related activities that lead to the displacement of indigenous peoples against their will from their traditional territories and environment, denying them their sources of nutrition and breaking their symbiotic relationship with their lands, has a deleterious effect on their health.

General Comment 15 (2002) on the right to water[258] requires states parties to give special attention to groups with traditional problems in relation to access to water, and explicitly mentions minorities, indigenous peoples and immigrants as such vulnerable groups (para 16). The Committee specifies the need for state parties to take steps to ensure that:

(d) *Indigenous peoples'* access to water resources on their ancestral lands is protected from encroachment and unlawful pollution. States should provide resources for indigenous peoples to design, deliver and control their access to water;
(e) *Nomadic and Traveller communities* have access to adequate water at traditional and designated halting sites.

The General Comment on the Right to Education,[259] and more particularly Art 13, notes that education has to be available, accessible, acceptable, and adaptable. In relation to acceptability the Committee highlights the obligation of states to 'fulfil (facilitate) the acceptability of education by taking positive measures to ensure that education is culturally appropriate for minorities and indigenous peoples, and of good quality for all' (para 50).

Finally the General Comment on the right to adequate housing[260] highlights that 'adequacy' is determined, inter alia, by cultural factors and goes on to specify that cultural adequacy requires that:

the way housing is constructed, the building materials used and the policies supporting these must appropriately enable the expression of cultural identity and diversity of housing. Activities geared towards development or modernization in the housing sphere should ensure that the cultural dimensions of housing are not sacrificed, and that, *inter alia*, modern technological facilities, as appropriate are also ensured. [para 8(g)]

In its concluding observations, the Committee also reveals considerable attention for effective access to socio-economic rights for minority groups, which is

[258] E/C12/2002/11.   [259] E/C12/1999/10.   [260] E/C12/1992/23.

linked to their right to identity and substantive equality. The parallels with the supervisory practice of other UN treaty bodies, as well as the FCNM's AC, will be obvious.

The Committee underscores for example the need to have comprehensive anti-discrimination legislation, which should definitely cover the areas of housing, health care, employment, education, social security, and access to services.[261] In this respect the Committee also suggests that contracting states ratify the 12th Additional Protocol to the European Convention on Human Rights which enshrines a general prohibition of discrimination.[262]

This acknowledgement that the prohibition of discrimination also encompasses a prohibition of indirect discrimination leads to critical assessments of de facto discrimination against 'foreigners, persons belonging to ethnic and national minorities, in particular migrant workers, Roma and Muslim community'.[263]

In relation to employment, the Committee not only urges states to counter de facto discrimination (inter alia through the strengthening of legal and institutional mechanisms aimed at combating racial discrimination),[264] but also calls explicitly for the adoption of positive action measures, 'introducing and effectively enforcing legal provisions requiring an ethnically balanced workforce in the public and private sectors'.[265] This kind of forward-looking positive action, and its focus on a civil service and an employment market that is representative of population diversity, has important symbolic, role-model repercussions with the potential to reinforce this representativeness.

Genuinely equal access to education is also addressed when the Committee notes the problems of the quality of classes in minority languages.[266] This should be improved, which might require appropriate textbooks and suitably qualified teachers for mother-tongue instruction.[267] This Committee also advocates a holistic approach to education, requiring the need to address the socio-economic difficulties of parents.[268]

In relation to access to services, the Committee warns against strict language requirements that might inhibit effective access to public services by minorities, while underscoring the need for supportive measures which would enable

---

[261] CESCR, Concluding Observations on the former Yugoslav Republic of Macedonia (n 244 above), para 11; CESCR, Concluding Observations on India, E/C12/IND/CO/5 (2008), para 52.
[262] CESCR, Concluding Observations on France, E/C12/FRA/CO/3 (2008), para 54.
[263] CESCR, Concluding Observations on Belgium (n 218 above), para 14.
[264] CESCR, Concluding Observations on France (n 262 above), para 16 and 36.
[265] CESCR, Concluding Observations on Costa Rica, E/C12/CRI/CO/4 (2008), para 39.
[266] CESCR, Concluding Observations on the former Yugoslav Republic of Macedonia (n 244 above), para 28, 48; CESCR, Concluding Observations on Hungary, E/C12/HUN/CO/3 (2008) para 28.
[267] CESCR, Concluding Observations on Hungary (n 266 above), para 51; CESCR, Concluding Observations on the former Yugoslav Republic of Macedonia (n 244 above), paras 28, 48.
[268] CESCR, Concluding Observations on France (n 262 above), para 28.

persons belonging to minorities to meet these linguistic requirements (insofar as they cannot be attenuated).[269]

In relation to effective access to health care, the Committee has promoted the protection of undocumented migrant workers as a vulnerable and disadvantaged group for which the state should adopt all appropriate measures so as to ensure their access to adequate health care facilities.[270] In a country with a caste system, like Nepal, the government is called upon to counter the discriminatory denial of access to public wells for persons belonging to the lower castes, as this will hamper their right to an adequate standard of living and their right to the highest attainable standard of health.[271]

The CESCR Committee confirms the trend of having rather extensive supervisory practice in relation to Roma, which is caused by their widespread, systemic discrimination in most areas of socio-economic life, leading to problems in access to employment, social assistance/social services, health care, and education.[272] Again the Committee does not shy away from formulating strategies that should be adopted, which are often of a supportive nature, such as (in relation to employment) enhanced professional training and sustainable employment opportunities, state obligations to encourage the private sector to provide adequate employment opportunities for the Roma,[273] and even state obligations to grant financial incentives to employers and assistance to Roma opening their own business.[274]

The housing problems of Roma should also be addressed by states, and the Committee is especially vigorous in relation to the obligation to fight residential segregation, including of a private nature.[275] In this respect, a holistic approach seems to have been favoured, for example when the Committee recalls the 'duty of state parties to ensure, by legalizing and improving the infrastructure and amenities of existing Roma settlements or through social housing programmes, that all Roma have access to adequate and affordable housing, security of tenure, electricity, adequate drinking water, sanitation and other essential services'.[276]

The typical educational issues relating to Roma also feature in the practice of the CESCR Committee, including the segregated education which needs to be countered,[277] and the acknowledgement that effective access to education might

---

[269] CESCR, Concluding Observations on Latvia, E/C12/LVA/CO/1 (2008) paras 12, 38.
[270] CESCR, Concluding Observations on Belgium (n 218 above), para 35.
[271] CESCR, Concluding Observations on Nepal, E/C12/NPL/CO/2 (2008), para 24.
[272] CESCR, Concluding Observations on the former Yugoslav Republic of Macedonia (n 244 above), para 12; CESCR, Concluding Observations on Hungary (n 266 above), para 11.
[273] CESCR, Concluding Observations on Hungary (n 266 above), para 34.
[274] CESCR, Concluding Observations on Ukraine, E/C.12/UKR/CO/5 (2008), para 37.
[275] CESCR, Concluding Observations on France (n 262 above), para 41.
[276] CESCR, Concluding Observations on the former Yugoslav Republic of Macedonia (n 244 above), para 43.
[277] CESCR, Concluding Observations on the former Yugoslav Republic of Macedonia (n 244 above), paras 28, 48; CESCR, Concluding Observations on Ukraine (n 274 above), para 54.

require special measures for Roma like recruitment of personnel from the Roma community,[278] as well as subsidies for textbooks and other education tools.[279] Finally, member states are urged to address the problems of Roma in relation to access to citizenship and the related problem of a lack of identity documents which inhibits their access to social services.[280]

In relation to indigenous peoples, the CESCR Committee confirms the trends already described in relation to the importance of the recognition of land rights for these groups and their right to exercise their traditional economic activities. Finland, for example, is criticized because of the lasting uncertainty of land ownership in the Sami homeland, which has negative repercussions for their right to maintain and develop their traditional culture and way of life, particularly reindeer herding.[281] The Committee goes as far as to urge states (especially when about half of the indigenous people do not have legal title to their lands) towards direct land restitution programmes that give due consideration to the right of indigenous peoples to their ancestral lands, which is qualified as being essential for their survival.[282]

Furthermore, the Committee underscores the widespread problems of indigenous peoples, and the way in which they are disproportionately affected by poverty and unemployment, illiteracy, limited access to water, to housing, to health care, and to education.[283]

The Committee also starts an important line of its own in relation to the effective enjoyment of the fruits of one's own traditional activities, like traditional medicine, by requiring authorities to develop a special intellectual property regime that protects the collective rights of indigenous peoples, including their scientific products, traditional knowledge, and traditional medicine.

A final point of synergy concerns the consistent suggestion that each and every contracting state ratify the UN Convention on Migrant Workers and their Families.[284]

An important recent development is the adoption by the General Assembly, at the end of 2008, of the long-debated and negotiated optional protocol which contains a complaints procedure for the ICESCR. It is anticipated that the justiciability of economic and social rights will be much strengthened,

---

[278] CESCR, Concluding Observations on Latvia (n 269 above), para 56.
[279] CESCR, Concluding Observations on Ukraine (n 274 above), para 54.
[280] CESCR, Concluding Observations on the former Yugoslav Republic of Macedonia (n 244 above), paras 12, 32.
[281] CESCR, Concluding Observations on Finland, E/C12/FIN/CO/5 (2008), para 11.
[282] CESCR, Concluding Observations on Paraguay, E/C12/PRY/CO/3 (2008), paras 18, 34. See also CESCR, Concluding Observations on Bolivia, E/C12/BOL/CO/2 (2008), para 36.
[283] CESCR, Concluding Observations on Costa Rica, E/C12/CRI/CO/4 (2008), paras 15, 35. See also CESCR, Concluding Observations on Bolivia, E/C12/BOL/CO/2 (2008), para 15.
[284] Eg, CESCR, Concluding Observations on Hungary (n 266 above), para 55; CESCR, Concluding Observations on Finland (n 281 above), para 31; CESCR, Concluding Observations on Latvia (n 269 above), para 60; CESCR, Concluding Observations on Belgium (n 218 above), para 41; CESCR, Concluding Observations on Ukraine (n 274 above), para 60.

d. Convention on the Rights of the Child (CRC)

In many respects, the supervisory practice of the Convention of the Rights of the Child takes up themes that were highlighted in the supervisory practices discussed previously. The need for comprehensive non-discrimination legislation, definitely covering the fields of social security, health care, education, and provision of goods and services,[285] are a recurrent theme, while it is again noted that legislation should go hand in hand with effective enforcement.[286] The Committee also acknowledges the importance and thus the need for states to adopt positive action measures for vulnerable groups of children like the Roma.[287] Indeed protection of the Roma is carefully monitored by the committee, not least because of the extensive socio-economic areas in which they suffer from discrimination.[288] In relation to education, this Committee also strongly resists any form of segregated education, highlighting a preference for integration into mainstream schools.[289] Authorities are called upon once again to adopt a holistic approach in relation to education, which would necessitate addressing the economic hardship of the parents.[290] The Committee also focuses upon the problematic living conditions of indigenous groups and demands that states address these, inter alia, through educational strategies and health care activities.[291]

The Committee is quite vocal about the need to protect non-citizens and immigrants (new minorities) against discrimination, and from anything that hampers their access to education, health care, and social services, which often leads to a minimal standard of living.[292] Finally, and related to the previous statement, it suggests that states ratify the UN Convention on the Protection of the Rights of All Migrant Workers and Members of their Families.[293]

B. Regional instruments

The evaluation of UN instruments was not intended to be totally exhaustive but, in the context of the multitude of regional instruments, only the

---

[285] CRC, Concluding Observations on Slovak Republic, CRC/C/SVK/CO/2 (2007), para 27.
[286] CRC, Concluding Observations on Georgia, CRC/C/GEO/CO/3 (2008), para 21.
[287] CRC, Concluding Observations on Slovak Republic (n 285 above), para 28.
[288] Ibid, paras 18, 59; CRC, Concluding Observations on Bulgaria, CRC/C/BGR/CO/2 (2008), para 71; CRC, Concluding Observations on UK, CRC/C/GBR/CO/4 (2008), para 25.
[289] CRC, Concluding Observations on Bulgaria (n 288 above), para 56.
[290] CRC, Concluding Observations on UK, CRC/C/GBR/CO/4 (2008), para 66.
[291] CRC, Concluding Observations on Venezuela, CRC/C/VEN/CO/2 (2007), para 79. See also CRC, Concluding Observations on Suriname, CRC/C/SUR/CO/2 (2007), paras 61–2.
[292] CRC, Concluding Observations on Dominican Republic, CRC/C/DOM/CO/2 (2007), paras 27, 77.
[293] Ibid, para 77.

highlights will be addressed. Considering the focus of this contribution on participation in social and economic life, the conventions and instruments with an explicit focus on socio-economic rights will be discussed somewhat more extensively.

The American Convention on Human Rights mostly enshrines civil and political rights,[294] the socio-economic ones were added later in the San Salvador Protocol. While there are no minority-specific norms in the Convention, it is important that indigenous peoples are recognized in the inter-American human rights system as a group requiring special protection, inter alia because of their poor socio-economic conditions resulting from the historical dispossession of their lands.[295] Due to the overlap between minorities and indigenous peoples,[296] minorities may actually receive protection, albeit indirectly.

In its annual reports, the Inter-American Commission on Human Rights has highlighted the kind of special protection required by indigenous peoples. One of the concerns that is often highlighted pertains to the socio-economic disadvantage of indigenous peoples because of the history of discrimination and their insufficient access to state services.[297] Furthermore, the Commission has become increasingly protective of indigenous peoples in the petitions (complaints) process, arguably surpassing the protection offered by the HRC. For example, in the case of the Yanomami Indians in Brazil, reminiscent in some respects of the Sami cases before the HRC, the Commission concluded that the authorities had not sufficiently protected the Indians against the destruction of their ancestral lands through settler invasion, and natural resource exploitation. This amounted to a violation of their rights (inter alia) to life, residence, and health. The authorities were required to adopt protective measures also pertaining to land tenure and control, which concerned fundamental aspects of group (minority) identity.[298]

---

[294] Art 26 requires states to take progressive measures to recognize the economic and social rights referred to in the Charter of the Organization of American States.

[295] See, eg, a recommendation of the Inter-American Commission to Colombia: in relation to its finding that the constitutional rights of Colombian indigenous communities to communal property and political participation were violated in practice, it recommended inter alia that the authorities take the necessary measures to enable ethnic and minority groups to survive and develop. Arguably a statement with socio-economic implications (Inter-American Commission on Human Rights, Second Report on the Situation of Human Rights in Colombia, 233–44, 251).

[296] The draft Declaration on the Rights of Indigenous Peoples sets out to address communal concerns regarding lands and resources. The 11th meeting of negotiations on this draft happened in Washington DC, 14–18 April 2008. It is not clear how much more time will be needed to finalize this draft.

[297] For a more extensive analysis see Thio, 'Battling Balkanization' (n 31 above), 431–2.

[298] Case 7615, Inter-American Commission on Human Rights, Annual Report 1996: Ecuardo: Yanomami Report, 9, OEA/SerL/\v/II66 Doc10 rev1, Res 12/85 (1986). See also Maya Indigenous Communities of the Toledo District of Belize, 12 October 2004, Report no 40/04, concerning the pollution and destruction of their ancestral lands through the grant of logging and oil concessions and failure to protect the lands appropriately.

The Inter-American Court on Human Rights has developed a strong jurisprudential line in which a progressive interpretation of the right to property is applied to indigenous communities so as to recognize and protect their communal use and communal ownership of land. In the first case on the rights of indigenous people, the Court followed this line immediately. *Mayagna (sumo) Awas Tingni Community v Nicaragua* concerned the impossibility for an indigenous group to secure collective ownership and enjoyment of their cultural lands because the government had not demarcated indigenous lands, as well as the negative impact of construction and logging activities on their lands.[299]

In the case on the *Indigenous Community of Yakye Axa v Paraguay* the Court not only concluded a violation of the right to property because the state had not adopted adequate legal means to guarantee the effective use and enjoyment of the ancestral lands to the community, but found that the forced relocation of the community also entailed a violation of the right to life, understood as a right to a dignified life. The community had to live in extreme misery with lack of adequate food, housing, and basic services.

The Court furthermore pronounced an important advisory opinion on undocumented migrants, and their right not to be discriminated against, thereby providing substantial protection for the participation of this new minority in social and economic life. The Court underscored that, considering the vulnerability of migrants, the international community recognized the need to adopt special measures of protection to ensure their human rights. States may adopt distinctions between documented and undocumented migrants, and between nationals and migrants, but this distinction must be proportional and respect the principle of equality. States may not be bound to offer work to undocumented workers, but once they perform remunerated activities, they are entitled to the same labour rights as those enjoyed by other workers. States also have to ensure respect for these rights by private employers.[300]

The African Charter on Human and Peoples' Rights is remarkable because it codifies the three generations of human rights and thus provides for socio-economic rights as well as several third-generation rights of peoples, which in turn have important socio-economic connotations. Once again a minority-specific provision is conspicuously absent.[301] While no explicit definition of 'people' (including its relation to the concept 'minority')[302] can be found in the Charter or in the case law of the African Commission on Human and Peoples Rights, the Commission does apply these peoples' rights to ethnic communities

---

[299] *Mayagna (sumo) Awas Tingni Community v Nicaragua*, 31 August 2001, Series C no 79. See also *Moiwana Village v Suriname*, 15 June 2005, Series C, no 124, para 133.
[300] American Court on Human Rights, Advisory Opinion 18 on the legal conditions and rights of undocumented migrants, 17 September 2003.
[301] Thio, 'Battling Balkanization. (n 31 above), 459.   [302] Ibid, 447.

that can be considered minorities,[303] eg the black population in Mauritania,[304] the Ogoni people in Nigeria,[305] and the Katangese people in Zaire.[306]

The *Ogoni* case in particular has received considerable attention in relation to the protection of socio-economic rights through an open interpretation of the peoples' right to development and a healthy environment.[307] The Commission criticized the authorities for not having prevented the oil exploitation in the Ogoni territory from being extremely detrimental to Ogoni health, their land (contamination), and their environment more generally. Furthermore, and this picks up a line of thought visible in the UN Minorities Declaration, the Ogoni should have been entitled to a share of the benefits accruing from development operations in their territory.

The latter point is also picked up in its Reporting Guidelines,[308] when Art 20 states that 'all communities are allowed full participation in political activities and are allowed equal opportunities in the economic activities of the country both of which should be according to the choices they have made independently'.[309]

These Guidelines also contain minority-specific language relating to education and, more particularly, to compulsory primary education: the full realization of the rights of everyone to receive primary education might necessitate special provisions for specific groups, like children belonging to linguistic, racial, religious, or other minorities and children belonging to indigenous sectors of the population (para 48(a)).

The European Convention on Human Rights is the Council of Europe convention that focuses on civil and political rights, while the European Social Charter focuses on socio-economic rights. Nevertheless the progressive and teleological interpretation by the European Court of Human Rights has entered the domain of socio-economic rights in several ways.[310]

---

[303] See also SA Dersso, 'Peoples' Rights of the African Charter: Interrogating their applicability to minority situations', unpublished, on file with the author, 22; and S Slimane, 'Recognizing minorities in Africa', MRG Briefing, 2003, 7.

[304] African Commission HPR, Communications 54/91, 61/91, 98/93, 164/97, 196/97, and 210/98; *Malawi African Association and ors v Mauritania*, 13th Activity Report African Commission (1999–2000).

[305] African Commission HR, Communication 155/96, *The Social and Economic Rights Action Centre and the Centre for Economic and Social Rights v Nigeria*.

[306] African Commission HR, Communication 75/92, 8th Annual Activity Report (1994–5). See also Report of the African Commissions Working Group of Experts on Indigenous Populations/Communities, 2005, 72–9; Slimane, 'Recognizing minorities in Africa' (n 303 above), 3–4.

[307] For a more extensive discussion, see F Coomans, 'The Ogoni case before the African Commission on Human and Peoples' Rights' (2003) 52 ICLQ (2003) 749–60.

[308] Note that there are two sets: the first one dating from 1998 and a later one which is kind of a summary but without there being clarity of the relationship between the two sets.

[309] Guidelines for National Periodic Reports, Second Activity Report of the African Commission on H and P Rights, Annex XII, Guidelines para III.14.

[310] The steady line of jurisprudence according to which Art 8 enshrines a right to a healthy environment is not expanded upon here because the existing case law does not concern persons belonging to minorities.

There are a whole multitude of cases concerning Roma. Whereas the ones on racist violence by public authorities or private parties fall outside the ambit of this study, several of the Roma cases concern questions that can be translated in terms of participation in social and economic life. In its Grand Chamber judgment in the *DH and ors v Czech Republic* case,[311] the Court sanctioned the disproportionate sidelining of Roma to special classes or special schools for mentally disabled children. The fact that the policy was not intended to be detrimental for Roma was said to be irrelevant. In many respects this judgment promised to be the new keynote judgment concerning the essential prohibition of indirect discrimination against minorities. The long list of cases concerning the lack of stopping places for Roma, or restrictions on the use of their own land for that purpose because of planning regulations, is well known. In *Chapman*[312] the Court acknowledged for the first time that Art 8 enshrines a right to a traditional way of life and identifies a positive state obligation to facilitate the gypsy way of life. Notwithstanding the important potential of these rulings, their application to the facts has been disappointing as the Court has tended to give precedence to the arguments of states.

The now defunct European Commission of Human Rights had already recognized, in *G and E v Norway*, that minorities have a right to exercise and benefit from traditional economic activities (under Art 8 of the ECHR). Again this important principle has not led to extensive protection because in the weighing process of the respective interests (when evaluating whether an interference amounts to a violation or not) state interests (captured within the context of the economic wellbeing of the country at large) tend to outweigh those of the minority group.[313] This is obviously reminiscent of the quasi-jurisprudence of the HRC in terms of Art 27 of the ICCPR.

Another judgment that should be mentioned is the famous *Thlimmenos v Greece* case.[314] In that judgment, the Court held for the first time that the prohibition of discrimination also encompassed an obligation to adopt differential measures for persons that found themselves in substantively different situations. Clearly, this theoretical principle is in itself of great importance to minorities. However, furthermore, this particular case concerned the problems experienced by a Jehovah's Witness in accessing the job of a chartered accountant because of his refusal to undertake military service (intrinsically bound up with his freedom of religion).

Sometimes the Court addresses the housing problems of minorities on the basis of the Art 3 prohibition of torture, and inhuman and degrading

---

[311] ECtHR, *DH and ors v Czech Republic*, 13 November 2007, no 17325/00.
[312] ECtHR, *Chapman v UK*, 18 January 2001, no 27238/95.
[313] ECommHR, *G and E v Norway*, Appl 9278/1981 and 9415/1981 (joined), *DR* 35, para 2.
[314] ECtHR, *Thlimmenos v Greece*, 6 April 2000, no 34369/97.

treatment.[315] According to the Court, the unlawful destruction of the houses of persons belonging to minorities, and especially the horrendous living conditions that the Roma and Kurds were subsequently forced to endure for long periods of time, amounted to prohibited inhuman and degrading treatment.

Finally, the access of migrants to social and economic benefits is also protected by the European Court, especially since the *Gaygusuz v Austria* judgment in which it indicated that differentiations on the basis of nationality were to be met with heightened scrutiny.[316]

The collective complaints procedure under the European Social Charter regularly addresses the problems of Roma and the difficulties they experience in accessing socio-economic rights, and thus participation in social and economic life. In the context of this Convention, the non-discrimination guarantee is key for the protection of the Roma. Several of the Roma-related cases concern matters pertaining to housing,[317] but one relates to health insurance coverage,[318] and one to a lack of adequate social assistance to unemployed persons without adequate resources which notably affects Roma.[319] A general theme in the assessment by the supervisory body is the positive duty on the part of the state to adopt special measures, adapted to the situation of the Roma, to ensure effective, substantively equal enjoyment of rights. From a conceptual perspective, it is important that the Committee establishes an explicit link between these duties of positive action/differential treatment on the one hand and the prohibition of indirect discrimination on the other: 'such indirect indiscrimination may arise by failing to take due and positive account of all relevant differences or by failing to take adequate steps to ensure that the rights and collective advantages that are open to all are genuinely accessible by and to all'.[320]

The Committee has, for example, acknowledged that the deficient implementation of legislation on stopping places for Travellers, which pushes them to make use of illegal sites and thus run the risk of forcible eviction, amounts to a violation of the prohibition of discrimination in relation to housing. This was further constructed as a failure to take their specific needs properly into

---

[315] ECtHR, *Selcuk and Asker v Turkey*, 24 April 1998, no 23184/94; ECtHR, *Moldovan and ors v Romania*, 12 July 2005, 41138/98 and 64320/01.
[316] ECtHR, *Gaygusuz v Austria*, 16 September 1996.
[317] European Committee of Social Rights, *ERRC v Greece*, 7 February 2005, no 15/2003; European Committee of Social Rights *ERRC v Italy*, 21 December 2005, no 27/2004; European Committee of Social Rights, *ERRC v Bulgaria*, 30 November 2006, no 31/2005; *European Committee of Social Rights, Interights v Greece*, no 49/2008, still pending; European Committee of Social Rights, *ERRC v France*, no 51/2008, still pending.
[318] European Committee of Social Rights, *ERRC v Bulgaria*, no 46/2007, still pending.
[319] European Committee of Social Rights, *ERRC v Bulgaria*, no 48/2008, still pending.
[320] European Committee of Social Rights, no 31/2005, *ERRC v Bulgaria*, para 40. See also European Committee of Social Rights, no 27/2004, *ERRC v Italy*, paras 21–36, 46; European Committee of Social Rights, no 33/2006, *International Movement ATD Fourth World v France*, paras 154–5.

account.³²¹ This theme was also taken up in relation to Italy's practice of placing the Roma in camps, where the Committee held that the 'failure to take into consideration the different situation of Roma or to introduce measures specifically aimed at improving their housing conditions, including the possibility for an effective access to social housing, means that Italy is in violation' of the Charter.³²² A duty to adopt special measures for Roma was also highlighted in the case against Bulgaria. Bulgaria's failure to adopt special measures for the Roma aimed at the legalization of their dwellings amounted to a violation of the prohibition of discrimination in relation to housing, because the particularly high risk of eviction was partly due to the lack of state intervention over a protracted period of time.³²³

C. European Union documents[324]

In relation to minority protection and the EU it should be borne in mind that the EU can only exercise those competences that are specifically assigned to it by its member states. So far, there is not an explicit EU competence in relation to minority protection. However, this has not stopped the EU from demanding from third states that an adequate system of minority protection is in place. The most visible and sustained action has been in its demands towards countries aspiring towards membership of the EU. The political Copenhagen criteria indeed included the requirement to respect the rights of minorities.³²⁵ As the EU has no benchmarks of its own,³²⁶ it refers back to the OSCE standards and especially to the FCNM.

Nevertheless, through the increasing attention devoted to minority issues as a result of the accession³²⁷ process and the monitoring of the ever-growing list of

---

³²¹ *International Movement ATD Fourth World v France* (n 320 above), paras 154–5.
³²² European Committee of Social Rights, no 27/2004, *ERRC v Italy*, para 46.
³²³ European Committee of Social Rights, no 31/2005, paras 40–2.
³²⁴ For an extensive analysis of minority protection in the EU see the various contributions in the edited volume by GN von Toggenburg, *Minority Protection and the Enlarged EU: The way forward* (2004). See also de Witte and Horvath, 'The many faces of minority policy in the EU' (n 15 above), 365–84.
³²⁵ Copenhagen European Council, 21–2 June 1993, *Bulletin EU* 6–1993, Conclusion 7(iii).
³²⁶ GN von Toggenburg, 'The protection of minorities at EU-level: A tightrope walk between (ethnic) diversity and (territorial) subsidiarity' in E Lantschner et al (eds), *European Integration and its Effects on Minority Protection in South Eastern Europe* (2008), 84. See also EU Network of Independent Experts on Fundamental Rights, *Thematic Comment No 3: The protection of minorities in the European Union* (2003), 29. In this respect it is also questioned whether the EU could establish an EU law notion of minorities using the national level as parameter of reference: P Hilpold, 'Minderheiten im Unionsrecht' (2001) 39 Archiv des Volkerrechts 432–71, 434.
³²⁷ F Hoffmeister, 'Monitoring minority rights in the enlarged EU' in von Toggenburg, *Minority Protection* (n 324 above), 93. For a critical and in-depth analysis, see also D Kochenov, *Commission's Approach to Minority Protection during the Preparation of the EU's Eastern Enlargement: Is 2 better than the promised 1?* EDAP Papers 02/2007; G Pentassuglia, 'The EU and the protection of minorities: The case of Eastern Europe' (2001) 12 EJIL 3–38; J Hughes and G Sasse, 'Monitoring the monitors: EU enlargement conditionality and minority protection in the CEECs' (2003) 1 *JEMIE* 1–28; A Wiener and G Schwellnus, 'Contested norms in the process of EU enlargement: Non-discrimination and minority rights', ConWEB no 2/2004.

candidate countries,[328] the minority discourse became internalized. Eventually this resulted in the inclusion in the Lisbon Treaty (as was the case for the defunct Constitution) of 'respect for human rights, including the rights of persons belonging to national minorities' as one of the foundational values of the EU.[329] Be that as it may, the Lisbon Treaty does not change anything in terms of competences: there is still no explicit competence for the EU in the field of minority protection. Arguably this implies that the least that could and should be done is to mainstream minority protection (concerns), ie to take minority protection into consideration whenever the EU exercises its competences.[330] In this respect, it is interesting to note that since the activities of the EU still mostly play out in the socio-economic field, the effects of minority protection mainstreaming fall mainly within that domain.

Most of the constitutional building blocks or resources[331] identified for mainstreaming[332] have particular resonance within the socio-economic field,[333] namely an extensive focus on equality/non discrimination (mainly in the socio-economic domain) and the related strategy of social inclusion and the incipient integration policies.[334]

---

[328] GN von Toggenburg 'A remaining share or a new part? The Union's role *vis-à-vis* minorities after the enlargement decade', EUI Working Paper 2006/15, 1–5.
[329] Ibid, 8: 'a container provision which is the basic rock upon which a European notion of minority rights can gradually develop'.
[330] GN von Toggenburg, 'Who is managing ethnic and cultural diversity in the European Condominium? The moments of entry, integration and preservation' (2005) 43(4) *Journal of Common Market Studies* 717–38, 718: competences do matter—mainstreaming as European response to complex patchwork of competences.
[331] Cultural and linguistic diversity are to be supported by the EU and this could be a possible avenue for mainstreaming minority concerns. However, minority protection is not consistently considered or promoted when exercising competences in the cultural field as is visible in the *Framework Strategy for Multilingualism* (Communication from the Commission, COM(2005) 596, 22 November 2005). The strategy does not pay attention to linguistic minorities in the sense that they do not get earmarked funding: see, eg, De Witte and Horvath (n 15 above), 375. Furthermore in relation to diversity and diversity management of the EU, there are actually two kinds of diversity that need to be managed: diversity within states and diversity between states: eg, GN Toggenburg, 'Unification via diversification: What does it mean to be "united in diversity"?' *EUMAP online journal*, Enlargement Day, 1 May 2004, available at <http://www.eumap.org/journal/features/2004/bigday/diversity> (accessed 31 July 2009).
[332] B de Witte, 'The constitutional resources for an EU minority protection policy' in von Toggenburg, *Minority Protection* (n 324 above), 107. See also De Witte and Horvath who argue that 'to understand the role of the EU one must first mentally dismantle the idea of minority rights into its constituent elements, then reconstruct it by putting measures from a number of diverse, interlocking policy areas into comprehensive minority protection framework'. De Witte and Horvath, 'The many faces of minority policy' (n 15 above), 367.
[333] Note also in words of von Toggenburg, the 'overarching value of cultural diversity': von Toggenburg, *Minority Protection* (n 324 above), 717. See also Art 151(4) of the TEC, cultural policy funding programmes, educational policies, etc. This is also captured in Charter Art 22: duty to respect cultural, religious, and linguistic diversity.
[334] In the EU it is also acknowledged that respect for cultural diversity and thus for the cultures of minorities is important for integration and inclusion.

The following paragraphs will provide a succinct overview of developments in these respects. However, it is important to note first that, while the so-called 'new minorities'[335] (non-nationals, often immigrants)[336] are increasingly recognized as minorities, when discussing the EU a further subdivision needs to be made within that category: EC citizens living in another member state and third-country nationals (TCNs). While non-discrimination and social inclusion policies are potentially relevant for both, the EU's integration policies are targeted at TCNs.[337]

Regarding non-discrimination, the Treaty of Amsterdam made a very important leap by including Art 13, providing a legal basis for taking measures to combat discrimination based on racial or ethnic origin, and religion, two identity markers of particular relevance for minorities. Two important directives developed on the basis of that Article were the Racial Equality Directive (RED) and the Employment Equality Directive (EED),[338] with the Racial Equality Directive being hailed as the most efficient EU minority protection tools for years to come.[339] These directives are not minority-specific but since persons belonging to minorities are frequently victims of discrimination, these instruments are of particular relevance to them.[340] They both contain various measures focused on effective enforcement—a recurrent theme throughout this contribution—and have several innovative features. What makes the RED stand out is its extremely broad scope which extends way beyond the sphere of employment, deep into the social sphere, and includes themes like housing, social security, and education.[341] The EED is thus far confined to the

---

[335] von Toggenburg, *Minority Protection* (n 324 above), 102.
[336] As the Commission underscored in its report on immigration, integration and employment (COM(2003) 336, 32) immigrants are too often exposed to risks of discrimination.
[337] von Toggenburg points out in this respect that EU citizens have a sort of constitutional guarantee of integration: von Toggenburg, *Minority Protection* (n 324 above), 727. Nevertheless Cholewinski argues that the European Employment Strategy and the Social Inclusion Strategy can also be considered as integration activities, hence even including EU citizens: R Cholewinski, 'Migrants as minorities: Integration and inclusion in the enlarged EU' (2005) 43(4) *Journal of Common Market Studies* 695–716, 703–4, 711. He underscores in this respect that the social inclusion reports minorities and immigrants are used interchangeably (at 711).
[338] Directive 2000/43/EC of 29 June 2000, implementing the principle of equal treatment between persons irrespective of racial or ethnic origin, OJ L189, 22; Directive 2000/78/EC establishing a framework for equal treatment in employment and occupation, OJ L303/16.
[339] De Witte and Horvath, 'The many faces of minority policy' (n 15 above), 372; de Witte, 'The constitutional resources' (n 332 above), 116; GN von Toggenburg 'The Race Directive: A new dimension in the fight against ethnic discrimination in Europe' (2001–2) *European Yearbook on Minority Issues* 231–44; D Petrova, 'Racial discrimination and the rights of minority cultures' in S Fredman (ed), *Discrimination and Human Rights: The case of racism* (2001) 45, 45–76. See also Ombudsman on Ethnic Discrimination, *Discrimination of the Sami: The rights of the Sami from a discrimination perspective* (2008), 39, where the application of the RED is considered to be an important source for the protection of the Sami minority in Sweden.
[340] von Toggenburg, *Minority Protection* (n 324 above), 728.
[341] See also the prediction by de Witte that linguistic proficiency requirements that are not justified by the nature of the job could be considered as indirect racial discrimination irrespective of whether they are imposed by a private or public employer: de Witte, 'The constitutional resources' (n 332 above), 117.

employment sphere but even that makes it particularly pertinent, given its obvious relevance for participation in economic life. However, it is to be noted that the Commission has circulated a draft directive to expand the scope of application *ratione materiae* of the EED to that of the RED.[342]

While this all sounds very promising, a lot will depend on their actual interpretation, ultimately by the European Court of Justice (ECJ). For example, the extent to which the private sphere will be covered is not yet clear, nor is what will be done with the exclusion of differentiation on the basis of nationality from the scope of application of the RED, considering the possible indirect racial discriminatory effect.[343] In the latter respect, it should be recalled that nationality has become in itself a suspect ground of distinction,[344] heightening the protection of immigrants.[345]

So far, the ECJ has only given one substantive judgment on the RED. In the preliminary ruling from a Belgian court,[346] the essential point was that the mere statement that you would not employ persons belonging to a particular ethnic minority could constitute discrimination, even in the absence of actual rejection. This ruling is rather important for effective access to employment for minorities, and especially for immigrant minorities.

Finally, it should be noted that the Lisbon Treaty also adds a general duty for the EU to combat discrimination (inter alia) on the grounds of racial or ethnic origin and religion when defining and implementing EU policies and activities. Hence, following this duty to mainstream equality,[347] the Commission is expected to insert more and more non-discrimination clauses into secondary

---

[342] European Commission, 'Proposal for a Council Directive on implementing the principle of equal treatment between persons irrespective of religion or belief, disability, age or sexual orientation', 2008/0140(CNS).

[343] As Groenendijk points out: 'distinctions on the basis of nationality in immigration law and elsewhere are often used to hide distinctions on the basis of ethnic origin and thus may amount to a forbidden indirect discrimination on the ground of race': K Groenendijk, 'Citizens and TCN: Differential treatment or discrimination?' in JY Carlier and B Coulie (eds), *The Future of Free Movement of Persons in the EU: Analysis of Directive 2004/38 of 29 April 2004 on the rights of citizens to move and reside freely* (2006), 86. See also B Perchinig, 'EU citizenship and the status of third country nationals' in R Bauböck (ed), *Migration and Citizenship: Legal status, rights and political participation* (2007), 79.   [344] Groenendijk, 'Citizens and TCN' (n 343 above), 81.

[345] ENAR enumerates this exclusion ('an unacceptable derogation to the principle of non-discrimination') as an important factor that could limit the effectiveness of the proposal for a Directive on a single application procedure for a single permit for TCNs to reside and work in the territory of a member state and on a common set of rights for TCNs legally residing in a member state: ENAR, 'Contributing to a Europe without Racism? The Proposal for a Directive on basic socio-economic rights of TCN', 7.

[346] ECJ, *Centrum voor Gelijkheid van Kansen en Racismebestrijding v Firma Feryn NV*, C 54/07, 10 July 2008. It needs to be said that in several respects the judgment is flawed, not least by internal contractions and confusion about the model of review adopted.

[347] Mainstreaming can be defined as demanding 'the integration of an equality perspective into all aspects of law making, ... whatever the subject matter under consideration. ... Mainstreaming recognizes ... that all policies must be mobilized': M Bell, 'Mainstreaming equality norms into European Union asylum law' (2001) 26 *European Law Review* 20–34, 21.

legislation so as to translate this duty into concrete norms in the respective policy fields.[348]

Social inclusion is a strategy that is obviously closely related to non-discrimination, which goes back to the European Council of Lisbon of March 2000. As is clearly evident from the Joint Social Inclusion Reports and their analysis of the National Action Plans on Social Inclusion, the member states often acknowledge the need to improve the social integration of ethnic minorities, especially in relation to employment and education and language policies.[349] The integration of immigrants is also an important component of the fight against poverty and exclusion, while ethnic minorities are similarly identified as having a high risk factor of social exclusion. Consequently the Council and Commission have called for an increased emphasis on their situation.[350] When considering the various yearly reports on social inclusion it is not always easy to compare them as they are not all equally detailed, but there are in any event clear trends to be drawn out. There are numerous references to ethnic minorities, often in combination with immigrants, while there tend to be more references to immigrants and surely to Roma who seem increasingly accepted as needing special attention.[351] The general message throughout these reports is that ethnic minorities, immigrants, and especially the Roma[352] are special risk groups for poverty and require special measures to prevent the transmission of poverty to the new generation.[353] It is striking that while the assessment of member states in 2004 was rather critical (they would not do enough to realize genuine access to the labor market and adopt the social protection schemes for these groups),[354] by 2007 this had changed; the Council and Commission noted that most member states actually did prioritize the social inclusion of immigrants and ethnic minorities,[355] and acknowledged education as important for subsequent employment opportunities and access to quality services,[356] generally adopting a holistic approach.[357]

---

[348] Eg, the final wording of Directive 2004/38/EC (OJ L 158, 30 April 2004, 77) says that member states should implement this directive without discrimination on membership of an ethnic minority.

[349] European Commission, *The Aspect of Culture in the Social Inclusion of Ethnic Minorities* (2006), 9.

[350] European Commission and European Council, 'Joint Report on Social Inclusion' (2004), 8.

[351] EU Network of Independent Experts on Fundamental Rights, *Thematic Comment No 3* (n 326 above). See also O De Schutter and A Verstichel, 'The role of the Union in integrating the Roma: Present and possible future', EDAP 2/2005, 34.

[352] Within the disadvantaged groups, the Roma as particularly disadvantaged (burdened by multiple disadvantages): European Commission and European Council, 'Joint Report on Social Inclusion' (2008), 31; European Commission and European Council, 'Joint Report on Social Inclusion' (2005), 5, 7, 9.

[353] European Commission and European Council, 'Joint Report 2008' (n 352 above), 30–1, 80, 109.

[354] European Commission and European Council, 'Joint Report 2004' (n 350 above), 95–102.

[355] European Commission and European Council, 'Joint Report 2005' (n 352 above), 64.

[356] Ibid, 10.

[357] Ibid, 80–6; European Commission and European Council, 'Joint Report on Social Inclusion' (2007), 2, 7, 13, 66, 114,181, 201, 213.

A similar development of increasing or at least solidifying attention for minorities is visible in the European Employment Strategy and more specifically the employment guidelines to be followed by member states when outlining their national strategies.[358] Ever since 1999 one of these employment guidelines[359] included a reference to minorities.[360] The Joint Employment Reports of the Council and Commission were initially rather critical because of the limited impact of the measures undertaken by the member states, inter alia because no numerical targets were set.[361] Strikingly, this strategy focuses on immigrants and the special attention they require to gain access to education, special language courses, etc,[362] even though the Commission has explicitly called on member states to consider minorities with citizenship, eg the so-called 'traditional minorities'. [363]

The EU appointed a High Level Advisory Group[364] to undertake a study and issue recommendations on the Social Integration of Ethnic Minorities and their Full Participation in the Labour Market. This report, focusing once again on participation in social and economic life, was released in December 2007 and highlighted the importance of integration and the need for a holistic approach, with special focus on education. The curricula should not only be geared towards a multicultural society, but educational disadvantages should be redressed and special attention paid to language training.[365] The report further confirmed the importance of the results of the Employment Strategy and underscored that special attention for immigrants and ethnic minorities as categories of disadvantaged people should continue, since 'successful inclusion in the market is the most powerful catalyst for successful social integration of minorities'.[366] The report also highlighted another important avenue for integration, intrinsically connected to participation in economic life, and that is diversity management (as a component part of corporate social responsibility which has gained increasing recognition since

---

[358] Until 2005 these national strategies were called National Action Plans—since 2005, National Reform Programs.

[359] See for the most recent version: COM(2005) 141 final, 2005/0057 CNS 12 April 2005. For a critical assessment, see T Malloy, 'The Lisbon strategy and ethnic minorities: Rights and economic growth', ECMI Issue Brief, April 2005.

[360] Initially this explicit reference to minorities was to be found in Guideline 9, but since 2001 it has been included in Guideline 7.

[361] European Commission and European Council, 'Joint Employment Report' (2003–4), 49, 135, 136.

[362] European Commission and European Council, 'Joint Employment Report' (2007–8), 7169/08, 10–14; European Commission and European Council, 'Joint Employment Report' (2006–7), 6706/07, 7–13. [363] von Toggenburg, *Minority Protection* (n 324 above), 14.

[364] Note that in Art 2 of the Commission decision establishing the group (Decision 2006/33) 'minority groups' are defined as including 'recent migrants, established ethnic minorities, national minorities, Roma'. This would seem to lend credibility to the argument with regard to social inclusion reports, where the concept of 'migrants' is often used side by side with 'ethnic minorities'.

[365] EU High-level Advisory Group, *Social Integration of Ethnic Minorities and their Full Participation in the Labour Market* (2007), 47. [366] Ibid, 53.

the 1990s),[367] combining equality and diversity strategies.[368] Finally, the report focused on what was needed for the integration of TCNs, and again adopted a holistic approach[369] addressing access to education, to employment, and social inclusion more generally.[370]

Since the Treaty of Amsterdam, migration policy and policy towards TCNs more generally has come increasingly to the forefront of EU policy, even though the treatment of TCNs is still dominated by member states. Integration, with its strong socio-economic holistic approach, is indeed an essential pillar of the Union's migration policy.[371] More particularly, since the Tampere Council of 1999, there has been a pronounced focus on more vigorous integration policies aimed at granting to migrants the rights and obligations comparable to those of EU citizens.[372] Once again, the importance of equal treatment for proper integration is apparent. The Commission's Communication on Immigration, Integration and Employment of 2003[373] highlights as key elements in holistic integration policies: integration in the labour market and diversity management, education and language skills, housing, health, and social services.[374] The Hague Programme elaborated in 2004 also aims at integration of TCNs and acknowledges the importance of non-discrimination in this respect, while underscoring that it is essential to go beyond that.[375] Nevertheless, equality and non-discrimination in a wide range of social and economic matters are once again recognized as central to genuine integration.[376] In 2004 the eleven Common Basic Principles for immigrant integration[377] were identified, and again economic and social participation were found to be key: the importance of education, access to services, improved living conditions regarding housing, health care, etc were highlighted.[378] At the same time, the

---

[367] Ibid, 76.
[368] It should be noted that already in 2005 the Commission (DG Employment) had increased attention for the business case for diversity, combining diversity and equality strategies.
[369] We also noted this in relation to the social inclusion strategy, see above.
[370] EU High-level Advisory Group, *Social Integration* (n 365 above), 84–92.
[371] von Toggenburg, *Minority Protection* (n 324 above), 16; De Witte and Horvath, 'The many faces of minority policy' (n 15 above), 369–70. For a more extensive analysis see Cholewinski, 'Migrants as minorities (n 337 above), 697. Important documents from the European Commission include Communication on Immigration, Integration and Employment COM(2003) 336 final; Communication: A Common Agenda for Integration: Framework for the Integration of TCN in the EU, COM(2005) 389 final.
[372] European Council in Tampere, Council Conclusions, 16 October 1999, para 18.
[373] Communication on immigration, integration and employment, COM(2003) 336 final, 28–30.   [374] COM(2003) 336 final, 19–22.
[375] European Council Conclusions, 8 December 2004, Annex I (The Hague Programme), point II.1.5.
[376] See also Cholewinski, 'Migrants as minorities (n 337 above), 708, who refers to recitals 4 and 12 of the Long Term Resident TCN Directive.
[377] European Commission, Justice and Home Affairs, 'A common framework for integration of third-country nationals', available at <http://ec.europa.eu/justice_home/fsj/immigration/integration/fsj_immigration_integration_en.htm> (accessed 31 July 2009).
[378] See also Common Agenda for Integration: Framework for the Integration of TCN in the EU COM(2005) 389 final.

importance of respect for different identities, language and culture for adequate integration was also recognized.[379] The Annual Reports on Migration and Integration pay particular attention to access to housing, health care, social security, and education and, of course, to labour market integration. The overview of national policies aimed at improving integration often refers explicitly to (particular) minorities.[380]

The expansion of the rights of EU citizens also strengthened calls for stronger, equivalent rights for TCNs, especially those that are long-term residents in member states.[381] This resulted eventually in the adoption of Directive 2003/109/EC on the status of TCNs who are long-term residents.[382] The duty to grant permanent residency after five years of legal residency constitutes an important vessel for other (socio-economic) rights. Equal treatment with nationals of the state is envisaged in a broad range of matters, several of which pertain to the social and economic domain: access to employment (not exercise of public authority) and self-employment, education and vocational training, social security, social assistance, and social protection, including access to goods and services available to the public.[383] Nevertheless, in several respects the member states retain a considerable level of discretion, which reduces the actual level of protection of TCNs in relation to participation in socio-economic life.[384]

The socio-economic participation of EU citizens as new minorities in the host countries should also be evaluated. Many of the rights granted to EU citizens are of particular relevance to minorities, especially in relation to participation in social and economic life: freedom of movement and residence and related rights added through the jurisprudence of the ECJ. The ECJ increasingly

---

[379] Common Basic Principle (on integration) 4. It should be highlighted that the European Year of Intercultural Dialogue 2008 has great potential to enhance this mutual respect. Note that in the Third Annual Report on Integration COM(2007) 512 final, the intercultural dialogue year 2008 became an essential instrument to foster successful integration and counteract racism and extremism!

[380] Second Annual Report on Migration and Integration, SEC(2006) 892, 8–10; Third Annual Report on Migration and Integration, COM(2007) 52, 6–7.

[381] See also GN von Toggenburg, 'Who is managing ethnic and cultural diversity in the European condominium? The moments of entry, integration and preservation' (2005) 43(4) *Journal of Common Market Studies* 717–38, 725–6, who highlights that the Long-term Resident TCN Directive obliges states to grant TCNs a permanent residency status after five years of legal residency, a status which is intended to approximate their legal standing to that of EU citizens.

[382] OJ 2004 L16/44. See also De Witte and Horvath, 'The many faces of minority policy' (n 15 above), 370, who also highlight the importance Directive 2003/86/EC of 22 September 2003 on the right to family reunification OJ 2003 L251/14. In addition, reference can be made to the various directives concerning the rights and protection of special categories of TCNs like refugees and asylum-seekers: S Peers, 'Key legislative developments on migration in the EU' (2005) 7(1) *European Journal of Migration and Law* 87–115.

[383] Art 11(4) of the Long-term Resident TCN Directive allows member states to limit equal treatment with regard to social assistance and social protection to core benefits.

[384] See, eg, Arts 5, 11, and 14 of the Long-term Resident TCN Directive.

accords these rights of EU citizens a wide scope,[385] especially in the areas of welfare and education benefits, in other words the social sphere.[386]

The Court held on the basis of the citizenship provision of the EC Treaty in *Martinez Sala*[387] that a Spanish national was entitled to a child raising allowance in Germany, and in *Grzelczyk*[388] a French national could qualify for minimum subsistence allowance in Belgium. In *Bidar*,[389] the Court even recognized the (qualified)[390] right of EC citizens to benefit from student maintenance grants. Similar qualified[391] entitlements were confirmed by the ECJ in relation to job-seekers allowance in *Collins*[392] and to a tide-over allowance in *Ionnadis*.[393] The ECJ nevertheless maintained a certain balance by allowing member states to set certain conditions: a member state can legitimately make certain social advantages dependent on the EU citizen concerned having demonstrated a certain degree of integration into the society of that state, as long as this condition does not amount to a de facto denial of the advantage.[394] The process of broader equal treatment of European citizens in the socio-economic sphere is confirmed and further extended in Directive 2004/38/EC on the rights of EU citizens.[395]

In view of the importance of adequate protection against discrimination for effective participation in socio-economic life, it should be underscored that EU citizens do not only benefit from the RED and the FED, but also from the prohibition of discrimination on the basis of nationality.

---

[385] See also Directive 2004/83 of 29 April 2004 on the right of citizens of the Union and their family members to move and reside freely within the territory of the Member States (OJ L229), integrating the vast jurisprudence of the ECJ on this topic into one legal text.

[386] For a good analysis see FG Jacobs, 'Citizenship of the European Union: A legal analysis (2007) 13(5) *European Law Journal* 591–610, 593–6; and D Kostakopoulou, 'European Union citizenship: Writing the future' (2007) 13(5) *European Law Journal* 623–6, 633–42. For an extensive discussion, see the contributions in E Spaventa and M Dougan (eds), *Social Welfare and EU Law* (2005).

[387] ECJ, *Martinez Sala v Fraiestaat Bayern*, 12 May 1998, C 85/96, ECR 1998 I-02691.

[388] ECJ, *Crzelczyk v Le Centre public d'aide sociale d'Ottignies-Louvain-la-Neuve*, 20 September 2001, C 184/99, ECR 2001 I-6193.

[389] ECJ, *R (on the application of Dany Bidar) v London Borough of Ealing*, 15 March 2005, C 209/03, ECR 2005 I-02119.

[390] According to the ECJ the member states were allowed to require a certain degree of integration into the society of the state concerned (para 57).

[391] In *Collins* and *Ioannidis* the state could require a genuine link between the claimant of a job-seekers allowance and a tide-over allowance respectively on the one hand and the employment market on the other.

[392] ECJ, *Collins v Secretary of State for Work and Pensions*, 23 March 2004, C 138/02, ECR I-02703.

[393] ECJ, *Office Nationale de l'emploi v Ioannidis*, 15 September 2005, C 258/04, ECR 2005 I-08275. [394] ECJ, *Dany Bidar* (n 389 above), C 209/03, para 59–61.

[395] Directive 2004/38/EC of the European Parliament and of the Council of 29 April 2004 on the right of citizens of the Union and their family members to move and reside freely within the territory of the member states, OJ 2004 L 229. See also the European Commission's Fourth Report on Citizenship, COM(2004) 695 final.

V. Other Actors

A. UN – UNIEMI and the Forum on Minority Issues

The United Nations Independent Expert on Minority Issues is one of the special procedures of the Human Rights Council with an explicit mandate focused on minorities. Strikingly, the Independent Expert has revealed a pronounced focus on questions related to economic participation of minorities.[396]

Two of the three thematic priorities outlined by her are paradigmatic in this respect. One of these thematic priorities is to 'increase the focus on minority communities in the context of poverty alleviation, development and the [Millennium Development Goals]'. According to UNIEMI, minorities do not benefit sufficiently from work towards the Millennium Development Goals (MDGs),[397] and she wants to promote programmes, policies and activities that take fully into account the special needs of minorities. As poverty is both a cause and a manifestation of the disadvantages and lack of opportunities of minorities, members of minority communities are disproportionally affected by poverty. This implies that they obviously do not participate fully in the economic life of the state, and do not benefit from the economic development of the state. The other thematic priority relates to increasing the understanding of minority issues in the context of promoting social inclusion. This focus on questions of participation in economic and social life means that, when it is emphasized that 'full and effective participation of minorities in policies and decisions that affect them is a guiding principle of the UNIEMI's work', this also applies to decisions

---

[396] These thematic priorities and their connection with economic participation can also be related to mandate of the UNIEMI which consists, inter alia, of promoting the implementation of the UN declaration (Human Rights Commission Resolution 2005/79: see also 2008 Resolution HRC on the mandate of the IEMI: A/HRC/7/L.17). It was already highlighted that the Declaration contains provisions of relevance to participation in economic life.

[397] Another UN body which is critically concerned with the Development Millennium Goals is the UNDP, the UN's global development network, an organization advocating for change and connecting countries to knowledge, experience and resources to help people build a better life. The UNDP network links and coordinates global and national efforts to reach these goals. It is important that the organization considers human rights as a key strategy to reach development. While much of the UNDP's work is not minority-focused, several of its strategic goals—like poverty prevention and conflict reduction—are relevant for the economic participation of minorities. Furthermore, some of its programmes are actually focused on specific minority groups, particularly the Roma.

It is quite significant that the UNIEMI underscored in her second annual report that the UNDP is one agency taking the lead on working with minorities, in that it ensures that the MDGs are achieved in a way which also benefits minorities. The inclusion in the UNDP's new Global HR Programme of a budget line for pilot initiatives with minorities, amounts to de facto acknowledgement that within development issues, minority concerns have to be taken on board (A/HRC/4/9 Add 1, 12).

Finally it should be underscored that in December 2008 there was a consultation on a draft resource guide on minorities in development, in which the UNIEMI also participated. This guide is intended to serve as a first step towards a specific policy note on how to deal with minorities in UNDP programming processes and is partly based on a month-long UNDP-wide survey.

related to economic participation and takes up the 'procedural' branch of socio-economic participation.

In her first annual report, the IEMI justifies her strategic objectives in relation to poverty and social inclusion by pointing out that minorities are frequently excluded from fully taking part in the economic and social life of their country.[398] At the same time, she underscores that poverty reduction is also essential to promoting the full range of civil, political, economic, and social rights generally.[399] She ties this to the realization of the MDGs and underscores that in order for poverty reduction efforts to be successful, development programmes, activities, and policies should fully take into account the special needs of minorities.[400]

Her second annual report[401] goes on to focus on poverty reduction. She repeats her statement that minorities face high and disproportionate levels of poverty, often of a structural kind, revealing an urgent need to address the situation of minorities in efforts to alleviate poverty and achieve the MDGs.[402] Social inclusion is essential to counter the discrimination related to their separate identity, which is often a potent causal factor in the disproportionate poverty they experienced. In line with what emerged from the practice of the Advisory Committee of the FCNM and several UN treaty bodies, she underscores the vital importance and crucial role played by education, and more particularly equal access to education, in reducing poverty and the lack of economic participation more generally.[403]

Another parallel can be identified in relation to the call for a robust enforcement of anti-discrimination legislation, and for the adoption of (temporary) positive action measures in both the public and the private sector to redress long-term discrimination against minorities. Similar calls are made in relation to education.[404]

Furthermore, she is attentive to supportive measures (of which we saw some examples in the practice of the AC), like targeted skills training to promote minority access to employment.[405]

Finally, the first meeting of the UN Forum on Minority Issues of December 2008 also focused on the theme that is of particular relevance to economic and social participation, namely education. Importantly, the Recommendations on Minorities and the Right to Education[406] underscores that education is a primary means of enabling people to lift themselves out of poverty while a lack of education limits their participation not only in the economic life of the state but also in public affairs, linking back to political participation. In order to enable persons belonging to minorities to participate fully in society, it is said to be crucial that the curriculum promotes the preservation and defence of minority

---

[398] UNIEMI, Report, E/CN4/2006/74, 6 January 2006, 2, 16.   [399] Ibid, 17
[400] Ibid, 17, 20.   [401] UNIEMI, Second Annual Report, A/HRC/4/9 (2007)
[402] Ibid, 2, 8.   [403] Ibid, 13.   [404] Ibid, 20.   [405] Ibid, 25
[406] A/HRC/FMI/2008/2.

languages and identity. The crucial importance of equal access to quality education also entails strong condemnation of any form of segregation in this respect. Another important synergy is the adoption of a holistic approach imbued with substantive equality considerations that reach far into the socio-economic field: 'in order to ensure effective access to education for members of minority communities, authorities should address impediments resulting from poverty and child labor, low nutrition levels and poor health and sanitation among communities'.[407]

B. International Labour Organization[408]

The ILO[409] has adopted numerous instruments pertaining to the prohibition of discrimination, inter alia on the grounds of race, colour, and religion, as components of international labour standards. These norms are of potential relevance to minority economic participation. In addition to Discrimination (Employment and Occupation) Convention 1958 no 111,[410] special reference should be made to the two ILO conventions on migrant workers (no 97/1949 and no 143/1975). However the ratification record of both is still very low. Furthermore, the supervision of these standards through the complaints procedure is not accessible to individuals, so minorities will need particular trade union or employer organizations to take up their cause.

C. Organisation of Economic Co-operation and Development (OECD): Development Assistance Committee (DAC)[411]

At the global level, reference should also be made to DAC, a body which is concerned with the realization of sustainable development in developing countries. Importantly, when DAC consults civil society, it makes sure to include minority populations in these consultations so that their concerns are taken on board. Does this constitute further recognition of the procedural dimension of economic participation?[412]

---

[407] Ibid, 4.
[408] UN Guide for Minorities, Part II Pamphlets, Pamphlet no 10: 'Minorities and the International Labour Organization'.
[409] A second strand of ILO norms that should be highlighted are provisions for the protection of indigenous peoples (hence minority specific rights) in ILO Conventions no 169 and 107, once again with a pronounced focus on issues pertaining to the socio-economic participation of the minorities concerned.
[410] Similarly the Forced Labour Convention 1930, no 29 is of special relevance to minorities, since they tend to be more vulnerable for this kind of violation of human rights.
[411] UN Guide for Minorities, Part II Pamphlets: Pamphlet no 13: 'The Organization for Economic Cooperation and Development's Development Assistance Committee (DAC)'.
[412] Note that DAC adopted an action-oriented policy paper on human rights and development on 15 February 2007.

D. MRG: Minority Rights Group International

MRG is the leading international human rights organization working to secure rights for ethnic, religious, and linguistic minorities and indigenous people around the world.

The work of MRG has never been confined to cultural issues in the broad sense, but has also included participation in social and economic life.[413] Special attention has been accorded to countering the process of having damaging development policies imposed upon minorities, and discrimination in education, employment, health care, housing and land rights.[414] MRG also focuses on the right to development and its importance for minorities and the protection of their rights, as exemplified by its submission to the now abolished UN Sub-commission, entitled 'Minority Rights and Development: Overcoming exclusion, discrimination and poverty'.[415]

VI. Evaluation

While minority rights and minority protection are still mainly associated with cultural issues in the broad sense, the above review has revealed that a pronounced interest in the social and economic participation of persons belonging to minorities is taking root. This may not always be explicitly addressed in terms of participatory rights, but that does not distract from the reality that through the equality paradigm and the interpretation of general human rights and minority-specific rights, an ever-growing protection for socio-economic participation of minorities is materializing.

In terms of Art 27 of the ICCPR, a steady jurisprudential line exists to protect the right of minorities to exercise their traditional economic activities and benefit from them.

The minority-specific provisions of the Council of Europe and the OSCE may not be very explicit, let alone elaborate, on minority rights in terms of participation in social and economic life either, but their practice in relation to various Articles of the FCNM have clearly made up for that. Similarly, the

---

[413] Bedard, *Participation in Economic Life* (n 18 above), 11. One of the reports made in the framework of this organization is entitled, 'Participation in Economic Life'. While it is focused on minorities in South-eastern Europe, several of its analyses are also valid in a more general sense. In any event, it is clear that several of the core provisions it identifies under international law concern non-discrimination. The author also highlights (in line with the strategy of the UNIEMI) the importance of the Millennium Development Goals, which focus on reduction of poverty and improvement of quality of life is particularly important for minorities.

[414] Minority Rights Group International, official website at <http://www.minorityrights.org/469/programmes/programmes.html> (accessed 31 July 2009).

[415] E/CN4/Sub2/AC5/2002/WP6.

ongoing activities of the HCNM have begun to include these themes as well, particularly in relation to the Roma.

General human rights are being interpreted with adequate minority sensitivity, also pertaining to their special needs (often to non-discrimination) in the socio-economic field. Arguably the substantive clarifications of social and economic rights can be understood as explanations of what is important in terms of participation in social and economic life. The importance of the actual interpretation of general human rights in favour of persons belonging to minorities cannot be underestimated, especially as these seem to confirm the practice of minority-specific rights without this pronounced focus on socio-economic rights. The adoption by the UN General Assembly of the additional protocol on a complaints procedure to the ICESCR is bound to significantly enhance the justiciability of these rights, of particular relevance to persons belonging to minorities. The importance of non-discrimination in the realization of participation in social and economic life of persons belonging to minorities is also fully captured and furthered by the Racial Equality Directive.

The various supervisory bodies acknowledge the crucial importance of education, equal access to and enjoyment of the right to education, for optimal integration in society and subsequent access to higher education, adequate qualifications, and thus proper jobs. The disproportionate rates of unemployment among persons belonging to minorities are generally a cause for concern, and similar/related problems in relation to equal access to health care services, other social services and housing also illicit criticism and concomitant calls on the respective states to improve the situation. Several supervisory bodies also acknowledge the instrumental importance of proper access to naturalization processes and hence the nationality of the state concerned.

Notwithstanding these developments, also in relation to the UNIEMI and the UN Forum on Minority Issues (and other international actors), there is still ample room for improvement in the sense that theoretical principles still need to be effectively implemented and realized. In view of the weak nature of minority rights, a lot depends on the political will of states. Arguably, the constructive dialogue approach of the AC of the FCNM is rather promising in this respect. The mainstreaming of minority concerns within the decision-making process generally (as hinted at in Lund Recommendation 6) would also go a long way to securing the desired result of enhancing minority participation in social and economic life.[416]

---

[416] The importance should be underscored of statistical data broken down along the identity markers of relevance for minorities (ethnicity, language, religion), not only with the aim of highlighting a particular problem with regard to participation, but also to devise policies to counter such problems and monitor eventual progress. The crucial importance of statistical data is something recognized by AC–UN treaty bodies across the board: see, among others, Phillips, 'The Framework Convention (n 5 above), 291, 306.

20

International Benchmarks
A review of minority participation in the judiciary

Katherine Nobbs

I. Introduction	588
II. International Standards	590
III. Implementation Practice	592
A. According minorities an effective voice at the level of central government	592
B. Conflict resolution	599
C. Long-term credibility	605
IV. Conclusion	608

I. Introduction

To date, the discussion on political participation of minorities has focused primarily on issues such as conflict settlement, complex power-sharing arrangements, electoral systems, or the role of minority representation within, or influence upon, the legislative and executive organs of government. By contrast, comparatively little analysis has been undertaken of minority participation in the justice sector, perhaps because the judiciary—constitutionally mandated to embody independence and impartiality—is not generally regarded as an appropriate forum for political wrangling or ethnic and national power-sharing.

The doctrine of judicial independence imparts to judges the role of objective intermediary between competing political forces. While political debates are played out in the executive and parliamentary law-making process, any resulting legislation is to be applied in an equitable fashion by the neutral arbiter of the judiciary. By this logic, to entrench judicial representation along ethnic, national, religious, or linguistic social cleavages would be to undermine the liberal constitutional bedrocks of judicial impartiality and the equality of all citizens before the law.

However, in reality, there is a great deal of constitutional and practical overlap between the making and evolution of law, and its application by the courts. This intersection is especially pronounced in common law systems, where the value of case law and the doctrine of precedent are accorded additional weight. In such cases, there has been exhaustive debate over judicial activism, and whether judges and the laws that they apply are, or even should be, apolitical. Judges' refusal to toe the government line on a range of socially contentious issues—for example, gay rights in the US, aboriginal rights in Australia, or terror laws in the UK—has demonstrated the ability, and occasional desire, on the part of certain judges to shape the legal frameworks within which they operate.

Generally speaking, political and public resistance to attempts to increase or entrench minority representation in the judiciary stem from a fear that minority judges would use their position to advance a specifically 'pro-minority' agenda. As with other counter-majoritarian or civil individualist critiques of minority rights, such action is regarded as inherently disadvantageous to majority defendants and/or majority cultural, linguistic, or religious norms, a bias which is perceived as particularly unseemly in an institution professing political neutrality.

Furthermore, the perceived reinforcement of ethnic, linguistic, cultural, or national cleavages through the medium of quotas or guaranteed seats is contentious even in the context of governmental organs with an expressly political mandate. It is feared that state construction and the creation of power-sharing arrangements along overtly ethnic lines is not conducive to long-term social harmony, and positive discrimination measures are generally accepted only as an interim solution to a fragile and politically divided post-conflict society, with the long-term normative preference being for the development of a political and civil infrastructure which promotes a politics of ideology rather than one of ethnic, linguistic, cultural, or religious identity (although that is not to dismiss the potential for overlap).

These concerns notwithstanding, however, it is increasingly accepted by the organized international community that not only is representation of minorities within the judiciary disproportionately low in Europe when compared with other sectors, but that the negative implications of this are evident both with regard to the protection and advancement of minority rights, and to the development of the law more generally.

As evidenced throughout the remainder of this chapter, a shortage or absence of minority judges is arguably responsible, at least in part, for the demonstrated lack of judicial awareness of minority problems, the persistent failure to address cases of discrimination through the courts, and practical and administrative issues relating, among other things, to due process and language rights. Furthermore, underrepresentation of minorities in the judiciary may have damaged public confidence in the criminal justice system; if the judiciary is not seen as representing the interests of all groups—or, in worst cases, is itself actively discriminatory—this has long-term implications for minority–majority relations and the development of the rule of law. Although relevant to all jurisdictions, this concern resonates especially strongly in post-conflict societies, where relations between groups are already strained and the need for perceived judicial independence is especially pronounced.

More broadly, it has also been argued that the composition of a judiciary will shape its 'metapolitics'—that is, its overarching vision of what a society should look like and whose interests should prevail. Each judge brings to the bench a distinctive set of experiences and assumptions, producing related interpretations of what counts as meaningful or relevant in a particular case.[1] If judges are all of the same gender, or are drawn from the same ethnic, social or political background, it is argued that the law will develop in accordance with the interests of that narrow splinter of the population, and not with a more holistic understanding of diverse interests within society.

The next section will examine these general issues within the context of international instruments and standards, breaking down normative recommendations for minority judicial participation into three concrete policy areas. The third section will then undertake a broad survey of recent European state practice, drawing primarily on national laws and on the opinions of the Advisory Committee (AC) on the Framework Convention for the Protection of National Minorities (FCNM).

II. International Standards

Lund Recommendation 6 clearly articulates the need for an effective minority 'voice' at the level of central government, with the judiciary cited as one of a range of institutions in which such influence might be appropriate. In this context, it is noted that minority judicial representation should extend from the 'lower courts' to the very highest 'supreme or constitutional courts', indicating that minorities should not only influence the law within the jurisdictions in which they are territorially or numerically concentrated but should impact substantively on the development of the national legal framework.

As with most international normative standards, however, states are accorded very wide discretion when it comes to implementation, and guaranteed judicial seats are clearly noted as just one among many possible power-sharing options for ensuring minorities a voice in government. In this context, it is helpful to envisage a spectrum of potential application, spanning from 'harder' constitutionally entrenched judicial power-sharing mechanisms—analogous to Quebec representation on the Canadian Supreme Court bench, or the

---

[1] KJ Bybee, *Mistaken Identity: The Supreme Court and the politics of minority representation* (1998), 30–1, 41.

requirement in the UK that one Law Lord be from Scotland and one from Northern Ireland—to 'softer' procedural or informal social measures aimed at increasing accessibility to the judicial profession in very general terms. Section III.A below will contextualize this spectrum with reference to state practice, but it should be noted here that constitutional or legal guarantees of minority judicial representation are comparatively infrequent, and the preference has clearly been for less formal mechanisms for boosting participation.

This is due, at least in part, to the above-mentioned tension between according minorities 'an effective voice at the level of central government'—which imparts to judges an activist, or at least a political, role—and judicial independence and impartiality, suggestive of political neutrality. This tension is clearly articulated in the Council of Europe Advisory Committee's Thematic Commentary on Participation:

122. It is also important to promote participation of persons belonging to national minorities in the judiciary and the administration of justice. Measures in this respect should be implemented in a way which fully guarantees the independence and the effective functioning of the judiciary.

The role of the judiciary in providing an effective remedy for the violation of minority rights is also taken into account in international instruments. In this context, the Explanatory Note to the Lund Recommendations draws attention to other instruments of international relevance: for example, Art 2.3 of the International Covenant on Civil and Political Rights, or Art 11 of the European Charter of Local Self-government. It also cites para 30 of the 1990 OSCE Copenhagen Document, which declares that OSCE participating states must:

recognize that the questions relating to national minorities can only be satisfactorily resolved in a democratic political framework based on the rule of law, with a functioning judiciary.[2]

Clearly, the lack of effective remedies not only renders meaningless any attempt to legislate effectively, but might mean that cases are simply not brought before the courts in the first place. As will be discussed in more detail below, a lack of judicial representativeness clearly correlates in practice with a lack of awareness on the part of judges as to the particular causes and nature of minority problems, as well as the details of anti-discrimination or minority rights legislation, and the AC has repeatedly recommended measures to address this.

Another provision of the Lund Recommendations refers specifically to the role of the judiciary in the context of conflict resolution:

2) Section IV.B.24
Effective participation of national minorities in public life requires established channels of consultation for the prevention of conflicts and dispute resolution, as

---

[2] As quoted in the Explanatory Note to the Lund Recommendation on the Effective Participation of National Minorities in Public Life, Art 24, available at <http://www.osce.org/documents/hcnm/1999/09/2698_en.pdf> (31 July 2009).

well as the possibility of ad hoc or alternative mechanisms when necessary. Such methods include:

- judicial resolution of conflicts, such as judicial review of legislation or administrative actions, which requires the State possess an independent, accessible, and impartial judiciary whose decisions are respected; and

…

As noted above, the perceived neutrality of the judiciary—or at least the popular perception that it represents the interests of all parties equally—is especially pertinent in the context of post-conflict societies, where ethnic and national tensions may still run high, and there is an enhanced need not only for justice to be done, but for it to be *seen* to be done. A population fragmented by conflict must be confident that the juidiciary is both willing and able to take account of the needs and interests of all groups in society, an issue which is accorded even greater weight in the context of truth and reconciliation processes.

Taking account of these framework provisions, both their explicit statements and their implicit long-term goals, the following sections will examine state practice in relation to three main normative concerns. The first is the stated need to accord minorities an effective voice at the level of central government and, notably, to provide persons belonging to minorities with an effective judicial remedy in the event of violation of their legal rights (Section III.A). The second relates to the role of the judiciary in the resolution and prevention of conflict, notably the interplay between representative constitutional courts and majority-dominated lower courts within an ethnic federation (BiH), and the impact of actively blocking minority representation in the immediate post-conflict period (Croatia) (Section III.B). Finally, the third section will draw on the implicit assumption that the judiciary must be broadly credible if overarching societal goals of rule of law and diversity management are to be achieved (Section III.C). It will address general issues of public confidence in and perceptions of the judiciary, structural barriers to entry, and the effectiveness of broad policies aimed at improving longer term judicial representativeness.

III. Implementation Practice

A. According minorities an effective voice at the level of central government

The underrepresentation of minorities in the judiciary is pervasive, and is noted repeatedly by the AC in its opinions on state practice.[3] Figures for the UK, for

---

[3] AC, First Opinion on Albania, ACFC/INF/OP/I(2003)004, 12 September 2002, para 75; First Opinion on Croatia, ACFC/INF/OP/I92002)003, 6 April 2001, para 56; Second Opinion on Croatia, ACFC/INF/OP/II(2004)002, 13 April 2005, paras 10, 90, 154, 157, 185; Second

instance, where public authorities are under a statutory duty to monitor diversity among employees, indicate that ethnic minorities represent 9 per cent of the total population but account for just 4 per cent of judges.[4] However, it is not possible to assess the full scale of underrepresentation as many states simply do not collect data on diversity in employment, which is found by the AC to be persistently lacking.[5] This is especially true of states that have rejected a so-called 'multiculturalist' approach to their minorities in favour of an 'assimilationist' one, and have actively resisted attempts to develop a system of ethnic diversity monitoring (eg, France). The collection of data might also be limited by privacy legislation (Portugal) or an absence of resources. Where official information is lacking, analyses have attempted to determine ethnicity from anecdotal evidence and professional names listings; these have pointed to similar, if not more exacerbated, patterns of underrepresentation of minorities within the judiciary.[6]

Taken alone, the fact of underrepresentation might not be especially problematic, as the link between descriptive or 'mirror' representation and substantive representation is by no means conclusively established; no direct causal relationship has yet been clearly identified between increased judicial minority representation and case outcome or judicial reasoning.[7] However, a number of

---

Opinion on Moldova, ACFC/INF/OP/II(2004)004, 24 May 2005, para 143; First Opinion on Montenegro, ACFC/INF/OP/I(2008)001, 6 October 2008, para 95; First Opinion on Romania, ACFC/INF/OP/I(2002)001, 6 April 2001, para 71; Second Opinion on Romania, ACFC/INF/OP/II(2005)007, 23 February 2006, paras 19, 187; First Opinion on Serbia, ACFC/INF/OP/I (2004)002, 27 November 2003, paras 38, 103, 165, 175; First Opinion on the former Yugoslav Republic of Macedonia (fYROM), ACFC/INF/OP/I((2005)001, 2 February 2005, para 99, 145; Second Opinion on FYROM, ACFC/INF/OP/II(2007)002, 9 July 2008, paras 25, 189, 229; Second Opinion on United Kingdom, ACFC/INF/OP/II(2007)003, 26 October 2007, paras 24, 241; Opinion on the implementation of the Framework Convention for the Protection of National Minorities in Kosovo, ACFC/INF/OP/I(2005)004, 2 March 2006, at 4, paras 37, 114.

[4] AC, Second Opinion on United Kingdom (n 3 above), para 67.

[5] AC, Second Opinion on Croatia (n 3 above), paras 43, 156; First Opinion on Montenegro (n 3 above), para 95; Second Opinion on Norway, ACFC/INF/OP/II(2006)006, 16 November 2006, para 142; First Opinion on Portugal, ACFC/INF/OP/I(2006)002, 6 October 2006, para 28; Second Opinion on Romania (n 3 above), para 195; Second Opinion on the Russian Federation, ACFC/INF/OP/II(2006)004, 2 May 2007, para 12; First Opinion on Serbia (n 3 above), para 34; Second Opinion on the Slovak Republic; ACFC/INF/OP/II(2005)004, 26 May 2005, para 39; Second Opinion on Spain, ACFC/INF/OP/II(2007)001, 2 April 2008, paras 33, 65, 98; First Opinion on Switzerland, ACFC/INF/OP/I(2003)007, 20 February 2003, paras 27, 85; and Opinion on Kosovo (n 3 above), para 155.

[6] A Böcker and L de Groot-van Leeuwen, 'Ethnic minority representation in the judiciary: Diversity among judges in old and new countries of immigration', (2007) *The Judiciary Quarterly* 16, 18, available at <http://www.rechtspraak.nl/NR/rdonlyres/D4F40740-87CE-4B4D-85F6-70B3A5541599/0/RVR_RECHTSTREEKS_ENGELS_BW3.pdf> (accessed 31 July 2009).

[7] The impact of judges' identity on case outcome has long been a topic of academic discussion in, eg, the United States. There, however, meta-analyses of quantitative studies have not yielded any clear causal link between a judge's race or gender and case outcome. This is not to suggest that no such link exists; in fact, there is ample evidence to suggest the contrary. Rather, it seems as if the complexity of the factors involved and the dynamics between them (eg, non-disclosure of judicial reasoning; the 'compensatory' effect sometimes exercised by minority or women judges; the different effects of identity on individual and panel decision-making, and so on) have made it almost

enduring problems have been identified by the AC which can, at the very least, be correlated to an absence on the bench of persons belonging to national minorities.

The most serious judicial shortcoming identified in Committee opinions is that of ethnic bias. In its First Opinion on Ireland, for example, the AC noted with concern 'press reports of discriminatory comments by individual ... members of the judiciary', directed against the Traveller Community.[8] In its Second Opinion on Moldova, the AC again found evidence of systemic ethnic bias within the criminal justice system:

> The Roma are also subject to discrimination as regards access to the courts since the police and judicial authorities tend to be reluctant to conduct the necessary investigations and prosecute known perpetrators of violence against the Roma ...[9]

The Committee also noted discriminatory attitudes among members of the Norwegian judiciary, directed against persons of immigrant background.[10]

Perhaps most worryingly, it not only drew attention to the 'disconcerting' underrepresentation of minorities (especially Serb) in the Croatian judiciary, but noted that the ethnic origin of victims and defendants were found to have a direct effect on domestic war crimes proceedings.[11] However, although these findings are clearly a cause for serious concern, Croatia's post-conflict context has meant that the dynamics of the case are highly distinctive; its specificities will be discussed in more detail in section III.B below.

It is clear that the manifestation of overtly prejudiced attitudes is of particular practical concern within an institution designed to implement and safeguard anti-discrimination legislation. However, openly intolerant behaviour is of course widely held to be unacceptable, both in international normative standards and in national jurisdictions; examples are extremely isolated, and are generally confined to individuals rather than institutions.[12] Where it has been identified

---

impossible to draw general conclusions on the relationship between descriptive and substantive representation. CW Bonneau and HM Rice, 'Race and the politics of criminal cases on State Supreme Courts', Paper presented at the Annual Meeting of the Southern Political Science Association, New Orleans, LA, 3–6 January 2007; S Farhang, 'Institutional dynamics on the US Court of Appeals: Minority representation under panel decision-making' (2004) 20(2) *The Journal of Law, Economics, and Organization* 299–330.

[8] AC, First Opinion on Ireland, ACFC/INF/OP/I(2004)003, 22 May 2003, para 68. All AC Opinions are available from the Council of Europe website, at <http://www.coe.int/t/dghl/monitoring/minorities/3_FCNMdocs/Table_en.asp> (accessed 31 July 2009).

[9] AC, Second Opinion on Moldova (n 3 above), para 69.

[10] AC, Second Opinion on Norway (n 5 above), paras 36, 86.

[11] AC, First Opinion on Croatia (n 3 above), para 55; Second Opinion on Croatia (n 3 above), para 89.

[12] An interesting exception here is the UK, where the Stephen Lawrence Inquiry and resultant Macpherson Report, released in 1999, identified the Metropolitan Police as being 'institutionally racist' (a phrase very carefully and narrowly defined as indirect, rather than direct, discriminatory practices). The Stephen Lawrence Enquiry, Report of an Inquiry by Sir William Macpherson, February 1999, available at <http://www.archive.official-documents.co.uk/document/cm42/4262/sli-00.htm> (accessed 31 July 2009).

by the AC, national governments appear to have been proactive in their attempts to address it: the Irish government has taken very seriously the problems experienced by the Traveller community, citing programmes and initiatives designed to promote tolerance and understanding between the settled and travelling communities, and maintain multi-annual funding;[13] it was also noted that Moldova has increased its efforts to combat discriminatory behaviour, both at the central and regional level.[14]

However, beyond the more easily identifiable issue of direct discrimination, the underrepresentation of minorities within the judiciary presents a broader challenge. As noted above, regional and national courts are designed to provide persons belonging to national minorities with a legal remedy in the event of violation of their rights. However, a survey of AC opinions suggests that the main problem of judicial unrepresentativeness is not open ethnic bias but rather a consistent and pervasive lack of awareness of the specificities of minority issues.[15] The Committee articulates this concern in its Second Opinion on Albania:

> Moreover, the issue of indirect discrimination does not appear to have been given sufficient consideration by the judicial and non-judicial authorities ... Indeed, the Advisory Committee notes that the problems faced by some persons belonging to national minorities in areas such as social services, housing and education are generally considered ... to affect the population as a whole rather than just national minorities ...[16]

The AC has thus directly criticized certain national courts for taking too little account of discrimination in areas such as housing and education. It opposes an individualist interpretation of social policy, whereby the issues in question are regarded as affecting society as a whole, and their disproportionately negative impact on minority groups is not taken into account. Practically, the failure to designate such legislation as discriminatory means that persons belonging to national minorities will not be entitled to remedies.

---

[13] Republic of Ireland, State Report, ACFC/SR/II(2006)001, 3 January 2006, 6.

[14] AC, Second Opinion on Moldova (n 3 above), para 71. Note that the exclusion of Norway here is due simply to the fact that a follow-up state report or a third cycle Opinion had not yet been released at the time of writing.

[15] First Opinion on Albania (n 3 above), paras 40, 94; Second Opinion on Austria, ACFC/INF/OP/I (2007)005, 11 June 2008, paras 9, 43; Second Opinion on Azerbaijan, ACFC/INF/OP/II(2007)007, 10 December 2008, paras 16, 36; First Opinion on Bulgaria, ACFC/INF/OP/I (2006)005, 5 April 2006, para 60; Second Opinion on the Czech Republic, ACFC/INF/OP/II (2005)002, 26 October 2005, para 195; First Opinion on Lithuania, ACFC/INF/OP/I(2003)008, 21 February 2003, para 46; Second Opinion on Moldova (n 3 above), paras 16, 73; First Opinion on Portugal (n 5 above), para 26; First Opinion on Romania, ACFC/INF/OP/I(2002)001, 6 April 2001, para 9; Second Opinion on Romania (n 3 above), para 94; Second Opinion on the Slovak Republic (n 5 above), para 34; First Opinion on Slovenia, ACFC/INF/OP/I(2005)001, 12 September 2002, para 39; First Opinion on Spain, ACFC/INF/OP/I(2004)004, 27 November 2003, para 29; Second Opinion on Spain (n 5 above), paras 98, 173; First Opinion on the fYROM (n 3 above), para 88.

[16] Second Opinion on Albania, ACFC/INF/OP/II(2008)003, 1 December 2008, para 66.

Contextualizing this problem of indirect discrimination within the issue of underrepresentation, it is plausible that such an approach might be due, at least in part, to a majority-dominated judiciary which is not sufficiently sensitized to the particularly acute problems of minority groups.

Another problem stemming from long-term underrepresentation of minorities in the judiciary is a lack of public confidence in the courts and in the justice system as a whole (to be discussed in greater detail in section III.C below). If the courts are perceived by members of national minorities to be systemically biased, those persons will be reluctant even to lodge anti-discrimination claims, effectively gutting any legislative efforts to protect and promote minority rights. Such concerns are heightened in the context of post-conflict reconstruction.

The implication of AC opinions is that there is, at the minimum, a correlation between judicial unrepresentativeness and issues of direct, and indirect, discrimination and public confidence. However, as noted in the introduction, government strategies for addressing the shortfall vary widely. This is due perhaps to the fact that the underlying causes of judicial underrepresentation of minorities remain unclear. Commentators have questioned whether the roots of the problem are essentially 'supply-side' or 'demand-side'.[17] If the former, it would be recruitment and selection mechanisms that place ethnic minorities at an inherent disadvantage. A dominance of one ethnic or national group within the judiciary would thus be the result of indirect discrimination in examination procedures or recruitment procedures, or a lack of personal contacts within the profession. By contrast, the demand-side argument is that high levels of educational and professional qualifications required to achieve judicial standing have meant that there are simply not enough potential minority judges coming through the system. By this logic, the judiciary has been subject to the systemic exclusion of disadvantaged social, economic or political groups—including ethnic, linguistic, religious or national minorities—and has become the preserve of the (majority) elite. Issues relating to aspiration are also thought to be relevant in this context.

The relevance of this distinction is that, if causes are found to be primarily supply-side, then states can undertake positive constitutional, legislative, or programmatic action to redress an unfair imbalance. However, if low recruitment into the judiciary is the result of a lack of candidates with the requisite levels of training and experience, this problem can only be tackled by broader and longer-term education and employment policies. Thus, distinctive national understandings of the underlying causes, coupled with divergences in national integration models or ideologies, have given rise to a range of state practice as regards implementation. In this context, and as noted in section II above, it is helpful to conceive participation mechanisms along a broad policy spectrum,

---

[17] Böcker and de Groot-van Leeuwen, 'Ethnic minority representation in the judiciary' (n 6 above), 3.

ranging from 'harder' measures, such as constitutionally entrenched judicial power-sharing, to 'softer', overarching societal measures aimed at increasing accessibility to the judicial profession as a whole.

Given concerns regarding the perceived need for judicial impartiality and apolitical application of the law, it is reasonable to assume that the constitutional or legal entrenchment of minority representation will only be extended to the more overtly political sectors of governance, at least in a non-conflict environment. This hypothesis is borne out in practice. A survey of the constitutional design of established democracies suggests that the constitutional entrenchment of judicial representation of minorities is extremely rare.[18] Judicial nominations may be controlled by mechanisms which split power between different parliamentary chambers or between the judiciary and the legislature,[19] but there are no express provisions for nomination according to ethnicity, religion, language, etc (although that is not to say that such considerations might not be indirectly taken into account or governed by convention).[20] Within the Council of Europe area, it seems that constitutional entrenchment of minority representation within the judiciary has, to date, been reserved for (transitional) post-conflict arrangements.

However, a survey of AC opinions does turn up a few examples of harder, positive discrimination measures for increasing judicial representation of minorities in non-conflict states, usually at the recruitment stage. In Romania, for example, the Justice System Act[21] gives preference to minority graduates of the National Judicial Institute for recruitment to the judiciary, 'provided that their abilities are equivalent to other candidates'[22] However, the condition is clearly much affected by broader demand-side issues of socio-economic exclusion, and how successful the legislation is in actually improving representation remains to be seen; the AC has encouraged more comprehensive monitoring to assess this.

A similar example of positive discrimination at the recruitment stage can be found in the former Yugoslav Republic of Macedonia (fYROM), where the state has implemented a range of constitutional measures to help reflect the interests of persons belonging to minorities. Among these is the provision that the appointment of three of the nine Constitutional Court judges and three

---

[18] A notable exception here is Canada, where the region of Quebec is entitled to three representatives out of a total of nine constitutional court judges.

[19] See Constitution of Austria (consolidated 1983), Art 86; Constitution of Belgium 1970, Art 151; Constitution of Germany 1949, Art 94.

[20] Note that the exceptions here are post-conflict states, where constitutional design has been extremely sensitive to minority–majority power-sharing. In such cases, provisions are sometimes made for the guaranteed representation of minorities within the judiciary.

[21] Law no 247/2005.

[22] Second Opinion on Romania (n 3 above), para 181. Note that this provision applies only to areas where the population using the same language represents at least 50 per cent of the total number of inhabitants.

members of the Judicial Council must be approved by the majority of votes of representatives claiming to belong to communities not in the majority.[23]

However, these harder mechanisms remain the exception outside post-conflict state construction. In fact, very few European cases actually address the problem of judicial underrepresentation of minorities directly—that is, by seeking to increase descriptive or 'mirror' representation[24]—but approach it instead through indirect measures that seek to increase the capacity of existing judges to represent minority interests, for example through specialized training or awareness-raising measures. Moreover, this position is supported by the Advisory Committee, which consistently advocates indirect rather than direct measures for improving minority representation.[25] For example, the Committee has advocated specialized judicial training in cases where anti-discrimination legislation had recently been passed (for example, the 2004 amendments to the Austrian Equal Treatment Act) but where judicial awareness of the legislation was deemed insufficient.[26] Such measures were also advocated in cases where there was a lack of case law and claims of ethnic discrimination, for it was held that its absence was not necessarily due to an absence of discrimination (as is sometimes claimed by state authorities) but might also be the result of a lack of awareness among the population and the judiciary of existing legal remedies.[27] Even in the most extreme cases, eg where underrepresentation of minorities in the judiciary is so severe that the judiciary has been charged with ethnic bias (Croatia), the Committee is extremely reluctant to adopt a direct approach to increasing representation, opting again for enhanced awareness and specialized training.[28]

The Committee also highlighted other indirect measures which, while not targeting minorities directly, are nevertheless aimed at improving administrative

---

[23] First Opinion on FYRM, ACFC/INF/OP/I(2005)001, 2 February 2005, para 94.

[24] This distinction between 'descriptive' or 'mirror' representation and substantive representation is most authoritatively elucidated by Hanna Pitkin in her seminal work *The Concept of Representation* (1972).

[25] First Opinion on Albania (n 3 above), paras 40, 94; Second Opinion on Albania (n 15 above), para 69; Second Opinion on Austria, ACFC/INF/OP/II(2007)005, paras 9, 46; Second Opinion on Azerbaijan, ACFC/INF/OP/II(2007)007, 10 December 2008, paras 36, 43; First Opinion on Bulgaria, ACFC/INF/OP/I(2006)001, 5 April 2006, paras 30, 60.

[26] Second Opinion on Austria, ACFC/INF/OP/II(2007)005, DATE, paras 42, 43, 46.

[27] Second Opinion on Azerbaijan, ACFC/INF/OP/II(2007)006, 10 December 2008, paras 37, 38; First Opinion on Bulgaria, ACFC/INF/OP/I(2006)005, 5 April 2006, para 29; First Opinion on Spain (n 14 above), para 58; Second Opinion on Spain (n 5 above), para 34

[28] Second Opinion on Croatia (n 3 above), paras 14, 9; Second Opinion on the Czech Republic, ACFC/INF/OP/II(2005)002, 26 October 2005, para 195; First Opinion on Lithuania, ACFC/INF/OP/I(2003)008, 21 February 2003, paras 46, 96; Second Opinion on Moldova (n 3 above), paras 16, 73; First Opinion on Montenegro (n 3 above), para 34; First Opinion on Portugal (n 5 above), para 26; First Opinion on Romania (n 3 above), para 9; Second Opinion on Romania (n 3 above), para 94; Second Opinion on Slovenia, ACFC/INF/OP/II(2005)005, 26 May 2005, paras 29, 58, 91; Second Opinion on Spain (n 5 above), para 173; Second Opinion on Switzerland, ACFC/INF/OP/II(2008)002, 29 February 2008, para 56; Second Opinion on FYRM, ACFC/INF/OP/II(2007)002, 9 July 2008, para 88.

or procedural problems faced by minority groups in the context of the justice system. These are usually concerned, for example, with issues of language or access to court. Where measures are aimed directly at persons belonging to national minorities, these are targeted at those on the other side of the judicial process, namely victims and defendants, rather than judges; they usually entail awareness-raising among minority populations, for example with regard to anti-discrimination laws to which they might have recourse.

To conclude, when assessing state practice for 'according minorities an effective voice at the level of central government', it is clear at this stage that neither the governments in question nor the AC have been willing to interpret 'effective voice' directly, eg as the voice of persons belonging to national minorities. Instead, it is understood primarily as the indirect voicing of minority interests through existing (predominantly non-minority) judges. While the consequences of this for the development of minority rights law are unclear, improvements in awareness and training will have no impact whatsoever on the persistent exclusion of persons belonging to minorities from the ranks of the judiciary, and it is argued that this will have long-term implications for judicial credibility and diversity management. This issue will be addressed in general terms in section III.C, which will assess state practice in the field of demand-side policies. The next section, however, is concerned with the issue of judicial credibility in the more immediate context of post-conflict state (re)construction and peace-building.

B. Conflict resolution

As noted above, where there does seem to be a trend towards harder measures of constitutional entrenchment of judicial representation of minorities is in the context of post-conflict settlements/state construction. In states where majority–minority relations are strained, public confidence in judicial independence will plummet if exclusion is systemic or is seen to perpetuate conflict dynamics, notably the dominance of one ethnic, social, or national group over (other) national minorities. Where the broad social interests of two or more groups are directly competitive, it is crucial that the judiciary has the experience and skill to take into account all opposing interests; if it is not representative of minority groups, it is liable to incur charges of bias, thereby damaging the mediation process in the short-term and potentially exacerbating ethnic or national tensions in the longer term. Furthermore, where post-conflict settlements provide for the establishment of war crimes tribunals with the aim of redressing past wrongs, it is important not only that those tribunals take into consideration the minority perspective but that they are seen to do so.

However, even here, there is a reluctance to break with the doctrine of judicial impartiality and independence. Although interim judicial arrangements in post-conflict societies may reflect ethnic, social or religious divisions—for example, ad hoc war crimes tribunals or special chambers, or increased accessibility of minorities to existing human rights frameworks—international reluctance to entrench ethnic or national divisions within the judiciary is evidenced by the lack of conflict settlements or peace agreements which establish quotas or guaranteed minority seats in respect of the judiciary.

There are, however, some notable and interesting examples. Most recently, the Constitution of Kosovo has addressed the issue of judicial representation of communities[29] very comprehensively. The Constitution declares that the composition of the judiciary 'shall reflect the ethnic diversity of Kosovo', and in particular that the composition of any court must reflect the ethnic composition of the territorial jurisdiction of the respective court.[30] There are strong provisions for guaranteed representation on the Supreme Court:

At least fifteen percent (15%) of the judges of the Supreme Court, but not fewer than three (3) judges, shall be from Communities that are not in the majority in Kosovo.[31]

Similarly, in any other court with appeal jurisdiction, at least 15 per cent of judges, and a minimum of two judges, must be from communities.[32]

Furthermore, the Constitution establishes the Kosovo Judicial Council to ensure that courts at all levels reflect the multiethnic nature of the state (as well as ensuring professionalism, impartiality and independence). The Council is explicitly mandated by the Constitution to give preference to members of communities that are underrepresented in the judiciary in the appointment of judges.'[33] Furthermore, out of the thirteen members of the Judicial Council itself, two must be elected by the assembly deputies holding seats guaranteed for the Serb community, of which one must be a judge, and two other members must be elected by the deputies holding seats reserved for other communities, of which one must again be a judge.[34]

The requirement of representation in the Constitutional Court is solidified through the requirement of a double majority in the appointments procedure. According to Art 114.3, the decision to propose two out of the nine Constitutional Court judges requires the consent of community representatives in the Kosovo Assembly:

The decision to propose seven (7) judges requires a two thirds (2/3) majority of the deputies of the Assembly present and voting. The decision on the proposals of the other two (2) judges shall require the majority vote of the deputies of the Assembly present and voting, but only upon the consent of the majority of the deputies of the Assembly holding seats reserved or guaranteed for representatives of the Communities not in the majority in Kosovo.

---

[29] In Kosovo, the term 'communities' or 'miniority communities' is used in place of 'minorities'.   [30] Constitution of the Republic of Kosovo, Arts 102(4), 104(3).
[31] Ibid, Art 103(3).   [32] Ibid, Art 103(6).   [33] Ibid, Art 108(2).
[34] Ibid, Art 108(6).

For other judicial positions reserved for members of communities, candidates may only be recommended by a majority of the Judicial Council members who have been elected by Assembly deputies holding reserved seats.[35] Special procedures also apply for the appointment of judges to basic courts, the jurisdiction of which exclusively includes the territory of one or more municipalities in which the majority of the population belongs to the Kosovo Serb community.[36]

Although these provisions are extremely far-reaching, and clearly the result of Kosovo's particular history of ethnic tensions and contested statehood, similar mechanisms are also evident in other cases where ethnic conflict has rendered the issue of judicial representation especially sensitive. For example, regional arrangements for the autonomous territorial unit of Gagauzia in Moldova require that:

Judges of the judicial bodies of Gagauzia shall be appointed by a decree of the President of the Republic of Moldova on the recommendation of the People's Assembly of Gagauzia, with the agreement of the Superior Council of Magistrates.[37]

Although this legislation concerns appointment to regional, as opposed to national, judicial bodies, the principle of consent on the part of elected minority representatives is nevertheless still apparent.

The case of Bosnia and Herzegovina is especially interesting, given the jurisdiction of the Constitutional Court not only in its rulings on issues of constitutional relevance, but in mediating between the two ethnic entities: the Federation of Bosnia and Herzegovina, and the Serb Republic (SR). From 1 January 2001, it also took over the responsibilities of the interim Human Rights Chamber. It was thus essential that it was able to strike an appropriate balance between due consideration of ethnic issues and its duties as national legal arbiter and guardian of constitutional principles. Article VI.1.a of the BiH Constitution states that:

Four members shall be selected by the House of Representatives of the Federation, and two members by the Assembly of the Republika Srpska. The remaining three members shall be selected by the President of the European Court of Human Rights after consultation with the Presidency.

Article VI.1.b then specifies that:

The judges selected by the President of the European Court of Human Rights shall not be citizens of Bosnia and Herzegovina or of any neighboring state.

In theory, the potential for deadlock between the ethnic representatives of the state's 'constituent peoples' has been balanced by 'neutral' representation of non-BiH or neighbouring state nationals.

---

[35] Ibid, Art 108(9).   [36] Ibid, Art 108(10).
[37] Law on the Special Legal Status of Gagauzia, no 344-XIII, signed 23 December 1994, Art 22 (2), available at <http://www.intstudies.cam.ac.uk/centre/cps/documents_moldova_law.html> (accessed 31 July 2009).

Broadly speaking, this arrangement appears to have been successful in rising above ethnic cleavages,[38] and the Constitutional Court has made a number of decisions which have challenged the overtly ethnic politics of the composite entities and advanced the principles of collective equality of constituent peoples and the overarching understanding of BiH as a 'multi-national state'. For example, in its important Decision on the Constituency of Peoples, the Court held that the:

> Elements of a democratic state and society as well as underlying assumptions—pluralism, just procedures, peaceful relations that arise out of the Constitution— must serve as a guideline for further elaboration of the issue of the structure of BiH as a multi-national state. Territorial division (of Entities) must not serve as an instrument of ethnic segregation—on the contrary—it must accommodate ethnic groups by preserving linguistic pluralism and peace in order to contribute to the integration of the state and society as such. Constitutional principle of collective equality of constituent peoples, arising out of designation of Bosniacs, Croats and Serbs as constituent peoples, prohibits any special privileges for one or two constituent peoples, any domination in governmental structures and any ethnic homogenisation by segregation based on territorial separation. Despite the territorial division of BiH by establishment of two Entities, this territorial division cannot serve as a constitutional legitimacy for ethnic domination, national homogenisation or the right to maintain results of ethnic cleansing. Designation of Bosniacs, Croats and Serbs as constituent peoples in the Preamble of the Constitution of BiH must be understood as an all-inclusive principle of the Constitution of BiH to which the Entities must fully adhere, pursuant to Article III.3 (b) of the Constitution of BiH.[39]

Similarly, in its Decision on the Insignia of Entities, it defended the cultural rights of minorities within the entities, eg the rights of Serbs in the Federation, and those of Croats and Bosniaks in the SR.[40] In its Decision on the Names of Cities, it ruled that the changing of town and municipality names to designate their exclusively Serb affiliation constituted discriminatory action contrary to Art II.4 of the Constitution, and was in violation of the basic constitutional principle of equal treatment of constituent peoples throughout the territory of BiH.[41]

Although voting patterns of individuals judges are not explored here, the example remains a testament to the ability of constitutionally guaranteed, but carefully balanced, ethnic judicial representation to rise above ethnic and social cleavages, and to actively advance a multiethnic conception of the state. It

---

[38] Note that a study of the voting patterns of individual judges remains outside the scope of this paper. What is important in this context is the overall composition of the Constitutional Court and the resultant decisions.
[39] Constitutional Court BiH, U-5/98 III, Partial Decision, 1 July 2000, 36, available at <http://www.ccbh.ba/eng/odluke/index.php?src=2#> (accessed 1 July 2009).
[40] Constitutional Court BiH, U-4/04, Partial Decision, 31 March 2006, 60, available at <http://www.ccbh.ba/eng/odluke/index.php?src=2> (accessed 1 July 2009).
[41] Constitutional Court BiH, U-44/01, Partial Decision, Decision on Merits, 27 February 2004, 20, available at <http://www.ccbh.ba/eng/odluke/index.php?src=2> (accessed 1 July 2009).

should be noted, however, that the principle of judicial representation of all constituent peoples has only been extended to the Constitutional Court, and underrepresentation of minorities persists within lower municipal, cantonal and entity-level courts. In its First Opinion on BiH, the Advisory Committee noted that, within the entities, discrimination against persons not belonging to the locally dominant constituent people was evident in access to employment, and found the problem to be especially pronounced in the SR, 'where it remains excessively difficult for persons who are not Serbs to be recruited in the judiciary'.[42] It remains to be seen whether the constructed balance between national, minority-representative judicial structures and entity-level courts controlled by the locally dominant constituent people is effective in mediating between the distinctive interests of the constituent peoples and the overarching aims of a 'multinational' BiH state.

The example of Croatia is also interesting, as its immediate post-conflict strategy was not to improve minority representation within governmental structures, but rather to take measures actively to exclude it, albeit temporarily. It was argued in the First Croatian State Report to the AC that the 1991–5 war had resulted in fundamental changes to the country's structure and, in particular, in major demographic shifts, notably in relation to the ethnic Serb population. Consequently, it was held that until the actual demographic structure of Croatia could be discerned—through a census commissioned by the state[43]—the operation of the Constitutional Law on Human Rights and Freedoms and the Rights of Ethnic and National Communities and Minorities should be suspended.[44] In other words, the discriminatory legislation was aimed at actively curtailing the number of persons belonging to (Serb) minorities in various public bodies, including in courts.[45]

While the AC seemed to accept this justification, it was nevertheless very critical of the 'disconcerting' underrepresentation of persons belonging to the Serb minority in state administration, and noted that the situation with regard to some, but not all, other national minorities was 'very unsatisfactory'.[46]

However, by 2004–5, the situation was improving. In some regions, notably in Eastern Slavonia, Baranja, and Western Sirmium, measures were taken to ensure 40 per cent representation of Serbs among judicial authorities in the region.[47] Following the census of 2001—which found that the number of

---

[42] AC, First Opinion on BiH, ACFC/INF/OP/I(2005)003, 11 Mat 2005, para 43.
[43] Law on the Census of Population, Households and Dwellings, Law No. 64/2000, 27 June 2000, available at <http://www.dzs.hr/Eng/censuses/Census2001/census_law.htm> (accessed 31 July 2009).
[44] AC, First State Report on Croatia, ACFC/SR(1995)05, 16 March 1999, para 31.
[45] AC, First Opinion on Croatia, above note 3, para 56.
[46] AC, First Opinion on Croatia, above note 3, para 55.
[47] Agreement on reintegration of the judiciary, signed by Croatia and the United Nations Transitional Administration in Eastern Slavonia, Baranja and Western Sirmium, 30 September 1997.

members of national minorities in the territory had decreased significantly since 2001, especially among the Serb population[48]—Croatia's Second State Report seemed to indicate a genuine understanding of the need for minority representation in state administrative and judicial bodies.[49] Article 22.2 of the 2002 Constitutional Law on the Rights of National Minorities[50] stated that:

> Representation in the bodies of government administration and judicial bodies is being ensured to members of national minorities, consistent to the provisions of special acts, taking into consideration the participation of members of national minorities in the total population at the level on which the government administration or judicial body is operating, and taking into account their acquired rights.

However, in spite of overall progress in the legislative framework of minority protection, a subsequent Council of Ministers resolution noted that:

> the implementation of the Constitutional Law on the Rights of National Minorities has been regrettably slow in some key areas. Shortcomings are particularly manifest as regards the participation of persons belonging to national minorities in the state administrative and judicial bodies, where the monitoring of the current situation and the implementation of the legal guarantees are yet to be developed.[51]

These concerns were echoed by the AC's Second Opinion on Croatia which, while praising significant advances in legislation and dialogue with minority groups, noted with concern persistent problems relating to implementation of the new legal guarantees, especially as concerned the judiciary:

> Shortcomings are particularly manifest as regards the participation of persons belonging to national minorities in the state administration and judicial, bodies, where the monitoring of the current situation and the implementation of the legal guarantees are yet to be developed.[52]

It noted the central role of the courts in guaranteeing the proper implementation of national and international legislative initiatives to protect minority rights in the territory, and deemed it imperative that serious judicial shortcomings, ranging from ethnic bias in war crimes trials to significant backlogs and deficiencies in the provision of legal aid, be addressed without delay. However, once again, it did not advocate harder measures such as proportional minority representation in the courts, but called instead for softer measures such as 'training and other initiatives' and the development of comprehensive monitoring and accurate data.[53]

---

[48] Second State Report on Croatia, ACFC/SR/II(2004)002, 13 April 2004, at 54.
[49] Ibid, at 19. [50] Official Gazette, 155/2002.
[51] Council of Europe, Committee of Ministers, Resolution ResCMN(2005)5 on the implementation of the Framework Convention for the Protection of National Minorities by Croatia, 28 September 2005, 2 [52] AC, Second Opinion on Croatia (n 3 above), para 10.
[53] Ibid, paras 14, 89, 90, 156.

To conclude, post-conflict state design clearly bucks the pervasive and persistent trend towards softer measures to increase judicial representation of minorities, and a number of cases have entrenched judicial representation in higher law. However, context remains highly specific, and arrangements suited to one case (the post-conflict exclusion of minorities from the judiciary in Croatia) would have been entirely inappropriate for another (ethnic state construction in BiH). And as both settlements are still comparatively young, it is difficult to assess the long-term implications of either. Clearly, the temporary suspension of minority rights in Croatia in the immediate post-conflict period has impacted negatively on the current situation regarding judicial representation of minorities. However, the AC has accepted Croatia's justification of temporary necessity in the wake of dramatic post-war demographic shifts; furthermore, Croatia has demonstrated good faith in seeking to restore a more equitable balance, although this remains an ongoing process.

The composition and decisions of the Constitutional Court of BiH are perhaps the most telling rejection of the argument against guaranteed judicial representation of minorities in ethnically divided states. For it demonstrates that a carefully balanced court may in fact serve as a broadly credible and respected source for mediating between opposing group interests. The above-mentioned cases indicate that it has actively resisted the predominance of ethnic cleavages over a multiethnic conceptualization of the state. This may of course be due to the fact that no minority is dominant, and that the potential for conflict is buffered by a 'neutral' presence. However, it remains one of the few practical examples of guaranteed judicial representation, and the development of its case law over the coming years will be interesting to observe.

The following section will move from the rather specific issue of judicial credibility in the context of post-conflict state construction to the broader issue of public confidence and long-term diversity management.

C. Long-term credibility

As noted in section III.A above, in addition to concrete 'supply-side' barriers relating to entry procedures and training—particularly the cost and risk—there is also the 'demand-side' argument that the high level of educational and professional qualifications required to achieve judicial standing has resulted in the systemic exclusion of disadvantaged social, economic, or political groups, including certain ethnic, linguistic, religious, or national minorities. The UK recently undertook a review of its judicial accessibility policy, commissioning a working party aimed, among other things, at 'identifying and reducing barriers to entry for minority and socially and economically disadvantaged students'. The resultant Neuberger Report published fourteen months later noted that, as judges can only be selected from a pool of highly specialized and trained individuals, broad systemic social and economic inequalities, notably in relation to education, resulted in de facto exclusion of minority groups. The Final Report stated that:

> the opportunities for people to live and work in the ways they choose depend greatly on general social factors like access to education. The Bar is inevitably constrained by such factors, and can only select from those who excel and who present themselves as candidates.

A related argument is that if the judiciary is perceived as only being open to more privileged groups, this perception will be accompanied by a strong element of self-fulfilment;[54] persons from socially or economically excluded backgrounds will be indirectly discouraged from considering a career on the bench.

This section will address the impact of this exclusion on popular perceptions of the judiciary, its implications for long-term credibility and diversity management, and measures adopted by governments to improve general accessibility to the profession.

For people to have confidence in the legal system, and in the rule of law more broadly, they need to have confidence that the judiciary understands and represents their interests, and not merely those of a privileged (majority) elite. As with judicial credibility in a post-conflict context, long-term confidence in the judiciary in a diverse society seems to be contingent on descriptive representation. It has been suggested that this might be due to the high-profile nature of judicial work, or because of the central role occupied by the courts within the criminal justice system, in which defendants are often disproportionately representative of disadvantaged minority groups.[55]

The AC has noted with concern a lack of public confidence in the judiciary, notably among members of minority groups, repeatedly drawing attention to the issue in its opinions on state practice.[56] In addition to overarching concerns about public confidence, it also suggests that this might explain why cases of minority discrimination are not even brought before the courts in the first place.[57]

However, it is argued that the problem here is that, if the underrepresentation of minorities within the judiciary is genuinely the result of broader societal discrepancies in wealth, education, and training, then addressing the problem through harder measures such as positive discrimination or guaranteed seats may

---

[54] AC, Second Opinion on Croatia (n 3 above), para 5.   [55] Ibid, para 55.
[56] AC, Second Opinion on Croatia (n 3 above), paras 14, 90; First Opinion on Montenegro (n 3 above), para 34; First Opinion on the United Kingdom, ACFC/INF/OP/I(2007)003, 26 October 2007, para 72.
[57] AC, Second Opinion on Albania (n 15 above), para 65; Second Opinion on Azerbaijan, ACFC/INF/OP/II(2007)007, 10 December 2008, para 38; First Opinion on Portugal (n 5 above); Second Opinion on the Russian Federation (n 5 above), paras 12, 46; First Opinion on the fYROM (n 3 above), paras 53, 99.

be either impossible, if no suitable minority candidates are put forward, or may compromise the quality of judicial decision-making, if positive discrimination extends to cases where a less qualified minority candidate is recruited over a more qualified candidate from a majority background.

In many ways, this explains why state practice is often directed at softer awareness-raising and training measures, rather than at proportional representation or an appointments procedure contingent on the consent of minority representatives. In the UK, the Neuberger Report issued a list of ultra-soft recommendations including, among other things, school placement schemes, raising awareness via new media, improved careers advice, clearer marking systems, and mentoring. Although the more 'radical' ideas, such as the introduction of a law module onto the national curriculum or the use of a private or government-subsidized loan scheme for financially disadvantaged students, might have gone some of the way to levelling the playing field, these have yet to be implemented (and are unlikely to be in the near future). Moreover it can be argued that certain other measures, such as increased risk awareness at postgraduate level and a language proficiency test, would actively discourage minority candidates from pursuing career in the judiciary, without a parallel effort to remove barriers to entry.

That said, the Judicial Appointments Commission is already reporting that the number of applicants from ethnic minority backgrounds is increasing.[58] It should be noted though that, as it will take time for these new entrants to filter up to the ranks of the judiciary, the real impact of these measures will not be visible for another decade or so. Of crucial importance, however, is that their relative success or failure will be easy to track, given that diversity monitoring is now a mainstream process in the UK.

In France, although the debate relating to the 'ethnic' structure of the judiciary is concerned only with overseas *départements* and territories (DOM-TOM), the French Council for the Judiciary has repeatedly expressed concern about justice in the DOM-TOM where most judges are from continental France, arguing that non-indigenous judicial composition was not conducive to public acceptance of court decisions. A 2001 report considered measures such as special information for law students in the DOM-TOM, awarding scholarships and opening special measures for the competitive examinations for the judicial training programme.[59] Again though, these are all softer demand-side measures to increase the number of viable judicial candidates rather than positively discriminating in favour of those that already exist. Even measures such as these are

---

[58] Judicial Appointments Commission, Annual Report 2006–7, *Committed to Selection on Merit* (The Stationery Office, London: 2007), 27, available at <http://www.judicialappointments.gov.uk/docs/JAC_AR2006_07.pdf> (accessed 31 July 2009).

[59] Böcker and de Groot-van Leeuwen, 'Ethnic minority representation in the judiciary' (n 6 above), 28.

comparatively few and far between, and it is clear that promoting greater ethnic diversity among the judiciary is not a policy priority for many European states, especially those which have not undergone recent ethnic or national conflict. Most have yet to implement schemes even to *monitor* diversity in employment, which perhaps explains the cautious approach adopted by the AC in its opinions and recommendations.

IV. Conclusion

The above review has given rise to a number of core conclusions, which warrant recapping briefly here. First, although international standards have identified the judiciary as one of the key areas in which minorities should be granted 'an effective voice', in practice the broad margin of appreciation extended to state implementation has resulted, not only in a wide spectrum of potential application, but in a clear trend towards softer, demand-side initiatives as opposed to constitutionally or legally guaranteed minority judicial representation. Furthermore, in the few cases where states have adopted positive discrimination, these have generally been contingent on demand-side problems already having been resolved, eg in areas relating to education and training ('provided that their abilities are equivalent to other candidates').

A notable exception seems to be post-conflict states, where judicial credibility and legitimacy are accorded additional weight within the peace-building process. However, even a brief review of these cases points to their extremely context-specific nature: for example, the temporary minority exclusion from the judiciary in Croatia due to large demographic shifts would have been highly inappropriate to the Bosnian case, where the decisions of a constitutional court needed to be credible to an ethnically divided population. As such, few generalizations can be made in this context.

What the Bosnian example does show, however, is that the entrenchment of ethnicity quotas for constitutional court judges (in addition, of course, to requisite educational and professional qualifications) has not hindered the Court's ability to deliver decisions which have overcome ethnic politics and advanced a holistic understanding of a multinational state. Along with Canada, BiH is one very few examples of guaranteed minority representation at such a high level of judicial decision-making, and its role and development will be very interesting to observe over the coming years.

The main point to emerge from the above survey is actually how little is being done, or even recommended, to address the acknowledged shortfall of minority representation within the judiciary in Europe. Although some states, notably the UK, have taken measures to address demand-side problems in judicial recruitment, the practice is by no means widespread. Some states, for example Germany and France, have yet to acknowledge even the need for a debate surrounding ethnic diversity in the judiciary, and the AC has had no choice but to adopt a softly-softly tone in its recommendations.

In fact, as noted previously, the AC has at no point called for increased direct representation of minorities, but instead consistently articulates the need for greater awareness and training for existing members of the (predominantly non-minority) judiciary; in other words, it is calling for enhanced indirect representation. The minority 'voice' of the Lund Recommendations has thus been interpreted, not as the voice of persons belonging to minorities, but as that of non-minority judges who better understand and represent minority interests and anti-discrimination legislation.

As noted above, it is unclear whether non-descriptive substantive representation would be sufficient to protect and promote minority rights. However, what is evident is that a failure to address the persistent and pervasive shortfall of minority judges, especially through long-term demand-side measures, will do nothing to redress the current problem of a lack of public confidence in the judiciary, especially among members of minority groups. The implications of this for judicial legitimacy and diversity management are clearly important.

What is needed as a matter of urgency is for states to adopt comprehensive schemes to monitor data on ethnicity and employment in the public sector. To its credit, the Advisory Committee has been working tirelessly towards this end. Until the full extent of minority underrepresentation within the judiciary is properly evidenced and understood, it will be difficult to convince governments or their electorates of the need to address it. And broadly speaking, while constitutional traditions of judicial impartiality and independence will remain a barrier to guaranteed or entrenched minority representation, it is clear that demand-side measures aimed at improving accessibility to the profession would go a long way towards redressing current imbalances.

PART V

MINORITY SELF-GOVERNANCE

21

Participation as Self-governance

Yash Ghai

I. Political Participation	613
A. Participation as representation and as self-governance	616
B. Participation and self-government as rights	617
C. Distinction between autonomy and federalism	621
II. Framework for Participation in the Lund Recommendations	622
A. Ethnicity and identity	624
B. Ethnicity and human rights	627
III. Paradoxes of Self-government	628
IV. Conclusion	633

I. Political Participation

The Lund Recommendations reflect the contemporary understanding of the rights of minorities. In the last three decades there has been a significant shift from limited protection against discrimination towards more active engagement of the state in facilitating the development of minority cultures and promoting a political role for minorities. Previously perceived as passive recipients of the state's beneficence, minorities are now regarded as holders of rights that entitle them to an active role in the affairs of the state. The emphasis on identity has led, in various ways, to the constitutional recognition of minority or ethnic groups and their political and cultural rights. The adoption of democracy, understood as political pluralism, representation, freedom of speech, accountability, tolerance, and promotion of diversity, in most parts of the world have highlighted the active role of citizens and communities. As the foundations of democracy in human rights are explored, the salience of minority rights as an essential component of a democratic society is acknowledged. Increasingly the broad framework of human rights, grounded in equality and human dignity, is used to assess social and political progress, particularly that of minorities. The concern with the rights of minorities has also been stimulated by the capacity of disenfranchised minorities to create political instability and inflict great harm on society. Central to this new understanding of the rights of minorities is their entitlement to participate in the institutions of the state, and in the decisions they make. Apart from the function of participation to protect the rights of minorities and promote political integration, it encourages the greater interest of the minority in political and social issues, leads to the acceptance and empowerment of minorities, and brings them closer to other communities.

The right of participation has been implicit in most formulations of rights after the emergence of the new international order following the Second World War. The Universal Declaration of Human Rights proclaimed that the government is based on the will of the people, and the rights freely to participate in the cultural life of the community (Art 27). Both the human rights covenants specify the right to self-determination of the people to freely determine their constitutional and political order. Article 25 of the International Covenant on Civil and Political Rights guarantees every citizen the right and opportunity 'to take part in the conduct of public affairs, directly or through freely chosen representatives, to vote and to be elected at genuine periodic elections on universal franchise ... and to have access, on terms of equality, to public services'. Article 27 is concerned with the rights of minorities, 'in community with the other members of their group, to enjoy their own culture, to profess and practise their own religion, or to use their own language'. The International Labour Organization Convention on Indigenous Peoples (no 169) of 1989, reversing the paternalistic and assimilationalist approach adopted in the 1957 Convention, recognized the 'aspirations of these peoples to exercise control over their own institutions, ways of life and economic development, and to maintain and develop their abilities, languages and religions, within the framework of the States in which they live'.

These provisions have been interpreted by international or regional courts or treaty bodies to develop the rights of participation (the Human Rights Committee has read in even the parsimonious language of Art 27 of the ICCPR positive state obligations towards minorities and, by establishing the nexus between culture and land, draws out the necessity of group rights, and together with other rights, the implications for 'the effective participation of members of minority communities in decisions which affect them').[1] The entitlements of minorities and the positive obligations of the state have been emphasized in the UN declarations on the rights of minorities and of indigenous peoples. Regional instruments, particularly in Europe, have laid a detailed framework for the participation rights of minorities (these are fully noted in the explanatory note to the Lund Recommendations). The concept of self-determination of the 'people' has been interpreted by international, regional, and national tribunals as entitling minorities as such to participation rights and, in appropriate

---

[1] General Comment 23, para 6.2 (1994).

cases, to autonomy. Some national constitutions and laws now reflect these developments.[2]

Through these instruments and interpretations, various forms of participation have been established (although there is no formal definition of the term). The Explanatory Note explains participation thus: 'The essence of participation is involvement, both in terms of the opportunity to make substantive contributions to decision-making processes and in terms of the effect of these contributions' (s 6). Since the concept of participation is closely connected to Art 25 of the ICCPR,[3] we can gain some understanding of its scope and methods by examining the General Comment of the UN Human Rights Committee on the article. The Human Rights Committee has explained the significance of Art 25 rights in General Comment 25 (1996). It said that Art 25 'lies at the core of democratic government based on the consent of the people and in conformity with the principles of the Covenant'. No distinctions are permitted between citizens in the enjoyment of these rights on the grounds of race, colour, sex, language, religion, political or other opinion, national or social origin, property, birth, or other status. The conduct of public affairs is a broad concept which relates to the exercise of state power, in particular the exercise of legislative, executive and administrative powers. It covers all aspects of public administration, and the formulation and implementation of policy at international, national, regional and local levels. The allocation of powers and the means by which individual citizens exercise the right to participate in the conduct of public affairs should be established by the constitution and other laws. Participation in public affairs includes lobbying, and for this and other reasons the freedom of expression and of the media must be secured. Equal access to public service must be ensured, if necessary through affirmative action.

Participation can take many forms. Much depends on its objectives, and the institutions and procedures of the government. The functions of participation range from lobbying at one end to making decisions at the other. In between are the right to be informed, the right to be heard, the right to make comments on others' proposal, the right to make one's own proposals, the right to take part in

---

[2] These developments have been discussed in a number of publications. See Y Ghai, *Public Participation and Minorities* (2001, reprinted as 'Public participation, autonomy and minorities' in ZA Skurbaty (ed), *Beyond a One-dimensional State: An emerging right to autonomy?* (2005), 3–45. This volume contains a number of valuable theoretical discussions and case studies on autonomy, which is a principal focus of this chapter.

[3] Article reads:
Every citizen shall have the right and the opportunity, without any of the distinctions mentioned in article 2 and without unreasonable restrictions:
   (a) to take part in the conduct of public affairs, directly or through freely chosen representatives;
   (b) to vote and to be elected at genuine periodic elections which shall be by universal and equal suffrage and shall be held by secret ballot, guaranteeing the free expression of the will of the electors;
   (c) to have access, on general terms of equality, to public service in his country.

decisions, the right to veto decisions, and the right to be *the* decision-maker. An important element is access to the institutions of the state, including the institutions of justice. These can be translated into the language of the Lund Recommendations, as:

- special representation in organs of the state (executive, legislative, public service, etc)
- electoral systems which ensure adequate representation
- mechanisms to ensure that interests of minorities are considered in state agencies
- recognition of minority languages in public service
- institutions to advise on minority issues
- institutions for consultation
- control or dominance of decision-making processes.

Insofar as there is a hierarchy of forms of participation, the right to make decisions ranks high. The Lund Recommendations emphasize 'effective' participation—that is, participation that is not symbolic or formal, but achieves its objectives. Self-government comes closest to that criterion.

A. Participation as representation and as self-governance

The Lund Recommendations elaborate two principal forms of participation which we may call 'representation' and 'self-governance'.[4] The former is discussed in terms of a broadly unitary state and is based on the involvement of minority groups as such in the affairs of the state. The latter focuses on the control and administration by the minority of prescribed functions of government. There are various forms of self-governance, the principal distinction being between arrangements based on territory and those on the cultural identity of the group, across the entire state. In turn, territorial governance is divided into various categories, the most important for the purpose of this chapter being 'autonomy' and 'federalism'.

The Lund Recommendations do not give sufficient indication of the benefits and disadvantages of the two major types of participation. Territorial self-governance is of course possible only if there is a significant concentration of a community in one part of the country. From the point of view of the majority community, participation as representation would be preferable, as it retains control over the entire territory and its own members outside the majority areas would not suffer discrimination. Nor would awkward questions about the reorganization of the state, divided sovereignty, and the threat of secession arise.

---

[4] I have followed the Lund Recommendations on the use of the term 'self-governance' to indicate principles and arrangements for what is variously described as autonomy, federalism, self-government, or decentralization. The focus of this chapter is autonomy and federalism. Where the context requires it, I have used the more specific term for the type of 'self-governance'.

However, from the point of view of the minority, representation without self-government would serve limited functions, and the group would remain a minority, whereas self-governance would give it the right to conduct its own affairs in areas that matter deeply to it (such as culture). It is easier to nurture one language and culture if a group has territory over which it can exercise governmental powers. Having a base of its own gives it psychic pleasure as well as a feeling of security as a majority, and the ability to negotiate with the central government and sometimes also its neighbours. It can thus fundamentally change the relations between it and the national majority.

Consequently, although the Lund Recommendations see both representation and self-governance as serving the same functions of minority protection and state integrity, the majority and minority communities do not always see the matter in this way. Each approach is fraught with anxiety for one or the other group, with the fear that its fundamental rights will be under threat. Thus from another perspective, the form, scope, and degree of participation depend on the vision about the country, the relationship between the communities *inter se*, the type of democracy and political system, and the balance between ethnic and national identities. The approach in the Lund Recommendations to these dilemmas is to set out the framework within which participation rights must be structured—to which I turn in the next section after exploring the status of participation as a legal and constitutional right.

B. Participation and self-government as rights

The Lund Recommendations do not pretend to create new rights, nor can they. Instead, they make recommendations on how to both enhance the rights of minorities and strengthen national unity. Some recommendations may indeed be reflective of a human right, recognized at international, regional, or national law. Others, though consistent with the rights regime, may not have the status of rights. However, to discuss self-governance, it is useful to establish which ones are founded on a right—for the principal reason that there is considerable resistance to it on the part of the state. Laws on self-government are almost always negotiated, and the outcome of negotiations is partly dependent on the rights and obligations of the negotiating parties. And so, to some extent, is the durability of self-government.

It is fair to say that there is no general right to self-government in international law. Various European instruments noted in the Explanatory Note show some movement towards the requirement of self-government, but impose no specific obligations on the state.[5] However, there are multiple, general, or

---

[5] A proposal in 1993 to amend the European Convention of Human Rights to give national minorities the right to 'have at their disposal appropriate or autonomous authorities or to have a special status matching the specific historical and territorial situation and in accordance with the domestic legislation of the State', though carefully drafted to limit state responsibilities, was rejected by the Parliamentary Assembly of the Council of Europe.

specific sources for instances of self-government—under international or regional law, bilateral treaties or state constitutions. In addition to the above, Dinstein has identified seven ways in which self-government has been established: multilateral (Bosnia and Herzegovina) or bilateral treaties (Palestine); resolution of the League of Nations (Aaland) and the UN General Assembly (Eritrea); decisions by the Security Council (Kosovo); and national laws, sometimes based on international treaty (South Tyrol) or sometimes purely local initiative (Greenland)—for each of these one can give additional examples. To this list might be added what has been described 'treaty federalism' which encompasses autonomies in Canada and US based on treaties made with the indigenous peoples.[6] The result is that there is no one model for the purposes or institutions of self-government. No attempt is made here to discuss the various sources of self-government, other than briefly.[7]

The most general basis of self-government is the right to self-determination which forms the opening article in both the human rights covenants. Outside the case of colonies, self-determination is used to refer to the right of a people to decide on the internal organization of the state, the underlying principle being that of democracy. The people of each state are free to decide how they would wish to be governed, without external interference. This is now often referred to as an internal aspect of self-determination. The UN Human Rights Committee which supervises the implementation of the Covenant has stated that the right of self-determination is not restricted to the colonial situation, but has not defined what a 'people' is or suggested that it encompasses the right to secede.

The Canadian Supreme Court has pronounced more clearly on the matter in an advisory opinion on whether Quebec has a right to secede from Canada under international law. The Court's general conclusion, noting the great importance attached to state sovereignty, was that the principle of self-determination does not grant a community the unilateral right of secession. But the court added a rider: a state is entitled to the integrity of its territory only if it respects the right of the people, including minorities, to determine political, economic, social, and cultural issues. In other words, the principle of self-determination requires that the state be democratic and inclusive. The Court's conclusion on this point was that self-determination was normally to be achieved within the framework of the state. It said that only a 'state whose government represents the whole of the people or peoples resident within its territory, on a basis of equality and without discrimination, and respects the

---

[6] JY Henderson, 'Empowering treaty federalism' (1986) 58 *Saskatchewan Law Review* 241–329.
[7] There is considerable literature on the subject. See Y Dinstein, 'Autonomy (international guarantees of autonomy)' in Skurbaty, *Beyond a One-dimensional State* (n 2 above); M Suksi, 'Keeping the lid on the secession kettle: A review of legal interpretations concerning claims of self-determination by minority populations' (2005) 12 *IJMGR* 189–226; and Ghai, *Public Participation and Minorities* (n 2 above), for some recent contributions.

principles of self-determination in its own internal arrangements, is entitled to the protection under international law of its territorial integrity'.

The UN Human Rights Committee has interpreted public participation rights under the ICCPR in the context of 'self-determination', on the basis that 'self-determination' is a fundamental right on which other rights depend.[8] It interpreted the right to participate in public affairs (Art 25) in the context of representation when it emphasized the importance of proportionality of the population, and set out at length the institutional and procedural aspects of free and fair elections. On another occasion, it upheld the rights of full participation of all communities in the constitution-making process.

The Human Rights Committee has also read a great deal of self-determination issues into Art 27.[9] Although the state's obligations were intended to be limited, being restricted to non-intervention, in a series of decisions (particularly concerning indigenous peoples), the Committee has read it as imposing positive obligations for the benefit of minorities. In General Comment 23 (1994) it clarified that the culture of some communities may consist of a way of life which is closely associated with territory and the use of its resources, which in some cases may justify forms of self-government or autonomy. As these individual rights can only be exercised in the context of the community, the identity of the minority must be protected. Affirmative action may be justified in favour of the minority. Minority members must be encouraged to participate in decisions that affect them.

Two recent UN declarations have emphasized self-government. The Declaration on the Rights of Persons Belonging to National or Ethnic, Religious, and Linguistic Minorities (1992) places positive obligations on the state to protect the identity of minorities and encourage 'conditions for the promotion of that identity' (Art 11). Minorities must have the right to 'participate effectively in cultural, religious, social, economic and public life' (Art 22) and to participate in decisions on national and regional levels that concern them (Art 23). The other is the Declaration on the Rights of Indigenous Peoples (2008), which expanded the scope of rights under the ILO Convention on Indigenous Peoples (1989). It gives them 'the right to autonomy or self-government in matters relating to their internal and local affairs' and recognizes their 'collective rights' (Art 4) and 'to maintain and strengthen their distinct political, economic, social and cultural characteristics' (Art 5).

Several conclusions can be drawn from the above account. Not only is there no general right to self-government under international law, there is no one model of self-government. Self-government serves a variety of purposes, to

---

[8] General Comment 12 (1984)

[9] Art 27 reads: 'In those States in which ethnic, religious, or linguistic minorities exist, persons belonging to such minorities shall not be denied the right, in community with the others members of their group, to enjoy their own culture, to profess and practise their own religion, to use their own language.'

accommodate a variety of situations. The structure of self-government varies accordingly. Even when it is deployed to protect minorities, there can be considerable variation in the precise objectives, and correspondingly, in the scope of, and institutions for self-government.[10] Of course, the same can be said about federalism. In a way, this is both the strength and weakness of self-government. The strength is that it can be tailored to the needs of a particular situation, including where desirable, variations among sub-state entities ('asymmetry'). The weakness is that the details of each form of self-government have to be negotiated, which puts the weaker party at a disadvantage (as is obvious in Tibet's negotiations with China).[11]

Although not all groups are entitled to autonomy under international law, there is considerable international support for autonomy. In part, this is the result of a compromise: moral difficulties of supporting oppression, yet reluctance to sanction secession. Autonomy (by disaggregating a country) was supported in Bosnia as a way to keep the country together, and in Kosovo as a way to keep Yugoslavia together. International support for autonomy in East Timor (regarded by the UN as a colony) was a concession to Indonesia, to keep its territorial integrity. The international community has also supported autonomy in order to maintain regional stability—by developing norms, as by the Organization of Security and Cooperation in Europe, the European Union and the Council of Europe, and occasionally by direct intervention. The mutual willingness of former metropolitan states and their colonies to accept a special relationship, as between New Zealand and Cook Island and Niue, Britain and the Caribbean territories, and France with New Caledonia (overseas territories), also opens up possibilities of autonomy—and through delegating some critical but expensive tasks of statehood to another sovereign, to assume other responsibilities of the state. Autonomy has also facilitated the formation of larger states through state mergers by ensuring a corporate identity of the merging states (Czech and Slovakia, the former Yugoslavia, princely states in India, Ethiopia and Eritrea).

However, details of the division of powers and the structure of institutions and relationships (on autonomy and federalism) are critical in the national constitution and laws, as self-government has to be operationalized at the state level. Here there is also a great deal of variety, in purpose and structure, not only between states but also within states. The Lund Recommendations recognize the

---

[10] Markku Suksi says that public international law 'can, under the right of self-determination, tolerate almost any institutional arrangement at the sub-State level, provided that if a people is involved, it has determined its status in a free process' and quotes with approval the statement by Hannum and Lillich that autonomy is 'a relative term which describes the extent or degree of independence of a particular entity, rather than defining a particular level of independence which can be designated as reaching the status of "autonomy"', Suksi, 'Keeping the lid on the secessionist kettle' (n 7 above), 203–4.

[11] In this regard the ILO Convention and the GA Declaration on the Rights of Indigenous People are valuable in setting out in some detail what is entailed in self-determination for them, although not all the entitlements set out there would be necessary or feasible in all situations.

value of flexibility. But at the same time they seek to set out to a greater extent than in international instruments the framework for self-government.

C. Distinction between autonomy and federalism

The two major forms of self-governance are autonomy and federalism. Both involve a division of powers between the centre and the region, and separate governments at both levels. The difference is that in autonomy only one or two regions have a special status, while in federalism all parts of the country, divided into regions, take part in the system of divided powers and institutions. Autonomy is more appropriate when there are only one or two ethnic minorities who are concentrated in a region and wish to have a measure of control over it to preserve and promote their culture or protect some special interest (such as a specific form of economy or life style, as in Hong Kong in relation to China, or indigenous peoples in Canada or the US). It is possible to provide for autonomy within a largely unitary state (as for Aaland in Finland, South Tyrol in Italy, Hong Kong in China, Bougainville in Papua New Guinea, or Aceh in Indonesia) or within a federal state (as Nunuvat in Canada, Puerto Rico in the US, or Norfolk Islands in Australia). Where the concerns of a relatively small ethnic group can be met in this way, there is much to be said for it, for it entails only a limited reorganization of the state.[12] Autonomy is also regarded as less of a threat to the integrity of the state as a small minority is less likely to want, or be able, to secede.

The number of subjects over which the autonomous region would normally want control is likely to be small, concerned predominantly with cultural matters. A greater measure of institutional distance may be permitted in autonomy, for the region may prefer to be left alone. A full-blown federal system necessitates more complex arrangements for the division of powers and for institutional relationships. Autonomy can also be accommodated in the legal and constitutional framework without much difficulty (and even, if there is trust, through ordinary legislation, as for Greenland), but a federal system cannot be established without a new constitution. However, where a number of groups are dissatisfied with the national government, a federal system is more appropriate (as was the case in Nigeria and currently in Nepal).

---

[12] However, there is some resistance to it by the majority as it might imply a special status for one group. The response of the Sri Lanka government to autonomy for the Tamils in the north-east of the country was to generalize the system of provincial government throughout the country, although at a lower level of decentralized powers (see N Tiruchelvam, 'Accommodating self-rule: Sri Lankan dialects' in Y Ghai (ed), *Autonomy and Ethnicity: Negotiating claims in multi-ethnic states* (2000).

II. Framework for Participation in the Lund Recommendations

The Lund Recommendations begin with a statement of general principles as the framework for specific recommendations. The purpose of participation is expressed as a 'peaceful and democratic society' (which requires good governance and integrity of the state). This is to be achieved through the inclusion of minorities within the state system and the maintenance by them of their identity and characteristics (General Principles (1)). However an individual is free to choose, without penalty or discrimination, whether she or he wishes to be treated as member of the majority or minority or neither. The foundations of the recommendations are human rights, equality and non-discrimination, as regards the participation in public life and other political rights of minorities. Institutions for participation must respect the rights of 'all those who are affected'. Both the substance and process of institutions for participation are important, to 'maintain a climate of confidence', for which an 'inclusive, transparent, and accountable process of consultation' is necessary.

The Lund Recommendations also have a sub-set of principles for self-governance. Institutions of self-government must be based on democratic principles to ensure that they genuinely reflect the views of the affected population.[13] Rights of all persons within a region, including minorities, must be protected. The allocation of responsibilities between the centre and regions must recognize 'the need for central and uniform decisions in some areas of governance together with the advantages of diversity in others'. The principle of subsidiarity (ie, 'decisions are taken as close as possible to, and by, those most directly concerned and affected') should govern the allocation of powers. But para 21 says, 'Where powers may be devolved on a territorial basis to improve the effective participation of minorities, these powers must be exercised with due regard for the minorities within these jurisdictions'. And para 20 of the Explanatory Note says, 'At the same time, the central government must retain powers to ensure justice and equality of opportunities across the State.' As for determining boundaries or other arrangements, the prescription is that 'in no case is this to include any ethnic criterion for territorial arrangements' (para 14 of Explanatory Note).

This is a complex framework which requires a careful balancing of interests. This is especially the case with respect to devices of participation that are the subject of this chapter—autonomy or federalism. In designing autonomy or federal arrangements, a large number of decisions must be made; and within each matter, there may be several options. In principle and practice, the design is the result of negotiations, often bitter and lengthy, during which adherence to general

---

[13] 'When institutions of self-governance are needed or desirable, the equal enjoyment by everyone of their rights requires application of the principle of democracy within these' (para 16 of Explanatory Note).

principles becomes problematic. Federalism or autonomy based on the participation of minorities generally has a particular ethnic bias which also challenges some human rights and equality assumptions of the general principles. The concept of identity is elusive and malleable and its implications for the organization of public space are profound and controversial. But if the ultimate objectives of participation—'peaceful and democratic society' and 'integrity' of the state—are to be achieved, some similar framework is desirable, as the parameters within which the final settlement would be made. Some form of pre-determination may also help parties to begin negotiations.

Understandably, the Lund Recommendations are based on a European understanding of human rights and their connection to national and international peace; the notion of dignity in human rights which is universal; non-discrimination and effective equality; human rights, civil society and democracy; identity and choice about identity; and the voluntary nature of these arrangements (meaning presumably not voluntary for the state, but for minorities). The Lund Recommendations are also based on the European experience of nearly a century of stable states, with considerable domestic legitimacy, in which it has been possible to accommodate new communities within the parameters of the existing state. The state continues to play a role in mobilizing social consensus, but it is not its central role. The state in developing countries is highly contested, and most conflicts are about the structure of and access to the state. Many of these conflicts are about ethnicity and 'identity', which, for a variety of reasons, it has not been possible to resolve through the framework of human rights and democracy.

However, some principles of the framework would be hard to observe, at least in developing countries where ethnic relations are deeply troubled and some solution based on self-governance is sought. While the majority would favour the approach in the Lund Recommendations, the minority is likely to reject it. But equally, the majority is unlikely to appreciate the emphasis on identity (at least of the minority). Indeed there may be some contradictions in the approach of the Lund Recommendations: on the one hand, the paramountcy of equal rights and democracy and, on the other, the great importance attached to ethnic identity. The Lund Recommendations see the observance of human rights as fulfilling the quest for the preservation and promotion of ethnic identity. Others see a basic conflict between them. The debate about self-government in Asia and Africa is intimately tied to ethnic claims and counterclaims—which has made it extremely controversial. The link of ethnicity to self-government has produced great resistance to the latter, and on the whole has been more of an obstacle than assistance for claims of autonomy. In order fully to understand the dilemma inherent in the Lund Recommendations on self-government, it is necessary to explore the links between human rights and ethnicity.

A. Ethnicity and identity[14]

I use the term ethnicity to refer to a situation when a community goes beyond a mere consciousness of what binds it together (such as language, religion, race) and what distinguishes it from other communities, to claim that these differences are politically significant, and that it constitutes a 'people' or 'nation' which is entitled to special recognition as such. The process of the rise of political consciousness is not dissimilar to that of the stimulation and promotion of 'nationalism', which in earlier periods formed the basis of the 'nation state'. It generally begins with intellectuals or persons with political ambitions, who begin to give symbolic, emotional, and material significance to their differences from other communities in the state (cementing internal cohesion and distancing themselves from other communities). This therefore involves the presence of some objective factors like language or religion, but which increasingly take on a symbolic or political meaning. This subjective factor can arise from a consciousness of discrimination against, or social or economic exclusion of, the community, a rediscovery of history when the community existed as a political entity, and increasingly of demands and insurgencies happening in other places.

The political claims that it makes vary from a constitutional or legal recognition of some aspects of its culture (such as relations within the family or dispute settlement mechanisms), special measures to improve its social and economic situation, inclusion through representation, and state support for its religion or culture. Sometimes (especially when their claims are denied) there is progression from modest to the more substantial demands, including a fundamental redesign of the state or even secession (arguing that only through this radical reform can its legitimate demands be met). Increasingly, these claims are justified by reference to international norms of human rights.

However, the presence of diverse people does not necessarily lead to ethnicity. A distinguished Indian political scientist, Rajni Kothari, has argued that rise of ethnicity is due to the consequences of the centralization and monopolization of the state (comparing the modern state to pre-colonial polities in Asia which did not aim at centralization of all authority, recognized diverse communities with their religion and customary practices, and whose borders were porous).[15] The growth of market relations and globalization led to the marginalization, and subsequent disruption, of community cohesion, causing insecurities produced by economic changes over which the communities had no control. This also

---

[14] In writing this and the following sections I have drawn upon two papers of mine: 'Constitutionalism and the challenge of ethnicity' in J Heckman, R Nelson and L Cubbington, *Contemporary Reflections on the Rule of Law* (2009) and 'Understanding human rights in Asia' in C Krause and M Scheinin (eds), *Human Rights: A textbook* (2009), 547–74.

[15] In an article now re-printed in Rajni Kothari, *Rethinking Development: In search of humane alternatives* (1988) as 'Ethnicity'.

affects the nature of ethnic consciousness, turning it from a positive and inclusive form to negativity, exclusion and violence.

In the West, it is more fashionable to talk of the resurgence of ethnicity in terms of the imperatives of identity, based on Kant's emphasis on the autonomy of the individual (particularly the work of Charles Taylor[16] and Will Kymlicka[17]). The antecedents of this approach can be traced to the influential work of the anthropologist, Clifford Geertz, who argued that ethnicity flows from 'primordial' affiliations in the context of a state. Primordial links were based on what he called 'givens', the accidents of birth in a community, to which one may be connected by ties of religion, language, descent, history. 'These congruities of blood, speech, custom and so on, are seen to have an ineffable, and at times overpowering, coerciveness in and of themselves.' In new states, these primordial attachments are particularly strong and are in frequent tension with the affiliation with and expectations from the state—and deeply destabiliziling.[18]

Charles Taylor defines identity as 'a person's understanding of who they are, of their fundamental characteristics as a human being'. Identity is achieved through a person's search for their inner soul. At another point, he says, 'There is a certain way of being that is *my* way. I am called upon to live my life in this way ... If I am not true [to myself], I miss the point of my life.'[19] According to Taylor, this consciousness of the uniqueness of one's identity is the result of a breakdown of social hierarchies, which defined our roles and gave us our understanding of our place in society. But with democracy and the reordering of society, our identity comes from self-reflection and contemplation. Identity has become essential to our own sense of dignity, as an attribute of our being human. Thus dignity is closely related to equality. And equality in turn depends on recognition by others, in the form of demands for the equal status of cultures and gender.

Although identity understood in this sense is an intensely personal affair, achieving a satisfactory understanding of oneself and one's potential, and of orienting oneself, depends on our contacts with others. Kymlicka says that our orientation, the way we negotiate values and makes choices, comes from our membership of a cultural community. Thus, in their different ways, Taylor and Kymlicka place the individual securely within a cultural context, and interactions within a community. In an earlier period, Herder and other German philosophers had claimed uniqueness for these communities, a unique,

---

[16] This paper relies largely on his contribution, 'The politics of recognition' in the anthology Charles Taylor et al (edited and introduced by Amy Gutman), *Multiculturalism: Examining the politics of recognition*, expanded edition (1994), 180.

[17] This paper relies principally on his first, important book, *Liberalism, Community and Culture* (1989) and several subsequent articles.

[18] C Geertz, 'The integrative revolution' in C Geertz (ed), *Old Societies and New States* (1963).

[19] Taylor, 'The politics of recognition' (n 16 above), 30.

historically, even ethnically derived identity for each community, the nation. Thus Kant's emphasis on individual autonomy was given firm roots in the community. The politics of recognition, in public and private spheres, has become central to our quest for just political and social orders.

Although there is now wide acceptance of the recognition of identity, and its corollary of social and cultural diversity, there are acute controversies about the nature of identity and the forms of its recognition.[20] If in the West identity is a matter of psychic satisfaction, in Asia identity politics are important as a means to resources; although just as in the West material benefits are not irrelevant and, in Asia, pride in one's community is also an important factor (although Taylor's explanation of the importance of individual identity due to the disappearance of social hierarchy does not apply equally in Asia). Identity is more a matter of political mobilization than a precise delineation of a community's characteristics or beliefs. Ethnicity has become a way of dealing and bargaining with the state. Because electoral politics and government interventions respond to ethnic pressures, economic issues are transformed into issues of cultural survival. For example, in most cases, ethnic fighting is not about religion, but about jobs; religion is used as a pretext, emptying religion of its sacred and ritual aspects.

A community's entitlements may depend on how it and others perceive it. A self-conscious ethnic group can place itself in different categories, deriving from political science or legal discourse—it can be a cultural, religious, or linguistic group; or it can be a minority, a nation, a 'people', or 'indigenous peoples'. Each of these categories is associated with a specific set of claims—participation, representation, recognition of language, religion, education, land, autonomy, etc. How does one establish a claim to one or the other category? They are in part derived from political theory or practice, such as a 'nation', with a clear notion of the right to self-determination, including separatism or secession, or a minority or indigenous peoples, which derives more from legal norms or rules (eg, Art 27 of the ICCPR, or the Declaration on the Rights of Minorities, or the ILO Conventions on Indigenous Peoples). Perhaps the most significant of these are the concepts of 'nation' and 'indigenous peoples' as they carry a large or high set of entitlements. To this extent a community's self-definition is determined or at least influenced by international political or legal norms, and sometimes the characterization or classification under national law (as in Spain).

Minorities have an interest in bringing themselves under the category of 'people', for in this case they are entitled to self-determination. Although the political understanding of self-determination is still associated with the 'nation state' (and has political resonances as such), its contemporary legal meaning is for the most part restricted to the internal organization of the state, and the right

---

[20] See the critiques of A Sen, *Identity and Violence: The illusion of destiny* (2006); and A Appiah, 'Identity, authenticity, survival: Multicultural societies and social reproduction' in A Gutman (ed), *Multiculturalism* (n 16 above).

of all citizens and communities to participate in decisions on that organization, including the drafting of the constitution. The right of minorities to participate in public affairs and in state institutions as well as to enjoy their culture now ranks high in the lexicon of self-determination (as this chapter illustrates).

B. Ethnicity and human rights

Ethnicity both invokes and undermines human rights. The fundamental dilemma of rights and diversity is well captured by Charles Taylor when he writes:

Now underlying the demand [for recognition of diversity] is a principle of universal equality. The politics of difference is full of denunciations of discrimination and refusals of second class citizenship. This gives the principle of universal equality a point of entry within the politics of dignity. But once inside, as it were, its demands are hard to assimilate to that politics. For it asks we give acknowledgement and status to something that is not universally shared. Or, otherwise put, we give due acknowledgment only to what is universally present—every one has an identity—through recognizing what is peculiar to each. The universal demands powers and acknowledgement of specificity.[21]

These attacks highlight what seem to be various contradictions between human rights and ethnicity. Human rights seek to be colour-blind, aloof from religious or other affiliations; ethnicity makes these affiliations basic to identity and human existence. Human rights empower the individual; ethnicity the group. Human rights are the framework for relations between citizens *inter se* and between citizens and the state; ethnicity compels attention to and regulation of interethnic relations, and the relations of the group to the state. Human rights aim to be inclusive, ethnicity exclusive. Thus, ethnicity has posed problems for human rights in a way that nationalism did not. Nationalism did not seek accommodation of rights within an existing state, but sought its own state; ethnicity seeks accommodation within an existing state. It internalizes to the state problems that would otherwise dissipate on the formation of a new state; it brings problems of cultural relativism not as concerns between distant societies, but as basic to the very definition and existence of a state. Ethnicity seeks to reconfigure the state as the principal framework for the formulation and enforcement of rights, with fundamental implications for how the scope and nature of rights are perceived. If the quarter-century after the end of the Second World War saw the rise of the ideology of individual-oriented human rights, the last quarter saw a major challenge, in the name of the community, to that approach. If, in the first period, self-determination was the foundation of state sovereignty, in the second period it was mobilized to challenge that sovereignty.

---

[21] C Taylor, 'The politics of recognition' (n 16 above), 39.

III. Paradoxes of Self-government

Self-governance, particularly in the form of a federation, has particular advantages for the political organization of a multiethnic state (although most of the 'classical' federations do not have an ethnic foundation). It facilitates the division and distribution of the powers of the state in a number of ways, so that all regions, and in some cases all communities, can participate in their exercise. Some powers can be exercised at the regional level, which are particularly suitable at that level (the Lund Recommendations suggest the principles for the distribution of powers). Others can be exercised at the national level, through institutions in which all the regions participate. In matters over which joint policies are desirable, the machinery of intergovernmental relations can facilitate consensual decisions. In this way, separate and common interests can be accommodated and harmonized. Such arrangements, by dismantling the concentration of state power, can also promote human rights and democracy.

Most countries that have become federal have experienced a massive increase in political participation (for example, India, Spain, Ethiopia). Central institutions are organized to allow for the participation of all regions in central governance. Normally a second chamber is set up—or if there is one already, it is reorganized—composed of regional representatives, usually elected by the residents, as such, of the regions. In some federations each region has the same number of representatives, and in some it is based on population (with a minimum number for the smaller regions). Regions are also represented in the other national chamber, normally on population basis. The second chamber, where the regions are directly represented, plays a more important role in state affairs than in a unitary system. It gives the people of even remote regions the opportunity to bring to the attention of the central government their pressing problems and to influence national policies. They also get opportunities to influence policy and administration at local levels, for in a federation regions have their own, elected, legislatures and executives, with significant and independent powers. Here their participation or influence can be direct, for they live close to where these institutions operate and their members and officials reside (with few opportunities to run away to Kathmandu). At that level, quite small communities which cannot expect to participate, much less, influence national affairs, can wield considerable political clout.

These constitutional arrangements also impact on the organization and structure of political parties. They give rise to regional parties, giving people a greater choice among parties, and the ability to influence them. Political parties then have incentives to learn about local issues and establish an effective presence outside the capital city. In some federations regional parties play a significant role at the national level (as in India today), so that the national government has to pay proper attention to regional problems and needs. Through regional institutions, information about national affairs and policies is disseminated locally, and people become aware of them, and of how they themselves fit into the national scene. Their understanding of democracy and political processes grows.

Although it is not guaranteed, the establishment of regional governments often leads to more efficiency and accountability. Almost by definition the regional government will have greater knowledge of local circumstances, aspirations and obstacles to development, and is well placed to plan and execute appropriate policies. The regional government will have incentives to promote economic and infrastructural developments, exploring local opportunities, which would lead to the emergence of new growth centres and creation of employment opportunities, reducing dependence on Kathmandu. The federal scheme for the sharing of revenue and the lobbying of the national government by regional representatives should ensure greater resources to the region for economic and social development. And if the constitution adopts mechanisms for equalization of development across the country, the less-developed regions would receive a larger share of the national revenue. There should be improvements in the delivery of welfare services, due to the greater familiarity with local needs. And since the focus of most regional governments will inevitably be rural, disparities between rural and urban areas should begin to be eliminated.

It will be easier to involve people in development and other projects. The people will have easier access to local officials, and should be able to deal with them in local languages. The regional government will have an incentive to please the local people in a way that the central government seldom has. Persons who until now were ignored as candidates at elections due to their caste or region would now have opportunities to contest elections to regional legislature or appointment to other institutions. Proficiency in local languages, some of which will become official languages at the regional level, will enable persons hitherto handicapped by the lack of command of Nepali to compete in entrance examinations and to serve in the civil service. Participation in regional and local affairs will give people confidence in their ability to plan their own future.

People's confidence and self-respect will also grow if regional governments promote their culture and language. For many communities, one of the most valued results of federalism would be the recognition of the worth of these cultures. Centuries of the denigration of their culture and language by the ruling elites at first produced a sense of inferiority, and now anger. Regional governments will provide the framework for sustaining local languages and cultures—and reversing the imposition of the values and cultures of others. The flourishing of these languages, literature, poetry, dances, religions, and lifestyles enrich the cultural diversity of the country. And with the pride and confidence that this creates the marginalized communities will be able to participate in other public spheres, work together with members of other communities and strengthen national capacity and unity.

Federalism can also give voice to minorities at the national level, through arrangements for 'shared rule'. Mention has already been made of regional participation in the second chamber. If regional parties become important, they will be represented in the other chamber, and if the political system is parliamentary then they will have representation in the national government (as part of a coalition government, as is becoming the norm in India). There will also be pressures that regional diversity should be reflected in the civil service, judiciary, and armed forces (in accordance with the Nigerian constitutional rule of the 'federal principle'). Regions can maintain a presence at the capital through an office for lobbying federal authorities. Regional participation in national affairs also occurs through membership of bodies for intergovernmental cooperation (like fiscal commission, water authority, development planning, and dispute settlement). The broad federal structure thus becomes a mode of centre–regional negotiations on a host of matters.

The granting of regional powers often means that many problems between the region and the centre become intra-regional. The politics of language in India in the 1950s became the centre point of intense conflict between Delhi, bent on Hindi as the official language of the country, and southern states which wanted the proper recognition of regional languages, including through the reorganization of federal units on linguistic grounds. The issue united several states and their residents in a national campaign against the central government. But once the linguistic principle was granted and states reorganized, the pressure on Delhi was replaced by internal differences and competition within states, centre–state relations improved, and it is generally conceded that Indian unity was strengthened.

Because of these perceived advantages of self-governance, drawing considerably upon the experience of older federations, federalism has become a favoured solution to ethnic conflict among Western governments and the international organizations which they dominate (as demonstrated, for example, by their efforts in Sri Lanka, the Sudan, former Yugoslavia, Indonesia in respect of Aceh, Cyprus, and Northern Ireland). However, on the whole, the experience of these and other countries shows that federalism and other forms of self-government have not always solved problems, and in some instances have created additional problems.[22] The record is in fact mixed: in India and Spain, for example, the use of self-governance approaches has helped to resolve acute tensions, even persistent violence, and strengthened national unity, but in Pakistan, Sudan, Cyprus, and even Bosnia and Herzegovina, self-governance has failed to solve problems. The record in Northern Ireland is mixed; it certainly has not proved a panacea.

There are several reasons why federalism and autonomy have failed in so many countries. I start with two factors: the process by which the federations are formed, and the foundational basis for the organization of the state. A federation may be formed by the coming together of previously independent entities ('aggregation' as the US, Australia, Switzerland) or the restructuring of a unitary

---

[22] See M Boltjes, *Implementing Negotiated Agreements: The real challenge to intrastate peace* (2007).

state ('disaggregation' as Nigeria, Ethiopia, Spain, South Africa, and Belgium). The former has generally been easier to set up: it is based on the consent of the separate units, it involves the establishment of only one new unit—the federal government (with transfer of limited powers)—and the regions already have well-established systems of government and laws, identity and boundaries, which more or less guarantee their viability.

On the other hand, federalizing by disaggregation raises a much larger number of issues: the boundaries and number of the regions, the number of levels of government, the dismantling of (at least some) structures of the state, the establishment of numerous new governments and laws, the transfer of substantial powers and personnel to the new regions—compounded by the fact that this type of federation is often accompanied by controversy and has sometimes resulted from armed conflict.

The second distinction among federations is between those which are based on considerations of geography and economy ('geo-economic') or old boundaries ('territorial'), and those based on ethnic, linguistic, or religious criteria ('ethnic'). The rationales of the two are different: the first deals with distance, common defence, democracy, responsiveness, and accountability; the other with self-determination, identity, and culture. With different objectives and purposes, they may produce very different kinds of federations, in terms of the criteria for regions, the number and size of units, the relationship between the regions and the central government, the division of powers among different levels, the salience of culture, and the politics of internal mobility. The dynamics of the two kinds are also different, the ethnic perhaps more unstable and with a tendency towards the proliferation of regions, and towards strained relations between both the regions and the centre, and among regions themselves.

It would therefore seem that 'ethnic' federations face greater social and political problems than the 'territorial' ones. In a territorial federation, rights and obligations of individuals are based on residence in the region, and personal characteristics like language, religion, or culture are irrelevant. In an ethnic federation, the land has ethnic, cultural dimensions—perceived by a community as its 'homeland', vested with religious history or emotions, or in a mundane way, land where a community has a numerical majority. In some federal versions, members of that community have higher rights than others in the region (as in the former Soviet Union). The exercise of regional power is in some sense tied to ethnicity. It may be that the language of the dominant community in the region will be the language of the government (as in India) or that its religion will have a special status (as in Switzerland), or it will have superior land rights (as in Colombia and Brazil). Even if there are no special rights, the ethos and culture of the majority community will dominate the policies and practices of the government.

Several recent federations have an ethnic orientation; the precise rights related to ethnicity vary. The purpose of these federations is to acknowledge and provide for cultural diversity and to empower politically and economically a community which would otherwise be a permanent minority in the state. Federalism is a compromise between a highly centralized state and secession (as in the Oslo agreement between the Liberation Tigers of Tamil Eelam and the Sri Lanka government, north and south Sudan, and Bosnia-Herzegovina). It represents a form of power-sharing. It is often forced on warring communities by the international community, and therefore is less consensual than the older federations. It may have little support among the parties that negotiated the deal for federation and with the departure of outside powers, the impetus for implementation declines.

There are other reasons for failure as well, such as the lack of legitimacy of constitutional arrangements that were produced in a hothouse environment, under intense foreign pressure, a combination of incentives and sanctions, and the lack of commitment to the agreement among the key local groups who have signed it. This problem is aggravated by the lack of popular participation in the negotiations or decision on the formation or structure of the federation—and the people's resentment that a clique of 'warlords' have patched an opportunistic agreement without consideration of the national interests (many such federations are accompanied by other power-sharing devices à la consociation, which keep the warlords in power).

As a result of the hothouse environment, not much attention is paid to the precise structures of the federation or the mode of distribution of power. One particular failing is the lack of thoughtful institutions at the centre. The emphasis on the structure and powers of the regions at the expense of the national government means that little attention is paid to strengthening the basis of national unity; the primary concern is to accommodate claims of dominant ethnic groups. As most regions are now populated by a plurality of ethnic groups, the concerns of the smaller groups tend to be overlooked (such as the Muslim Tamil speakers in the north-east of Sri Lanka).

The lack of a perfect fit between ethnicity and geography means that in most regions the majority or dominant group is able to impose its own values and interests on all, and to disregard the rights of others (a common practice in many regions in Nigeria). In this way the fundamental problems of federalism shift from the relations between the centre and the state to relations within the region or between two regions. These conflicts often draw in the national authorities, and their resolution becomes very difficult, as the conflict takes a violent turn. One method for resolving this problem is the creation of new regions, based again on the ethnic factor, which leads to the proliferation of regions (India and Nigeria are obvious examples), with decreasing resources for all, and the lack of capacity to discharge the functions of government. A very careful design of institutions and their powers is necessary to avoid such situations or to resolve them—in few federations has this been done.[23]

---

[23] See the excellent doctoral thesis for Bern University by Andrea Iff, 'Federalism: Institutional device for conflict management?' (2009).

Another cause of failure is that, due to time pressure in negotiations, agreements for self-governance tend to be general, and even vague (as a strategy to ensure agreement). There is minimal experience on the ground of implementing federalist arrangements. And given that there is little trust among the previous warring groups who now constitute the government, the goodwill necessary to find solutions to implementation problems is frequently not forthcoming. This factor aggravates the considerable political and technical complexity of federalism.

IV. Conclusion

Underlying the Lund Recommendations is very properly the aim of protecting minorities and safeguarding the integrity of the state. In almost all countries this now requires the careful balancing of particular and national interests and identities. There are several political and legal devices available for this purpose. However, there is considerable controversy among scholars and policy-makers as to which are most desirable, derived from differences in ideologies of ethnic relations. The controversies turn in part on what value to place on identity. Where ethnic identities are considered critical, the solution is often a form of power-sharing between ethnic groups. Those who believe that identities are malleable and changing and that a national identity is critical for political stability and social solidarity, advocate non-ethnic solutions.

Federalism, with its numerous options for dividing powers and resources, establishing criteria for regional boundaries, structuring institutions at different levels of government and the relationship between them, offers an excellent mechanism for the careful balancing of interests and identities mentioned above. But even here the ideological controversies are relevant for, as we have seen, the foundational basis of a federation can either focus on ethnic considerations or transcend them. The Lund Recommendations are ambiguous on this, if not contradictory, as I have tried to show. It is perhaps for this reason, as well as the very Eurocentric nature of the approach, that it has not had much appeal globally. Even within Europe, with the rise of some kinds of fundamentalism, the preoccupation with identity and self-governance is giving way to more statist and integrative policies. The underlying objective of the Lund Recommendations is undoubtedly correct, and they have pointed to various principles, institutions, and procedures by which to achieve it. This chapter has represented a modest attempt to clarify some confusion in the Recommendations and to build on some key suggestions.

22

Cultural Minority Self-governance

Ephraim Nimni

I. The Relevance of Cultural Minority Self-governance within the Wider Area of Political Participation of Minorities	634
A. Is cultural minority self-governance necessary?	637
B. Cultural minorities and the nation state	639
C. Why cultural minorities?	641
II. The Implementation of the Lund Recommendations Standards	643
A. The architecture of cultural minority self-governance	643
B. Cultural minorities and asymmetrical forms of governance	644
C. The Lund Recommendations on minority education and languages	645
III. The Implementation Standards of Cultural Minority Self-government	647
A. Cultural minority self-government in Quebec	648
B. Cultural minority self-government in the Spanish state	651
C. A case for non-territorial cultural autonomy: the Sami parliament in Norway	655
IV. The Participation of Cultural Minorities in Self-governance: A Final Discussion and Evaluation	658

I. The Relevance of Cultural Minority Self-governance within the Wider Area of Political Participation of Minorities

The quality of democracy should be judged from the way minorities are treated.

Mahatma Gandhi

Necesse est omnes suam auctoritatem praestare, ut, quod omnes similiter tangit, ab omnibus comprobetur[1]

Corupus Iurus Civilis

The Lund Recommendations on the Effective Participation of Minorities in Public Life ('the Lund Recommendations')[2] are one of the most comprehensive international instruments in determining the standards and ground rules for cultural minority self-governance. Their importance and scope are clear just from the magnitude of the problem they address: the urgent need for a mutually acceptable accommodation between cultural majorities and minorities, at a time when the multiethnic and multicultural architecture of nation states is becoming a significant issue for their security and political stability. While the Lund Recommendations offer no comprehensive definition as to who constitutes a minority, there are several definitions available in the literature. This is not unusual. Because of definitional difficulties, many scholars have addressed issues relating to minorities without defining what a minority is.[3] For the purposes of this chapter I propose to use the definition of the Special Rapporteur of the United Nations Sub-commission on Prevention of Discrimination and Protection of Minorities, Francesco Capotorti,[4] with the important modification that it should also include refugees and migrant workers.

The term self-governance is discussed in detail in the Lund Recommendations and the Explanatory Note that accompanies them. Art 14 of the Explanatory Note explains that self-governance is a measure of control by a cultural community over matters affecting it. In a further clarification of the term, the Explanatory Note explicitly breaks with the age-old understanding of governance as a form of exclusive sovereign competence. This resembles the division of competences in the European Union, as in the Lund Recommendations the term governance does not imply an exclusive jurisdiction and might also subsume different administrative authorities.[5] Here, one important method for achieving this is through a system of autonomous administration that corresponds with the historical and cultural circumstances of the minority communities in tandem with the configuration of central governments.

---

[1] 'It is necessary that everyone exercise his own authority so that what touches everyone may be approved by everyone.' *Corupus Iurus Civilis* (Body of Civil Law, Justinian Code) 5.59.5.2.
[2] OSCE High Commission for National Minorities, 'The Lund Recommendations on the Effective Participation of Minorities in Public Life' (September 1999).
[3] J Packer, 'On the definition of minorities' in J Packer and K Myntti (eds), *The Protection of Ethnic and Linguistic Minorities in Europe* (1993), 24.
[4] 'A group numerically inferior to the rest of the population of a state, in a non-dominant position, whose members—being nationals of the state—possess ethnic, religious, or linguistic characteristics differing from those of the rest of the population and show, if only implicitly, a sense of solidarity, directed towards preserving their culture, traditions, religion or language.' Study on the Rights of Persons Belonging to Ethnic, Religious and Linguistic Minorities (1979) E/CN4/Sub2/384/Rev 1, UN Sales No E91XIV2, 96.
[5] S Hix, *The Political System in the European Union*, 2nd edn (2003), 18.

The understanding of self-governance presented by the Lund Recommendations follows some crucial recent advances in political theory in the area of sovereignty and multiple jurisdictions.[6] These advances decisively overcame the limitations of earlier liberal understandings of democratic governance. For a very long time and with the triumph of the democratizing egalitarian ideology of the liberal nation state, the dominant conception of nation building was that stable democracies could not be maintained in the face of cultural diversity.[7] The classical example of this was the well known assertion of John Stuart Mill that:

> Free institutions are next to impossible in a country made up of different nationalities ... Among people without fellow-feeling, especially if they speak different languages, the united public opinion, necessary to the working of representative government cannot exist.[8]

In a decisive break with this fruitless tradition, a momentous paradigm change over the last twenty-five years has given birth to a new, more pluralist, and multidimensional understanding of democracy and governance. A common element across the various versions of the new paradigm is that the dispersal of governance across multiple jurisdictions is both more efficient than, and normatively superior to, a central state sovereign monopoly.[9] This new paradigm emerged precisely in the area of conflict resolution and multiculturalism, advocating a system of governance based on the participation in governance of several democratically organized communities with multiple jurisdictions, one in which the governmental process was not of discrete centralized homogenous units as in the old nation-state model, but one in which governance is understood as a multilayered and multicultural mechanism, with regional and minority devolution and multiple jurisdictions.[10] The Lund Recommendations are perhaps the most accomplished policy expression of this dramatic paradigm change. This is not a fortuitous coincidence. These new forms of democratic administration emerged precisely because they came to terms with a problem that broke the back of the old versions of national sovereignty and centralized government, a problem that is simultaneously the main concern of the Lund Recommendations: the crying need to break with the oppressive governance of

---

[6] S Benhabib, 'Twilight of sovereignty or the emergence of cosmopolitan norms? Rethinking citizenship in volatile times' (2007) 11(1) *Citizenship Studies* 19–36, 23–4.

[7] A Gagnon, 'The moral foundations of asymmetrical federalism' in A Gagnon and J Tully (eds) *Multinational Democracies* (2001), 319.

[8] JS Mill, *Considerations of Representative Government* (1862), reproduced in HB Acton (ed) *Utilitarianism, On Liberty and Considerations on Representative Government* (1976).

[9] I Bache and M Flinders, *Multi-level Governance* (2005), 5.

[10] The proliferation of seminal ideas and works in this area is astonishing, to cite only just a few: W Kymlicka, *Multicultural Citizenship: A liberal theory of minority rights* (1995); B Parekh, *Rethinking Multiculturalism* (2000); Gagnon and Tully, *Multinational Democracies* (n 7 above); J Tully, *Strange Multiplicity: Constitutionalism in the age of diversity* (1995); C Taylor, *Multiculturalism: Examining the politics of recognition* (1994), M Keating and J McGarry (eds) *Minority Nationalism and the Changing World Order* (2001), and many others.

cultural minorities, avoid the pain and wanton destruction that results from the disaffection of these minorities, and to find ways to accommodate cultural minorities effectively within the areas of governance and political participation.

The multilateral acceptance of cultural minority rights, the international acceptance of some kind of power-sharing agreements, including the participation of cultural minorities in governance, are central questions for the peaceful accommodation of majorities and minorities in many troubled areas of the world.[11] The issue here is not only that states should recognize the autonomous rights of their cultural minorities, but that states should participate in the collective effort to internationally implement and enforce standards of cultural minority self-governance.[12] In the last few decades and mainly because of the gravity and urgency of ethno-territorial conflicts, a definite change has taken place in the way in which we understand and conceptualize conflicts between cultural minorities and states. Through the struggles of mainly indigenous peoples, linguistic and cultural rights are now seen as an acceptable part of the compromise necessary to reach equitable forms of governance.[13] While phrased in terms of participation, the Lund Recommendations effectively suggest that cultural minorities should enjoy the greatest degree of self-government that is compatible with their circumstances.[14] As in recent years, and mainly through the already mentioned paradigm shift, the complex position of cultural minorities is widely recognized and the Lund Recommendations must be seen as a significant effort to ensure good governance by incorporating cultural minorities to the political life of the state. But why should we centre our attention on cultural minorities?

A. Is cultural minority self-governance necessary?

Art 27 of the International Covenant on Civil and Political Rights states that:

In those states in which ethnic, religious, or linguistic minorities exist, persons belonging to such minorities shall not be denied the right, in community with other members of their group, to enjoy their own culture, to profess and practise their own religion, or to use their own language.[15]

---

[11] J Hughes and G Sasse, 'Monitoring the monitors: EU enlargement conditionality and minority protection in the CEECs EU enlargement and minority rights' (2003) 1 *Journal of Ethnopolitics and Minority Issues in Europe* 3.
[12] SC Roach, *Cultural Autonomy, Minority Rights, and Globalization* (2005), 27.
[13] See W Kymlicka, 'The (Re-)internationalization of state-minority relations, part 1' in W Kymlicka, *Multicultural Odysseys* (2007), 3–60
[14] H Hannum and E Babbitt, *Negotiating Self-determination* (2005), 73.
[15] General Comment 23 on The Rights of Minorities (Art 27), 08/04/94. CCPR/C/21/Rev1/Add5, available at <http://www.unhchr.ch/tbs/doc.nsf/0/fb7fb12c2fb8bb21c12563ed004df111?Opendocument> (accessed 31 July 2009).

But there is no reference to self-governance here. Before embarking on an analysis of the Lund Recommendations for the governance of cultural minorities and the standards of practice it elicits, a set of burning questions on the political status of cultural minorities need to be elucidated.

Some politicians, practitioners, and academics, by and large subscribers of the old paradigm, invoke foundational principles of the Western liberal tradition and ask: is cultural minority self-governance necessary? Why do we bother with intricate and sometimes contentious mechanisms to ensure the participation of cultural minorities in public life? Why cultural minority self-governance? Why not content ourselves with the principled application of democratic governance for all and with civil liberties? These questions are particularly relevant to the position of cultural minorities in contemporary liberal democracies. In fact, influential scholars and practitioners emphasize the equal value of every culture and dismiss the need to develop specific legislation to protect cultural minorities. They argue instead that the universal values of human rights and, in particular, the legal protections available in liberal democratic systems are sufficient to protect the rights of all, including cultural minorities. Jürgen Habermas for example, argues that if human rights and democratic principles are correctly understood, it is not necessary to enact separate cultural minority rights as these overtax a system of rights tailored to individual persons.[16] Similarly, Brian Barry argues that the idea that people can flourish only within their ancestral culture is a fallacy that belongs to an archaic nineteenth-century romantic nationalism.[17]

However, these scholars miss an important point: can citizens that are members of cultural minorities be fairly represented as equals if public institutions do not recognize their cultural identities?[18] A conservative estimate puts the number of national minorities in this world at well above 3,000, while with the admission of Montenegro in 2006, there are 192 states represented in the UN. Fewer than twenty states are ethnically homogeneous in the sense that cultural minorities account for less than 5 per cent of the population.[19] Clearly, cultural communities that have states are only a small fraction of all nations, and it is not an exaggeration to say that the term 'nation state'—understood as one (cultural) nation in one state—is a misnomer.[20] While the overwhelming majority of states represented in the UN are not culturally homogeneous, the configuration of their political institutions often gives the impression that they are, and this is particularly so in contemporary liberal democracies.

---

[16] J Habermas, 'Struggles for recognition in the democratic constitutional state' in C Taylor et al (eds), *Multiculturalism, Examining the Politics of Recognition* (1994), 130.
[17] B Barry, *Culture and Equality* (2000), 263.
[18] For a detailed discussion of this question see E Nimni, 'Constitutional or agonistic patriotism? The dilemmas of liberal nation states' in P Mouritsen and KE Jørgensen (eds), *Constituting Communities: Political solutions to cultural conflict* (2008), 95.
[19] ME Brown, *Ethnic Conflict and International Security* (1993), 6.
[20] T Govier, *Social Trust and Human Communities* (1997), Ch 10, 269, n 1.

Multiethnic societies have existed since time immemorial and are a reflection of the cultural plurality of human life, but it is only with the advent of modernity, and specifically with the democratization of nation states, that cultural minorities have become a problematic dimension of governance and of political participation in the broadest sense of the term. If 'the people' is the sovereign, modern democracies require that peoples are vested with common cultural attributes to generate their cohesion and solidarity. As cultural majorities have an assured hegemony in democratic nation states by virtue of their numbers, there are no clear mechanisms to protect the rights of those who are part of a cultural minority from the hegemony of majority communities. This is a 'blind spot' of contemporary majoritarian democracies. The exclusive system of 'one person–one vote' cements by default the hegemony of the cultural majority, for the equality offered is between individuals and not between cultures.[21] This inbuilt inequality between cultural communities leads at best to the alienation of minority communities, and at worst to their marginalization and collective disadvantage. In the very worst, and mercifully few, cases this alienation leads to expulsion and ethnic cleansing. Michael Mann argues that ethnic cleansing is the dark side of democracy: the ideal of rule by the people tends in some cases to convert *demos* into *ethnos*, when belonging to the dominant culture is the sole criterion for citizenship, thus generating a culturally organic nationalism that encourages the cleansing of minority cultures.[22]

These problems are not easily resolved in majoritarian liberal democracies for their legal systems are primarily designed for the nourishment and protection of the rights of individuals and not necessarily the collective cultural rights of minority groups.

B. Cultural minorities and the nation state

Prima facie, this problem could be resolved by the reorganization of the nation state into multination states with enshrined collective rights for all participant cultural communities. The National Cultural Autonomy (NCA) model and consociationalism use this organizational logic in deeply divided societies when the abode of the constituent cultural communities overlaps. The NCA model has its origins in the twilight of the Habsburg Empire and the attempt by Austrian socialists to convert the decaying empire from a conglomerate of squabbling cultural communities into a democratic federation of nationalities.[23] In sharp contrast to most other forms of national autonomy, the NCA model rests on the idea that autonomous cultural communities could be organized as

---

[21] E Nimni, 'The sovereign predicament of dispersed nations' in E Nimni (ed), *National Cultural Autonomy and its Contemporary Critics* (2005), 241.
[22] M Mann, *The Dark Side of Democracy: Explaining ethnic cleansing* (2005), 3.
[23] See my introduction to the English reading audience, in O Bauer, *The Question of Nationalities and Social Democracy* (2001), xxii–xxiii.

autonomous collectives whatever their residential location within a multi-national state. As in the millet system in the Ottoman Empire, peoples of different cultural identities can coexist in a single polity without straining the principle of national autonomy, but in sharp distinction from the millet system, these communities are organized in accordance with the principles of liberal-democratic representation of nations.[24]

Consociationalism is a better-known form of governance that requires collective (group) representation. It presents an alternative to the principles of majoritarian democracy and for that reason it is normally used to manage conflict in deeply divided societies. The term was popularized by Arend Lijphart[25] and was further developed by John McGarry and Brendan O'Leary in a series of seminal works on conflict resolution and on Northern Ireland.[26] It is more elite-centred than the NCA model, and is based on the principles of a grand coalition across cultural divides, mutual veto on matters vital for the continuity of minority communities, proportionality in representation, and the segmental autonomy of each community. As with the NCA, the aim is to make government more responsive to the concerns of minorities and offer alternative outcomes to territorial nationalism and secession. In this way, secessionist groups are neutralized and cultural minorities are encouraged to feel confident of representation and protection for their vital concerns.[27]

As will be seen below the Lund Recommendations incorporate some important prescriptions derived from these two models, without endorsing them completely. At the time of their drafting, it was deemed impractical and not feasible to endorse *tout court* the model of a multination state advocated by consociationalism and by the NCA model. Key international players—nation states—are unlikely to willingly concede wide-ranging demands for the restructuring of the sovereignty of states. Even if the power of the nation state as an institution has diminished in the contemporary world with the development of multilateral institutions such as the European Union, nation states still remain the principal focus of political power and institutional organization. Instead, the purpose of the Lund Recommendations is to set standards that

---

[24] On the contemporary validity of the model see D Smith and K Cordell (eds), *Cultural Autonomy in Contemporary Europe* (2008); SC Roach, *Cultural Autonomy, Minority Rights, and Globalization* (2005) and E Nimni, 'Nationalist multiculturalism in late imperial austria as a critique of contemporary liberalism: The case of Bauer and Renner' (1999) 4(3) *Journal of Political Ideologies* 289–314.

[25] A Lijphart, *Democracy in Plural Societies: A comparative exploration* (1997).

[26] B O'Leary, 'Debating consociational politics: Normative and explanatory arguments' in S Noel (ed), *From Power Sharing to Democracy: Post-conflict institutions in ethnically divided societies* (2005); J McGarry and B O'Leary, 'Consociational theory, Northern Ireland's conflict, and its agreement: What Critics of consociation can learn from Northern Ireland' (2006) 41(2) *Government and Opposition* 249–77.

[27] IS Lustick, D Miodownik, and RJ Eidelson, 'Secessionism in multicultural states: Does sharing power prevent or encourage it?' (2004) 98(2) *The American Political Science Review* 208–29, 210–11.

facilitate the adoption by nation states of specific measures that alleviate tensions related to the presence of cultural communities, and ensure the coherence of their implementation.

In a world of nation states, two remedies are available for cultural minorities that feel alienated by the hegemony of the national majority. The first is secession and the constitution of separate nation states. This route is clouded with difficulties, for it almost always incurs the veto of the dominant nation[28] and, moreover, the abode of different cultural-national communities often overlaps. When cultural grievances become entangled with territorial disputes they become bitter, protracted, bloody, and extremely difficult to resolve. Cultural-territorial conflicts are classic zero-sum situations: the gain of one is by definition the loss of the other. It will be impossible in the contemporary world to find sufficient 'portions of real estate' to allow for each and every cultural community to have a territorial state of their own.[29] The UN Charter offers contradictory advice here: on the one hand, it sees the right of self determination as the right to constitute separate states, but on the other it opposes the dismemberment of it members.[30]

The second route is the one advocated by the Lund Recommendations. The central aim is to find solutions to the difficult problems of cultural minorities that are compatible with the system of nation states. For this reason, the Lund Recommendations provide a far-reaching set of specific recommendations that are designed to encourage and facilitate the adoption by states of concrete and specific measures aimed at overcoming the alienation of minority communities and alleviating the tensions inherent in situations of territorial cohabitation.[31] The recommendations for cultural minority self-governance are crucial ingredients in this formula, because they set the standards for a different interpretation, away from secession and towards forms of cultural self-determination. The Lund Recommendations also provide models of minority accommodation that can be followed by all states, and are applicable to autochthonous and migrant cultural communities alike.[32]

C. Why cultural minorities?

At this point a sceptical reader might ask: why such a fuss about cultural minorities? After all, there are many ways of dividing humanity and culture is but one of them. What is so special about cultural diversity?

---

[28] Rare exceptions are Singapore and Slovakia.
[29] For the difficult problems that result from minority secession see S Dion, 'Why is secession difficult in well-established democracies? Lessons from Quebec' (1996) 26(2) *British Journal of Political Science* 269–83.
[30] See TD Musgrave, *Self-Determination and National Minorities* (2000), 69–77.
[31] J Packer, *The Origin and Nature of the Lund Recommendations on the Effective Participation of National Minorities in Public Life* (2000) 29(4) *The Helsinki Monitor* 29–45, 41–2.
[32] IM Young, 'Two concepts of self-determination' in S May, T Modood and J Squires (eds), *Ethnicity, Nationalism, and Minority Rights* (2004), 180.

Culture occupies an important position in the formation of human identity. In an abstract sense, culture is constitutive of social mores because it informs and helps to shape individual identities through social relations and institutions.[33] For example, citizens' legal status is associated with particular cultural forms of law in a given society, which in turn informs notions of person, property, or status.[34] It is also constitutive because it provides the parameters within which individuals construct their identity and preferences. This does not mean that it is the only causal factor, but other general economic and social factors, such as class or status, require a concrete cultural form to become credible in a particular milieu.[35]

It is important to note that culture is not interpreted in the same way by all members of a cultural community, and thus becomes an arena of struggle between different interpretations.[36] For these reasons, in democratic societies, when individuals cannot find some expression of their culture in the governing institutions, they experience a sense of loss, of estrangement, of social distance, which leads to disenchantment and the desire to break away or to remain marginal within the governmental process. Hence, an examination of the role of culture in the political participation of citizens is not only concerned with minorities, but with the place of culture in a multitude of governance processes. One cannot discuss minority rights without asking why minorities are politically relevant and this in turn requires a considered theory of the role of culture in political life.[37]

Consequently, a crucially important way of enhancing the integration of cultural minorities is to encourage their participation in governance and to do so, as the Lund Recommendations suggest, through the political representation of minority communities. As it will be shown below, in places where this is implemented, minority representation strengthens intercultural links, fosters more positive attitudes toward the common government, and encourages individual political participation.[38] This helps to overcome the alienation of national minorities by integrating them, not only as the individuals foreseen by the apostles of liberal democracy, but also as communities that partake in joint governance of public institutions. In a multicultural democracy, the demand for recognition is often articulated as a claim for self-governance and for the equality of status of different cultural groups.[39] For the system to work and to overcome the alienation of minorities, intercultural recognition has to be based on mutual

---

[33] A Kane, 'Cultural analysis in historical sociology: The analytic and concrete forms of the autonomy of culture' (1991) 9(1) *Sociological Theory* 62.

[34] BS Turner, *Outline of a General Theory of Cultural Citizenship* in N Stevenson (ed), *Culture and Citizenship* (2001), 11.

[35] B Parekh, *Rethinking Multiculturalism, Cultural Diversity and Political Theory* (2006), 124.

[36] I develop this point in my forthcoming book, *Multicultural Nationalism*.

[37] Parekh, *Rethinking Multiculturalism* (n 35 above), 346.

[38] S Banducci, T Donovan, and J Karp, 'Minority representation, empowerment, and participation' (2004) 66(2) *The Journal of Politics* 534.

[39] R Baubock, 'Cultural minority rights for immigrants' (1996) 30(1) *International Migration Review* 212.

trust and built through autonomous self-governing participation. In this regard, the aim of the Lund Recommendations is to create a level playing field between majority and minority communities, so that everyone feels that the cultural values and the sense of self imbedded within them are institutionally relevant, appreciated, and welcomed. The trust, confidence, and resulting sense of belonging that are brought about by these self-governing measures go a long way towards securing minority integration. We shall now examine the relevant provisions put forward by the Lund Recommendations in pursuit of these aims.

II. The Implementation of the Lund Recommendations Standards

A. The architecture of cultural minority self-governance

The third section of the Lund Recommendations spells out in considerable detail the provisions it makes for the self-governance of cultural minorities. Given the wide range of circumstances in which cultural minority self-governance can occur, the Lund Recommendations suggest a number of alternatives for different situations and this flexibility is one of their important strengths. As will be seen below, there are many different cases that fall within this category, and the Spanish case illustrates that it is counterproductive to set standards that are too restrictive.

Arts 14–15 of the Lund Recommendations suggest territorial arrangements, non-territorial arrangements, or a combination of the two. The devolution of power to minorities is balanced by the argument that devolution must operate in tandem with the recognition by members of the devolved government that some types of decision are best exercised centrally and these are spelled out in some detail. The intention is clearly that minorities should have a say and that their point of view, as expressed by their autonomous governance organs, should be taken seriously.[40] The Lund Recommendations and its Explanatory Note present in some detail the various modes of autonomy available to cultural minorities. This helps to avoid the confusion outlined by Hans-Joachim Heintze, between the terms 'autonomy', 'self-government', and 'self-determination'.[41] Nevertheless, while this confusion might have been understandable under the 'old' paradigm—when sovereignty was closely associated with concepts of self-determination—under the new circumstances, it is possible to talk, as most indigenous groups do, about self-determination, autonomy, and self-government without intending or aiming to constitute separate nation states.[42]

---

[40] K Henrard, '"Participation", "representation" and "autonomy" in the Lund Recommendations' (2005) 12 *International Journal on Minority and Group Rights* 149.
[41] HJ Heintze, 'Implementation of minority rights through devolution of powers: The concept of autonomy reconsidered' (2002) 9 *International Journal of Minority and Group Rights* 328.
[42] Ibid, 335.

Self-determination as a strong right to sovereignty and a separate state is no longer as compelling or plausible as it was thought to be in the nineteenth century. Nowadays, it is not only possible, but normatively desirable to have a different meaning for self-determination, namely the need for democratic and autonomous self-government. In this way, self-determination remains central to incorporating cultural minorities within the governance frameworks of contemporary states.[43]

Here the Lund Recommendations touch upon the central claim of the new paradigm mentioned above and furthermore, resemble the NCA model. Here, a discussion of the performance of this model will help refine the application of this standard.[44] In Art 17 of the Explanatory Note to the Lund Recommendations, the use of national cultural autonomy is especially recommended in cases when cultural communities are geographically dispersed. These minorities rarely press for self-determination, understood as sovereignty. They aspire instead for greater recognition and inclusion within the mainstream social and political structures, as well as recognition of their cultural specificity.[45]

This is an important and growing cluster of cultural minorities, as the phenomenal migration of the last few decades has diluted the territorial base of many cultural communities. This growing cluster has particularly affected migrant religious communities and indigenous peoples, albeit for different reasons, and this will be discussed below.

B. Cultural minorities and asymmetrical forms of governance

There is an innovative reference to asymmetrical forms of governance in Art 15 of the Lund Recommendations, one that echoes the new paradigm break with older notions of sovereignty. Here, the desirability to grant asymmetrical devolved power to regions or communities that exhibit a distinct cultural identity is not taken to imply the desire to constitute separate states. Asymmetrical decentralization along territorial or cultural lines (or both simultaneously), is an increasingly common form of territorial autonomy in cases of deep cultural diversity. The concept of sovereignty as total and indivisible power has been significantly eroded and borders are no longer seen as dividing lines between states and societies.[46]

Under the old paradigm, an important principle derived from the egalitarian ethos of popular democratic sovereignty was that when governance is devolved

---

[43] CC Gould, 'Self-determination beyond sovereignty: Relating transnational democracy to local autonomy' (2006) 37(1) *Journal of Social Philosophy* 52.
[44] See in particular the debate generated by the NCA model in E Nimni (ed) *National Cultural Autonomy and its Contemporary Critics* (2005); and Smith and Cordell *Cultural Autonomy* (n 24 above).   [45] M Deveaux, *Cultural Pluralism and Dilemmas of Justice* (2000), 9.
[46] SJ Henders, 'Cantonisation: Historical paths to territorial autonomy for regional cultural communities' (1997) 3(4) *Nations and Nationalism* (1997) 521.

to lower units, rules and regulations are devolved uniformly to all constituting units. This egalitarian ethos however, militates against the autonomy of cultural minorities, particularly those that have a different culture that acts as a marker of difference. This point is continuously refuted by doctrinaire liberals,[47] which led Charles Taylor to state that this kind of doctrinaire liberalism is inhospitable to difference because it insists on a uniform application of the rules defining rights and is suspicious of collective goals.[48] Asymmetrical self-governance of cultural minorities is also seen by those who oppose it as incompatible with the equality of citizens.[49] However, this has been challenged by recent literature on devolution that argues that symmetrical governance fails to correctly understand the core characteristics of most contemporary nation states, namely, that they are plurinational and not simply national.[50] Without asymmetrical arrangements these plurinational states will simply stop functioning and groups within them will fall into protracted bickering over competences. Asymmetrical autonomy has merit not only wherever a state's different communities seek different levels of self-government,[51] but also in circumstances where the cultural needs of different communities vary.

C. The Lund Recommendations on minority education and languages

Art 18 of the Lund Recommendations notes the importance of minority languages for the participation of cultural minorities. This is an important standard, as language is often a crucial artefact for the transmission of minority culture and, conversely, one of the principal sources of alienation of cultural minorities is a restriction in the use of their vernacular.[52] It would be a mistake to say that the use of language is a question of individual preference. Rather, it is a collective act that affects every user in that particular cultural *community*. Language is thus instrumental in defining and circumscribing cultural minorities.[53]

Cultural minority members should have the right to use their vernacular names while addressing state institutions, and to be addressed through their vernacular names. Members of cultural minorities must also have the right to

---

[47] See Barry, *Culture and Equality* (n 17 above), 300.
[48] C Taylor, *Multiculturalism, Examining the Politics of Recognition* (1994), 60.
[49] A Stepan, 'Federalism and democracy: Beyond the US model' in LJ Diamond and MF Plattner, *The Global Divergence of Democracies* (2001), 217.
[50] M Keating, *Plurinational Democracy: Stateless nations in a post-sovereignty era* (2004), Ch 4, 102–33.
[51] J Mcgarry, 'Asymmetrical autonomy and conflict regulation' (2007) 6(1) Ethnopolitics 133.
[52] R Bernard, 'Les contradictions fondamentales de l'école minoritaire' (1997) 23(3) *Revue des sciences de l'éducation* 510–11; and F Grin, 'Towards a threshold theory of minority language survival' (1992) 45(1) *Kyklos* 69–97.
[53] H-J Trenz, 'Reconciling diversity and unity language minorities and European integration' (2007) 7(2) *Ethnicities* 159.

petition the central government in their vernacular language, and to receive a response in the same language. Historically, the obligation to speak a common language in a state is a recent phenomenon, closely associated with the ascendance of nation states as the prime form of political organization.[54] Since the French Revolution it has been used by centralizing states as a tool to assimilate minority communities.[55] Very often, monolingualism is considered an issue of practicality and expedience, as well as an expression of the normative equality of all citizens, something that inflicts cultural violence upon those who speak different languages. With the onset of modernity, monolingualism became concomitant with 'nation building' (or nation destroying)[56] and as such was the dominant trend that closely followed the egalitarian ethos of nascent national democracies.[57] However, with the proliferation of demands for recognition of different cultures and languages, it is now increasingly accepted that linguistic standardization is no longer politically viable, particularly in those areas where cultural minorities have shown strong resistance to it.[58] In this regard, the situation of minority languages parallels that of minority cultures. There are about 7,000 spoken languages in the world, but only a small minority of them are afforded the protection of state institutions.[59]

As a result of this complex renaissance of minority languages, and in particular the strong alienation and resistance to the pattern of linguistic standardization, a new approach is necessary for the accommodation of cultural minority languages to the nation state. Benedict Anderson's 'fatal diversity of human language',[60] is now the lively asset of a multicultural renaissance, and the provisions of the Lund Recommendations on the use of minority languages play a crucial role in protecting minority languages. This protection is not only an important mechanism for ensuring the participation of cultural minorities in state governance and for rectifying an historical injustice, but is also an important codified catalyst for accommodating the languages of cultural minorities, autochthonous or migrant, within increasingly de facto plural nation states.

Likewise, education is an important mechanism for the transmission of language and culture to subsequent generations, and is key instrument for the intergenerational continuity of the cultural minorities. Art 15 of the

---

[54] S May, 'Uncommon languages: The challenges and possibilities of minority language rights' (2000) 21(5) *Journal of Multilingual and Multicultural Development* 370.

[55] I develop this argument in detail in 'Constitutional or agonistic patriotism?' (n 18 above), 96–8. See also G Nootens, 'Le modèle de l'état nation' in *Désenclaver la démocratie, Des huguenots a la paix des braves* (2004), 29–60.

[56] W Connor, 'Nation building or nation destroying?' in *Ethnonationalism, the Quest for Understanding* (1994), 28–66.

[57] S Gal, 'Contradictions of standard language in Europe: Implications for the study of practices and publics' (2007) 14(2) *Social Anthropology* 163–81.

[58] W Kymlicka and A Patten, 'Language rights and political theory' (2003) 23 *Annual Review of Applied Linguistics* 3–21.

[59] T Skutnabb-Kangas, *Linguistic Human Rights: Overcoming linguistic discrimination* (1995).

[60] B Anderson, *Imagined Communities* (1983), 46.

Explanatory Note to the Lund Recommendations defines education as one of the areas susceptible to cultural minority self governance and refers to Art 5.1 of the UNESCO Convention against Discrimination in Education, which argues, *inter alia*, that it is essential to safeguard the liberty of parents or guardians to choose educational institutions for their children that comply with the minimum requirements of the educational system in question. Art 15 furthermore recognizes the rights of cultural minorities to carry out their own educational activities and to teach in their own vernacular language.

One of the key methodologies advocated by education experts on minority cultures is what they call 'culturally relevant education'. This is a pedagogical method that empowers students in different educational dimensions by using cultural referents to impart knowledge, skills, and attitudes.[61] In this way the students gain an appreciation of their cultural referents because they are seen as connected to more universal values and goals in education, establishing a balance between universal educational needs and the promotion of their vernacular cultures. For example, a group of educational practitioners developed a curriculum for teaching mathematics to Mexican-American students, in such a way that they not only learned mathematics but also the connection between mathematics and the cultural markers of their community.[62] These pedagogical methods are not only good practice but dovetail and reinforce the principles of autonomous education of cultural minorities advocated by the Lund Recommendations.

III. The Implementation Standards of Cultural Minority Self-government

How has the praxis of cultural minority self-governance performed in recent years? Following the explosion of cultural minority demands for self-governance, it will be interesting to discuss briefly the application of different models of cultural minority self-governance and see how they responded to the standards advocated by the Lund Recommendations. We shall briefly review a small selection of cases, although there are many others that also exemplify the validity of the Lund Recommendations. Two of the cases reviewed here relate to territorial autonomy of cultural minorities, and one to non-territorial autonomy. I hope to show how these cases square with the Lund Recommendations.

---

[61] G Ladson-Billings, 'Culturally relevant teaching: The key to making multicultural education work' in CA Grant (ed) *Research and Multicultural Education: From the margins to the Mainstream* (1992), 9.

[62] E Gutstein et al, 'Culturally relevant mathematics teaching in a Mexican American context' (1997) 28(6) *Journal for Research in Mathematics Education* 709–37.

A. Cultural minority self-government in Quebec

The case of Quebec is interesting, for the autonomy granted by Canada was the result of a remarkable and sophisticated debate between advocates of different theories of governance. In some ways, events in Quebec set the tone for the shift of paradigm that informs the new modalities of territorial devolution, and the trajectory of Quebec can be interpreted as an example of best practice of the territorial autonomy advocated by the Lund Recommendations, with the proviso that a few question marks remain open with regards to the relationship of Quebec with its immigrant minorities and with its indigenous peoples (First Nations). Demands for the recognition of the cultural uniqueness of Quebec within the Canadian federation play a central role in the politics of the Canadian province and, as a result, provincial political parties have sought greater autonomy for Quebec and recognition of its unique status.

Briefly, Quebec is a large province in eastern Canada. While there are French speakers in other parts of Canada, Quebec is the only Canadian province with a predominantly French-speaking population whose official provincial language is French. This differentiates Quebec from the rest of English-speaking Canada. The French-speaking settlers of Quebec came into existence in a colony called *Nouvelle France* in the mid-seventeenth century, long before the Canadian federation was created. When the British Empire acquired the colony of *Nouvelle France* in the Treaty of Paris in 1763, they called this newly acquired territory the Province of Quebec.[63] However, the history of contemporary Quebec began in 1960 with the death of Maurice Duplessis, the conservative provincial prime minister, and the transformations that resulted from *La révolution tranquille* (The Quiet Revolution) of the 1960s. This was characterized by the secularization of society and the division of Québécois nationalism into autonomist and separatist factions. This nationalist awakening witnessed the implementation of new language laws aimed at improving the position of the French language in the government and private sector, giving exclusive official status to French and stipulating its use in business and education, albeit with a special dispensation to the English-speaking minority.[64]

Initially, relations between the Canadian central government and Quebec were fraught with difficulties during a series of constitutional crises. *The Parti Québécois* of Premier Rene Lévesque, who introduced Bill 101, ran for election under the goal of secession from Canada. Secession was defeated in a Quebec

---

[63] L Balthazar, 'The Quebec experience: Success or failure?' in F Aldecoa and M Keating (eds), *Paradiplomacy in Action: The foreign relations of subnational governments* (1999), 156.
[64] See Charte de la Langue Française, loi 101, Gouvernement du Québec, in English Bill 101 available at <http://www.publicationsduquebec.gouv.qc.ca/accueil.fr.html> (accessed 31 July 2009); M Keating, 'Stateless nation-building: Quebec, Catalonia and Scotland in the changing state system' (1997) 3(4) *Nations and Nationalism* 701. See also C Taylor, *Rapprocher les solitudes écrits sur le fédéralisme et le nationalisme au Canada* (1992).

referendum in 1980. The matter was further complicated by the devolution of the Canadian Constitution from the UK, and the enactment of the Canada Act in 1982, approved by all Canadian provinces except Quebec, which demanded its recognition as *une société distincte* (a different society); this was a political neologism that gave legal currency to the legal, cultural, and linguistic difference of Quebec. In 1987 a convention at Lake Meech attempted to give Quebec the cultural recognition it demanded, but this was not ratified by two provinces. A similar attempt was made in the Charlottetown Accord in 1992 which was put to a referendum and defeated. The French-speaking population of Quebec grew visibly angry at the refusal of the rest of Canada to recognize them as *une société distincte* and in 1995, in a new referendum on secession in Quebec, the secessionist motion was only defeated by a whisker (50.6 to 49.4).[65] In 2006, the Canadian House of Commons passed the following motion: 'This House recognizes that the Québécois form a nation within a united Canada' (*Cette Chambre reconnaisse que les Québécois forment une nation au sein d'un Canada uni*).[66] The vote was passed 266 to 16. Interpretations of the value of this resolution vary, but its symbolic value in defusing the Quebec crisis is undeniable.

In view of the reconciliation with English Canada and the multiethnic composition of the population of Quebec, a commission was established to study interethnic relations on 8 February 2007 by Quebec Premier Jean Charest, which has the status of a Royal Commission. Its official name was 'The Consultation Commission on Accommodation Practices related to Cultural Differences' (*Commission de consultation sur les pratiques d'accommodement reliées aux différences culturelles*),[67] best known as the Bouchard–Taylor Commission. It was led by the noted philosopher Professor Charles Taylor and no-less noted sociologist Professor Gérard Bouchard. The final report was made public on 22 May 2008. Its mandate was (a) to take stock of accommodation practices in Québec; (b) to analyse the attendant issues bearing in mind the experience of other societies; (c) to conduct an extensive consultation on this topic; and (d) to formulate recommendations to the government to ensure that accommodation practices conform to the values of Quebec society as a pluralistic, democratic, and egalitarian society.[68]

With regard to relations with the indigenous peoples, in 2001 the Quebec government and the Cree indigenous nation signed the James Bay Agreement or

---

[65] I discuss this in *The Sovereign Predicament of Dispersed Nations* (n 21 above), 248–9.
[66] Hansard, Canadian Parliament, 27 November 2006.
[67] See the English site of the Commission, <http://www.accommodements.qc.ca/index-en.html> (accessed 31 July 2009).
[68] G Bouchard and C Taylor, 'Building the future a time for reconciliation', abridged report of the consultation Commission on Accommodation Practices Related to Cultural Differences (English), Gouvernement du Québec, Publications du Québec, 2008, 7, available at <http://www.accommodements.qc.ca/index-en.html> (accessed 31 July 2009).

La Paix des Braves (The Peace of the Braves, reminiscent of the 1701 peace treaty between the French settlers and the indigenous Iroquois).[69] The agreement recognized the ancestral rights of indigenous peoples to their lands and allowed Hydro-Québec to exploit hydroelectric resources in exchange for a financial settlement to be given to the indigenous Cree Nation.[70] *La Paix des Braves* brought to the Cree Nation considerable advantages in the fields of development of education, social and sanitary issues, as well as tourism.[71]

The agreement states, inter alia:

2.1 Both the Cree Nation and the Québec Nation agree to place emphasis in their relations on those aspects that unite them as well as on their common desire to continue the development of Northern Québec and the self fulfilment of the Cree Nation.

2.2 The Cree Nation must continue to benefit from its rich cultural heritage, its language and its traditional way of life in a context of growing modernization.

2.3 This Agreement marks an important stage in a new nation-to-nation relationship, one that is open, respectful of the other community and that promotes a greater responsibility on the part of the Cree Nation for its own development within the context of greater autonomy.

2.4 Québec will promote and facilitate the participation of the James Bay Crees in forestry, hydroelectricity and mining development in the territory through partnerships, employment and contracts.[72]

There is no space here to discuss in detail the recommendations of either the Bouchard–Taylor Commission, or *La Paix des Braves* and the agreements with the First Nations, other than to say that they are very similar, in spirit and letter, to the Lund Recommendations. In the future, it would be very interesting to compare notes and experiences between the two.

As far as the Lund Recommendations are concerned, there is little doubt that the Canada–Quebec accommodation, and the accommodation of Quebec with the indigenous Cree Nation has to be understood as one of the best practice examples in terms of territorial and non-territorial autonomy for cultural minorities. The effort of the government of Quebec to reach out to its immigrant cultural minorities through the Bouchard–Taylor Commission is also an example of good practice. In conclusion, the autonomous power of the government of Quebec, its multicultural provisions, the recognition by

---

[69] For the text of the agreement, see <http://www.saa.gouv.qc.ca/relations_autochtones/ententes/cris/entente-020207_en.pdf> (accessed 31 July 2009).

[70] J Maclure, *Quebec Identity: The challenge of pluralism* (2003), XIV; Nootens, *Désenclaver la démocratie, Des huguenots a la paix des braves* (n 55 above), 165–7.

[71] A Bargès, 'Culture, territories, and confidence in food: An anthropological view on health in the context of environmental pollution and socio-political tension' (2008) 51(1) *Appetite* 33.

[72] Agreement Concerning a New Relationship Between le gouvernement du Québec and the Crees of Québec, 6, available at <http://www.saa.gouv.qc.ca/relations_autochtones/ententes/cris/entente-020207_en.pdf> (accessed 31 July 2009).

the Canadian state of the distinctiveness of the Québécoise nation, the treaties of the Quebec government with its indigenous peoples and reconciliation with the First Nations all fall within the best practice of the Lund Recommendations.

B. Cultural minority self-government in the Spanish state

The Autonomous Communities in Spain present another opportunity for testing the praxis of cultural minority self-governance, this time in Europe.

Franco's dictatorship ended with his death in 1975. The dictatorship created a highly centralized state, with no room for cultural autonomy, and even less for the use of minority languages. However, the idea of a strong homogeneous state was a recurrent idea of Madrid's conservative elites and was implemented for a long period with the imposition of the Castilian language,[73] despite the fact that Spain has a long history of different forms of autonomy for minority communities.[74]

Following the death of Franco, a process of democratic transition took place which culminated with the enactment of the Constitution of Spain after a referendum in 1978. With the transition to democracy, Spain moved from an authoritarian centralist state into a quasi-federal polity in which the seventeen autonomous communities were awarded considerable political autonomy.[75] The Constitution created a system of autonomous government, which catered in part to the clamour from the cultural minorities for self-governance and the use of their vernaculars. The section of the Constitution that dealt with the autonomies was marred from the start by controversy because it was a compromise between opposing views that left no one entirely happy. However, Spain was transformed from being a highly authoritarian and centralized state into a relatively (albeit limited) federal constitutional monarchy.[76]

The Spanish Constitution outlines a rigid territorial model for self-government (the Autonomous Communities). It establishes the sovereign (the Spanish Nation) and the character of that sovereignty (indissoluble).[77] However, the

---

[73] D Conversi, *Autonomous Communities and the Ethnic Settlement in Spain* in Y Ghai (ed), *Autonomy and Ethnicity: Negotiating competing claims in multi-ethnic states* (2000, at 124).

[74] The *fueros* (local jurisdictions or municipal charters), were a set of rules, rights and privileges granted by rulers usually to protect the way of life of a particular community. Eg, the incorporation of Navarre within Castile, following the 1512 defeat, was undertaken on the grounds that Navarre would retain its status as a kingdom and its own institutions. There are many similar forms of collective rights, which in Spanish constitutional history take the name of *fueros*.

[75] TA Börzel, 'From competitive regionalism to cooperative federalism: The Europeanization of the Spanish state of the autonomies' (2000) 30(2) *Publius* 17.

[76] D Conversi, 'The smooth transition: Spain's 1978 Constitution and the nationalities question' (2002) 4(3) *National Identities* 223.

[77] JJ Jiménez Sánchez, 'Nationalism and the Spanish dilemma: The Basque case' (2006) 34(3) *Politics & Policy* 540.

second article of the Constitution recognizes the rights of 'regions and nationalities':

> The Constitution is based on the indissoluble unity of the Spanish Nation, common and indivisible homeland of all Spaniards, and recognizes and guarantees the right to autonomy of nationalities and regions that make it up and the solidarity among them.[78]

The autonomies may use vernacular languages (Basque, Valencian, Catalan, and Galician depending on the case) as the language of government and administration even if there is some dispute as to whether Valencian is a language or a Catalan dialect. However, Castilian Spanish is the official language of the state.

Article 3 states that:

1. Castilian is the official Spanish language of the state. All Spaniards have the duty to know it and the right to use it.
2. The other Spanish languages are also official in their respective Autonomous Communities in accordance with its Statute.[79]

According to the 1978 Constitution, autonomies are created when a single province can define or claim an historical identity or status, when two or more contiguous provinces define common historical and cultural characteristics, and when they come into existence in insular territories. By conceiving Spain as a single nation, the Autonomous Communities system lacks a procedural mechanism for resolving disputes and mediating between the regional and state authorities.[80]

Over the period 1978–96 the seventeen Autonomous Communities were constituted with clearly delimited jurisdictions: Andalucía, Catalonia, the Basque Country, Galicia, and later Valencia were defined as 'historical nationalities', communities that were considered to carry a common cultural baggage. Aragon, Castile, and Castile-La Mancha, and the Extremadura community were granted autonomy as communities integrated by provinces with common historical characteristics. The Canary Islands and the Balearic Islands were granted autonomy as insular territories; Cantabria, Asturias, La Rioja, and the Region of Murcia were granted autonomy as single provinces, as was Navarra, even though a section of its population speaks Basque and wishes to be part of the Basque Country.[81]

---

[78] Art 2 of the Spanish Constitution: 'La Constitución se fundamenta en la indisoluble unidad de la Nación Española, patria común e indivisible de todos los españoles, y reconoce y garantiza el derecho a la autonomía de las nacionalidades y regiones que la integran y la solidaridad entre todas ellas.' My own translation from Castilian-Spanish.

[79] Art 3 of the Spanish Constitution: '1. El castellano es la lengua española oficial del Estado. Todos los españoles tienen el deber de conocerla y el derecho a usarla. 2. Las demás lenguas españolas serán también oficiales en las respectivas Comunidades Autónomas de acuerdo con sus Estatutos.' My own translation from Castilian-Spanish.

[80] SC Roach, 'A constitutional right to secede? Basque nationalism and the Spanish state' (2007) 8 *International Studies Perspectives* 454.

[81] M Balado Ruiz Gallegos, 'La España de las Autonomías. Reflexiones 25 años después', Editorial, *Bosch*, Barcelona, 2005.

The criteria used to create the autonomous regions were derived on the one hand from the desire to appease centralist tendencies, and on the other hand to appease more radical demands from minority nationalists. These criteria included all territories in Spain, whether they had a common cultural characteristic or not. This alienated minority nationalists. They called the autonomous arrangement *café para todos* ('coffee for all')[82] indicating that in the collective division of the Spanish state into symmetrical autonomies, the cultural specificity of the historical nationalities was lost.

However, problems have resulted from the difficulties of the central government in recognizing the specificity of the cultural status of minority communities for fear of secession. This is especially difficult in the Catalan and Basque cases as politicians from these two autonomous communities demand from time to time an enlargement of their autonomous competences. The latest and most important such occasion, because of its repercussions, was a plan put forward under the title Political Statute of the Community of the Basque Country but better known as the 'Ibarretxe' Plan, named after the President (Lehendakari) of the Basque autonomous community, Juan José Ibarretxe. The plan was the result of wide consultation, including with a large number of civil society stakeholders. Although it did not call for secession from Spain, it challenged the basis of the Spanish state (symmetrical) sovereignty as enshrined in 1978 Constitution.[83] The plan aimed to find, in accordance with the new paradigmatic understandings of self-determination, an alternative arrangement to the old fruitless dilemmas of nation state sovereignty or secession and full-blown independence. The plan was narrowly approved in the Basque parliament in 2004, then submitted to the Spanish parliament and rejected because it was deemed unconstitutional. The Basque government called for a referendum in the Basque Country in October 2008, but this was again deemed unconstitutional by the Spanish Constitutional Court.

The Ibarretxe Plan aimed to constitute the Basque community as freely associated with the Spanish state (as Puerto Rico is with the US). Basque citizenship was to be based on Spanish citizenship rules, and open to all residents of the Basque Country with the provision that no one would be subject to discrimination on the basis of belonging or not belonging to the Euskal Herria (Basque Cultural Community). The Spanish Constitutional Court would interpret bilateral relations between the governments of Spain and the Basque Country. According to the ancient tradition of the *fueros*, the King of Spain would remain head of state.[84] The proposal to establish a status of 'free association' between the Basque Country and Spain was strongly rejected by the

---

[82] NG Jesse and KP Williams, *Identity and Institutions: Conflict reduction in divided societies* (2005), 38–9.
[83] M Keating and Z Bray, 'Renegotiating sovereignty: Basque nationalism and the rise and fall of the Ibarretxe Plan' (2006) 5(4) *Ethnopolitics* 348. [84] Ibid, 354.

centrist parties, and was viewed by the Spanish parliament as non-debatable due to its perceived breaching of the framework of the Constitution.[85] Even if the Ibarretxe Plan proposed a form of asymmetric federalism, it was nonetheless identified by the conservative government in Madrid as a 'definitive leap towards independence'.[86]

The problem here results from the difficulties of accommodating the needs of the cultural territorial minorities within the context of the Spanish state, which has very fixed notions of state sovereignty, and of finding a compromise between the old and new understandings of self-determination. While the Spanish Constitution has gone a considerable way towards de facto recognition of the cultural diversity of the Spanish state, it still needs to come to terms with the idea that this recognition is (*de jure*) incompatible will the old version of governance and state sovereignty. The central government has failed to understand that recognition of these new forms of self-determination would not foster secession but, on the contrary, would prevent it from occurring. The not-so-unspoken assumption behind the Ibarretxe Plan was that it put an end to ETA terrorism. However, Spanish socialists and conservatives stand by Arts 1–2 of the Spanish Constitution, which they believe are incompatible with the Ibarretxe Plan, and appear to stand in the way of a more flexible solution to the Basque problem.[87]

Here, the Lund Recommendations could be of considerable help in overcoming the impasse, as they contain detailed suggestions on territorial and non-territorial arrangements which could be the basis for a compromise between the respective positions of the Basque parliament and the Spanish state. This compromise could be reached with the help of some small symbolic gestures to alleviate the tension between cultural minorities and the cultural majority in the Spanish state. In line with Art 18 of the Lund Recommendations, the use of all vernacular languages in Spain should be permitted in the Spanish parliament (Cortes). The visibility and representation of cultural minorities should be increased, for example through reform of the upper house, so that it acts as a sole representative of the autonomous governments. Furthermore, in line with the Lund Recommendations, a more asymmetrical system of representation should be permitted at the level of the central executive and legislative, so that cultural minorities can enjoy more effective participation in the public life of the Spanish state.

---

[85] P Kennedy, 'Phoenix from the ashes: The PSOE government under Rodríguez Zapatero 2004–2007: A new model for social democracy?' (2007) 20(3) *International Journal of Iberian Studies* 199.

[86] P Ibarra and I Ahedo, 'The political systems of the Basque Country: Is a non-polarized scenario possible in the future?' (2004) 10(3) *Nationalism and Ethnic Politics* 366.

[87] M Heiberg, B O'Leary, and J Tirman, *Terror, Insurgency, and the State: Ending protracted conflicts* (2007), 405.

C. A case for non-territorial cultural autonomy: the Sami parliament in Norway

The Sami people are one the largest indigenous ethnic groups in Europe, inhabiting the north of Sweden, Norway, Finland, and Russia. Indigenous disadvantage is prevalent in many parts of the world and this includes not only the settler societies of the American continent and Australasia, but some parts of Europe. There is a huge diversity of indigenous peoples, but most share common predicaments derived from their history of invasion or rule by a settler society.

According to the Special Rapporteur on Indigenous Peoples, Professor Rodolfo Stavenhagen, one of the areas that most clearly illustrates the vulnerable nature of indigenous peoples' human rights is the administration of justice and the failure to recognize customary indigenous law in governance and self-determination.[88] Faced with a state based on an alien and violent intrusion into their ancestral homelands—an intrusion that rendered them scattered minorities in the first place—indigenous peoples demand national autonomy and public recognition of their way of life.[89] Bearing in mind the special circumstances of indigenous peoples, the UN General Assembly approved in 2007 a declaration on the Rights of Indigenous Peoples that states inter alia:

Article 3

> Indigenous peoples have the right to self-determination. By virtue of that right they freely determine their political status and freely pursue their economic, social and cultural development.

Article 4

> Indigenous peoples, in exercising their right to self-determination, have the right to autonomy or self-government in matters relating to their internal and local affairs, as well as ways and means for financing their autonomous functions.

Article 5

> Indigenous peoples have the right to maintain and strengthen their distinct political, legal, economic, social and cultural institutions, while retaining their right to participate fully, if they so choose, in the political, economic, social and cultural life of the State.[90]

---

[88] R Stavenhagen, Special Rapporteur, General Assembly of the United Nations Document no A/59/258, 12 August 2004, (2005) 17 *Australian Indigenous Law Reporter*.
[89] Nimni, 'Nationalist multiculturalism' (n 24 above), 297.
[90] United Nations Declaration on the Rights of Indigenous People, Official Records of the General Assembly, Sixty-first Session, Supplement no 53 (A/61/53), Pt 1, Ch II, s A, 13 September 2007.

The UN General Assembly Declaration on the Rights of Indigenous Peoples dovetails perfectly with the Lund Recommendations on the rights of self-governance of cultural minorities, particularly in the areas of non-territorial self-governance. The development of a parliament for the Sami peoples in several Scandinavian countries, over which the Sami exercise their right to non-territorial self determination, is of particular interest to our discussion. Because of space constraints, we shall only discuss the Sami parliament in Norway.

The Sami, like many other indigenous peoples cannot sustain forms of territorial autonomy because their areas of residence overlap with others. Territorial organization cannot serve as a means for self-determination without crucially affecting the rights of other inhabitants.[91] The flexible system of Sami villages, *siidas*, adopts a fundamentally different approach to territoriality than states, with the latter's conception of fixed boundaries.[92] For this reason, Norway has adopted a special constitutional provision with regards to the Sami people. Article 110a of the Constitution of Norway states that 'It is the responsibility of the authorities of the State to create conditions enabling the Sami people to preserve and develop its language, culture and way of life.'[93]

In discharging its obligations towards its indigenous people, the Norwegian government has implemented a series of measures to advance the education of the Sami people in their vernacular language. The Sami language was already being used in primary schools when legislation extending language and cultural rights to Norway's Sami people was enacted in 1992. Sami is both a medium of instruction and is taught as a subject in secondary schools. The Sami College is an important institution, providing a model from which other countries might borrow in many aboriginal settings.[94] Here again we encounter a constitutional statement and legal provisions that are entirely in line with the principles established by the Lund Recommendations on the protection and preservation of the way of life of cultural minorities, and they should be commended as good practice.

The *Sámediggi* (the Sami parliament) in Norway is elected through general elections every four years by all members of the Samis in the country, normally in conjunction with Norwegian general elections. The *Sámediggi* is elected by a non-territorial electoral system that resembles the NCA model of Otto Bauer and Karl Renner.[95] It is an independent political organ and is the highest representative body of the Samis in Norway. The Sami parliament was

---

[91] AJ Semb, 'Sami self-determination in the making?' (2005) 11(4) *Nations and Nationalism* 542–3.

[92] K Karppi, 'Encountering different territorialities: Political fragmentation of the Sami homeland' (2001) 92(4) *Tijdschrift voor Economische en Sociale Geografie* 394–404.

[93] Constitution of the Kingdom of Norway, English translation available at <http://www.stortinget.no/en/In-English/About-the-Storting/The-Constitution/The-Constitution/> (accessed 31 July 2009).

[94] D Corson, 'Norway's Sámi Language Act: Emancipatory implications for the world's aboriginal peoples' (1995) 24(4) *Language in Society* 499.

[95] Semb, 'Sami self-determination' (n 91 above), 543.

inaugurated by King Olav in 1989 and consists of forty-three elected representatives from thirteen electoral districts. The Sámediggi's legal base is found in s 12 of the Sami Act of the *Storting* (Norwegian parliament), which states that the Samis shall have their own National Sami parliament elected by and among the Samis in Norway. The establishment of the *Sámediggi* is the result of the implementation of s 110a of the Norwegian Constitution, which was adopted by the *Storting* on 21 April 1988. The political mandate of the Sámediggi includes all issues that relate to Sami interests, including language, education, and mass media.[96]

All members of the Sámi community of Norway that are registered in the Sámi census regardless of area of residence are entitled to vote for the Sámediggi (the Sami parliament). This participation is personal and not territorial. The Sami Act of 1987 defines entitlement for registration in the Sami census according to a combination of linguistic and self-definition criteria:

Everyone who declares that they consider themselves to be Sámi, and who either has Sámi as his or her home language, or has or has had a parent, grandparent or great-grandparent with Sámi as his or her home language, or who is a child of someone who is or has been registered in the Sámi census, has the right to be enrolled in the Sámi census in the municipality of residence.[97]

Sami elections are lively and present voters with a choice, as there are contrasting interpretations of the Sami position in Norwegian society which are constructed through a combination of Sami cultural markers with various other issues.[98] This suggests that the Norwegian Sami parliament has been a success, as it is a constant among cultural minorities that they close ranks to present a united image when they feel threatened, but open up for internal debate when they feel that their circumstances are favourable to expressing their cultural identity. The Sámediggi has the formal responsibility for development and protection of the language, culture, and heritage sites. It also took over the functions of the Sami Educational Council from the Ministry of Education.[99]

The Sámediggi exemplifies almost precisely the non-territorial arrangements stipulated in Lund Recommendations 17 and 18, and as such should be considered one of the best practices of non-territorial autonomy applied to an indigenous community for their effective participation in public life. The example of the Sami parliament in Norway can be replicated in other areas of the world where indigenous peoples wish to exercise their right of self-determination.

---

[96] 'The Sámi People: A handbook', Official publication of the Sami parliament in Norway, Karasjok 2006, 1, available at <http://www.galdu.org/govat/doc/eng_sami.pdf> (accessed 31 July 2009).   [97] Ibid.
[98] L Gaski, 'Contesting the Sami polity: Discursive representations in the Sami electoral campaign in 2005' (2008) 25(1) *Acta Borealia* 1–21.
[99] *Lander Arbelaitz*, 'The Silent Revolution', *Gáldu*, Resource Centre for the Rights of Indigenous Peoples, <http://www.galdu.org/web/index.php?artihkkal=344&giella1=eng> (accessed 31 July 2009).

IV. The Participation of Cultural Minorities in Self-governance: A Final Discussion and Evaluation

The previous discussion has shown how cultural minority self-governance has progressively gained currency among academics, practitioners and, above all, among states and international organizations. The paradigm shift towards flexible and accommodating forms of self-determination, self-government and shared competences has helped immensely in the cumulative expansion of models of cultural minority self governance. With the rebirth of minority rights,[100] territorial and non-territorial cultural minorities are finding it easier to develop suitable models for accommodation within the context of states' increasing readiness to recognize cultural diversity. In this regard, the Lund Recommendations have done well, not only by achieving new landmarks, but also by being part of an era during which the recognition of cultural diversity has flourished across the world.

However, isolated from this phenomenal progress, there remains a missing dimension, namely the position of mainly immigrant non-Christian religious minorities in the Western world. A symptomatic example is the position of Islamic minorities. After the terrorist attacks in the United States in 2001, and similar attacks in the UK and Spain, the large European Islamic population (estimated at around 17 million) has come under intense scrutiny and suspicion, making their diverse cultural and legal traditions the subject of debate and criticism. This hostile scrutiny has singled out Islam as a closed and dogmatic civilization[101] and ignores the common Abrahamic origin of many of the Islamic facets under scrutiny. Moreover, the Islamic faith is often presented as a single monolithic and static tradition, ignoring the dynamic plurality of interpretation of this vast faith, which has consistently demonstrated its ability to adapt to vastly different cultural and geographic environments.[102]

The problem was highlighted by the European Commission against Racism and Intolerance (ECRI) of the Council of Europe, when it issued General Policy Recommendation no 8 on combating racism while fighting terrorism[103] which argues *inter alia*:

As a result of the fight against terrorism engaged since the events of 11 September 2001, certain groups of persons, notably Arabs, Jews, Muslims, certain asylum seekers, refugees

---

[100] Kymlicka, *Multicultural Odysseys* (n 13 above), 30–8.
[101] An influential work on this regard is SP Huntington, 'The clash of Civilizations?' (1993) 72(3) *Foreign Affairs* 22–49; see the reply by EW Said, 'The clash of ignorance', *The Nation*, 22 October 2001, available at <http://www.thenation.com/doc/20011022/said> (accessed 31 July 2009).
[102] SB de Sousa, 'Towards a multicultural conception of human rights' in M Featherstone S Lash (eds) *Spaces of Culture: City – Nation – World* (1999).
[103] ECRI General Policy Recommendation no 8 on Combating Racism while Fighting Terrorism, 17 March 2004, available at <http://www.coe.int/t/dghl/monitoring/ecri/activities/GPR/EN/Recommendation_N8/recommendation_N%C2%B0_8_eng.pdf> (accessed 31 July 2009). See also 'Muslims in the European Union: Discrimination and Islamophobia', EUMC 2006. Islamophobia is a neologism was coined by a well-known NGO, The Runnymede Trust, to explain this surge of anti-Islamism: see 'Islamophobia: A challenge for us all', available at<http://www.runnymedetrust.org/uploads/publications/pdfs/islamophobia.pdf> (accessed 31 July 2009). The phenomenon shows marked similarities with interwar European anti-Semitism.

and immigrants, certain visible minorities and persons perceived as belonging to such groups, have become particularly vulnerable to racism and/or to racial discrimination across many fields of public life including education, employment, housing, access to goods and services, access to public places and freedom of movement.

This situation, combined by the presence of large groups of religious minorities in Europe, requires the development of special procedures that encourage effective participation of (non-Christian) religious minorities in public life. On this matter, there is a need to incorporate into the Lund Recommendations procedures and standards to encourage the effective participation of religious minorities in public life, as their needs and characteristics are different from those of other cultural minorities. In the case of Islamic minorities, it is necessary to carve out an autonomous space in which some aspects of Islamic jurisprudence—particularly on personal issues such as marriages, divorces, births and so on—are recognized by the secular legal system as valid for those who practise this faith willingly and without coercion, so that they in turn can recognize themselves as participating in the public lives of their societies. As will be shown below, there is precedence in a similar arrangement for the orthodox Jewish community in the UK.

The Archbishop of Canterbury, the head of the Anglican Church, Dr Rowan Williams recently suggested in a much misunderstood lecture[104] that there is a need for the incorporation of certain aspects of Islamic jurisprudence, Sharia law,[105] particularly on family matters and in such a way that it does not contradict human rights values, to allow for better participation of British Muslims in British life. The Archbishop asks:

> How are we to relate to religious communities which, while no less 'law-abiding' than the rest of the population, relate to something other than the British legal system alone?[106]

In response to this question, the Archbishop calls for the incorporation of carefully considered aspects of Islamic law under the rubric of 'supplementary jurisdictions'.[107] These supplementary jurisdictions are compatible with human rights values and chime very much with the spirit and letter of the Lund Recommendations on the autonomy of minority cultures, for they create an

---

[104] R Williams, 'Civil and religious law in England: A religious perspective' (2008) 10 *Ecclesiastical Law Journal* 262–82. This is the full transcription of a lecture delivered on 7 February 2008. The lecture was part of a series of discussions on Islam in English law.

[105] There are considerable misunderstandings about Sharia Law. It not is a single, codified body of law. It is the human interpretation of the Revelation applicable to different spaces and circumstances. Sharia is a human interpretation of religious teachings and, as such, changeable and subjected to different interpretations in different circumstances, such as, eg, an interpretation that is attuned to the values of Western liberal democracies.

[106] Williams, 'Civil and religious law in England' (n 104 above), 262.

[107] The term is derived from the work of the Israeli political theorist, A Shachar, *Multicultural Jurisdictions, Cultural Differences and Women's Rights* (2001).

autonomous jurisdiction over which freely consenting Muslims can exercise their religious beliefs and customs. Moreover, there are an increasing and varied number of Islamic theological works that call upon the adjustment of Islamic teachings to Western societies, to allow for more effective Muslim participation. There is nothing unusual about this, as it happens in other contexts where the Islamic tradition is operative.[108]

It is therefore justifiable to incorporate a recommendation to include these supplementary jurisdictions for consenting members of these religious minorities into the Lund Recommendations. This will see the expansion of these spheres of autonomy to some aspects of religious law, and therefore allow for the full and effective participation of members of minority religious communities in public life.

In British law, these supplementary jurisdictions can already be found in recent acts of parliament to accommodate Orthodox Jewish religious marriages and divorces (Divorce (Religious Marriages) Bill 2001),[109] which recognizes rulings of the *Beth Din* (Jewish Rabbinical Court) on individuals that freely consent to be guided by these rulings. The aim of the bill is to alleviate the position of *Agunoth*, Orthodox Jewesses that are not accorded a divorce by their husbands.

In 1999, Lord Irvine, the British Attorney-General, issued a formal apology to a Sikh solicitor whose ritual dagger (*kirpan*) was confiscated as he entered the High Court. This incident resulted in a formal order that allowed *kirpans* in court if they were carried by bona fide Sikhs and authorized by their religious authorities.[110] These supplementary jurisdictions are also present in the recent parliamentary direction that allows Sikhs, under the certification of Sikh religious authorities (mainly *Gurduwara Sahibs*, Sikh temples), to carry *kirpans* into security enclosed areas of Heathrow airport and into schools.[111] These are very good standards and should find their way into the second decade of the Lund Recommendations for cultural minorities self-governance.

---

[108] See, among many, T Ramadan, *Western Muslims and the Future of Islam* (2005). From a different perspective see M Arkoun, 'Rethinking Islam today', (2003) 588(1) *Annals* 18–39; and for yet another perspective see S Fishman and F al-Aqalliyyat, 'A legal theory for Muslim minorities', Centre for Islam, democracy and the Future of the Islamic world, Monograph Hudson Institute (2006), available at <http://www.futureofmuslimworld.com/docLib/20061018_MonographFishman2.pdf> (accessed 31 July 2009).

[109] Divorce (Religious Marriages) Bill, 23 October 2001, available at <http://www.publications.parliament.uk/pa/cm200102/cmbills/035/2002035.htm> (accessed 31 July 2009).

[110] G Singh, D Singh Tatla, *Sikhs in Britain: The making of a community* (2006), 136.

[111] See House of Commons Hansard, Airport and Aircraft Safety Debate, 23 October 2001.

23
Enhanced Local Self-government as a Means of Enhancing Minority Governance

Bill Bowring

I. Introduction	661
II. Conceptual Issues	662
III. Standards	669
IV. Case Study: Russia and Other FSU and CEE Countries	674
V. Conclusion	681

I. Introduction

In this chapter I focus on the role and importance of local government in enhancing the political participation of minorities—ethnic and 'national' minorities—in public life. If I may be forgiven an autobiographical note at the start, I myself served as an elected councillor for a central London borough from 1978 to 1986,[1] representing a substantial black population. From 1985–6, I served alongside a number of black councillors under the first black—Afro-Caribbean—Mayor of the borough, Lloyd Leon.[2] It is my own view that the opportunity to participate in local government (as distinct from local administration) is of crucial significance to all minorities, and 'national minorities' especially.

---

[1] When on grounds of 'wilful misconduct'—a protest against the policies of Margaret Thatcher—we were all subjected to administrative proceedings by the Audit Commission, 'surcharged' a very large amount of money, and banned from public office for five years—see the intervention of the local MP at <http://hansard.millbanksystems.com/commons/1986/mar/05/lambeth-and-liverpool-surcharge-of> (accessed 1 July 2009).

[2] See <http://www.lambeth.gov.uk/Services/CouncilDemocracy/ElectedRepresentatives/Mayors MetropolitanBorough1900To2007.htm> (1 July 2009).

The structure of this chapter is as follows: under the heading 'Conceptual Issues' I first explore the definition of local government. Europe has the European Charter of Local Self-Government (ECLSG), of which more later, and in the Council of Europe space local government is—with the exception of the jurisprudence of the European Court of Human Rights—regarded without qualification as a good in itself. It should not be forgotten, however, that the USA is a leading member of OSCE, and that 'localism' is a matter of intense controversy there. Secondly, therefore, I present some of the arguments. Thirdly, I have something to say about local government as against local governance (if that is an issue). I turn fourthly to questions of privatization and marketization, as tending to the fragmentation of local government in Europe. Finally, local and central government do come into conflict, the clearest example being the UK, which took a long time to ratify the ECLSG, and was reluctant to participate in the EU's Committee of the Regions.[3]

The second section of this chapter deals with 'standards'. Here I look in more detail at the enormous amount of standard-setting since 1990. I start with the Lund Recommendations themselves—they have less to say about local government than might be expected. Then I turn to the UN Declaration on Minority Rights, following which I consider the ECLSG; the relevant provisions and case law of the European Convention on Human Rights; and the Framework Convention for the Protection of National Minorities (FCNM).

The third section explores some empirical considerations. Here I turn in particular to the Russian experience. Russia now has its third post-communist law 'On Foundations of Local Self-government in the Russian Federation', and has made, in aspiration at least, a very serious attempt to comply with the ECLSG. I must ask the question, therefore, whether this has any impact on Russia's highly complex institutional—and other—relationships with its national minorities. I also present and update some of the findings of an excellent collection published in 2002.[4]

II. Conceptual Issues

Local self-government is not at the centre of discussions on enhancing minority governance. Steven Wheatley, for example, who focuses on democracy in relation to minorities, does not (as far as I can see) consider local government at all.[5]

---

[3] See B Bowring 'The Committee of the Regions: Europe and British local government' (1995) 1(3) *European Public Law* 395.
[4] V Tishkov and E Filippova (eds) *Local Governance and Local Empowerment in the CIS* (Local Government Institute: Budapest, 2002).
[5] S Wheatley *Democracy, Minorities and International Law* (Cambridge University Press: Cambridge, 2005); S Wheatley, 'Minorities under the ECHR and the construction of a "democratic society"' (2007) *4 Public Law 770*.

Nor does Tove Malloy in the section on 'Models of Accommodation' in her excellent book.[6] In a later chapter she devotes a section to the Congress of Local and Regional Authorities of the Council of Europe (CLRAE), to which I turn below.[7] Yash Ghai, in his contribution to his collection *Autonomy and Ethnicity*, does have the following to say:

Local government can also be an effective way to give certain powers to a group, as the geographic scale is small and the prospects of its inhabitants being ethnically homogenous are better. Some federations now constitutionally protect local government as a third tier of government for this very reason (Nigeria and Spain: but constitutional protection was rejected in India).[8]

However, the remainder of the collection, including a wide range of country case studies, does not return to the theme. The present chapter, in its third section, does attempt an analysis of the situation in the Russian Federation.

For a more rigorous attempt at a definition, we should turn to an article written on the basis of long experience of work with the United States Agency for International Development (USAID) by Harry Blair. He provides the following definition:

Democratic local governance ... combines the devolutionary form of decentralization (in which real authority and responsibility are transferred to local bodies) with democracy at the local level. Accordingly, it can be defined as meaningful authority devolved to local units of governance that are accessible and accountable to the local citizenry, who enjoy full political rights and liberty.[9]

He contrasts this with previous approaches:

It thus differs from the vast majority of earlier efforts at decentralization in developing areas, which go back to the 1950s, and which were largely initiatives in public administration without any serious democratic component.[10]

Representation is thus a key issue. This is the question of giving citizens a meaningful role in local decisions that affect them. Blair points out that many new constituencies can gain representation: 'businessmen, local notables, large farmers, professionals, and possibly some labor leaders will quickly find a place on local councils'.[11] Significantly for this chapter, he adds that in his study[12] 'two other constituencies have gained representation: minority ethnic groups

---

[6] T Malloy *National Minority Rights in Europe* (2005), 40–4.   [7] Ibid, 240–7
[8] Y Ghai 'Ethnicity and autonomy: A framework for analysis' in Y Ghai (ed), *Ethnicity and Autonomy: Negotiating competing claims in multi-ethnic states* (2000), 9.
[9] H Blair 'Participation and accountability at the periphery: Democratic local governance in six countries' (2000) 28(1) *World Development* 21.   [10] Ibid, 21.
[11] Ibid, 23.
[12] Two cases in Latin America (Bolivia and Honduras), two in Asia (India and the Philippines), and one each in Eastern Europe (Ukraine) and Africa (Mali).

and women'. However, in his own paper he does not have much to say about the latter.

The other vitally important and complementary issue is accountability. It is essential that people will be able to hold local government responsible for how it is affecting them. Blair notes that 'democratic governance at the local or national level can succeed only if public servants are held accountable—government employees must be accountable to elected representatives, and representatives must be accountable to the public'.[13] Accountability can take a number of forms, as he points out:

(a) Bureaucratic accountability to elected officials. Blair notes that Ukraine transferred far more authority to local authorities than the other countries in his study did, largely because the central government was unable to do more on its own.[14]
(b) Elected officials' accountability to the public.

This accountability can be secured in several ways: (a) elections, (b) political parties, (c) civil society, (d) the media, (e) public meetings, (f) formal grievance procedures, and (g) opinion surveys. Blair comments that 'Ukraine had essentially no civil society at the local level at the time of the USAID study, nor was there much sign of social capital—the trust that facilitates people working together toward a common purpose—which would help build civil society'. The main reason, of course, is the country's recent Soviet history, in which the state controlled almost all organized social activity. The whole web of organized life collapsed with the communist system, leaving families and individuals autonomous and without social moorings. The USAID study found people in the major cities were just beginning to organize in their apartment buildings for such purposes as maintaining common areas, providing security, and dealing with outsiders encroaching on public space.[15]

This is a very useful framework for analysis. And Blair is quite right to conclude that:

Viability for the democratic component of Democratic Local Governance (and for much of its local governance component as well) depends in the final analysis on participation and accountability—bringing as many citizens as possible into the political arena and assuring that local governors are responsible to the governed for their actions.[16]

Indeed, this is a truism. His survey has very little to say about minorities—not even in Ukraine, where issues of language and ethnicity are of great importance.[17]

---

[13] Blair, 'Participation and accountability' (n 9 above), 27.   [14] Ibid, 27.
[15] Ibid, 28.   [16] Ibid, 35.
[17] See B Bowring 'Language policy in Ukraine: International standards and obligations, and Ukrainian law and legislation' in J Besters-Dilgers (ed), *Language Policy and Language Situation in Ukraine: Analysis and Recommendations* (2008), 57; there are also excellent chapters in this collection by an anthropologist, sociologists, socio-linguists, linguists, and a political scientist.

The themes developed by Blair are also explored in the OSI collection *Diversity in Action*, published in 2001.[18] Tony Verheijen points to the fact that 'the creation of local self-governing authorities, often with rather broad competencies, has been completed in virtually all Central and East European States' since the collapse of communism.[19] In his view, this is 'highly important for the creation of sustainable democratic systems of governance'. For him also participation is all-important, and the factor which distinguishes present experience from the communist past, with its 'legacy of dual subordination and democratic centralism'.[20] He compares reforms in Poland, Hungary, Slovakia, and the Czech Republic; in all of these, it is plain that considerable progress has been made, using a variety of different forms. He concludes that local self-governing institutions provide 'the roots for any democratic system of governance'.[21]

Tomila Lankina goes further. She is one of the few scholars to focus on minorities, and observes that: 'The peculiar feature of local government, its contact with the citizenry, provides local governments with unique mobilisational opportunities.'[22]

Another is the well-known anthropologist and former minister of nationalities in Russia, Valerii Tishkov. However, in the introduction to his impressive 2002 collection *Local Governance and Local Empowerment in the CIS*, Tishkov plainly does not consider the notion of 'local self-government' to require further explication: he refers to its purpose as an effort 'to empower the populace through local self-government'.[23] There are in fact serious reasons for reflecting critically on local government as an unproblematic good.

But he makes an important and valuable point with regard to the Soviet experience:

In Soviet times, the notion of local self-government, usually referred to as 'the local power', had a special connotation and was part of the mechanism of control of the totalitarian state. But the contradictory nature of the Soviet heritage is such that the local self-governments also genuinely served the citizens. The comprehensive system of Soviets (councils) was, at least formally, designed to distribute power through elected bodies at all levels—all the way down to villages and townships. This form of government actually performed a variety of essential functions of management and representation and involved a great number of people, both elected deputies and civil servants. Much of the old system of management is preserved to this day, and many aspects of this past experience are still valuable.[24]

---

[18] A-M Biro and P Kovacs (eds), *Diversity in Action: Local public management of multi-ethnic communities in Central and Eastern Europe* (2001).
[19] T Verheijen, 'Public administration reform: A mixed picture' in Biro and Kovacs (eds) *Diversity in Action* (n 18 above), 30. [20] Ibid, 36.
[21] Ibid, 42.
[22] T Lankina, 'Local administration and ethno-social consensus in Russia' (2002) 54(7) *Europe-Asia Studies* 1037.
[23] Tishkov and Filippova (eds), *Local Governance and Local Empowerment in the CIS* (n 4 above), xxi. [24] Ibid, xxii.

I can confirm this from my own experience. My first regular visits to Russia (the USSR) were, from 1983 to 1986, undertaken in the context of town twinning—that is, a formal relationship created in the Second World War between the London Borough of Lambeth in London, and the elected Moskvoretsky Rayon, its counterpart in the centre of Moscow. It was plain that while, ultimately, the Communist Party was in charge, a great number of people were actively involved in many aspects of local governance, from housing, to education, to town planning. The level of popular participation then was much greater than it is today, when elected local authorities no longer exist within the city of Moscow; it is now divided into purely administrative units.[25] There was even a degree of accountability, despite the fact that elections in a one-party state were a formality. The elected deputies were required to report back to regular public meetings, and could be and were removed in case of public dissatisfaction.

I should not leave this topic without reporting a singular curiosity: Sidney Webb's article on Soviet local governance, published in 1933.

> What, then, beyond a verbal 'sovereignty' do the constituent parts of the Union retain in their own hands? Here we may see how very differently the Bolshevists have, from the first, handled the problem of 'national minorities' ... To the seven Union republics, and as far as practicable to all of the thirty-five other 'autonomous areas' is conceded, in the first place, complete 'cultural autonomy'. They may use their own vernacular languages to the fullest extent, even to a severe subordination of Russian; they may keep, and vary as they choose, their own religious rites and racial customs; they may conduct and staff their own schools, colleges, universities, hospitals and medical services; they may have their own newspapers and magazines, and their own government publishing houses; they may provide and control their own theatres and cinemas, concert halls and stadiums. In the second place, they may have their own local police and magistracy (apart from the State Political Department, with its special political police—the dreaded OGPU ...) and their own courts of justice, enforcing their own laws, so long as these are not contrary to those of the federation. In the third place, they can, if they choose, with insignificant exceptions, staff their own governments ... with their own local citizens, speaking their own languages, accustomed to all the local conditions and imbued with all the local patriotism and other particularisms. Substantially, these three great classes of autonomous action include everything that stirs the emotions of "national minorities," or that touches their *amour propre*. The result is that, after ten years' experience, it is not too much to say that Soviet Russia today ... has no 'national minorities problem'.[26]

---

[25] Moscow is divided into ten administrative *okrugs*, which are in turn subdivided into districts (*rayons*). See <http://government.moscow.ru/ru/capital_russia/executive_authority/> (accessed 31 July 2009).
[26] S Webb, 'Soviet Russia as a federal state' (1933) 4(2) *The Political Quarterly* 182–200, 185–6.

I have cited this passage at length, not simply for its historical curiosity, but because in tone and content it is so similar to the official line of the Russian government in its reports to the FCNM.

Nowhere in the world is local government and governance accorded such importance as in the USA (this honour once belonged to Britain, before the era of rate-capping, privatization, and the evisceration of local democracy). I now turn, therefore, to US 'localism', which has found severe critics, including Sheryll D Cashin. She argues that:

> ... our nation's ideological commitment to decentralized local governance has helped create the phenomenon of the favored quarter. Localism, or the ideological commitment to local governance, has helped produce fragmented metropolitan regions stratified by race and income.[27]

She cites Richard Briffault,[28] and continues:

> Permissive state laws reflecting a popular bias toward local authority have contributed to the proliferation of new, homogeneous local polities, particularly in outer-ring developing suburbs. In turn, the balkanization of the metropolitan population into separate jurisdictions increasingly stratified by income and usually stratified by race has changed the nature of political discourse at the local, state and national level.[29]

She sets out the US debate as follows:

> The normative debate on localism reflects a scholarly tension regarding the equity impacts of fragmented local government. One school of thought, most prominently advocated by Gerald Frug, is that local governments are powerless and that more authority ought to be vested in them in order to promote certain values. For Frug and others, local autonomy is justified first and foremost because it maximizes 'democratic participation in public affairs'.[30] In addition, proponents of local autonomy argue that it promotes the efficient allocation of goods and services and that it creates and reinforces a salutary concept of community. These three values—democratic participation, efficiency, and community—form the basis of an entrenched predisposition toward localized authority in legislative and judicial decision making concerning local government law. As a result, general purpose municipal governments typically have great

---

[27] S Cashin, 'Localism, self-interest and the tyranny of the favored quarter: Addressing the barriers to new regionalism', (1999) Georgetown University Law Center Working Paper Series in Law in Business and Economics, Working Paper no 194751, 4, available at <http://papers.ssrn.com/paper.taf?abstract_id=194751> (accessed 31 July 2009); also S Cashin, 'Localism, self-interest, and the tyranny of the favored quarter: Addressing the barriers to new regionalism'(2000) 88 Georgetown Law Journal 1985–2048; and S Cashin, 'Federalism, welfare reform and the minority poor: Accounting for the tyranny of state majorities'(1999) 99 *Columbia Law Review* 552.

[28] R Briffault, 'Our localism, part I: The structure of local government law' (1990) 90(1) Columbia Law Review 1–115, 1, 113: 'Local autonomy is to a considerable extent the result of and reinforced by a systemic belief in the social and political value of local decision making.'

[29] Cashin, 'Localism, self-interest and the tyranny of the favored quarter' (n 27 above), 6.

[30] G Frug, 'The city as a legal concept' (1980) 93 Harvard Law Review 1057, 1151.

autonomy in matters of zoning, land use, property taxation, and the provision of public services.

She concludes that the 'extreme degree of decentered power that currently exists in metropolitan America may in fact be undermining the value of citizen participation, *inter alia*, because of the way fragmentation disenfranchises non-residents of powerful suburban localities'.[31] To put it simply, the affluent and predominantly white suburbs increasingly assert their independence from the city; and the city is the home of the disenfranchised and poor blacks and Hispanics.

Local government is not treated as an unmixed blessing by all European commentators. Some criticisms of trends in Western European policy towards local governance have drawn a useful distinction between 'local government' and 'local governance'. Thus, Caroline Andrew and Michael Goldsmith reported in 1998 that:

In many countries the local level is marked by fragmentation of institutions, or the rise of what has been called in Britain 'local governance'. Another way of thinking about this process is in terms of marketization of the public sector, whether through the creation of special agencies or of special purpose bodies (well known in major North American cities), processes of contracting out or compulsory competitive tendering (CCT), or privatization. This process of 'reinventing government'[32] has been undertaken in the name of efficiency and effectiveness and has been very much dominated by market values.[33]

I would add that this process has continued under the Labour governments first elected in 1997. They continue by observing that:

Furthermore, in some countries—and Britain is a notable example, but New Zealand and Australia are others—changes have been imposed on local government from above. The United Kingdom is the 'brand leader of local governance' in many respects, introducing a whole raft of new bodies at the local level, mainly special purpose bodies, all appointed, whilst removing functions from elected local governments at the same time.[34] These two processes reflect the loss of legitimacy at the local level and give rise to the fragmented structures referred to by the generic title of local governance.

The reader should thus bear in mind that while local government is in this author's view a mainstay of the whole democratic edifice, the term 'local

---

[31] S Cashin, 'Localism, self-interest and the tyranny of the favored quarter' (n 27 above), 21.
[32] D Osborne and T Gaebler *Re-inventing Government: How the entrepreneurial spirit is transforming the public sector* (1992).
[33] C Andrew and M Goldsmith, 'From local government to local governance: And beyond?' in 'New trends in municipal government' (1998) 19(2) *International Political Science Review/Revue internationale de science politique* 101, 104.
[34] A Cochrane, 'From theories to practices: Looking for local democracy in Britain' in D King and G Stoker (eds) *Rethinking Local Democracy* (1996), 193.

governance' can signal decisive moves away from democracy—at least in the sense outlined above of participation and accountability.

III. Standards

I will start at the end, as it were, with the Lund Recommendations themselves,[35] since they are based on the preceding instruments and standards, to which I will then turn. In fact, the Recommendations have little to say explicitly about local government (or governance). However, in Part II, on 'Participation in decision-making', they state:

C. Arrangements at the Regional and Local Levels
  11) States should adopt measures to promote participation of national minorities at the regional and local levels such as those mentioned above regarding the level of the central government (paragraphs 6-10). The structures and decision-making processes of regional and local authorities should be made transparent and accessible in order to encourage the participation of minorities.

While Recommendations 6–10 are directed primarily to central and regional government, there are also provisions applicable to local government. Recommendation 6 calls for 'effective voice', including 'special representation of national minorities, for example, through a reserved number of seats'; the other provisions are only applicable to central government. Recommendation 7 provides for the electoral process, including the rights to vote and stand for elections. Recommendation 8 deals with political parties: 'the freedom to establish political parties based on communal identities as well as those not identified exclusively with the interests of a specific community' is clearly relevant to local government. Recommendation 9 on the electoral process contains recommendations for 'single-member districts'. It is unlikely however that proportional-representation systems, preference voting, or lower numerical thresholds will be so relevant. Recommendation 10, finally, recommends that the 'geographic boundaries of electoral districts should facilitate the equitable representation of national minorities'.

Part III, on 'Self-governance', provides in Recommendation 14, that '[e]ffective participation of minorities in public life may call for non-territorial or territorial arrangements of self-governance or a combination thereof'. It is however mainly concerned with regional arrangements, as in Recommendation 19. On the other hand, Recommendation 20 does provide that '[a]ppropriate local, regional, or autonomous administrations that correspond to the specific historical and territorial circumstances of national minorities may undertake a

---

[35] The Lund Recommendation on the Effective Participation of National Minorities in Public Life and Explanatory Note, available at <http://www.osce.org/documents/hcnm/1999/09/2698_en.pdf> (accessed 31 July 2009).

number of functions in order to respond more effectively to the concerns of these minorities'. But this formulation is so general and bland as to be almost meaningless.

The Explanatory Note makes it clear that Recommendation 11 applies to local government, and continues that 'the criteria used to create structures at the regional and local level may be different from those used at the level of the central government. Structures may also be established asymmetrically, with variation according to differing needs and expressed desires.' Indeed, if one takes only the CEE and FSU members of the OSCE, there is an enormous variety of models, symmetrical and asymmetrical. I turn to some of these in the third section.

The note to Recommendation 14 is not simply self-referential; it does point to the Preamble to the European Charter of Local Self-government (ECLSG),[36] which stresses 'the principles of democracy and the decentralisation of power' as a contribution to 'the safeguarding and reinforcement of local self-government in the different European countries'. It continues: 'In this last connection, the [ECLSG] provides in Article 9 for the entitlement of adequate financial resources for the exercise of such decentralized authorities.'

Furthermore the Explanatory Note insists (20) that:

Autonomous authorities must possess real power to make decisions at the legislative, executive or judicial levels. Authority within the State may be divided among central, regional and local authorities and also among functions. Paragraph 35 of the Copenhagen Document notes the alternatives of 'appropriate local or autonomous administrations corresponding to the specific historical and territorial circumstances'. This makes clear that there need not be uniformity within the State. Experience shows that powers can be divided even with respect to fields of public authority traditionally exercised by central government, including devolved powers of justice (both substantive and procedural) and powers over traditional economies. At a minimum, affected populations should be systematically involved in the exercise of such authority. At the same time, the central government must retain powers to ensure justice and equality of opportunities across the State.

The international starting point is, however, the UN's 1992 Declaration on the Rights of Persons Belonging to National or Ethnic, Religious, and Linguistic Minorities.[37] Art 2(3) provides:

Persons belonging to minorities have the right to participate effectively in decisions on the national and, where appropriate, regional level concerning the minority to which they belong or the regions in which they live, in a manner not incompatible with national legislation.

---

[36] Strasbourg, 15 October 1985, CETS no: 122, available at <http://conventions.coe.int/Treaty/EN/Treaties/Html/122.htm> (accessed 31 July 2009).
[37] Adopted by General Assembly resolution 47/135 of 18 December 1992, available at <http://www.unhchr.ch/html/menu3/b/d_minori.htm> (accessed 31 July 2009).

Marc Weller made the following comment in 2005, while laying the ground for a General Comment of the UN Sub-commission:

> At the lower end of the spectrum, one may consider cases of local autonomy. These would be instances where provision for local government that applies throughout the state is improved in cases of certain municipalities, given their demographic composition. An example is the case of 'enhanced' local self-government that was provided in the Ohrid settlement for Macedonia. While it was not felt politically prudent to designate the areas concerned as autonomous units, significant special provision was made in relation to them in view of their ethnic composition.[38]

As already noted the Council of Europe formulated relevant standards as early as 1985, with the ECLSG. Art 4(3) states that:

> Public responsibilities shall generally be exercised, in preference, by those authorities which are closest to the citizen.

As of 26 February 2009, the ECLSG had been ratified by forty-four of the forty-seven member states of the Council of Europe; that is, every member state which has a system of local government.[39] Russia, for example, ratified in 1998, within two years of joining the Council. The UK ratified in the same year—it was only when the Labour Party came to power in 1997 that ratification became possible. The ECLSG was anathema to the Conservative governments of Margaret Thatcher and John Major.[40] France did not ratify until 2007.

Tove Malloy, as indicated earlier in this chapter, comments on the CLRAE, the Congress of Local and Regional Authorities of the Council of Europe.[41] It was responsible for Recommendation 43 (1998) on 'Territorial autonomy and national minorities'.[42] She starts with the Preamble, which provides: 'Considering that the principle of subsidiarity takes concrete form in the recognition

---

[38] M Weller, 'Towards a general comment on self-determination and autonomy', 25 May 2005, Sub-commission on the Promotion and Protection of Human Rights, Working Group on Minorities 11th Session, 30 May–3 June 2005, E/CN4/Sub2/AC5/2005/WP5, 7, available at <http://www2.ohchr.org/english/issues/minorities/docs/2005-wp.5-eng.doc>(accessed 31 July 2009). [39] Thus, Andorra, Monaco, and San Marino have neither signed nor ratified.
[40] See B Bowring, 'The Committee of the Regions: Europe and British local government' (1995) 1(3) European Public Law 395.
[41] Malloy *National Minority Rights in Europe* (n 6 above), 240–7.
[42] CLRAE Recommendation 43, sent to the Committee of Ministers on 27 May 1998, Appendix, eighth recital, CLRAE Rec 43 (1998), GR-H(2001)3 revised, CM/Del/Dec(2001)747/1.1 and 796/10.7, available at <https://wcd.coe.int/ViewDoc.jsp?id=853855&Site=Congress&BackColorInternet=e0cee1&BackColorIntranet=e0cee1&BackColorLogged=FFC679> (accessed 31 July 2009).

Draft reply of the CM of 2002 available at <https://wcd.coe.int/ViewDoc.jsp?id=285963&Site=COE&BackColorInternet=DBDCF2&BackColorIntranet=FDC864&BackColorLogged=FDC864> (accessed 31 July 2009).

and the institution of territorial autonomy, which may consist in local or regional self-government'; and:

Bearing in mind the fact that the concept of territorial autonomy does not necessarily imply that the powers assigned to a particular level of government—local, provincial or regional—are the same, but that, in relation to the same level of self-government, powers may be distributed differently in accordance with economic, geographical, historic, social, cultural and linguistic requirements.

Malloy comments as follows:

It was therefore an effort to include co-nations in a system of subsidiarity already existing in some states and to make sure that post-1989 democracies take the principle of subsidiarity seriously.[43]

Resolution 52 (1997) on 'Federalism, Regionalism, Local Autonomy and Minorities'[44] also reaffirms a central Council of Europe principle that 'the legal forms of federalism, regionalism and local autonomy are nothing more than various applications of the principle of subsidiarity', as defined by the ECLSG as noted above. It also provides (para 8) that:

self-government can be defined in accordance with the principles of the European Charter of Local Self-Government as the right and the ability of territorial authorities, within the limits of the law, to regulate and manage a substantial share of public affairs under their own responsibility and in the interests of the local population.

As to the European Framework Convention for the Protection of National Minorities (FCNM), I note Weller's comments, in the same work for the Sub-commission:

Yet, in the context of the legally-binding [FCNM] the situation is somewhat different. The final version of Article 15 FCNM, as adopted, does not fully reflect the emphasis on local self-governance found in other documents. In contrast to the corresponding provision in the *UN Declaration*, the rather cautious reference to decisions specially affecting 'regions where they live' was struck from the final version of Article 15 of the FCNM.

Nevertheless, when addressing Article 15, the official FCNM Explanatory Report encourages governments to consider, for instance, decentralized or local forms of government as a means of achieving effective participation.[45] This is fully in accordance with Article 4(3) of the European Charter of Local Self Government, which emphasizes that 'public responsibilities shall generally be exercised, in preference, by those authorities which are closest to the citizens'.[46]

---

[43] Malloy, *National Minority Rights in Europe* (n 6 above), 242.
[44] Resolution 52 (1997) on Federalism, Regionalism, Local Autonomy, and Minorities, 4th Plenary Session of the Congress, 3 June 1997, available at <https://wcd.coe.int/ViewDoc.jsp?id=848841&Site=Congress&BackColorInternet=e0cee1&BackColorIntranet=e0cee1&BackColorLogged=FFC679> (accessed 31 July 2009).
[45] Framework Convention for the Protection of National Minorities, Strasbourg, February 1995, para 80, available at <http://www.coe.int/t/dghl/monitoring/minorities/1_AtGlance/PDF_H(1995)010_FCNM_ExplanReport_en.pdf> (accessed 31 July 2009).
[46] Weller, 'Towards a general comment on self-determination and autonomy' (n 38 above), 14.

He notes in his Commentary on Art 15 to the FCNM[47] that proposals to include a reference to subsidiarity were opposed in CAHMIN as these 'would touch upon the constitutional systems of the Parties'.[48] He points out, however, that 'the official FCNM Explanatory Report encourages governments to consider, for instance, decentralised or local forms of government as a means of achieving effective participation'.[49] And he notes that this is fully in accordance with Art 4.3 of the ECLSG.

I turn finally to one peculiarity of the Council of Europe edifice, which is the exclusion of local government from the protection given to electoral democracy in Art 3 of Protocol 1 to the European Convention on Human Rights (ECHR). For this we must turn to the jurisprudence of the European Court of Human Rights.[50] Article 3 of Protocol 1 (P1-3) states as follows:

Right to free elections
    The High Contracting Parties undertake to hold free elections at reasonable intervals by secret ballot, under conditions which will ensure the free expression of the opinion of the people in the choice of the legislature.

In 1985 in *Clerfayt, Legros and ors v Belgium* the former Commission explained that the term 'legislature' in P1-3 must be interpreted in the light of the legislative institutions established by the member states' constitutions.[51] In 1987 the Court followed suit, and held that although this term 'does not necessarily mean only the national parliament … it has to be interpreted in the light of the constitutional structure of the State in question'.[52]

Thus, the Court recognized that regional parliaments in certain countries 'have competence and powers wide enough'[53] to make them constituent parts of the respective state's legislature. This applied to federal and regionalized states such as Austria,[54] Belgium,[55] Germany,[56] Italy,[57] and Spain.[58] In 2004 the Court explained the applicability of P1-3 to an Italian regional council in *Vito Sante Santoro* by the fact that, under the Italian Constitution, 'the regional councils are competent to enact, within the territory of the region to which they

---

[47] M Weller, 'Article 15' in M Weller (ed), *The Rights of Minorities: A commentary on the European Framework Convention for the Protection of National Minorities* (2005), 436–7.
[48] CAHMIN, 1st meeting, CAHMIN (94) 13, meeting report, 25–8 January 1994, para 46.
[49] Weller, 'Article 15' (n 47 above), 429.
[50] This section draws from the excellent work of S Golubok, 'Right to free elections: Emerging guarantees or two layers of protection?', draft in the possession of the author. This is forthcoming in the *Netherlands Quarterly of Human Rights*.
[51] *Clerfayt, Legros and ors v Belgium*, no 10650/83, Commission decision of 17 May 1985, 42 DR, 218, 222–3.
[52] *Mathieu-Mohin and Clerfayt*, no 9267/81, 2 March 1987, Series A no 113, para 53.
[53] Ibid, para 53.
[54] *X v Austria*, no 7008/75, Commission decision of 12 July 1976, 6 DR, 120, 121.
[55] *Mathieu-Mohin and Clerfayt* (n 52 above), para 53.
[56] *Timke v Germany*, no 27311/95, Commission decision of 11 September 1995
[57] *Vito Sante Santoro v Italy*, no 36681/97, ECHR 2004-VI, para 52.
[58] *Federación Nacionalista Canaria v Spain* (dec), no 56618/00, ECHR 2001-VI.

belong, laws in a number of pivotal areas in a democratic society, such as administrative planning, local policy, public health, education, town planning and agriculture'.[59]

Should the same not apply to representative bodies of local self-government? Such bodies have in fact been treated by the Court for other purposes as a 'State organisation', that is, an 'authority which exercises public functions'.[60] But the Court has tended to answer the question of applicability of P1-3 to local government in the negative.[61] The Court refers to the local government body's legal status under national law and basically follows the Commission's earlier approach, according to which what matters for the purposes of P3-1 is whether the authority in question possesses 'an inherent primary rulemaking power',[62] that is a power (a) deriving from the Constitution (b) to enact laws, as the latter term is understood in the domestic legal order. In other words, what is decisive is not whether a local authority actually regulates one or more of 'pivotal areas' in the sense of the judgment in *Vito Sante Santoro*, but whether it is designated as a law-making (legislative) body in the national constitution. It follows that the term 'legislature' in P1-3, at least for the time being, is closely linked to its national interpretation and does not constitute, unlike some other terms used throughout the Convention, an 'autonomous concept'.[63]

IV. Case Study: Russia and Other FSU and CEE Countries

The Russian Federation is the largest and most complex in the world. When the author wrote about this topic previously, in 2000,[64] it was composed of no less than eighty-nine 'subjects of the Federation'. As of 1 March 2008, it had eighty-three subjects. The reasons for this surprising 'shrinking' are explored by the author elsewhere; it is plain that since 2004 there has been a premeditated assault on the foundations of Russian federalism, with profound consequences for the potential for ethnic conflict.[65] Is this also the case for local government?

---

[59] *Vito Sante Santoro* (n 57 above), para 52.
[60] See, eg, *Mikryukov v Russia*, no 7363/04, 8 December 2005, para 21.
[61] *Xuereb v Malta* (dec), no 52492/99, 15 June 2000; *Cherepkov v Russia* (dec), no 51501/99, ECHR 2000-I; *Gorizdra v. Moldova* (dec), no 53180/99, 2 July 2002; *Mółka v Poland* (dec), no 56550/00, 11 April 2006.
[62] *Booth-Clibborn and ors v United Kingdom*, no 11391/85, Commission decision of 5 July 1985, 43 DR, 236, 248.
[63] G Letsas, 'The truth in autonomous concepts: How to interpret the European Convention on Human Rights', (2004) 15 *European Journal of International Law* 282.
[64] B Bowring, 'Ancient Peoples and New Nations in the Russian Federation: Questions of Theory and Practice', in S Tierney (ed), *Accommodating National Identity: New Approaches in International and Domestic Law* (2000), 211.
[65] This is explored further in B Bowring, 'The Russian Constitutional System: Complexity and Asymmetry' in M Weller and K Nobbs (eds), *Asymmetrical Autonomy and the Settlement of Ethnic Conflicts*, forthcoming.

Local government is intended to have a special status in Russian constitutional law. Art 12 of the 1993 Constitution, in Chapter 1, on Fundamentals of the Constitutional System, states:

Local self-government shall be recognized and guaranteed in the Russian Federation. Local self-government shall be independent within the limits of its competence. Bodies of local self-government shall not form part of the system of State government bodies.[66]

Furthermore, there is a separate chapter, Chapter 8, dealing with Local Self-government. This contains the following:

Article 130

1. Local self-government in the Russian Federation shall provide for the independent resolution by the population of issues of local importance, and the possession, use and management of municipal property.
2. Local self-government shall be exercised by citizens by means of referendum, elections and other forms of direct expression of their will, and through elected and other bodies of local self-government.

Article 131

1. Local self-government shall be administered in urban and rural settlements and on other territories with due consideration to historical and other local traditions. The structure of bodies of local self-government shall be determined by the population independently.
2. Changes of borders of the territories in which local self-government is administered shall be permitted with due consideration to the opinion of the inhabitants of the relevant territories.

This would appear at first sight to be an excellent basis for enhancing minority governance.

Furthermore, Russia ratified the ECLSG on 5 May 1998 (it came into force for Russia on 1 September 1998). This provides as follows:

Article 3 – Concept of local self-government[67]

1. Local self-government denotes the right and the ability of local authorities, within the limits of the law, to regulate and manage a substantial share of public affairs under their own responsibility and in the interests of the local population.
2. This right shall be exercised by councils or assemblies composed of members freely elected by secret ballot on the basis of direct, equal, universal suffrage, and which may possess executive organs responsible to them. This provision shall in no way affect recourse to assemblies of citizens, referendums or any other form of direct citizen participation where it is permitted by statute.

---

[66] Official English translation on the Russian President's web-site at: <http://www.kremlin.ru/eng/articles/ConstEng1.shtml> (accessed 31 July 2009).
[67] European Charter of Local Self-government, Strasbourg, 15 October 1985, available at <http://conventions.coe.int/Treaty/en/Treaties/Html/122.htm> (accessed 31 July 2009).

Local government is a field which has attracted considerable legislative activity in Russia. Post-communist Russian legislation on local self-government commenced with the Law of the USSR of 1990 and the Law of the RSFSR of 6 July 1991 both entitled 'On Local Self-government'. Two further laws, the Law of 28 August 1995 'On General Principles of Organisation of Local Self-government in the Russian Federation'[68] and, following ratification of the ECLSG, the Law of 6 October 2003 'On General Principles of Local Self-government Organization in the Russian Federation'.[69] Both represent attempts to bring Russian legislation into line with European standards.[70] The law was originally meant to come into force on 1 January 2006 but in October 2005 the Duma passed legislation postponing full implementation until 2009.[71]

Aleksei Sergeev notes, in his contribution to a leading recent Russian collection on local government in Russia, that according to the ECLSG local authorities should have freedom of activity within the limits of the law, and that most foreign countries have enacted legislation to that effect.[72] In particular, the 2003 law was intended to strengthen the legislative activity of local self-government.[73] Throughout his lengthy chapter, Dr Sergeev constantly uses the ECLSG as the yardstick against which the new Russian legislation is to be measured. Igor Babichev also notes that since the beginning of the 1990s Russians have studied the practice of European local government, which evolved over centuries of struggle between towns and central royal and regional feudal power, and is enshrined in the ECLSG.[74] Thus, work on the 2003 Law started in 2002 with a commission headed by VV Shipov, and was firmly centred on the 1993 Constitution and the principles of the ECLSG.[75]

The issue of the *Sratnitelnoye Konstitututsionnoye Obozrebniye* (*Comparative Constitutional Review*) just received by the author at the time of writing

---

[68] V Gelman, 'The politics of local government In Russia: The neglected side of the story' (2002) 3(3) *Perspectives on European Politics and Society* 495.

[69] Law no 131-FZ, in the wording of Federal laws of 19 June 2004 no 53-FZ, of 12 August 2004 no 99-FZ, of 28 December 2004 no 183-FZ, of 28 December 2004 no 186-FZ, of 29 December 2004 no 191-FZ, of 29 December 2004 no 199-FZ, with change brought by the Federal law of 30 December 2004 no 211-FZ.

[70] A Ivanenko, 'Introduction' in A Ivanenko (ed), *Konstitutsionniye i zakonodatelniy osnovy mestnovo camoupravleniya v Rossiiskoi Federatsii* (*Constitutional and Legislative Foundations of Local Self-government in the Russian Federation*) (2004), 3.

[71] C Ross, 'Municipal reform in the Russian Federation and Putin's "electoral vertical"' (2007) 15(2) *Demokratizatsiya. The Journal of Post-Soviet Democratization* 191, 193.

[72] A Sergeev, 'Mestnoye samoupravleniye v Rossiiskoi Federatsii: pravovaya teoriya i sotsialnaya praktika' ('Local self-government in the Russian Federation: Legal theory and social practice') in A Ivanenko (ed), *Konstitutsionniye i zakonodatelniy osnovy mestnovo camoupravleniya v Rossiiskoi Federatsii* (*Constitutional and Legislative Foundations of Local Self-government in the Russian Federation*) (2004), 56.

[73] Ibid, 57.

[74] I Babichev, 'Mestnoye samoupravleniye v postsovetskoi Rossii: nekotoriye itogi i prognozy' ('Local Self-government in post-Soviet Russia: Some conclusions and prognoses') in A Ivanenko (ed), *Konstitutsionniye i zakonodatelniy osnovy mestnovo camoupravleniya v Rossiiskoi Federatsii* (*Constitutional and Legislative Foundations of Local Self-government in the Russian Federation*) (2004), 175.

[75] Ibid, 200–1.

(March 2009) contains three important articles under the rubric *Munitsipalnaya demokratiya: traditsii i novatsii* (Municipal democracy: Traditions and innovations). The authors are Armen Dzhgaryan,[76] an adviser to the judges of the Constitutional Court of the Russian Federation; Nikolai Mironov,[77] a senior adviser of the state civil service of the Russian Federation; and Vladimir Gelman,[78] a professor of the European University in St Petersburg. Although Dr Dzhgaryan provides an authoritative review of the important judgments of the Constitutional Court in relation to local government, he nowhere mentions either the ECLSG or the problems of Russia's national (ethnic) minorities. The same is true of Dr Mironov. Gelman notes the work in Russian of Lankina,[79] as criticizing the approach of the 2003 law as 'technocratic' and complaining that its drafters 'had a contemptuous attitude to elections, as to all the most important components of democracy, giving preference to the professional administrative hierarchy'. But he does not follow Lankina in her interest in the effect of local government reform on minorities.

Indeed, for a more critical review it is necessary to turn to international scholars. The US commentator Jeffrey Hahn rightly observes that:

> Whereas federal and regional political institutions are part of a single system of state power, local government is not ... The law was a product of a commission set up by Putin in September 2001 ... [its] task was to establish a uniform and universal system of local government throughout Russia and to delimit the functions of the federal, regional and municipal levels of government. However, the rather closed process by which the Law was drafted and adopted tended to favour those with a vested interest in strengthening the executive vertical by making local government more effective and more accountable to the central authorities.[80]

Thus, three levels are created by Art 2: first, rural and urban settlements such as towns, villages and small cities; secondly, the municipal district (*rayon*) which

---

[76] A Dzhagaryan 'Mestnoye samoupravleniye v Rossiiskoi Federatsii: osnovy konstitutsionnoi kontseptsii I tendentsii razvitiya v kontekste natsionalnoi munitsipalno-pravovoi traditsii' ('Local self-government in the Russian Federation: Foundations of constitutional conceptions and tendencies of development in the context of the national municipal legal traditions') (2008) 6(67) *Sravnitelnoye konstitutsionnoye obozreniye* (*Comparative Constitutional Review*) 111.

[77] N Mironov, 'Modernizatsiya cherez detsentralisatsiyu: K voprosu o 'vertikali', balanse i znachenii mestnovo samoupravleniya v sovremennoi Rossii' ('Modernization against decentralisation: Towards the question of "verticals", the balance of power and significance of local self-government in contemporary Russia') (2008) 6(67) *Sravnitelnoye konstitutsionnoye obozreniye* (*Comparative Constitutional Review*) 127.

[78] V Gelman, '*Reforma vlasti v gorodakh Rossii: mery, siti-menedzheri i mestnaya demokratiya*' ('The reform of power in the cities of Russia: Mayors, city-managers and local democracy') (2008) 6(67) *Sravnitelnoye konstitutsionnoye obozreniye* (*Comparative Constitutional Review*) 143.

[79] T Lankina, 'Reformy mestnovo samoupravleniya pri Putine' ('Reform of Local Self-government under Putin') in N Petrova (ed), *Federalnaya reforma 2000-2004 Tom. 2 Strategii, instituty, problemy* (*Federal Reform 2000-2004*, ii: *Strategies, institutions, problems*) (Moskovskiy obshchestvennyy nauchnyy fond: Moscow, 2005).

[80] J Hahn, 'Have Putin's policies on local government changed the way Yaroslavl is governed?' (2008) 16(4) *Demokratizatsiya. The Journal of Post-Soviet Democratization* 383, 389.

will include several adjacent settlements; and thirdly the city district (*gorodskoi okrug*), limited to larger municipalities. As Young and Wilson note, generally speaking, '[u]nder the new law, local governments will have fewer responsibilities and will receive less funding'.[81] The number of municipalities will more than double. Referring to data from the Central Electoral Commission, Cameron Ross estimates that they have already grown from about 12,000 to around 24,000 since 2006.[82]

As I have noted above, Tomila Lankina focuses on the effect of local government reform on ethnic minorities. Her findings in 2002, across a number of ethnic republics, showed that:

Local governments—both their executive and representative branches—maintain control over local societies through a system of appointments to local institutions, and through incorporating notables from large social and professional networks into the regime by 'selecting' them into the local councils.[83]

In 2005 she added that:

Although the rhetoric surrounding the reform stressed its democratic aspects, the institutional changes suggest that the authors were more concerned with centralizing power and strengthening vertical institutional accountability. Ideas normally associated with decentralization, such as developing civil society, respecting the diversity of local contexts, and increasing popular participation and initiative in local decision making, receive little attention in the law.[84]

Most seriously for the purpose of this chapter, she notes the following:

Respect for diversity should have been a crucial element of the legislation, considering Russia's multiethnic nature. Instead, the law appears to be an extension of the overall tendency to disregard the needs of minority ethnic groups in Putin's Russia, manifested in the withdrawal of ethnic republican privileges, the curbing of powers of ethnic autonomies, and the introduction of language legislation and nationality policy concepts implicitly privileging the majority ethnic Russian group—a tendency that only serves to encourage nationalist extremism.[85]

I am in complete agreement with Lankina. In my recent work on asymmetric federalism in Russia, I concluded that 'recent "reforms", while ostensibly designed to strengthen the Russian state and its unity, have the potential for re-opening past conflict and creating new ones'.[86]

---

[81] J Young and G Wilson 'The view from below: Local government and Putin's reforms' (2007) 59 (7) *Europe-Asia Studies* 1071.
[82] Ross, 'Municipal reform in the Russian Federation' (n 71 above), 193.
[83] T Lankina, 'Local administration and ethno-social consensus in Russia' (n 22 above), 1047.
[84] T Lankina, 'President Putin's local government reforms' in P Reddaway and R Ortung (eds), *The Dynamics of Russian Politics: Putin's reform of federal–regional relations* (2004), vol. 2, 145, 165–6. [85] Ibid, 166.
[86] B Bowring, 'The Russian constitutional system: Complexity and asymmetry' in M Weller and K Nobbs (eds) *Asymmetrical Autonomy* (n 65 above).

Russia may be compared with some of the Central and Eastern European states, where the experience would seem to be a great deal more positive. Kinga Gal commented that:

Especially important is the minority representation in the local self-governments where these communities live. In several cases (Hungary, Romania, Poland, Slovenia) the application of laws on local self-government or electoral laws enabled the parties, alliances representing minority communities to hold power. This actually means that at least in certain municipalities the principle of subsidiarity can be implemented.[87]

For Bulgaria, for example, it is reported that the Bulgarian Turks have since 1991 enjoyed significant representation in local government authorities in areas where they live compactly.[88] The Czech experience is also mixed. Michael Illner commented in 2005:

Size and spatial distribution of ethnic minorities is a geo-demographic factor which can be relevant in designing territorial administrative structures, particularly at the regional level. Large, spatially concentrated and politically active minorities may demand territorial autonomy or some other form of special administrative and political status. In the Czech decentralization reform (its second stage dealing with intermediary government) this has not been a relevant issue. Nowhere, in the ethnically fairly homogeneous country are at present large and, at the same time, spatially concentrated ethnic groups deserving or demanding politico-administrative autonomy. The 1992 constitution defined the country as the unitary state.[89]

Hungary since 1994–5 had its own system of minority self-governments, according to the Minority Act of 1993.[90] According to Gábor Soós:

Minorities in Hungary live dispersed in the country, so the system of minority local representation cannot be based on territorial units. Ethnic and national minority groups have the right to form minority self-governments through a special electoral procedure. Municipality councils must obtain the consent of minority self-governments for decisions that affect interests in minority education, culture, etc. The law on minority self-government recognizes the right of individuals to choose identities and, therefore, the choice of identity is absolutely free and confidential. Candidates can run and voters can

---

[87] K Gal, 'The Council of Europe Framework Convention for the Protection of National Minorities and its impact on Central and Eastern Europe' (2000) *JEMIE - Journal on Ethnopolitics and Minority Issues in Europe*, available at <www.ecmi.de/jemie/download/JEMIE05Gal30-07-01.pdf> (accessed 31 July 2009).

[88] E Gyurova, 'Emerging multi-ethnic policies in Bulgaria: A central-local perspective' in Biro and Kovacs (eds) *Diversity in Action* (n 18 above), 116.

[89] M Illner, 'Thirteen years of reforming sub-national government in the Czech Republic', paper delivered at the conference 'Reforming local government: Closing the gap between democracy and efficiency', 26–7 September 2002, Stuttgart, available at <www.uni-stuttgart.de/soz/avps/rlg/papers/CZ-Illner.pdf> (accessed 31 July 2009), 4.

[90] J Kaltenbach, 'From paper to practice in Hungary: The Protection and involvement of minorities in governance' in Biro and Kovacs (eds) *Diversity in Action* (n 18 above), 182

vote in minority elections without needing to prove membership in the ethnic or national minority that they represent and vote for.[91]

And Gwedolyn Sasse comments:

Most of Hungary's minorities are quite small and not politically mobilised. On the whole, they had little impact on the 1993 Act. Instead, the historical resonance of the Treaty of Trianon (1920), which left large Hungarian territorialised minorities in neighbouring states (Slovakia, Romania, Serbia, Ukraine), has underpinned the political will in favour of minority protection both at home and abroad.[92]

And there are doubts as to whether the system really assists the minority most in need of support, the Roma. Poland, despite its overwhelming ethnic homogeneity, has had some experience of success in German and Ukrainian minorities obtaining representation in local government.[93] In Slovakia, the Mečiar coalition attempted, in 1998, to introduce a Local Election Act which would, in municipalities with ethnically heterogeneous populations, have provided for obligatory distribution of councillors according to the ethnic composition of the population. This measure, which never came into force as the result of a decision of the Constitutional Court, was strongly criticized by, among others, Max van der Stoel, then HCNM, on the ground that it would have prevented candidates for local councils from having equal access to local seats.[94] In local elections in 1994 and 1998, the Hungarian minority was well represented; the Roma were not.[95] This pattern is repeated throughout the region.

I should add that I represented the Strasbourg applicant in *Ždanoka v Latvia* (Grand Chamber Judgment of 16 March 2006).[96] She had been denied the right to stand either for local or national elections; but only the latter complaint was justiciable by the Court.[97] A further irony is that despite Latvia's accession to the European Union, there remains a large population of stateless persons, mostly Russian-speakers, many of whom were born and have paid taxes all their lives in Latvia, but are granted only 'Alien Passports'. They are denied the right to vote in local elections, a right enjoyed by all EU citizens resident in Latvia.[98]

---

[91] G Soós, 'Local government reforms and the capacity for local governance in Hungary', paper presented at the Conference 'Reforming local government: Closing the gap between democracy and efficiency' (n 89 above) available at <www.uni-stuttgart.de/soz/avps/rlg/papers/Hungary-Soos.pdf> (accessed 31 July 2009).

[92] G Sasse, 'EU conditionality and minority rights: Translating the Copenhagen criteria into policy, (2005) Robert Schuman Centre for Advanced Studies Working Paper 2005/16, available at <www.iue.it/RSCAS/WP-Texts/05_16.pdf> (accessed 31 July 2009).

[93] P Bajda, M Syposz and D Wojakowski, 'Equality in law, protection in fact: Minority law and practice in Poland' in Biro and Kovacs (eds), *Diversity in Action* (n 18 above), 223–4.

[94] J Buček, 'Responding to diversity: Solutions at the local level in Slovakia' in A-M Biro and P Kovacs (eds), *Diversity in Action* (n 18 above), 290.   [95] Ibid, 291.

[96] Application no 58278/00, 16 March 2006.

[97] See B Bowring, 'Negating pluralist democracy: The Strasbourg Court forgets the rights of the electors' (2007) 11 KHRP *Legal Review* 67.

[98] See text at <http://www.greens-efa.org/cms/default/dok/105/105215.htm> (accessed 31 July 2009).

As set out in a recent English language booklet,[99] a series of international bodies including the CLRAE, the Council of Europe's Commissioner on Human Rights, and others have condemned this failure to comply with the accession requirements. The Commissioner stated in 2007:

> The exclusion of non-citizens from political life does nothing to encourage their integration. The Commissioner stressed this point in the previous report, recommending that Latvia examine the possibility of granting them, among other things, the right to vote in local elections. It should be highlighted that the overwhelming majority of non-citizens belong to minorities, and that this status debars them from participating in the political life of their country. They can neither vote nor be elected, even at the local level.[100]

I need make no further arguments in order to demonstrate the crucial importance of local government for national minorities.

V. Conclusion

This chapter has noted the fact that local government is given little attention in the Lund Recommendations or indeed in the other relevant documents and instruments. It is frequently conflated with regional government and many recommendations, especially as concerns autonomy, are clearly better suited to regions.

Yet the ECLSG, to which I have turned throughout this analysis, and which is plainly of central importance, is one of the cornerstones of the Council of Europe edifice, of which, of course, multi-party democracy is one of the three pillars. The jurisprudence of the European Court of Human Rights appears, therefore, to stand in contradiction to the principles set out so clearly in the ECLSG.

Russia has proved to be an extraordinarily interesting case study, especially in comparison with the experience of several Central and Eastern European states. There have now been two serious attempts to enshrine the ECSLG's principles into Russian legislation on local self-government. Yet among the many shortcomings of the latest version, the 2003 law, is its glaring neglect of the challenge of representation of national minorities.

---

[99] Latvian Human Rights Committee, 'Citizens of a non-existing state: The long-term phenomenon of mass statelessness in Latvia' (2008), available at <http://www.pctvl.lv/i/doc/citizens_nonexisting.pdf> (accessed 31 July 2009).

[100] Commissioner for Human Rights, Memorandum to the Latvian Government: Assessment of the progress made in implementing the 2003 recommendations of the Council of Europe Commissioner for Human Rights, CommDH(2007)9, 16 May 2007.

24

Minority Associations

Issues of representation, internal democracy, and legitimacy

Peter Vermeersch

I. Defining the Role of Minority Associations	684
A. Conceptual and normative considerations	684
B. What kind of associations? Locating different types of association on a spectrum of public participation	686
II. Representation and Participation through Non-governmental Minority Associations and Specialized State Bodies: Opportunities and Limits	688
A. Effective representation and participation	688
B. Non-elected consultative bodies	690
C. Elected bodies	695
III. Conclusion	700

While most of the contributions in this volume assess the institutions and mechanisms that grant minorities access to political decision-making processes, this chapter turns to the minorities themselves and how they interact with existing institutions and mechanisms. How are minorities organized? In particular, how are they organized in response to the opportunities created by the institutions and mechanisms that allow them some level of access to political decision-making processes?

This question follows implicitly from current international standards on national minority protection in Europe. As the other chapters in this volume clearly show, these standards go beyond issues of protection per se and encourage states to adopt institutional models that foster and regulate the political participation and representation of minorities. In the Lund Recommendations, for example, participation is considered 'an essential component of a peaceful and democratic society'. Moreover, international norms usually see participation not simply as a matter of individual political involvement but as something that should be realized by minority associations and organizations. Para 33 the OSCE's 1990 Document of the Copenhagen Meeting on the Human Dimension, for example, states that the ethnic, cultural, and religious identity of national minorities should be protected 'after due consultations, including contacts with organizations or associations of such minorities'. In practice, minority associations are often included in official consultative bodies, and these associations themselves select (or elect) individual members for these bodies.

But how do minority associations ensure that they are representative of a larger group of minority citizens? How do governments know which minority organizations are representative of a particular minority group? And, once organizations have been selected (or elected) to form an official body, what does such a selection (or election) say about the *extent* to which these organizations are representative and legitimate? Moreover, how do organizations choose candidates for their representation in public bodies? How do minority organizations ensure internal democracy, transparency, and legitimacy? And how can these be gauged and monitored by governments?

The topic raises many questions, and they all warrant complex answers. The issue is complex for several reasons, including the fact that the concepts of democracy, transparency, and legitimacy in general remain open to debate and interpretation. In the case of minority protection arrangements more specifically the complexity is exacerbated by the fact that international standards are not completely clear as to which types of minority associations should be supported in order to promote legitimate forms of minority representation and participation. Minority representation and participation are part of a broad and often vaguely defined field of political action, a field that falls partly within and partly outside of the established institutional frameworks for minority protection. International standards recommend consultation with minority associations, but they do not define the term 'minority association'. To gain better insight into what international standards might mean when they mention minority associations as pivotal actors in minority participation, the first part of this chapter is a conceptual exploration of the subject. It discusses the normative ideas behind the promotion of the role of minority organizations. And it distinguishes the concept of non-governmental organizations (NGOs) from other, related concepts, such as minority self-governments, specialized state bodies for minority representation, minority supportive organizations, ethnic political parties, informal ethnic structures, and transnational advocacy networks. These are different types of organizations, and the political and participatory role of each different type should be assessed differently.

The latter half of the chapter offers a more empirical treatment of the phenomenon. It provides a comparative study of a number of crucial cases in new as well as old EU member states. Several European countries have, for a number of years, implemented institutional arrangements aimed at establishing, fostering, and monitoring the ways in which minorities are organized and the ways in which these organizations are allowed access to government structures. By exploring similarities and differences in these arrangements, I will offer a number of tentative conclusions about their opportunities and limitations. In particular, the chapter will examine two relationships: that between minority populations and the organizations that are meant to represent them, and that between these representative organizations and the monitoring institutions of the state.

The cases examined include the government's consultative body for national minorities in the Czech Republic, the Sami parliament in Norway, the Hungarian minority self-government system, the consultative bodies for race relations in the UK, and the board of minority self-government organizations in Flanders (Belgium). This sample obviously could have been composed differently, but it is wide enough to reflect some of Europe's diversity in this field. It includes cases from the East and the West of Europe, and it explores elected quasi-governmental minority bodies (Hungary and Norway) as well as non-elected consultative bodies based on civil society organizations (Czech Republic, UK, Belgium).

I. Defining the Role of Minority Associations

A. Conceptual and normative considerations

When international standards on minority protection turn to issues of representation and participation they often focus on the role of minority associations. Protection systems should not only be devised *for* minorities, as these documents imply, they should also be created, at least in part, by minorities themselves, and this should happen through the work of their associations. What are the reasons behind the idea that associations should play an essential role in fostering political representation and participation?

One reason is conceptual: minority groups are not individual actors, they are comprised of numerous citizens who do not necessarily have a connection apart from the fact that they are seen as belonging to the same minority group. Minority associations on the other hand *are* actors. They are formally organized, they often have membership criteria, and they usually have leaders and spokespersons. While it is not possible to engage in meaningful policy dialogue with a minority as a whole, it is possible to have such a discussion with a limited number of organizations representing a minority.

This point may seem self-evident, but its implications for the policy-making process need to be carefully considered. Every form of democratic government, including minority governance, relies to some extent on the cooperation of those who are governed. In order to foster the representation and participation of minorities, states have to communicate and collaborate with the people who affiliate themselves with particular minority groups. In practice this is less straightforward, since there is usually no way of knowing exactly who feels connected to which group. It is not possible to 'talk' to a national minority as a whole because a minority is not a single, clearly identifiable political protagonist. The term national minority does not describe a pre-existing, pre-political reality so much as it is a label that creates such a reality. People can be grouped under a particular minority label, or they may choose to affiliate themselves with it. Yet people may be grouped under other, competing categories at the same time. People may be seen, or see themselves, as members of a gender group, a nation, a family, a socio-economic class, a religious collective, a language group, a territorially defined unit and so on. People who, from one particular perspective, belong to the same community may in other important ways stand in opposition to each other. The existence of a minority group is thus not a given, but rather is the result of the act of making one label more prominent and more relevant as a frame for identification and affiliation. The making of a national minority is something that is actively pursued (through discrimination or through emancipation) not by the abstract collective of a national minority itself, but by particular actors, including organizations and individual ethno-political activists. To formulate this more provocatively, one could say that national minority activists or ethno-political entrepreneurs 'produce' national minorities, not the other way around. Brubaker has made the point that:

[W]e can think of a national minority not as a fixed entity or a unitary group but rather in terms of the *field of differentiated and competitive positions or stances* adopted by different organizations, parties, movements, or individual political entrepreneurs, each seeking to 'represent' the minority to its own putative members, to the host state, or to the outside world, each seeking to monopolize the legitimate representation of the group.[1]

Minority organizations are central to the political endeavour of ensuring a collective voice for a minority because they are identifiable, registered entities that can act as negotiating partners for policy-makers and because they may be seen (or at least may present themselves) as representative of a larger population. Indeed, a state cannot ensure a voice for national minorities without ratifying particular organized national minority activists. These activists may have competing conceptions about who belongs and who does not belong to 'their' group.

There is also a normative background to the matter. Implicit in the recommendation of minority protection standards is the idea that citizens should form independent organizations in order to participate more fully in the cultural, economic, social, and political fields of interaction that make up a democratic society. Since the fall of communism in Central and Eastern Europe, the democratic value of minority participation has increasingly been regarded as a

---

[1] R Brubaker, *Nationalism Reframed: Nationhood and the national question in the new Europe* (1996), 61.

crucial ingredient of democracy. In part this is linked to the particularities of history in this region. In Central and Eastern Europe, the emergence from below of 'a highly articulated, organized, autonomous, and mobilizable civil society'[2] was the cornerstone of the popular protests that undermined the communist regimes. Hence, also after 1989, non-governmental organizations were increasingly recognized as the region's 'connective tissue of democratic culture'.[3] The idea that minority organizations could play a crucial role in the realization of minority protection mechanisms has to some extent also been the result of the growing prevalence of the principle of deliberative democracy. In sum, according to a theory of civil society (as promoted for example by Cohen and Arato[4]), democracy can be deepened through various forms of voluntary associative activity, including the activity of minority associations.

B. What kind of associations? Locating different types of association on a spectrum of public participation

Participation in politics is usually associated in the first place with electoral politics and political parties. Mainstream parties in the multi-party systems of most European countries often identify themselves by an ideological label. Yet, in the same way as there are nationalist parties or identity-oriented parties for cultural or ethnic majorities, in elections national minority activists may decide to stand not on an ideological platform but on an ethnic basis, and form political committees as part of a larger party or as independent political parties. The Framework Convention for the Protection of National Minorities (FCNM) has sought to secure the rights of freedom of peaceful assembly; freedom of association; freedom of expression; and freedom of thought, conscience, and religion, which is a provision sometimes interpreted by the Advisory Committee of the FCNM as a stand against prohibiting the establishment of national minority parties organizing on an ethnic basis.

But while international documents may implicitly suggest that states should permit the existence of national minority parties, international institutions are often wary about the value of ethnically defined parties. The Explanatory Note by the experts of the Lund Recommendations shows awareness of the potential dangers of isolation and fragmentation posed by the establishment of political parties along ethnically defined lines. But it nevertheless argues that it might—sometimes temporarily—be a good solution:

While full respect for equal rights and non-discrimination will reduce or eliminate the demand and need for political parties formed on the basis of ethnic ties, in some

---

[2] JL Cohen and A Arato, *Civil Society and Political Theory* (1997), 32.
[3] JR Wedel, 'US aid to Central and Eastern Europe, 1990–1994: An analysis of aid models and responses' in JP Hardt and RF Kaufman (eds), *East-Central European Economies in Transition* (1995), 323.   [4] Cohen and Arato, *Civil Society and Political Theory* (n 2 above).

situations such communal parties may be the only hope for effective representation of specific interests and, thus, for effective participation. [Article II.b.8]

Besides political parties, however, all kinds of other organizations and groupings, which are rather part of the realm between the private and the public sphere, may function as a form of minority representation. These civil society associations include registered associations with names and activities that suggest a strong concern with the formulation and defence of the interests of particular national minorities. They may also include more informal and episodic gatherings that might not necessarily have a political aims, such as ad hoc protest groups, religious gatherings, and cultural groups. Of course, the boundary between these categories is blurry: a group may find itself in the hybrid area between episodic and more established, or it can shift from one category to the other. The role, function, and value of a particular minority organization should be judged on the basis of what these organizations themselves put forward as a goal. Not all organizations can or will aim to speak in the name of a minority, but those organizations that do claim to be representative of the entire minority should be expected to be transparent about how such level of representation is reached.

Although minority organizations may vary in terms of stated goals, representative quality, or political commitment, as a category they are to be distinguished from supportive organizations. Minority support organizations are typically NGOs that stand up for minority interests but do consider themselves to be part of a minority. Such organizations may work together across state borders and form a transnational advocacy network. Transnational advocacy networks have attracted the attention of scholars who study the diffusion and power of international norms. One of the arguments proposed in this literature contends that through emphasizing the norms of universal human rights, international NGOs are able to support domestic opposition movements demanding political change in norm-violating states. For example, Risse and Sikkink argue that international NGOs advocating human rights have played a crucial role in mobilizing domestic opposition and legitimating the claims of local social movements in such diverse regions as Latin America, Africa, and Eastern Europe.[5] Since the beginning of the 1990s, a growing transnational advocacy network has focused on the situation of national minorities in Central and Eastern Europe. A number of international NGOs have criticized the lack of minority protection mechanisms in these countries and conducted campaigns aimed at changing government behaviour, educating citizens, and raising awareness of rights within minority communities. The political initiatives of advocacy organizations that focused on Central and Eastern Europe was greatly

---

[5] T Risse and K Sikkink, 'The socialization of international human rights norms into domestic practices: Introduction' in T Risse, SC Ropp and K Sikkink (eds), *The Power of Human Rights: International norms and domestic change* (1999), 1–38.

helped by the EU's conditionality policy. Since the EU demanded that its prospective members adhere to the principles of minority protection, transnational advocacy groups had an opportunity to pressure states into taking particular commitments seriously.

Besides political parties, non-governmental minority associations and supportive organizations, there are also state bodies specifically aimed at representing minorities. These special public bodies usually involve delegates from non-governmental minority organizations or experts from supportive organizations. The character and composition of these bodies may differ from country to country. In some states expert bodies have been set up with the sole purpose of consultation. In other cases an elected minority self-government or minority parliament has been established with some structural power of influence. These bodies can operate at the level of central, regional, or local government. Minority self-governments can take the form of non-territorial or territorial autonomy bodies. In the latter case, they are sometimes part of a federalization, devolution, or regionalization process. In themselves these constitutional arrangements ensure the participation of various recognized regional entities in public affairs. But in turn, the regional entities may also themselves become responsible for the promotion of civil society activity among regional minority groups, for example through subsidizing non-governmental minority associations at the regional level.

II. Representation and Participation through Non-governmental Minority Associations and Specialized State Bodies: Opportunities and Limits

A. Effective representation and participation

The idea behind the Lund Recommendations is to encourage states to adopt measures that might foster the participation of minority representatives in organized civil society, including media, and in decision-making and governing institutions in order to alleviate tension between minorities and majorities and thus to prevent conflict. Such participation should ideally be achieved both in cultural affairs as well as at the level of politics. The Recommendations suggest a number of areas where such increasing representative participation ideally should be achieved:

1. at the level of central government through reserved seats in parliament, cabinet and civil service positions, or in local government structures (ss II.A and II.C)
2. in politics more broadly through electoral arrangements (s II.B), advisory and consultative bodies (section II.D)
3. through territorial or non-territorial self-governance arrangements (s III).

What underpins all of these options is that there should be an 'inclusive, transparent, and accountable process of consultation in order to maintain a climate of confidence' (Art I.5). The Explanatory Note to the Recommendations expands on the democratic value of an inclusive dialogue:

In the framework of democracy, the process of decision-making is as important as the substance of decisions made. Since good governance is not only of the people but also for the people, its processes should always be inclusive of those concerned, transparent for all to see and judge, and accountable to those affected. Only such processes will inspire and maintain public confidence. Inclusive processes may comprise consultation, polling, referenda, negotiation and even the specific consent of those directly affected.

It is, in other words, important to find actors who can be considered representative of 'those concerned'. How can the effectiveness of such minority-interest representation in politics be guaranteed? When the issue pertains to the field of democratically elected minority citizens in mainstream institutions (eg, minority politicians who have been elected to the parliament on a mainstream ticket, as candidates of a national minority party or through special procedures such as reserved seats or lower thresholds) then there is no real problem. Or at least, effectiveness here is seen simply as the responsibility of those democratically elected; they are accountable to their voters and can be evaluated by those voters in elections.

The issue is more complex when interest representation does not happen through mainstream electoral procedures but through specialized bodies for consultation. As the Advisory Committee of the FCNM noted in its 2008 Report: 'Consultation alone does not ... constitute a sufficient mechanism for ensuring *effective* participation of persons belonging to national minorities' (emphasis in original).[6] One might consider the word 'effective' here to refer not only to the outcome of the process of participation but also to the process itself. How does one ensure there is a form of participation that is capable of bringing the right interests to the attention of policy-makers. Especially when consultation is done through a single body with members of different representative organizations per minority, there might be disagreement about what the interests of each minority are. And even minority organizations representing the same minority might have competing demands. In other cases, taking into account only one representative per minority group does not always do justice to the diversity within minority groups. The example of the Roma comes to mind here. While the Roma are recognized as a single national minority in many countries (and some international bodies increasingly see them as a transnational

---

[6] Advisory Committee on the Framework Convention for the Protection of National Minorities, 'Commentary on the effective participation of persons belonging to national minorities in cultural, social, and economic life and in public affairs,' ACFV/31DOC(2008)001, 2008, 28.

ethnic group), the situation in which they find themselves differs from country to country and might even vary regionally within countries.[7]

What do states do to deal with this problem? Obviously the possibilities are not unlimited. The prerequisite for any democratic participation through minority associations is that states protect the liberties of association and assembly. On the other hand, states will try to interfere through monitoring or even organizing the mechanisms that allow organizations to elect or delegate representatives. Possibilities include procedures for the evaluation of organizations' internal election or appointment procedures, demands for transparency, and the establishment of formal contacts with the organization's members, or with the wider group, through public activities. Appointment procedures may be defined from the top down, but the state may also organize special elections in order to create minority representative institutions. Let me examine a number of examples in detail.

B. Non-elected consultative bodies

The Czech Republic is a country with a small number of relatively small minority groups, but as a result of the EU's conditionality policy (and in response to growing international attention to the plight of the country's largest minority group, the Roma) the Czech government has increasingly relied on special consultative institutions that facilitate discussion with delegates from minority organizations. The most important state institution for minorities is the Government Council for National Minorities (*Rada vlády pro národnostní menšiny*), a consultative body that brings together representatives of the largest national minorities and representatives of various ministries and the government administration. In addition, there is also a special consultative body for the Roma, the Interministerial Commission for the Affairs of the Roma Community (*Rada vlády pro záležitosti romské komunity*), an advisory team for national minority cultures at the Ministry of Culture, and an advisory team for national minority education at the Education Ministry. At the regional and municipal level there are national minority committees or boards.

These institutions are meant to organize and represent the voice of a large and diverse field of minority organizations. They continue to struggle, however, with the issue of input representation. This is most clearly the case at the level of central government. One problem, for example, is that the Government Council for National Minorities does not automatically cover all potential national minority groups. The Jews are not considered to be a national minority, rather a religious group, but in practice the problems they face are not entirely dissimilar from those of recognized *national* minorities. Although Czech Jews are not

---

[7] P Vermeersch, *The Romani Movement: Minority politics and ethnic mobilization in contemporary Central Europe* (2006).

officially represented in the Government Council, the Czech government has devoted special attention to this group.⁸ Moreover, the Czech Republic has realized that in order to secure the representative character of the Council, the body has to be open to certain changes. After its inception in 1994 the Council comprised just six minority representatives,⁹ although it later included representatives of the Bulgarians, Croats, Hungarians, Germans, Poles, Roma, Ruthenians, Russians, Greeks, Slovaks, and Ukrainians. In 2004, the Serbians were de facto recognized as a national minority and Serbian representatives were included in the Council.

Since the Council is not elected, the issue of representation is dealt with through a number of alternative measures. At the beginning of the process a request to nominate a candidate for the Council is sent to all officially registered minority organizations. These nominations must be confirmed by the statutory organ of the relevant associations. Then, the nominations are approved or amended by the chairperson of the Council. The Council's report describes how this procedure worked during the last nominating round:

> In particular, information had to be disclosed about the nominating organization, with a focus on how representative it is of the given community (number of members, the duplicity of membership of a nominee put forward by multiple organizations, the body making the decision on the nomination, the level of support enjoyed by the nominee within the organization, etc.). At the same time, the definition of an entity eligible to nominate a candidate to the Council was expanded to take into account the needs of traditional minorities with an unfavourable population structure and lack of means to carry out their activities.¹⁰

The last sentence means that the Council for National Minorities takes into account the possibility that minorities might not have the appropriate organizations to secure representation. Moreover, the Council's secretariat is also 'in contact' with the organizations for national minorities that do not have a seat in the Council. It is likely that minority organizations will start to adapt to this procedure since it creates a political opportunity for interest representation. Some minority groups are well represented and have minority umbrella organizations that have the specific purpose of defending the interests of the group (thus in a sense making the group a special target of national minority policy). Other minority groups (the Croats and the Serbs), however, do not yet have a formal umbrella association. Although this is a nomination process specifically for organizations (and not an electoral procedure among minority citizens), it is, according to the secretariat of the Council, widely accepted among the

---

⁸ Advisory Committee on the Framework Convention for the Protection of National Minorities, Second Opinion on the Czech Republic, ACFC/INF/OP/II(2005)002, 24 February 2005, 9.
⁹ Vermeersch, *The Romani Movement* (n 7 above), 81.
¹⁰ Office of the Government of the Czech Republic Secretariat of the Council for National Minorities of the Government of the Czech Republic, 'Report on the situation of national minorities in the Czech Republic in 2006', Prague, 2007, 7.

participating organizations as a fair and transparent way of dealing with the issue. The government has tried to ensure such transparency by stimulating the formation of a unified platform for the representation of minority organizations. At the end of the 1990s, an Association of National Minority Organizations was established. This, however, did not prove to be a success: there remains a low level of coordinated action among organizations from the different minorities.[11]

Summarizing the case of the Czech Republic, one might say that the main quality challenge has been to ensure that the people who are selected as members of officially sanctioned minority representative bodies are indeed regarded as representatives by the group they claim to represent. Other countries face additional challenges. For example, the need to make sure that the *composition* of the minority consultative body actually reflects the situation on the ground. In the case of the Czech Republic there may not have been a complete consensus on which organizations should send delegates to the Council for National Minorities, but at least there has been a rather high level of agreement among political actors and independent organizations about which groups should be regarded as 'national minorities'. In the case of countries with a much more complex recent history of migration—post-colonial or otherwise—the situation is rather different. The UK and Belgium are good examples of the latter category.

While it is clear, and officially acknowledged, that the UK is a multicultural society, and that the recognition of minority groups plays an important role in the fostering of such a workable multicultural society, there is some confusion as to how exactly to single out groups for special representation as the country's national minorities. Obviously one element of guarding and fostering peaceful societal relations among citizens with different cultural, ethnic, national, or religious affiliations is the introduction of anti-discrimination legislation and anti-racism campaigns. The basis of anti-discrimination legislation in the UK was laid mainly by the 1976 Race Relations Act—which makes discriminating against particular groups unlawful in various fields of life, including employment, housing, education, and the provision of goods, facilities and services—and the amendment of that act in 2000, which has placed 'numerous public bodies under a specific positive duty to promote equality of opportunities and interracial relations'.[12] Yet one issue that has remained permanently unresolved within this legal context is: which groups are considered minorities? The Race Relations Act has offered a legal framework to define 'racial groups', but recognition as a racial group does not necessarily coincide with recognition of the status of what the Lund Recommendations or other international instruments have called 'national minorities'.

---

[11] I thank Milan Pospíšil of the Secretariat of the Council for National Minorities for providing me with the necessary information.
[12] J Turner, 'Minority rights protection in the United Kingdom' (2001–2) 1 *European Yearbook of Minority Issues* 395–424, 399.

Within this context, the UK has not chosen to establish a consultative body that claims to represent all national minorities and, hence, no electoral procedures for such a consultative body have been installed. But there have been attempts to include members from particular target groups in the policy discussion on minority issues. The emphasis has clearly not been placed on representation but on expert consultation. In 1999, for example, a twenty-eight member Race Relations Forum was established at the Home Office. It served to provide ethnic-minority communities with a new channel of communication with the government. It was explicitly meant to serve the Home Secretary. The idea was to make the government consider the Forum's recommendations when formulating new policies on minority issues. Although the members of this forum were chosen on the basis of their expertise as well as their being prominent members of particular target communities, the issue of representation was not dealt with in any direct way.

Later, ad hoc measures for the recognition of minority organizations ratified their role as official minority delegates in (informal) consultative bodies. Such consultation rounds have been time-limited and have been aimed at offering advice to the government on specific priority issues. One such project group has been the REACH group, established in February 2006, aimed at 'raising the aspirations and achievement among Black boys and young Black men'.[13] It consists of twenty-five members, including not only people who might be seen as representative of the target population but also people from support organizations and foundations, from education, local authorities, academia, and law enforcement. Useful as such short-term consultative groups might be, something seems to have been lost through the abolition of the forum as a standing consultation group. In 2007, the Advisory Committee of the FCNM publicly regretted the closure of the Race Relations Forum and the Lawrence Steering Group, two standing committees of minority representatives. The Advisory Committee noted that:

standing consultative structures can play a particularly important role in facilitating the effective participation of persons belonging to minorities in public life by providing a regular forum for dialogue between minorities and government representatives.[14]

Belgium is another instructive example because there, too, discussions about the recognition and representation of minorities have emerged and have had an effect on minority policy consultation methods. Although Belgium has signed the FCNM it has, for reasons related to the ongoing process of federal state reform and the delicate political equilibrium between political representatives of

---

[13] REACH, 'An independent report to government on raising the aspirations and attainments of Black boys and young Black men' (2007), available at <http://www.communities.gov.uk/documents/communities/pdf/reach-report.pdf> (accessed 31 July 2009).

[14] Advisory Committee on the Framework Convention for the Protection Of National Minorities, Second Opinion on the United Kingdom, ACFC/OP/II(2007)003, 6 June 2007, 45.

the two main language groups that are needed to push this process forward, not found a parliamentary majority to ratify it. Because of its political history, Belgian state authorities distinguish between the main linguistic groups and smaller immigrant groups. Minority policies in Belgium mainly pertain to these latter groups, but they cannot be understood entirely out of the context of the development of the relationship between the former.

Since the early 1970s, Belgium has undergone a number of profound constitutional changes that increasingly paved the way for the institutionalization of linguistic difference. As a result Belgium now has three regions: Flanders, with about 6 million inhabitants; Wallonia, with a population of almost 3.5 million; and the Brussels Capital Region, with a population of just under 1 million. Only the latter region has bilingual status. The official language communities in Belgium are not considered minorities, even if people are present in a region where their language is not the official administrative language.[15] But besides these major language divisions, there are divisions between Belgian citizens who are seen as autochthonous and citizens coming from a variety of foreign national backgrounds, who often also come from another linguistic background. The presence of these groups is in large part the result of immigration waves in the 1950s and 1960s. About 8 per cent of the Belgium population is officially seen as belonging to what is called an ethno-cultural minority, a term which is mainly reserved for people with roots in African or non-EU Mediterranean countries.[16] A wide range of organizations claim to represent one or several of these groups.

The status of these organizations has been different in different parts of the country. In Wallonia the individualist republican model of France is adopted and therefore no ethnically defined organizations can be recognized or subsidized in that region.[17] Policies there focus on youth work, the fight against economic inequality, and anti-discrimination. In Flanders, however, associations established on the basis of ethno-cultural affiliation have been subsidized since 1995. The Flemish government has also stimulated the formation of umbrella associations; these bring together a broad field of local organizations, usually organizations from the same minority group. In the case of the Moroccans and the Turks there are several umbrella groups per minority, which reveals regional

---

[15] In twenty-seven municipalities, however, linguistic facilities are offered to people who are affiliated with another linguistic community. These facilities provide a possibility for communication with the local or federal administration in an official language that is not the language of the territory to which the municipality belongs. See W Swenden, 'Personality versus territoriality: Belgium and the Framework Convention for the Protection of National Minorities' (2002–3) 2 *European Yearbook of Minority Issues* 331–56.

[16] M Hooghe, 'Ethnic organisations and social movement theory: The political opportunity structure for ethnic mobilisation in Flanders' (2005) 31(5) *Journal of Ethnic and Migration Studies* 975–90, 976.

[17] D Jacobs and M Swyngedouw, 'Het verenigingsleven van allochtonen van Marokkaanse en Turkse origine te Brussel' in B Khader, M Martiniello, A Rea and C Timmerman (eds), *Immigratie en integratie anders denken* (2006), 131–52.

divisions within minority groups. A large number of local organizations have not become members of any umbrella association and, hence, do not receive subsidies.

All of this has its bearing on processes of political representation and consultation. While ethnic minority representation is not possible in Wallonia, the Flemish government has established a Forum for Ethno-cultural Minorities, which is an umbrella organization that serves as the contact point between the government and fourteen umbrella associations of ethnocultural minorities in Flanders and Brussels. Especially in the field of education and employment, the forum formulates demands and seeks to influence policy developments. The composition of the forum is based on an internal election procedure: the member organizations have the opportunity to elect a limited number of board members. The forum only has umbrella associations as members and it can therefore not claim to represent all minority associations in Flanders and Brussels. Through the umbrella organizations, however, it does maintain contact with more than 700 such associations. The views of the forum appear in the media and are represented at meetings of the thematic commissions that formulate advice for the Flemish government, such as the Flemish Education Council (*Vlaamse Onderwijsraad*) or the Social-economic Council of Flanders (*Sociaal-Economische Raad van Vlaanderen*).

C. Elected bodies

Some countries have opted for popularly elected minority representation. The introduction of such a special electoral system for minorities should perhaps not be seen as a substitute for the creation and fostering of voluntary associations, but it can be an important tool for the creation of a legitimate representative body at the level of local or central policy-making. In a number of cases, such a system is embedded in the larger context of either a personal or a territorial autonomy regime. In federal states, where minority groups form an entity of the federation, the election of minority representatives is simply a feature of the electoral system. Special elections as part of non-territorial autonomy arrangements are less common and deserve special attention. The Lund Recommendations place special emphasis on the positive potential of such non-territorial autonomy arrangements. Two examples illustrate its potential, but also its limits: the Sami parliament in Norway and the Hungarian national minority self-governments.

The Sami parliament is a body of currently forty-three representatives and functions mainly as an institution that must guarantee cultural autonomy for the citizens of Norway who affiliate themselves with the Sami heritage. The institution should be seen as part of a larger effort by the Norwegian government to recognize the Sami as an aboriginal population and grant them major language and cultural rights.[18] Finland and Sweden have similar bodies for indigenous populations. In Norway, the Sami parliament first convened in 1989 and has, since then, accumulated political responsibilities.[19] It mainly has competence over the distribution of funds allocated to foster Sami culture and education.

The Sami parliament is a body for minority interest representation and minority governance that shares important features with officially appointed minority institutions in other European countries, but it differs from the advisory bodies discussed above in that its composition is not dependent on voluntary associations and its representatives are elected and not appointed. The Sami parliament is elected by direct vote from thirteen electoral constituencies. Although such a system bypasses to some extent the debate about whether civil-society organizations should be considered an essential component of a democratic society, it can ensure its representative quality in more transparent ways than a system of appointed bodies. While appointed bodies might be imputed with being established through a procedure that does not involve minority citizens themselves (only a selection of organizations), a system of elected minority bodies can claim to have avoided this democratic deficit. Yet minority elections do not solve all the problems linked to the establishment of a system of minority representation.

One of the problems it does not entirely solve is the issue of legitimacy. In the case of elections to the Sami parliament, for example, the question of whether the results can be accepted as legitimate depends on how well the number of registered voters reflects the number of citizens of Sami origin. Since these are elections in which not all Norwegian citizens can automatically vote, the registration process itself becomes politically charged. To what extent is the population registered as Sami seen as a good approximation of the Sami population as a whole? Observers point out that in recent elections the number of people who were registered as Sami in the Sami electoral roster (a prerequisite for participation in the elections) was much lower than the number of people who could linguistically be defined as belonging to the Sami population.[20] In 2001, estimates suggested that as many as 45,000 people could theoretically be identified as Sami, but less than 10,000 people registered for the Sami electoral roster.[21] The introduction of a system of ethnic registration, needed to establish an elected minority body, may thus open up new avenues for contestation within the minority population. According to research by Anne Julie Semb, in the case

---

[18] D Corson, 'Norway's "Sámi Language Act": Emancipatory implications for the world's aboriginal peoples' (1995) 24 *Language in Society* 493–514.
[19] C Smith, 'The development of Sami rights since 1980' in T Brantenberg, J Hansen and H Minde (eds), *Becoming Visible: Indigenous politics and self-government* (1995).
[20] AJ Semb, 'Sami self-determination in the making' (2005) 11(4) *Nations and Nationalism* 531–49.
[21] Ibid, 534.

of the Sami the discussion about the need for registration is part of a wider contestation over the Sami parliament among Sami organizations:

> The largest Sami organisation in 1987, the Norwegian Sami Union (*Samenes Landsforbund*), strongly opposed the establishment of the Sami Parliament, as the organisation believed that the Sami Electoral Roster would create tensions between registered and non-registered Sami and increase tensions between Sami, ethnic Norwegians and descendants from early Finnish-speaking immigrants, who are called Kvens (*kvener*). The Association of Norwegian Sami Reindeer Herders, (*Norske Reindriftsamers Landsforbund*) also opposed the proposed Sami Parliament, fearing that they would not be adequately represented by the proposed electoral system.[22]

There is clearly a rationale for states to introduce minority elections: they can hope to circumvent the problem of having to select one or several minority organizations as the only acknowledged representative of the wider minority population. As noted earlier, minority organizations often compete among themselves not only over who is more representative of a given minority population but also about how a minority population should be defined. Often the two issues go hand in hand. Once an organization is able to make its own definition dominant, it can more easily claim to be an organization that best represents that minority. In an electoral contest, however, minority citizens choose their own representatives, and these representatives go uncontested as long as the procedure is accepted by all those who participate in the elections. In theory, voluntary associations are not needed to create any form of political representation. In practice, however, it is hard to imagine a system of democratic minority representation that would not involve some sort of participation by minority organizations. As is clear from the Sami example, elections do not really solve the problem of democratic legitimacy. Every minority election will be preceded by a decision as to how minority citizens must be registered. Even in the case of the Sami, where there has generally not been much debate over the voting rules for the Sami parliament, the introduction of a particular registration procedure was a process that opened new avenues for contestation.

In the end, it is often the case that elected minority bodies coexist with non-elected non-governmental organizations that seek to represent the same group. In the case of the Sami, one such non-elected group is the Sami Council, a transnational association that since 1956 has represented voluntary Sami associations from Finland, Russia, Norway, and Sweden and seeks recognition for the rights of the Sami as a nation, the boundaries of which would cut across existing state borders.[23]

---

[22] Ibid, 534–5.
[23] See official website of the Sami Council, available at <http://www.saamicouncil.net> (accessed 31 July 2009).

A similar debate concerning the legitimacy and representative quality of elected and non-elected minority organizations has taken place in Hungary.[24] Through Law LXXVII of 1993 on the Rights of National and Ethnic Minorities, Hungary granted its thirteen officially recognized 'historical' minorities (twelve 'national minorities' with external kin states and the Roma (Gypsies) as an 'ethnic minority') a far-reaching form of cultural autonomy. This autonomy was realized through a system of elected local and national self-government. Since the mid-1990s members of *local* self-governments in Hungary can be elected by the population of towns and villages where minorities are sufficiently present, while the members of *national* minority self-governments (representing the minority at the country-wide level) are elected by an electoral body that consists of the members of local minority self-governments. In 2006, 1,118 local Roma minority self-governments were formed.[25] According to the Minorities Law, local minority self-governments are fully responsible for the development and management of local minority educational and cultural institutions. The national self-governments were created to regulate consultative rights for these minorities.

After the system was put into effect it did not take long before the legislation became the target of serious criticism. The election of the 'Gypsy self-governments' in particular highlighted a number of problems. Although the minority self-government system was not established with the specific aim of improving the living conditions of Hungary's largest and most marginalized minority group, the Roma soon became the single most important topic in the discussion about the value and functioning of the minority self-government system. One of the controversies over the Roma related to the question of legitimate representation.

Here the problem was not that too few people voted in the minority elections and that therefore the elections could be diagnosed as non-representative; the problem here was that there were rather too many voters. In the local elections of December 1994 almost 900,000 people voted for Roma self-governments all over the country, while the number of Roma electors in even the most optimistic estimates was not higher than 200,000.[26] The fact that so many additional voters had participated in the election was officially explained by reference to 'sympathy voters'.[27] Many Roma activists and independent observers felt that this explanation was implausible, or at least insufficient. In their view, the high voter turnout illustrated a major weakness of the system, namely, the lack of

---

[24] My discussion of the Hungarian case draws on a more detailed analysis in Vermeersch, *The Romani Movement* (n 7 above), 72–9.

[25] National Democratic Institute for International Affairs, 'The Hungary minority self-government system as a means of increasing Romani political participation', Assessment Report, 2007.

[26] M Kovats, 'The development of Roma politics in Hungary 1989–95', Unpublished doctoral dissertation, University of Portsmouth, 1998, 129.

[27] T Doncsev, 'Minorities: Recent changes in the condition of national and ethnic minorities', Lecture at the conference of the Hungarian Academy of Sciences and the Office for National and Ethnic Minorities, 8–9 April 1999, Budapest, 3.

voter registration. According to the law, every voter in the 'regular' local elections could decide to vote for a candidate on the list of the minority self-government, independently of whether that voter identified herself or himself as a member of a minority. The openness of the system made it vulnerable to manipulation and led some Roma organizations to question the legitimacy of some of the elected candidates. Were they really elected by 'the Roma'? As one activist said:

> The electoral system is ... absolutely ill-devised. Everyone can vote for the minority self-government. It is as if the prime minister [of Hungary] would be elected in Germany. How should a non-Roma who is not involved in the Roma communities be able to decide who is a good representative and who not?[28]

Some even went as far as to question the value of the existence of the National Gypsy Minority Self-government. This distrust was exacerbated by the fact that the first election for the National Gypsy Minority Self-government was held in Szolnok, stronghold and home base of one of the main Roma organizations contending in the elections, Lungo Drom. The success of the Lungo Drom coalition—it won all fifty-three seats in 1995 and 1999—raised the suspicions of many Roma that its advancement had been patronized by the Hungarian government.[29] Moreover, doubts about the legitimacy of the elected Roma candidates on the local level were further triggered by the fact that—as the Hungarian press pointed out—some of the elected candidates had no clear link to the local constituencies where they were elected. Some observers even reported problems with people standing as candidates for two minorities.[30] At the time of the 2002 local minority self-government elections, the results could be compared with recent census data. Such comparison revealed that there were some municipalities where minority elections had been initiated despite the fact that according to the census data nobody there had professed to be a member of a minority community.[31]

At that time, parliamentary minority ombudsman Jenő Kaltenbach argued that the only real solution to this problem was the introduction of some kind of ethnic registration of minority voters. Only voters who are registered as minority members, he contended, should be allowed to cast a vote on a minority self-government list. This solution was reluctantly contemplated by Hungarian politicians since it was deemed to contradict one of the basic principles of the

---

[28] Quoted in Vermeersch, *The Romani Movement* (n 7 above), 73.
[29] M Kovats, 'The political significance of the First National Gypsy Self-government (Országos Kisebbségi Önkormányzat)' (2001) 1 *Journal of Ethnopolitics and Minority Issues in Europe* 9, available at <http://www.ecmi.de/jemie/download/Focus11-2001Kovats.pdf> (accessed 31 July 2009).
[30] I Riba, 'Minority self-governments in Hungary' (1999) 40(155) *The Hungarian Quarterly* 80–99.
[31] J Kaltenbach, 'Report 2002', Budapest: Parliamentary Commissioner for National and Ethnic Minority Rights, 2003.

minority protection system, the freedom to choose one's own ethnic identity. In 2005, however, next to a number of other changes in the self-government system, a registration procedure was introduced. After years of negotiations on the subject, the Hungarian parliament introduced an amendment to the law that now requires candidates for minority self-governments, including the Roma, to be nominated by a minority association. In addition, voters now need to declare their ethnicity and register before they can vote in the minority self-government elections.

The basic competencies and powers of local and national self-governments did not change however, which, according to many observers, is the main cause of the lack of increased legitimacy of the system among the Roma. One report commissioned by the OSCE notes the following:

Lack of voter education and registration, segregated polling places, and required declaration of ethnicity are all problematic. While the amendments may have resolved the previous problem of non-minorities 'hijacking' the [minority self-government] system, they also seem to depress voter turnout and further de-legitimize [minority self-government] representatives who are elected by only a fraction of their community's voters.[32]

The report further recommends reconsidering the role of non-elected voluntary associations. The Hungarian self-government system might not be enough to ensure a legitimate form of minority participation and it seems reasonable to expect a reappraisal of the role of non-elected minority associations. The latter might be involved, together with elected minority bodies, in monitoring the policies of local and national governments.

III. Conclusion

The purpose of this chapter has been to illustrate the fact that discussions about issues of minority political representation, internal democracy among minorities, and legitimacy of minority associations are to be found in a wide variety of forms. While political participation of minorities clearly benefits from systems that offer some sort of power to elected or selected minority members of minority organizations, the election and selection procedures in themselves usually cannot completely avoid the fact that the representative quality of the established minority bodies is often questioned. For a number of years, several European countries have implemented institutional arrangements aimed at establishing, fostering, and monitoring the political representation and participation of minorities through increasing their control over elected or selected self-governing

---

[32] National Democratic Institute for International Affairs, 'The Hungary minority self-government system' (n 25 above), 7.

organizations. By exploring similarities and differences in these arrangements, this chapter has demonstrated the opportunities that might be available to minority activists in these arrangements, but also the limits. Indeed, the promotion of elected or selected consultative or governing bodies for minorities proves to be an option that is often welcomed by minority activists. It clearly has its advantages. But it would be an illusion to think that it can solve *all* the problems of political participation and representation facing our contemporary multicultural democracies.

PART VI

IMPLEMENTATION ISSUES

25

Minority Participation in Bilateral and International Reporting and Monitoring Processes

Emma Lantschner

I. Introduction	705
II. Relevance of the Issue within the Wider Area of Effective Participation	707
III. Analysis of the Relevant Provisions in International or Bilateral Documents	708
A. The documents of the CSCE/OSCE	710
B. The Framework Convention for the Protection of National Minorities	714
C. The UN Declaration	718
D. Bilateral agreements	719
IV. Implementation Practice	721
A. Monitoring and reporting on the FCNM	721
B. Practice of the Advisory Committee	721
C. State practice	723
V. How Do Minorities Steer their Destiny	727
A. Monitoring practice of bilateral agreements	728
B. Practice of the Advisory Committee	728
C. State practice	729
VI. Overall Assessment	734

I. Introduction

Persons belonging to national minorities are very often sidelined in purely domestic decision-making processes; consequently, most of the existing studies on minority participation focus on the national context. However, the international dimension should not be neglected. This chapter will aim to fill this lack of analysis by focusing on the final element of a chain that starts with negotiations on a bilateral or international treaty related to the protection of minorities, continues with the drafting and the adoption of such a treaty, and ends with its implementation and monitoring. The 'protected subjects' of such treaties, persons belonging to national minorities, should be part of this process from the beginning through to the end.

Within that process, this chapter will focus on a very specific aspect of minority participation in international and bilateral relations: the *monitoring* of treaty obligations related to the protection of minorities and, if applicable, respective *reporting* obligations.

Treaties provide for different mechanisms to oversee their implementation. While some provide for a complaints procedure,[1] others oblige states parties to regularly deliver reports on the state of implementation of the respective treaty which are then evaluated by a specific body.[2] A combination of these two procedures—complaints and reporting procedures—is also possible.[3] Other treaties establish a monitoring body with the aim of evaluating the implementation of the treaty in its states parties without previously receiving a report by the respective states.[4] Leaving out the complaints procedure, this chapter provides an analysis of how persons affected by the treaty provisions, persons belonging to national minorities, are involved in the work of international and bilateral monitoring bodies, and in the respective reporting processes where these exist.

At the international level, this chapter focuses on minority participation in the reporting and monitoring processes of the Framework Convention for the Protection of National Minorities (FCNM). This is primarily for two reasons. First, because the main actor in the monitoring of the Convention, the Advisory Committee (AC) on the FCNM has, in its recent Commentary on Participation,[5] established 'standards' for how states should involve minority representatives in their reporting obligations and these rules can also be considered *mutatis mutandis* applicable to other treaties with reporting obligations. The second reason for focusing on the FCNM is because the practice of the AC offers comprehensive illustrative material on how it involved minorities in its own monitoring.

No reporting procedures exist for bilateral agreements and therefore the focus will be on the involvement of minorities in the activities of the monitoring bodies of these agreements, the Joint Intergovernmental Commissions.

---

[1] Eg, European Convention on Human Rights.
[2] Eg, the European Charter for the Protection of Regional or Minority Languages; the Framework Convention for the Protection of National Minorities.
[3] Eg, the International Covenant on Civil and Political Rights; the International Convention on the Elimination of All Forms of Racial Discrimination.
[4] Eg, the European Convention for the Prevention of Torture and Inhuman or Degrading Treatment or Punishment; most bilateral agreements on good neighbourly relations or bilateral agreements concerning the protection of minorities.
[5] AC, Commentary on the Effective Participation of Persons Belonging to National Minorities in Cultural, Social, and Economic Life and in Public Affairs (hereinafter 'Commentary on Participation'), adopted on 27 February 2008, ACFC/31DOC(2008)001.

The following, more general, considerations will locate the relevance of the issue of minority participation in bilateral and international reporting and monitoring processes within the wider area of effective participation. In section III the relevant provisions in international and bilateral documents are presented in order to subsequently analyse in section IV the implementation practice of various actors with regard to the FCNM and bilateral agreements. Finally, the last section will provide an overall assessment on minority participation in bilateral and international reporting and monitoring processes.

II. Relevance of the Issue within the Wider Area of Effective Participation

The area of effective participation can be subdivided into at least two sub-dimensions. The most obvious is that which focuses on the *substance side* of effective participation. The question here is: in which fields should minorities be involved? The first answer that comes to mind is: public life. Only recently has increased attention been paid to participation in cultural, social, and economic life, although all these fields are strongly interlinked and mutually interdependent.[6]

This chapter deals with the second dimension: the *procedural side* of effective participation. The question to be asked in this case is: how can minorities be involved and how can it be assured that participation is not only symbolic, but effective? The indicator for the effectiveness of participation is the degree of pluralism of procedures.[7] This is valid for all stages of a process, from the drafting of governmental policies and legislation to implementation and monitoring, be it on the national or the bilateral/international level. A multi-directional dialogue during the monitoring of bilateral and international instruments has a good chance of resulting in the beneficial implementation of the instruments. During the monitoring phase, it is essential that the subjects protected by the instruments are given the opportunity to say whether the measures adopted by the government, with whichever intentions, have had the desired or anticipated effect. This is the phase in which minority concerns can be brought to the attention of the government and/or a monitoring body and discussed; in a best-case scenario, solutions will be found. In this sense, consulting minorities in the monitoring phase not only has the potential to prevent conflicts by giving minorities the feeling that their rights and interests and being respected and their views included, but it also presents a chance for resolving a dispute where conflict has already erupted. This conflict preventive or resolving function has even

---

[6] F Palermo, 'The dual meaning of participation: The Advisory Committee's Commentary to Article 15 FCNM' (2008) 7 *European Yearbook of Minority Issues* (forthcoming).   [7] Ibid.

bigger potential in the monitoring of international agreements, due to the involvement of international monitoring bodies as neutral third parties.

So what are the means and instruments for ensuring effective participation in the procedural sense? And which are those most relevant to minority participation in bilateral and international monitoring and reporting processes? To answer these questions, it is useful to recall the distinction between instruments of representation, in the sense of mechanisms that facilitate or guarantee representation in (elected) bodies, and instruments of participation in the narrower sense—meaning consultation mechanisms or veto powers.[8] The element of consultation is clearly the central type of participation in the context of this article.[9] The monitoring bodies, be they at the international or at bilateral level, can in many cases be understood as consultative bodies. This is obviously the case of the Advisory Committee on the FCNM, which, according to the text of the Convention, assists the Committee of Ministers in the evaluation of the states' performance in the implementation of the FCNM.[10] This is also the case of the Joint Intergovernmental Commissions, established to monitor bilateral agreements, as they are supposed to recommend to their respective governments measures concerning the implementation of the respective agreements. Persons belonging to minorities should, of course, be appointed to these bodies. The legal entrenchment of such representation is clearly preferable to mere practice. But independent from the presence of persons belonging to minorities in the monitoring bodies, it is essential that dialogue and consultation with those concerned take place. This goes for both the state, in the fulfilment of its reporting obligations, and the monitoring body, in the fulfilment of its supervisory function. This contributes to pluralism in the process and thus to a more effective participation.

III. Analysis of the Relevant Provisions in International or Bilateral Documents

The general issue of participation of minorities in public life is expressly mentioned only in four international documents: para 35 of the 1990 Document of

---

[8] For a typology of legal instruments in the field of participation see J Marko, 'Effective participation of national minorities: A comment on conceptual, legal and empirical problems', Report prepared for the Committee of Experts on Issues Relating to the Protection of National Minorities, DH-MIN(2006)014, Strasbourg, 20 October 2006, 4–5.

[9] On consultation mechanisms see M Weller, 'Consultation arrangements concerning national minorities', Report prepared for the Committee of Experts on Issues Relating to the Protection of National Minorities, DH-MIN(2005)011, Strasbourg, 24 February 2006. Among the functions of consultative bodies Weller mentions, among other issues, the 'participation in the reporting to international mechanism' (at 12). See further, Committee of Experts on Issues Relating to the Protection of National Minorities, 'DH-MIN Handbook on minority consultative mechanisms', DH-MIN(2006)012, 20 October 2006. [10] Art 26 of the FCNM.

the Copenhagen Meeting on the Human Dimension of the (then) CSCE (hereinafter 'Copenhagen Document'), para 24 of the 1992 CSCE Helsinki Document: The Challenges of Change (hereinafter 'Helsinki Document'), Art 2 of the Declaration of the General Assembly of the UN on the Rights of Persons Belonging to National or Ethnic, Religious, and Linguistic Minorities of 1992 (hereinafter 'UN Declaration'), and Art 15 of the FCNM. However, none of these provisions explicitly addresses the international or bilateral dimension of participation of minorities in monitoring states' obligations. Yet, there is no reason to believe that this sphere is of less importance to minorities. In decisions and activities affecting them, minorities must be involved; otherwise, no confidence will be developed, and suspicion and insecurity will be engendered, promoting or perpetuating conflict.[11]

From the outset, the scarceness of express international provisions on effective participation made it a difficult for the drafters of the Lund Recommendations on the Effective Participation of National Minorities in Public Life (hereinafter 'Lund Recommendations') to come up with 'a meaningful set of recommendations'.[12] It is therefore no surprise that in the Lund Recommendations there is also, at first sight, no specific reference to participation of minorities in monitoring beyond the national scene. Considering the origins of these recommendations, it is clear that they flowed from considerations that were focused primarily on accommodating conflict situations in which minorities sometimes claimed the right to self-determination, in the sense of secession from a state. The purpose was therefore to find ways and means to ensure effective participation of minorities within the boundaries of the state, so as to dissipate such claims.[13] The interstate dimension only came to the fore later, and culminated at the level of OSCE into the Bolzano/Bozen Recommendations on National Minorities and Inter-state Relations (hereinafter 'Bolzano/Bozen Recommendations') of June 2008.[14]

In the following section, the relevant provisions in various international documents are analysed. The approach followed in this exercise is not the usual 'top-down' one, starting with instruments of universal nature (UN documents), and continuing with instruments at the regional European level (OSCE, CoE) to end up with bilateral documents; nor a 'bottom-up' one, detailing the instruments in reverse order. Instead, this analysis will progress from documents with the least specific provisions—both concerning international and bilateral monitoring and reporting—to documents with a more precise focus. Therefore, the more general documents within the realm of the

---

[11] J Packer, 'The origin and nature of the Lund Recommendations on the effective participation of national minorities in public life' (2000) 11(4) *Helsinki Monitor* 29, 31.   [12] Ibid, 36.
[13] Ibid, 31.
[14] For a detailed discussion of the Bolzano/Bozen Recommendations, see N Sabanadze, 'National minorities in interstate relations: Turning menace into promise' (2008) 7 *European Yearbook of Minority Issues*, forthcoming.

OSCE, in particular the Copenhagen and the Helsinki Documents as well as the Lund and Bolzano/Bozen Recommendations will be analysed first. The latter recommendations, the most specific document of the OSCE in the field, will then lead over to the FCNM, which will be examined both from the perspective of which possibilities minorities have to participate in the monitoring of the Convention, and form that of what the FCNM says with regard to the participation of minorities in bilateral bodies. After this, our focus will turn to the UN Declaration as it provides an interesting connection with the bilateral level and the participation of minorities in the relevant bodies, to be dealt with at the end of the chapter.

A. The documents of the CSCE/OSCE

At the level of the OSCE there are two major documents that address explicitly the issue of participation of national minorities in public life. First, there is the Copenhagen Document of 1990 and, second, the Helsinki Document of 1992. Both documents state very generally that participating states must respect the right of persons belonging to national minorities to effective participation in public affairs and, in the latter document, that they must promise to intensify their efforts to ensure the free exercise of this right. The Helsinki Document further clarifies that this right includes democratic participation in decision-making and consultative bodies at the national, regional and local levels.[15]

The provisions refer to participation in decision-making and consultation, under which one typically subsumes not only the stages of drafting and adopting of governmental policies and legislation but also the implementation and monitoring phases. However, the Helsinki Document explicitly refers to the 'national, regional and local level', excluding thereby the bilateral and international level. However, if this paragraph is read in conjunction with para 25 of the Helsinki Document, by which participating states stipulate that they 'will continue through unilateral, *bilateral and multilateral efforts* to explore further avenues for *more effective implementation* of their relevant CSCE commitments',[16] one can conclude that the participatory approach extends also to the bilateral and multilateral level.

---

[15] Para 35(1) of the Copenhagen Document; Pt VI, para 24 of the Helsinki Document. In terms of standard-setting, the activities of the OSCE in the years immediately following the collapse of communism and before the adoption of the Helsinki Document have exhausted the possibilities for further steps on major issues, such as the protection of national minorities. Therefore the substantive content of the paragraphs on political participation of the Copenhagen Document and of the Helsinki Document do not vary considerably. See A Bloed, *The Conference on Security and Co-operation in Europe: Analysis and basic documents, 1972–1993* (1993), 64.

[16] Emphasis added.

A further relevant passage in the Helsinki Document is contained in para 26, which provides that participating states 'will address national minority issues in a constructive manner, by peaceful means and *through dialogue among all parties concerned* on the basis of CSCE principles and commitments'.[17]

If this provision is set within a bilateral or international context, the 'parties concerned' that are to be included in the constructive dialogue are governmental authorities of two or more states, international monitoring bodies and, first and foremost, persons belonging to national minorities and their organizations. This interpretation is confirmed by the Explanatory Note to Lund Recommendation 5, which points out that 'in connection with "all parties concerned", paragraph 30 of the Copenhagen Document recognizes "the important role of non-governmental organizations, including political parties, trade unions, human rights organizations and religious groups".'

This is the first example of a paragraph of the Lund Recommendations, which at first glance is not related to international monitoring but, when put into context, is also of clear importance for this field. Recommendation 5 underlines that, in the creation of institutions and procedures, 'both substance *and process* are important'.[18] It further states that both governmental authorities and minorities 'should pursue an inclusive, transparent, and accountable process of consultation in order to maintain a climate of confidence'. Applying this recommendation to a state's obligation to report to an international monitoring mechanism it means that in the 'process' of writing a state report, an inclusive approach should be pursued so as to involve 'all parties concerned' in the dialogue, meaning representatives of minorities and their organizations.

Also relevant for the purposes of this article are Recommendations 12–13, concerning advisory and consultative bodies. According to Recommendation 12, such bodies 'serve as channels for dialogue between governmental authorities and national minorities'. Although Recommendation 13 provides that 'authorities should consult these bodies regularly regarding minority-related legislation and administrative measures', these channels of communication can and should be used, not only when it comes to the decision on laws and policies, but also when it comes to evaluating their results, eg the monitoring of their implementation, and particularly if there is a link to international obligations. In this sense, Recommendation 13 points out that these bodies should be able to 'monitor developments'.

Further, these provisions are relevant also for the participation of minorities in bilateral bodies. As the Explanatory Note to Recommendation 13 points out, '[t]he possibilities for constructive use of such bodies vary with the situations'. Thus, in a bilateral context, the joint intergovernmental commissions established to monitor the implementation of bilateral agreements could be qualified

---

[17] Emphasis added. [18] Emphasis added.

as consultative bodies.[19] The bilateral agreements that define the mandate of these commissions lay down that they have the task to discuss current issues of the minorities concerned, to evaluate the implementation of the obligations under the agreement and finally prepare and adopt recommendations for their respective governments concerning the implementation of the agreement. The commissions thus 'consult' or 'advise' the governments as to what measures should be taken in order to achieve appropriate implementation of the agreement.

The explanatory note to Recommendation 12, which suggests that '[t]he composition of such bodies should reflect their purpose and contribute to more effective communication and advancement of minority interest', specifies that for these bodies to be effective, they 'should be composed of minority representatives and others who can offer special expertise'. Therefore, the participation of national minorities in joint commissions should also be guaranteed in those cases where it is not explicitly foreseen in the bilateral treaty. The Explanatory Note further suggests that these bodies should be 'provided with adequate resources, and given serious attention by decision-makers'. This latter provision is of utmost importance for both bilateral and domestic consultative mechanisms. As practice shows, however, financing is a particularly pronounced problem within these bodies:

> [I]n all cases, good governance requires positive steps on the part of the authorities to engage established advisory and consultative bodies, to refer to them as needs may arise and to invite their in-put.[20]

That this is particularly relevant at the bilateral level has been demonstrated by tensions that arose in the context of the adoption of the Hungarian status law,[21] particularly between Hungary and Romania, when the involvement of the joint commission finally led to resolution of the conflict.[22] It goes without saying that the need to refer to joint commissions arises not only when conflict has erupted. In fact, if such a commission is regularly engaged, such conflicts may even be avoided.

Both the qualification of joint commissions as advisory and consultative bodies, as well as their usefulness in addressing potential conflicts is confirmed by Recommendation 19 of the Bolzano/Bozen Recommendations, which reads as follows:

---

[19] When providing national practice examples for the application of Recommendations 12–13, Myntti focuses only on national commissions. No example of a bilateral commission is given. K Myntti, *A Commentary on the Lund Recommendations on the Effective Participation of National Minorities in Public Life* (2001), 30–40.   [20] Explanatory Note to Recommendation 13.

[21] The Act LXII of 2001 on Hungarians living in neighbouring countries. For details see S Constantin, 'The Hungarian "Status Law" on Hungarians living in neighbouring countries' (2001–2) 1 *European Yearbook of Minority Issues* 593.

[22] B Aurescu, 'Bilateral agreements as a means of solving minority issues: The case of the Hungarian Status Law'(2003–4) 3 *European Yearbook of Minority Issues* 509.

States should make good use of all available domestic *and international instruments* in order to effectively address possible disputes and to avert conflicts over minority issues. This may include *advisory and consultative bodies* such as minority councils, *joint commissions* and relevant *international organizations*. Mediation or arbitration mechanisms should be established in advance through appropriate bilateral or multilateral agreements.

This recommendation draws primarily on Lund Recommendations 12–13, as shown by the wording of its Explanatory Note. It literally repeats the comments made in the Lund Recommendations about advisory and consultative bodies concerning composition, financing, and the need for decision-makers to give these bodies serious consideration.

Another example of where the Bolzano/Bozen Recommendations have simply amplified the focus of a paragraph of the Lund Recommendations from a domestic focus to a bilateral and multilateral one concerns the involvement of persons belonging to minorities in dispute resolution mechanisms. Recommendation 24 of the Lund Recommendations provides that 'additional dispute resolution mechanisms [in addition to the judicial resolution of conflicts], such as negotiation, fact finding, mediation, arbitration, an ombudsman for national minorities, and special commissions, which can serve as focal points and mechanisms for the resolution of grievances about governance issues' should be established as 'channels of consultation for the prevention of conflicts and dispute resolution'. As has been seen, according to Recommendation 19 such mechanisms should be established through bilateral and multilateral instruments, as the combined use of these instruments 'can lead to a more dispassionate discourse and remedial action'.[23]

Overall it can be concluded that with the exception of the Bolzano/Bozen Recommendations, and Recommendation 19 in particular, including its Explanatory Note, there is no explicit reference in the documents of the OSCE concerning the participation of national minorities in the monitoring of bilateral and international obligations or their role in reporting procedures. However, from a combined reading of different provisions it is possible to deduce the applicability of the commitment to also involve national minorities in public life in the area of bilateral and international monitoring. Furthermore, it is interesting to note that the issue of cross-border bodies is, again with the exception of the Bolzano/Bozen Recommendations and one paragraph contained in the Helsinki Document (Pt VI, para 25), quite underdeveloped within the framework of the OSCE. As will be seen in the following section, this situation is different to that of the Framework Convention for the Protection of National Minorities, which contains specific provisions concerning cross-border contacts and bilateral agreements.

---

[23] Explanatory Note to Recommendation 19.

B. The Framework Convention for the Protection of National Minorities

As stated above, the FCNM is of particular interest because of its provisions concerning interstate relations, discussed below. Another reason why it is interesting to take a closer look at the provisions of the FCNM and its monitoring is the fact that the Framework Convention is the only legally binding document that explicitly foresees the participation of national minorities in public life. Thus, it is particularly relevant to see how this obligation is put into practice during the Convention monitoring process, not only by states parties during the fulfilment of their reporting obligations, but also by the key player of the monitoring mechanism, the Advisory Committee.

When it comes to the *states*, bona fide implementation of Art 15 would imply that state authorities have to involve persons belonging to national minorities in all phases of monitoring: first, minorities would have to be consulted when the reports for submission to the Council of Europe were drafted. Secondly, minority representatives would be given the chance to comment on the opinion of the Advisory Committee. The ACFC considers it good practice to include the views of minority representatives in the governmental comments on the opinions. And, last but not least, they would be involved in the final follow-up meetings to discuss the results of the monitoring of the Framework Convention. Such an inclusive approach would contribute to the transparency of the monitoring process, something which is mandated by the Explanatory Report concerning Arts 24–6 of the FCNM, dealing with its monitoring.[24] How these steps translate into practice, and how states have acted in this regard, is discussed in the next section of this chapter.

Which are the possibilities formally foreseen for the involvement of minorities by the Advisory Committee in the course of its monitoring? The provisions for monitoring the FCNM, contained in Arts 24–6, focus on three actors: the Committee of Ministers, the Advisory Committee and, of course, the states parties. The participation of minorities in the monitoring process is not touched upon at all. And with regard to the Advisory Committee, the provisions are very limited; it is only foreseen that the Committee of Ministers will be assisted by such a committee in evaluating the adequacy of measures taken to implement the FCNM, and that its composition and procedure will be determined by the Committee of Ministers.[25]

Resolution 97(10) adopted by the Committee of Ministers contains, among other things, rules relating the composition and election of the members of the AC and to the procedure to be followed in performing the monitoring functions.[26]

---

[24] Para 97 of the Explanatory Report.   [25] Art 26 of the FCNM.
[26] Resolution (97)10, Rules adopted by the Committee of Ministers on the monitoring arrangements under Arts 24–6 of the Framework Convention for the Protection of National Minorities, adopted by the Committee of Ministers on 17 September 1997.

This resolution contains relevant provisions concerning the participation of minorities in the monitoring process. The most interesting ones are laid down in rules 30–2.

Rules 30–1 provide that the AC 'may receive information from sources other than state reports' and it may even 'invite' such information 'after notifying the Committee of Ministers of its intention to do so'. The first part obviously implies that persons belonging to national minorities and their organizations are free to submit information to the AC either on specific aspects of the implementation of the FCNM or on its overall implementation. In the second case the AC is allowed to adopt an active approach and can directly address persons or organizations with the invitation to provide information on actual practice in a certain country, provided the AC has previously notified the Committee of Ministers of its intention. As the AC is of the opinion that it is its duty to get as complete a picture as possible of the state of implementation of the FCNM in a certain country, it also considers it essential to take into consideration the information provided by minority representatives and other civil society actors. Consequently, it can receive information 'of the ways in which minorities themselves view the implementation of the Framework Convention'.[27] The AC thus notified the Committee of Ministers of its intention to seek information through sources other than the state, without limiting this notification to a specific country. The Committee of Minister 'took note' of this.[28]

Rule 32 of Resolution (97)10 is of central importance to the entire monitoring process of the AC, and for the participation of minorities within this process. The rule foresees in para 1 that the AC will hold meetings with the government if a government so requests and, in para 2, that the AC can obtain a specific mandate from the Committee of Ministers if it wishes to hold meetings for the purpose of seeking information from sources other than state authorities. It therefore provides for the possibility of carrying out on-the-spot visits, including meeting with minority representatives or minority consultative bodies.[29] In the experience of the AC, these country visits provide an excellent

---

[27] Advisory Committee, Meeting Report of the 3rd Meeting, 22–5 March 1999, ACFC/MR/INF(1999)009, para 11.

[28] Concerning the first monitoring cycle it took note of this notification at its meeting on 19 May 1999. See R Hofmann, 'Review of the monitoring process of the Council of Europe Framework Convention for the Protection of National Minorities' (2001/2) 1 *European Yearbook of Minority Issues* 435, 439–40. In the Renewal of Authorizations granted to the Advisory Committee for the first monitoring cycle of 8 April 2003 (CM/Del/Dec(2003)832/4.1, 833/4.3 and GR-H (2003)2), the Committee of Ministers 'took note of the Advisory Committee's intention, as from the second reporting cycle and for subsequent cycles, to seek where appropriate information from international organizations, ombudsmen and national institutions for the promotion and protection of human rights, as well as from representatives of civil society and non-governmental organizations'.

[29] See M Weller, 'Article 15' in M Weller, *The Rights of Minorities in Europe: A commentary on the European Framework Convention for the Protection of National Minorities* (2005), 448.

opportunity for engaging in direct dialogue with various sources.[30] As regards the additional information from sources other than the state, the Committee of Ministers has provided the Advisory Committee with a blanket authorization 'to hold meetings with non-governmental bodies and independent institutions in the context of visits conducted by the Advisory Committee to the State Parties concerned'. When this authorization was renewed for the second monitoring cycle, the Committee of Ministers also extended it to all subsequent cycles.[31] By contrast to the very open approach of the Committee of Ministers and the AC towards country visits, the UN High Commissioner for Human Rights endorsed guidelines which *discouraged* experts from undertaking such country visits, as 'such invitations may be perceived as an attempt to influence the outcome of the consideration of the report'. The secretariat of the OHCHR is thereby not involved in the preparation or conduct of such visits, nor does it provide for administrative or financial support.[32] This is thus an aspect which clearly distinguishes the monitoring process under the FCNM from the monitoring of other international human rights instruments.[33]

In addition to the possibility of meeting with non-governmental bodies and independent institutions during country visits, during the second monitoring cycle the Committee of Ministers also authorized the AC to hold such meetings outside the context of country visits, provided it informed the state concerned prior to the meeting. Such meetings have the stated purpose 'to ensure that the Advisory Committee is provided with a balanced range of opinion'.[34]

Only recently, the Committee of Ministers adopted an important amendment to Resolution (97)10. It concerned the rule that the opinions of the AC have to be made public at the same time as the conclusions and recommendations of the Committee of Ministers.[35] This rule has been interpreted by the Committee of Ministers to allow states to publish opinions earlier.[36] The recent

---

[30] In literally all opinions of the first monitoring cycle, with the exception of course of opinions on states in which no country visit has taken place (Portugal and Spain), the AC used a similar wording in order to underline the usefulness of the country visits. See, eg, paras 7 of the First Opinion on Albania, Armenia, Azerbaijan, Bosnia and Herzegovina, Bulgaria, Croatia, Czech Republic, Germany, Ireland, Montenegro, Poland, Slovenia, Ukraine, available at <http://www.coe.int/t/dghl/monitoring/minorities/3_FCNMdocs/Table_en.asp/> (accessed 31 July 2009).

[31] For the first cycle the decision was taken by the Committee of Ministers on 17 May 2000. For the second and subsequent cycles see, Renewal of Authorizations granted to the Advisory Committee for the first monitoring cycle of 8 April 2003 (CM/Del/Dec(2003)832/4.1, 833/4.3 and GR-H(2003)2).

[32] UN, Report on the Working Methods of the Human Rights Treaty Bodies Relating to the State Party Reporting Process, HRI/MC/2006/4, 17 May 2006, Annex, 40.

[33] See R Hofmann, 'Minorities, European protection', *Max Planck Encyclopedia of Public International Law* (2008), no 39.

[34] Ibid. See also C Pekari, 'Review of the monitoring process of the Council of Europe Framework Convention for the Protection of National Minorities' (2003/4) 3 *European Yearbook of Minority Issues* 347, 349.

[35] Committee of Ministers, Resolution (97)10 (n 26 above), Rule 26.

[36] Decision adopted by the Committee of Ministers in June 2001 (756th meeting of the Ministers' Deputies).

amendment modifies this provision completely in that it foresees an automatic publication of the opinions 'four months after transmission of the opinion to the State Party concerned, unless that State Party submits a reasoned objection in writing to the Secretariat'. At the latest, however, opinions must be published twelve months after the transmission of the opinion to the state concerned.[37] This early publication allows for greater transparency within the monitoring process and represents an important improvement for those who would like to be actively involved in the process.

While there are thus important rules providing for the involvement of persons belonging to national minorities and their organizations in the FCNM reporting procedure, apart from the positive development concerning the publication of the opinions there are no provisions concerning the role of minorities in the follow-up to the adoption of AC opinions and Committee of Ministers resolutions. There is also no provision, either in the FCNM or in the Resolution (97)10, to the effect that representation of persons belonging to national minorities in the Advisory Committee itself should be fostered and having the necessary requirements.[38] As a matter of fact, most states have so far been rather reluctant to include persons belonging to national minorities in their list of names to be submitted to the Secretary General of the Council of Europe for election of members of the AC by the Committee of Ministers. Despite this fact, there have always been a small number of AC members who belonged to national minorities in their countries.

As already mentioned, the FCNM is also relevant in the context of this article, as it contains a substantive provision which encourages states to conclude bilateral agreements, 'in particular with neighbouring States, in order to ensure the protection of persons belonging to the national minorities concerned' and to take measures for the fostering of cross-border cooperation.[39] Neither the Article nor the Explanatory Report says anything specific about the monitoring bodies of such agreements, or about the participation of minorities in such bodies. However, as this type of agreement would affect minorities it is clear that, on the basis of Art 15, the participation of minorities is required not only in decision-making on the content of such agreements but in their monitoring. In other words, while the Article and the Explanatory Report focus on the substance and the purpose of such agreements, the procedural side of effective participation, as covered by Art 15, cannot be neglected.

Furthermore, arrangements on transfrontier cooperation can be negotiated directly between territorial communities or authorities. As there is often a concentration of minorities in border regions this would provide another

---

[37] New rule 26bis, introduced by Resolution CM/Res(2009)3 amending Resolution (97)10 on the monitoring arrangements under Arts 24–6 of the Framework Convention for the protection of National Minorities, adopted by the Committee of Ministers on 16 April 2009.
[38] Rules 5–6 of Resolution (97)10.   [39] Art 18 of the FCNM.

opportunity for them to engage in cross-border bodies, established by such arrangements. But transfrontier cooperation is not limited to territorial communities or authorities but may also extend to the activities of non-governmental organizations (NGOs) and informal working arrangements.[40]

Thus, the FCNM offers a broad range of possibilities for persons belonging to national minorities of being involved in cross-border bodies and in the monitoring and reporting procedure.

C. The UN Declaration

The UN Declaration on the Rights of Persons Belonging to National or Ethnic, Religious, and Linguistic Minorities of 1992 is quite progressive in the area of interstate relations, in particular considering the fact that this domain only began to receive increased attention from European institutions and instruments after 2001. However, the UN Declaration also does not explicitly require the participation of minorities in cross-border bodies and it is again necessary to interpret the provisions on interstate cooperation (Arts 5–7) in the light of the Art 2(2) which stipulates the right of persons belonging to minorities to participate effectively in cultural, religious, social, economic, and public life. Art 5(2) reads as follows:

Programmes of cooperation and assistance among States should be planned and implemented with due regard for the legitimate interests of persons belonging to minorities.

In his commentary on the Declaration, Eide identifies in the wording of this article a dual task for actors involved in international cooperation: first, to ensure that the legitimate interests of minorities are not negatively affected by programmes of cooperation and assistance; secondly, to ensure that persons belonging to minorities can benefit from cooperation as much as members of the majority. An assessment of the likely impact of cooperation programmes on affected minorities should be an integral part of any feasibility study.[41] While the focus of Eide's assessment is on the impact of international cooperation and not specifically on the involvement of minorities, it is clear that minorities need to be involved in the process of decision-making on such programmes in order to reach the two goals.

Art 6 contains another interesting provision concerning interstate relations. It says that '[s]tates should cooperate on questions relating to persons belonging to national minorities, inter alia by exchanging information and experience, in

---

[40] See J Jackson-Preece, 'Article 18' in Weller, *The Rights of Minorities in Europe* (n 29 above), 516–17. For a an interesting sample of case studies on cross-border cooperation and minorities in Eastern Europe, see the Special Focus entitled 'Crossborder cooperation and minorities in Eastern Europe: Still waiting for a chance?' (2006–7) 6 *European Yearbook of Minority Issues* 137.
[41] As Eide, Commentary to the Declaration on the Rights of Persons Belonging to National or Ethnic, Religious, and Linguistic Minorities, 2 April 2001, E/CN4/Sub2/AC5/2001/2, para 74.

order to promote mutual understanding and confidence'. As one of the means of attaining the goals of non-intervention on one hand, and the promotion of conditions for minorities on the other, Eide mentions bilateral treaties and the necessity of the inclusion of provisions for the settlement of disputes regarding their implementation.[42] Again the procedural side of the coin concerning the involvement of minorities in the monitoring process is not explicitly mentioned, but is assumed to be covered by Art 2.2.

And finally, Art 7 provides that states should cooperate in order to promote respect for the rights set forth in the Declaration. In his Commentary, Eide focuses on European and UN bodies established for that purpose,[43] again neglecting to mention that states or the bodies they have created should involve persons belonging to national minorities as much as possible in their endeavours.

Overall, the UN Declaration can be considered quite progressive where bilateral and multilateral cooperation on minority issues is concerned. However, the role of persons belonging to minorities in bodies created for such transfrontier cooperation or in the monitoring of agreements concluded remains rather underdeveloped.

D. Bilateral agreements

Intergovernmental joint commissions—established within the framework of special bilateral agreements on national minorities, or general bilateral treaties on good neighbourliness and cooperation that contain extensive provisions on the protection of minorities—are considered the most effective mechanisms for implementation and monitoring of these bilateral agreements.[44]

Their mandate is to discuss the current issues of relevance to the two minorities concerned; to evaluate the implementation of obligations under the respective agreement; and to prepare and adopt recommendations for their respective governments concerning the implementation and, if necessary, the modification of that agreement.[45]

The participation of persons belonging to national minorities in these commissions is in most cases the consequence of a specific provision in the treaty.[46]

---

[42] Ibid, para 77.   [43] Ibid, para 78–9.

[44] K Gál, 'Bilateral agreements in Central and Eastern Europe: A new inter-state framework for minority protection?', ECMI Working Paper 4, 1999, 13, available at <http://www.ecmi.de/download/working_paper_4.pdf/> (accessed 31 July 2009).

[45] This mandate is explicitly spelled out like this in the Hungarian Conventions with Slovenia and Croatia (Arts 15–16, respectively), but also the other commissions, where the mandate is not spelled out in the agreement, have the same tasks.

[46] Art 16 of the Hungarian–Croatian Convention and Art 15 of the Hungarian–Slovenian Convention stipulate: 'The members of the Committee from the respective minorities shall be appointed upon the proposal of minority organizations'; Art 15 of the German–Ukrainian Agreement says: 'Ukraine shall ensure that representatives of the German minority are included in

In a few cases, their presence is agreed later, in the First Protocol that establishes the Joint Commission.[47] In other cases, their presence had no textual basis but arose in practice. This was the case for the German–Romanian Commission. Neither the treaty nor any protocol explicitly foresaw the representation of minorities in the commission. However, in the view of the German authorities, such minority involvement was in the spirit of the agreement.[48] However, although minority representatives are invited to attend the proceedings they are not full members of the Commission and participate instead only as observers with a consultative role.[49] In general, it can be said that if minority participation is not foreseen by a treaty or agreement, but rather is agreed upon later or arises simply from practice, their representatives are normally accorded only a consultative role.

Thus, persons belonging to national minorities are generally represented to different degrees within bilateral monitoring bodies. However, this is not the only way in which they can participate in the monitoring of bilateral obligations. Other possibilities include the consultation of minority organizations and their representatives by the individual (members of) delegations of joint commission, either in between or before meetings or the organization of 'country visits' during which the joint commissions would hold meetings with minority representatives that are not members of the commission. Of course, it is also relevant to see how minorities are involved in the follow-up to the adoption of Recommendations. For example, are persons belonging to national minorities aware of the existence of the agreement and its monitoring? For all these

---

the Ukrainian delegation, and shall appoint these representatives'; Art 16 of the Hungarian–Ukrainian Declaration is speaking about a 'Joint Committee composed of representatives from the two Parties' state bodies and national minorities'. Also the agreements stipulated by Serbia and Montenegro with various neighbours contain provisions on the representation of minorities in the Joint Commissions: Art 16 of the agreement with Hungary: 'The Governments of the Contracting Parties shall appoint equal numbers of Commission members, with the mandatory participation of representatives of the national minorities'; Art 11 of the agreement with Romania: 'The Commission ... shall also include representatives of associations of persons belonging to national minorities'; Art 16 of the agreement with Croatia: 'The Parties shall appoint equal numbers of representatives to the Joint Committee, including members of the minorities'; Art 14 of the agreement with Macedonia: 'The Contracting Parties shall appoint equal numbers of representatives [in the intergovernmental Joint Commission], with the mandatory participation of representatives of national minorities.'

[47] Polish–Lithuanian Commission (Protocol of the Inaugural Meeting); Romanian–Hungarian Commission (Rules of Operation and Protocol of the First Meeting)

[48] See German answer to question 4.e. of a questionnaire sent out to the members of joint intergovernmental commission in the framework of a project of the Council of Europe on the work of these commissions, carried out in cooperation with the European Academy Bolzano. A comparative summary of the answers to the questionnaire (by Emma Lantschner and Sergiu Constantin) as well as the full text of the answers are available on the website of the Council of Europe, Doc SP/BA(2003)002, Strasbourg, December 2003.

[49] See Romanian answer to question 4.a. of the questionnaire referred to above (n 48). It needs to be stressed, however, that since the conclusion of the treaty on 2 June 1997, only one meeting took place until 2006. For more on this commission see section below, on monitoring practice of bilateral agreements.

questions no specific rules are foreseen in the texts of the agreements, and they will be dealt with in the next section, which is concerned with implementation practice.

IV. Implementation Practice

In this section I will focus on two major fields: first, minority participation in the international monitoring and reporting practice of the FCNM; and secondly, their participation in the monitoring practice of bilateral agreements.

A. Monitoring and reporting on the FCNM

When analysing the participation of persons belonging to national minorities in the reporting and monitoring process on the FCNM, three perspectives have to be taken into account. First, did the *AC* involve the minorities concerned in its monitoring and in what ways? How should states in the view of the AC involve minorities in the reporting? Secondly, how are these ideas reflected in the *state practice*? Did the states involve the minorities concerned during the fulfilment of their reporting obligation and during the follow-up of the Committee of Ministers recommendations? And thirdly, in what ways did *minorities* themselves play an active role in the whole monitoring exercise?

B. Practice of the Advisory Committee

According to Art 15 of the FCNM, the AC requires that states create the conditions necessary for the effective participation of persons belonging to national minorities in all fields of life, and in particular in relation to issues that affect them. It is only reasonable to expect that the AC itself would strive for an inclusive approach during its monitoring exercise.

Within the framework of the rules and regulations presented in the previous section, the AC has in fact done as much as possible to involve persons belonging to national minorities in its monitoring process. Apart from those very few cases where it was not invited to a country,[50] the AC visited all states parties and regularly came to the conclusion that the additional information supplied by the government and 'other sources, especially the representatives of national minorities', was most valuable, particularly in connection with the practical implementation of the relevant norms. It felt that these visits were an excellent opportunity for direct dialogue 'with various sources.'[51] During its country visits, the AC had meetings not only in state capitals but in areas

---

[50] In the first cycle these countries were Portugal and Spain.
[51] See paras 7 of almost all first-cycle opinions.

inhabited by minorities. This practice was first observed in 2001 and has since developed into a constant feature of the country visits.[52] The AC further welcomed the submission of alternative reports, which it viewed as being 'of considerable relevance' for the final drafting of opinions, and actively sought further additional information from non-state sources.[53]

The AC adopted an inclusive approach, not only when considering the situation in individual countries, but in its elaboration of thematic commentaries. For the purpose of this chapter, the Commentary on the Effective Participation of Persons Belonging to National Minorities in Cultural, Social, and Economic Life and in Public Affairs[54] is interesting in two respects: first, concerning its drafting process and, secondly, concerning its comments on the reporting and monitoring process.

Unlike the first AC Commentary on Education, the Commentary on Participation has been drafted with the involvement of external partners, in particular representatives of national minorities. A draft commentary was sent out to a wide range of minority NGOs and organizations as well as to experts in minority issues. The organizations addressed were primarily those that had already been in contact with the AC in the course of earlier country visits or had submitted 'shadow reports' or other relevant information to the AC. These organizations were further invited to a two-day round table, hosted by the European Academy Bolzano/Bozen (Italy) in October 2007. This seminar gave the minority organizations the opportunity to discuss the draft together with members of the AC and academics. After incorporating a number of the suggestions made during the seminar, the AC adopted the Commentary in February 2008.[55]

In terms of content, the executive summary to the Commentary makes it clear, that '[w]hile the Commentary *primarily focuses on participatory mechanisms at the domestic level*, it is crucial that persons belonging to national minorities are *also involved at all stages of the monitoring and implementation process of international instruments*, and in particular the Framework Convention, in order to achieve a balanced and quality outcome'.[56] The Commentary therefore also

---

[52] Hofmann, 'Review of the monitoring process' (n 28 above), 403; Pekari, 'Review of the monitoring process (n 34 above), 348–9; A Korkeakivi, 'Frameworking: Review of the monitoring process of the Council of Europe Framework Convention for the Protection of National Minorities' (2005–6) 5 *European Yearbook of Minority Issues* 255, 258.

[53] Hofmann, 'Minorities, European Protection' (n 33 above), no 39.   [54] See n 5 above.

[55] For more details on the Commentary see F Kempf, 'Review of the monitoring process of the Council of Europe Framework Convention for the Protection of National Minorities' (2008) 7 *European Yearbook of Minority Issues* (forthcoming); Palermo, 'The dual meaning of participation' (n 6 above). This participatory approach has been continued also recently when a process of assessing the impact of the FCNM in its state parties has been launched. A draft study on indicators to measure this impact has been prepared by researchers of the European Academy Bolzano/Bozen and has been widely circulated among minority organizations, NGOs and experts on minority issues with the request to provide comments on how to improve these indicators. For the draft of the study see <http://www.coe.int/t/dghl/monitoring/minorities/6_Resources/PDF_IAConf_Report_Bolzano_en_12nov08.pdf> (accessed 1 July 2009).

[56] Executive Summary to the Commentary on Participation (n 5 above), 4 (emphasis added).

contains a specific section on the participation of persons belonging to national minorities in the monitoring of the FCNM.[57] Its main elements can be summarized as follows: first of all, it follows from Art 15 of the FCNM that states should consult persons belonging to national minorities '[w]hen preparing state reports and other written communications required under the Framework Convention or other international treaties pertaining to minority issues', thereby also supporting an inclusive approach beyond the FCNM. However, certain types of interlocutors, such as consultative bodies, should not be perceived as exclusive interlocutors. State authorities should 'also include other actors, especially minority or/and non-governmental organizations in the consultation process'. The AC encourages states to include comments made by minorities and civil society in their state reports and their comments on the opinion of the AC.[58] The AC also welcomes the 'shadow reports' submitted by minority organizations or NGOs, which often constitute a valuable additional source of information.[59] Transparency and publicity are two essential aspects of an inclusive approach to the monitoring process as a whole. The AC is therefore of the opinion that all documents related to monitoring should be made available to minorities and the public at large, as early and as widely as possible, including in local languages.[60] Finally, the AC encourages states to set up a system of regular consultation to discuss their concerns between the monitoring cycles. The AC believes this dialogue to be crucial in building trust and confidence and in creating a climate of tolerance.[61] 'The Advisory Committee considers that the monitoring mechanism set up under the Framework Convention is in itself a valuable process to facilitate dialogue between persons belonging to national minorities and the authorities.'[62] Indeed, monitoring under the FCNM has contributed, in some countries, to the establishment and/or strengthening of communication channels between minorities and authorities around implementation of the Convention. In some cases, this has led to the setting up of institutionalized bodies for consultation and dialogue.[63]

The next section on state practice will analyse the extent to which this 'ideal' involvement of persons belonging to national minorities in the reporting process has been applied by states in the first two monitoring cycles.

C. State practice

The main sources for the following comments are the first- and second-cycle opinions of the Advisory Committee, as published to date. In all its opinions, the AC comments on the degree of minority involvement in the drafting of state

---

[57] Paras 142–5 of the Commentary on Participation (n 5 above).
[58] Commentary on Participation (n 5 above), para 142.   [59] Ibid, para 143.
[60] Ibid, para 144.   [61] Ibid, para 145   [62] Ibid, para 12.
[63] Kempf, 'Review of the monitoring process' (n 55 above).

reports, as well as in preparation of state comments to the AC opinion. In the second-cycle opinions there is even a special section dedicated to the monitoring procedure. A similar approach might be also expected from the third-cycle opinions, as the new reporting scheme places increased emphasis on requesting information from the states on measures taken to promote the participation of minority organizations and NGOs in the monitoring process.[64]

From a survey of these opinions it seems that, in the first cycle of monitoring, only slightly more than half of the states involved minority organizations and their representatives in the drafting of state reports. And even among these countries, only about half completely satisfied the expectations of the AC, while the other half were sometimes criticized by the AC where it appeared that consultation did not extend to all groups concerned—in some cases, a number of prominent NGOs dealing with minority issues were not even informed about the process—and where dialogue with local and regional organizations and authorities was limited. In these cases, the AC urged or recommended (depending on the cases) further, more extensive and in-depth consultations.[65] More positively, the good practice of some states should be mentioned, whereby the comments made by minority organizations were appended to the state report.[66] The Polish authorities attached to the state report the remarks of minority organizations which were not incorporated in the state report and provided reasons for adopting this approach.[67] Germany sent the comments made by minority organizations along with its own comments.[68]

Comparing the attitudes of old EU member states (including Norway and Switzerland) in the first cycle with that of newer EU member states, the western Balkan countries and the post-Soviet states Armenia, Azerbaijan, Moldova, Ukraine, and Russia,[69] it seems that there is a clear tendency towards an inclusive approach among the Western European states,[70] while in the new EU member states as well as in the Western Balkans only half of the countries or less consulted their respective minority organizations; out of the post-Soviet states, only Armenia carried out consultations with minority organizations during the preparation of the state report.

The situation improved considerably during the second monitoring cycle.[71] More than three quarters of all states involved their minorities in the reporting

---

[64] Ditto.
[65] See para 8 of the First Opinion on Austria; para 8 of the First Opinion on Bulgaria; para 8 of the First Opinion on Croatia; para 7 of the First Opinion on Finland; para 8 of the First Opinion on Montenegro; para 8 of the First Opinion on Norway; para 8 of the First Opinion on (then) Serbia and Montenegro; para 6 of the First Opinion on Sweden. For the full text of all opinions see n 30 above.
[66] See, eg, para 6 of the First Opinion on Austria; para 6 of the First Opinion on Sweden (n 30 above). [67] See, para 6 of the First Opinion on Poland (n 30 above).
[68] See, para 6 of the Second Opinion on Germany (n 30 above).
[69] Georgia is not taken into consideration here, as the first opinion has not yet been adopted.
[70] Nine of twelve involved minority representatives in the reporting period, at least partly.
[71] Korkeakivi, 'Frameworking' (n 52 above), 258.

process, although there was still some criticism by the AC of the fact that minority representatives were given only limited time to comment on the state report,[72] or that some relevant NGOs maintained that consultation should have been more inclusive and their concerns should have been more fully reflected in the state report.[73]

While the Western European states managed to keep their level of involvement high, other states also evidence a much better record of consultation. In only two out of seven opinions adopted on new EU member states, the AC found that minority representatives were not given sufficient opportunities to effectively influence the state report.[74] In Moldova and in the Russian Federation the situation improved, but minority representatives were still unsatisfied with the extent to which their concerns were reflected in the state report.[75]

Next to involving minorities in the drafting of the state report and of the comments on the opinion of the AC, states have other possibilities by which they can foster the participation of minorities in the monitoring process.

Awareness-raising is a precondition for minorities to be able to influence the monitoring process in the first place. Minorities need to be informed about rights contained in the Framework Convention and the possibilities they have to express their views about the implementation of the Convention during the course of monitoring process. For that purpose, the FCNM and its Explanatory Report should be made available to minorities, possibly in their own languages. But this alone is not enough. They also need to have access, as soon as possible, to all other monitoring-related documentation, be it the state report, the opinion of the Advisory Committee or the resolution of the Committee of Ministers. Again, these documents should be available at least in the official language of the state, and preferably in minority languages, in order to make the whole monitoring process more accessible to minorities. In the first monitoring cycle, the AC encouraged state authorities in almost all of its opinions to take further measures to improve awareness of the Framework Convention and its related documents. In some cases, the AC realized that the FCNM had not been widely known about or used by the relevant authorities or the public at large prior to the monitoring process,[76] or even that numerous interlocutors were only hearing

---

[72] See, eg para 7 of the Second Opinion on Austria; para 7 of the Second Opinion on the United Kingdom.

[73] See, eg para. 7 of the Second Opinion on Croatia. Similar also in para 6 of the Second Opinion on Cyprus; para 8 of the Second Opinion on Denmark; para 7 of the Second Opinion on Hungary; para 7 of the Second Opinion on Moldova; para 7 of the Second Opinion on Norway; para 6 of the Second Opinion on the Russian Federation (n 30 above).

[74] Para 6 of the Second Opinion on Romania; para 6 of the Second Opinion on Slovenia (n 30 above).

[75] Para 7 of the second opinion on Moldova; para 6 of the second opinion on the Russian Federation (n 30 above).

[76] Para 8 of the Opinion on the implementation of the FCNM in Kosovo; para 9 of the First Opinion on Romania (n 30 above).

about it for the first time when they were contacted by the AC.[77] In the second cycle, the AC focused much more on the translation and dissemination of first-cycle opinions and resolutions into official and minority languages.

In this context, the earliest possible publication of AC opinions contributes to the transparency of the monitoring process, by facilitating the access of minority representatives to the monitoring process. Until the amendment of April 2009, the rules foresaw that opinions would be made public at the moment when the resolution of the Committee of Ministers was published.[78] The Committee of Ministers has, however, made use of the addition: 'unless in a specific case the Committee of Ministers decides otherwise'. In fact, in general the Committee of Ministers decided to allow states parties to publish the AC opinion concerning them, 'together with their written comments if they so wish, before the adoption of the respective conclusions and possible recommendation by the Committee of Ministers'.[79] An increasing number of states chose to do so in the first monitoring cycle and this was welcomed by the Advisory Committee.[80] Some states published the opinions concerning them even before the adoption of their own comments.[81] The recently introduced rule that opinions are to be made public four months after the transmission of the opinion to the respective state[82] still allows a state to publish an opinion immediately upon transmission or at any time thereafter, unless the state submits a reasoned objection in writing to the secretariat of the FCNM. This amendment further contributes to improved access to the monitoring process for persons belonging to national minorities.

Of further relevance to the participation of minorities in the monitoring process is their involvement in follow-up seminars. While the AC meets various interlocutors separately during the country visits, these follow-up seminars 'provide an opportunity to bring all actors together around the same table to express their views on how best to advance the implementation of the monitoring findings'.[83] A survey of second-cycle opinions indicates that the majority

---

[77] Para 8 of the First Opinion on Denmark (n 30 above).

[78] Rule 26 of Resolution 97(10) of the Committee of Ministers.

[79] Committee of Ministers, Framework Convention for the Protection of National Minorities: General issues related to the monitoring of the Framework Convention, (GR-H(2001)7, 12, CB6 and CB8), 756th meeting, 12–14 June 2001, Pt 6 of the decisions.

[80] See on this issue, eg, R Hofmann, 'Review of the monitoring process of the Council of Europe Framework Convention for the Protection of National Minorities' (2002–3) 2 *EYMI* 401–33, 405–6; C Pekari, 'Review of the monitoring process' (n 34 above), 351; E Jurado and A Korkeakivi, 'Completing the first decade of monitoring: Latest developments under the Framework Convention for the Protection of National Minorities' (2006–7) 6 *European Yearbook of Minority Issues* 373, 377.

[81] In the first cycle, this was the case of (then) Serbia and Montenegro. In the second cycle this practice has been followed already by Finland, Romania, Ireland and Norway (which has, however, decided to submit no comments). Jurado and Korkeakivi, 'Completing the first decade' (n 80 above), 377.

[82] Four months from transmission of the opinion is also the deadline for submission of written comments on the opinion by the state concerned.

[83] Korkeakivi, 'Frameworking' (n 52 above), 259.

of states organized such seminars with the involvement of minority representatives and members of the AC. Only a very limited number of states that have already published their second-cycle opinion have not held a follow-up session. In particular, larger states should also make sure that the findings of the monitoring cycles are also disseminated throughout the more peripheral regions.[84]

V. How Do Minorities Steer their Destiny

Of course, minorities can also become active of their own accord, without being invited by the state or the AC. As seen above, the most common method is to submit an alternative or shadow report to the AC at the same time as the respective state report is due, in which they present their own views of the implementation of the FCNM in their respective state. Shadow reports can follow a similar structure to state reports, and give an article-by-article description of implementation for all minorities in a country. However, they can also focus on specific issues or on the situation of specific minorities.

It is also possible to submit ad hoc information to the secretariat of the AC, irrespective of the monitoring phases. If such information reports serious developments in a country, the AC could even start an ad hoc contact procedure that allows for consistent and timely reaction to disconcerting information in situations where none of the regular contact with the authorities concerned is forthcoming.[85]

Minority organizations and NGOs can also organize awareness-raising campaigns and seminars with the aim of informing persons belonging to national minorities about their rights under the FCNM and the possibilities they have to articulate their views during the course of its monitoring.[86]

In practice, the AC 'has continued to draw extensively on information and other types of input provided by NGOs and minority associations'.[87] The Secretariat of the FCNM, together with international NGOs (such as Minority Rights Group International) organizes training sessions for NGOs on the use of the FCNM as an advocacy tool. These training sessions normally focus on countries in which the next monitoring cycle is about to begin.[88]

---

[84] Para 6 of the Second Opinion on the Russian Federation.
[85] For more on this procedure see Korkeakivi, 'Frameworking' (n 52 above), 260–1.
[86] These and other possibilities are described also on the website of the FCNM, where a particular page is dedicated to the role of NGOs. See<http://www.coe.int/t/dghl/monitoring/minorities/2_Monitoring/NGO_Intro_en.asp> (accessed 31 July 2009).
[87] Jurado and Korkeakivi, 'Completing the First Decade' (n 80 above), 385.
[88] Ibid. For a guide on the preparation of shadow reports and additional information see M Syposz, 'Framework Convention for the Protection of National Minorities: Opportunities for NGOs and minorities', Minority Rights Group, April 2006, available at <http://www.minorityrights.org/?lid=876> (accessed 31 July 2009).

A. Monitoring practice of bilateral agreements

Art 18 of the FCNM provides that the parties 'shall endeavour to conclude, where necessary, bilateral and multilateral agreements with other States, in particular neighbouring States, in order to ensure the protection of persons belonging to the national minorities concerned'. In combination with Art 15 on effective participation of minorities in public affairs, in particular those affecting them, it seems obvious that persons belonging to national minorities are to be involved in the monitoring of such bilateral treaties. Interestingly, the AC paid relatively little attention to this aspect in the first two monitoring cycles; however, before describing state practice in this context, the few comments made by the AC made will nevertheless be presented.

B. Practice of the Advisory Committee

Generally, the AC has provided only a few comments on the implementation of Art 18 of the FCNM. As this article is not formulated as an obligation but rather recommends that states pursue a certain conduct,[89] it is not too surprising that the AC mainly limits itself to ascertain whether a state has concluded bilateral agreements[90] or not.[91] At times, it encourages states to take into consideration the conclusion of further bilateral agreements.[92] The AC underlines the importance of involving minorities in the elaboration and amendment of such agreements[93] and, more generally, in initiatives and activities in the context of trans-frontier cooperation.[94]

---

[89] J Jackson-Preece, 'Article 18' (n 40 above), 510, 516.
[90] See eg para 79 of the First Opinion on Albania; para 85 of the First Opinion on Armenia; para 74 of the First Opinion on Austria; para 84 of the First Opinion on Azerbaijan; para 68 of the First Opinion on Croatia; para 46 of the First Opinion on Cyprus; para 74 of the First Opinion on the Czech Republic; para 70 of the First Opinion on Germany; para 57 of the First and para 121 of the Second Opinion on Hungary; para 106 of the First Opinion on Macedonia; para 93 of the First Opinion on Poland; para 74 of the First Opinion on Romania; para 116 of the First Opinion on the Russian Federation; para 116 of the First Opinion on Serbia and Montenegro; para 51 of the First and para 128 of the Second Opinion on the Slovak Republc; para 79 of the First Opinion on Slovenia; para 79 of the First Opinion on the Ukraine (the listing is not complete). For the full text of the opinion, see n 30 above.
[91] Eg para 115 of the First Opinion on Bosnia and Herzegovina (n 30 above).
[92] Eg, para 68 of the First and para 180 of the Second Opinion on Croatia; para 106 of the First Opinion on Macedonia (the listing is not complete) (n 30 above).
[93] Para 94 of the First Opinion on Poland. AC commented positively on the drafting of the Sami Convention but did not say anything about the involvement of the Sami in the drafting of this document. See paras 163–4 of the Second Opinion on Finland; paras 175 and 178 of the Second Opinion on Sweden (n 30 above).
[94] Paras 151–2 of the Second Opinion on Cyprus; paras 172–5 of the Second Opinion on Denmark; para 64 of the First and para 172 of the Second Opinion on Estonia. Para 173 further states: 'Estonia should continue to introduce initiatives to facilitate cross-border contacts between Estonia and the Russian Federation and involve persons belonging to national minorities in relevant bilateral initiatives.' See further, para 152 of the Second Opinion on Norway; paras 163–5 of the Second Opinion on Spain (n 30 above).

Only very few comments are concerned with the monitoring of bilateral agreements. Once, the AC welcomed the attempts of two states to improve the functioning of their joint commissions.[95] In other cases, the AC recommended that states make better use of existing bilateral mechanisms.[96]

The opinions of the AC could have made a much stronger link between Arts 15 and 18 of the FCNM and commented more extensively on the involvement of persons belonging to national minorities in the monitoring process of bilateral agreements. Generally, it can be said that the AC has not sought enough information on the monitoring of these agreements, be it in the form of written documentation or in the form of meetings with members of the joint commissions during its country visits. This is a pity, as information received in this respect would, in the first place, be an indicator of the inclusive or exclusive approach adopted by a state and, second, be an interesting source of information for the monitoring of the AC.

C. State practice

As already mentioned, most of the bilateral agreements concluded since the early 1990s, particularly by countries of Central, Eastern, and South-eastern Europe, provide for the representation of minorities in the body established for monitoring implementation of the agreement. Generally, they are proposed by the minority organizations and appointed by the government. These representatives can be members of parliament or of a local government.[97] In the case of the Hungarian–Serb Commission, the bodies responsible for the appointment of minority members are already mentioned in the agreement. Art 16 provides that members of the Commission who are representatives of the Hungarian national minority in Serbia and Montenegro are to be appointed at the proposal of the Hungarian National Council of Serbia and Montenegro, and representatives of the Serbian minority in Hungary at the proposal of the National Self-government of the Serbs in Hungary.

More interesting than the appointment procedure of minority members in commissions where their presence was provided for in the underlying treaty, is to look at those cases where representation was provided for only later. In the case of the Polish–Lithuanian Commission, for instance, the Commission decided at its inaugural meeting that 'in further meetings representatives of the Polish minority in Lithuania and of the Lithuanian minority in Poland shall take part in discussing selected problems'. It was decided that if the Commission held

---

[95] Para 57 of the First Opinion on Hungary; para 51 of the First Opinion on the Slovak Republic (n 30 above).
[96] Para 80 of the First and para 182 of the Second Opinion on Slovenia; para 114 of the First Opinion on Bulgaria; paras 122–3 of the Second Opinion on Hungary; para 150 of the Second Opinion on Moldova; paras 129–30 of the Second Opinion on the Slovak Republic (n 30 above).
[97] See answers to question 4.d. of the questionnaire mentioned in n 48 above.

its meeting in Lithuania the Polish minority in Lithuania would participate, and if the Commission met in Poland the Lithuanian minority of Poland would participate. The representatives of minority groups were selected from a list drawn up by the Polish and Lithuanian Ministries of Foreign Affairs, in consultation with their consulates in the other state. As they are not full members of the Commission, minority representatives are only able to express their opinion on certain issues in meetings, and do not have any decision-making power.[98]

The situation in the Hungarian–Romanian Commission should also be mentioned. In the treaty the parties only agree to establish an intergovernmental expert commission, without mentioning minority participation. In the founding session of the Commission, the parties agreed on their involvement. The Protocol, containing the Rules of Operation, foresees under Art 4 that the Romanian co-president of the Commission 'may invite' to its sessions a representative of the Hungarian community in Romania and the Hungarian co-president may invite a representative of the Romanian community in Hungary. The parties reiterated this commitment in the protocol of the first meeting of the Commission, agreeing that, as of the following meeting, one representative of the Hungarian minority in Romania and one of the Romanian minority in the Republic of Hungary should be invited. The minority representatives would participate as permanent invited members, but would formally have only a consultative role. It seems, however, that it is not appropriate to speak about the 'decision-making power' of the Joint Commission's members, as all decisions are taken by consensus and no decision can be taken against the wishes of a concerned minority representative who is participating at the sessions.[99]

The fact that the Rules of Operation only provided for the possibility of an invitation to participate in the meetings (the co-presidents 'may invite') and not for an institutionalized guarantee caused concern among minority representatives. They feared that their membership in the Commission would depend too much on the will of the government in office to invite minority representatives to take part in the meetings.[100] Since the existence of the Joint Commission, the Democratic Alliance of Hungarians in Romania (DAHR) was either part of the governmental coalition (between 1996 and 2000 and between 2004 and 2008),

---

[98] See E Lantschner and S Constantin, 'Comparative summary: Bilateral agreements for the protection of national minorities and the work of the Joint Commissions in the field of minorities, established in the frame of bilateral agreements in Central and South-Eastern Europe' in *Kin-State Involvement in Minority Protection: Lessons learned*, The Works of the Seminar held in Bucharest, on 12 February 2004, 70–1. This information was reverified during the course of writing this chapter.

[99] Ibid, 71. See the Hungarian and Romanian answers to question 4.g. and the Romanian answer to question 5.j. of the questionnaire mentioned above (n 48).

[100] Opinion expressed by a representative of the Hungarian minority living in Romania during the Meeting of Representatives of Joint Commissions on 'The implementation of bilateral agreements in the field of minorities in Central and South-Eastern Europe', Poiana Brasov, Romania, 18–19 November 2002.

or supported the government. Therefore this issue was not really problematic. Since late 2008, however, the Hungarian Alliance has been in opposition and the question might arise as to whether the practice of inviting a minority member will be continued. However, according to official rhetoric, the fact that they have not become part of the coalition, even though one of the parties was very much in favour, can be ascribed more to political power play between the two major parties than to ethnic reasons. It is therefore anticipated that the involvement of minority representatives in the Joint Commission will also continue in the future.[101]

However, the question is: even if persons belonging to national minorities are represented in the joint commissions, is that participation effective? Is the opinion of one or a few members representative of the overall opinion of the minority group? Sometimes, there are several minority organizations with different views that cannot all be represented in the commission. Practice seems to suggest that the secretaries of the delegations (alone or together with the secretary of the counterpart), or the delegations separately, hold written or oral consultation with representatives of both minorities—the minority living in their own state as well as the 'kin-minority'—but in most cases there is no standardized procedure and talks are carried out irregularly as the need arises.[102] This might lead to a situation in which minorities have the feeling that commissions rely very much on the input provided by its minority members and do not seek sufficient contacts with other minority organizations.[103] It can happen, therefore, that a commission adopts a recommendation and finds out in the next meeting that there was no real interest in the issue among the relevant minority concerned.[104] In order to ensure that the recommendations adopted by the commissions are of real benefit to those concerned, prior consultation should be as wide as possible.

For example, the secretaries of the Hungarian Commissions with Croatia prepare their Commission meeting as follows: the secretaries of the two delegations meet with the minority representatives of their respective country to get their evaluation of the current situation and suggestions on what could be improved and how. They also seek input from relevant line ministries and other

---

[101] Interview with Sergiu Constantin, researcher at the European Academy Bolzano, expert on minority issues in Romania, on 29 January 2009.

[102] See answers to question 5.a.-e. of the questionnaire mentioned above (n 48).

[103] Conclusion to which the minority representatives came during the meeting in Poiana Brasov, mentioned (n 100 above): Commissions rely on the information they receive from the minority representatives sitting in the Commission. They have to ensure consultation with their group and also have to report back to the group, informing its members about the decisions that have been taken during the meeting.

[104] Linda Schweiger notes the example of Hungarian-Slovak Commission which recommended the establishment of a Slovak faculty in Hungary, although the Slovak minority did not show real interest in this. See L Schweiger, 'Bilateral agreements: A political tool complementary to international minority protection', E.MA thesis European Master's Degree in Human Rights and Democratization, 2001, 47.

authorities. They then meet in a preparatory session to develop a draft of the protocol which is then submitted to minority representatives to grant them the possibility of commenting on the proposed recommendations. The Commission thus ensures the involvement of the persons concerned, and decisions that are in the interest of the minorities.[105]

The procedure adopted for the preparation of the meeting of the Joint Commission between Hungary and Slovenia in 2008 is also interesting. In the run-up to the meeting, the Hungarian and Slovene delegations received contradictory information from within the Slovene minority living in Hungary. To clarify the situation, the secretaries of the two delegations went together to visit the area in which the Slovene minority of Hungary lived and met with different representatives of that minority. Through this direct consultation it was possible to obtain a more precise picture of the situation on the ground which in turn contributed to a successful meeting of the Joint Commission.[106] This shows that a fruitful meeting of the Commission is dependent on good preparation, including the direct contact with the minorities concerned.

A similar example of good practice is provided by the Romanian–Ukrainian Joint Commission. In 2006, the two countries agreed on a methodology for carrying out monitoring missions in areas inhabited by the respective minorities.[107] For this purpose they requested the presence of experts from the Council of Europe[108] and the Office of the High Commissioner on National Minorities of the OSCE.[109] Three monitoring cycles were planned which are all supposed to follow the same structure and preparatory works.

The procedure is as follows: each state nominates a delegation composed of members which are, at least partially, also members of the respective delegation to the Joint Commission. They normally come, among other places, from the Ministry of Foreign Affairs, the departments responsible for Romanians and Ukrainians abroad, departments responsible for minority issues, diplomatic offices and/or regional administrations. The two delegations go together to visit regions in which minorities live: first in one state and then in the other state. These 'fact-finding missions' normally last for about a week. During this mission, the joint delegation meets with representatives of the local administration, of the school administration (principals, teachers, students) and minority cultural

---

[105] Information provided by the Department for National Policy at the Hungarian Prime Minister's Office in February 2009.

[106] Information provided by the Department for National Policy at the Hungarian Prime Minister's Office in March 2009.

[107] Government of Romania, Ministry of Foreign Affairs, Department for Relations with Romanians Abroad, 'Activity Report of the Department for Relations with Romanians Abroad during January–December 2006', 6.

[108] See Council of Europe, 'Human Rights Information Bulletin', no 69, 1 July–31 October 2006, 60.

[109] For both, the CoE and the OSCE HCNM it was the first time to be involved in this type of monitoring.

organizations. The issues discussed follow the principles and standards of the FCNM, and try to cover as much of the situation on the ground as possible. At the end of the mission, the joint delegation drafts a protocol which summarizes the results of the visit and transmits it to the Joint Commission. The Commission then discusses the problematic issues identified during the monitoring missions and decides on further steps to be taken by formulating recommendations to the respective governments. To date, two cycles have been completed, one in 2006 and one in 2007.[110] The third cycle was interrupted during a monitoring mission of the joint delegation in Ukraine in May 2008, due to differences concerning the personal scope of the application of the agreement.[111] At present, it appears that monitoring will be resumed in April/May 2009.[112]

Although the process has temporarily ground to a halt, this example shows how close bilateral agreements and, indirectly, the FCNM can be brought to the persons concerned, and how they can be involved in the monitoring process of bilateral agreements, independently of whether a person belonging to the respective minority is represented in the Joint Commission. Ideally, of course, both possibilities are combined. Other commissions, although they do not involve the respective minority population so closely, have decided to hold their meetings not in the capitals but in the regions where minorities live.[113] All these measures potentially increase the awareness of persons belonging to minorities of their rights, as laid down in international and bilateral agreements, and the opportunities they have to influence the monitoring process.

Another innovation of the approach taken by the Romanian–Ukrainian Commission is the involvement of external experts from the OSCE and the Council of Europe. These experts participated as observers in the monitoring missions of the joint delegation, but not in the meeting of the Joint Commission. Their presence was highly appreciated and is envisaged for future activities of this kind.[114]

By involving experts on the Framework Convention, it would be possible to create mutually beneficial synergies between the monitoring of the bilateral agreement and the FCNM. It would also be desirable that other commissions follow a similar approach, both with regard to the involvement of persons

---

[110] Information provided through the Permanent Representation of Romania to the Council of Europe in March 2009.

[111] See 'Kiev claims Bucharest's "non-constructive" position on the minority issue', *Divers Bulletin* 65 (308), 2 June 2008.

[112] Information provided at the website of the Ukrainian embassy in Romania available at <http://www.mfa.gov.ua/romania/ua/4725.htm> (accessed 31 July 2009).

[113] This is, eg, the case of the Hungarian-Croatian Joint Commission which met in Osjek, the Hungarian–Romanian Commission which met in Gyula and Sfîntu Gheorghe, the Hungarian–Serb Commission which met in Subotica, and the Hungarian-Slovenian Commission that met in Lendava and Szentgotthard.

[114] Information provided through the Permanent Representation of Romania to the Council of Europe in March 2009.

belonging to national minorities in their monitoring activities, and in the involvement of external experts of the Council of Europe and the OSCE.

VI. Overall Assessment

Provisions for the participation of persons belonging to national minorities in the reporting and monitoring processes attached to international instruments are very scarce, and even in the context of the FCNM it would not be correct to maintain that the monitoring process is 'characterized by a kind of *equality of arms* between the governments and national minorities'.[115] However, the resolutions and decisions of the Committee of Ministers, as well as the practice of the AC, have meant that it is now possible to say that the 'monitoring process is indeed characterized by quite a strong factual involvement of representatives of national minorities'.[116] The comparison between the first and the second monitoring cycle has shown that the level of involvement of minorities has improved considerably. It is to be hoped that this tendency will continue, and that states will make increasing use of the possibility to publish the opinions of the AC at an earlier stage. It is also important to underline that standards applied in minority involvement in the reporting process under the FCNM should also be applied in the context of other international human rights treaties.

The AC has also exhibited a more inclusive approach in the drafting of its second thematic commentary, which has resulted in a document in which minorities can have a feeling of co-ownership.

Shortcomings in the practice of the AC can be identified when it comes to the monitoring of bilateral agreements. By seeking more information on the monitoring of these agreements, be it in the form of written documentation or of meetings with members of joint commissions during its country visits, it could improve its level of knowledge of the implementation of the FCNM and could give better visibility to the activities of the Joint Intergovernmental Commissions.

When it comes to minority participation in bilateral monitoring processes, it can be concluded that minorities are widely represented in the monitoring bodies, even if it seems that explicit legal entrenchment is preferable to mere practice in some cases. In addition, to ensure a high level of pluralism, and thus effectiveness of participation, it is necessary to explore possibilities for a more in-depth consultation with minorities beyond their representation in the monitoring body. The procedure used by the Romanian–Ukrainian Commission has been cited as an example of good practice. But as noted above, not even the most advanced method of consultation is immune from setbacks and problems, and all require constant reconsideration and negotiation among the relevant partners.

---

[115] Hofmann, 'Minorities, European Protection' (n 33 above), no 39.   [116] Ibid.

26

Legal Entrenchment and Implementation Mechanisms

Alain Chablais[1]

I. Introduction	735
II. Main International Norms and Standards	736
A. The Lund Recommendations	736
B. The Framework Convention for the Protection of National Minorities (FCNM)	737
C. Other sources	738
III. Political Participation: State Practice under the Scrutiny of International Monitoring Bodies	739
A. Legal entrenchments	739
B. Implementation mechanisms	747
IV. General Assessment	750

I. Introduction

The present contribution aims to embrace a rather particular aspect of the issue of political participation of persons belonging to national minorities, which may seem at first glance to be of a purely procedural character: it is actually about examining how the existing guarantees promoting such participation are entrenched in the domestic legal order, but also how these guarantees may be implemented in practice through appropriate legal safeguards.

Although it is true that it is essentially through a procedural prism that arrangements promoting the political participation of minorities will be analysed, one must not forget that for them to be fully workable in practice, such arrangements must be applied in good faith by the authorities and fully used by the persons concerned and/or their associations. It is only in this way that

---

[1] The views expressed herein are solely those of the author.

proper participatory mechanisms, coupled with adequate legal entrenchment and implementation mechanisms, are likely to result in truly effective participation of persons belonging to national minorities. The purpose of this chapter will, however, limit itself to the first aspect and not consider the whole set of conditions which must be met in order to ensure that participatory mechanisms are indeed fully operational in practice.

II. Main International Norms and Standards

A. The Lund Recommendations

Although several international norms and standards come into play in the context of the promotion of political participation of national minorities, the Lund Recommendations clearly represent the most articulate source in international law which governs the question of entrenchment and implementation mechanisms. The Lund Recommendations are generally labelled as 'soft law' and are therefore not legally binding, but they clearly draw inspiration from a range of existing international treaties like the International Covenant on Civil and Political Rights (ICCPR), the International Covenant on Economic, Social and Cultural Rights, the International Convention on the Elimination of all Forms of Racial Discrimination and, not least, the Framework Convention for the Protection of National Minorities (FCNM). The Lund Recommendations also take due account of the commitments undertaken by all OSCE participating states, in particular those of the 1990 Copenhagen Document of the Conference on the Human Dimension. Their content is therefore meant to complement that of other relevant sources due to their close interconnection.

The Lund Recommendations contain a specific subheading entitled 'Guarantees' (Chapter IV), which sets out in Recommendations 22, 23, and 24 a range of principles aimed at articulating detailed guidance on 'Constitutional and Legal Safeguards' on the one hand, and 'Remedies' on the other hand. Without expressing a clear preference for a particular solution, the recommendations intend to provide a list of possible forms of entrenchment,[2] ranging from constitutional to legal or sub-legal norms, as well as a variety of remedies,[3] essentially divided into judicial and non-judicial resolution of conflicts. Although they take due account of the variety of national situations and therefore do not favour a particular model, they provide a limited number of more specific requirements. This is notably the case with regard to questions of

---

[2] The Lund Recommendations on the Effective Participation of National Minorities in Public Life (hereinafter 'Lund Recommendations'), Recommendation 22, available at <http://www.osce.org/documents/hcnm/1999/09/2698_en.pdf> (accessed 1 July 2009).

[3] Lund Recommendations (n 2 above), Recommendation 24.

'stability' and 'flexibility'. As spelt out in the Explanatory Note to Lund Recommendation 22, it is indeed of utmost importance that existing arrangements providing for self-governance are properly entrenched in legal norms since stability is required to assure some security for those affected, especially persons belonging to national minorities. At the same time, it may be useful to specify some reconsideration at fixed intervals to achieve the desired balance between stability and flexibility.[4] Recommendation 23 even encourages the testing of new and innovative regimes, rather than specifying terms for altering existing arrangements.

B. The Framework Convention for the Protection of National Minorities (FCNM)

Art 15 of the FCNM represents the most relevant legally binding provision promoting the effective participation of national minorities in public affairs and hence their political participation. It would be wrong, however, to consider it in isolation from the other provisions of the FCNM since participation is also a key to the full enjoyment of other rights protected under the FCNM.[5] In that sense, Art 15 of the FCNM has sometimes been described as a 'foundational right', closely linked to other types of minority rights provisions.[6]

Although the FCNM was certainly a source of inspiration for the Lund Recommendations, it is striking that Recommendations 22–24 under the heading 'Guarantees' make no explicit mention of Art 15 of the FCNM. The main reason for this is that Art 15 of the FCNM itself says nothing on legislative entrenchment and remedies, and nor does its Explanatory Note which only lists a number of possible measures states are invited to consider. Another reason is that at the time of the adoption of the Lund Recommendations (September 1999), the accumulated practice by the monitoring bodies was still non-existent given that the first country-specific opinions were only adopted by the Advisory Committee in 2000.

In the meantime, a number of developments have taken place: altogether, the Advisory Committee has adopted more than sixty country-specific opinions in the course of two monitoring cycles and it has also finalized a comprehensive thematic Commentary on Effective Participation, which

---

[4] See Explanatory Note to Recommendation 22 (n 2 above).
[5] See Advisory Committee Thematic Commentary no 2 on 'The effective participation of persons belonging to national minorities in cultural, social, and economic life and public affairs' adopted on 27 February 2008, Art 13: 'The relation between Article 15 and Articles 4 and 5 is, in this context, particularly important. In fact, Articles 15, 4 and 5 can be seen as the three corners of a triangle which together form the main foundations of the Framework Convention.'
[6] See M Weller, 'A critical evaluation of the first results of the monitoring of the framework convention on the issue of effective participation of persons belonging to national minorities' in *Filling the Frame: Five years of monitoring the Framework Convention for the Protection of National Minorities* (2004), 71

largely builds upon this experience. A closer analysis of these documents, which represents the authoritative interpretation of Art 15 of the FCNM formulated by the monitoring mechanism of this Convention, can now shed further light on the way in which states and other stakeholders should address the question of legal entrenchments and implementation mechanisms. Indeed, the practice has shown that even though the text of the FCNM was silent on this, the Advisory Committee has considered it warranted in a number of national contexts to give concrete guidance on how better legal safeguards were necessary and how the introduction of effective remedies was important.

C. Other sources

In addition to the Lund Recommendations and the FCNM, there are obviously several other sources which are relevant to the issue of entrenchment and remedies to promote political participation of persons belonging to national minorities. Hard law sources include the European Convention on Human Rights and, more specifically, its Art 13 (Right to an Effective Remedy) and Art 3 of the Protocol (Right to Free Elections); the International Covenant on Civil and Political Rights, essentially its Art 2(3) (Right to an Effective Remedy) and Art 25 (Right to Participation); as well as the European Charter of Local Self-government, in particular its Arts 2 and 11. The case law under the European Convention on Human Rights and the ICCPR is rich and on a number of issues has established concrete requirements also relevant to minorities,[7] but it has certainly not resulted in the obligation of states to develop a comprehensive scheme to advance minority participation in all areas of public life. The text of the European Charter of Local Self-government is important in this context, especially its Art 2, which is devoted to the constitutional and legal foundations of local self-government,[8] and its Art 11 which governs legal protection of local self-government.[9] This instrument does not deal with minority self-government, but with local self-government. It is nevertheless true that local self-government has in many instances been instrumental in promoting the participation of national minorities in public affairs, especially where minorities are geographically concentrated. The relevance of this treaty must therefore be borne in mind. Hard law sources also include International Labour Organization

---

[7] For a detailed review of this case law, see A Moucheboeuf, *Minority Rights Jurisprudence Digest* (Council of Europe Publishing, Strasbourg 2006), 259–93; see also Venice Commission Report on Dual Voting for Persons Belonging to National Minorities, CDL-AD(2008)013, 13–14 June 2008, Arts 47–54.

[8] Art 2 reads as follows: 'The principle of local self-government shall be recognised in domestic legislation, and where practicable in the constitution.'

[9] Art 11 reads as follows: 'Local authorities shall have the right of recourse to a judicial remedy in order to secure free exercise of their powers and respect for such principles of local self-government as are enshrined in the constitution or domestic legislation.'

Convention 169 concerning Indigenous and Tribal Peoples in Independent Countries, which contain several provisions on participation. However, since these concern only indigenous peoples, they will not be addressed in this chapter.

In addition to hard law, a number of soft law standards promote—directly or indirectly—the participation of minorities in public life. This is in particular the case for the 1948 UN Universal Declaration of Human Rights and the 1992 UN Declaration on the Rights of Persons Belonging to National or Ethnic, Religious, or Linguistic Minorities, although they are not as elaborate as the Lund Recommendations on this topic.

III. Political Participation: State Practice under the Scrutiny of International Monitoring Bodies

A. Legal entrenchments

1. Constitutional Guarantees

There seems to be a limited number of arrangements promoting the political participation of minorities for which a constitutional entrenchment would be strongly recommended if not required. Without pretending to be exhaustive, one can certainly identify two main such arrangements, ie territorial arrangements of self-governance as well as right to special representation in parliament.

Although territorial arrangements like autonomy or devolution are not directly aimed at improving the opportunities of minorities to exercise authority over matters concerning them, they have often been regarded as conducive to effective participation of at least those national minorities who live in compact settlements.[10] Since such arrangements concern the organization and the exercise of state power over (part of) its territory and although their mode of entrenchment varies considerably among the existing models, it is generally admitted that they should preferably be couched in the constitution or at least in constitutional laws, so as to ensure fuller democratic endorsement and stability for the future. Although there is no right to autonomy under the FCNM[11] or

---

[10] See Advisory Committee Thematic Commentary (n 5 above), Art 134: 'The Advisory Committee found that, in the State Parties in which territorial autonomy arrangements exist … they can foster a more effective participation of persons belonging to national minorities in various areas of life.'

[11] See Advisory Committee Thematic Commentary (n 5 above), Art 133: 'The Framework Convention does not provide for the right of persons belonging to national minorities to autonomy, whether territorial or cultural. Yet, the Advisory Committee has examined the functioning and impact of territorial and cultural autonomy arrangements on participation of persons belonging to national minorities in State Parties where they exist.'

under general international law[12] one can infer, from the Advisory Committee's comments in relation to some of the autonomy regimes it was given to address, a call for—or at least a positive appreciation of—explicit constitutional safeguards in this respect.[13] This seems to be in line with the opinions of various authors on this question, although they usually take care to recall that the degree of entrenchment may vary considerably between existing models of autonomy.[14]

As is the case with autonomy arrangements, there is no right to special representation of minorities in parliament under Art 15 of the FCNM.[15] This being said, the Advisory Committee has had occasion to comment on such electoral arrangements in those countries which have decided to introduce them. In this context, a call seems to have emerged for clear and strong entrenchment, possibly at the constitutional level. However, this is generally not considered sufficient since implementing legislation is indispensable to regulate the technicalities in electoral legislation. Telling instances have in particular been analysed in Hungary, Montenegro, Croatia, and Romania.[16] This has subsequently been reaffirmed in the

---

[12] See T Benedikter, *The World's Working Regional Autonomies: An introduction and comparative analysis* (Anthem Press: London 2007), 372; M Suksi, 'On the entrenchment of autonomy' in *Autonomy: Applications and implications* (1998), 152.

[13] Advisory Committee First Opinion on Moldova, ACFC/INF/OP/I(2003)002, 1 March 2002, para 92: 'The Advisory Committee appreciates the intention announced by the authorities to include in the Constitution a provision recognizing the status of autonomy of Gagauzia and encourages the authorities to examine the situation, in co-operation with those concerned'; Advisory Committee First Opinion on Italy, ACFC/INF/OP/I(2002)007, 14 September 2001, paras 61 and, especially, 62: 'The Advisory Committee appreciates the various institutional arrangements in aid of effective participation in all areas, public affairs especially, for persons belonging to the German-speaking and Ladin minorities resident in the Trentino-Alto Adige autonomous region. It especially welcomes the recent changes made by Constitutional Law No. 2 of 31 January 2001 which improves representation of Ladins in the legislative and executive bodies of both the region and the province.'

[14] See, eg, M Weller, 'Article 15' in *The Rights of Minorities: A commentary on the European Framework Convention for the Protection of National Minorities* (2005) 437; Suksi, 'On the entrenchment of autonomy' (n 12 above), 151–2, 168–9; also Benedikter, *The World's Working Regional Autonomies* (n 12 above), 364–5, 368.

[15] See Advisory Committee Thematic Commentary (n 5 above), Art 81: 'Bearing in mind that State Parties are sovereign to decide on their electoral systems, the Advisory Committee has highlighted that it is important to provide opportunities for minority concerns to be included on the public agenda. This may be achieved either through the presence of minority representatives in elected bodies and/or through the inclusion of their concerns in the agenda of elected bodies.'

[16] Advisory Committee First Opinion on Montenegro, ACFC/INF/OP/I(2008)001, 6 October 2008, paras 93–4; Advisory Committee First Opinion on Hungary, ACFC/INF/OP/I(2001)004, 22 September 2000, paras 49: Advisory Committee Second Opinion on Hungary, ACFC/INF/OP/II(2004)003, 9 September 2004, paras 109–12; Advisory Committee First Opinion on Romania, ACFC/INF/OP/I(2002)001, 6 April 2001, para 65; Advisory Committee First Opinion on Slovenia, ACFC/INF/OP/I(2005)002, 12 September 2002 paras 69–72; Advisory Committee Second Opinion on Slovenia, ACFC/INF/OP/II(2005)005, 26 May 2005, paras 165–8; Advisory Committee Second Opinion on Croatia, ACFC/INF/OP/II(2004)002, 1 October 2004, paras 160–3; see also the HCNM approach on this issue summarized by A Verstichel, 'Special measures to promote minority representation in elected bodies: The experience of the HCNM' in *The Participation of Minorities in Public Life*, Reports of the

Advisory Committee's Thematic Commentary on Participation.[17] It is interesting to note that the Venice Commission has also stressed, on different occasions, the need for clear constitutional provisions on minority representation in parliament, which seems to corroborate the trend towards the proper requirement for constitutional entrenchment.[18]

Apart from territorial arrangements of self-governance as well as a right to special representation in parliament, there are certainly other mechanisms promoting the political participation of minorities which may enjoy some form of constitutional entrenchment. Examples include non-territorial forms of self-governance,[19] exemption of electoral thresholds, veto rights,[20] qualified majority requirements in parliament,[21] etc. These are, however, isolated forms of enhanced entrenchments which are not supported by a clear pattern in comparative constitutional law. Furthermore, the findings of the international bodies monitoring human and minority rights do not necessarily call for the generalization of such practices,[22] even though they may be deemed laudable in a given national context.

2. Legislative Guarantees

A variety of measures intended to advance the political participation of national minorities exist in Europe and, in many cases, have been anchored in ordinary law. This may be the case in a comprehensive law protecting national minorities in all aspects of life and/or in sectoral legislation. It would be too cumbersome to enter into a casuistic analysis of such measures, which are often so specific to a given country that they can hardly be compared to another national context. It seems that there are nevertheless a few main areas which deserve legislative entrenchment and for which a meaningful practice has been developed by the

---

UniDem Seminar organized in Zagreb on 18–19 May 2007, Venice Commission (ed) (Council of Europe Publishing: Strasbourg 2008), 57–8.

[17] See Advisory Committee Thematic Commentary (n 5 above), para 83: 'Constitutional guarantees for the representation of persons belonging to national minorities in elected bodies need to be coupled with effective implementing legislation and accompanying measures within reasonable time'; see also Weller, *The Rights of Minorities* (n 14 above), 442–3.

[18] See Venice Commission, Opinion on the Constitution of Serbia, CDL-AD(2007)004, 17–18 March 2007, para 52; Venice Commission Opinion on the Constitution of Montenegro, CDL-AD(2007)047, 14–15 December 2007, paras 53–4; Venice Commission interim Opinion on the Draft Constitution of Montenegro (CDL-AD(2007)017), 1–2 June 2007, paras 11 and especially 65: 'International standards require that appropriate electoral arrangements are made to ensure effective participation of minorities in public life. Several options exist, and the necessary details should be set out in ordinary law, but it is essential that the Constitution provides in general terms the necessary guarantees ...'   [19] See, eg, Art 68(4) of the Constitution of Hungary

[20] See, eg, Art 64 (5) of the Constitution of Slovenia.

[21] See, eg, Art 81 of the Constitution of Kosovo and Advisory Committee First Opinion on Kosovo, ACFC/INF/OP/I(2005)004, 25 November 2005, para 110; Advisory Committee Second Opinion on 'the former Yugoslav Republic of Macedonia', ACFC/INF/OP/II2005)001, 23 February 2007, para 193.

[22] See Advisory Committee Thematic Commentary (n 5 above), para 97–9 which is somewhat cautious on 'veto rights'.

international bodies, namely cultural autonomy and positive measures in elections and functioning of elected bodies (other than cultural autonomy).

Models of cultural autonomy are considered non-territorial arrangements of self-governance by the Lund Recommendations and they are deemed to be instrumental particularly for dispersed national minorities.[23] Such models of cultural autonomy were mostly operational during the inter war period but there has been a certain revival of these arrangements, especially in Eastern European countries, following the fall of the Berlin Wall. Examples include re-establishment of old cultural autonomies as well as recent introduction or attempts to introduce new models in countries such as Estonia, Romania, Hungary, and Croatia. These models usually involve the election of bodies of cultural autonomy.

Whereas it is clear that the system of cultural autonomy as such needs to be entrenched in a law, a review of the findings and opinions of international bodies reveals that there are a number of important questions which also need to be entrenched in a legal basis with a view to making the system fully operational in practice. A case in point is offered by the Romanian Draft Law on the Statute of National Minorities Living in Romania, which aimed to introduce a new and ambitious model of cultural autonomy involving real decision-making powers for the institutions of cultural autonomy. Certain key issues were, however, left unanswered in the draft law at issue, which generated serious doubts as to the workability of the system as a whole. For example, it was apparent that the relationship between the institutions of cultural autonomy and the state authorities—including from a budgetary perspective—were not sufficiently regulated in detail in the law itself so as to avoid subsequent conflicts of competences, overlap in duties and legal uncertainty. These deficiencies, which were concerned with the weak entrenchment of the system of cultural autonomy, were identified by the Advisory Committee in the context of its second monitoring cycle in Romania.[24] They were also largely addressed by the Venice Commission, which undertook a detailed analysis of the Draft Law at the request of the Romanian government,[25] and considered by other commentators who

---

[23] See Recommendation 17 and related Explanatory Note.
[24] Advisory Committee Second Opinion on Romania, ACFC/INF/OP/II(2005)007, 24 November 2005, paras 71–2: 'With regard to the mechanism of "cultural autonomy" introduced by the Draft Law on the Status of National Minorities, the Advisory Committee considers that, in order to become operational, the legislature needs to provide additional clarifications. Eg, to avoid an overlap of responsibilities and the taking of conflicting decisions, special attention should be focused on relations between the institutions of cultural autonomy and other decision-making actors, particularly those state bodies which have the same or similar responsibilities in the fields covered by cultural autonomy …'
[25] See Opinion of the Venice Commission on the Draft Law on the Status of National Minorities Living in Romania of 21–2 October 2005, CDL-AD(2005)026, paras 66–73.

highlighted at the same time the difficulty of adopting a detailed law fully integrated into the constitutional order.[26]

In the case of Hungary, and notwithstanding the already significant experience gathered during almost fifteen years of implementation of the system of minority self-governments as provided for in the 1993 Law on the Rights of National and Ethnic Minorities, a number of somewhat similar problems have been identified: the Advisory Committee has therefore also called for clearer legislative norms to govern, inter alia, duties and jurisdictions of minority self-governments, as well as regulations pertaining to financial contributions by the state and by local authorities.[27] The OSCE HCNM also supported legislative amendments to address these shortcomings.[28]

In the case of Croatia, the 2002 Constitutional Law on the Rights of National Minorities fundamentally changed the organizational structure, resulting in important new bodies at the local, regional, and central level and increasing the voice of representatives of national minorities in what resembles a system of cultural autonomy. In this context, the election procedures of the minority councils in particular were deemed to justify more detailed legislative regulations.[29]

Building on these various country-specific experiences related to malfunctioning models of cultural autonomy,[30] the Advisory Committee has recently come up with a relatively clear call for stronger and clearer legislative guarantees in this field, as spelled out in its second thematic commentary.[31]

Another set of measures, which could be grouped under the heading 'positive measures in elections and in the functioning of elected bodies' could give rise to

---

[26] See C Decker, 'Contemporary forms of cultural autonomy in Eastern Europe: Recurrent problems and prospects for improving the functioning of elected bodies of cultural autonomies' in *The Participation of Minorities in Public Life* (n 16 above), 95.

[27] Advisory Committee Second Opinion on Hungary (n 16 above), paras 113–8 and especially 119: 'Clearer rules on state and local authority funding and support for the minority self-governments could help to improve relations between the local minority self-governments and local authorities.'

[28] See Verstichel, 'Special measures to promote minority representation in elected bodies' (n 16 above), 59.   [29] Advisory Committee Second Opinion on Croatia (n 16 above), paras 168–9.

[30] For another telling example of malfunctioning, see the Serbian councils, the establishment of which was problematic as it was based on a ministerial decree rather than a law, as was foreseen in the 2002 Federal Law, and see F Bieber,'The role of the FCNM in selected countries of South-eastern Europe after two monitoring cycles', Report prepared for the Conference: Enhancing the Impact of the FCNM, 9–10 October 2008, Strasbourg, 11, available at <www.coe.int/minorities> (accessed 1 July 2009).

[31] See Advisory Committee Thematic Commentary (n 5 above), para 136: 'Where State Parties provide for such cultural autonomy arrangements, the corresponding constitutional and legislative provisions should clearly specify the nature and scope of the autonomy system and the competencies of the autonomous bodies. In addition, their legal status, the relations between them and other relevant State institutions as well as the funding of the envisaged autonomy system, should be clarified in the respective legislation. It is important that persons belonging to national minorities be involved and that their views be duly taken into account when legislation on autonomy arrangements is being prepared or amended.'

the possible emergence of an international requirement for entrenchment of a legislative nature. It is again not possible to undertake in the present contribution a thorough country-by-country review of such positive measures, the variety of which renders comparison difficult at times. A few instances have, however, been addressed by international bodies and it may be worth considering them under the specific standpoint of their legal entrenchment.

By nature, electoral rules—be they general or specific to enhance minority representation—are to be found in a law, which is in most cases an election law or an electoral code. Electoral systems may, as such, of course facilitate minority representation in a given domestic context as can number, size and magnitude of electoral districts, but specific positive measures—or electoral affirmative action rules—can do it more directly.[32] One such example is the provision of reserved seats, but it was shown earlier in this chapter that the related requirement seems to be that of a constitutional rather than mere legal entrenchment. There are, however, other such specific measures, such as threshold exemptions for candidate lists or parties representing national minorities. The existence of such threshold exemptions is generally seen as a means of enhancing minority participation in elected bodies[33] and it is logical that such a measure is to be codified in a law, as is the case in several states such as Poland, Germany, and Serbia.[34] The introduction of a double voting right for persons belonging to national minorities is another specific measure enhancing the political participation of minorities. Although this measure has existed in a very limited number of states and despite doubts expressed as to its compatibility with the principle 'one person–one vote',[35] there is agreement that it can prove instrumental in

---

[32] Such measures are explicitly provided for by the Code of Good Practice in Electoral Matters of the Venice Commission of 18–19 October 2002, CDL-AD (2002)23rev, which states under item 2.4 lit. b): 'Special rules guaranteeing national minorities reserved seats or providing for exceptions to the normal seat allocation criteria for parties representing national minorities (for instance, exemption from a quorum requirement) do not in principle run counter to equal suffrage'; for a list of the most frequently used affirmative action electoral rules, see Venice Commission, Report on Electoral Rules and Affirmative Action for National Minorities' Participation in Decision-making Process in European Countries, CDL-AD(2005)009, 11–12 March 2005, para 16.   [33] See Advisory Committee Thematic Commentary (n 5 above), para 82.
[34] See Venice Commission Report on Electoral Rules (n 32 above), paras 39, 45; Venice Commission/ODIHR Joint Recommendations on the Laws on Parliamentary, Presidential and Local Elections, and Electoral Administration in the Republic of Serbia, CDL-AD(2006)013, para 82: 'As noted earlier, Article 81 of the Law on Parliamentary Elections creates an exception to the legal threshold for mandate allocation for "political parties of ethnic minorities and coalitions of political parties of ethnic minorities" ... the OSCE/ODIHR and the Venice Commission recommend that consideration be given to providing a similar provision in the Law on Local Elections'; Advisory Committee First Opinion on Poland, ACFC/INF/OP/I(2004)005, 27 November 2003.
[35] See Venice Commission Report on Dual Voting for Persons Belonging to National Minorities, CDL-AD(2008)013, 13–14 June 2008, paras 55–72.

advancing minority representation in some very specific circumstances, it being understood that such a measure clearly requires legal entrenchment.[36]

An important way of advancing minority participation consists of promoting the representation/participation of persons belonging to national minorities in public administration, in the judiciary and/or in the executive. Indeed, it is generally viewed as good practice to involve persons belonging to national minorities in various aspects of public life, and especially in state bodies, as this is an important factor in their integration. This is a general requirement which derives from Art 15 of the FCNM, and the Advisory Committee has consistently encouraged states parties to identify ways and means to make sure that state authorities reflect, to the extent possible, the diversity of society. In practice, a wide range of measures exist which aim to achieve this result and a number of countries have developed their own measures.[37] Whatever the mechanism chosen, however, international bodies have often been preoccupied by their efficiency and, consequently, called for entrenching them in a legislative basis, as well as for coupling them with adequate implementation measures.[38]

Finally, against the background of introducing positive electoral measures in favour of persons belonging to national minorities, mention must be made of the need for states to provide for clear and efficient legislative guarantees ensuring protection of ethnic data. Admittedly, electoral systems providing for facilitated representation of minorities may necessitate a certain identification of voters belonging to a minority. These systems must, however, be accompanied by legal guarantees ensuring the confidentiality of the information given, which constitutes data of a sensitive nature as this is a requirement stemming inter alia from Art 3 of the FCNM.[39]

---

[36] See Venice Commission Opinion on the Draft Law on Rights of National Minorities of Bosnia and Herzegovina, CDL-INF(2001)12, 6–7 July 2001, ad item 17; Venice Commission Opinion on the Constitutional Law on the Rights of National Minorities in Croatia, CDL-AD (2002)30, 18–19 October 2002, paras 29–32; Venice Commission Opinion on the Constitutional Law on the Rights of National Minorities in Croatia, CDL-AD(2003)009, 14–15 March 2003, para 22: 'The Commission recalls that the election law still has to solve several important issues, such as the issue of double vote for members of national minorities and the issue of additional seats in Parliament in derogation of the number of seats fixed in the Constitution …'.

[37] Eg, the Statute of Autonomy of South Tyrol requires that the Executive authority of the Province (*giunta*) be composed of members from the linguistic groups in proportion with the linguistic composition of the Provincial Council. See F Palermo and J Woelk, *Diritto costituzionale comparato dei gruppi e delle minoranze* (2008), 56; see also Art 79 of the Constitution of Montenegro, which includes a right to 'proportionate representation' in public services, state authorities and local self-government bodies.

[38] See Advisory Committee Thematic Commentary (n 5 above), paras 120–8 and especially 121; Advisory Committee Second Opinion on Romania (n 24 above), para 195; Advisory Committee Second Opinion on Croatia (n 16 above), paras 155–9; Advisory Committee First Opinion on Montenegro, 28 February 2008, ACFC/OP/I(2008)001, paras 95–6; Venice Commission Opinion on the Draft Law on Amendments to the Law on National Minorities in Lithuania, CDL-AD(2003)013, 14–15 March 2003 paras 23–4.

[39] See Advisory Committee First Opinion on Russia, ACFC/INF/OP/I(2003)005, 13 September 2002, para 104; Advisory Committee First Opinion on Italy (n 13 above), para 21; Venice

Minority consultative bodies constitute another area where a growing requirement of legislative entrenchment has emerged in recent years, notably through the interpretation and implementation of Art 15 of the FCNM. The establishment and functioning of such bodies differs greatly from one state to another and the related state practice is consequently extremely diverse, bearing in mind also that no specific model is prescribed by the relevant international standards.[40] Today, it is nevertheless considered important to ensure that consultative bodies have a clear legal status, that the obligation to consult them is entrenched in law, and that their involvement in decision-making processes is of a regular and permanent nature. It is also important to ensure that relevant regulations are detailed enough to provide for efficient and consistent consultation.[41] It is even the status, competences, and working practices of these bodies which should preferably be anchored in a law and be clearly defined.[42]

3. Sub-legislative Guarantees

While genuine minority consultative bodies should be given a clear legal status, there is a range of less formal mechanisms which may play a (more limited) role in the promotion of a full and effective participation of minorities in public affairs. This is notably the case for specialized consultative bodies or ad hoc structures, which can be set up to address the situation of a particular national minority or a given question, such as the development of a draft law. Such mechanisms exist in many states and although they can play a useful role in certain contexts, they are certainly not generally encouraged and less demanding forms of entrenchment seem perfectly admissible in this regard. Good practice would perhaps suggest consolidating their status and competences, and consequently their entrenchment, if they have proved useful tools and calls have been voiced in this direction in respect of different countries.[43]

Commission Opinion on the Constitutional Law on the Rights of National Minorities in Croatia, CDL-AD(2002)30, 18–19 October 2002, para 32; Venice Commission Opinion on the Constitutional Law on the Rights of National Minorities in Croatia, CDL-AD(2003)009, 14–15 March 2003, para 22; Opinion of the Venice Commission on the Draft Law on the Status of National Minorities Living in Romania of 21–2 October 2005, CDL-AD(2005)026, para 53; Code of Good Practice in Electoral Matters of the Venice Commission of 18–19 October 2002, CDL-AD (2002) 23rev, ad item 2.4 lit. c.

[40] See Verstichel, 'Special measures to promote minority representation in elected bodies' (n 16 above), 58–9. [41] See Advisory Committee Thematic Commentary (n 5 above), para 107.

[42] Ibid, para 116; DH-MIN Handbook on Minority Consultation Mechanisms, DH-MIN (2006)012, 20 October 2006, paras 34–8; Advisory Committee First Opinion on Azerbaijan, ACFC/INF/OP/I(2004)001, 22 May 2003, para 74; and Second Opinion on Azerbaijan, ACFC/INF/OP/II(2007)007, 9 November 2007, paras 153, 155; Advisory Committee Second Opinion on Norway, ACFC/INF/OP/II(2007)007, 5 October 2006, para 140; Advisory Committee Second Opinion on the Czech Republic, ACFC/INF/OP/II(2005)002, 24 February 2005, para 174; Weller, *The Rights of Minorities* (n 14 above), 448.

[43] See Advisory Committee Second Opinion on Finland, ACFC/INF/OP/II(2001)002, 2 March 2006, paras 148–51; Advisory Committee First Opinion on Norway, ACFC/INF/OP/I (2003)003, 12 September 2002, para 61; Advisory Committee Second Opinion on Switzerland, ACFC/INF/OP/II(2008)002, 29 February 2008, para 180.

In addition to minority consultative bodies, including less formal mechanisms, many governments have also introduced governmental coordination bodies. These bodies comprise mainly governmental representatives but also frequently include invited representatives of national minorities in their membership, usually without them forming the numerical majority. The role of these coordination bodies often appears subordinate to the aim of interministerial coordination and they can therefore not be equated with genuine minority consultative bodies, which usually have a wider mandate.[44] The distinction, however, is not always easy to draw in practice.[45] In any case, their aim is essentially to facilitate the design, coordination, and monitoring of governmental policies. Consequently, it largely falls within the prerogative of a government, which can decide on the organization of its own work, usually through the adoption of decrees or other sub-legislative guarantees. This makes them less likely to survive any government change but they can, on the other hand, easily be established and may help streamline minority policies while not substituting genuine minority consultation bodies.

B. Implementation mechanisms

Implementation mechanisms, or remedies, are essential to ensure that arrangements designed to enhance the political participation of minorities are respected in practice. Not surprisingly, there is a correlation between the type of legal entrenchment on the one hand, and the level of guarantee on the other hand. In other words, the higher the hierarchical level of entrenchment, the stronger the guarantee. Constitutional entrenchments are usually coupled with powerful judicial review, whereas legislative or sub-legislative guarantees may sometimes be left with a weaker judicial remedy, or simply non-judicial mechanisms.

1. *Judicial or Quasi-judicial Mechanisms*

In a democratic state, the judicial resolution of conflicts remains the strongest guarantee for redressing possible violations of legal entrenchments promoting minority participation. It is therefore logical that the Lund Recommendations mention this avenue at the outset, while stressing that judicial resolution of conflicts, such as judicial review of legislation or administrative actions, requires that the state possess an independent, accessible, and impartial judiciary whose decisions are respected.[46]

---

[44] See M Weller, 'Consultation arrangements concerning national minorities', Report prepared for the DH-MIN on 24 February 2006 (DH-MIN(2006)011), 20.
[45] See Advisory Committee Second Opinion on Italy, ACFC/INF/OP/II(2005)003, 24 February 2005, paras 127–31. [46] See Lund Recommendation 24, para 1.

As far as territorial arrangements like autonomy or devolution are concerned, it can be noted that, in most cases, a judicial remedy is in place to ensure that the state does not unduly reduce or even withdraw the competences exercised by the devolved entities. This may take the form of a review undertaken by the constitutional court, at least for those autonomies which have been anchored in the constitution or in a constitutional law.[47] Furthermore, although it is not strictly speaking a remedy, mention should also be made of the numerous guarantees which usually accompany the amendment procedure of arrangements like autonomy or devolution: such amendments frequently include an obligation to consult the devolved entity—and thereby at least indirectly the minority which benefits from it—before deciding on any change. In a number of cases, the central government must in fact even obtain the consent of the devolved entity or a qualified majority possibly entailing the consent of the minority concerned.[48] The findings of international bodies monitoring human and minority rights tend to corroborate this duty of the central state to take into careful account the views of the minorities concerned when (re)designing territorial arrangements[49] and even when carrying out administrative territorial reforms that can adversely impact on the possibility to enjoy effective participation in public affairs.[50] Finally, one should also be mindful of the principle that once such autonomy arrangements have been introduced, a state may be under a general obligation not to worsen or abolish them without the consent of the inhabitants concerned.[51] Admittedly, this doctrinal principle may be questioned but it can play a safeguarding role, especially for those somewhat weaker autonomies that enjoy no constitutional entrenchment.

As is the case with territorial arrangements, special electoral rights for minorities—or more specifically their right to a special representation in parliament—are usually also matched by a strong judicial review system, which has, in some instances, materialized through landmark rulings by constitutional courts. The most interesting judicial statements in this regard come from countries providing for high standards of preferential political representation of their minorities, such as Slovenia and Croatia.[52] Even in countries where

---

[47] Concerning the autonomy of the Basque Country in Spain, see, eg, EJ Ruiz Vieytez, 'The evolution of autonomy in the Basque country: Experiences and trends' in *Constitutions, Autonomies and the EU Report from the Aland Islands Peace Institute* (2008), 9.

[48] See Verstichel, 'Special measures to promote minority representation in elected bodies' (n 16 above), 60; Palermo and Woelk, *Diritto costituzionale comparato dei gruppi e delle minoranze* (n 37 above), 59.

[49] See, eg, Advisory Committee First Opinion on Serbia and Montenegro, ACFC/INF/OP/I (2004)002, 27 November 2003, para 112, which concerns the case of Vojvodina.

[50] See, eg, Advisory Committee Second Opinion on Denmark, ACFC/INF/OP/II(2004)005, 9 December 2004, paras 158–68, where the German minority is affected by the planned administrative reform in the Southern Jutland County.

[51] See Suksi, 'On the entrenchment of autonomy' (n 12 above), 164; Benedikter, *The World's Working Regional Autonomies* (n 12 above), 369.

[52] See F Palermo, 'Domestic enforcement and direct effect of the FCNM' in *The FCNM: A useful pan-European instrument?* (2008), 207–9.

minority representatives have challenged their alleged lack of access to elected bodies, constitutional or supreme courts have occasionally delivered interesting rulings, such as in Poland, and Bosnia and Herzegovina.[53]

2. Non-judicial Mechanisms

Entrenchment that consists of sub-legislative guarantees is in most cases not compounded by judicial remedies in the sense that its alleged violation cannot be reviewed by courts. For example, it is possible, and in fact rather frequent in practice, that the structure of existing governmental coordination bodies, specialized consultative bodies or ad hoc structures is changed through a simple decision from the executive.[54] Even minority consultative bodies, *stricto sensu*, can easily be suppressed or institutionally weakened if they do not benefit from legislative entrenchment. In such cases, best practice would certainly encourage the establishment of some form of negotiation, or at least mediation, with the minorities concerned in order to comply fully with the spirit of Recommendation 24 of the Lund Recommendations.

That being said, non-judicial mechanisms of dispute resolution should not necessarily be construed as alternative ways to existing judicial avenues: in fact these two types of dispute resolution can coexist in practice. Indeed, it is in the interest of any democratic society to try and resolve possible conflicts with minorities through negotiation, mediation or arbitration if this can prevent the systematic use of court adjudication. It is, however, essential that such non-adversarial means of dispute resolution are used in good faith by the authorities with a view to finding constructive solutions and not just *pro forma*. The monitoring of the FCNM offers some examples of such non-judicial mechanisms of dispute resolution[55] and a number of countries in the Western Balkans have for example established committees charged with mediating between majorities and minorities,[56] but it seems that states parties tend to overlook the importance of non-judicial means in their reporting obligations.[57]

---

[53] See Polish Supreme Court, 18 March 1998 (Gorzelik), followed by ECHR [GC] judgment of 17 February 2004, *Gorzelik and ors v Poland*; Constitutional Court of Bosnia and Herzegovina, AP 2678/06, 29 September 2006, followed by Venice Commission Amicus Curiae Brief (CDL-AD(2008)027), 17–18 October 2008.

[54] See, eg, Advisory Committee First Opinion on Romania (n 16 above), para 69.

[55] See Advisory Committee First Opinion on Hungary (n 16 above), para 47, which states that 'the Parliamentary Commissioner for National and Ethnic Minority Rights may be best placed to review these complaints and provide guidance in remedying shortcomings'; Advisory Committee First Opinion on Austria, ACFC/INF/OP/I(2002)009, 16 May 2002, para 51; see also Advisory Committee Second Opinion on Austria, ACFC/INF/OP/II(2007)005, 8 June 2007, paras 124–9, which illustrates the possible interrelation between judicial and non-judicial mechanisms of dispute resolution and at the same time the need to resort to the latter in good faith and not just to avoid implementation of binding rulings.

[56] See Bieber, 'The role of the FCNM in selected countries of South-eastern Europe' (n 30 above).

[57] See Weller, *The Rights of Minorities* (n 14 above), 450–1.

IV. General Assessment

Entrenchment and implementation mechanisms are needed to contribute to ensuring that the effective participation of minorities in public life becomes a tangible reality in European states. It is indeed through strong legal guarantees and efficient means of dispute resolution that minorities can advance their claims to take a more active part in political life. The importance of guarantees and remedies must therefore be borne in mind since participatory rights are a *sine qua non* for a democratic society to fully respect the rights of its minorities.

The existing international standards are not very prescriptive as to the level of entrenchment and the types of remedies which are expected from the states, in contrast to their importance for making political participation more than a slogan. In fact, apart from the Lund Recommendations, which devote a specific chapter to them, they are mostly to be inferred from more general guarantees promoting effective participation, which necessarily entail a wide margin of appreciation for the national authorities. This margin of appreciation refers not only to the models of participation, but also to the entrenchment and the remedies chosen.

Notwithstanding this somewhat weak international legal framework, it is striking to note that, in the last ten years or so, an evolving state practice, which is subject to increased scrutiny through various European bodies, clearly shows a tendency to reinforce the entrenchment of domestic measures to promote minority participation in public affairs. This is at least apparent for mechanisms such as cultural autonomy, minority consultative bodies, and positive measures in elections and in the functioning of elected bodies. It is therefore to be expected that in the future, the interpretation of existing standards will be more demanding in terms of entrenchment and, possibly, remedies, since a growing number of states understand them in such a way.

The reinforcement of entrenchment is not supposed to mean that existing measures promoting minority participation in public affairs shall become more difficult to revise. As expressed in the Lund Recommendations, it is indeed essential that measures can be reviewed periodically in order to take account of changing legal, social, and other circumstances. The minorities and their representatives must however be closely associated with any review exercise and it is good practice that their consent is sought before implementing reforms in this field.

Finally, it can be noted that the question of remedies merits closer attention by states, as well as by international bodies. Whereas in most cases, any reinforcement of the entrenchment of a guarantee would be accompanied by corresponding progress as regards remedies, more effort should be made to report on domestic practice in this field and more attention should be given to evaluating the effect, in practice, of non-judicial means of dispute resolution.

APPENDIX I

The Lund Recommendations on the Effective Participation of National Minorities in Public Life (OSCE)

Introduction

In its Helsinki Decisions of July 1992, the Organization for Security and Cooperation in Europe (OSCE) established the position of High Commissioner on National Minorities to be 'an instrument of conflict prevention at the earliest possible stage'. This mandate was create largely in reaction to the situation in the former Yugoslavia which some feared would be repeated elsewhere in Europe, especially among the countries in transition to democracy, and could undermine the promise of peace and prosperity as envisaged in the Charter of Paris for a New Europe adopted by the Heads of State and Government in November 1990.

On 1 January 1993, Mr. Max van der Stoel took up his duties as the first OSCE High Commissioner on National Minorities (HCNM). Drawing on his considerable personal experience as a former Member of Parliament, Foreign Minister of The Netherlands, Permanent Representative to the United Nations, and long-time human rights advocate, Mr. van der Stoel turned his attention to the many disputes between minorities and central authorities in Europe which had the potential, in his view, to escalate. Acting quietly through diplomatic means, the HCNM has become involved in over a dozen States, including Albania, Croatia, Estonia, Hungary, Kazakstan, Kyrgyzstan, Latvia, the Former Yugoslav Republic of Macedonia, Romania, Slovakia and Ukraine. His involvement has focused primarily on those situations involving persons belonging to national/ethnic groups who constitute the numerical majority in one State but the numerical minority in another State, thus engaging the interest of governmental authorities in each State and constituting a potential source of inter-State tension if not conflict. Indeed, such tensions have defined much of European history.

In addressing the substance of tensions involving national minorities, the HCNM approaches the issues as an independent, impartial and cooperative actor. While the HCNM is not a supervisory mechanism, he employs the international standards to which each State has agreed as his principal framework of analysis and the foundation of his specific recommendations. In this relation, it is important to recall the commitments undertaken by all OSCE participating States, in particular those of the 1990 Copenhagen Document of the Conference on the Human Dimension which, in Part IV, articulates detailed standards relating to national minorities. All OSCE States are also bound by United Nations obligations relating to human rights, including minority rights, and the great majority of OSCE States are further bound by the standards of the Council of Europe.

Through the course of more than six years of intense activity, the HCNM has identified certain recurrent issues and themes which have become the subject of his attention in a number of States in which he is involved. Among these are issues of minority education and use of minority languages, in particular as matters of great importance for the maintenance and development of the identity of persons belonging to national minorities. With a view to achieving an appropriate and coherent application of relevant minority rights in the OSCE area, the HCNM requested the Foundation on Inter-Ethnic Relations - a non-governmental organization established in 1993 to carry out specialized activities in support of the HCNM - to bring together two groups of internationally recognized independent experts to elaborate two sets of recommendations: The Hague Recommendations regarding the Education Rights of National Minorities (1996) and the Oslo Recommendations regarding the Linguistic Rights of National Minorities (1998). Both sets of recommendations have subsequently served as references for policy- and law-makers in a number of States. The recommendations are available (in several languages) from the Foundation on Inter-Ethnic Relations free of charge.

A third recurrent theme which has arisen in a number of situations in which the HCNM has been involved is that of forms of effective participation of national minorities in the governance of States. In order to gain a sense of the views and experiences of OSCE participating States on this issue and to allow States to share their experiences with each other, the HCNM and the OSCE's Office for Democratic Institutions and Human Rights convened a conference of all OSCE States and relevant international organisations entitled 'Governance and Participation: Integrating Diversity', which was hosted by the Swiss Confederation in Locarno from 18 to 20 October 1998. The Chairman's Statement issued at the end of the conference summarized the themes of the meeting and noted the desirability of 'concrete follow-up activities, including the further elaboration of the various concepts and mechanisms of good governance with the effective participation of minorities, leading to integration of diversity within the State'. To this end, the HCNM called upon the Foundation on Inter-Ethnic Relations, in co-operation with the Raoul Wallenberg Institute of Human Rights and Humanitarian Law, to bring together a group of internationally recognized independent experts to elaborate recommendations and outline alternatives, in line with the relevant international standards.

Appendix I 753

The result of the above initiative is The Lund Recommendations on the Effective Participation of National Minorities in Public Life—named after the Swedish city in which the experts last met and completed the recommendations. Among the experts were jurists specializing in relevant international law, political scientists specializing in constitutional orders and election systems, and sociologists specializing in minority issues. Specifically, under the Chairmanship of the Director of the Raoul Wallenberg Institute, Professor Gudmundur Alfredsson, the experts were: Professor Gudmundur Alfredsson (Icelandic), Director of the Raoul Wallenberg Institute of Human Rights and Humanitarian Law, Lund University; Professor Vernon Bogdanor (British), Professor of Government, Oxford University; Professor Vojin Dimitrijevi (Yugoslavian), Director of the Belgrade Centre for Human Rights; Dr. Asbjørn Eide (Norwegian), Senior Fellow at the Norwegian Institute of Human Rights; Professor Yash Ghai (Kenyan), Sir YK Pao Professor of Public Law, University of Hong Kong; Professor Hurst Hannum (American), Professor of International Law, Fletcher School of Law and Diplomacy, Tufts University; Mr. Peter Harris (South African), Senior Executive to the International Institute for Democracy and Electoral Assistance; Dr. Hans-Joachim Heintze (German), Director of the Institut für Friedenssicherungsrecht und Humanitäres Völkerrecht, Ruhr-Universität Bochum; Professor Ruth Lapidoth (Israeli), Professor of International Law and Chairman of the Academic Committee of the Institute for European Studies, The Hebrew University of Jerusalem; Professor Rein Müllerson (Estonian), Chair of International Law, King's College, University of London; Dr. Sarlotta Pufflerova (Slovak), Director, Foundation Citizen and Minority/Minority Rights Group; Professor Steven Ratner (American), Professor of International Law, University of Texas; Dr. Andrew Reynolds (British), Assistant Professor of Government, University of Notre Dame; Mr. Miquel Strubell (Spanish and British), Director of the Institute of Catalan Socio-Linguistics, Generalitat de Catalunya; Professor Markku Suksi (Finnish), Professor of Public Law, Åbo Akademi University; Professor Danilo Türk (Slovene), Professor of International Law, Ljubljana University; Dr. Fernand de Varennes (Canadian), Senior Lecturer in Law and Director of the Asia-Pacific Centre for Human Rights and the Prevention of Ethnic Conflict, Murdoch University; Professor Roman Wieruszewski (Polish), Director of the Poznan Human Rights Centre, Polish Academy of Sciences.

Insofar as existing standards of minority rights are part of human rights, the starting point of the consultations among the experts was to presume compliance by States with all other human rights obligations including, in particular, freedom from discrimination. It was also presumed that the ultimate object of all human rights is the full and free development of the individual human personality in conditions of equality. Consequently, it was presumed that civil society should be open and fluid and, therefore, integrate all persons, including those belonging to national minorities. Moreover, insofar as the objective of good and democratic governance is to serve the needs and interests of the whole population, it was presumed that all governments seek to ensure the maximum opportunities for contributions from those affected by public decision-making.

The purpose of the Lund Recommendations, like The Hague and Oslo Recommendations before them, is to encourage and facilitate the adoption by States of specific measures to alleviate tensions related to national minorities and thus to serve the ultimate conflict prevention goal of the HCNM. The Lund Recommendations on the Effective Participation of National Minorities in Public Life attempt to clarify in relatively straightforward language and build upon the content of minority rights and other standards generally applicable in the situations in which the HCNM is involved. The standards have been interpreted specifically to ensure the coherence of their application in open and democratic States. The Recommendations are divided into four sub-headings which group the twenty-four recommendations into general principles, participation in decision-making, self-governance, and ways of guaranteeing such effective participation in public life. The basic conceptual division within the Lund Recommendations follows two prongs: participation in governance of the State as a whole, and self-governance over certain local or internal affairs. A wide variety of arrangements are possible and known. In several recommendations, alternatives are suggested. All recommendations are to be interpreted in accordance with the General Principles in Part I. A more detailed explanation of each recommendation is provided in an accompanying Explanatory Note wherein express reference to the relevant international standards is found.

General Principles

I. General Principles

1) Effective participation of national minorities in public life is an essential component of a peaceful and democratic society. Experience in Europe and elsewhere has shown that, in order to promote such participation, governments often need to establish specific arrangements for national minorities. These Recommendations aim to facilitate the inclusion of minorities within the State and enable minorities to maintain their own identity and characteristics, thereby promoting the good governance and integrity of the State.

2) These Recommendations build upon fundamental principles and rules of international law, such as respect for human dignity, equal rights, and nondiscrimination, as they affect the rights of national minorities to participate in public life and to enjoy other political rights. States have a duty to respect internationally recognized human rights and the rule of law, which allow for the full development of civil society in conditions of tolerance, peace, and prosperity.

3) When specific institutions are established to ensure the effective participation of minorities in public life, which can include the exercise of authority or responsibility by such institutions, they must respect the human rights of all those affected.

4) Individuals identify themselves in numerous ways in addition to their identity as members of a national minority. The decision as to whether an individual is a member of a minority, the majority, or neither rests with that individual and shall not be imposed upon her or him. Moreover, no person shall suffer any disadvantage as a result of such a choice or refusal to choose.

5) When creating institutions and procedures in accordance with these Recommendations, both substance and process are important. Governmental authorities and minorities should pursue an inclusive, transparent, and accountable process of consultation in order to maintain a climate of confidence. The State should encourage the public media to foster intercultural understanding and address the concerns of minorities.

II. Participation in Decision-Making

A. *Arrangements at the Level of the Central Government*

6) States should ensure that opportunities exist for minorities to have an effective voice at the level of the central government, including through special arrangements as necessary. These may include, depending upon the circumstances:
   - special representation of national minorities, for example, through a reserved number of seats in one or both chambers of parliament or in parliamentary committees; and other forms of guaranteed participation in the legislative process;
   - formal or informal understandings for allocating to members of national minorities cabinet positions, seats on the supreme or constitutional court or lower courts, and positions on nominated advisory bodies or other high-level organs;
   - mechanisms to ensure that minority interests are considered within relevant ministries, through, e.g., personnel addressing minority concerns or issuance of standing directives; and
   - special measures for minority participation in the civil service as well as the provision of public services in the language of the national minority.

B. *Elections*

7) Experience in Europe and elsewhere demonstrates the importance of the electoral process for facilitating the participation of minorities in the

political sphere. States shall guarantee the right of persons belonging to national minorities to take part in the conduct of public affairs, including through the rights to vote and stand for office without discrimination.

8) The regulation of the formation and activity of political parties shall comply with the international law principle of freedom of association. This principle includes the freedom to establish political parties based on communal identities as well as those not identified exclusively with the interests of a specific community.

9) The electoral system should facilitate minority representation and influence.
   - Where minorities are concentrated territorially, single-member districts may provide sufficient minority representation.
   - Proportional representation systems, where a political party's share in the national vote is reflected in its share of the legislative seats, may assist in the representation of minorities.
   - Some forms of preference voting, where voters rank candidates in order of choice, may facilitate minority representation and promote inter-communal cooperation.
   - Lower numerical thresholds for representation in the legislature may enhance the inclusion of national minorities in governance.

10) The geographic boundaries of electoral districts should facilitate the equitable representation of national minorities.

C. Arrangements at the Regional and Local Levels

11) States should adopt measures to promote participation of national minorities at the regional and local levels such as those mentioned above regarding the level of the central government (paragraphs 6-10) The structures and decision-making processes of regional and local authorities should be made transparent and accessible in order to encourage the participation of minorities.

D. Advisory and Consultative Bodies

12) States should establish advisory or consultative bodies within appropriate institutional frameworks to serve as channels for dialogue between governmental authorities and national minorities. Such bodies might also include special purpose committees for addressing such issues as housing, land, education, language, and culture. The composition of such bodies should reflect their purpose and contribute to more effective communication and advancement of minority interests.

13) These bodies should be able to raise issues with decisionmakers, prepare recommendations, formulate legislative and other proposals, monitor

developments and provide views on proposed governmental decisions that may directly or indirectly affect minorities. Governmental authorities should consult these bodies regularly regarding minority-related legislation and administrative measures in order to contribute to the satisfaction of minority concerns and to the building of confidence. The effective functioning of these bodies will require that they have adequate resources.

III. Self-Governance

14) Effective participation of minorities in public life may call for non-territorial or territorial arrangements of self-governance or a combination thereof. States should devote adequate resources to such arrangements.
15) It is essential to the success of such arrangements that governmental authorities and minorities recognize the need for central and uniform decisions in some areas of governance together with the advantages of diversity in others.
    - Functions that are generally exercised by the central authorities include defense, foreign affairs, immigration and customs, macro-economic policy, and monetary affairs.
    - Other functions, such as those identified below, may be managed by minorities or territorial administrations or shared with the central authorities.
    - Functions may be allocated asymmetrically to respond to different minority situations within the same State.
16) Institutions of self-governance, whether non-territorial or territorial, must be based on democratic principles to ensure that they genuinely reflect the views of the affected population.

A. Non-Territorial Arrangements

17) Non-territorial forms of governance are useful for the maintenance and development of the identity and culture of national minorities.
18) The issues most susceptible to regulation by these arrangements include education, culture, use of minority language, religion, and other matters crucial to the identity and way of life of national minorities.
    - Individuals and groups have the right to choose to use their names in the minority language and obtain official recognition of their names.
    - Taking into account the responsibility of the governmental authorities to set educational standards, minority institutions can determine curricula for teaching of their minority languages, cultures, or both.
    - Minorities can determine and enjoy their own symbols and other forms of cultural expression.

B. Territorial Arrangements

19) All democracies have arrangements for governance at different territorial levels. Experience in Europe and elsewhere shows the value of shifting certain legislative and executive functions from the central to the regional level, beyond the mere decentralization of central government administration from the capital to regional or local offices. Drawing on the principle of subsidiarity, States should favourably consider such territorial devolution of powers, including specific functions of self-government, particularly where it would improve the opportunities of minorities to exercise authority over matters affecting them.

20) Appropriate local, regional, or autonomous administrations that correspond to the specific historical and territorial circumstances of national minorities may undertake a number of functions in order to respond more effectively to the concerns of these minorities.
    - Functions over which such administrations have successfully assumed primary or significant authority include education, culture, use of minority language, environment, local planning, natural resources, economic development, local policing functions, and housing, health, and other social services.
    - Functions shared by central and regional authorities include taxation, administration of justice, tourism, and transport.

21) Local, regional, and autonomous authorities must respect and ensure the human rights of all persons, including the rights of any minorities within their jurisdiction.

IV. Guarantees

A. Constitutional and Legal Safeguards

22) Self-governance arrangements should be established by law and generally not be subject to change in the same manner as ordinary legislation. Arrangements for promoting participation of minorities in decision-making may be determined by law or other appropriate means.
    - Arrangements adopted as constitutional provisions are normally subject to a higher threshold of legislative or popular consent for their adoption and amendment.
    - Changes to self-governance arrangements established by legislation often require approval by a qualified majority of the legislature, autonomous bodies or bodies representing national minorities, or both.
    - Periodic review of arrangements for self-governance and minority participation in decision-making can provide useful opportunities to

Appendix I 759

determine whether such arrangements should be amended in the light of experience and changed circumstances.

23) The possibility of provisional or step-by-step arrangements that allow for the testing and development of new forms of participation may be considered. These arrangements can be established through legislation or informal means with a defined time period, subject to extension, alteration, or termination depending upon the success achieved.

B. *Remedies*

24) Effective participation of national minorities in public life requires established channels of consultation for the prevention of conflicts and dispute resolution, as well as the possibility of ad hoc or alternative mechanisms when necessary. Such methods include:
- judicial resolution of conflicts, such as judicial review of legislation or administrative actions, which requires that the State possess an independent, accessible, and impartial judiciary whose decisions are respected; and
- additional dispute resolution mechanisms, such as negotiation, fact finding, mediation, arbitration, an ombudsman for national minorities, and special commissions, which can serve as focal points and mechanisms for the resolution of grievances about governance issues.

Explanatory Note to the Lund Recommendations on the Effective Participation of National Minorities in Public Life

I. General Principles

1) Both the Charter of the United Nations (hereafter the 'UN Charter') and the foundational documents of the CSCE/OSCE seek to maintain and strengthen international peace and security through the development of friendly and co-operative relations between equally sovereign States respecting human rights, including the rights of persons belonging to minorities. Indeed, history shows that failure to respect human rights, including minority rights, can undermine stability within the State and negatively affect relations between States, thus endangering international peace and security.

Beginning with Principle VII of the decalogue of the 1975 Helsinki Final Act, the OSCE participating States have emphasised the fundamental link between respecting the legitimate interests of persons belonging to national minorities and the maintenance of peace and stability. This link has been reiterated in subsequent basic documents such as the 1983 Concluding Document of Madrid (Principle 15), the 1989 Concluding Document of Vienna (Principles 18 and 19), and the 1990 Charter of Paris for a New Europe, in addition to subsequent Summit Documents, e.g. the 1992 Helsinki Document (Part IV, paragraph 24) and the 1996 Lisbon Document (Part I, Lisbon Declaration on a Common and Comprehensive Security Model for Europe for the Twenty-First Century, paragraph 2). At the level of the United Nations, the link between protection and promotion of minority rights and maintenance of peace and stability is expressed, inter alia, in the preamble to the 1992 UN Declaration on the Rights of Persons Belonging to National or Ethnic, Religious and Linguistic Minorities (hereafter the 'UN Declaration on Minorities'). Moreover, following adoption of the Charter of Paris for a New Europe, all OSCE participating States are committed to democratic governance.

Full opportunities for the equal enjoyment of the human rights of persons belonging to minorities entails their effective participation in decision-making processes, especially with regard to those decisions specially affecting them. While situations vary greatly and ordinary democratic processes may be adequate to respond to the needs and aspirations of minorities, experience also shows that special measures are often required to facilitate the effective participation of minorities in decision-making. The following international standards commit States to take such action in such situations: according to paragraph 35 of the 1990 Document of the Copenhagen Meeting on the Human Dimension (hereafter the 'Copenhagen Document'), OSCE participating States 'will respect the right of persons belonging to national minorities to effective participation in public affairs, including participation in the affairs relating to the protection and promotion of the identity of such minorities'; according to Article 2, paragraphs 2 and 3, of the 1992 UN Declaration on Minorities, '[p]ersons belonging to minorities have the right to participate effectively in [¼] public life' and 'the right to participate effectively in decisions on the national and, where appropriate, regional level concerning the minority to which they belong or the regions in which they live'; and, according to Article 15 of the Council of Europe's 1994 Framework Convention for the Protection of National Minorities (hereafter the 'Framework Convention'), States Parties 'shall create the conditions necessary for the effective participation of persons belonging to national minorities in cultural, social and economic life and in public affairs, in particular those affecting them'.

The creation of opportunities for effective participation takes for granted that such participation will be voluntary. Indeed, the underlying notion of social and political integration is distinguished from processes and outcomes which constitute coerced assimilation, as cautioned in

Article 5 of the Framework Convention. Only through voluntary processes may the pursuit of the legitimate interests of persons belonging to minorities be a peaceful process which offers the prospect of optimal outcomes in public policy- and law-making. Such inclusive, participatory processes thus serve the objective of good governance by responding to the interests of the whole population - weaving all interests into the fabric of public life and ultimately strengthening the integrity of the State. The international standards referring to effective participation of minorities in public life underscore the fact that they do not imply any right to engage in activities contrary to the purposes and principles of the United Nations, OSCE or Council of Europe, including sovereign equality, territorial integrity and political independence of States (see paragraph 37 of the Copenhagen Document, Article 8(4) of the UN Declaration on Minorities, and the preamble of the Framework Convention).

2) In the spirit of paragraph 25 of Part VI of the 1992 Helsinki Document, these recommendations build upon the relevant commitments insofar as they offer OSCE participating States 'further avenues for more effective implementation of their CSCE commitments, including those related to the protection and the creation of conditions for the promotion of the ethnic, cultural, linguistic and religious identity of national minorities'.

Article 1(3) of the UN Charter specifies that one of the purposes of the organisation is 'To achieve international co-operation in solving international problems of an economic, social, cultural, or humanitarian character, and in promoting and encouraging respect for human rights and for fundamental freedoms for all without distinction as to race, sex, language, or religion' - which is further specified in Article 55(c) as including 'universal respect for, and observance of, human rights and fundamental freedoms for all without distinction as to race, sex, language, or religion'. The Charter is based upon the intimate relationship between respect for human rights and international peace and security, and the fundamental value of human dignity is further expressed in Article 1 of the 1948 Universal Declaration of Human Rights and the preambles of the 1966 International Covenant on Civil and Political Rights, the 1966 International Covenant on Economic, Social and Cultural Rights, and the 1965 International Convention on the Elimination of All Forms of Racial Discrimination. Such dignity is equally inherent in all human beings and accompanied by equal and inalienable rights.

Following from the premise of equal dignity and inalienable rights is the principle of non-discrimination as expressed in virtually all international human rights instruments, including notably Article 2 of the Universal Declaration of Human Rights, Articles 2 and 26 of the International Covenant on Civil and Political Rights, and Article 2 of the International Covenant on Economic, Social and Cultural Rights. Article 1 of the

International Convention on the Elimination of All Forms of Racial Discrimination makes clear that this instrument prohibits discrimination also on the basis of 'descent, or national or ethnic origin'. Article 14 of the 1950 European Convention for the Protection of Human Rights and Fundamental Freedoms (hereafter the 'European Convention on Human Rights') also expressly extends the principle of non-discrimination to cover grounds of 'national or social origin, [or] association with a national minority', whenever the rights and freedoms guaranteed by the convention are engaged. Indeed, the constitutions of most OSCE participating States incorporate these affirmations and principles.

Insofar as persons belonging to national minorities are entitled to the right to effective participation in public life, they are to enjoy this right without discrimination, as expressed in paragraph 31 of the Copenhagen Document, Article 4 of the Framework Convention, and Article 4(1) of the UN Declaration on Minorities. However, according to Article 4(2) of the Framework Convention, concern for equal dignity extends beyond the principle of non-discrimination towards 'full and effective equality between persons belonging to a national minority and those belonging to the majority' for which States should 'adopt, where necessary, adequate measures ... in all areas of ... political ... life' in respect of which 'they shall take due account of the specific conditions of the persons belonging to national minorities'.

The connection made in the recommendation between respect for human rights and the development of civil society reflects the call for an 'effective political democracy' which, according to the Preamble of the European Convention on Human Rights, is intimately related to justice and peace in the world. OSCE participating States have further affirmed in the Charter of Paris for a New Europe that democratic governance, including respect for human rights, is the basis for prosperity.

3) When specific institutions are established to ensure the effective participation of national minorities in public life, this must not be at the expense of others' rights. All human rights must be respected at all times, including by such institutions which may be delegated authority by the State. According to paragraph 33 of the Copenhagen Document, when participating States take measures necessary for the protection of the identity of persons belonging to national minorities, 'Any such measures will be in conformity with the principles of equality and non-discrimination with respect to the other citizens of the participating State concerned'. The Copenhagen Document further stipulates at paragraph 38 that OSCE 'participating States, in their efforts to protect and promote the rights of persons belonging to national minorities, will fully respect their undertakings under existing human rights conventions and other relevant international instruments'. The Framework Convention has a similar stipulation in Article 20: 'In the exercise of the rights and freedoms

flowing from the principles enshrined in the present framework Convention, any person belonging to a national minority shall respect the national legislation and the rights of others, in particular those of persons belonging to the majority or to other national minorities.' This addresses in particular the case of 'minorities within minorities', especially in the territorial context (see recommendations 16 and 21 below). This would also include respect for the human rights of women, including freedom from discrimination in relation to 'the political and public life of the country' as stipulated at Article 7 of the 1979 Convention on the Elimination of All Forms of Discrimination against Women.

4) The principle of self-identification of persons belonging to minorities is based on several fundamental commitments. Paragraph 32 of the Copenhagen Document specifies that 'To belong to a national minority is a matter of a person's individual choice and no disadvantage may arise from the exercise of such choice'. Article 3(1) of the Framework Convention provides similarly that 'Every person belonging to a national minority shall have the right freely to choose to be treated or not to be treated as such and no disadvantage shall result from this choice or from the exercise of the rights which are connected to that choice'. Article 3(2) of the UN Declaration on Minorities includes the same prohibition against any disadvantage resulting 'for any person belonging to a minority as the consequence of the exercise or non-exercise of the rights set forth in the present Declaration'.

An individual's freedom to identify oneself as one chooses is necessary to ensure respect for individual autonomy and liberty. An individual may possess several identities that are relevant not only for private life, but also in the sphere of public life. Indeed, in open societies with increasing movements of persons and ideas, many individuals have multiple identities which are coinciding, coexisting or layered (in an hierarchical or non-hierarchical fashion), reflecting their various associations. Certainly, identities are not based solely on ethnicity, nor are they uniform within the same community; they may be held by different members in varying shades and degrees. Depending upon the specific matters at issue, different identities may be more or less salient. As a consequence, the same person might identify herself or himself in different ways for different purposes, depending upon the salience of the identification and arrangement for her or him. For example, in some States a person may choose a certain language for submission on tax forms, yet identify herself or himself differently in a local community for other purposes.

5) In the framework of democracy, the process of decision-making is as important as the substance of decisions made. Since good governance is not only of the people but also for the people, its processes should always be inclusive of those concerned, transparent for all to see and judge, and

accountable to those affected. Only such processes will inspire and maintain public confidence. Inclusive processes may comprise consultation, polling, referenda, negotiation and even the specific consent of those directly affected. Decisions resulting from such processes are likely to inspire voluntary compliance. In situations where the views of the public authorities and the affected community may differ substantially, good governance may suggest using the services of a third party to assist in finding the most satisfactory arrangement.

In relation specifically to national minorities, paragraph 33 of the Copenhagen Document commits OSCE participating States to take measures to 'protect the ethnic, cultural, linguistic and religious identity of national minorities on their territory and create conditions for the promotion of that identity [...] after due consultations, including contacts with organizations or associations of such minorities'. In Part VI, paragraph 26, of the Helsinki Document, OSCE participating States further committed themselves to 'address national minority issues in a constructive manner, by peaceful means and through dialogue among all parties concerned on the basis of CSCE principles and commitments'. In connection with 'all parties concerned', paragraph 30 of the Copenhagen Document recognizes 'the important role of non-governmental organizations, including political parties, trade unions, human rights organizations and religious groups, in the promotion of tolerance, cultural diversity and the resolution of questions relating to national minorities'. Inclusive processes require conditions of tolerance. A social and political climate of mutual respect and equality needs to be assured by law and also taught as a social ethic shared by the whole population. The media have a special role in this regard. Article 6(1) of the Framework Convention provides that 'the Parties shall encourage a spirit of tolerance and intercultural dialogue and take effective measures to promote mutual respect and understanding and co-operation among all persons living on their territory, irrespective of those persons' ethnic, cultural, linguistic or religious identity, in particular in the fields of education, culture and the media'. In particular, States should act to stop the public use of derogatory or pejorative names and terms and should take steps to counteract negative stereotypes. Ideally, the representatives of the affected community should participate in the choice and design of any steps taken to overcome such problems.

II. Participation in Decision-Making

A. *Arrangements at the Level of the Central Government*

6) Building upon paragraph 35 of the Copenhagen Document, paragraph 1 of Part III of the 1991 Report of the CSCE (Geneva) Meeting of Experts

Appendix I 765

on National Minorities underlines that 'when issues relating to the situation of national minorities are discussed within their countries, they themselves should have the effective opportunity to be involved ... [and] that [such] democratic participation of persons belonging to national minorities or their representatives in decision-making or consultative bodies constitutes an important element of effective participation in public affairs'. Paragraph 24 of Part VI of the Helsinki Document committed OSCE participating States to 'intensify in this context their efforts to ensure the free exercise by persons belonging to national minorities, individually or in community with others, of their human rights and fundamental freedoms, including the right to participate fully, in accordance with the democratic decision-making procedures of each State, in the political, economic, social, and cultural life of their countries including through democratic participation in decision-making and consultative bodies at the national, regional, and local level, inter alia, through political parties and associations'.

The essence of participation is involvement, both in terms of the opportunity to make substantive contributions to decision-making processes and in terms of the effect of those contributions. The notion of good governance includes the premise that simple majoritarian decision-making is not always sufficient. In terms of the structure of the State, various forms of decentralization may be appropriate to assure the maximum relevance and accountability of decision-making processes for those affected, both at the level of the State and at sub-State levels. This may be accomplished through various ways in a unitary State or in federal and confederal systems. Minority representation in decision-making bodies may be assured through reserved seats (by way of quotas, promotions or other measures), while other forms of participation include assured membership in relevant committees, with or without voting rights. Representation on executive, judicial, administrative and other bodies may be assured through similar means, whether by formal requirement or by customary practice. Special bodies may also be established to accommodate minority concerns. Meaningful opportunities to exercise all minority rights require specific steps to be taken in the public service, including ensuring 'equal access to public service' as articulated in Article 5(c) of the International Convention on the Elimination of All Forms of Racial Discrimination.

B. *Elections*

7) Representative government through free, fair and periodic elections is the hallmark of contemporary democracy. The fundamental objective is, in the words of Article 21(3) of the Universal Declaration of Human Rights, that 'The will of the people shall be the basis of the authority of

government'. This basic standard is articulated in universal and European treaties, namely Article 25 of the International Covenant on Civil and Political Rights and Article 3 of Protocol I additional to the European Convention on Human Rights. For OSCE participating States, paragraphs 5 and 6 of the Copenhagen Document specify that, 'among those elements of justice which are essential to the full expression of the inherent dignity and of the equal and inalienable rights of all human beings', 'the will of the people, freely and fairly expressed through periodic and genuine elections, is the basis of the authority and legitimacy of all government'.

While States have considerable latitude in choosing the specific manner in which to comply with these obligations, they must do so without discrimination and should aim for as much representativeness as possible. Indeed, within the context of the United Nations, the Human Rights Committee has explained in paragraph 12 of its General Comment 25 on Article 25 (57th Session 1996) that 'Freedom of expression, assembly and association are essential conditions for the effective exercise of the right to vote and must be fully protected. [...] Information and materials about voting should be available in minority languages'. Moreover, paragraph 5 of General Comment 25 clarifies that 'The conduct of public affairs [...] is a broad concept which relates to the exercise of political power, in particular the exercise of legislative, executive and administrative powers. It covers all aspects of public administration, and the formulation and implementation of policy at international, national, regional and local levels'.

Insofar as no electoral system is neutral from the perspective of varying views and interests, States should adopt the system which would result in the most representative government in their specific situation. This is especially important for persons belonging to national minorities who might otherwise not have adequate representation.

8) In principle, democracies should not interfere with the way in which people organize themselves politically - as long as their means are peaceful and respectful of the rights of others. Essentially, this is a matter of freedom of association, as articulated in a wide variety of international instruments including: Article 20 of the Universal Declaration of Human Rights; Article 22 of the International Covenant on Civil and Political Rights; Article 11 of the European Convention on Human Rights; and paragraph 6 of the Copenhagen Document. Freedom of association has also been guaranteed specifically for persons belonging to national minorities under paragraph 32.6 of the Copenhagen Document and Article 7 of the Framework Convention. More specifically, paragraph 24 of Part VI of the Helsinki Document commits OSCE participating States 'to ensure the free exercise by persons belonging to national

minorities, individually or in community with others, of their human rights and fundamental freedoms, including the right to participate fully, [...] in the political [...] life of their countries including [...] through political parties and associations'.

While full respect for equal rights and non-discrimination will reduce or eliminate the demand and need for political parties formed on the basis of ethnic ties, in some situations such communal parties may be the only hope for effective representation of specific interests and, thus, for effective participation. Of course, parties may be formed on other bases, e.g. regional interests. Ideally, parties should be open and should cut across narrow ethnic issues; thus, mainstream parties should seek to include members of minorities to reduce the need or desire for ethnic parties. The choice of electoral system may be important in this regard. In any event, no political party or other association may incite racial hatred, which is prohibited by Article 20 of the International Covenant on Civil and Political Rights and Article 4 of the Convention on the Elimination of All Forms of Racial Discrimination.

9) The electoral system may provide for the selection of both the legislature and other bodies and institutions, including individual officials. While single member constituencies may provide sufficient representation for minorities, depending upon how the constituencies are drawn and the concentration of minority communities, proportional representation might help guarantee such minority representation. Various forms of proportional representation are practised in OSCE participating States, including the following: 'preference voting', whereby voters rank candidates in order of choice; 'open list systems', whereby electors can express a preference for a candidate within a party list, as well as voting for the party; 'panachage', whereby electors can vote for more than one candidate across different party lines; and 'cumulation', whereby voters can cast more than one vote for a preferred candidate. Thresholds should not be so high as to hamper minority representation.

10) In drawing the boundaries of electoral districts, the concerns and interests of national minorities should be taken into account with a view to assuring their representation in decision-making bodies. The notion of 'equity' means that no one should be prejudiced by the chosen method and that all concerns and interests should be given fair consideration. Ideally, boundaries should be determined by an independent and impartial body to ensure, among other concerns, respect for minority rights. This is often accomplished in OSCE participating States by means of standing, professional electoral commissions.

In any event, States should not alter electoral boundaries, or otherwise alter the proportions of the population in a district, for the purpose of diluting or excluding minority representation. This is expressly prohibited by Article 16 of the Framework Convention, while Article 5 of the European Charter of Local Self-Government stipulates that 'Changes in local authority boundaries shall not be made without prior consultation of the local communities concerned, possibly by means of a referendum where this is permitted by statute' (see recommendation 19 regarding territorial arrangements).

C. Arrangements at the Regional and Local Levels

11) This Recommendation applies to all levels of government below the central authorities (e.g. provinces, departments, districts, prefectures, municipalities, cities and towns, whether units within a unitary State or constituent units of a federal State, including autonomous regions and other authorities). The consistent enjoyment of all human rights by everyone equally means that the entitlements enjoyed at the level of the central government should be enjoyed throughout the structures below. However, the criteria used to create structures at the regional and local level may be different from those used at the level of the central government. Structures may also be established asymmetrically, with variation according to differing needs and expressed desires.

D. Advisory and Consultative Bodies

12) Paragraph 24 of Part VI of the Helsinki Document commits OSCE participating States 'to ensure the free exercise by persons belonging to national minorities, individually or in community with others, of their human rights and fundamental freedoms, including the right to participate fully [...] in the political [...] life of their countries including through democratic participation in [...] consultative bodies at the national, regional, and local level'. Such bodies can be standing or ad hoc, part of or attached to the legislative or executive branch or independent therefrom. Committees attached to parliamentary bodies, such as minority round tables, are known in several OSCE participating States. They can and do function at all levels of government, including self-government arrangements. In order to be effective, these bodies should be composed of minority representatives and others who can offer special expertise, provided with adequate resources, and given serious attention by decisionmakers. Aside from advice and counsel, such bodies can constitute a useful intermediary institution between decisionmakers and minority groups. They can also stimulate action at the level of government and among minority communities. Such bodies may also perform specific tasks related to the implementation of programs, e.g. in the field of education. In addition, special purpose

committees may hold particular significance for certain minorities who should be represented therein.
13) The possibilities for constructive use of such bodies vary with the situations. However, in all cases, good governance requires positive steps on the part of the authorities to engage established advisory and consultative bodies, to refer to them as needs may arise and to invite their input. An open and inclusive approach on the part of the authorities vis-à-vis these bodies and their members will contribute to better decisions and to greater confidence of the wider society.

III. Self-Governance

14) The term 'self-governance' implies a measure of control by a community over matters affecting it. The choice of the term 'governance' does not necessarily imply exclusive jurisdiction. In addition, it may subsume administrative authority, management, and specified legislative and judicial jurisdiction. The State may achieve this through delegation or devolution, or, in the case of a federation, an initial division of constituent powers. Among OSCE participating States, 'self-governance' arrangements are variously referred to as delegations of autonomy, self-government, and home rule. In no case is this to include any ethnic criterion for territorial arrangements.

In paragraph 35 of the Copenhagen Document, OSCE participating States have noted 'the efforts undertaken to protect and create conditions for the promotion of the ethnic, cultural, linguistic and religious identity of certain national minorities by establishing, as one of the possible means to achieve these aims, appropriate local or autonomous administrations corresponding to the specific historical and territorial circumstances of such minorities and in accordance with the policies of the State concerned'. Following upon this, the Report of the CSCE (Geneva) Meeting of Experts on National Minorities noted in paragraph 7 of Part IV 'that positive results have been obtained by some [participating States] in an appropriate democratic manner by, inter alia:[...] local and autonomous administration, as well as autonomy on a territorial basis, including the existence of consultative, legislative and executive bodies chosen through free and periodic elections; self-administration by a national minority of aspects concerning its identity in situations where autonomy on a territorial basis does not apply; decentralized or local forms of government; [...] provision of financial and technical assistance to persons belonging to national minorities who so wish to exercise their right to establish and maintain their own educational, cultural and religious institutions, organizations and associations [...]'. Of a more general nature, the Preamble to the European Charter of Local Self-Government stresses 'the principles of democracy and the decentralisation of power' as a contribution to 'the safeguarding and reinforcement of local self-government in the different European countries'. In this last connection, the European Charter of Local Self-Government provides in Article 9 for the entitlement of adequate financial resources for the exercise of such decentralized authorities.

15) Insofar as the State holds responsibility in certain fields affecting the whole State, it must assure their regulation through the central authorities of the State. These typically include: defense, which is essential to maintain the territorial integrity of the State; macroeconomic policy, which is important insofar as the central government serves as a sort of equalizer between economically disparate regions; and the classical affairs of diplomacy. Insofar as other fields may have important national implications, these too must be regulated at least to some degree by the central authorities. Regulation in these fields may also be shared, including with specially affected territorial units or minority groups (see recommendations 18 and 20). Such sharing of regulatory authority must nevertheless be consistent with human rights standards and be managed in a practical and coordinated manner.

One field which is well-established as being shared on either a territorial or a non-territorial basis, or both, and holds special importance both for the State as a whole and also for minority groups, is education. Article 5.1 of the UNESCO Convention against Discrimination in Education spells out in some detail how such sharing in this field should be achieved: 'The States Parties to this Convention agree that: [...]

(b) It is essential to respect the liberty of parents and, where applicable, of legal guardians, firstly to choose for their children institutions other than those maintained by the public authorities but conforming to such minimum educational standards as may be laid down or approved by the competent authorities and, secondly, to ensure in a manner consistent with the procedures followed in the State for the application of its legislation, the religious and moral education of the children in conformity with their own convictions; and no person or group of persons should be compelled to receive religious instruction inconsistent with his or their conviction;

(c) It is essential to recognize the right of members of national minorities to carry on their own educational activities, including the maintenance of schools and, depending on the educational policy of each State, the use or the teaching of their own language, provided however: (i) That this right is not exercised in a manner which prevents the members of these minorities from understanding the culture and language of the community as a whole and from participating in its activities, or which prejudices national sovereignty; (ii) That the standard of education is not lower than the general standard laid down or approved by the competent authorities; and (iii) That attendance at such schools is optional.'

16) The principle of democratic governance, as articulated in Article 21 of the Universal Declaration of Human Rights, Article 25 of the International Covenant on Civil and Political Rights, Article 3 of Protocol I to the European Convention on Human Rights and in OSCE standards is applicable at all levels and for all elements of governance. When institutions of self-governance are needed or desirable, the equal enjoyment by everyone of their rights requires application of the principle of democracy within these institutions.

A. *Non-Territorial Arrangements*

17) This section addresses non-territorial autonomy - often referred to as 'personal' or 'cultural autonomy' - which is most likely to be useful when a group is geographically dispersed. Such divisions of authority, including control over specific subject-matter, may take place at the level of the State or within territorial arrangements. In all cases, respect for the human rights of others must be assured. Moreover, such arrangements should be assured adequate financial resources to enable performance of their public functions and should result from inclusive processes (see Recommendation 5).

18) This is not an exhaustive list of possible functions. Much will depend upon the situation, including especially the needs and expressed desires of the minority. In different situations, different subjects will be of greater or lesser interest to minorities, and decisions in these fields will affect them to varying degrees. Some fields may be shared. One area of special concern for minorities is control over their own names, both for representative institutions and individual members, as provided in Article 11(1) of the Framework Convention. With regard to religion, the Recommendation does not advocate governmental interference in religious matters other than in relation to those powers (e.g. concerning personal civil status) delegated to religious authorities. This Recommendation also does not intend that minority institutions should control the media - although persons belonging to minorities should have the possibility to create and use their own media, as guaranteed by Article 9(3) of the Framework Convention. Of course, culture has many aspects extending to fields such as welfare, housing and child care; the State should take into account minority interests in governance in these fields.

B. Territorial Arrangements

19) There is a general trend in European States towards devolution of authority and implementation of the principle of subsidiary, such that decisions are taken as close as possible to, and by, those most directly concerned and affected. Article 4(3) of the European Charter of Local Self-Government expresses this objective as follows: 'Public responsibilities shall generally be exercised, in preference, by those authorities which are closest to the citizen. Allocation of responsibility to another authority should weigh up the extent and nature of the task and requirements of efficiency and economy.' Territorial self-government can help preserve the unity of States while increasing the level of participation and involvement of minorities by giving them a greater role in a level of government that reflects their population concentration. Federations may also accomplish this objective, as may particular autonomy arrangements within unitary States or federations. It is also possible to have mixed administrations. As noted in recommendation 15, arrangements need not be uniform across the State, but may vary according to needs and expressed desires.

20) Autonomous authorities must possess real power to make decisions at the legislative, executive or judicial levels. Authority within the State may be divided among central, regional and local authorities and also among functions. Paragraph 35 of the Copenhagen Document notes the alternatives of 'appropriate local or autonomous administrations corresponding to the specific historical and territorial circumstances'. This makes clear that there need not be uniformity within the State. Experience shows that powers can be divided even with respect to fields of public authority traditionally exercised by central government, including devolved powers of justice (both substantive and procedural) and powers over traditional economies. At a minimum, affected populations should be systematically involved in the exercise of such authority. At the same time, the central government must retain powers to ensure justice and equality of opportunities across the State.

21) Where powers may be devolved on a territorial basis to improve the effective participation of minorities, these powers must be exercised with due account for the minorities within these jurisdictions. Administrative and executive authorities must be accountable to the whole population of the territory. This follows from paragraph 5.2 of the Copenhagen Document which commits OSCE participating States to assure at all levels and for all persons 'a form of government that is representative in character, in which the executive is accountable to the elected legislature or the electorate'.

IV. Guarantees

A. Constitutional and Legal Safeguards

22) This section addresses the issue of 'entrenchment', that is, solidifying arrangements in law. Very detailed legal arrangements may be useful in some cases, while frameworks may be sufficient in other cases. In all cases, as noted in recommendation 5, arrangements should result from open processes. However, once concluded, stability is required in order to assure some security for those affected, especially persons belonging to national minorities. Articles 2 and 4 of the European Charter of Local Self-Government express a preference for constitutional arrangements. To achieve the desired balance between stability and flexibility, it may be useful to specify some reconsideration at fixed intervals, thereby depoliticizing the process of change in advance and making the review process less adversarial.

23) This Recommendation differs from Recommendation 22 insofar as it encourages the testing of new and innovative regimes, rather than specifying terms for alteration of existing arrangements. Responsible authorities may wish to follow different approaches in different situations among central authorities and minority representatives. Without compromising final positions, such an approach may yield good experiences, not least through the processes of innovation and implementation.

B. Remedies

24) In paragraph 30 of the Copenhagen Document, OSCE participating States 'recognize that the questions relating to national minorities can only be satisfactorily resolved in a democratic political framework based on the rule of law, with a functioning independent judiciary'. The idea of effective remedies is also provided in Article 2(3) of the International Covenant on Civil and Political Rights, while 'a judicial remedy' is specified in Article 11 of the European Charter of Local Self-Government.

Judicial review can be performed by constitutional courts and, in effect, by relevant international human rights bodies. Non-judicial mechanisms and institutions, such as national commissions, ombudspersons, inter-ethnic or 'race' relations boards, etc., may also play critical roles, as envisaged by paragraph 27 of the Copenhagen Document, Article 14(2) of the International Convention on the Elimination of All Forms of Racial Discrimination, and paragraph 36 of the Vienna Declaration and Programme of Action adopted by the World Conference on Human Rights in 1993.

APPENDIX II

Strasbourg, 5 May 2008

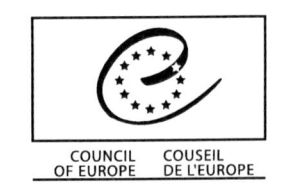

ADVISORY COMMITTEE ON THE FRAMEWORK CONVENTION FOR THE PROTECTION OF NATIONAL MINORITIES

COMMENTARY ON

THE EFFECTIVE PARTICIPATION OF PERSONS BELONGING TO NATIONAL MINORITIES IN CULTURAL, SOCIAL AND ECONOMIC LIFE AND IN PUBLIC AFFAIRS

Adopted on 27 February 2008

Table of Contents

EXECUTIVE SUMMARY	777
PART I INTRODUCTION	782
PART II PRELIMINARY REMARKS	783
1. INTERNATIONAL STANDARDS FOR EFFECTIVE PARTICIPATION OF PERSONS BELONGING TO NATIONAL MINORITIES: THE FRAMEWORK CONVENTION AND OTHER INTERNATIONAL INSTRUMENTS	783
2. CORE CONSIDERATIONS ON ARTICLE 15 OF THE FRAMEWORK CONVENTION	784
a) Effective participation, full and effective equality and promotion of national minorities' identity and culture	785
b) Effective participation on 'issues affecting national minorities'	785
c) 'Effectiveness' of participation	786
d) Effective participation of national minorities and intercultural dialogue	787
PART III KEY FINDINGS ON PARTICIPATION OF PERSONS BELONGING TO NATIONAL MINORITIES IN CULTURAL, SOCIAL AND ECONOMIC LIFE AND IN PUBLIC AFFAIRS	787
1. PARTICIPATION IN ECONOMIC AND SOCIAL LIFE	787
a) Availability of statistical data on the socio-economic situation of persons belonging to national minorities	788
b) Legislation prohibiting discrimination in socio-economic life	789
c) Capacity of public service to deal with socio-economic needs of persons belonging to national minorities	789
d) Participation of persons belonging to national minorities in socio-economic life in depressed regions	790
e) Participation in socio-economic life of persons belonging to disadvantaged national minorities	791
f) Access to land and property as a condition for participation in socio-economic life	792
g) Residency, language and other requirements as a condition for participation in socio-economic life	793
h) Housing standards and participation in socio-economic life	794
i) Health care and participation in socio-economic life	794

776   *Appendix II*

   2. PARTICIPATION IN CULTURAL LIFE   795
   3. PARTICIPATION IN PUBLIC AFFAIRS   796
      a) Participation of persons belonging to national minorities in legislative process   797
         i. Political parties   797
         ii. Design of electoral systems at national, regional and local levels   798
         iii. Administrative and constituency boundaries   800
         iv. Reserved seats system   800
         v. Parliamentary practice   801
         vi. 'Veto' rights   801
         vii. Citizenship requirements   802
         viii. Language proficiency requirements   802
      b) Participation of persons belonging to national minorities through specialised governmental bodies   803
      c) Participation of persons belonging to national minorities through consultative mechanisms   803
         i. Setting-up consultative mechanisms   803
         ii. Representativeness of consultative mechanisms   804
         iii. Types of consultative mechanisms   804
         iv. Role and functioning of consultative bodies   805
      d) Representation and participation of persons belonging to national minorities in public administration, in the judiciary and in the executive   806
      e) Participation of persons belonging to national minorities through sub-national forms of government   807
      f) Participation of persons belonging to national minorities through autonomy arrangements   808
      g) Availability of financial resources for minority-related activities   809
      h) Media as a source for the effective participation of persons belonging to national minorities in public affairs   809
      i) Participation of persons belonging to national minorities in the monitoring of the Framework Convention   810
PART IV CONCLUSIONS   811
APPENDIX RELEVANCE OF OTHER ARTICLES OF THE FRAMEWORK CONVENTION FOR THE INTERPRETATION OF ARTICLE 15   812

Executive Summary

Article 15 of the Framework Convention for the Protection of National Minorities stipulates that State Parties 'shall create the conditions necessary for the effective participation of persons belonging to national minorities in cultural, social and economic life and in public affairs, in particular those affecting them'.

The purpose of this Commentary is to set out the Advisory Committee's interpretation of the provisions within the Framework Convention relating to the effective participation of persons belonging to national minorities, drawing on the Advisory Committee's country-specific Opinions adopted between 1999 and 2007. The Commentary aims to provide a useful tool for State authorities and decision-makers, public officials, organisations of minorities, non-governmental organisations, academics and other stakeholders involved in minority protection.

While the Commentary primarily focuses on participatory mechanisms at the domestic level, it is crucial that persons belonging to national minorities are also involved at all stages of the monitoring and implementation process of international instruments, and in particular the Framework Convention, in order to achieve a balanced and quality outcome.

Participation in Economic and Social Life

Effective participation of persons belonging to national minorities encompasses their economic and social life as well as their engagement in the political and public sphere

Effective participation requires States not only to remove the barriers preventing minorities' equal access to economic sectors and social services, so as to establish equal opportunities, but also demands that States promote their participation in the delivery of benefits and outcomes.

Reliable and easily accessible data is an essential precondition for developing effective measures to address socio-economic discrimination and encourage effective equality. Therefore, State Parties should regularly collect up-to-date data on the socio-economic and educational situation of persons belonging to national minorities in order to compare it with the situation of the majority population. The collection of such data should be made in accordance with international standards on personal data protection.

Effective participation in socio-economic life requires the existence of comprehensive legislation prohibiting discrimination on ethnic grounds, by public and private actors. This legislation should extend to employment, housing, health care and social protection. It is also important that appropriate legal remedies are available in cases of discrimination, and that particular attention is paid to multiple discrimination against women belonging to national minorities.

The participation of national minorities in socio-economic life is sometimes hampered by administrative obstacles, and by an institutional lack of sensitivity to their cultural background and specific needs. State Parties should develop training programmes for public service staff to enable them to adequately respond to the needs of national minorities.

Information on public services and welfare institutions needs to be easily accessible and, where appropriate, available in the languages of national minorities. Public institutions should promote the recruitment and retention of persons belonging to national minorities.

Those persons belonging to national minorities living in economically depressed regions, e.g. rural, isolated and border areas, war-damaged areas or regions affected by deindustrialisation, should be the target of specific measures to enable effective socio-economic participation. Such measures could be promoted through bilateral and cross-border co-operation where appropriate.

Furthermore, specific social and economic measures are often required for persons belonging to disadvantaged minority groups to ensure their effective equality.

In order to promote effective integration of Roma and Travellers in socio-economic life, comprehensive and long-term strategies should be designed and effectively implemented. The implementation of these strategies should be monitored, and the effects evaluated in close co-operation with those concerned.

State Parties should remove undue obstacles and excessive regulations hindering the practice of economic activities specific to certain minority groups, and which are under threat.

In order to guarantee full and effective equality for persons belonging to national minorities in privatisation processes, the authorities should not only ensure transparency, but also set up monitoring and evaluation mechanisms. Following armed conflicts, State Parties should ensure that property claims made by persons belonging to national minorities are processed and implemented in an efficient, transparent and non-discriminatory manner.

Land traditionally used by persons belonging to certain groups, such as indigenous peoples, should be given particular and effective protection. Representatives of these groups should be closely involved in any decision-making on land rights and land usage in their traditional areas of residency.

Access to the labour market, basic social benefits and public services should not be restricted by undue residency or language requirements, which particularly affect persons belonging to some national minorities. At the same time, State Parties should ensure that residency registration processes are easily accessible and do not discriminate—directly or indirectly—against persons belonging to national minorities and that they are regularly monitored.

In the housing sector, State Parties should take resolute measures to put an end to discriminatory practices that lead to segregation and marginalisation of persons belonging to certain national minorities. Moreover, they should develop comprehensive sectoral policies to remedy problems of substandard housing and lack of access to basic infrastructure, which particularly affect persons belonging to some minorities.

In the health care sector, State Parties should ensure the effective involvement of persons belonging to the minorities concerned, in the design, implementation and evaluation of measures taken to address health care issues, so as to better respond to their specific needs. Medical and administrative staff employed in health services should receive adequate training, and the recruitment of health care mediators belonging to national minorities should be encouraged.

Moreover, policies promoting equal opportunities should not be limited to access to health care only. They should also aim at the provision of quality services to persons belonging to national minorities, which have the same impact as the provisions for the rest of the population.

Participation in Cultural Life

When designing and implementing cultural policies that affect persons belonging to national minorities, it is essential that the authorities adequately consult those national minorities and involve them in the decision-making process to meet their needs effectively. This applies equally in the allocation of public support for minority cultures.

Processes of decentralisation, and the delegation of competences to cultural autonomies, can play an important role in enabling national minorities to participate effectively in cultural life.

The media play a pivotal role in cultural life; with this in mind, persons belonging to national minorities need to be able to create and make use of their own media. It is equally important that they are represented in the mainstream media, in order to present their views on issues of interest to the society at large.

Participation in Public Affairs

Persons belonging to national minorities can be involved in public affairs through a number of arrangements, such as representation in elected bodies and public administration at all levels, consultative mechanisms or cultural autonomy arrangements. Particular attention should be paid to the balanced representation of women and men belonging to national minorities.

Notwithstanding that minority representation in elected bodies can be achieved by means other than the formation of specific political parties, legislation prohibiting the formation of political parties on an ethnic or religious basis can lead to undue limitations of the right to freedom of association. Any limitation should be in line with the principles embedded in the norms of international law. Parties representing, or promoting the interests of persons belonging to national minorities should have adequate opportunities to campaign during elections.

Following due consultation, constitutional guarantees should be coupled with effective implementation of legislation to ensure the effective participation of persons belonging to national minorities. Whatever the arrangements chosen, it is advisable to carry out a periodical review in order to ensure that they adequately reflect developments in society.

As a rule, measures facilitating the representation of persons belonging to national minorities in elected bodies should be supported. Exemptions from threshold requirements, reserved seats or veto rights have often proved useful to enhance their participation in elected bodies. However, the mere introduction of such arrangements does not automatically provide persons belonging to national minorities with a genuine and substantial influence on decision-making. In certain specific circumstances, a system of 'veto' or 'quasi veto' rights can even lead to a paralysis of State institutions. In such cases, alternative ways of enabling persons belonging to national minorities to take part in the decision-making should be identified.

The introduction of parliamentary committees overseeing minority issues can contribute to keeping the concerns of persons belonging to national minorities high on the parliamentary agenda. These concerns should also, however, be highlighted in other parliamentary committees.

The way in which constituency or administrative boundaries are drawn may have an impact on minority participation. States should ensure that constituency changes do not reduce the opportunities for election of persons belonging to national minorities.

Citizenship is an important element which can influence minority participation in public affairs. While it is legitimate to impose certain restrictions on non-citizens concerning their right to vote and to be elected, they should not be applied more widely than is necessary. States are encouraged to provide non-citizens with an opportunity to vote and to stand as candidates in local elections. Language proficiency requirements imposed on candidates for parliamentary and local elections are not compatible with Article 15 of the Framework Convention, in so far as they have a negative impact on the effective participation of persons belonging to national minorities in public affairs.

Consultation mechanisms are an additional way to enable persons belonging to national minorities to take part in decision-making processes. However, just as representation in elected bodies alone may be insufficient to ensure substantial influence on the decision-making, mere consultation does not constitute a sufficient mechanism for ensuring effective participation of persons belonging to national minorities. Bearing in mind the need to take into account national circumstances, States should be encouraged to design a system that provides for both representation of and consultation with national minorities.

Consultative bodies should have a clear legal status and the obligation to consult them should be entrenched in law. Furthermore, the involvement in decision-making processes should be of a regular and permanent nature. Due attention should be paid to ensuring that consultative bodies are inclusive and representative. Appointment procedures should be transparent and designed in close consultation with national minority representatives. They should be periodically reviewed to ensure that the bodies concerned represent a wide range of views amongst persons belonging to national minorities. Consultative bodies should also regularly address issues of concern to numerically smaller minorities and persons belonging to national minorities living outside areas with traditional or substantial minority populations.

Public administration, judiciary, law-enforcement agencies and executive bodies should, to the extent possible, reflect the diversity of society. The recruitment of persons belonging to national minorities in the public sector should therefore be promoted. Measures aimed at reaching a rigid, mathematical equality in the representation of various groups should, however, be avoided. State language proficiency requirements placed on public administration personnel should not go beyond what is necessary for the post or service at issue. Increased attention should be given to Roma and Travellers and numerically smaller national minorities, who are often strongly under-represented in public administration.

States are encouraged to establish governmental structures dealing with national minorities. The role of these structures should be to initiate and coordinate governmental policy in the field of minority protection. Coordination between these structures on the one hand, and minority consultative mechanisms and other governmental structures on the other, is essential. Such arrangements can help ensure that minority concerns are prioritised in governmental policies.

The constitutional design of a State can have a decisive impact on the effective participation of persons belonging to national minorities in public life. Bearing in mind the need to take account of national circumstances, sub-national forms of government and minority autonomous self-governments can be valuable tools to foster effective participation of persons belonging to national minorities in many areas of life. Irrespective of the constitutional design of a State, the central authorities should remain committed to their responsibility towards persons belonging to national minorities resulting from the international and national legislative framework.

Adequate human and financial resources should be made available to enable bodies involved in minority issues to effectively carry out their work.

It is essential that the public is adequately informed, both by mainstream and minority media, about political issues relevant to persons belonging to national minorities. Hence it is important to ensure adequate participation of persons belonging to national minorities in various media-related bodies, such as supervisory boards and independent regulatory bodies, public service broadcast committees and auditors' councils.

Part I Introduction

1. The effective participation of persons belonging to national minorities in various areas of public life is essential to ensure social cohesion and the development of a truly democratic society. The Framework Convention for the Protection of National Minorities[1] (hereinafter 'the Framework Convention') therefore stipulates in its Article 15 that State Parties "shall create the conditions necessary for the effective participation of persons belonging to national minorities in cultural, social and economic life and in public affairs, in particular those affecting them".
2. In view of the importance of effective participation for the protection of persons belonging to national minorities, the Advisory Committee on the Framework Convention (hereinafter 'the Advisory Committee') decided to devote its second thematic commentary to the participation of persons belonging to national minorities in social, economic and cultural life and in public affairs. The main objective of this commentary is to highlight the interpretation given by the Advisory Committee, mainly in its country-specific Opinions adopted between 1999 and 2007, to the provisions of the Framework Convention relating to effective participation of persons belonging to national minorities. The commentary aims to provide a useful tool for State authorities and decision-makers, public officials, organisations of minorities, non-governmental organisations, academics and other stakeholders involved in minority protection.
3. The Preliminary Remarks to the Commentary introduce a reflection on the importance of participation and its relevance for the effective enjoyment of other rights guaranteed by the Framework Convention. The Commentary itself analyses a number of key findings on effective participation of persons belonging to national minorities, as identified in particular in the country-specific Opinions under various Articles of the Framework Convention (Part III). In its Conclusions, the Commentary highlights the main challenges which remain in this field and identifies areas which will need to be given further attention by the Advisory Committee in the future country-by-country

---

[1] The Framework Convention for the Protection of National Minorities, which was adopted in 1994, is the main Council of Europe instrument to protect persons belonging to national minorities. It entered into force in 1998 and it has so far been ratified by 39 Member States.

Appendix II   783

monitoring. The Appendix contains an analysis of the relations between Article 15 and other articles of the Framework Convention. This Commentary is to be understood as a living document, which will need to be further developed as monitoring under the Framework Convention progresses.

4. In elaborating this Commentary, the Advisory Committee carried out extensive consultations with national minority representatives and organisations, academics and other stakeholders in order to ensure that the Commentary be as comprehensive as possible and that it adequately reflects the main challenges facing national minorities.

Part II Preliminary Remarks

1. International Standards for Effective Participation of Persons Belonging to National Minorities: The Framework Convention and Other International Instruments

5. The protection of national minorities and of the rights and freedoms of persons belonging to national minorities, as embedded in the Framework Convention for the Protection of National Minorities, forms an integral part of the international protection of human rights.[2] Hence the right to effective participation of persons belonging to national minorities in cultural, social and economic life and in public affairs, as spelled out in Article 15 of the Framework Convention, forms also part of the international protection of human rights.

6. Although the Framework Convention protects the rights of individual persons belonging to national minorities,[3] the enjoyment of certain rights, including the right to effective participation, has a collective dimension. This means that some rights can be effectively enjoyed only in community with other persons belonging to national minorities.[4]

7. Besides the Framework Convention, there are other international documents that are relevant for the participation of persons belonging to national minorities. The Advisory Committee has taken into account the standards contained in these international texts when preparing this Commentary. They range from legally binding standards to recommendations and guidelines. Legally binding standards include those contained in the European

---

[2] See Article 1 of the Framework Convention.
[3] See Explanatory report to the Framework Convention on Article 1 of the Framework Convention, paragraph 31.
[4] See Article 3 paragraph 2 of the Framework Convention: 'Persons belonging to national minorities may exercise the rights and enjoy the freedoms flowing from the principles enshrined in the present Framework Convention individually as well as in community with others'.

Convention for the Protection of Human Rights and Fundamental Freedoms and the related case-law of the European Court of Human Rights, the revised European Social Charter or the European Charter for Regional or Minority Languages. The Lund Recommendations on the Effective Participation of National Minorities in Public Life published by the OSCE High Commissioner on National Minorities, have also been carefully considered by the Advisory Committee in its analysis of Article 15 of the Framework Convention. The United Nations also contributed to developing norms in the field of participation, notably through the Declaration on the Rights of Persons belonging to National or Ethnic, Religious and Linguistic Minorities (adopted in 1992), the Declaration on the Rights of Indigenous Peoples (adopted in 2007) and, on a more general level, in the International Convention on the Elimination of all forms of Racial Discrimination.

2. Core Considerations on Article 15 of the Framework Convention

8. Article 15 is a central provision of the Framework Convention in many respects. The degree of participation of persons belonging to national minorities in all spheres of life can be considered as one of the indicators of the level of pluralism and democracy of a society. Creating the conditions for effective participation of persons belonging to national minorities should, therefore, be considered by the State Parties as forming an integral part of the implementation of the principles of good governance in a pluralistic society.
9. Effective participation of persons belonging to national minorities is also crucial for enhancing social cohesion, as keeping national minorities on the periphery of society can lead to social exclusion and tensions among groups. Marginalising persons belonging to national minorities in socio-economic life also has implications for the country as a whole, with the risk of losing their contribution and additional input to society.
10. Article 15, like other provisions contained in the Framework Convention, implies for the State Parties an obligation of result: they shall ensure that the conditions for effective participation are in place, but the most appropriate means to reach this aim are left to their margin of appreciation. This Commentary aims to provide the State Parties with an analysis of existing experiences so as to help them to identify the most effective options.
11. Promoting the effective participation of persons belonging to national minorities in the society requires continuing and substantive dialogue, both between persons belonging to national minorities and the majority population and between persons belonging to national minorities and the authorities. These two dimensions of dialogue can be achieved only if effective channels for communication are in place.

12. The Advisory Committee considers that the monitoring mechanism set up under the Framework Convention is in itself a valuable process to facilitate dialogue between persons belonging to national minorities and the authorities.

a) *Effective participation, full and effective equality and promotion of national minorities' identity and culture*

13. While Article 15 is the Framework Convention's central provision devoted to the right to effective participation, participation is also key to the full enjoyment of other rights protected under the Convention.[5] The relation between Article 15 and Articles 4 and 5 is, in this context, particularly important. In fact, Articles 15, 4 and 5 can be seen as the three corners of a triangle which together form the main foundations of the Framework Convention.
14. Article 4 requires States to promote full and effective equality for persons belonging to national minorities in all areas of life. This implies the right of equal protection of the law and before the law and the right to be protected against all forms of discrimination based on ethnic origin and other grounds. Furthermore, full and effective equality also implies the need for the authorities to take specific measures in order to overcome past or structural inequalities and to ensure that persons belonging both to national minorities and to the majority have equal opportunities in various fields. Article 5 implies for State Parties an obligation 'to promote the conditions necessary for persons belonging to national minorities to maintain and develop their culture and to preserve the essential elements of their identity, namely their religion, language, traditions and cultural heritage' in order to guarantee *effectively* their right to identity.
15. The right to effective participation, as enshrined in Article 15, makes it possible that the concerns of persons belonging to minorities regarding full and effective equality, and regarding their right to preservation and development of their specific identity, are heard and effectively taken into account.

b) *Effective participation on 'issues affecting national minorities'*

16. Article 15 requires States to create the conditions necessary for the effective participation of persons belonging to national minorities on various issues, *in particular those affecting them*. This part of Article 15 requires that State Parties pay specific attention to the involvement of persons belonging to national minorities in decision-making processes on issues of particular relevance to them. The Advisory Committee has made extensive comments

---

[5] See Appendix to the Commentary.

on the various mechanisms which have been established by States to involve national minorities' representatives in consultative and decision-making processes on issues of relevance to them. These comments focus on mechanisms for involving national minorities in decision-making on specific cultural, social and economic policies as well as in public affairs.

17. At the same time, the Advisory Committee has often underlined that persons belonging to national minorities should also have a say on issues which are not of exclusive concern to them but affect them as members of the society as a whole. Participation in public affairs is indeed essential not only to ensure that the particular concerns of persons belonging to national minorities are taken into account, but also to make it possible for them to influence the general direction of development in society.

c) *'Effectiveness' of participation*

18. Another central issue in relation to Article 15 is the meaning of 'effectiveness' in the context of minority participation. 'Effectiveness' of participation cannot be defined and measured in abstract terms. When considering whether participation of persons belonging to national minorities is effective, the Advisory Committee has not only examined the means which promote full and effective equality for persons belonging to national minorities: it has also taken into account their impact on the situation of the persons concerned and on the society as a whole. This impact has qualitative and quantitative dimensions and may be viewed differently by different actors, depending on their engagement in the processes.

19. Hence it is not sufficient for State Parties to formally provide for the participation of persons belonging to national minorities. They should also ensure that their participation has a substantial influence on decisions which are taken, and that there is, as far as possible, a shared ownership of the decisions taken.

20. Similarly, measures taken by the State Parties to improve participation of persons belonging to national minorities in socio-economic life should have an impact on their access to the labour market as individual economic actors, their access to social protection and, ultimately, their quality of life. Full and effective equality may, in this context, be seen as a result of effective participation.

21. It may be a challenge for representatives of national minorities to participate effectively in decision-making. It implies the allocation of time and resources, not only to participate, but also to try to reflect accurately the variety of views among persons belonging to their national minority. Consequently, national minorities require both capacity building and resources to ensure that their representatives can contribute effectively.

d) *Effective participation of national minorities and intercultural dialogue*

22. Article 15 is also intended to facilitate intercultural dialogue by making it possible for national minorities to be visible, have their voice heard and participate effectively in decision-making, including participation on issues of relevance to the society at large. In fact, dialogue should not be limited to representatives of the national minorities and the authorities, but it should be extended to all segments of society. The Framework Convention intends to provide persons belonging to national minorities with increased possibilities to participate in the mainstream society and at the same time for the majority population to become better acquainted with the culture, language and history of the national minorities, in a spirit of intercultural dialogue.[6]

Part III Key Findings on Participation of Persons Belonging to National Minorities in Cultural, Social and Economic Life and in Public Affairs

1) Participation in Economic and Social Life

23. The Advisory Committee has frequently pointed out that *effective* participation of persons belonging to national minorities cannot be restricted only to their participation in public affairs, and that effective participation in economic and social life is of equal importance to their participation in public affairs, in conformity with the principles of the European Social Charter and the Revised European Social Charter.
24. Participation in social and economic life covers a wide range of issues, from access to adequate housing, health care, social protection (social insurance and social benefits), to social welfare services and access to work. Participation of persons belonging to national minorities in economic life implies both access to the labour market, public and private, and access to business and other self-employment opportunities. These are, in turn, closely linked to property rights and privatisation processes.
25. It is also important to recall that persons belonging to different minority groups face different obstacles to their participation in socio-economic life. Persons belonging to some groups, such as the Roma and Travellers or indigenous peoples, are more at risk of suffering forms of exclusion from socio-economic life than persons belonging to other national minorities or the majority population. These groups may require specific measures to address their needs.

---

[6] See also Article 6.1 of the Framework Convention.

26. Effective participation in social and economic life requires, *inter alia*, that State Parties remove barriers which prevent persons belonging to national minorities from having equal access to various spheres of economic life and social services and to promote their equal access to employment and market opportunities and to a range of public services, including social housing and health care.
27. Moreover, equal opportunities should not be limited to giving equal access to markets and services. Effective participation also requires that State Parties promote participation of persons belonging to national minorities in economic and social life and in benefits and outcomes in the social and economic spheres, which includes, among others, the right to benefit from economic development, health services, social security and other forms of benefits.
28. Therefore, the Advisory Committee findings which are presented below are the result of a combined analysis of findings in respect of Article 15 (effective participation) and Article 4 (equal treatment).
29. Some of the findings are relevant for most of the State Parties; these include the lack of statistical data on the socio-economic situation of national minorities and the sometimes inadequate response of public service to the needs of persons belonging to national minorities. Others specifically relate to some countries or regions or minority groups, such as difficulties resulting from land privatisation processes, obstacles in pursuing traditional activities by persons belonging to some national minorities.

a) Availability of statistical data on the socio-economic situation of persons belonging to national minorities

30. State Parties should regularly collect data and gather up-to-date information on the socio-economic and educational situation of persons belonging to national minorities in order to compare the latter with the situation of the majority population. The availability of reliable data, disaggregated by age, sex and geographical distribution, is an important condition for the development of well-targeted and sustainable measures, which meet the needs of the persons concerned. It is also crucial for the formulation of effective policies and measures to tackle discrimination in areas such as access to employment and housing. Data collected as a result of population census are, in general, insufficient to serve as a sound basis for these policies and measures.
31. The collection of data on the situation of national minorities should be made in accordance with international standards of personal data protection,[7] as well as respecting the right for persons belonging to a national minority freely to choose to be treated or not to be treated as such. Wherever possible, representatives of the national minorities concerned should be

---

[7] See for instance the Convention for the Protection of Individuals with regard to Automatic Processing of Personal Data (ETS 108) and the Committee of Ministers Recommendation (97) 18 on the protection of personal data collected and processed for statistical purposes.

involved throughout the process of data collection, while the methods of collection of such data should be designed in close co-operation with them.

b) Legislation prohibiting discrimination in socio-economic life

32. The Advisory Committee has frequently observed that some national minorities have proportionally higher unemployment rates, sometimes lower employment rates, and a generally lower participation in the labour market than the majority population. They can be faced with direct and indirect discrimination, inequalities in career development and often with structural obstacles (e.g. a ceiling to the level of their promotion within an organisation).
33. The existence of comprehensive legislation prohibiting discrimination on grounds of belonging to a national minority, covering the fields of employment, housing, health care and social protection by public and private actors, is a precondition in any policy aimed at promoting participation of persons belonging to national minorities in various spheres of socio-economic life.
34. The Advisory Committee has, therefore, repeatedly insisted on the fact that anti-discrimination legislation should be enacted or, as appropriate, further developed and fully implemented with a view to eliminating discrimination against persons belonging to national minorities, especially in the labour market, in the field of housing and by health care providers. This also implies that adequate measures should be taken to raise awareness in the society at large and provide training for all stakeholders, including law-enforcement bodies.
35. It is also important that appropriate legal remedies are available in cases of discrimination. State Parties should raise awareness among persons belonging to national minorities on existing remedies and ensure that these are easily accessible.
36. Moreover, the Advisory Committee has often underlined that racism and discrimination can have a disproportionate impact on women and girls belonging to some minority groups in particular. They can experience multiple discrimination because of their ethnic origin and gender. Targeted measures should, therefore, aim to remedy specific forms of discrimination faced by women belonging to national minorities.[8]

c) Capacity of public service to deal with socio-economic needs of persons belonging to national minorities

37. Participation of persons belonging to national minorities in socio-economic life is sometimes hampered by administrative obstacles and by a lack of

---

[8] See for example second Opinion on Ireland, adopted on 6 October 2006, paragraphs 50 and 51.

sensitivity to the specific needs and difficulties encountered by these persons on the part of administrations and public services. In some cases, difficulties arise from the insufficient capacity of the administrations concerned to cater for the specific needs of persons belonging to national minorities. Administrations and public services include education and social institutions, such as employment services, social services and social benefits providers, health and housing services, public transports and utilities, sports and recreation services.

38. State Parties should therefore take measures to better prepare the staff of public services and welfare institutions to provide adequate responses to the needs of persons belonging to national minorities. Specialised training may be required on the specific needs of persons belonging national minority communities as well as on the specific social and economic problems which may affect persons belonging to some national minorities in particular. In fact, persons belonging to some minority groups are more at risk of social exclusion and their integration in socio-economic life often requires targeted approaches, which fully take into account cultural and other specific circumstances.

39. Public services and welfare institutions need to be made easily accessible and available to national minorities. This may require a range of outreach activities and an adaptation of these services and institutions to ensure that they meet the specific needs of national minorities in practice as effectively as they meet the needs of the general population.

40. Information and advice on public services and welfare institutions need to be made easily accessible and available, where appropriate, in the languages of national minorities.

41. Moreover, State Parties should promote the recruitment, promotion and retention in the administration and public services of persons belonging to national minorities, both at national and local levels.

d) *Participation of persons belonging to national minorities in socio-economic life in depressed regions*

42. Persons belonging to national minorities often live in border areas and other regions at a distance from political and economic centres of activity. Hence they can be confronted with more difficult socio-economic situations than the majority population. State Parties should take specific measures to increase the opportunities for persons belonging to minorities living in peripheral and/or economically depressed areas, such as rural, isolated and border areas, war-damaged areas or regions affected by de-industrialisation, to participate in socio-economic life.[9]

---

[9] See for example 1st Opinion on Ukraine, adopted on 1 March 2002, paragraph 73 and 2nd Opinion on Estonia, adopted on 24 February 2005, paragraph 160.

43. Where appropriate, this could result from bilateral or cross border co-operation. Trade and other economic activities across borders can be an important factor of economic and social development for persons belonging to national minorities. State Parties should, therefore, ensure that cross border co-operation is not limited by any undue obstacle.
44. State Parties should ensure that economic rehabilitation programmes and regional development initiatives targeting depressed regions, including some inner city areas, are designed and implemented in a manner that also provides benefits to those in need among persons belonging to national minorities who live in such regions. In order to ensure this, studies should be undertaken to assess the possible impact of development projects on persons belonging to national minorities. Particular attention should be paid to the situation of women and youth from national minority backgrounds.
45. The authorities should ensure that persons belonging to national minorities are fully involved in the planning, implementation, monitoring and evaluation of policies and projects likely to have an impact on their economic situation and the situation of the regions where they live in substantial numbers.
46. In post-conflict situations, particular attention should be paid to the socioeconomic situation of persons belonging to minorities who have been discriminated against on account of their national minority background and were barred from employment. Specific measures should be taken to redress the consequences of past discrimination and promote these persons' participation in socio-economic life.[10]

e) *Participation in socio-economic life of persons belonging to disadvantaged national minorities*

47. Persons belonging to certain minority groups, among others the Roma and Travellers and indigenous peoples, often face more significant difficulties than others in accessing the labour market, education and training, housing, health care and social protection. Difficulties in the various sectors are often connected and mutually reinforcing and they can lead to a spiral of exclusion from socio-economic participation. Women belonging to these groups are often particularly vulnerable to poverty and social exclusion.
48. Furthermore, a certain number of persons belonging to these groups continue to occupy specific economic niches and pursue traditional activities and trades, which are sometimes difficult to maintain in a rapidly changing economic context. State Parties should remove undue obstacles, including excessive regulations, which hinds the practice of economic activities which

---

[10] See for example 2nd Opinion on Croatia, adopted on 1 October 2004, paragraphs 60 to 62.

are specific to certain minority groups. This concern should be borne in mind when new regulations in this area are developed.

49. In order to promote effective integration of persons belonging to disadvantaged minority groups in socio-economic life, comprehensive and long-term strategies should be designed and implemented. Where such strategies are in place, particular attention should be paid to their effective implementation. Adequate resources need to be provided in a timely manner at all levels of operation, especially locally. Furthermore, the implementation of such policies should be carefully monitored and their impact evaluated, in close co-operation with representatives of the minorities concerned, with a view to adapting and strengthening them over time. Effective coordination of measures undertaken by the various bodies involved should be a key concern.

f) Access to land and property as a condition for participation in socio-economic life

50. Obstacles to obtaining access to property (whether residential, commercial or agricultural) can have a disproportionate effect on persons belonging to national minorities, aggravating their economic difficulties and unemployment.

51. The unequal access to property, including land property, is sometimes connected with privatisation processes and processes of property restitution which, in some cases, have had a disproportionate impact on persons belonging to vulnerable minority groups. State Parties should therefore ensure equal and fair access to privatisation and property restitution processes, as these have long-term implications for the effective participation of persons belonging to national minorities in economic life. In order to enhance full and effective equality for persons belonging to national minorities, the authorities should, in particular, ensure that the privatisation process is transparent and set up mechanisms to monitor and, in due course, evaluate the impact of privatisation. Moreover, persons belonging to national minorities should participate effectively in these monitoring and evaluation processes.[11]

52. Substantial difficulties in gaining access to property can also result from armed conflicts and the subsequent displacements of populations. State Parties should ensure that property claims by persons belonging to national minorities are processed and implemented in an efficient and transparent manner and do not result in discriminatory outcomes.[12]

---

[11] See for example Opinion on Kosovo (UNMIK), adopted on 25 November 2005, paragraph 115. [12] See for example Opinion on Kosovo (UNMIK), paragraph 116.

53. Violations of land rights or limitations imposed on the use of land by certain groups such as indigenous peoples, whose economic situation is closely connected to land usage, can significantly undermine their participation in socio-economic life. Therefore, land traditionally used by them should be given particular and effective protection. Furthermore, the representatives of indigenous peoples should be closely involved in any decision-making affecting the use of land in their traditional areas of residency.

g) Residency, language and other requirements as a condition for participation in socio-economic life

54. In some State Parties, residency requirements are imposed by some employers or by the State as a prerequisite for recruitment,[13] or for registering and running private business; these practices can affect in a disproportionate manner persons belonging to certain national minorities. They can face specific difficulties in registering their residency, due to administrative or other obstacles. Residency requirement problems can also hinder their access to basic social rights, such as healthcare, unemployment services and pension entitlements. Persons belonging to national minorities which have a nomadic lifestyle also face obstacles to participation in socio-economic life when residency-related requirements are not adapted to their lifestyle.
55. Moreover, undue or disproportionate language proficiency requirements in order to access certain jobs or in the provision of goods and services, especially in the private sector, can hamper access to employment and social protection of persons belonging to national minorities.[14] State Parties should therefore take effective measures to remove any undue restrictions in the access to the labour market, which particularly affect persons belonging to certain national minorities. In situations where language proficiency requirements are a legitimate condition for access to certain jobs, notably in the public service, language training courses should be made available to prevent discrimination of persons belonging to national minorities. Access to basic social benefits and to certain public services should not be hampered by undue language or residency requirements.
56. At the same time, State Parties should ensure that residency registration processes are accessible and do not discriminate, directly or indirectly, against persons belonging to national minorities. Where needed, assistance for registration should be available for persons belonging to national minorities and, finally, regular monitoring of the registration processes should be carried out by the authorities.

---

[13] See for example 2nd Opinion on the Russian Federation, paragraphs 59, 272 and 273.
[14] See for example 1st Opinion on Azerbaijan, adopted on 22 May 2003, paragraph 79.

h) Housing standards and participation in socio-economic life

57. Substandard housing conditions, often coupled with the physical/spatial separation of persons belonging to certain national minorities, in particular Roma and Travellers, considerably affect their ability to participate in socio-economic life and can result in their further poverty, marginalisation and social exclusion. This is frequently made more acute by the lack of legal provisions securing their residency rights and by their vulnerability to forced evictions, including as a consequences of processes of property restitution.[15]
58. State parties must take effective measures to put an end to discriminatory practices which lead to segregation and marginalisation of persons belonging to certain national minorities.[16] Particular attention should be paid to ensuring full respect for the human rights of persons belonging to national minorities in housing matters.
59. Moreover, State Parties should develop comprehensive sectoral policies to address problems of substandard housing and lack of access to basic infrastructure, which affect persons belonging to certain minorities. State Parties should also promote their equal access to adequate housing, in particular by improved access to subsidised housing.
60. In doing so, the authorities should provide for adequate participation of the persons concerned in decision-making on housing and related programmes designed to improve their socio-economic situation, in order to ensure that the needs of these persons are adequately catered for. Such policies should be adequately funded. It is equally important for State Parties to ensure that local authorities comply with existing anti-discrimination legislation in housing matters as measures which perpetuate segregation are often taken locally.

i) Health care and participation in socio-economic life

61. Persons belonging to certain national minorities face particular difficulties in their access to health care, a situation which results from different factors, such as discrimination, poverty, geographical isolation, cultural differences or language obstacles. Difficulties in the access to health care have a negative impact on the participation of persons belonging to national minorities in socio-economic life.

---

[15] See for example 2nd Opinion on Romania, adopted on 24 November 2005, paragraphs 80 and 82.
[16] See for example 2nd Opinion on the Czech Republic, adopted on 24 February 2005, paragraphs 52 and 57, 2nd Opinion on the Slovak Republic, adopted on 26 May 2005, paragraph 46 and 2nd Opinion on Slovenia, adopted on 26 May 2005, paragraphs 67 and 68.

62. State Parties should ensure the effective involvement of persons belonging to the minorities concerned in the design, implementation, monitoring and evaluation of measures taken to address problems affecting their health care. These are necessary to enable health services to respond more effectively to their specific needs.
63. Medical and administrative staff employed in health services should receive training on the cultural and linguistic background of national minorities, so that they can adequately respond to the specific needs of persons belonging to national minorities.[17] The employment of health mediators or assistants belonging to national minorities can contribute to improved communication and more appropriate approaches.[18]
64. Particular emphasis should be put on providing equally effective services to persons belonging to national minorities in the health care system.[19] Equal opportunity policies should not be limited to access to health care only. They should also aim at the provision of quality services to persons belonging to national minorities, which have the same impact as the provisions for the rest of the population.

2) PARTICIPATION IN CULTURAL LIFE[20]

65. The effectiveness of the participation of persons belonging to national minorities in cultural life is in most State Parties closely connected to their level of participation in public affairs and in social and economic life. The Framework Convention protects both the right for persons belonging to

---

[17] See also remarks in part c) above.

[18] See for example 2nd Opinion on the Czech Republic, adopted on 24 February 2005, paragraph 55, and 2nd Opinion on the Slovak Republic, adopted on 26 May 2005, paragraphs 56 and 57.

[19] See for example 2nd Opinion on the Slovak Republic, adopted on 26 May 2005, paragraphs 56 and 57.

[20] See also other Council of Europe reference texts on cultural diversity and on the media, such as:
  - *The Faro Declaration on the Council of Europe's Strategy for Developing Intercultural Dialogue*, adopted by the Ministers responsible for Cultural Affairs of the States parties to the European Cultural Convention, meeting in Faro on 27 and 28 October 2005.
  - *The Declaration on Intercultural Dialogue and Conflict Prevention*, adopted by the Conference of the European Ministers of Culture on 22 October 2003.
  - 7th European Ministerial Conference on Mass Media Policy: *Integration and diversity: the new frontiers of European media and communications policy*. Texts adopted (MCM(2005)005).
  - Recommendation No. R (97) 21 of the Committee of Ministers *on the media and the promotion of a culture of tolerance and its Explanatory Memorandum*.
  - Parliamentary Assembly of the Council of Europe: Recommendation 1773 (2006): *The 2003 guidelines on the use of minority languages in the broadcast media and the Council of Europe standards: need to enhance co-operation and synergy with the OSCE*.
  - Parliamentary Assembly of the Council of Europe: Recommendation 1277 (1995) *on migrants, ethnic minorities and media*.

minorities to preserve and develop their own cultural heritage and identity and the right for them to take part effectively and interact in mainstream cultural life, in a spirit of tolerance and intercultural dialogue. Therefore, the findings presented in this chapter result from a combined analysis of Articles 5, 6 and 15.

66. When designing and implementing cultural policies affecting persons belonging to national minorities, it is important that the authorities carry out adequate consultations with them so as to meet their needs effectively. National minorities, through their representatives, should also be effectively involved in processes of allocation of public support for their cultural initiatives. Moreover, when specific institutions exist for channelling such support, persons belonging to national minorities should be adequately represented and should be able to take part in the corresponding decision-making.[21]

67. Processes of decentralisation can play an important role in creating the conditions necessary for persons belonging to national minorities to participate effectively in cultural life. In particular, cultural autonomy arrangements, whose aim is *inter alia* to delegate competences to persons belonging to national minorities in the sphere of culture and education, can result in increased participation of minorities in cultural life.[22]

68. Additionally, when analysing the participation of minorities in cultural life, it is important to assess their level of participation in the media. It is important that minorities have the possibility to create and use their own media. It is, however, equally important that they have access to and are present in mainstream media so as to be able to present their views on issues of interest to the society at large.

3) PARTICIPATION IN PUBLIC AFFAIRS

69. The Advisory Committee, while considering whether persons belonging to national minorities effectively participate in public affairs, has examined their overall involvement in decision-making. It has not only examined their representation and participation in various mechanisms, but also devoted particular attention to the effectiveness of their influence on decision-making processes. The different decision-making arrangements which exist in the State Parties should take into account the composition of society and reflect its diversity.

---

[21] See for example 2nd Opinion on Norway, adopted on 5 October 2006, paragraphs 60 and 69.
[22] See also paragraphs from 133 to 137 below on autonomy arrangements.

70. Effective participation includes a wide range of possible forms, such as an exchange of information, dialogue, informal and formal consultation and participation in decision-making. It can be ensured through different channels, ranging from consultative mechanisms to special parliamentary arrangements. Particular attention should be paid to equal participation of women and men belonging to national minorities.
71. Whatever the mechanisms chosen, persons belonging to national minorities should be given real opportunities to influence decision-making, the outcome of which should adequately reflect their needs. According to the Advisory Committee, mere consultation is, as such, not a sufficient means to be considered effective participation.
72. Representation and participation of persons belonging to national minorities in elected bodies, public administration, judiciary and law-enforcement agencies is an essential but not sufficient condition for effective participation. Their inclusion in elected bodies at different levels largely depends on the constitutional traditions and guarantees provided for by electoral legislation. The choice and modalities of the electoral system often has a direct impact on the effectiveness of minority participation in decisionmaking. Besides the possibilities provided for by the two main types of electoral systems (majoritarian and proportional), special mechanisms, such as reserved seats, quotas, qualified majorities, dual voting or 'veto' rights, may be introduced. In addition, cultural autonomy arrangements can reinforce minority participation in public affairs.
73. Specialised governmental structures dealing with minority issues contribute to ensuring that the needs of minorities are consistently integrated into governmental policies. Minority-related issues should, however, not remain exclusively in the domain of specialised governmental bodies. The minority perspective needs to be mainstreamed in general policies at all levels and procedural steps by the actors involved in policy-making.
74. The media should inform the society at large of minority-related issues with a view to promoting a spirit of tolerance and intercultural dialogue.

a) Participation of persons belonging to national minorities in legislative process

i. Political parties

75. The right of every person belonging to a national minority to freedom of peaceful assembly and freedom of association as stipulated in Article 7 of the Framework Convention implies, *inter alia*, the right to form political parties and/or organisations. Legislation which prohibits the formation of political parties on an ethnic or religious basis can lead to undue limitations of this right. Any limitation should, in any case, be in line with the norms of

international law and the principles embedded in the European Convention on Human Rights.[23]

76. The registration of national minority organisations and political parties may be subject to certain conditions. Such requirements should, however, be designed so that they do not limit, unreasonably or in a disproportionate manner, the possibilities for persons belonging to national minorities to form such organisations and thereby restrict their opportunities to participate in political life and the decision-making process. This concerns, *inter alia*, numerical and geographical conditions for registration.[24]

77. State Parties should ensure that parties representing or including persons belonging to national minorities have adequate opportunities in election campaigning. This may imply the display of electoral advertising in minority languages. The authorities should also consider providing opportunities for the use of minority languages in public service television and radio programmes devoted to election campaigns and on ballot slips and other electoral material in areas inhabited by persons belonging to national minorities traditionally or in substantive numbers.[25]

78. Political parties, both mainstream and those formed by persons belonging to national minorities, can play an important role in facilitating participation of persons belonging to national minorities in public affairs. Internal democratic processes of selection of their candidates by mainstream parties are crucial in ensuring participation of persons belonging to national minorities. Inclusion of minority representatives in mainstream political parties does, however, not necessarily mean the effective epresentation of the interests of minorities.

79. In countries where prominent minority parties exist, it is important to ensure that other minority parties or political organisations wishing to represent the interests of other persons belonging to the same national minorities have opportunities to do so.

ii. Design of electoral systems at national, regional and local levels

80. The participation of persons belonging to national minorities in electoral processes is crucial to enable minorities to express their views when legislative measures and public policies of relevance to them are designed.

---

[23] Article 11 of the European Convention for the Protection of Human Rights and Fundamental Freedoms (ECHR), which guarantees the right to freedom of peaceful assembly and of association, provides that no restrictions shall be placed on the exercise of these rights other than such as are prescribed by law and are necessary in a democratic society in the interests of national security or public safety, for the prevention of disorder or crime, for the protection of health or morals or for the protection of the rights and freedoms of others.

[24] See for example 2nd Opinion on Moldova adopted on 9 December 2004, paragraphs 74 to 77, 2nd Opinion on the Russian Federation adopted on 11 May 2006, paragraph 261 and 1st Opinion on Bulgaria, adopted on 27 May 2004, paragraphs 61 to 63.

[25] See for example 1st Opinion on Estonia adopted on 14 September 2001, paragraphs 55 and 56.

81. Bearing in mind that State Parties are sovereign to decide on their electoral systems, the Advisory Committee has highlighted that it is important to provide opportunities for minority concerns to be included on the public agenda. This may be achieved either through the presence of minority representatives in elected bodies and/or through the inclusion of their concerns in the agenda of elected bodies.
82. The Advisory Committee has noted that when electoral laws provide for a threshold requirement, its potentially negative impact on the participation of national minorities in the electoral process needs to be duly taken into account.[26] Exemptions from threshold requirements have proved useful to enhance national minority participation in elected bodies.
83. Constitutional guarantees for the representation of persons belonging to national minorities in elected bodies need to be coupled with effective implementing legislation and accompanying measures within reasonable time.[27] The Advisory Committee considers it essential that persons belonging to national minorities participate or are consulted in the process of drafting such legislation and monitoring its implementation.
84. State Parties are encouraged to strengthen the participation of persons belonging to national minorities, including those in a disadvantaged position, in local elected councils. In this respect, the Advisory Committee has underlined that due attention should be paid to the possible negative impact of certain residency requirements on the participation of persons belonging to national minorities in local elections.[28]
85. Electoral provisions aimed at promoting a balanced presence of women in elected bodies can be designed to have a positive impact on the participation of women belonging to national minorities in public affairs.
86. Whatever the arrangements chosen, it is in general advisable to carry out a periodical review in order to ensure that they adequately reflect developments in the society and the needs of persons belonging to national minorities.
87. Where possibilities for persons belonging to national minorities to be represented in elected bodies are in practice limited, alternative channels, such as specific arrangements to facilitate minority representation, need to be considered in order to enhance their participation.[29]

---

[26] See for example 2nd Opinion on the Russian Federation adopted on 11 May 2005, paragraph 262 and 1st Opinion on Serbia and Montenegro, adopted on 27 November 2003, paragraph 102.
[27] See for example 1st Opinion on Hungary adopted on 9 December 2004, paragraph 48.
[28] See for example 2nd Opinion on Ireland, adopted on 6 October 2006, paragraph 104.
[29] See 2nd Opinion on Denmark adopted on 9 December 2004, paragraph 154.

iii. Administrative and constituency boundaries

88. Changes of electoral constituencies may affect efforts to ensure effective participation of persons belonging to national minorities in public affairs, including in elected bodies. When considering reforms leading to constituency changes, State Parties should ensure that they do not undermine the opportunities of persons belonging to national minorities to be elected.[30]
89. When considering reforms which aim to modify administrative boundaries, the authorities should consult persons belonging to national minorities and carefully consider the possible impact of such reforms on their participation in public affairs.[31]
90. In any case, State Parties should not adopt measures which aim to reduce the proportion of the population in areas inhabited by persons belonging to national minorities or to limit the rights protected by the Framework Convention.[32] On the contrary, administrative reforms in such areas should aim *inter alia* to increase opportunities for minority participation.

iv. Reserved seats system

91. Arrangements involving reserved and/or shared seats for representatives of national minorities have in a number of cases proved to be a useful means to enhance participation of persons belonging to national minorities in decision-making. The provision of reserved seats, whether shared between various national minorities or designed for one group, is one of the ways in which the representation of persons belonging to national minorities can be ensured in elected bodies.
92. The 'shared seats' system is particularly adapted to the needs of numerically small minorities. For such an arrangement to have a significant impact on the participation of all the national minorities represented through the shared seat(s), it is important that the minorities concerned agree on a common strategy and shared goals to be reached through the representation in the electoral body at stake. Elected representatives occupying shared seats should take due care to represent the concerns of all persons belonging to national minorities in the constituency. A rotation of the representatives of the different national minorities may help create the sense of a shared seat.
93. In order to ensure that a guaranteed seat arrangement contributes substantially to effective participation, it is important that the minority representatives elected are effectively involved in decision-making processes.

---

[30] See for example 2nd Opinion on the Slovak Republic adopted on 26 May 2005, paragraph 115 and 1st Opinion on Ukraine adopted on 1 March 2002, paragraph 69.
[31] See for example 1st Opinion on "the former Yugoslav Republic of Macedonia" adopted on 27 May 2004, paragraph 103.   [32] See Article 16 of the Framework Convention.

Moreover, they should have a real possibility to influence decisions taken by the elected body, including those not strictly related to national minorities. It is therefore important that they have speaking and voting rights in the elected body and that their role is not limited to a mere observer status.[33]

94. However, the Advisory Committee is of the opinion that the mere establishment of such arrangements does not automatically provide persons belonging to national minorities with a genuine and substantial influence in decision-making.[34]

v. Parliamentary practice

95. In those State Parties where there are special parliamentary committees to address minority issues, these bodies have, in a number of cases, helped take into account concerns of national minorities in decision-making processes. The possibility of using minority languages in these committees has proved particularly effective. Nonetheless, the importance of effective participation in other parliamentary committees also involved in aspects of minority protection should not be neglected. Co-operation across party lines within the parliamentary committees strengthens efforts conducive to mainstreaming minority issues into policies.

96. For the work of such committees to be effective, it is essential that appropriate attention be given to their recommendations, particularly when drafting or amending legislation concerning national minorities. In addition, regular dialogue should be minorities or of persons small of that the through shared to national national means to enhance -making. The pursued between the committees and the relevant authorities as well as between them and minority associations.

vi. 'Veto' rights

97. In some State Parties, members of parliaments representing national minorities have a 'veto-type' right over draft legislation directly affecting them. This mechanism, which may constitute a valuable tool in certain circumstances, has been introduced by some State Parties in order to ensure that minority representatives have a possibility to accept or reject legislation on matters directly affecting them.

98. The Advisory Committee has noted, however, that 'veto' rights can usually be invoked only in relation to legal acts concerning *exclusively* the rights and status of persons belonging to national minorities.[35] Hence, it might not be

---

[33] See 1st Opinion on Cyprus adopted on 6 April 2001, paragraph 41.
[34] See for example Opinion on Kosovo (UNMIK) adopted on 25 November 2006, paragraph 110.
[35] See 1st Opinion on Slovenia adopted on 12 September 2002, paragraph 71.

sufficient to guarantee the proper involvement of minority representatives in issues which do not concern them directly or exclusively.
99. There are also concerns that such a system of 'veto' right or a 'quasi veto' right on some matters can, in specific circumstances, lead to a paralysis of State institutions.[36] In such cases, other and/or additional ways of enabling persons belonging to national minorities to voice their views in legislative processes can be identified as a substitute or a complement to the 'veto' system.

vii. Citizenship requirements

100. Citizenship is an important element that can substantially influence participation in public affairs. Experience has shown that citizenship requirements can hamper effective participation in certain fields of public affairs. When examining the personal scope of application of the Framework Convention, the Advisory Committee has, in a number of cases, called for flexibility and inclusiveness in the approach taken by the State Parties.[37] Moreover, the Advisory Committee has consistently emphasised the fact that the application of the Framework Convention to non-citizens belonging to national minorities can enhance a spirit of tolerance, intercultural dialogue and co-operation.

101. Although it is legitimate to impose certain restrictions on non-citizens concerning their right to vote and to be elected, such restrictions should not be applied more widely than is necessary. While citizenship requirements can be applied in relation to parliamentary elections, State Parties are encouraged to provide non-citizens belonging to national minorities with a possibility to vote and to stand as candidates in local elections and governing boards of cultural autonomies.[38] Citizenship should not be a condition for persons belonging to national minorities to join trade unions and other civil society associations. This is particularly important in State Parties where citizenship policy has been in a state of flux.

viii. Language proficiency requirements

102. Language proficiency requirements imposed on candidates for parliamentary and local elections are not compatible with Article 15 of the Framework Convention. They negatively affect the effective participation of persons belonging to national minorities in public affairs.[39]

---

[36] See 1st Opinion on Bosnia and Herzegovina adopted on 27 May 2004, paragraphs 100 and 101.
[37] See also remarks in respect of Article 3 of the Framework Convention in the Appendix to this Commentary.
[38] See for example 1st Opinion on Estonia, adopted on 14 September 2001, paragraph 55.
[39] See 1st Opinion on Estonia, paragraph 55.

b) Participation of persons belonging to national minorities through specialised governmental bodies

103. The establishment of specialised governmental structures dealing with national minorities within national, regional or local authorities can help improve minority participation in public affairs. Where such bodies have not been set up, State Parties are encouraged to establish them or, at a minimum, to identify contact points for minority issues within public services.
104. Specialised bodies should not substitute but complement national minorities' consultative mechanisms. Their effectiveness depends to a great extent on the level of coordination and complementarity with consultation bodies. The recruitment and retention of staff with national minority background and/or minority language skills in these specialised bodies can contribute to their effective functioning.
105. Specialised governmental bodies should not substitute the work of mainstream government institutions on minority-related issues. The main role of specialised bodies is to initiate and coordinate governmental policy in the field of minority protection. They are therefore seen as important channels of communication between the Government and minorities. It is essential that the relevant governmental institutions be aware of the needs of persons belonging to national minorities and that minority issues be mainstreamed in the work of other governmental services.[40]

c) Participation of persons belonging to national minorities through consultative mechanisms

i. Setting-up consultative mechanisms

106. Consultation of persons belonging to national minorities is particularly important in countries where there are no arrangements to enable participation of persons belonging to national minorities in parliament and other elected bodies. Consultation alone does not, however, constitute a sufficient mechanism for ensuring *effective* participation of persons belonging to national minorities.
107. It is important to ensure that consultative bodies have a clear legal status, that the obligation to consult them is entrenched in law and that their involvement in decision-making processes is of a regular and permanent nature. While there are various models as regards the functioning of such structures,[41] it is important to ensure that relevant regulations are detailed enough to provide for efficient and consistent consultation.

---

[40] See for example 2nd Opinion on Armenia adopted on 12 May 2006, paragraph 122.
[41] See also the DH-MIN Handbook on minority consultative mechanisms (www.coe.int/minorities).

108. The authorities may also organise joint consultations with representatives of different national minorities and/or enter into a direct dialogue with representatives of individual national minorities. While the former is an important method to address common issues and to enhance dialogue between various national minorities, the latter is appropriate, for example, to consider those issues which concern only a specific national minority. The Advisory Committee has noted that, in some cases, consultation with umbrella bodies of national minorities only is not sufficient to adequately take into account the concerns of individual national minorities.

ii. Representativeness of consultative mechanisms

109. Appropriate attention should be paid to the 'inclusiveness' and 'representativeness' of consultative bodies. This implies, *inter alia*, that where there are mixed bodies, the proportion between minority representatives and officials should not result in the latter dominating the work. All national minorities should be represented, including numerically smaller national minorities.[42]
110. Representativeness of consultative bodies also depends on minority organisations and their appointment procedures. Moreover, when specific consultative mechanisms in respect of an individual national minority are set up, due regard should be paid to the diversity within this group.[43]
111. For the credibility of consultative bodies, it is essential that their appointment procedures be transparent and designed in close consultation with national minorities. State Parties are encouraged periodically to review the appointment procedures to make sure that the bodies concerned are as inclusive as possible, maintain their independence from governments, and genuinely represent a wide range of views amongst persons belonging to national minorities. It is important to ensure that women belonging to national minorities are involved in consultative bodies.
112. Consultation should not be limited to the concerns of persons belonging to national minorities who live in areas with traditional or substantial minority population. This also implies that the agenda should not only reflect the concerns of the numerically largest minorities.

iii. Types of consultative mechanisms

113. While *ad hoc* consultations can be useful to address a particular issue, State Parties are encouraged to establish regular consultative mechanisms and

---

[42] See for example 2nd Opinion on Ireland adopted on 6 October 2006, paragraph 112.
[43] See for example 2nd Opinion on Germany adopted on 1 March 2006, paragraph 152.

bodies with a view to institutionalising dialogue between the governments and minority representatives.[44]

114. Consultative mechanisms with persons belonging to national minorities should not exclude, where appropriate, parallel consultation with independent experts. The Advisory Committee has noted in some cases that expertise is a useful complement to the consultation procedure.

115. In addition to national structures, regional and local consultative mechanisms have, in some circumstances, proved to be a useful additional channel for the participation of persons belonging to national minorities in decision-making, especially in areas of competencies where decision-making powers have been decentralised. In such situations, it is important that local and regional authorities regularly involve these consultative bodies in their decision-making processes, when dealing with minority issues.[45]

iv. Role and functioning of consultative bodies

116. It is essential that the legal status, role, duties, membership and institutional position of consultative bodies be clearly defined. This includes the scope of consultation, structures, rules governing appointment of their members and working methods. It is important to ensure that consultative bodies have a legal personality, as a lack of this may undermine their effectiveness and their capacity to fulfil effectively their mission. Working methods of consultative bodies should be transparent and their rules of procedures clearly defined. Publicity of the work of the consultative bodies should be promoted so as to enhance transparency.

117. State Parties are invited to take measures to enable persons belonging to national minorities to be aware of the existence, mandate and activities of such consultative bodies. In addition, it is important that the meetings of these bodies are convened frequently and on a regular basis.[46]

118. Consultative bodies need to be duly consulted in the process of drafting new legislation, including constitutional reforms that directly or indirectly affect minorities. State Parties should also consult persons belonging to national minorities and their consultative structures in relation to obligations arising under international treaties, including in respect of reporting obligations of interest to them.

119. Adequate resources should be made available to support the effective functioning of consultative mechanisms.[47]

---

[44] See for example 2nd Opinion on Finland adopted on 2 March 2006, paragraphs 148 to 151.
[45] See for example 2nd Opinion on the Czech Republic adopted on 24 February 2005, paragraphs 171 and 172.
[46] See for example 1st Opinion on Ukraine adopted on 1 March 2002, paragraph 72 and 1st Opinion on Azerbaijan adopted on 22 May 2003, paragraphs 73 and 74.
[47] See also remarks in paragraphs 137 and 138 below.

d) Representation and participation of persons belonging to national minorities in public administration, in the judiciary and in the executive

120. Public administration should, to the extent possible, reflect the diversity of society. This implies that State Parties are encouraged to identify ways of promoting the recruitment of persons belonging to national minorities in the public sector, including recruitment into the judiciary and the law enforcement bodies. Participation of persons belonging to national minorities in public administration can also help the latter better respond to the needs of national minorities.[48]
121. One way of pursuing this aim is to provide a legal basis for promoting the recruitment of persons belonging to national minorities in public administration. It is important that such guarantees are coupled with adequate implementation measures.
122. It is also important to promote participation of persons belonging to national minorities in the judiciary and the administration of justice. Measures in this respect should be implemented in a way which fully guarantees the independence and the effective functioning of the judiciary.[49]
123. Measures which aim to reach a rigid, mathematical equality in the representation of various groups, which often implies an unnecessary multiplication of posts, should be avoided. They risk undermining the effective functioning of the State structure and can lead to the creation of separate structures in the society.
124. Roma and Travellers, indigenous peoples and numerically small national minorities are often particularly under-employed in public administration and this issue requires specific attention from the authorities. Their employment in public administration can contribute to a better image and increased awareness of such minorities in the society at large, which in turn is likely to improve their participation at all levels.
125. Targeted measures can be designed to address the specific circumstances of past inequalities in employment practices of some national minorities, including the most marginalised. This implies that all employees need to be sufficiently trained and competent to perform their work effectively.[50]
126. State language proficiency requirements placed on public administration personnel should not go beyond what is necessary for the post or service at issue. Requirements, which unduly limit the access of persons belonging to national minorities to employment opportunities in public

---

[48] See for example 1st Opinion on the United Kingdom adopted on 30 November 2001, paragraphs 96 to 99.
[49] See for example 2nd Opinion on Croatia adopted on 1 October 2004, paragraphs 154 to 159.
[50] See also remarks in paragraphs 36 and 37 above.

administration, are not compatible with the standards embedded in the Framework Convention.[51] Where necessary, targeted support should be provided to facilitate the learning of the official language for applicants or personnel from national minorities.

127. Comprehensive data and statistics are crucial to evaluate the impact of recruitment, promotion and other related practices on minority participation in public services. They are instrumental to devise adequate legislative and policy measures to address the shortcomings identified. The collection of data on the situation of national minorities should be made in accordance with international standards of personal data protection,[52] as well as the right for persons belonging to a national minority freely to choose to be treated or not to be treated as such. Representatives of the national minorities concerned should be involved in the entire process of data collection and the methods of collection of such data should be designed in close co-operation with them.

128. Attention should also be paid to the participation of persons belonging to national minorities in the executive. Effective participation can be advanced by various means such as the introduction of posts assigned for minority representatives in the executive at all levels. Measures excluding persons belonging to national minorities from accessing public posts are potentially discriminatory.[53]

e) *Participation of persons belonging to national minorities through sub-national forms of government*

129. Sub-national forms of government can play an important role in creating the necessary conditions for effective participation of persons belonging to national minorities in decision-making. This is particularly relevant for regions where persons elonging to national minorities live compactly.

130. In order to ensure that, in practice, decentralisation and devolution processes have a positive effect on the participation of persons belonging to national minorities in public life, it is crucial to clearly define the respective competencies of sub-national and central authorities. Lack of clarity in this respect can reduce the level of participation of persons belonging to national minorities and may also hamper minority access to the public funds needed for their activities. It is also important to provide local

---

[51] See for example 1st Opinion on Azerbaijan adopted on 22 May 2003, paragraph 79.
[52] See Council of Europe Convention for the Protection of Individuals with regard to Automatic Processing of Personal Data (ETS 108) and the Committee of Ministers' Recommendation 97 (18) concerning the protection of personal data collected and processed for statistical purposes.
[53] See for example 1st Opinion on Bosnia and Herzegovina adopted on 27 May 2004, paragraph 98.

authorities with appropriate resources to enable them to carry out their tasks effectively.[54]

131. Where reforms relating to sub-national forms of government are considered, it is essential that their impact on the protection of persons belonging to national minorities be carefully analysed. To this end, State Parties are encouraged to provide ways of involving regional institutions as well as minority representatives in reform processes. Attention should be paid, in particular, to the potentially negative consequences of these measures for the protection of national minorities, notably as regards minority access to decision-making processes and financial resources.[55]

132. Irrespective of the territorial structure adopted by State Parties, the central authorities should remain committed to their general responsibility resulting from their international obligations and the national legal framework regarding participation of persons belonging to national minorities in various spheres. In this respect, State Parties are encouraged to ensure that sub-national authorities respect the obligations arising from the Framework Convention. Specific awareness-raising at the local and regional level is often needed to ensure this outcome.

f) Participation of persons belonging to national minorities through autonomy arrangements

133. The Framework Convention does not provide for the right of persons belonging to national minorities to autonomy, whether territorial or cultural. Yet, the Advisory Committee has examined the functioning and impact of territorial and cultural autonomy arrangements on participation of persons belonging to national minorities in State Parties where they exist.

134. The Advisory Committee found that, in the State Parties in which territorial autonomy arrangements exist, as a result of specific historical, political and other circumstances, they can foster a more effective participation of persons belonging to national minorities in various areas of life.

135. The Advisory Committee commented more extensively on cultural autonomy arrangements in those State Parties in which they have been established. These cultural autonomy arrangements are granted collectively to members of a particular national minority, regardless of a territory. They aim *inter alia* to delegate to national minority organisations important competences in the area of minority culture, language and education and can, in this regard, contribute to the preservation and development of minority cultures.

---

[54] See also remarks in paragraphs 138 and 139 below.
[55] See for example Opinion on Kosovo (UNMIK) adopted on 25 November 2005, paragraph 113.

136. Where State Parties provide for such cultural autonomy arrangements, the corresponding constitutional and legislative provisions should clearly specify the nature and scope of the autonomy system and the competencies of the autonomous bodies. In addition, their legal status, the relations between them and other relevant State institutions as well as the funding of the envisaged autonomy system, should be clarified in the respective legislation. It is important that persons belonging to national minorities be involved and that their views be duly taken into account when legislation on autonomy arrangements is being prepared or amended.

137. When designing electoral systems for autonomous bodies, the representativeness of the national minority concerned should be a key consideration. Electoral systems for self-government arrangements should entail protection against possible abuse.[56]

g) Availability of financial resources for minority-related activities

138. Availability of financial resources for bodies involved in minority protection is essential to enable them to carry out their mission. This implies the availability of funding for consultative mechanisms, cultural autonomy arrangements and government bodies involved in minority issues at all levels.

139. The resources allocated should be proportionate to the responsibilities of the bodies in question. Funding and budgetary arrangements for minority autonomy bodies should be designed so that they do not undermine their operational autonomy.[57] Consultative bodies also need to be provided with adequate resources, including staff and financial means, to support their effective functioning. Resources are also needed to enable them to communicate effectively with their constituencies and to monitor and evaluate the implementation of legislation and policies which affect them.

h) Media as a source for the effective participation of persons belonging to national minorities in public affairs

140. It is essential that the public be adequately informed about issues relevant to persons belonging to national minorities, which should also be part of mainstream media reporting. It is essential that both mainstream and minority media play a key role in this process, not only by means of transmitting information, but also by promoting tolerance.[58] At the same time, excessive politicisation of minority issues through the media should be avoided. Moreover, the media, in particular electronic media, can

---

[56] See 1st Opinion on Hungary adopted on 22 September 2000, paragraph 52.
[57] See 2nd Opinion on Hungary adopted on 9 December 2004, paragraphs 116 to 119.
[58] See also paragraphs 68 and 74 above.

facilitate consultation processes with persons belonging to national minorities.

141. The participation of persons belonging to national minorities in supervisory boards of public service broadcasts, auditors' councils and other media-related bodies, as well as in production teams, is essential to ensure adequate dissemination of information on national minorities. In the private sector, providing incentives for broadcasting in minority languages or on minority-related issues can contribute to increasing participation of persons belonging to national minorities in the media.

i) Participation of persons belonging to national minorities in the monitoring of the Framework Convention

142. Participation of persons belonging to national minorities in the monitoring process of the Framework Convention is crucial for achieving a balanced and quality outcome. When preparing State Reports or other written communications required under the Framework Convention or other international treaties pertaining to minority issues, State Parties should respect the principles enshrined in Article 15 of the Framework Convention and consult persons belonging to national minorities. In this and other contexts, it is important that interlocutors, such as consultative bodies, be not perceived as exclusive interlocutors but that State authorities also include other actors, especially minority or/and non-governmental organisations in the consultation process. The Advisory Committee welcomes the inclusion of comments made by minorities and civil society in State Reports, as well as in the Comments on the Advisory Committee's Opinions.

143. The Advisory Committee also welcomes alternative reports prepared by nongovernmental actors. They often constitute a valuable additional source of information. They are also an evidence of a desire of non-governmental actors to engage in a constructive dialogue based on international human rights norms.

144. It is essential that transparency of the consultation process be ensured and that State Parties make the full text of the Opinions of the Advisory Committee and the Resolutions of the Council of Europe Committee of Ministers available to persons belonging to national minorities and to the public at large as early and as widely as possible. The authorities should ensure that these, and other monitoring documents, including the State Report, are made available in local languages so that minorities can take part in the process in an inclusive manner.

145. The Advisory Committee has encouraged State Parties to set up a system of regular consultation providing an opportunity for minority representatives to discuss their concerns between the monitoring cycles of the

Framework Convention, be it follow-up seminars or other modalities. This dialogue is crucial to respond to specific concerns and also to build trust and confidence in the implementation of the Framework Convention. It creates a climate of tolerance and dialogue which enables diversity to be a source and a factor, not of division, but of enrichment for each society.

PART IV CONCLUSIONS

146. This Commentary is the result of the Advisory Committee's effort to provide a summary of its interpretation of Article 15 and related articles of the Framework Convention for those involved in the implementation of this Convention. The ultimate aim is to help advance participation of persons belonging to national minorities in various areas of life, to improve the implementation of the principles of the Framework Convention and to help State authorities build up a more integrated and better functioning society.
147. Based directly and indirectly on the country-specific work of the Advisory Committee, the Commentary is providing decision-makers, public officials, nongovernmental organisations, academics and other stakeholders, not least among minorities themselves, with an analysis of possible options to enable them to make adequate and informed choices when designing legislation and policies to improve minority participation. Choices to be made should be agreed upon by the authorities and the national minorities if they are to be sustainable. It is also important that they take into account the views of the majority population and the type of relations prevailing among various groups in society.
148. It is obvious that different solutions can be applied to different national minorities as well as to different situations prevailing in the State Parties. Measures taken in some State Parties have been considered by the Advisory Committee as an adequate implementation of Article 15 of the Framework Convention in given circumstances. Yet, it is important to recall that a measure that leads to effective participation in one State Party does not necessarily have the same impact in another context. State Parties therefore need to assess, in the light of their own domestic situation, the applicability and effectiveness of measures that have, elsewhere, resulted in increased participation of national minorities. The Advisory Committee's objective, in this Commentary, is to highlight those experiences out of which meaningful conclusions can be drawn for the benefit of all State Parties.

149. Additionally, the fact that actions taken by State Parties may be considered satisfactory in given circumstances and at a given stage of the monitoring process does not mean that they will be sufficient to ensure compliance with the standards of the Framework Convention in the future. This Commentary, therefore, also attempts to help State Parties set up conditions enabling them to comply, in a sustainable way, with the provisions of the Framework Convention in the future and adopt longer-term perspectives on minority protection and the type of relations in society they want to achieve.
150. Moreover, the situation of minorities and majorities alike is in constant evolution and new issues will develop or arise over time. Some of the issues mentioned in this Commentary, notably in the field of participation in socio-economic life, have not yet been fully explored and analysed, neither by the Advisory Committee in its country-by-country work nor by other actors involved in the protection of minority rights. Further attention needs to be given to a range of such issues, in particular concerning effective participation in economic, social and cultural life. Examples of issues to be further explored range from the impact of environmental problems on participation of persons belonging to vulnerable minorities, to access by persons belonging to national minorities to credit and banking services.
151. Other issues will have to be reassessed by the Advisory Committee in subsequent cycles of monitoring, when a longer term perspective on their impact on participation will be available. As already mentioned in the Introductory Remarks, this document is to be seen as a living instrument, which should be developed as monitoring under the Framework Convention progresses.

APPENDIX

RELEVANCE OF OTHER ARTICLES OF THE FRAMEWORK CONVENTION FOR THE INTERPRETATION OF ARTICLE 15

Article 3[59]

152. In its Article 3, the Framework Convention stipulates the right of persons belonging to national minorities to freely choose to be treated or not to be

---

[59] 3(1) Every person belonging to a national minority shall have the right freely to choose to be treated or not to be treated as such and no disadvantage shall result from this choice or from the exercise of the right which are connected to that choice.

3(2) Persons belonging to national minorities may exercise the rights and enjoy the freedoms flowing from the principles enshrined in the present framework Convention individually as well as in community with others.

treated as such. Inclusion in the personal scope of application of the Framework Convention is important for the enjoyment of the minority rights contained in the Framework Convention, including the right to effective participation in all areas of life. In its examination of the personal scope of application of the Framework Convention, the Advisory Committee has consistently recommended that State Parties avoid arbitrary or unjustified exclusions from the protection of the Framework Convention and that they opt for an 'inclusive' approach. On many occasions, it has invited State Parties to review and consider extending the personal scope of application of the Framework Convention as circumstances have changed over time.

Article 6[60]

153. Article 6(1) of the Framework Convention invites State Parties to encourage 'a spirit of tolerance and intercultural dialogue' and promote 'mutual respect and understanding' among all persons living on their territory. As already mentioned above,[61] effective participation of persons belonging to national minorities in various spheres of life is an important tool to enhance intercultural dialogue.
154. At the same time, the effectiveness of the participation of persons belonging to national minorities depends on the existence of a climate of mutual respect, tolerance and recognition in the society. It is therefore essential that State Parties take measures to encourage intercultural dialogue between the majority and minorities, as well as between various minorities and, more generally, among all persons living on their territory. In this context, the Advisory Committee has often stressed the importance of integration policies, both as a way of promoting equal opportunities and preventing tensions in society.
155. Furthermore, the Advisory Committee has often underlined the importance of the participation of persons belonging to national minorities in decision-making concerning activities to promote a better knowledge of minority cultures in the society at large. This includes the field of education, particularly when deciding on the inclusion of elements concerning national minorities in educational material, the media and the design and implementation of cultural policies.

---

[60] 6(1) The Parties shall encourage a spirit of tolerance and intercultural dialogue and take effective measures to promote mutual respect and understanding and co-operation among all persons living on their territory, irrespective of those persons' ethnic, cultural, linguistic or religious identity, in particular in the fields of education, culture and the media. 6(2) The Parties undertake to take appropriate measures to protect persons who may be subject to threats or acts of discrimination, hostility or violence as a result of their ethnic, cultural, linguistic or religious identity.

[61] See paragraph 21.

Article 7[62]

156. State Parties are requested to ensure that the right of every person belonging to a national minority to freedom of peaceful assembly and of association, as embedded in Article 7 of the Framework Convention, is respected. This includes the right to form minority associations and political parties, which are important forms of participation. State Parties should refrain from any unjustified interference with the exercise of this right, and create conditions allowing minority associations and parties to acquire and enjoy legal personality, and to operate freely. The right to freedom of assembly and association is a prerequisite to the enjoyment of the provisions of Article 15, even though it is not sufficient in itself to ensure effective participation.

Article 9[63]

157. Article 9 (1) protects the right of persons belonging to national minorities to freely receive and impart information and ideas in the minority language, and therefore, the possibility for them to participate in public debates and public affairs in general, notably through the media. Moreover, Article 9 (1) requires that State Parties ensure respect for the prohibition of discrimination in minorities' access to the media. Under Article 9 (4) of the Framework Convention, the authorities are required to adopt appropriate measures to facilitate access to the media of persons belonging to national minorities.
158. The access to and participation in the media of persons belonging to national minorities involves various dimensions: they should have access to the media as part of the audience, as owners of media outlets and as representatives of minorities in the mainstream media.
159. Adequate access to mainstream and minority media by persons belonging to national minorities considerably contributes to their effective participation in society, in particular in cultural life. It facilitates awareness-raising of the society at large about minorities' culture and identity. Moreover, the possibility for national minorities to create and use their own media is in itself an effective form of participation, in particular in public affairs and cultural life. This may also have direct and indirect social and economic benefits for persons belonging to national minorities.

---

[62] The Parties shall ensure respect for the right of every person belonging to a national minority to freedom of peaceful assembly, freedom of association, freedom of expression, and freedom of thought, conscience and religion.

[63] 9(4) In the framework of their legal systems, the Parties shall adopt adequate measures in order to facilitate access to the media for persons belonging to national minorities and in order to promote tolerance and permit cultural pluralism.

Article 10[64]

160. The right to use freely minority languages orally and in writing, in private and in public, as well as in relations with administrative authorities is a significant factor enhancing the participation of persons belonging to national minorities. This is particularly relevant for persons belonging to national minorities who live in areas inhabited traditionally or in substantial numbers by national minorities.[65] For example, policies of recruitment of civil servants favouring those with minority language proficiency are a positive way of promoting and enhancing minority participation in public administration. Likewise, the possibility of using minority languages in relations with administrative authorities can contribute to more effective communication with the authorities by persons belonging to national minorities. In local elected bodies, the possibility to use minority languages can allow persons belonging to national minorities to participate more effectively in decision-making. In contrast, strict language requirements may seriously hamper participation of national minorities in certain areas of life, in particular in socio-economic life and electoral processes. Yet, the importance of proficiency in the official language should not be underestimated as it also contributes to the effective participation of persons belonging to national minorities.[66]

Article 12, 13 and 14

161. Articles 12, 13 and 14 of the Framework Convention encapsulate wide-ranging provisions in the field of education, which have been extensively analysed by the Advisory Committee in its Commentary on Education adopted in 2006.[67]
162. Article 12 (1) requires that State Parties take measures to foster knowledge of the culture, language, history and religion of national minorities and of the majority population. Together with Article 6 (1),[68] Article 12 thus sets the objective for State Parties to promote a climate of mutual understanding and intercultural dialogue, which is a precondition for effective

---

[64] 10(2) In areas inhabited by persons belonging to national minorities traditionally or in substantial numbers, if those persons so request and where such a request corresponds to a real need, the Parties shall endeavour to ensure, as far as possible, the conditions which would make it possible to use the minority language in relations between those persons and the administrative authorities.

[65] 10(1) The Parties undertake to recognise that every person belonging to a national minority has the right to use freely and without interference his or her minority language, in private and in public, orally and in writing.   [66] See also the remarks below concerning Article 14.

[67] See Commentary on education under the Framework Convention for the Protection of National Minorities, adopted by the Advisory Committee on 2 March 2006.

[68] See paragraph 152 above.

participation of persons belonging to national minorities. In order to meet this objective, there is a need for adequate teaching and other material to be made available, for teachers to be adequately trained and for exchanges between students and teachers to be promoted, as highlighted under Article 12 (2). Moreover, under this Article, the Advisory Committee has often recommended that the authorities provide for the participation of persons belonging to national minorities in the preparation of legislation on education, as well as in the monitoring and evaluation of educational policies and programmes, in particular those concerning them.

163. Article 12 (3) of the Framework Convention is of particular relevance when analysing Article 15 as it requests State Parties to promote equal opportunities for persons belonging to national minorities in access to education at all levels, including in vocational training and adult education.

164. Article 14 (1) and (2),[69] on the one hand, sets the right for persons belonging to national minorities to learn their minority language and provide that State Parties should, under certain conditions, endeavour to provide adequate opportunities for receiving instruction or for being taught in a minority language. This is an important means to preserve and develop their identity and culture, as also stipulated in Article 5.[70] Article 14 (3) on the other hand, specifies that this should be implemented without prejudice to the learning of the official language. Adequate knowledge of the official language by persons belonging to national minorities is indeed essential for their participation in various spheres of life and their integration in mainstream society.[71] Therefore, the main foundations underlying the Framework Convention, already described in paragraphs 13 to 15 above on the connection between Articles 4, 5 and 15, are also fully reflected in Article 14.

165. The Advisory Committee has in many cases stressed the importance of effective participation of persons belonging to national minorities for the implementation of the rights contained in Article 14. It is, in particular, crucial to involve persons belonging to national minorities in decisions taken with regard to the organisation of minority language education[72] to

---

[69] 14 (1) The Parties undertake to recognise that every person belonging to a national minority has the right to learn his or her minority language. 14 (2) In areas inhabited by persons belonging to national minorities traditionally or in substantial numbers, if there is sufficient demand, the Parties shall endeavour to ensure, as far as possible, and within the framework of their education systems, that persons belonging to those minorities have adequate opportunities for being taught the minority language or for receiving instruction in this language.
14 (3) Paragraph 2 of this article shall be implemented without prejudice to the learning of the official language or the teaching of this language.
[70] See paragraphs 13 and 14 above. [71] See also remarks under Article 10 above.
[72] See also the Commentary on Education under the Framework Convention for the Protection of National Minorities, adopted by the Advisory Committee on 2 March 2006.

ensure that this type of education caters for the needs of national minorities.

Article 17 and Article 18[73]

166. Article 17 (1) of the Framework Convention stipulates that State Parties shall not prevent persons belonging to national minorities from establishing and maintaining free and peaceful contacts across frontiers, in particular with persons belonging to the same national minorities. Article 17 (2) aims to ensure that persons belonging to national minorities can make an active contribution to civil society, at the national and international levels.
167. Like Article 17, Article 18 (2) encourages a proactive approach to transfrontier co-operation, but between States. Cross-border co-operation can significantly contribute to developing participation of persons belonging to national minorities in public affairs and in social, economic and cultural life.

---

[73] 17 (1) The Parties undertake not to interfere with the rights of persons belonging to national minorities to establish and maintain free and peaceful contacts across frontiers with persons lawfully staying in other States, in particular those with whom they share an ethnic, cultural, linguistic or religious identity, or a common cultural heritage. 17 (2) The Parties undertake not to interfere with the right of persons belonging to national minorities to participate in the activities of non-governmental organisations, both at the national and international levels. 18 (2) Where relevant, the Parties shall take measures to encourage transfrontier cooperation.

Index

accountability
  effective participation 82–3, 89
  Framework Convention 89, 108
  local self-government 664, 666, 669
  parliaments 409–13
Advisory Committee of FCNM (ACFC)
  see also **FCNM Commentary**
  ad hoc contact procedure 727
  autonomy 244–5, 739–41
  awareness-raising 725–6
  best practices 229
  bilateral agreements, monitoring of 717, 728–34
  Committee of Ministers 226, 254, 708, 714–17, 721, 725–6
  composition 226, 714–15
  consultation 240–1, 478–81, 486–9, 493–8, 501, 714, 723, 725
  cooperation 717–18, 728
  country visits 715–16, 721–2, 726
  customary law of minority protection 229
  dialogue-related perspective 228, 229–30
  education 722
  effective participation 74–7, 87, 88–90, 92
  election of members of ACFC 714–15
  elections 235–6, 271–2
  equality of arms 734
  European Convention on Human Rights 220
  European Union 724
  experts 733–4
  follow-up seminars 726
  hard law 227
  identification requirements 247–8
  implementation of Framework Convention 708, 714–18, 721–34
  indigenous people 310
  information, submission of 715–16, 727
  joint intergovernmental commissions, membership of 729–34
  judiciary 592–9, 603–6, 609
  language 248–9, 725–6
  legal approach 229–30
  legal entrenchment of participation 737–43, 745
  meetings 715–16
  minimum standards 229, 230, 254
  minority associations 686, 689
  monitoring 254, 706, 714–18, 721–34

  multiple discrimination 250
  non-governmental organizations (NGOs) 718, 724–5, 727
  OSCE High Commissioner on National Minorities (HCNM) 284
  opinions 716–17, 724
    dual legal and political effect of 225–30
    legal entrenchment of participation 737–8
    normative power 227
    publication 726–7
  persuasive authority 230
  political approach 229–30
  political parties 233–4
  power-sharing 416–17
  practice 721–3
  publicity 723
  recommendations 230, 254, 721, 724
  reports 706, 722–7, 734
  reserved seats systems 236–7
  residency 246
  rights-oriented approach 229
  Roma 238, 512, 522
  shadow reports 727
  social and economic life, participation in 249–50, 526–8, 535–53, 587
  soft jurisprudence 225–30
  standards 108–9, 229–30
  state parties 714, 716–17
  state practice 721, 723–34
  statistic data, collection of 248
  thematic commentaries 226, 722–3, 734, 737–8, 741
  transparency 714, 723, 726
  Travellers 238
  UN High Commissioner for Human Rights 716
  veto rights 417
  visits 715–16, 721–2, 726
advisory mechanisms *see* **consultative and advisory mechanisms**
affirmative action *see* **positive or special measures**
Afghanistan 170–2
African Charter on Human Rights (AfrCh) 104, 110, 570–1
African descent, participation of persons of 289, 290, 291
agenda setting in parliament 401–5

Albania 427, 447 518
alternative vote (AV) systems 169–70, 374–5, 383–5, 392–4
American Convention on Human Rights 104, 110, 569–70
Argentina 324
Armenia 93
Asian descent, participation of persons of 290
assimilation 39–40, 56–7, 67, 312
associations *see* minority associations
Australia 317, 325, 327, 388
autonomy
  Advisory Committee of FCNM (ACFC) 244–5, 739–41
  communitarian autonomy 334–6
  competencies 244
  consultative and advisory mechanisms 478
  cultural autonomy 57–8, 244–5, 643, 645, 647, 650–1, 655–6
  decentralization 244
  democracy 205–6
  drafting legislation, consultation on 244
  discrimination 143–5
  effective participation 232, 245–7
  electoral systems, design of 364, 366, 383
  European Convention on Human Rights 205
  FCNM Commentary 244–7
  federalism 619–23, 630–1
  Framework Convention 232, 245, 739–40
  gender 152, 160–1
  implementation mechanisms 748
  indigenous people 312, 328–34, 338, 341–2
  legal entrenchment of participation 739–42, 750
  minimum standards 245
  nationalism 160–1
  peace settlements 464, 465, 468, 472
  power-sharing 478
  private autonomy 205–6, 208
  public autonomy 205–6, 208
  self-governance
    cultural autonomy 643, 645, 647, 650–1, 655–6
    discrimination 143–5
    federalism 619–23, 630–1
    indigenous people 338
    territorial arrangements 217–18, 328–9
  territorial arrangements 68, 155–6, 215–17, 329–34
  territorial domination for minorities 57–8
  UN Declaration on Minorities 291

women's movements and nationalism 160–1

Balkans, civil service in the 446–50
Bangladesh 336
Belgium
  consociational model of power-sharing 167–8
  cultural identity 168
  linguistic communities 167–8, 425–6, 430–1, 693–4
  minority associations 693–5
  power-sharing 425–7, 430–1
  quotas for women 167–8
  Roma, special contact measures (SCMR) for 520
belief, thought, conscience and opinion, freedom of 354–5
bilateral agreements 708, 719–21, 728–34
birth rates 43
block votes 380–1
Bolivia 316–21, 323, 334
Bolzano/Bozen Recommendations 709–10, 712–13
Bosnia and Herzegovina
  coalition governments, partners in 10–11, 33
  Dayton Agreement 193–4, 244
  judiciary 601–3, 605, 608
  mobilization 10
  power sharing 10–11, 30, 33, 141–3, 426–7, 430, 433
  secessionist conflicts 15
  Serbs 10–11
  stand for office, right to 193–4
  veto rights 244
boundaries *see* gerrymandering
Bulgaria 427–9, 433, 679
Burma, repression in 37

Canada 165–7, 330–3, 380, 618–19, 648–51
Central and Eastern Europe *see also* particular countries
  Central European Initiative Instrument 480
  conflicts 259–60
  consultative and advisory mechanisms 480
  domination of minorities in democracies 37–9, 64–5, 71
  local self-government 679–80
  minority associations 685–8
  OSCE High Commissioner on National Minorities (HCNM) 259–60
  Roma, special contact measures (SCMR) for 504–5, 519–20
Chechnya 64
children, rights of 568

Index 821

Chile 318, 324, 326
China, repression in 37
citizenship
  Armenia 93
  civil service, access to 93
  definition of minority 90–1
  demographic domination 43
  discrimination 113, 550–1, 561–2
  effective participation 90–3, 245–7
  elections 113, 245–6, 318
  Estonia 43
  European Union 579, 582
  FCNM Commentary 245–7
  Framework Convention 92–3, 246
  indigenous people 318
  International Covenant on Economic, Social and Cultural Rights 567
  Latvia 43
  new and immigrant communities 246
  non-citizens 91–2, 245–6
  old minorities 246
  political rights 91–2
  social and economic life, participation in 550–1, 556, 561–2, 579, 582
  standards 103–4
  UN Declaration on Minorities 293, 556
  Venice Commission 245–6
  vote, right to 245–6
civil service 439–52
  Albania 447
  Armenia 93
  Balkans 446–50
  citizenship 93
  Croatia 448–50
  discrimination 109, 113, 147–8
  effective participation 93, 439, 440–1, 451–2
  enhanced minority participation 441–52
  equitable representation 447–8, 451
  guaranteed participation 441–2, 449–51
  linguistic communities 444–6
  Lund Recommendations 447
  multinational states 442–4
  power-sharing in executive 442–6
  promotional states 443–4
  proportional representation 444, 448
  quotas 441–2, 444–8
  second-generation representation clauses 446–51
  social and economic life, participation in 534
  South Tyrol 444–6, 448
  standards 104, 105
  Western Balkans 446–50
civil society organizations 201–3, 687, 696
civil wars 4, 6–8, 16–17, 21–4, 31, 455

coalitions 10–11, 33, 53–4, 402–3, 420–2, 428
coercive assimilation 39–40, 67
coercive domination 58–60, 66–7
Colombia 316, 329–30
colonialism 15, 20–1, 160–1, 329–30, 369, 373
Commentary on Framework Convention *see* FCNM Commentary
commissions 708, 719–21, 729–34
committees 400–5, 412, 514–16, 519–20
competition, exclusion and 17
conditionality principle 350–1
Conference for Security and Co-operation in Europe *see* Organization for Security and Co-operation in Europe (OSCE)
conflict resolution and prevention
  Afghanistan 171–2
  Bolzano/Bozen Recommendations 713
  cultural minority self-governance 636
  democracy 262
  gender 151–2, 158, 171–2
  human rights 262
  implementation mechanisms 747–9
  indigenous people 336
  intersectionality, theory of 158
  judiciary 591–2, 599–605, 608
  long-term and short-term 262
  Lund Recommendations 261–3, 454
  OSCE High Commissioner on National Minorities (HCNM) 259–61, 267–8, 280–1
  political parties 275–7
  social and economic life, participation in 534–5
conflicts *see also* conflict resolution and prevention
  Central and Eastern Europe 259–60
  civil wars 4, 7–8, 16–17, 21–4, 31, 455
  configurations of power 12–17, 32
  definition of armed conflict 19
  democratic deficit 459–60
  distinguishing ethnic conflicts from non-ethnic conflicts 19
  diversity, politics and 4–17, 22–3, 31–2
  effective participation 459–61
  elections 459–60
  ethnic politics and ethnic conflict 4–17, 22–3, 31–2
  Ethnic Power Relations, dataset on 19–20
  ethno-nationalist wars 4
  exclusion 461–4
  infighting 5–6, 14–16, 19–20, 26–30, 32–3
  languages 456–8, 459, 462–3
  large minorities 462
  Lund Recommendations 455, 457–8, 461

conflicts (*cont.*)
  Mexico, Chiapas uprising in 10, 30, 33
  non-neutrality of states and
    minorities 455–60
  power, configurations of
  quantitative analysis of ethnic diversity and
    armed conflict 3–34
  reasons 22–6, 454–64
  rebellions 14–16, 19–20, 26–30
  religion 455–6, 457
  secession 14–16, 28–30
  secularism 456
  separatist and non-separatist conflicts 20
  Sri Lanka 462–5
  state neutrality 455–60
  state preferences 458–61
  territorial conflicts 641
  types of ethnic conflict 12–17, 32
  Uppsala/PRIO Armed Conflict Dataset
    (ACD) 17, 19
  war-prone configurations, hypotheses
    on 14–17
**Congress of Local and Regional Authorities
  (Council of Europe)** 663, 671–2, 682
**conscience, belief, opinion and thought,
  freedom of** 354–5
consociationalism 84–6, 167–8, 415–16,
  420, 640
**constitutionalization of international law
  regimes** 219
consultative and advisory mechanisms
  477–502
  activities, areas and types of 486–8
  Advisory Committee of FCNM (ACFC)
    240–1, 478–81, 486–9, 493–8, 501,
    714, 723, 725
  appointments 240–1
  areas of activities 486–8
  Australia 325, 327
  autonomy 478
  Bolzano/Bozen Recommendations 713
  Central European Initiative Instrument 480
  co-decision mechanism 483
  communication-participation-
    integration 278
  complex systems 488
  consultative councils 483–7, 494, 496–500
  contact offices 485
  co-ordination measures 243, 485–6, 501
  culture 481, 486
  Czech Republic 495
  definition of minority 495
  democratic deficit 279
  development projects 313–14
  different, right to be 212
  drafting of legislation, involvement in
    491, 494

economic issues 479
education 327
effective participation 231, 239–43,
  477–80, 490, 500
establishment 240–2, 277–9
expert bodies 485–7
FCNM Commentary 239–43, 481
Finland 493–4, 496, 500
Framework Convention 231, 479, 480–1,
  489–90, 501
functions 489–93
funding by government 499–500, 502
Germany, Sorbian minority in 494
groups, mechanisms focusing on
  particular 487–8
human rights 278–9, 482, 497
Human Rights Committee 482, 497
Hungary 489
ILO Convention 169 on indigenous
  people 482
implementation mechanisms 748–9
Independent Expert on Minority Issues
  (UN) 302
indigenous people 313, 324–8, 482, 486
international organizations, relations
  with 492–3
languages 481
Latin America 324
legal entrenchment of participation
  746–7, 750
legal establishment 488–9, 495
legal framework 479–82
legislation, drafting of 244
Lithuania 495
local development 327
Lund Recommendations 277–9, 324, 489,
  493–4, 501
mandates 489–93, 501
Maori, economic activities of 555
membership 278, 493–7
minority associations 689, 690–5
minority councils 240–2
mixed bodies 240–1
monitoring 708
multilevel consultation 486–7
Nepal, National Foundation for Indigenous
  Development of 325
organizations representing national
  minorities, functions of 490–1
OSCE Copenhagen Document 479, 480
OSCE High Commissioner on National
  Minorities (HCNM) 277–80,
  282, 481
Philippines, National Commission on
  Indigenous Peoples in 325
pluralism 278
policy sectors 326

power-sharing 478
programming, involvement in 491–2
quality of outcomes 500
regular basis, consultation on 243
reports 492–3
resourcing 499–500, 502
Roma 487, 488, 516–20, 522–3
Sami parliament 493–4, 500
self-government 477–8, 486
Slovakia 494–5
social and economic life, participation in 528–9, 533, 537, 555–6
social issues 479
social welfare 327
specialized consultative mechanisms 487
specialized government bodies 243
treaties, drafting of 493
types of activities 483–6
types of bodies 482–8
UN Declaration on Minorities 479–80
veto, right of 500
working methods 497–9, 501–2
contact offices 485
Convention on the Rights of the Child 568
co-ordination measures 243, 485–6, 501
Council of Europe *see also* **Advisory Committee of FCNM (ACFC); Framework Convention for the Protection of Minorities (FCNM)**
conditionality principle 350–1
Congress of Local and Regional Authorities 663, 671–2, 682
Convention on Participation of Foreigners in Public Life 92
elections 92, 358
local self-government 662, 663, 671–2, 675–7, 681
OSCE High Commissioner on National Minorities (HCNM) 88
Roma, special contact measures (SCMR) for 512–13, 522
country visits
Advisory Committee of FCNM (ACFC) 715–16, 721–2, 726
Independent Expert on Minority Issues (UN) 302–3
UN Declaration on Minorities 299
Croatia
civil service 448–50
cultural autonomy 743
effective participation 83, 84
expulsions 42
judiciary 603–5
power-sharing 421
Roma, special contact measures (SCMR) for 518

CSCE *see* **OSCE Copenhagen Document**
culture
autonomy 244–5, 643, 645, 647, 650–1, 655–6, 742–3, 750
Belgium 168
coercive assimilation 40
consultative and advisory mechanisms 481, 488
Croatia 743
destruction of culture 40
democracy 206–7, 639–40, 642–3, 646
different, right to be 211
discrimination 96–7
domination 38–9, 67
education 545, 646–7
effective participation 254
essentialism 157
FCNM Commentary 254–5
Framework Convention 106, 254–5
gender 151, 161–2, 166–7, 168
human rights 638, 655
Hungary 743
importance of cultural diversity 641–3
indigenous people 329, 338, 637, 649–50, 655–7
International Covenant on Civil and Political Rights 288, 637–8
International Covenant on Economic, Social and Cultural Rights 294, 306, 563–8, 587, 738
interpretations of culture 642
intersectionality, theory of 157, 158
Islamic minorities 658–60
Jewish marriages and divorces 660
language 645–9, 652
multiculturalism 154–9, 172, 636
multi-ethnic societies 638–9
names 645–6
nation states, cultural homogeneity of 7
National Cultural Autonomy (NCA) model 639–40, 644
non-territorial self-government 218
Nunavut, gender balance in legislature in 166–7
privatization of culture 67
religious minorities 658–60
resources, consent to preservation of 294
Roma 560
Romania 742–3
self-determination 641, 643–4, 655–6, 658
self-governance 629, 634–40
Sharia law 659–60
Sikhs, kirpans and 660
social and economic life, participation in 249–53, 532, 539, 545, 553, 560
sovereignty 643–4, 654
Spain, Autonomous Communities in 651–4

culture (cont.)
  supplementary jurisdictions 659–60
  territorial arrangements 643, 650–1, 656
  territorial conflicts 641
customary law 98, 109, 229, 329
Cyprus 118–19, 247–8, 516
Czech Republic 495, 518–19, 521, 690–2

data protection 248
decentralization 54–5, 108, 244
decision-making
  discrimination 97
  effective participation 75–6, 84–5
  Helsinki Document 710
  indigenous people 314, 315–27
  Lund Recommendations 107
  veto rights 239–40
Declaration on Minorities *see* UN Declaration on Minorities
definition of minorities 90–1, 495, 635
deliberation in parliament 405–9, 413
democracies *see* democracies, domination of minorities in; democracy
democracies, domination of minorities in
  coercive assimilation 39–40, 67
  coercive domination 58–60, 66–7
  control 39–41
  cultural domination 38–40, 67
  demographic domination 40–3
  discrimination 39, 67–8
  Eastern Europe 37–9, 64–5, 71
  economic domination 38, 39
  electoral domination 44–51, 66, 67–70
  employment, discrimination in 39
  end of domination 64–70
  equality 67
  ethnic cleansing 40–1
  European Union 64–5
  freedom of expression and association 67
  genocide 40–1
  hierarchies of privilege within political systems 36–7, 64–5
  instability 40–1
  institutional basis of ethnic domination 41–64, 70–1
  integrationist policies 68–9
  international law 35–6, 65, 71
  land 39
  language 38–9, 40, 65, 66
  legal domination 60–4
  liberalism 67–71
  Lund Recommendations 35–6, 64, 65
  majority rule 65–6
  minority rights 35–6, 64–8
  names 39
  policy basis of ethnic domination 41–64, 68
  political domination 38, 51–4, 67–71
  regions, funding for 39
  religion 38–9, 67
  republicanism 66, 68–70
  stability 40–1, 69
  symbolic domination 38
  territorial domination 54–8, 66, 68–9
democracy *see also* democracies, domination of minorities in
  autonomy 205–6
  conflict prevention 262
  conflicts, reasons for 459–60
  consultative and advisory mechanisms 279–80
  cultural minority self-governance 639–40, 642–3, 646
  cultural rights 206–7, 639–40, 642–3, 646
  deliberation in parliament 406
  deliberative democracy 204–8, 214, 686
  democratic civil peace theory 21
  democratic deficit 204, 279–80, 459–60
  different, right to be 207–8
  effective participation 436
  elections 180–1, 185–7, 204, 372
  European Convention on Human Rights 179–208, 348
  Framework Convention 436
  gender 151–2, 171–2
  internal democracy of minority communities 108
  legitimacy 204–7
  Lund Recommendations 262, 279–80
  minority associations 686
  Office for Democratic Institutions and Human Rights (ODIHR) 269–71, 282, 505–6, 509, 523
  Organization for Security and Co-operation in Europe (OSCE) 258, 265, 350
  OSCE High Commissioner on National Minorities (HCNM) 265
  peace settlements 459–60
  political parties 125–6
  religion 206–7
  Roma, special contact measures (SCMR) for 507–8, 511
  self-governance 613, 623, 628–9
  South Africa 163–4
  undemocratic political parties 125–6
  unreasonable others 207
denaturalization 43, 44–5
Denmark 240, 52–2
development
  African Charter on Human and People's Rights 571
  consultation 313–14
  Dublin Convention against Racism 290
  human rights-based approach 296–7

indigenous people 313–14
infighting 15
institutions, encouragement of development 290
local development 327
OECD Development Assistance Committee (DAC) 585
rebellions 15
social and economic life, participation in 571
UN Declaration on Minorities 306
UN Declaration on the Right to Development 289, 297
UN Development Program 297, 306–7
UN standards and practices 289, 297
different, minority right to be 207–14
differential treatment 100–2, 121–2, 130, 135, 435–6, 572
discrimination *see* non-discrimination and equality
displacement of persons 252
dispute resolution *see* conflict resolution and prevention
districting 394–5
diversity
  diversity breeds conflict tradition 4–7, 23, 31
  Guidelines and Good Practice for Policing in Diverse Societies (OHCHR) 296, 304, 306
  quantitative analysis of ethnic diversity and armed conflict 3–34
domination of minorities *see* democracies, domination of minorities in
downsizing minorities 42–3
Dublin Conference against Racism 289–91, 294–6, 303–6

Eastern Europe *see* Central and Eastern Europe
economic domination of minorities 38, 39
economic life *see* social and economic life, discrimination in; social and economic life, participation in
Ecuador 320, 323, 327
education
  Advisory Committee of FCNM (ACFC) 722
  African Charter on Human and People's Rights 571
  culture 545, 646–7
  discrimination 39, 540–1, 559–62, 571
  economic domination of minorities 39
  International Covenant on Economic, Social and Cultural Rights 294, 564, 565, 566–7

judiciary 596, 605
language 544–5, 557, 565, 571
positive or special measures 545–6, 560, 568
Roma 509–10, 545, 559–62, 566–7, 568, 572
segregation 559, 562
social and economic life, participation in 530–1, 538, 540–7, 557, 559–62, 571
UN Forum on Minority Issues 584–5
effective participation 73–94, 280–5 *see also* Lund Recommendations; positive or special measures
accountability 82–3, 89
African descent, persons of 290
aims of participation 77–81
Asian descent, persons of 290
autonomy 232, 244–5
best practices 232
citizenship 90–3, 245–7
civil service 93, 439, 440–1, 451–2
conflicts, reasons for 459–50
consociational mechanisms 84, 85–6
consultative and advisory bodies 84, 231, 239–43
cultural diversity 254
decision-making processes 75–6, 84–5
definition 75–7
democracy 436
differential treatment 435–6
discrimination 78–82, 95–149, 288
Dublin Convention against Racism 289–291, 294–6, 303–6
elected bodies, participation in 243–4
elections 82–5, 92, 132, 234–6, 359
electoral systems, design of 234–6
equality 78–81
essentialism 83–6
FCNM Commentary 230–49, 254–5
formal approaches 254–5
forms of participation 230
Framework Convention 74–7, 87–90, 92–3, 222–5, 230–49, 254, 350
full and effective participation 95–149, 307
gender 288, 290
goal of integration, instruments with 232
government 76, 82, 237–9
group proliferation 86–7
identification requirements 247–8
identity, promotion of 78
indigenous people 310–11, 315
influence on decisions 75–7, 85, 239
institutional measures 231
instruments and measures which enable, foster or guarantee participation 231

effective participation (*cont.*)
  International Covenant on Civil and
      Political Rights 349
  international organizations, accession criteria
      to 73–4
  judiciary, representation in the 76, 80, 82,
      237–9, 439–41
  language requirements 248–9
  legal instruments 232
  legal restrictions and problems 245–9
  legislative process, representation in 232–7
  minimum standards 231–2
  ministries, creation of specific 237
  minority associations 688–90
  mirror representation 81–3, 89
  monitoring 76, 87–8, 707–8
  multiple identities 83–6
  normative deficit 263–7
  OSCE Copenhagen Document 74, 77
  OSCE High Commissioner on National
      Minorities (HCNM) 74, 88,
      90, 283–4
  parliamentary representation 298, 437
  participation, instruments of 708
  peace settlements 464–73
  pluralism 435–7
  political parties 232–4, 246–7
  procedures 231, 265–7, 707–8
  public administration, representation in
      the 237–9
  racism 288
  representation
      institutions of 708
      without participation 239–40
  reserved seats 236–7, 240
  residency 246
  results-oriented approach 239
  rights versus security perspective 77–8
  Roma, special contact measures (SCMR) for
      504, 522–3
  security versus rights perspective 77–9
  social and economic life, participation in
      249–53, 533, 537–8, 542, 549–50
  social cohesion 86–7, 90
  socio-economic inequality 78
  specific obligations 254
  stability 77–8
  standards 106, 286–307
  statistical data, collection of 248
  substantive approaches 78–81, 254–5, 707
  UN Declaration on Minorities 74, 76, 77,
      292–3, 296, 298–9, 304, 349
  United Nations standards and practices
      286–307
  universal principles of political
      participation 345–8
  Venice Commission 87, 93
veto rights 239–40
will of people, selecting and
    determining 436
elected bodies, participation in 243–4,
    695–700 *see also* **parliaments**
elections 348–57 *see also* **electoral systems,
    design of; gerrymandering; political
    parties**
  Advisory Committee of FCNM
      (ACFC) 271–2
  age requirements 187
  anti-competitive practices 47–9
  Bolivia 318–20, 321
  campaigns 355
  citizenship 113, 245–6, 318
  civil society organizations 201, 203
  codification of practices 360–2
  conditions on participation 117–21
  conflicts, reasons for 459–60
  Cyprus, Turkish-Cypriot community
      in 118–19
  democracy 180–1, 185–7, 204
  demographic domination 43
  denaturalization 44
  discrimination 67–70, 97, 109–13, 116–23,
      147–9, 188, 349–53
  domestic elections 180–195, 220–1
  domination of minorities 44–53, 66, 67–70
  Draft Convention on Election Standards,
      Electoral Rights and Freedoms 360–1
  dual voting 44, 67, 139, 274–5, 282, 745
  effective participation 82–5, 92
  elections 187–8, 191–2
  equal and universal suffrage 351–3,
      354, 360
  Estonia 51
  European Convention on Human Rights
      180–95, 201, 203–4, 220–1, 347–8
    discrimination 118–23, 149
    domination of minorities 69–70
    Roma 511
    standards 105
  European Court of Human Rights 181
  FCNM Commentary 120–1
  Framework Convention 92–3, 107–8,
      271–2, 353
  fraud 347
  freedom of association and assembly 203,
      318, 357
  freedom of expression 182–3, 355–6, 367
  freedom of information 355–6
  gender 165, 169–70, 353
  genuine elections 353–4, 362
  Germany, Danish minority in Schleswig-
      Holstein 73
  historical factors 123
  Human Rights Committee (UN) 117

Human Rights Council (UN) 352
implementation mechanisms
    358–60, 748–9
individual country approach 269–70
Indonesia 48
International Covenant on Civil and
    Political Rights 104, 348, 353
Israel 45, 48–9
language 120–1, 318, 459
Latin America 319–22
Latvia 51, 120–1
legal entrenchment of participation 743–5
legislative bodies, elections to 180–1
legitimization of arrangements 272–5
literacy tests 44, 51, 66, 67
local considerations 120, 122
Lund Recommendations 69, 107, 181,
    268–75, 282, 318
majority electoral formulae, under
    representing minorities through 45–7
margin of appreciation 182, 184–7
media, access to 147–8, 354–5
military law, imposition of 50
monitoring 103–5, 107, 269–71
Nicaragua 314, 318–21
Northern Ireland 45–7, 49–50, 67, 134
observation missions 269–71, 358–62
Office for Democratic Institutions and
    Human Rights (ODIHR)
    269–71, 282
OSCE Copenhagen Document 271–2,
    273, 347
OSCE High Commissioner on National
    Minorities (HCNM) 268–75, 282
pluralism 45–7, 184, 354
political factors 123
poll tax payments as pre-condition for
    voting 49
polling places, access to 361
positive or special measures 123, 132, 134,
    137–41, 273–5, 353, 361–2, 745
post-election methods that penalize minority
    politicians 49–51
prisoners 187
proportionality 120, 137–41
quotas 322
radio and television air time 147–8, 354–5
reducing the minority vote 44–5
registration of voters 113
reserved seats 141–3, 236–7, 240, 268–9,
    295–6, 395–6, 514, 744–5
residence requirements 117
Roma, special contact measures (SCMR)
    for 510–11
Russia 48
secret ballots 182, 214–19
segmented states 32

Slovakia 46–7
Sri Lanka 48
stand for office, right to 181, 188–95
standards 103–5, 107, 358–60
subscription groups 319–20
thought, conscience, belief and opinion,
    freedom of 354–5
threshold systems 46–7, 69–70, 73,
    123, 184–7
Turkey, Kurds in
    discrimination 70, 123
    domination of minorities 46, 50, 69–70
    threshold system 46, 69–70, 184–7
United States 44–5, 49–51, 63–7, 69
Universal Declaration on Human
    Rights 346
universal principles of political participation
    346, 347
Venice Commission 93, 137–42, 272–5
Warsaw Guidelines 270–1
electoral systems, design of see also
    proportional representation (PR)
adversarial cycles 377
Advisory Committee of FCNM
    (ACFC) 235–6
alternative vote 170, 374–5, 383–5, 392–4
anti-plurality vote 397
apparentement 366
approval voting systems 397
authoritarian governments, interests
    of 372–3
autonomy 364, 366, 383
ballot structure 366
block vote 380–1
Borda methods 397
boundaries 364–5
categorical or X votes 368–70
classification of systems by formula 367–97
Colomer's law 389–90, 394, 395
colonial background 369, 373
Coombs rule 397
Condorcet winners 383–4
corporate or reserved systems 395–6
cube rule 376
decolonization 373
democratization 372
district magnitude 365
districting 394–5
double-ballot run-offs 369
effective participation 234–6
electoral formula (seat allocation rule)
    365, 367
ethnic political parties 399
European Convention on Human Rights
    181–7, 364
FCNM Commentary 234–6
first-past-the-post 375

electoral systems (*cont.*)
  France 381
  geography 370, 374, 394–5
  gerrymandering 235, 366, 374, 377–8, 398
  hybrid systems 371
  imperial or Hegemon-effects 370
  independent electoral commissions 365
  Jenkins Commission (United
      Kingdom) 398
  Lund Recommendations 364–5, 369,
      374–5, 378–9, 383, 385, 395, 397–9
  majoritarianism 170, 367–9, 370–6, 380–2
  malapportionment 366, 376, 378, 398
  method majoritaire 396
  mixed or hybrid systems 367, 387
  non-monotonic elections 383–4
  non-preferential systems 368–9, 372
  Northern Ireland 373–5, 380
  number of persons elected 369
  origins of electoral systems 369
  OSCE Copenhagen Document 364
  parallel systems 368, 369, 371, 374–5, 387
  participation goals 364
  party block votes 381
  plurality or winner takes all (WTA) 364,
      367–71, 373–80
  population density 370–1
  positive or special measures 234–6
  preferential systems 368–9
  psychological effects 378–9
  Quebec 380
  regulations 364
  relative majority formula 376
  reserved seats 395–6
  seat allocation rule (electoral formula)
      365, 367
  secession 373, 379–80, 399
  single member districts (SMD) 364, 370–1,
      373–80, 410
  single transferable vote (STV) 170,
      373–4, 394
  site of elected body 366
  small political parties 234–5 tactical
      voting 378
  thresholds 234–5, 366, 394–5, 398
  two-party systems 379
  two-round systems (TRS) (double-ballot
      majoritarianism) 369, 370, 374–5,
      381–2, 384
  two-tier systems (parallel systems) 367–8
  UN Declaration on Minorities 293
  UN Electoral Assistance Unit 365
  United States 365, 374
  Universal Declaration of Human
      Rights 364
  untried systems 396–7
  wasted votes 376
  winner-takes-all (WTA) 364, 367–71,
      373–80, 394
  winner-takes-all (WTA)/ single member
      districts (SMD) 375–80, 394
emergency powers 62
employment *see also* civil servants; public
      employment
  discrimination 39, 543–4, 558–9, 561, 565
  economic domination of minorities 39
  Employment Equality Directive 576–7, 582
  European Employment Strategy 579
  International Covenant on Economic, Social
      and Cultural Rights 565
  judiciary 596
  language 39, 544, 558–9, 561
  public sector 39
  social and economic life, participation in
      531, 538–9, 541–4, 558–9, 561, 565
  urban-rural divide 249–50
enhanced local self-government 661–81
entertainment, access to places of 548
equal and universal suffrage 351–3, 354, 360
equality *see* non-discrimination and equality
Estonia
  citizenship 43
  cultural autonomy 57
  denaturalization 43, 44
  domination of minorities 39, 43, 51, 59, 64–5
  electoral domination 51
  employment, discrimination in 39
  European Union 64–5
  land 39
  language 249
  security service domination of minorities 59
ethnic cleansing 40–1, 252
ethnic diversity, politics and 4–17,
      22–3, 31–2
ethnic nepotism 7
ethnic political parties 232–4
  agenda setting in parliament 403
  coalitions 403
  elections 318–19, 399
  electoral systems, design of 399
  European Convention on Human Rights
      199–201
  indigenous people 318–19
  Lund Recommendations 275–7
  minority associations 686
  UN Declaration on Minorities 292–3
Ethnic Power Relations, dataset on 4,
      5, 17–20
  access to executive power 17–18
  codings 18–20, 22–3
  infighting 19–20
  politically relevant groups and access to
      power 17–18, 19
  rebellions 19–20

Index

secession 20
Uppsala/PRIO Armed Conflict Dataset (ACD) 17, 19
war coding 19–20
ethnicity, definition of 17–18
European Charter for Regional or Minority Languages 481
European Charter of Local Self-Government 662, 670–1, 675–7, 681, 738
European Commission against Racism and Intolerance (ECRI) 658–9
European Commission for Democracy through Law *see* **Venice Commission**
European Committee of Social Rights 130
European Convention on Human Rights 177–221
  absolute rights 179–80
  Advisory Committee of FCNM (ACFC) 220, 229
  autonomy 205
  balancing interests 180
  civil society organizations 201–2
  conditional rights 180
  conflicts with Lund Recommendations 219
  constitutionalization of international law regimes 219
  democracy 125–6, 179–207, 214, 348
  democratic society and need for democratic law 204–8
  different, minority right to be 207–14
  differential treatment 121
  discrimination 110–23, 148–9, 572–3
  elections 180–195, 201, 203–4, 220–1, 347–8
    design of systems 181–7, 364
    discrimination 118–23, 149
    domination of minorities 69–70
    Roma 511
    standards 105
  European Court of Human Rights
    Advisory Committee of FCNM (ACFC) 229
    different, right to be 212–13
    elections 181, 220–1
    Framework Convention 226
    role 180, 220–1, 213–14, 348
  fragmentation, benefits of 220
  Framework Convention 220, 225–30
  freedom of association 195, 197–9, 202–3
  freedom of expression 195, 196–8, 348
  governance 178–80
  hard law, as 179–80
  housing 573, 574
  inhuman or degrading treatment 572–3
  interpretation 212–13
  language 249
  legal entrenchment of participation 738
  legislative bodies, elections to 180–1
  local self-government 675
  Lund Recommendations in global governance 178–80, 199, 219
  margin of appreciation 180, 196, 199, 200, 203
  Muslim parties in Turkey 200–1
  object and purpose 213–14
  pluralism 195, 197, 199–222
  political parties 124–8, 196, 198–201, 203, 232–4
  positive or special measures 133–6, 141–3, 148–9
  power-sharing 141–3
  proportionality 196, 197
  Protocol 12 111–12, 142, 149
  right of political participation in democratic politics 195–203
  Roma 511, 572–4
  secret ballots 348
  self-governance 214–19
  social and economic life, participation in 571–4
  social services, access to 573
  stand for office, right to 188–95
  standards 105
  universal principles of political participation 347–8
European Social Charter 250, 571, 573
European Union
  accession conditions 350, 574–5
  Advisory Committee of FCNM (ACFC) 724
  citizenship 579, 582
  competences 574–5
  Copenhagen criteria 574
  discrimination 114–15, 576–8, 580
  domination of minorities 64–5
  Employment Equality Directive 576–7, 582
  elections, observation of 358
  Estonia 64–5
  European Court of Justice 114–15, 577, 581–2
  European Employment Strategy 579
  Framework Convention 574
  High Level Advisory Group 579
  integration 578–81
  Latvia 64–5
  Lisbon Treaty 575, 577–8
  mainstreaming 575, 577
  migration policy 580
  new and immigrant minorities 576, 579–82
  Race Equality Directive 576–8, 582, 587
  Roma 578
  Slovakia 64
  social and economic life, participation in 574–82

European Union (*cont.*)
  social inclusion 578–9
  social security, access to 582
  Tampere Council 580
  third country nationals 576, 580–1
  traditional minorities 579
  universal principles of political
    participation 348
exclusion, conflicts and 4–5, 11–17,
  20–3, 26–34
executive *see* **government**
experts
  Advisory Committee of FCNM
    (ACFC) 733–4
  bilateral agreements, monitoring of 733–4
  consultative and advisory
    mechanisms 485–7
  Independent Expert on Minority Issues
    (UN) 302–3, 305–7, 584
  indigenous elders 317
  Intergovernmental Committee of Experts on
    Issues relating to Protection of National
    Minorities (DH-MIN) 87
  Office of High Commissioner of Human
    Rights (OHCHR) 306
  UN standards and practices 291–8, 304–7
expulsion 42–3

FCNM Commentary
  advice-related perspective 228
  agenda setting in parliament 404–5
  autonomy 244–5
  bilateral agreements, monitoring of 728
  binding effect of FNCM 227
  cabinet meetings 408–9
  committees 405
  consultative and advisory mechanisms
    239–43, 481
  cultural diversity 254–5
  dialogue-related perspective 228, 255
  discrimination 112
  displacement of persons 252
  economic, social and cultural life,
    participation in 255
  effective participation 230–2,
    234–48, 254–5
  elected bodies, participation in 243–4
  elections 120–1, 271–2
  electoral systems, design of 234–6
  ethnic cleansing 252
  government, representation in 237–9, 438
  group-oriented dimension 254–5
  health care 252
  housing standards 252
  identification requirements 247–8
  influence 239, 243–4

  intersectionality, theory of 153
  judiciary, representation in the 237–9
  land 252
  language 248–9, 253
  legislative process, representation in
    the 232–7
  minimum standards 231–2, 254
  ministries, creation of specific 237
  OSCE High Commissioner on National
    Minorities (HCNM) 255
  parliamentary practice 243–4, 401
  political parties 232–4, 246–7
  positive or special measures 254
  power-sharing 416
  public administration, representation in
    the 237–9
  representation without
    participation 239–40
  reserved seats 236–7, 240
  residency 246
  results-oriented approach 239
  social and economic life, participation
    in 250–3
  specific measures 238–9
  standards 108–9
  statistical data, collection of 248
  targeted measures 238
  text 774–89 (App II)
  veto rights 239–40, 243–4
federalism 54, 619–23, 628–33, 654, 674–6
feminism 159, 160–3
Fiji 168–70
Finland
  consultative and advisory mechanisms
    493–4, 496, 500
  power-sharing 422–3, 425, 433
  Roma, special contact measures (SCMR) for
    520, 521–2
  UN Declaration on Minorities 299
first-past-the-post electoral systems 375
floor voting, records of 412
Forum on Minority Issues (UN) 305–6,
  584–6, 587
fractionalization indices 7–8
**Framework Convention for the Protection of
  Minorities (FCNM)** 222–55 *see also*
  **Advisory Committee of
  FCNM (ACFC)**
  accountability 89, 108
  adequate measures 224
  autonomy 232, 245, 739–40
  best practices 232
  binding effect 226
  citizenship 92–3, 246
  Committee of Ministers 226, 254
  consultative and advisory mechanisms 231,
    479, 480–1, 489–90, 501

contextual interpretation 230–49
culture 106, 234, 254
decentralization 108
democracy 108, 436
different, right to be 211
differential treatment 435–6
direct effect 226–7
discrimination 112, 149
effective participation 222–5, 230–49, 254, 350
elections 92–3, 107–8, 353
European Convention on Human Rights 220, 225–30
European Court of Human Rights 226
Explanatory Report 226
forms of participation 230
full and effective equality 224
government, participation in 438
identification requirements 247
identity and culture, promotion of 234
implementation 226–7, 708, 714–18, 721–34, 749
indigenous people 310
institutional measures 231
instruments and measures which enable, foster or guarantee participation 231
integration 224, 232
interpretation 230–49
interrelatedness between identity, equality and participation 224
legal entrenchment of participation 737–40, 745–6
legal instruments 232
local self-government 667, 672
Lund Recommendations
  comparison with 225–30, 254
  minimum standards 254
media 109
minimum standards 231–2
minority associations 686
monitoring 87, 88, 706, 709–18, 721–34, 749
national courts, judgments on status of FNCM by 226–7
normative power 226–8
OSCE High Commissioner on National Minorities (HCNM) 284
parliamentary representation 437
pluralism 435–7
positive or special measures 108, 132–4, 224–5, 231–2
power-sharing 416
programme-type principles 226, 254
religion 106
reporting 706, 721
Roma 512, 522, 549
self-governance 143

social and economic life 106, 535–42, 549, 574, 586–7
social cohesion 90, 224
soft law, as 226
standards 231–2
subsidiarity 108
transparency 108
will of people, selecting and determining 436
France 153, 381, 520, 607–8
fraud 153, 347
free, prior and informed consent to state measures (FPIC) 313–14
freedom of assembly and association
  discrimination 123
  elections 203, 318, 357
  European Convention on Human Rights 195, 197–9, 202–3
  indigenous people 318
  Lund Recommendations 125
  margin of appreciation 203
  political domination of minorities 67
  political parties 67, 124, 198–9, 203, 232–3, 275–7, 357
  privileges which follow the fact of association 202–3
  proportionality 197
  restrictions 357
freedom of expression
  challenging existing order 197
  discrimination 123
  domination of minorities 67
  elections 182–3, 355–6, 357
  European Convention on Human Rights 195, 196–8, 348
  International Covenant on Civil and Political Rights 356
  language 562
  margin of appreciation 196
  media 356
  OSCE Copenhagen Document 356
  pluralism 197
  political expression 196–8, 356
  political parties 196, 198–9
  proportionality 196, 356
  public interest 356–7
  restrictions 356
  thought, conscience, belief and opinion, freedom of 355
freedom of information 355–6
freedom of thought, conscience, belief and opinion 354–5

gender 150–73
  Advisory Committee of FCNM (ACFC) 151
  Afghanistan 170–2

gender (*cont.*)
  African descent, participation of persons of 290
  Asian descent, participation of persons of 290
  autonomy 152
  Belgium 167–8
  collective action 151–2, 159
  collective identity 166
  Committee on Elimination of Discrimination against Women 301
  conflict resolution 151–2, 158, 171–2
  consociational model of power-sharing 167–8
  cultural identity 166–7, 168
  democratic theory 172
  democratization 151–2, 171
  differential treatment 101–2
  discrimination 110–11, 114, 145, 149, 288, 301
  effective participation 290
  elections 165, 169–70, 353
  Fiji 168–70
  governance arrangements 152, 165–73
  International Convention on the Elimination of All Forms of Discrimination against Women (CEDAW) 110–11, 114, 129, 149, 156, 288, 301
  International Covenant on Civil and Political Rights 353
  intersectionality, theory of 151–9, 160, 170, 172
  Lund Recommendations 150–1
  minorities within minorities 151
  multicultural theory 154, 172
  multiple discrimination 151, 250–1, 295
  Muslim women 159–60
  nationalism 152, 159–66, 172
  nation-building 170–2
  Nunavut, gender balance in legislature in 165–7
  patriarchal culture 151, 161–2
  Roma, special contact measures (SCMR) for 506, 507
  self-governance 145, 165–7
  'targeted' approach to group rights 151, 154–9, 172
  women's movements and nationalism 159–65
genocide 40–2, 43
genuine elections 353–4
Germany 73, 494
gerrymandering
  decentralization 54–5
  design of electoral systems 235, 366, 374, 377–8, 398
  domination of minorities 47, 54–6, 69
  elections, observation of 358–9
  indigenous persons 320–1
  Northern Ireland 47, 55–6
  positive or special measures 361–2
  reserved seats systems 236
  United States 47, 73
  Venice Commission 362
governance *see also* **self-governance**
  European Convention on Human Rights 178–80
  gender 152, 165–73
government *see also* **self-governance**
  assemblies 439
  civil service, minority participation in the 439, 440–52
  coalitions, partnership in 10–11, 33
  effective representation 76, 82, 237–9, 439–41
  Ethnic Power Relations, dataset on 17–18
  FCNM Commentary 237–9, 438
  Framework Convention 438
  indigenous people 315–18
  judiciary 590–9
  Lund Recommendations 438
  Maine, United States 318
  non-territorial self-government 218
  participation in government 434–5, 438–52
  political domination of minorities 38, 51–4
  positive or special measures 438–9
  powers 440–1
  power-sharing 414–33, 444–6
  representation of minorities 438–51
  South Tyrol 444–6
greed and grievance theories 16–17
greed and opportunity perspective of conflict 4–6, 7, 23, 31
Greenland 332–3
Guidelines and Good Practice for Policing in Diverse Societies (OHCHR) 296, 304, 306

health care 252, 540, 543, 547, 563–4, 566
Helsinki Document 257–9, 709–11
historical factors 123, 127–8, 13, 143, 189–90, 193
housing 531, 540–3
  discrimination 252, 540–1, 547, 558–9
  inhuman or degrading treatment 573
  International Covenant on Civil and Political Rights 564, 566
  International Covenant on Economic, Social and Cultural Rights 564, 566
  Roma 547, 566, 574
human rights *see also* **European Convention on Human Rights; Human Rights**

Committee (UN); International
Covenant on Civil and Political
Rights; non-discrimination and
equality
African Charter on Human Rights (AfrCh)
104, 110, 570–1
American Convention on Human Rights
104, 110, 569–70
conflict prevention 262
consultative and advisory
mechanisms 278–9
cultural minority self-governance 638, 655
development, human rights-based approach
to 296–7
Human Rights Council (UN) 291, 301, 352
inhuman or degrading treatment 194–5
International Covenant on Economic, Social
and Cultural Rights (UN) 294, 306,
563–8, 587, 738
Lund Recommendations 262, 278–9
Office for Democratic Institutions and
Human Rights (ODIHR) 269–71,
282, 505–6, 509, 523
Office of the High Commissioner for
Human Rights (OHCHR) 296,
298–9, 304, 306, 716
Organization for Security and Co-operation
in Europe (OSCE) 259
peace settlements 467
power-sharing 416
private and family right, right to respect for
209–10, 217–18
Roma, special contact measures (SCMR) for
504, 520, 523
self-governance 613–15, 617–18,
623, 627–8
social and economic life, participation in
528, 552, 553, 557, 587
thought, conscience, belief and opinion,
freedom of 354–5
Universal Declaration of Human Rights
103, 207, 210–11, 346, 364, 510,
7 739

Human Rights Committee (UN)
consultative and advisory mechanisms
482, 497
discrimination 98, 145–7
elections 117
indigenous people 310
International Covenant on Civil and
Political Rights 288, 300–1
jurisprudence developed by HRC 310
positive or special measures 98, 128,
131, 136
self-governance 145–7, 615, 618–19
social and economic life, participation in
528, 553–6, 561–3

humanitarian issues 259
Hungary
consultative and advisory mechanisms 489
cultural autonomy 57, 743
local self-governments 82, 83, 679–80
minority associations 698–700
Roma 519, 520–2, 698–700

identification requirements 247–8
identity
collective identity 166
definition 625–6
different, right to be 211
discrimination 97
effective participation 78
ethnicity 624–7, 633
Framework Convention 234
gender 166
interrelatedness between identity, equality
and participation 224
multiple identities 83–6
political parties, communal identities and
199–200
recognition 625–6
Roma 551, 567
self-governance 624–7, 633
social and economic life, participation in
525–6, 532, 536, 538
ILO *see* International Labour
Organization (ILO)
immigration *see* new and immigrant
minorities
implementation mechanisms
autonomy 748
complaints 706
consultation 748–9
cultural minority self-governance 643–57
devolution 748
dispute resolution 747–9
elections 358–60, 748–9
Framework Convention 226–7, 708,
714–18, 721–34, 749
Helsinki Document 710
international organizations 357–8
judicial or quasi-judicial mechanisms 590,
592–608, 747–9
legal entrenchment 747–50
Lund Recommendations 534–5, 747, 749
monitoring 706
non-judicial mechanisms 749
power-sharing 417–18
reporting 706
Roma, special contact measures (SCMR)
for 514–22
social and economic life, participation
in 251

implementation mechanisms (*cont.*)
standards 357–60
territorial arrangements 748
UN standards and practices 304–7
incitement to ethnic hatred 125–6
incohesive states 4, 16, 20–1, 26, 31 4, 20–1, 26, 31
Independent Expert on Minority Issues (UN) 302–6, 583–4, 587
India 316, 630
indigenous peoples
advisory and consultative bodies 324–8
Advisory Committee of FCNM (ACFC) 310
American Convention on Human Rights 569
Argentina 324
assimilation 312
Australia 317, 325, 327
autonomy 312, 328–34, 338, 341–2
Bangladesh 336
Bolivia 316, 317–20, 321, 323, 334
Canada 330–3
central government 315–18
Chile 318, 324, 326
citizenship 318
Colombia 316, 329–30
communitarian autonomy 334–6
conflict prevention 336
consulted, right to be 313, 324–8
cultural and spiritual values 329, 338
cultural minority self-governance 637, 649–50, 655–7
customary laws 329
de facto arrangements 329
decision-making, participation in 314, 315–27
Declaration on the Rights of Indigenous Peoples (UN) 309–13, 328, 655–6
decolonization 329–30
development projects, right to participate in and be consulted on 313–14
economic activities 553–5, 560
Ecuador 320, 323, 327
effective participation 310–11, 315
elections 318–22
ethnic political parties 318–19
expert witnesses, indigenous elders as 317
forced incorporation and assimilation 312
Framework Convention 310
free, prior and informed consent to state measures (FPIC) 313–14
freedom of association 318
Greenland 332–3
health care 563–4
Human Rights Committee, jurisprudence developed by 310

ILO Convention (ILO 169) 313, 482, 614
India 316
Indonesia 336–8
Inter-American Court of Human Rights 314
International Covenant on Civil and Political Rights 301
International Covenant on Economic, Social and Cultural Rights 563–4, 567
judicial decision-making 317–18
justice systems 328
land 310, 319–20, 326–7, 560, 567, 568–70
language 318
Latin America 314–24, 327, 329–36
local development, consultation on 327
local levels, arrangements at 322–3
Lund Recommendations 308–11, 315, 318, 324, 336, 340, 342
Maine, United States 316
Maori in New Zealand 315, 317, 321, 327, 554–5
Mexico 318, 323, 324, 333, 335
minority rights approach 309–10, 340–1
national minorities concept, application of 308–9
natural resources 326–7
Nepal, National Foundation for Indigenous Development of 325
Nicaragua 314, 318–22, 326–7, 332, 336, 341
non-territorial arrangements 338–40
Nunavut 165–7, 333
Panama, *comarcas* system in 331–2, 336
parliaments 338–9
Philippines, National Commission on Indigenous Peoples in 325
political parties 318–19
positive or special measures 315
post-conflict arrangements 336–7
Quebec, Canada 649–50
quotas 322
recognition as part of state administrative machinery 335
regional and local levels, arrangements at 322–3
reservation system in United States 330–1
Sami parliaments 338–9, 493–4, 500, 553–4, 655–7, 695–7
self-determination 312, 328, 655–6
self-governance 145–6, 312, 314, 328, 341–2, 637, 649–50, 655–7
self-government plus 328
social and economic life, participation in 532, 550–5, 560, 562–4, 567–9
social welfare services 327
standards 309–15, 328, 341

subscription groups 319–20
Surinam 335
territorial arrangements 329–38, 339–40
traditional knowledge and medicine 567
traditional systems 312, 342
UN Declaration on Minorities 309
United States 326, 330–1
Venezuela 316, 323
Waitangi Tribunal 317
water, right to 564
Indonesia 48, 336–8
infighting 5–6, 14–16, 19–20, 26–33
influence on decisions 75–7, 85, 239, 243–4
information technology 411–12
inhuman or degrading treatment 194–5, 572–3
institutional incentives to favour co-ethnics 11–12
insurgency model 6–7, 21
integration 68–9, 224, 293, 525, 536–7, 578–81
Intergovernmental Committee of Experts on Issues relating to Protection of National Minorities (DH-MIN) 87
International Convention on the Elimination of All Forms of Discrimination against Women 110–11, 149
  Committee on Elimination of Discrimination against Women 301
  effective participation, no guarantee of 288
  indirect discrimination 114
  intersectionality, theory of 156
  positive or special measures 129
International Convention on the Elimination of All Forms of Racial Discrimination 110–11, 149
  Committee on Elimination of Racial Discrimination (CERD) 299–300, 350
  definition of racial discrimination 116
  education 559–62
  effective participation, no guarantee of 288
  elections 349–50
  indirect discrimination 114–15
  nationality 560–1
  positive or special measures 129, 558, 560
  public service, representation in 558–9
  Roma, special contact measures (SCMR) for 510
  segregation 559
  social and economic life, participation in 558–61
  state reports 300
International Covenant on Civil and Political Rights *see also* **Human Rights Committee (UN)**
  cultural life, right of everyone to participate in 288
  cultural minority self-governance 637–8
  different, right to be 211
  discrimination 99, 100, 149, 288, 349, 561
  effective participation 349
  elections 104, 348, 353–4
  freedom of expression 356
  gender 353
  housing 564, 566
  indigenous rights 301
  judiciary 591
  legal entrenchment of participation 738
  positive or special measures 131, 288
  Roma, special contact measures (SCMR) for 510
  self-governance 146, 614–15, 619
  social and economic life, participation in 528, 553–4, 561–3, 586
  standards 103–4
  UN Human Rights Committee 288, 300–1
  universal principles of political participation 346
International Covenant on Economic, Social and Cultural Rights
  citizenship 567
  Committee on Economic, Social and Cultural Rights (CESCR) 294, 306
  complaints procedure 567–8, 587
  cultural life, right to participate in 306
  cultural resources, consent to preservation of 294
  design and implementation of laws and policies 294
  education 564, 565, 566–7
  employment 565
  health care 563–4, 566
  housing 564, 566
  indigenous persons 563–4, 567
  languages 565–6
  legal entrenchment of participation 738
  monitoring 306
  positive or special measures 565
  Roma 566–7
  services, access to 565–6, 567
  social and economic life, participation in 563–8
  traditional knowledge and medicine 567
  water, right to 564
International Labour Organization (ILO)
  consultative and advisory mechanisms 482
  indigenous people 313, 482, 614, 738–9
  legal entrenchment of participation 738–9
  self-governance 614
  social and economic life, participation in 585

international organizations 73–4, 357–8, 492–3 *see also* **particular institutions**
international standards *see* **standards**
intersectionality, theory of
  conflict prevention 158
  culture 157, 158
  differentiation 156–7
  essentialism 157
  FCNM Commentary 153
  gender 151–9, 160, 170, 172
  Lund Recommendations 152, 156–7
  minorities within minorities 145, 151
  multicultural theory 154–9
  multiple discrimination 151, 295
  Muslim headscarf ban in France 153
  national minorities, territorial autonomy and 155–6
  nationalism 160
  quota movement 157–8
  race discrimination 152–3
  'targeted' approach to group rights 154–7
  territorial autonomy 155–6
  United States regulations on marriage fraud 153
  women's movements and nationalism 160
Iraq 10–11, 33, 37, 64, 395–6
Ireland 519
Islamic communities *see* **Muslim communities**
Israel
  cultural autonomy 57
  domination of minorities 37–9, 42–3, 45, 48–9, 56–8, 60, 62, 64
  demographic domination 42–3
  electoral domination 45, 48–9
  emergency powers 62
  expulsions 42
  judges 60
  land 39
  legal domination 60, 62
  political domination 51
  Right of Return 42–3
  security service domination of minorities 58
  settlements 56–7
  status quo, limiting participation to parties that endorse 48–9
  symbolic domination 38
  territorial domination of minorities 56–7
Italy, South Tyrol region in 247, 430–1, 444–6, 448

Jewish marriages and divorces 660
joint intergovernmental commissions 708, 719–21, 729–34
judiciary, minority participation in 76, 80, 82, 588–609
  Advisory Committee of FCNM (ACFC) 592–9, 603–6, 609
  bias 594–5, 597–9
  Bolivia 318
  Bosnia and Herzegovina 601–3, 605, 608
  central government, giving minorities an effective voice in 590–9
  common law 589
  conflict resolution 591–2, 599–605, 608
  constitutional entrenchment 590–1, 597, 599, 605, 608–9
  credibility 605–8
  Croatia 603–5
  demand-side barriers 596–7, 608
  discrimination 589–590, 595–9, 602, 606–9
  domination of minorities 60–1
  education 596, 605
  effective participation 237–9, 439, 440–1
  effective remedies for breach of minority rights 591–2, 595
  employment 596
  ethnic bias 594–5, 597–8
  expert witnesses on indigenous issues 317
  FCNM Commentary 237–9
  France 607–8
  implementation practice 590, 592–608, 747–9
  independence 588, 591, 599–600
  indigenous people 317–18
  indirect discrimination 595–9
  International Covenant on Civil and Political Rights 591
  Israel 60
  judicial activism 589
  Kosovo 600–1
  law-making 589
  legal entrenchment of participation 747–9
  long-term credibility 605–8
  Lund Recommendations 590–2, 609
  monitoring 593
  Northern Ireland 60–3
  OSCE Copenhagen Document 591
  positive or special measures 597–8, 606–8
  power-sharing 590–1, 597
  pro-minority agenda 589
  public confidence 596, 599, 606
  quotas 589, 597–8, 600, 608
  recruitment or selection 596–7, 605–6
  rule of law 590
  shortages or absences of minority judges 589–90, 592–609
  Sri Lanka 61
  standards 590–2, 608
  supply-side barriers 596, 605, 608
  under-representation 589–90, 592–609

United Kingdom 605–7
United States 60–1

kin-states 54–5, 275, 551
Kosovo 34, 82–3, 427, 433, 600–1
Kurds *see also* **Turkey, Kurds in**
    domination of minorities 40, 65
    electoral systems, design of 395–6
    Iraq 295–6
    language 40, 65

land and property
    economic activities on indigenous land 560
    economic domination of minorities 39
    Estonia 39
    FCNM Commentary 252
    indigenous people 310, 319–20, 326–7, 560, 567–70
    Israel 39, 56–7
    Maori people in New Zealand 327
    settlements 56–7
    social and economic life, participation in 252, 550, 560, 568, 569–70
language
    Advisory Committee of FCNM (ACFC) 248–9, 725–6
    Belgium 167–8, 425–6, 430–1, 693–4
    civil service 444–6
    coercive assimilation 40
    conflicts, reasons for 456–8, 459, 462–5
    consultative and advisory mechanisms 481
    cultural domination 38
    cultural minority self-governance 645–9, 652
    deliberation in parliament 408–9
    discrimination 120–1, 251, 462–3
    domination of minorities 38–9, 40, 65, 66
    education 544–5, 557, 565, 571
    effective participation 248–9
    elections
        codification of practices 361
        conflicts, reasons for 459
        discrimination 120–1
        indigenous people 318
        observation 360
        stand for office, right to 188–9, 190–2
    employment discrimination in public sector 39
    Estonia 249
    European Charter for Regional or Minority Languages 481
    FCNM Commentary 253
    freedom of expression 562
    incohesion 29–30
    India 630
    indigenous people 318

    International Covenant on Economic, Social and Cultural Rights 565–6
    Israel 38
    Kurds 40, 65
    Latvia 65, 120–1, 188–9, 190, 248–9
    Lund Recommendations 645–7
    Macedonia 360
    minority associations 695–6
    official languages 456–7
    positive or special measures 131
    power-sharing 423–6, 430–1
    proficiency requirements 249, 253
    proportionality 249
    quantitative analysis of ethnic diversity and armed conflict 21, 29–30
    Quebec, Canada 648–9
    Russian in post-Soviet parliaments 409
    Sami parliaments 695–6
    secessional conflicts 29–30
    self-governance 629–31
    services, access to 548, 550, 565–6
    Slovakia 38, 64
    social and economic life, participation in 251, 253, 535, 538, 544–5, 548, 550, 557–9, 561–2, 565–6, 571
    South Tyrol 444–6
    Sri Lanka 38–9, 462–5
    stand for office, right to 188–9, 190–2
    state neutrality 456–8
    Switzerland 423–4
    Thailand 457
    Trentino-South Tyrol, language affiliation declarations in 247
    Turkey 40, 65, 457
Latin America *see also* **particular countries**
    consultative and advisory bodies 324
    elections 319–22
    indigenous people 314–24, 327, 329–36
    regional and local levels, arrangements at 322–3
Latvia
    citizenship 43
    denaturalization 44
    discrimination 120–1
    domination of minorities 51, 59, 64–5
    elections 44, 51, 120–1, 188–90, 248–9
    European Union 64–5
    language 65, 248–9
    local self-government 680–1
    security service domination of minorities 59
    stand for office, right to 188–9, 190
legal domination of minorities 60–4
legal entrenchment of participation 735–47
    autonomy 739–42, 750
    constitutional guarantees 739–41, 747
    consultative bodies 746–7, 750
    cultural autonomy 742–3, 750

legal entrenchment of participation (*cont.*)
  devolution 739
  elections 743–5
  European Charter of Self-Government 738
  European Convention on Human Rights 738
  Framework Convention 737–40, 745–6
  guarantees 739–47, 749, 750
  International Covenant on Civil and Political Rights 738
  International Labour Organization (ILO) Convention on Indigenous People 738–9
  judicial or quasi-judicial mechanisms 747–9
  legislative guarantees 741–6
  Lund Recommendations 736–7, 750
  margin of appreciation 750
  monitoring 738, 739–47
  non-judicial mechanisms 749
  public administration, employment in 745
  remedies 750
  reserved seats 744–5
  self-government 738, 741
  soft law 739
  standards and norms 736–9, 750
  sub-legislative guarantees 746–7, 749
  UN Declaration on Minorities 739
  Universal Declaration of Human Rights 739
legislation
  accountability of parliament 409–13
  agenda setting in parliament 401–5
  committees 404–5
  consultation 244, 491, 494
  design and implementation of laws and policies 294
  discrimination 99–100, 251, 239–42
  effective participation in legislative process 232–7
  legal entrenchment of participation 741–6
  legislative offices 403–5
  monitoring performance of legislators 409–10, 411–13
  social and economic life, participation in 251, 539–42
  sponsorship 412
  symbolic domination 38
legislature *see* **parliaments**
liberalism 67–71
linguistic communities *see* **language**
Lisbon Treaty 575, 577–8
Lithuania 59, 495, 519
local considerations
  development, consultation on 327
  discrimination 120, 122, 127–8, 148
  elections 120, 122
  indigenous people 322–3, 327
  Latin America 322–3
  political parties 127–8
  proportionality 120
local government *see* **enhanced local self-government; regional arrangements; self-governance**
Lund Recommendations 74, 76, 90, 256–7
  alternative vote system 383, 385
  amendments 284–5
  civil service 447
  committee membership 400–1
  conflict prevention 261–3, 454
  conflicts, reasons for 455, 457–8, 461
  consultative and advisory mechanisms 277–9, 324, 489, 493–4, 501
  contents 281
  cultural minority self-governance 635–8, 640–8, 654, 656–60
  decision-making, participation in 107
  delegated or implementing legislation 280
  democracy 262, 279–80
  different, right to be 211–12
  domination of minorities 35–6, 64, 65, 69
  elections
    design of systems 364–5, 369, 374–5, 378–9, 383, 385, 395, 397–9
    domination of minorities 69
    European Convention on Human Rights 181
    indigenous people 318
    OSCE High Commissioner on National Minorities (HCNM) 268–75, 282
    standards 107
  European Convention on Human Rights 178–80, 219
  Framework Convention 225–30, 254
  freedom of association 125
  gender 150–1
  good practice, framed as 179
  government, participation in 438
  human rights 262, 278–9
  implementation mechanisms 534–5, 747, 749
  indigenous people 308–11, 315, 318, 324, 336, 340, 342
  interpretation 285
  intersectionality, theory of 152, 156–7
  Islamic minorities 659–60
  judiciary 590–2, 609
  language 645–7
  legal entrenchment of participation 736–7, 750
  list of agreements mirroring Lund Recommendations 469–71
  local self-government 662, 668–70, 681
  minimum standards 254

minority associations 682–3, 686, 688–9, 695
monitoring 709–13
multi-ethnic states, viability of 262
normative deficit on national minority standards 263–7, 280
objectives, progressive realization of 281
OSCE High Commissioner on National Minorities (HCNM) 179, 257, 261–85
peace settlements 454, 465–73
pluralism 278
political parties 125, 199, 275–7
power-sharing 417
procedural dimensions 265–7
proportional representation (PR) 393
Quebec, Canada 648
Roma, special contact measures (SCMR) for 504–7, 514, 520
self-governance 107, 144–5, 214–15, 613, 616–17, 620–8, 633, 737
social and economic life, participation in 526–7, 533–5
soft law, as 178–9
standards 107, 254, 263–7
substantive standards, normative deficit in 263–5
text 751–73 (App 1)
UN Declaration on Minorities 292
UN standards and practices 305

Macedonia 38, 43, 55, 360, 419–25, 429, 433, 464–5
mainstreaming 304, 575, 577
majoritarianism
  alternative vote system 170
  cultural minority self-governance 639–40
  domination of minorities 51–3, 65–6
  electoral systems, design of 170, 367–9, 370–6, 380–2
  political domination of minorities 51–3, 66
  proportional representation (PR) 390–1
Malaysia 37, 38, 39, 53–4
manifest beliefs, freedom to 355
Maori in New Zealand 315, 317, 321, 327, 554–5
margin of appreciation
  different, right to be 210
  discrimination 124, 148–9
  elections 182, 184–90, 193
  European Convention on Human Rights 180, 196, 199, 200, 203
  freedom of association 203
  freedom of expression 196
  legal entrenchment of participation 750
  political parties 199, 200

positive or special measures 133, 138–9, 143
stand for office, right to 188–90, 193
Venice Commission 138–9
marriage fraud in United States 153
Mauritius
media 109, 253, 354–6
Mexico
  Chiapas uprising 10, 30, 33
  excluded groups 10–11, 30, 33
  indigenous people 318, 323, 324, 332, 336
Migrant Workers Convention 561, 568
military law, imposition of 50–1
ministries, creation of specific 237
Minorities at Risk (MAR) dataset 8–9
minorities, definition of *see* definition of minorities
minorities within minorities 145, 151
minority associations 682–701
  Advisory Committee of FCNM (ACFC) 686, 689
  advocacy 687
  appointment procedures 690, 691–2
  Belgium 693–5
  Central and Eastern Europe 685–8
  civil society organizations 687, 696
  conceptual and normative considerations 684–6
  consultation 689, 690–5
  Czech Republic 690–2
  definition 683
  deliberative democracy 686
  discrimination 124–5, 692–3
  effective participation 688–90
  elected bodies 695–700
  ethnic political parties 686
  Framework Convention 686
  Hungary 698–700
  language 695–6
  legitimacy 683, 696–8
  Lund Recommendations 682–3, 686, 688–9, 695
  monitoring 690
  non-elected consultative bodies 690–5
  non-governmental organizations (NGOs) 683, 686–7
  OSCE Copenhagen Document 683
  political parties 686
  race discrimination 692–3
  role, definition of 684–8
  Roma 689–90, 698–700
  Sami parliament in Norway 695–7
  standards 682–4
  supportive organizations 687
  types of associations 686–8
  umbrella associations 691–5
  United Kingdom 692–3

minority mobilization school 4–5, 8–9, 31
Minority Rights Group International
 (MRGI) 586
mirror representation 81–3, 89
monitoring
 Advisory Committee of FCNM (ACFC)
  254, 714–18, 721–34
 bilateral agreements 717, 720, 728–34
 Bolzano/Bozen Recommendations
  709–10, 712–13
 consultation 708
 effective participation 76, 87–8, 707–8
 elections 105, 269–71, 359–60
 equality of arms 734
 Framework Convention 87, 88, 709–10,
  713–18, 721–34, 749
 Helsinki Document 709–11
 implementation mechanisms 706
 International Covenant on Economic, Social
  and Cultural Rights 306
 judiciary 593
 legal entrenchment of participation
  738, 739–47
 legislators, performance of 409–10, 411–13
 Lund Recommendations 709–13
 minority associations 690
 Organization for Security and Co-operation
  in Europe (OSCE) 109, 259,
  261, 708–11
 social and economic life, participation
  in 250
 UN Declaration on Minorities 298–9,
  709, 718–19
 UN standards and practices 298–301, 307
multiculturalism 154–9, 172, 636
multiple identities 83–6, 151, 250–1, 295
Muslim communities
 cultural self-governance 658–60
 European Commission against Racism and
  Intolerance (ECRI) 658–60
 France, headscarf ban in 153
 Lund Recommendations 659–60
 Norway 159–60
 political parties in Turkey 200–1
 terrorism 658–9
 women's movements and
  nationalism 159–60

names 39, 645–6
nation states
 Afghanistan, nation-building in 170–2
 co-ownership in state 95
 cultural homogeneity 7
 cultural minority self-governance 638–41
 formation 11–12, 170–2
 gender, nation-building and 163–5, 170–2
 institutional incentives to favour co-
  ethnics 11–12
 nation-building 163–5, 170–2
 non-neutrality 455–60
 preferences 458–61
nationalism 9, 152, 159–66, 172, 624, 627
nationality discrimination 63, 560–1
natural resources 21–2, 30, 54, 326–7
Nepal, National Foundation for Indigenous
 Development of 325
neutrality of states and minorities 455–60
new and immigrant communities
 citizenship 246
 European Union 575, 579–82
 Migrant Workers Convention 561
 migration policy, European Union and 580
 OSCE High Commissioner on National
  Minorities (HCNM) 284
 social and economic life, participation in
  532, 557, 561, 575, 579–82
New Zealand, Maoris in 315, 317, 321,
 327, 554–5
Nicaragua 314, 318–22, 326–7, 341
non-discrimination and equality *see also*
 racism; social and economic life,
 discrimination in
 African Charter on Human and People's
  Rights 110
 American Convention on Human
  Rights 110
 associations, restrictions on minority 124–5
 citizenship 113, 561
 civil service, equal access to 109, 113, 147–8
 conditions and restrictions 113–15,
  123–8, 148
 co-ownership in state 95
 cultural diversity, value of 96–7
 cultural identity 96
 customary international law 98, 109
 decision-making 97
 definition of discrimination 115–16
 differential treatment 100–2, 121–2, 130
 domination of minorities in democracies
  39, 59–60, 67–8
 economic domination of minorities 39
 education 39
 effective participation 78–81
 elections 67–70, 97, 109–13, 116–23,
  147–9, 188, 194–5
 employment in the public sector, access to
  39, 109, 113, 147–8
 European Commission against Racism and
  Intolerance (ECRI) 658–9
 European Convention on Human Rights
  110, 148–9
  accessory provision 111
  differential treatment 121

elections 111, 118–23, 149, 188
free elections, right to 111
independent non-discrimination
  provision 111–12, 149
indirect discrimination 114, 120–1
justification for discrimination
  116, 119–21
Protocol 12 111–12, 149
public affairs, conduct of 111
right to political participation 133–6
European Court of Justice 114–15
fact, obligation to ensure equality in 99–100
FCNM Commentary 112
Framework Convention 112, 149
freedom of assembly and association 123
freedom of expression 123
full and effective equality 95–149, 224
gender 145
housing 252, 540–1, 547, 558–9
human rights 96, 145–7
identification of discrimination 100
identity rights 97
illegality of regulations, procedures, criteria
  or other factors 99
indirect discrimination 59–60, 67, 113–16,
  120–4, 148, 595–6
International Convention on the
  Elimination of All Forms of
  Discrimination against Women
  (CEDAW) 110–11, 114, 149, 288,
  301
International Covenant on Civil and
  Political Rights (ICCPR) 99, 110,
  149, 288, 349
international law 98–9, 109
interrelatedness between identity, equality
  and participation 224
judiciary 589–90, 595–9, 602, 606–9
justification for discrimination 116, 119–22
language 462–3
laws, regulations, criteria and policies and
  other factors 99–100
liberalism 67
local conditions 120, 122, 127–8, 148
margin of appreciation 124, 148–9
minority associations 692–3
minority mobilization school 31
nationality 53, 560–1
Northern Ireland 63
not to discriminate, obligation 99,
  113–28, 147
OSCE Warsaw Guidelines 113
other political rights 123–8
particular situations, application to
  115–16, 148
peace settlements 464
plurality, value of 96–7

political parties 124–8
politically relevant groups and access to
  power 18
positive or special measures 79–81, 102,
  112, 122, 128–43, 148–9
proportionality 116
public affairs, conduct of 109, 113, 147
public resources, access to 39, 109,
  113, 147–8
public sector, access to employment in 39
right to political participation 103–49
second legal test of discrimination
  121–3, 148–9
security service domination of
  minorities 59–60
self-governance 143–7, 218–19
special facilitation of minority
  representation 97
Sri Lanka 463–5
stability 95
stand for election, right to 147–8, 194–5
standards 287–8
tests 116, 121–3, 148–9
UN Declaration on Minorities 112
UN Human Rights Committee (HRC) 98
voter registration 113
non-governmental organizations (NGOs)
  103, 299, 683, 686–7, 724–7
Northern Ireland
boycotts 45
Catholic middle class, mobilization of 9, 30
demographic domination 42, 43
domination of minorities 37–8, 42–6,
  49–52, 55–64, 67
dual voting 44, 67
elections 44–6, 49–50, 67, 134, 373–5, 380
emergency powers 62
emigration of Catholics 43
excluded groups 9, 10–11, 30
family allowance policy 43
gerrymandering 47, 55–6
judges 60
Leech Commission 55–6
legal domination 60–3
nationalism 9
oaths of allegiance 49, 50
peace settlements 459, 465
pluralism 46, 67
political domination of minorities 51–2
political opinion and national identity,
  discrimination on grounds of 63
post-election methods penalizing minority
  politicians 49
positive or special measures 134
power-sharing 431–2
proportional representation 134, 429,
  430, 431–2

Northern Ireland (*cont.*)
  religion 37, 38, 42, 43, 64
  secessionism 30
  security service domination of minorities 58–60
  symbolic domination 38
  territorial domination for minorities 55–6
Norway 159–60
Nunavut, Canada 165–7, 333

observation of elections 269–71, 358–60, 362
OECD Development Assistance Committee (DAC) 585
Office for Democratic Institutions and Human Rights (ODIHR) 269–71, 282, 505–6, 509, 523
Office of the High Commissioner for Human Rights (OHCHR) 296, 298–9, 304, 306, 716
opinion, thought, conscience and belief, freedom of 354–5
opting out 83–6
Organization for Security and Co-operation in Europe (OSCE) *see also* Lund Recommendations; OSCE Copenhagen Document; OSCE High Commissioner on National Minorities (HCNM)
  Conference on Security and Cooperation in Europe (CSCE), change of name from 257
  democratic governance, attainment of 258
  economic and environmental dimension 259
  elections, observation of 358–9
  Helsinki Document 257–9, 709–11
  human dimension 259
  human rights 259
  humanitarian issues 259
  institutionalization 258
  interpretation 258
  monitoring 259
  OCSE Copenhagen Document 259
  political commitments 258
  politico-security dimensions 259
  Roma, special contact measures (SCMR) for 508–11
  Warsaw Guidelines 113, 270–1
OSCE Copenhagen Document
  consultative and advisory mechanisms 479, 480
  democracy 350
  effective participation 74, 77
  elections 271–2, 273, 347, 364

  judiciary 591
  language 102
  local or autonomous administrations 109
  minority associations 683
  monitoring 105, 708–11
  positive or special measures 132
  Roma, special contact measures (SCMR) for 508–9, 512
  self-governance 144–5
  standards 104–5, 109
  universal principles of political participation 346–7
OSCE High Commissioner on National Minorities (HCNM) 259–61
  Advisory Committee of FCNM (ACFC) 284
  Central and Eastern Europe, conflicts in 259–60
  comprehensive security 261
  conflict prevention 259–61, 265, 267–8, 280–1
  consultative and advisory mechanisms 277–80, 282, 481
  Council of Europe 88
  early warnings 90
  effective participation in public affairs 74, 88, 90, 283–4
  electoral arrangements 268–75, 282
  establishment 259
  failure of Lund Recommendations 283
  FCNM Commentary 255
  Framework Convention 284
  freedom of expression 356
  general approach 268
  human dimension approach 260–1
  inter-agency consultation, cooperation and coordination 283
  language 535
  Lund Recommendations 257, 261–7
  mandate 260–1, 265, 284
  monitoring 261
  new minorities 284
  normative deficit on national minority standards 263–7
  peace settlements 465, 473–4
  political parties 275–7
  positive or special measures 139
  recommendations 264, 266–7
  Roma 506, 534–5
  self-governance 144
  social and economic life, participation in 533–5
  social cohesion 90
  standards 107, 280–1, 283
  thematic approach 268, 280–1, 283–4
Ottoman Empire, millet system in 54–5

Panama, *comarcas* system in 331–2, 336
parliaments
  accountability 409–13
  agenda setting 401–5
  coalitions 402–3
  committees 403–5, 412
  deliberation 405–9, 413
  effective participation 298, 437
  European Convention on Human Rights 180–1
  FCNM Commentary 243–4, 401
  Framework Convention 437
  law-making 401–5
  Nunavut, gender balance in legislature in 165–7
  partisan control 402–3
  political domination of minorities 51–4
  regional parliaments 673–4
  Roma, special contact measures (SCMR) for 514–16
  rules and procedure 401–2
  Sami parliaments 338–9, 493–4, 500, 553–4, 655–7, 695–7
  UNDP and Inter-Parliamentary Union (IPU) Project 298
participation *see* effective participation
patriarchal culture 151, 161–2
peace-building 32, 170–1
peace settlements 453–4, 464–73
  autonomy arrangements 464, 465, 468, 472
  Dayton Agreement 194–5, 244
  democratic deficit 459–60
  discrimination 464
  effective participation 464–73
  human rights 467
  list of agreements mirroring Lund Recommendations 469–71
  Lund Recommendations 454, 465–73
  Macedonia 464–5
  Northern Ireland 459, 465
  Ohrid Framework Agreement 464–5
  OSCE High Commissioner on National Minorities 465, 473–4
  power-sharing 464–8, 474
  territorial autonomy 472
  under-representation and under-participation 465–7
Philippines, National Commission on Indigenous Peoples in 325
Poland 126–7, 162–3, 680
policing 58, 296, 304
political domination of minorities 38, 51–4, 67–71
political factors
  elections 123, 189–90, 193
  ethnic diversity, politics and 4–17, 22–3, 31–2

politico-security dimensions 259
security service domination of minorities 60
stand for office, right to 189–90, 193
Turkey, elections in 123
political institutions, domination by 38, 51–4, 66–7
political parties
  accountability of parliament 410
  Advisory Committee of FCNM (ACFC) 233–4
  bans 48
  communal identities 199–200
  community-based parties 275
  democratic pluralism 125–6
  discrimination 66, 67, 68–70, 124–8
  domination of minorities 48–9, 50, 66–70
  dual pluralism 234
  effective participation 232–4, 246–7
  electoral systems, design of 399
  ethnic parties 232–4, 318–19
    agenda setting in parliament 403
    coalitions 403
    electoral systems, design of 399
    European Convention on Human Rights 199–201
    indigenous persons 318–19
    Lund Recommendations 275–7
    minority associations 686
    UN Declaration on Minorities 292–3
  European Convention on Human Rights 124–8, 196, 198–201, 203, 232–4
  FCNM Commentary 233–4, 237–9, 246–7
  freedom of assembly and association 67, 124–5, 198–9, 203, 232–3, 275–7, 357
  freedom of expression 67, 196, 198–9
  incitement to ethnic hatred 125–6
  independents, minority politicians running as 50
  indigenous people 318–19
  Israel 48–9
  kin states 275
  large parties, rules which favour 66, 67, 68–70
  local and historical circumstances 127–8
  local self-government 665–7, 678–81
  Lund Recommendations 125, 199, 269, 275–7, 282
  margin of appreciation 199, 200
  minimum standards 233–4
  minorities, membership restricted to 126–7
  minority associations 292–3, 686
  Muslim parties in Turkey 200–1
  national parties, requirement for 48
  organization and structure 628–9
  OSCE High Commissioner on National Minorities (HCNM) 275–7

political parties (*cont.*)
 pluralism 199
 Poland, Silesian minority in 126–7
 political domination of minorities 67
 positive or special measures 138
 prohibition 124–8, 199, 233–4
 promotion and protection of minority identity 125
 proportionality 127
 public order 125
 registration 124–8, 203, 246–7
 Russia 199–200
 secession, advocating 126
 self-governance 628–9
 Sharia law, introduction of 200–1
 small parties 66, 67, 68–70, 234–5
 status quo, limiting participation to parties that endorse 48–9
 temporary bans 199
 Turkey 198, 200–1
 two-party systems 379
 UN Declaration on Minorities 292–3
 undemocratic parties 125–6
 United States 49
 violence, advocating 125–6
positive or special measures 78–81, 86–7, 89
 children 568
 differential treatment 102, 130, 135
 discrimination 79–81, 102, 112, 122, 128–43, 148–9, 254
  elections 123
  gender 129
  racial discrimination 128–9, 558, 560
  social and economic life 251, 529–30, 540–4, 551, 560–1, 565, 584
 dual votes for minorities 139–41
 Dublin Convention against Racism 289, 291
 education 545–6, 560, 568
 elections 132, 134, 137–41, 353
  design of systems 234–6
  discrimination 123
  dual votes for minorities 139
  equal voting power and rights 137–41
  equality of opportunity 137–48
  gerrymandering 361–2
  legal entrenchment 745
  legality of measures 137
  Lund Recommendations 273–5
  Northern Ireland 134
  proportionality 137–41
  radio and television air time 147–8
  Venice Commission 137–41
 European Committee of Social Rights 130
 European Convention on Human Rights 133–6, 141–3, 148–9
 fact, equality in 128–30

 FCNM Commentary 254
 Framework Convention 108, 132–4, 224–5, 231–2
 gender 129
 gerrymandering 361–2
 government, participation in 438–9
 historical, local and political factors 133, 143
 Human Rights Committee (UN) 128, 136
 indigenous people 315
 International Court of Justice 130
 International Covenant on Civil and Political Rights 131, 288
 International Covenant on Economic, Social and Cultural Rights 565
 judiciary 597–8, 606–8
 language 131
 law, equality in 128
 legality of measures 137–43
 Lund Recommendations 273–5
 margin of appreciation 133, 138–9, 143
 media 147–8, 354–5
 Northern Ireland, proportional voting system in 134
 OSCE Copenhagen Document 132
 OSCE High Commissioner on National Minorities (HCNM) 139
 pluralism 133–4
 political parties 138
 power sharing systems, reserved seats in 141–3
 proportionality 135–43
 racial discrimination 128–9, 558, 560
 radio and television air time 147–8, 354–5
 reserved seats systems 236
 Revised European Social Charter 130
 right to political participation 133–6
 Roma 129
 social and economic life, participation in 250–2, 529–30, 540–6, 551, 558, 560–1, 565, 568, 584
 socio-economic inequality 78
 stand for office, right to 141–2
 substantive equality 134–6
 temporary measures 79–80, 133
 UN Declaration on Minorities 131–2, 349
 UN Independent Expert on Minority Issues (UNIEMI) 584
 Venice Commission 137–42, 273–5
poverty 78, 250–2, 583–4
power, configurations of 12–17, 32
power-sharing
 Advisory Committee of FCNM (ACFC) 416–17
 Albania 427
 autonomy 478
 Belgium 425–6, 427, 430–1

Bosnia Herzegovina 10–11, 30, 33, 141–3, 426–7, 430, 433
Bulgaria 427–9, 433
civil service 442–6
coalitions 402–3, 420–2, 428
complete consociational executives 420
concurrent consociational executives 420
consociational democracies 415–16, 420
consociationalism 84–6, 167–8, 415–16, 420, 640
constitutional executive power-sharing 425–7
consultative and advisory mechanisms 478
Croatia 421
cultural minority self-governance 637
definition of power-sharing 415
duration 415, 433
elites, number of power-sharing 14
ethnic political parties 403
European Convention on Human Rights 141–3
executive power-sharing 414–33
FCNM Commentary 416
Finland 422–3, 425, 433
forms of power-sharing 419–32
Framework Convention 416
human rights 416
hybrid or transitional systems 427–9
implementation of minority rights 417–18
infighting 14
judiciary 590–1, 597
Kosovo 427, 433
linguistic communities 423–6, 430–1
Lund Recommendations 417
Macedonia 419–20, 422, 424–5, 429, 433
minority representation 419–21, 428, 432–3
Northern Ireland 429, 430, 431–2
number of partners 20–1, 26, 32–3
quantitative analysis of ethnic diversity and armed conflict 20–1, 26, 32–3
parliament 403
peace settlements 464–8, 474
positive or special measures 141–3
post-communist countries 424
rebellions 16, 26–7
regional executive power-sharing 429–32
reserved seats 141–3
Romania 427–9, 433
self-determination 418
Serbia 421
Slovakia 419
small minorities 416, 423, 427
South Tyrol 430–1, 444–6
standards 416–18
Switzerland 422, 423–4, 425

transitional systems 427–9
Venice Commission 142–3
veto rights 417, 423
weak consociational executives 420
presidential systems 52–4, 66
prisoners, elections and 187
private and family right, right to respect for 209–10, 217–18
proportional representation (PR)
  accountability of parliament 410
  alternative vote 392, 393
  Australia 388
  civil service 444, 448
  Colomer's law 389–90, 395
  Condorcet tail 392
  design of systems 234–5, 364, 367–74, 387–94, 398
  d'Hondt method 389–90
  Droop quota 389–90, 391
  geography 394
  Hagenbach-Bischoff quota 389
  Hare quota 390, 391
  Jefferson method 389
  List-PR systems 390–2
  locking in 398
  Lund Recommendations 393
  majoritarianism 390–1
  micro-mega rule 389–90
  MMP (mixed member proportional) 392–4
  Northern Ireland 134
  quota-preferential 391
  quotas or divisors 387–92
  reserved seats systems 236
  Sainte-Laguë rule 390
  single transferable vote (STV) 170, 373, 387–8, 391–2
  thresholds 234–5
  V/M 389
proportionality
  discrimination 116, 530
  elections 120, 137–41, 191, 193–4
  European Convention on Human Rights 196, 197
  freedom of association 197
  freedom of expression 196, 356
  language 249
  political parties 127
  positive or special measures 135–43
  social and economic life, participation in 530
  stand for office, right to 191, 193–4
protest movements 15, 28
public employment *see also* **civil service; judiciary, minority participation in**
  discrimination 39, 558–9
  Dublin Convention against Racism 290

public employment (*cont.*)
  legal entrenchment of participation 745
  social and economic life, participation in 531, 542–3, 550, 558–9
  UN Declaration on Minorities 293

quantitative analysis of ethnic diversity and armed conflict 3–34
  centre segmentation, degree of 20, 23, 26–8
  civil wars 4, 6–8, 16–17, 21–4
  configurations of power and types of ethnic conflict 12–17, 32
  data sources 20–2
  democratic civil peace theory 21
  direct rule, short history of 5–6
  diversity breeds conflict tradition 4–6, 7
  ethnic politics and ethnic conflict 4–17, 22–3, 31–2
  Ethnic Power Relations, dataset on 4, 5, 17–20
  excluded people 4, 5, 13–14, 20–3, 26, 30–4
  explaining armed conflict 22–3
  explaining ethnic conflict 23–6
  fractionalization indices 7–8
  greed and opportunity perspective 4–6, 7
  imperial history, measure of past 20–1
  incohesive states 4, 20–1, 26, 31
  infighting between elites 5–6, 14, 26–30, 32–3
  insurgency model 21
  intervention 31–2
  Iraq 33
  linguist diversity 21, 29–30
  Minorities at Risk (MAR) dataset 8–9
  minority mobilization school 4–5, 8–9
  models and findings 22–8
  natural resources, availability of 21–2, 30
  peacemaking 32
  power-sharing partners, number of 20–1, 26, 32–3
  prevention 31–4
  rebellion, explaining 26–30
  segmented states 4, 26, 32–3
  state cohesion 20–1, 32
  state power, distribution of 5
  variables 20–2
Quebec, Canada 380, 618–19, 648–51
quotas
  Belgium 167–8
  civil service 441–2, 448–9
  elections 322
  gender 167–8
  indigenous people 322
  intersectionality, theory of 157–8
  judiciary 589, 597–8, 600, 608

racism *see also* **International Convention on the Elimination of All Forms of Racial Discrimination**
  Dublin Convention against Racism 289–291, 294–6, 303–6
  effective participation, no guarantee of 288
  elections 349–50, 352–3
  European Commission against Racism and Intolerance (ECRI) 658–9
  intersectionality, theory of 152–3
  judiciary 594–5, 597–8
  minority associations 692–3
  Race Equality Directive 576–8, 582, 587
  Roma, special contact measures (SCMR) for 504–5, 507, 510
  social and economic life, participation in 558–61, 576–8, 582, 587
  state reports 300
  Trust Fund for the Programme of the Decade to Combat Racism 291
  United Kingdom 692–3
radio and television air time for political parties 147–8, 354–5
rebellions 6–7, 14–16, 19–20, 26–30
regional arrangements
  funding 38
  indigenous people 322–3
  Latin America 322–3
  parliaments 673–4
  power-sharing 429–32
  self-governance 628–30
religion
  conflicts, reasons for 455–6, 457
  cultural domination 38–9
  cultural minority self-governance 658–60
  democracy 206–7
  domination of minorities 38–9, 67
  France, headscarf ban in 153
  freedom of religion 67
  Islamic minorities 153, 159–60, 200–1, 658–60
  Jewish marriages and divorces 660
  liberalism 67
  Northern Ireland 9, 30, 37, 38, 43, 64
  Poland, Catholic Church in 162–3
  political parties 200–1
  secularism 456
  Sharia law 200–1, 659–60
  Sikhs, kirpans and 660
  social and economic life, participation in 563
  Sri Lanka 38–9
  state neutrality 456, 457
  supplementary jurisdictions 659–60
  terrorism 658–9

thought, conscience, belief and opinion, freedom of 354–5
women's movements and nationalism 159–60
republicanism 66, 68–70
reservation systems in United States 330–1
reserve and auxiliary security forces 59
reserved seats systems
  Advisory Committee of FCNM (ACFC) 236–7
  Denmark 240
  design of electoral systems 395–6
  effective participation 236–7, 240
  emerging standards 237
  FCNM Commentary 236–7, 240
  gerrymandering 236
  Iraq, Kurdistan Region of 295–6
  legal entrenchment of participation 744–5
  Lund Recommendations 268–9
  pluralism 237
  positive or special measures 236
  power-sharing 141–3
  proportional representation 236
  Roma, special contact measures (SCMR) for 514
  thresholds 236
  Ukraine, Crimea in the 236
residency 92, 117, 246, 253
Revised European Social Charter 130, 250
right-peopling the state 42–3
right-sizing the state 41–2
Roma
  advisors 516–17
  advisory bodies 517–20, 522–3
  Advisory Committee of FCNM (ACFC) 238, 512, 522
  Albania 518
  Belgium 520
  best practices 506
  Central and Eastern Europe 504–5, 514–19
  committees 514–16, 519–20
  consultative and advisory mechanisms 487, 488, 516–20
  Council of Europe 512–13, 522
  Croatia 518
  culture 560
  Cyprus 516
  Czech Republic 518–19, 521
  democracy 507–8, 511
  Denmark 521–2
  Dublin Convention against Racism 290
  education 509–10, 545, 559–62, 566–7, 568, 572
  effective participation 504, 522–3
  elections 510–11
  European Convention on Human Rights 511, 572–4
  European Roma and Travellers Forum (ERTF) 506–7, 513–14, 523
  European Union 578
  Finland 520, 521–2
  Framework Convention 512, 522, 549
  France 520
  health care 547
  housing 547, 566, 574
  human rights 504, 520, 523
  Hungary 519, 520–2, 698–700
  identity documents 551, 567
  implementation practice of states 514–22
  International Covenant on Civil and Political Rights 510
  International Covenant on Economic, Social and Cultural Rights 566–7
  Ireland 519
  Lithuania 519
  local and regional level
    arrangements at 520–2
    recommendations at 507, 520–1
  Lund Recommendations 504–7, 514, 520
  minority associations 698–700
  Office for Democratic Institutions and Human Rights (ODIHR) 505–6, 509, 523
  Organization for Security and Cooperation in Europe (OSCE) 506, 508–12
  OSCE Copenhagen Document 508–9, 512
  OSCE High Commissioner on National Minorities (HCNM) 506
  parliamentary committees 514–16
  parliamentary representation as SCMR 514–15
  participatory democracy 507–8
  positive or special measures 129
  racial discrimination 504–5, 507, 510
  reserved seats 514
  Slovakia 521
  Slovenia 521, 522
  social and economic life, participation in 534–5, 540–9, 551–2, 559–62, 566–8, 572–4, 578
  social services, access to 562
  special contact measures (SCMR) 503–23
  Sweden 519–20
  UN Declaration on Minorities 510–11
  Universal Declaration of Human Rights 510
  women 506, 507
Romania 427–9, 433, 742–3
rule of law 590
Russia 48, 64, 199–200, 408–9, 665–7, 678–81

Sami parliaments 338–9, 493–4, 500, 553–4, 655–7, 695–7

Index

secession
  Bosnia and Herzegovina 15
  cohesion, amount of 15
  conflicts 14–16
  cultural minority self-governance 641, 653
  electoral systems, design of 373, 379–80, 399
  Ethnic Power Relations (EPR), dataset on 20
  imperialist pasts 15
  incohesive states 16, 31
  indirect rule, long history of 14–15
  infighting 28–30
  institutional cohesion 15
  language 29–30
  large states 15
  natural resources, availability of 21–2, 30
  Northern Ireland 30, 380
  political parties advocating secession 126
  power, configurations of 14
  Quebec 380
  rebellions 28–30
  territorial boundaries 14
  territorial domination for minorities 54–5
  war-prone configurations 14
secret ballots 182, 348
secularism 456
security service domination 58–60, 67–8
security versus rights perspective 77–9
segmented states 4, 26, 32–3
segregation 33, 559, 562
self-determination
  Canary Islands, legislature of 216
  cultural minority self-governance 641, 643–4, 655–6, 658
  indigenous people 312, 328, 655–6
  New Caledonia, legislature of 216–17
  power-sharing 418
  self-governance 215–17, 328, 614–15, 618, 626–7
  territorial self-government 215–16
  UN Declaration on Minorities 291
self-governance 613–33
  architecture of self-governance 643–4
  asymmetrical forms of governance 644–5
  autonomy
    cultural autonomy 643, 645, 647, 650–1, 655–6
    discrimination 143–5
    federalism 619–23, 630–1
    indigenous people 338
    territorial arrangements 217–18, 328–9
  consultative and advisory mechanisms 477–8, 486
  culture 629, 634–60
  de facto arrangements 329

  definition of self-governance 635
  democracy 613, 623, 628–9, 639–40, 642–3, 646
  developing countries 623
  discrimination 143–7, 613–33
  enhanced local self-government 661–81
  ethnic federations 631–2
  European Charter of Local Self-Government 662, 670–1, 675–7, 681, 738
  European Convention on Human Rights 214–19
  federalism 619–23, 628–33, 654
  forms 143–4, 616, 618–20
  Framework Convention 143
  gender 145, 165–7
  governance, meaning of 214–15
  human rights 613–15, 617–18, 623, 627–8, 638, 655
  Human Rights Committee 145–7, 615, 618–19
  identity and ethnicity 624–7, 633
  indigenous people 145–6, 312, 314, 328–42, 637, 649–50, 655–7
  International Covenant on Civil and Political Rights 146, 614–15, 619, 637–8
  International Labour Organization Convention on Indigenous Peoples 614
  Islamic minorities 658–60
  Jewish marriages and divorces 660
  language 629–31, 645–9, 652
  legal entrenchment of participation 738, 741
  Lund Recommendations 107, 144–5, 214–15, 613, 616–17, 620–8, 633–48, 654–60, 736–7, 750
  majoritarianism 639–40
  minorities within minorities 145
  multi-ethno societies 638–9
  nationalism 624, 627
  non-territorial self-government 215, 217–19, 338–40
  OSCE Copenhagen Document 144–5
  OSCE High Commissioner on National Minorities (HCNM) 144
  paradoxes of self-government 628–33
  political consciousness 624
  political parties, organization and structure of 628–9
  power-sharing 637
  Quebec 618–19, 648–51
  regional governments 628–30
  regional parliaments 673–4
  religious minorities 658–60
  representation, participation as 616–17

rights, participation and self-government as 617–21
Sami parliaments 338–9, 655–7
secession 641, 653
self-determination 215–17, 328, 614–15, 618, 626–7, 641, 643–4, 655–8
self-government plus 328
Sharia law 659–60
Sikhs, kirpans and 660
social and economic life, participation in 534
sovereignty 643–4, 654
Spain, Autonomous Communities in 651–4
subsidiarity 622
supplementary jurisdictions 659–60
territorial self-governance 215–18, 329–40, 616, 620, 631, 643, 650–1, 656
UN Declaration on Minorities 144, 619
Universal Declaration of Human Rights 614

separation of powers 52
separatist and non-separatist conflicts 19–20
Serbia 42, 421
services, access to *see also* social services, access to
　International Covenant on Economic, Social and Cultural Rights 565–6, 567
　language 548, 550, 565–6
　social and economic life, participation in 534, 543, 548, 550, 565–6
　standards 103
settlements 56–7
Sharia law 200–1, 659–60
Sikhs, kirpans and 660
single-member district (SMD) electoral systems 364, 370–1, 373–80, 410
single transferable vote (STV) 170, 373–4, 387–8, 391–4
Slovakia
　consultative and advisory mechanisms 494–5
　domination of minorities 38, 46–7, 55, 64
　effective participation 84
　electoral domination 46–7
　European Union 64
　language 38, 64
　local self-government 680
　power-sharing 419
　Roma, special contact measures (SCMR) for 521
　territorial domination for minorities 55
Slovenia 84, 521, 522
social and economic life *see* social and economic life, discrimination in; social and economic life, participation in

social and economic life, discrimination in 251–3, 525, 527, 529–30, 538–44
　capacity building 251
　children, right of 568
　citizenship 550–1, 562
　differential treatment 572
　education 540–1, 559–62, 571
　employment 543–4, 558–9, 561, 565
　European Convention on Human Rights 572–3
　FCNM Commentary 251–3, 255
　formal equality 529
　health care 252, 540, 566
　housing 252, 540–1, 547, 558–9
　implementation of legislation 251
　indirect discrimination 530, 540–2, 565, 572
　International Convention on the Elimination of All Forms of Racial Discrimination 558–61
　International Covenant on Civil and Political Rights 561
　International Covenant on Economic, Social and Cultural Rights 565–6
　International Labour Organization (ILO) treaties 585
　intent 530
　justification 529–30
　land 550
　languages 251
　legislation 251, 539–42
　Minority Rights International (MRG) 586
　multiple discrimination 250–1
　nationality discrimination 560–1
　outreach 251
　positive or special measures 251, 529–30, 540–4, 551, 560–1, 565, 584
　proportionality 530
　public service, representation in the 558–9
　racial discrimination 558–61
　Roma 540–1, 543–4, 547–9, 552, 559–60, 566–7, 573
　segregation 559
　substantive equality 529–30, 534
　UN Independent Expert on Minority Issues (UNIEMI) 584
　undocumented migrants 570
social and economic life, European Union documents on 574–82
　accession, conditions on 574–5
　citizenship 579, 582
　competences 574–5
　Copenhagen criteria 574
　discrimination 576–8, 580
　Employment Equality Directive 576–7, 582

social and economic life, European Union documents on (*cont.*)
  European Court of Justice, interpretation by 577, 581–2
  European Employment Strategy 579
  Framework Convention 574
  High Level Advisory Group 579
  integration 578–81
  Lisbon Treaty 575, 577–8
  mainstreaming 575, 577
  migration policy 580
  new and immigration minorities 576, 579–82
  Race Equality Directive 576–8, 582, 587
  Roma 578
  social inclusion 578–9
  social security, access to 582
  Tampere Council 580
  third country nationals 576, 580–1
  traditional minorities 579
social and economic life, participation in 249–53, 524–87 *see also* **social and economic life, discrimination in**
  Advisory Committee of FCNM (ACFC) 249–50, 526–8, 535–53, 587
  African Charter on Human and People's Rights 570–1
  American Convention on Human Rights 569–70
  areas of concern 251–3
  capacity building 251
  children, rights of 568
  citizenship 550–1, 556, 561, 562, 579, 582
  civil service 534
  conflict prevention 534–5
  consultative and advisory mechanisms 479, 528–9, 533, 537, 555–6
  Convention on the Rights of the Child (UN) 568
  culture 249–53, 532, 539, 545, 553, 560
  data collection 549–50
  definition of minorities 532–3
  detailed assessments 542–51
  development, right to 571
  differential treatment 572
  discrimination 676–8, 680
  economic activities 538–9, 544, 553–7, 571, 572, 586
  economically depressed regions 250, 251–2
  education 530–1, 538, 540–7, 557, 559–62, 566–8, 571–2, 584–5
  effective participation 249–53, 533, 537–8, 542, 549–50
  employment 531, 538–9, 541–4, 558–9, 561, 565, 576–7, 579, 582
  entertainment, access to places of 548
  European Committee of Social Rights 130
  European Convention on Human Rights 571–4
  European Court of Human Rights 571
  European Social Charter 250, 571, 573
  European Union 574–82
  facilities, access to 548
  FCNM Commentary 250–3
  Framework Convention 106, 535–42, 549, 574, 586–7
  health care 252, 540, 543, 547, 563–4, 566
  housing 252, 531, 540–1, 543, 547, 558–9, 564, 566, 573–4
  human rights 528, 552, 553–7, 561–3, 587
  Human Rights Committee (UN) 528, 553–6, 561–3
  identity, right to 525–6, 532, 536, 538
  indigenous people 532, 550, 551, 553–5, 560, 562–4, 567–9
  inhuman or degrading treatment 572–3
  instrumental issues 549–51
  integration 525, 536–7
  Inter-American Commission on Human Rights 569–70
  International Covenant on Civil and Political Rights 528, 553–4, 561–3, 586
  International Covenant on Economic, Social and Cultural Rights (UN) 294, 306, 563–8, 587, 738
  International Labour Organization (ILO) treaties 585
  interpretation 531
  kin states, cross-border cooperation with 551
  land and property 252, 560, 568, 569–70
  language 253, 535, 538, 544–5, 548, 550
    education 544–5, 557, 565, 571
    employment 544, 558–9, 561
    freedom of expression 562
    proficiency 253
    FCNM Commentary 253
    services, access to 548, 550, 565–6
    social services, access to 550
  legal requirements and obstacles 253
  Lund Recommendations 526–7, 533–5
  mainstreaming 575, 577
  Maori, economic activities of 554–5
  media 253
  Migrant Workers Convention 561, 568
  Millennium Development Goals (MDGs) 583
  Minority Rights International (MRG) 586
  monitoring 250
  multiple discrimination 250–1
  new or immigrant minorities 532, 557, 561, 576, 579–82

norms in non-minority conventions 557–82
OECD Development Assistance Committee (DAC) 585
OSCE High Commissioner on National Minorities (HCNM) 533–5
political participation 249–53, 526
positive or special measures 250–2, 529–30, 540–6, 551, 558, 560, 565, 568, 584
poverty 583–4
procedural economic participation 555–6
public service, employment in 531, 542–3, 550, 558–9
Race Equality Directive 576–8, 582, 587
recommendations 533–5, 551
regional instruments 568–74
religion 563
residency 253
Revised European Social Charter 250
Roma 534–5, 540–1, 543–7, 548–9, 552, 578
  culture 560
  education 545, 559–62, 566–7, 568, 572
  European Convention on Human Rights 572–4
  housing 547, 566, 574
  identity documents 551, 567
  International Covenant on Economic, Social and Cultural Rights 566–7
Sami community, economic activities of 553–4
scope of participation 527–42
self-governance 534
services, access to 534, 543, 548, 550, 565–6
social cohesion 536–7
social inclusion 578–9, 583–4
social security, access to 582
social services, access to 543, 548, 550, 562, 573, 582
standards 525–7, 532–3, 553
structural obstacles 251–2
traditional knowledge and medicine 567
travelling and nomadic people 564, 573–4
treaty bodies, supervision by UN 557–82, 587
UN Declaration on Minorities 556–7
UN Declaration on the Right to Development 289
UN Forum on Minority Issues 584–5, 587
UN Independent Expert on Minority Issues (UNIEMI) 583–4, 587
undocumented migrants 570
United Nations 289, 527, 557–85, 587
urban-rural divide, unemployment and 249–50
utilities, access to 548
water, right to 564

social cohesion 86–8, 90, 224, 536–7
social services, access to
  consultative and advisory mechanisms 327
  European Convention on Human Rights 573
  European Union 582
  language 550
  Roma 562
  social and economic life, participation in 543, 548, 550, 562, 573
socio-economic inequality 78, 250–2, 583–4
soft law 178–9, 225–30, 739
South Africa 37, 163–4
South Tyrol 247, 430–1, 444–6, 448
Spain, Autonomous Communities in 651–4
special contact measures for Roma (SCMR) 503–23
special measures *see* positive or special measures
sponsorship of legislation 412
Sri Lanka
  conflicts, reasons for 462–5
  constitutional review 61–2
  demographic domination 43
  denaturalization 44
  discrimination 39, 463–5
  domination of minorities 37–9, 43–4, 48, 51–2, 56, 58, 60–4, 68
  electoral domination 44, 48
  emergency powers 62
  employment, discrimination in 39
  judges 61
  language 38–9, 462–5
  legal domination 61–3
  political domination of minorities 51–2
  presidential systems 52
  religion 38–9
  security service domination of minorities 58, 60, 68
  settlements 56
  symbolic domination 38
  territorial domination for minorities 56
stand for office, right to
  Bosnia and Herzegovina, Dayton Peace Agreement and 193–4
  democracy 193
  discrimination 147–8, 194–5
  dual or multiple nationalities, persons with 192
  European Convention on Human Rights 181, 188–95
  historical and political factors 189–90, 193
  inhuman or degrading treatment 194–5
  language 188–9, 190–2
  Latvia, language requirements in 188–9, 190, 248–9
  legitimate expectations 188

stand for office, right to (*cont.*)
  limitations 189–94
  margin of appreciation 188–90, 193
  positive or special measures 141–2
  proportionality 191, 193–4
  removal from office 188
  standards 103, 105
  vote, right to 191–2
standards
  access to public service 103
  Advisory Committee of FCNM (ACFC) 108–9, 229–30
  African Charter on Human and Peoples' Rights (AfrCh) 104
  American Convention on Human Rights (ACHR) 104
  autonomy 245
  citizenship 103–4
  civil service, right of equal access to 104, 105
  conditions 104
  cultural, religious, social, economic and public life 106
  definition 103
  effective participation 106, 230–2, 286–307
  elected, right to be 103, 105
  elections 103–5, 107
  enhanced protection, need for 106
  European Convention on Human Rights 105
  FCNM Commentary 108–9, 230–2
  forms of participation 104, 106, 108–9
  Framework Convention 106, 107–8
  indigenous people 309–14, 328, 341
  International Covenant on Civil and Political Rights 103–4
  judiciary 590–2, 608
  legal entrenchment of participation 746–7, 749
  local self-government 682, 669–74, 676
  Lund Recommendations 107, 263–7
  media 109
  minority associations 682–4
  non-citizens 103
  non-governmental civic associations, social movements and advocacy groups 103
  OSCE Copenhagen Document 104–5, 109
  OSCE High Commissioner on National Minorities (HCNM) 107, 280–1, 283
  political parties 233–4, 247
  positive or special measures 105, 108
  power-sharing 416–18
  public affairs, conduct of 103–4, 105, 107
  public life, definition of 107
  self-government 328, 682, 669–74, 676
  social and economic life, participation in 525–7, 532–3, 553
  subsidiarity 108
  UN Declaration on Minorities 106–7
  UN Human Rights Committee (HRC) 103
  UN Declaration on Minorities 286–307
  Universal Declaration of Human Rights 103
  vote, right to 103, 105
statistical information 248, 303
status quo, limiting participation to parties than endorse the 48–9
subscription groups 319–20
subsidiarity 622, 673
Sudan 64
supplementary jurisdictions 659–60
Surinam 335
Sweden 519–20
Switzerland 422–5
symbolic domination of minorities 38
Syria, Alawite minority in 37

'targeted' approach to group rights 151, 154–9, 172
television and radio air time for political parties 147–8, 354–5
temporary measures 133
territorial boundaries, conflict and 13–14
territorial domination 54–8, 66, 68–9
territorial arrangements
  autonomy 68, 155–6, 215–17, 329–34
  Bangladesh 336
  Bolivia 334
  Canada 330–3
  Colombia 329–30
  communitarian autonomy 334–6
  conflict prevention 336
  cultural and spiritual values 329, 338
  cultural minority self-governance 643, 650–1, 656
  decolonization 329–30
  federalism 631
  Greenland 332–3
  implementation mechanisms 748
  indigenous people 329–40
  Indonesia 336–8
  intersectionality, theory of 155–6
  Iraq 68
  Latin America 329–36
  Lund Recommendations 336
  Mexico 333, 335
  Nicaragua 332, 336
  Nunavut 333
  Panama, *comarcas* system in 331–2, 336
  peace settlements 472
  post-conflict arrangements 336–7

recognition as part of state administrative machinery 335
Sami parliaments 339–40
self-determination 215–16
self-governance 215–17, 616, 620, 631
Surinam 335
United States, reservation system in 330–1
terrorism 658–9
Thailand 457
Thematic Commentary of Framework Convention *see* FCNM Commentary
thought, conscience, belief and opinion, freedom of 354–5
token inclusion 38
traditional knowledge and medicine 567
travellers and nomadic communities *see also* Roma
  Advisory Committee of FCNM (ACFC) 738
  Dublin Convention against Racism 290
  European Convention on Human Rights 573–4
  residency 246, 253
  social and economic life, participation in 573–4
  stopping places 573–4
  water, right to 564
treaty bodies, supervision by 557–82, 587
Trentino-South Tyrol, language affiliation declarations in 247
Trust Fund for the Programme of the Decade to Combat Racism 291
Turkey 60, 200–1 *see also* Turkey, Kurds in
Turkey, Kurds in
  coercive assimilation 40
  discrimination 70
  domination of minorities 40, 62, 65
  elections 46, 50, 69–70, 184–7
  emergency powers 62
  European Convention on Human Rights 69–70
  European Union 65
  freedom of association 198
  historical and political factors 123
  independents, running as 50
  language 40, 65, 457
  legal domination 62
  military law, imposition of 51
  settlements 57
  territorial domination for minorities 57
  threshold requirement for elections 46, 69–70, 184–7
two-party systems 379
two-round systems (TRS) (double-ballot majoritarianism) 369, 370, 374–5, 381–2, 384
two-tier systems (parallel systems) 367–8

Ukraine 236, 664
umbrella associations 691–5
UN Declaration on Minorities
  autonomy 291
  checklist of rights 295–6
  citizenship 293, 556
  Commentary of Working Group on Minorities 288, 291–3, 295–6, 305–6
  consultative and advisory mechanisms 479–80
  contents 288
  cooperation 718–19
  country visits 299
  development 306
  different, right to be 211
  discrimination 112
  Dublin Convention against Racism 290
  effective participation 92, 292–3, 296, 298–9, 304, 349
  electoral systems 293
  ethnic political parties 292–3
  examples of participatory mechanisms 292
  Finland, country visit to 299
  indigenous people 309
  integration 293
  international level, participation at 305, 718–19
  interpretation 288
  interstate cooperation 718–19
  legal entrenchment of participation 739
  local self-government 662, 670–1
  Lund Recommendations 292
  Mauritius, country visit to 299
  Minority Profile and Matrix 295–6
  monitoring 298–9, 709, 718–19
  non-governmental organizations (NGOs), monitoring by 299
  Office of the High Commissioner of Human Rights (OHCHR) 298–9
  positive or special measures 112, 131–2, 349
  public sector employment, access to 293
  Roma, special contact measures (SCMR) for 510–11
  self-determination 291
  self-governance 144, 619
  social and economic life, participation in 556–7
  standards 106–7
  Working Group on Minorities 92, 288, 291–3, 295–6, 299, 556–7
UN Declaration on the Right to Development 289, 297
undocumented migrants 570
United Kingdom 398, 605–7, 692–3 *see also* Northern Ireland

United Nations (UN) *see also* **Human Rights Committee (UN); UN Declaration on Minorities**
  Afghanistan, Security Council resolution on 171
  constitutional and legal safeguards, lack of 305
  Declaration on Right to Development 289, 297
  discrimination 287–8
  Dublin Convention against Racism 289–291, 294–6, 303–6
  effective participation 286–307
  Electoral Assistance Unit 365
  expert advice 291–8, 304–7
  Forum on Minority Issues 305–6, 584–6, 587
  human rights-based approach to development 296–7
  Human Rights Council 291, 301, 352
  implementation 304–7
  Independent Expert on Minority Issues 302–3, 305–7, 584
  indigenous people 309–10, 312–13, 328
  Lund Recommendations 305
  monitoring 298–301, 307
  norms and standards 287–8, 304–7
  Office of the High Commissioner for Human Rights (OHCHR) 296, 298–9, 304, 306, 716
  recommendations and expert advice 291–8, 304–7
  social and economic life, participation in 289, 527, 557–68, 587
  special procedures 302–3
  standards 286–307
  substance of right, advancing the 304–7
  treaty bodies 299–301
  UN Development Programme (UNDP) Resource Guide on Minorities in Development 297, 306–7
  UNDP and Inter-Parliamentary Union (IPU) Project 298
  Universal Periodic review (UPR) 301–2, 307
United States *see also* **United States, elections in**
  indigenous people 326
  intersectionality, theory of 153
  judges 60–1
  legal domination of minorities 60–1 63–4
  local self-government 662, 663, 667–8
  localism 662, 667–8
  Maine 316
  marriage fraud 153
  political domination of minorities 52–3
  presidential systems 52–3
  reservation system 330–1
  settlements 56
  territorial domination for minorities 56
United States, elections in
  Deep South 37, 44–5, 47, 49–51, 66–7, 69
  design of systems 365, 374
  domination of minorities 37, 47, 49, 63–4
  gerrymandering 47, 73, 378
  ghettoization 69
  independent electoral commissions 365
  intimidation and violence 56
  literacy tests 44, 51, 66, 67
  poll tax payment as prerequisite 44, 51, 67
  post-election methods penalizing minority politicians 49–50
  status quo, limiting participation to parties which endorse the 49–50
Universal Declaration of Human Rights 103, 207, 210–11, 346, 364, 510, 739
Universal Periodic Review (UPR) 301–2, 307
universal principles of political participation 345–8
Uppsala/PRIO Armed Conflict Dataset (ACD) 17, 19
utilities, access to 548

Venezuela 316, 323
Venice Commission
  citizenship 245–6
  constitutional law 272–3
  effective participation 87, 93
  elections 93, 137–41, 272–5
  gerrymandering 362
  margin of appreciation 138–9
  positive or special measures 137–42, 273–5
  power-sharing 142–3
veto, right of 239–40, 243–4, 417, 423, 500
Vienna Convention on the Law of Treaties 212–13
violence, political parties advocating 125–6
visits
  Advisory Committee of FCNM (ACFC) 715–16, 721–2, 726
  Independent Expert on Minority Issues (UN) 302–3
  UN Declaration on Minorities 299
voting *see also* elections

Waitangi Tribunal 317
wars *see* conflicts
Warsaw Guidelines (OSCE) 113, 270–1
water, right to 564
Western Balkans, civil service and 446–50
Western individualism 160
will of people, selecting and determining 436

winner-takes-all (WTA) election systems 364, 367–71, 373–80, 394
winner-takes-all (WTA)/ single member districts (SMD) electoral systems 375–80, 394
women *see* gender; women's movements and nationalism
women's movements and nationalism 159–65
  autonomy 160–1
  collective action 159
  colonialism 160–1
  feminism 159, 160–3
  intersectionality, theory of 160
  mobilization 160–3
  nation-building 163–5
  Norway, Muslim women in 159–60
  patriarchal culture 161–2
  Poland, Catholic Church in 162–3
  political agency of women 159–60, 164–5
  sequencing 160
  South Africa, transition to democracy in 163–4
  Western individualism 160
World Conference on Racism 289–91, 294–6, 303–6